# THE WRITER'S HANDBOOK

# The Writer's Handbook

Edited by

## SYLVIA K. BURACK

*Editor, The Writer*

*Publishers*      THE WRITER, INC.      Boston

# CONTENTS

## BACKGROUND FOR WRITERS

1 IS THERE A SECRET
TO GETTING PUBLISHED?.......... Katherine Paterson 1
2 TAKING THE PLUNGE............... Mary Higgins Clark 8
3 WRITE IT DOWN!....................... Barnaby Conrad 10
4 RECREATING REALITY: MAKING IT HAPPEN FOR YOUR
READER ........................ Ursula K. Le Guin 14
5 A WRITER'S EDUCATION ................ Rick DeMarinis 18
6 PURSUING YOUR DREAM ............ Margaret Chittenden 21
7 A WRITER'S HABITS ................. Donald M. Murray 25
8 ARE YOU READY FOR A
WRITING COURSE? .............. Madeena Spray Nolan 32
9 THE WRITER'S EYE...................... Randall Silvis 35
10 MUCH ADO ABOUT PROCESS .............. Candice Rowe 38
11 WAITING FOR INSPIRATION .................. Peggy Rynk 41
12 SIX MYTHS THAT HAUNT WRITERS ... Kenneth T. Henson 44
13 KEEPING A WRITER'S JOURNAL
Marjorie Pellegrino, Lynne Weinberg-Hill, and Tama White 48
14 BRING YOUR IMAGINATION
BACK TO LIFE ...................... Cynthia K. Jones 52
15 CRITICISM: CAN YOU TAKE IT? ......... Lance E. Wilcox 55
16 CORRESPONDENCE COURSES—
ANYWHERE, ANYTIME............ Joan E. Juskie-Nellis 58

## HOW TO WRITE—TECHNIQUES

### GENERAL FICTION

17 PLOTTING FROM A TO Z ............... William F. Nolan 65
18 ACHIEVING A SENSE OF REALITY
IN YOUR NOVEL ................... LaVyrle Spencer 69
19 DIALOGUE: THE MEANING BEYOND
THE WORDS......................... Tim Sandlin 73
20 GETTING STARTED ........................ John Irving 79
21 NOVEL IDEAS
An Interview by Billie Figg .... Barbara Taylor Bradford 86
22 ANSWERS TO QUESTIONS ABOUT
FICTION WRITING .................... Sidney Sheldon 91
23 HOLD THAT EDGE OF EXCITEMENT... Phyllis A. Whitney 96
24 WHERE DOES YOUR FICTION "LIVE"? ..... Shelby Hearon 103
25 EVERYONE IS A STORYTELLER ............. Herbert Gold 107
26 FICTION OPENINGS: FIVE MUSTS.......... F. A. Rockwell 111

27 The Essence of Storytelling:
    Dramatize, Dramatize . . . . . Elizabeth Forsythe Hailey  119
28 Going for the Jugular . . . . . . . . . . . . . . . Eileen Goudge  124
29 A Writer's Characters . . . . . . . . Elizabeth Jordan Moore  130
30 Why I Write Novels . . . . . . . . . . . . . . . T. Alan Broughton  135
31 Dialogue That Works . . . . . . . . . . . . . . . . . Ann Harleman  140
32 That Crucial First Draft . . . . . . . . . . . . . John Dufresne  147
33 Memory and the "I" . . . . . . . . . . . . . . . . . . Sidney Sulkin  152
34 Breaking the Rules . . . . . . . . . . . . . . . . . . . . . John Lutz  157
35 Emotion in Fiction . . . . . . . . . . . . . . . Rosamunde Pilcher  163
36 The Missing Piece Syndrome . . . . . Richard Martin Stern  167
37 Where Do Your Stories Come From? . . . . . . Rick Hillis  170
38 When Is a Story a Short Story? . . . . . Susan R. Harper  176
39 Rewriting Your Novel . . . . . . . . . . . . . . . . . . S. L. Stebel  181
40 Too Good To Be True:
    The Flawless Character . . . . . . . . . . . . . Mary Tannen  185

SPECIALIZED FICTION

41 Writing Novels About the Past . . . . . . Thomas Fleming  191
42 Having Something to Say . . . . . . . . Patricia D. Cornwell  197
43 Creating Series Characters . . . . . . . . . . . . . Anne Perry  202
44 Dick Francis: An Interview . . . . . . . . . . . . Dick Francis  206
45 Free-Form Plotting
    the Mystery Novel . . . . . . . . . . . . . . . . . Marcia Muller  209
46 Grilling Ed McBain . . . . . . . . . . . . . . . . . . . Evan Hunter  215
47 Writing Science Fiction:
    Where to Begin . . . . . . . . . . . . . . . . . . Paula E. Downing  223
48 Characterization and Story . . . . . . . . . . . L. R. Wright  228
49 How to Write the Police
    Procedural Novel . . . . . . . . . . . . . . . . . O'Neil De Noux  233
50 Plot and Character in Suspense Fiction . . Joan Aiken  239
51 Horror Fiction: Time for Some
    New-Fangled Fangs . . . . . . . . . . . . . Graham Masterton  246
52 Living With Series Characters . . . . . . . James Melville  253
53 Setting Is More Than Place . . . . . . . . William G. Tapply  258
54 Creating a Credible Alien . . . . . . . . . . . . Jerry L. Stern  263
55 Meanwhile, Back at the Ranch . . . . . . . Warren Kiefer  269
56 Character: The Key Element
    in Mystery Novels . . . . . . . . . . . . . . . . . James Colbert  276
57 Writing the Short Whodunit . . . . . . . Richard Ciciarelli  281
58 Writing "True" Crime: Getting Forensic
    Facts Right . . . . . . . . . . . . . . . . . . . . Steven Scarborough  287
59 The Mystery Is in the Writing . . . . . . . William Murray  292
60 Science Fiction Writing at Length . . . . Roger Zelazny  295

NONFICTION: ARTICLES AND BOOKS

61 Writing the Newspaper Travel
    Article . . . . . . . . . . . . . . . . . . . . . . . Arthur S. Harris, Jr.  301

62 WRITE SHORTS THAT SELL ................ Selma Glasser 307
63 A BIOGRAPHER'S TALE ..................... Bettina Drew 311
64 THE MARKET FOR OP-ED ARTICLES ..... Genie Dickerson 317
65 GIVE READERS WHAT *THEY* WANT—
     AND NEED ...................... Samm Sinclair Baker 320
66 TRUE CRIME THAT PAYS ............... Krist Boardman 324
67 WRITING THE NON-CELEBRITY PROFILE ...... Erna Holyer 330
68 THERE'S A MARKET FOR SERVICE ARTICLES! ... Don Ranly 334
69 GETTING STARTED IN BOOK REVIEWING .... Bryan Aubrey 340
70 SELL YOUR HIDDEN GOLD WITH A QUERY .. Tom Jenkins 345
71 WRITING THE PRO/CON ARTICLE . Barbara McGarry Peters 351
72 YOU DON'T HAVE TO GO TO SPAIN TO WRITE TRAVEL
     ARTICLES .................. Barbara Claire Kasselmann 355
73 THE ART OF INTERVIEWING .......... Wendell Anderson 361
74 HOW TO WRITE AND SELL A SPORTS
     ARTICLE ................................. Tol Broome 366
75 WRITING A PUBLISHABLE HEALTH ARTICLE .. Joan Lippert 371
76 HOW TO WRITE A PROFILE ............. Lou Ann Walker 377
77 WRITING BIOGRAPHIES: THE PROBLEMS
     AND THE PROCESS ............... Katherine Ramsland 383
78 HOW TO WRITE A HOW-TO THAT SELLS ..... Gail Luttman 388
79 MASTERING THE CRAFT OF
     CRAFT WRITING .............. Beverly L. Puterbaugh 392
80 WITH DEFERENCE TO REFERENCE: A BIBLIOMANIAC'S
     TALE ........................... Robert M. Weaver 396

POETRY

81 THE SHAPE OF POETRY .................... Peter Meinke 403
82 YESTERDAY'S NOISE: THE POETRY OF CHILDHOOD
     MEMORY ............................... Linda Pastan 408
83 EMOTION AND THE LANGUAGE
     OF POETRY ....................... James Applewhite 415
84 WRITING POETRY: THE MAGIC
     AND THE POWER .................. T. Alan Broughton 422
85 HOW TO WRITE A FUNNY POEM .......... Jack Prelutsky 428
86 RECEIVING A POEM ................. Donald M. Murray 434
87 STALKING THE POETIC IMAGE ............. Miriam Sagan 441
88 THE POET WITHIN YOU .................... David Kirby 446

JUVENILE AND YOUNG ADULT

89 WHAT'S AHEAD FOR CHILDREN'S
     BOOKS? ........................ James Cross Giblin 453
90 WRITING "HIGH" FANTASY: ONCE UPON A TIME
     TOO OFTEN ...................... Patricia A. McKillip 461
91 IS IT GOOD ENOUGH FOR CHILDREN? .. Madeleine L'Engle 467
92 CALLING IT QUITS ....................... Lois Lowry 471
93 PUTTING YOUR CHARACTERS TO WORK IN MYSTERY
     FICTION ...................... Mary Blount Christian 475

94 DIALOGUE: LET YOUR CHARACTERS
   DO THE TALKING . . . . . . . . . . . . . . . . . . . . . . . Eve Bunting 479
95 WRITING THE WESTERN NOVEL FOR
   YOUNG ADULTS . . . . . . . . . . . . . . . . . . Joan Lowery Nixon 484
96 DISCOVERING STORIES FOR PICTURE
   BOOKS . . . . . . . . . . . . . . . . . . . . . . . . . Barbara Abercrombie 488
97 TEN COMMON ERRORS IN WRITING FOR
   CHILDREN . . . . . . . . . . . . . . . . . . . . . . . Linda Lee Maifair 492

PLAYWRITING

98 BEFORE YOU TRY BROADWAY . . . . . . . . . . . . . Anna Coates 499
99 TEN GOLDEN RULES FOR PLAYWRIGHTS . . Marsha Norman 506
100 NEW WRITING FOR THE THEATRE
   . . . . . . . . . . . . . . . . . . . . . Shelley Berc and Robert Hedley 508
101 AN OBJECT LESSON FOR PLAYWRIGHTS . . . . . Jeffrey Sweet 514
102 CONFLICT: THE HEARTBEAT OF A PLAY . . . D. R. Andersen 519

EDITING AND MARKETING

103 AN EDITOR SPEAKS FROM THE TRENCHES . . . . Peter Rubie 529
104 THE AUTHOR/AGENT RELATIONSHIP . . . . . Jonathan Dolger 535
105 DEBUNKING THE WRITING-FOR-CHILDREN-
   IS-EASY MYTH . . . . . . . . . . . . . . . . Stephanie Owens Lurie 541
106 WHEN *NOT* TO TRY, TRY AGAIN . . . . . . Wendy Corsi Staub 546
107 COMMON QUESTIONS ABOUT COPYRIGHTS
   . . . . . . . . . . . . . . . . . . . . . . . . . . . . . . . Howard Zaharoff 552
108 GETTING STARTED IN THE LITTLE AND LITERARY
   MAGAZINES . . . . . . . . . . . . . . . . . . . . . . . . . . . . James Plath 558
109 WHY IT'S HARDER TO FIND AN AGENT THAN A
   PUBLISHER . . . . . . . . . . . . . . . . . . . . . . . . . Edward Novak 563
110 WHEN YOU WRITE FOR *ALFRED HITCHCOCK'S
   MYSTERY MAGAZINE* . . . . . . . . . . . . . . . . . . . . Elana Lore 569

WHERE TO SELL

INTRODUCTION . . . . . . . . . . . . . . . . . . . . . . . . . . . . . . . . . . 575
ARTICLE MARKETS . . . . . . . . . . . . . . . . . . . . . . . . . . . . . . . 578
   General-Interest Publications . . . . . . . . . . . . . . . . . . . . . 578
   Current Events, Politics . . . . . . . . . . . . . . . . . . . . . . . . . 587
   Regional and City Publications . . . . . . . . . . . . . . . . . . . 590
   Travel Articles . . . . . . . . . . . . . . . . . . . . . . . . . . . . . . . . 604
   Inflight Magazines . . . . . . . . . . . . . . . . . . . . . . . . . . . . . 608
   Women's Publications . . . . . . . . . . . . . . . . . . . . . . . . . . . 609
   Men's Publications . . . . . . . . . . . . . . . . . . . . . . . . . . . . . 613
   Home and Garden Publications . . . . . . . . . . . . . . . . . . . . 613
   Lifestyle and Family Publications . . . . . . . . . . . . . . . . . . 616
   Sports and Recreation . . . . . . . . . . . . . . . . . . . . . . . . . . 619
   Automotive Magazines . . . . . . . . . . . . . . . . . . . . . . . . . . 631
   Fitness Magazines . . . . . . . . . . . . . . . . . . . . . . . . . . . . . 632
   Consumer/Personal Finance . . . . . . . . . . . . . . . . . . . . . . 633

Business and Trade Publications.................... 634
In-House/Association Magazines.................... 647
Religious Magazines............................... 650
Health........................................... 662
Education........................................ 665
Farming and Agriculture.......................... 667
Environment and Conservation..................... 669
Media and the Arts .............................. 671
Hobbies, Crafts, Collecting ...................... 676
Popular & Technical Science, Computers............ 682
Seniors Magazines ............................... 685
Animals.......................................... 686
Military.......................................... 688
History .......................................... 689
College, Careers ................................. 691
Op-Ed Markets ................................... 692
Adult Magazines ................................. 695
FICTION MARKETS ................................. 696
Detective and Mystery ........................... 702
Science Fiction and Fantasy....................... 704
Confession and Romance .......................... 706
POETRY MARKETS.................................. 707
Poetry Series .................................... 710
GREETING CARD MARKETS.......................... 712
COLLEGE, LITERARY, AND LITTLE MAGAZINES......... 714
Fiction, Nonfiction, Poetry ....................... 714
HUMOR, FILLERS, AND SHORT ITEMS ................ 737
JUVENILE, TEENAGE, AND YOUNG ADULT MAGAZINES.. 744
Juvenile Magazines............................... 744
Teenage and Young Adult......................... 749
THE DRAMA MARKET ............................. 752
Regional and University Theaters.................. 752
Play Publishers .................................. 762
The Television Market............................ 763
Television Script Agents .......................... 764
BOOK PUBLISHERS ................................ 765
UNIVERSITY PRESSES ............................. 798
SYNDICATES...................................... 800
LITERARY PRIZE OFFERS........................... 802
WRITERS COLONIES............................... 814
WRITERS CONFERENCES............................ 822
STATE ARTS COUNCILS ............................ 831
ORGANIZATIONS FOR WRITERS...................... 836
LITERARY AGENTS ................................ 845
INDEX TO MARKETS ............................... 855

# Background for Writers

# §1

# IS THERE A SECRET TO GETTING PUBLISHED?

## BY KATHERINE PATERSON

ONCE UPON A TIME THERE WAS A WOMAN who wanted to write. No, delete that first sentence. Once upon a time there was a Maryland housewife with first two, then three, then four children under the age of six who was constantly composing in her head and furiously writing down the bits whenever she had a moment, who wanted desperately to publish. She became a celebrated, award-winning commercially successful writer of books for children and lived happily ever after. The end.

What a minute! That's no story.

What do you mean "that's no story"? You have "once upon a time" and "happily ever after." What more could anyone want?

A middle! A story must have a beginning, a middle, and an end.

But that's the boring bit. Delete "boring," insert "depressing." Besides, it's a story the audience will know all too well. The slogging away at manuscripts she has no hope will ever see the light of day—the wistful attendance at writers' conferences—the seven dismal years of self-addressed envelopes jammed into the mailbox—the coffee-stained manuscripts that have to be painfully retyped before they can be submitted to yet another seemingly heartless editor—the drawers of printed rejection slips—the wondering if it is worth the headache, not to mention the postage. She doesn't think about the time—her time evidently has no value.

Through the years, she tries everything—stories, poems, articles, fillers—but nothing sells except one story and one poem. The tiny magazines that buy them immediately fold.

She is, obviously, not meant to be a published writer. She doubts that she has any talent at all. In all other ways, she is a fortunate woman—she has a good husband and four happy, healthy children. Isn't that

1

enough? Why can't she be content?

But if she'd been content in the middle, the happily ever after wouldn't have happened.

What you've just read is an internal debate between my creative side and my business side. The business side is, frankly, a bit surprised that anyone would ask me to speak about "writing for the market." Years ago she made noble efforts to steer me toward writing something that might be marketable, but it became sadly evident that I was simply incapable of that kind of writing. The creative side wants me to tell the middle of the story, hoping it might help other weary writers, though she's not quite sure how. . . .

So, I pulled myself together and called my editor to tell her that I'd been asked to speak on writing for the market. "What are you planning to say?" she asked nervously. "Well, that's what I'm trying to figure out," I said. "What do *you* think I should say?"

"Well," she said, "I'm right now reading through the slush pile, and I wish everything weren't so market driven. I think people should write what they need to write."

"Can I quote you on that?" I asked.

"No, wait a minute. I have to phrase this very carefully. Writers have to know what's being published today and what's selling. It's not enough to go to libraries. Writers have to go to bookstores to find out what's being published and what's selling. But, having said that, I believe they should write what they need to write."

"Do you think new writers have a chance today?"

"It's harder," she admitted, "though it's always been hard. But today there are fewer editors willing to read slush-pile submissions. Though I can't understand it. How are they going to find good first novels if they don't read slush-pile submissions?"

No wonder my story turns out well. Does anyone in the world have such a terrific editor?

But back to the middle of the story. The question I suppose I need to address is how I got from there to here—how the frustrated, practically unpublished housewife became, if not exactly a household name, at least a respected and well-paid writer.

Let me say first of all that no one has been more surprised by my success than I have. But everyone seems a bit surprised. When people first meet me, I watch them make a mental adjustment. I don't look the way they think I ought to. Here's this woman, not nearly so clever as I, they're thinking, and she's supposed to be this well-known writer. Then often, surprise moves to questioning—or to be more specific, to what is sometimes known as the "trick" question. Which is, what is your trick? There must be some trick, some secret that you know that I don't. So, be generous, tell me your secret, so I can be rich and famous like you.

It doesn't do to say that there is no trick. The person will just think you're being selfish. And advice, even good advice, comes without a guarantee. It reminds me of the Mother's Day card I got from one of my sons this year: "Mom," it says, "all the advice you gave me growing up is still as clear in my mind as the day you gave it—And to this day, I always look both ways before accepting candy from strangers. . . ." Hm-m.

But, anyhow, for what it's worth, here it is: The middle of the story—the trick—the secret—the advice. It boils down to what my editor suggested: I did read what was being written in the field of children's books, but when I sat down to write, I wrote what I *needed* to write, I wrote what I *wanted* to write, what, as it turned out, I *could* write.

There is a wonderful story about the writer Conrad Aiken who during his lifetime received awards and critical respect, but very little in the way of actual money. During the 1920s and 1930s, he was a struggling writer with a house full of children to support. He was publishing, but only in toney little literary magazines too high class to insult contributors by paying them for their work. But what Aiken needed most of the time was cold, hard cash.

He decided to change his ways. Forget literature. Write something that would put groceries on the table. He went about his assignment scientifically. Taking most of the almost non-existent family budget, he bought copies of all the magazines that paid real money to writers for their stories. There were a lot more of them in those days than there are, alas, now: *The Saturday Evening Post, Liberty, Collier's.* He studied and analyzed all the stories in these publications until he figured out the key. Then he deliberately wrote a *Saturday Evening Post* story, one he was sure the editors would not be able to resist.

Well, of course, the *Post* rejected his "perfect" story, as did all the other high-paying magazines. (His "Silent Snow, Secret Snow" was eventually published in some obscure place, but it has been repeatedly anthologized in the years since Aiken's death as an example of a great literary short story.)

The moral of this cautionary tale is, you can study the market to a fare-thee-well, but in the end, you write what you can.

When children ask me where I get my ideas, I turn the question back on them. Ideas are everywhere—a dime a dozen. But before I write a book, I look at the idea, or rather, the complex of ideas I am proposing to turn into a story, and I ask two questions: Is it worth all the trees? And, the second question, which gets more relevant for me with every passing year—is it exciting enough, important enough for me to live with it for the year, two years, maybe three years of my ever-shortening life that it will take me to write it?

You may wonder why I ever write a book—so do I. And yet I do, because, like you, somehow I must. It's what I do. But I only write books that I truly need to write—that matter deeply to me.

I began to write my first novel back in those grim days when nothing I wrote was getting published. A lady in the church where my husband was pastor felt sorry for me, home with all those little children. She took me on as a kind of good work. "How about attending a writing class through the county adult education program?" she asked. She knew I was trying to write, but without success. It sounded great—Mom's night out. I started in a general writing course. Then the next year I took a course on Writing for Children. I was writing something—a story or a poem—every week, and publishing nothing, when it occurred to me that if I could write a story a week, I might be able to write a chapter a week. And at the end of the year I would have a book.

I wanted to write a story set in Japan, because I had lived there for four years, back when I was a competent single woman, and I was a little bit homesick for Japan. If I wrote a story set in Japan in the past, I would have an excuse to read Japanese history, something I loved doing. I don't think I ever knew that if I did that I would be committing historical fiction. I wasn't thinking about genre, I was thinking about story. I'm sure I didn't know that a book for children set in 12th-century Japan would be for all practical purposes totally unmarketable.

But a novel has to have more than fascinating setting and well-paced plot. It has to have an emotional core. It has to be written out of passion. And the heart of this novel set in 12th-century Japan came

4

from an unexpected source. It came to me from my then five-year-old daughter.

Lin was born in Hong Kong in the fall of 1962. When she was about three weeks old, she was found on a city sidewalk by a policeman and taken to an orphanage out in the New Territories, where she lived for more than two years before she came to be our daughter. Her initial adjustment was horrendous, and again when we moved from New Jersey to Maryland in 1966, a lot of it came unglued and had to be redone. But by 1968 when she was five, life had settled down pretty well for her. Still, there were times when for no reason we could discern, the bright, happy little daughter she had become would disappear. And in her place would be a silent waif. It was as though the child we knew had simply pulled down a curtain that we could not reach through, often for several days at a time. And it scared me to death. Where had she gone? What was going on behind that blank stare? And how on earth could I reach her? I had tried everything—cajoling, begging, holding her. Nothing worked. One evening I was in the kitchen making supper and she came in. Without a word she climbed up on a high kitchen stool and sat there, her tiny body present, but the rest of her completely closed away. I tried to chat with her in a normal tone of voice. There was no answer, no indication that she even heard. The harder I tried, the more tense I became.

Finally, I did what any good mother would do under the circumstances, I lost my temper and screamed. "Lin," I yelled, "how can I help you if you won't tell me what's the matter?"

She jerked to life, her eyes wide open. "Why did that woman give me away?" she demanded.

And then it all began to pour out. Why had she been given away? We'd never told her that she was a foundling. It seemed too harsh—just that her mother had not been able to keep her and wanted her to have a home. I repeated this, adding that I was sure her mother hadn't wanted to give her away, and wouldn't have if there had been any possibility that she could take care of her. Was her mother alive? Was she all right? I couldn't answer her questions, but she let me try to comfort and assure her. She never again, even in adolescence, pulled down the curtain in just that way.

She is a mother herself now—a wonderful, loving, funny mother, giving our baby grandchild all the care that she herself never had but

5

that somehow she knows how to give. She is a wonder, and I cannot tell you how I admire her.

But what she gave me that day was not only herself, but the emotional heart of the story I wanted to write. What must it be like, I wondered, to have a parent somewhere that you do not know?

I look at this book—*The Sign of the Chrysanthemum* is its title—and it's no marvel to me now that I had difficulty finding a publisher. It is set in the midst of the civil wars of 12th-century Japan. The central character is a thieving bastard who is searching for the father he never knew. The girl he cares about ends up in a brothel; I didn't put her there because I wanted to scandalize my readers, but because a beautiful thirteen-year-old girl in 12th-century Japan who had no one to protect her would, most likely, end up in a brothel, and the penniless teen-age boy who loved her would be powerless to save her.

Now at some point I must have realized that I hadn't seen a lot of books for young readers along this line, but when I wrote *The Sign of the Chrysanthemum* I wasn't, to be honest, worrying about readers. I was writing a story I needed and wanted to write, as honestly and as well as I knew how.

For those of you who have been wondering about the difference between novels for young readers and adult novels, the adult bestseller at about the same time my book was published—a bestseller that was breaking every sales record since *Gone With The Wind*—was the sentimental tale of an overachieving seagull [*Jonathan Livingston Seagull*, by Richard Bach]. Then how on earth did my book ever see the light of day?

It almost didn't. It made the rounds of various publishers for more than two years. And then a miracle happened. It was taken out of the seventh or eighth publisher's slush pile by a young woman just out of college who read it and loved it. She took it to the senior editor, who had just come back from a visit to Japan and who was and is a woman of vision in the field of children's books. She has always dared to publish books that she feels will open up unknown worlds for children. She had no illusions that the book would sell well, but she wanted young readers to have a chance to read the book, and she wanted the writer to have the chance to write more books.

Though *The Sign of the Chrysanthemum* has never sold well in hardback, it sells remarkably well in paperback. This is particularly

6

satisfying to me, because children and young people buy paperbacks, and it means that the book is reaching the people I am writing for.

Well, that's pretty much the middle of the story. It is harder to place a first novel now. The corporate giants who control most of the New York publishing houses do not have the vision of my first editors. Fewer chances are being taken.

There was a depressing article a few years ago in *Harper's Magazine* entitled, "Reading May Be Harmful to Your Kids." It included the twenty best-selling paperback children's books of 1990. Nine of the top ten had the words "Teenage Mutant Ninja Turtles" in the title. There were only two genuine books on the whole list. One of these, number fifteen, was E. B. White's *Charlotte's Web*, published in 1952, and the other, number twenty, was Maurice Sendak's *Where the Wild Things Are*, published in 1963.

So those of us who haven't the patent on Ninja Turtles might just as well devote our energies to writing something we really care about. And which, not incidentally, may be the only thing we really can write.

It is well to remember that by the time you write a book for the market and that manuscript has gone through the long process of selling itself to an editor and being published, the market may have long before gone somewhere else and left your book far behind. But a beautifully written book, a well-crafted story, a work of honest human feeling and deep passion, like the stories of Conrad Aiken, E. B. White, and Maurice Sendak, will never go out of style. And I still believe there will be a few horribly underpaid, sensitive, unjaded young people ploughing through the slush pile who will find your manuscript and take it to one of the rare remarkable editors left in the business, who will dare against all trends to put it between covers.

It will take a miracle, of course. But who am I to deny the existence of miracles?

# 2

## TAKING THE PLUNGE

### BY MARY HIGGINS CLARK

I ALWAYS COMPARE BEGINNING A BOOK with standing on a cliff. A very high cliff. Way below, looking less like an ocean than a damp washcloth, is the water. I am about to take the plunge. I debate about whether the least painful way is to close my eyes and freefall or point my hands, spring forward and attempt to hit that damp object. I elect for the latter.

And here we go again.

I have ardent admiration for the blessed who can write quickly, the ones for whom words do not drip-drip like the legendary Chinese torture but waterfall upon the computer screen, a generous flow that once present can be manipulated, expanded, snipped, or deleted.

Some years ago, after having seen Barbara Cartland interviewed on television, I rushed to check out her modus operandi. Ms. Cartland claimed that when she began a new book, she sat in her garden, absorbing the beauty of the flowers and trees and sky and sun. Instantly, her mind began to weave stories, and she would dreamily vocalize her fantasies. Her secretary, crouched behind a nearby bush, took down the verbalized stream of consciousness.

Unfortunately when I languish outdoors for any period of time, the one mosquito within a radius of five miles rushes to my side, nestles on my neck or arm, brushes my forehead, and savagely bites the spot on my shoulder that I can't reach. My stream of consciousness becomes a sullen attack on this winged pest, this least of God's creatures. Neither have I found anyone willing to crouch in the bushes and take down my golden prose.

Some writers plan a book to the last detail before beginning the actual process of writing. They can honestly announce that the book is finished even though not one word has been set on paper.

Alas, when I begin, 'tis always the same: An idea. The only comparison I can offer is the slogan: *Bring us a button, and we'll build a suit*

8

*around it.* A realization of who did it and why comes next. A broadly outlined final scene follows. And then, like Ronald Coleman trying to return to Shangri-La, I hack my way through the wintery afternoons of the cold, cold screen, the sessions of white-heat output that the next day reads like drivel, the writing and the rewriting, the eventual sense that the divining rod is jumping. I'm on the right track.

One way or t'other, a manuscript grows. One glorious day the book is finished.

Two weeks pass. Deferred lunch dates are rescheduled and kept. Luxurious salon days are thoroughly enjoyed. Closets are straightened. And then a sense of loss sets in. Something is wrong. Time's a-wastin'.

A few days more and my reluctant footsteps begin the climb. I'm on the cliff again. Aiming at the damp object hundreds of feet below.

# ⧢ 3

# WRITE IT DOWN!

## BY BARNABY CONRAD

THE DAY ARNOLD BENNETT'S BELOVED MOTHER WAS BURIED, he made his daily entry in his notebook as usual.

"Some bricks dry before others," he noted before the funeral; apparently it had rained earlier. Then, after a detailed impression of the ceremony, he added: "Long walk from cemetery gates to region of chapel. By the way, the lodge at gates is rented as an ordinary house to a schoolmaster. John Ford's vault next to Longson with records of his young wives ('The flower fadeth' etc.). This could be exaggerated into a fine story."

There was no disrespect or less loving of his dead mother here; it was simply the professional writer at his never-ending job. Like most writers, Bennett knew that an important part of his job was his notebook. Perhaps he never found the right niche into which he could slip his comment about the bricks, but the mere fact that he had observed it and then made a note of it made him a better writer by furthering his habit of *seeing* instead of just *looking*. Perhaps he never pursued the idea of the young wives, but it was a manifestation of the habit of constantly searching for story ideas around him.

If you, as an embryonic writer, are not keeping notes regularly, you deserve the guilty feeling that is oozing into your body right now!

Someone has said that stories are not written, they are rewritten. That is where I find the notebooks or file most valuable. After finishing the first draft of a story, I diabolically run through my files to see if I can find anything that could be slipped into the context to help make it sparkle. Sometimes nothing is found which could become an integral part of the story, help to develop character, advance the plot, or aid in setting the scene in an interesting manner. Naturally, one shouldn't throw in a *bon mot* or a clever simile where it doesn't belong, just because it is *bon* or clever.

The file is especially helpful for minor characters whose functions are necessary for the advance of the story, but whose faces and bodies remain unaccountably blurred. Once I had to have a barber come up to my hero's room and shave him. He was in the story for only three sentences, but I wanted to give the reader some sort of hook to hang his imagination on. I ran through my files under "mannerisms, walk, etc." and found:

A timid little sparrow of a man who put each foot down on the rug as though apologizing for stepping on it.

I don't know who inspired the observation originally, but it fitted this minor character perfectly and also indirectly helped to characterize my big-shot hero by showing the effect he had on the people around him.

And in finding that card I came across another which I stuck in ten years before but never could find a place for. "He looks like an undriven nail," put in the mouth of a minor character, helped me to individualize my main character. In the file, it was sandwiched in between "eyes as washed out as a teabag in a boarding house" and "his grinning monkey face looked like one of those clay heads you put seeds in to grow grass hair," which will probably find their niches in stories sometime within the *next* ten years.

On a trip down the Thames River I made a note: "Black and white cows along the back drinking their reflections," stuck it in an article for a travel magazine, and *Reader's Digest* picked it up last year for their "Toward a More Picturesque Speech and Patter" page.

It is impossible to remember that wonderful bit of conversation you heard on the bus, or the special ear-tugging, nose-twitching mannerism the mailman has, no matter how indelible the first impression seems. Get it down on paper as soon as possible! You can't expect your memories to come flooding back magically whenever you sit down to write and need those details. And why should you try to rely solely on memory? Sinclair Lewis, Scott Fitzgerald, Steinbeck, Maugham, and Hemingway all kept notebooks.

As Sinclair Lewis's secretary in 1947, I saw how meticulously he kept his notes. He always carried a twice-folded piece of typewriter paper in his wallet, which he'd take out many times a day.

I remember once walking with him around his farm in Massachusetts when we heard an unusual evening sound. Mr. Lewis stopped a home-ward-bound farmer and asked:

"What's that—a cricket? A frog?"
The man laughed. "Oh, no, sir, that's a tree toad."

Lewis jotted it down immediately; sometime the fact that a tree toad makes a different noise from an ordinary toad might be important, and he knew he'd forget it if he didn't make a note of it right away.

And I would have forgotten that whole incident if I hadn't made a note of it that same evening and come across it recently in my "S. Lewis" file!

Mr. Lewis always tried to make his notes surreptitiously. Nothing is as disturbing and ostentatious as a writer violently pursuing his craft at a social gathering. Mr. Lewis often would excuse himself from a party and in the privacy of the bathroom would make a note of some par-ticularly good dialogue, an observation, or perhaps a random idea that came to him while unlistening to a long-winded bore. Later, the day's gleanings would be transferred to "Ebenezer," his corpulent notebook, under its proper classification.

We all have different vocabularies. People in special trades have special vocabularies. Prizefighters, jockeys, and baseball players use their own special terms, just as tailors, musicians, and bankers do. Unless you've actually practiced the trade of the character you're writing about, it's hard to impart authenticity without associating with a member of that profession and recording the flavor of his speech. Witness Arnold Bennett's journal again. His single entry for October 20th, 1924, was:

Collins the tailor, trying on new trousers on Saturday, asked me whether I wanted a "break" at the foot. As I hesitated he said, "Just a shiver." I said yes. "Shiver" is a lovely word for this effect.

On another day he records:

Chiropodist yesterday. He congratulated me on my toenails. Said they were strong—a sure sign of a good constitution. He said in a sort of ecstasy: "It's a grand thing, a nail is!"

On another day, he records random phrases he heard from a conductor rehearsing his orchestra. Notice how authentic the instructions sound, even though we might never have heard how a conductor talks, how unusual and basically interesting in themselves they are, and how they individualize the speaker.

"I want a savage staccato."
"Nice and limpid."
"Nice and stormy."
"Nice and gusty."
"Nice and manifold."
"Weep, Mr. Parker, weep. (Mr. Parker weeps.) That's jolly."
"Press that A home."
"Can we court that better?"
"Now, side-drum, assert yourself."
"Everyone must be shadowy together."

There is a wonderful, unfakable, authentic ring to every one of those phrases, and if used in a story, they would immediately tell your readers and, more important, the editor, "Here is somebody who knows music and knows how his characters talk."

But suppose Arnold Bennett had not written them down right after hearing them? How many could he have remembered when it came time to use them? Try it yourself. See how many of them you can remember even half a day after reading them. And they should be exact. "Bring that A home" or "Carry that A home" is not as good as "Press that A home." "Can we play that better?" is insipid next to "Can we court that better?"

John Cheever's notebooks show a lifetime habit of recording observations and insights and ideas on paper. And *habit* is the operative word there.

The late Stewart Edward White, author of over forty books, advised me when I was very young: "If you can possibly not be a writer, don't be one. But if you cannot help yourself, if you have to write, learn your craft and be a professional in all things connected with writing. And professional writers keep notes!"

13

# 4

# Recreating Reality: Making It Happen for Your Reader

## By Ursula K. Le Guin

I don't know how many times I read or was told, "Write what you know. Write about what you know."

And it is certainly good advice.

On the common sense level, it keeps you from looking foolish. For instance, when I was a very young writer, I wanted very much to put an Englishman in the story I was writing. But I didn't know any Englishmen, didn't really know how the English talk, except in movies; all I knew was that there were lots of people who *did* know—including the population of England. And if they read my story, they'd notice every mistake I made. I had read stories by English writers who had characters from Brooklyn saying things like "Aw, shucks, podner, I reckon 'tain't so," and I knew that a story can never recover from what you might call the Shock of Ignorance. So, until I really knew some Englishmen, I'd better stick to American characters.

If you take it in its deepest meaning, "Write about what you know" means write from your heart, from your own real being, your own thoughts and emotions. It means what Socrates meant when he said, "Know yourself." If you don't know who you are and what you know, if you haven't worked to find out what you yourself truly feel and think, then your work will probably be imitation work, borrowed from other writers. It may be brilliant, full of meanings and ambiguities and symbols and all that stuff they teach in literature courses, but it won't be the real goods. It won't wash. There won't be any wear in it, and the colors will run. . . .

See, I know quite a lot about doing the wash. I know what you can put in the dryer and what you have to line-dry, and what happens to rayon if the water's too hot. Doing the wash has been a notable part of my life experience. I could write plenty about it.

14

So I can draw on it for a metaphor. Or if a character in a story is doing the wash, I can describe what she does (or, less probably, what he does) without having to do any research on it—at least, if my washerwoman is modern American. If she lives in Borneo, or in 1877, then I know only part of what doing the wash involves for her. I may well have to go read up on it—literally go to the library to find out how to do the laundry.

And this is where the advice about writing what you know begins to get a little tight at the seams. How much does any of us really know?

Writers who start out young often feel they really don't know *anything;* but those who begin writing later in life know that you can only get so much into a few decades. Most of us have not wrangled cattle, piloted a jet, been a midwife, managed an insurance office, nursed in a burn ward, or visited Saskatchewan; none of us has done all those things. Even if we've traveled, changed jobs, changed spouses, had adventures, there's no way we can experience everything, and if we tried, we'd be so busy rushing about "getting experience" that we'd never write anything.

"Write what you know" doesn't mean you have to know a lot. It just tells you to take what you have, take who you are, and *use it.* Don't try to use secondhand feeling; use yourself. Stake your claim, however small it may seem, and dig your own gold mine.

Artist-writers are miners, digging deeper and deeper to get to the true gold—to find out what it is they really know about themselves, about their life, about other people, about life.

But their shovel, their pick, the tool they use, *is their writing.* Writing itself, writing fiction or poetry, is a learning device—a means of knowledge, self-knowledge, knowledge of life.

So how can you write what you know, if you use your writing to find out what you know?

If you truly limited yourself to "what you know," you would have to write only about people of your gender, living during your lifetime in places where you have lived, doing and thinking and feeling just what you do, think, and feel.

Is that so bad? Well, it rules out fantasy, romance, historical novels, and science fiction, but still, don't most real novelists write from their own experience? Isn't that what Jane Austen did? Isn't that what Dickens and Tolstoy and Woolf did?

I don't think so. Jane Austen was never a man, Dickens never was a hunted murderer, Tolstoy didn't fight in the Napoleonic Wars, and Virginia Woolf was not a spaniel. Yet they wrote about those experiences. In using what they knew, using *everything* they knew about their own incredibly intensely lived/thought/felt lives, they also used their imagination.

Aha, what is this stray sock that's come up as the wash goes round? Is it a red one? Will it turn everything else pink? Yes, it will! Once you get the imagination in, all the colors of everything change. And the color never fades.

Jane Austen couldn't experience what it was to be a man. All she—a shy, unmarried woman—could do was watch the men who came into her narrow, limited life—father, brothers, brothers-in-law, clergymen—listen to them, think about them, and imagine her way into their minds and hearts, until she knew what a certain kind of man would think and feel, would say and wouldn't say—knew it with the knowledge of the imagination. And so created proud, stubborn, honorable, lovable Mr. Darcy, a real man, a true man.

What distinguishes imagination from wishful thinking is truthfulness. Heroes in romances aren't meant to be true men, but dream-men—boytoys. Women in novels by men all too often are mere objects of desire or of terrified hatred, stereotypes: sexpots, witches, the fair maiden, the bad mother, etc. Here both knowledge and imagination have failed.

If fiction is to be truthful about what human beings really are and do, we have to define knowledge as a goal of the imagination. After all, when I go down to the library and find out about doing the laundry in Borneo or in 1877, I'm not learning through experience, but through the imagination: I read, and recreate the reality in my mind till I know it. That's what writing, fact or fiction, is for. What I "know" comes to me maybe from experience, maybe from hearsay, maybe from books or other arts. What matters is what I make of it—what I do with it.

Let's say that there is something you know, an experience, a fact: When you were a kid, Mrs. Brown next door put so much bleach in the wash that her family's clothes disintegrated. This event has stuck in your mind ever since. Did she mean to pour in a gallon of Clorox? Did she know she was doing it? Did she think about it beforehand? You don't *know,* but you begin to *imagine* how it happened . . . and a story begins to grow around that memory and those imaginings.

16

So the fact becomes a nucleus of a story. Maybe it's one small event in the story, maybe it's the climax, depending on how you imagine it. That's the imagination using knowledge to create deeper knowledge. And the story is how you arrive at and how you tell that new understanding.

But then a very upsetting thing can happen when other people read your story. They say, Oh, wow, this is great, but listen, there's this one part that I just don't believe. It's where she pours a whole gallon of Clorox into the washing machine. It just isn't convincing.

Hey! you say. But that's the true part! It happened! I was there!

And your reader looks at you and says, So what? You have to make it happen for me. You have to make *me* be there.

That is the trick hidden in "write what you know." Just knowing isn't enough. You "know it for a fact"—but your job as a writer is to "make it true." The writer makes it *seem* true (so that the reader won't question it), and also finds out the *truth* of it (so that telling matters).

A gallon of Clorox in the wash is the fact.

Making it seem true is imagining the scene: the way the Clorox gurgled out of the heavy plastic jug, the way the white, white shirts tore and shredded away from the clothesline as the wind tugged them. . . .

Finding the truth in it is imagining what Mrs. Brown thought and felt: how she picked up her husband's overalls from the floor where he'd dropped them and looked at the oily filth ground into them, while she heard him in the other room turning the pages of his porn magazine. . . .

If we look at "writing what you know" in this way, we can even put fantasy and science fiction back in the tub. The whole wash has turned rainbow-colored anyhow. If Dickens can kill Nancy (in *Oliver Twist*), Virginia Woolf can be a spaniel (in *Flush*), and Tolstoy can be Napoleon (in *War and Peace*), and yet all of them are writing from real knowledge given them by the imagination, then you and I can be tentacled purple dweebdorks from the Planet Fsrxki. If we think about the dweebdorks, if we listen to them, feel what they feel, get into their purple skins, if we *know* them, if we even know how dweebdorks do their laundry . . . then we can show our readers that they, too, can be dweebdorks for as long as the story lasts, and that, though it never happened and never will, it matters—it is true.

17

# 5

# A Writer's Education

## By Rick DeMarinis

I WASN'T RAISED IN A FAMILY of book readers. My mother worked in a fish cannery, and my stepfather drove a bread truck. There were a few books in the house—a library copy of *Forever Amber* no one had bothered to return, some mildewed paperbacks with racy covers, an ancient encyclopedia, and, amazingly, a beautiful, gold-embossed, wonderfully illustrated copy of the Koran! (My mother was Lutheran, my stepfather Baptist, and I, at sixteen, was a fallen-away Catholic.) This small and exotic collection of books didn't make much sense, but it contained an essential message for a young aspiring writer: don't expect things to make sense. Expect surprise.

In high school English class, we were introduced to something called, with unmistakable reverence, Literature. I hated it. I remember having to read novels such as *Silas Marner*. But the nebulous minds of sixteen-year-old California kids were hardly prepared for such fare. We traded copies of Mickey Spillane out in the parking lot, away from the snooping eyes of teachers. A novel about gang warfare called *The Amboy Dukes* was hugely popular with us. We saw reading as an extension of our internal lives, and could not make the great leap to the world of George Eliot.

Something happens to people destined for a life of writing that has nothing to do with Literature. It happens early in life, and is probably the psychological equivalent of scarlet fever. It has to do with pain. In answer to the question, "How does one become a writer?" Ernest Hemingway is said to have replied, "Have a lousy childhood." I believe this, but I also know that people who have had wonderful childhoods— on the surface at least—have become, in spite of this handicap, first-rate writers. Even so, something happened to them. Maybe *birth* happened to them and that was disaster enough. Someone sensitive to his or her surroundings, sensitive in the sense of always being aware, of noticing the details, and of being affected imaginatively by the force of these impressions—i.e., a person destined to be an artist—will find trauma waiting around every corner. A childhood doesn't have to be lousy to be traumatizing. As Flannery O'Connor said, ". . . anybody who has survived his childhood has enough information about life to last him the rest of his days."

Then something else happens. We find that words can be an escape from the pain of social impotence. Words became, for me, a bright mantle of power. I discovered that pressing a #2 pencil into a sheet of clean white paper was a sensual experience. And as that pencil moved, a world was created. What power *that* was! Creating fictional worlds is a natural refuge for the powerless, since it *confers* power. There, on the clean white page, all power is restored. My English teachers (except for that one fine teacher all of us seem to encounter, that mythic "helper" who appears just at the right time with the right kind of encouragement) had no perceivable passion for words. It was as if the Literature we were asked to read were made of rarefied ideas breathed directly onto the page by pure mind from the slopes of Olympus. It was the rock solid clatter and bang of our raucous and flexible language that moved me like small earthquakes. Rarefied ideas were a vapor that would be condensed in college and graduate school much later on. Besides, at sixteen I had no apparatus for absorbing serious ideas, and surely none for expressing them. Writing was a physical exercise, as pleasureful as bench pressing heavy weights, but not as socially acceptable. There was something shameful about a strong, healthy boy spending long hours in his room *writing stories*. And so writing, like all suspect activities, had to be done in secret. But how lovely it was, putting down those blocks of words until I and my perplexing, misperceived world were redefined on *my* terms. I became a middleweight boxer, on his way to the championship, when a beautiful girl (who looked remarkably like Jean Simmons in one of her Christian epics) convinced me that boxing was brutal and inhuman—hours before my title fight! Or I became a jet fighter pilot, touring MIG alley in Korea with a vengeance unknown to modern warfare, or a professional quarterback playing in the NFL title game against a team who had dropped me from their roster.

My English teachers and I regarded each other through the wrong ends of our private telescopes. We shied away from each other, and yet they gave me an occasional B or A for my awkward but imaginatively untethered "essays" that twisted the world out of its expected shapes. This habit of twisting the world persisted. If you twist hard and long, it surrenders its truths. George Eliot knew that. All writers know that. Too often, English teachers, even college English teachers, don't know that or they don't see it as the central mission of fiction writing.

Is the writer therefore anti-intellectual? Not necessarily. The intellect, however, wants to be "right." It wants answers and it wants certainty. A writer operates in a different atmosphere, an atmosphere charged with uncertainty and surprise. I heard E. L. Doctorow say, in a recent speech, that the writer, *as* a writer, is someone who places equal value on the objects of his experience. The latest cosmological theory is of no more intrinsic importance than the way sunlight passes through a Japanese fan. This democracy of the objects of experience is a necessary state of mind for the writer. It opens the gates and lets a whole world in where things won't necessarily make sense. For example, you might find your mother in such a world, just home from the cannery and smelling like fish—your mother who quit school at fourteen—sitting at the kitchen table reading a gold-embossed, illustrated edition of the Koran.

# 6

## PURSUING YOUR DREAM

### BY MARGARET CHITTENDEN

WHEN I WAS A VERY SMALL CHILD, I believed, sincerely and absolutely, that a lot of little people lived inside the radio. I believed that when you turned the switch to off, they knew to shut up.

Now I'm grown up, and I still believe in all those little people, though now they live inside my head. I know they are there because they talk to me.

Lots of people hear voices. Some of them are called mad and are shut up in rooms where they stare at the walls all day. Some of them are called writers, and mostly they do the same thing.

So here I am, a writer, staring at the walls of my office, trying to come up with something wise to say about pursuing the dream of becoming a writer. The room is silent. The voices aren't talking. The brain is dead. I've obviously burned out. I've said everything that is in me to say. This, by the way, is the same ritual of despair I go through when trying to start a new novel.

But always, quite suddenly, one of the little people in my head wakes up and starts talking to me, and my fingers start rattling the computer keys. In this case, the voice said, "Define the dream."

What exactly is the dream? What is *your* dream? If it's to be a writer, then you've got it made. Anyone can sit down with a typewriter, a pencil and paper, or a word processor, and write away, all day, every day.

If your dream is to be a *good* writer, then we've added a level of difficulty. And if your dream is to be a good *published* writer, we've added a steep hill to climb.

I'm going to tell you three very short stories.

The first, which I've always hoped was apocryphal, deals with a famous writer who was asked to speak at a writing seminar. He stood up in front of the microphone and said, "How many of you want to be writers?" All the hands went up. And the famous writer said, "Then go home and write," and sat down again.

21

The second story I *know* is apocryphal because I made it up. It concerns a young man who graduated from M.I.T. and decided he didn't want to be an engineer after all; he wanted to be a violinist. He hadn't ever played an instrument, but he thought it looked pretty simple. So he went to a music store and bought a violin and came home and tuned the strings and put rosin on the bow and tucked the violin under his chin and played the "Intermezzo" from *Cavalleria Rusticana*.

The third story is about the Greek geometrician and mechanician, Archimedes, who once lowered his body into a filled bathtub, spilled a lot of water out onto the floor, and then jumped out and ran naked through the streets of Athens yelling "Eureka"—"I have found it." He had discovered the law of hydrostatics, which states that a body surrounded by a fluid is buoyed up by a force equal to the weight of the fluid it displaces.

It seems to me that the first two stories say the same thing, that if you want to do something badly enough, all you have to do is to go home and do it. I don't believe this for a minute.

The third story tells the truth. Archimedes was not visited by divine inspiration. He had devoted his entire life to research and experiment in plane and solid geometry, arithmetic and mechanics. In short, Archimedes had studied his subject. So when the water spilled over, he could go with the flow, so to speak.

We've all heard that we should study the type of writing we want to do. This is very good advice. But why not go a step beyond that? I spend a lot of very pleasurable time studying Sue Grafton and Sara Paretsky's mysteries for pace and suspense techniques; Joyce Carol Oates for atmosphere and anticipation and interesting story structure, as well as characterization in depth; John le Carré for good clean writing and a broad sweep to the story; Anne Tyler for storytelling techniques as well as terrific writing and characterization and style; Anne Perry for her command of historical detail. I study science fiction to stretch my imagination, newspapers for immediacy, and my favorite romance authors for sensual atmosphere, tight plotting, and the tensions that can occur between a man and a woman.

I study these various types of writing, not to copy those writers' techniques, but to develop and improve my own and to stimulate my imagination and creativity. The problem is, you see, that if we read only one type of writing, we may fall into the trap of writing in a way that we *think* is the proper way to write in that particular genre, rather than writing in a way that is natural to us and to our own style.

What we are after is a way to create writing that has what, for want of a better word, I call sparkle. I've read a lot of beginners' manuscripts in workshops and contests. Some were terrific. Some weren't. A lot weren't. They reminded me of my cake baking. I'm a good cook if I stick to dinners, soups, and pies. When I try to make a cake, it's disaster time. I don't know why this is. I use all the proper ingredients and utensils, but my cakes still turn out like flabby pancakes. So it is with some of the manuscripts I've read. The ingredients are all there, but the whole is not equal to the sum of the parts. There's no sparkle.

What exactly is sparkle? I don't know. It's rather like the judge's definition of pornography—I don't know how to define it, but I certainly know it when I see it. I'm willing to bet you do, too.

While pursuing the dream, it's a good idea to cultivate insomnia. I decided to learn how to write during the middle of a sleepless night, and I've had some of my most creative ideas while staring wide-eyed at the shadowed ceiling of my bedroom. Scott Fitzgerald talked about the real dark night of the soul, where it is always three o'clock in the morning. I've had many a real dark night of the soul. And I've learned that at such times I'm incapable of dishonesty. I can see with crystal clarity everything that is wrong with the novel I've been working on for four months. I'm reminded here of one of my favorite quotes, from H. G. Wells. "If you are in difficulties with a book, try the element of surprise: attack it at an hour when it isn't expecting it." Try three o'clock in the morning, run your latest manuscript through your mind and see if it tests positive for sparkle.

My old friend Archimedes would tell you that the shortest distance between two points is a straight line. But in the active pursuit of our particular dream, that's not always true. During the first two years of my writing career, I took a very circuitous approach. I wrote humor articles for my local newspaper's Sunday magazine, I wrote short stories for Sunday school papers, trade magazines, school publications. I suspected, rightly I'm sure, that I wasn't ready to write a novel. Nobody can really pick up a violin for the first time and play the "Intermezzo" from *Cavalleria Rusticana*. It makes sense to practice scales and finger exercises and try to master "Twinkle, Twinkle, Little Star" before plunging headfirst into more difficult works.

23

Persistence pays. Put the emphasis on the pursuit rather than on the dream. Active pursuit. We have to look upon the road to publication as a journey. We have to resolve to have the patience and the stamina to stay with it, to persist in the face of rejection.

In my opinion, the only way to handle rejection is to meet it head on and leap over it. We should never interpret rejection as meaning we're no good; we should look upon it as a challenge. (I'm going to show *them*!)

Literary history is full of stories about great books that were rejected umpteen times and finally sold. My own first children's book was turned down by 25 publishers before finding a home. John Creasey, a prolific English writer who created several popular mystery series—altogether under 28 pseudonyms he published 600 books—collected 743 rejections before selling a single book.

It is very easy to get discouraged when you are a writer. Rejection slips do not drop upon us as the gentle rain from heaven, they come at us sideways from publishers' offices, arrows shooting straight to our hearts. Belief in yourself as a writer isn't always easy to sustain.

So I would offer this final thought for you to ponder. If the pursuit of the dream seems endless, if you receive more rejection than encouragement, if the road to publication seems impossibly long, bear in mind two very important words that were given to us by the ancient Romans. *Nil Desperandum,* which very loosely translated means, hang in there. Define the dream; pursue it actively, professionally, studying, learning, writing, rewriting, looking at your work with three-o'clock-in-the-morning honesty, trying at all times to make your work sparkle. Don't give up. Don't *ever* give up!

# 7

# A WRITER'S HABITS

## BY DONALD M. MURRAY

HABIT IS THE WRITER'S BEST FRIEND: the habit of the notebook, the habit of placing the posterior in the chair at the writing desk, the habit of using the mail.

I am surrounded by neighbors and friends who want to write and know more than I do, have more to say than I do, are blessed with more talent than I have, but they do not yet have writers' habits.

In trying to help some of them become productive writers recently, I found myself taking inventory of the habits that make me a published writer. I was not born with these habits. They were all acquired years ago for a practical rather than an aesthetic reason: Baby needs shoes.

I suppose I hungered for fame, but I wrote to eat. Over the years I have discovered joy in my craft. I delight in my hours alone at my desk when I am surprised by the words that appear on my computer screen. But to arrive at joy I had to develop writing habits.

The following ten habits are essential to my practice of the writer's craft.

## The habit of awareness

I am never bored, because I am constantly observing my world, catching, out of the corner of my eye, the revealing detail, hearing what is not said, entering into the skin of others.

I look out my window at snowy woods illuminated by the moon, and the trees seem to move apart: I have a poem. I hear what someone says visiting a sick room: I have a column. I taste my childhood in a serving of mashed potatoes and have a food page feature. I hear Mozart's 16th piano concerto on the FM, hear it again as I heard it when I lay in intensive care, and have another column.

Some of the observations taken in by eye, ear, fingertip, taste bud, or nose are recorded in my daybook or journal, but many more are held in memory. In practicing the habit of awareness, I record more than I know, and that inventory of filed away information surprises me when I write and it appears on the page.

It is almost half a century ago that I was a paratrooper taught how to make myself invisible while crawling forward in a field of grass, bush, and ledge, and, on my last furlough before going overseas, I demonstrated this strange skill for a girl standing at the top of a New Hampshire field. I had forgotten that until a character in my novel edged up that field, and I realized I was not making it up; I was reporting what had rested in a file drawer in my brain all these years.

## The habit of reacting

I am aware of my reaction to my world, paying attention to what I do not expect, to what is that should not be, to what isn't that should be. I am student to my own life, allowing my feelings to ignite my thoughts.

That sounds normal, but I have found beginning writers do not value their reactions to their world. They think other people have thought the same way or felt the same way. Perhaps they have, but writers need an essential innocence or arrogance that says, "This experience—observation, thought, or feeling—has not existed until I write it." As writers we must value our response to our world.

I notice my writing habits, and from that grows this article. I see young soldiers poised for combat and write the reactions of an old man who survived combat. I see signs for a house tour, feel an unexpected anger at the smugness of those who invite tours into their homes and end up writing a humorous piece about an imaginary tour through a normally messed up house, ours. I put down my holiday thoughts about the daughter we lost at twenty and find, from readers, that my private reactions speak for them.

I have taught myself to value my own responses to the world—and to share them with readers. I build on my habit of reacting.

## The habit of connecting

My wife thinks that my habit of making unexpected connections is my most valuable talent as a writer. Writers see the universal in the particular, they delight in anecdote and parable that reveals a larger story. They treasure metaphor; as Robert Frost said, "Poetry is metaphor, saying one thing and meaning another, saying one thing in terms of another."

26

I study a painting, read what the artist said about its making, and connect that with a technique essential to effective writing; observe the relationships between the way a child plays and a nation makes war.

Usually, these connections come in a special form I call a "line," that is usually more than a word but not yet a sentence. The line contains an essential tension that will release a text when it is developed in writing. When I have that fragment of language I know I have something to write.

Years ago I wrote in my daybook that "I had an ordinary war," realized what becomes ordinary in combat and began the novel I am writing. More than 20 years ago I wrote "a writer teaches writing" and that phrase became both a book and the title of my first textbook on teaching writing. I wrote "I remember silence," and wrote a poem that recreated the loneliness of my childhood and the way we inflicted pain by turning away. The remembered warning "step on a crack and break your back" turned me into a woman on a circus high wire, and I told her story in a poem.

## The habit of rehearsal

The most important part of my writing day may be the twenty-two hours or so when I am *not* at my writing desk. As I leave my writing desk, I start to mull over next morning's writing in my head, and during the hours when I am asleep and awake my conscious, subconscious and unconscious minds combine to prepare next day's pages. I am always rehearsing what I may write.

I walk down the street and I am Melissa confronting Iain in the kitchen of a New Hampshire farmhouse. I see them and hear them. At a stop light I play with the strange, often ironic terminology of financial managers—"redemption," "yield," "trust"—and realize I am writing a column. Sitting in the living room watching the Boston Bruins play Montreal, I am actually weaving an argument for a chapter in a textbook. I am always in the world and out of it, writing what will be written the next morning.

## The habit of disloyalty

Graham Greene once asked a profound question—"Isn't disloyalty as much the writer's virtue as loyalty is the solider's?"—that I often used to describe the relationship of writer to subject, but recently I have realized that I must practice the habit of disloyalty toward myself.

27

I must be disloyal to what I have written on the same subject before, seeing the familiar anew, willing to contradict what I have said and how I have said it. Writing is an experimental art, and I must conduct new experiments on old questions, digging deeper and deeper into the subject which is often myself. I must be disloyal to the most comforting beliefs and myths of my life.

I find myself, after writing strong columns against war, creating a pastoral poem celebrating a peaceful moment during combat. A character in my novel believes the opposite of what I believe when I am not in that character's skin. I record the anger I feel against my daughter who died early—a rare but momentarily true feeling most survivors experience. I revise my textbooks, changing some of the principles for which I argued strenuously in the last edition.

## The habit of drafting

~~nulla dies sine linea. Never a day without a line.~~
~~Each morning I~~
~~I draft~~
~~I write drafts~~

Those who do not write wait until what they want to say is clear in their minds, and when they see it perfectly they write it down. Remember I said that is what those who do *not* write do; writers follow the counsel of Andre Gide:

Too often I wait for the sentence to finish taking shape in my mind before setting it down. It is better to seize it by the end that first offers itself, head and foot, though not knowing the rest, then pull: the rest will follow along.

As a trained journalist, I tend to write the first sentence first because it contains the voice, the subject, my point of view toward the subject, the form, the seed from which the writing will grow, but I do it by drafting, grabbing it by "the end that first offers itself," as I did at the beginning of this section, drafting leads until I get one I can follow.

## The habit of ease

I live in a community of writers, and I became bored by their grumping, groaning, whining about how hard it was to write. And then I realized I was the leading whiner. If I really felt that way, I told myself, I

28

should take up something more pleasant, perhaps embalming or selling real estate.

The fact is I have to write, need to write, love—admit it—to write. In recent years I have worked hard to make writing easy. I study the conditions that make it easy to write—a laptop computer I keep by my living room chair and take on trips, my music on the CD player that helps me concentrate, the information stored on my hard disk to which I can refer in seconds, the community of writer/readers I call on the phone when I need support or stimulus, counsel or a listener for a draft.

I start early, well ahead of deadlines, and when the writing doesn't flow, I step away from it, returning again and again until it comes easily. Unlike the schoolteacher's dictum, "Hard writing makes easy reading," for me, easy writing makes easy reading.

## The habit of velocity

I write fast. On a good day I am the boy on the bicycle wobbling downhill so fast his feet are off the pedals, and he is out of control. That's how I want to write, with such velocity that my typing is bad, my grammar ain't, and my spelling is worse; I want to write what I do not know in ways I have not written. I need to speed ahead of the censor and write so fast that my velocity causes the accidents of insight and language that make good writing.

I might write:

There is tak of land war and I am sitt in a wrm room in my house stil surprised that the dancing shells passed by me [me by?]. Outsde winter woods like the snow woods in whch I fout and I fd my fingers rubb together nervously. What are they doing? I know. It is that bone, smooth, [by yrs?], I find when I dig a foxhole under shell fire, digging like md, crujnhing dwn. It is human, a kull, leg, some part of a man. I remember a txtbk. This was a battlefield in the First World War and this the bone is part of a soldier who fell was killed, shlld?, here in this fld in that war.

I know all that is wrong with that chunk of prose—the typing, the spelling, the awkward language—but it is leading me toward meaning, making me go deeper and deeper into experience. The switch to the present tense, for example, commands me to go back in time until it is immediate and take the reader with me.

I wrote that fast and the speed took me where I did not expect to go. Now I have some writing to do.

29

## The habit of revision

I am in the habit of revision, but I do not try to correct error as much as I try to discover the strength of the draft and try to make it stronger. One of the habits that is most successful for me these days is to layer or overwrite, putting the draft on the computer screen and then writing over it. Here I will demonstrate that technique by saving, with a line drawn through it, what I would simply delete.

~~There is tak of land war and I am sitt in a wrm room in my house stil surprised that t~~ The dancing shells passed by ~~me [by me?].~~ this time. I dig faster, deeper. The shells will return. My shovel hits a rock, no something else. I pull it free it is ~~Outsde winter woods like the snow woods in wheh I fout and I fd my fingers rubb together nervously. What are they doing? I know. It is that~~ bone. I put my entrenching tool down and rub my hand over it, it is curved, **smooth, [by yrs?], I find when I dig a foxhole under shell fire, digging like md, crujnhing dwn. It is human, a kull, leg, some part of a man.** the back end of a human skull and suddenly I am back in school listening to the professor drone through European History. **I remember** a place on a map and realize I am there. It is a ~~txtbk. This was~~ a **battlefield in the First World War and** in **this** lonely hour in combat I have found my companion ~~the bone is part of a~~ soldier ~~who fell was killed, shlld?, here in this fld in that war.~~ with whom I share the shell's return.

When I copy it out, you can share the text I found:

The dancing shells pass by this time. I dig faster, deeper. The shells will return. My shovel hits a rock, no, something else. I pull it free. It is bone. I put my entrenching tool down and rub my hand over it. It is curved, smooth, the back end of a human skull and suddenly I am back in school listening to the professor drone through European History. I remember a place on a map and realize I am there. It was a battlefield in the First World War and in this lonely hour in combat I have found my companion soldier with whom I share the shell's return.

That may develop into a column, find a place in the novel, become a poem, but now that I have rediscovered that fragment of bone I am sure it will develop into a piece of writing—and be revised again to fit its purpose.

## The habit of completion

I wrote but did not submit. Then I met Minnie Mae Emmerich. She is of German descent and does not believe in waste. She sent off something I had thrown away, and it was published. I learned the lesson of completion: A piece of writing is not finished until it is submitted for publication as many times as is necessary for it to appear in print.

I learned the lesson, but I need to relearn it. Forty years later, the poet Mekeel McBride read some poems I had discarded, commanded me to submit them, and some were published. Now I am rededicated to the habit of completion—and submission. I use the mails, submitting what I write to the best market first and, when it comes back, to another and another and another.

Consider my habits, but develop your own by studying what you did when the writing went well, and make what you discover your own writing habits.

# 8

## Are You Ready for a Writing Course?

### By Madeena Spray Nolan

IF YOU ARE NOT SURE WHETHER YOUR FORTE IS poetry or prose, or whether you want to write for fun or find a market fast, no course can teach you much that will be of use to you. Your first step, therefore, must be to decide on your own what you want to write. Take some time to explore this, to see if your interest is in poetry, or fiction, or perhaps serious or humorous essays.

What if, having dabbled on your own, you still are not sure whether it is poetry or essays that you most enjoy? In that case, take a course in each, first one, then another. For the duration of each course, concentrate on that field. Immerse yourself in various poetic modes, or in the various possibilities of a well-written essay. You don't have to settle on one field: Many writers have written poetry and prose. But you should give yourself an opportunity to explore the different fields extensively, not just switch every time the going gets a bit sticky and never quite finishing anything.

Let's assume you have settled on one category. You love to read novels and to make up stories about the people you see on the street. You even have a story in the back of your mind, wanting to be told. Obviously, you decide, fiction is your field. You start out bravely. Then, along about Chapter Three, you can't figure out what's wrong, what should happen next. Now, you are ready for a writing course. But, as John Gardner says, "About all that is required is that the would-be writer understand clearly what it is that he wants to become and *what he must do to become it*" (emphasis mine).

A writing course can help you motivate your characters, but it cannot supply you with motivation. Even though you have settled on the field you want to pursue, if you can't get yourself to sit at the typewriter or word processor and put words down on paper, day after day, no writing course can provide a miracle cure. You have to come up with ways of spurring yourself on. It isn't easy in the beginning, and it doesn't really get any easier. No magic secret drives a writer to his or her desk, brain seething with ideas. It takes hard work.

Set aside time each day, even if only an hour, and put some words on paper. Use the fact that you want to have something to read in class as an initial motivating factor. Pin these words by Flannery O'Connor over your desk, or where you will see them daily: "I'm a full-time believer in writing habits, pedestrian as it all may sound. You may be able to do without them if you have genius, but most of us only have talent, and this is simply something that has to be assisted all the time by physical and mental habits, or it dries up and blows away." If you are serious, you must supply your own motivation: It might as well be now.

To repeat, a writing course can help you with the problems, the techniques, and the basics of whatever field you are working in; it can help you sharpen your skills, but it cannot tell you what to write.

One way a writing course *can* help you most is in exposing your work to intelligent criticism. Many writers, perhaps most, begin by showing a relative or close friend what they've written. It is usually someone who will think everything they write is marvelous. But if you are serious about writing, you must move out of this uncritical, comfortable atmosphere to where you can hear some truths about your weaknesses as well as your strengths.

Some years ago, when I finished reading a short story I'd written to the class, I waited through the painful moment of silence that always follows. Finally, one member asked politely, "Are we supposed to like these people?" I was devastated. I felt my characters—who were, of course, supposed to be likable—had been insulted. I vowed I would never subject myself to such abuse again. I was, however, back at the next session, ready for more.

Criticism hurts. The idea of holding your deeply felt writing up for criticism by strangers can be terrifying. Yet, submitting your work to such criticism is one of the best ways to pinpoint problem areas. There is a myth that true writers work in total isolation, until the day their work is ready to be sent to the publisher. But, in fact, most writers have had at least one respected contemporary to whom they showed their writing along the way.

F. Scott Fitzgerald regularly showed works-in-progress to his friends.

And, as their letters of reply make clear, he chose as critics friends—such as Hemingway—who were quite willing to tell him if they did not like what they read. Sylvia Plath took a class from Robert Lowell and sought the advice of Lowell and of Anne Sexton.

We do not all have the opportunity of getting a Robert Lowell or an Anne Sexton or Ernest Hemingway to criticize our efforts. But students in a serious writing class can be an excellent audience. They know they can learn from your mistakes as well as from their own, and from your strong points, as well.

Of course, if the criticism you receive is sniping, petty, or personal, you should leave the group. Having your work held up to ridicule will not help the work, and it can only hurt you. But for the most part, you will find your instructor and your fellow students to be sincere in their comments.

Listen to the criticism offered with all the objectivity you can muster. Take notes. You may love your main character and initially feel hurt that no one else can see her extraordinary qualities from the character sketch you wrote. However, it might be true that you know her so well you neglected to add all the details—some negative but human—that would have made her convincing to others. After a critical session, put your work away and reread it the next day, keeping the criticism in mind. You will be surprised how often you find at least some truth in it.

Listen with a critical ear to what is read by others in the course. Does the writer capture place particularly well? How does he or she do that? Are you suddenly aware of an awkward shift in viewpoint or tone? After several sessions, you will find yourself reading everything you come upon—including your own work—with a more acute sense of what effective writing is and what makes it so.

Writing courses can be of immense help to the beginning or practicing writer. But they can only *help*. Becoming a writer—someone who works at writing regularly, who sets a goal and works steadily toward it, who welcomes and can profit by constructive criticism—can be accomplished by no one but you.

# 9

# The Writer's Eye

## By Randall Silvis

A PART of every successful writer is, and must be, amoral. Detached. Unfeeling. As nonjudgmental as a tape recorder or camera. It is this capacity to stare at pain or ugliness without flinching, at beauty without swooning, at flattery and truth without succumbing to the lure of either, which provides the mortar, the observable details, to strengthen a story and make it a cohesive unit. This capacity I call the writer's eye.

As a child, I was and still am fascinated by the peaks and valleys of people's lives. I was blessed—or cursed—with what was often referred to as "morbid curiosity." At the scene of a funeral, I would be the one trying to inch a bit closer to the coffin, one ear turned to the dry intonations droning from the minister; the other to the papery rustle of leaves overhead. I would take note of how the mourners were standing, where they held their hands, if there were any clouds in the sky, who wept and who did not even pretend to weep, which shoes were most brilliantly shined, the color of the casket, the scent of smoke from someone's backyard barbecue, a killdeer whistling in the distance.

This is how I would remember and record the day, the event. In the details themselves, unbiased, unvarnished and pure, was every nuance of emotion such a tragedy produced. The same held true for weddings and baptisms, for joyous moments as well as sad. Almost instinctively I seemed to know that every abstraction had an observable form: To remark that my neighbor, a tired and lonely man, was drunk again, said nothing; to say that he was standing by the side of the road, motionless but for his gentle, oblivious swaying even as the cars zipped by and blasted their horns at him, his head down, eyes half-closed, hands shoved deep in his pockets as he sang a mumbled "Meet Me Tonight in Dreamland," said it all.

The writer's eye discriminates. It does not and cannot record every detail in a particular scene, only the most telling ones. It is microscopic

35

in focus, telescopic in intent. If, for example, you wish to depict a woman who is trying to look poised despite her nervousness, does it deepen the depiction to say that she wears a two-carat diamond ring on her left hand? Probably not. But if she is shown sitting very straight, knees and feet together, a pleasant smile on her lips as her right hand unconsciously and repeatedly pulls at and twists the diamond ring on her left? These details are in and of themselves emotionally pallid, but in sum, they add to a colorful, revealing whole. In such a description, the word *nervous* need never be uttered. Yet the conclusion is inescapable, and all the more acute because the reader has not been informed of the woman's uneasiness but has witnessed it for himself.

In my novel *Excelsior* (Henry Holt, October, 1987), one of the most important scenes is a moment of closeness between an inept father and his six-year-old son. The scene takes place in a YMCA locker room minutes after the father accidentally knocked the terrified boy, who cannot swim, into the pool. Bloomhardt, the father, despises himself for his own incompetence, and believes that his son does, too. But during a rare moment of openness, six-year-old Timmy admits *his* feelings of frustration and failure. At this point, it would have been quick and easy to state simply that Bloomhardt was relieved, grateful that his son did not despise him, and was filled with a fervent, though awkward, desire to reassure the boy. Instead, I chose to show his state of mind as evidenced in observable details:

Bloomhardt blinked, his eyes warm with tears. He leaned sideways and kissed his son's damp head. . . . He faced his open locker again, reached for a sock and pulled it on. He smiled to himself.

Bloomhardt's actions are elemental and, on their own, nearly empty of emotional value. But in the context of this passage and in relation to the man's and boy's characters as defined prior to this scene, these details are all that are needed to show the beginnings of a mutual tenderness, trust, and love.

The writer's eye is not merely one sense, but every power of observation the writer possesses. It not only sees, but also smells, tastes, feels, and hears. It also senses which details will paint the brightest picture, which will hint at an unseen quality, which will allow the reader to see beneath the surface of a character to the ice and fire of emotion within.

Think of each phrase of description, each detail, as a dot of color on a Seurat landscape. Individually, each dot is meaningless, it reveals nothing, neither laughter nor sorrow. But if you choose your dots carefully and arrange them on the canvas in their proper places, you might, with luck and practice, compose a scene to take the breath away.

# 10

## MUCH ADO ABOUT PROCESS

### BY CANDICE ROWE

THE PROCESS OF WRITING IS AS DISTINCTIVE to a writer as voice, word choice, world view, in essence, all those elements that add up to a writer's finished work. In addition to being highly personal and idiosyncratic, process is flexible. A writer can write one piece quite successfully with one process and find that another approach is more workable with another. In this spirit of individuality and flexibility, here's a partial list of different approaches to the process of writing intended only to suggest the range employed by creative writers.

*The shopping list compiler:* This writer has down the basic shape of the work, whether it be a short story or novel. The writer then fills in the gaps in a haphazard or logical way until the project is completed. Vladimir Nabokov writes, "The pattern of the thing precedes the thing. I fill in the gaps of the crossword at any spot I happen to choose. These bits I write on index cards until the novel is done." Amy Tan revealed in an interview that her agent asked her to write a proposal for a book, so Tan spent "a few hours creating a two-sentence summary of each chapter." After the book was placed, she went back, and with alternating voices of a mother and a daughter, fleshed out those lines into *The Joy Luck Club*.

*The planner:* This writer knows exactly where he or she is going every step of the way. Planners are rigorous to various degrees. Some plan or outline an entire novel in a couple of pages. Others make extensive outlines that detail development of the work scene by scene. More preparation is done by the planner than by the shopping lister. For example, these writers include actual bits of dialogue, descriptions, and so forth. Where the writer "begins" is also flexible. Aristotle recommends that the writer begin in the middle of things. John Irving emphatically states that writing process is not an unfolding mystery. Irving explains, "I not only know the end of the novel, but the end of the chapter before I begin the chapter, the end of the scene before I begin the scene." This knowledge gives the writer what Irving calls "absolute authority."

*The blind faith believer:* These writers just do it. They sit down at the machine or with a pad of paper and there is no fear of the white page. In fact, this phrase and its connotation of drawing a freezing blank puzzles them. The white page is an opportunity, a fresh snowfall ready for footprints. Ann Beattie has said that she writes five or six pages, and if it doesn't work, she trashes it without recrimination. Likewise, Raymond Carver explained how he started a story with a perfect opening line and worked confidently from that point.

*Kitchen sinkers:* These madcaps throw in everything and worry about editing another day. No problem with the editor leaning too heavily on the shoulder here. Frank O'Connor explains this approach: "I write any sort of rubbish which will cover the main outlines of the story, then I can begin to see it."

*The explorers:* Closely related to the sinkers are the explorers. For these writers, process is a journey of discovery. Joyce Carol Oates illuminates process when she states that writers throw themselves into their work, "writing eight or ten hours at a time, writing in our daydreams, composing in our sleep, we enter that fictional world so deeply that time seems to warp or to fold back in upon itself." And in an article appearing a few years ago in *Esquire,* John Gregory Dunne explores "How to Write a Novel," by detailing how everyday events, observations, and sensations become part of the writer's creative world and fodder for work immediately.

*Excessive drafters:* Susan Sontag wonders if your first draft has "only a few elements worth keeping." And Joy Williams, recalling Isaac Babel, talks about removing every speck of mud from a manuscript through excessive revision.

*The incredibly confident writer:* These writers write quickly a draft that does not need changes. John Updike is an example. He has never been one, as he puts it, for "agonizing much."

*The writer/editor in concert:* Here is a different species from the sinkers. This poor soul writes one page, slowly, painfully, word by word. Anthony Burgess explains that this process is one way of producing a novel "that doesn't . . . need any revision." Lynn Emanuel, who won the National Poetry Series Award, writes about how revision "confronts us moment to moment in writing as composition, a vision. And that is all vision is: revisions coming at the speed of light."

*The one-sitting-wonder:* "I always write a story in one sitting," Katherine Anne Porter is quoted as saying. Richard Bausch explains how after one false start, "The Fireman's Wife" wrote itself in "fewer than six days."

As we consider these approaches to the process of writing, perhaps what we should take away from our cursory look here is that the process is distinctive to the writer and distinctive to the individual project. The best advice to offer a writer new to this whole business of creating is to try everything and see what works. Try free writing and sinking. Then try to be more structured and organized. If a writer is producing and is satisfied (within normal human bounds, of course), why tamper with success? Process is indeed idiosyncratic and most importantly flexible. Whatever works, works.

# 11

## Waiting for Inspiration

### By Peggy Rynk

MANY WRITERS, ESPECIALLY BEGINNERS, OFTEN HAVE the notion that to write well they must be inspired.

That notion is wrong.

The belief persists that simply sitting down and writing without feeling inspired is not real writing, but hack work.

That notion is also wrong.

The truth is that most of what we read on the printed page, whether in books, newspapers, magazines, or whatever, was written by someone who just sat down and wrote it. That's the way the work gets done.

Do we have to feel inspired to pass an exam, get a degree, parent our children, do brain surgery, or fix a leaky faucet? Of course not. Neither must we feel inspired in order to write and write well. A good part of writing well depends on practice. If you wait to practice until you feel inspired, you will write very little.

One writer I know pens stories with well-rounded characters, plot lines that move the reader happily along and that are a pleasure to read. But in the years I've known her, she's finished few of them. Why? She says she runs out of inspiration before she reaches the final page. Her unfinished, unpolished manuscripts gather dust, not checks. At the rate she's going, she'll never see her byline anywhere.

What makes this "inspiration" nonsense even worse is that some writers have decided that inspiration is something mysterious that can't be harnessed. They think of it as some irresistible, magnetic force that draws them to the typewriter or keyboard where they then have no choice but to get it down on paper. And what happens when this force is missing? Why, of course, they can't do anything!

You're welcome to wait for inspiration if you prefer to, but you must recognize that waiting is an excuse not to write, not a reason. Why not write something while you're waiting and see how it turns out? Nobody

41

says you have to send it anywhere, or even keep it. You can toss it later if it turns out limp, lifeless, and dull.

But maybe when you read the work over later, it will contain something good, something unexpected, something you hadn't even realized you were thinking when you wrote it. Maybe it'll be worth polishing and submitting. Maybe an editor will buy it.

It's true that sometimes when you write, you feel as if you're being guided by some influence outside yourself. The words seem to flow onto the page almost by themselves, and they give you a warm glow of satisfaction. The next day when you read over what you've done, your writing may live up to your hopes and be a truly fine piece of work. This can be a heady experience—something like falling in love. It's great when it happens, but don't count on it to be an everyday occurrence.

More often, the writing you produce on demand is just as good, just as salable, and certainly more abundant because your creative energies are always flowing on one level or another, whether you're conscious of feeling those energies or not.

"But if I don't *feel* anything," you might ask, "what am I supposed to write about? What if my mind is a blank?"

These are good questions, and they have good answers. One is to read widely, copiously, so that your mind is constantly packed with facts, thoughts, questions, characters, suppositions, and what-ifs. Writing comes from what you know, what you think, and what you imagine, and these come from your store of information.

Another answer is to keep an idea file. When something occurs to you—a subject for an article, a plot twist for a novel or short story, an interesting character trait, an appealing phrase, even a question you'd like an answer to—jot it down. Keep these ideas and snippets on index cards, bits of scrap paper, scribbled in a notebook—whatever suits you. Then on days when you can't think of anything to write about, you will have something to work on. All you have to do is sit down and write. You're in business again.

A writing teacher I know gets his students off and writing with an exercise that piques the imagination. He'll ask the class for possible story titles—ordinary or odd, sane or lunatic—then writes them on the board. Out of those listed, he selects five. Each student then picks one and writes a story using it as a starting point. The story can move in any direction; it can be funny, serious, poignant, sassy. But by the next week each student must have written a story.

42

Come up with your own list of titles, right off the top of your head. Don't dig for them. Then use the list as a springboard to write a story, an article, a poem, an essay, or anything else. The results may surprise you.

If one title turns out to be a dead end, try another. Soon one will click. In the meantime, you'll gain practice and discipline, both of which are necessities for writers.

Each day set yourself a realistic goal—to write five pages, for example—and don't quit until you've reached it. If one page is more reasonable for you because of other responsibilities, that's fine, too. Don't set your goal as minutes or hours spent working; it's too easy to waste that time looking up one last fact, changing your margins, or when desperate, searching for a new pen.

If you meet this goal every day, five days a week, at the end of a month you'll have completed a substantial amount of work, an accomplishment you can see and touch, review and polish, not because you waited for inspiration, but because you didn't.

The more experience you have at practicing your craft, the easier the words and ideas will flow—much like learning to type, to play tennis, or to drive a car. Before long, you'll be able to produce high quality writing almost anywhere, almost anytime, and under almost any circumstance.

# 12

# SIX MYTHS THAT HAUNT WRITERS

## BY KENNETH T. HENSON

AMONG THE MANY THINGS I have learned in conducting writers workshops on campuses across the country is that there are several false ideas, myths, that haunt most writers and often impede and/or block beginners. The following are six of these myths—and some suggestions for dealing with them.

1. *I'm not sure I have what it takes.*

I have found that on each campus, coast to coast, there is a superstar writer who, I am assured, has only to put his fingers to the keyboard or pen to paper and, presto, words, sentences, and paragraphs—publishable ones—flow. And, it is thought, these creations are effortless.

These tales are as ridiculous as ghost stories, but more damaging, since most people *believe* them. And like ghost stories, their purpose is to frighten.

If I were a beginning writer and believed that writing comes so effortlessly to some, I would be totally discouraged.

You admit that you, too, have heard of such a superwriter? You may even know such a person by name. Well, don't believe it. It's probably the creation of a person who doesn't intend to write and therefore would prefer that you don't either. The next time someone mentions this super-person, think of Ernest Hemingway, who wrote the last chapter of *Farewell to Arms* 119 times. Or think of the following definitions of writing: "Writing is 10 per cent inspiration and 90 per cent perspiration" and "Successful writing is the ability to apply the seat of the pants to the seat of the chair." Contrary to the myth, all writers perspire; some even sweat!

2. *I don't have time to write.*

You have heard this many times, and if you're like most of us, you have even said it yourself: "If only I had time to write." Ironically, most would-be writers have more time to write than most successful writers do. Some writers even have 24 hours a day to do as they please. But they represent only a small fraction of all writers. The vast majority of writers are free lancers who have either part-time or full-time jobs and pick up a few extra dollars, a little prestige, and a lot of personal satisfaction through writing articles.

The reason behind the bold statement that you have more time than most successful writers have to write is that, probably like you, most of them must earn a living some other way. Yet, these individuals have allotted themselves some time for writing: they took it away from their other activities. Good writers don't *make* time, and they don't *find* time. Rather, they reassign part of their time to writing. And that part of their lives is usually some of their leisure time.

I don't suggest that you stop golfing or fishing or jogging or watching TV, but if you are to be a successful writer, you must give up part of the time you spend (or waste) in the coffee room or bar and you must also give up the idea that you are too tired to write or that watching a mediocre TV show relaxes you. Writing is far more relaxing to most of us who return from our work emotionally drained; it provides an outlet for frustrations, a far more effective release than our more passive attempts to escape from them.

The next time you hear people say, "I don't have time to write" or "I would write for publication if I had time," observe how those persons are spending their time at that moment. If writing is really important to you, replace the activities that are less important with writing. Let your friends and family know that this is your writing time and that you're not to be disturbed. Then tell yourself the same thing. Disciplined people have much more time than do undisciplined people.

3. *I don't have anything worth writing about.*

We've all heard this for years. A significant percentage of aspiring writers really believe that they don't know anything that is worthy of publication. If you are one of them, you're not learning from your experiences: either you don't make mistakes or you don't adjust your behavior to avoid repeating them.

The truth is that you possess a lot of knowledge that would be valuable to others. And you have the abilities that successful writers have to research the topics you wish to write about. I don't know any successful writers who don't feel that they need to research their topics. Start with the subjects that are most familiar, then enrich your knowledge of these subjects by periodic trips to the library, or by interviewing people, or by conducting surveys on these topics.

4. *The editors will reject my manuscript because my name isn't familiar to them.*

Of all the excuses that would-be writers give for not writing, none is weaker than, "If my name were James Michener or Stephen King, editors would listen to me."

But these people don't consider the fact that the Micheners and Kings didn't always have famous names; they started as unknowns and made their names known through talent and hard work. And they would probably be first to say that they have to keep earning their recognition through hard work. Of course, these writers have unusual talent, but you can be equally sure that they work hard and continue to do so to sharpen their skills, research their topics meticulously, and to create and invent new, fresh ways to express their ideas.

There's no guarantee that any of us can earn similar status and acclaim, but we can improve our expertise in our areas of interest and improve our communication skills.

5. *My vocabulary and writing skills are too limited.*

Many people equate jargon, unfamiliar words, complex sentence structure, and long paragraphs with good writing. Actually, though a good vocabulary is a great asset to writers, so are dictionaries and thesauruses, for those who know how to use them and who are willing to take the time to do so. Jargon and long sentences and unnecessarily complex paragraphs harm writing more than they help it.

The sooner you replace words like *utilize* and *prioritize* with words like *use* and *rank,* the faster your writing will improve. Remember, your job is to communicate. Don't try to impress the editor. Editors know what their readers want, and readers seldom demand jargon and complexity.

6. *In my field there are few opportunities to publish.*

If your area of specialization has few professional journals (actually, some fields have only one or two), you may feel trapped, knowing that this uneven supply/demand ratio drives up the competition for these journals.

You might deal with this by searching for more general journals that cover your field, or journals whose editors often welcome articles written by experts in outside but related fields. For example, a biologist or botanist might turn to wildlife magazines, U.S. or state departments of conservation publications, forestry magazines, hunting and fishing publications, or magazines for campers and hikers.

Again, you could consider writing for other audiences, expanding your areas of expertise by taking courses in other disciplines, reading widely, and doing research in other fields to help you develop a broader range of subjects to write about.

Some fields have more journals than others, and some writers are luckier (and more talented) than others. But for those who are willing to work hard at their craft, writing offers a way to reach many professional and personal goals.

# 13

## KEEPING A WRITER'S JOURNAL

### BY MARJORIE PELLEGRINO, LYNNE WEINBERG-HILL, AND TAMA WHITE

FOR MANY WRITERS, THE JOURNAL IS MORE THAN A DIARY recording life's events. It is an essential tool resulting in deeper thinking. Writing about things outside yourself from an introspective point of view allows you to reach into your core to discover untapped resources. The journal is a place to find your voice, to experiment and play, to be alone with yourself.

Here are some suggestions—not rules—on how to keep a journal, what to write in it, and how the raw material you produce can be transformed into nonfiction, fiction, and poetry.

Use a notebook that doesn't restrict your writing. A loose-leaf offers more freedom than a small, dated diary. You can insert pages from your computer, magazine articles, letters, excerpts from books, even notes made on the backs of envelopes.

Date your entries, but don't worry about writing every day. Read aloud what you have written to discover the emotion beneath the words, but keep your journal private. If you decide to share what you have written, make a copy.

Here are some ideas to stimulate and enrich your journal writing.

- Dig deep. Sit in silence a few moments before you begin, and record what you really care about.
- Tell the truth, even if you have to write in code.
- Write quickly, so you don't know what's coming next.
- Turn off the censor in your head.
- Learn to be observant. Write down six things you notice each day.
- Write from different points of view to broaden your sympathies.
- Collect quotations that inspire you, and jot down a few notes on why they do.

48

- Set goals, and keep track of your progress.
- Record your dreams. Ask what the symbols remind you of, and describe what you think the dream is telling you.
- Use your journal as a non-judgmental friend to listen to your angry or confused thoughts.
- Make a list of the things you love. Note how often you make time for them.
- When words won't come, draw something—anything.
- Dedicate an entry to your muse or to a person you admire.
- Don't worry about being nice, fair, or objective. Be selfish and biased; give your side of the story from the heart.
- Write even what frightens you, *especially* what frightens you. It is the thought denied that is dangerous.
- Don't worry about being consistent. You are large; you contain multitudes.

## Nonfiction

Well-crafted nonfiction excites and informs. The reader is drawn into the piece by an edge, an undercurrent, and kept involved by the flow of ideas. For nonfiction writing that sparkles, journal writing offers the essential ingredients, capturing the emotion of an idea, theme, or event. It locks in details that would otherwise vanish over time.

Two of my strongest nonfiction pieces, "September Sunday" and "Reunion," grew directly from journal entries. During a three-month period when my brother faced a life-threatening illness, I wrote in my journal every day to keep myself centered. Those pages resulted in a published poem, an article, an inspirational piece, and a nonfiction book proposal. Organizing, filling out, and editing came later, but the part that moved the reader found its voice in my journal.

While sometimes I pull an essay from my journal, other times I have a work-in-progress and use the journal process to edit, organize, or find a focus. I might ask myself, "Why am I writing this article? What is it about? What are the most important things the reader should know?" Through this exploratory writing, the thread of a meandering piece becomes clearer, and I'm more aware of excess baggage that needs to be lightened, or an essential point that needs to be moved to the forefront.

I also use my journal to focus nonfiction ideas that I will then develop

49

into queries. A remark by a neighborhood child about my family's bike helmets resulted in several journal pages. I then decided to write a piece on bike safety, feeling that if as a parent I was concerned about how children could learn to be safe bike riders, other parents would probably be concerned as well.

## Creating fiction

Fiction grows from the writer's imagination, but the seeds of the story can often be found in the writer's life. A scene, an event, a character, a remark overheard, can start those seeds growing.

Long before I became a fiction writer, I began keeping a journal. I recorded events of the day, feelings, settings, scenes, even dialogue. I didn't write in my journal every day, sometimes not even every week.

As I began taking my writing seriously, I used my journal as a compost heap, throwing in everything I wanted to recycle. Now when I'm writing a story and need fresh details from a long-ago scene, I can locate that memory in my journal.

For instance, when I went to court for a traffic violation, I described the courtroom in my journal, noting the high ceiling, wood paneling, flags, and signs on tables. In my first published story, "Walkers and Other Tribes," I used those details in a pivotal scene. Epi, an older Hispanic woman, has chosen to go to court alone and plead "not guilty" for having her dog off-leash in the park. Details enhanced the tension:

In the courtroom, Epi takes a seat on a low pew. The room is huge under a 30-foot-high ceiling, outlined by wood paneling. The judge faces into the room, behind a large bench, an American flag to his right and an Arizona flag on his left. Two large tables separate him from the wooden pews. The first table has a sign reading *plaintiff*. The second table says *defendant*.

Along with everything else I put into my journal, I record my dreams. While I was writing my second published story, "Roadrunner," I recorded this dream:

I was captured by Palestinian terrorists. Other captives and I were being driven in a mini-van. . . . Then I realized none of the terrorists were in the car. I suggested we not drive to the destined spot, but flee instead. Everyone agreed. I felt a moment of relief. When the driver turned the van in another direction, the terrorists shot him.

In my story, the character receives an unsettling call late in the evening. I framed the dream passage with, "I had a hard time falling asleep and then dreamed an odd dream," and ended with, "I found a microphone hidden on the front seat and wondered at my naivete. To think I could do combat with terrorists."

Not only does your journal help you understand what is currently going on in your life, it offers perspective on the past. As you dig through your journals, you rediscover old friends, buried feelings, past events, and forgotten details. With distance and insight, your life, as recorded in your journal, can yield many fiction possibilities.

## Inventing poetry

Half of my journal entries are records of dream or waking reverie and are full of images and symbols coming directly from the unconscious. Capturing these images in a journal is the first step in the writing of poetry.

I use this type of journal entry in several ways. Most often I take an index card and lay it vertically on the left side of my journal pages, cutting off the first two to four words of each line. Reading down the page gives me such phrases as "standing at the top of my head." (You can use these in one poem, or you may choose just one as a jumping-off point or poem title.) That's how I came up with the titles "This Dream, A Road in the Mirror" and "This Elevator Could Be Considered." The middle of lines can be isolated using two cards, one on either side, and, of course, the ends of lines are equally useful.

A related method involves photocopying a page from my journal and tearing it into small pieces, each containing a few words that can be used together, as in the index card method. In that way, I created the title of my first published poem, "Grandmother, Do You Think Like Roses?"

"What I did today" journal entries can be used in similar ways or can serve as take-off points for longer, narrative poems, and even for a series of related poems revolving around a group of characters (suitably disguised, of course). A loose-leaf notebook is again useful, allowing you to remove pages and set them side by side, so that new lines can be constructed by reading across from one page to the next.

Journal writing is what keeps me going during dry spells. Even when I am producing little finished work, the time spent on my journal entries is not a total loss, as I have produced dozens and dozens of pages of raw material to work from when inspiration strikes anew.

# 14

## BRING YOUR IMAGINATION BACK TO LIFE

### BY CYNTHIA K. JONES

YOU ROLL A CLEAN SHEET OF PAPER into your typewriter, then sit staring at it, your mind a total blank. Frustration begins to build as minutes tick by and not one fresh idea comes to mind. The minutes stretch into an hour, and still nothing. In other words, your imagination is dead. To bring it back to life—almost instantly—take a stroll through a graveyard.

Yes, a graveyard. It needn't be large, but it should be old. Wander among the headstones, and don't just read what's written on them; study them, and ask plenty of questions, for every headstone is a story, somebody's story that could become your story with just a little probing.

In an old church cemetery rests Jonathan David West, who died at age 18 months. His headstone reads "John-John, gone so soon." And although he died over 40 years ago his grave is neat, cared for, and boasts fresh flowers. The work of the mother? The father? The still grieving sister who took care of him after their mother's death in childbirth? Or could it be the doing of a remorseful person who felt responsible for the baby's death?

In that same cemetery, there is another grave—small, crude, neglected, at least in appearance. But on several Sundays you notice a woman—old, unkempt, obviously poor—who comes to visit it. She always takes a creased and faded photograph out of the pocket in her frayed sweater and holds it to her heart as she stands silent over the grave. What is *her* story? But more important, what do you *imagine* is her story?

Why is James Johnson buried beside his first wife while his second wife and widow is buried alone 30 feet away? Did his children so hate her that they refused to allow her to be laid to rest beside their father? Or did the widow come to so hate her husband—who continually praised his first wife—that she insisted on not being buried with him—and *her*?

Why did sisters Lucy, Jane and Mary never marry although they lived into their eighties? Too good for the rural boys of that small town? Or would no one have them in spite of their money?

And can you imagine the life of "Red," whose 1884 headstone declares that he was "legally hanged"? And was Anna Lee Smithson really a traitor at the age of 17, as her headstone claims? Or is her coffin empty, and her "death" was only a ploy designed to smoke out the real traitor? If so, what happened to Anna?

Even a seemingly ordinary headstone can set the imagination flying. Mary Ann Jones died in Virginia in 1926, just two weeks shy of her sixteenth birthday. Her headstone is large and very elaborate, suggesting that she was from a wealthy family. Think back over the years. Can you see Mary Ann, her mother, and grandmother, as they excitedly plan her "coming-out" party—an expected event for girls of wealthy families during that period. Can you imagine Mary Ann as she lies awake at night dreaming of her party—only two weeks away now! Do you feel her girlish excitement as she dreams of a certain young man, hoping he will ask to court her? For a novelist, Mary Ann doesn't have to die, and the party doesn't have to be canceled. In fact, Mary Ann could and should have a future far beyond anything she could have dreamed of.

Bring the dead back to life. Three-year-old Jennie died in 1893. Imagine her on her deathbed, feverish and weak, her small hand clasped in her 20-year-old mother's already work-roughened one, pleading in a small tired voice, "Mama, help me." The mother knows there's nothing she can do for her daughter. Can you see her valiant, reassuring smile? Can you feel the constriction in her throat as she answers, "Drink some water, dear, then get some sleep. You'll feel better soon. Mama loves you." We know the child dies, but how did her death affect her mother and the rest of the family? If you're a writer, you know they didn't just carry on as before.

Gravestone names can stir the imagination in many ways. Abraham McBain died at the age of 71, a bachelor. With a name like that he might have had a Jewish mother and an Irish Catholic father. Would neither group accept him and allow him to marry their daughters? Did he spend his life embittered, self-pitying, resigned, or well-adjusted? What kind of life did his parents have together?

In Montana in 1823 Kitty Morgan died, along with her two-year-old

53

twins. What might have happened to them? Were they killed fighting Indians, disease, starvation, or by bandits? What were they doing that far West so early in our nation's history? Were they on their way back East, or firmly settled?

Captain David Wilson, a veteran of the Revolutionary War, is buried in a small fenced-in section of a tiny graveyard in South Georgia, along with his three wives and five infant daughters. What might their story be? Anything you want it to be, and if you're imagining, you can imagine anything.

Family graveyards can be especially interesting, particularly to those writing multi-generational novels. What would your imagination conjure up if you found a family graveyard neatly divided in half, the immediate family on one side and the daughters- and sons-in-law on the other? You might not want to be a part of such a family, but you might want to write about them.

Don't just read the engravings on the headstones, read *into* them. Tom Johnson's headstone claims he was a veteran of the Spanish American War, which ended when he was fourteen years old. What about the headstone that says, "He was ninety years old, and it was time for him to go"? A family glad to be rid of a burden or a compassionate family relieved to see a loved one released from pain and suffering?

Is there a poem or scripture engraved on the headstone or just the bare facts? Compare, "Nancy Smith, beloved wife of David," to "Nancy Smith, wife of David Smith, born 1932, died 1967."

Question the dead, pry open their secrets, don't take anything you see at face value, and your imagination will come to life.

# 15

## CRITICISM: CAN YOU TAKE IT?

### BY LANCE E. WILCOX

WE WRITERS OFTEN FANCY OURSELVES THE loneliest of lone wolves. We delight to picture ourselves hidden away in our dusty garret or our remote New Hampshire cabin, giving birth to our works in sublime isolation. But this is curious when you consider that the business we're about is furiously social. We're trying to communicate. In our splendid solitude, we write and rewrite, polish and repolish, all in hopes of breaking through that solitude into the lives and minds of other people. Because writing is so social, it makes sense now and then to gather up our papers, leave our garret, and seek out other people's reactions to our work before even thinking of sending it to an editor. How best can we go about doing this?

Whenever you seek others' reactions to your work, your attitude toward your writing is especially important. Don't hand your manuscript to your reader and cry, "Here it is! Unworthy, presumptuous trash, I know! Tear it to pieces!" This sounds like humility, but it's really manipulation. It's a desperate and dishonest plea for mercy, and mercy is precisely what you don't need.

What you want to cultivate is a poised, matter-of-fact objectivity about yourself and your work. You already know, if you think about it, that everything you've ever written, and ever will write, could be better. There is always room for improvement. And once you get this firmly in your head, you won't be tempted to ask (a hopeful quaver in your voice), "Is it. . . . O.K?" but simply, "How does this work for you? What do you like and dislike? What parts catch your attention or give you trouble?" Then, when your reader does point out strengths and weaknesses, you won't be devastated. In fact, you'll probably face the task of rewriting with more confidence and energy than usual.

You're not obliged to get an expert's opinion. What you're after is a sample audience—not a brilliant, scholarly, authoritative critic, but just people who like to read, who are reasonably bright, and who won't either coddle or attack you. You're not seeking The Indisputable Truth about your piece, but simply how it works. Where is it interesting? Where is it confusing? Do your readers feel as if they're skiing down the slopes or trudging uphill through the sand?

You may, in fact, have to help your readers here. They may feel pressured to play English teacher, and you don't need that. All you ask is that they report their real felt reactions in as clear and honest a manner as possible. When your reader tells you, "I was really enjoying it up to this point, but right around here somewhere I started to bog down," or, "Edward intrigued me, but I never really knew what he wanted," that's when you know where to put your efforts in revision.

Your readers also at first may offer reactions that are vague, global, impressionistic. This isn't a bad place to start, but you will want to press them further. Try to draw them out on their reactions. Point to specific passages you yourself aren't sure about and get their reactions to those. Try to get them to pinpoint, as precisely as possible, what in your draft attracted them or turned them off, and why.

You will find as you do this striking differences among your acquaintances as to how much they actually help you. Some are nitpickers. Others are incapable of anything but diffuse, unhelpful praise. But still others will prove level-headed, frank, at once encouraging and incisive, and adept at saying just how they felt paragraph by paragraph as they were reading. Keep them around!

Finally—and this should go without saying—*never, under any circumstances, defend your work to your readers.* If your work bored them, it bored them. Don't try to convince them that, dullards as they are, they simply failed to see how fascinating it really is. If something on Page Three confused them, it confused them. Don't insult them by pointing out the perfectly lucid explanation on Page Two that they must have overlooked. When you're actually discussing your work, you're on a fact-finding mission. What did these words do for them or to them? You want to see the work through *their* eyes, not bully them into seeing it through yours.

So then, you've sought, listened to, and taken note of the reactions of a few capable readers to the draft you worked on so carefully. Now what? Well, first you curl up, whimper a bit, and lick your wounds. Secretly, we always hope we've written the loveliest sonnet since Yeats, the suavest essay since E. B. White, the truest story since Hemingway—and we haven't, and every time it's a disappointment.

Then dust yourself off, roll up your sleeves, and start back to work, rewriting again what you've already labored over so long. You needn't take all your readers' suggestions, but you should probably take most of them. As a rule, whatever flaws they report are really there—as you'd see for yourself if you were to file the piece away for six months and read it then. But the final responsibility is always yours and yours alone.

For the beginner, nothing makes real the sense of an audience . . . like an audience. For the pro, it's Continuing Education. But perhaps best of all, it continually reminds you that you're really not alone. You can hide in an igloo at the North Pole, and your readers are all huddled in there with you. Sometimes they may terrify you. But if you genuinely wish to do well by them—that is, to provide them good reading matter—you'll find, after all, that they're ready and able to help.

# § 16

## CORRESPONDENCE COURSES—
## ANYWHERE, ANYTIME

### By Joan E. Juskie-Nellis

I'VE BEEN TAKING CLASSES IN WRITING nonfiction and poetry part time for the past year and a half. One course in poetry taught by a widely published poet provided detailed critiques of my poetry. (I live in a small city that doesn't even have a college!) Too good to be true? No, it was by correspondence study!

Over 10,000 correspondence classes are offered by universities around the country, according to *The Independent Study Catalog,* a bible for people who wish to take correspondence classes. This catalog defines correspondence study as "individual instruction by mail" (also sometimes referred to as "independent study" or "home study"). Courses are listed by subject (look for writing classes under English or Journalism) and course title, and there are numerous possibilities for those who wish to learn to write, or improve their talent. Writing classes range from the introductory level to the more advanced critique-based workshops through the mail. You can find writing classes in fiction, poetry, and nonfiction (including some special genre areas like writing for children and journal writing), as well as in such supportive areas as grammar, editing, and expository writing.

Classes are offered noncredit, for undergraduate credit, and sometimes even for graduate credit. Tuition costs vary among institutions and programs: They range from about $70 for a short noncredit workshop to about $350 for a credit class at one of the more expensive institutions (some private schools may be even higher). Most programs

---

*The Independent Study Catalog, published by Peterson's Guides, for the National University Continuing Education Association. May be ordered directly from Peterson's, P.O. Box 2123, Princeton, NJ 08543-2123, (1-800-EDU-DATA), for $16.95, plus $4.75 for shipping and handling.

allow you to sign up any time of the year, but an occasional one will go by the academic year and allow you to sign up only during registration time. Most give you a year to complete the course, but some run for shorter periods. I'd recommend the same process I went through when I decided to enroll in correspondence classes:

(1) Get a copy of *The Independent Study Catalog* *(I.S.C.)*.

(2) Find out which institutions offer courses in subjects in which you are interested.

(3) Send for their catalogs (addresses are in *I.S.C.*). Some institutions have a separate course description sheet or a syllabus for specific classes. Ask for one when you request the catalog.

(4) Evaluate which course seems right for your current needs. Introductory or advanced? (You may want to write to the instructor if the catalog doesn't specify.) Some advanced courses, like good writing programs, may require you to submit a writing sample to be admitted to the class. How many submissions does the class require? I found one with eleven submissions a lot more valuable than one with only five. Also find out if they have a page limit per submission. In one, all my prose submissions were limited to three typed pages; it's hard to develop an article within that limitation. Make sure you're getting *writing* rather than *literature*.

(5) After you get your first assignment back, reevaluate the course. Is this the type of feedback you are looking for? Having the right instructor is a very important part of the process. If the teacher has a writing slant very different from yours, you may have trouble accomplishing your objectives. In this case, consider changing courses before you continue. Check the catalog for the institution's policy for dropping a course. Most allow you to drop out within the first month or so, and will refund the charge (minus a slight processing fee). I made the mistake once, when I was very disappointed with the quality of critique, to continue throughout the entire course. It made me less motivated to put everything into it, and consequently I learned less. I should have dropped the class after the first lesson.

When I first began to take correspondence classes, I sent for about twenty catalogs from different schools (and there are still a lot more out there to investigate). Here are some of the highlights of my research into writing classes. Because details of course cost and availability continually change, it is essential to write for the most recent catalogs.

59

- Indiana State University offers *Intro to Photojournalism,* a subject not often available through correspondence.
- Indiana University offers the usual creative writing classes in poetry, fiction, prose, and drama, some requiring twelve submissions.
- Oklahoma State University offers fiction writing (three credits) for $139.95, and poetry writing (three credits) for $148.00. (These prices may have increased since I did my research, but I found them among the lowest for credit classes.)
- Texas Tech University had some interesting noncredit classes for only $44.00: *Creative Autobiography; Write and Publish Stories, Books & Articles;* and *Express Yourself in Poetry.*
- University of California, Berkeley, offers the largest selection of writing classes I've found. In addition to all the usual ones, they have a number of unique classes: *Editorial Workshop* "develops your skill in copyediting reports, newsletters, journals, books, and other nonfiction." *Individual Projects in Writing* is very individualized: "Design your own writing projects and determine form, content, and purpose." They also have a *screenwriting* course and genre writing in *romance, mysteries,* and other popular categories. A professional manuscript reading service is available for advanced writers. *Perfecting Your Poem: A Guide to Revision* caught my eye, along with *Poetry of the Self: The Writers Within,* described not as a poetry writing class, but a way to "explore your own ideas and experiences." The instructor has a background in Gestalt and Jungian psychology.
- The renowned University of Iowa offers correspondence courses in creative writing, often critiqued by participants in the Iowa Writer's Workshop.
- University of Minnesota has a *Journal and Memoir Writing* course, as well as the interesting-sounding *Topics in Creative Writing: Journaling into Fiction.* Their courses sometimes use cassette tapes.
- University of Wisconsin offers an outstanding variety of courses (almost as many as UC Berkeley), high-quality instruction, and affordability. Look for classes in both English and Journalism Departments. *Attack on Grammar* is a fun review class!
- Western Washington University offers *Journal Writing I* and *II,* open to beginning and experienced writers. Ask for a catalog and syllabus.

Writing works especially well in correspondence study because some of the most important skills required for correspondence study are also required for writers. First, strong reading skills are needed—and since most writers are also avid readers, they have an advantage here. Second, you must be able to work alone, make your own deadlines, set your work habits and follow them closely, and turn out material regularly. Again, this is part of a writer's life. I found that having to churn out new material for correspondence-course assignments increased my productivity. Finally, correspondence courses can increase your motivation to submit for publication. Having your manuscript come back with an "A" creates a strong incentive to make corrections and submit it to a magazine. You can learn to write by writing—it's a fun way to improve your skills.

# How To Write—Techniques
## General Fiction

# 17

## PLOTTING FROM A TO Z

### BY WILLIAM F. NOLAN

PLOT HAS A DOUBLE PURPOSE IN FICTION. Actively, it's the driving force of any story or novel, the locomotive that pulls the train of characters and incidents from point A, the start, to point Z, the ending. Passively, it's the spine of a story, the structure around which the story is told.

A strong, surprising plot is essential if you are to capture and hold readers. The plot must keep them engaged and draw them deeper and deeper into the narrative.

The most important element in plotting, in my opinion, is the uniqueness of the writer. Each writer is wholly individual, and it is through the process of exploring one's own individuality that the best plots are written. Find the elements within yourself that make you unique. Explore your inner beliefs, loves, fears, and experiences and use these as the source of your plotting.

No matter how fanciful your story, its plot should contain elements of reality, of the truth that can be found *only* within yourself.

There are certain basic elements of plotting that must be kept in mind as you explore your own inner landscape.

*Forward movement:* Set a course of action and propel your characters along this course. Each scene or chapter must move your narrative forward along a rising arc of drama. Characterization and incident should always contribute to this forward movement. Your story or novel must have a goal that your characters strive to reach.

The beginning of your arc of drama should set your characters on course for the goal. Your center section should see them in conflict, confronting problems that must be overcome in order to reach that goal. The climax should see them arriving, for better or worse, at the end of their quest.

*Twists and surprises:* Readers enjoy being thrown off balance; they love to encounter the unexpected, to discover that you, the writer, are always a step ahead of them in providing twists and surprises they didn't anticipate. In my first novel, *Logan's Run,* I had my hero and heroine pursued through the book by an individual they (and the reader) thought to be a young hunter named Francis. At the climax, when they reach their goal (safety, or as I called it in the book, Sanctuary), Francis is revealed to be Ballard, a much older man who has secretly been working to help them achieve Sanctuary. Although this is a big surprise to the reader, it's not out of context, since I carefully planted my clues throughout the narrative. A writer must always play fair with readers.

In my novel, *Helltracks,* I set up the situation of a "death train" on the plains of Montana, which is somehow responsible for several murders. But not until the climax do I reveal that it is the train *itself* that is the killer, that it is a creature of organic life with an appetite for human flesh. A shock—and a surprise for every reader.

*Logic and reality:* In plotting any type of story or novel, you must create a sense of logic and reality. The forward-moving events must involve characters with whom the reader can identify and believe completely. The secret of Stephen King's plotting is the sense of reality he brings to his characters. King has often pointed out that if the people in a story are realistic, then the reader will follow them anywhere— even into the most fantastic situations. The actions of your characters, whether they are in conflict with a vampire or a Mafia gangster, must be logical, based on what such characters might actually do in a given fictional situation.

*The darkest hour:* Every plot, but particularly plots for novels, must have its darkest hour, the moment at which all seems lost for the protagonist, when the goal that has been sought seems hopelessly beyond reach; the moment at which, depending on the level of danger in the story, death itself might threaten. You must bring your characters to this moment, always very late in the story, and then you must devise a *logical* way to reverse the situation and have the dangers and conflict resolved before reaching the story's windup. Naturally, not *all* stories end happily for your characters. Some characters may have been defeated or (depending on the *type* of story you are telling) even killed before your final resolution.

66

It's easier to provide unhappy or tragic endings in a short story. In a novel, an ending that's a "downer" is generally not welcomed by readers who have invested a great deal of themselves in your characters. The novelist must work to achieve an ending that is emotionally satisfying.

*Character change:* The events of your plot must have an *effect* on the character or characters involved. You must structure your story in a way that allows your protagonist to emerge from the various incidents of the plot with a new perspective on his or her life. The emotional or physical trials he or she has endured should act upon your protagonist in a manner that results in a basic character change. This is especially true in novels. Without such a character change, your plot will lack depth and maturity.

*Dialogue:* One of the key elements in building a proper plot is dramatic dialogue. Dialogue should never be static. It must help keep the plot moving as well as serve simultaneously to build character and keep your readers informed. What your characters say to one another must lead them to become involved in actions that propel the story along its arc.

Analyze the dialogue in any successful suspense novel, and you'll see that it is always *active,* never passive.

*Research:* Unless you're writing about a totally imaginary place, plotting requires research. Readers must believe in your backgrounds, locales, and in the general arena your characters inhabit. When writing *Helltracks,* I had to deal, in part, with a sheep ranching family in Montana. When I got the idea for this novel, I knew nothing about the business of raising sheep, but by the time I was into the actual writing of the book, I had researched this subject extensively and so was able to handle the sheep-raising background with conviction. Study the novels of Dean R. Koontz and note how he uses realistic backgrounds. Koontz is a master plotter; he utilizes all of the elements I've discussed to stunning effect. Note, in particular, how he builds suspense within the arc of the story, how he leads the reader relentlessly along his plotted road, and how he always provides a host of new twists and surprises.

Koontz has written over 60 novels. As a beginning writer, he set out to learn his craft the way a medical student sets out to learn medicine.

Each new book he wrote reflected what he'd learned from the previous one. I've been writing fiction for three decades, and I'm still learning.

To develop your plotting ability I recommend a simple method. Pick up a book of stories in the genre that holds special interest for you as a writer. Read the *first half* of each story, put the book aside, and finish plotting the narrative. Then go back and read the second half of the story. How does your plot compare with the one as published? What elements did the author have in the story that you failed to include? If you're really good, you may even feel that your plot is superior to the one the author created. Using this method, you can learn a lot about how a good plot is constructed.

Should you make a plot outline before you write your story? Absolutely. It's your blueprint, your map to guide you along the road. It can be as long or as short as you feel necessary, provided the main story line is sketched out from beginning to end. Without an outline, it is far too easy to become bogged down, or to take wrong turns that will lead your characters away from their goal rather than toward it.

The elements I've described here are all tools for solid plotting. They are vital to the art of taking the reader with you on your fictional journey from A to Z.

With a good plot, you're well on the way to achieving the goal of every fiction writer: an excellent story.

# 18

## ACHIEVING A SENSE OF REALITY IN YOUR NOVEL

### BY LaVYRLE SPENCER

"HOW DO YOU MAKE THINGS SEEM SO REAL?" When an author is asked this question it is a compliment. If he is told, further, "I felt as if I were there. I could hear and smell and feel the places as if I had stepped onto the page," he has truly given the reader something special.

When I'm asked how I make things seem real I answer, "By appealing to the five senses." What writers don't always realize is that reality is achieved by appealing to the reader's five senses. It is simple enough to appeal to the visual sense, but how often do we include a smell, a sound (other than in dialogue), something tactile, or a taste?

I've been writing since 1976, yet I still keep on my office wall a list of five words: SEE, HEAR, FEEL, TASTE, SMELL. As I work on a scene, I refer to this list and consciously *plan* to put into it something with scent. It need not be a good smell; indeed, some offensive smells are wonderfully effective in creating reality. Consider the smell of spoiled fruit, as a character opens a refrigerator door; of rancid fat, as a man skins a bear; of gasoline on a woman's gloves after she fills her tank at a self-service station.

It is not enough to mention the scent at the outset of the scene; to get the most mileage out of it, you must refer to it again and again as you move your characters around. Let us suppose a man and woman are having an argument; he storms into the kitchen, shouting at her from the doorway, "I've had all I can stand of your mother living with us. The old lady better be out by the time I get back, or I'm packing my bags!" In setting up such a scene, I could easily have the woman baking a pumpkin pie (sweet, homey scent reminiscent of loving times like Thanksgiving), but the scene takes on a much more effective tang if accompanied by the acrid smell of pickling spices and vinegar from the relish she is making. If the dialogue goes on for half a page, at one point

69

I might remind the reader of the smell by a line such as this: *"I'm warning you, Nora, it's either her or me!" he said, looking as sour as the smell in the room.*

It is effective to turn that same sour smell into something sweet by *intentionally* having it accompany a tender scene. In such a situation, the addition of humor would most commonly be used.

Don't forget, as you go on writing a scene such as the one above, to show Nora continuing her canning as the argument goes on. As she's shouting a line of dialogue, she can burn her hand, then thrust it under cold running water. This, of course, heightens the sense of feel, again, not a pleasant feeling, but *real,* nonetheless. She can be pouring brine over the pickles and spill some, then have to wipe it up (wet). She can dry her hands on her apron (coarse cotton). She can feel sweat trickling down her forehead (heat, tickle). She can brandish a slotted spoon at him (hard, wooden handle) while shouting.

As the arguing grows louder, what other sounds might be heard? Does a dog saunter in and drink from the tin pie plate on the floor? (Slurp, slurp, slurp . . .) Does an old car chug by on the street outside? Are children's voices heard as they play in the yard next door? As the water boils in a canner on the stove, do the glass jars clink together?

How hot is it? Have you told the reader it's 95 degrees? If so, does your heroine have a glass of iced tea or iced coffee on the counter beside her pickling jars? When the argument ends, unsettled, with the man stomping out angrily, does she pick up the glass and take a swig of iced coffee, find it bitter, and make a face?

As you can see, it is possible to evoke all five senses in a scene such as the one sketched above, but to make this happen, the scene must be carefully planned. Most scenes will not lend themselves to using all five senses (taste is the most difficult to work in), but by using props, you can easily evoke four senses, and surely three in most scenes.

In dialogue, too, writers must work to create a sense of believability. Forgetting to use contractions, for example, will produce stilted dialogue. Contemporary Americans simply *don't* say *do not* very often, nor do they say *will not* when they can say *won't,* or *have not* in place of *haven't.* When in doubt about the reality of your dialogue, read it aloud, pretending you're an actor, speaking with the inflections that would be used on a movie screen or stage. If it sounds forced or unnatural, change it. Don't forget, people speak unfinished thoughts, so let some of your characters' sentences trail off. People ask questions of one another, so remember to make your characters do so, especially when they are getting to know one another. People sigh, chuckle, scratch their heads, puff out their cheeks, study their fingernails during a conversation. Make your characters do these kinds of things, too. People continue conversations as they go about their work. Use tag lines to create motion in a scene. Consider the following two:

> "You never liked my mother!" Nora shouted. She slammed the kettle down.
> "You never liked my mother!" Nora slammed the kettle down.

The second example increases tension, moves the scene along faster, and eliminates excess words, showing rather than telling the reader that Nora was shouting.

This is the perfect time to mention the rule by which I gauge all of my writing:

*A moment of tension requires an economy of words.*

I learned it from my tenth-grade English teacher many years after high school graduation. I'd written my second book but couldn't get several scenes to work. Something was wrong with the rhythm, and I couldn't figure out what, so I gave her the manuscript and asked for her comments and suggestions. Once she told me the rule and I applied it to the novel manuscript, everything became clear. In a tense scene, use shorter sentences, shorter words within those sentences, and fewer tag lines. Be brusque. When you do this, tension becomes inherent.

By contrast, in languid scenes in which a sense of tranquility prevails, use longer sentences, longer words, longer paragraphs, and more tag lines. Doing so automatically relaxes tension.

Realism is also established when you plan your novel before the first paragraph is written. Only through research can you paint accurate pictures of believable people performing their daily work amid the sights, sounds, smells, touches, and tastes that are indigenous to their surroundings. In researching my most recent novel, *Forgiving*, I learned much from books about old hand-printing presses, but only from a man who'd used them could I learn that a typesetter's efficiency (in 1889) was judged by listening to the *snick-snick-snick* of the metal type hitting his composing stick. Only from him could I learn that ink left out in the air on a brayer turns sticky and ruins the tool. Only from him could I learn that printers' ink and turpentine are the scents that pervade the air of an old-time newspaper office. Only by printing some sheets on his venerable old Washington Hand Press could I feel the thump of it against my hip, and realize a hip is used as much as a hand during this operation. Oh, you see what I've been doing again—now, let me see. . . .

snick, snick, snick (hear)
turpentine and printer's ink (smell)
thump on the hip (feel)
press, brayer, ink, office, composing stick (see)

Uh-oh! No taste. (Short sentences, short words, increased tension.)

Well, as I said earlier, taste is the toughest one to include, but four out of five isn't so bad.

Appealing to the senses and creating (or relaxing) tension with sentence structure will help you write stories that readers won't be able to put down because they're so real.

# 19

## DIALOGUE: THE MEANING BEYOND THE WORDS

### BY TIM SANDLIN

THE FIRST NIGHT OF MY FICTIONAL FICTION CLASS, I walk to the front of the room, open the roll form conveniently provided by Central Wyoming College, and begin.

"George Singleton."

"Yo."

"Irene Bukowski."

"Present."

One by one, I call their names and they respond.

"Here."

"You got me."

"Yes."

"It is I."

One girl doesn't say anything, just raises her hand a half-inch off the desk.

"Accounted for."

"Sorry, I'm late."

And with each response, I learn something about the characters. The "Yo" guy will write comic pieces that start with the hero waking up hung over. The girl who won't speak will write a poem featuring death. The "It is I" girl won't take criticism, "You got me" is sneaky, and "Sorry, I'm late" will drop out after we read his first story.

Your snap judgments based on one or two words of dialogue may not match mine, but the point is that each member of the class gave a different response. And they stayed in character.

In real life, half the class would say "Here" and the other half raise their right hand about chin high, but this is fiction, and fiction is not real life. Don't forget that. If you write so realistically you can't stand the thought of that much diversification in a group, skip calling the roll and go right to the scene where each student says a few words on "Why I'm taking this creative writing class."

Won't be any repeat answers there.

In fiction with energy, no two characters put any one thought the same. There are four primary ways to build a character—description, dialogue, and action, plus thought in your viewpoint people. To pass up the smallest opportunity to differentiate and build on your fictional people is a waste. Worse, it's stagnant. Even a story about stagnation can't be stagnant.

Several years ago in a show called "Charlie's Angels," three women with teeth and hair brought bad guys to bay with perkiness and spunk. But without dialogue. As far as the lines went, the women were interchangeable. Mostly, they took turns saying, "Come on, Charlie."

In putting words on paper, no one has enough teeth or hair to get away with this sloppiness. P. G. Wodehouse believed every sentence in a book must have entertainment value. That may or may not be true with every style of book, but it sure is true of dialogue. If the reader doesn't learn something new every time he ventures between the quotation marks, the writer has botched his or her job.

So what are these gems the reader is supposed to learn between the squiggly floating marks? Oversimplified, dialogue must do four things— show character, advance plot, give information, and set the voice, tone, and scene.

**Show character.** There are people in the English-speaking world of a certain cultural and educational background who actually say, "It is I." Imagine that. The secret is to nail down a character as quickly as possible. If you have her say "It is I," then follow up with a tight bun on her head and dark purple nail polish, you've pretty much done the job. Give her some matching action and send her down the road.

The idea is to supply one or two details that are so distinct, the reader can fill in all the others. A character who says, "I'm going to snatch you kids baldheaded," won't wear the same clothes or drive the same car as a character who says, "I have difficulty interfacing with children."

Even non-dialogue is dialogue. The girl who wouldn't answer but held up her hand a half-inch revealed character by not speaking. From there, you can have her go with the grain by keeping her in sweaters four sizes too large and afraid to ride on an elevator unless it's empty, or you can blast against the grain—and be almost as trite—by turning her into a sex-crazed tigress when she lets down her hair.

Not speaking often says more than speaking, especially in tense climactic showdowns. It's a lot easier to write a scene where a man punches out his boss than a scene in which his anger is beyond words, and he walks away. That makes sense. By definition, "beyond words" is harder to put into words than a punch in the nose.

Here's a trick for keeping your characters in character. When I wrote a book about two 13-year-olds and their awkward struggles to overcome strange upbringings, I found my old junior high yearbook from 1963. Whenever one of my kids said something precocious, wise, or cornball, I looked at a photo of my 13-year-old classmates, and said, "Could this have come from Ronnie Craig's mouth, or Ann Humphrey's, or Annette Gilliam's?" The answer was usually "No," and the line got thrown out.

**Advance action.** This one should be self-explanatory. Story is how characters react to conflict, and much of the conflict between people in our modern world is caused by words. Communication—the thing that is supposed to resolve problems—actually causes more than it resolves.

We advance action by arguing, seducing, planning, slighting, gossiping, giving ultimatums—I could go find a thesaurus and stretch this into twelve column inches, but you get the idea.

Here's another place where fiction differs from real life. Most of those heart-to-hearts you have with your mother/husband/wife go in circles and dead-end. The same thoughts are constantly reported in slightly different ways, and when all this communicating is done, nothing has changed.

You don't have time for this jive in fiction. Each conversation must end with some condition different from what it was at the beginning. The relationship between the speakers has been slightly altered, or someone has grown wiser, or the speakers—at the very least, the readers—have information they didn't know before. Your viewpoint character is in more trouble or thinks he is moving closer to the solution to the conflict. Or maybe all she's done is order lunch. Ordering lunch reveals more about a character than his or her resumé.

A sidetrack on dialect. Anyone who tries it is braver than I am. Mark Twain pulled it off. John Kennedy Toole pulled it off. People think Eudora Welty pulls it off, but if you read her work carefully, you'll see she does it more with sentence rhythm and word choice than by dropping g's off walkin' and talkin'.

Check this out from her "My Life at the P.O.":

I says, "Papa-Daddy, you know I wouldn't any more want you to cut off your beard than the man in the moon. It was the farthest thing from my mind. Stella-Rondo sat there and made that up while she was eating breast of chicken."

Not a misspelled word in the quote, yet after I read this story to my class, they all swore it was written in Deep Mississippi dialect.

**Give information.** This is the easiest one to mess up. The worst example I can think of in conveying information through dialogue happens on the soap operas.

MAMA: "I saw Mildred Kinnicknick at the grocery store yesterday."
DAUGHTER: "Is that the same Mildred Kinnicknick whose father was tried for murder, then he got off by claiming insanity because he'd eaten too many Twinkies and whose mother used to be married to Doc Watson, then she divorced him and married his brother Spud, only now she's back with Doc but carrying the baby of his older brother Bubba?"
MAMA: "Yes."

Uh-uh. Dialogue doesn't work that way. To get information across, you have to be sneaky. This is part of the Show-Don't-Tell lesson you've heard 200 times. Don't say, "I see you wear glasses." Do say, "Your glasses are always dirty." This gets across that the character does wear glasses, and it also says something about his personality that they're always dirty and it says something about the speaker's personality that she notices the dirt and is brazen enough to comment on it.

This is especially true when you use dialogue to foreshadow. In mysteries by unskilled writers, there's always a line where someone says, "I notice you have a gun in your closet," or "We're spraying the rose bushes with Fetadetamiacin today, so don't stick any petals in your mouth or you'll die." Right then, I know that 200 pages from now, the gun or the Fetadetamiacin will pop up and kill somebody.

Foreshadowing, especially in mysteries, has to be done so when readers come to the place where the gun is used, they're totally surprised, but then they think about it and say, "Gee, that makes sense."

Anticipated surprises—they're what make endings fun. And the sneakiest way to foreshadow without getting caught is in dialogue.

**Set the voice, tone and scene.** Choosing the tone may be the most important decision you make when starting a story. I was once assistant editor at a literary magazine, and I read something like 200 stories in a weekend. Every one of those stories was competent—not a total loser in the batch—but what made an exceptional story rise above the others were the voice and tone.

The Holy Trinity of fiction is plot, character, and voice—Father, Son, and Holy Ghost. And, like the Holy Ghost, voice is the hardest to understand. Voice is that attitude of the writer to the story. It's the attitude of the writer toward his or her readers.

Sometimes I have my students write a two-page story, then rewrite it Erma Bombeck-style, then Edgar Allan Poe-style, then Louis L'Amour. The growth of these stories is amazing. And the easiest place to establish these styles is in the dialogue. People in Valley Girl High School speak differently from people in 1880s Bitter Creek or Transylvania. People about to be murdered on the moors speak differently from people chasing down the blue light special at K Mart. Doesn't take a Guggenheim grant to figure out that one.

Not everything to do with dialogue happens between the quote marks. The reader has to know who is talking and in what tone of voice. For this we use dialogue tags.

Dialogue tags seem to come in styles, like hats. What worked in 1932 looks slightly ridiculous now. There are no absolute rules in writing dialogue tags or anything else. If it works, you got away with it. But there are certain ways to playing it that work more often than not.

The easiest tag is none. Compare—Laurie crossed her arms on her chest. "Why do you say that?" to— "Why do you say that?" Laurie asked defensively.

If you can set the tone of the speech with a bit of action, you're better off than "Blah-blah," he said, adverb. If it isn't crystal clear who is speaking, use *he said* or *she said*. Once every couple of pages, sneak in a *he asked*. Don't, under penalty of personal castigation, use *he stated, she observed, the boy piped, George groaned,* or any other word for *said*. If you want George to groan, have him do it first.

George groaned. "I can't get up this morning."
Not—"I can't get up this morning," George groaned.

Trust me on this. You can't groan and talk at the same time.

77

And, if at all possible, avoid adverbs in dialogue tags. In the 1950s, riding the wave of the Hemingway revolution, adverbs were words to be avoided like the plague. I look at them as tools, and no tool should be banned forever.

However, use them with care. Hand grenades don't kill—people who throw hand grenades do kill. Pretend the adverb, when used in a dialogue tag, is a hand grenade. Don't play with it.

A word about typographical tricks. Say your character is really hacked off.

"GET OUT OF MY HOUSE." "Get out of my house!"

*"Get out of my house."*

Every editor in America is going to hate two of those three sentences, but I can't tell you which two, because it depends on the editor. Personally, I'd rather snort barbwire than use an exclamation point, and I can't even think of a metaphor disgusting enough to compare to dialogue in ALL CAPS, so I'm stuck with italics. Some editors can't stand italics. It's a pet peeve deal. If possible, work it into the action.

> George smashed a glass on the linoleum floor.
> "Get out of my house."

If that isn't strong enough for you, try one of the other three. I highly recommend against any combinations. *"GET OUT OF MY HOUSE!"*

And the worst, absolutely bottom-of-the-barrel method of expressing quoted frenzy is multiple punctuation.

"Get out of my house!!?!"

This was once Batman-style, but no more. I just looked in one of my son's *Ghost Rider* comic books, and do you think Mephisto himself screams questions!? Heck, no @#%&!

Of course, as soon as I say that, someone will mail in an example of James Joyce and the double exclamation point. Which brings us back to rule number one: There are no rules.

# 20

## GETTING STARTED

### BY JOHN IRVING

IT IS USEFUL WHEN YOU BEGIN A NOVEL to invoke certain guidelines if not actual rules that have given you aid and comfort during the periods of tribulation that marked the beginnings of your Novels Past. You are never, of course, so given to imperatives as when you don't know what you're doing and, therefore, haven't begun. This helps to explain an obvious contradiction in most book reviews: a notable absence of any understanding of the examined work in tandem with a flood of imperatives regarding what the work ought to have been. First novelists, especially, are afflicted with the need to give advice—witness Tom Wolfe's advice to us all, regarding our proper subject matter (lest we end up bantering among ourselves, like so many poets). But I digress— a common weakness with all beginnings.

Beginnings are important. Here is a useful rule for beginning: Know the story—as much of the story as you can possibly know, if not the whole story—before you commit yourself to the first paragraph. Know the story—the whole story, if possible—before you fall in love with your first *sentence,* not to mention your first chapter. If you don't know the story before you begin the story, what kind of a storyteller are you? Just an ordinary kind, just a mediocre kind—making it up as you go along, like a common liar. Or else, to begin a novel without an ending fixed in your mind's eye, you must be very clear, and so full of confidence in the voice that tells the story that the story itself hardly matters. In my own case, I am much more plodding; confidence comes from knowing the story that lies ahead—not in the limited powers of the voice that tells it. This calls for patience and for plotting.

And most of all, when beginning, be humble; remember that your first, blank page has this in common with all other blank pages: It has not read your previous works. Don't be enthralled by the sound of your own voice; write with a purpose; have a plan. Know the story, *then* begin the story. Here endeth the lesson.

The authority in the storyteller's voice derives from foreknowledge. In my opinion, a novel is written with predestination—a novel being defined as a *narrative; a good* narrative has a *plot.* If you're not interested in plot, why write a novel? Because plot provides momentum, plot is what makes a novel better on page three hundred than it was on page thirty—*if* it's a good novel. A good novel, by definition, keeps getting better. Plot is what draws the reader in—plot *and* the development of characters who are worthy of the reader's emotional interest. Here endeth another lesson.

Is this advice for everyone? Of course not! "Plot" isn't what compels many novelists to write, or some readers to read. But if you choose to write a novel without a plot, I would hope three things for you: that your prose is gorgeous, that your insights into the human condition are inspirational, and that your book is short. I am directing my remarks, of course, to those writers (and readers) of *long* novels.

Would a film director begin to shoot a picture without a screenplay? I would never begin a novel without knowing the whole story; but even then, the choices for how to begin are not simple. *You* may know exactly where the story begins, but choosing where you want the *reader* to begin the story is another matter. And here cometh another lesson for the writer of long novels: Think of the reader. Who is this reader? I think of the reader as far more intelligent than I am, but a child—a kind of hyperactive prodigy, a reading wizard. Interest this child and he will put up with anything—he will understand everything, too. But fail to seize and hold this child's attention, *at the beginning,* and he will never come back to you. This is your reader: paradoxically, a genius with the concentration span of a rabbit.

I am amazed that mere consideration of the reader, nowadays, often marks a writer as "commercial"—as opposed to "literary." To the snotty charge that Dickens wrote what the public wanted, Chesterton replied, "Dickens *wanted* what the public wanted!" Let us quickly clear up this name-calling regarding "commercial" and "literary": It is for artistic reasons, in addition to financial wisdom, that *any* author would prefer keeping a reader's attention to losing it.

Three obvious but painstaking components either succeed in making a novel "literary," or they fail and make it a mess: namely, the crafts-manlike quality of the storytelling (of course, in my opinion, a novel should be a story worth telling); the true-to-life quality of the characters (I also expect the characters to be skillfully developed); and the meticulous exactitude of the language (discernible in every sentence and seeming to be spoken by an unmistakable voice).

What makes a novel "commercial" is that a lot of people buy it and finish it and tell other people to read it; both "literary" novels and failed, messy novels can be commercially successful *or* unsuccessful. The part about the reader *finishing* a novel is important for the book's commercial success; both good reviews and the author's pre-existent popularity can put a book on the bestseller lists, but what keeps a book on the list for a long time is that a lot of those first readers actually finish the book and tell their friends that they simply must read it. We don't tell our friends that they simply must read a book we're unable to finish.

In my own judgment, as a reader, the faults of most novels are the sentences—either they're unambitious or they're so unclear that they need to be rewritten. And what's wrong with the rest of the novels I don't finish is that the stories aren't good enough to merit writing a novel in the first place.

One of the pleasures of reading a novel is anticipation. Would a playwright *not* bother to anticipate what the audience is anticipating? The reader of a novel also enjoys the feeling that he can anticipate where the story is going; however, if the reader actually does anticipate the story, he is bored. The reader must be able to anticipate, but the reader must also guess wrong. How can an author make a reader anticipate—not to mention make a reader guess wrong—if the author himself doesn't *know* where the story is going? A good beginning will suggest knowledge of the whole story; it will give a strong hint regarding where the whole story is headed—yet a good beginning must be misleading, too.

Therefore, where to begin? Begin where the reader will be invited to do the most anticipating of the story, but where the reader will be the most compelled to guess wrong. If anticipation is a pleasure, so is surprise.

My last rule is informed by a remark of the late John Cheever—from his journals—that he was "forced to consider [his] prose by the ignobility of some of [his] material." My advice is to consider—from the beginning—that *all* of your material suffers from ignobility. Therefore, *always* consider your prose!

In the past, I have deliberately loaded my first sentences with all these admonitions in mind. The first sentence of *The World According to Garp:* "Garp's mother, Jenny Fields, was arrested in Boston in 1942 for wounding a man in a movie theater." (The sentence is a shameless tease; "wounded" is deliberately unclear—we want to know *how* the man was "wounded"—and that the person "arrested" was somebody's *mother* surely suggests a lurid tale.) The first sentence of *The Hotel New Hampshire:* "The summer my father bought the bear, none of us was born—we weren't even conceived: not Frank, the oldest; not Franny, the loudest; not me, the next; and not the youngest of us, Lilly and Egg." (Well, what is shameless about this is that *anybody* bought a bear—the rest of the sentence is simply an economical means of introducing the members of a large family. In fact, this family is so large, it is cumbersome; therefore, a few of them will die deaths of convenience rather early in the novel.) The first sentence of *The Cider House Rules:* "In the hospital of the orphanage—the boys' division of St. Cloud's, Maine—two nurses were in charge of naming the new babies and checking that their little penises were healing from the obligatory circumcision." (This beginning operates on the assumption that orphanages are emotionally engaging to everyone; also, how people are named is always interesting, and the matter of "obligatory circumcision" suggests either religion or eccentricity—or both. Besides, I always wanted to put "penises" in an opening sentence; the word, I suppose, sends a signal that this novel is *not* for everyone.) And the first sentence of *A Prayer for Owen Meany:* "I am doomed to remember a boy with a wrecked voice—not because of his voice, or because he was the instrument of my mother's death, but because he is the reason I believe in God; I am a Christian because of Owen Meany." (When in doubt, or wherever possible, tell the whole story of the novel in the first sentence.)

All of those first sentences were not simply the first sentences I ended up with; they were, with one exception, the first sentence of those books that I wrote. (In the case of *Garp,* the *first* first sentence was the sentence that is now the last sentence of the book: "But in the world according to Garp, we are all terminal cases.")

In the case of the novel I am now writing, I have narrowed the possible beginning to three choices; I haven't made up my mind among these choices—so it is still possible that a fourth alternative will present itself, and be chosen, but I doubt it. I think I shall proceed with something very close to one of these.

1. "A widow for one year, Ruth Cole was forty-six; a novelist for twenty years (counting from 1970, when her first book was published), she'd been famous only a little longer than she'd been a widow—in fact, in Mrs. Cole's mind, her husband's death and her literary success were so closely associated that her grief overshadowed any enjoyment she could take from the world's newfound appreciation of her work."

This is a plain, old-fashioned beginning: It holds back more than it tells, and I like that. The character is a woman of some achievement; we may therefore expect her to be a character of some complexity, and—as she is a recent widow—we can be assured that we enter her life at a vulnerable moment. This beginning continues to build on our impression of Mrs. Cole *at this moment:*

"Furthermore, she'd always perceived any recognition of her writing—both when the praise had been spotty and now that it was profuse—as nothing more than a seductive invasion of her privacy; that such sudden and so much attention should come to her at a time when she most sought to be alone (and most needed to grow accustomed to being alone) was simply annoying. Fame, to Mrs. Cole, was merely a trivial vexation among the more painful torments of her loneliness. She wanted her husband alive again, she wanted him back; for it was only in her life with him that she'd been afforded the greatest privacy, not to mention an intimacy she'd never taken for granted."

We stand on solid ground with this beginning; we already know a lot about Mrs. Cole and her situation. We may be interested in such a woman, at such a time in her life, but there is no hook; the beginning is *too* plain—it lacks even a hint of anything sensational.

Try again.

2. "Dr. Daruwalla had upsetting news for the famous actor, Inspector Dutt; not sure of the degree to which Inspector Dutt would be distressed, Dr. Daruwalla was impelled by cowardice to give the movie star the bad news in a public place—young Dutt's extraordinary poise in public was renowned; the doctor felt he could rely on the actor to keep his composure."

This, of course, is the beginning of a novel by Ruth Cole; it is one of *her* beginnings. Mrs. Cole continues in a tone of voice that promises us she will, occasionally, be funny. "Not everyone in Bombay would have thought of a private club as a 'public place,' but Dr. Daruwalla believed that the choice was both private and public enough for the particular crisis at hand." And the second paragraph provides the "hook" I feel is missing from my first beginning.

"That morning when Dr. Daruwalla arrived at the Duckworth Sports and Eating Club, he thought it was unremarkable to see a vulture high in the sky above the golf course; he did not consider the bird of death as an omen attached to the unwelcome burden of the news he carried. The club was in Mahalaxmi, not far from Malabar Hill; everyone in Bombay knew why the vultures were attracted to Malabar Hill. When a corpse was placed in the Towers of Silence, the vultures—from thirty miles outside Bombay—could scent the ripening remains."

This is certainly a more mysterious beginning than my first—not to mention more foreign. The language (that is, Mrs. Cole's) is more lush and dense than my own—this beginning is altogether more exotic. But pity the poor reader when he discovers that this is *not* the novel he is reading—rather, it is a novel *within* the novel he is reading. Won't the poor reader feel misled too much? (To mislead is divine, to *trick* is another matter!) However, I am aware that I will never get the reader to read Mrs. Cole's Indian novel as closely as I want him to *if* the reader knows it is merely a novel within a novel; by beginning with Mrs. Cole's novel, I make the reader read it closely. What a choice! And so I come, cautiously in the middle, to the third possibility.

3. "*Son of the Circus,* the seventh novel by the American novelist Ruth Cole, was first published in the United States in September, 1989; the excitement was mitigated for the author by the unexpected death of her husband—he died in his sleep beside his wife, in a hotel in New York City; they had just begun the promotion tour."

This is not yet quite the blend I want—between what is plain and old-fashioned, and what is exotic—but this comes close to satisfying me, *provided that* I begin the so-called Indian novel quickly, before the reader becomes *too* involved in poor Mrs. Cole's widowhood (not to mention the bad timing of her husband's demise). And that last line— "they had just begun the promotion tour"—hints at a tone of voice that will prevail both in Ruth Cole's fiction and in my telling of her actual story; any consideration of one's prose must include a consideration of the tone of voice.

But what I miss (from Mrs. Cole's beginning) is greater than the kind of purity gained by the third possibility. Both the first and third beginnings tell the reader what *has* happened to Ruth Cole; Mrs. Cole, on the other hand, tells us what Dr. Daruwalla is *going to* do—he's going to give an actor named Inspector Dutt some bad news. What *is* this news? I want to know. And Dr. Daruwalla may be so used to vultures that *he* does "not consider the bird of death as an omen," but we readers know better: Of *course* the vulture is an omen! *Anyone* knows that! Therefore, at this writing, I am inclined to begin my novel with Mrs. Cole's first chapter, or part of it. If Mrs. Cole's story is good enough, the reader will forgive me for my trick.

Even as I write, a fourth opportunity presents itself to me: Instead of starting with Mrs. Cole's novel or with Mrs. Cole, it is possible to begin with someone else reading her novel—perhaps her former lover.

"At that moment, the German stopped reading; he was a golfer himself, he did not find dead-golfer jokes amusing, and he was overwhelmed by the density of the description—the pace of this novel was unbearably slow for him, not to mention how little interested he was in India. He was not much of a reader, especially not of novels, and he despaired that he was less than halfway through the first chapter of a very long novel and already he was bored. (The last book he'd read was about golf.) But special interests, none of them literary, would compel him to keep reading the novel he'd momentarily put aside.

"He knew the author; that is, he had briefly been her lover, many years ago, and he was vain enough to imagine that in her novel he would find some trace of himself—that was what he was reading for. Once he penetrated the story—past the dead golfer—he would find much more than he'd bargained for; his imagination simply wasn't up to the task he'd set for himself, but he didn't know that as he sat fingering the German translation and smiling boorishly at the author photograph, which he found faintly arousing."

And by the time you read this, I may be considering a fifth possibility. Anyway, once the beginning is locked in place, it is time to invite similar scrutiny of the next chapter and then the next. With any luck, you will hear from me (and Mrs. Cole) in about four years.

# 21

## NOVEL IDEAS

### By Barbara Taylor Bradford
### An Interview by Billie Figg

**Timing**

A finger on the public pulse is vital. When I wrote *A Woman of Substance* twelve years ago, I was obsessed by an urge to write about strong women. It was what felt important then and the character Emma Harte was the right woman at the right time.

Since then many surrogate Emmas have been created, not just by me, but by other authors, too. I had kicked off the decade of the "matriarchal dynastic saga."

In 1988 I was about to embark on a novel about a woman who creates a great shipping empire when a new book landed on my desk for comment.

To my dismay I saw it was yet another "woman of substance" story. Everyone was writing about women heading great businesses. It simply wasn't new any more.

That's when I decided that strong women books were over and it was time to write about a man.

The fact that *The Women in His Life* was number one on the bestseller lists for five weeks shows that readers feel as I do. A good hero is *in*.

And it demonstrates that if you are going to produce bestsellers on a regular basis, you've got to feel along with the public. Call it a sixth sense, if you like. The point is: Have *you* got it?

**Motivation**

A burning desire to write novels must be paramount. If you don't feel driven, I would say forget it. I was writing stories in childhood, usually about an imaginary friend named Sally who shared my games and tea-parties because I was an only child.

By the time I was sixteen I knew I wanted to be a novelist, but realized I wasn't ready. It was thirty years before I was!

## Creating characters

Creating believable characters is the hardest part. That was what I had to get to grips with and, if you're serious about novel writing, so will you. You will be a close people watcher, observant of mannerisms, susceptible to inner reactions, a bit of a psychologist and emotionally able to get under their skin.

I always start my novels with the character. For instance, faced with the switch from dominant heroine to powerful hero, the crucial question was: What kind of man should he be?

I thought hard about it. Then one day as I was passing my favorite house set on a corner in London's Mayfair, it suddenly struck me—he's a tycoon and that's where he lives. As I walked on, it came in a rush. He has to be top of the pile, successful on a Gargantuan scale, because he must be larger than life to live on paper.

He has to be special, too. I couldn't write about a struggle to succeed, as that's not interesting enough now. He has to have a conflict within himself.

## Imagination

You have to indulge a lively imagination. For instance, when my husband Bob and I were in Berlin a few years ago, we were walking down the Unter den Linden looking at the Brandenburg Gate when I suddenly had a sense of déjà vu. I felt I had stood at the same place before—during the war.

I really did hear the metallic click of jackboots, the voice of Hitler screaming and crowds applauding. It was like a bit of film unrolled in my head with the sound-track running.

And I saw a woman's face. She had big, luminous eyes, pale, blonde hair and was standing in a reception room under chandeliers, wearing a white, satin gown with diamond necklace and earrings.

Her image stayed in my mind's eye when I got home to New York, but it wasn't until two years later when I was determinedly discarding matriarchal dynastic sagas that this image came back very strongly.

By this time, I had built up the personality of my tycoon, Maximilian West. So it was easy to work out his childhood trauma.

I thought: He's a German Jew who escaped, but was wrenched from his mother and never saw her again. And that's who that woman is, his mother.

Suddenly the character sprang to life and from him the plot. The conflict arose from the fact that he always goes after women who remind him of his mother. He's the little boy lost.

How did he become a tycoon? It occurred to me that as a child growing up in England, he determines he is not going to be a victim ever again, but a victor trampling over the graves of those who persecuted him and his family. So he builds a citadel of power and wealth.

That's how my stories shape up. Character first, then plot, welded together by a healthy dose of imagination.

## Research

Sound research gives a novel reality. A lot of people can string words together, but you are not a novelist unless you are able to tell monumental lies around invented people and make them seem believable.

That's what I failed to do in my earliest attempts in the Sixties. I set tales in exotic places I hardly knew—and my fibs failed to convince even me. Result: I scrapped them.

It wasn't until I wrote about Yorkshire, where I was born and bred, that my fairy tales rang true and *A Woman of Substance* was born. The strength of *The Women in His Life* is that I have related personal lives to political reality and researched it carefully.

## Curiosity

Getting the atmosphere accurate takes a strong streak of curiosity. I had always been fascinated by Nazi Germany, so it was a coincidence that twenty-eight years ago I married a man who escaped as a child from East Berlin to France, never to see his family again.

Not that this book is my husband's story. But, of course, his background enhanced my interest in how Hitler's evil regime held power.

Now I had to understand the climate of those times. I read about thirty books including diaries of the era and looked at pictures showing the chilling theatrical effects the Nazis created with giant columns topped by floodlit eagles down the Unter den Linden boulevard. I got hold of prewar maps and walked the rebuilt streets, trying to sense the daily life in Berlin in those days.

That's how deeply you have to immerse yourself in your subject.

## A sense of drama

Character, plot, and research work only with a sense of drama. Mine was sharpened as a cub reporter on the *Yorkshire Evening Post*. The police beat and the coroners' courts showed me plenty of drama in everyday situations.

You've only to read the papers to pick up ideas. Nothing is more dramatic than real life. And watching television, going to the cinema or reading books and plays shows you how to present a story and what makes it click.

## Organization and a quick eye

You need to be organized with memories and papers. I've trained myself so that I can tell you what's in a room in the flash of an eye—and then keep a mental note of it to put in my computer.

As for research, three quarters has to be thrown away and the vital information filed. My desk has just a typewriter, telephone, pens, photo of Bob, yellow notepad and immediate research. I can't stand stuff around me—mistakes lurk in mess.

## Tenacity

So now it's down to tenacity, a must for any novelist. If you can't stick at things, try stories, not books. Sometimes, though, a promise to someone will keep your nose to the grindstone.

That's what finally got me through over six hundred pages and two years' hard slog to the end of *A Woman of Substance*. I had interested an agent and vanity would not let me fail.

Even if you can't get taken on professionally—and remember, I had years of journalistic work to show—it might help if someone you trust declares confidence in your idea. Your pride is then on the line.

## Writer's block

Writer's block is no excuse for giving up. I admit that at the start of a book I might not know what I'm going to say. But if the going gets tough, I always put something down—even if it's rubbish!

By the time I have been to a bookstore, done some more research or had a hair-do, I feel refreshed and at least I've something to polish up.

## Relationships

Finally, never forget, relationships are what the reader cares about.

To get them on the page in a way that reads true, you have to know and feel what they are made of.

I treasure my friends—most of them date from thirty or more years ago. I see them regularly between novels or when I'm on promotion tours for the books or the television mini-series my husband makes of them.

But you can't be a social butterfly *and* a successful novelist: I have to cut off from people when I'm writing, which can mean months locked in my Manhattan room with just Gemmy, my dog, for company.

But that's what I want to do. In the depressed Thirties, when my father was out of work, my mother went back to nursing to enable me to go to a private school. I still remember what she used to say to me: "Never waste your gifts. Pursue your dreams."

# 22

## ANSWERS TO QUESTIONS ABOUT FICTION WRITING

### BY SIDNEY SHELDON

**Q.** *Do your books ever take unexpected twists as you are writing them? How far should a beginning writer follow a tangent when it presents itself in the course of writing a novel?*

**A.** The twists in my books are constantly surprising me. I never know what is going to happen next, since I don't work with an outline. If a beginning writer finds himself thinking about an unexpected tangent, he or she should follow it. That's the character talking.

**Q.** *How thoroughly developed are your characters and your plot before you begin to write?*

**A.** When I begin a novel, I start with a character. I have no idea what the plot is going to be. Incidentally, this method of working is not one that I would recommend to an inexperienced writer because there are too many pitfalls along the way. I dictate the first draft of my novels and as I talk, the characters come to life and the plot begins to take shape. When I have finished the first draft, which can run to 1,500 pages, I take the typed pages and begin to rewrite, to polish and cut and shape. I do a dozen complete rewrites and spend two years on each book.

**Q.** *Though a protagonist in a novel may be bold, self-possessed, ambitious, attractive, it is also important that he/she have certain flaws in order to be a believable, three-dimensional character. How important is it for readers to care about the major character and what happens to him or her?*

**A.** I don't believe it is important for the reader to necessarily like every character, but it is important for the reader to understand and empathize—even with the villains—so that they at least have an understanding of their motivations.

**Q.** *How often are characters or events in your novels based on an autobiographical trait or event? When something interesting or particularly moving happens in your own life, do you automatically begin thinking of how it would work in a novel?*

**A.** I don't use real characters or historical events in my novels, except occasionally as a background, i.e., *The Other Side of Midnight* character, Constantin Demiris, was based on Aristotle Onassis, and I did create a character in *Bloodline* based on Cary Grant. There are no topics that I will not write about. The most painful scenes I wrote were the death scenes in *Windmills of the Gods.* My wife had died shortly before I wrote the book and writing the scenes was a catharsis for me.

**Q.** *Do you think a writer's natural tendency to fictionalize what he sees—even as his experiences unfold before him—necessarily distorts what he's really witnessing?*

**A.** I believe that a writer can get wonderful material by what he witnesses around him, but I don't think his imagination would destroy what he witnesses—only embellish it.

**Q.** *Do you write regularly, on a fixed schedule, whether you feel like it or not?*

**A.** I work from 9:30 in the morning until 6:00 in the afternoon every day during the week. Sometimes I'll continue the same schedule over the weekend, or use that time to edit and make additional notes for future chapters. I write every day because I enjoy it.

**Q.** *New writers often encounter false starts in writing a novel. What causes this, and should they start over, even to the point of creating a new outline?*

**A.** John D. MacDonald told me that he worked without an outline, and when he came to a place where he found the novel was no longer working, he backed up to the point where it did work, then took the character on a different tangent. I think it's very important for new writers to work with a complete outline before they start a book.

**Q.** *Was there any aspect of writing* The Doomsday Conspiracy *that particularly set it apart from your other writing experiences?*

**A.** Writing *The Doomsday Conspiracy* was a departure for me in several ways. I had never done anything approaching science fiction before. I talked to a dozen astronauts, among other experts, and was rather startled by the experiences they recounted to me. The question in my mind is: Is *The Doomsday Conspiracy* science fiction?

**Q.** *Today's standards for the extent to which some types of sexual behavior and violence are acceptable in mainstream novels differ from those of two or three decades ago. Can you give examples of how such standards have affected your writing throughout your career?*

**A.** Today's standards of sexual behavior and violence are radically different from the standards of not too many years ago. In the 1940s, I was at MGM, writing a movie for Cary Grant. The Breen Office, which was then the censorship office for motion picture studios, sent a man to tell me that I would have to change a scene in my screenplay. Cary Grant and a woman were about to leave a room. Cary pointed at two characters and said they would want to be alone. He turned out the lights and Cary Grant and the woman left. The censor said, "The scene has a sexual connotation. You'll have to change it." I thought the man was joking. The two characters Cary Grant pointed to were two goldfish swimming in a bowl. I changed the scene.

**Q.** *What do you do when your story just doesn't seem to work?*

**A.** When you no longer believe in your book, try to find out what went wrong. If you can't solve whatever the problem is, it may be time to abandon it.

**Q.** *If lengthy descriptions are less acceptable in today's novels than they were, say, 100 years ago, just how important is setting to the success of a novel, and what elements of a setting should a writer strive to convey with present constraints?*

**A.** Lengthy descriptions are not less acceptable today if they are well done. Any good writing is appreciated, whether it's the description, the characterization, or dialogue.

**Q.** *How can dialogue best be used to differentiate characters, so they reflect who they are, what their background is, and what role they play in a novel?*

**A.** If you understand your characters, you don't have to think about how they would talk. A mobster uses one language, a socialite another. If the characters are clear in your mind, you don't even have to think about it.

**Q.** *What characteristics do novels and films have in common? What has to be left out when a novel is turned into a film? What does a novel gain from becoming a film?*

**A.** Novels and films both tell stories. What has been left out when a novel is turned into a film is a lot of description, extraneous scenes, and extraneous characters. When a novel is turned into a film, it's usually wonderful publicity for the book, and will gain a wider audience for the author.

**Q.** *Your novels have been translated into many languages and have also been made into TV miniseries. Have you ever been unhappy with the changes in scenes or intent that can often occur when others interpret your work?*

**A.** Because I began writing for the dramatic form, rather than the narrative form, I am aware of the problems in transferring a novel to the screen. Since I am Executive Producer of most of my projects, I have a great deal of input as to how the transition is made.

**Q.** *How to stimulate the imagination is a niggling problem for many writers. What tactics do you recommend for overcoming the dreaded block?*

**A.** One of the most practical suggestions I have for trying to prevent writer's block is to end each day's work with the beginning of the following day's scene, so that when you sit down to write the next morning, your scene has already been started.

**Q.** *Many books today seem to read like movies—with short scenes where one can almost see camera angles and close-ups, followed by dialogue never heard outside a cinema. Do you feel that writers and readers have shorter attention spans than when you first started writing? Do you think a decreased tolerance for lengthy description and observation will have an effect on what publishers are willing to consider?*

**A.** I think the world has a shorter attention span, largely because of TV and "news bites." On the other hand, if another Thomas Wolfe comes along with his love of language, I think publishers would be very happy to publish such a book.

# 23

# Hold That Edge of Excitement

## By Phyllis A. Whitney

THERE ARE A GOOD MANY EXCITING MOMENTS IN a writer's life. These happenings are all the more gratifying because of the rejections and discouragement that have gone before. I will never forget my first encouragement from an editor, or the first acceptance and appearance of my words in print. Of course I felt ecstatic when I held my first book in my hands.

However, I'm sure that the true "high" for any writer of fiction lies elsewhere. Fortunately, it is something that can come again and again, and we learn to treasure and encourage it. I mean that magical moment when the first glimmer of an idea for a story stirs in our minds. There can be a sense of marvelous "shimmer" around the flashing of those early indications of a story (or novel) to come. We always feel that *this* will be the best thing we've ever written.

While this miracle can occur for me in an instant—perhaps when I'm not even searching—it is something I may carry about with me for days or weeks, while the shining nucleus in my mind gathers more of its special sparkle, developing as if by magic. Perhaps creativity in any field is one of life's most satisfying experiences. That it doesn't last must be accepted and dealt with, so that it can be transferred to something that exists in the real world.

At first, the experience can be so invigorating that I need to hold back and not run around telling everyone what a remarkable book I am going to write. After seventy-three books, I can still be eager and even naive, though I know by this time that too much talking is a sure way to dampen the glow—and possibly even kill my own interest in what is happening.

Getting the idea down on paper in some form is much safer than bragging about it. Even a few words can capture it sufficiently so it won't get away for good. I do know, by now, that this glimmer is only that, and it won't be ready to become a full story or novel for quite a while. So, impatient though I may be, I have learned to wait.

When I was twelve years old, I discovered that I enjoyed making up stories. I could tell exciting stories to neighborhood children, making them up as I went along and delivering them with a dramatic flair that made up for their shortcomings. But I wanted something more permanent that could be read over again—by others, and by me.

My young brain teemed with stories, and I began to set them down on paper. I started out gloriously with story after story, but only now and then did I finish one. Whatever I wrote was never as wonderful as the dream. I was in too much of a hurry, and when I found I had created only the beginning of a story and must then find out where I was going, I lost interest. The magic disappeared and I gave up repeatedly.

There are two kinds of writers. I envy the writer who *can* run with the initial idea and develop it into a story or novel. (I have a private theory that these writers may need even more revision than I want or expect to do.) But my mind doesn't work that way; I can't find my story by writing it immediately, so I will deal here with my sort of writer. *We* need to find out where we're going before we attempt to write. I have developed a few methods that I use to hold onto that early shimmer and help it to grow. Or to be reborn. Somehow, in the course of three hundred pages or more, I must keep the initial excitement going so my interest will stay high until I finish the project.

How long that first edge of excitement will last differs with each book. I spend time with my notebook, developing my characters, collecting odds and ends of plot, discovering my direction, simply jotting down whatever comes to me—until the moment I *must* write. This always arrives before my planning is complete, and I know better than to deny the urge. At least I may get the opening for my story down. So I reward myself by writing several pages. My actors come onstage and begin to live. This is good for future planning, and I don't mind when the desire to write dies and I must go back to work on my characters and plotting.

When I read over what I've written, exhilaration runs high again, and I want to share this remarkable piece of writing with a reader. I never seem to learn, but perhaps it doesn't matter, since one part of my brain is being realistic and doesn't expect too much too soon. Of course, what I want is warm applause, approval—the same response to the "shimmer" that *I* have been feeling, even though I know that I am the worst possible judge of my own work when I am too close to the creative phase to see its faults.

Usually, my chosen reader, knowing the game, provides encouragement, with a hint of gentle suggestion that brings me down to earth. Sooner or later, I take another look at the first chapter and see if I can do a better version with a little more thought. For the beginner, there may be a danger in asking for criticism too soon. Our excitement over that first shining vision can be damaged all too easily. It's a lot safer to get the work done before we call on that necessary reader/critic.

Though I no longer expect that high point of excitement to last, I know it will return to engage and delight me—and keep me going. The writing of several hundred pages cannot be achieved on a single wave of exhilaration. Still, I can manage to lose myself in individual scenes that I feel are good. Along the way, wonderful new ideas attach themselves, and I take unexpected turns that lift me to the heights again. Fiction writers are allowed to be emotional people. If we write coldly and automatically, it will show.

It isn't wise to wait for these spurts of inspiration to come from out of the blue. I ask myself deliberate questions: What unexpected action can a character take at this point? What surprise event can I supply that will be logical and lift the story? I dream, see pictures in my mind, invent—and encourage lightning to strike repeatedly.

Let's consider three types of excitement that are involved in fiction writing. First and most important is the author's feeling about the story he or she is going to write. That's what I've been talking about. The second is the excitement the characters themselves feel as they play their roles in the story. If you examine what will excite each character and move him or her to action, you'll raise the excitement level.

The third type concerns the reader. If your interest and the interest of the characters remain high, the reader will live your story and take satisfaction from the experience. As writers, our purpose is to make the reader feel emotion along with the characters. But how does a writer retain that high interest level, often so difficult to achieve, when it's necessary to work on the same novel for months, or even years? Boredom for what we're writing and loss of perspective remain a real threat.

To avoid this and keep a certain freshness about the work, I make it a rule not to go back very far over what I've written. When I start work each day, I read only the last finished pages before moving ahead. This gives me a needed impetus to continue. Though I am dying to know what I've done and whether it's any good, I never allow myself to look back for more than a few pages—not for a while, anyway.

Eventually the time comes when I begin to feel sure that what I've written is a mess. I lose interest and courage. Since I expect this to happen, I now go back and read all those earlier pages that I'd stayed away from—read them up to the point where my writing stalled. They always seem much better than I expected, and I'm caught up again in the excitement of the story and can move ahead. I find that I even know my characters better after that rereading. This can be repeated a number of times in the course of writing a novel.

Often I receive letters from young writers—or even older ones who are still beginners—who are experiencing "writer's block." "Writer's block" is not a label I believe in. These pauses and stoppages are never incurable. We learn to set aside the "real" world with its worries and sorrows that can pull us away from our fictional scenes. The healing that results from our writing can be remarkable. We learn to turn the blows life gives us into stories, thus helping not only ourselves, but perhaps our readers as well. Nothing that happens to a writer ever needs to be wasted. We adapt and change and *use,* whether a happening is good or bad. For me the only writer's block occurs when excitement over my creation dies and my interest is suddenly gone. That could be fatal if I accepted the condition!

The problem came home to me repeatedly in the writing of my Charleston, South Carolina, novel, *Woman Without A Past.* I found myself breaking one of my own major rules: *to give my main character a strong, life-or-death drive*—a struggle she must engage in and deal with in order to save herself. In the course of writing this novel, I often failed to achieve this and my excitement for the story died along the way.

In the early stages of the novel, my heroine took action only when she was forced to by the characters around her. *They* all had plenty of drive and purpose, much of it tremendously important to them. My heroine's one goal was to solve the mystery of her birth. But that wasn't strong enough in itself and she drifted along without much drive behind her actions. I worried about her, but couldn't seem to correct the flaw. When I asked myself what she was striving for, fighting for, I came up with nothing strong enough. I ploughed through dull (to me) transition

99

scenes, hoping I could fix them later. (Transition scenes are always hard for me to make interesting, so that was nothing new.)

During this struggle (on my part, if not on my heroine's) I called in every device I knew to keep myself interested in a character who wasn't fighting for her life, or for much of anything else. I examined my other characters—interesting enough—to discover how they would challenge my heroine and force her to act. This worked pretty well. My own interest quickened, and my excitement level rose—at times.

When the action sagged, I worked on emotion. It is all too easy in the middle deserts of a novel to lose contact with the main character's feeling. Each writer must find a way to recover lost emotion. Some play music that moves or stirs them; others take long walks that seem to free the creative mind. Or you may have a trusted friend—not necessarily another writer—with whom to discuss the problem. There are times when talking helps.

My own method is to read. Certain fiction speaks to me. I read, not to imitate or to get ideas, but to find a mood. My attention will wander from the page as something touches some emotion in me. Then I can write, because I have transferred that feeling to my main character. I rewrite the wooden love scene, and this time it works. Once you evoke your memories, they are endlessly useful and can be adapted to the needs of the scene you are working on. My heroine, I find, has a good deal to worry about.

I have also discovered that a good way to cure my loss of interest is to feed something new into my mind. Long ago, when I was teaching writing at New York University, I adopted a slogan: *Interest follows action.* When students would look at me blankly, with not a story idea stirring, I'd tell them to go out and *do* something new. Study something they knew nothing about—have fresh experiences. These need not be earthshaking, but just something to open the possibility of exploring a new field. They were always surprised that their own interest came to life when they took this sort of action, and very quickly they found themselves filled with fresh story ideas. First, you *do* something, and then you get interested. It never fails. While writing *The Singing Stones,* I went up in a hot air balloon. I had no idea how I could get that into a story—but it churned away at the back of my mind and gave me a lovely climax scene.

So when I was baffled by my problems with *Woman Without A Past,* I investigated a new subject, for me: what is known in the psychic field as "channeling," when a voice (from another dimension?) speaks through a living person. Or through a story character! My interest came to life, and I was able to develop several scenes that tied in with the plot. I even investigated cats for this novel, reading several books about them so I could understand and write about the cat in my story. Research about practically anything that will fit in can give you more material than you can handle. You, your characters, and your readers will profit from what you learn.

Nevertheless, when I finished the book, I had no great confidence in what I'd written. I knew there were some good dramatic scenes, and my Charleston setting offered wonderful material. Yet, my heroine's drifting continued to worry me, and I waited anxiously for editorial response. To my surprise, my agent and my daughter thought the story strong, exciting, satisfying. No one seemed to notice that my main character was more done-to than doing. By all the rules I know, it wasn't supposed to work—but it did. Why?

It took me some time to find the answer, and it's a useful one. I discovered the explanation in a book by Dwight Swain: *Creating Characters.* One of the goals he lists for a character is "relief from. . . ." Now I knew why my heroine had succeeded in spite of the author! I had written about a sympathetic young woman who is much put-upon (that's important) and who deserves to win out in the end. The goal of *relief-from-adversity* is legitimate and can be very satisfying to the reader.

A great deal of anxiety can be involved, in spite of having the main character take only minor action on her own. Often she is afraid, and this helped with my own interest as I became aware of her desperate, threatened state. She certainly needed relief from a number of unpleasant actions by other characters.

Anxiety can be a good tool to think about and use. However, I don't recommend that this rather negative goal be the sole direction of your main character. In my next novel, I shall make sure that my main character has a strong drive against tough opposition, though I'll certainly use the element of "relief-from" as well.

All such methods and devices are part of a writer's tool kit. We use them to keep our characters in a state of excitement that will convey itself to the reader and will grow from our own effort to hold that first shimmer of an idea alive—that edge of magical excitement that is the best reward of all to the fiction writer.

# 24

## WHERE DOES YOUR FICTION "LIVE"?

### BY SHELBY HEARON

ON MY EARLY MORNING WALKS, I pass a rural cemetery with a sign offering: PLOTS FOR SALE. My Oxford dictionary defines *plot* as "a small portion of any surface differing in character and aspect from the rest." And this seems to me to be a fine way to think about where fiction begins: with that plot, that parcel of ground, that place that you make yours and no one else's.

I always begin a novel with place. I might choose somewhere I have lingered or left, somewhere I took a fresh turn or turned my back, but when I step on the actual streets of my past, it is as if my story comes unbidden through the soles of my feet.

Sometimes you cannot go back to an actual place you have lived. Times change; houses and neighborhoods are not what they were. In these cases, I find a stand-in locale that has the deep emotional tug that the original had for me. For instance, in a novel called *A Small Town,* I moved a number of scenes from my childhood in Kentucky across the Mississippi River to Missouri, to a tiny town that once had coal-burning furnaces and felt then as my now-prosperous, bustling hometown had felt so many years before. Similarly, in a novel I'm researching now, I've picked a small town in the Blue Ridge Mountains of western South Carolina in which to set an important year when I was five and my daddy was mapping gold mines in north Georgia. I switched location because where we once lived in a rustic cabin has become a busy artists' colony and is no longer the site of my pine-scented memories. (I'm using small towns as examples, because so many of my novels are set there, but the same techniques would apply in choosing one neighborhood over another in any large city.)

Once I've selected my retrospective spot, I'm ready to get to know it from the ground up as it is today. I like to think of a place as having three faces: its history, its view of itself, and its significance to the people who live there. For the first, how it sees its past, I go to the local library's historical archives for clippings, photos, letters, first-hand accounts of earlier times; I investigate the geology and geography. Then, to get a picture of how the community sees itself now, I subscribe to the local newspaper, so I can follow the town through its civic seasons, learn its concerns, hear how it speaks of itself.

When I was working on my novel, *Hug Dancing*, which is set in Waco, Texas (a town that reminds me sharply of the smaller, more insular Austin of my child-rearing years), a lot of my plot grew out of a close reading of the paper. For example, when I saw that the front page of the sports section had a daily fishing column, giving the latest on lures and bait, river and lake conditions, I knew I must have a fisherman as a character. And when I read that the high schools were offering Japanese as a second language, I got a glimpse of what it meant for a little conservative city that had once supplied the whole confederacy with cotton to find itself on the burgeoning science corridor between Austin and Dallas.

But helpful though libraries and newspapers are, the only way you really get what a community is for its people, its voice, habits, ways of giving approval and disapproval, sanctions and prohibitions, is to walk the ground of the town yourself. I like to start my present-day acquaintance with a place by eating and eavesdropping. Meals tell a lot. For instance, in South Carolina on my last trip I had pork chops for breakfast, lunch, and dinner. Then, later that month, checking out the east Texas location where the other part of my fictional family lives, I was served a luscious morning meal of wild Russian hog sausage and batter-fried bacon. Knowing that hickory, pecan, and walnut trees go with such pork economies, I hunted out the rich aromas of green nut husks that will serve to tie my two locations together.

Eating leads to overhearing, of course; food and conversation go together. I always write down every interchange I hear, wanting to get the exact language of how, in this place, women and men talk together, parents and children, old-timers and outsiders. When I was working in Missouri on *A Small Town*, in my back booth at a Mom and Pop cafe, I kept hearing about "when we got the b'ar pit," and the "level of water in the b'ar pit." After a bit, curious, since the bare marshy river bottoms did not seem to me to be bear country. I asked the owner to explain. It seems the word was *borrow*. A borrow pit was a depression, filled up after the topsoil had been sold (borrowed), just as, years before, lumber companies had "borrowed" the region's stand of trees. From these conversations I gained a sense both of the area's language and of its way of dealing with loss.

Being on location in the place you have chosen, you can also see, with your own special vision, the sudden object or juxtaposition or absence you did not expect or did not recall. For example, in setting a novel called *Five Hundred Scorpions* in the small Mexican village of Tepoztlán, I was choosing a place that reminded me of how I'd felt the first time I went into a foreign-speaking country: a stranger in a strange land. I'd read seven books on the much-studied mountain village, and even had a map of the town when I arrived. But when I actually found myself on its steep tropical streets, I was struck at once by the fact that there was *no wood* anywhere. The rich homes had tile floors and metal doors and chrome chairs; the poor homes had dirt floors and hide chairs and rush doors. The local industry was charcoal—all the trees were burned before they reached lumber potential. At once I knew that my main character, who had left his wife and law practice behind in Virginia to come to Mexico, had left behind more than he counted on: handcrafted furniture, old oak doors, burnished hardwood floors. And this became a symbol of all that he missed that he had not expected to. Again—as happens every time I arrive on the streets of a chosen place—my story changed in response to what I saw.

Once you've picked a real place from your past or a stand-in place that conjures up the sounds, smells, and sights that remind you of old times and fuel your story, once you have been there and seen and heard what's there today, the final step is to make sure your setting is singular and significant for the reader. For you, it is special because you were there; for the reader, meeting it for the first time, it must be made memorable. In choosing Missouri for the setting of my childhood scenes, I selected a town that had fallen into the Mississippi River in 1811 in the worst earthquake of the western hemisphere—so that the reader would have a sense of shaky ground, of being in a spot that might at any moment disappear. Again, for my Carolina town, I have picked a community that before the Civil War was the site of the grandest artesian spa in the country, so that the reader will enter an area that feels itself to have been wiped out by history, will get to know people who feel their past has been taken away. And, in my Mexican village, I

105

didn't select the locale I had actually visited before, but instead chose a place that had been studied by male social scientists from the Twenties through the Sixties, and I thought readers would enjoy the idea of two female social scientists studying the place in the present.

Having made your place particular for the reader, you are ready, by repetition, accrual, exaggeration, to do what I call "turn up the volume," so that the reader can hear what you have to say. Working on *Hug Dancing*, for example, I noticed that every day the newspaper had some big item about the weather. Reading up on record highs and lows, heaviest ice storms, floods, tornadoes, all the major acts of nature in Texas, I found that Waco was always right in the middle, getting hit with the worst of whatever was blowing in, most notably the tornado of '53, which leveled the entire downtown. So, after experiencing the gusty winds and sudden storms myself, I made sure that some of the most important parts of my plot hinged on the weather: a mother's drowning in a flash flood, a father's crash in an ice storm, lovers taking cover from hail, my fisherman stuck at home in a heavy duster. And also, weather became a central metaphor for the book: my characters' feelings reflecting those of the child-raising time in my life when everything seemed out of control.

Texas naturalist Roy Bedichek once said of the cabin where he worked: "The sights, sounds, odors and especially the feel of this place stimulate in me memories so warm and intimate that taking up residency here seems a homecoming." That is the feeling I set out to recapture when I select a location for a story: that feeling about place which is where fiction begins.

# 25

## EVERYONE IS A STORYTELLER

### BY HERBERT GOLD

AT AGE 13, MY HORMONES BUSY WITH THE USUAL FRANTIC RUSH ORDER, fate dealt me one of the wild cards of adolescence. An older woman—she was 15—chose to giggle, surprise me with a kiss, and then dash in her saddle shoes down the romantic February bleakness of a school stairway. I was lost to love.

Pattie's kiss ignited a fantasy that may seem insane to someone who doesn't remember the beginnings of adolescence. I was a bit nuts.

What rescued me? I began to write poems and stories, lyrical yawps, melodramatic tales of lost love, fatal love, abandoned love, even miraculously fulfilled love.

Like other writers, I use my work to approach the outskirts of sanity. I imagine galaxies of love out of a teasing kiss. When Freud suggested storytellers need love to function properly, he surely meant to add: *and everyone is a storyteller*. We all dream, exploring in dreams our need for love, freely indulging fears and lusts, sometimes awakening in a sweat from this serious work. What artists do is master their dreams, partially anyway, and express them in a form that brings a moment of communion. It's a religious experience that may even elicit applause.

Now let me modestly pretend I'm writing about someone else. That's how writing becomes objective, isn't it?

As an adolescent he believed he was not really his Cleveland parents' child but the son of Feodor Chaliapin, the great Russian basso. Just as mental power could oblige the girl he loved to climb out of her window and into his arms, so he believed he could sing Boris Godunov or at least write poetry and stories. This last delusion saved him. Thinking made it so. He spun out a dream about being the illegitimate son of a Russian giant, singing *basso profundo* about true love under a tree growing in some vague geography near Lake Erie, not far from Moscow. He learned to treat his delusions as comedy to be shared.

Otherwise, had he not been able to turn fantasies into stories, he might have been an inmate, a drunk, or a morose old mumbler. Being a novelist is an improvement, no matter what the reviews say. The storyteller masters his nuttiness and burns it as fuel for the communication of dreams.

To master experience, at least temporarily, is the ultimate success of art. The French philosopher-mathematician Poincaré said he put his problems under his pillow, slept on them, and the solution cooked together, problem and head, while he dreamed.

Not every sleeper finds the secret of the universe. But waking or sleeping, below the reverie line, we are all continually trying out new possibilities. If we can find a way to express them, we take control of a piece of our lives.

Even following the lead of an artist, being audience or appreciator, means we share the work of putting still another perspective on what the artist offers. I may not be able to carry a tune, but when I hear music, it changes my metabolism. And when Mose Allison sings, "If your phone ain't ringin', it's me that ain't callin'," we know there is someone like us out there, overcoming vengefulness after hurt at the hands of a beloved. His art helps us take control of our chaos.

Mad Alex, a nonstop talker at the Co-Existence Bagel Shop during my early beatnik days in San Francisco, lectured to the seen and the unseen. Surely he was a little off, a lot off, telling folks, "I got the bucket if you got the water." But his power to dip into his soul and come up with this insidiously suggestive poetry gave him some status. People tended to listen. His value on earth was confirmed. It was better than just exploding or dying, which will come soon enough anyway.

The psychologist Selma Fraiberg described Franz Kafka's genius as his ability to capture his dream life, a kind of booty that he brought back from sleep. By the discipline of prose, he preserved himself. Otherwise, she suggested, he might have been a schizophrenic. He nailed his demons by naming them with initials.

Fantasy has us all in its grip. We can't live without dreaming. The scholars of sleep suggest that dreamtime is as important as the physical regeneration that takes place, and that deprived of dreamtime, we become disoriented, psychotic. We are all storytellers—it's a required course.

So if everybody dreams, defanging dreads, practicing possibilities, why should we need the waking exercise of art? That one essential quality is missing in mere dreamwork: communication. Look at the response on the face of a significant other when you stumble out with your dream at breakfast. Boredom and bewilderment. The dream says little unless the listener is a professional or the teller shapes it into a vision.

The dreamer is alone with his urgings. The writer communicates with those others out there. The effort of shaping, finding a way of sharing, is profoundly gratifying and healing. It brings the dreamer back into the family.

When I go through a period of not telling stories, my dreams become frightening. I wake out of nightmare, grinding my teeth. My dyslexic dentist says: For the sake of your mandibular joint, keep writing, fella.

And everyone can do something like it, needs to. Everyone is crazy at 13 and every other age. We yearn, have fantasies, our desires are unique, we correct and anticipate our daily lives. Some go out of control, but some make furniture. Some only drink or dope and some write (and drink, too). Some grieve for lost possibilities and some shape the world by painting, sculpting, making music, or just telling lies with a glitter in their eyes. We all need to ride our energies. The artist needs it a lot, and during those moments of a lifetime when he is doing it, knows a happiness very much like that of lovemaking. So does my fanatic friend, endlessly constructing a sailboat in his garage. He'll never sail in it, he'll probably never get it out of the garage—that's not the point. In his dream, he's an ancient mariner with sun-baked, salt-basted gaze. In reality, he can admire his skill at caulking and shaping while his friends murmur, "Hey! Good work!" and his body makes love with tools he has learned to control.

My dyslexic dentist expresses his soul through beautiful carpentry; it gives shape to what he cannot express with words or by a water-cooled drill. Music as the wonder of sound and time, painting as the shock of color, sculpture as celebration of the miracle of space, volume, and weight—all the arts turn mysteries into consolations and exhilarations. Theater brings communion; the artist's creation relieves loneliness; and my *aha* when I am persuaded to share your dream makes it not mere craziness. You have given me something like a work of art, a thing made.

THIS IS THE LAW: You don't commit suicide in the middle of writing the note.

Here are the amendments: After you've finished, if you're proud of

109

your note, you tend to wait around to see how the audience receives it. And if the reception is enthusiastic—What cunning melancholia! How brilliantly you express your grief!—you offer yourself up for further preening purposes. Your coat gets glossy. You feel knitted back together.

When the distraction and trouble build up again, the nightmares and anxieties grow pernicious, you start to construct your next suicide novel (or poem or story). This one will *really* do the trick.

In fact, of course, some poets commit suicide. But not when the poem is coming good. The trouble is, as E. E. Cummings said, the poet is only a poet during a few hours of his lifetime. The rest of the time he's a would-be poet and it's hard to remember what he can do.

The artist's work of mastering madness, bringing comfort out of grief, is never completed. To make the unreal of dreams into the real of art is a job and a half. It works for those whose passion survives distraction and makes it work.

F. Scott Fitzgerald described an embrace with words like a romantic ballad: Out of her kiss, I built a stairway to the stars. Well, we all know such a stairway tends to topple and leave the kisser tumbling lost in space. Imagination, undaunted hope, discipline, and a sense of rhythm may keep the image alive in the worlds of if.

Pattie, magic lady of my 13th year, look what you've made of me.

# 26

## Fiction Openings: Five Musts

### By F. A. Rockwell

In fiction as in life, first impressions are the strongest, or, as a management consultant tells his sales personnel: "If you don't strike oil in two minutes, stop boring."

There are five "musts" that the beginning of a story, novel, or chapter should have to make your readers read on.

(1) It should capture attention with a fresh, original hook.

(2) It should arouse expectation with a promise of more to come.

(3) It should let the reader in on the *Who, What, When, Where,* and *Why,* with telling clues as to how the problem will be solved. Jules Pfeiffer updates these classic "fives" this way: Wake 'em Up, Wind 'em Up, Whip 'em Up, Whoa! and Wind Down." (But you should save the last two for later, not for the opening, which should never wind down.)

(4) It should include a cliffhanger that makes us read on.

(5) It should set the tone for the story or chapter.

Plot your fiction all the way through. Decide what is its strongest feature, and present this in your opening. If you are writing a predominantly character story, begin with one character (or more); if it's an atmosphere piece, take your reader to a certain place; if action, start with something active; if emotion, start with a strong feeling. A philosophical opening should prepare your reader for deep reflections on life; a situation opening should plunge your reader into an intriguing story, one that will be the focus; and a dialogue opener should promise that the emphasis will be on communication between people.

No matter which type of opening you start with, it must establish the style, arouse *suspense,* and imply that something dramatic has happened, and there will be more to come.

Even if the author works with a canvas broad enough to accommodate a 50,000-word novel, he usually begins with sharp brush strokes that grab the reader's attention quickly. Law enforcement training stresses immediate reactions, as found in the novel openings of works by writers like Dorothy Uhnak. Look at the *in medias res* beginning of her *False Witness:*

*Prologue:*

As she lay near death, Sanderalee Dawson was spared the pain of her terrible injuries by shock.

She swallowed the salty, thin blood that filled her mouth. It was an instinctive attempt to keep the life force inside of her, as was her attempt to breathe in small, short, careful gasps rather than in huge, lung-filling expansions, which she might then be unable to exhale.

*Chapter One starts:*

She had been left for dead. Had Sanderalee Dawson been, in fact, dead, a great many lives and reputations and careers and ambitions and relationships would now be quite different. Including mine. Especially mine.

How's that for a running start? Here are a few professional examples of each type of opening:

## Character opening

Fay Morgan never had any money. Never had had any money, in fact. But, then, she'd always *known* she'd never had any money, and that helped, really it did. More than you'd think.

The other thing Fay had always known was what was going to happen. Where things were. Who was coming into who else's life and when and why.
—*The Fortune Teller,* by Marsha Norman

According to the wall, he was dead. Keith Johnson stood at the Vietnam Veterans Memorial and saw himself reflected in the polished black granite, a tall, powerfully built man with prematurely gray hair and borderless black eyes. Inscribed in stone was his own name, *Keith Everett Johnson,* one of thousands who died in Vietnam.

But he was not dead.

—*Crux,* by Richard Allen

Barbara Taylor Bradford's *Act of Will* opens with three characters who will be equally important in her novel:

Audra Crowther sat on the sofa in the living room of her daughter's Manhattan penthouse. She held herself tense and clenched her hands together so hard that the knuckles shone white as she looked from her daughter Christina to her granddaughter Kyle.

The two younger women stood in the middle of the room, their faces pale, their eyes blazing as they glared at each other. Their angry words of a few minutes ago still reverberated on the warm afternoon air.

Here's character in action plus atmosphere:

Chloe Carriere strode swiftly through the Heathrow departure lounge, trying with little success to escape the inquisitive lenses of the familiar throng of paparazzi. As photographers buzzed around her, several businessmen waiting for their flights lowered their morning newspapers to stare at one of Britain's most famous and sexiest singing stars.

—*Prime Time*, by Joan Collins

## Atmosphere opening

Chapter 1 of Thomas Harris's *The Silence of the Lambs* takes us out of our usual environment into an ambience that promises unusual happenings. It also includes characterization, action, and a cliff-hanger.

Behavioral Science, the FBI section that deals with serial murder, is on the bottom floor of the Academy building at Quantico, half-buried in the earth. Clarice Starling reached it flushed after a fast walk from Hogan's Alley on the firing range. She had grass in her hair and grass stains on her FBI Academy windbreaker from diving to the ground under fire in an arrest problem on the range.

No one was in the outer office, so she fluffed briefly by her reflection in the glass doors. She knew she could look all right without primping. Her hands smelled of gunsmoke, but there was no time to wash—Section Chief Crawford's summons had said *now*.

Here's a different atmosphere and a hint of a vital decision:

There is a small village high in the mountains of Ethiopia. I can't tell you its name. But often I dream of my village high in the Simien mountains, and when I wake up my face is wet with tears.

In the dream I stand with my *shamma* wrapped tightly around me, for the wind is chill. I wait for someone—perhaps for the spirits of my mother and father, both dead, to lead me away. I hear the sudden loud call of an eagle, and I cannot decide: Shall I follow? Or shall I stay? How can I leave my home and those I love?

—*The Return*, by Sonia Levitin

## Action opening

The reader who wants action fiction should be clued into this with some visual movement in the very beginning.

The fright came later. At the moment that the first attempt was made on Tom

113

Costigan's life, I was immobilized by the crazy unexpectedness of it—a live hand grenade dropping on the carpeted floor between Costigan and myself. My first fuzzy thought was that it was a joke concocted by one of the cartoonists. Their idea of humor was quite primitive. The grenade hissed. I half expected the infernal thing to pop open and wave a flag, saying "BANG!" If it didn't, well, then all three of us were going to be blown to kingdom come bloody and disheveled. I stared at the grenade, unable to move.

> —*The Hell's Kitchen Connection,*
> by Robert B. Gillespie

Here it was, some action finally—an armed hold-up of a town bus—and Craig Rollins was in urgent need of a toilet! Nevertheless, Craig raised his camera once again and snapped, just as a scared-looking man was hopping down the steps of the halted bus. Then Craig ran, heading for Eats and Take-Away, where he knew there was a men's room by the phones.

Craig was back in under a minute, but by then the action seemed to be over. He hadn't heard any gunshots. A cop was blowing a whistle. An ambulance pulled up . . .

> —"Where the Action Is,"
> by Patricia Highsmith

## Dialogue opening

Conversation at or near the beginning promises fiction that will be mainly about interactions. This is doubly true in the first chapter of *The Celestial Bed,* by Irving Wallace: Dr. Arnold Freeberg has set up a sex surrogate clinic in Tucson, Arizona, which has cured impotence in several patients, including Timothy, the son of Ben Hebble, the city's most successful banker. The banker tells the doctor:

". . . In two months you did it. After that, Timothy played the field for a while until he fell in love with a pretty young lady from Texas. They tried living together, and it was such a success that they're getting married. Because of you, I expect to be a grandfather yet!"

He backs up his gratitude by setting up a foundation that will guarantee one hundred thousand dollars a year for the doctor and his staff. But there is a problem, as we learn from City Attorney Tom O'Neil's dialogue with Dr. Freeberg:

"I've been officially informed by—by several other therapists that you're using a sex surrogate to cure patients. Is that true?" Freeberg squirmed uneasily. "Why, yes, it—it is true. Because I've found that it's the only means that works with many dysfunctional patients."
O'Neil shook his head. "It's against the law in Arizona, Arnold."

This proves the plus-minus dynamism necessary in good plotting. Dr.

114

Freeberg is elated by the banker's generous donation (+), and then is deflated when O'Neil tells him that surrogacy is illegal in Arizona (–). Not only is this a powerful (and necessary) reversal, but it prepares the reader for the tremendous conflicts later on.

## Emotion opening

Most romance novels begin with emotional reactions, often blended with characterization, atmosphere, or action. Elizabeth Forsythe Hailey's *Joanna's Husband and David's Wife* is an emotional portrait of a marriage written like a journal. What's unique about this format, continued throughout the book, is that after each entry written by the wife, the husband inserts his feelings printed in italics:

Her opening:

I did something today I've never done before—asked a boy for a date. I can't fall asleep for wondering why. Maybe if I write down what's happening between us I won't be so frightened. I promise this won't turn into another of my mushy high school diaries. That phase of my life is behind me! Besides, I don't feel mushy about him at all.

His comments:

*Well, thanks. I had never felt so mushy about a girl in my life. And what's wrong with a little mush? Hate the word, love the feeling. In fact, I still feel mushy about her even now. Are there tears in these old eyes?*

## Situation opening

I held the telephone tensely as I listened. The woman from the Center sounded compassionate, kind, considerate—all those good things that I'd needed so desperately in the past. Only now I dreaded the opening of old wounds. Seven years had gone by since Debbie was three, and the chances of finding my lost daughter grew slimmer all the time.

"It's a very long shot, Mrs. Blake," the voice said, "but I know you want to follow up on the slightest lead, so perhaps you would talk to this woman in British Columbia. It isn't a matter for the police yet, and she seems a responsible person with good credentials."

Clear across the country in Canada! But then, Debbie could be anywhere.

—*Feather on the Moon,*
by Phyllis A. Whitney

The men who wanted to kill Ahmet Yilmaz were serious people. They were exiled Turkish students living in Paris, and they had already murdered an attache at the Turkish Embassy and firebombed the home of a senior executive of Turkish Airlines. They chose Yilmaz as their next target because he was a wealthy supporter of the military dictatorship and because he lived, conveniently, in Paris.

—*Lie Down with Lions,*
by Ken Follett

I am sitting by the coffin watching him. They have drawn up the lid so that nothing of him is visible except his face . . . I am watching him, as once he watched me.

I wanted his death. I think he wanted mine.

—"Tomorrow I Will Clean the Brass,"
by Victoria Holt

## Philosophical opening

People who still believe in good surprises are always young; the ones who have come to believe surprises can only be bad, or that there will no longer be any surprises at all, are old—no matter what their real age is. The phone rings late at night and the old ones think immediately of disaster: an accident, illness, death. The young ones simply think "I hope it's for me." Of course there are bad surprises; this is life after all, a grab bag. But there are also the other kind. They exist. They do.

—*After the Reunion,*
by Rona Jaffee

Fairy tales, we have been told, have within them the content of all fiction. As an exercise, write the same story as a fairy tale, and then as the kind of fiction we are more used to.

—"A Writing Lesson,"
by Mary Gordon

The principal trouble with being married is that being single never prepares you for it. The initiated members never tell you beforehand; no college course provides a proper introduction.

—"The Uninvited Guest,"
by Eileen Herbert Jordan

Try writing a "get-up-and-go" opening of each category: perhaps a brief, attention-grabbing opening paragraph like the one that starts the novel, *Blind Trust,* by Susannah Bamford:

It was either leave him or kill him. It had come down to that.

While it may be true that you shouldn't write the real opening of any fiction until after you have worked out the whole plotline and have decided what the emphasis should be, many professional writers keep files of exciting but unused openings they wrote as they thought of them. Later, they serve as inspiration for other works. The major ingredient is *suspense,* so tease and titillate, but never give away the conclusion. It may help to keep in mind the opening of W. Somerset Maugham's story, "The Romantic Young Lady":

One of the many inconveniences of real life is that it seldom gives you a complete story. Some incident has excited your interest, the people who are concerned in it are in the devil's own muddle, and you wonder what on earth will happen next. Well, generally nothing happens. The inevitable catastrophe you foresaw wasn't inevitable after all, and high tragedy, without any regard to artistic decency, dwindles into drawing-room comedy. Now, growing old has many disadvantages, but it has this compensation . . . that sometimes it gives you the opportunity of seeing what was the outcome of certain events you had witnessed long ago. You had given up the hope of ever knowing what was the end of the story, and then, when you least expected it, it is handed to you on a platter.

You might say that telling or even hinting at the ending in your opening is like wishing for old age while you're still young.

Other guidelines for openings:

1) Start either *in medias res* or just before or after a crisis, but never on a dull plateau.

2) Introduce the main characters before bringing in secondary ones either by direct onstage action or by referring to them. Present the main problem before introducing minor problems.

3) Establish a specific emotional reaction and the characters' emotional attitudes toward one another (even though they may change convincingly later). Strive for variety, so that the reader doesn't *like* or *dislike* everyone. Use character clues, action, and dialogue to help the reader choose whom to root for and vice versa.

4) Do not open with a single character just thinking or reminiscing or feeling sorry for himself or herself. If alone, he should be in the midst of a crucial, active situation or making a momentous decision.

5) Plant any clues or information that will be important later, but not too deeply or so apparent that the reader could guess too much, too soon.

6) Never be satisfied with a rough draft. Prune and polish every sentence so that it's the very best to rivet the attention of the reader and lure him on.

7) To produce a real page-turner, be sure that there's some unsolved mystery in the beginning and a cliffhanger at the end.

8) Use a quicker pace for the opening of a short story than for a novella or a novel.

9) Don't telescope the ending or give the impression that everything's going to be fine before the actual resolution comes. When your reader stops guessing, he'll stop reading, so always keep one step ahead.

# 27

# THE ESSENCE OF STORYTELLING: DRAMATIZE, DRAMATIZE

## BY ELIZABETH FORSYTHE HAILEY

DRAMATIZE, DRAMATIZE" IS THE ADVICE Henry James gave to writers of fiction.

His advice was reinforced in my own case by marriage to a novel-hating playwright who is not only my first audience but also my first editor. I knew when I started my first novel I would have to find a form that would engage and hold his attention—which is why I chose in *A Woman of Independent Means* to show the life of a woman from childhood to old age through the letters she writes, leaving the audience to imagine what her correspondents say to her in reply.

One of the keys to dramatizing is enlisting the imagination of your audience, forcing them to do some of the work and in effect making them accomplices in the conspiracy that is fiction.

Drama is the essence of storytelling. Wanting to know what happens next is what keeps a viewer in his seat or a reader turning the pages of a novel. But telling a story—like starting a fire—requires friction, two different elements striking against each other. Like natural combustion, the dramatic conflict that ignites a work of fiction requires antagonists.

In *A Woman of Independent Means* the main antagonist—the arch villain, if you will—is time. My heroine Bess, a character based on my own grandmother, was a woman with an extraordinary appetite for life. She wanted to see and do it all, and a single lifetime was not nearly long enough. She asked that her epitaph read "to be continued."

This central conflict was heightened when I adapted the novel into a one-person stage play. Thanks to a tour-de-force display of acting by stage and film star Barbara Rush, the audience was able to witness a lifetime in the space of two hours. Without benefit of makeup or costume changes, relying only on the most subtle adjustments in speech and movement, she was able to transform herself from a young girl of eighteen into a frail old woman facing death. The message of the book—to show how quickly even a long, full life passes—was translated into heightened dramatic terms on the stage.

The experience of adapting my first novel into my first stage play continues to serve me well when I return to the novel form.

I had no problem finding points of conflict and dramatizing them in my novel *Joanna's Husband and David's Wife*. It's the chronicle of a marriage over twenty-five years from a dual perspective—the point of view of both husband and wife.

Joanna starts a diary the day she meets David, determined to have a complete record of her relationship with the man she plans to marry. On their twenty-fourth anniversary, she returns to her parents, leaving the diary to her daughter, who has fallen in love for the first time. The diary is her way of showing her daughter what marriage is like (my characters have learned the secret of dramatizing: show, don't tell). But David discovers the journal first and decides to add his side of the story before their daughter reads it.

The device of the diary—and David's later discovery of it—allowed me to make use of two techniques that reinforce dramatic conflict: passage of time and point of view. The narrative spine of the novel is from Joanna's point of view—her diary entries. But David, looking back at an event, often remembers it differently—and there are times when he has no memory at all of what Joanna is describing. Using two points of view and locating them at different moments in time not only allows the characters to express hidden conflicts (those hidden from each other as well as those hidden from the reader), but encourages them to keep secrets. Sometimes what is unsaid between them can be more explosive than what is said.

However, in transforming *Joanna's Husband and David's Wife* into a two-character stage play, I had to write some of the novel's unwritten scenes, exploring the conflicts anew and allowing the characters to confront each other in the same time frame.

With my novel *Home Free*, my heroine took shape in my head a full year before I could come up with a story for her. I wanted to write about a middle-aged woman from a conventional, middle-class background who finds herself alone (I wasn't sure in the beginning whether her husband would die or desert her for another woman) and is forced to redefine her ideas about home and family.

I had some vague idea that she would sell the house she had shared with her husband and, instead of finding another permanent residence, would become a housesitter for friends who traveled a lot or divided their lives among houses in different places. My idea was to make her a member (at least through marriage) of the moviemaking community—work that keeps people on the move. I saw her becoming involved in the lives of the different families for whom she served as a housesitter.

But even though I made a lot of notes on possible characters and situations, I knew in my heart of hearts I did not have the makings of a novel: The elements of conflict were missing. At best what I had was a book of interrelated short stories with my main character serving as a connecting device. But that was not what I wanted to write. My heroine, Kate Hart, was real and full to me, and I wanted to write a novel in which her actions would be focal.

Then three years ago at Thanksgiving I read a magazine piece on a homeless family in Los Angeles. The faces in the accompanying photographs seared my consciousness. There was a husband, a wife, a son, a daughter, even a dog—the all-American family—but they were living in their car. The article describing their ever more desperate plight changed all my comfortable assumptions about why and how people found themselves living on the street. Suddenly I saw my heroine opening the front door of the house where she now lived alone to a fictional family very much like the one whose faces now confronted me in the magazine. And I knew I had found the missing half of my novel. My heroine, who had a home but no family, was going to get involved with a family who had no home.

The story fell into place very quickly. I saw it in scenes, like a film, and used a device screenwriters often employ when constructing a movie script. I took a pack of index cards and, allotting one card for each scene, made notes of what I imagined happening between characters. The test of whether a scene deserved to be written was the strength of the potential conflict at the core of it.

I have a tendency in my first draft to spend too much time establishing characters and setting before zeroing in on the central conflict. But using the index card system forces a novelist to think in terms of scenes rather than endless chunks of prose.

When I first started plotting *Home Free,* I planned to show my two main characters in their separate settings before bringing them together. I wrote on my first index card: "Christmas Eve. Kate and her

121

husband fight. He leaves." And on my second card: "Christmas Eve. Homeless man panhandles outside supermarket to buy presents for his family." Staring at my third index card, wondering how they would meet, I realized I had started the book too soon. The point of the novel was to make their two very separate worlds collide, and the sooner that happened, the more compelling and original my novel would be. So I put aside my first two index cards and started over. Notes for my new opening read: "Kate sees homeless man's car stall in front of her house as her husband walks out the door." Those two abandoned index cards saved me hundreds of unnecessary words.

Index cards are a terrific way to construct anything—novel, screenplay, magazine article, possibly even a poem (though I've never tried it)—much less cumbersome and rigid than a prose outline. You can shift scenes around or delete them with ease, and whenever a random idea occurs to you—a line of description, a scrap of dialogue— you can jot it down where you think it might fit.

The novel is such an open-ended form (running anywhere from several hundred pages to several thousand), it does not encourage disciplined dramatic construction. In contrast, the length of a play or film (with some well-known exceptions) is pretty much decided by the patience of the audience, and usually takes place within a two- or three-hour time frame. Also, economics can dictate the number of characters and settings.

But the novel is wide open—choices of scenes, characters, points of view limited only by the imagination of the novelist. The intoxicating possibilities of so much freedom can easily overpower a latent sense of dramatic economy. The task of the novelist is to practice from within the discipline imposed on the playwright from without.

It is not a coincidence that a lot of best-selling authors—Sidney Sheldon is a notable example—began by writing for the screen. They developed the craft of storytelling by learning how to construct scenes—scenes that would advance the action by entangling the characters in conflict.

In plotting your novel, try to see it as a film or play. Watch the story unfold before your eyes. Listen as your characters talk and argue.

My friend, the late Tommy Thompson, was a distinguished journalist and author of such nonfiction bestsellers as *Blood and Money* and *Serpentine* when he embarked on his first novel. Several chapters into it, he found himself for the first time in his life paralyzed by a massive case of writer's block. He had churned out hundreds of thousands of words under unrelenting deadline pressure as a journalist, but he was not prepared for the terror that comes from facing a blank page when the story is taking place only inside your own head.

Fortunately, he had a very wise editor who said to him, "Just because you're writing fiction doesn't mean you've stopped being a reporter. What you have to do is what you always do when you cover a story. Look at what's going on, listen to what people are saying, and report it—report all of it. The only difference is that the story you're reporting now is taking place in your imagination. But the process is the same."

I can imagine no better advice for a writer of fiction, whether novelist, playwright, or screenwriter. First see the scene, then report it. From that point on, you're home free.

Home free. Good title.

# 28

## GOING FOR THE JUGULAR

### BY EILEEN GOUDGE

IMAGINE YOU'RE IN AN AGENT'S OR EDITOR'S OFFICE and you're describing the plot of the novel you're writing. It goes something like this: A kid comes home from college and discovers his father has been murdered. He's crazed with grief, and now Dad's ghost is urging him to avenge his death by nailing the murderer, who just happens to be the kid's uncle, who's now married to the kid's mother. Sound farfetched? You bet. And yet who would dispute *Hamlet* as one of the greatest, and most enduring, literary works of the English language?

Often, in my own novels, I'm accused of being "over the top." Far from feeling criticized, I take it as a compliment! Just as, in fiction, characters must be larger than life in order to capture the reader's interest and sympathies, so, too, must plots be larger than life for their ultimate denouement to truly satisfy.

There's a wonderful line in one of my favorite old movies, *Miracle on 34th Street,* in which Edmund Gwen says to the young Natalie Wood, "You've heard of the British nation . . . and the Indian nation . . . well, this [pointing to his head] is the imagi-nation." I like that metaphor of the mind as an actual place, a country unto itself filled with limitless possibilities. Imagine then, in the midst of this vast country with its teeming populace, a story so big it captures the front-page headline of every major newspaper and is featured on every television news show. A government ousted by a military coup. A mafia don on trial. A former heavyweight boxing champion accused of rape. The stuff of real life, but not *everyday* real life—not what Joe Smith in Terre Haute had for breakfast, but whom Jackie Onassis dined with last night at the Four Seasons. It's what sells newspapers and magazines, what makes you stay tuned to the evening news after bedtime. The same with fiction—it's those larger-than-life characters reacting to the larger-than-life situations they're thrown into that make for busy cash registers in bookstores.

124

In my first hardcover adult novel, *Garden of Lies* (I'd written twenty-five paperback novels for young adults), a very pregnant Sylvie Rosenthal is shopping in Bergdorf Goodman's when her water breaks. She's in a panic. She has good reason to suppose the child she's about to give birth to is that of her swarthy Greek lover rather than of her light-complected husband. When her worst fears are realized, she finds salvation of sorts in a fire that rages through the hospital that night, and claims the life of her ward mate. In the confusion, Sylvie rescues the dead woman's baby . . . only to have the infant girl later mistaken for her own. A mistake she decides to go along with—with disastrous results.

Over the top? Undoubtedly. O.K., but let's suppose I'd written *Garden of Lies* another way: Sylvie's husband is with her when she goes into labor. One look at his newborn daughter and he realizes he's been cuckolded. Sylvie must then spend the rest of the book working her way back into his good graces.

More realistic, perhaps, but not as exciting. For one thing, a woman yearning for her child—a child she herself, in a moment of impulse, had given up—is far more compelling than that same woman merely eating crow for four hundred and fifty pages. And what about the two daughters? Suppose they'd merely been neighbors, or friends in school? Again, not nearly as dramatic as a pair of women who have never met and whose destinies are as closely linked as those of two trains hurtling down the same track from opposite directions. When Rose discovers that the love of her life, Brian, has married another woman—and that woman is none other than Sylvie's changeling, Rachel—credibility is stretched a bit, but, oh boy, just sit back and watch the fireworks! And if the million copies that placed *Garden of Lies* on the top 10 paperback list for 1989 is any testament, then I'm sure countless readers would agree.

In my novel, *Such Devoted Sisters,* it was the theme of sibling rivalry that I took to extremes. In real life, what does a woman do when she's jealous of her prettier, more accomplished sister—snitch the sister's favorite earrings? Flirt with her boyfriend to get back at her? But what if you took it several steps further, as I did in *Sisters*—which kicks off in 1954—and had that jealous woman actually mail a letter containing evidence of her sister's "unAmerican" activities to Senator Joe McCarthy? An act of betrayal which results in her sister's suicide, and leaves a second generation of sisters virtually orphaned. How can Dolly *ever* absolve herself of a sin of such magnitude? And how do Annie and Laurel, two teenaged girls, alone in the world and nearly penniless, manage to survive when they subsequently run away to New York City?

Let's back up a bit, and start at the beginning. "What if?"—the seed from which every plot is germinated. The trick is to raise the ante, increase the stakes, so that "What if?" becomes "If only . . ." If only Sylvie can find and reconcile with her true daughter. If only Dolly can fulfill her desire to win the love and forgiveness of her nieces. If only Annie, in love with Laurel's husband, will realize in time that it's really Emmett she needs. "If only . . ." is the clock that keeps the plot ticking, and the reader turning the pages; it's the internal combustion that fires that story, and, if the stakes are high enough, propels it at a breakneck pace right through to the very last page.

Now that I've told you some of the ingredients that go into writing a page-turner, the question is *how*? How do you go about fashioning a plot that will hook a reader and keep him or her glued to the pages?

*Don't be afraid to take risks.* Outrageous, outlandish, over-the-top—it's the stuff of our most beloved books, plays, movies. A girl whisked from the Kansas prairies by a cyclone to a magical, mythical land. A pair of teenagers so passionately in love with one another they defy their warring families and even follow one another into death. A southern belle who singlehandedly holds together her crumbling plantation in the wake of the Civil War. Trust in the power of storytelling at its grandest—and in the reader's capacity for suspension of disbelief—and you may be rewarded, as I was, by letters like the one I received from a friend who had given his dying mother a copy of *Garden of Lies* and reported that it was the only book, during her last pain-wracked days in the hospital, that held her attention to the end.

*Put the horse before the cart.* If your characters are fleshed out, their motives and modus operandi clearly established, almost any situation they are placed in can be made plausible. When Sylvie, in *Garden of Lies,* switches her baby for another, you believe a mother could really do such a thing because Sylvie is not merely reacting to a set of circumstances, she's acting out of her own insecurities, doubts, and past experience—all of which have been firmly established earlier in the chapter. And in *Such Devoted Sisters,* when Dolly mails the damning letter to McCarthy, one can even sympathize with her to some extent.

126

We know, for instance, how much she truly loved her sister, and how hurt she was by Eve's callow disregard of her feelings. Even as the letter slips from her fingers into the mailbox, we understand her motives and can see ahead into her future; we know how tormented she'll be. Most of all, the reader feels that, yes, given the same situation, *she* might have reacted in the same way.

Character development, then, in essence, is the key to making outrageous plots stick. Had Juliet come across as drab and one-dimensional, would anyone have believed Romeo would want to die for her? Had Scarlett not rescued Melanie and her baby from the flames of Atlanta, would we have believed her capable of saving Tara?

Often, it's the plot that is blamed when a novel fails to capture our imagination. But, really, almost *any* plot, even one truly outrageous, will work if you can make the reader fall in love with your characters. Ask any one of the millions of readers who gobble up Stephen King novels!

A word about character development—one trick I learned early in the game, when I was writing paperback novels for teens, which were set in high school and therefore teeming with characters, was how to keep the reader from confusing all those names. I always try and introduce characters within context, that is, doing something that makes them unique, sets them apart from everyone else. As in this excerpt from *Too Much, Too Soon:*

> Alex was nowhere in sight. Then Kit spotted a pair of tanned, muscular legs sticking out from underneath the back end. They were soon followed by a T-shirt-clad chest and a head capped by sleek mahogany-colored hair. Kit wasn't a bit surprised to see her friend this way—Alex, to say the least, was hardly the conventional type. While her hobby wasn't fixing cars or anything, she did know a little about them and saw no reason for getting someone else to do a job she was perfectly capable of doing herself. . . .

With main characters, it's best to bring them on stage one at a time, as I did in *Too Much, Too Soon* by having each of my four heroines arriving at a slumber party separately. That way they're firmly established as individuals—each one complete with her own individual set of interests, quirks, conflicts. I suggest devoting a chapter to each point of view character—or at least a whole scene in which your hero/heroine/villain is introduced along with his or her *raison d'être*. In a novel of any

127

length, five or six point of view characters are ideal. Introduce a cast of thousands and unless you're James Michener, you'll have trouble drumming up as many readers!

How many times have you heard someone say about a book or a movie, "I couldn't keep all those characters straight!" Usually it's not because there are literally too many characters but because too many characters means too little space for proper development of each one. And besides, who wants to wait until Chapter 13 to find out what happened to a character we last heard from in Chapter 3?

Now that you've got all these wonderful characters, what are you going to do with them? What sort of plot can you develop that will be worthy of them? In Hollywood, there's a phrase you hear bandied about a fair bit—"high concept." A producer friend once explained it to me as, "A plot that can be effectively summed up in the space of a *TV Guide* blurb." Publishers, too, are frequently seduced into paying big money for a book with a "high concept," or what is also known as a "hook." Of course, no idea, no matter how wonderful, can take the place of good writing and meticulous plot development. But taking into consideration the ocean of manuscripts submitted to agents and editors every day of the week, it doesn't hurt to have a concept, a hook, that will grab someone's attention and make *your* well-written, tightly plotted novel stand out from all the rest.

Take the famous example of Peter Benchley's first novel, which can be summed up in one breathtaking sentence: Shark terrorizes New England seaside town. It is perhaps unfair to a fine author to note that none of Benchley's subsequent novels has come close to matching the tremendous success of *Jaws*—which, if you'll pardon the pun, had one terrific hook.

Does this mean you need to lie awake nights attempting to conjure up an idea so revolutionary it will knock everyone's socks off? Not necessarily. It's enough, I think, merely to open yourself to the possibilities strewn on our everyday paths like diamonds disguised as dross—the "big" story that lies just beyond every little one; the extra twist that turns an ordinary event or emotion into something extraordinary. It's a little like turning up the volume on your radio—the music that a minute ago was putting you to sleep now has you pumped up, ready to rock and roll.

Recently, I was doing an autograph signing at a bookstore in Boston, and who should appear but an old boyfriend I hadn't seen in more than twenty years. He was older, heavier . . . I didn't even recognize him at first, and truth to tell we had never been much of an item to begin with. But suppose he *had* been the love of my life; suppose I had borne his child without ever having told him I was pregnant. Suppose this had been just the twist of fate we needed in order to rekindle our affair. . . .

Oh, dear, here I go again!

# 29

## A Writer's Characters

### By Elizabeth Jordan Moore

Some stories originate in setting, some arise from plot, some from theme. I always begin with character, because for me, character is the most interesting, the most magical, and the most liberating element in fiction writing. It's the engine that starts the story moving, brings it through the woods, and home again.

Where or how does a writer find characters? I believe characters come not directly from life, but from the imaginations of writers. The writer is painting with words on a page the portrait of a being who's been riding around in his or her mind for a while.

In her biography of Paul Scott, Hilary Spurling quotes her subject as saying that writing comes from emotion, not ideas, and I think that's precisely correct. Characters are born because the writer's emotions were engaged fiercely, in the present or long ago, by a person or event.

Characters arise from emotions evoked in the writer by seeing or hearing about people: a miserable child in a store; a man and woman swimming in the sea; somebody in the check-out line at the grocery; a small item in the newspaper about a couple who got married in their local 7-Eleven. Something in these people attracts the writer, and they become the starting point of a character in a story or novel. Although they are strangers, they are familiar in some way; the writer knows them, and that is why they can be made real on the page. What makes them real is the imagination, and imagination is based on attraction. Which isn't to say necessarily that the writer is drawn only to people who appear especially colorful or exotic; the writer is attracted to people because they will meet his or her purpose, although the writer may not yet be consciously aware of that purpose.

For instance: There was a man in the K-Mart housewares department who fascinated me. He was square: his head, his jaw, his body. He moved very precisely, and his expression was always droll. He wasn't handsome, but I always noticed him when I was in the store, and much later he formed the beginning of one of the main characters in my novel. Characters are chosen and developed to dramatize the writer's passions, to tell the story that is in the writer to tell at that time.

I think it's always best to be fearless with characters, to trust one's instincts. Good characters—by which I mean characters that live—have a way of leading the writer forward. And one should trust and follow. One of the most exciting things about writing is discovering your own mind, what you feel and know, what you can do. It often turns out that you know more than you may have realized, and you have forgotten little.

How does one make characters live? Characters exist in the world the writer makes for them, and like real people, they experience the world through the senses. If characters are rendered through what they hear and feel and see and smell, the reader can experience their world with them, and so will begin to believe in and care about them. Other elements work to make characters vivid and real in their contexts. Well-drawn characters have distinctive ways of speaking. Their dialogue is their own and tells much about how they see their world. As they talk to other characters, as they talk inside their own heads, they are defining themselves. The speech of a character—his own words and expressions—can reveal much of his history, his sense of fate, and can expose who he is. Dialogue is important.

The writer may like to create characters who are unusual or who do things that make them interesting or compelling. However, these singular details must be as integral to the character as bones, not just hung on like jewelry or chains. The writer might want, for instance, to give someone a bad habit or obsession, a scar or fear, such as becoming absolutely speechless when required to speak in public or even answer the telephone. But these things must, of course, deepen character, not be a substitute for it.

To illustrate: I gave a character a limp because in my mind he was spiritually crippled, and I wanted his body to symbolize that. But people who read it asked me, "What happened to him? How'd he get that limp?" This was a good reaction, because it meant they were interested in him. But I had other problems at the time, and I thought, "I have no idea why he limps, and I don't care; the guy is a spiritual cripple." But as in real life, the reader cares: The reader wants the

131

details, wants the drama, wants to know what happened to that leg. So I had to enlist my character in the Navy, arrange an accident for him, deal in the story with the consequences of that (which is plot). So it turned out, as it often does, that my problem was a blessing, because in unknotting it I found my way forward with my novel. Flannery O'Conner said, "You can do anything you can get away with, and you can't get away with much." I was awfully grateful that I couldn't get away with using a bad leg merely as a symbol.

I also feel that setting is terribly crucial to creating believable characters. In and out of fiction, people live in a particular place at a particular time, and this shapes their lives and informs their values. Setting is a big part of what makes characters real to the reader, and to the writer. If I, as a reader, can believe in the physical world the writer creates on the page, I am ready to believe in the characters he or she puts into that world.

Iris Murdoch, for example, describes rooms that you want to go sit in, feel the sun on your legs where it falls through the long windows. When Carolyn Chute (in *Letourneau's Used Auto Parts*) describes a field of snow, you see it, and you taste the cold rising from it, and when a character comes from the woodline and starts across that field, you are already believing in the reality of that character.

Setting is real to the reader when it is carefully and specifically described, and this is the result of the writer's really having *looked,* either at a particular piece of the world, or into the picture in his mind's eye. But setting must be an integral part of the story and not just something external that is crammed into it because the writer thought setting was obligatory. When setting comes as a result of a deliberate concession, it shows, as, for instance, when writers fall into the habit of balancing adjectives, two per object: "a *large, green* tree beside an *old, white* house." This feels very artificial and lumbering to the reader and is, I suspect, an outcome of the writer's having failed really to *look.* As a final caveat, I would urge writers to avoid using brand names, except for a very specific reason.

I want to say something about minor characters. I believe that no character should be "minor" to a writer. And no character should be put into a story as a sort of dummy to provoke revealing dialogue from the characters we think *are* important. Each character deserves—requires—the writer's full effort and should be created as realistically as possible, with his or her own distinctness, his or her own reality within the world of the story.

Sometimes, if a character is troubling you—"irritating" might be more precise—and you don't know what to do, you might be tempted to kill him or her off. But you can't get away with it. You know it's wrong even as you write it. You feel uncomfortable, but you go forward into what you know is the wrong territory, because you are stuck, and you have to go somewhere. Fine—for the moment. But trust your instinct: The solution is the wrong one, and eventually you will have to write a much better one. Maybe you can't at that time, so work on some other problem, knowing that before you have finished you must bring these murdered characters back from the dead and deal with them in a way that is right for the story.

When I say "right for the story," what I mean is dramatic events and outcomes that satisfy the expectations and limits you have established in the reader's mind by what has gone before. You really can't avoid any of the issues that you yourself have raised.

Writing is artifice, so characters don't have to behave like real people: They "simply" have to be true to the reality created within your story. This means they must be consistent within themselves so that the reader, who has come to believe in them and to care about their fate, isn't pulled up abruptly to puzzle over the fact that the villain in the story has inexplicably ceased her wicked ways.

I don't mean one can't surprise the reader, but the reader must enjoy being surprised and not be made uncomfortable. Whenever the reader is made so uncomfortable that he or she stops believing in the reality of the fiction, the writer has cheated in some way.

The writer may have felt compelled to cheat by having an insurmountable problem to which he or she could find no other solution, but then the fiction has faltered. Or the reader may be feeling uncomfortable because the writer is attempting not to solve a difficult problem but to force something on the reader, some personal wish or agenda. In forcing this tyranny of meaning over the integrity of character, the fiction is distorted, and such distortion always shows, always disfigures, is always damaging to the relationship between the reader and the work. The writer's values and passions will inevitably emerge if the writing is good, but characters who are forced to carry the writer's quirky opinions and personal quests will stumble like overburdened donkeys. Characters who are left unimpeded to struggle in their vulnerability and their moments of grace will live in the reader's mind after the story is finished. The writer loves his characters because he made them, and if they are made well, the reader will care about them also, because in this, their story, they are real, and they matter.

# 30

## WHY I WRITE NOVELS

### BY T. ALAN BROUGHTON

ONE OF THE REASONS I KEEP WRITING NOVELS is to try to find out why I do it. The vexations are so daunting: all those years of struggling through versions that may go dead at any moment, a concentration so absorbing that family and friends become less real than imagined characters and their plights, a world of publishing that remainders one's efforts in such a short time that each new novel is a "first" novel. What kind of fool would accept a job with such a description?

One answer is in the process itself. Writing can be a journey of discovery to learn whether the right words will be found to reveal what I did not know I knew. This involves a tension between the knowledge I want to hold on to and a new understanding the work will reveal to me. If I am to defeat my own ignorance, I must be as open to the work as I am to my own raw experience.

Reader and writer meet, if all goes well. The writer hopes the reader will be unaware of all the discarded novels one book represents, but certainly a reader aware of craft and technique stands very close to the writer. Much of writing is in revision, a process in which I am struggling to see the work for itself, and when all the things I have learned are helpful. But even though I need to know how to construct the illusions that dramatize character, or how to manipulate point of view, I am also trying to reach that confusing, chaotic part of the mind that is in all of us, but which I want to hear because it can speak with the wider voice of the species.

That area is not limited to the more narrow, daily self, and fortunately it remains largely untutored. Because of this, it can offer us new and unbiased approaches. We all have that area of the mind and must deal with it. But an artist seems driven by talent and obsessive persistence to make things with its help, hoping to share them with others.

If I take my third novel, *The Horsemaster,* and try to recall how it happened, I can tell you about incidents that helped to start it and about some landscapes that I felt needed a story, but why I should want to write about horses and abandoned daughters and familial relationships, I know only vaguely. I think most stories or novels originate in something so deeply personal that the writer can never fully know why that image or incident insists on words. But if that connection has been effectively explored, the image or symbol is the private doorway of re-entry to the magic garden of the species.

When I was a child visiting a farm belonging to relatives in Canada, horses always fascinated me. But once I saw how dangerous they could be when I watched my father being dragged by a runaway team, the reins tangling his arms, the disk harrow nearly running over him as he struggled for control. Much later, the occurrence that started my novel was narrated to me in a letter from my father. Both of these incidents were violent, and I know that writing stories has often been a way for me to circumscribe violence I find hard to understand or accept.

In a first draft, I have only an inkling. I make some notes. Perhaps a character, a name. I pause, take a deep breath. Look again. I cannot make a clear diagram or outline. All is dim. If I could make that outline, I probably would not proceed. Without the excitement of discovery, why bother? Am I saying I really don't know what the book will be, or am I saying I prevent myself from knowing so that I can keep working every day for the year or so that the first draft will take me? What I do know is that I have a faith in the mind's form—maybe a sense that the book is all there in the mind, but it will be paid out to me only from slowly unraveling, tangled skeins. And part of the problem is that sometimes what I am being given is false matter, a test by that surly gnome far below to see how determined I am to find the secrets out. The only way to find the form that is embedded in the material is to let it grow, then look—pruning, redirecting, finding out what really made it grow.

There is a farm at the bottom of the hill near our summer place in the Adirondack Mountains of New York State. It was owned for a while by wealthy visitors who bought some Percheron horses. All this was a hobby for them, but for their hired hand it was a return to the best times of his youth—a time when he and his father had worked with draft horses.

When the summer people divorced each other and then their farm,

136

the caretaker bought the horses and rented one of the fields. One night after a party on a nearby estate, some rowdies decided it would be fun to ride the horses. The horses were not happy; they had never been subjected to the indignity of carrying men on their backs. They panicked and broke out into the highway where they were hit by a passing truck. The handyman had to shoot them. That is the incident my father described to me and it appears in the middle of *The Horsemaster,* although it is transformed by the necessities of imagined characters, plot, and altered landscape.

After I heard about the incident, I could not stop thinking of the horses and a man who cared for horses as much as he cared for anything. I found a name for the horseman—Lewis Beede. I gave him a cabin. I found him a job caring for someone else's horses. I decided that he was single but not unattached, that he was middle-aged and about to learn what that entailed. I made him forty-five because I was forty-three and figured I'd finish the novel when I was forty-five. Lewis and I could arrive together.

I thought I was ready to start. But for the first time in anything I'd written, I knew I had to know something else.

Facts. I could describe horses, but how could I pretend to know them? Research, or the gathering of facts for a specific piece of writing, can be dangerous for a writer. After all, the book was not about horses, but living in a world in which horses also lived—the difference between facts as knowledge and facts as experience. But what a writer must know is the vocabulary. I had better be able to pretend to be as knowledgeable as Lewis.

I read veterinary texts. I read books on raising and breeding draft horses. I read texts on farm machinery, a book on the language of horses, and even one on the magic and folklore of horses. Whenever I saw horses, I would stop the car and watch them, or I trudged to the fence and tried to talk to them. I promised myself a trip north where friends were raising horses, but I never made it. I began writing instead. I was losing Lewis in all that information. I decided that I would send portions of the book to horse people when I finished it. I did, and I passed inspection, even in the descriptions of a birth and copulation, neither of which I had observed.

It pleased me after the book came out that my uncle in Canada who had spent much of his life farming and on whose farm I had met some horses in my childhood, said, "I couldn't but wonder how you learned so much about horses and their care, things like the pitman shaft of mowing machines." Or that a reviewer in *The Evener,* a draft horse journal, said, "There is a detailed description of breeding a Percheron stud to a mare that might be as useful as any found in a veterinary guide."

Now, after the book is done and my obsession with that world is over, I dread a conversation with my uncle in which he will be puzzled to discover I no longer know any of that. It's gone, learned and held onto for as long as I needed it, knowledge as illusory as the world it was used for. I want these worlds to seem real and possible, but I don't raise and breed horses, only characters. Fiction depends on our willingness to listen to illusions in order to hear truths, and art is a world of permissible lies. But a good liar gets his facts straight.

I began writing the novel in September, 1979. I write every day when working on a first draft and am very nervous or unhappy to miss a day. The people, places, events gradually become as real as, if not more real than the lives around me. I dream about them. I have to run home halfway through jogging to get a snippet of conversation down or note the direction the next scene must go. But I am hardly ever more than a day or so ahead in my mind. I like to stop when I can vaguely hear the next words coming. I finished the first draft five months later, a very short time for me.

What followed were four complete revisions, innumerable revisions of certain passages here and there that remained stubborn to the end. There were alterations when my editor read and commented. At no point in all of this was there—or is there now—a sense of completion. Maybe more certainty—that is, I became more and more sure what the characters could do, what the world would do to them—but there is no end to what I could tell you about them, have them do or reveal. I left them finally with mingled regret and weariness. I'd never see them again or enter their lives with such intimacy, and that was a kind of death, but I had tired of them.

The hardest part for me is that perilous strait between the wish and the reality. I am often too soft-hearted, and in the end of the first version of the book I gave Lewis back his woman Annie, his daughter Miriam, a new horse farm, and just about everything he might have wanted, even if not in quite the way he would have liked to obtain it.

In a letter of complaint to my editor, I wrote:

*I have been working hard every day. I am only just beginning to separate myself from the characters sufficiently to see them. In my daily life, I am always struggling to control angers or frustrations, to treat the people around me with the kindness and understanding they deserve. Even in my writing I want to give my characters harmonious lives. I want them to find blessings, and bless each other.*

*But what I want in my life has little to do with what must happen in a book. A good novel shows that rub between what we want and what we are—what we are going to get whether we want it or not. If the book is to suggest the wholeness of this man's specific life, the final destination cannot be what I desire for Lewis any more than what he desires for himself.*

*Working through this book again in the last weeks, I have sensed how hard it is both to love a character and be totally objective. Thank God we can't do that in life!*

*But this isn't the first novel I've blundered through, so I know that a year from this fall I'll look at it (as I have with all the others) and say, "Damn it, what a book this could have been."*

The novel was published, but it is not finished and never will be. I wonder if someday I will feel pleasure in picking up that book and reading a paragraph or two rather than merely seeing all the ways it should be revised. At this point *The Horsemaster* seems to have been merely a good way of learning a little more about how to make a novel.

# 31

## DIALOGUE THAT WORKS

### BY ANN HARLEMAN

OF ALL THE ELEMENTS OF FICTION, dialogue carries the heaviest burden. It must simultaneously reveal character and advance the plot. Dialogue that does both is a powerful device for realizing the fiction writer's maxim of "Show, don't tell." It creates tension and drama, expresses theme, establishes and develops the relationships among characters, and contributes to mood, tone, and setting. No wonder Elizabeth Bowen said that "dialogue requires more art than does any other constituent of the novel"!

"Art" is the key word here. Most of us have acquired the skill to fulfill the purpose of dialogue—revealing character. We know how to use diction, dialect, and syntax to show the relatively static attributes of our characters: their class, age, sex, education, intelligence, neuroses. We know how to create speech. But dialogue is speech *in motion*. It is characters acting on each other. The art of dialogue lies in showing what happens *between* characters—because that's where the drama is.

We've all read—and, worse, written—dialogue like this:

"How did it go at the unemployment office today, George? What a shame that someone like you, with a master's degree and six years' experience as a systems analyst, has to collect unemployment!"

"Dammit, Louise, you always say the wrong thing. It's been the main problem with our marriage all along."

"Well, Dr. Grundy, the counselor we've been seeing for nine weeks, doesn't think so!"

"I've had it with her—and you, too. I'm taking our twelve-year-old Mustang with the faulty brakes and getting out!"

This exchange reveals character: George's quick temper, his tendency to put the worst interpretation on what is said to him, his impulsiveness; Louise's self-righteousness and lack of tact. It also advances the plot, by showing George's decision to leave, and provides the

140

background information we need in order to grasp the relationship between Louise and George, their problems, and the ominous potential of George's proposed action. But this exchange isn't believable; and it doesn't move us. What has gone wrong?

In fiction, the reader is always an eavesdropper. The passage we've been looking at, stuffed full of information aimed at the reader, ignores that fact. The characters aren't speaking to each other, but over their shoulders to a third party. As a result, their speech is clumsy and unemotional, and their conflict—the ingredients for which are certainly present—is flattened.

So we arrive at the first principle of effective dialogue: *Characters engage only with each other.* David Huddle's story "The Undesirable"* offers an exchange between father and son:

> "Dad?"
> He grunted.
> "Dad, are you listening?" I asked him. "What?" he said, still in that preoccupied tone of voice.
> "Why'd you ask me if you didn't want to hear?" I shouted at him. I went upstairs to my room, stomped on the stairs and shut the door hard.

Here tension and drama are not diluted by even a sidelong glance in the reader's direction. We are on the outside looking in, and must glean what we can from that position. The writer's job—*your* job—is to give us the help we need without "stuffing" the characters' speech. You must create dialogue so believable that its form, as well as its content, advances the plot.

Once you have your characters fully engaged with each other, and only each other, you are ready to implement the second principle of effective dialogue. In the words of novelist Jean McGarry, *Characters always say less than you think they say.* Start by eliminating small talk. With the double burden it must carry, fictional dialogue is always Large Talk. Cut out ritual exchanges, formulas, and conversational fillers like "uh" and "well." Use your blue pencil on the following passage:

> "Hey, Fred!"
> "Well, hi there, James."
> "How've you been? Haven't seen you around for a while."

*Published in *Only the Little Bone,* by David Huddle (David R. Godine Publishers)

141

"Yeah, well, I've been sick. You know how it is. So, have you got the bomb?"
"Sure, it's right here in my lunch pail. But I want the money now, you know?"

You should end with something like this:

"Fred! Where've you been?"
"Sick. Have you got the bomb?"
"In my lunch pail. But I want the money now."

To achieve an even livelier, more natural sound you can lop off grammatical elements as well— "a/an," "the," "has" and "did," and (as Elmore Leonard does so effectively) "if." "Man who don't like huntin, he's no man at all." "Moon's full tonight." "He put the car in the garage yet?" "Tommy! You don't come inside this minute, I'll whip you good!" These sentences sound more like real people talking than the fuller, grammatical versions would. And they read faster, creating a sense of forward movement that intensifies the dramatic impact of the scene.

There is another kind of dialogue situation when less is more. When people feel strongly, or when there is a strong bond between them— either one of affection or one of conflict—they say less. What they do say conceals as much as it reveals. They talk about anything but what is on their minds; sometimes they say nothing at all. The third principle of effective dialogue, then, is: *The more intense the feelings, the less articulate the speaker.*

To show a character in the grip of strong emotion, you can have him or her break off in midsentence or speak in one-word sentences or phrases. This increases dramatic tension and at the same time draws the reader in, since the temptation to complete the character's sentences is irresistible.

To show intense intimacy between characters, you can use a device I call "gapping." In my novel, *The River Upside Down,* I have one of the protagonists, a fourteen-year-old girl named Lil, talk with her great-aunt Clesta, the only person in the family to whom Lil lets herself get close:

On the other side of Clesta, the dog Chinky curled his lip. "It's the heat," Clesta said. "Makes him morose."
"It's hotter in Aruba."
Clesta sighed. Her wide, flat breasts rose and fell under her nightgown. "Your father loves life. He's just— I've often thought, James is just one of the naturally joyful."

Here Lil makes an apparently disinterested comment about the weather in Aruba. Communication takes place in the gap between Lil's words and Clesta's, so that Clesta responds to Lil's underlying, unstated concern. In Aruba, we know from information given earlier in the chapter, Lil's parents are on a second honeymoon in a last-ditch attempt to salvage a marriage damaged by her father's frequent infidelities. *We* figure out Lil's meaning by the same process that Clesta does, and at the same time. "Gapping" draws us into the exchange between Lil and Clesta so that we experience their emotional bond. Yet it allows the characters to remain completely engaged with each other. There are no over-the-shoulder glances in the reader's direction.

The negative feelings—fear, envy, jealousy, hate—that bond characters to each other emotionally lend themselves to the same treatment. Broken utterances, gapping, saying the opposite of what is meant, and complete silence can all express intense feeling between characters. In his story, "Surprised by Joy,"* Charles Baxter makes effective use of silence to create tension and move the plot along.

"My son would like to read to you," the man said, glancing down at the boy. "Do you have time to listen for a minute?"

Jeremy said nothing. . . .

"For thou art the God of my strength," the boy read. "Why hast thou put me from thee?" . . .

Jeremy said, "Who sent you here?" The father heard what he said, but his only reaction was to squint through the screen. . . .

Both characters repeatedly use silence as a response, building tension so that later in the scene, when Jeremy finally says what's on his mind, it has explosive force.

Twice the father in Baxter's story, by means of a gesture, reveals more than he says: his pride in his son; his lack of interest in Jeremy. This brings us to the fourth principle of effective dialogue: *Actions speak.* In real life, the nonverbal behaviors accompanying speech—tone of voice, facial expression, gesture, body language—offer continual clues to the speaker's true meaning. Like every other aspect of reality that finds its way into fiction, this one must be heightened and made larger than life. The art of creating effective dialogue involves the insightful selection and deft placement of nonverbal clues.

---

*Published in *Through the Safety Net,* by Charles Baxter (Viking Penguin)

You can have characters refuse to meet each others' eyes, wring their hands, rub their foreheads, lick their lips, tap a foot, tug at an ear, scratch their heads, frown, widen their nostrils—the list is endless. These more-or-less stock gestures are best used to contrast with what a character is saying rather than to reinforce it. This reduces their stereotypical quality and creates tension as well. Better still, find a more individual gesture that grows out of the particular character and the particular situation. Here are some examples from Mavis Gallant, a master of the telling gesture: "She folded her arms under her cape and kicked at the Maginot Line instead of kicking herself, or Al, or Lottie"; "His gesture of licking snow from her hands was as formal as a handshake"; "Leopold, who never touched anyone, pressed lips to his father's hand." Each of these gestures is unusual, has special significance coming from that particular character, and is closely bound to the setting.

Besides revealing character and advancing the plot, the nonverbal element in dialogue supplies a scene with movement and injects variety into long exchanges. And nonverbal responses can be a way for your characters to "talk" to *you*. Sometimes what begins as a simple nonverbal response turns into an indispensable action in the story. It may become part of the plot, embodying climax or resolution; or it may become a symbol for the story's theme. At the end of Grace Paley's "Dreamer in a Dead Language," for example, the protagonist says, "So bury me," and lies down in the October sun at Brighton Beach while her two young sons cover most of her with sand.

Suppose you've succeeded in creating an effective dialogue—one in which characters who are fully engaged with each other speak with dramatic spareness, convey intense feeling, and express themselves through vivid gestures as well as speech. Now you have a fairly long stretch of conversation. What can you do to make it less daunting? How can you make sure that your eavesdropping reader will stay put, absorbed in the passage, letting it carry him or her further into the story?

"Open up" the passage and invite your eavesdropper in. One way to do this is to avoid a steady beat of "he said/she said," which acts as a reminder that the dialogue is an artifact and so breaks the illusion of reality you are trying to create. Omit dialogue tags whenever you can do so without creating confusion about who is speaking. Try your blue pencil on the following passage:

She picks up the phone on the second ring. "Hello?" she says.
"Hi, babe," Juan says. His voice is frayed from too many cigarettes too late at night."
"I'm sorry. You have the wrong number," Maude says. She hangs up.

You should end with something like this:

She picks up the phone on the second ring. "Hello?"
"Hi, babe." Juan's voice is frayed from too many cigarettes too late at night.
"I'm sorry. You have the wrong number." Maude hangs up.

Describing the character's actions is enough to show who is talking. Giving the characters distinct voices and having them use each other's names occasionally would also help. Don't try to achieve variety by using alternative dialogue tags *(he grimaced, she chortled, he testified)* or by loading up with adverbs *(she said puzzledly, he asked chafingly, she said distractedly)*. Whatever you're thinking of expressing as an adverb, build that quality into what your character says, instead. Stick to a simple, unadorned *said,* with an occasional *asked,* and eliminate even those where you can.

Another way to "open up" a dialogue is to vary its texture by putting some of what your characters say into indirect discourse. Instead of having one character reply to another's question about the weather with a full report, you can say "I told her what I'd heard on the radio that morning." "He asked why she no longer loved her husband," "Darlene told Max what her students were saying about him," "They talked about the Yankees' hopes for the pennant"—all vary the texture and rhythm of a long, direct conversation. This is especially important if your reader already knows what one character is telling another—if, say, you have an earlier scene in which Darlene's students discuss Max's drug habit.

Finally, make sure that your characters react to each other. Remember, dialogue is something characters *do* to each other—an interaction on the same level as a fist-fight or lovemaking. By the end of a conversation, the characters ought to have changed, just as, by the end of a scene, their situation should be different from what it was at the beginning. The change can be small—as small as one character realizing that the other hasn't really heard him, as in David Huddle's story—but it must be significant *for them.* Any dialogue that does this sustains narrative tension and, ultimately, advances the story.

145

The art of dialogue is the art of seeing through your characters, first to discover, and then to reveal, their true feelings and their deepest motives. It is the art of showing what you've seen, in the form of an exchange so believable, dramatic, and lively that your reader feels he or she is there, invisible, watching and listening.

# 32

## THAT CRUCIAL FIRST DRAFT

### BY JOHN DUFRESNE

*It's one of the things writing students don't understand. They write a first draft and are quite disappointed, or often should be disappointed. They don't understand that they have merely begun, and that they may be merely beginning even in the second or third draft.*

—Elizabeth Hardwick

GIVEN THAT STORIES AND NOVELS DO NOT GET WRITTEN BUT RE-WRITTEN and that all matters of consequence in fiction are addressed in the revisions, it is not surprising that writers' magazines and writing classes are packed with advice on plotting, characterization, dialogue, point of view, and so on. These discussions of narrative technique can be extremely valuable. They can help writers fine-tune their manuscripts, clarify the story's vision, add texture and significance to their fictive worlds.

This is not one of those profitable articles on methodology. This is about what goes on before you cut and polish your gem, about the dirty and rigorous work of mining the imagination. I want to examine the writing process and not the finished product because the most essential fact about revision is this: You must have something to revise. The first draft.

Frank O'Connor explained a first draft this way. He said he followed Maupassant's advice to get black on white. "I write any sort of rubbish which will cover the main outlines of the story, then I can begin to see it." Writing a first draft should be easy because, in a sense, you can't get it wrong. You are bringing something completely new and strange into the world, something that did not exist before. You have nothing to prove in the first draft, nothing to defend, everything to imagine. And the first draft is yours alone; no one else sees it. You are not writing for an audience. Not yet. You write the draft in order to read what you have written and to determine what you still have to say.

You begin a draft of your story at the same place everyone else begins. That is, you begin the journey not knowing where you'll end up. You may have a destination in mind, and you may well set off in that direction, but what you encounter along the way will likely alter your course. This uncertainty, though daunting, is crucial to the writing process. It allows for, even encourages, revelation and surprise, while it prevents the manipulation of character or plot to suit a preconceived, and usually ill-conceived, notion of what the story must be. In writing the first draft, you begin to work through all the uncertainty and advance toward meaning.

All that should be reassuring, but it is not easy. It takes perseverance to write fiction; it takes that and more to write a first draft. It takes faith and tenacity. "The first draft," according to Bernard Malamud, ". . . is the most uncertain—where you need guts, the ability to accept the imperfect until it is better." You must have the courage to allow yourself to fail. The first draft is where the beginning writer most often finds himself blocked, to use a conventional, though perhaps misleading, verb.

The novice I'm thinking of is the person who claims to have dozens of brilliant, compelling ideas for stories. He can describe his story to you in elaborate detail; it's often about his own experiences. He can articulate theme, explain how he'll go about revealing character, lay in symbols, build tension. But he never gets the story written, though he feels an urgency to do so. Often it is this very urgency that aborts the narrative. He wants to dodge the drafting process and write the story immediately. He doesn't know what every experienced fiction writer knows—that the story does not exist before the act of writing, that it emerges through the flow of images and the rhythm of words. He fails to understand that while life may be spontaneous, art is not.

And so he makes mistakes. He sets unrealistic goals for what he may not acknowledge to be, but is in fact, the first draft. He undermines his effort by holding unrealistic expectations of his own imaginative and organizing powers. And so he becomes discouraged when the people in his head are unrecognizable on the page, when the intense emotion he felt in real life is unrealized in what he writes. The beginning writer who has read a great deal is even more susceptible to this kind of dejection. She knows that the Chekhov story she just read did not flounder the way hers seems to. She loses confidence and hope, becomes intimidated by the magnitude of the problem that is the nascent story, is humbled by her vaulting ambition. What had seemed like an exciting and noble undertaking now seems foolish and impossible.

Do not try to write beyond what the first draft is meant to accomplish: Do not demand or expect a finished manuscript in one draft. The worst thing you may do in writing the first draft may be to focus on the form or content of the story. Do not even consider technical problems at this early stage. And do not let your critical self sit at your desk with your creative self. The critic will stifle the writer within.

Use the first draft to explore the world of your story and to spend some time getting to know these people you've made up. If you want to care about your characters (and if you don't, your readers won't), you have to know them, and to get to know them, you have to hang out with them, talk to them, listen to them. Engage that part of yourself that you may ignore in the analytical, task-oriented world of your real life. You can do that by free-writing—writing quickly without concentrating on any subject for a designated time. Do not lift the pen from the paper or fingers from the keyboard. If you're stuck, write, "I'm stuck. I'm supposed to be writing about grief, but I can't." Whatever you do, don't stop.

If you're having trouble, that means you're thinking. You can free-write on any emotion, on any character, on any place. If you are blocked, write a character's name, say, on a blank page and free-write for five, ten, or however many minutes you need to prime the pump. Or free-associate. Write a word, an emotion, a city, and then write the first word that comes into your head, then the next, and the next. Again, don't think. Associate. Continue until your unconscious mind makes the critical connection.

I brainstorm lists whenever I feel stuck. As fast as I can, I'll scribble all the possible choices that my character has or I think he has at that moment in the story. I never go with the first item; it's always too obvious. I'll try another, and if I don't feel excited by where it leads me, I'll try again. I'll ask why would he do this and not that. Sometimes he'll tell me, and then I know I'm on track. I'll look at the room my characters are sitting in, and I'll describe everything in it, from the cabbage rose wallpaper to the clanging cast iron radiator to the chipped cornice above the dining room door. Even the smell of the bananas darkening in a wooden fruit bowl on the window sill. Now I'm there

149

with my characters, and though the wallpaper won't appear in the story, something else that I might have otherwise overlooked will. Just before he tells his wife he's leaving her, my fictional husband notices their child's pacifier under the coffee table. What does he do? Time to make a list.

Out of the blue, have your narrator (first- or third-person, it doesn't matter) make a declarative statement about your central character. It's better if the statement contains quirks or even a desperate action, and it should come as a surprise to you. Perhaps the character's action is one that you had considered her incapable of performing. And then ask the natural questions suggested by the statement. The answers to those questions will provide the raw material for the rest of the narrative.

The narrator of my story "The Fontana Gene" said this:

> When Billy Wayne Fontana's second wife, Tami Lynne, left him for the first time, he walked into Booker T. Washington Elementary School, interrupted the fourth grade in the middle of a hygiene lesson, it being a Thursday morning and all, apologized to Miss Azzie Lee Oglesbee, the substitute teacher, fetched his older boy Duane, and vanished for a year and a half from Monroe.

The line was a gift that appeared because I pushed the narrator to tell me something about Billy Wayne that I didn't already know. Suddenly I had a father, a ten-year-old boy, at least one other male child, two wives, a town, submerged trouble, an eventual reconciliation, a second split, a kidnapping, a disappearance.

I began to ask questions. What made Billy Wayne do something so desperate? Why take just the one boy? Why would Tami Lynne take him back? What would he do to make her leave again? What did he do and where did he go for a year and a half? Why did he come back? And what about that voice? Who is it telling this story? I answered the questions, fiddled with structure; three months later I had an unwieldy first draft, but one that interested me immensely. Six months later, I finished the story.

Your first draft is an exploration. You invent characters and wonder what they'll do. You watch them, and they surprise you. You gather information, do research, generate scenes. You write it all down with a temporary disregard for logic, transitions, and grammatical conventions. In the process, you learn that the story you set out to write is not so interesting as the one that surfaces on the page. The purpose of

150

exploration is discovery, and what you discover in writing that first draft are character, structure, plot, theme. In short, you begin to discover what it is you have to say about what it is you're writing about.

Trust in the writing process. It may take you on tangents, lead you astray more than once; it might cost you reams of paper and days of your time, but none of it is wasted. All the work you put in on one story is put in on all the stories you'll ever write. In the first draft, rely on spontaneity, trust in inspiration, follow your accidents. Don't want to say something so badly that you can't hear what the story is trying to tell you. All first drafts are experimental, chaotic, messy, and all take time, energy, patience, and persistence. You won't get it right the first time, and that's as it should be. The purpose of the first draft is not to get it right, but to get it written.

# 33

## MEMORY AND THE "I"

### BY SIDNEY SULKIN

FOR SOME YEARS, THE IDEA FOR A STORY about a group of characters I had once worked with rattled around in my head, a memory out of youth so clear that putting it on paper, I was sure, would be no effort at all, if only I could get to it. I had the setting: a taxi stand in Boston's Dorchester; the time: a stormy winter night in the years of the Great Depression; the characters: a group of hard-drinking drivers, their cadging hangers-on, and a young dispatcher; and the story: the drivers, whipped on by drink, the storm, the emptiness of their lives, turn on the cadgers in a rising frenzy of sadism that ends in tragedy. Everything was there, vividly real in recollection. And that was what misled me.

What I found as I wrote my early drafts was that I had it all a bit too fully, too exactly, too intimately. These were in truth the people I had worked with, each with his own traits, colorful and interesting, and the events were, with a bit of shading and highlighting and reorganizing, pretty much what happened. But the story didn't work; it was grounded in reality but it had no life. The difficulty is common. Characters that spring whole from real life often have no fictional reality; they suppress imagination; they are memories, and that is what they remain.

The problem obviously was one of "distancing." The solution brought a surprise. The story as it stood was seen through the eyes of the young switchboard dispatcher and told in the third person, which is, of course, the time-honored way to achieve separation between author and story. But a switch to first-person narration produced an unexpected and interesting change of tone. A new authenticity was introduced, a special kind of intimacy, quite different from the intimacy of recollection, in the relationship between the "I" narrator and the other characters. The "I" became one of the actors, and the outside amorphous third-person voice (burdened by my loyalty to memory) began to fade. To put it another way, I liberated the story by surrendering the telling of it to one of the participants. The effect was a more concentrated vision, a clearer dramatic shape.*

This, of course, sounds paradoxical. Use of the first-person voice usually raises the question of limited point of view, sending authors twisting and turning to explain how it is that their narrator knows so much. Furthermore, you would expect it to exacerbate rather than solve the problem of distancing. The answer lies in how the "I" is used. In his otherwise beautifully written Faulkneresque novel *The Wind,* French Nobelist Claude Simon distracts us with an anonymous narrator who pops up from time to time simply to say, "He told me." We have no notion who the narrator is, nor do we care. Fitzgerald's Nick Carraway, in *The Great Gatsby,* is a semi-participant. His role is the standard one of the narrator who, fascinated by the central character, has decided to tell his story by gathering information and reporting it as a thorough detective might, down to the discovery of a handwritten schedule showing how Gatsby as an ambitious boy planned to spend the minutes of the day. He acts as mediator or stage manager for the action but has no emotional stake in it.

Hemingway, in *The Sun Also Rises,* places the "I" at the center of the emotion. The story is, precisely, how the narrator, his sexual capacity destroyed by the war, sees and feels. Everything is colored by his special point of view. Distancing is achieved in the patented Hemingway manner by letting the emotion rise as if on its own between simple but carefully calibrated sentences.

There are other ways to use the first-person point of view: the sly device of the unreliable narrator, for example, through whom the reader is being deliberately misled until he realizes what's going on; the "I" of the interior monologue, the most famous being, I suppose, Molly Bloom's marvelously earthy ruminations at the end of *Ulysses;* the old-fashioned introducing narrator who sets up the character and the story and then lets the third-person voice take over (nothing creaky about this when it is skillfully used as, for example, in Edith Wharton's *Ethan Frome*).

In "Like the Whiteness of the World,"* the story's narrator is endowed with a lively poetic sensibility; thus the risk of limited point of

*The story, "Like the Whiteness of the World," was published in *The Virginia Quarterly Review,* Winter, 1991.

view dissolves, as surmise and imagination come creatively and credibly into play.

Still, something more was required, something to give the "I" an integral role in the story, a relationship between him and the characters he was telling about that would create tension and in effect give him an emotional involvement in the story's outcome. And so attention is focused on the boy's fascination with one of the drivers, and his developing sense of a paradoxical, reciprocal identification between them.

In the very first paragraph the narrator, his memory jogged by a snow storm, has a sharp memory of Finney: ". . . the thin smirk with all the pain in the corners of the cruel self-despising mouth . . . ," and a "vision of him as he looked at the wake . . . relaxed at last, the Finney he had wanted to be, the wild frustrations gone out of him. Francis Xavier Finney. I never knew the full name until I saw it in the paper." The character of Finney is concentrated there as seen through the creative imagination of the narrator. The final tragedy is foreshadowed and made credible.

Another couple of paragraphs, and we have the setting—a freezing winter weekend in Boston in the midst of the Great Depression—and the young part-time dispatcher "slumped lazily at the switchboard gazing through the plate-glass windows at the rows of icicles that rimmed the library eaves. I was a poet, conjuring metaphors. Fingers of frozen sky. Spears of winter breath."

The hangers-on begin to arrive looking for warmth and a drink. The storm begins to build. The drivers slowly get drunk and begin to center their frustration on the cadgers. The metaphor-minded Boston Latin School boy takes in the detail: The old inebriate Croak, whose "chin and cheeks were the color of cement. He had probably just finished sleeping off a drunk; but he had shaved before coming out as he always did and in spite of the frayed sleeves and drab tie managed somehow to suggest the dapper dude they say he once was . . . His face was Finney's face ten years older." And Gimpy, the cripple, with his "brass yellow hair and massive shoulders that seem to have grown around his crutches." Later he and Croak are forced to dance for their drinks, Croak balancing a quarter placed on his head by Pete Waller, "his fat fingers curling out like feathers"; Gimpy doing a handstand on his crutches, "crumpled legs flopping. Limp tassels, I thought automatically. Windless pennants."

154

But it's Finney the boy centers on. He drinks and smokes "in hard quick tugs . . . angrily." He switches from a black leather cap to visored chauffeur's cap when he drives one of the two Cadillac limousines. He is often irritated, "though it was not always clear why." From time to time, when he takes off his hat, he suddenly looks "as if his anger or whatever the hardness was that lay stored up in him had melted." And "I imagined that it was the wife and kids he never saw that had come into his thoughts. It was always a surprise to remember that he was married." And now the narrator freely improvises a dialogue—as in a play by "O'Casey? Synge?"—between Finney and his Sheila, who is pretty and whom he loves and drunkenly abuses and who "turned her back on him and shut him out." Later he imagines Finney as a vicious kid, "forever aching for a fight with someone he could lick. . . . Rage curled like smoke in his eyes from the first grade on, still did, showed in the snarl on his thin mouth, sprang out like the swipe of an animal's claw. I knew him, others like him . . . the hostile eyes, and the whispers floating behind me like a foul breath down the aisles, into the toilets. . . . I feared him, more than I feared Waller."

And then the narrator detects an ambivalence in Finney's contempt and in his own fear. Finney harbors, he thinks, "a kind of sneering envy, and maybe even a contemptuous patronizing sympathy: I had hold of possibilities—and he was the older brother, failed, self-hating, vicious, and yet, perhaps, in a pinch, the kid's protector."

The story and its drama depend on, spring from, the narrator's vision. The details, as noted by him—and this is where memory and invention based on memory come into play—anchor the story in reality, giving it a time and place and a convincing concreteness. They delineate the characters and, more, suggest the narrator's feelings about them and recognition of the push and pull within each of them. It is not only in Finney that he perceives a sense of loss, but also in crude Waller, who, later in the story, if only for a brief competitive moment, seems to feel a wistful pang for a wasted past, as he thrusts out the names of books he has read. In the final scenes, as Finney comes to recognize himself as "riffraff" no better than the others and goes out into the snow to his death, it is through the boy narrator as participant that we experience a "sadness like the whiteness of the world."

From time to time, if you're lucky, a fiction will set its own tone and point of view from the first line, or seem to. In this case it was necessary for me to overcome that first deception and play the words back again and again before the right key sounded. The leftover notes, mostly based on memories, are nearly as long as the final manuscript. The job was to break free of them and, as Van Gogh told his brother Theo, try to make something "truer than truth."

# 34

## BREAKING THE RULES

### BY JOHN LUTZ

YOU'VE PROBABLY HEARD OR READ IT: The rule is there are no rules, and that's the only reliable rule for writing good fiction.

However, over the years and from countless creative writing classes, panels, and seminars, there has evolved what is known as the conventional wisdom. Beginning writers pay close attention to the various pearls of advice dropped by those established in the fields of writing or teaching fiction. Many of the pearls are false.

Writing is a uniquely individualistic endeavor, not for the most part mystical, and to a large degree teachable and learnable. But since it is, more than most activities, individual and personal, there are dangers in embracing what seems to be the soundest advice.

When aspiring writers attend seminars or read instructional books or articles, they should select very carefully what methods might work for their particular way of writing, then experiment with them before adopting them. Professional writers understand the difficulties involved in learning to write, and almost all of them are empathetic and really do want to share what they know to help others hone their craft or make that first sale. But advice given with wholehearted sincerity by established pros can sometimes harm more than it helps, in the way of strong medicine wrongly prescribed. I'm not saying it's always, or even usually, wise to reject the conventional wisdom, but I *am* saying you should always question it. Be extremely selective before incorporating it into your personal and distinctive method of writing.

The first piece of advice offered, even crammed down throats, in creative writing classes is to WRITE ABOUT WHAT YOU KNOW.

Wrong. Don't write about things of which you are entirely ignorant, but don't hesitate to build on scant knowledge and explore unknown territory. The fact is that no one "knows" enough about enough subjects to write expertly on the many elements that make up most stories or

157

novels. Probably you'll exhaust your expertise long before you learn how to write effectively. The trick is to learn to research in a way that complements your writing and to select which facts to use to capture the essence of the subject. Not so much the hard facts, but the nuances, the mood and character. In some instances, the reader will sense and share your pleasure of discovery when you've explored and chosen what's useful and representative and incorporated it in your fiction.

It's possible to know *too* much about a subject. For instance, I learned recently that many Revolutionary War battles weren't fought mainly at a distance with muskets and bayonets, but fought at close quarters with knives, hatchets and weapons known as spontoons. A spontoon is a sort of combination spearhead and axe head fitted to a staff about six feet long. Revolutionary War officers carried them rather than firearms because George Washington didn't want his field commanders concentrating on loading the inaccurate and time-consuming powder weapons of the era rather than paying attention to strategy and the ebb and flow of battle. However, the spontoon hardly fits the average reader's concept of Revolutionary War skirmishes, so were I writing fiction set in that period, I'd deliberately leave out that morsel of fact and probably arm my officers with muskets. Let's leave spontoons to the historians.

ALL GOOD FICTION IS ROOTED IN REALITY.

This is true only up to a point. Reader concept of reality is as important as the reality itself. We write fiction, not travelogues or instructional manuals. Your streets are not made to seem real because you've made sure the traffic is flowing in the right direction, or the street signs are spelled correctly, or the addresses match genuine house numbers, etc. Fictional streets are made real when your character bruises a heel stepping on a sharp stone, or stumbles over a raised section of concrete, or is made uncomfortable on sunbaked concrete by heat radiating through thin soles; when on a certain level the reader *feels* what the character feels.

It's a mistake to rely heavily on trying to create plausibility by impressing readers with a deluge of details and facts. You might educate them right out of suspension of disbelief. Of course, essential, widely known facts should be portrayed accurately so a glaring inaccuracy (a mountain in Florida, a subway system in St. Louis) won't puncture the illusion you're trying to create, but they have little do to with the actual creation of the illusion.

Using reality is fine unless carried to the extreme of emphasizing irrelevant or esoteric details rather than writing to engage the reader emotionally. That's what fiction's really about: engaging the reader's emotions. If you do everything else wrong but manage that, you've succeeded. Fiction isn't about facts, and sometimes facts need to be ignored, twisted, or embellished. Like Mark Twain's prematurely reported death, the importance of truth in fiction is greatly exaggerated.

### CREATE AN OUTLINE BEFORE YOU BEGIN TO WRITE.

Here's another piece of conventional wisdom that can be a mistake. Most writers need some kind of map to lend their story sure-footedness and direction, but a rigid outline can lead to rigid, mechanical writing. It can be constricting as well as defining. I think it's best to keep the work fluid as long as possible, not close doors in the mind even before you sit down and begin writing. My own method is to work from a loose and free-flowing synopsis that provides general direction but at the same time leaves room for improvisation; maybe a clever new plot twist, expansion of the role of a previously minor character who's evolved surprisingly well, exploration of a subplot that's taken on life and interest, or a romance that's created more heat than anticipated. We cannot, and should not, know *everything* before we write the first word. If nothing else, that would take some of the fun out of writing.

### KNOW THE ENDING OF A STORY BEFORE YOU WRITE THE BEGINNING.

Now, while I find this one to be generally true, and certainly true in my case, I know a few writers who begin without the slightest idea of the tail of their tale. Possibly this has to do with the way story concept takes root in their minds. Some writers seem to start with an interesting slant, startling incident or powerful theme, then charge ahead and somehow find not only direction, but a powerful and meaningful ending. Or they begin with some sense of direction, maybe even an outline, but project the ending only in simple or vague terms. That's fine if it works for them.

Each writer possesses a unique creative process, often not thoroughly understood even by the writer.

This rule is definitely one you should experiment with. Begin at least one story without any ideas as to how you'll end it. See what happens, the better to know thyself.

REVISE, REVISE, REVISE.

Again, this is true of me. But I've observed that there are writers who write "long" and writers who write "short" and then add (not pad) as well as cut and tighten. I fall into the "short" category unfortunately, and the more I embellish and revise the better the result. A well-known science fiction writer often told me he didn't revise at all, which I doubted until I went to his home and watched him sit at his typewriter and in a burst of creativity reel out one excellent page after another. Go figure. The point is, had he been following the conventional and usually correct advice to revise his work extensively, he'd probably still be unsold.

BASE YOUR CHARACTERS ON PEOPLE YOU KNOW.

This one can get you into serious trouble. While it will be easier to remember your characters' eye and hair color and little eccentricities, you should also take into account that your fictional characters must fit the requirements of your novel or story.

If you populate your fictional world with non-fiction people, it could cause you problems in character delineation and motivation. Your real Aunt Millie (the one you know so well) might indeed have done something your fictional Aunt Tillie does, though in the case of Aunt Tillie it might be totally out of character in the eyes of your readers, who've never met Millie.

The "real" person might in a number of ways get in the way of his or her fictional counterpart, might even behave in some fashion during the course of your writing that alters your perception of him or her. And the fact that someone does something in real life doesn't mean such behavior has been qualified to occur in fiction. Real people don't always behave logically, but fictional people almost always do. I've heard even professional writers complain, when an editor objected to a character behaving implausibly, that no revision was necessary because the real person on whom the fictional person was modeled actually behaved that way, so it *must* be in character. This often prompts the editor, who has heard this before, to sharpen a blue pencil.

160

CHOOSE A SUCCESSFUL WRITER WHOSE WORK YOU ENJOY AND AD-
MIRE, AND COPY HIS OR HER STYLE.

I've heard this dubious piece of advice a lot lately, and I'm sure it
works for some. But then some people like eggplant. It seems to me
that this game is supposed to be about originality. Publishers won't pay
real money for imitation books or stories. Following this advice is
rather like a singer or actress building her career on imitating Madonna.
Lots of performers can do that, but there's still only one Madonna, and
she tends to get the bookings.

Maybe you can imitate someone else's work long enough and ex-
haustively enough so that somehow your own style finally emerges. On
the other hand, maybe your own style will be suppressed.

If I were you, I'd think hard about this one.

STUDY MAGAZINES SO YOU KNOW WHAT KIND OF FICTION THEY
PUBLISH.

Well, if you were to read issue after issue of a magazine and then
write a story almost exactly like most of the stories that had appeared
in it, your story would probably be rejected for not being fresh. No
editor wants to buy a story that reads too much like every other story.
So much familiarity breeds rejection. Study the magazines again and in
each story you'd probably find some unique angle or strength, something arresting, that made it different from all the others. That is why it
was published.

A better approach might be to read a magazine to learn what it
*doesn't* publish. Try to determine editorial taboos, then avoid them, and
write the story *you* want to write. It will automatically fall within the
parameters of what the editor's looking for, and at the same time be
fresh.

As an example, one of the leading mystery magazines seldom publishes stories that feature diseases, denigration of the old, or subject
matter that might even remotely risk legal action. Nor will you find in its
pages graphic violence or sex (though a certain measure of subtle
eroticism is acceptable), or stories involving spouse murder. These
taboos, shaped by taste as well as marketing considerations, are for the
most part reasonable and easy enough to avoid, and they leave a wide
range of subjects for good fiction.

These are only a few of the maxims launched the beginner's way when he or she seeks advice. Also heard are: "Set aside a certain amount of time each day to write." "Show your work to a friend whose judgment you trust before you submit it for publication." "Read some poorly written but strongly plotted 'formula' fiction so you can clearly see how it's constructed." And so on. There are many such standard pieces of advice floating around writers' conferences and creative writing classes. All of them are wrong at least some of the time.

While writers do have much in common, the odds on finding two who are alike are longer than with snowflakes. There are writers who require silence and writers who work with the radio blaring. Some who demand solitude and some who forge successful careers working in the company and din of a growing family. Some can't work without cigars or cigarettes in their mouths, or cups of coffee at hand, or cats in their laps. Some write in longhand, some type, some use word processors. Probably somewhere there is one who uses mud and a sharp stick.

Despite the established rules of creativity and marketability, writing remains an intensely personal and unique exercise, as mysterious as the labyrinth of the human mind. That might very well be why we write.

Before you wrap yourself too tightly in the security of the rules, ask yourself if a measure of daring might not be more valuable than any of them.

# 35

## EMOTION IN FICTION

### BY ROSAMUNDE PILCHER

I WAS, AS A CHILD, extremely emotional. Almost anything or anybody could make me cry. I wept copiously as I listened to Paul Robeson singing "Ol' Man River." Soggy with sentiment, I begged my Scottish mother to oblige me with a rendering of "Loch Lomond," swearing that I wouldn't blub. But when she got to the bit, "But me and my true love will never meet again," my good resolutions went with the wind and the tears poured down.

There were books as well. A dreadful Victorian drama for children called *A Peep Behind the Scenes*. I have no recollection of the plot, but I know that almost everybody, in some way or another, died. Mother had tuberculosis, and a saint-like child who crossed the road in order to pick buttercups in a field was squashed flat beneath the wheels of a passing cart. When I found myself with an empty afternoon and no one to play with, I would find myself drawn, with hideous inevitability, to the bookshelf, and the dismal book. Sitting on the floor, I would turn the pages, scarcely able to see the print for weeping.

In other words, I, like an awful lot of other people, enjoyed a good cry.

The poem, "The Raggle, Taggle Gypsies" had the same effect on me, and, oddly enough, so did Beatrix Potter's "Pigling Bland." I say "oddly enough," because Beatrix Potter was always marvelously unsentimental and thoroughly practical about the seamy side of life. Jemima Puddleduck, laying her eggs in the wrong places, was deemed a simpleton. Squirrel Nutkin, teasing the owl, got his deserts and lost his tail. And right and proper, too. But Pigling Bland was different. He and his little girlfriend Pig Wig finally escaped the dreadful fate of being sent to market, and sent off on their own, running as fast as they could.

> They came to the river, they came to the stream,
> They crossed it, hand in hand,

163

Then over the hills and far away,
She danced with Pigling Bland.

It made me cry, not because it was sad, but because it was beautiful. I still think it is beautiful, and I still get a lump in my throat when I read it aloud to my grandchildren.

The most subtle form of arousing emotion is to slip the reader, with little or no warning, from laughter to tears. James Thurber wrote a piece entitled "The Dog That Bit People." It was about an Airedale called Muggs. He didn't simply bite people, but terrified the life out of deliverymen and was regularly reported to the police. Told in Thurber's laconic style, it was marvelously funny.

But in the last paragraph, Muggs dies, quite suddenly, in the night. He is duly buried, in a grave alongside a lonely road. Mother wants a marble headstone erected, but finally settles for a smooth board, on which Thurber wrote, with an indelible pencil, "Cave Canem," and his mother was pleased with the simple classic dignity of the old Latin epitaph.

All right; so the death of any faithful animal is a sure-fire tear-jerker, but it still gets to me, every time I read it.

Emotion, conveyed by the written word, is a delicate business. Like humor, it cannot be pushed, or it slips into sentimentality. Hemingway, that master of reported speech, could wring the heart by the bare bones of his painful dialogue. He never stressed the fact that he was telling you something that went beyond ordinary feelings, and yet you read the mundane, oft-used words, and hear his voices, and recognize the poignancy of the frailty of man, and there comes the lump in the throat and the sting of incipient tears.

Some years ago, I wrote a three-act play, with a single set; not a very accomplished piece of work, but it was produced by our local repertory theater, and for a few weeks I enjoyed a mild local fame. For the first time in my life, I was invited to open fetes, judge competitions, and hand out prizes for various contests. I found none of this too daunting. But then I was approached by a woman famous for her good works, and asked if I would make an appeal on radio to raise funds for her pet project—a training center for young mothers (scarcely more than schoolgirls) unfit to care for their unwanted babies. Touched by the plight of these little families, I agreed. Only then was I told that not only would I have to deliver the appeal, but would have to write the message myself.

It was the first time that I had been faced with a situation in which I deliberately had to drag emotion out of the bag. For without emotion, I should not touch hearts, and if I didn't touch hearts, I would not touch pockets. I engaged the help of a bright girl who was involved in the project, and for two days we sat at our typewriters, finally bashing out five minutes' worth of heartbreak, sentiment, and crying need. I duly read this out over the radio one Sunday morning, and by the end of the week the center was about a hundred and fifty pounds to the good. It wasn't much, and it wasn't enough. They struggled on for a month or two, and then closed down. We had tried, but it hadn't worked.

Much more recently, the very opposite occurred. In Dundee, Scotland, a small boy was desperately ill. Specialized neurosurgery was required, but the Dundee Royal Infirmary did not have the necessary equipment. In Boston, Massachusetts, however, the equipment was available, and this was flown, in some urgency, to Scotland. The two neurosurgeons had never used the device before, but they operated, with total skill, and the small boy's life was saved.

The story appeared the next day in our local paper, *The Dundee Courier and Advertiser*. A plain, factual account of what had taken place. We learned that the reason the equipment had had to be borrowed was that the Infirmary could not afford the £60,000 necessary to purchase it. With some idea of expressing my gratitude and admiration for the two doctors, I put five pounds in an envelope and posted it to the Infirmary. So did just about everyone else, who, that morning, took the paper. A fund had to be hastily set up, without an appeal ever having been launched, and within the next two weeks, the £60,000 target had been achieved. Which proves that if you've got a good story to tell, you don't need to play your sobbing violin at the same time.

Sadness, bravery, beauty, all touch our heart strings. Great happiness can be deeply touching, else why do we sometimes weep at weddings, or that moment when an old gentleman heaves himself to his feet at his Golden Wedding party and raises his champagne glass to his wife?

My novel *The Shell Seekers* covered a span of fifty years, and because of this, the varying ages of the characters, and the intrusion of two terrible wars, I found myself writing, more than once, about death. The demise of an elderly person I do not, in fact, find particularly sad. A

165

shock and a loss, certainly, to be followed by a period of grieving, but death is part of life, and just about the only thing we can all be certain of.

However, the death of the young officer, Richard Lomax, killed on Omaha Beach, with all his life ahead of him, I found quite agonizing to set down. And worse was endeavoring to describe the reactions of Penelope Keeling, who when told of his tragic end, knew that their brief love was finished, and that the rest of her life would have to be lived without him. Struggling, as she struggled, for words, I gave her only the most banal of sentences to utter. And then cheated, and instead let her recall the final passage of the Louis MacNeice poem which they had both known and loved.

> . . . the die is cast
> There will be time to audit
> The accounts later, there will be sunlight later,
> And the equation will come out at last.

Cheating, perhaps. But it seemed to me to say it all.

To sum up, an analysis of what touches the writer is what will eventually get through to the reader. Understated, underplayed, unexaggerated, and yet totally sincere. There has to be rapport, a chime of instant recognition, clear as a bell. If you don't produce tears, you will at least kindle understanding, identification, and so forge a bond with the reader. And, at the end of the day, perhaps this is what writing is all about.

166

# ❦ 36

## THE MISSING PIECE SYNDROME

### BY RICHARD MARTIN STERN

NO PROFESSIONAL WRITER I KNOW will challenge the need for discipline. It is the *sine qua non* of the trade, craft, business, call it what you will, of setting thoughts and ideas down on paper and selling them. A writer's place is at his desk facing his typewriter or word processor, *not* finding reasons why today he cannot write. And yet. . .

I speak here only of and for writers of fiction. Writers who deal with facts have, or should have, the facts in front of them before they sit down to write. The fortunate ones can wrestle with those facts, arrange and rearrange them, in effect play with their material as with the pieces of a jigsaw puzzle until the picture finally becomes whole and clear and ready to be presented as effectively as the writer can manage.

Fiction writers are in a somewhat different situation. We deal not with facts but with dreams and smoke and mirrors, and these *on occasion* refuse to fit together in a way that will make the illusion you are attempting to create, the illusion of reality, even inevitability in your tale, come off.

It is always possible that somewhere along the way your hand has slipped, and the picture you have presented of this character or that has thrown your entire story out of whack. Reading and rereading and frequently rereading again can usually turn up the cause of this aberration. You can then stifle the guilty character's propensity for taking center stage and shove him or her back into his proper niche in the story.

Or you may have made the mistake (all too easy to make) of putting certain scenes in the wrong sequence, thereby destroying the effect of building suspense, and what you intended to be a crashing climax fizzles like a wet match because you have told too much too soon.

167

It is also possible that in the delicately tangled web of your narrative you have overlooked a complete contradiction and, say, had Character A behaving on the basis of knowledge he could *not yet have had*. It does happen. You might even have already killed off a character you now bring on stage to catch your reader's attention with his brilliant performance.

These, of course, are only a few of the possible flaws in your tale that have brought you to the discouraging but unavoidable conclusion that the story as written will not wash. To return to the jigsaw analogy, what I am talking about is the *missing* piece syndrome, the missing twist of plot, the character emphasis, the single, cohesive fact of feeling or force that can bring the entire story into sharp focus. In short, you do not yet have the handle, and this is when discipline, that *sine qua non* of writing, as I said, simply does no good at all.

This is one of the most discouraging of times for a writer. You *know* something is wrong, badly, basically, damnably wrong, but you don't know what it is. Reading and rereading what you've written turns up nothing but emptiness. You sit and stare at the machine and the blank page or screen. You go over and over the entire story as it first appeared in your mind—that shining, whole, flawless concept—and you realize that it does not even vaguely resemble what you have put down on paper, but you don't know why.

All of the characters are there, and the situations, the conflicts, the interplay of emotions and even the drama, carefully contrived. But the whole picture is askew, out of focus, whopperjawed, simply *not right*.

If you plow on, you tell yourself, it will all come out the way it should. If at first you don't succeed . . . But there also comes to mind the conclusion W. C. Fields put to that dictum: "Give up; stop making a fool of yourself." And sometimes W. C. Fields was right; a small voice tells you so, and *sometimes* you had better listen to that small voice, because if you do not, you are headed for nothing but disaster.

In every successful story there is something—and I will not even try to put a name to it because it is too nebulous, no more than a feeling— that binds the story into a whole, brings it alive, draws the reader into it page after page and in the end lets him put the tale down, satisfied.

Without that feeling, that binder, that whatever it may be called, there is nothing. And until you have found that essential force and have it firmly in mind, you will do well to throw discipline out of the window and wait for something within you, perhaps your unconscious, to come up with what is needed.

Only then, after balancing conscience against reality, is apparent sloth not only justified, it is mandatory.

I have recently begun the third complete revision of a new 135,000-word novel, and it has struck me with stunning force that I do not yet have the handle; in short, I do not know yet what the hell I am doing. I will now do nothing until the answer appears out of nowhere, as it will, bright and clear and good, tying everything together, bringing the story off the paper and into reality, making the entire tale *alive*.

Then, and only then, will I be able to proceed with confidence.

# 37

## WHERE DO YOUR STORIES COME FROM?

### BY RICK HILLIS

WHEN YOU TAKE YOUR FIRST EXPLORATORY STEPS onto a blank page, you're probably farther ahead if you're treading on something a tad more concrete than an idea. I'm talking about nuts and bolts: scene, character, tone of voice. As many short stories sprout from an interesting character you want to follow around for a bit, a curious image, a musical line of description, or even a mysterious title you keep scribbling onto cocktail napkins, as from any idea you might have.

Pre-formulated thoughts and politically correct opinions are not good short story fodder. Issues such as homelessness, child abuse, racial or sexual discrimination seem at first to be exactly the sort of topic a short story writer should take on. These ideas matter. You think they will make the kind of art that moves people to action!

But trying to cram big issues into seventeen pages is a lot like trying to shoehorn a whale into a wetsuit. In order to get your point across you have to manipulate the story's components so they add up right. Characters spout dialogue that sounds suspiciously like ventriloquism. They creak robotically, predictably, through moments more didactic than delicate and poetic. No mystery. No surprise. No discovery. The "epiphany" at the end clanks down like a hobnail boot.

Why? How come the story failed? Can't be the idea. There's nothing wrong with a noble idea.

In the real world, maybe not. But in the world of fiction, trying to dramatize conventional wisdom makes for a story that's too broad, too easy, too uncomplicated. None of the messy gray area that is the heart of most stories.

But now that a writer has this ball and chain of an idea and has invested time in a story, has something, no matter how lifeless, on the page, he or she will revise and rework and polish in a vain attempt to

170

breathe life onto the page, changing everything *except* the idea. During the course of writing a story, things change. You make discoveries. Patterns emerge that weren't in your original game plan. In the end, the story may be about something totally different from what you intended, maybe something wholly different from what you believe at the moment.

In order for the story to become itself, characters, images, whole passages of prose you have sweated over often have to be sacrificed for the good of the story. Don't worry—these are spare parts to be used in another story. But knowing this doesn't help. Parting is always tough, especially parting with an idea. The idea *is* the story, right? That, in a nutshell, is the trap. An idea makes you want to create literature *before* you've built a story.

The best "idea" you can have for a story is to think in scenes. Stories are composed largely of scenes. The camera in close-up, paying close attention to detail, and the action unfolding dramatically at about the same pace as the time it is taking you to read it. Many stories are one long scene.

"Limbo River," the title story in my collection, is a good example of how a writer may build a story from image to image, discovering through these images and the scenes they spark, the story's central theme.

"Limbo River" came out of an image I had of a boy swirling around in a ride at a cheap fair. It was a cage. He was upside down, could see the stars between his running shoes. I'd just been at such a fair, and the experience triggered a memory of riding upside down on a similar ride when I was a kid.

On a napkin, I jotted down the image of the boy's "screaming at the stars between his shoes." I didn't know what the image suggested or why the boy was screaming, but it felt right to me, enough so that I not only thought about it, I wrote a mini scene to go with it, getting down as much detail as I could remember from the fair (broken bolts and nuts, cigarette butts, popcorn, change flying out of pockets on a ride, the sense of night). Here's the tail end of it:

It was a mesh cage that spun and orbited around a greasy hub like a planet around a star. There were broken bolts and nuts in the popcorn and cigarette butts scattered around the base, but we didn't care. "We're here for a good time, not a long time," Marcel laughed. And as he said this our cage jerked, lifted us into the night sky, and we spun upside down, and Marcel's change flew out of his pockets, whizzed past our ears like shrapnel. My heart tore free of my chest and I felt it in my mouth. We dove toward the ground, but at the last minute were scooped up, swirling through the blackness, me and Marcel, screaming at the stars between our shoes.

This could be the ending to any number of stories dealing with any number of ideas. But the important thing to me was that it seemed to *be* an ending, part of a climactic scene. Everything suggested a past history: It was night; there seemed to be a complicated bond built over time between the characters; the broken-down ride through the darkness seemed like the end of a journey; and the "stars between our shoes" suggested the arrival of some sort of personal philosophy. Something had changed in the boy to get to the point where he felt whatever he felt on that ride. Now all I had to do was find the rest of the pieces to fit the puzzle.

About the same time as I wrote the fair ride scene, another image came to mind, something I'd seen. Because of drought, a stream was drying up, and down river from a dam, huge fish were captive in isolated pools. You couldn't catch them because it was illegal to fish within a hundred yards of the dam.

Somehow I thought this image fit with the fair ride image. There seemed to be a connection between the freedom of the ride and the flowing river, and the same way that the ride's cage was a prison image, so were the shrinking, isolated pools in the river.

I could say it was intuition that made me link these images, and that intuition is a large part of writing fiction. And it is. But the truth is the images were linked because I wanted them to be. They were good material, and I wanted to use them in a story, so I made them fit.

Images that reinforce and build upon what's come before, like everything in short fiction, can accomplish several things at once. They can serve as events, flashbacks, humor, description. They are often the phrases that close out or open scenes, loaded with implication and beauty and tension. They are the joints of the skeleton of a story. And often, both for the writer and the reader, they hold the seed of what will become the story's idea. Throughout "Limbo River," I consciously remained on track, by reinforcing the basic ideas of the first images with more images that worked similarly:

"The Trip took so long, we felt like bugs trapped in a jar"; "Ralph was

172

swimming back and forth across the dark blue cage, slamming the windows, the wire mesh"; "The pen was located out where the blue vein of river wound through scrub prairie land"; " I went and nosed my car into a creek"; "By then the (drowning) victims were misshapen balloons hung up in the debris after spending all winter locked in their frozen bodies under the ice. . . ."

All but one of the stories in *Limbo River* came about in this way. The one exception is "Blue," which, ironically, is one of my better stories. From the beginning, "Blue" was an idea. And I thought the idea was a winner. It had to be; it was all I had. Here it is: A woman gets hired on a pipeline construction crew. It's her one chance to have a solid, good-paying job. Her redneck coworkers are theatened. Sparks fly. O. K. It doesn't sound that great, but reduce any idea to a phrase or two, and it's going to sound idiotic. I think I liked this idea because it was the only one I'd ever had for a story—that, and I'd done pipeline work, so I had imagery stockpiled, ready to use when the story took shape.

But, it wouldn't take shape. In the first version of the story I tried to save my idea (the woman encountering the rednecks) so I could spring it on the reader in a climactic shootout. No matter how hard I revised, scenes seemed toenailed together, characters moved as if I were jiggling marionette strings. I was killing time until about page fourteen—*voila!* I could finally make this cardboard woman appear in the welding shop. And then, boy-oh-boy, the welders are not thrilled. Change had visited the men's traditional workplace, but dammit, it was time things changed!

Horrible, and I knew it was horrible, but I didn't know why.

One of the terrible things about an idea-driven story is that once the idea has hold of you, it won't let go. The more trouble you have doing the idea justice, the more precious and important it seems. It takes over. It haunts you.

About three or four years after I first started taking runs at "Blue" (I was calling it "The Wobble" then), it finally dawned on me that everybody knows that if a woman joins a pipeline, sparks will fly and things will be tough. That's no climax scene, no epiphany . . . it's a *beginning.*

So I wrote:

Lubnickie slams the truck door and leaps up the ramp to the shop. Nothing new about that, but this morning Murdoch grabs his arm as soon as he steps inside, gives him a shake, gets his goddamn attention.

173

"You seen them yet?"

"Don't even think like that," says Lubnickie.

But when his eyes get used to the dark and he sees them, it's true. Three of them, two in their early twenties with faces like they got off at the wrong bus stop, the other one older, maybe thirty or so, and hard looking. She's got on men's jeans and dirty running shoes with the toes worn through on top. Her hair is reddish, tied from her face with a green scarf. One of the younger ones has on dress shoes with pointed heels and keeps lifting her feet one at a time like a flamingo . . .

By beginning with what I thought would be the climactic scene, exposing the idea on the first page, I stumbled on the prime short story axiom:

*Start as close to the main action as you can. If your story is about a guy being stood up at the prom, don't begin in kindergarten.*

Great. On the other hand, what happens next? Now that I'd opened with Norma encountering Ed in the welding shop, I'd written the sum of what I knew about the story by the end of the first page. I had no idea what was going to come next until out of nowhere:

Norma, the older of the women, fixes her eyes on a spot on the wall where no one is leaning. She is nervous, more frightened than she would ever admit, especially to herself. But seeing these cocky men with their pressed jeans and polished boots makes her think, *screw everybody*. Screw the younger ones with the muscle cars and designer jeans that cost more than the parka she's worn through at the elbows. Screw the older guys with their grade-eight educations, color TVs, second cars, houses with nice lawns, big weddings for their daughters, holidays in the summer. She knows who they are, because she's seen their wives in the mall, spending money their husbands made. . . .

So Norma had some real anger in her. Maybe even a chip on her shoulder. I hadn't realized that about her until I wrote it. Not only that, *I was in her mind, telling the story through her experience* as well as Ed's!

Which leads to a couple more axioms—or close to it: *Stories are not about issues or events* (sexism on the job, for example); they are about how these events affect *people*. Also when writing about a gathering of people, an outsider forced to be on the inside will provide an interesting point of view. For example, Norma can observe details Lubnickie would overlook. Everything is old hat to him.

By dispatching the rigid idea on the first page, I let myself be surprised and discover the natural structure of the story. Juxtaposing parallel moments between characters, each from their own points of view, came out of the blue. But once I had it, I knew the characters would drive the narrative. A day later the story was finished.

By setting out to dramatize an idea, it's unlikely you'll get beyond it. Three of a writer's chief tools—intuition, risk, and playfulness—will be left in the toolbox, and you won't enjoy one of a writer's great highs: discovery. Unless, in the end, you manage to say more than you intended (or even knew you knew), writing is just painting by numbers. It's not the idea you begin with that matters. It's the one you come away with.

# 38

# WHEN IS A STORY A SHORT STORY?

## BY SUSAN R. HARPER

"THIS IS ON ITS WAY TO BEING a powerful short story," I once wrote on a manuscript—in fact, I've written something like that on any number of them, over the years. "But it isn't a short story yet," is how the second sentence goes, followed by sentences that offer thoughts on how it might become one.

The author of the piece I'm recalling right now asked to have his story read in class; he wanted it judged by a jury of his peers. I had to think about that for a minute; I never deliberately leave students open to embarrassment. But there's nothing inherently embarrassing about an early draft that falls short or isn't working—at least, there shouldn't be. Not in a workshop, anyway. That's what workshops are for. Besides, perhaps I'd been wrong: judged the story too harshly, missed its point. I've been crashingly wrong about stories at times.

I read the story out loud to the class, as I almost always do. That way the authors remain anonymous, and the criticism is directed toward the work, not the writers. I was careful to present the story as well as I could, as if I myself had written it. Then I asked for comments, first on what was working well (we usually begin with that), and then on what seemed not to work.

There was a lot to like in the story, everyone agreed: The characterizations were strong, the point of view consistent and convincing, the setting well evoked. . . . But? The comments suddenly became vague: "I didn't care for the ending."—a useless observation except that it did point to a problem area and got the group talking about it. "I wasn't ready for it to end."—a *bit* more helpful. "I don't know," said one young man. "Are we sure it *had* an ending? I felt more as if it had just quit. Like a plane that's supposed to come in for a landing, but instead just drops out of the sky."

176

"But did you have any idea *where* it would land?" asked another student.

"No," the first admitted.

"I didn't either. There wasn't any sense of a destination, or any suspense about whether or not the character would get there—wherever 'there' is."

"Right," someone else said. "It isn't that you don't care. The main character's too real for that; you can't be indifferent to him. But you don't know where he's headed, or what really matters to him. So when things happen to him, you don't know how you're supposed to feel about them."

## Tell me a story

What's interesting to me about those comments is the way they spontaneously and almost innocently reveal what readers expect from a short story. There wasn't anything hifalutin' about the remarks—nothing technical or showoffy. People were just groping around for how they felt about that story.

Their feelings, I think, go all the way back to childhood, and beyond, to the beginnings of the human race. As we learned in high school biology, each of us repeats, in our individual lives, the whole history of our species. A lovely and intriguing thought! It assigns each generation more to absorb; it makes the "front ends" of our lives seem (in the abstract, at least) like speeded-up movies; and it offers one explanation, at least, for why things seem more frantic and more complicated with each succeeding generation.

When we sit around a long table in a seminar in San Francisco and listen to a story, we are doing something almost as old as humankind: gathering around a fire. And we are doing something we probably did when we were children. As soon as we became truly verbal, one of our requests was "Tell me a story."

What did we mean by that? I think that in a funny way I had a chance to find out as a kid. My parents came from a long line of raconteurs, and my father in particular was and is a very good storyteller. He has led an adventurous life, so he's continually adding to his repertoire, but the old stories are the ones we've heard the most and know the best. Even now, when we get together for a holiday or a reunion, we ask for these old stories by name. "Tell us 'Punk's Hack,'" we say. "No, how about 'Ham and Eggs and Gravy Legs'?" They are stories we've heard from childhood.

But I was a child of the forties and fifties, the era of the "shaggy-dog story"—a long, rambling narrative, the point of which was that it had no point. This type of story was, for some perverse reason, hilarious to my dad. So once in a while, if we asked for a story, we got a shaggy-dog story, told by him with great amusement and greeted by us with something close to mutiny. "That wasn't a *story*," we'd protest. I'm sure my father thought we were a pretty humorless bunch. But I can still remember my real disappointment, the sense of having been cheated. I wanted something with a *point*, something that started at A and went to B (or G, or Z). It was this desire, in fact, that the shaggy things exploited and mocked. So we weren't wrong in feeling that we were somehow being laughed at.

Were our desires different from most people's? Look at what the class members were implicitly looking for in the story I read aloud. They wanted an ending, certainly: an ending they were prepared for. "A destination," one of them called it—implying a journey: a shape of the whole story, as if it were a trajectory. "Suspense," one of them mentioned. Another talked about getting a sense of "what really matters," so that "when things happen to [the character], you . . . know how to feel about them."

## The slice-of-life question

The key question in a short story workshop is: "What was the author's intention?" That is what we as readers must divine, if we are to do justice to the writer's work. In the last analysis, the writer may not do what we want, but has he achieved what *he* wanted?

That was the question at which our discussion arrived, and we were up in the air about answering it. "Since I couldn't tell where the author was going with this story," said the woman, "I never knew whether he or she got there."

Then a new voice joined the discussion. "I had the feeling that we were being shown something—like, say, a snapshot," he said, "and being asked to draw our own conclusions." And how had he felt about that? Was that a valid thing for a story to do?

178

"I guess anything is valid," he said (a true child of the seventies). "But how I felt was, well—it was as if I'd been given a test and had never found out if I'd passed. I always want to know the *author's* conclusions. Otherwise, why read an author's stuff, right?"

At that point, we turned to the author, who could hardly wait to speak. "That was the whole *idea,*" he said. "The story did just what I wanted it to do. It presented a slice of life. Period. The rest is up to the reader. It's *supposed* to make you feel frustrated; it's *supposed* to bring you face to face with life, and with the inevitability of making decisions and drawing conclusions and being alone in your judgments."

"O.K.," I said. "The author has done what he set out to do. His story affected us as he hoped it would. In that sense, he's entirely satisfied.

"The basic question now is: Has he written a short story? Does this piece have the hallmarks of what we call by that name? Or is it something else?"

"What else could it be?" someone asked.

## If it's Tuesday, this must be fiction

One of the assumptions people fall into sometimes is that if a piece of writing is "creative" (as opposed to purely factual and expository) and if it's prose, it must be a short story. "What else could it be?"

The answer is that it could be a prose poem, or a novella, or a "short short story," or a vignette, or a character sketch. Each of these has particular attributes that distinguish it from the others. So-called slice-of-life stories usually turn out to be vignettes—brief incidents or scenes, or short descriptive sketches; moments, places in time, rather than trajectories—and I felt that the piece we were considering was probably a vignette. Because they're static, vignettes can't stand alone. And in that sense, they don't fulfill our expectations of the short story.

The short story, in fact, like the sonnet, can inspire (and fulfill) the most extravagant expectations. And even in its simplest, purest form, it is as rigorous, as rigidly circumscribed by "rules," and as demanding as the sonnet, though it doesn't have a prescribed number of lines or words or syllables, or a rhyme scheme with a name. But it has been interpreted—by writers, readers, and critics alike—with wide latitude. It flows between broad banks, retaining its fluidity and grace. Yet, like any chemical compound, including water, it has a specific structure that can be diagrammed, and a specific set of elements that go to make it up.

179

These aren't arbitrary, and they aren't optional; they are what make a short story a short story rather than a vignette or a prose poem or a shaggy-dog story.

Like the child in the old television advertisement who is playing in the snow while waiting for his mother to make soup for lunch, we have certain definite expectations. "Is it soup yet?" the child calls in to his mother as she stands at the stove, stirring something in a pot. The child is expecting a hot liquid to be set before him in a cup or bowl. But if, when he sits down, his mother serves him tea—a hot liquid in a cup or bowl—he will protest, "This isn't soup!" We will expect the same response if she offers him oatmeal or chili. Soup is soup.

## Call me a short story

We don't just decide that a piece of prose is a short story because we want it to be or wish it could be or don't know what else it is. We *know* whether a piece of prose is a short story by what is in it.

I'm thinking now of the injured man lying in the street, who cried out to a nearby hippie, "Call me an ambulance." Nodding, the hippie responded, "Like, man, you're an ambulance." I realize that the fact that this is one of my favorite awful old jokes shows the extent to which I am my father's daughter. But it's still true that if we dub something a short story without even thinking about it, we're as bad as the hippie. We're discouraging the author from understanding his or her work, and from confronting the standards by which it is measured. The short story is called a demanding form for good reason. And we don't write one by accident. Look at what Edgar Allan Poe wrote when he offered—more than 150 years ago—the critical definition of the short story that still stands today:

In the whole composition there should be no word written, of which the tendency, direct or indirect, is not to the one pre-established design. And by such means, with such care and skill, a picture is at length painted which leaves in the mind of him who contemplates it with a kindred art, a sense of the fullest satisfaction.

*Pre-established design? At length?* This is not the description of a casual process, but of a painstaking and specific (and perhaps lengthy) one. A rewarding one, too, for at its best it leads to that "sense of the fullest satisfaction" for reader and writer alike.

# 39

## Rewriting Your Novel

### By S. L. Stebel

LET'S SUPPOSE YOU'RE ONE OF THOSE HAPPY FEW who have filled enough intimidatingly blank pages to flesh out a book, and have actually been able to write those magical words: THE END!

The novel may have ended. That's the good news. But is it finished? Alas, more than likely not.

How to know? Fortunately, there are some simple yet effective procedures that I've developed to help a writer determine, first, whether a novel meets the standards deeming it "publishable," and second, whether it has achieved all the possibilities inherent in the material.

It's important to let the book "settle" for a time. Put it away—out of sight, out of mind—long enough to enable you, when you pick it up again, to read it "cold," giving you a reasonably fresh and objective look. Do not despair if you then discover that your story line is murky, that your beginning, which seemed lively enough at the time you wrote it, soon slacks off, and that your ending seems to be overly abrupt and (dare you admit it?) not quite as powerful as you had intended.

What has gone wrong? The guideposts of your outline (assuming that you had one) seem to have disappeared underneath an avalanche of words; your scenes sprawl randomly and without point; your characters wander like underutilized actors in search of a drama in which they may act out their parts.

But no doubt there are also scenes you do not even recall writing that have sprung brilliantly to life, and one or more characters that have become so vivid and uniquely individual they surprise even you. (Let's hope one of them is your protagonist!) Keep those wonderful moments ready at hand; they are products of your writing partner—your unconscious—and are key clues to the solving of any problems your novel may have.

But wait. Don't start rewriting yet. Instead, write a glowing review of

181

the novel you had hoped you were writing. Putting modesty aside, imagine that you're the leading reviewer of the most influential book reviewing publication in the country, and you're going to do your utmost to convince readers that they must go out and buy your novel immediately!

"Let's not mince words," you may write. "This is a stunning novel, written by (your name here), a master of his/her craft, who has produced as enthralling, if not profound, work that keeps the reader engrossed from first page to last."

O.K. so far: You've tantalized your audience. But in order to get them to rush out to the bookstore, you first have to give them a reason, and that involves telling them who and what your book is about. Seems easy enough. . . .

"The protagonist," you continue enthusiastically, "with a *dominant attribute* (i.e., *ambitious* young priest, *melancholy* Dane, *risk-taking* wife, *greedy* stock manipulator, *frightened* soldier), encounters *another character with a dominant attribute* (see examples above), who offers a fatal temptation. In a momentary lapse, for reasons buried deep within his psyche, the protagonist steps from the straight and narrow and in a series of harrowing events discovers (blank) about life and (blank) about him/herself."

Pause a moment here. Have you found it easy to describe a dominant trait about each of your characters? If not, why not? Could it be they're not well enough defined, even in your own mind? If so, it's imperative for you to learn more about them. Do a little creative snooping into each character's history. You may discover hidden motivations that can surprise you, that must surprise you before you can surprise your readers.

And how clearly have you been able to describe the basic conflict? How determined is your protagonist to achieve some goal? What, or who, stands in his/her way? Does *every* character you've created contribute to the dramatic action? If not, what are they doing in your story?

If those questions prove difficult to answer, try listing all the emotional and historical baggage your leading characters carry. I'll bet you'll find some things you didn't expect. Now chart your main characters' emotional journeys from the beginning to the end of your novel. Examine the result: Do your leading characters grow and develop?

One way readers know they've been told a story is by seeing that a character has changed, or has at least been enlightened in some important, revelatory way. In any relationship story (is there any other kind?), the characters should change or enlighten each other.

What about the dramatic action? As you continue writing your review, do you find it easy to sketch the narrative line (sometimes called plot) in a gripping way, yet clearly enough for a reasonably intelligent person to understand it?

If the story line—even in an episodic, metaphorical novel—does not possess some kind of interior logic, or if the events, sparse as they may be, only "happen," without any motivation except the author's recognition of the need for some kind of "action," it may be necessary to take a more practical, hands-on approach. To do this effectively, there is nothing better than borrowing from the past and taking a "classical" approach to the material.

A very useful technique is to break your novel down arbitrarily into three acts. (It may be a book of many acts, unnatural and otherwise, but for the purpose of this exercise, assume there are only three.) We'll further assume, in the interests of simplification, that Act One states the problem, Act Two complicates the problem, Act Three resolves the problem.

Next, do a "step" outline. We'll take it for granted that each of your chapters deals with a separate event. But it can be extraordinarily helpful simply to write a sentence for every time something actually happens in your novel. That can be a *physical* happening—one character murders another, or merely enters or leaves a room—or it can be an *emotional* happening, in which, for example, one character professes love for another, threatens another, or breaks down and weeps.

Though in this step outline you may write a sentence when one character newly engages another character in dialogue for the first time (not mere conversation), you may not write another sentence, no matter how long they talk or how many pages of exquisite descriptive prose goes on, unless something *else* happens: a sudden lie, say, or an unexpected idea in the mind of one of the characters that has the potential for action (i.e., a mental vow for revenge). If you find that there are a great number of pages for which you are not able to add another sentence to your step outline, you'd better investigate: Has your material become static, and in all likelihood, boring?

When you've finished this step outline, examine it, then revise it, and keep revising it until you have a story line that moves, clearly and dramatically, in a slowly ascending scale of intensity. Obscurity is not a virtue. Neither is ambiguity, unless deliberate. The author should always know what is going on, even if at some point the object will be to keep the characters and/or readers in the dark.

This brings us to what I believe is the underlying purpose of the writing process: a search for the thematic statement. The thematic statement can, and should, be simple. "Oh, what a tangled web we weave when first we practice to deceive." "Love can transform the most savage beast." "Revenge, at first though sweet, bitter ere long back on itself recoils." A writer can ring as many changes on a theme as are within his or her inventive powers. He can rebut the theme, reinforce it, complicate it, but he must never deviate from it. If in writing your review, you find yourself saying that your novel is about this, and it is also about that, and it may well be also about another thing, be assured that your thematic statements will contradict rather than reinforce one another, leaving readers frustrated and confused.

Once you've discovered and clarified your thematic statement, you'll be able to approach the actual rewriting of your text with the kind of assurance that will convince your readers that they are in the hands of a confident and skilled writer. "Author" is (or should be) short for authoritative.

The Greeks, especially Aristotle, had a word for it. Their attitude toward the writing of drama—in which I include all forms of fiction—is worthy of emulation. Every line you write, they believed, should do one of three things (or, in the best of all possible worlds, all three things simultaneously): (1) define character (2) create atmosphere (3) advance the action.

All else is redundant. It may be writing for the sake of writing, a form of intellectual pretension that may delude some into believing they're in the presence of artistry. Or it may be misguided hope on the author's part that the reader will fill in the gaps, supply the missing motivations.

With this approach, however, your novel will become coherent, its underlying theme, or subtext, suddenly all of a piece. Knowing your theme will make rewriting a delight and give you the freedom to be as inventive as you're capable of being. Try it. You have everything to gain, and nothing to lose.

# 40

## Too Good To Be True: The Flawless Character

### By Mary Tannen

My mother once bought a new table that came with a card printed on buff-colored heavy stock explaining that the table had been "distressed" with artful gouges and well-placed worm holes to give it a patina of age. We (her four children) thought this was hilariously funny and said that if we had only known she wanted distressed furniture we would have been happy to oblige and that clearly we had misinterpreted her screams of anguish every time we left a soda bottle on the coffee table or ran a toy car up the leg of the Duncan Phyfe chair.

The very phrase "character flaw" makes me think of that distressed table, as if characters were naturally shiny new and perfect and needed only the addition of a flaw or two, artfully placed, to make them more realistic. To me, a personality, whether actual or fictional, is not solid but liquid, not liquid but airborne, as changeable as light. What looks like a flaw might turn out to be a virtue. Virtue might, under certain circumstances, prove to be a fault.

When my daughter was reading *Billy Budd* and having a hard time with it, she came storming into my room to protest, and seeing the book I was working on in galleys, took it into her room to read. She brought it back the next day and announced that it was "better than *Billy Budd*."

"Better than *Billy Budd*!" I could see it emblazoned across the book jacket. Actually, my novel isn't better than *Billy Budd*, but the style was a lot more congenial to my daughter. She was appalled by Melville's heavy symbolism, by the way Billy Budd was the representation of an idea, not an actual man.

Billy Budd had no flaws, physical or moral (except for his stutter). He was illiterate, of noble but unknown birth, untainted by the corrupting influence of either family or literature. He was a myth, "Apollo with his

185

portmanteau"! Melville never intended to create a realistic character. Billy Budd was Adam before the fall.

Sometimes when reading over a draft of a fiction piece I am working on, I realize that one of my major characters is suspiciously lacking in flaws. She is usually a person like me, but she is lacking in defects as well as in color and definition. When this happens in a piece of fiction I'm writing, it is a sign that I am identifying too closely with her. Just as I try to show my good and hide my bad, I am protecting this fictional person.

Recently I discovered a trick that helped me correct this. I was working with a character, Yolanda, a woman my age who ran a book-store. Yolanda was nice. She was good. A nice good woman, and very bland. I couldn't get a grip on her or who she was. I went to my local swimming pool to do a few laps and take my mind off my troubles, when I saw a woman I'd seen many times before but don't know very well—a tall skinny woman with short elfin hair and wide-awake eyes. I decided to steal this woman's body and give it to Yolanda.

It worked miracles because now Yolanda was no longer me. She was this woman I didn't know very well. She began to exhibit all kinds of personality traits. She was allergic to almost everything and purchased her meals at the New Age Take-Out Kitchen. This explained why she was so thin. She spent lonely nights watching the families in the apartments across the street. The strange thing was that although Yolanda had many more weaknesses than she did before I discovered she wasn't me, I liked her better.

Another way to break the spell of the flawless character is to elicit the opinion of another character in the novel or story, one who dislikes, resents, or holds a grudge against the paragon of virtue. In *Second Sight*, I had a perfectly lovable older woman, Lavinia, who refused to believe that her philandering husband, Nestor, had left her for good. Instead of selling the house and investing the proceeds in order to live off the income, she managed on very little so that she could keep the house intact for Nestor's return.

Nestor (who had flaws to spare) had another version of the story. Lavinia's loyalty enraged him. He saw it as a ploy to make him feel guilty and remain tied to her. Indeed, at the end when Nestor asked Lavinia to take him back, Lavinia realized she no longer wanted to return to her old life with Nestor. She wondered if perhaps instead of being noble and true all those years, she hadn't actually been taking out a genteel and subtle revenge.

A character without flaws has nowhere to go. He can't change or grow. In Philip Roth's *The Counterlife,* the novelist Zuckerman, who used himself as a character in his books, was writing about his younger brother Henry. Because Zuckerman had given all the faults to himself-as-character, he had doomed his brother-as-character to a life of virtue. Henry had always been the good son, the good husband, father, dentist. Writing about Henry at thirty-nine, Zuckerman imagined him as the suffocating prisoner of his perfect but shallow life. The only way Henry could break the pattern was to escape altogether, leave his family and practice in New Jersey and begin anew in Israel. Zuckerman went to visit Henry in his kibbutz on the West Bank and found that his younger brother had simply exchanged one slavish system for another. He was still the good brother. He could change the scene, but he couldn't change himself because he was a character without flaws.

I realize I have been using the term "flaw" as if it could mean anything from nail-biting to one of the Seven Deadly Sins. I think of a flaw as a personality trait I wouldn't confess to, except on a dark and stormy night to a stranger passing through. And then there are the flaws we hide from ourselves, or lack the insight to see, but which help determine the course of our lives.

When I'm writing, the flaws that interest me are not the ones I assign ("Q kicks small dogs"), but those that emerge in the course of the story. Take Yolanda, who tries to be good, to be virtuous, to do no harm to others: I was amazed to discover, somewhere near the end of the first draft, that she had used someone, a man, a friend, to get over a wound suffered long ago, and in using him had hurt him. Yolanda didn't see how she could hurt this friend whom she considered much more powerful and attractive than she. The more I work on that novel, the more I see that Yolanda's major flaw is her modesty. She lets people down because she cannot conceive that she means as much to them as they do to her.

In *Second Sight,* the opposite was true: a character's flaw proved to be her saving grace. Delia, the widowed mother of a twelve-year-old son, lacked all marketable skills. She lived on welfare and whatever she could make telling fortunes over the phone. Everyone, but especially

Delia's career-minded sister Cass, faulted her for not taking her life in hand and finding a way out of the dead-end life of poverty she and her son had fallen into.

But Delia operated on another level from her more rational friends and relatives. She was watching for signs and portents, for signals that the time was right. She refused to force the unfolding of her life.

Delia did manage finally to bring about a change for herself and her son, to the amazement of the others, who began to see a glimmer of wisdom in her otherworldliness. Cass, however, could never accept that Delia's passivity had enabled her to recognize and receive love when it came her way. Cass would continue to take charge of her life, as Delia said, captaining it as if it were a ship, but never allowing for the influence of wind or tide or current.

People, fictional and real, are not perfect, like fresh-from-the-factory tables. They come with their faults built in, mingled and confused with their virtues. Whenever I find I am dealing with a character without flaws, and I am not intending a twentieth-century rewrite of *Billy Budd*, I take it as a sign that I have not done my work. I have not imagined my character fully, have not considered her through the eyes of the other characters. Finally, I have not cut the umbilical cord. I am protecting her, shielding her, and, at the same time, imprisoning her in her own virtue. It is time to let her go so she can fail and change and grow.

# SPECIALIZED FICTION

# 41

## WRITING NOVELS ABOUT THE PAST

### By Thomas Fleming

THE SOCIETY OF AMERICAN HISTORIANS, one of the country's best known and most exclusive historical organizations (its membership is limited to 250), recently created a new award: the James Fenimore Cooper Prize for historical fiction. It is a sign of the growing importance of the historical novel, not merely as a source of reading pleasure, but as a communicator of serious knowledge about the past.

In the final decade of this century (as in the previous one), the number of historical novels on publishers' lists is likely to increase; readers are inclined to look back and try to understand the years through which they and their parents have lived. The 1890s saw a veritable explosion of historical fiction on American subjects, as well as a great deal of biography and narrative history. There are strong grounds for expecting the 1990s to follow the same trend. The dramatic events of the 20th Century—World War I, the Great Depression, World War II, Vietnam, the collapse of the Communist empire—cry out for the kind of exploration good historical novelists can provide.

There will, of course, be equally vigorous explorations of these subjects by historians, both amateur and professional. What does the historical novel offer the reader that entitles its practitioners to claim a fellowship with historians? What must a writer do to be able to sustain that claim to importance?

Both historians and historical novelists construct *narratives,* that crucial word whose Latin stem means *knowing.* Both are in the business of helping readers understand the past with fresh insights and information. That means the historical novelist must know as much about the period and the subject as an historian—and then some. The novelist must not only grasp the big issues and main events, he must acquire a feel for the everyday life of the period, the minutiae that will enable him to bring characters to life.

Especially valuable for the historical novelist are diaries or biographies of secondary figures. From them you can acquire attitudes and opinions that major figures either conceal or ignore. For *Over There,* my novel set during World War I, I found a wealth of material in the diaries of two of General John J. Pershing's lesser generals, Robert Lee Bullard and James Harbord. The pessimistic Bullard made me realize, for the first time, the embarrassment and dismay that enveloped Americans during their first twelve months in France, when troops arrived in a pathetic trickle and the British and French contemptuously tried to get rid of Pershing and his generals and seize the doughboys as replacements for their exhausted armies.

Even better, if possible, is a visit to the scenes of the book. For *Over There,* I drove across the vast valley of the Argonne; I prowled the murderous dimness of Belleau Wood; I stood on the banks of the Marne near Chateau Thierry at twilight and imagined what raw American soldiers felt in June of 1918, knowing there were 500,000 German veterans in the steep hills on the other side of that swift river, poised to make their final lunge toward Paris.

For my previous novel, *Time and Tide,* set aboard a cruiser in the South Pacific during World War II, I flew to Guadalcanal and chartered a boat to explore Ironbottom Sound, where thousands of Japanese and American sailors fought to the death in some of the most ferocious sea battles in history. I continued to Australia, where the crew of my symbolic ship, the *USS Jefferson City,* went on wild liberties.

Ph.D. dissertations provide another rich source of material. For a modest fee, University Microfilms International Dissertation Information Service in Ann Arbor, Michigan, will do a computer search that can turn up reams of unpublished information on all aspects of your subject. You can buy the dissertations on microfilm for roughly the price of a book and read them at your local library.

Speaking of microfilm, *The New York Times* has a company that will sell you microfilms of old newspapers. For about $200, I obtained day-by-day copies of the Paris Edition of *The New York Herald* for the years 1917–18. It was a gold mine of information about the mood of people in France during those years. I could not have written *Over There* without it.

Interviews are not to be scorned by the historical novelist. For *Time and Tide,* I attended a reunion of the cruiser *USS Columbia* and spent

192

hours talking to the officers and enlisted men about their experiences off Guadalcanal, the Philippines, and Okinawa. The enlisted men told me things that dramatized how ferociously they resented the Navy's class system—for instance, how the engine room gang "persuaded" the stewards to feed them hams and steaks from the officers' mess. One ex-lieutenant gasped: "That couldn't have happened aboard the *Columbia.*" I need hardly add that this insight went into my novel.

Ditto for another item that I got from an interview with the former engineering officer of an aircraft carrier: The fact that some ships in the fleet were "wet"—the Captains allowed the officers to bring liquor aboard and drink it in the wardroom. This became a crucial part of the plot of *Time and Tide*.

For *Over There* interviews, I had a built-in source—my father, who had been a lieutenant in 78th Division. I made extensive notes on the stories he told me before he died. I also visited several reunions of the 78th Division at Fort Dix to talk to other ex-doughboys.

Important as research is for establishing the authority and authenticity of the historical novel, it is by no means the essence of the book. At the heart of every important historical novel is the *historical imagination,* a term that makes some people nervous. Imagination is too often associated with make-believe, with illusion. The historical imagination sounds as if the historical novelist has a license to rewrite history, to make up a different, erroneous version of the past.

On the contrary, the historical imagination is rooted in a knowledge of history, the more intimate and more detailed, the better. In every historical novel I have written, I have begun with an imaginative penetration of an actual historical situation. *Over There* began with the discovery that nineteen months before John J. Pershing was appointed to command the AEF, his wife and three daughters were killed in a fire in their quarters at the Presidio in San Francisco.

Into my imagination leaped a West Point classmate of Pershing's, Malvern Hill Bliss, who has lost his wife and son to a Moro guerilla in the Philippines. Pershing takes Bliss to France with him, because he understands what is happening in his soul. Only to him can Pershing say: "We can't let Death break us." Only to him can he explain the meaning of the 23-year-old mistress he took in Paris.

Next came another act of the historical imagination, rooted in research. I discovered that an astonishing 25,000 American women went to France to participate in the war. Most of them were feminists. Many were pacifists, until Woodrow Wilson's rhetoric turned the war into a moral crusade. General Bliss meets one of these women on the *USS Baltic*, en route to France. "Intelligent violence wins wars. And war is the engine of history," he says, summing up his professional soldier's creed.

"Bunk!" says red-haired Polly Warden, instantly defining their relationship.

*Time and Tide* began with a similar act of historical imagination. I was reading an account of the battle of Savo Island, the disastrous American defeat off Guadalcanal in August 1942. I was suddenly riveted by the realization that the *USS Chicago* had sailed *away* from the Japanese without firing a shot, abandoning her four sister cruisers to destruction. A quick check in the records revealed the *Chicago's* captain was relieved from duty and later shot himself.

What if the Captain's best friend, his Annapolis roommate, took over the ship—with orders to find out what had happened on that disgraceful night? A novel, eventually embedded in a painstakingly researched, realistic narrative of the Pacific war, had been born. A novel that enabled me to write nothing less than major revisions of many conventional scenarios of the war, revealing inept admirals by the dozen, weapons that did not work, a Navy riven by feuds.

*Over There* has similar historical surprises for the reader. Malvern Hill Bliss denounces Belleau Wood as a brainless slaughter. A mortified Polly Warden, an ambulance driver in the VADs, the British Voluntary Aid Detachment, watches three massive German offensives rampage through the British and French armies in the spring of 1918 while the AEF sits on the sidelines, not firing a single shot.

At the same time, in both these books—as in every good novel, historical or contemporary—the focus is on the emotions of the imagined characters. Readers share the anguish and the courage, the anger and the joy of men and women struggling to cope with the vortexes of history. Here lies the real importance of the historical novel—its ability to blend knowledge and deep feeling to create what Thomas De Quincy called the literature of power.

Inevitably, because history is never neat, the historical novelist may have to telescope events or rearrange some minor facts to maintain the narrative focus. But if the writer has a solid grasp of the history, he need never worry about altering historical truth in a fundamental way. The creator of the American historical novel, James Fenimore Cooper, put his finger on the key idea, when he insisted that historical fiction should be "probable." To know what is probable requires a grasp of the historical facts.

For instance, toward the end of *Time and Tide*, Arthur McKay, the captain of the *Jefferson City*, discussed the atomic bomb with Admiral Raymond Spruance, a real historical character. Spruance tells McKay he loathes the idea of dropping it on a Japanese city. One reviewer of the novel, a nonfiction writer, criticized this scene because he said there was nothing in the historical record to support Spruance's words.

True. But it is a matter of historical record that most of the Navy's top admirals disapproved of the use of the bomb, though they made no official protest. From my study of Spruance's character, and his intimate friendship with McKay, it was probable, plausible, that he would say such a thing—adding that, of course, he had no intention of going public with his opinion.

The Cornell University critic, Cushing Strout, has coined a phrase that goes a long way to solving the fact-versus-fiction conflict in historical novels. The good historical novelist, Strout says, is always guided by a "veracious imagination." He or she operates within a broad hemisphere of truthful probability. Strout contrasts this to the "voracious imagination," which consumes both the truth and art in the name of some febrile political emotion. His prime example of this misuse of the genre is E. L. Doctorow's *Ragtime*, which inserts a black activist from the 1960s into early 1900s America, attributing to him rhetoric and a militancy he could not possibly have possessed at that time.

It is this *veracious* historical imagination that separates the historical novel from the docudrama, that atrocious version of history that television has foisted upon us. The docudrama claims it is telling the literal truth about a subject, such as the Cuban Missile crisis. The focus is always on the subject; there are no imagined characters or scenes, no plot beyond the history itself. In the film, *JFK,* director Oliver Stone has demonstrated how recklessly this form can mangle rather than reveal historical truth.

Good historical novels can and do mingle real and imaginary characters. The more attention the writer gives to the real characters, the more careful he must be not to exceed the bounds of probability. Another strategy, followed by Robert Penn Warren in *All The King's Men,* is to create an imaginary character, Willie Stark, who is a virtual mirror image of the real character, Huey Long. I used this device with several minor characters in *Over There.* Douglas Fairchild, a wildly ambitious colonel with a dragon for a mother, is obviously modeled on Douglas MacArthur. But changing his name enabled me to use him with more fictional freedom.

The more I write historical novels, the more attractive becomes the advice of architect Louis Sullivan, who said it was the artist's task to "grasp the largeness of things." History adds a dimension to fiction that it too often lacks—and fiction gives a dimension to history that helps us appreciate its power and significance in everyone's life. No one put it better than the greatest of our century's historical novelists, William Faulkner. "The writer's duty is to . . . help man endure by lifting his heart, by reminding him of the courage and honor and hope and pride and compassion and pity and sacrifice which have been the glory of his past."

# 42

## HAVING SOMETHING TO SAY

### BY PATRICIA D. CORNWELL

I REMEMBER TAKING LITERATURE AND CREATIVE WRITING CLASSES AT Davidson College in North Carolina and being struck by a frustrating dilemma. It seemed that the best stories were told by the worst writers and the best writers had nothing to say. I have decided by now that this is a common problem, if not THE problem.

The sad reality is, talent does count. You cannot muscle your way to the top simply by doing enough research and spending twelve hours a day in your office. An example is my tennis ability. My pipe dream when I was a child was to play at Forest Hills. I practiced six hours a day, watched matches on TV, and kept *The Inner Game of Tennis* on the table by my bed. The highest I was ever ranked, I think, was fourteenth in North Carolina. The only way I was ever going to make it to Forest Hills was to sit in the stands.

Though you can improve your writing skills, just as you can improve your tennis skills, you cannot learn the inner poetry and descriptive brilliance that extraordinarily gifted writers seem to conjure up without trying. But instead of dwelling on the unsurprising revelation that few of us are geniuses, I'd rather assume that most of us fall into the category of the *good writer who has nothing to say.*

### Your voice

I decided to write crime novels not because I liked to read them but because I had been a crime reporter for *The Charlotte Observer.* Beyond that, I cannot fully explain my fascination with violence, but I suspect it has to do with my fear of it.

In my college days, I think I imitated whomever I was reading at the time. This is fine when you are in your formative stages as a writer. But in order for you to write successfully, you must discover your voice and your story. Your voice is what you sound like when you no longer are consciously trying to imitate someone else. Perhaps your voice is dry and quite funny, like Sue Grafton's. Or it may be melancholy and richly poetic, like Pat Conroy's. When you really tap into your own voice, you are discovering a layer of yourself that is not necessarily apparent in the personality other people see when they meet you. For example, my writing is dark, filled with nightscapes and fear. Isolation and a sense of loss whisper throughout my prose like something perpetually stirring in the wind. It is not uncommon for people to meet me and find it incongruous that I write the sort of books I do.

Finding your voice requires endless writing, and you may discover your voice at the same time you discover your story.

## Your story

What draws you in? When you read the newspaper in the morning, what do you look at first? Sports, comics, crime stories, or politics? My eye has always caught crime stories first, and that's been true for as long as I can remember. Ask yourself other questions, as well. Or maybe you already know your story. Maybe you're a lawyer like Scott Turow or know as much about horse racing as Dick Francis. Maybe you fought in Vietnam or work in law enforcement. Maybe your life has been a series of tragic romances—or no romances—and that's the song you want to sing.

Whatever your story is, if you write enough, certain themes will reappear. Watch for them. Don't be afraid to face them. Writing is an intensely psychological experience, or it should be, and the words don't have to be born of wounds, but they might be. My story is violence. I finally figured that out after years of failed manuscripts. My story is people who carry on in a world that is hard and cold and sharp around the edges. My story is not Southern or "clever" or derivative. It is an eyewitness account, the framework starkly wrought from what I see, the flesh and soul nurtured by my own experience and personality. I've done and continue to do a lot of research. Could I redesign my life, I would have been a chief medical examiner with a law degree who somehow found time to write novels featuring a chief medical examiner with a law degree. Then I would have discovered that my true gift was writing and could have lived off my intellectual investments for the rest of my literary life. But had I been a forensic pathologist with a law degree, I would have been far too busy and burned out to feel creative after hours. The truth is, I am a former journalist who majored in English in college. I hated chemistry and math, did not want to touch a computer, and was indifferent toward biology. By the time I was twenty-five I'd never been to a funeral because I was afraid of death.

I began work on my first murder mystery in the fall of 1984. A physician I knew recommended that I interview a medical examiner since forensic medicine is so important in modern criminal investigation. I was fortunate enough to get an appointment at the Office of the Chief Medical Examiner in Richmond, Virginia. I spent three hours talking with Dr. Marcella Fierro, the deputy chief. I was utterly fascinated, and I was horrified by how ignorant I was. I thought, "How can you write crime novels when you don't even understand what these people are talking about?"

I began to discover that subjects I had fled from in college not only fascinated me now, but I had an aptitude for them. Without realizing it, I had just embarked upon a grim and peculiar journey that, oddly, would lead me to my voice and story.

## Authentic credibility

If you are interested in a particular field or intend to address a particular subject, you must learn something about it. Being a master at stringing words together or describing sunsets is not enough. If your story lacks credibility and authenticity, no one will care how exquisite your metaphors are.

For example, if your knowledge of journalism is limited to what you read in the paper or see in movies, don't decide to create a protagonist who is a journalist. Or if you do, start educating yourself. Get someone to introduce you to a journalist. Ask him if you can ride with him on his beat one day. Or see if you can do any sort of volunteer work in the newsroom on your day off from your regular profession.

For me, it is essential to experience directly what I'm writing about (within reason). I want to know what it looks like, feels like, smells like, sounds like. Writers are pests. We drive everybody crazy with our cries for help when we're getting started, and I've decided that you might just get what you want if you abandon any notion of entitlement. Don't think some harried reporter is going to be thrilled about having you ride shotgun while he rushes around on his beat. A lot of cops or other experts would get tired of you, too. Forget a medical examiner warming up to the idea of your hanging around the morgue. If you're determined to master a subject, apply the same rules that work in good business: You give me something, I give you something.

What would you like to master? Is there something you can do to help? Let's say you want to create a protagonist who is a gardener, yet you live in a fourteenth-story apartment in Manhattan. Find a greenhouse and go to work or volunteer. Expose yourself, somehow, to whatever it is you wish to understand. But never forget—if you want, you also must give. The irony is that when you're P. D. James, everybody wants you doing research at their facility when you no longer need it. When you're just getting started, you have to pay your dues because nobody cares.

I wanted to understand police work better, so I signed on as a volunteer police officer in Richmond City. I dressed in uniform. I took dog bite reports, directed traffic, and worked parades. I gave the city hundreds of hours of my time, but I got something extremely valuable in return. I know how to drive an unmarked car, get free coffee at 7-Elevens, talk on the radio and light flares. I've been to numerous homicide scenes and I know homicide detectives because I've ridden with them on their four to midnight shifts more times than I can count.

I know how Pete Marino, the homicide detective in my series, thinks. To learn how Dr. Scarpetta thinks, I went to work for the medical examiners. At first I assisted in technical writing. Eventually, I became their computer analyst. Though I work only as a consultant for them now, I was down there constantly for more than six years. I would place myself on the extreme end of the spectrum. Not everyone could or would throw himself into research to this extent. Most writers have other professions. Moderation for all things, but if you have a passion for westerns, at least go ride a horse.

## Seeking advice

In the early days, I used to have friends read chapters as I wrote them. I wrote letters to P. D. James. I did everything most fledgling writers do, and now I know why. I thought I wanted advice. What I really wanted was assurance. What I got was a lot of confusion.

If it works better for you to discuss constantly a current project with someone, then do it. I can't. If meeting with groups of aspiring writers and commiserating and sharing ideas works for you, do it. I can't. In the first place, I feel that my ideas are private. I'm not going to tell you about this great plot I've devised. That places a burden on you to keep my secret, and the more I talk about my great plot, the more I relieve the tension necessary to drive me into my office. I have about concluded that the more someone talks about a book, the less he's working on it.

Writing is solitary. You can't write unless you are willing to spend a lot of time alone. I'm not saying you should never meet with groups or go to conventions. Much depends on your personality type. Some writers like crowds and derive much from panel discussions. Others, like me, choose to confide in a friend, but in the main, figure it out on their own. I believe trial and error is the best teacher, and that you can learn most about what makes a novel or story work by reading the best authors.

# 43

## CREATING SERIES CHARACTERS

### BY ANNE PERRY

THE BEST SERIES CHARACTERS are those that readers come to know and like, that they enjoy meeting again and again. Some—Miss Marple, Poirot, or Columbo, for example—do not noticeably progress or have any personal life outside the plot of the current story. Others, whom I personally admire more, grow, have changing relationships, and inhabit a world of places and events that also develop. Dorothy Sayers's Lord Peter Wimsey is an excellent example of the latter type, with his World War I experiences as an officer in France, his family, his courtship and marriage of Harriet Vane. One wishes to read the next book not only for its mystery, but to know what happens next in *his* life.

I have never created a series character intentionally. I began with Charlotte and Pitt when they met in *The Cater Street Hangman,* and I rather lurched from one book to another for at least the first half dozen of my novels, always hoping the next one would be accepted but never sure in advance. After that, when I might have been confident enough to plan, it was far too late. The personalities and their histories and relationships were thoroughly established.

My second series character, Monk, was something of an accident, but I now realize, as I am beginning the fourth Monk novel, *The Gardener in White,* that by the greatest good luck, I have endowed him with many of the characteristics that make keeping him in a series relatively easy. I say "relatively," because there are still many pitfalls.

However, on thinking about it, I have come up with a list of qualities I would have given him, had I planned it, and why. (I will use the masculine simply to avoid saying "he" or "she" each time.)

When creating the past for a series character, leave plenty of spaces for events you may wish to put in later. I mean not only spaces in time, but also emotional spaces, unresolved ideas, brief mentions of experiences that may have been important. Be careful about too many unexplained hints; they can be very irritating to the reader. It is better simply to leave a space in your own mind with a possible way to account for it: service in a war, a period of living in a different country or a difficult social environment, a very unusual job, or anything else that allows for a variety of references in future stories.

With Monk, I have in my mind his entire past, which is unknown country to him because of his amnesia *(Face of a Stranger),* and slowly he is discovering past love affairs, people to whom he owes immense debts of gratitude, cases in which he failed and the consequences were very painful to him *(Defend and Betray).* Charlotte is very well known, but Pitt's youth is still largely unexplored, and I have plans for it in a future novel. But there are also all the subsidiary characters like Great Aunt Vespasia, who since she is eighty, must have a past with interesting adventures.

Relationships over time are very complex, and people are changed by closeness to one another. There are periods of intimacy and of distance, mutual injuries, misunderstandings, debts, dependencies, and all these will change and leave their mark on the characters. The people from the past can greatly contribute to your hero's personality, and later on you can introduce them if you wish, or insert such powerful experiences as a failure and the character's resultant sense of guilt; the death of someone close; a bitter injustice; or anything relevant to the story you are currently telling.

When inventing your hero's past, think hard about his family and other relationships—mentors, loves, professional rivals or friends, adversaries, etc. Do not draw him in such detail at the outset that you leave no room for layers of personality, conflicts, even contradictions to be revealed later on. People change from day to day, let alone from year to year, but we are all the sum of everything we have been. Our past, whether we remember it consciously or not, leaves its mark on us one way or another.

Show how your hero has been affected by the people he has known: those he loved, hated, feared, admired, or whatever. If you don't say too much to begin with, you will leave yourself room to bring in other people in later books. Suggest their existence with a sketch or a single reference or memory, then you may use them as key figures in a later story. This will not only provide a character for the plot, but will also affect your hero far more profoundly than a stranger might.

Let your hero be moved by the events of each story, and consequently be slightly changed, whether wiser, gentler, more compassionate; or if you prefer, more foolish, more arrogant, more cynical, whatever you feel would work for you. But remember, if *you* do not like your hero, your readers may not either, in which case they are unlikely to want to follow him through a series of novels.

I am not suggesting he become a saint, but simply that his adventures engage his emotions and that he will grow because of that. He may well have failings he never conquers, battles he wins, but wars he loses. Be careful of weaknesses like alcoholism or drug dependency, or a permanently bad marriage, or the inability to sustain a relationship. Such things can become very boring to readers after a while. Also, self-pity is tedious in real people, and not really any better in fictional ones. A short-lived problem can be interesting, but after two or three novels, it loses its appeal. Readers will begin to feel the hero should have dealt with his shortcomings or come to terms with them. I know that is not always the case in life, but if we wish our readers to continue to read and enjoy our stories, we have to make them enjoyable. I don't suggest a Pollyanna ending, but if a problem cannot be solved, be quiet about it. No one *has* to read our novels; we must write so readers will be eager to, and that means that the cardinal sin is to be boring.

Think how you yourself have grown, changed your feelings, your views; allow your hero or heroine to do the same. If you write a series over a ten- or twenty-year period, you will not be the same as when you started; neither should your characters be. Your readers should be able to trace the course of your characters as they mature from one novel to another—the development of their relationships; their skills; their inner spiritual life (if relevant).

For example, Charlotte's marriage to Pitt, a man of lower social status and income, changed her a great deal. She became more practical, learned to be less outspoken and to modify many of her previous judgments. That may be a reflection of my own friendships with a wide variety of people!

Monk has faced *much* more violent change in his discovery of his own past, his acts, and the character they portrayed. He was obliged to see himself as others had, without any knowledge of his motives at the time; his consequent assessment of himself shook him to the core. The examples are legion, and you can create them for yourself.

Beware of having a specific ending in mind when you start building a character, or you may find you reach the end before you mean to and have nowhere further to go.

In creating your series characters, try to create friends for yourself and others, people your readers will like so much they will not want you to let them die or disappear.

# 44

# DICK FRANCIS: AN INTERVIEW

**Q.** *Did your journalistic training provide a good background to novel writing?*

**A.** Journalism was a wonderful school for book writing. Newspapers will never print an unnecessary word because they're always pushed for space. I used to think I was a pretty good editor and, in the end, it annoyed me intensely if I took my article up to Fleet Street and the sub found an unwanted word.

**Q.** *Why didn't you write your first thriller until five years after your autobiography?*

**A.** Writing for the *Sunday Express* was quite hard and I didn't think I had a story to tell. But as we passed the book stands in a railway station once I suddenly said to my wife, "I'm going to write one of those thrillers one day."

Some time later, the carpets were wearing out and we had two sons to educate. Although I had a good job on the newspaper, it wasn't as lucrative as being a successful jockey had been. Mary said, "Well, you always said you were going to write a novel. Now's the time." So I sat down and wrote *Dead Cert,* which took about a year.

**Q.** *Do you carry a notebook around and jot down ideas?*

**A.** Before I go to bed, I sometimes put a note down about something. But my wife Mary and I have quite good memories. Mary especially. I'm always asking her to reel off what happened at such and such an event.

Mary also takes photos of things like telephone kiosks and buses. These help to describe the scene when I am writing a story.

**Q.** *How do you plan your books? Do you know how they will end when you start?*

**A.** I have a good idea of the main crime upon which I'm basing the story. But I create many sub-plots as I go along. I often describe things I hadn't thought of before or introduce new characters.

I do only one draft. I hear of people doing two or three but I couldn't possibly do that. I write it all in longhand in a notebook and then put it onto a word processor. My procedure hasn't changed in the past 25 years. Even when I wrote the racing articles, I only ever did one draft.

**Q.** *As you write one chapter, then, you can't know what will happen in the next.*

**A.** That's right. I can't really be sure. But when I'm halfway through a chapter, I know I've got to start warming it up. I try to finish at an exciting spot, so that the reader can't put the book down and starts the next chapter.

**Q.** *There's a good balance in the scenes between action pieces—full of shocks and climaxes—and descriptive pieces. How do you create this?*

**A.** I don't know. I suppose it comes from experience. I like to grab the reader on the first page. It's rather like riding a race. You keep your high moments until the last furlong and then you produce your horse to win. When you're jumping the big fences, you're placing your horse to meet that fence. When you're writing your story, you're placing your words so that the reader will be excited at the right moment and, then, easing off after you've jumped the fence.

**Q.** *All your novels are written in the first person. Are there any limitations with this?*

**A.** I write in the first person because that's how I like to describe things. I had great difficulty in writing the Lester Piggott biography because I had to write in the third person.

I think this is one of the reasons no films have been made of the books, although options have been taken on them all. As they're written in the first person, a lot of each book describes what's in the hero's mind. It would be difficult to portray on screen.

**Q.** *Do you identify with your heroes?*

**A.** Probably, yes, though I'm not as tough and brave as my main characters are. They usually have some cross to bear but I try to make them compassionate and likeable, with a sense of humor and a lively eye. I wouldn't want to write about a miserable, depressing character. I get on well with people myself and I try to make my hero do the same.

My heroes aren't like James Bond superstars throughout. I try to make them human and make them develop in the book.

**Q.** *Do you ever get writer's block?*

**A.** Not really. Nowadays I do most of my writing in Florida, sitting on the balcony looking out to sea. I spend hours looking at the ocean, thinking. Often I've got a character in a certain position and I don't know how I'm going to get him out of it. I think out all the pros and cons of one way and then another and, eventually, find the right one.

# 45

# FREE-FORM PLOTTING THE MYSTERY NOVEL

## BY MARCIA MULLER

PLOTTING THE MODERN MYSTERY NOVEL is a complex task that bears as little resemblance to so-called formula writing as Miss Jane Marple does to Lew Archer. One of the questions most often asked by aspiring mystery writers (frequently in tones of frustration, after being outfoxed by one of their favorite authors) is, "How on earth do you complicate your plots and still get them to hang together?"

Unhappily for those who seek instant solutions, there is no one sure-fire method of plotting. The techniques vary from writer to writer along a continuum that stretches from detailed, extensive outlining to what I call winging it (writing with no planning whatsoever). Writers adopt the type of plotting that best suits their working styles and personalities. Some hit on the appropriate type immediately, others gradually make their way toward it through experimentation—plus hard work and practice. There are no major shortcuts, but there are *little* shortcuts. Tiny ones, actually. What I'm about to tell you about plotting is only my highly individualized technique; all, some, or none of my suggestions may help.

I've learned my craft the hard way. In the past fifteen years I've made every attempt to "reinvent the wheel," especially where plotting is concerned. I began by making detailed character sketches, outlines, and time charts, a method distilled down to a lengthy storyline synopsis. I've tried winging it, with unsatisfying results. What I've finally settled into is a technique that I call "free-form plotting"; as the term implies, its key ingredient is flexibility.

Before we go on, however, let's discuss the concept of plot. If someone were to ask you what a novel's plot is, you'd probably say "the story." But if you examine a given *plot,* you'll see it's somewhat different from the *story.* The story is linear; it is the events that happen,

209

both on and off scene. The plot is the *structure* you impose on those events. You select which to include, in what order, and how to tell each one. You shape your plot from the raw material—the story.

Here's an example of a crime story, simplified for our purposes:

1. Killer meets victim; they interact.
2. Killer murders victim.
3. Murder is discovered; detective enters case.
4. Detective investigates.
5. Detective solves murder; killer is apprehended.

Taking the raw material of this particular story, you could plot in a number of ways. You could tell it in a linear fashion, from step one to step five (although that's not likely to be surprising or dramatic). You could start with the discovery of the murder, continue through to the killer's apprehension, explaining in flashback or dialogue what went on in steps one and two. You could start with the actual murder, masking the identity of the killer. The steps may be ordered any whichway, depending on what kind of book you want to write. It is up to you to decide how this simple story is told; the question we are addressing here is how you make and follow through on your decision.

What I like about free-form plotting is that it allows me to defer the decision, feeling my way as I write. It saves me from becoming locked into an inflexible plot outline that may, in the end, not suit my purposes. I can start a novel with a minimal idea of where I'm going, develop some ideas and characters, experiment with them, keep what fits, discard what doesn't. An example of this is how I plotted my most recent Sharon McCone novel, *There's Something in a Sunday*.

When I started I had in mind a beginning situation, a few characters, a background, a theme, and a hazy idea of the ending. The situation has Sharon McCone being hired to follow a man who came to San Francisco every Saturday night and stayed through the early morning hours on Monday. The characters were the man, Frank Wilkonson; Sharon's client; a woman the man was looking for; and a married couple who were friends of the woman's. The background was dual: neighborhood activism and the plight of San Francisco's homeless people. The theme was the relationships between men and women, and how they go awry. And the ending—well, I won't reveal everything.

When I start a mystery novel, I like to set the situation in the first one or two chapters. In this case, it was Sharon following Wilkonson, observing his eccentric Sunday activities, and wondering if the client had told her the entire truth about his interest in Wilkonson. Because she observed Wilkonson's movements closely for nearly twenty-four hours, she feels that she knows him—and so did I, although he had not as yet uttered a single word of dialogue. In these two chapters, I had developed his character in some depth, and had begun to consider him a real person. As he developed, I began to think differently about Wilkonson and what I intended to do with him later on.

I employed the rule of flexibility very early. When I read my first two chapters, I found something was wrong: Taken together, they moved too slowly. So I broke them up, inserting a flashback chapter between them, in which I introduced the client, Rudy Goldring, and showed how Sharon had come to spend her Sunday tailing Wilkonson. By the time I finished the scene, both Goldring and the derelict who served as "door-man" at his office building had come alive for me, and I began to see new ways they could be used in the plot.

My next step was to introduce the supporting characters: the people at All Souls Legal Cooperative, where Sharon works. Again, something was wrong with the scene I'd planned. I was tired of writing about the co-op in the same old way. If I had to write the scene with Sharon sitting in her boss's office discussing the case one more time. . . . My solution was to introduce a new attorney and an assistant for Sharon, to give more prominence to an old character, the secretary, and to create personal problems for the boss, whose previous life had been placid. Now I had a situation that I was eager to write about, and a fast-developing personal subplot that (because the life of Sharon and the people at All Souls is an ongoing story from novel to novel) didn't necessarily have to be wrapped up at the end.

Of course, what happened in the scene at All Souls required going back and making minor adjustments in the first three chapters; the new attorney, for instance, was now the person who had handed Sharon the Goldring assignment, rather than her boss. This is a time-consuming necessity of free-form plotting but, as we'll see later, it has its advantages.

At this point I was ready to establish my other characters. And, while a lot had happened and a number of questions about Wilkonson and Goldring had been raised, I needed something more dramatic—the murder.

At the scene of the crime I was able to introduce another of the main characters, an unnamed woman who appeared suddenly and then vanished. In the next few chapters, as Sharon followed up on the case for reasons of personal satisfaction, I brought in the other characters who would figure prominently: the married couple, Wilkonson's wife, and his employer.

Most of these characters had turned out differently from what I'd first envisioned. A character "taking over" the story is a phenomenon that writers often discuss. No one knows exactly why or how this happens, but I suspect it has to do with the writer's being relaxed and "into" the story. As you sit at the keyboard, new ideas start to flow. Characters take on fuller identities as you allow them to speak and act and interact with one another. When this happens to me, I simply go along with whatever is developing; often I write pages and pages of dialogue or action, then pare them down or toss them out entirely. It's easier to cut or eliminate your prose than to go back and add material later. By setting down these free-flowing scenes on paper, you will avail yourself of the opportunity to create something that may vastly improve your novel. And (impossible in real life) you can always rip up the pages or hit the delete key.

One example of this phenomenon is the development of the married couple that I've mentioned—Vicky and Gerry Cushman. Originally, I'd seen them in a strictly functional sense, as friends of the woman who appears at the murder scene and then vanishes—the pivotal character in the plot. But, as Vicky began to take shape, what emerged was not the coolly efficient neighborhood activist I'd planned, but a woman with severe emotional problems. And in response to this development, her husband Gerry emerged as a selfish man who exacerbated her problems. I had created an unexpected conflict that wove nicely into the theme of the novel—and I was able to use it to further complicate my plot.

At this point—the end of your primary development stage—you can take full advantage of free-form plotting. You have your characters in all their individuality and richness; you have a situation that is ripe for additional complication; you have an idea of where you're going. Now is the time to find out exactly where that is—and how you're going to get there.

The way I accomplish this is to read what I have on paper. Then I play the game of "what if." The game is a question-and-answer process: "What if such-and-such happened? How would that work?"

In *Sunday,* I reached this point just as Frank Wilkonson disappeared. He had gone to an abandoned windmill in Golden Gate Park; Sharon was following him, but lost him in the darkness and fog; Wilkonson never returned to his car. This was an unplanned development; the setting of the windmill had occurred to me while driving by it one day, and it seemed a perfect place for an eerie, late-night scene. The scene wrote easily, but at its conclusion I had to admit I had no idea why Wilkonson had gone there or where he'd gone afterwards. Time for "what if. . . ."

Why did he? I asked myself. The obvious answer was that he planned to meet someone there. Sometimes the obvious choice is the best. But who? I could think of one character who would have reason to be there, but no reason to meet Wilkonson. But what if he was asked to contact Frank? By whom? I knew who that might be. But then, why hadn't Sharon seen Frank meet the other person? What if Wilkonson had. . .?

By the end of this question-and-answer session I found myself in possession of a new plot twist: an eventual second murder and a killer who hadn't even been on my list of primary suspects. Because of my accidental choice of a setting and the manner in which I wrote the scene, my plot had taken on greater complication—and greater mystery.

A few chapters later I was faced with another situation calling for "what if." Sharon had finally located the woman from the murder scene. The woman had ties to all the major characters, but they were as yet nebulous. In a few cases, they were nebulous even to *me.* So I considered the connections among all six of these people. What if the client was an old friend of the woman? What if they had once been lovers? No, friends was better. But what if she had had a lover? What if it was Frank? Or Gerry? Or Frank's boss? Or. . .? Because the characters were well established at this time, I was able to come up with a logical answer.

As I've said, free-form plotting requires constant readjustments of scenes and details to make them consistent with one another. This is laborious at times, often necessitating extensive rewriting. But I'm convinced that it is also extremely beneficial. As you rewrite, you are forced to pay great attention to detail, to polish your prose, to reexamine your logic.

Logic is crucial to a mystery novel. If it is flawed, the whole plot—no matter how original your premise, fascinating your characters, or vivid your settings—simply falls apart. I advise frequent rewriting and rereading. Check every detail; make sure every place is described properly, especially if the action depends on the lay of the land. As I was preparing the final draft of an earlier McCone novel, *Eye of the Storm*, I found that I'd handled a description of a boathouse in two different ways. In the early chapters, it had been a building on pilings over the water; later on, it had a concrete foundation and boat wells. Since near the end something happened in one of those wells, the initial description made no sense whatsoever!

This may sound like an incredible error, but, believe me, things like this happen to professionals, too. When I discovered it, I had read the manuscript numerous times. A friend and frequent collaborator had read it twice. Neither of us had caught the discrepancy. So check your copy. Recheck. Publishing houses have copyeditors to catch the little things, but the big things are your responsibility.

There you have the basics of free-form plotting. Develop a general situation, background, theme, characters, and ending. Set the situation. Allow your characters to act and interact with one another. When the primary development stage is complete, complicate by playing "what if." Write some more. Be flexible; play "what if" again and again. Rewrite, reread. Check, recheck. And as you write, take advantage of the surprising things that develop—they will often point the way to a truly baffling plot!

# 46

## GRILLING ED MCBAIN

### BY EVAN HUNTER

**Evan Hunter:** I'm often asked why I chose to use the name Ed McBain on my crime fiction. I always respond that when I first started writing the 87th Precinct novels . . .

**Ed McBain:** I thought *I* was the one who wrote the 87th Precinct novels.

**EH:** The point is . . .
**McB:** The point is, *we* chose the McBain pseudonym because we didn't want to mislead people.

**EH:** Mislead them how?
**McB:** Into believing they were buying a mainstream novel, and then opening the book to find a man with an ax sticking out of his head.

**EH:** Yes. But in addition to that, mysteries back then were considered the stepchildren of literature, and . . .
**McB:** They still are, in many respects.

**EH:** You surely don't believe that.
**McB:** I believe that a grudging amount of respect is given to a good mystery writer. But if you want to win either the Pulitzer Prize or the National Book Award, stay far away from corpses among the petunias.

**EH:** You've been writing about corpses among the petunias . . .
**McB:** Other places, too. Not only in flower beds.

**EH:** For thirty-three years now. You've remarked that you begin work at nine in the morning and quit at five in the . . .
**McB:** Don't you?

215

**EH:** Exactly.

**McB:** Just like an *honest* job.

**EH:** But I wonder if you can share with us how you manage such a regimen. It must require a great deal of discipline.

**McB:** No. Discipline has nothing whatever to do with it. Discipline implies someone standing over you with a whip, *forcing* you to do the job. If you have to be *forced* to write, then it's time to look for another job. If you don't *love* every minute of it, even the donkey work of endless revisions, then quit.

**EH:** Do you make endless revisions?

**McB:** Not endless, no. One of the most important things about writing is to know when something is finished.

**EH:** When is it finished?

**McB:** When it works.

**EH:** But how many revisions *do* you make?

**McB:** As many as are required to make the thing *work*. A good piece of fiction *works*. You can read it backward and forward, or from the middle toward both ends, and it will *work*. If a scene isn't working, if a passage of dialogue isn't working . . .

**EH:** What do you mean by working?

**McB:** Serving the purpose for which it was intended. Is it supposed to make my hair stand on end? If my hair isn't standing on end, the scene isn't working. Is it supposed to make me cry? Then there had better be tears on my cheeks when I finish it.

**EH:** Do you make these revisions as you go along, or do you save them all up for the end?

**McB:** I usually spend the first few hours each morning rewriting what I wrote the day before. Then, every five chapters or so, I'll reread from the beginning and rewrite where necessary. Happily, nothing is engraved in stone until the book is published. You can go back over it again and again until it works.

216

**EH:** There's that word again.

**McB:** It's a word I like.

**EH:** How do you start a mystery novel?

**McB:** How do *you* start a mainstream novel?

**EH:** With a theme, usually.

**McB:** I start with a corpse, usually. Or with someone about to become a corpse.

**EH:** Actually, though, that's starting with a theme, isn't it?

**McB:** Yes, in that murder is the theme of most mysteries. Even mysteries that start out with blackmail as the theme, or kidnapping, or arson, eventually get around to murder.

**EH:** How do you mean?

**McB:** Well, take a Private Eye novel, for example. When you're writing this sort of book, it's not necessary to discover a body on page one. In fact, most private eyes—in fiction *and* in real life—aren't hired to investigate murders.

**EH:** Why are they hired?

**McB:** Oh, for any number of reasons. Someone is missing, someone is unfaithful, someone is stealing, someone is preparing a will, or inheriting money, or settling his son's gambling debts, or what-have-you. But hardly any of these reasons for employment have anything to do with murder. In fact, the odd thing about private-eye fiction is that the presence of the p.i. on the scene is usually what *causes* a murder. Had the p.i. not been hired, there'd have been no body.

**EH:** What about other categories of mystery fiction?

**McB:** Such as?

**EH:** Well, Man on the Run, for example. Is it necessary to start with a body in this type of story?

**McB:** That depends on why the guy is running, doesn't it?

**EH:** Why *would* he be running?

**McB:** Because he did something.

**EH:** Like what?

**McB:** Anything but murder. If he's done murder, you can hardly ever recover this guy; he's already beyond the pale, so forget him as a hero. I would also forget rape, kidnapping, terrorism, child abuse, and arson as crimes to consider for your hero. But if he's committed a less serious crime—such as running off with a few thousand dollars of the bank's money—then the police are after him, and he must run. And running, he meets a lot of different people, one of whom he usually falls in love with, and experiences a great many things that influence his life and cause him to change—for the better, we hope.

**EH:** That's what fiction is all about, isn't it? Change?

**McB:** I like to think so.

**EH:** But surely there are dead bodies in a Man-on-the-Run novel.

**McB:** Oh, sure. Along the way. I'm merely saying that in this sub-genre of Man on the Run, it isn't essential to *start* with a corpse.

**EH:** Are there other sub-genres?

**McB:** Of Man on the Run? Sure. We were talking about a man who'd actually *done* something. But we can also have a man who'd done absolutely *nothing*.

**EH:** Then why would he be running?

**McB:** Because the something he didn't do is usually murder. And that's where we *do* need a corpse. Immediately. For the police to find. So that they can accuse our man and come looking for him, which prompts him to flee, fly, *flew* in order to solve the murder and clear his name while of course falling in love with someone along the way.

**EH:** A Man on the Run can also be a person who *knows* something, isn't that so?

**McB:** Yes. Where the body is buried, or who caused the body to become a body, or even who's about to *become* a body. Dangerous knowledge of this sort can cause a person to become a man who knows too much and who must flee north by northwest in order to escape becoming a body himself.

EH: On the other hand, it isn't necessary that he *really* be in possession of dangerous knowledge, is it?

McB: No. As a matter of fact, he can know absolutely nothing. In which case, he merely *appears* to know something which the bad guys think he actually *does* know.

EH: And this semblance of knowledge becomes even more dangerous to him than the knowledge itself would have been because he doesn't even know *why* someone wants him dead.

McB: In either case, a body is the essential element that sets the plot spinning.

EH: A body, or a substitute for one. The body doesn't have to be an *actual* stiff, does it?

McB: No, it can be what Alfred Hitchcock called the MacGuffin. I prefer the real thing, but there are many successful thrillers that utilize to great effect a substitute corpse.

EH: Can you give us some examples?

McB: Well, the classic Woman-in-Jeopardy story, for example, may very well be *Wait Until Dark*, where a *blind* woman unknowingly carries through customs a doll in which the bad guys have planted dope. They want the dope back. So they come after her.

EH: That's a woman in jeopardy, all right.

McB: In spades.

EH: A gender reversal of Man on the Run.

McB: Which all Woman-in-Jeopardy stories are. In this case, the substitute corpse is a doll—a graven lifeless image of a human being. The woman doesn't *know* where the body is buried, but they think she does. Without the doll—that is, without the corpse—there'd be no reason to stalk and terrify this woman, and there'd be no thriller.

219

EH: And in much the same way that our Man on the Run learns and changes from *his* hair-raising escapes, so does our Woman in Jeopardy become stronger and wiser by the end of *her* ordeal.

McB: Leaving the reader or the viewer feeling immensely satisfied.

EH: Let's get back to the way you begin one of your mysteries.

McB: With a corpse, yes. Well, actually, before the corpse, there's a title.

EH: I find titles difficult.

McB: I find them easy. I look for resonance. A title that suggests many different things. For example, the title *Ice* seemed to offer limitless possibilities for development. Ice, of course, is what water becomes when it freezes. So the title dictated that the novel be set during the wintertime, when there is ice and snow . . . ah. Snow. Snow is another name for cocaine. So, all right, there'll be cocaine in the plot. But in underworld jargon, to ice someone means to kill him. And ice also means diamonds. And, further, ice is the name for a box-office scam in which tickets to hit shows are sold for exorbitant prices. The title had resonance.

EH: A lot of people had trouble with one of my titles.

McB: Which one?

EH: *Love, Dad*.

McB: That's because it's a terrible title, very difficult to say. You have to say "My new book is called Love Comma Dad." Otherwise, no one will know what you're talking about.

EH: Most people thought the title was *Dear Dad*.

McB: Why?

EH: I don't know why. Actually, I thought *Love, Dad* was a wonderful title.

McB: You should have called it *No Drums, No Bugles*.

EH: Why?

McB: Were there any drums or bugles in it?

220

EH: No.
McB: There you go.

EH: Tell me where *you* go after you've got your title and your corpse.
McB: I write the first chapter. Or the first two or three chapters. As far as my imagination will carry me until it gives out.

EH: Then what?
McB: I'll outline the next few chapters ahead.

EH: Not the whole book?
McB: No.

EH: Why not?
McB: Because in mystery fiction, the reader never knows what's going to happen next. It helps if the *writer* doesn't quite know, either. If what happens is as much a surprise to him as it is to the reader.

EH: Isn't that dangerous?
McB: *If it doesn't work, you can always go back and change it.*

EH: As I understand it, then, you keep outlining as you go along.
McB: Yes. Whenever I feel a need to move things along in a certain direction. Which, by the way, may change the moment the characters *get* there and discover things I didn't know they'd discover.

EH: I always love the moment.
McB: Which moment?

EH: When the characters do just what the hell they *want* to do.
McB: When they come alive, yes.

EH: That's when you know you've got a book. That's when you know these aren't just words on paper.
McB: A lot of writers talk about how *awful* it is to be a writer. All the suffering, all the pain. Doesn't anyone find *joy* in it?

221

**EH:** I do.

**McB:** So do I.

**EH:** You once said . . . or *we* once said . . .

**McB:** *We* once said . . .

**EH:** . . . when asked which qualities we considered essential for a writer of fiction today . . .

**McB:** Yes, I remember.

**EH:** We said . . . a head and a heart.

**McB:** Yes. The head to give the work direction, the heart to give it feeling.

**EH:** Would you change that in any way now?

**McB:** I would say only please, please, please don't forget the heart.

# 47

## WRITING SCIENCE FICTION: WHERE TO BEGIN

### BY PAULA E. DOWNING

IN THE PAST FORTY YEARS, SCIENCE FICTION has matured from its pulp-magazine origins into a genre that is attracting some of the best young writing talent today. SF is openly receptive to new writers: Approximately ten percent of all SF novels published each year are first novels, significantly higher than other writing fields. SF also has a wide field of magazines for short fiction, including many small-press publications. Moreover, SF editors are actively interested in discovering new talent, and they find most of that new talent in their slushpiles. They are easily accessible at science-fiction conventions, will write you personal notes just to be friendly, and will encourage the almost-there new writer. Writing SF is a great way to break into print.

## What SF Editors Look For

### Character-oriented stories

SF is a genre of ideas about the future, with an emphasis on technology and space, future societies, and future choices. At the same time, it is strongly oriented toward character: SF fans are as interested in the people in your story as in the future you present—and editors follow that strong reader interest. So focus on your characters as genuine people, and find ways to make them come alive in your story. Don't litter your story with dozens of people; choose a strong protagonist, and keep the story focused on him or her.

### How much science?

You don't need a formal scientific education to write science fiction. Many professional SF writers have non-scientific backgrounds. I majored in history in college and later became a lawyer; other SF professionals are college English teachers, small businessmen, homemakers, librarians, and social workers. My scientific education is almost wholly self-taught; I've had a lifelong fascination with astronomy and years of reading general-science books. You *can* research the science for your story effectively at the library, and science magazines (*Science, Scientific American,* and *Science News,* etc.) have wonderful topical articles written at a layman's level.

At the same time, science fiction is *science* fiction. SF editors actively look for stories with solid scientific content, and you are more likely to sell your story if it has a strong science focus. Your science should be intrinsic to the story and play some significant role in its development, be it a future world, spaceship technology, or a future society extrapolated from current times. The science must be *accurate:* Don't imagine Eden-like gardens on Venus. Do your research, and then spin out your story from what you've learned.

## A strong plot

Genre fiction is defined in part by its strong and vivid plotting. Most genre readers, including SF fans, like a compelling and active story that moves along briskly. "Briskly" is *not* a pell-mell race from crisis to crisis without attention to scenery or character, but it *is* active. Try to avoid long-winded passages about the scenery or other background; you should have some background information to flesh out the story, but keep it at a minimum. Watch out for characters who talk too much: Dialogue is a wonderful means for characters to interact, but keep it in proportion. Remember the action.

Your story should begin with a strong "narrative hook" that catches the reader's attention and a character with a compelling problem that forces him or her into immediate action. Once you've decided where to start your story, look for key events in your overall narrative, then build scenes or chapters around them for a beginning, middle, and end. Present your character with an ultimate choice, something that winds up the entire story at the end. You don't have to know everything that will happen while you write—some of your best ideas will occur during the writing itself—but don't wander to little purpose. Keep on track in telling your story.

## Good writing

When I edited for *Pandora,* a small-press SF magazine, I read many short stories by novice writers which had interesting characters, a fairly good plot, and intriguing ideas—written in a plodding, tedious style that blunted everything the story had to offer. Overwritten prose, poor pacing, misused words, bad dialogue, and weaknesses in style can make your writing less than it can be. When the style problems become pervasive, your story crosses the line of what an editor is willing to fix, however interesting the story. Good style can carry a somewhat weak story, but the reverse is rarely true. To succeed in SF, you must learn to write well.

Good representative stylists in SF are Connie Willis, a multiple-Hugo winner; Robert Silverberg; Lucius Shephard, especially known for his short stories; C. J. Cherryh; and Pat Murphy and Karen Joy Fowler, who have won great acclaim for their short fiction. Such writers not only tell a good story, but tell it exceptionally well in terms of craft.

## Originality

One of the hallmarks of science fiction is its intense originality. SF has few limits on topics or scope, and has wandered far into speculation about the future, future societies, and technological change. Along the way, SF writers have explored fiction's classic themes of life and death, human failure, and challenges intrinsic to any worthwhile story. To catch an editor's eye, you must have something different in your story, something you handle especially well—a vivid character, an intriguing background, a compelling theme.

For example, in a recent Hugo-winning novel, *Hyperion,* Dan Simmons wrote a haunting reprise of *The Canterbury Tales* set in the far-future. Lois McMaster Bujold has won both Nebula and Hugo awards for her Miles Vorkosigan stories, because of the strength of her vivid hero and magical writing. Most SF novels published today have something special, something drawn from the writer's individual talent and vision.

Originality comes from experience. As you work with your story ideas, you will gradually develop your own voice and style. But remember that in considering marketability, editors tend to be conservative about first novels. Until a writer has a readership that will buy anything the writer writes, editors look for well-written novels solidly in the middle of SF's range, the area that will likely generate the highest sales. As a result, editors often impose an unwritten list of "good points" on their selections, such as "no first person," "convincing plot," "proper length," and other generic comments that appear in rejection letters. You don't have to stifle your creativity, but keep these factors in mind.

## How to Prepare Yourself to Write SF

### What to read

Science fiction now has a wide readership, stimulated by *Star Wars* and *Star Trek* fandom, but modern SF is much more than movie-SF. To find the better SF writers and to pick up clues about the kind of short fiction that is currently selling in the field, read the short stories and book reviews in *Analog, Isaac Asimov's Science Fiction Magazine, Fantasy & Science Fiction, Pulphouse: A Fiction Magazine,* and *Science Fiction Review.* The major SF magazines are generally available in bookstores, and subscription prices are quite modest—about $18 to $25 a year. SF's two trade magazines, *Locus* and *Science Fiction Chronicle,* also publish extensive book reviews, as well as lists of upcoming books, news about SF editors and writers, market and bestseller lists, and essays about SF as a writing field and trade. In addition, SF has a host of small-press magazines that publish fiction, such as *Pandora, 2 A.M. Magazine, Figment, Argonaut,* and *Tales of the Unanticipated,* again at a modest subscription cost. Small-press markets that pay receive scores of quality submissions, so you will have strong competition.

Finally, read the Hugo and Nebula award-winners, the current bestsellers, a sampling of the newer writers, and SF classics by authors such as Robert Heinlein, Roger Zelazny, and Ursula K. Le Guin. Modern SF is a wide-ranging and innovative genre, and reading extensively will give you a good idea of what current SF writers are doing with the wide-open horizons of science fiction.

For tips and advice on how to write science fiction, a little study of such books as the *Science Fiction Writers of America Handbook* (Pulphouse Publishing, 1990) and *On Writing Science Fiction,* by George Scithers, et al. (Owlswick Press, 1981), can reduce the time wasted in trial and error. In addition, you should buy or borrow from the

226

library good general books on fiction writing. And most important of all, write regularly.

## Attend SF conventions

By attending science fiction conventions you can hear directly from professional science fiction writers all about SF as a business and a craft. Nearly all SF conventions have panel discussions on writing, and many also have writers' workshops led by professionals in the field—writers and editors who are very accessible and willing to help the new generation of writers and pass along what they have learned from other pros and from their own experience.

## Join an SF workshop

You can also join the Science Fiction & Fantasy Workshop, 1193 South 1900 East, Salt Lake City, UT 84108, a nationwide correspondence group of aspiring and professional SF writers. Its members critique each other's stories, publish a newsletter about markets and writing, and have several special-interest groups for other exchanges. The camaraderie is wonderful; I've made dozens of writer friends through the Workshop, people who love SF as much as I do; who aspire to the same goals; who face the same craft problems, career irritations and disappointments; and who find the same intense joy in writing. A good alternative is a local workshop: Try to find other beginning writers in writer's groups or at SF conventions. One of the best sources of encouragement you can find is in reading other novices' stories.

Science fiction is a popular and energetic genre, with wide-open possibilities, fine talent, and unlimited horizons. I've wanted to write SF since I began reading it in my very early teens. After several years of wishing and then several years of trying, I finally sold my first novel and have since sold three others, with more to come. My SF writing is my proudest and hardest-won accomplishment; it can be for you, too. There is nothing quite like the writing life, and SF is a great place to begin the adventure.

# 48

## CHARACTERIZATION AND STORY

### BY L. R. WRIGHT

THE BULLETIN BOARD IN MY OFFICE is studded with pieces of paper bearing aphorisms. Most are typed on index cards, the authors' names noted at the bottom. But some are scrawled on paper torn from whatever lay handy, written in ink now faded, and of these, a few lack attribution. One of these unintentionally orphaned maxims reads as follows: "It's the way we are that makes things happen to us."

The relationship between character and story is so close as to render the two indistinguishable: Each story must seem inevitable, given its characters. Writers are often asked where their stories come from, and my answer is, from our characters. The better defined we make our characters—the better we know them—the stronger the stories they tell.

But where do these people come from?

They emerge, gradually, from a conglomeration of memory, observation, and imagination. Some emerge easily, and some only with great difficulty.

Each of my novels, except one, evolved from a visual image of somebody doing something. *Among Friends,* for example, began as an image of a woman in an alley, at night, staring at something lying on the ground. When I started to write it, I knew absolutely nothing about this character, except that she was female. I began work on the novel by describing the picture that had lodged itself in my head. The character then began to come to life. (More accurately, by describing the scene in the alley, I began creating that character.) She developed into a woman in her late fifties who lives alone and works as a secretary-receptionist for a small news magazine. Because of the kind of person she is—reserved, proud, solitary—she doesn't ask for help when the underpinnings of her life give way. And because she is also frightened, and possesses an extravagant imagination, she conjures up a terrifying hallucination upon which to focus her fraying powers of concentration.

Although the following lines were written as the first paragraphs of the first draft of the book (there were at least three rewrites), in the completed novel they don't appear until page 132, at the beginning of Emily's crisis:

A few minutes later Emily stood immobile in a dark downtown lane, her concentration fixed on something lying on the ground. The blank surface of the lane looked wet and slick, and it shone dully in the light from the streetlamp at the end of the lane. Huddled against a brick wall, away from the light, an old man lay on his stomach with his knees pulled up; like a baby asleep in its crib. His right cheek was cuddled into the pavement, and his left hand clutched an empty wine bottle. His grey hair stood up in spikes and his eyes were tightly closed. A white shirt collar poked up from the old grey coat in which he was wrapped. He wore hiking boots and a pair of dark pants.

Emily turned slowly, holding her purse in both hands. She sighed, a soft, barely perceptible sound, and walked back toward the street. . . .

Any other night, she was sure, if her eye had been caught by something moving and glinting in a late night downtown lane, she would not have entered it but walked on. She couldn't understand what had possessed her to go in there. She remembered a feeling of detachment, and a sensation that she was invisible, or at least invincible.

Emily was a character who came easily.

Karl Alberg, though—that's another story. Alberg is the Royal Canadian Mounted Police staff sergeant in my three mystery novels, and perhaps it's because he was so difficult to "get" that I am especially fond of him.

Initially, I didn't know that my fourth novel, *The Suspect,* was going to be a mystery, even though it opens with the murder of one octogenarian by another. I had expected that once I'd written the crime (the visual image with which the book opens) and created the criminal, I would become immersed in a long flashback that would reveal the reasons for the murder, and this flashback, I thought, would constitute the book. But I became so caught up in the deed and its effects upon George, the elderly murderer, that momentum swept me along until the next thing that had to happen was a police investigation.

So I needed a policeman.

It was easy enough to decide upon his physical characteristics, his age, his marital status; but as hard as I tried, I simply could not make the man real.

Finally, somewhat desperate, I took him out of the book. I wrote about him in all manner of situations: in the middle of a funeral; grocery shopping; in conversations with people I know—fictional and real. All

229

this is a painful, laborious attempt to breathe life into him. Nothing worked. He remained stiff, awkward, utterly unbelievable, until . . . One morning I armed him with pruning implements and dispatched him into his overgrown backyard to cut back the greenery. Then, who knows why, he suddenly became authentic.

It is because of the kinds of people George and Alberg are that *The Suspect* develops as it does. George feels no guilt about trying to evade punishment for his crime, because he knows that his suffering for earlier "crimes" far outweighs anything the law can do to him. Alberg grows, reluctantly, to admire George even as he suspects him; but he can't stand the thought of anybody—including George—getting away with murder.

*A Chill Rain in January* is the only one of my novels that didn't begin for me with a visual image and some sense of a central character, however vague and fuzzy.

I became curious about people who lack a conscience, who are incapable of distinguishing between right and wrong; sociopaths. For them, I thought, life must be complicated and hazardous—rather like trying to walk when lacking a sense of balance. They are also very dangerous people, because they are impervious to guilt. Psychiatrists differ about what causes this condition. Some think it is learned behavior, and others believe it is the result of a physiological abnormality, a chemical imbalance in the brain. I opted for the latter. My sociopath would be born that way.

For a while I struggled with a male character, because the books say that sociopaths are almost always male. But I soon decided that it would be more interesting if the character were female. A great deal of anger attends this condition, and a female sociopath would have to place stronger controls on her anger than would a male.

The process of creating her was different from anything I'd experienced before, since I had no picture in my head to get me going. I began by recalling events in my childhood that I associated with the emergence of my own sense of morality, and I described them, in the first person, as if I were another person, a child incapable of understanding "morality." Some of this work survived to become a part of the novel. Here's how it developed:

One day when I was very young, I scissored away some of the fur on my cat's back. In my memory, the cat (whose name was Myrtle) screeched and howled, tore herself from my grasp, ran out the door, and was never seen again. (My mother assures me that Myrtle, although she avoided me for a few days, didn't run away.) I remember a feeling of absolute amazement as it dawned on me that I had done something that caused another creature anguish, and that it was something I had had no right to do. I used this incident to create an imaginary one:

. . . The cat screamed and bashed around among the burning leaves and finally rolled out of the flames: it looked as if it had smoke coming out of it. It got to its feet and fled drunkenly across the park. . . .
Zoe's mother looked as if she felt dizzy or something. She kept staring at Zoe and saying her name, over and over again, as though she couldn't believe Zoe was really standing there, as if Zoe had just suddenly appeared, out of nowhere. . . .
"What did you do?" said Zoe's mother.
"I put Myrtle in the fire."
"But why? How could you do such a terrible thing?" She was staring at Zoe and hanging on to her purse with both hands. The purse had a couple of new scratches on it—places where the leather had been made less brown. Zoe thought Myrtle had probably done that, with her stupid claws.
"I don't know. She made me angry."
Her mother turned around so that her back was to Zoe, and then she turned the rest of the way around, so that she was looking straight at her again. "Didn't you hear it screech? Don't you know how much it must hurt?"
"But—it wasn't me," said Zoe.
"But you just said—you just said, I heard you, 'I put Myrtle in the fire.' You just told me that."
"Yes," said Zoe. "I mean, it wasn't me that hurt."

Again, it is what Zoe *is* that generates the story. When she feels threatened, the only "right" thing to do is the thing most likely to re-establish order in her world. The cost to others is irrelevant to her.

Situations of crisis, danger, dread, or distress are not hard to imagine; we've all survived a few. And it's amazing what's stored in our memories just waiting to be used—not the events themselves, but the ways in which we experienced them.

When I was about eight years old, I was attacked by a guard dog chained up behind a warehouse. He and I were friends, I thought. But on that day I approached him while he was eating, and that turned out to be a big mistake. Thirty years later I wrote a novel called *The Favorite,* in which a little girl gets beaten up by one of her schoolmates. While writing that scene, I used "sense memories" from the day the dog attacked me:

231

. . . she stood feeling small on the playground, blood running slowly from her nose, a bruise on the side of her head, ragged with dust, hair full of it, tangled and wild. . . .

Sarah aimed herself toward the sidewalk and started to move her feet, one after the other. She knew her body must be broken into hundreds of pieces. It wasn't falling apart because of her skin. She was grateful to her skin. It would have been awful if her whole body had fallen apart right there on the public sidewalk.

She struggled up the street and past the neighbors' houses and if she saw anybody she knew, she didn't remember it later. . . .

She walked up to her front door and hoped Muriel would know what to do about something like this. She knew her father would know what to do, but he was at work, and so was her mother. She put her hand out to take hold of the doorknob and saw that her hand was shaking, her whole body was shaking, she thought her skin wouldn't be able to hold in all the broken pieces if it kept on being shaken around like that and she opened the door and started to scream.

If you allow yourself time to develop characters who are concrete and substantive, you can, by making use of your own personal memories as well as your imagination, put these characters into any imaginary situation, into confrontations with any other fictional people, and discover, as you write, how they must react.

It is these stage-managed collisions—character with character, character with life events—that produce for me the best and often the most unexpected results in storytelling; the thing that everyone calls plot.

# 49

## HOW TO WRITE THE POLICE PROCEDURAL NOVEL

### BY O'NEIL DE NOUX

A PROMINENT CITIZEN IS MURDERED. The police are called in and find that clues are few, if any. So who's going to solve this baffling case? The gifted amateur; the college professor who moonlights as a P.I. on weekends; the spinster convenience-store clerk who is secretly a master sleuth? Unlikely. The case will be solved by hard-working homicide detectives.

Like its first cousin, the mystery novel, the police procedural novel features a well-structured, fast-paced chronicle of crimes and punishments. Unlike the mystery, the police procedural stresses the step-by-step procedures always followed by professional detectives in solving these cases: processing the crime scene to collect physical evidence; canvassing the neighborhood for witnesses or suspects; postmortem examination of the body to determine the cause and manner of death; identifying the victim; tracing the background of the victim; investigating associates of the victim, and those who reside or work near the scene of the crime; examining the method of operation of the perpetrator; and the continuing follow-up investigation.

These steps, although mandatory, can be described briefly or in detail by a writer, depending on the dramatic effect of the story. Don't let the specialization scare you away from writing police procedurals. There are seven basic guidelines that one should follow to write the successful police procedural novel.

### Plot well

The *plot is the backbone* of the police procedural. A well-plotted scenario will allow the writer to create memorable characters, unforgettable scenes, uniquely described settings, so long as the writer does not forget to follow normal police procedures. Deviation from the norm removes credibility from your story. Strive for believability.

Although the hero or heroine travels step by step along a predetermined road, a good writer will fill that road with pot holes. The hero must then hurdle these obstacles. There are always complications, one damn thing after another, sequences of rising dangers relieved by moments of release, followed by increased danger. Remember the goal in fiction is to elicit an emotional response from the reader.

So where do you get your plots? Try the daily newspaper or the evening news. Murder has become an American pastime. Recently, I wrote a story based on a newspaper article about a rapist who served his time, and when released went straight out and kidnapped his original victim and raped her again. This story was filled with emotion and anger and irony.

## Keep the novel action-oriented

*Action is the flesh and blood* of your story. Watch your pacing. Ask yourself if each scene moves the story forward. If it doesn't, toss it out. Do not go off on tangents or take vacations in the middle of working a case. Blend dialogue and descriptions with action, and you'll have no problem.

Although real police investigations include long, sometimes grueling days of unending canvasses, surveillances and dead-end leads, you should be selective. Short scenes with crisp dialogue can streamline the most mundane parts of an investigation. Leave out the boring parts.

Yet your story doesn't have to be all police work. Cops have private lives, too. A great deal of the action in Charles Willeford's Hoke Moseley series (*Miami Heat, Sideswipe,* and *New Hope for the Dead*) takes place at Hoke's home, with his family and friends.

In my novels, I include a strong ancillary plot revolving around my main character's relationship with the twin sister of a victim from his first murder case. That action, consequently, takes place away from the office.

## Create well-rounded characters

As in all fiction, *character is the heart* of the police procedural. Although the hero/heroine of the police procedural is usually a police officer or someone closely associated with the criminal justice system,

234

they are real people existing in a familiar world. What happens to them is extraordinary. Their reactions are usually courageous or clever.

In *The Silence of the Lambs*, Thomas Harris' heroine is FBI trainee Clarice Starling. Although only a trainee, Clarice exhibits extraordinary maturity and rare courage in her dogged pursuit of her villain. The hero of my novels is Dino La Stanza, a New Orleans homicide detective, a man with a perfect solution record who pursues his perpetrators with the tenacity of a hungry leopard. These characters are professional lawmen working within an admittedly imperfect legal system.

Joseph Wambaugh, perhaps the dean of police proceduralists, has focused on revealing, through his sometimes poignant characters, the pressures under which police officers live twenty-four hours a day. In *The Black Marble*, *The Glitter Dome*, and *The Secret of Harry Bright*, Wambaugh documents the ravages police work can inflict on the best of officers.

There is room to maneuver with your characters. They can ponder. They can do things against the grain. They can make profound statements and explore the secrets of the human heart. This is where you can insert your theme—your statement of the human condition. Unlike mainstream fiction, whose characters are sometimes obsessed with the discovery of their interior lives, police procedural characters have a crime to solve.

Your characters must think *with* action as opposed to pondering without action. You, the writer, must remain devoted to the sequence of the story.

## Create a distinctive setting

The *setting is the skeleton* your story is built around. It is more than just the description of a place or time period; it is the feeling of that place and time.

Give the reader a distinct, vivid setting stressing sensory details: the acrid smell of gunpowder, the salty taste of blood, the tacky feeling of rubber grips on a .357 magnum when the hero's hand is sweating, the sexy sound of nylon when a woman crosses her legs, the way a culprit, when he is lying, will look away from the detective.

Your setting must be so realistic that the readers will be convinced the elements of your story could really happen. Charles Willeford, in his Hoke Moseley stories, paints a vivid picture of south Florida with

235

snapshot descriptions mixed with plenty of action. Willeford once explained that capturing south Florida's fascinating society was a primary aim of his series.

In my series, set in New Orleans, I have attempted to make the setting equal in importance to character and plot. Reviewers have consistently commented on the richness of the setting and the interplay between my characters and the city, and their effects on one another.

Tony Hillerman places the hero of his Navajo police series, Lieutenant Joe Leaphorn, in a vividly rendered social and cultural environment, using the panorama of the west as a backdrop. James Lee Burke, a winner of the Edgar Allan Poe Award from the Mystery Writers of America, is a master of setting. His Detective Dave Robicheaux adventures, beginning with *The Neon Rain* (also *Heaven's Prisoners, Black Cherry Blues, A Morning for Flamingos,* and *A Stained White Radiance*) is an excellent example of a writer not only giving a visual description of a setting, but the feel, taste, and smell of the place through strong sensory details.

## Use language accurately

Ever walk into a police station? If you do, be prepared to cover your ears. Policemen talk in harsh street language salted with profanity and jargon, particularly among each other. Criminals are worse. Neither uses flowery passages, and rarely speaks in complete sentences.

Through dialogue, you have an excellent opportunity to create emotion, from scintillating nails-on-the-blackboard passages uttered by creepy serial killers, to the soft whispers spoken to an overworked detective by a sympathetic lover.

Real cops, from Bangor to San Diego, from Seattle to Miami, verbalize their frustrations through black humor. Rope off a crime scene, fill it with policemen seasoned by years of sarcasm, and someone is bound to make derogatory or ludicrous remarks about the condition of the body of the murder victim. Describing a shot between the eyes as a perfect bulls-eye or viewing brain matter splattered on a wall and asking if anyone wants pizza later is nothing more than a release, an escape-valve reaction to the horrors of murder.

## Be realistic

Make sure of your facts. Revolvers do not have safeties, nor can a silencer be used on one. Police do not have "Ballistics Labs," or ballistics examiners. They have firearms examiners. Ballistics is the study of objects in flight. Policemen are concerned with matching projectiles to weapons.

Do not depend on television or movies for accurate portrayals of police procedures. How many times have you seen chalk lines around bodies, or cops shooting suspects and then walking away for a couple of beers? Investigators never alter crime scenes with chalk. If an officer shoots someone, he is quickly spirited away by investigators who secure his weapon for analysis, who interview him in isolation, who secure his formal statement. In many departments an officer must endure a Superintendent's Hearing before he goes home. The officer must then face a Grand Jury investigating the death and the inevitable civil lawsuit automatically filed by overeager attorneys, no matter how justified the shooting.

Detectives take notes. How many times have you seen a movie or read a book and actually observed a detective taking notes? I was a detective for nine years. I never shot anyone, but I certainly killed a lot of pens. A pen is the detective's most useful tool and mightiest weapon. Every killer on death row began his long trek through the criminal justice system with a homicide detective taking notes at a crime scene.

Real detectives use *inductive* reasoning, conclusions from observations of facts, to arrive at a solution that fits all of the evidence. Amateurs, including many fictional detectives, use *deductive* reasoning, arriving at a specific conclusion from a general assumption. In other words, inductive reasoning involves relying on facts and only facts until only one conclusion is possible.


## Have a definite resolution

Don't cheat the reader out of an ending to your story. Police cases end, usually with an arrest and trial, sometimes with a shootout. This is a natural climactic event. Even cases that are suspended or closed without a solution have a climactic moment, when the investigators come face to face with the nightmare of someone getting away with murder. There have been successful stories written about The Zebra Killer and The Green River Killer, as well as about the ultimate un-solved murders by Jack The Ripper.

In your resolution, remember that something must be affirmed. Good triumphs over evil, or at least goes the distance.

So how does one learn the steps taken by lawmen in their pursuit of criminals or the procedures used by lawmen in the nineties? What is DNA or genetic fingerprinting, for instance? How does one learn that this scientific breakthrough, which may be more important than fingerprints, gives investigators the ability to isolate, identify and catalogue an individual's genetic fingerprint from a drop of blood, a tiny amount of semen, or a piece of skin found beneath a victim's fingernail? How does one learn that no two individuals have the same DNA fingerprint pattern, unless they are identical twins?

As a veteran homicide detective, I find that these procedures come second nature to me. But there are sources out there. The best is direct information from police officers or former police officers, who rarely shun the opportunity to share their war stories. Other sources can be found in your public library: *The Crime Writers' Handbook of Technical Information,* edited by John Kennedy Melling and *The Writer's Complete Crime Reference Book* by Martin Roth are two good examples.

Remember you are still writing a genre novel. The police procedural, like the mystery, science-fiction, or romance novel, will not have the prime space in bookstores, nor will it usually get the featured spot in your local paper's book section. But the sales will come. There is a large audience concerned about crime.

Mickey Spillane once said of crime fiction, "Those big shot writers can never dig the fact that there are more salted peanuts consumed than caviar."

# 50

## PLOT AND CHARACTER IN SUSPENSE FICTION

### BY JOAN AIKEN

WHICH CAME FIRST, the chicken or the egg? Does plot arise from character, or character from plot? The question is in many ways an artificial one; most writers have felt, at one time or another, the heady excitement of knowing that a whole story, or at least its basic elements—plot, character, and development all tangled together—is struggling to emerge from the dark.

But if this does not happen?

"What is character," says Henry James in *The Art of Fiction* (1884), "but the determination of incident? What is incident but the illustration of character?" And the Old Master goes on to add (several pages later), "The story and the novel, the idea and the form, are the needle and the thread, and I never heard of a guild of tailors who recommended the use of the thread without the needle, or the needle without the thread."

Perfectly true, and you have to have both before you can begin. But, suppose you have only half of the combination?

Characters are generally the problem. *Plots* come a dime a dozen, they are easy to pick up. We read them every day in the papers. A mother, even after several years, remains positive that the death of her teenage son, classified as suicide, was not so; but whenever she pushes her inquiries about it, other unexplained deaths take place. The pet poodle of a notorious Chicago mobster is stolen. The CIA sets up a spurious marine engineering firm in an effort to salvage a sunken Soviet submarine. A middle-aged woman demands a daily love poem from her browbeaten husband. A descendant of one of the twenty-one victims of the Boston Molasses Disaster is still seeking compensation. A convention of magicians plans to meet in an Indian town, but the citizens raise strong objections. . . .

Any of these incidents, all culled from the daily press, might trigger a

239

story, might produce that wonderful effervescent sensation, familiar to every writer (it really is like the working of yeast in one's mind), when different elements begin to ferment together and create something new. The best plots, of course, instantly create their own characters. That wife, that domineering wife, compelling her husband to produce a new love lyric every evening: we know at once what she would be like. And the cowardly put-upon husband, submitting to this tyranny, trudging off to the library for new rhymes and new verse forms, until the climactic moment when he rebels, and supplies you with the start of your story. Or the grieving, brooding mother, worrying on and on about her son's death, gradually acquiring little bits of information. It would be very easy to tell her story.

But if you have the plot without the characters?

There's nothing so frustrating for the reader as a potentially interesting, intricate story, full of turns and twists, in which the characters are so flat, machine-made, and lifeless that they form a total barrier to following the course of the narrative, because it is impossible to remember who is who. Is Miranda the actress or the secretary? Was it Wilmost whose car was stolen, or Harris? Is Casavecchia the gangster or the millionaire? Why *does* Kate hate Henry?

In murder mysteries and procedural detective novels, character portrayal is not so important. The reader won't expect great depth among the victims and suspects, while the detective probably has a number of well-established peculiarities, built up over a series of books: he is Spanish, wears elegant grey silk suits, and carries his exclamation point upside down; or he is very fat and drinks a pint of beer on every page; or he is a rabbi; or she is female, karate-trained, and has a huge wardrobe, which is just as well, since the vicissitudes of her job frequently reduce her clothes to tatters. We know all these and love them as old friends.

The problem of character arises most particularly—and can be a real handicap—in suspense novels.

Suspense novels are deservedly popular, but very hard to define. They are not murder mysteries. They are not just straight novels, because something nasty and frightening is bound to happen. That is the promise to the reader. They are not spy stories, and they are certainly not procedurals. One of the very best suspense novels ever written, *A Dram of Poison,* by Charlotte Armstrong, had no murder in it

240

at all, not even any death (except a natural one in the first chapter, setting off the whole course of events), but it possesses more riveting tension than any other story I can recall.

In a suspense novel, the element of character matters very much indeed. The hero/heroine is pitted, not against organized crime or international terrorism, but against a personal enemy, a personal problem; the conflict is on an individual, adversarial level. And so, if either hero or hero's enemy is not a flesh-and-blood, fully rounded, recognizable entity, the tension slackens, the credulity drops.

In *A Dram of Poison,* all the mischief is caused in the first place by the arrival of the hero's sister, one of those terrible, self-satisfied, know-it-all characters (plainly Charlotte Armstrong wrote the story in the white heat of having recently encountered one of them) who can always interpret other people's motives and give them some disagreeable psychological twist. By her confident assertions, she soon has the heroine paralyzed with self-distrust and the hero downright suicidal. Then, in between the breathless excitement of trying to find what he did with that wretched little bottle of poison he had meant to swallow, the reader has the fearful pleasure of knowing that, in the end, odious Sister Ethel is bound to receive her comeuppance.

Charlotte Armstrong was particularly skilled at villains; the frightful parasitical pair of sisters who, in *Mask of Evil,* (originally published as *The Albatross*) come and prey on the two central characters are particularly memorable, with their sweet saintly selfishness. The sense of being *invaded,* taken over, in their own home, by repulsive aliens, was particularly well conveyed in that story.

The suspense novel is often a closed-world plot. The hero/heroine must battle it out against the adversary in a situation that, for some reason, allows for no appeal to outside help. There must be valid reasons for this. If not a snowstorm, with all phone lines down, then the villain has bruited it around that the hero is hysterical, unbalanced, alcoholic, a drug abuser, or just traumatized by recent grief so no call for help will be heeded or believed.

Ursula Curtiss had a particular gift for these enclosed-world situations, and she had a masterly touch with villains as well. It is an interesting exercise to compare some of her stories with others, for she was a very fertile creator of creepy domestic-suspense plots. Many of her ideas were brilliant, but some of them succeeded far better than

241

others. Why? Because of the characters with which they were animated. *Voice Out of Darkness,* which has a fine snowy Connecticut setting and an excellent basic idea—harking back to the long-ago question of whether the heroine did or did not push her very unpleasant adoptive sister under the ice when they were both eleven—yet somehow fails to come off because it is peopled with rather stock characters: two handsome young men, two pretty girls, and some recognizable small-town citizens, the drunk writer, the gossipy lady. Her novel, *The Stairway,* however, is pure gold from the first page to the last. Why? Because of its villainness, the repulsive Cora. Judged dispassionately, the plot is simple and only just credible. Madeline, the heroine, is married to Stephen, an intolerable man whom she is about to divorce, a monster of tyranny who terrifies her small son. But Stephen falls downstairs and breaks his neck. Cora, the humble cousin, the poor relation, by pretending to believe that Madeline pushed him, gradually assumes more and more dominance over the household and seems all set to stay for the rest of her life. Madeline, in a bind because *she* believes that *Cora* pushed Stephen, feels that she can't betray her and is helpless. All this, given a moment's cool thought, seems hard to swallow. Why had Madeline married the horrendous Stephen in the first place? Why should she submit to Cora for a single moment? But Cora is made so *real,* with her greediness, her anxious, reproachful air, her dreadful clothes, her fondness for eating candy out of a paper bag and rustling the sheets of the newspaper, that all she does and says is instantly, completely credible.

Playwright Edward Albee once observed that the test he had for the solidity of his characters was to imagine them in some situation other than the play he had in mind and see if they would continue to behave in a real manner. The character of Cora would be credible and recognizable whether we saw her in a hospital ward, a supermarket, or a graveyard.

*The Stairway* was an early Curtiss novel, but one of her later ones, *The Poisoned Orchard,* contains the same terrifying claustrophobic, inturned quality, again because of its hateful and convincing villainness, the heroine's cousin Fen, and her accomplice, the cleaning lady, Mrs. List. This sinister pair have Sarah the heroine hog-tied, especially clowning, ugly, self-assured Fen, who continually manages to force her much nicer, much better-looking cousin into the unenviable role of straight man refusing to laugh at Fen's jokes. The relationship between the two is beautifully and most credibly realized, so that the reader is prepared to swallow the fact that Fen and her evil ally seem to be omniscient and omnipresent, able to anticipate Sarah's efforts to combat their plots almost before she can make a move. And what is it all about? We hardly know. A wicked deed, way back in Fen's past, that is catching up with her. And anyway, what can they *do* to Sarah? It hardly matters. The point is that they are menacing, and that she is more and more at their mercy. Fen is a wholly convincing monster, the more so because she is quick-witted and amusing, as well as being unprincipled. *Fear* is the essential ingredient of a suspense novel, and fear can be achieved only if the reader thoroughly sympathizes with the main character and thoroughly believes in the villain.

If the villain is less convincing, then the main character must be made more so.

Dick Francis, the English writer of deservedly best-selling mysteries with horse-racing backgrounds, wrote an interesting early novel, *Nerve,* in which all the jockeys on the turf were being persecuted by a well-known TV personality who secretly spread malicious gossip about them, prevented their getting to races on time, and had their horses doped. Why does he do this? Because he, son of a famous racehorse owner, is terrified of horses, and therefore psychotically jealous of all who succeed in the horsey world.

What a preposterous theme it sounds, set down in cold blood. And the villainous TV star, Maurice Kemp-Lore, somewhat sketchily depicted, only just makes his murderous obsession credible to the reader. What does give the book immediate life, great energy and plausibility, so that it moves at a rattling pace and carries the reader along, completely hooked by the story, is the treatment of the hero. As always in Dick Francis novels, the hero tells the story in the first person; in common with other Francis heroes he is an odd man out, who has fallen into the racing world by a series of accidents. Descended from a family of professional musicians, he is the only non-musical one; despised by his kin, he has had to justify himself in some other direction. The contrast between the hero's elegant relations conducting Beethoven at the London Festival Hall, while he gallops through the mud at Ascot, is bizarre enough to be convincing, so that we are passionately on the hero's side as he struggles to combat what he begins to recognize as a sinister plot against his whole *raison d'être*. The villain remains shadowy, but the hero, in this case, carries enough weight to sustain the story.

Given a satisfactory plot, it should not be too hard to equip it with characters. But what if the boot is on the other foot?

Some writers are compulsive character collectors. Wherever they go, they watch, listen, record, jot down notes and descriptions: the fat woman in the black-striped dress at the rail station with two elegant little pig-tailed girls, also in black-and white striped outfits, hanging on her arms. The lanky, unshaven six-foot male in the subway, with a shock of red hair and gold rings in his ears. The professional portrait painter, met at a party, who has produced a portrait every two months for the last twenty years, and has a photographic eye for a face. The woman who, though courteous and well-mannered, is an obsessive corrector, so that she can never hear a sentence spoken without chipping in to put the speaker right—politely, but *oh*, so firmly. . .

Character collecting is an excellent habit, because sooner or later some of these characters will start to move.

You have a whole cast of characters, but no plot. So: Make extensive notes about them—their preferences, dislikes, habits, childhood history. Like Edward Albee, set them in different environments, confront them with crises. What would the woman in the black-striped dress do if she were in charge of forty school children on a sinking cruise liner? Make them encounter each other. Suppose the portrait painter were sitting in a subway train, drawing lightning sketches, and the man with red hair and gold earrings, unaccountably angry at being drawn, grabs the sketchbook and gets out at the next stop? A character may suddenly get up and walk away, pulling a skein of plot behind him. Suppose they then meet by chance, somewhere else?

Imagine Jane Austen saying to herself, "Now, let's tell a story about a sensible practical sister and a self-indulgent, overemotional sister. What sort of men shall they fall in love with?"

Suppose in writing *Sense and Sensibility,* she turned her story the other way round. Suppose sensible Elinor had fallen in love with handsome, romantic Willoughby, and susceptible Marianne had been bowled over by reliable, prosaic Edward? But, no, it won't work. Marianne could never have fallen for Edward, not in a thousand years. Jane Austen, even at a young age (she was twenty-two), had her characters

244

and plot inextricably twined together, one growing out of the other; there is no separating them. But it is fun to probe and investigate and reconsider; fun, after all, is what writing is all about. Jane Austen took huge pleasure in writing *Sense and Sensibility*. The fact is evident; she knew these characters entirely before she put pen to paper.

What is the best way of displaying your characters?

There are, of course, hundreds, but the worst way is to describe them flatly.

My recent novel, *Blackground,* has the theme of two characters who marry in romantic haste, and then, on a winter honeymoon in Venice where they are, as it were, suspended together in a vacuum, they discover that they had in fact met long ago and aren't at all the people each thinks the other to be. To make this as much of a shock as I intended, both of them and, hopefully, for the reader, I had to be familiar with their life stories right back to childhood. In order not to a) begin too early or b) bore the reader with too much flashback, I make Character A tell his story to Character B on the honeymoon, while hers is disclosed to the reader in snatches throughout the narrative.

Michael Gilbert, a writer of several different kinds of mysteries, whose characters are always remarkably individual and three-dimensional, adopts a very swift and vivid method of displaying his quite large cast of characters in his suspense novel *The Night of the Twelfth* (about sadistic murders in a boys' school). Sometimes a whole chapter is divided into blocks of conversation, often only about half a page—between A and B, between B and C, between C and A, between A and D—these fast-moving dialogues equally convey character and advance the action.

Sometimes you know your character *too* well; you could write volumes about his quirks and complications. But how do you get all this across to the reader without being pompous, or overexplicit?

How about portraying this person as seen through the eyes of another narrator, quite a simple soul (like Nelly Dean, the housekeeper in *Wuthering Heights,* who tells much of the story), or even a child? *What Maisie Knew,* by Henry James, can be an example to us all.

"Try to be one of those people on whom nothing is lost," said Henry James.

Perfect advice for a writer!

245

# ⸮51

# HORROR FICTION: TIME FOR SOME NEW-FANGLED FANGS

## BY GRAHAM MASTERTON

ABOUT SIX OR SEVEN YEARS AGO, horror started to become a very popular genre for new, young authors just starting out on a writing career.

This was partly because of the huge and obvious success of Stephen King, and partly because a new young generation of writers was coming of age, a generation brought up on horror comics, TV's *Twilight Zone*, and even books by me. They had a comprehensive reading background and a natural interest in horror.

But it was also because the horror market was rapidly expanding. Publishers were demanding more and more horror titles, and quite simply it was easier for a new writer to get his or her work published in the horror genre than almost any other.

So long as the fiction market in general and the horror genre in particular were expanding, this was fine, and in those six or seven years, many excellent new authors found their way into print. Only a couple of years ago, almost every major publisher had a horror list, and in almost every case that I know of, that list was administered by a young, enthusiastic, and dedicated editor. It was New Author Heaven.

But when recession struck the publishing industry, those horror lists were among the first casualties. Within a dramatically short space of time, opportunities for new horror writers have been considerably reduced, and it is now much harder for a new horror writer to get started in the genre, harder . . . but by no means impossible. More demanding, yes . . . but *because* it's more demanding, much more rewarding, too.

In fact, I can let you into a secret: If you have real faith in your writing skill and a deep and genuine interest in the development of yourself as a horror writer and horror fiction in general, it may even be a *better* time than ever before. But, you must be prepared to accept the challenge of a much tougher market, and be prepared to commit yourself to a considerable amount of preparation, writing, rewriting, and polishing. More than anything else, though, you must be prepared to stretch your imagination to the utmost. To succeed in horror fiction today, you must not only write skillfully, but you must come up with some *very* new ideas.

If you can invent a totally novel and unexpected terror, and present it with style and quality, then you have the chance not only of breaking into the horror market, but breaking into it at a time when it is much less flooded with other horror books . . . giving *your* book a better chance of standing out.

If there was ever a chance of your becoming the next Stephen King, it's now.

You see, one of the effects of a quickly expanding market was that publishers tended to bring out far too much category horror, much of it deficient in invention and quality of writing. Even some of the very best horror writers seemed to run short of new ideas and began to regurgitate themes that had lost much of their surprise, their shock value . . . and thus all of their *terror,* too.

Quite apart from the problems of recession, horror fiction began to show signs of creative exhaustion, the same kind of tiredness that, thirty years ago, affected the western. In particular, many leading writers seemed to forget that readers buy horror to be scared half to death and started to indulge in political and philosophical waffle along with the horror. There's nobody like a well-established horror writer for indulging in political and philosophical waffle.

An infallible sign of literary arthritis in *any* genre is when the books start getting thicker and thicker and thicker . . . as if length and verbosity can somehow make up for a fundamentally thin idea.

Publishers frequently send me new horror manuscripts to read, for the purpose of giving endorsements. In the past two years, I have seen nothing but the old, old stories. Vampires, werewolves. More vampires, more werewolves. Mutant babies. Children with unusual psychic powers. Children with *usual* psychic powers. *Exorcist III* asks, "Dare you climb these steps again?" and the answer is yes, we dare, but who cares? We know what's up there and it doesn't frighten us any more.

Even the recent books by the market leader, Stephen King (*The Dark Half* and *Misery*) have, quite simply, lost their power to scare. Whereas, after rereading some of *'Salem's Lot* the other day, I still believe that it's frightening.

Clive Barker has become (by his own admission) more of a "fantasist" than a horror writer and the splatter-punk brigade (John Skipp and Craig Spector) are straining harder to think of new ways of being disgusting, to the point where the suspension of disbelief becomes stretched beyond breaking-point. A novel that you can't believe in is no longer frightening, by definition.

So what is a new horror writer supposed to do? He or she is faced with the very difficult task of creating a story that goes beyond the bounds of acceptable taste, as well as, with the seemingly impossible task of creating a totally new terror—totally new, but believable, too.

How can this be done? Well, in my opinion, by rethinking the entire framework of modern horror fiction, by rejecting the patterns and devices and themes developed over the past two decades by Stephen King and John Farris and Rick McCammon (*They Thirst,* et al.) and, yes, by me, too. The way I see it, the future of modern horror fiction lies in far greater believability, and in the development of stories that are far less gimmicky and outré—stories that come closer to the quirks of real human psychology.

Stories, too, that are well-written, soundly constructed, and obey the fundamental principles of good novel-craft. That is: that they have engaging and three-dimensional characters, an interesting and credible setting, a strong forward movement, a heart-clutching beginning, a sound middle, and a huge mind-expanding climax. Easy, *ja*?

We have all tried to stretch the boundaries of the supernatural as far as we can. One of the most implausible stories that I recently attempted was *Walkers,* a novel in which the inmates of an asylum for the dangerously insane had escaped from captivity by disappearing into the walls. They traveled *inside* the bricks and out through the ground, and made good their getaway.

Of course, the basic notion of *Walkers* was utterly wacky. We all know Newton's Law that two objects cannot occupy the same space at the same time, which is one of the reasons that we have traffic accidents and bump into other shoppers in the supermarket. But I worked hard to develop a locale and an atmosphere that would make the reader want to believe that such a thing *could* happen. And that's the difference: *want* to believe.

It's comparatively easy to create a horror scenario in which the reader *doesn't* want to believe that such hideous events can take place. But it requires much more skill and much more thought to create a horror scenario in which the reader is actually working *with* you, rather than against you, a horror scenario in which the reader actively helps you to frighten them.

Enlisting the reader's support requires acute observation, writing discipline, and a strong empathy with other people's feelings. It requires not only believability, but a certain degree of *likability*. Your characters have to be not only real people, but *enjoyable* real people, people your readers wish they could spend some time with, whether they get involved in the Horror Beyond The Grave or not.

It also requires a fast, strongly constructed plot; a plot that trots; a plot that never allows your reader to get ahead of it. Sometimes, if your characters are really strong, you can get away with a certain amount of predictability. But you shouldn't take the risk. A horror novel should be a novel of sudden shocks and surprises, right to the end. It's better to make an unexpected change in your story line (unexpected even for *you*, the author) than allow your reader to guess what's going to happen next. The worst response a horror writer can hear is "I *knew* that would happen."

So let's take a look at all the demands that I've made. First, you need a startling new premise: an idea that's fundamentally frightening, but which nobody has ever thought of before. Here's a paragraph from *Walkers* that might give you a taste:

A little farther away, a *face* had emerged from the floor, too. A man's face, with a heavy forehead and a strong jaw, and a fixed triumphant grin. It looked as if it had been smothered in dry cement. There were powdery wrinkles and cracks around its mouth. Its eye sockets were totally black—*black*, like night, no whites at all, as if the inside of its head were empty. But it was alive, there was no question about that. It had risen straight out of the concrete floor, in the way that a swimmer emerges from the dust-covered surface of a lake.

*It was alive and it was grinning at him and it was gleefully trying to drag him under the surface of the concrete, too.*

No vampires, no werewolves. Something different. But something that can appear at any moment and threaten your hero or heroine with total fear.

It can be very fruitful to delve into occult archives to learn what demons and devils and odd monsters frightened people in the past. Many of the olden-day demons were created out of very strong and primitive fears—fears to which people can still be remarkably sensitive, even today. I used legendary Red Indian demons in *The Manitou* and *Charnel House*; Mexican demons in *The Pariah*; and stories about the real Scottish witch Isabel Gowdie in the third and last of my Night Warriors triology *Night Plague*. I altered many of the mythical details of their malevolent powers in order to suit my stories, and in some cases I changed their names. But they were all characterized by their elemental threat to human stability and human security; and this elemental threat was worth analyzing and translating into modern terms.

Demons and ghouls were created by the earliest storytellers as a way of giving shape and meaning to their most deeply seated anxieties and superstitions. Because they were the imaginary embodiment of such very basic terrors as fear of the dark, fear of inanimate objects changing into vicious creatures, fear of one's own reflection in a mirror, fear of children, they have a lasting potency that you can adapt and exploit, even today. Alternatively, you can use a modern artifact as a demon: a car *(Christine)* or a motorcycle, or a building, or a subway train. But I must warn you: Demonic possession of inanimate objects recently reached a nadir with a British horror-flick entitled *I Bought A Vampire Motorcycle,* and you will probably find it hard to have any similar ideas taken seriously after that.

Personally, I believe that a strong social theme has always been essential to a good horror novel (though beware waffle). In *The Burning,* a novel of fiery reincarnation, I attempted to deal with the issues of materialism, prejudice, and personal responsibility. So my characters had to deal with their own conscience and their own part in a larger society, as well as with horrific and supernatural terrors.

In his interview for horror-anthologist Stanley Wiater's collection of interviews, *Dark Dreamers,* David Morrell (author of *Rambo*) very correctly said that "when you're talking about a breakthrough book, it's not so much the field you're working in, it's the 'canvas.' I hate to use that overworked word, but it's one we all understand. The scope and breadth of a book."

He added (and I really can't put it better): "Most horror novels tend to be inbred: They rely on the ideas and concepts of others who have gone before them. Of course, a horror writer must be aware of the history of the genre. But to sell a lot of copies, a horror writer also has to find a large idea and head toward uncharted territory, announcing, in effect, that this book is *different* from other horror fiction."

The challenge to new horror writers is enormous. But it's a challenge that you *must* address if you're going to make your mark. When I wrote *The Manitou* in 1974, the horror market was Dennis Wheatley and me. Jim Herbert hadn't yet written *The Rats*; and Stephen King was unheard of. But now, many years later, a whole new generation of writers has emerged who were brought up on King and Straub and McCammon and me . . . and instead of being a field of four or five horror writers, as it was then, it's literally a field of thousands.

The next Stephen King will have to be a writer so innovative and striking that his (or her) talent spans many fields of thought and social relevance and be twenty times better than Stephen King—much more stunning than *'Salem's Lot* ever was. I really can't wait for this to emerge. That new writer could be you.

I discussed the necessity for characters who are both likable and real. The problem with many horror manuscripts that I've read recently is that the hero or heroines have been weak or corrupt or plain obnoxious or (even worse) unbelievable. I can understand why horror writers bring such characters into their stories. They have difficulty in dealing with the extremity of the threat their characters have to face. They don't attempt to imagine *how it actually feels* to witness a loved one having her head cut off in front of them, or *how it actually feels* to see a roaring demon emerging from their root-cellar.

Just because their fictitious threats are wild and imaginary doesn't mean that their characters should be wild and imaginary. In fact, totally the opposite. The more real the characters' response, the more frightening the threat turns out to be.

I can understand that, nervous of failure, many writers try to distance themselves from the raw emotions that any horrific or supernatural crisis would evoke. Have you ever witnessed a serious traffic accident? Have you tried to describe how you really felt about it? You should recognize that a horror novel will work well only if the characters react in a credible, true-to-life manner. So many horror movies flop because teenage girls keep screaming whenever a monster appears. Watch the

251

newsreels. Watch the way people really behave when they're desperately frightened. They don't scream. The way they really act is far more disturbing than the way so many writers make their characters act.

The characters in a horror novel should be as detailed and believable as the characters in any other novel. I've read so many horror novels in which the protagonists have no parents, no wives, no children, no job, even. They seem to be rootless, floating dummies, just waiting to have something Horrible inflicted on them. Just remember: Their *raison d'être* isn't to be victims in your novel; they have their own *raison d'être*. And if you have a struggle making them believe in your horrific threat, and in making them respond to it, then so much the better. You will end up with a far more convincing story.

Make sure that even your minor characters are real. Bob Tuggey, a McDonald's grillman who witnesses the first ghastly immolation in *The Burning,* was described in three dimensions, even though his part in the novel was comparatively small:

. . .balding and overweight and by far the oldest employee at McDonald's Rosecrans Street. When his left eye looked west, his right eye looked nor-nor-west. . . . He had drifted through one menial government clerkship after another, black coffee, brown offices. He had started to drink, a bottle of Ricard a day, often more. Days of milk-white clouds and aniseed.

Make sure that your locations are real. Choose somewhere you know, or visit somewhere specially. I set *Walkers* in Milwaukee, which is an energetic city of varied weather and distinctive character, but which also suited the blue-coller personality of the hero. In contrast, I set *The Burning* in La Jolla, which was a perfect setting for the fashionable upwardly mobile restaurant owner who was the protagonist of *that* novel. Each setting in its own way was fascinating to discover and describe, and added to the depth of the novel.

Out of a strong combination of believability and daring imagination, I believe the next generation of horror fiction will eventually be born. The challenge is enormous; the creative task is very great. However, I am looking forward with considerable relish to the day when the advance manuscript arrives through the mail that will tell me somebody has given horror fiction the sharp new teeth it needs.

252

# §52

## LIVING WITH SERIES CHARACTERS

### By James Melville

WHEN I DECIDED SOME FIFTEEN YEARS AGO to send Superintendent Tetsuo Otani to investigate reports of odd goings-on at a Buddhist temple in an out-of-the-way part of Hyogo prefecture in western Japan, I never supposed that he, his wife Hanae, and Inspectors "Ninja" Noguchi and Jiro Kimura would still be the daily companions of my imagination today. That much may easily be inferred by anyone who glances through *The Wages of Zen,* which was published in 1979. In that first book, I made two thumping mistakes that could serve as awful warnings to any writer creating a character who might develop a will of his or her own and refuse to fade away after the words "The End" are typed.

First, I made Otani much too old for his and my own good, by suggesting that he was approaching retirement age. Worse, I fixed him in historical time by stating that he had seen brief service in the Imperial Japanese Navy as a very young and junior intelligence officer at the end of World War II. Assuming therefore that he was 19 years old in 1945, Tetsuo Otani was well into his fifties when he made his debut, an age when senior Japanese police officers do as a matter of fact retire. Moral: If you want to begin a series without making trouble for yourself, either create a young hero or heroine with reasonable career prospects, or avoid being too specific about dates.

My problem was that in addition to writing my first murder mystery, I wanted to describe and try to communicate to fellow westerners some of my own fascination with various aspects of Japanese society and culture as they were when I encountered them during the sixties, when I lived for seven years in Kyoto. Moreover, I've been trying in an amateurish sort of way to record the changing face of modern Japan ever since. Well and good: All the pundits agree that one should write about what one knows, but it does mean that Otani has had to age to the point at which he's distinctly long in the tooth for a working police officer.

Needless to say, there are plenty of detective Methuselahs in the mystery field, compared with whom Otani is a mere stripling. Already retired from the Belgian police when first sighted, Poirot must have been nudging his centennial by the time Agatha Christie eventually pulled the plug on him. The great Nero Wolfe was a game old survivor, too, while (admittedly at the hands of Hollywood writers) Sherlock Holmes himself was still going strong in the mid-nineteen-forties, nearly sixty years after he first captivated Victorian readers.

There's no point in getting upset about this. I can testify from personal experience that mystery fans and even critics are tolerant souls, more than willing to suspend their disbelief and grant generous extra time to characters they approve of. My novels have sometimes been praised and sometimes panned, but no reviewer has complained that both Otani and Noguchi should have been pensioned off by now, or that the indefatigably randy Kimura really can't go on being a playboy for much longer. I'm not about to tempt providence, but there may perhaps be just a little life still left in my team.

Certainly I have no intention of killing any of them, as Conan Doyle killed Sherlock Holmes, and Nicholas Freeling terminated Van der Valk. Look what happened to them: Both characters demanded to be resuscitated. Besides, I'm much too fond of Otani & Co. to see any of the inner circle off, even though the Chief is becoming more and more crusty and contrary as we grow old together.

Like any other long-term relationship, the one between a durable fictional character and his creator has its ups and downs, and any author contemplating putting one or more into several books needs to be aware of the delights and pitfalls ahead. As it seems to me, these balance out pretty evenly. First, I'll consider the advantages for the author.

The first and most important of these from the severely practical point of view is that publishers of mysteries and thrillers like series characters. All other things being equal, they are more likely to accept a first novel featuring a strong central character if there is the prospect of more appearances to come. In my own case, it was made clear to me (with urbane, iron-hand-in-velvet-glove courtesy) that *The Wages of Zen* would be accepted for publication only on the understanding that

Otani would take center stage in at least three further books. After all these years, I still sometimes break out into a cold sweat when I remember my euphoria as I accepted the obligation, and the pure panic that supervened an hour later when the cold reality of what I'd let myself in for dawned on me. In the event I instinctively adapted the excellent advice given to alcoholics, by persuading myself that I could surely write *one* more book, and then perhaps one after that . . . and who knows how many more?

Readers of crime fiction like series characters, too. At least, I do, and I think I belong to the majority. We enjoy a judicious mixture of the familiar and the unfamiliar. I sigh with pleasure every time Nero Wolfe opens his pre-prandial bottle of beer after coming down from his morning session in the plant rooms, and I settle back with satisfaction when Perry Mason lumbers to his feet and starts working his courtroom magic for the umpteenth time. Such repetitive formulae, like the much-loved catch-phrases of an established comic, would, however, soon stale if new material weren't also forthcoming every time.

The most successful serial characters are people with whom a majority of readers can in some respect or degree identify; and that means they must be fallible and imperfect. Even Sherlock Holmes was a delightfully *flawed* superman, after all. His weaknesses were appealingly human (and we must remember that in Victorian times the drug habit that would damn him nowadays was viewed rather differently). The writer who creates a paragon as a serial character will soon find that there's no scope for development as book follows book. The protagonist who is exactly the same in the fourth novel as the first is going to disappoint readers. He or she must be seen to change and grow, to face dilemmas, problems, frustrations, and temptations that we can imagine cropping up in our own lives. In short, the series character must be credible and command both sympathy and a degree of affection; which also means that a character can be moderately naughty and self-indulgent, but shouldn't be in thrall to any wildly aberrant vices.

A well-established series character offers both opportunity and challenge to an author. When I embark on a new Otani book, it is often on the basis of a newspaper cutting sent to me by one of a number of kindly friends in Japan. Not always: My novel *The Bogus Buddha* had its origins in an eye-catching headline in the London *Financial Times*. "Japanese Fund Manager Buried in Concrete," it announced baldly, and I immediately asked myself how Otani and his associates would cope with that. Because I now know them so well, after a comparatively short period of reflection I had the basis of a plot to work on. My regular characters, therefore, act as pegs for me to hang ideas on; between books they are always there in the wings, made up and in costume, waiting patiently to walk on. However, I would stress again that, while many a well-loved film or stage actor can get away with playing himself or herself over and over again, when it comes to crafting a novel, a writer should try to keep his characters moving and show new sides to them from time to time.

Thus, Otani has from the outset been a Rotarian and a mystery fan, but only after several years did I discover that he is really quite serious about *bonsai,* or that he has an unlikely crony in the person of a trendy author and TV personality. Hanae and he have become grandparents, and their daughter Akiko has had quite an eventful married life. I often fill in details of my characters' biographies by references to past events, and one recent book *(A Haiku for Hanae)* is based on an account of a twenty-year-old case.

At this point, a little more needs to be said about conveying information in novels whose principal purpose is to entertain. In my capacity as a reviewer, all too often I come across authors who undoubtedly write about what they know, but who lecture me. Their narratives frequently grind to a shuddering halt while they supply great blocks of unadulterated information. Professional journalists trying their hands at thriller writing are particularly liable to offend in this way, and it simply won't do. Any passage that doesn't either help the story along or serve to round out a character should be excised ruthlessly. The reader should ingest information almost unconsciously *while* enjoying the story.

I was faced with a particular problem in this context while writing *A Haiku for Hanae,* and anyone who wants to decide whether or not I managed to solve it should read the chapter in which Otani calls on the eccentric lawyer Mori. I might want to use Mori again in another book, because it goes without saying that minor series characters can come and go. I was rather sorry to part with the chilly martinet Inspector Sakamoto at the end of *The Death Ceremony,* but his erudite successor Inspector Hara is fun to work with. Another occasional character, Hanae's formidable sister Michiko Yanagida, seems to be demanding a lot more of the limelight these days, while I'm expecting great things of female detective Junko Migishima.

If a series is to be successful over a long period, the right ratio of familiarity to novelty must be achieved with reasonable consistency. One must always respect readers and never take their good will or loyalty for granted. Above all, therefore, the author must be ever alert for signs of boredom or listlessness in himself. If and when they are manifest, it's time to think seriously about abandoning a series or at least trying something completely different for a while in order to put a bit of fizz back into the creative juices; because if the author's bored you can bet your life his readers will be. I've taken time off from Otani to write two political thrillers (*The Imperial Way* and *A Tarnished Phoenix*), and an invitation to write three new lighthearted Miss Seeton tales around some of the late Heron Carvic's English village cozy characters was very welcome. I enjoyed being "Hampton Charles" for a year or so, and while I'm currently once more mentally in Japan, I won't necessarily stay there.

# 53

## SETTING IS MORE THAN PLACE

### BY WILLIAM G. TAPPLY

AN INTERVIEWER RECENTLY ASKED ME WHY I choose to set my mystery novels in New England instead of, say, Nebraska. I was tempted to answer with the old vaudeville punchline: "Everybody's got to be somewhere." Every story has to have a setting.

Instead I told the interviewer the simple truth: My choice of New England was easy—New England is where I've lived my entire life. It's what I know best. I couldn't write about Nebraska.

I define setting broadly. It's more than place. Setting comprises all the conditions under which things happen—region, geography, neighborhood, buildings, interiors, climate, weather, time of day, season of year.

I feel fortunate. My New England provides me with a rich variety of settings from which to select. I can send my narrator/lawyer/sleuth Brady Coyne from the inner city of Boston to the wilderness of the Maine woods, from the sand dunes of Cape Cod to the farmland of the Connecticut Valley, from exclusive addresses on Beacon Hill to working class neighborhoods in Medford. New England has whatever my stories might call for.

New England also gives me the full cycle of the seasons and all the weather and climate that accompany them. It gives me Locke-Ober and pizza joints, museums and theaters, factories and office buildings, mansions and apartments, skyscrapers and fishing lodges, condominiums and farmhouses.

I don't know about Nebraska. I suspect that if I lived there and knew it as intimately as I know New England I'd find a similar wealth of possibilities. I have, in fact, sent Brady to parts of North Carolina and Montana that I'm familiar with. What's important is knowing my settings well enough to invoke the details that will bring them to life and be useful in my stories.

Settings must strike our readers as realistic. A realistic setting persuades readers to suspend their disbelief and accept the premise that our stories really happened. The easiest and best way to do this is to write knowledgeably about real places, places where our readers live or have visited, or, at least, places they have read about or seen pictures of. Readers, I have learned, love to find in a novel a place they know. They enjoy comparing their impressions of Durgin Park or the New England Aquarium with Brady Coyne's. They like to hear what strikes Brady as noteworthy about Newbury Street, the Combat Zone, the Deerfield River, or the Boston Harbor.

You must get actual places precisely right or you risk losing your readers' trust. No matter how much you might dislike it, you cannot avoid research. You *must* hang out in the places you intend to write about. Observe the people, listen to the sounds, sniff the smells, note the colors and textures of the place. I have spent hours loitering in Boston's Chinatown and prowling the corridors in the East Cambridge courthouse. I've wandered around the Mt. Auburn Hospital and the Peabody Museum, looking for the telling detail that makes the place unique and that will allow me to make it ring true for every reader who has been there.

Research need not be unpleasant, in fact. I make it a point to eat in every restaurant I write about, no matter how familiar it already is to me, at least twice—once just before writing the scene to fix it in my mind, and once again afterward to make sure I've rendered it accurately.

A realistic setting doesn't really have to exist, however, and the fiction writer shouldn't feel limited to using actual places if doing so will alter the story he wants to tell. A fictional setting can still be true. My rule of thumb is this: If the setting you need exists, use it; if it doesn't exist, make it up but make it true. I built Gert's on the North Shore and Marie's in Kenmore Square—where no such restaurants stand—because my stories demand there be restaurants like them there. Readers are continually asking me how to find Gert's and Marie's, which I take to mean that I have rendered them realistically.

I made up a hardscrabble farm in Lanesboro and a horse farm in Harvard—fictitious but realistic places in actual Massachusetts communities. In my first Brady Coyne novel, I moved a rocky hunk of Rhode Island coastline to Massachusetts, committed a murder there, and named it Charity's Point because that storyline required it. I've had readers tell me they believe they have been there. In *The Vulgar Boatman*, I invented the town of Windsor Harbor. Had I tried to set that tale in a real community north of Boston, too many readers would have known that no events such as the ones I invented actually happened there. They would have been unable to suspend their disbelief.

Gert's and Marie's, the farms in Lanesboro and Harvard, Charity's Point, and Windsor Harbor were like the characters that populated the books. Although they were not *real*, they were all *true*—places like them exist, and they *could* be where I put them.

Setting can—and should—serve as more than a backdrop for the action of the story. The conditions under which the action occurs should do double or triple duty for you. Setting can create mood and tone for your fiction. The places where they live and work can reveal the personalities and motivations of your fictional characters. Places, weather, climate, season of year, and time of day can cause things to happen in a story as surely as characters can.

Shakespeare and Conan Doyle understood how setting can establish mood and foreshadow events. The "dark and stormy night" had its purpose, as did the spooky mansion on the remote moor or the thick fog of a London evening. Contemporary writers can use thunderstorms and abandoned warehouses and the barrooms and alleys of city slums in the same way. Robert Louis Stevenson once said, "Some places speak distinctly. Certain dank gardens cry aloud for murder; certain old houses demand to be haunted; certain coasts are set apart for shipwrecks." Find such places. Use them.

But be wary. Such obvious settings can too easily become literary clichés. Misuse them, or overuse them, and they lose their punch. Clever writers understand the power of going against stereotypes. Seek subtlety and irony. Murder can be committed on a sunny May morning in a suburban backyard, too, and when it does, the horror of it is intensified by the contrast.

Carefully selected details of setting can delineate the characters who populate the place. Match the pictures or calendars that hang on every office wall with some trait of the man who works there. Is the policeman's desk littered with half-empty styrofoam coffee cups? What kind of tablecloths does your restaurant use? What music is piped into the elevator of the office building? Does a week's worth of newspapers litter the front porch of that Brookline mansion? Does a specimen jar containing a smoker's lung sit on the desk of the forensic pathologist? Does the lawyer keep a bag of golf clubs in the corner of his office? Does a stack of old *Field & Stream* magazines sit on the table in the dentist's waiting room? Such well-chosen particulars can reveal as much about a character as his dress, manner of speech, or physical appearance.

Think of your settings as characters in your stories. Settings need not be passive. They can act and interact with your characters. Rainstorms cause automobile accidents. Snowstorms cover footprints and stall traffic. Laboratories contain chemicals that spill and release toxic fumes. The bitter cold of a Boston winter kills homeless people. Water released from a dam raises the water level in a river and drowns wading fishermen.

Your choice of setting may, at first, be arbitrary and general—the city where you work, the village where you live. But as you begin writing, you will need to search out particular places where the events of your story will unfold. Visit them often enough to absorb them. If you're lucky, you'll find that your real settings will begin to work for you. You'll see a person whose face you'll want to use. You'll overhear a snatch of conversation that fits a storytelling need. You'll note a detail you didn't expect that suggests a new direction for your plot. On one background-ing mission to a rural farmyard, I came upon a "honey wagon" pumping out a large septic tank. This suggested to me an unusually grisly way for a villain to dispose of a dead body; this murder method found its way into my story.

The secret of a successfully rendered setting lies *not* in piling ex-haustive detail upon repetitive particulars. There's no need to lug your typewriter around a room describing the designs of the furniture, the colors of the rugs and drapes, the brands of the whiskey on the sidebar. Extended descriptive passages, no matter how poetic and clever, only serve to stall the momentum of your story and bore your reader.

Setting is important. It serves many purposes. But don't get carried away. It *is* only a setting, the conditions in which your characters can play out their conflicts. The key to creating effective settings lies in finding the *exactly right* detail that will suggest all of the others. Be spare and suggestive. Look for a water stain on the ceiling or a cigarette burn on the sofa. You may need nothing else to create the picture you want in your reader's imagination. As Elmore Leonard says, "I try to leave out the parts that people skip."

# 54

## CREATING A CREDIBLE ALIEN

### BY JERRY L. STERN

AS SCIENTISTS HAVE EXPANDED OUR KNOWLEDGE of physics, biology, and astronomy, writing science fiction has become more difficult. An alien character that would have been believable fifty years ago might now be rejected as either impossible or unreasonable. Modern fans of science fiction have far more expertise in the sciences than the fans of those early years. They love searching stories for scientific errors, and they are very good at finding them!

These modern science fiction readers won't tolerate a bug-eyed monster as the bad guy from outer space. They won't watch the hero of a story be ripped to shreds by an alien character who talks like a human, stalks like a hunter, pounces like a cat, screams like a banshee, or sniffs out your hero like a bloodhound. How terrestrial. How boring. If you can't do better than that, write a werewolf story instead, and set it in London in 1880.

Building a truly alien character is difficult. It takes a lot of work, a lot of thought, to design an alien's physical characteristics, home planet environment, and language. But without taking that time, a writer may create only an alien costume, or a man in a creature suit. That alien shell would behave exactly like a human. If the alien in your story behaves like a human, then *make it a human!* Your story gains nothing by the addition of an anthropomorphic alien. Science fiction readers can tell the difference between good and bad aliens, and they will tell you quite emphatically when you've made a mistake.

Science fiction fans constantly play "the game." Their part of the game is to find all of an author's science errors. An author's job in the game is slightly more difficult. The author must decide on the basic characteristics of a story. Are the characters performing on a oddball planet? Is the hero reptilian, or is the story about the consequences of a new invention? The game will allow nearly any combination of these factors as starting points. Once that initial premise has been established, however, every other detail in that story must be consistent not only with all the details of that premise, *but also with the reasonable extrapolations of those ideas, within the limits of current scientific knowledge.*

But you can write science fiction if you don't know every last fact about the science of the nineties. There is a method. Limit your science to the minimum necessary for your plot, and the logical extrapolations of that scientific premise. It may not be necessary to use an alien in every story. If your story really *needs* an alien for plot reasons, here are some things to consider while developing the concepts needed for building a believable alien. . . .

## Biochemistry

Does the alien have our basic body biochemistry? Does it use the carbon-based system of converting sugars and water and oxygen to carbon dioxide? Then it must breathe oxygen and come from a planet that has photosynthesis, or an equivalent, to cycle that process backward. That limits its livable temperature range basically to that of liquid water. A "hot" alien, from a desert planet, where the temperature is always above 250 degrees, couldn't share our body chemistry no matter how strange its anatomy. If you choose a different chemical basis for life, be sure it is theoretically possible, or the readers will say, "Ahhh! Another inconsistency! Bad science!" Bad alien, too.

## Physics

Maybe you would like to write "hard" science fiction. The "hard" applies to the science involved. It's easy to determine if a piece of science fiction writing is classified as "hard." If there is a lot of mathematics involved in proving a premise, that's hard. Unless you have a lot of science background, you might want to leave such subjects to the experts. For example, the subject of living on a neutron star has been explored by the science fiction novelist Robert L. Forward, who is also a consultant on scientific matters such as solar sails, deep space exploration, and anti-matter. His novel *Dragon's Egg* speculates how life might evolve on a neutron star, and how we could communicate with it.

264

Without going quite to a neutron star, you can still describe a strange environment. Think about how a heavy gravity planet would affect the development of a culture. Or maybe, how would living in the zero gravity environment of an interplanetary trading ship be different from the life on a ship limited not to space, but bound to an ocean.

## Anatomy

How many arms does an alien need to work on a space-faring vessel? How many joints should there be in an arm? Or should your alien have arms? Should it be he or she? Or maybe there is a realistic story reason to use three sexes, or some other system that could only evolve under conditions that would have to be scientifically explained.

These are just some of your choices in building an alien body. You are not necessarily limited to what would look familiar or reasonable on Earth. Anything that can be explained as a reasonable evolutionary development is fair play.

Say, for the sake of a thought experiment, that you've devised an alien. We'll call this one a *he*, although we suspect some quirky adaptive bits in his biology. He comes from a planet under a sun similar to our own, although his planet is just slightly warmer than the Earth, and has considerably stronger gravity. But the creatures on his planet have evolved shaped like barrels, with five double-jointed arms and matching legs and feet, each with five smaller appendages that we'll call fingers and toes for lack of better terms.

## Psychology

If something that grew up on a heavy gravity planet came to Earth, and saw the skyline of New York, what would be its reaction? In three gravities, a skyscraper could not be built with the methods and materials used on Earth.

Science fiction fans will carry this analysis much further. If you jump off a building, the factor that determines how badly you will be injured is not the height of the building; it is the speed that you're traveling when you hit the ground. On Earth, that speed is always the same for a given height off the ground. The higher the gravity, the more quickly a falling object increases in speed. On a heavy gravity planet, a drop of only a few inches would be fatal. Our alien is probably afraid of heights.

If you think that's a minor point in developing the cultural codes of a civilization, take a look at Hal Clement's novel, *Mission of Gravity*. Clement's planet Mesklin is a great example of a strange planetary environment, a flattened spheroid with variable gravity and a day of seventeen and three-quarter minutes. The gravity is strongest at the poles of the planet, where the aliens each weigh over 900 pounds. At the equator of their planet, the Mesklinites have a weight of only a few pounds each, and are understandably worried about the strong winds carrying them away.

Clement's Mesklinite aliens are sailors and explorers on a sea of liquid methane. Certainly humans could not live in such cold, so the cultures of humans and Mesklinites will have very different structures.

## Culture, personality, and language

Culture and personality are the most important parts of alien characterizations. Given a background of the basic premise of the story and descriptions of the environment, chemistry, and anatomy of an alien, as a science fiction author you must develop a feel for what an alien's social culture could be like. What reasonable personality could develop from these starting points? After the third chapter, creatures that merely look strange will no longer hold the attention of a science fiction reader. There must be an *alien persona* resident in an alien, matching what should reasonably have evolved in such a creature.

Next decision: Will the alien be able to learn our language fairly well, or just a pidgin dialect? It may become difficult to convince your readers of the intelligence of an alien that has only a limited vocabulary; it may become impossible to express ideas through that alien that relate to real concerns of fully developed characters.

You'll have to watch your language when talking to aliens. The verbal shortcuts that we have developed may not be understandable. Sure, we can assume that once they learn English they will understand some of our expressions, but will symbols make any sense at all? *We* may understand "dropping pennies into a piggy bank," but our five-sided alien will not understand why we place coins in livestock.

Just as some English might not be understandable to your alien, some of his language may not be translatable into English. You'll need to make up an alien language. Fortunately, you won't need an entire vocabulary and grammar, but you will need words for the basic concepts of the alien society, including names and titles of aliens. Words for

266

those concepts that are not translatable will be useful, as will terms of respect and admiration. Don't go overboard on language, though. The more details present in a fictional language, the more likely it is for a fan to find an inconsistency and tear your work apart. So, before you throw in alien language words, decide if those concepts really cannot be said in English.

When designing your alien's language, look out for pronunciation and phonemes. If your alien has a different mouth structure from ours, the phonemes he uses, or cannot use, will be different from ours. Could an alien with a bird beak say, "*Friend* or *Foe*"? An alien language does not need to be verbal, but look out! A tonal or sung language, or a language based on body movement, will be difficult to convert into words; don't approach it casually. Your readers will not appreciate being unable to pronounce character names or alien terms. If necessary, invent a subtle way to sneak in an explanation of pronunciation, maybe as an aside comment of a human character.

Human body language is a set of visual codes. Our alien is five-sided. When he nods his head, does it mean yes? Think about it. Isn't nodding or shaking your head side to side the same motion to this creature? So his body language will not be based on anything we could understand easily. Any gestures he makes will have to be explained, or translated into our own visual codes, at least the first time each gesture is made.

To see how an expert creates aliens and language and social structures, read C. J. Cherryh's novel, *Cuckoo's Egg*. Cherryh does the best aliens in the science fiction genre. She has managed to incorporate enough alien concepts to make the aliens come alive and not seem to the reader like costumed humans, and yet she has not made the aliens so strange that communication is lost.

An alien and a human must have something in common if there is to be any competition or friendship or even hate beyond pure xenophobia. There must be enough jointly held concepts to keep a conversation moving, a joint exploration traveling, or a colonial trader running from planet to planet.

Just because you've created a creature that, to human eyes, appears strange, don't assume that you've created an alien being. Even a bug-eyed monster can become a believable alien. Just use some empathy, a touch of psychological strangeness, and some good extrapolation from a purely biological description of the alien to the planet, evolution, and

267

culture that created it. As a writer, build up a picture for yourself of the kinds of events that could trigger your alien character's responses, and you'll soon have an alien writing his own action and dialogue for you. Once that happens, writing science fiction is like any other fiction. Just let the characters do what they must, and hang on for the ride through space and time.

# 55

## MEANWHILE, BACK AT THE RANCH . . .

### BY WARREN KIEFER

A FULL-SCALE NOVEL ABOUT THE WEST is as different from a formula Western as a satellite view of the Great Plains is from a county roadmap. Although elements of "formula" writing may be used in both, the dynamics are significantly altered. But it is the formula Western and its perpetuation of the Western myth that people generally mean when they speak of Western fiction.

A "formula" Western is as structured as a sonnet, and as stately as a minuet, and any writer who breaks the rules does so at his peril. Simplicity and violent action are what matter. Humor and sex are rarely allowed, and only on the periphery of the story.

One theme, justice, is central to the plot, although there are endless variations on the righting of wrongs which include certain classic, immutable elements readers of the genre have come to expect and rely on.

Most of us are familiar with these elements, if not from the books themselves, from films and television screenplays that follow similar patterns. Good and evil, black and white, right and wrong must be clear from the start.

The hero must be single, rootless, and reluctant to be drawn into conflict. He is embarrassed about his deadly skills and tries to hide them, while the villain can brag or show off as long as he is absolutely villainous. His greed, sadism, lust or avarice should be as obvious as a sandwich board.

At the beginning, the reader of the formula Western only has to know who wants what and why he can't get it, while evil must appear to be winning. By the middle of the story, reader interest may shift to the question of who's doing what to whom, and how long can they stand it.

Everyone knows what must happen at the end, but nobody knows exactly how it will happen; this is the kind of suspense that invites the reader to gallop along behind.

The climax comes only after the clamor for the hero's services has peaked, and not one page earlier, when even his friends are beginning to doubt his courage. He then shows us what we suspected all along, that heroes shoot only when provoked, but are fearless, tough, and implacable even when outnumbered.

Other characters adhere to certain rules or standards, too. Wives and daughters are chaste and virtuous while dance hall girls can be "loose," but not mean or vindictive. The town drunk, gambler, or any other non-combatant can betray the hero, but only out of fear or weakness. Never for money, which only interests villains.

In the past, if blacks appeared at all, they were cast as servants, Chinese were cooks or laundrymen, and the Native American Indian passed successively from his original role as Bloodthirsty Savage to Noble Redman to Tragic Victim, all of which have mercifully bitten the dust over recent years.

But with the elimination of old racial (and racist) stereotypes, Native Americans have become as invisible as blacks in the formula Western. Action, not opinion, moves this kind of story, and dialogue works only when it complements that action. The format is visual and visceral rather than verbal, with images as precisely circumscribed as those of a fairy tale.

The prose must be lean, fast and sinewy as the hero, but with more obvious direction and control. Stylistic no-nos include such avoidable sins as intransitive or compound verbs, the passive voice, and unwieldy dependent clauses; a list that would find a place in any chapter on clear, concise writing.

Above all, the formula Western is a commentary on universal justice and on the time-honored principle of virtue triumphant as wrongs are redressed. Although its tested structure is fairly rigid and unforgiving, it is not necessarily confining.

This may sound a little like painting by the numbers, but it doesn't have to be. Within limits, one may write anything. But to tamper with those limits is to court disaster.

How does a writer go about it then, if he wants to break the pattern? How can he write about a kindly cattle thief, an Indian policeman, a black cowboy or a near-sighted hero who drinks too much? How does he escape the old restrictive clichés to write what he believes to be a story closer to historic truth?

He abandons the formula Western entirely and writes a novel about the historic West. Only in that way is he free to create a gallery of offbeat, even eccentric characters who would never be allowed inside the Western myth. Here he can deal with sex as well as violence, and may even attempt the subtlest nuances of character without necessarily losing his reader.

Such unlimited creative freedom, however, like the wide open spaces the writer writes about, is attended by high risk. What he is attempting flies in the face of the Western myth, and he will not be easily forgiven if he fails. He must be very good and extraordinarily careful not to fall between two stools.

Verisimilitude is the hallmark of the Western novel, and a sloppily researched fact or an off-pitch line of dialogue can shatter a reader's trust. The novelist who abandons all pretense of formula writing is saying, "I will not lie." The West was a challenge, and maybe some men did fight for justice, but mainly it was a hostile, desolate place, full of danger, dirt, and disease, with greed, violence, and corruption as common as they are today. Spectacular scenery abounded, but little civilized comfort reached people except where the railroads passed, in themselves a mixed blessing. The Great Plains swarmed with buffalo, and the forests teemed with deer, but few towns boasted potable water, plumbing, street lights, or any reliable public transportation.

The historic West, as opposed to the mythic West, is exciting territory for the novelist. By abandoning the safe confines of the traditional form, he gains plenty of creative elbow room. He can be funny, bawdy, original, and clever, as well as historically accurate. But in order to make it to the end of his chosen literary trail, he will probably need as much stamina and luck as the best of his characters.

Unlike the familiar terrain of the formula Western, this strange and difficult frontier must be explored with no maps. The writer is now free to gallop ahead of a prairie fire, cross the Rockies in winter, and shoot the rapids in the Grand Canyon. But he must never forget that in his special private wilderness he is the only guide the reader can follow.

What is often the hardest task for the writer—research in depth—begins long before he starts to write. For example, when I chose turn-of-

271

the century New Mexico for *Outlaw,* I already knew a lot about the people and politics of the place, having gone to school there. But twenty more years of research were needed for a cumulative laying up of facts.

A general interest in the period gave me a working knowledge of everything from railroad timetables and sexual mores, to the state of the art in medicine and mining. I learned about horses and jails and military meals, about oil, wars, and tropical diseases. About trolley lines and rodeos, and women's skirt hems and Gatling guns.

I read or studied hundreds of books, documents, letters, diaries, military manuals, court records, and newspapers. I pored over old photographs and even looked up a few surviving people who had been young in those days, and who remembered.

To avoid historical anomalies, every writer should acquire a feel for the workaday lives of ordinary people, the tensions between competing groups, the dreams and scams and prejudices of the time. And once he's done all that, he must find the best voice to use in telling his story.

Mark Twain once said, "I only write about what I know and then blame it on somebody else in case they catch me out." He was being facetious, but what I'm sure he meant was that every author has to find the right voice, one that is both authoritative and unique, and which the reader implicitly trusts.

For *Outlaw,* I invented eighty-nine-year-old Lee Oliver Garland, a cowboy with scant education and total recall, who began life as an orphan, became successively a cattle rustler, soldier, banker, oil millionaire, and ambassador to Mexico.

Lee Garland's story is the story of New Mexico, our third youngest state, and much of 20th-century America as well. Shards of the mythic West survive in his tale, but he soon takes it far beyond anything in formula fiction. Lee is a decent man who is faster than most with a gun. He is bigger than life, as a Western hero should be, but he is also truer to life, as no mythic hero can ever be.

Lee's own view of his exploits and crimes is succinct. He tells us:

"I wasn't no hero, even if the army did give me a medal, and I wasn't no villain, even though I did commit a murder."

I knew all about the mythic West and formula writing before I began *Outlaw,* having written scripts for Western films and television. But my involvement with Garland was an entirely new experience. I knew his was the right voice, yet two or three hundred pages into the story, I nearly abandoned it, thinking I had been too ambitious. But Garland was no quitter and gave me no sleep until I resumed the writing. Since then, the critical and commercial success of the book more than justified his persistence.

As fast with his tongue as with his Colt, Garland could never have been squeezed into any kind of formula fiction, and I was glad I had not tried to do it. But he tells it better than I do. Trying to reassure a frightened woman during an attack by Pancho Villa's bandits, he brags about his marksmanship:

"Where are you from, ma'am?"
"P-p-port Huron, Michigan."
"Back there, maybe my name ain't a household word yet, but around these parts it is. You heard of Kit Carson? Jesse James? Billy the Kid?"
She nods, tiny tears of fear watering her eyes.
"You might say I'm in the same category."
"But they're all dead," she says, with that stubborn kind of logic some females got a talent for.

His view of his own actions is summed up thus:

"Sometimes there's principles more important than the law . . . It ain't easy for a man to know where he stands anymore. Today everything's more complicated, watered down, lacks salt."

On blacks:

"A colored man's got as much right to be what he wants as me, but nobody admits that. If he's lazy like me, they call him no-account and say what do you expect? If he's smart and hardworking and educated, they say he don't know his place."

On Indians:

"We pass some Apache . . . poor as mice, walking along barefoot . . . they don't go near the ranches or towns because some folks will shoot an Apache same as a coyote. . . . It's hard to believe these was the people gave the white man the hardest run for his money. They never surrendered, never signed no treaty and never stayed put on no reservation. The poor devils kept their pride, but they sure didn't keep much else . . . you got no right to expect gratitude from an Indian."

And on love for his wife:

"As many years as we was together, we never got everything said we had to say to each other . . . She showed me when you love somebody enough, you never really lose them."

This is the same Lee Garland who earlier in the story hunts down the man who has murdered his friend Cody, wounds him and stands over him with a gun, thinking:

"I feel no pity for him . . . mocking my weakness, so goddamn cocksure I lack the guts to shoot him. . . . Who cares about Cody, he says? . . . There's only one answer to that and I got it . . . I fire the last shot into Sorenson's face while he's looking at me, and pull the trigger on the empty chambers until Mountain takes the gun away."

I did not plan to have Garland fight in the Battle of San Juan Hill, but after he joined Roosevelt's Rough Riders to avoid jail, I could not keep him off the battlefield:

"Our infantry starts up the other slope, their blue shirts against the green grass in the sun. Little pinpoints of fire pick at them from the Spanish trenches, and they look pitiful and disorganized, scrambling around, spread out, holding their rifles across their chests, slipping in the grass. There don't seem to be very many, not nearly enough for what they're trying to do.
"I'm thinking there's been a terrible mistake here. Somebody gave the wrong order and the poor dumb bastards don't know it. It ain't heroic or gallant or brave, just pathetic. The only thing you can admire is the stubborn way they keep going, slipping and sliding and falling. I want to call out to them to come back, not even try it."

He says about our victory in the Spanish American War:

"As wars go, it wasn't much. A couple of battles and the surrender of a third-rate power to an army of scarecrows. There was more mistakes than glory and more misery than action. None of us asks if it was worth it. Wars never are, I guess, to the men that fight them."

On his son's death during the 1918 influenza epidemic:

"I couldn't deal with it, just plain couldn't. Couldn't believe it, couldn't accept it and couldn't understand it . . . Like he forgot his manners and just left us. Like he didn't know how much we loved him and how much our own happiness depended on his staying around. . . . I spent days locked in the library with my Colt in my lap, drunk a lot and feeling sorry for myself, cocking and uncocking that old revolver as I tapped the barrel against my teeth. Until one day I looked up and saw how Caroline was suffering, and realized I was the only one could help her."

In that way, Lee told his own story for me, as surely as if he had elbowed me aside while I wrote. It is a Western all the way, but as far removed from traditional mythology and formula writing as a story can be.

His was not an easy voice to catch at the beginning, and I was never sure I could sustain him throughout a rambling account of his long and exciting life. But I did not have to, really. He helped me get away with it. Like a lot of fascinating old geezers I've known, once I got him talking it was hard to shut him up.

# 56

## CHARACTER: THE KEY ELEMENT IN MYSTERY NOVELS

### BY JAMES COLBERT

BY DEFINITION, TO BE A MYSTERY a novel must have a murder at the beginning that is solved by the end. And by convention there must be a solution, whether or not there is an apprehension. This is the contract assumed by the reader when he or she picks up a book classified as a mystery. Yet despite this murder-solution requisite, mysteries offer the writer great freedom, a basic structure around which to work plot, setting, and most important, character.

Without doubt, character is the most important element of a mystery. A clever plot helps, certainly, as does a strong sense of place, but those elements are secondary, best used to show how the central character thinks and responds to events and environment. One writer may have a native Floridian solving murders while another may send a New York City detective to Florida. While Florida, of course, remains the same, the interesting thing for the reader is to see how the character responds, how he or she integrates the sense of the place into an overall experience. The same is true of the plot. No matter how interesting, unless uncovered by a central character readers find engaging, events take on a flat, two-dimensional quality. "Just the facts, ma'am. Just the facts" has its place, all right, but that place is in a newspaper, not a mystery.

So how does a writer go about portraying an engaging character? The answer to that is as multi-faceted and as complex as the character must be, and it is accomplished one small step at a time. Think of a police artist putting together a composite sketch of a suspect. Thin sheets of transparent plastic, each with slightly different lines are laid one over another, composing different parts of the face until a whole picture emerges. While the medium is different, the technique is not dissimilar to the one a writer uses. First sheet: How tall is the character, and how much does he weigh? How is he built? Second sheet: What color hair

276

does he have? What are his distinguishing characteristics? Third sheet: What is the setting, and what is the character thinking? Small elements are put together, one over another, until a whole picture emerges.

Where the police artist leaves off with the physical portrait, however, the writer is just beginning because the reader wants to know, well, what's this guy really *like?* Is he threatening or non-threatening? Well-read or illiterate? Optimistic or pessimistic? What kind of car does he drive? What does he eat? The nuances, eccentricities, habits, way of thinking and quirks are what separate a description of a character from one who starts to *live*; and all those things are revealed as the character responds to his surroundings and reacts to events—in a very good mystery, dynamic events make the character *grow*.

Growth and change are intrinsic, inevitable elements of the human condition. The growing and the changing, however, usually occur very slowly, day by day, not very noticeably. Within the usually limited time frame of a novel, this change is often very difficult to portray, but the mystery has the advantage of a dynamic structure. A murder occurs at the beginning and is solved by the end. Events, feelings, new understandings are speeded up, compressed into a very short time. As a result, it is credible that the characters change fairly quickly in response. Really successful mysteries allow the reader not just to know a character but to grow with him, to learn his lessons as he did, without actually having to endure the violent crime. Observe Burke in Andrew Vachss's novel, *Blossom,* or listen to the first-person narrator in Scott Turow's *Presumed Innocent.* Notice how they change during the course of the book. Observe what they learn and how the new understandings affect them. And watch how, with the characters firmly in hand, the authors thrust them into the events that form the respective plots.

Plots are usually very simple ideas extended. Even the most complex plot can be described briefly. (Excellent examples of this can be found in your Sunday paper, in the film listings where even very involved movies are summarized in a line or two.) But unlike the step-by-step development of characters, plots appear complex at the outset and become more and more simple. Elements are stripped away rather than added. What appears confusing, even chaotic, at the start makes sense later on when other motives and actions are revealed: In retrospect, all the twists and turns make sense. The reader is left with a clear sense of order, a good sense of character, and, one hopes, a strong sense of place.

Evoking a place is stage setting in its most basic form. Remember, it is crucial to have the stage set for the central character—and not the other way round. Overlong descriptions of a place and a recitation of facts about it are best left to travel guides, which is not to say that setting is *un*important. But it *is* secondary. When successfully used, setting becomes the character and helps to reveal his or her foibles and way of life. In John D. MacDonald's Travis Magee novels, Travis Magee's houseboat, for example, is very much a part of Travis Magee, accommodating, even making possible, a way of life that is so much a part of him that when he travels, he seems to embody one *place* confronting another. Readers envy Travis the beachbum freedom of his life, and we understand how it feels to leave the beach and go, say, to New York City or to Mexico—or, for that matter, just to go to work. The setting is integral to Travis Magee and enriches the whole series; but while it may be difficult to imagine him anywhere else, the fact is, readers can. (MacDonald even tells us how to go about it whenever Travis considers his options.) For the writer, however, the single most important facet of technique, as important in its own way as making character primary, is to make use of what you know.

If presented well, there is no human experience that is uninteresting. Very good books have been written about what might, from all appearances, be very mundane lives. Yet mystery writers too often feel the need to write not what they know but what they perceive they *should* be writing about. As a result, the characters they create do not ring true, or in particular, they are tough when they should not be, or have no real sense of what violence is really like. But despite the hard-boiled school of detective fiction, it is *not* necessary for a central character in a mystery to be either tough or violent—the book can, in fact, be just as interesting when a character conveys some squeamishness or distaste for violence. Not all detectives have to be built like linebackers and display a penchant for brutal confrontation.

The simple fact is, what you know is what will ring true. Andrew Vachss writes about violence and violent people because he knows his subject; but Tony Hillerman eschews that and writes about Navajo Indians, which is what *he* knows. Scott Turow, the lawyer, writes about legal proceedings. All three have written very good books. But since Dashiell Hammett's *Continental Op,* far too many mystery writers have felt it mandatory to make their investigators tough, even when the writer has no notion of what real toughness is all about. The result is facade rather than substance—and the reader will sense it. In fiction, certainly, there is a need for imagination, but the imagination must spring from knowledge, not speculation. The most credible, most substantive books are those in which the author's grasp of his or her subject shows through. Allow your character to know what you know and do not attempt to impose on him what you feel he *should* know. Your character will appear shallow if you do, shallow, and most damning of all, contrived. With respect to that, it is important, too, that you consider your story first, *then* the genre it happens to fall into.

With my first novel, *Profit and Sheen,* I wasn't even aware that I had written a mystery until the first review came out. What makes me appear rather dense in one way worked to my advantage in another: I told my story as well as I knew how and was completely unencumbered by any feeling of restriction. The point is, tell your story as well as you know how and see how it comes out. *Then* worry about genre. If you start out with the expressed intent of writing a mystery, well and good; if you follow the rules. But if what you have in mind is a story with only some elements of a mystery, tell your story first and do not try to change it to conform to some vague idea of what a mystery should be. Your publisher will classify your book for you; genre classification is a subjective thing, nothing more than a handle, really, an easy and convenient way of breaking down different works into groups more for marketing purposes than for readers.

There are, of course, other aspects of writing a mystery to consider, but these are more difficult to pin down. Most notable among them, however, are point of view and voice. Selecting the right point of view is extremely important, because it determines what the reader will and will not learn. Voice is, really, the application of point of view to a consistent rhythm, a *voice* the reader hears. More often than not, point of view is intrinsic to the writing itself (the writer will begin "I . . ." or "He . . ."), but voice requires a certain conscious effort on the writer's part, an attempt to convey the story consistently through or around the central character—even when that central character's vision is rather limited or, to the writer, unattractive. The success of the voice is directly related to how true the writer remains to his character and how willing the writer is to remain "transparent."

If you work within the given structure, writing a mystery is not so different from writing any other kind of novel. Good mysteries do, in fact, have all the elements common to all good fiction: engaging characters, strong sense of place, compelling plot, believable voice. Allow the structure to work for you, write as honestly as you know how, and everything else will fall into place.

# 57

## WRITING THE SHORT WHODUNIT

### BY RICHARD CICIARELLI

EVERY WHODUNIT HAS TO PLAY FAIR WITH THE READER, and the short mystery story is no exception. Whether or not they actually solve the mystery, readers at least want to know that they had a fair chance to match wits with the detective—that the detective was not privy to any secret information not given to them.

To this end, the writer must create a challenging puzzle for readers to solve and then work in all the clues that point to its solution—but this must be done in a way that doesn't make these plants too easy to spot, or readers will be disappointed.

Using different kinds of clues—verbal, physical, habitual, or "missing"—will help writers accomplish this goal.

A favorite type of *verbal* clue is the murder victim's enigmatic last words that the detective must interpret. I used such a device in "Tony Libra and the Killer's Calendar" *(Alfred Hitchcock's Mystery Magazine),* in which an English professor who is frightened for his life says, "In case anything happens to me, check up on the calendar." Since the dying statement clue has been overdone in mysteries, I had the professor say this very early in the story. When he dies, the detective realizes the importance of the statement and focuses on it.

I got the idea for that clue by accident. When I was looking something up in a dictionary, I noticed that there were two ways to spell calendar: *calendAr,* meaning the rotation of days, weeks, and months, and *calendEr,* which is a Hindu fakir. It was actually this latter word the professor meant.

In the same story, I used another type of verbal clue, in which the guilty person makes a statement that no one except the crime's perpetrator would understand. When the suspects were being questioned, the murderer said that the victim had turned down a drink offer and had gone home. Since that drink offer had been made in private, the only way the suspect could have known about it would have been if he had been eavesdropping, which is exactly what he had done because he was afraid the professor might say something to incriminate him.

A *physical* clue is just that: a physical object. It may be something like lipstick on a cigarette butt to indicate a woman was present, or it could be a scratch on the floor, indicating that the suspect who uses a metal-tipped cane was present.

A *habitual* clue is something that a character does by habit. In "Heavy Bet" *(AHMM)*, the victim is a baseball player who has a habit of wiping his lips with his wrist sweatbands before every pitch. Someone gets the idea that an ingenious way to poison him would be to soak those wristbands in a solution of strychnine. Of course, it isn't until the end of the story that this murder method is discovered, but earlier in the story the player's habit is mentioned. (Remember: Play fair.)

Finally, there is the *"missing"* clue—an object that should be present but isn't, and its absence becomes the basis for the mystery's solution.

In "Death of a Recluse," detective Drake Robbins has to determine if a reclusive millionaire really died of an accidental gunshot wound or if the wound was inflicted by a murderer. In describing the eccentric's house, I omitted any mention of lamps or electric lights of any kind. This leads the detective to the conclusion that the recluse was blind and would therefore never own a rifle. His death, then, could hardly have been accidental.

The most satisfying mystery puzzles use combinations of two or three kinds of clues. Since all the pieces of the whodunit puzzle must fit together precisely, I must know before I begin to write a mystery story what clues point to the culprit.

Some mystery writers claim that they start writing with no idea of who the guilty person is until one of the suspects slips up and is found out. I can't do that. For me to plant clues properly and give the readers a fair chance, *I* have to know at the outset what those clues are and what they mean. This is especially important when using the *missing* clue. How can a writer know what object to omit if he doesn't know in advance that it will be important?

Usually, I begin with the problem and its solution and work backward. With "The Toymaker's Troubles," for instance, I wanted to create a seemingly impossible crime, in which someone steals a company's plans for best-selling toys and sells them to a competitor.

282

First, I had to decide how to make the crime "impossible." That was the easy part. All the workers were thoroughly searched as they left work every day, and there would be no physical means (doors, windows, air vents, etc.) of getting the plans out of the building.

Then came the hard part: determining how the crime *would* be committed. I tried to imagine myself as the person who searched the suspects. How would I proceed? Where would I look?

After eliminating every normal possibility, I then asked myself what was left. Where would I never think to look? The answer came to me—behind someone's glass eye. The criminal would hide a microdot photograph of the toy plans behind his artificial eye.

Once I had the solution, I worked backward and established the crime and the suspects. I included a detailed description of each suspect's background, and in one of them I mentioned the man who had one glass eye.

In "When the Lights Go Out" I again began at the end of the story and worked backward. This story, too, was a *how*dunit as well as a *who*dunit. As a change of pace from murder, the crime was the theft of a $250,000 necklace owned by Sarah McClure. She hired Drake Robbins to arrange for security for her apartment when she had to go away for a short while.

Robbins placed a trustworthy guard at the apartment's entrance and had all the locks on the apartment doors changed. To complicate the problem, there were only two ways to reach the apartment: by elevator and by stairs. At the time of the robbery, Robbins, Mrs. McClure, and her two personal bodyguards would be on the stairs (she has a deathly fear of elevators), and the maintenance man who had just changed the locks, Sam Tailor, would be trapped between floors in the elevator because of a power failure.

Once I had the situation in my mind, I had to decide how someone could get to the apartment in the dark, chloroform the guard, get into the apartment, and steal the necklace.

I started with the *how*dunit part of the story, and as I did, the *who*dunit part fell into place easily.

The power failure was a part of the plot to steal the necklace. Sam Tailor had an accomplice waiting in the basement to throw the master power switch, plunging the entire building into darkness and trapping him between floors, thereby making it seem impossible for Tailor to be guilty. What Tailor did, however, was climb out the emergency door of the elevator, shinny up the elevator cables to the floor of Mrs. McClure's apartment, and chloroform the guard.

He then entered the apartment using a duplicate set of keys he had made when he purchased the new locks. He stole the necklace and returned to the elevator after scratching the lock to make it look as though it had been picked. He then hid the necklace in his tool box.

Now I had to decide how Tailor could signal his accomplice at the precise moment he wanted the power turned off. The answer—walkie-talkies.

Once I had the solution, I needed clues to point to Tailor as the guilty party. Early in the story I described him in his work uniform. Later, after he emerged from the elevator, I mentioned his coveralls were greasy, hinting at his cable-climbing escapade. I also mentioned that Tailor and the hotel manager communicated via walkie-talkie, but the manager, who was a bit forgetful, had misplaced his handset. Actually, of course, Tailor had taken it and given it to his accomplice.

A final clue was the fact that when the power went off, Robbins could hear many hotel guests commenting about the darkness, but he never heard Tailor, who was trapped in the elevator, call out for help. Also, when the power was restored, Tailor rode the elevator to the main floor, got off, and went casually about his work, not the least bit curious or concerned about the power failure—behavior most unnatural unless he knew all along the blackout would occur.

With the clues and solution before me, I could then create the necessary characters and plot line to form the robbery puzzle.

Another trick I've learned in writing the whodunit is to spread the clues throughout the story. If possible, I don't have two clues on the same manuscript page, so readers have to work a little harder to gather all the pieces of the puzzle.

An example of this is my story "Like a Dull Actor." In this story, egotistical actor Jason Ferrars has been receiving anonymous threatening letters, so he hires Drake Robbins as a bodyguard. As he is rehearsing a scene from his one-man play about Leonardo DaVinci, Ferrars is shot by an arrow fired from a crossbow that was part of a display in the foyer of the theater. The only people present during the rehearsal were Robbins; Ferrars' manager, Ted VanHorne; his publicity agent, Sally White; and his gofer, Louie Marley. All four were seated when the attack occurred.

On page seven of the manuscript I introduced Sally White as a petite woman who sat in the middle of the auditorium.

On page eight VanHorne entered. He was described as a large man who wore thick glasses because he's extremely nearsighted. He sat in the balcony.

One page later, Louie Marley arrived with Jason Ferrars' trademark mink coat "hung neatly on a hanger." (Marley had just retrieved the coat from the cleaners.) He sits right next to Robbins and drapes the coat over the seat in front of them.

On page ten, Ferrars is shot by the crossbow arrow. The crossbow is found at the rear of the theater, but Robbins can't explain how it got there. When he last saw it, it was in the foyer.

Drawing back a crossbow requires a great deal of strength, which VanHorne possesses, but shooting it demands excellent eyesight, so that eliminates him as a suspect.

On page sixteen, it's revealed that Sally White is an army colonel's daughter and that she learned to shoot at a very early age. But because of her slight build, she could not have drawn back a crossbow.

Eventually Robbins puts all these clues together and realizes it was a conspiracy. Louie Marley brought the crossbow into the theater disguised as the coathanger for Ferrars' coat. Then, as Marley distracted Robbins, Ted VanHorne drew back the bow, locked it into place, and Sally White shot it.

Spread out over the course of a dozen or so pages, then, are the clues needed to solve the mystery.

Keep in mind that in every story I've described, readers could see every clue, but my problem was to conceal these clues in seemingly innocent places and to include false clues designed to throw readers off the track.

To sum up, remember to start with your solution and work backward. Once you've determined who the guilty person will be and how the crime will be committed, decide what kinds of clues you will use. Make some verbal, some physical, some habitual, and some "missing." Then work out a story line in which the clues can be scattered throughout the story.

Remember, too, that your solution can't be too complicated. In a short whodunit, there isn't enough time to go into a five-page explanation of how the mystery was solved. And don't have your solution depend on magic, the supernatural, or anything extraterrestrial. That's just not fair—and rule number one is, always play fair. Give your readers a chance. Don't have your detective pick up "something" and put it in his pocket. If that "something" is important, tell what it is.

Your readers will respect you more for it.

# 58

## WRITING "TRUE" CRIME: GETTING FORENSIC FACTS RIGHT

### BY STEVEN SCARBOROUGH

THE STORY READS LIKE THIS: Mitch Sharp, the skillful detective, solves the "Casino Slasher Case" by tracing cloth fibers and a drop of saliva found at the murder scene to the stealthy criminal.

What's wrong with the facts in this scenario? This simply can't be done. The evidence is scientifically dubious. When is a case plausible, and when does it stretch reality? A writer can know only by examining the type of forensic evidence necessary for the events of the story and then by doing the appropriate research.

### Fingerprints

Fingerprints are the most conclusive form of forensic evidence; they are the only type of evidence that does not require corroborative proof. Though the probability of finding that elusive fingerprint or that single strand of hair is low, it can be woven into your story if you include the proper background. Fingerprint processing of a toenail and an eyeball of a murder victim in the *Red Dragon* is not only technically correct, but it also lends a gritty credence to Thomas Harris's novel.

Fingerprints command the most attention in court, and they should get equal billing in your crime story. In a city of about 300,000, fingerprints lead to the identification, arrest, or conviction of nearly one person every day.

While fingerprints are readily retrieved from glass, shiny metal, and paper, they are difficult to recover from fabric, textured objects, or finished furniture. Surface to surface, the methods of recovery differ, so the writer should know the proper processes for recovering incriminating fingerprints. It will make a story both interesting and accurate.

In *Presumed Innocent,* Scott Turow gives us an impressive account of

287

the questioning of a fingerprint witness in court. His only lapse is in describing blue fingerprints developed on glass with ninhydrin powder. Ninhydrin, a liquid chemical brushed on paper, produces a purplish fingerprint. The common graphite powder method is used on slick surfaces such as glass.

A dramatic punch to your story might be to recover prints from one of your victims, and it can be done. Iodine fumes are blown over the body with a small glass tube and a silver plate is pressed against the skin to lift the print. However, at this time prints can be recovered only within two hours from a live person and within about twelve hours from a deceased one.

Is your antagonist trying to incriminate someone else? Maybe he has considered forging a fingerprint? Forget it; his attempts are sure to be futile. It is nearly impossible to recreate an accurate die of someone's fingerprint. A cast can be made, provided he has a willing or dead hand to cast. Yet, even then the resulting print will be reversed or backward if transferred to an object.

A fingerprint expert cannot testify to how long a fingerprint will last on an object. General rules suggest that a fingerprint will last days, not weeks, outside in the weather; weeks but not months in a residence; and a month would not be long for a fingerprint left on a mirror, especially if encased in a drawer or a safe. Fingerprints have been chemically recovered years later on the pages of a book.

When tracing someone from latent fingerprints, the investigator must have the suspect's name and fingerprint record on file to make a positive match. Lawrence Block captures the essence of fingerprints in *The Burglar Who Painted Like Mondrian*:

. . . you can't really run a check on a single print unless you've already got a suspect. You need a whole set of prints, which we wouldn't have, even if whoever it was left prints, which they probably didn't. And they'd have to have been fingerprinted anyway for a check to reveal them.

Historically, fingerprints have been filed using a ten-print classification system; without recovering latent fingerprints of all ten fingers, a person could not be identified. In the 1980s, the AFIS (Automated Fingerprint Identification System) computer was introduced, enabling jurisdictions with access to the computer to link a single latent fingerprint to a suspect previously fingerprinted. Writers should remember

288

that AFIS computers cost over a million dollars, and your quaint Vermont village will not have one. The well-connected fictional investigator should know someone at a large agency or the FBI for a record check.

## Body Fluids

Fingerprints may be the most positive form of identification, but what if your perpetrator does not leave any? In the absence of fingerprints, body fluids are a common type of evidence found at a crime scene. If an intact sample of adequate size is recovered, body fluids can be analyzed to obtain a DNA genetic profile that can be compared with the suspect's or examined for blood type.

Blood, semen, and saliva are all excellent media for determining a DNA match. DNA (deoxyribonucleic acid) is the blueprint of a person's genetic makeup and is absolutely unique for each individual.

Contrary to common belief, hair will not reveal a person's DNA pattern. Have your victim yank out a clump of hair with the skin cells to make a DNA match.

The equipment necessary to analyze DNA is highly specialized and costly. Again, if your story is set in a quaint village, it may not be feasible to run a DNA check. It also may take months to get results from one of the few laboratories that do DNA analysis. This need not be a negative; think of the desperation, the agony, of waiting for results while your killer still stalks.

Body fluids can be analyzed by the local crime lab to help your detective. An important factor associated with body fluids, including blood types, is secretor status. A secretor puts out, i.e., secretes, his ABO blood type into peripheral body fluids such as semen, perspiration, etc. It is possible for your fictional serial rapist to avoid any link to his body fluids by being one of the 15 per cent that are non-secretors.

What does blood type tell the investigator? Normally a blood type places a person in a broad portion of the general population. A community might have 45 per cent of its members with O blood, 40 per cent with A blood, and so on. Therefore, if standard ABO typing is done, the results are of little value because of the large population with that blood type.

Additional blood grouping techniques, specifically enzyme and protein analyses, enable the forensic chemist to assign a suspect to a narrower population. Your fictional crime lab should not give your detective a match on blood from the crime scene. They can limit only the number of people in your town that have that type of enzyme blood group.

The special equipment needed for thorough blood analysis is costly, and it is probable that numerous crimes go unsolved because sufficient testing is either too expensive or neglected.

## Other evidence

Hair can be of forensic value. Strands found at the scene of the crime can be compared to a suspect's for similarities in color, shape, and texture, but it is difficult to determine race or even sex. An author can write that some of the suspects were eliminated because analysis concluded that their hair was not similar or consistent with the hair found at the crime scene.

Footwear prints, recovered by photography, fall into the class category. Except for the exceptional case, shoeprints can only be said to be made by the same type of shoe. Footwear, or any class type evidence (hair, fiber, ABO blood type) by itself would normally not be enough to convict your suspect in a court of law.

Handwriting cases rarely get into court. A handwriting expert renders an opinion after examining several varying factors such as letter height ratio and slant. If the writing is similar, then degrees of match probability are reported.

Criminals usually disguise their writing. It is unlikely that a kidnapper's ransom note, written in block letters will lead to the identity of your brutish villain. Words in blood dribbled on a wall may provide a strong clue and add color to your story, but they will not enable a handwriting examiner to point to your murderer.

Striations on a bullet are unique, much like the ridges of a fingerprint. Therefore, a bullet can be traced to a gun using the scratches or lands and grooves imprinted on it by the barrel of a gun. Unfortunately, if the barrel is damaged or changed, or if the bullet is mangled, the examination will be inconclusive. Careful scrutiny is necessary before including a firearms match in your murder mystery.

Thomas Harris was very skillful in weaving his forensic research throughout his novel. FBI Agent Will Graham explores the gamut of forensic evidence from fingerprints to blood typing to bite marks. *The Red Dragon* could be used as a forensic model for crime writers.

The increasing sophistication of today's readers is a two-edged sword: Readers are no longer satisfied with, "He was the only one tall enough who had a motive." A writer trying to add more realism to a story need not shy away from scientific evidence, but he must check his forensic facts for accuracy. Credibility is the key to a successful crime novel. Just as a character's action may lead the reader to say, "He wouldn't do that," an erroneous forensic fact can turn off the reader. Do your research well, and you will be rewarded by readers clamoring to pick up your latest authentic crime story.

# 59

## THE MYSTERY IS IN THE WRITING

### BY WILLIAM MURRAY

WE TEND IN THIS COUNTRY TO PIGEONHOLE and compartmentalize everyone and everything, which saves us the trouble of thinking. I don't consider myself an author of mysteries per se. I chose the mystery genre only because it seemed to me to be the only way I could find an immediate audience for myself and my stories. It also made it easier for publishers to launch them into an increasingly precarious market.

Being identified as a genre author has its drawbacks (one tends not to be taken seriously by the highbrows), but the best way to handle the situation is simply to write the best books one is capable of and wait for the critics to catch up. They are usually well behind the reading public in these matters. One could argue, for instance, that Haydn was a genre composer, as was Verdi in his early operatic years, since they both composed in established forms and for a particular audience. The safest approach is to tell a good dramatic story as well as possible and not worry about genres and whether, in the publishing jargon of the day, it will turn out to be "the breakthrough" book.

I'm not primarily a reader of mysteries, but it seems to me that there are two kinds of detective stories. One is the pure whodunit, which is constructed like an elaborate puzzle and in which the primary interest centers on the old question of Who Killed Cock Robin. The great practitioners in the field, most notably Agatha Christie, have ennobled the form and become stars in the process. The second kind consists of the novels of such writers as Dashiell Hammett, Raymond Chandler, Ross Macdonald, and Ross Thomas, which illuminate the darker corners of an entire society and portray a particular world. The latter are the writers who, in my opinion, have used the genre as a legitimate literary form and who can be considered artists as well as storytellers.

The world I deal with in my novels is the circumscribed one of the racetrack, with its large floating population of horsemen, grifters, speculators, aristocrats, pimps, prostitutes, addicts, gypsies, and hustlers of all varieties. Its great appeal to me is that of an ambience I understand and which I think of as a metaphor for life itself. One of its great fascinations derives from the fact that it is a world of new beginnings. No matter how disastrous events have proved, there is always tomorrow. Or, as an old racetrack adage goes, "Nobody ever committed suicide who had a good two-year-old in the barn." What could be more appealing to a novelist than that?

The reviewers of my books seem to be pretty much in agreement on one aspect of my writing—an ability to create vivid and believable characters. I think this may be because I always begin with the people in my stories, never with the story itself. I detest outlines, mainly because I find the idea constricting. I generally have only a vague idea of what my story will be about and what might eventually happen, but nothing more. Once I have this concept, then I start thinking about the characters in the piece, because I know that ultimately it is they who will dictate the outcome of events. Very often, in fact, characters I haven't even envisioned or who appeared as minor ones suddenly take on a life of their own and become major players.

In my book, *I'm Getting Killed Right Here,* a minor female character named May Potter becomes, by the end of the story, a major one, with a history and a life all of her own, one that I hadn't conceived at all when I sat down to write. For some mysterious reason, I gave her a scar on her neck. It wasn't until three-quarters of the way through the novel that the reason for the scar became clear to me and turned into a plot revelation. I don't pretend to understand this process of creation, but it is the reason I keep writing. Every novel becomes an adventure and a process of discovery.

These stories are all told by my narrator and alter ego, Shifty Lou Anderson. When I first decided to write them, I knew only that I wanted a narrator who was not a private eye or a cop. I also wanted one who was an artist in a profession that paid poorly, so that he would have to supplement his income either as a bettor or, during the inevitable losing streaks, by temporary employment in a variety of other jobs. A close-up magician was the ideal solution, because, whatever his skills, he works in a profession that cannot earn him a great deal of money. I had written several articles about magic and magicians and had become friends with a few, most notably Michael Skinner, a master prestidigitator who works at the Golden Nugget in Las Vegas. I myself have no talent for magic, and I'm the sort of person who can't put tacks into a piece of cork without stabbing himself. But I do know what it takes to be a great sleight-of-hand artist, and I've used that knowledge to create Shifty, who has become almost as real to me as my own children.

In the writing workshops that I now teach at the University of California at San Diego, I urge my students not to think of fiction as a form entirely separate from other kinds of writing. Novelists need to acquire reportorial and research skills and should cultivate them in order to increase their knowledge of society and its workings. I also stress discipline and a regular pattern of work, the adoption of a rhythm into which the writer can lose himself every day. Ivory-tower writing and waiting for inspiration are anathema to me and result in an elitist, self-defeating attitude toward one's work. The computer will not do the work for you nor is it essential to the process. I myself work on lined yellow pads with No. 2 pencils and don't get around to typing the material up until I've rewritten and polished the text so that I feel it's ready to be read by someone else. Rewriting is the key to good writing. As for writer's block, my answer to that problem is a quick glance at my bank statement.

294

# 60

## SCIENCE FICTION WRITING AT LENGTH

### BY ROGER ZELAZNY

IN THIS BOLD NEW AGE OF LITERARY EXPERIMENT and scientific breakthrough, how do the old rules apply? In science fiction the answer requires some knowledge of the field itself.

Science fiction is an interesting literary phenomenon not only because it has evolved rapidly through a great number of forms during the past 60 years—space opera, the "hard" sf tale, social sf, experimental sf, a fusion of all of the above—but because every one of these forms is itself alive and well today. Fashions come and go. New scientific gimmickry may come into prominence and be overworked, the social focus may shift from the middle or upper class of a hypothetical society to its underside. The introspective may for a time become more fashionable an emphasis than the external. But the field has grown to the point at which it can support all of these categories today, so that a writer need not indulge in archaeology to find good examples of any sort of science-fiction story told in any fashion. And all of them are still fair game for series development. Writers of science fiction should be aware of the variety of forms available, and, in considering a possible series, should select the type closest to their interests and abilities.

The sequel, the trilogy, the series, or whatever represents a continuation of a story from one novel to another—all of these have become particularly prominent in science fiction in recent years. They have come into being for a variety of reasons, in a variety of forms, and represent a mixed bag of results.

First, it should be noted that this is not a new phenomenon. For an interesting, well-written story as well as a reasonably authentic picture of the British publishing scene of over a century ago, I recommend George Gissing's *New Grub Street,* a novel by a man intimately acquainted with the Victorian marketplace, where the "three-volume novel" was the publisher's mainstay. Readers who enjoy a certain group of characters are likely to come back for more of the same. And with a series, the appearance of each successive volume gives a boost to the sales of the previous novels. So there is a definite commercial incentive for their production.

Not all series were originally intended as series, though. Often an author will write a novel that sells well beyond expectation and leaves a sufficient number of characters alive at its conclusion for an editor to see future possibilities and suggest, "Couldn't you do something more with these people/that idea/this place?"

But my longest series—novels dealing with Amber and its royal family—came about in a somewhat different manner from this. When I began to write the first novel in that series, *Nine Princes in Amber,* I had no idea where it was headed. There was actually a point at which I thought it would be a single book. I forget where I was in its telling when I realized that I had more story than I'd at first thought, and that a sequel would probably be required for its completion. So a series was born. When the second volume failed to resolve things, I decided simply to keep going till I came to the end. And it took five volumes to do it.

With my Dilvish series, on the other hand, I intentionally created a situation from which I could generate fresh stories whenever the need arose. I did this so I would never be caught short of material if I needed to produce a story in a hurry.

The stories of my nameless detective, collected in *My Name is Legion,* came about in a similar fashion.

My novel *Madwand* was written at editorial request because its predecessor, *Changeling,* had been well-received.

These are all valid means, all valid ways of going about the business. Valid, because they worked.

I have been told that the difference between a series and a serial lies in the serial's being a single, continued story, carried out through a number of volumes—as I did with Amber—whereas a series is tied together by continuing characters of a common setting, but generally possesses brand-new plots for each successive story. This is often the case in the mystery field. It is certainly a consideration in plotting. Are you setting out to write, say, a trilogy, requiring you to conceive and execute a big, three-part story with appropriate build-up and climax for each part? Or are you attempting to create characters sufficiently interesting that there may be an indefinite demand for their adventures?

Both require that build-up and a climax in each book—the rhythm of the novel—but the serial needs an overall crescendo as well. The most common distinction between serial and series, however, lies in characterization. Characters are supposed to develop, or at least change, in a story. If they're pretty much the same coming out as going in, the entire action seems, in a sense, wasted. In a series, though, you don't want the characters to change too much unless you're willing to risk losing those readers who liked them just as they were in the first place, and only want more of the same. In its worst form, such a story represents comic-book-type heroes who revert to precisely the same situation and attitude after each adventure. There are tricks, though, for providing excitement and maintaining interest in the series without creating such a blatant flatness of character. Sherlock Holmes, for example, remained pretty much the same throughout his adventures, but a) he was seen through the eyes of another (Dr. Watson), one who was constantly amazed by his intellectual prowess and who talked about it at length; b) the magician's trick of misdirection drew part of the reader's attention from the protagonist to the puzzle that he faced; and c) there was a process of "slow revelation," allowing the reader a few new tidbits about the protagonist every now and then. These are all useful tricks to bear in mind to keep a continuing character from seeming too flat through a long series of tales.

And whenever we're talking of fiction at length, another practical consideration involves the amount of material to be used. If we're thinking in terms of a quarter-million-word story, rather than one of 85,000 words, how are we to maintain the pace and hold reader interest, while achieving the length, without "padding?" The answer is in the second step of plotting.

After the writer has worked out what is to happen in a story, he must consider how it is to be told. Using the point of view of a single character is rewarding in that it provides constant opportunity for characterization in depth; on the other hand, it is often inappropriate when dealing with a "broad canvas" story. A writer might consider using third-person viewpoint, with subplots featuring a number of point-of-view characters, maintaining suspense by separating these characters and then following and departing from them at crucial moments—in effect, telling several stories, a piece at a time, all of them fitting together into the greater whole. William Gibson's *Mona Lisa Overdrive* is an excellent example of this technique, as it is when used by writers as diverse as J. R. R. Tolkien and Edgar Rice Burroughs. This presupposes a single, long story spaced out over a number of books.

Another method, found in the mystery area, is to use the same character in a sequence of totally different stories, as I did with my futuristic detective in *My Name Is Legion*. I could still bring him back—same character, same world, same methods of operation—in a new story which could stand independent of the earlier ones. Unlike Dilvish, there was not a continuing thread, a kind of "overstory" lurking in the background—one which finally got told in a novel *(The Changing Land)*. In such a case, it is easier to find some new wine with which to fill such a bottle than to nurture a fresh grape crop. Knowing when to quit may well be the hardest part of such an enterprise.

I feel that once an entertainment ceases to be fun, you should stop. I've seen too many good stories dragged out beyond the point of no return just for the earnings. Don't do it. There are plenty more stories waiting to be written in the place where that first, good impulse arose. If it isn't there, don't be persuaded to force it. Quit entertaining and go write something new and different.

# NONFICTION: ARTICLES AND BOOKS

# 61

# WRITING THE NEWSPAPER TRAVEL ARTICLE

## BY ARTHUR S. HARRIS, JR.

YOU'RE NOT EXACTLY A PRO, BUT YOU'VE SOLD A FEW TRAVEL ARTI-CLES to daily newspapers and are encouraged. But with a change of luck, almost all your submissions are now being returned.

Note I used the verb *returned*. After one reaches a certain level of competence, articles are *returned* more than *rejected*. Here's why:

1. *You used first person and sent it to a newspaper that prefers articles in the third person.*
Other papers are addicted to first-person "experiential" writing: adventuresome couple hiring a guide and trying for the summit of Mt. Kilimanjaro, river rafting near Kuusamo, Finland, taking a desert camel safari at Nefta in Tunisia. Generally, these papers are not located in retirement areas such as Florida but are likely to be in university cities—Boston, Madison, Denver/Boulder, the Bay Area of California. A Florida editor wrote me, "Our readers are simply not going to risk getting lost on unmarked, winding dirt roads of Vermont, although the idea sounds sublime to me."

If uncertain what approach a travel section takes, I pop several dollars in an envelope and mail it to the paper's circulation department requesting a recent Sunday paper (or a Saturday paper in Canada), a prudent end run around a busy travel editor.

Once I examine the travel section, it's apparent how much is free lance, syndicated, or staff-written copy. Do the stories tilt toward first, second, or third person? Too often free lancers are ignorant of a market and unimaginative (not to mention penurious) in checking it out.

Another advantage of having a recent travel section in hand should be obvious. When you submit an article to the same paper, your covering letter can immediately show the editor you're familiar with the travel

301

pages: "Loved that article last Sunday on Boston, which is my hometown. You caught the spirit of the place."

Such a covering letter fairly cries out: Here's a pro at work, one who's taken the trouble to examine the travel pages.

### 2. *Timing is off.*

Many papers maintain an inflexible schedule, having planned a year's travel themes in advance: foliage pieces after Labor Day (accepted in early or mid-summer), followed by ski and winter sports, then Christmas, followed by off-season bargains in Europe. After New Year's, look for even more Caribbean and Mexico subjects.

These themes differ geographically. Thus most papers in the North feature the Caribbean and Mexico in the winter, whereas those in the South spotlight the Caribbean in, say, June because their readers are in the habit of going to the islands during the inexpensive "off season." Texas papers run Mexico articles year round since for their readers it's often merely a day's drive to interior Mexico.

Some editors might hold a good piece, hoping that when a Far East travel section rolls around again in ten months, they'll be able to fit in "Inexpensive Inns of Japan," but this is rare.

Some newspapers won't reveal their travel theme schedules, regarding them as semi-confidential; after all, they're established primarily for advertising purposes. But others cheerfully send out a year's schedule if requested. No matter—after a while the sharp free lancer who reads a lot of travel sections develops a sense of when, ideally, a manuscript on a given subject or area should arrive on an editor's desk.

By late May a travel editor may return your "Placid Barge Vacations on French Canals" with a note: "Sorry, I'm all Europed out." Although articles on European travel may well appear in the paper in the next several issues, they were accepted months before. By mid-May it could be too late to sell a piece on a domestic destination or the Canadian Atlantic provinces.

### 3. *Are the photos (called "art" in the trade) acceptable?*

Most professionals submit photos with their articles: color slides to a newspaper that uses lots of color, black-and-white glossies to those that use little. Often a travel writer will send both slides *and* b/w prints along with the manuscript, hoping that color will run on the front page of the travel section, black and white inside. Not only does good art help sell the manuscript, but most papers pay extra for photos.

Today the average travel editor opens up a manila envelope and looks first, and sometimes *only,* at the art. Is there variety? Are photos carefully labeled, well exposed? The black and whites printed with plenty of contrast? Also, most editors like to see people in the fore-ground of scenics—tourists gazing at a pyramid, for instance, instead of just the stark pyramid.

Please believe me: More than one editor has confessed that if the art (photos, line drawings, etc.) isn't up to scratch, the article may not even be read! Sad but true. Travel editors are notoriously overworked and understaffed. Sometimes they return from a lengthy press trip and have to produce weekend travel sections immediately. Naturally, they have to cut a corner here and there.

That's why editors generally dislike receiving a note explaining that photographs to illustrate "Bountiful Budapest" are available. Too much writing, phoning, faxing. A busy editor told me once: "Just give me the complete package at one time so if I want to, I can run it in the weekend paper without follow-up phone calls."

Most profitable newspapers accept articles without art, then use staff photos or buy costly photographs from a stock house such as Image Bank. Others phone a country's tourist office or public relations firm to request a selection of no-cost visuals to accompany a piece, say, on Lapland. Stock house photos will be originals and exclusive to the purchaser, whereas the PR firm will submit adequate art but often photos which have appeared elsewhere, sometimes even in a brochure glamorizing the destination.

Or a newspaper may ask its art department to draw a map or make a line drawing. (I sometimes hire an artist to do a map for me, then send along a copy with my article—anything to encourage a sale.)

4. *The paper likes your story but wants it submitted via modem or floppy disk.*

Keying a free lancer's article into a newspaper's computer is, in business jargon, *labor intensive.* Consequently, more and more news-papers (*The Boston Globe, Chicago Tribune, Montreal Gazette, Grand Rapids Press, Birmingham News,* etc.) are asking writers, once their copy has been accepted, to submit the piece electronically. There's no need to own or even operate a word processor to satisfy these requirements. Small business firms can feed your story into a word processor, then run off floppy disks. I hire such work out and find it reasonable. Also, it helps the sale because you've made things easier for a harried editor. After all, the free lancer's biggest competition is syndicated copy, which can be fed into a newspaper electronically.

5. *Multiple submissions may not be welcome.*

A handful of large-circulation newspapers (such as *The Washington Post* and *The New York Times,* which are carried at newsstands on both coasts) insist on exclusivity and won't consider pieces being submitted to other newspapers, a common procedure for hard-working free lancers who, in effect, syndicate themselves. In other words, these newspapers buy first North American rights.

However, many papers accept manuscripts that are submitted elsewhere so long as there's no conflict with their circulation area. Thus a submission to *The Boston Globe* with its 800,000 Sunday circulation throughout the six New England states had better not be sent to Providence, Springfield, Worcester, Portland, etc., but rather to the midwest, south, or west.

Similarly, the *Los Angeles Times* is distributed over a wide area, including San Diego. Submitting to this Los Angeles paper *and* the *San Diego Union* would be a no-no. Try elsewhere.

Of course, if *The Miami Herald* buys your article, forget all other Florida newspapers, as the *Herald* is widely sold throughout the state, and even in the Caribbean and Mexico. Watch out also when you submit to Texas; Ft. Worth and Dallas are in the same metro area.

Early in your career, you may wish to tell editors where your article has already been published. But for the prolific travel writer, who at any time has forty submissions afloat, it's just too much unnecessary work. All travel writers of my acquaintance simply state "Exclusive to your circulation area," and leave it at that.

6. *Budget problems.*

It's hardly a secret that in the last few years, newspapers have experienced a decline in income: advertising is off, sales, too. Consequently, budgets for various departments (lifestyle, sports, travel) have been curtailed. A conscientious editor when returning your submission may write, "They've cut my budget. Try me next year."

Too often an article is returned with no explanation and the frustrated free lancer indulges in self-pity. But—really—what great powers of observation are required to note that a travel section which formerly ran 20 pages is now reduced to 10 or 12? Or that it's largely made up with syndicated copy?

7. *Conflict with newspaper staffer.*
Sometimes a kind editor will write, "Sorry, we have a staffer who's going to this destination shortly." Or: "We cover Paris with our news bureau there."
Often an editor is sitting on an article with superb art hoping for a chance to run it. So still another submitted article on the same subject could be automatically ruled out. Your article wasn't read, but was simply returned.

8. *The paper accepts no articles resulting from free or subsidized travel.*
Travel articles in which the writer was accommodated in any way— with free or reduced airfare or hotels—are not acceptable at some newspapers. A handwritten note may accompany your return: "To judge by the five-star hotels and expensive restaurants you mention in this article, to say nothing of the paean to a *particular* airline among *many* flying to Japan, we suspect a free trip. Sorry, strictly against our policy."

9. *Editorial whims.*
Free lancers naturally have mixed feelings when an editor they've dealt with retires or moves to another section of the newspaper. What an effort to start in again with someone who doesn't know you at all!
Yet other writers are delighted, especially if the first editor has been hard to crack. The new editor may not know any of the paper's "regulars" (too many travel editors develop a little stable) and might try other writers.
Since a particular person, not the periodical itself, returned "Enchanting Edinburgh," here's a chance to try it on a new editor. Most of us get considerable satisfaction when a newspaper accepts a yarn that has previously made one round trip to the very same desk. Perhaps the previous editor was on automatic pilot: The article on Scotland simply hadn't come from a regular, and therefore wasn't acceptable.

305

An interesting situation arose for me not long ago at a well-known Florida newspaper which for years had been publishing unremarkable articles from a hometown coterie of writers known personally by the editor. A new editor (a splendid writer, by the way) came in seeking fresh talent. Suddenly, here was a market opening up for writing with verve and texture. "I don't really *see* this French ski village at twilight after the ski lifts have closed for the day," the editor phoned me after I sent him my first story—thus giving me a chance to rewrite it.

Such helpful editors are not that rare once a writer gets rolling. "You tell me Europe is a great bargain off-season," scrawls an editor on the margins of my covering letter (I don't take offense; it's a common editorial time-saving procedure), "but I don't see *any* specifics. Give me particulars and costs out of O'Hare, and you've got a sale."

A few hours of work and $20 worth of phone calls, and I had indeed made another sale. I don't begrudge the phone charges. As in any business, one must spend money to make it. I help keep two photo labs (one color, one b/w) afloat, not to mention a home word processing firm. To a busy (say 60 hours weekly) writer, such costs are offset by multiple sales, often from inventory, to periodicals all over the U.S.A. and Canada. There's plenty of satisfaction in that.

# 62

## WRITE SHORTS THAT SELL

### By Selma Glasser

TURNING A SHORT PHRASE, ORDINARY WORD, or current expression into something humorous, original—and salable—is easy and fun. It can be a gold mine for writers who master this technique. Overworked clichés, songs, proverbs, or often straight quotes are ideal source material. Simply with a twist or change of a letter or sound, you can get published. You can utilize old standbys to create short items that sell because they are quickly recognized in their adapted forms. And best of all, you need not be a mental giant or genius with words: The only qualifications required are alertness, perseverance, and adaptability. The words are all in the dictionary. It's how we choose to "doctor them up" that counts.

Writing shorts is the name of my game. There's no need for me to squirrel myself away for endless hours of writing. It's possible to write on the run, when inspiration hits, wherever I am or whatever I'm doing. Ideas are everywhere, just waiting to be converted, adapted, condensed, parodied, or reversed—with or without embellishment. Major magazines such as *Reader's Digest, The New Yorker,* and even *Playboy* will accept short material, as long as you give the original source and date of publication. While some experts advise writers to start at the bottom, I aim for the big league right from the start, because it pays well. Why not start at the top? You can always go down, if necessary. If you're observant and discerning, you can earn money and bylines from misprints, signs, bumper stickers—plus a little ingenuity.

Be alert and ready to jot down inspirations. You can add your own touches, a new title, or interpretations later. As an example, a trip to Florida enabled me to earn $50.00 for this sign, which I titled, HISTOR-ICAL LANDMARK:

"On this site, exactly nothing happened."

Sometimes a straight sign that we see often can be worked into a filler. What would you do with these two? AVOID HOME ACCIDENTS. WATCH OUT FOR CHILDREN. Here's how I sold them to *Medical World News:*

SIGNS OF THE TIMES: Planned parenthood isn't anything new. For years, we've observed signs and seen warnings like:
"AVOID HOME ACCIDENTS" and "WATCH OUT FOR CHILDREN"

We hear talk about car pools almost daily. Here's how I used it for a *Good Housekeeping* item:

Where should folks take their cars swimming? IN CAR POOLS.

I thought of a few other commonly used phrases like the "cold war," and my question was:

What do antibiotics fight? THE COLD WAR.

How many times have we heard the expression: "something new under the sun"? A new cleaning product added blue to its formula. I started a prize-winning statement this way:

"First with something blue under the sun . . ."

I usually have pad and pencil with me when I'm driving. It was lucky I did on the day I saw this bumper sticker on the car in front of me:

ANSWER MY PRAYERS, STEAL THIS CAR.

*Reader's Digest* accepted it for its Bumper Snicker Section of their "Picturesque Speech" page.

When a local radio station offered cash for a reason you'd want to jump back into bed, I thought of someone who was good for nothing. I improved on that hackneyed phrase by submitting:

"Because I'm good for NODDING!"

This is what I did with proverbs to make a sale:

"He who hesitates is last."

"A fool and his money are soon partying."
"Every cloud has a silver airliner."

My favorite fun pursuit is giving unusual or unexpected meanings to ordinary words or phrases. I called a column I sold to *The Saturday Evening Post* "DeFUNitions":

I Do—State of the Union message
English Channel—British TV station
Unmanned vehicle—Car driven by a female
Syntax—Money collected from sinners

I'm not a poet, and I know it. However, by dreaming up all sorts of simple "sound" techniques, I have managed to produce eye-appealing, pun-concealing, rhyme-revealing fillers in the form of light verse, terse verse, or prize-winning rhymes for contests. I changed the spelling and the meaning of the word "deserter" and it served as a pun ending for this poem:

### War on Food
No matter how I try
I find dieting pure murder.
It seems there's no amnesty
For this desserter!

Another time, I thought of weather forecasters, and how incorrect they can be, at times. This suggested to me "weather flawcasters," while another popular phrase reworked gave me the punch line I needed. I wrote this light verse:

### Weather Flawcasters
Predicting weather they're so wrong,
With each and every scoop;
That's why forecasters all belong
To a non-prophet group!

I write a column I call PHRAZE CRAZE or RIME TIME, which is simply terse verse. For example:

What's a pink flower?        Rosy posy
What's a cheap nose job?     Frugal bugle
What's a matchmaker?         Knotter plotter

In writing a contest entry for a hair product that called for a statement, I used rhyme to win the prize:

With Protein 21 care,
I've sheen-clean, wash-'n'-wear hair.

In a Royal Cola contest, I created a pun on the sponsor's name, in this way:

I get more energy from this soft drink because it offers me more Royal ColawATTS per glassful.

My short cut for creating epigrams is describing subjects in terms borrowed from an entirely different field. For example: Here are two epigrams of mine that *Playboy* published:

A guy with money to *burn* usually meets his *match.*

(Note the words "burn" and "match," which sparked the idea for this epigram.)

A man with a *chip* on his shoulder is an indication of *wood* higher up.

You can readily see how the italicized words add interest and creativity here.

There are hundreds of other fields from which you may adapt appropriate words to help you create similar epigrams. For example, ELECTION *(candidate, favorite, platform, win)* or FISHING *(reel, catch, hook, net).*

I hope these examples of the various kinds of short items I've written and had published will help set the stage for you to write shorts that sell.

310

# 63

## A Biographer's Tale

### By Bettina Drew

I FIRST FOUND NELSON ALGREN IN 1983, after reading about his posthumous novel, *The Devil's Stocking,* in *The New York Times Book Review.* His lifelong interest in the outcasts and his depression wanderings fascinated me; and I soon realized, after scouring the library reference section and writing a letter to his archivist at Ohio State University, that no one was working on Algren at all. In the forties Algren's name appeared next to Dreiser, Farrell, Wright, and Bellow, but most people I knew had never heard of him. Hemingway had ranked Algren next to Faulkner, and his work was translated into dozens of languages, but the academics had left him alone. There had been a couple of intermittent dissertations and a tiny Twayne series biography, but Algren seemed to have disappeared. The last of American naturalists like Twain, Crane, and Dreiser, Algren had lived through the Depression, served in World War II, and covered Vietnam as a journalist; he'd had a long romantic love affair with this century's great feminist writer, Simone de Beauvoir. Terrific material? Absolutely, so I naïvely embarked on a biography, one of the most underpaid, tedious, and nerve-wracking nonfiction projects possible. A Texas librarian mentioned to a friend that I'd written for some Algren letters, and not long afterwards the University of Texas Press offered me a contract on the basis of ten pages. I sensed possibilities. I wrote to one New York agent and within eight weeks he got me a contract with a major publisher.

In the writing, I found that I could, curiously, make use of my own experiences while discovering the imaginative possibilities of history. I found great pleasure, for instance, in recreating the Depression. Looking for work as a journalist after college, Algren wandered across the Southwest much as I had done in my early twenties, in the 1970s, when so many lost young people tramped out to Boulder or Santa Fe or

Berkeley looking for some vague idea of meaning. I had lived in vans and sometimes in the forests of furnished rooms in run-down hotels; and writing Algren's Depression life I felt again the mood of being adrift in a vast indifferent country whose centers of civilization were connected only by highways and a history not quite long enough to offer direction. Like Algren, who learned through the crash that everything he'd been taught about America was a lie, I, too, was disillusioned with the American dream expressed in the suburbs. Fortunately, these episodes of emotional transference occurred early in the book; through them I learned how to place myself into scenes as a silent observer, by which I mean simply to imagine them.

I did so much background reading on the Depression that I almost got stuck there, but I soon discovered that each era had its charms. When I finally finished the long sad night of the 1930s and 40s which for Algren had included more than five years of joblessness, a suicide attempt, a failed marriage, a good novel, an excellent one, and what felt like prison in the army, Algren entered the happiest time in his life. "Oh, Night, Youth, Paris, and the Moon!" I wrote to a friend when, after 1947, Algren had his own place in the Chicago slums and enough time to observe the junkies, produce his best work, fall deeply in love with Simone de Beauvoir, travel to Paris, and win the National Book Award. It was that short time when, with the Nazis defeated, so much felt possible—i.e., before the heavy boom of the Cold War came crashing down.

In the rational universe of the library, I found that I loved investigative work. I spent many hours poring over Algren's papers at Ohio State, afternoons at a beat-up desk in the airless stacks of the archive, oblivious to everything except reconstructing a time even Algren had not remembered clearly. I learned, through interviews, how fallible the average person's memory is when recalling events of twenty or thirty years ago. I loved reading Algren's letters for the laconic references to events of tremendous psychological importance. My discoveries about Algren were all the more rewarding since, though he sometimes kept a reporter's notebook, he never wrote diaries—except once, at Beauvoir's instigation. He was, in fact, a thoroughly guarded individual, who presented to the world a tough-guy face that only just managed to conceal the incredibly sensitive and vulnerable person beneath.

As I've suggested, Algren first interested me as a product of the

312

Depression, and I'm amused now at the reasons I was drawn to him. I saw him as a heroic radical championing the causes of the underdog and social justice. He was that, of course, but more tangentially than one might suppose; if he was first a poet, he was also a gambler, prone to terrifying depressions, and destructive of love relationships. In fact, the very thing that began to horrify me about him in the end made him such a good subject, and that was, of course, the darkness of his inner vision and psychology. For though I believe strongly in the influence of social and economic circumstance on human development, I don't see how anyone could come to biography without being fundamentally interested in the inner man—that is, the place inside each of us where we live life most of the time. "Not to idolize, not to deify, but to humanize, is the supreme task of creative psychological study; not to excuse with a wealth of far-fetched arguments, but to explain, is its true mission," wrote Stefan Zweig, in my mind this century's greatest biographer.

I sometimes felt that people around me, usually my fellow adjuncts teaching subjects and verbs at the City College of New York, wondered—how did *she* get to see Simone de Beauvoir? or some other well-known person, but there really wasn't much to it. I merely wrote saying what I was doing and asking for an interview, and it was usually granted. I met people I would otherwise never have seen, and I managed to avoid feeling intimidated by convincing myself that the famous aren't so different from other people. They were, for instance, fallible. In Paris, almost all the people of color I saw were sweeping the streets, yet when petite, turbaned Simone de Beauvoir opened the door of her quiet, sunny apartment to me, she let me know right off how conformist *Americans* were. In her living room, surrounded by mementos from her travels, she regurgitated what she'd already put in print until I probed a subject that still infuriated her after twenty-five years. Sometimes I would go to an interview, knowing the person had had an affair with Algren, and hear it denied against all evidence. Studs Terkel, friend of the working man, seemed offended by my Radio Shack tape recorder. These glimpses into lives we read about were lucky little educations for me, but I was more impressed, for instance, to meet the deeply insightful late New York City homicide detective Roy Finer, aka "The Big Cop," or Roger Groening, a friend of Algren's who is one of the most well-read individuals I've known. There were many others, three especially who remain among my closest friends today.

Naturally, I encountered sexism, mostly from men twice my age who wondered how this "little girl"—as one Pulitzer-Prize winning author and champion of liberal causes described me when I was thirty—could possibly write accurately about a tough guy. Another American writer, male, questioned every opinion I held about Algren, until, exasperated, I responded to a question by saying that since he'd corrected everything I'd said, I hardly knew how to respond. Fortunately, the interview was just about over. I was later surprised when the same writer wrote two very generous reviews of my book, even saying in one that I had a keen eye for the phony and fatuous. Though a number of professional academics who'd been sitting on Algren material for ten years or more didn't want to share it because they were "planning to do something with it" or demanded free books or placed nit-picking restrictions on speaking to me, most of the hundred or more people I contacted for information were extremely generous with their time and letters, pictures, and memorabilia.

Because Algren lived among and wrote about junkies, prostitutes, gamblers, and others who lived less than legitimate lives, I also wanted to find some of the underworld people who had so inspired him. It was largely impossible. I got tantalizingly close to an army buddy who was the inspiration for Frankie Machine in Algren's *The Man with the Golden Arm,* finally reaching his brother in Blue Island, Illinois. But he told me the man was drunk and homeless, and had just gotten out of the hospital in very poor shape. After a lot of work that included a trip across the decimated slum of West Chicago to the suburban enclave of River Forest, Illinois, I reached, by telephone to California, a former narcotics addict and prostitute who has lived clean for decades. She was suspicious and I had been warned to play dumb about her past. Thus I questioned her about Algren as if I did not know her; then I put all the evidence I had together.

Nothing ever made sense until I wrote it. I worked chapter by chapter, never moving on to the next one until the chapter was finished—which usually meant, with constant revision, I don't know how many drafts; I suppose eight or ten or so. Only when I put down exactly what I wanted to say out of the material at hand could I go on, because only then did I understand what had happened to Algren. A case in point was a letter he wrote in the fifties saying he had "played poker" with $32,000. Since Algren was a compulsive gambler, I took the letter at face value when I first found it; later I realized that he had merely seen his business situation through the gambling metaphor. And so on. Although I had originally begun with the twenty-two-chapter outline used to sell the book, I found that chapter breaks had to be changed to accommodate dramatic content. Wherever I could sacrifice to style I did so, until the facts became the starting point around which the narrative was wrapped.

There were many times when I hated Algren, his sexism, his peevishness and paranoia, but through him I came to understand a great deal about human contradiction, even though sometimes continuing work only by summoning up large doses of compassion. In fact, Algren, whose work is so drenched in compassion, demanded it of me, and I am very, very grateful for that. About halfway through the book, the writing lost its magic because I had learned how to do it. Then sometimes it seemed that my work consisted merely of grouping ideas into paragraphs and finding transitions. But I had too much invested not to go on, and it became, actually, another challenge to hide this from the reader, to hide also that I could not make sense of Algren's last twenty-five years even after writing them, until Algren's friend Roger Groening made me see that the themes I had carried through the book earlier actually did continue later on, a feat of insight for which I dubbed him Roger "The Savior" Groening. I only barely restructured the final sections in time, and it was done so quickly I can't really believe I managed it.

The cuts and editorial and legal revisions, all completed against a rather tight deadline, were, to say the least, physically exhausting. Worry over money, the expense of permissions, and the loss of cordial relations with people who'd helped me, only to be infuriated with what I'd written—a letter from an ex-wife's lawyer comes to mind here—drained me emotionally. In fact, the task of preparing the 500-page manuscript for publication was so overwhelming that, though I accomplished it, I was scarcely able to appreciate the American publication.

For a long time after the book came out, I heard floating in my head James Taylor's words, "I'd have to be some kind of natural-born fool to want to pass that way again." However, *Nelson Algren* appeared in Britain in January 1991 to very positive reviews. *The Spectator* called it "magisterial"; *The London Times,* "first-rate." While Americans, with a sort of hangover from a Cold War culture when criticism about capitalism couldn't be tolerated, felt uneasy about embracing or pro-

315

moting a man who spoke for and lived among the lost, the British saw Algren's as a quintessentially American life.

I've been working on some essays, but have found that I miss the security of the big project, of waking up in the morning with no doubt about what to work on, of getting out of the house to meet people, of traveling here and there. I haven't been opening anyone's mail, but I have to admit that I've been looking into various lives and snooping around libraries. So who knows?

# § 64

# THE MARKET FOR OP-ED ARTICLES

## BY GENIE DICKERSON

THERE'S A LOT OF CONFUSION ABOUT OP-ED articles, the free-lance essays that newspapers publish opposite their editorial pages. Papers buy two kinds of op-ed pieces: personal experience and opinion or analysis. Most op-ed rejections result from the writer's confusion and blending of the two types.

Let's take the personal experience piece first. This offers writers the best and easiest way to get published by a newspaper. All that's required is 1) simple, clear, tight writing, and 2) an experience in some segment of public affairs.

Included in this type might be first-person narratives by a foreign defector, for example, or by personal victims of some horror. The whistleblower, the disaffected union worker, the member of an ethnic minority who has been discriminated against—all these may have special stories they want to tell. Any topical firsthand experience will work.

I've had op-ed articles published on my problems with neighborhood squirrels and on a conversation I overheard while having breakfast at a restaurant. Virtually everyone has at least one personal story that would interest newspaper readers.

## Analysis or opinion op-eds

The analysis type of op-ed article usually sheds light on a public concern, or expresses a new point of view or opinion, but it does not involve personal experience. Here the writer uses the third person and turns out an impersonal commentary. The tone of an analysis should be firm and somewhat formal; its vocabulary is more likely to use polysyllabic words from the Latin, and the style is more sophisticated and knowledgeable. Facts and statistics must be verifiable. For instance, just because a person is sick and tired of the government's budget deficit doesn't necessarily mean he should get paid to have his opinion set into print. The reader deserves more.

In dollars, how big was the deficit last year? Who is to blame? When did the problem begin? Do the United Kingdom, Germany, and Japan also run budget deficits? What evidence is there for these statements? The writer must present the facts in a logical essay and tie them together with an answer to one more question: What's the solution?

Experience is helpful but not necessary. I've sold opinion pieces on income tax, freedom of the press, and public funding for the arts, without having any special knowledge. Research at the library can fill in. Telephone inquiries to such sources as government bureaus and senators' offices are another good option.

With analytical op-eds, it's especially important to stick to one subject. Tossing in gratuitous comments on secondary issues may alienate readers needlessly. Avoid blanket criticisms of large groups like conservatives, liberals, ethnic groups, teenagers, college students, etc. Try to lead readers to look at an issue from a new angle without insulting any person or class. Balance should permeate the piece.

Writers of analytical op-eds should omit unnecessary personal facts: age, religion, race, political party preference, lifestyle choices, etc. If the writer seems to have an ax to grind, he'll lose the reader. The greatest pitfall in op-ed writing is mixing the personal, emotional narrative type with the impersonal, intellectual analytical type.

The first sentence is the most important part of any op-ed. It should be clever and concise, telling just enough about what is to come to hook the reader. The next most important sentence is the last one of the article, which should summarize the main point.

Humor is another valuable element in an op-ed. If the article can raise a smile or a laugh, so much the better. Although op-eds aim basically to provoke thought and discussion, the writer should offer readers some frosting on the cake. Although this sort of writing cannot be used in hard news reporting, it sells op-ed articles. But don't go too far. Fluff, purple prose, and padding will only bring rejections.

## Titles and headlines

Newspaper headlines run longer than most magazine titles and often contain a verb. Also, individual newspapers use their own capitalization styles. Follow the style of the paper to which you submit. The paper may change your heading, but at least you have suggested a workable one and have shown your knowledge of the newspaper's style.

Follow normal manuscript form—typed, double-spaced—and include an SASE. Payment rates for op-ed pieces range from nothing to several hundred dollars, with larger-circulation papers paying the higher rates. Op-eds longer than the usual 700 to 800 words also command the higher-range fees, but few papers buy long pieces.

The best op-ed markets are hometown papers. Some newspapers refuse to buy from out-of-area writers, but most op-ed editors of metropolitan papers welcome the freshness brought by writers outside their region. Address the manuscript to "Op-Ed Editor" or to the editor by name. A few op-ed editors prefer queries, but many topics would be cold before the query was answered. Check the query policy of your targeted paper.

Whether or not to send a cover letter with the manuscript depends on what you've got to say in it and who the editor is. If you have relevant expertise, then a cover letter (or a bio line at the end of the manuscript) is in order. Rarely do op-ed editors welcome footnotes or a bibliography. If you have tearsheets on the same subject as the submitted manuscript, include them as support for your knowledge of the subject. Generally, however, the editor would rather just get to your manuscript without spending time reading extras.

If you prefer to test the waters before jumping into op-ed writing, try a short letter to the editor, similar in content to pieces published on the op-ed page. A success or two will build your self-confidence.

# 65

## GIVE READERS WHAT *THEY* WANT— AND NEED

### BY SAMM SINCLAIR BAKER

BEST-SELLING NOVELIST Stephen King was quoted in *Publishers Weekly* as saying, "Don't give them what they want—give them what you want." In my opinion, that statement should be reversed if you want to write nonfiction that will sell. Your basic guideline—which can make the difference between sale and rejection—is: *Give them [readers] what they want, not what you [the writer] want.* You must concentrate on serving the reader. That doesn't mean you're greatly restricted in your subject matter: Your articles can inform, elevate, entertain, and teach.

As with every type of writing, you want to attract and involve readers in your articles quickly and personally. A sure way to accomplish that is to appeal to readers' *self-interest,* and show them how they will benefit from what you are telling them in your piece. Keep in mind always the old saying: "Feed your pets what *they* want, not what *you* prefer to eat."

To make your articles most effective, keep the readers' problems and needs foremost and write the best you can, clearly and simply. Above all, focus on the stated or implied you-you-you. In articles and nonfiction books, too much I-I-I is likely to trigger no-no-no from editors. When you recheck and revise your manuscript, cut out every extraneous "I"; insert "you" wherever it fits. That's what will grab and hold editors and readers.

### How the YOU-factor works

The superior value of "you" over "I/me" in most nonfiction was proved to me beyond doubt by an ad I worked on years ago for a then new gardening product, "Miracle-Gro." In a preliminary test, the ad was headlined, "How to Grow a Miracle Garden"—a general appeal. The resulting orders were satisfactory, but not great.

320

We then reran the ad in the same publication, making the headline just one word longer: "How *you* can grow a Miracle Garden." The seemingly minor change increased by many times the draw of the first ad. That dramatic experience taught me the enormous power of the YOU-factor, which I then applied to writing my thirty nonfiction books (including three blockbuster best sellers) and many articles on a variety of subjects.

Since then, the actual word "you" or the implied you has been the guiding sell-word for all my nonfiction. I urge you to consider that in what you write from now on. Also, check your rejected manuscripts for sufficient stress on the YOU-factor. You'll see how even minor changes can often enliven and increase the power of the piece, grab your reader, and sell. Emphasis on *you* can be a significantly valuable guideline in your nonfiction writing.

## Concentrate on the reader

Here are two devices I use that you can try for yourself: First, I print the word YOU on a small card and set it up on my desk where I see it intermittently as I write.

Second, I find a newspaper or magazine photo of a person who represents the reader I'm aiming to reach. For a diet article or book, I focus on a photo of an overweight couple. If you are writing about health topics, choose a photo of individuals of varying ages, depending on the market you are addressing.

Whatever the subject, you must make sure that it has an appeal that will grab the reader in a personal way. An article in *Smithsonian Magazine* started this way:

> You really feel your age when you get a letter from your insurance agent telling you the car you bought slightly used the year you got out of college can now be considered a "classic." "Your premiums will reflect this change in your classification," the letter said. I went out to look at the car and could almost hear my uncle's disapproving voice. "You should never buy a used car . . ."

Check how many times "you" and "your" keep the reader bound closely to the page. Also note that most individuals are involved at some time in buying a car, new or used, so the topic has universal appeal.

An article on golf in *Modern Maturity* states:

321

Sharpen your game with seven points from senior pros . . . that will give you power and accuracy. . . . Whatever your problem, you can take the solutions we recommend straight to the practice ground or the course.

Again, note the lure of a popular subject—golf—and how the reader is then brought in intimately by the use of "you" and "your." See how this personalizing technique is far more effective than a general approach.

In the first of my three diet book bestsellers, *The Doctor's Quick Weight Loss Diet,* the reader is hooked in the opening paragraph this way:

The prime aim of this book is to help you take that weight off quickly, and then to help you stay slim, healthy, and attractive. Here you'll learn exactly how in clear, simple, proved ways never told before.

Because the subject of diet is of deep concern to tens of millions of people, I was able to sell dozens of diet articles. The field is wide open for you today. Another point: Never bypass the possibility of milking a subject on which you've scored.

In my inspirational book, *Conscious Happiness,* I had to establish a special, close personal connection with the reader quickly. The opening lines were:

Conscious happiness is free. It can enrich your life tremendously—yet it doesn't cost you a cent from now on. But nobody else can pay for it and give it to you as a gift. You must earn it yourself by wanting it enough so that you work at it daily. Once you attain it, you can keep and enjoy its great benefits for the rest of your more rewarding life.

Note again how the variations of "you" linking the reader to the text repeatedly serve to reach and hold the reader's attention. As for the subject, who doesn't want to be happy?

Convinced more than ever by results I gained in my writing from the selling power of "you," I used those writing techniques for *The Complete Scarsdale Medical Diet,* which started selling immediately after publication and zoomed to become the bestselling diet book of all time.

Right near the start, the writing captured readers this way:

Most meaningful for you are reports from overweight people. Their statements, which came unsolicited through the mail, are all-important as proof that the diet that worked wonderfully for them can do the same for you too. . . .

The clear lesson you can derive from this boils down to three words: *Involve the reader*. Heed this advice and you'll have a far better chance of receiving acceptances instead of rejections on your future nonfiction submissions.

Captions on the covers of major magazines are good examples of the emotional connection that the writer must evoke in the reader. For example, from *Ladies' Home Journal:* "When Your Man Doesn't Give You What You Need." The opening of an article in *McCall's* reads:

Quick! Can your toddler swim? Has your five-year-old expressed an interest in a musical instrument? Does your 12-year-old keep up socially? . . . No? Well, what are you doing wrong?

Note carefully for your future guidance that in another issue of *Ladies' Home Journal*, there are several pages with "you" in the overall headings; *YOU—Relationships & More*, with subsections: *High Anxiety, Ways to Make Your Weekends More Fun . . . Five Things Never to Say in the Height of an Argument*. This is followed by *FINANCE: How Safe is Your Money?*

This is succeeded by an article: "Barbra's New Direction" that starts, "When you first walk into Barbra Streisand's large but cozy apartment . . ." See how the sentence leads *you* personally on the guided tour.

Consider how the following *Reader's Digest* article projects the YOU-factor in the opening line: "Your thoughts influence feelings and behavior and therefore the state of your body. Awareness of this can be an important difference in treating problems of overweight. *Study yourself . . .*" Note the repetition: "*your* thoughts . . . *your* body . . . study *yourself.*"

In short, study the market you are trying to sell to, the subjects that are most timely for that readership, and the best ways to attract the interest of those readers intimately.

Seeking to reach the reader deeply, Walt Whitman wrote, "The whole theory of the universe is directed unerringly to a single individual— namely to You." That wise and enduring concept applies just as effectively today.

The all-important pointers offered to you here will help you profit from your writing now, and from now on.

# 66

## TRUE CRIME THAT PAYS

### BY KRIST BOARDMAN

FOR THE ASPIRING WRITER, CRIME DOES PAY. If you're willing to do some research and master the techniques of detective magazine writing, you can develop a market for yourself that will pay frequently and reasonably. Detective magazines specialize for the most part in true homicide cases. Sold on newsstands, these magazines feature criminal cases in the United States and other countries where police and court records are accessible to the public and journalists.

Usually, these stories are about *closed cases*. This means that a suspect has been arrested, tried, convicted, and sent to prison. There are exceptions to the closed case rule, but beginning true crime writers need not be concerned with them until they have mastered the craft and are contributing to the magazines regularly.

Where do you find a crime story to write about? Any old murder will not do. Though the annual murder rate in the United States now approaches 25,000, you must be selective. To find out what murders have been committed in your area, read the local or metropolitan sections of your newspaper. When you find a case that involves a homicide, clip and date it. Continue to gather clippings. With some practice, you will be able to separate good prospects for true crime features from those that will not work. If the case involves a lot of detective work and has some interesting and unusual twists, it is probably a good possibility for a crime magazine article.

You will notice that crime coverage in metropolitan newspapers usually differs from that in county weeklies. Reading the major dailies—which often publish news of major criminal cases in their home states, not just in their metropolitan areas—is an excellent way to gather leads on cases from all over the state, but those news accounts may be very tersely written, without the details you need for a good true crime article. County weeklies, on the other hand (which cover a smaller area), frequently carry in-depth coverage of particular cases being tried in their communities.

Having identified a good magazine possibility, send a query to a detective magazine editor. Detective magazine editors are usually receptive to new writers who have had some previous writing experience or demonstrate a keen interest in learning how to write these articles. In your query, include the type of crime, names of the victim and suspect, approximate date of the crime, locale, weapon used (if any), a short description of what happened, and the outcome of the case if it has already gone on trial. You can do this prior to the trial, but in that event, don't work on your piece until you get the editor's approval to do it and unless there is a conviction.

The best true crime features are well researched. Go to the courthouse where the criminal case was tried and look up the court file or official record. You can skip over the tedious legal deliberations and go right to what happened, as outlined in the original complaint by the police or prosecutor. Also take careful note of important evidentiary material, such as medical examiner reports, testimony of forensic experts and lab results requested by the police.

In addition, check the files of the county's newspaper of record in the county library. Photocopies of news reports will be helpful when you're describing what happened during the trial.

If the murder case was solved easily, you probably won't have enough material for a 5,000-word story. In that event, remember that there are many other good crimes for you to look into; refocus your efforts on them. More than once, I've found that though my original article never panned out, I nevertheless established new contacts that led me to other publishable ones I was previously not aware of.

Before leaving on a research trip, review your news clips and, if necessary, call ahead to the police department or prosecutor in the jurisdiction concerned to ask if they will talk to you about the case. Your chances of having them cooperate are considerably better if you approach them when their case has already been tried and the criminal has been convicted. An advance call also saves you unnecessary time and expense on trips. Another way to economize is to target several cases in a particular geographical area, so that you can do all your research on them at the same time.

In your research, you want to touch all of the bases, if you can. You may find that interviews are hard to come by, or that court officials are not cooperating in making key documents available, or that the case was not covered in the local media. By consulting all your sources, you will usually be able to get enough material for your story without compromising accuracy.

There is no hard-and-fast way to gain the cooperation of police and prosecutors, but it's always worth a try. Frequently, they appreciate having their firsthand perspectives recorded in a detective magazine. (Police and prosecutors are among the most avid readers of these publications.) Sometimes, police and prosecutors will roll out the red carpet and give you excellent, detailed, accurate accounts of crimes that even their local newspapers missed.

If they can't or won't help you, don't be discouraged; they often operate in highly political environments and under bureaucratic constraints that prevent them from talking to you. You have to learn to take this kind of rejection in stride.

When you have completed your research, you are ready to write your article.

To create a compelling narrative that will keep readers and editors asking for more, there are important techniques to follow.

Begin your manuscript with the commission of the crime, or the events leading up to its discovery. For example: It is five o'clock on a February morning in a medium-sized city. The air is chilly, and the sun has not yet risen. The trash man who comes into the alley to empty a dumpster is shivering and moving quickly to stay warm, exhaling clouds of dimly seen vapor. He notices a body on the ground in front of his truck, and thinking a homeless person is sleeping there, he nudges the body with his foot, but there is no response. He then rolls the body over, and in the murky rays of dawn, sees a bloody, battered face at the head of a lifeless torso. In the headlights of the trash truck, he sees a bloody hammer on the pavement several feet away.

As an editor of a group of detective magazines used to say, there is no need for a true crime writer to write dramatically. Murder is inherently dramatic, without literary embellishment. Just write the facts; in my opinion, understatement is a most powerful form of writing and is appropriate for this medium.

Your article may then explain something about the town where these events occurred, either before or after discovery of the body, to establish setting and also to indicate the frequency of crime in that locale. Perhaps the police have very few homicides to deal with, or maybe murder is commonplace in the area. Either situation will affect the behavior and attitude of the responding investigator and his coworkers.

A uniformed officer arrives first, followed by a detective and a crew of evidence technicians. Usually, the detective takes charge and becomes the central character in your narrative. You adopt him as the protagonist in your account and follow him through his paces until the defendant is apprehended and goes to court.

What kind of identification was on the body? If there was none, what clues were used to establish identity? What about that bloody hammer nearby? Whose fingerprints—if any—were on it? Whose blood? What type? What does the medical examiner establish as the probable time of death, and is the investigator able to find witnesses who saw or heard anything unusual in the area at that estimated time of death? What else did the detective find? How did he respond? These are questions that your investigator will be asking and to which you will want to provide your readers answers all along the investigative trail.

You should also tell your readers something about the primary investigator and his close associates. If you were able to interview the detective, you will have a feel for him, as well as for some specific details about his life and career. The detective may have a partner or a supervisor, and all three may have played unique roles that you will want to explain.

An important element of the police inquiry is the identity of the victim—not just name, address, and occupation, but what in the life of the victim led to his or her murder. Through interviews with his or her friends, coworkers, employers, acquaintances, boyfriends, girlfriends, spouses, the detective will try to reconstruct what the victim's life was like just prior to his death. These different angles produce a profile of the victim's life and world and help narrow the field of suspects to those who interacted with him.

Always remember that except for the victim, suspect, police, and court officials—judges and attorneys—you should not use actual names in your story. A witness identified by name in court documents should be described in your story only as the trash man, a neighbor, a girlfriend, or a relative. The same rule applies to the names of businesses. *This restriction is a must for detective magazines,* because it protects them from lawsuits from persons claiming invasion of privacy.

Avoid revealing the identity and motive of the suspect until you have exhausted every other aspect. I call this style "writing backwards," or backing into the denouement of your story; it prolongs the suspense and pulls the reader along. You want to focus on the clues, the blind alleys of the investigation, other possible suspects, and even possible red herrings, until it's virtually impossible to avoid giving up the identity of the suspect. This keeps the reader in suspense about the resolution of the case until the very end.

This technique is totally different from straight newspaper reporting, which tends to explain the outcome first and then goes back and fills in the details.

Frequently, the most interesting character is the perpetrator of the crime. Once he's been identified as a suspect, you will want to tell more about him and the motivations that led him to commit his crime. His personality often has a direct bearing on the outcome of the case: Is the suspect an abused, mentally disturbed person simply acting in self defense, or is he a vicious and calculating repeat offender who enjoys making his victims suffer? Is he someone in between these extremes? The judge usually takes all of these factors into account when determining a sentence, and the defendant's character might become a point of contention that should be mentioned in your article.

The court trial can be as dramatic as the steps that led up to it. Significant quotations from court testimony, interviews, and news articles can be used to illustrate how the case was resolved.

Now that you have written your 5,000-word manuscript and checked it for factual and grammatical accuracy, get whatever photos you can. This is not always easy, and you must be resourceful. You should ask official sources for crime scene photos, photographs of key evidence, pictures of defendants and suspects. Take your camera to interviews and ask the prosecutor and detectives for permission to photograph them. If they can't give you pictures, ask if you can make copies of their pictures. This is less than ideal but much better than nothing. If official photos are totally unavailable, take your own photos of the scene of the crime and the courthouse where the case was tried. Try to find some pictures of the defendant and victim from local newspapers. Sometimes local newspaper photographers or their newspapers will be willing to share pictures in exchange for a credit line in a national magazine or for nominal payment. If possible, do all this when you are gathering material; being able to mention to an editor that you have photographs or artwork available will increase your article's salability.

The true crime magazine story offers the serious and committed writer the opportunity to get published regularly, and to hone his craft in a market that constantly looks for new material. I also feel that the true crime writer has a mission: to let the world know that the unfortunate victims of murder have not been forgotten, and that serious efforts were made to bring the criminals to justice.

# 67

# WRITING THE NON-CELEBRITY PROFILE

## BY ERNA HOLYER

IF YOU HAVE NOT WRITTEN PROFILES because you lack access to "celebrities," you may be missing a good source of income. Not only modest suburban newspapers, but major magazines and many publications in between are on the lookout for profiles of seemingly "ordinary" citizens.

Who makes a good profile subject? Look for some unique happening or a combination of unusual factors in the life of a little-known person. Dig for the odd, strange, and curious that will make readers exclaim, "Amazing!" not "So what?"

Profiles are written to *inspire, instruct,* or *inform.*

**Inspiration.** Do you know somebody who is going strong despite advanced age? I sold several profiles featuring an 82-year-old widow who wrote 125 letters a month to "pen-pals" all over the world and received thousands of gifts from correspondents who appreciated her sage advice. I learned about this extraordinary lady from seeing her picture in the newspaper and then found her name in the phone book.

Perhaps you know somebody who has shown great courage in the face of a personal handicap; profiles of a poster boy born without arms and hip sockets and a polio-stricken artist who won a national award resulted in three sales for me. All it took was a call to the March of Dimes.

**Instruction.** Do you know a collector or craftsperson? A neighbor with a teddy bear collection and a student who made collectors' dolls gave me how-to-do-it instruction, which I incorporated into profiles about them.

A farmer whose land was taken to build a freeway; a "cowboy" who sold out to a subdivision; and a guitar maker who moved his shop provided me with news pegs for articles. Other information they gave about gardening, raising horses, and guitar buyers represented a bonus for readers. In my profile of a hospital volunteer who won a Citizen of the Year award I was able to include instruction for would-be volunteers.

**Information.** A teacher aroused my interest in historical profiles. Rather than having to interview strangers—which I was reluctant to do—I wrote about personalities long dead and passed on information about their lives and times. I even sold an article on my history teacher, and in the profile of a Candy Striper, I included information for teenagers interested in medical careers.

Once you have found your subject, prepare a list of questions and set up the interview. Whether you aim for magazines or newspapers, you need to include the following elements to satisfy readers and editors:

- Quotes from the subject 1) explaining how and why success was achieved; 2) giving advice to the reader; 3) imparting his or her personal motto or philosophy of life
- Biographical data
- A general account of the achievement, told in your own words, the subject's words, or in statements by his friends, family, associates

Portray the person in a sympathetic manner, working in characteristic gestures, mannerisms, speech patterns. Describe the person and his or her surroundings. Answer the question, "What kind of person is this?"

Unless you are writing an as-told-to, write in third person. Put the spotlight on your "star" and keep yourself in the wings; readers want to learn about the person, not about you.

Before beginning your profile, ask yourself, "What is the purpose of this story?" "At whom is it aimed?" "What is the benefit for the reader?"

Note the difference between magazine and newspaper writing. Magazines feature well-rounded stories—lead, body, conclusion. Newspapers use inverted pyramid style, putting the most important information first, then other details in descending order of importance; a newspaper editor may lop off your conclusion in favor of an ad!

Comparison and contrast will get your profile off to a good start. In "Cowboy Moves Doggies for Final Time," I started this way:

331

Dick Miller's base station for cattle operations has been alive with the sights, sounds, and smells of animals for twenty years. But soon all this will end.

Early on, tell the reader how it all started. Give the person's motivation. Answering the question of how the hospital volunteer became interested in her work, I quoted the subject:

"I wanted to become a doctor, but money was tight and I didn't get into medical school. I did the next best thing—I volunteered for hospital work and it makes me feel like a million dollars."

After your opening, briefly foreshadow the story. Stick to a single storyline. Indicate the person's struggle with his shortcoming, or how he overcame poverty, sickness, lack of education.

Bridge the lead and body of your profile with as much biographical data as seems necessary—place and time of birth, what milieu?—then continue in chronological order. In "Farmer Loses Land to Freeway" I used the following opening:

Born in Los Gatos, California, to Wackichi and Sakae Jio, the boy traveled with his parents and eight siblings to Japan prior to World War II.

Give examples, showing setbacks, triumphs, and close calls. Take the reader on the scene. Work in humor, if possible. In "Dollmaker Creates Wonder, Excitement," I used the following illustration:

When the average woman opens the oven door and wails, "Oh, no!" she's probably looking at a fallen cake. When Hedy Katin wails, "Oh, no!" she's looking at a batch of dolls' eyes melted. "A year's work shot down!" she comments. "Now I'll miss my deadline for the Christmas sales."

In "Poster Boy Travels for Birth-Defected Children," I included this incident to show the boy's spunk:

While recruiting volunteers, the energetic youngster developed hip pains and the doctor ordered him off his feet. But Marty was not ready to quit. Four men manufactured a portable chair and the poster boy rode in style—to the applause of thousands of cheering walkers.

Include details your target readers may want to know. Reveal secrets (with the person's permission). Dramatize. Give your readers uplift and encouragement. Your profile should be vivid, memorable. Readers should feel they have met the person.

Profiles of unknowns can carry tremendous human interest appeal; reader identification accounts for much of the popularity. A story of Jane Smith in Smalltown, USA, who saw her baby through a major tragedy, will be read by mothers anywhere.

I ended the profile of my history teacher with his philosophy, "If you have knowledge, let others light their candles by it." You can light your own candles by discovering non-celebrities whose examples *inspire, instruct,* or *inform.* Find that child, mother, or volunteer who triumphed over unusual obstacles. Observation and carefully thought out interview questions will yield that well-balanced profile readers and editors look for.

# §68

# THERE'S A MARKET FOR SERVICE ARTICLES!

## BY DON RANLY

TAKE A LOOK AT THE MAGAZINE STANDS. Look at the range of service articles highlighted on the covers. A *Woman's Day* cover has the following blurbs:

"How to Pay Your Bills When You Can't"

"Create a New Wardrobe With Clothes You Own"

"Learn to Cook Low-fat Recipes"

"Save $$ Hundreds on Housewares, Food, Drugs"

"Best Brownies of the Year"

No, not every magazine features this type of piece, but they probably comprise the majority of articles in the majority of magazines.

Some magazines have regular departments called "news to use." *Woman's Day* calls its department "Quick—News You Can Use Now!" Even a news magazine, *U.S. News & World Report,* has a department called "News You Can Use."

You'll find service articles in corporate, association, university, and specialized business magazines—some of which accept free-lance articles. The same is true of the style, food, travel and entertainment sections of newspapers.

All these publications are becoming more useful and usable to readers. Many call it service journalism.

## What is service journalism?

Any subject can become service journalism, since it's not really a separate category of writing. It's simply a different approach to writing. The one word that best characterizes a service article is the word "useful." That word implies two things for the writer:

1. The reader must find the subject personally useful.

334

2. The writer must present the article in the most useful way. That may mean text, but it could also mean using pictures, charts, and illustrations.

Service articles do more than just inform or entertain—though they surely can be informative and entertaining. They provide information readers can use; they move people to do things. Often service articles report on and evaluate goods and services, and tell readers how to improve something.

Service articles put the reader first. Think of your audience, find subjects they want to know about, and present them simply and clearly. A good service article is one that the reader would tack on the refrigerator. You have done your job even better if the reader takes some action as a result of the information and advice you give.

## Working principles of service articles

Here are some working principles to make your service articles effective.

1. *Cut the copy.* Then cut the copy again. You can't always be brief, but you can always be concise. Don't waste a second of the reader's time.

2. *Be clear.* Remember when you bought that outdoor cooker and couldn't follow the directions to put it together? How-to, practical articles must be clear and easy to follow.

3. *Involve the reader.* There are three ways to do this effectively.

a) The "how-I" approach. You are the expert; you speak with authority and experience. If you are well-known as an expert in the subject, your credibility and effectiveness are increased.

However, you don't have to be an expert. Subjects such as "How I Conquered My Crabgrass," or "How I Saved $200 on Air Fare to Europe," may be based on a one-time experience.

b) The "how-you" approach. Talking directly to the reader works best for most kinds of writing. John Caples, author of *How to Make Your Advertising Make Money,* has a list of "how-to" titles. Here's that list changed to "how-you."

How you can have _____
How you can keep _____
How you can start _____

335

How you can become _____
How you can improve _____
How you can develop _____
How you can get the most out of _____
How you can avoid _____
How you can end _____
How you can get rid of _____
How you can conquer _____
   c) The "how-Jane Doe" approach.

● Find the expert. Because you are not the expert on this subject, find someone who is.

● Find a celebrity. People love celebrities. The celebrity need not be an expert on the "how-to" topic. Sometimes it is more interesting when the celebrity is not.

● Find an amateur. Again, the amateur may be an expert at something else but not at what the article is about. If a stockbroker found an old barn in the country and turned it into a country estate, readers may well enjoy finding out how she did it. How much did it cost? What advice does she have for others who would like to try it? What mistakes did she make?

4. *Think "useful."* This means that in writing service articles, you should use vocabulary that suggests usefulness, as you would in writing ads. Here is a list of words John Caples suggests to accomplish this purpose:

| | | | |
|---|---|---|---|
| handy | usable | reversible | versatile |
| helpful | practical | serviceable | powerful |
| useful | washable | workable | reliable |

You can add to that list. In today's environment-conscious world, you may use the words "reusable" or "recyclable."

5. *Think "new" or "news."* You know how important new is to the news. "Now" is also key to service writing. What is the best and most up-to-date advice on how to avoid high cholesterol? Here are some other words from Caples indicating news:

announcing   today   modern

introducing   novel   recent
presenting   latest   suddenly

But not everything has to be new. People are hungry for the nostalgic. Look for new ways to recycle and enjoy old things.

6. *Think money.* One of the first questions readers ask is: How much is this going to cost? Everyone likes to make or to save money. Everyone likes a bargain. The only thing people like more than a bargain is something free.

Because for most people the cliché "time is money" happens to be true, you should tell them how much time it will save or take to do something. The words "quickly," "immediately," "soon," and "easily" are key words to successful service articles.

## Devices and writing techniques of service articles

Here are some devices and techniques that make service articles quick and easy to use.

1. *Lists.* Whenever you can, make a list. Sometimes you can summarize the key points of a service article with a "do" and "don't" list or "advantages" and "disadvantages." Also, think of "five ways," "the ten best," or "the six worst."

Using numbers gives structure and organization to the article. Because it is organized clearly, logically, sequentially, readers can grasp and retain the information more readily.

2. *Subheads.* Subheads should do more than break up the copy and make it visually appealing. They should show the organization and structure of the article so that the reader in a hurry can grasp the essence of the story by scanning the subheads. Subheads should provide entry points for the reader who needs or wants only certain parts of the article.

3. *Blurbs.* There are two types:

a) External blurbs. These are crisp, clear summaries of what the article is about. Think of them as "contents blurbs," a few words that give readers the benefit they will gain from reading the piece.

Busy readers need to know immediately how they can gain by reading the article. Tune them in to WIIFM—"What's In It For Me?"

b) Internal blurbs. Internal blurbs are used to break up the copy and to entice the reader. In service articles, try to give useful information in the blurbs.

4. *Sidebars and boxes.* A sidebar contains information that complements or is related to the main piece. Sometimes you will box that information. Readers are often more likely to read the sidebar than they are to read the story itself. Also, if you get readers to read what's in the sidebar or box, they are more likely to read the article.

With good sidebars, you need not worry as much about having an article that is so long readers will be scared away. A long piece broken into three shorter pieces will attract more readers. It's all a matter of presentation. For every three pages of double-spaced copy, you should have at least one sidebar or box. For example:

*References*—Service articles should always include a box that tells the reader how and where to get more information on the topic. The box should contain a short bibliography, addresses, and phone numbers.

*Notes*—Also consider a box that gives a short summary of all the most important information in the article—information you are sure readers should have. Think of it this way: If you were taking notes on the article to prepare for an exam, what would you write down? Readers don't have time to take those notes. Why don't you do it for them?

*Glossaries*—You might also include in a box technical terms used in your article, rather than defining such terms within the article and breaking the flow of the piece, to increase your readers' vocabulary. Also, if the words are difficult to pronounce, give the phonetic pronunciation.

5. *Charts.* Writers often act as if the only way to give information is to write. Many times a chart can replace pages of copy, and the information will be much easier and quicker to grasp and to retain.

A chart may simply supplement or complement what the article says, or it may present the same information visually. But sometimes, the bulk of the story can and should be the chart. In other words, the chart is not simply decoration or additional information. The graphic does all the informing.

A chart showing the nutrients, calories, fat, etc., of breakfast cereals need not be just words and bars and lines. It may be constructed in such a way that cereal boxes or cereal replace simple bars and lines. The graphic becomes more graphic.

Not every service article has to contain all of these elements. But the more you include, the more usable your information becomes. Besides, you'll have more fun writing the piece. You'll soon find ways to use these principles and techniques in other kinds of writing.

Remember, service article writing is not a separate category of writing. It is an approach to writing that you can use to attract editors and readers.

# 69

## GETTING STARTED IN BOOK REVIEWING

### BY BRYAN AUBREY

IF YOU LOVE BOOKS, AN ENJOYABLE AND REWARDING way of following your hobby and building up your writing credentials at the same time is to become a book reviewer. A few simple guidelines can help you get started. The first thing to decide is the type and genre of the book you are going to review. If you are interested in nonfiction, start with a book connected with any area of expertise, or hobby, you might have. You do not always need a specialist's knowledge of the subject to write a review, but it helps to be well informed. If your choice is fiction, it's advisable to select a novelist whose work you are familiar with.

Your review needs to be timely. By the time a book appears on the bestseller list, it is usually too late to review it, except possibly for a small weekly paper. So consult *Library Journal* or *Publishers Weekly*, both of which review upcoming books, as well as *Forthcoming Books* (R. R. Bowker), which gives up to five months' advance notice of new books. These may be found in the reference department of a good library.

In selecting the book you want to review, decide where you are going to submit the review. First find out which magazines and newspapers carry book reviews. Useful reference sources found in most large public libraries are *Working Press of the Nation* (published by the National Research Bureau) and *Editor and Publisher International Yearbook*, both published annually. They list every newspaper in the United States, with the names of book review editors. *The International Directory of Little Magazines and Small Presses* (published annually by Dustbooks, California) lists nearly 300 publications that carry book reviews. Try to obtain sample copies of the publications that are likely markets for reviews so you can see what type of books they review and how long the reviews run, then query the appropriate editor about the specific book you want to review. (First, verify by telephone the name

340

of the editor, as they change frequently.) Give some information about the book, and say why you think the readers of that particular magazine or newspaper would be interested in it. Enclose some sample reviews (if you have any), whether published or unpublished, with your query.

Another approach is to make a general inquiry, stating your desire to review books for that particular publication, and the type of books you wish to review, but leaving the choice of book to the editor. Opportunities will certainly come your way if you are persistent. Early in your reviewing career, you may have to buy the book yourself, but when you have had a few reviews published, you can write to the publicity department of the publisher and request a review copy, mentioning the publication to which you will be submitting the review. Also indicate that the publication has shown an interest in your review (if such is the case).

At first, your best markets may be local. Have a look at the "recent additions" shelf at the library, then ask the editor of the local paper if he is interested in an occasional review of one or more of the new books acquired by the library. Suggest a specific book title or two. You can present this idea as a service to the community—something to encourage people to use their library. After all, not everyone reads *The New York Times Book Review,* and many library users would welcome a reliable guide to the books they find on the shelves. This may lead to your doing a regular book review column. Always be on the alert for books by local authors; these are more likely to arouse the interest of a local newspaper.

With a specific book and market in mind, how do you go about writing the review? When you start reading a book, it's a good idea to note the page numbers on which major characters first appear, where important incidents take place or significant things are said. It will save you time when you come to writing your review.

If the book is nonfiction, keep track of key statements, statistics, summaries, conclusions, and anything else that you may want to use in your review. As you read, write down some of your own thoughts, impressions, and reactions to the book. Don't rely on your memory to recapture all your best ideas to use in the review when you need them. If you're reviewing fiction, subjective impressions are a good place to start. Ask yourself some simple questions: Do you like the novel? Did it move you—if so, how and why? In addition, there are various elements you should consider, although you won't have space to include them all.

341

In reviewing a novel you should first give some indication of the plot and characters. What is the main conflict that propels the narrative? How are the main characters contrasted with each other, and what are their relationships? Are the characters fully developed as individuals, or do they seem to be only stereotypes? How do the characters change during the course of the novel, and why do they change? Do they change for better or worse?

You will also need to comment on the theme: Is the main theme optimistic or pessimistic? Does it give any insight into the human condition? Is it deep (you're still reflecting on it the next day) or shallow (it's gone from your mind within an hour of finishing it)? Does the novel contain any symbolism or archetypal imagery? If so, how does it add to the impact of the work? What about the author's style? Is the language colloquial, formal, realistic, or poetic and figurative? How does the setting contribute to the impact of the novel? What difference would it make if it were set somewhere else?

It is advisable to know something about the author's previous work. You can consult *Contemporary Authors, Dictionary of Literary Biography, Contemporary Literary Criticism,* or one of the many other reference books available in libraries, where you may find overviews of an author's work, biographical sketches, and sometimes excerpts from reviews of his or her earlier work. In your review you may wish to make some allusion to or comparison with the author's previous books. Is the new novel different from her other books, or does it deal with similar themes? Is it the author's best work to date, or is it less impressive than her earlier novels? If you are going to comment on previous work, make sure you are familiar enough with it to avoid a comment that may be unfair to the author or misleading to the reader. If it is a first novel, make note of that in your review and comment on its quality and promise for future novels.

Your review should certainly include some evaluation of the overall quality of the book.

If all this seems an intimidating amount of material to cover in one review, you should be aware that many publications do "round-up" review columns, in which, for example, several books of poetry, or mysteries, or children's books are covered. Obviously, these reviews are shorter and mostly descriptive, although they generally include some evaluative comment also.

If the book you are reviewing is nonfiction, you should be sure to indicate its scope and content. What is its thesis? Is it likely to be controversial? What are the author's qualifications? Is the book on new research? Is the book aimed at a popular or professional readership? How does it compare to other books on the same subject? The *Subject Guide to Books in Print* can help you here. If you cannot obtain the relevant books listed, the annual *Book Review Digest* may contain several extracts from reviews. Or you can check the *Book Review Index,* which will guide you to periodical reviews, as will *The Readers' Guide to Periodical Literature,* which will also alert you to relevant articles. Some careful research, which need not take up much time, can make your review sound authoritative. For example, I recently reviewed a book about holistic health, a subject in which I have no particular expertise. But a quick bibliographic search led me to three recently published articles that were highly relevant to the book in question. Armed with this background knowledge and having carefully read the book, I was able to turn out an informed review.

How much can you expect to be paid for a review? You are certainly not going to get rich through book reviewing. Local newspapers will pay very little, possibly nothing at all. Larger newspapers will pay anything between $35 and $250. Some of the better literary journals or magazines may not pay a fee, but if they have commissioned the review, you will receive a copy of the book. Although rates of pay are generally fairly low, you can make your book reviews more financially rewarding if you sell them over and over again. As long as you select noncompeting publications, repeat sales are a strong possibility. A California newspaper is not going to mind if your review has already appeared in, say, a newspaper in Baltimore. But before sending your review out, it is advisable to contact the editor directly and ask whether he or she is interested. Be sure to mention where your review was first published. If you get a favorable response, send the review with a covering letter that says something about who you are. Tell the editor that you are a free lancer and have no connection with the author.

Finally, a few quick "don'ts" about reviewing. If you're reviewing fiction, don't just retell the story. This may seem too obvious to mention, but I recently read a review that did just that—and only that. Remember that a review is not a plot summary, although of course you should summarize enough of the plot to ensure that your reader can understand your review. But don't give away too much of the ending.

Don't read other reviews of the book you're reviewing. It's tempting, of course, particularly if you don't yet feel fully confident of your own judgments. But reading a review in, say, *The New York Times Book Review* may be more intimidating than helpful, and in the case of a novel will almost certainly interfere with the originality of your own response.

Don't review books written by your friends. It is difficult, if not impossible, to approach the work of a friend objectively. Remember that you are writing for your readers' benefit, not for the benefit of the author.

If you enjoy books, you'll enjoy reviewing. You'll be performing a useful service for others and enhancing your own writing skills and career at the same time. Once you get started, the possibilities are endless.

# § 70

# SELL YOUR HIDDEN GOLD WITH A QUERY

## BY TOM JENKINS

A ONE-PAGE QUERY LETTER IS THE FIRST step in selling your article to a magazine or newspaper. No matter how well you write, you need to market your work; otherwise, it may remain hidden gold.

A written query shows you respect the editor's time—it can be answered at his or her convenience—and indicates your trust that the editor can judge your worth as a writer by reading your writing sample: the query letter.

A query letter should do the following: (1) grab interest; (2) summarize your idea; (3) show you can organize and write simply; (4) sketch your qualifications; and (5) make it easy for the editor to respond.

### 1. *Grab interest*

No one knows the magazine better than its editor, so in reading a query letter, how long does it take him to know if an article idea fits his publication? The first few words of your query, therefore, are crucial: You may not get another chance. It is obvious you need to grab his interest immediately and keep it throughout the letter. If you can do it in the query, the editor will know you can probably do it in the article you are proposing.

The opener should be brief, arouse a bit of curiosity, and at times suggest a point of view.

Bamboozlement. That was the cry of an English teacher recently as advertising copy writing, a favorite target of the ignorant, became the subject of attack.

This was the opener of my query for an article intending to show the effectiveness of written advertising copy. Acknowledging the flaws and

345

gimmickry of "adblat," I went on to give examples of good advertising copy. The result was an article that appeared in a local newspaper.

Sometimes you can get attention with a single and accurate superlative: "The oldest living organism on earth is alive and well in California: the bristlecone pine." This query opener led to an article published in *Garden* magazine. That was ten years ago.

Since that time, horticulturists have learned that a drab and common shrub growing in the Southwest deserts is older: the creosote bush, one of which is believed to be 11,700 years old. I queried *Garden* again with an opener comparing the bristlecone with the creosote bush, and that led to an article that the magazine bought and published.

Sometimes you can arouse interest and give information at the same time, often in presenting a query about an unusual person. I came across a 52-year-old man whose past nervous condition had caused ulcerative colitis resulting in surgery to remove eight inches of his colon. My query to *Signs of the Times* opened with the following:

He rides a bicycle, bowls, flies an ultralight and skydives, but he also carries his own portable toilet with him everywhere. This is not a gag but the truth about a courageous man. Robert Kidwell is an ostomate.

The article was published under the title, "Faith Can Fly."

### 2. *Summarize your idea*

Your query letter should reflect your careful study of the readership, editorial needs, and style of the magazine to which you are writing. A query letter is specific; it is not a form letter sent to multiple publishers simultaneously, hoping for a lucky hit. You are not just proposing an article; you are proposing an article for a particular publication.

Your letter should give an overview of your topic and treatment with just enough details to show the editor you not only know your material but also how to present it.

In a query to *Desert* magazine, I wrote:

Misunderstood, maligned, and condemned throughout the West, the nation's cleverest wild animal is a needed predator: the coyote.

With hair-trigger reflexes and superbly sensitive senses, the coyote's ability to adjust and survive in the wilds is uncanny. It can sprint at 40 mph and cover 200 miles in a single day in search of food.

A social animal, attached to family and clan, the coyote has been undaunted by the growth of communities, suburban sprawl and compound 1080. Once concentrated almost entirely in the West, the coyote has turned up as far east as Maine, replacing the larger but less intelligent wolf as a wildlife predator.

The response was favorable, asking for the manuscript on speculation. The article appeared under the title, "The Controversial Predator."

Occasionally, a brief listing (but not a separate or complicated outline) in the body of the one-page query letter can give a structured overview some editors prefer. In a query to *Computer Decisions,* I suggested an article about how computerizing geographic data can save money for public utilities that depend upon large numbers of cumbersome, manually controlled maps.

The query included the following list:

With your approval, the article could be organized as follows:
1. Identify the basic problems of costly, nonintegrated and outdated maps that are manually controlled by a gas, electric, telephone or water utility company.
2. Explain how integrating and automating the maps can save money.
3. Give the details of a particular public utility, probably a telephone company, that saves money by using this kind of map management.

The associate editor responded with handwritten comments on the query letter itself, and I wrote the manuscript accordingly. "Big Saving in Computer Management of Maps" appeared in the magazine six months later.

Usually, your article idea is presented—in a kind of extended summary—in the opener and throughout the entire letter. When I read a newspaper item about a local college professor involved in an excavation project in downtown Mexico City, I perked up. I arranged an appointment with him and was impressed, both by him and the article possibilities. My query opened as follows:

Beneath the busy streets of downtown Mexico City, another city is buried. It is the sacred center of an entire empire, including the Great Temple of Tenochtitlan of the Aztec people (circa 1521), a 15-story architectural marvel incongruously devoted to human sacrifice.

I went on to summarize the quest of the University of Colorado's Dr. David Carrasco and his students to accumulate a priceless archive of ritual findings for the college. The managing editor of *Westways* liked

347

the idea, but gave me the assignment only if I collected better photos than those I had submitted with the query. I did so, got an O.K., and the resulting article, "Digging Up a Dynasty," appeared in *Westways*.

3. *Show you can organize and write simply*

Organize your query letter in discrete but related parts, all contributing to the unity of your idea. Then say it simply. Don't try to impress an editor with multisyllabic words and elaborate phrases. Occasionally, you can use a quote to get attention and stress your point. In one query letter, I began with a two-word quote:

"Money walks."
This was the caption of a full-page photo in a national magazine. It was an Easter Seals advertisement showing a small boy, a polio victim, resting on his crutches and looking down at his dog at his side as the dog looked up at him.

The boy's desire to walk was depicted by the photo; the reader's opportunity to give money for research to help make his walking possible was conveyed by the two simple words. The photo by itself was incomplete; the copywriter's words made it complete. I added:

A picture isn't always worth a thousand words. No photo can do what the two words, "Money walks," can do. Those words grab more than the eyes. They grip the mind.
Such use of language is copywriting at its best.

This part of the query became part of the published article, entitled, "In Defense of Advertising Copywriting."
You can use plain words and write a query about a common subject:

It's a simple thing, really. It happens every year. In the fall, aspen leaves turn from green to gold. But the spectacle is stunning no matter how many times you've seen it.

This opener to my query to *Travel & Leisure* became part of the first paragraph of the article as published. The piece described a one-day aspen-viewing trip in the high country of Colorado. After one of the editors made some helpful suggestions, I included side roads, places to eat, and practical advice on what to bring and wear.

4. *Sketch your qualifications*

An editor wants to know if you can handle the article you are

348

proposing. Although you can demonstrate your control of language in the query letter, your past success in published articles, as well as your education and work experience, are reasonable indicators of your ability to deal with a chosen subject.

Indicate your qualifications in the query. You can list them or combine the information with your proposed topic in the same paragraph. In a query that proposed a piece about an unorthodox inventor, I wrote as follows:

Frederick Fisher has built a prototype for a solar-powered crematorium. Yes, a device to make after-the-fact use of the same sun that gave life.

This kind of irony fits in with other articles I have written about paradox and the oddities of human nature. They include an acre of coffins, an automobile with a 1937 license plate parked in a driveway, untouched for 32 years, and a freelance cartoonist who draws 60 cartoons a week for 60 different newspapers with no written contract for payment.

The article, entitled "Burn Me Up," was accepted and appeared in an alternative newsweekly, *Westword*.

If you have not published anything yet and therefore have no "official" publishing credentials, let your choice of an appropriate idea targeted to a particular magazine contribute to your credibility as a writer. Refer to whatever applicable background you have as a worker, researcher, traveler, collector, hobbyist or adventurer. Remember that your credentials also encompass your imagination, creativity, and intuitive powers. Be alert and observe carefully. You will find article ideas everywhere. An example: An item on a televised news broadcast about a missing railroad train engine caught my interest. I drove to the search site and became even more interested. This led me to the library and an eventual query:

On a proverbial dark and stormy night in 1878, Kiowa Creek flooded, washing out bridges and sending a Kansas-Pacific railroad train into the raging waters. Afterward, train cars were found, some smashed and almost entirely buried in the sandy creekbed.

But the locomotive was never recovered.

Today, 100 years later, a search is taking place.

I went on to tell about the excited people behind the search, including novelist Clive Cussler *(Raise the Titanic)*. The query to *True West* brought a go-ahead. I sent in the article and two weeks later a check came in the mail.

## 5. *Make it easy for the editor to respond*

It's an old but valid story. Always include an SASE or a self-addressed postcard for the editor who may not want to send a letter back to you. What could be simpler than a self-addressed postcard? You can even type on the reverse of it: Yes _____ No _____ Deadline _____ Photos preferred _____. Or variations of this. All the editor needs to do is make a check mark or two and perhaps indicate a word count. Nothing to dictate or write, no letter or envelope to type, and no stamping or metering. The editor will appreciate your thoughtfulness and assume you are organized and considerate.

I am not without my share of rejections; who isn't? It is unlikely that any of us can be 100 percent efficient in free-lance letter queries, but with practice you can come close. If you can query successfully, you will become a published writer.

There is no shortcut. It isn't an easy process, but it is a workable one. You need to know as much as you can about the publication you are querying. You need to know what articles it has published during the past year; you need to study them. Then you can write a query letter that will reveal your hidden gold.

# 71

## WRITING THE PRO/CON ARTICLE

### BY BARBARA MCGARRY PETERS

SKILLED WRITERS WHO TYPICALLY SAIL THROUGH FACTUAL NEWS reports or how-tos often shy away from controversial subjects. It's easy to understand why. Pro/con articles have inherent perils and pitfalls and so are tricky to do well.

Why then enter the fray? A well-written pro/con piece brings several rewards. One payoff is the insight you gain from successfully thrashing out a complex problem with no obvious answer. Another is the satisfaction of helping your readers make a difficult choice. A third is the challenge of writing an honest article that's fit to print—and getting paid for it.

Here are seven guidelines that might help you, as they've helped me, with the writing process.

1. *Choose a point of view.* This will be your story line. This doesn't mean you should come down hard on one side or the other. That would be courting rejection. Your point of view comes from an organizing principle—a point at which the two sides meet or at least brush by one another. From this unifying thread or central idea, you can move in either direction, and your article takes shape.

Without this strong theme, you may end up with a string of ideas not clearly linked to a developing story line. This happened to me when I was trying too hard to write a well-balanced piece. To the editor, my article appeared "disjointed and choppy—jumping back and forth abruptly without moving in a particular direction." Wanting to present both sides of the argument without taking sides and keep within the word limit, I had cut the connective tissue that held the article together. As a result the editor was as perplexed about the problem at the end of the article as he was at the beginning. But, thanks to his detailed

351

rejection letter with suggestions for revision, I refashioned my article, and it appeared in print a month later.

2. *Get to the point quickly and stick to it.* Don't stumble or back your way into the article. Use punchy words and snappy, short sentences to capture your readers' interest. Your lead should announce your theme. Make it clear who your target audience is: for example, women or men of a special age group. Soon after you present the pro side, acknowledge the con position.

After you state your theme, tell readers your reason for writing the piece, and why you are writing it now. Has there been a fresh development that makes the article newsworthy? Your "angle" or "hook" could be a report from a recent conference, a political speech, a public announcement, or the publication of a scientific study.

Begin with general statements, then zoom in on details. But don't tell the readers anything they don't have to know. Irrelevant or tangential facts clutter the page and mask the story line. Scrutinize each sentence of your draft, and ask yourself: "Can my reader make a decision without knowing this?"

3. *Give evidence of thorough research.* Steep yourself in the subject, and interview experts from a wide range of disciplines. Controversies often affect people in a variety of ways: physical, emotional, social, political, and spiritual. It's important to include quotes on all aspects of a complex problem because one part of the problem might have a bearing on another. For instance, an article on the pros and cons of postmenopausal hormone treatment might include specialists in disease prevention and health promotion, gynecology, heart and bone disease, breast and uterine cancer, and genetic research. An article on the abortion controversy might include specialists in law, sociology, women's and children's health, psychology, medical research, religion, and ethics. Weave the experts' quotes into the article with smooth transitions, so that they reinforce your idea without slowing the pace.

Devote at least one paragraph to every argument. Imagine your reader asking you to clarify a point. What could you do to make the idea clearer, more understandable, persuasive?

4. *Keep your focus on general guidelines.* Don't overwhelm your reader with statistics related to the arguments, such as figures on

mortality, disease, or divorce rates or voter preferences. Statistics are virtually meaningless in a complex problem, especially one that involves more than one person. Even if risks were certain, making a choice between options would still be difficult, because there is always a trade-off between benefits and risks. And too many numbers confuse readers and slow the pace of the article.

5. *Keep your tone neutral.* A "let's reason together" tone is most likely to keep a reader's attention. Use concrete words for emotional effect. Avoid inflammatory words. If you're trying to remain objective and an angry tone slips into your writing, you'll lose most editors fast. It's tempting to use colorful, emotion-packed quotes, but your editor may become convinced you're promoting one side and will reject your article.

Avoid judgmental words or phrases; specious reasoning; unfair or weak arguments; uninformed, offensive remarks of unknown origin; questionable, simplistic, or vague accusatory comments.

6. *Save your strongest pro and con arguments for last.* It is the end of your article that will stick in your reader's mind. Don't discount the fact that many readers habitually take a peek at the end before they even finish the lead. A strong conclusion gives the reader something to think about—a clinching bit of evidence, a promising resource, a challenging question.

Wrap up your article by rephrasing your theme, and then leave readers with a new, provocative idea that invites them to weigh the implications of their decision.

7. *Ask a colleague or friend who is objective to read the manuscript for clarity,* to make sure it is not condescending, preachy, or insulting to your readers' intelligence. What questions have not been answered about the subject that should be? This step will help root out ambiguous sentences and unconvincing arguments.

Following these seven tips will greatly improve your chances of acceptance, but there still may be some frustrations along the way when you write about a controversial topic. The only writers who seem to have an easy time with it are those who refuse to consider both sides of the question.

What if you tackle a hot issue and find yourself with a pile of conflicting research, all supposedly valid arguments from leaders in the field? You must try to put things into perspective and consider the humorous aspects. As Bertrand Russell said, "The most savage controversies are those about matters . . . to which there is no good evidence either way."

# 72

# YOU DON'T HAVE TO GO TO SPAIN TO WRITE TRAVEL ARTICLES

## BY BARBARA CLAIRE KASSELMANN

NO, I'VE NEVER BEEN TO SPAIN. OR PARIS, OR TAHITI OR TIERRA DEL FUEGO, for that matter. But I have been to Dayton, Woods Hole, Ludowici and Pittsburgh. And I do write travel articles and sell them.

I can assure you, you don't really have to travel to exotic locales and stay in fabulously expensive resort hotels to be a travel writer. If you can make the corner ice cream store come alive with your lively writing style, you can write and sell travel articles. I can show you how, by regaining that old childhood sense of wonder and carrying a notebook everywhere you go, you can turn any place, even the county fair or the local shopping mall, into a trip. And of course, a trip means a travel article. I have learned to make the most of where I can afford to go. And I have come rather to like that. With the travel writer's approach, I see the colors and hear the songs much more vividly, which leads not only to writing more travel articles, but it also makes life richer and more fun.

To be a successful travel writer, the first thing you have to do is to think like a travel writer. See every beach, every historical marker, every museum or restaurant as a possible destination or stop along the way for the curious tourist. Then experience that place and take notes on it. (No serious writer of any type should ever be caught without a notebook and a pen.)

Is the beach lonely or lively? Who swims or sunbathes here? Does it have palm trees or rocky cliffs, crashing waves or dramatic sunsets? Would you come here for peaceful meditation, great fried clams or to watch the beautiful people? If it's a historical site, make a note of what happened where and when. If you have time, visit the museum and eat at one of the restaurants.

Once you've found and explored that undiscovered little clam shack or archaeological wonder, check out the surrounding area. Are there other restaurants around? Budget motels or grand old hotels? Unusual gift stores or antique shops? And how about access? Is it near a major highway, public transportation or an airport? Travelers want to know how to get there, where they can stay, and if there's anything more to do when they get there than read one brass plaque. When you get ready to write your article, you'll want to combine a number of places and activities into a varied, interesting package for your reader.

Two very important lessons I learned the hard way are that my memory might not always be quite as clear as I thought it would be, and that I might not be able to go back again next week to get additional information. Hence, I carry not only my trusty notebook, but a big old canvas bag as well for items that might be pertinent to any article I may want to write: schedules of upcoming exhibits, festivals, or other special events, brochures, menus, local maps, business cards from hotels, restaurants, gift shops, bargain outlets, museums, theaters, and historical sites. If an establishment doesn't seem too busy, I say I am a travel writer and ask to speak to the manager to get some basic information. This personal contact makes it easy for me to call back later for more information.

When I get home, I immediately file all my literature by region, state, city and/or specific topic. The more deeply I get involved in travel writing, the more refined and explicit my files must become.

I also expand my files by reading, clipping, mailing, and calling information centers, convention and visitors' bureaus. I am an inveterate reader of the travel section of Sunday newspapers, as well as travel and airline magazines. Newspapers in particular are filled with 1-800 numbers, coupons, or addresses from which you can obtain travel packets of brochures, rates and information. I send for those from a place I might want to visit and write about within the next year or two. I also clip articles that might be related in some way to an area I am interested in exploring. All this literature helps me tremendously in making my travel and writing plans.

My budget limitations help curtail my files. I know there is no point in my accumulating massive files on Tahiti or Bora Bora this year. I stick mostly with literature about hidden treasures of New England (my home) and nearby Canada, which is also a possibility. I also consider the areas of the country I can visit because friends or relatives live there; my old hometown, and an occasional dream place like New Orleans or Montreal.

In general, I firmly believe that to write authentic, interesting travel articles, a writer must, in most cases, actually visit a place and experience it. I could write a good encyclopedia entry about Morocco or Melbourne without ever going there, but I probably couldn't write a great travel article that would make people want to hop the next plane and go there. So I write about Newburyport, which is a favorite old haunt of mine, 45 miles up the road from Boston, or Vidalia, just a lazy half-day's drive through the tall Georgia pines from my daughter's house.

It is possible, however, to write good travel articles without ever leaving the farm. It takes extra effort at traveling through research material, corresponding with possible sources and surveying markets. Target publications that prefer third person, informational pieces rather than personal accounts. Use your imagination and creativity to add spice, but be careful never to embroider the facts.

To be an effective travel writer, it's critical to maintain a childhood sense of wonder about the places you visit. Allow this funky little town, these rolling fields of graceful pecan trees or that musty old museum to sink into your senses.

Take a table at a little café or enjoy a picnic on the river bank, and absorb the world around you. Listen to the sounds of the street life, smell the aromas from the barbecuing ribs, feel the cool fog on your arms. Order a regional specialty dish—Maryland crab cakes, Cincinnati chili, Gulf shrimp. Relax, enjoy, and record. As you sit there soaking up the scene, take notes on the sights, the sounds, and the tastes. Make a list of shops you see up and down the street you will want to visit before you leave.

I always like to talk to the people in a region to get the flavor of their accents, their interests, and the styles that make that part of the country or the world special. If you make these people come alive in your writing, it will pique the prospective traveler's interest in the destination about which you will be writing. From the residents you can often pick up fascinating bits of local lore or find out about the best places to visit or dine, those little secrets and haunts not found in the tour books.

How important are photos? For me, they have been very important, but they are not essential. I took my first travel photo in the Smoky Mountains when I was five years old, and I have been clicking away ever since. While I do not have extensive photographic equipment, I do have a good quality camera and an eye for what will make a good picture. Along with my notebook, my camera is a permanent part of my gear. I never know when or where I will see that perfect hideaway to suggest to travelers. When I am proposing an article to a travel editor, I include a few color slides or mention their availability, which is definitely a plus.

If you are not a photographer, however, don't force it. Check with the information officer at local tourist sites and convention and visitors' bureaus to see what photos they have available, so you can mention specific photo possibilities when you query an editor. It is advisable to establish contact with good photographers; you can get their names from local newspapers, photographers' organizations, or the yellow pages.

When visiting an area, learn to look for the unusual. Why should readers want to visit this museum of art when they have a fine museum in their own city? Why should they travel 1,000 miles for an Italian dinner when they can get great ravioli right around the corner? Anticipate the questions your readers are going to be asking; it's your job to answer them. Show what things set a particular area apart from similar places to prove that it's worth the time and money to visit. Make a site come alive on the pages, and make it a special place worthy of a vacation, big or small.

To be a published travel writer, you have to learn about more than just the places you plan to write about. As with any article writing, you must study your markets and your readers. Read travel pages in the newspapers to which you'd like to submit, and study travel magazines, as well as the many general, regional, and women's magazines that use travel articles. *The Writer's Handbook* (see "Where to Sell") and *The Writer* Magazine are important guides for free-lance writers seeking publication. They give practical, precise information on where to send your manuscripts, who is buying, and how much they pay.

Select three or four publications that seem appropriate for your work. If you have an impressive line-up of clips from major magazines or newspapers, you can afford to start with the bigger markets, but if you are just getting started, small regional publications or the Sunday travel sections of small city papers are good places to start. Pay may not be high at first, but you will be compiling clips so you can gradually move up the ladder to bigger and better.

Get a feel for the style and editorial requirements of the publication to which you plan to submit your article. Are the articles 300 or 3,000 words long? Are they written in first, second, or third person? Do they feature local one-day trips, weekend getaways or exotic world tours? Are they aimed at wealthy world travelers, singles looking for an exciting weekend or families on a budget? Don't waste your time or the editor's by proposing an article on budget getaways to a decidedly upscale magazine, or suggesting a New York City weekend to a magazine for recreational vehicle owners.

Develop a query letter as soon as possible after visiting a place, while the sensations and sights are still fresh in your mind. As with all queries, make it vivid, but to the point. Make the travel editor want to go where you've just gone, and he or she will be hooked on your idea.

If you have kept all those brochures and menus and interview notes, you have the battle well under control when you actually begin to write the article. I like to peruse my literature, take a look at the slides I took of the region, and get back into the mode of the vacation place I am preparing to write about. This is much easier to do if I have visited a place within the past few weeks, rather than five years ago.

I organize my notes and write down every topic and angle I plan to cover. Then I number the topics in the general order I plan to use, highlighting points that might make a good lead and an effective conclusion. For most "on-the-move" travel articles, chronological order seems to work best. However, if you have stayed in one locale for a week, you might want to group and compare dinners, sports activities, beach days or evenings on the town. If you are a strict outliner, which I am not, use that approach; it will save you a great deal of grief.

Throughout the article, include specifics on places to stay, where to dine, how to get there. Give locations for historic sites or other points of interest. Some publications prefer a box or sidebar at the end of the article, with a wrap-up of hotels, event schedules and addresses or telephone numbers for travel and visitors' bureaus. Consider these points when surveying publications to which you plan to submit.

Many readers of travel articles do just what I do: clip them and use them in travel plans. Accuracy is vital: Make sure you've listed the correct addresses and phone numbers for hotels, restaurants, and other

359

places mentioned in your article. Check and double-check your spelling, and the dates for any event that you include. If you're not positive about any piece of information, make a quick phone call to verify or update it.

If you're very lucky, you might sell your first travel article. However, it's more likely you will have to be determined, hard-working, persistent, and a reasonably good writer to crack the travel writing market eventually. If you have good skills and are willing to accept editorial criticism, it will only be a matter of time before you get a letter saying, "Yes, we would like to see your proposed article about visiting the sand dunes of western Michigan."

Of course, as soon as you get your first positive response from an editor, you'll stay up all night writing the dunes article. Then you'll start exploring and considering other towns or lakes you know and love, to get ready to write your next travel piece. Once you're on a roll, keep the momentum going, keep your writing alive, fresh, vivid, real, and full of sensations and specifics. Develop and hone your own style, and make the most of it.

These are the rules I follow, and they have paid off for me. I love traveling; I love travel writing. If you do, too, it will show in your writing, and before you know it, you, too, will be collecting checks for doing what you love to do.

As I continue to write and teach, I still keep one eye on my mailbox. I don't want to miss that letter saying, "We have continued to read and follow your travel articles, and we want to send you to a fantastic beach in Tahiti for a month so you will write an article for us." You say the plane leaves in an hour?

# 73

# The Art of Interviewing

## By Wendell Anderson

Interviews are a helpful research tool for the nonfiction writer. Information obtained firsthand from experts adds credibility and authenticity to an article. I've sold articles on ways to enjoy a stress-free Christmas, how to grow popcorn, how to decorate the office with house plants, ways to raise money to start a business, and many other topics—all based on research conducted through interviews.

Interviews are the best way to gather anecdotes and quotes that enliven and add color to nonfiction writing. An engaging anecdote or quote can make an article memorable, but quoted material requires careful handling. Should every word uttered by the subject be taken down verbatim? What about grammatical errors, slang, or obscenities? When can you change the subject's words?

Magazines, newspapers, and individual writers differ on only one point regarding quoted material: whether to "clean up" a quotation. Some won't, for fear it could change the picture one gives of a subject. Other writers will make changes if direct quotes may embarrass a subject. The standard practice is to correct grammatical errors and to omit obscenities unless you are including them to benefit the reader. Otherwise, there is universal agreement that only the subject's exact words may be enclosed in quotation marks. So, if you quote indirectly, not using the exact words but giving only the gist of what your subject says, quotation marks are not used. In fairness to your subject and your readers, however, make sure the indirect quotations are accurate restatements of the subject's original words, and use language as similar to the subject's in tone and meaning as possible, taking care to keep the statements in proper context.

If you have questions about a quotation, verify its accuracy with the subject or don't use it. Misquoted material can never really be corrected and could close off future interviews with that subject—and further publication in the magazine that ran it.

While the only way to be sure of capturing quotes verbatim is to use a tape recorder, you can jot down a few ideas, impressions, observations, or additional questions as the interview progresses. Always ask the interviewee for permission to tape the conversation; taping without the interviewee's knowledge or permission is unethical and an invasion of privacy.

To record telephone interviews, you can use a special, inexpensive device available at stores like Radio Shack. Otherwise, you will have to take quick, but careful, notes. (You may want to learn a simple shorthand system, or devise one of your own.)

Before you go to an interview, do your homework. Knowing as many facts as you can about your subject is flattering and encourages him or her to respond better to you. At a minimum, learn your subject's title and background, and be sure to spell his or her name correctly—including middle initials.

Also, learn all you can about your topic in advance. Don't ask the interviewee for information you can easily get elsewhere beforehand, and don't rely on the interviewee as your sole reference. Experts can sometimes be out of touch or simply wrong. Statistics, in particular, can be troublesome. If you can, verify numbers you get from an interviewee with another source or from published material in the library.

When you've done your research, you're ready to prepare your questions. Thorough research will help you develop questions that appear spontaneous, conversational, and natural. Writing down your questions will help you keep the interview focused. Always ask open-ended questions that require an answer other than "yes" or "no." For example, instead of *Did you really fall into a vat of chocolate?* ask, *What was it like to fall into a vat of chocolate?*

Avoid leading questions. Instead of, *Was the UFO shaped like a saucer or like a cigar?*, ask, *What was the UFO shaped like?* Let subjects use their own words.

Save difficult or controversial questions for the end of the interview; you want to put the subject at ease before you ask tough questions, and when you do, be prepared to explain why.

Rely on your written questions, but remain flexible. Watch for ideas that flow naturally from the conversation, and follow tangents that lead down productive paths.

When setting up the interview, let the subject know approximately how long the interview will take. People are usually willing to talk within a specified time. Be punctual and respect the subject's schedule. Choose an environment in which your subject will be most comfortable. I like to interview people where they are most natural and relaxed, in their homes or in their places of work. I once interviewed a florist in his truck as he drove around picking up supplies and making deliveries.

Good interviewers are courteous but assertive, professional and objective, but interested and determined. Show your professionalism by having your questions and equipment organized ahead of time. Have your tape recorder loaded and ready before you go to the interview, and have blank tapes and back-up batteries on hand. Fumbling with a tape recorder makes you look like an amateur.

Be honest with subjects about your work. Let them know if you're working on spec or on assignment. Tell them that what they say may or may not be quoted in print. Some people want to be quoted or referred to by name and may feel slighted if they're not.

Whether you agree or disagree with what your subject says, keep your opinions to yourself. Even though you are—as you should be— well informed about the topic under discussion, let your subjects feel that *they* are the experts, leading you through a complex topic or issue.

Follow the basic rules of listening. Wait until the subject finishes speaking before asking the next question. You can't talk and listen at the same time. Occasionally, you may interject a brief comment to show you are paying attention. But don't talk too much; the subject's comments are more important than yours. The idea is to control the conversation without dominating it. Looking at your watch or staring into space are sure signs of boredom.

Of course, not all interviews run smoothly. It's up to you to keep an interview on track and get the information you want.

When the subject goes off on an innocent tangent, try to get him or her back on track by asking your prepared questions. If the subject says he doesn't understand a question, repeat or rephrase it. When the subject answers in monosyllables, try to draw him or her out by saying something like, *I'm still not quite clear about. . . ,* or, *I don't mean to repeat myself, but. . . ,* then repeat the question. Or ask questions that begin with "why" or "how." This forces the subject to define a position or to elaborate on it.

With wary subjects, you can use what some reporters call the "Columbo technique" (named for the TV detective): As you're headed for the door, turn around and say, *Oh, by the way. . . .* The subject is often disarmed at this point and may offer further information.

A technique that sometimes works well with reluctant subjects is the third-person technique: Instead of asking questions, say, *I suppose you've heard that your opponent said. . . ,* or, *I suppose your critics could say. . . .*

Sometimes you may have to go "off the record" to get an interviewee to open up. Doing so can provide leads or facts that you verify with other sources. While off the record, you can say, *I like what you just said; can I use that part?* If you've established a good rapport, the subject will often consent.

Professional ethics dictate that if you promise to go off the record, you keep your promise. If you publish facts or opinions that you agreed not to, you may be infringing on privacy rights, and, at the least, betraying a trust.

End your interview by asking, *Is there anything else you'd like to tell me?* Give the subject a chance to help you. And be sure you can get in touch with your subject if you have questions that arise while you're writing the article. When working on a piece for which the subject is the main resource, I usually refer to it as "our article," establishing a feeling of collaboration. Then if at some later time I have to return for further information or confirmation, the subject is usually more willing to continue working with someone viewed as a collaborator, rather than an interviewer.

Review your notes as soon as possible after the interview, while it's still fresh in your mind; many valuable quotes and facts have been lost because writers couldn't read their own scribbles.

Generally, it's a mistake to show subjects your article before it's published. Most people will want to edit it. They will say things like, "I didn't say that," or, "I didn't really mean to say that." Their perspective may be distorted by their own self-interest. Check with your subject if you have any doubts about facts, direct quotes, or paraphrases, but not for tone or style. But in the end, the finished piece is your responsibility.

Keep in mind that an interview is a conversation between two people. The better you relate to your subject, the better your interview, and ultimately, your article.

# 74

# HOW TO WRITE AND SELL A SPORTS ARTICLE

## BY TOL BROOME

WHAT WOULD YOU SAY ABOUT A MARKET THAT IS HUNGRY for quality writing and for which most free lancers can write? A market that includes books, newspapers, newspaper weeklies, annuals, programs and promotional material, as well as more than 600 regularly published magazines?

You may be surprised to learn that the market to which I am referring is the sports market. The arena of sportswriting has broadened considerably in recent years and now includes opportunities for publication not only in the big three sports—baseball, basketball and football—but also on a host of other topics: hockey, running, boating, skiing, sports medicine, and sports-card collecting, to name just a few.

Here is a step-by-step approach that I have used to publish several dozen sports articles in a variety of publications over the past six years:

## The game plan

There are two key rules of thumb to follow to generate ideas. First, be a fan. You will come up with a healthy number of ideas from attending or participating in sporting events, watching sports on television, and reading about athletic events.

A couple of years ago while I was watching a 49ers game on television, the commentators began to discuss Roger Craig's amazing year in 1985. That made me wonder how that sensational season stacked up against superlative performances by other running backs. A good bit of research answered my question and resulted in the publication of an article, " Running For Glory: The Greatest Seasons Ever For Running Backs," in *Sports Collectors Digest*.

The second "rule" is to keep current and be aware of sports anniversaries. For example, in 1991 on the 50th anniversary of Joe DiMaggio's 56-game hitting streak and the 30th anniversary of Roger Maris's 61 homers, interesting pieces appeared in publications all over the country. But after that, these articles were no longer timely or salable.

In choosing your angle, avoid covering a sporting event strictly from a news angle, as editors have staff writers who do that. What angles are in demand? Personal experience pieces, particularly for specialty magazines (i.e. boating, skiing and soccer), are marketable, and a fresh statistical analysis angle will often draw editor interest.

Additionally, editors need interviews and player profiles. Find out if any current or retired athletes live in or near your hometown off-season. You need not limit yourself to professional athletes. Many publications are just as interested in material on such amateurs as an outstanding Little Leaguer or a successful disabled athlete.

## Pre-game warm-up (research)

I cannot stress enough the importance of thorough research. A good place to start is your local library, where you will find reference books, magazines, newspapers, biographies, clipping files, and a wealth of other sources. You can also get needed information from interviews, letters to Halls of Fame (the major sports halls have extensive libraries, and the information in them is readily available to the public), daily newspapers, television announcers, and even the backs of sports cards.

If you plan to write sports articles regularly, buy some good reference books, such as sports encyclopedias. Not only will this save time, but they will also come in handy when you get an idea at midnight, and you just have to know how many touchdown passes Joe Montana threw from 1984–87.

The accuracy of your research can either help establish or weaken your credibility. If you aren't sure about a statistic or fact, look it up. Sports article readers (and editors) are notorious for their close scrutiny of facts and figures. If you guess wrong about the number of races won by Secretariat, the editor will notice it, and the likelihood of publication will be greatly diminished.

## The first quarter (title and lead)

Your article's title is its calling card, so make it count. The title can be a good place for a pun or alliteration. For instance, for a player profile on Isiah Thomas, how about, "There's No Doubting This Thomas," or "Isiah Profits From His NBA Success."

The lead is at least as important as the title. I have been successful with different approaches, including quotes, questions, word definitions, little-known facts and anecdotes. Your lead will often tell the editor whether or not it's worth his or her time to read on, so be innovative.

### The second quarter (theme)

This is easy to overlook. Your theme statement may be one short transitional paragraph or it may be part of your lead. Just be sure you inform the reader of your slant before you proceed to the body of the article.

### The third quarter (the body)

In a closely contested sports event, the third quarter is often the key in determining the outcome. The team that is most effective in carrying out its game plan will nearly always gain the upper hand in the critical third quarter.

The same holds true in sportswriting. If the editor likes your title, lead, and slant enough to keep reading to this point, a well-organized presentation of your key points in the third quarter may determine whether or not your piece is accepted.

Begin with your strongest point first—a "scoop" about an athlete in a player profile or one or two key facts in a statistical analysis piece.

Editors like quotes, anecdotes, examples, and analogies interspersed throughout a manuscript. And the use of some jargon in a sports article is a plus, because it demonstrates "inside" knowledge of your subject. But don't overdo it, or your article will seem trite and will likely doom your chances of acceptance.

### The fourth quarter (the conclusion)

Your conclusion is a good place to use a quote, a pun, or an anecdote. For instance, if you have written a player profile on James Worthy, try something like, "James's three championship rings and 18.6 career scoring average should some day make him Worthy of induction into the Basketball Hall of Fame." A clever conclusion will help the reader and the editor remember your article.

## Overtime (sidebars)

Sidebars are used extensively in sportswriting. They are particularly effective for statistical information that might otherwise "clutter" your article—charts, rankings, graphs, and lists.

For example, for the article on the greatest years for running backs, I used sidebars to present the extensive statistical comparisons. This allowed me to provide the reader with "user-friendly" visual aids in comparing the campaigns.

## Post-game wrap-up (editing)

Contrary to popular belief, all sports publication editors pay very close attention to diction, grammar, spelling, style, length, transitions, and flow. Therefore, before you attempt to submit your article for publication, read it over several times, and don't be afraid to slash, change, add, and rewrite. You may also want to consider letting someone else edit your piece, whether or not he or she is a sports fan. This can help you hone language, grammar, and even spelling.

As in other markets, it is a good idea to obtain writers' guidelines from sports publications for which you hope to write, and to query them with prospective ideas.

The sports market is extensive, ranging from *Sports Illustrated* (with a circulation of 3.6 million) to specialized publications with circulations of only a few hundred. Most use some free-lance material, but many of the national publications require agent representation, references and/or extensive experience.

For this reason, I recommend that you start with relatively small markets. My first sports article, published in a now-defunct local sports weekly, brought me $10.00. But it was a start, and led to bigger and better sales. Other possible markets for entry-level writers include minor league baseball programs (there are 177 nationwide), college annuals and programs (try your alma mater), and specialty publications. Newspapers are not a good market, because they use staff writers and extensive national wire services.

The best source of potential markets is *Sports Market Place,* a reference guide (available in major libraries) which lists 478 sports publications in 53 specialty markets, as well as 142 general sports publications. You may also want to try obtaining information about or even joining a writers' association, such as the Outdoor Writers' Association of America (2017 Cato Avenue, Suite 101, State College, PA 16801-2768).

# 75

## WRITING A PUBLISHABLE
## HEALTH ARTICLE

### BY JOAN LIPPERT

IF ONLY YOU WERE A DOCTOR, RESEARCHER, DIETITIAN, OR OTHER HEALTH PROFESSIONAL—you would be truly qualified to write about health, right?

If you're none of these, you have a delightful surprise coming: Your very lack of expertise in the health field may make you ideal as a health writer. You wonder about the same things your readers wonder about, and you express the answers in simple words the reader can understand. Consider well-known health writer Jane Brody. She is not a doctor, nor does she have a doctorate in any medical subject; she's just a journalist like you and me, a very thorough reporter who knows how to translate the esoterica of medicine into language that Aunt Enid in Hicksville can understand. She is a professional writer who thinks of her audience first. It's qualities like these that can endear you to editors.

What besides a sense of your audience will you need to write about health? With an objective and intense interest in the way the body works, a good medical dictionary, and the pointers that follow, you can probably find an opening in the health-writing field.

***Start small.*** If you have not written about health before, consider a short news item as your first project. Fortunately, proposing one health news item or even a group of them does not have to mean a big investment of your time or the time of a busy doctor. You can write a few sentences about a medical advance—enough to get a go-ahead from an editor—simply from reading a health journal, an abstract (article summary or preview), press release or speech. Once you have a go-ahead from an editor for the subject you propose, you can go after the interview. (Many doctors will not take the time to speak with you until you have an actual assignment, and many editors prefer a short query to an unsolicited submission.) Magazines typically pay little for news items, and newspapers even less, but it is a good place for a novice to start.

Another way to break into the health-writing field is with a personal experience piece: how you lost the weight, climbed the mountain, figured out what was ailing you, for example. A number of magazines publish first-person articles. On the down side, you will probably need good photography to illustrate your story, and most of us do not have a Leica loaded with slide film as a constant companion. Also, your personal experiences suitable for such articles are probably limited.

A few magazines—those with a low editorial budget—will let a beginner start with a full-length article. You will probably have to do the piece on spec, and you will not make a lot of money, but if all goes well, you will get a few credits you can use to open other doors. Make your article query specific about the subject you are proposing. A common error new health writers make is vagueness: "How about an article on sugar?" is not enough to sell your idea. It's very likely that the editor has already published an article on the subject you are proposing and will want to know what makes your approach new and different.

*Seek out the newest and the best information.* The highest level health magazines—*American Health, Health, Men's Health*—are looking for news on the cutting edge, available in news reports or by attending the meetings that many professional associations hold. The American Cancer Society, the American Academy of Ophthalmology, the American College of Allergy and Immunology, and a hundred other associations have meetings each year to which the media are invited, and magazines cannot possibly send staffers to cover them all. You can also call up experts you know or who live close by and ask about new developments in their field. It takes real expertise to recognize and report health news gathered on the spot.

A beginner may have better luck combing the newspapers for health news or getting information where the newspaper reports get it: from the medical journals. These can be impenetrable, but do not be discouraged. Get out your medical dictionary and look up unfamiliar terms and words. Read and reread until you understand the study's hypothesis and conclusions. Even top medical writers wipe their brows frequently when reading medical journal articles. And remember that you do not have to limit yourself to heavy medicine. The health field also includes nutrition, psychology, fitness, pediatrics, even beauty science. Journals dealing with these subjects are often more readable.

If your local library has no medical or health journals, try a hospital or university library. For a fee, some libraries can hook you up with Medline, a computer service that gives instant access to a large medical index.

Cable TV is another window on the medical world. On Sundays in New York, Lifetime Medical Television airs health shows all evening. Among the subjects are obstetrics and gynecology, cardiology, pediatrics, and a roundup called "Physicians' Journal Update." These programs are not always up to the minute in terms of news, but if you have never seen streptokinase dissolve a blood clot in a coronary artery or witnessed a knee operation, shows like these offer viewers a great education.

Another approach is to read a roundup of medical journal articles. Two good ones are *Medical Abstracts,* a monthly four-page newsletter that reviews about thirty journal articles per issue, and *Science News,* which publishes fewer journal reviews but includes meeting coverage. Since these are secondary sources, they are not as up to date as journals themselves.

Major organizations such as the American Dental Association, the American Society of Plastic and Reconstructive Surgeons, the American Academy of Dermatology, and the American Academy of Pediatrics issue press releases regularly, and these are usually written in delightfully plain language. The catches are that getting yourself on the mailing lists can take time, and the current economic crunch has made some groups reluctant to add new names to their free lists.

Books are not good information sources for health articles, because the health field is dynamic. A new finding can supplant an old one before a book is in galleys. A few years ago, studies called oat bran a cholesterol-lowering miracle food—remember? In the short time since, oat bran fell from favor, was resurrected, and was then challenged by several other foods. (The jury is still out.) If you use books for research, do so only for background for your item or article. Avoid medical books more than five years old, and use journal studies more than a year old with caution.

***Study the publication you are aiming for.*** It's essential to examine a magazine's audience to understand the "voice" used to address them. How much do the editors assume the readers already know? Is the presentation newspaper-style direct, focusing strictly on *who, what, why, when,* and *where*? Or is it lighter? Is there room for outright humor? Is the writing geared to men, women, or both? What age and demographic group does the publication serve? These factors should be taken into account in any interviews you conduct, and in the way you write.

***Think up smart questions.*** Do *not* begin your interview expecting a researcher to spoon-feed you a basic course, or you will lose your source's good will fast! Study all available print material in advance, and ask only the questions you have been unable to answer for yourself.

***How to get the experts.*** Some health professionals are more interested in fame and fortune than in fact. Some have axes to grind or prey upon people's desperation. Public relations firms can give you access to luminaries who might otherwise be unavailable, but you can find more accessible sources by working with the researchers listed at the head of an article in a medical journal. You can also find reputable experts to interview through well-known universities, major hospitals, established organizations, and famous research centers—for example, the American Heart Association or the Memorial Sloan-Kettering Cancer Center. The Encyclopedia of Associations can help you locate referring groups; when you call, ask for Communications, Public Affairs, or Public Relations.

***Find the real science.*** The best health reporting is based on studies and research; the worst is based on anecdote, or one person's story. Say someone's malignant tumor disappears after he ate half a pound of dandelions vinaigrette every day. You could draw two conclusions from this "anecdotal evidence": 1) dandelions vinaigrette cure cancer, or 2) the remission of the cancer and the eating of the salad were coincidental. (The correct answer is probably 2!) Look for studies that involve large numbers of people and a control group.

***Hedge.*** It is far wiser to say that a therapy "may help" or that "in this study, the treatment was effective in four of every five patients" than to trumpet a new finding as the cure-all. Careful wording of findings can save you a lot of grief later, particularly when a new study may come out that proves your current study false. Just a few years ago, polyurethane-covered breast implants were state of the art. When I wrote about them back then, my editor and I inserted wording to the effect that their safety had not yet been thoroughly evaluated, and that a woman considering them should discuss all the options with her doctor. A good thing, too, since now these breast implants have been linked with cancer. A wise health editor will include a simple sentence that leaves room for change, uncertainty, or new information.

***Do a rigorous spell-check.*** As an editor, I once received manuscripts with the words "ophthalmology" and "wheal" misspelled (as "opthamology" and "wheel"). While I was not at liberty to throw these manuscripts into the garbage—they were assignments—in my alarm and distrust I gave the careless writers a rough going-over of facts and figures. It was clear to me that neither writer had ever looked carefully at appropriate print materials. An editor may tolerate a typo or two, but misspelling a key medical word should ring an alarm bell.

***Complete your project ahead of deadline.*** If you can, finish your item or article early and set it aside. A few days later, pick it up and read it from a reader's viewpoint. Is the writing clear, logical, accessible? Have you defined terms the reader might not understand? Have you written for the publication's specific audience? Health writing, particularly, benefits from this kind of distancing because it is so easy for a writer to slip into the "medicalese" your sources speak.

***Go with your gut.*** If after you have finalized your piece an inner voice tells you that something seems wrong with what you have written, pay careful attention to it. Have you left something out? Have you contradicted yourself? Do you not quite understand what you have heard and written down? Did you get strange vibes from a source? Edit or reinterview at this point. Better that you ask questions of yourself than have an editor spot weaknesses in your work.

Economic times are tough; magazines, including health magazines, have been known to die suddenly. But it may hearten you to consider that health information is something people cannot live without. Many of the magazines that survive will carry health columns because readers like them. So giving health writing a try may turn out to be a worthwhile investment.

375

Another reason to try your hand at health is more personal: The field is fascinating. Unlike other areas of reporting, in which we repackage the same old information and human situations, health is a science that really is advancing into the unknown. Just think of the changes in the field over the last decade or two: We have seen the benefit of aerobic exercise, the harm of cholesterol, the potential of organ transplants, the promise of new diagnostic techniques like Doppler ultrasound (which allows you to see blood moving through the vessels). In the decades to come, you could be reporting on findings that are just as exciting and truly new, and may have a chance to do some futurecasting: to guess what is coming next and be there when the story breaks. You could have the privilege of speaking with some of the greatest thinkers of our time. You could be an educator who helps people.

That short news item, article, or personal experience piece you take a chance on today could mark the beginning of a long and satisfying career.

# 76

# How to Write a Profile

## By Lou Ann Walker

One of the first profiles I ever read was of Candice Bergen. I remember every detail vividly: what her room looked like, how she was dressed, the ideas she found frivolous, what mattered to her. As a teenager, I thought young Bergen was a wonderful role model. She believed in hard work and challenge, and ignoring her detractors. Not long ago, *New York Woman* magazine asked me to write a cover story on Bergen. I became very nervous. She was too glamorous to talk to, I thought. After the reams of copy that had been written about her, how could I make her come alive on paper? And then I reminded myself that I was curious about how she had developed over the years. I realized the challenge was to capture her essence, to rediscover what had enthralled me before, and to present Bergen in a new way.

To write a profile, you don't have the muss or fuss of figuring out what your topic is. You have a finite number of facts, and you can't get lost in too many subplots. Your job is to make the reader think that he or she has had a long, candlelit dinner full of shared intimacies and revelations. And, yes, usually laughs. Using your interview and research materials can be a far more creative and enriching process than writing most journalistic stories. After all, you're a detective, a psychologist, and a sage all rolled into one. The more talents you have, the better. Getting a *good* interview is 75% of the battle. Here are some tactics for making a profile come alive.

### Getting the interview right

The interview, I've come to realize, is really a skillfully crafted performance, a *pas de deux*. Here are some tips for making the "dance" work.

1. Be creative in setting up an interview. Sometimes, particularly

with celebrities, I'll have an intermediary, a press agent, or a magazine editor tell me some of the activities the subject likes. Then, if I call the subject directly, I'm armed with a notion of the kind of article I'll do, and some of the topics I'll focus on. Usually home turf for the person is best. An office is all right, but often people are stiffer in that setting. Hollywood child star and comedienne Jane Withers taught me that if you're going to a restaurant, call ahead and ask the maitre d' for the quietest table.

One of the best tactics is to stay with a person all day, particularly on a movie set. Academy Award winning actress Marlee Matlin allowed me to tag along on a free day, and we had a most illuminating time. I let her drive me all over Los Angeles. (Frankly, it was a death-defying stunt. She's so excitable that when she uses her hands to sign, she often takes both of them off the steering wheel.) She took me to visit her elderly grandmother in a nursing home, and I could see the family affection. We went to a Beverly Hills restaurant where she used her TTY (telecommunications device for the deaf) on the phone at our table to have a conversation with her boyfriend, an actor on location in Canada. It was these small moments that made our interview memorable.

2. Become friendly with the people who work with the person you're interviewing. Charming a secretary who is snooty can lead to important revelations. One such secretary confided in me that the actress I was interviewing was just breaking up with a man and dating someone new. I never would have found that out if I hadn't done a little buttering up.

3. Research, research, research. *Before* you meet the person, you need to know everything you can. There is a warmth, a relaxation, that subjects undergo when writers have done their homework. Knowing background can help you read deeper meanings into answers.

4. Make a list of questions. For days before an interview, I ask myself what I want to know about the subject. Why does this politician care so much about drug task forces? Was someone in his family mugged? I think up questions while I'm driving around, or jogging. I rarely look at my list during the interview, but it's there just in case there's an awkward silence or the subject freezes up.

5. Don't be afraid to ask dumb questions. I've gotten many of my best answers that way. Keep a few stock questions in reserve for dry spells. "What are your best qualities? What are your worst?" might not

seem to have Pulitzer-winning potential, yet you'd be surprised where they may lead. Don't be afraid of silences, by the way. People often free associate in riveting ways. My favorite question is: "Why?"

6. Go with the conversational flow. If someone starts opening up about the worst day of his or her life, don't suddenly say, "What year were you born?"

7. The number one worst sin of interviewers: Talking too much. Many interviewers are really more interested in talking about themselves than they are in the subject. Your time with a person is precious. Use it to find out what you need for your profile. Being a bit forthcoming is useful, but Joe DiMaggio would probably not be terribly interested in your son's Little League score.

8. Play poker. In other words, don't pounce on perceived indiscretions on your subject's part. Stay cool, and later on bring up that name your subject dropped to find out what response you get. Don't get testy if there are interruptions. You might get revealing material from an overheard phone conversation.

9. Be compulsive. I use a tape recorder and write notes at the same time. I know of too many instances when batteries died, and I've also discovered that background noise drowns out a person's voice. It's better to have notes than nothing at all. But develop the technique of writing while looking your subject square in the eye as much as possible. Also, at some point, you must be compulsive about facts; you have to figure out if the explorer moved to New Zealand before or after he lived in Timbuktu.

10. Don't waste time. The best interviews aren't necessarily the longest. Use your judgment. Several shorter interviews are probably better for the subject than one marathon. Too much information can be hard to sift through. And you'll repeat yourself. But don't be shortchanged. Before leaving an interview, ask the person for a number where he or she can be reached if you have more questions or need to check some facts.

11. Ask about friends or acquaintances you can talk to. It's useful to interview other well-known people about a celebrity, but they'll probably give you pat answers. An old high school pal or college roommate will often provide more illuminating material. Ask to look at photo albums. Or places where certain events took place.

12. Never be intimidated. Remember, the subject, no matter how

important, had traumas and defeats as well as successes. And whether it was good or bad, most people like talking about their childhood. You don't have to be ingratiating. Sometimes winning a subject's trust means shaking the person up a bit or disagreeing with a point. As an interviewer, you're like a psychologist, figuring out what makes that person tick. Use your knowledge of human nature every way you can. There are times when you need to be confrontational, say with a senator who has been stripped of his congressional seat. But you don't need to be argumentative while interviewing a puppeteer for the local paper. Have a good understanding of what your editor wants.

13. Some time ago *The New Yorker* ran a two-part article by Janet Malcolm about the relationship between a writer and his subject. Malcolm's premise is that an interviewer is a seducer, then betrays the subject with what is written. Certainly there's an element of that in a story. But it's also true that many subjects are seducing writers, trying to manipulate the portrait. Be prepared for such seduction. If someone says: "You're going to write a nice article, aren't you?" don't dissemble. Be ready to say: "I'm going to write a fair piece."

14. Get people to be specific. Ask for examples. Most people talk in generalities to reporters. They think they sound more intelligent when, in actuality, it just makes for a dry story. You need anecdotes and details. If someone says, "I'm a very poor storyteller," your retort should be, "Give me an example." That, surprisingly enough, can turn out to be, "Well, when I met Winston Churchill . . ."

15. Observe and make notes about everything. Jot down the person's eye color, what photos are on the desk, the type of decor. After I walk out the door I usually stand in the hallway or sit in my car writing down impressions while they're still fresh.

## Capturing the person on paper

1. Get reacquainted with the person. I generally type out all my notes, even if it takes a lot of time, as a way of imagining myself with the subject again. Usually when I'm typing, lines or images stand out, and I can tell immediately what the beginning and end of the piece will be.

2. Play around with structure. You're telling a story. Make it entertaining. Read other profiles for techniques for weaving together background with the present. It's just plain boring to write: "So-and-so was born in 1946. . . ." You want bounce and verve in your writing, even if

your subject was dry as dust. Make a dateline for the person. Or a chart to show the ups and downs of someone's career. Or maybe make a list of memorable quotations. I recently interviewed a 91-year-old woman doctor who still sees patients every day. She had so many crusty quotes, I couldn't possibly fit them all in. So I settled on a box with her "prescriptions" for modern man. It worked wonderfully well.

3. Make associations. Do some free-floating thinking about figures in history whose careers parallel your subject's. Or that your character looks like Meryl Streep but acts like Madonna. Push your creative buttons. Otherwise, you're a quotation box.

4. Examine the text closely. Throw out the canned responses immediately—unless you're making the point that someone is in a rut. Having read published articles about your subject, you know what is really fresh. Scan the answers for themes. For example, a television producer I recently interviewed used the word "control" over and over again. Having won a battle with cancer, she was re-establishing dominion over her own life. From the opening sentence, I built the piece around this producer's tug-of-war with life.

5. Give your analysis. The reader wants you to explain how or why the subject said what he or she said. You are the guide in this expedition. So lead.

6. Vary the tone. No life is all happy or sad. No profile should sound the same note again and again.

7. An infallible rule: You can never, ever tell how people are going to react to what you write. I did a tough portrait of a well-known actress. It was not a puff piece, but I was absolutely scrupulous in telling the truth about her failures and successes. She later wrote me it was the best article ever written about her. Her husband thought so, too. Intelligent subjects don't want to come off sounding like Milquetoasts. They want you to come up with original angles, not press release rehashes. It's balance you're after.

Finally, advice no one else will give you: Don't be afraid to turn down an assignment if you have negative feelings about the subject. I'm not saying you have to like the person you're interviewing. Tension can be good. But if you have no respect for the person's work or beliefs, then the interview will suffer.

The best way to be true to an interview subject is to be true to yourself. An editor I often write for recently told me that she realized my secret. I'm wide-eyed and non-judgmental, so people just open up to me. It can be a curse in a supermarket line or on a long plane trip, but I've come to realize it's one of my strong suits. If you're an enthusiastic person, there's no sense trying to mask that with a somber demeanor. If you're serious, don't try for the jollies. Just channel your interests and your behavior to get and write the best story you can.

Over the course of time, the people who write the best profiles are the ones who are, quite simply, captivated by others: That's what makes almost all wonderful writers. Simple fascination with humankind.

# 77

# WRITING BIOGRAPHIES: THE PROBLEMS AND THE PROCESS

## BY KATHERINE RAMSLAND

BIOGRAPHERS ARE FIXED ON THEIR heroes in a very peculiar manner," said Sigmund Freud. By that he meant that writing a biography is motivated by some psychological preoccupation. It is difficult for biographers to sustain such demanding work without intense emotional involvement with their subjects. Biographers must be prepared to make a major commitment, to immerse themselves totally in the point of view of another person so they can recreate that person's life with accuracy.

### Choosing the subject

Most biographers write about their subjects because they know them, admire them, or believe a biography will make a contribution. Some biographers rework old material in new ways, and much of the "detective work" is already done. Those who introduce the subject for the first time must spend considerable effort collecting data. Writers of "authorized" biographies have access to private papers, while others have to struggle along without such cooperation. If the subject is living, the biographer faces problems not a factor when the subject is dead.

The choice of subject is also dictated by publishers' criteria. An academic publisher may want a scholarly book on an existing body of information, emphasizing literary criticism, while a commercial biography must demonstrate its market value, i.e., its readability and appeal to the general reader.

### Dealing with research

Basically, there are two methods for dealing with facts. One is to collect them first, and organize them later. This prevents premature interpretations from highlighting some facts over others. The second method involves collecting just enough facts to set up a general guide for future directions. Your own personality will dictate which one you choose.

Both methods benefit from an active and passive phase. After a flurry of fact-gathering, allow your unconscious mind to go to work to reveal meaningful patterns as well as gaps in research. To be understood, facts must be absorbed and digested in the context of other information.

Inevitably you will be faced with an inordinate amount of data that needs careful organization and interpretation. Facts are malleable; they can be magnified out of proportion, interpreted out of context, minimized or suppressed. The first rule is to resist the impulse to appear omniscient. No person's life can be known completely. At best, a biography is a *perspective* based on the biographer's vision. Undocumented conjecture, while sometimes necessary, should be so acknowledged. The point is to create from raw data an organic portrait that reveals the significance of the subject's life or work. Not all of the facts will contribute to this goal. However, an abundance of facts must still be gathered to pinpoint those that give shape to how the subject's life was lived. There are many sources for locating that material.

1. Information may already be written in archives, letters, diaries, media profiles, unpublished manuscripts, and in earlier biographies.

2. Interviewing people who had personal acquaintance with the subject is essential. If the subject is living, he or she may give you a list. Otherwise, surviving family members can be helpful. Friends and relatives provide perspectives that can corroborate or broaden your understanding. Sometimes these contacts will be made over the phone or by mail, but often they will be face-to-face. Some people will be eager to cooperate; others may be reluctant. Friends will seek to protect, enemies to malign. You need tact, patience, persistence and discernment to obtain as many perspectives as possible. Prepare questions ahead of time. In the immediacy of an interview it is easy to forget points you wanted to raise.

All comments should be recorded, if possible. Do not count on being able to reconstruct a conversation later, especially as you begin to accumulate data. Biographies evolve. Your first impressions may not correspond to later insights. I am constantly surprised as I read over transcripts how items jump out at me that I had earlier overlooked. Had I just taken notes, those items would have been lost to me. Always ask permission to record, even over the phone. Be prepared to take notes if they say no.

3. Visit places that have meaning for the subject. Anne Rice lived in New Orleans. In writing her biography, I walked the streets she walked, and experiencing some of the same sensory impressions as she did—the smell of magnolias, the noise of rattling streetcars—gave me a perspective on her childhood.

4. You should have some grasp of the social and cultural influences that affected the subject.

5. General reference books on relevant subjects are helpful. I read books on psychology, sociology, alcoholism, and creativity to enhance understanding. Also, reading short profiles of other personalities can suggest new directions and help the writer create vivid impressions.

6. Reading books that influenced your subject can yield surprising insights.

7. Your own intuition is important. Note your emotional connections. You may have to make reasonable guesses about the subject's motivations, and using the facts you *do* have along with your intuition can help you make logical associations.

8. Photographs can reveal a great deal about a person's character and emotional development.

The idea of research is to find unifying themes among seemingly contradictory events or actions. Keep your eyes open for ideas or events that changed the person's *perspective* so you can monitor his or her emotional pulse. The points at which subjects' lives are most vivid to them are the points with which readers will identify most.

There is no end to the amount of factual data you can accumulate. One way you can organize and focus this research is to make an outline that provides logical progression and continuity. And you can structure your outline by choosing a biographical model.

**Choosing a model**

Biography involves both content and form. The form is like the plot of a novel: it makes the diverse elements work together to serve the purpose of the whole. Facts and quotes must be accurate, and critical interpretations interesting, but there is a consensus among contemporary biographers that there be enough flexibility of form to allow a biographer to make a work unique. In other words, biographers are free to give their books an *aesthetic* unity and to interpret the stages of this subject. The choice of a model is important to this process.

1. Interpretive models guide readers, typically through psychological explanations, to reveal the motives that make sense of the subject's choices.

2. Objective models use all the known facts to document how the subject lived. This method is viewed more as historical than artistic.

3. Dramatic models *show* the subject through fictional devices, telling the life story through a series of vignettes and events. Virginia Woolf first coined the term "creative fact" to describe a fact that suggests or creates mood and character, even as it provides information. In such biographies, the "facts" are interpreted by the writer's imagination, thus replacing objectivity with intimacy. These biographies read more like novels than factual nonfiction.

The strength of a biography lies in creating the moments that reveal the most profound psychological truths—the motivations, transformations, and points of conflict—in the life of the subject. Biographers make choices in their writing as did the subjects in their lives. The writer's goal is to enable readers to *see* the subjects and to grasp how they acted and reacted, intentionally and unconsciously.

Many biographers make use of fictional devices, constructing their books with "plots," and paying special attention to creating tone and mood. Chapter endings may be "cliff-hangers," and using anecdotes with dialogue can provide details.

Ask yourself how closely you should stick to "just the facts." Dramatic styles take more license than objective styles. However, even the most fact-oriented biography can utilize fictional devices to create tension, advance the story, give information and reveal character.

For example, dialogue and physical impressions can be constructed from memory or from recordings to create scenes at important moments in the lives of the subjects. You can write dialogue by quoting from an exchange of letters, or if the subject is living, use what he or she recalls in dialogue.

Short chapters can give the feeling of tension, impatience, and urgency, as does Gerald Clarke's *Capote*. Metaphors and imagery deliver powerful impressions. The idea is to reveal the essence of the person, and to accomplish this, figurative language is sometimes superior to facts.

### Uncomfortable discoveries

You may be confronted with information about your subject that gives you pause: sexual misconduct, cruelty, bigotry or marital discord. Perhaps the subject has even created a false picture of his or her life to manipulate public opinion. If the subject is still alive, and especially if he or she is cooperative, such information will raise important questions. How much must be revealed to facilitate an understanding of the person's life and how much is really just gratuitous gossip?

Arguments can be made for either side. Advocates of full revelation might consider one of the following points:

1. On the "objective" model, suppressing anything is an interpretation; to achieve objectivity, *all* facts must be revealed.

2. The dramatic model feeds on personal information—the more personal the better—to make the work truly vivid.

3. Some biographers idealize their subjects and justify avoiding the "dark" areas as unimportant in order to keep to their view of the person. For example, it was once thought that biographies of women should not disclose (for the "higher purposes" of society) information that detracted from their femininity. Carol Heilbrun, in *Writing a Woman's Life,* disagrees. She urges biographers of women to include "unfeminine" anger, dissatisfaction with roles, and quests for sensuality and power. Presenting the *whole* person takes priority.

Yet there are also arguments *against* full disclosure. For example:

1. People still alive may be harmed by the revelations.

2. Gossip detracts from scholarship. If the biographer reveals the information only to play up scandal, then he or she is not playing fair—(though including this type of information often adds to the readability of the book).

There are no easy answers to writing biography, and authors must decide for themselves what information will best serve their purpose. The purpose of biography is not to "spill the beans," but to deliver an interesting and comprehensive portrait guided by principles, imposed partly by the author and partly by the need for continuity, accuracy, depth, and focus.

387

# 78

# How to Write a How-to That Sells

## By Gail Luttman

Any activity that interests you—from canoeing to cooking to collecting Civil War relics to cutting your own hair—is a potential how-to article. And whether you are an expert or a novice, you are qualified to write about it.

**Where to start**

The most successful introductions to how-to pieces state a problem and then propose one or more possible solutions, perferably those relating to the seven basic human motivators.

**Ego**—Does your solution to the problem improve the way you look, the way you feel about yourself, your ability to relate to others?

**Economy**—Does it save money, protect the environment, improve quality without increasing cost?

**Health**—Does it give you more energy, promote safety practices, increase your psychological well-being?

**Romance**—Does it enhance sex appeal, create a cozy atmosphere, improve personal relationships?

**Family**—Does it entertain children, foster loyalty, help research family history?

**Leisure**—Does it enliven holiday activities, provide an engrossing hobby, help plan exciting vacations?

**Individuality**—Does the activity appeal to the universal desire for uniqueness by offering something new, different or better?

These motivators often overlap. A hobby may bring in income. Dieting may improve both health and self-image. An inexpensive bungalow of unusual construction may serve as a romantic retreat. The more motivators you appeal to, the greater interest you will generate in your how-to.

**Moving on**

After piquing the reader's interest, offer a brief explanation of what the activity involves, couched in enthusiastic words that inspire confidence. Can the skill be learned in five easy steps? Fifteen minutes a day? Does it require a special setting, or will a corner of the garage do? What special tools or materials are needed?

Rather than barrage readers at the beginning with a large number of tools or materials required, you may want to list them in a sidebar, a separate boxed-off article that accompanies the main story. Sidebars are a great way to include data or lengthy explanations without interrupting the narrative flow. Some editors favor articles with one, two, or even three sidebars if the article is very long or complex.

Definitions of unfamiliar terms might go into a vocabulary sidebar, especially when they are numerous; on the other hand, if special words are few or are easy to define, it is better to explain their meanings as you go along.

Whenever possible, describe new concepts by drawing a comparison with something familiar. In a piece about building stone walls, for example, a description of the proper consistency of mortar as "buttery" sparks instant recognition.

Complicated procedures don't seem quite as confusing when written up in short, uncomplicated sentences of the sort found in cookbooks. Explicitness also ensures clarity. Vague directions such as "measure out six to eight cups of water" or "cut two to three yards of string" leave the reader wondering which of the two stated amounts to use.

Clarity is also improved by separating general principles from specific procedures. If you are writing about how to build a chicken coop, for example, after the introductory remarks, explain how the layout and dimensions are established, then include some specific plans. In a how-to about cooking a Christmas goose, first describe how to roast the goose, then offer some favorite recipes. In that way you'll satisfy both the creative reader who likes to improvise and the less adventuresome reader who feels more comfortable with step-by-step instructions.

The final and best way to ensure clarity is with illustrations. The less commonplace the subject, the more important photographs and sketches become, and they are essential when dimensions are involved. In addition, the market is more receptive to illustrated how-tos. But don't despair if you are not an accomplished photographer or artist; many how-to magazines have illustrators who will enhance your article with clear, easy-to-follow illustrations.

## Organization

The subject of a how-to usually dictates whether to organize the steps chronologically or to start with simple procedures and work toward difficult ones. If two steps are to be taken at the same time, it is important to make that clear. In bread baking, for instance, point out that yeast should be softening in warm water while the other ingredients are being measured.

Repetition can help or hinder reader understanding. Too much repetition causes readers to lose interest. In a short article, a brief reference to the original explanation is usually all that's needed. But if the article is very long or complex and the explanation is relatively short, repetition is better than asking readers to flip pages back to find the required information.

Include a timetable for each step to help readers gauge their progress. How long does concrete take to set? Eggs to hatch? Wine to ferment? Do varying conditions influence timing? Can or should any deliberate measures be taken to speed things up or slow them down? What specific signs might the reader watch for as the project nears completion?

Finally, what can go wrong? Think twice before including a separate how-not-to section or a trouble-shooting sidebar. Faced with a long list of things that can go wrong, a reader might understandably wonder whether the whole thing is worth the bother. But, in general, as long as a how-to is clearly written and well organized, it doesn't hurt to point out danger spots along the way.

Research, including interviews with appropriate experts, supplies background that adds depth and authority to how-tos, thereby increasing reader interest and credibility. It also helps a writer discover whether his experiences are typical or not. If not, avoid making sweeping or questionable generalizations.

When consulting authoritative sources, watch out for regional variations in the terms and methods you plan to describe, especially when you're writing for a national magazine. Mention chicken wire and a southerner is likely to picture what the westerner calls lifestock fencing. Talk about reupholstering a divan or davenport, and there are readers who won't realize you are discussing a couch or a sofa. Before you write your article, look up alternative terminology from other areas.

## Voice

Of course, the target audience determines how to approach your subject. If you are describing a new weaving technique to experienced weavers, you may use standard terms freely without defining them. But you should define any words that are specific to the new technique and you should definitely explain why the new technique is worth learning.

It is your job as a how-to writer to make certain that all readers achieve the same level of information by the time they reach the heart of your piece, and to do it without talking down. You can manage this by pretending you are writing a detailed letter to an interested friend.

You will find your most effective how-to voice by writing your article as if you were addressing a particular person who engages you in especially lively conversation. If you can't think of anyone suitable, invent someone. By writing expressly for that single reader, real or fictitious, you will delight all your readers with the personal tone of your how-to.

## 79

# MASTERING THE CRAFT
# OF CRAFT WRITING

## BY BEVERLY L. PUTERBAUGH

A WRITER WHO CROCHETS, KNITS, QUILTS, PAINTS, CARVES, or performs any number of creative crafts as a hobby, may develop a new pattern or an original idea in the process. The original design and instruction are salable. The first question is: What is and what isn't an original design?

Any design that is truly your own from beginning to end is an original. It can be a design taken from two or more patterns of different sources and combined to make something completely new and different from either of the patterns used.

It cannot be a simple color or stitch change or a pattern from a previously published or printed source altered by merely adding or subtracting buttons, ribbons, or trims. Changing a painted or sewn design on something does not make it an original, even if it does improve the design.

You cannot give instructions for another person's original design unless you share the byline and the payment with her.

Do not submit items that use copyrighted characters. In other words, you cannot design an original craft and then paint or sew a Snoopy, Charlie Brown, Mickey Mouse, or Sesame Street figure on to your design. It is illegal to do so, and magazines cannot legally use these.

Most craft magazines like the personal touch—one crafter to another—and prefer articles in the active rather than the passive voice. Your manuscripts should be neatly typed, double-spaced; instructions must be accurate, simple and use the correct terms and abbreviations for each step. One way to make sure that your instructions are accurate is to make the object, following the directions in your typed manuscript.

All craft publications ask for a list of materials and tools needed for the project. For example, if a crochet hook or knitting needle is used, you must list the size of the needle. This is also true of a paint brush type and size or a saw blade. The list should include the amount of each type of material required, and an estimate of the cost (in round figures); for example, "under five dollars." The "less than" or "under" helps sell the idea. It's the old principle of $2.99 seeming less expensive than $3.00 to a buyer. After all, you must sell the editor first if you want to get the piece published. Then you must sell it to the readers so they will want to make the item.

If the materials are hard to find, tell the readers where they may be purchased, and make sure that any address or telephone number you list is accurate. It is discouraging to a crafter to be unable to locate the materials needed. The only thing worse is to have a mistake in the directions. Double-check before you submit your manuscript.

You must not assume or overestimate your reader's ability. Many of the people who will be making your item may never have tried that particular craft and know nothing about it. Craft people are known for trying different things, and therefore the instructions must be written for the knowledgeable reader as well as the novice.

Write each step so that the reader can follow the instructions from beginning to end without difficulty. Do not confuse the reader with complicated words or misplaced information.

Like many other magazines, craft publications have deadlines and lead times. If you have a piece about an Easter craft, for example, it should be in the mail by October. Christmas articles should be mailed no later than June.

Some craft publications require the completed sample of the object. Others ask for a good photograph, either in black and white or color. "A picture is worth a thousand words" isn't just a cliché; in the craft business, it's true. Photos or illustrations often "sell" an article. Make sure they are clear. You may want to hire a professional to take pictures or ask a friend who is a good photographer. Take several shots to make sure you have a few good ones. If after seeing the photo, an editor asks to see the completed object, send the one in the picture. Some publications keep the object, while others return it. Check the guidelines to be sure how each magazine handles submissions.

Besides their regular features, many craft magazines offer contests or "Pattern of the Month" opportunities. This is a good way to start. I once sent an article, photos, and illustrations to a magazine that offered $50 for patterns, if used. My article was accepted and the magazine asked if I had more. I ended up writing for them on a regular basis at $150 per article.

If you are a beginning writer, the national exposure in a craft magazine can lead you to other fields. After publishing a few craft-related articles, you will have clips that may help you sell to other types of publications. The first magazine article I had published was craft-related, and from there I have gone on to other fields. Because the instructions must be correct, writing craft articles will teach you to be accurate in all types of writing.

Payment varies from publication to publication: Some pay only in subscriptions, while others pay from $25 to $300, depending on the articles and such extras as photos, illustrations, and sidebars that you supply. Illustrations should be in black ink on white paper. Always write for guidelines. They will tell you what the editors need and want and how much they pay.

Check through several back issues of the magazine to see what kind of crafts are preferred. Also check for lengths of published articles. Length can vary from a few words (filler) up to a couple thousand words. Knowing this in advance could mean the difference between a sale and a rejection.

Some craft magazines cover a variety of crafts while others specialize in plastic canvas, crochet, needlepoint, woodworking, or some of the latest craft fads. Check these to see where your interest lies, and then craft your original object and manuscript to fit the need. Perhaps you already have an original design. Type it up and send it out.

Other topics that some craft magazines are interested in are: craft fairs, craft museums, craft villages, bazaar news, safety tips while crafting, marketing tips, organization of craft materials, craft rooms, and crafting as a business.

As a writer, you can use your "craftiness" and "creativity" to write a craft-related article. There is a need for people who can make things and who can also write about a particular craft. The sooner you learn the tricks of the trade, the sooner you will be selling to today's growing craft magazine market.

## Craft Writer's Checklist

- Have you included all the steps in the process to complete the product?
- Have you listed all materials and tools needed?
- Did you list the size of needles, hooks, brushes, or saw blades?
- If pattern pieces are illustrated, are they precise and will they fit together properly?
- Are measurements correct? Did you measure them with a standard measuring device?
- If using wood or fabric, should your instructions include grain lines?
- If using fabric or carpeting, should your instructions include nap directions?
- If using yarn or thread, did you list weight, amount, and color needed?
- Have you made a sample of the object from your directions?

Send a self-addressed, stamped envelope for writer's guidelines before submitting. Also check women's, juvenile, senior or retirement, city and regional, and general-interest magazines that use craft-related material.

# 80

## WITH DEFERENCE TO REFERENCE: A BIBLIOMANIAC'S TALE

### BY ROBERT M. WEAVER

I'M NOT ASHAMED TO ADMIT IT. I am a reference-book junky. Word books, fact books, phrase books, book books—if it's shelved in the reference section of the local bookstore, I start for my wallet. According to -*Ologies & -Isms,* edited by Laurence Urdang, Anne Ryle, and Tanya H. Lee (Gale Research Company), it's a textbook (or reference book) case of *bibliomania.*

When I decided to pursue the study of English literature and writing in college, the tools of my trade became words, phrases, and shelves of reference books; or, to be more accurate, a *shelf* of reference books. A quick inventory of my personal reference library at the time disclosed a collegiate dictionary, an ancient copy of Bartlett's *Familiar Quotations,* a three-volume paperback set consisting of a thesaurus, an abridged dictionary, and an antonym-and-synonym finder, Strunk and White's *Elements of Style,* and a 10-year-old Rand McNally *U.S. Road Atlas.* That basic collection sufficed well into my adult professional life as a corporate public relations writer. But, when I set out to become a free-lance magazine writer, I faced the sobering realization that my written words had to prove themselves all over again.

I tried to crush my creative insecurities with a battery of word books and other reference materials. At first, additions to my home library were reasonable enough: a quality, unabridged thesaurus, a 20th-century compendium of quotations, and a stylebook for occasional reference. I bought two: *The Associated Press Stylebook* was necessary for its journalistic viewpoint and The University of Chicago's *Manual of Style* for its academic slant.

Subsequent visits to the local bookstore produced a new world atlas, *Harper Dictionary of Foreign Terms,* and (perhaps thinking I still lacked enough style, or because it was on sale) *Webster's Standard American Style Manual.*

Warning lights should have been flashing. Slowly, but unequivocally, my selections began to stray from the standard reference materials and enter a vague realm of fringe classifications. I was becoming hooked on the endless varieties of occasionally quite helpful, but more often merely amusing, volumes of published information. My first expenditures in this twilight area were the most extravagant, but also the most justifiable: *The New York Public Library Book of Chronologies* and its *Desk Reference* have proved both useful and entertaining.

From there, I began to spin out of control, reaching out hungrily and desperately to other books that promised answers to all the whos, whats, whys, whens and wheres of the world: Joel Achenbach's *Why Things Are* (Ballantine); David Feldman's *Why Do Dogs Have Wet Noses, When Do Fish Sleep* and *Why Do Clocks Run Clockwise* (Perennial Library); David Macauley's *The Way Things Work* (Houghton Mifflin); Reginald Bragonier and David Fisher's *What's What* (Ballantine); Charles Panati's *The Browser's Book of Beginnings* (Houghton Mifflin), and later, his *Extraordinary Origins of Everyday Things* (Perennial Library).

Gleaning page after page of nugatory trivia, my lack of self-confidence, rather than subsiding, grew at a furious rate. So paranoid did I become about my gaps in knowledge, I added Judy Jones and William Wilson's *An Incomplete Education* (Ballantine) to my personal catalogue, as well as Kenneth C. Davis's *Don't Know Much About History* (Crown).

Collections of historic and contemporary utterances began to crowd my shelves and desk, beginning with major compilations—an updated version of Bartlett's *Familiar Quotations* and Tripp's *The International Thesaurus of Quotations*—and quickly expanding to include innumerable volumes of idioms, aphorisms, quotes, and anecdotes.

I then turned to *Publishers Weekly* and found listed there over forty new hardcover and nearly twice as many new paperback reference titles scheduled to appear. But that, I soon learned, was a trifle.

The public library held the mother lode. There, I could spend aimless hours picking up books at random and idling through their pages. The daily stock prices for 1968 were available at my fingertips, as were those from '64 through '91; in the aisle opposite was an intriguing five-volume looseleaf collection of *Surgery on File*. Several centuries could easily be spanned in the space of the few thin volumes separating *The Mozart Compendium*, by H. C. Robbins Landon (Schirmer Books), from the *New Age Music Guide*, by Patti Jean Biroski (Collier Books).

All one had to do was imagine the category—pick any subject out of the air—and there was at least one reference book covering the field. There were even reference books on reference books, including my favorite: *General Reference Books for Adults: Authoritative Evaluations of Encyclopedias, Atlases, and Dictionaries*, edited by Marion Sader (R. R. Bowker Company). This bible for reference-book afficionados lists, describes, and critiques 215 in-print encyclopedias, world atlases, word books and large print reference works. Beginning with a history of general reference books, *GRBFA* goes on to review 11 encyclopedias, 32 atlases, 75 general dictionaries, 19 etymological dictionaries, 12 synonym-and-antonym dictionaries, 17 thesauruses, and 45 usage dictionaries and related word books.

"There are over 8,700 books in this room," a reference librarian told me. I imagined the high-minded scholarly puzzles she'd surely helped solve over the years.

"A student called once," she said, "wanting to know the name of Lewis and Clark's dog. (She found the answer in *The Animals' Who's Who*, by Ruthven Tremain [Charles Scribner's Sons].)

"Another caller wanted to know if we have a list of all people who have deceased relatives. I asked him if he wanted a regional list or national list." Who says librarians don't have a sense of humor?

I had only one last question to ask this reference guru. How, I wondered, could I get my hands on her 225-city set of Yellow Pages?

## A Writer's Personal Reference Library

If you are building a reference library from the ground up, you should begin with two basic cornerstones: a quality dictionary and thesaurus. There are dozens of versions of each in print, and choosing among the top four or five in each category is a matter of personal preference. An excellent place to compare them—as well as atlases, encyclopedias, and other word books—is your public library. There, in addition to finding most of the books, you'll likely find a copy of *General Reference*

*Books for Adults,* a thorough study of the pros and cons of comparable works.

After choosing your dictionary and thesaurus, the other components for your ideal personal reference library will depend on your experience, subject matter, and again, personal preference. Mystery and medical writers might find *Gray's Anatomy* indispensable, while writers of verse would likely want a rhyming dictionary; speech writers undoubtedly would require several volumes of anecdotes, aphorisms, and idioms.

My library has a little (no, a *lot*) of everything, but I can count on my fingers the titles that do yeoman's share week after week. The books listed below are as vital to my daily work as are the keyboard, monitor, and computer that help me put words to paper.

1. Dictionary and thesaurus of choice.
2. *The Address Book,* by Michael Levine (Perigee Books)
3. *The Art of Readable Writing,* by Rudolf Flesch (Harper & Row)
4. *The Associated Press Stylebook and Libel Manual* (Addison-Wesley Publishing Company, Inc.)
5. *Harper Dictionary of Foreign Terms,* edited by Eugene Ehrlich (Harper & Row)
6. *The International Thesaurus of Quotations,* compiled by Rhoda Thomas Tripp (Harper & Row)
7. *The New York Public Library Book of Chronologies,* by Bruce Wetterau (Simon & Schuster)
   *The New York Public Library Desk Reference* (Simon & Schuster)
   *The New York Public Library Book of How and Where to Look It Up,* edited by Sherwood Harris (Simon & Schuster)
8. *The Times Atlas of the World* (Times Books)
9. *World Almanac and Book of Facts* (Pharos Books)
10. *The Writer's Handbook,* edited by Sylvia K. Burack (The Writer, Inc.)

Two books not on this list because they aren't specifically writing tools but are great fun to wander through anyway are *An Incomplete Education,* by Judy Jones and William Wilson (Ballantine Books), and *An Exaltation of Larks,* by James Lipton (Viking).

# POETRY

# § 81

# The Shape of Poetry

## By Peter Meinke

There's been a lot of interest lately among young writers in the New Formalism, which is basically a good thing—writers should know what form has to offer, which forms their voice might be compatible with—just as painters and musicians benefit from working with a variety of materials and instruments.

But New Formalism is not an interesting subject, because it's irrelevant to the main question: Are the poems good or not? Writing a villanelle or a sonnet is neither a virtue nor a sin. The point is, does it work? Just as "free verse" often disguises laziness of thought and execution, "formal verse" often sugar-coats a bloodless triviality.

My theory is that every poem, formal or free, has an ideal shape, and the job of the poet is to find it. (I suppose this is partly what Gerard Manley Hopkins meant by his term "inscape"—the "pattern" of a poem.) There is no limit on these shapes but I believe some poems truly want to be free and all over the page, and some want to be haiku or sestinas. A poet, as he or she is working on the early drafts of a poem, has to recognize which way the poem is leaning (of course, to do that, you have to acquaint yourself with the possibilities—no one can write poetry who doesn't spend a lot of time reading it).

Here's the title poem of my book, *Liquid Paper:*

## Liquid Paper

Smooth as a snail, this little parson
pardons our sins. Touch the brush tip
lightly and—abracadabra!—a clean slate.

We know those who blot their brains
by sniffing it, which shows
it erases more than ink
and with imagination anything

can be misapplied . . . In the Army,
our topsergeant drank aftershave, squeezing
my Old Spice to the last slow drop.

It worked like Liquid Paper in his head

until he'd glide across the streets of Heidelberg
hunting for the house in Boise, Idaho,
where he was born . . . If I were God
I'd authorize Celestial Liquid Paper
every seven years to whiten our mistakes:
we should be sorry and live with what we've done
but seven years is long enough and all of us

deserve a visit now and then
to the house where we were born
before everything got written so far wrong.

In the first few drafts of this poem, it was all in one stanza, a regular
(or irregular) free verse poem, about half again as long as the final
version. I think it's best to write uncritically for as long as you can, until
you come to a stopping point or run out of steam. When I had done
that, I began to think about what was the best structure for the poem; it
was clear that although the lines tended to be about the same length, it
wasn't going to be regularly rhymed or metered: no clusters of rhymes
or near-rhymes looking to get organized, no iambic pentameter motor
throbbing below the surface.

The next thing I noticed was that the line, "It worked like Liquid
Paper in his head," was more or less in the middle, so I isolated it. I
liked the idea of its being by itself (like Liquid Paper clearing a little
space). Dropping lines and phrases here and there, I shaped the poem
so the same number of lines preceded and followed that line.

Now I had a funny-shaped poem, with two stanzas of about a dozen
lines surrounding a skinny one-line stanza. It was a little hard to read, to
follow. I looked for the first natural break, which came after "a clean
slate" in the third line, so I made that a three-line stanza (that seemed
right: it *was* a clean slate). I then tried writing the poems with three
three-line stanzas surrounding the middle line. That wasn't bad, but
never quite worked just right. The poem didn't want to be in three-line
stanzas.

It took me a while to recognize that this was a poem with a religious
thrust. I had begun just by staring at this familiar little black and white
bottle and seeing what I could think about it, where it would lead me

(poems are seldom really about their ostensible subject, which is just an excuse to enter the poet's mind). When I realized I had used the number "seven" twice, that led me to the symmetrical final shape of three/seven/one/seven/three—those numbers all having religious significance. The point about all this shifting around is to find the shape in which your poem most clearly and vividly expresses itself. Few readers will notice what you've done—just as no one can see the backbone that holds up your body—but it's extremely important that you've done it: It supports your poem.

One advantage of working in this way is that it's easier to know when you're finished. Although it may be true that poems are not so much finished as simply abandoned, there's a greater chance that the poem will feel finished when you put the last touches on a satisfactory shape. As I stared at "Liquid Paper" in its final stages, I could see that in the (now) second stanza there was a leap of imagination between "misapplied" and "In the Army"; and this was more or less balanced by a similar leap in the fourth stanza, between "born" and "If I were God." I wouldn't have noticed this if I hadn't already broken the poem down into these particular stanzas, but now that I did, I worked on creating a mirror image, dropping a few words, and adding the ellipses, making a sort of four/three: three/four split within the seven-line stanzas. So who cares? I care, the way a painter may stare with dissatisfaction at his painting, and then add a little touch of red to the bottom left hand corner and say, "That's it!" Though no one else will notice, the painter knows he has finished his painting.

I hope when you read "Liquid Paper" it seemed perfectly natural, as if this is just the way it popped out of my head. As Yeats wrote:

> A line will take us hours maybe;
> Yet if it does not seem a moment's thought,
> Our stitching and unstitching has been naught.

The sound of the poem is shaped, too, from the beginning alliterations to the combination at the end of "done," "long," "all," "then," "born," "wrong." Of course, some of these were present in the very first draft, but many were added, and—more importantly—much was jettisoned to outline the sound that I saw already imbedded there.

I hope also the poem sounds "true"—I think it's a true feeling. But some "facts"—as opposed to "truth"—had to be sacrificed for the shape of the sound. For example, my poor old sergeant really did drink my Old Spice, and that fit perfectly well because "Old Spice" goes nicely with "misapplied." But I was stationed in Schweinfurt, not Heidelberg—and I think the sergeant was from Orlando. Obviously, for all kinds of "sound" reasons, Heidelberg and Boise, Idaho, work a lot better here. "Until he'd glide across the streets of Schweinfurt" might have been "true," but the sound is so awkward it breaks up the thought.

Another, maybe simpler, example is the following poem:

### Soldiers With Green Leggings
*Villa Schifanoia, 1987*

Father and daughter marched between
the erect cypresses, moss turning

the dark trunks green
on the north side

like soldiers with green leggings
and he wanted to say

Let us lay down our swords
(how pompous like a father!)

and she wanted to say
Let's open our doors

(how sentimental like a daughter!)
but the music in their heads

kept playing so they held
their chins high, stepping

together left right left right
smart as any parade and soon

the trees marched with them
ground rumbling like distant cannon

birds whirling like bewildered
messengers until a white flag

rose from the castle
and they fell to their knees

to sign the treaty:
any treaty—my treaty, your treaty.

This poem went through many "shapes" until I came up with those couplets, marching unpunctuated side by side down the page, mirroring the two people in the poem. An early draft began like this:

406

Father and daughter walked between the erect cypresses, moss turning the trunks green on the north side, like soldiers with green leggings. He wanted to say, Let us lay down our swords and she wanted to say, Let us open our doors . . .

Changing it into couplets focused the poem and led to the parenthetical additions, as well as other changes which were much clearer to see with the new structure (i.e., the military emphasis).

There will always be disagreement between those who favor "spontaneity" and little rewriting (Allen Ginsberg, for example), and those (like Yeats) who "labor to be beautiful." Nothing wrong with this. Every poem is a mixture of lines that have just been "given" to us—the inspiration—and those that we have worked on to fulfill the great promise of the original lines—the perspiration. Of course, we tend to be "given" more lines when we're well prepared. Ginsberg began by writing Blakean rhymed poems. As Alexander Pope wrote:

> True ease in writing comes from art, not chance,
> As those move easiest who have learned to dance.

If you are one of those writers whose lines (mostly) come out best on the first try—God bless. I'm jealous. And of course, this happens to everyone, even me, once in a while, like being dealt four aces. But as advice to writers, I'd be lying if I didn't say that I think ninety-nine percent of first drafts benefit from rewriting. Severe rewriting, serious shaping. An inspiration is not a poem, but if it's a real inspiration, with hard work and an eye to the shape it's struggling to be, it can become one.

# 82

# YESTERDAY'S NOISE: THE POETRY OF CHILDHOOD MEMORY

## BY LINDA PASTAN

*How sweet the past is, no matter how wrong, or how sad.*
*How sweet is yesterday's noise.*
—Charles Wright, "The Southern Cross"

I WROTE AN ESSAY TEN YEARS AGO CALLED "Memory as Muse," and looking back at it today I am struck by the fact that in the poems I write about childhood now the mood has changed from one of a rather happy nostalgia ("Memory as Muse") to a more realistic, or at least a gloomier, assessment of my own childhood and how it affects me as a writer ("Yesterday's Noise"). Let me illustrate with a poem called "An Old Song," from my most recent book.

### An Old Song*

How loyal our childhood demons are,
growing old with us in the same house
like servants who season the meat
with bitterness, like jailers
who rattle the keys
that lock us in or lock us out.

Though we go on with our lives,
though the years pile up
like snow against the door,
still our demons stare at us
from the depths of mirrors
or from the new faces across a table.

And no matter what voice they choose,
what language they speak,
the message is always the same.
They ask "Why can't you do
anything right?" They say
"We just don't love you anymore."

408

As A. S. Byatt said about herself in an interview: "I was no good at being a child." My mother told me that even as a baby I would lie screaming in the crib, clearly terrified of the dust motes that could be seen circling in the sun, as if they were a cloud of insects that were about to swarm and bite me. By the time I was five or six, I had a series of facial tics so virulent that I still can't do the mouth exercises my dentist recommends for fear I won't be able to stop doing them. I'm afraid they'll take hold like the compulsive habits of childhood that led my second-grade teacher to send me from the room until I could, as she put it, control my own face. There was the isolating year (sixth grade) of being the one child nobody would play with, the appointed victim, and there was the even more isolating year (fourth grade) of being, alas, one of the victimizers. There was my shadowy room at bedtime, at the end of a dark hallway, and, until some worried psychologist intervened, no night light allowed.

I thought about calling my last book *Only Child* because something about that condition seemed to define not only me, but possibly writers in general who sit at their desks, necessarily alone, for much of the time. In some ways, of course, it defines all of us, born alone, dying alone, alone in our skins no matter how close we seem to be to others. I tried to capture my particular loneliness as a child, my difficulty in making friends, my search for approval, in what I thought would be the title poem of that book:

## Only Child*

Sister to no one,
I watched
the children next door
quarrel and make up
in a code
I never learned
to break.

Go Play!
my mother told me.
Play! said the aunts,
their heads all nodding
on their stems,
a family of rampant
flowers

and I a single shoot.
At night I dreamed
I was a twin
the way my two hands,
my eyes,
my feet were twinned.
I married young.

In the fractured light
of memory—that place
of blinding sun or shade,
I stand waiting
on the concrete stoop
for my own children
to find me.

At a reading I gave before a group of Maryland PEN women, some-one who had clearly not read beyond the tables of contents of my books introduced me as a writer of light verse. I remember thinking in a panic that I hardly had a single light poem to read to those expectant faces, waiting to be amused. Did I have such an unhappy life, then—wife, mother, grandmother, with woods to walk in, books to read, good friends, even a supportive editor?

I am, in fact, a more or less happy adult, suffering, thank God, from no more than the usual griefs age brings. But I think my poems are colored not only by a possibly somber genetic temperament, but also by my failure at childhood, even when I am not writing about childhood per se. And more and more, as I grow older, those memories themselves insist upon inserting themselves into my work. Perhaps it is the very way our childhoods change in what I called "the fractured light of memory" that make them such an inexhaustible source of poetry. For me, it is like the inexhaustible subject of the seasons that can be seen in the changeable light of the sun, or the versatile light of the imagination, as benign or malevolent or indifferent, depending upon a particular poet's vision at a particular moment.

I want to reflect a little then on those poems we fish up from the depths of our childhoods. And for any teachers reading this, I want to suggest that assigning poems to student writers that grow out of their childhoods can produce unusually good results, opening up those frozen ponds with what Kafka called the axe of poetry.

Baudelaire says that "genius is childhood recalled at will." I had a 19-

410

year-old student once who was not a genius but who complained that he couldn't write about anything except his childhood. Unfortunately, his memory was short, and as a result, all of his poems were set in junior high school. He had taken my course, he told me, in order to find new subjects. I admit that at first glance junior high doesn't seem the most fertile territory for poems to grow in. On the other hand, insecurity, awakening sexuality, fear of failure—many of the great subjects do exist there. It occurred to me that when I was 19, what I usually wrote about were old age and death. Only in my middle years did I start looking back into my own past for the subjects of poems. This started me wondering about the poetry of memory in general. Did other poets, unlike my young students, come to this subject relatively late, as I had? As I looked rather casually and unscientifically through the books on my shelves, it did seem to me that when poets in their twenties and thirties wrote about children, it was usually their own children that concerned them, but when they were in their late forties or fifties or sixties, the children they wrote about tended to be themselves.

Donald Justice, in an interview with *The Missouri Review,* gave as good an explanation of this as anyone. He said, "In the poems I have been thinking of and writing the last few years, I have grown aware that childhood is a subject somehow available to me all over again. The perspective of time and distance alter substance somewhat, and so it is possible to think freshly of things that were once familiar and ordinary, as if they had become strange again. I don't know whether this is true of everybody's experience, but at a certain point childhood seems mythical once more. It did to start with, and it does suddenly again."

There are, first of all, what I call "Poems of the Happy Childhood," Donald Justice's own poem "The Poet At Seven" among them. But for poets less skilled than Justice, there is a danger to such poems, for they can stray across the unmarked but mined border into sentimentality and become dishonest, wishful sort of recollections. When they are working well, however, these "Poems of the Happy Childhood" reflect the Wordsworthian idea that we are born "trailing clouds of glory" and that as we grow older we are progressively despiritualized. Even earlier than Wordsworth, in the mid-17th century, Henry Vaughan anticipated these ideas in his poem, "The Retreat."

I mention Wordsworth and Vaughan because in looking back over the centuries at the work of earlier poets, I find more rarely than I expected

411

poems that deal with childhood at all. Their poems are the exceptions, as are Shakespeare's 30th Sonnet and Tennyson's "Tears, Idle Tears." Perhaps it wasn't until Freud that people started to delve routinely into their own pasts. But nostalgia per se was not so rare, and in a book called *The Uses of Nostalgia: Studies in Pastoral Poetry,* the English critic Laurence Lerner comes up with an interesting theory. After examining pastoral poetry from classical antiquity on, he concludes that pastoral poems express the longing of the poets to return to a childhood arcadia, and that in fact what they longed to return to was childhood itself. He then takes his theory a step further and postulates that the reason poets longed for childhood is simply that they had lost it. He writes, "The list is varied of those who learned to sing of what they loved by losing it. . . . Is that what singing is? Is nostalgia the basis not only of pastoral but of other art too?" Or as Bob Hass puts it in his poem "Meditation at Lagunitas," "All the new thinking is about loss./ In this it resembles all the old thinking."

But though there are some left who think of childhood as a lost arcadia, for the most part Freud changed all of that.

We have in more recent times the idea of poetry as a revelation of the self to the self, or as Marge Perloff put it when describing the poems of Seamus Heaney, "Poetry as a dig."

The sort of poems this kind of digging often provides are almost the opposite of "Poems of the Happy Childhood," and they reflect a viewpoint that is closer to the childhood poems I seem to be writing lately. In fact, a poem like "Autobiographia Literaria" by Frank O'Hara actually consoles the adult by making him remember, albeit with irony in O'Hara's case, how much more unpleasant it was to be a child. If the poetry of memory can console, it can also expiate. In his well-known poem, "Those Winter Sundays," Robert Hayden not only recreates the past but reexamines his behavior there and finds it wanting. The poem itself becomes an apology for his behavior as a boy, and the act of writing becomes an act of repentance.

If you can't expiate the past, however, you can always revise it—and in various and occasionally unorthodox, ways. Donald Justice in the poem "Childhood" runs a list of footnotes opposite his poem, explaining and clarifying. Mark Strand in "The Untelling" reenters the childhood scene as an adult and warns the participants of what is to occur in the future.

Probably the most ambitious thing a poem of childhood memory can accomplish is the Proustian task of somehow freeing us from time itself. Proust is perfectly happy to use random, seemingly unimportant memory sensations as long as they have the power to transport him backwards. When he tastes his madeleine, moments of the past come rushing back, and he is transported to a plane of being on which a kind of immortality is granted. We can grasp for a moment what we can never normally get hold of—a bit of time in its pure state. It is not just that this somehow lasts forever, the way we hope the printed word will last, but that it can free us from the fear of death. To quote Proust: "A minute emancipated from the temporal order had recreated in us for its apprehension the man emancipated from the temporal order." Proust accomplished his journey to the past via the sense of taste, but any sense or combination of senses will do. In my poem "PM/AM," I used the sense of hearing in the first stanza and a combination of sight and touch in the second. Here is the second:

## AM**

The child gets up
on the wrong side of the bed.
There are splinters
of cold light on the floor,
and when she frowns
the frown freezes on her face
as her mother has warned her it would.
When she puts her elbows roughly
on the table her father says:
you got up on the wrong side of the bed;
and there is suddenly
a cold river
of spilled milk.
These gestures are merely formal,
small stitches in the tapestry
of a childhood she will remember
as nearly happy. Outside
the snow begins again,
ordinary weather
blurring the landscape
between that time and this,
as she swings her cold legs
over the side of the bed.

413

But did I really say: "A childhood she will remember as nearly happy"? Whom are you to believe, the poet who wrote that poem years ago or the poet who wrote "An Old Song"? As you see, the past can be reinterpreted, the past can be revised, and the past can also be invented. Sometimes, in fact, one invents memories without even meaning to. In a poem of mine called "The One-Way Mirror Back," I acknowledge this by admitting: "What I remember hardly happened; what they say happened I hardly remember." Or as Bill Matthews put it in his poem "Our Strange and Lovable Weather"—

> . . . any place lies about its weather,
> just as we lie about our childhoods,
> and for the same reason: we can't
> say surely what we've undergone
> and need to know, and need to know.

This "need to know" runs very deep and is one of the things that fuels the poems we write about our childhoods.

But the simplest, the most basic thing such poems provide are the memories themselves, the memories for their own sakes. Here is the third stanza of Charles Simic's poem "Ballad": "Screendoor screeching in the wind/ Mother hobble-gobble baking apples/ Wooden spoons dancing, ah the idyllic life of wooden spoons/ I need a table to spread these memories on." The poem itself, then, can become such a table, a table to simply spread our memories on.

Looking back at some of my own memories, I sometimes think I was never a child at all, but a lonely woman camouflaged in a child's body. I am probably more childlike now. At least I hope so.

---

*"An Old Song" and "Only Child" appear in *Heroes In Disguise,* Norton, 1991.
**"AM" is from *PM/AM:New and Selected Poems,* Norton,1982.

# 83

## EMOTION AND THE LANGUAGE OF POETRY

### BY JAMES APPLEWHITE

AS I MEDITATE ON THE WAYS THAT LANGUAGE in a poem evokes emotion in the reader, I'd like to recall the writing of a particular lyric—one that involved location in landscape, in time and atmosphere, and in the psychological circumstances of my life. When I begin a poem in response to a place, it is more than just a record of impressions. I am engaged by such details as fall leaves, an overcast sky, and the lateness of an afternoon. I seek language for the qualities of tone and color that circumstances seem to create. But for the poem to be interesting, the details must appeal to something in me, establishing a connection with a world outside. Thus, I feel a bit of good luck when a location, and an atmosphere and event, correspond to an emotion and give it form. I might note that this *form* of landscape-encounter may shape poems even if wholly from imagination or memory. It is the structure of significant experience, simplified for contemplation: an example of how inner and outer, past and present, meaning and image, align themselves in the psyche and in language.

I was returning from a late afternoon hike in the Eno River State Park, which is next to my home. I passed through a familiar, partially cleared site where an abandoned homestead had left the sky open above a chimney pile of stones. As I crossed this wild room, brown-floored with grass and crumpled leaves, an owl shouldered his soft noiseless flight across the sky and alighted to my left, in an attic-like corner made by pines. His crossing stopped me, made the self-bounded spot of the vanished homestead the space of my thought that moment.

The browns and grays of the owl and of the leaf-rug made me think of wool. I wanted such yarn colors in words, to sew in his palpable, puffed texture—to render the snowflake beat of his wings, and to suggest the downy tip feathers that dampened all whistle from his flight. Already, the two sounds of *owl* and *wool* had fascinated my ear. These seemed to me woolly, brown sounds, puffed like the bird with soft volume. Here are the first lines of a two-stanza poem, as I composed them in my head while walking along the ridge and crossing Seven Mile Creek toward my house:

> An owl over my head shouldered
> like wool—coasting, a quietness.
> Perched in his overcoat,
> he browned the twilight.

I wrote another stanza after hearing the owl's eerie *whoo, whoo* when I was already on my own lot, passing through the open hardwood trees toward the yellow-lighted windows of my house. I remember feeling a solemn pleasure in the sound-tones of the words in my head and in the owl's cry—as well as in the sense of colors around me. There seemed a blueness in the darkening air, like water, with the yellow window squares of the house beyond, where I knew my wife was waiting. The second of the original two stanzas wished at this time to *play* with sound and color, but not to bear much burden of narration:

> Later his echo-halloo shadowed
> the air blue, like water.
> I was not far enough from home
> to hear any lonelier color.

I'd written the first two stanzas of my owl poem a few months after my mother's funeral. The mood had been spare, and the writing rather minimal. Later, when I saw the poem's bent toward emotional coloration, I wrote another draft overemphasizing sound and sensory imagery, acknowledging in effect the memory and grief and partial solace hidden behind the plain description of the first draft. The key was in what the owl had reminded me of. Why had the branches he perched in seemed so rafter-like, why had he seemed a kind of ghost in an attic? And why did I find his overcoat-gray and vagrant, hunched look so moving? Here are two of the overwrought stanzas I wrote while trying to grasp the owl's emotive resonance for me:

> Softer than a hawk, not
> black as crow or raven it

> interrogated thought with its beak's
> immortal incision. Underneath

> sight it questioned, asking if
> ever even the cleft and loss of
> a house and its past could sink
> like light into the night's deep lake.

Clearly, I am pressing, trying too hard. I have associated the owl with Poe's Raven, for in another of these intermediate, discarded stanzas I see it/him "as in a niche with its idol." I'm not likely to use nineteenth-century echoes, or the word *immortal,* in poems I take seriously. This illustrates how a touch of the magical may be used to gloss over a lack of psychological understanding. Yet I was beginning to realize that the owl and the abandoned home site had to do with my own past.

As I worked on the poem further, the pleasure of sound-echo seemed to console me and help release my sense of grief and loss. The relation between *wool* and *owl* and the image of the overcoat brought in by *wool* finally led me to realize the ramifications of my initial response to the real bird. The poem's formal wordplay, like Freudian free association, led me to the discovery that the owl in his woolly, vagrant, overcoated aspect had reminded me of my dead uncle. The vanished farmhouse of the clearing had been a ghostly replica of my childhood home, with tree limbs as rafters and the owl as Almon, my mother's older brother, a bachelor school teacher who had perched upstairs in our house during his summer vacations. It was Almon who had helped awaken my interest in language, by telling me stories from *The Odyssey, Huckleberry Finn,* and from his own wandering life as teacher in wild, out-of-the-way places along the North Carolina coast. His horn-rimmed glasses had made him look owlish. His penchant for tales of war, physical suffering, and situations of terror had made him rather a Gothic figure. I put my uncle into a new version of the poem:

> My uncle upstairs on holidays
> once whooed his loss of home:
> a vagrant teacher on solitary
> Halloweens, his coat like *owl's.*

The connotations of *owl* and my childhood associations suggested *Halloween*—a word that lightens the Gothic darkness, acknowledging the fun and playfulness with which this man told his stories of fright.

Almon had been a kind of quasi-father, there for me those summers because of what seemed to me in my harsh child's judgment his ineffectuality as a man, because he had not an all-season job, like my busy father—who seemed sometimes too busy for me.

The losses hardest to accept, I think, are not the lives cut short by accidents or illness, but the things we feel we could or should have had. The poem is really about my partial loss of father, and the substitution by this uncle, who was a man of language more than of action. The poem is thus, indirectly, about the psychological dislocation whereby I became a poet.

For a space in the new version of the poem, I seemed to myself as useless as Almon, shiftlessly wandering the twilight woodland, when all regular men were raking leaves or stuffing down pot roasts. The owl had become a version of myself, a fatherless image I'd picked up from a teacher-uncle. Vagrant and wordy. Alone in evening. Masculine in his overcoat of feathers but solitary and introverted. The next draft of my poem began with a title that acknowledged a death. Not able to include the whole complexity of my mother's death having called up that of my uncle, I named the poem "Riverwalk with Owl, After the Funeral." Before I'd gotten the beginning and middle of the poem to suit me, a fuller description of the initiating time and place and events seemed to offer hope for a new ending. I described coming down the ridge and crossing the creek toward my present home, which was marked in gathering darkness by the yellow-lighted windows which reminded me my wife was nearby. I had felt good returning from the blue water of memory, even if followed by its echo in the owl's *whoo, whoo.*

Just as *atmosphere* can mean both weather and aesthetic aura, so does the word *color* include both sensory fact and literary effect. *Color* in both senses had been an important part of the poem from the beginning. The aqua sky, refracted in the damp air of the clearing, had seemed a lake, a reflecting surface that the owl had crossed. The melancholy, reflective colors of the gray-brown bird and bluish twilight seemed to me carried into the end of the poem by the owl's final call. I'd felt a tension between a loneliness like that of Almon's, and a sense of being at home—between grief for the lost past and the warmth of my present house and marriage. I tried to render this tension in spatial terms, and through contrasts of color.

I climbed down the ridge to
  the stream, seeing across and
into my own life, where a yellow
  window meant my wife.

There, an echo-halloo shadowed
  the air blue, like water.
I was not far enough from home
  to hear any lonelier color.

The present is made warmer, with yellow window and wife, to stand against the chill call from the past, wherein sound and color seem fused. Here is the whole poem in its final form.

## Riverwalk with *Owl*, After the Funeral

I followed the snowflake beat
  of a wool owl's flight
falling wing by wing on
  the coming night—as if circling

a seeming surface of air,
  its aqua reflection. He perched
in pine branches cleft like
  rafters of a vanished house,

then ruffled up his overcoat,
  a ghost, charring that site
where attic and chimney had gone
  and briars grew over the stones.

My uncle upstairs in our house
  his summers as vagrant teacher
once whooed his Halloween travels
  no more alone than *owl*.

I whispered *Almon, Almon*
  as a charm against his breath's
mistake. The sound alone rounded
  the clearing, mirroring light.

Consoled by the sky's slick
  lake, I felt his loneliness
and hurt cease to haunt.
  Words were our common lot.

I climbed down the ridge to
  the stream, seeing across and
into my own life, where a yellow
  window meant my wife.

There, an echo-halloo shadowed
the air blue, like water.
I was not far enough from home
to hear any lonelier color.

Curiously, the very words that indicate emotive qualities in writing also help to embody those qualities: *texture,* as in *wool owl; color,* as in *aqua reflection* and *yellow window;* and *atmosphere,* as the pervasive quality of weather, light, color, and sound. Sound repetitions like *wool* and *owl,* connotative connections like *overcoat* and *vagrant,* color relations such as "air blue, like water," and "yellow/window," are elements that act on a partially unrealized, irrational level. It is as if the emotional unconsciousness of the poet operates subliminally through the poem's form to influence the reader, who meantime, may be more aware of rhyme scheme or meaning than of emotion.

How does one learn or develop this style of writing? Not by logic but by cultivating the habit of thinking with the voice and making associations. The poet makes sounds echo against one another, using rhythm within a narrative context. He learns to do this by noticing the play and the feeling in the works of great poets. Remember W. H. Auden's alliterations in "Seascape": "Look, stranger, on this island now/The leaping light for your delight discovers. . . ." Meditate on the fragile, pointed brilliance of Wallace Stevens' "spruces rough in the distant glitter" of January sun in "The Snow Man."

Be sensitive to assonance and consonance and unexpected connotation. Against the habit of our age, which treats language as mainly a conveyor of information, the poet must recollect that words in poetry form an art whose colors are chosen by feeling and whose sounds echo from chords deep in the psyche. In this way, the poet returns language to its first condition, as a medium for play and pleasure, and a means of embodying emotion along with thoughts and facts.

Having gone from Innocence into Experience (to use William Blake's categories), the poet needs to attain the simple sense of language as a child has it, of reading with moving lips, of an openness to nonsense combinations. Often I start my poetry classes with Lewis Carroll's "Jabberwocky." Words such as *brillig* and *slithy* perfectly convey the union of sound-suggestions and connotation. The chief point is to notice that language as art is very different from language as argumentation or information. The resources within the writer that charge word combinations with emotion are preconscious, partially hidden even from the poet in the act of composing. Poetry, therefore, requires a strange balance between skill and intuition, and a reliance on formal devices. If, despite all the necessary, acquired knowledge, poets can revive the frolic and inventiveness of babbling and fantasy, then the musical, tone-colored stories they feel can revive in the reader a wisdom, which is pleasure.

# § 84

## WRITING POETRY: THE MAGIC AND THE POWER

### BY T. ALAN BROUGHTON

SPRING—WHICH IN VERMONT is a form of late winter. My four-year-old son and I are taking advantage of a pocket of sunshine to blow bubbles on the front lawn. He likes to wave the wand, then see if he can recapture one of the larger bubbles, perching it on the tip where he can watch it make oily, transparent shifts through the colors of the rainbow. Sometimes, with a wave of generosity, he will free the bubble again to rise into its ultimate journey. Today an uncertain breeze is blowing whatever he makes straight up, or sideways, or into our faces.

He holds out his wand, stares at me through the soapy hole that will become a bubble, and says, "I am magic even though the bubbles have the power."

"What?"

But like any professional oracle he does not repeat or explain. The hand waves, the bubbles coalesce out of air, he dips again and runs across the lawn, trailing a cloud behind him.

I have begun to write down such statements when I can, although I swear I will try not to embarrass him with them when he is older, if he finds them so. An only child has enough self-consciousness to deal with. But this statement won't let go. It snags me the way an image, a word, an incident—glimpsed through my own eyes or vicariously—will when they demand to become a poem. But this time I'm going to blow it off in prose, here, in a brief essay about the making of bubbles that are poems.

Write a poem. That is the first, terrifying instruction I often give my students in a writing class. Ninety percent, if not more, of the instruction in such a course is concerned with revision. Skill, technique, examples of fine poems and some of their drafts, assignments based on specific objectives—these are matters that can be taught consciously with the hope that they will become so well learned that they are innate. But that first assignment, its terror and, if it works, its joy, is directed toward that other part of the process—the unknown, the constantly new, the unlearned that can be learned only in the moment of doing. I give the assignment not to discourage or crush a shaky talent, but to let each of those writers know what every writer feels like, no matter how experienced, when sitting down to make a new poem.

I read poetry not only to find out more of its secrets, even if I cannot use them, but also to remind myself that poems can be written. In the silence of one's mind, no matter how many stacks of books have been filed there, no matter how much knowledge about line-lengths or figures of speech has been stored away, the image of the blank page or screen is fitting metaphor for the fearful ignorance of beginning. By now I have written thousands of poems, only a handful of which I would want anyone to read, although, sometimes to my embarrassment, more than a handful have been published. But no one *wants* to write the same poem again and again, even if some of us are doomed by the limits of talent to do so. The resistance writers so often describe as being present each morning (or evening if they are night-writers) is inevitable. "Momentum" is perhaps an appropriate term to use in sports where a team is melding into a tribe rather than being a mere gathering of disparate individuals, but for the single writer in the solitude of study or park bench, each poem is discovering again that poems can be written.

Which is where the joy resides, and probably also where the need to do it again and again, even for a whole lifetime, originates. Words begin to happen. Perhaps the first few are brutally and impatiently crossed out, the pen for a moment thrown down in impatience. Try again. The next few stick like burrs—at least through this first version. Later one may delete them without regret. But it is happening, whether line by line, image by image, sound by sound, or all together. Each writer will do it in her or his own way—out loud, standing up, lying down, in notebooks, on scraps of paper, on the greenish glow of a screen.

It is a moment that no one can take away from the writer, no matter how fiercely some critic will respond later to the object made. At least my premise is that this is what makes the difference between the writer who persists and the one who gives it a try and goes on to prefer real estate or engineering or the teaching of literature. It is not just the hope that the next poem will be the best poem that keeps the poet going, but also the simple surprise that more poems are there and that the magic is available.

Which is not to say that the process is without its practical side. The distortion in my description so far is that even if "momentum" is not the right term, there is some accumulation of experience. Those students who find the first assignment so daunting that they return with deep circles under their eyes and one of those poems about "how I am trying to write a poem and not succeeding and this is it" can be helped along. Such help can be only tentative and personal, but like any talisman, once used to enter the next level in the cave, it can be thrown away and that person can find his or her own better means.

1. For the moment, forget what any other poet has written about. Write out of your own experience. Despite the anxiety that we are just like everyone else, the fear that we are lost in the *pluribus* rather than standing out as *unum*, the miracle of existence is that each one of us is uncloned, comes piled with genes never before accumulated in quite the same pattern. Enjoy. Now. Because the price for that, of course, is that you must die. What you have done, seen, reacted to, absorbed, dreamed, imagined is not exactly like anyone else's experience. Because you are a member of the human species, the larger patterns are similar—which does enable you to hope that what you write sufficiently incarnates those patterns to be accessible to others. But the intensity will come from those fine, small differences that make you and your poem an-other.

2. So the corollary is be concrete, be specific, sing out of the sensuous facts of your own body. Large abstract terms are the voice of the herd lowing to itself—Love, Hope, Joy, Defeat. We need them—the smoothed objects of ritual naming that help us believe we know what we have done and seen. But to journey into them, we need a map of their huge domains as detailed as the description of their hedges and weeds, the sound a specific woman's voice makes when it calls from the window of a particular house. Perhaps the sound will add up to Loneliness or Loss, but your reader will believe that only when he is tricked into hearing the voice, and he will believe what he has heard is much richer and more complex than the single term.

3. And that complexity is what the words poems use can give us—

especially in Metaphor, that yoking of the disparate or opposite, the comparison that is known but often unacknowledged until the poet shows it to us.

Translated loosely, and for a New England readership, Moritake's haiku could be "A fallen leaf returning to the branch." It is meaningless without its title: "Butterfly." Two utterly known, utterly common objects. A leaf, a butterfly. They are superimposed. The delight may be small—a leaf seen as a butterfly, a butterfly seen as a leaf. The basis of comparison is motion—that faltering, fluttering, seemingly indeterminate flight of both. The poet's ability to defy gravity is the surprise. Small effect. But is it so small if, after having read the poem, one always sees the two objects in their flights differently from before?

The yoking of disparate elements is a larger pattern of poems, that incorporation of the Yin and Yang of the world. In writing through the first drafts, part of the struggle is in keeping the mind open to illogic, to prevent all the training we have had since childhood in being "reasonable" from taking over. At the moment of writing, the mind is not so much concentrating on belief as admitting that whatever the poem has started to say, is saying at this very moment I am putting down words, it may be about something else, a something else I could never have imagined without doing what I am doing now—writing it into existence. Perhaps in the first draft that "otherness" will show only in glints, and then revision will be in sleuthing, trying to find those unexpected moments.

Bear in mind that metaphor does not reside in images alone, but in situations also. I remember once trying to write a poem that I thought was a story about a boy falling from a flagpole. He had come to a place with his father to fix the pole. The narrator was a man watching, describing the event that happened to virtual strangers even if he had hired them. What I discovered was a poem that was really about the man and his marriage, the terrible descent he and his wife and his own small son were going through. The foreground remained the death of the boy climber, but the foreground was the way to present the other descents. In another instance, a poem I thought was to be about stopping by the side of the road and hearing Mozart coming through the air from the open window of someone's truck becomes yoked with a death in the nearby woods, a suicide and its investigation that might seem to be as far removed from a Mozart Serenade as possible.

# Serenade for Winds

*We know life so little that it is very little in our power to distinguish right from wrong, just from unjust, and to say that one is unfortunate because one suffers, which has not been proved.* (Van Gogh, to his brother Theo and sister-in-law Jo.)

Clustered beside the road are a van,
pick-up, two sedans. In another season
we might imagine hunters tracking deer
or lugging sixpacks away from their wives.
But the Seal of State on one door warns
a new fact has burned its brand on the landscape.

From the vacant truck a radio plays
Mozart into the summer breeze.
Now an oboe floats above
the bass of bassoon, a clarinet
lures the horn to join
this conversation on the waves.

We have stopped to check the map
but might believe that only this
was why we drove for hours—
leaves lifted in a freshet,
all else forgotten and offstage
when air and music are one.

In the forest a trooper stops
a witness from cutting the rope
with his knife. Procedures require
cameras and tape, a careful report.
A man's body, halted by noose
and gravity, slowly swings
from the maple's limb.
In an hour or two a wife
and elder son will try
through taut jaw to say
they're not surprised, blame him,
the State, or bank, or all.

Only a few bars remain.
Cut him down. Let him drop
on the layered leaves.
The notes rise into the silence of air
through which the body must descend.

That's enough for starters, at least for me when I sit down to try to find a new poem. Everyone who knows poets intimately has to learn to forgive them for their metaphor-hounding. Any little act or word can be snatched up and transformed by poems. I hope my son, if he sees this years from now, will forgive my plagiarizing. But I couldn't have found a better way to say it—that moment of sharing between poet and poem when the day's last word announces itself, when that bubble called a poem begins to take its translucent form. "I am magic, even though the bubbles have the power."

# 85

# HOW TO WRITE A FUNNY POEM

## BY JACK PRELUTSKY

WRITING HUMOROUS VERSE is hard work. For the humor to succeed, every part of the poem must be just right: It requires delicacy. If the poet uses too heavy a hand, the poem goes beyond being funny and turns into something disquieting or even grotesque. Conversely, if the poet doesn't push the idea far enough, the incongruities that are supposed to make the poem funny bypass the reader.

Humorous poetry is often highly underrated. The reader responds easily to humor with laughter, often unaware of the mental and technical gymnastics that the poet has performed to elicit this response. Physiological studies have shown that the body has a much easier time laughing than getting angry. Since humor is such a facile emotion, the reader assumes that the funny poem is also a simple poem—about as complicated as slipping on a banana peel.

How do I make a poem funny? Exactly what are these gymnastics? I'll start with one that is a favorite, and then continue with several others that should be standard in any humorist's repertoire.

I love the technique of asking serious questions about a silly idea. You can make almost anything funny by starting with an absolutely nonsensical premise, and asking common sense questions about it. I once was in a supermarket selecting some boneless chicken breasts for dinner, and it suddenly occurred to me to ask the question, "What about the rest of the chicken—was that boneless, too?" And if so, where did it live, what did it do, and what did the other chickens think of it? When I'd finished answering my "serious" questions, I had the groundwork for a poem, "Ballad of a Boneless Chicken," which appears in *The New Kid on the Block.*

While I was writing the poem, one last question occurred to me: Exactly what sort of egg does a boneless chicken lay? The answer provided me with a surprising, yet somehow logical conclusion.

428

## Ballad of a Boneless Chicken

I'm a basic boneless chicken,
yes, I have no bones inside,
I'm without a trace of rib cage,
yet I hold myself with pride,
other hens appear offended
by my total lack of bones,
they discuss me impolitely
in derogatory tones.

I am absolutely boneless,
I am boneless through and through,
I have neither neck nor thighbones,
and my back is boneless too,
and I haven't got a wishbone,
not a bone within my breast,
so I rarely care to travel
from the comfort of my nest.

I have feathers fine and fluffy,
I have lovely little wings,
but I lack the superstructure
to support these splendid things.
Since a chicken finds it tricky
to parade on boneless legs,
I stick closely to the hen house,
laying little scrambled eggs.

Another of my tricks is to find that one small special something in the ordinary, or to add something unexpected to the apparently mundane. For example, in *The New Kid on the Block*, I have a poem called, "Euphonica Jarre." Euphonica would be unexceptional, were it not for one preposterous talent—she's the world's worst singer. In this poem, I applied another device, one familiar to all humorists—*exaggeration!* To make Euphonica outlandishly funny, I decided that her vocalizing should cause unlikely events, such as ships running aground, trees defoliating themselves, and the onset of avalanches.

## Euphonica Jarre

Euphonica Jarre has a voice that's bizarre,
but Euphonica warbles all day,
as windowpanes shatter and chefs spoil the batter
and mannequins moan with dismay.

Mighty ships run aground at her horrible sound,
pretty pictures fall out of their frames,
trees drop off their branches,
rocks start avalanches,
and flower beds burst into flames.

When she opens her mouth, even eagles head south,
little fish truly wish they could drown,
the buzzards all hover, as tigers take cover,
and rats pack their bags and leave town.

Milk turns into butter and butterflies mutter
and bees look for something to sting,
pigs peel off their skins, a tornado begins
when Euphonica Jarre starts to sing.

In *The New Kid on the Block,* there's another poem called, "Forty Performing Bananas," which illustrates the tactic of making something extraordinary out of the ordinary. On the surface, there's nothing unusual about bananas. They're found in every food market, and we take them for granted when we slice them over our breakfast cereal. However, they become uniquely foolish when imbued with the skill to sing and dance. Some inanimate objects are just naturally amusing when they're anthropomorphized. Performing bananas are among them; airborne hot dogs, which appear in my newest book, *Something Big Has Been Here,* are another.

By the way, I use a lot of wordplay in the banana poem: their features are "appealing" and their fans "drive here in bunches." It's probably already occurred to you, but I'd like to mention that I routinely combine several techniques in a poem and can wind up with some complex results. Another way to find humor in the ordinary is to take this item or idea and keep amplifying it until it reaches a totally absurd conclusion. When I was writing *Something Big Has Been Here,* I was struck with the notion of an uncuttable meat loaf. It's an old joke, and there are dozens of examples on TV and film. I searched for an approach that would allow the reader to experience that old joke in a new way. In this case, the meat loaf in question resists all attempts to slice, hammer, drill or chisel it. The implements become more and more exotic, the speaker resorts to bows and arrows, a blowtorch, a power saw, and finally a hippopotamus to trample it. Nevertheless, the meat loaf remains intact. Though I could have ended the whole business here, I decided to employ an additional tactic, that of combining two different ideas that normally don't belong together, further stretching credulity. I conclude the poem by accepting the meat loaf for what it is (indestructible) and reveal that additional meat loaves are now being manufactured as building materials. Of course, no builder would use meat loaves to erect a house, but by making such an absurd leap, I made the poem even funnier.

I'd like to touch on a rather obvious resource for any poet who writes humor: letting the humor grow out of the words themselves. There are numerous kinds of wordplay: puns, anagrams, spoonerisms, and malapropisms. I love puns, and in *Something Big Has Been Here,* I expanded on the sayings that children write to each other in their autograph books when I composed the poem, "I Wave Good-bye When Butter Flies." In this list of puns, you can watch a pillow fight, sew on a cabbage patch, dance at a basket ball, etc.

## I Wave Good-bye When Butter Flies

I wave good-bye when butter flies
and cheer a boxing match,
I've often watched my pillow fight,
I've sewn a cabbage patch,
I like to dance at basket balls
or lead a rubber band,
I've marveled at a spelling bee,
I've helped a peanut stand.

It's possible a pencil points,
but does a lemon drop?
Does coffee break or chocolate kiss,
and will a soda pop?
I share my milk with drinking straws,
my meals with chewing gum,
and should I see my pocket change,
I'll hear my kettle drum.

It makes me sad when lettuce leaves,
I laugh when dinner rolls,
I wonder if the kitchen sinks
and if a salad bowls,
I've listened to a diamond ring,
I've waved a football fan,
and if a chimney sweeps the floor,
I'm sure the garbage can.

Another common technique to achieve humor is the surprise ending. My use of this device is the result of being so astounded and delighted by the O. Henry stories I read as a child. One of my most successful uses of a surprise ending is in the title poem of my book, *The New Kid on the Block*. I recite a complaint about a neighborhood bully, the new kid who punches, tweaks my arm, pulls my hair, likes to fight, is twice my size, and just at the point when everyone has conjured up an image of some big, loutish boy, I end the poem with the following lines:

". . . that new kid's really bad, I don't care for her at all."

I admit that the punch line's humor depends heavily on the shameless use of one of contemporary society's most common stereotypes, but it has never failed to draw laughter whenever I've recited the poem to an audience. This is a good place to remind everyone that much of our humor is culture bound. Very often, what may be hilarious to an American audience may draw blank looks from residents of the Himalayas. Actually, I don't have to go as far as Tibet to make an apt comparison; there are many moments on the British "Benny Hill" television show that draw blank looks from me.

One last device I'll mention is irony. It can be as simple as in my poem, "My Dog, He is an Ugly Dog" (from *The New Kid on the Block*), where I list all the things wrong with my dog: He's oddly built, sometimes has an offensive aroma, has fleas, is noisy, stupid, and greedy. Nevertheless, despite this litany of his drawbacks, I declare that he's the only dog for me.

In my poem, "I Met a Rat of Culture" (from *Something Big Has Been Here*), the irony becomes a bit more sophisticated when I describe a learned and highly skilled rodent; he's handsomely attired, recites poetry (a bit of irony within irony), speaks many languages, is knowledgeable about all the arts and sciences, and so on, but at the end of the poem, he reveals his true nature: ". . .but he squealed and promptly vanished at the entrance of my cat, for despite his erudition, he was nothing but a rat."

There are several other methods I incorporate, but I'll leave them to some desperate graduate student to uncover. A few involve simple observation and focusing on incongruities. That's what happened when I was squirrel-watching, and noticed that their tails looked like question

432

marks. I wrote a poem in which I concluded that it's pointless for them to wear question marks, inasmuch as "there's little squirrels care to know." ("Squirrels," from *Something Big Has Been Here*.) And there's always the riddle trick, when you start with the punch line and work backward, as I did in "A Wolf is at the Laundromat" from *The New Kid on the Block*. You learn in the last line that the unusually polite wolf doing its laundry is not to be feared, since it is nothing more than a "wash-and-wear-wolf."

So much for the mechanics of making a poem humorous. What do you do when you're stuck for a really funny idea? Watch an "I Love Lucy" rerun—it hasn't failed me yet.

# 86

## RECEIVING A POEM

## By Donald M. Murray

I AM WRITING THIS ARTICLE AS I AM IN THE PROCESS of making myself receptive to poetry: I can command myself to write non-fiction or fiction but I have to receive poetry.

This is not *the* way to write poetry. There is no correct way to write anything, certainly not poetry. This is merely an honest account of the writing of a poem that has not yet arrived with the promise to record precisely what happens.

Last night I knew I would attempt this experiment of writing an article *about* writing poetry *while* writing poetry. I often make my brain aware of the next day's writing. I don't think about the writing but create a climate of awareness.

The morning started badly. I woke too early, slept a bit late, had no time for my morning walk when lines of what may become poetry are often received. I felt this project hopeless, but as I drove back from the store—we were out of juice; I wanted muffins; I had to get the paper—I spotted a neighbor, a forestry expert walking his teenager somewhere. The boy carried a cooler, the father a stool and I made a strange speculation, "He was going out to watch a tree grow." That line might become a poem.

And it was that line that released another line: "August is the month of leaving." I sat in the garage for a moment, not yet speaking silently to myself of the full meaning of August in our family, instead forcing myself to think the line came because of a humorous column I was thinking of writing about what polite lies we speak as dreadful summer guests depart. But I knew that August was the month, fourteen years ago, when our middle daughter died at 20.

Now I will attempt some writing that *may* become a poem, following that fragment—"August is the month of leaving"—to see where it will lead, what connections it will make. The result is usually a clump of

434

half-poetry, half prose in which I write fast, paying some, but not too much attention to line breaks.

I start to censor myself. I do not want to write about Lee's death; I do not want to think about her premature departure. But I may have no choice. I will write about August and see what happens.

## ~~The tide at Ocean Park~~
The morning tide at Ocean Park is out
and I run toward the sun to make my last
collection: razor clam shell, seaweed collar,
driftwood cane. Look back and draw,
with my big toe, this summer's cottage
and myself running toward me, knowing the tide
will return

In August my wool uniform itched as I saw
    Grandma
for the last time. She thought I was leaving
for Waterloo where her great-uncle for whom
I was named had taken a ball in the leg. But
I limped from football and would dance on air
swinging from the parachute kite and discover
all wars are the same.

In August I first learned to swim, took my first
wife blueberrying and in August, the month of
    buzzing
~~and~~ heat, we had the fight over vichyssoise my
    second
wife will not forget. In those last slow days
of August when summersun (paints?) pools of
    brightness
on the lawn and I watch the maple's shadows record
the breeze, we got that call that made us drive madly
home.

Lee told us how sweet her sisters had been in her
    fevered
hours, smiled and gently shut us out of her
                          **[interrupted by phone call]**
slow dying. [anger/rage] My woods are filled with
    leaves,
daisies, tall swaying trees but I walk to the rock
wall, [calm?] not touching the vulnerable blossom
    of the
daylily that opened this hour and will not last
the night.

435

I followed the poem wherever it took me, and, as it so often happens, my writing took me where I did not want to go. I felt physically ill toward the end of its writing, but I also felt I must write it. This not-yet-poem demanded to be heard.

I tried to stay in the poem, not to think but to record. I was on the beach, then—for no reason outside the poem—at Grandma's bedside, then in other Augusts before and after my war without understanding their meaning or connection, and then at Lee's bedside.

I put a parenthesis and question mark around "paints" that I thought a cliché, but I did not want to stop and interrupt the flow. When the phone rings or someone comes by, I stop in mid-line as many writers do, so I can pick it up and re-enter the writing. I was aware in the corner of my eye that the poem seemed to be in stanzas but did not know there were 7-7-8-7 lines until I now count them. I don't like many of the line breaks that seem to end on weak words and do not flow into the next line or stanza, but all that is a matter for the next draft.

I have never made bracketed notes to myself—"anger/rage" and "calm?"—within a draft before but went back and inserted them today to indicate a change of mood that *may* take place in the revision of the poem. I do think I have a text to work on and will let it sit for a while.

This was written on my computer. Usually the first drafts are written by hand in my daybook, but today I paste a printout of the poem in my daybook. I have to visit my laptop in computer hospital in Massachusetts, and the poem keeps on writing a new third stanza in my head. Finally, I stop by the road and scribble down:

It was my ninth August when I drowned, crystal bright spray, the sudden roof of water, blue warm then cold green. My 13th August I learned to swim underwater, daring the blackgreen death. The sudden rising. It was Vermont August, pools of brightness on lawn, the dance of maple leaf shadows when we heard the phone ring ring and suddenly drove home.

It was pretty bad but maybe there was something going on. I tossed the censor and my daybook on the back seat and drove on. In Massachusetts I stopped in a Friendly's, asked for a back booth, and while waiting for my soup and sandwich, played with what I had, trying not to be critical but to see what was working, to release the poem if one was on the page. I put what was inserted in bold type and show what I crossed out.

# August is the Month of Leaving

The morning tide at Ocean Park is out
and I run toward the sun to make my last
collection: razor clam shell, seaweed collar,
driftwood cane. Look back and draw,
with my big toe, this summer's cottage
and myself running toward me, knowing the tide
will return.

~~In August m~~My wool uniform itched **in August** as
   I saw Grandma
for the last time. She thought I was leaving
for Waterloo where her great-uncle ~~for whom~~ **wore**
**my name into battle. He took** ~~I was named had~~
   ~~taken~~ a ball
      in the leg. But **saved the flag his brother**
   **dropped.**
I ~~limped from football and~~ would dance on air,
swinging from the parachute, ~~kite~~ and discover
   all wars
are the same.

~~In August I first learned to swim, took my first~~
~~wife blueberrying and in August, the month of~~
   ~~buzzing~~
~~and heat, we had the fight over vichyssoise my~~
   ~~second~~
~~wife will not forget. In those last slow days~~
~~of August when summersun (paints?) pools~~
   ~~of brightness~~
~~on the lawn and I watch the maple's shadows record~~
~~the breeze, we got that call that made us drive~~
   ~~madly~~
~~home~~.

~~It was~~ my ninth August ~~when~~ I drowned, crystal
   bright
spray, the ~~sudden~~ **rising** roof of water, blue warm
   then cold
      **blackgreen sinking down.**
My 13th August I learned to swim underwater
   **(laughing?)**
      **holding my breath,** ~~daring the blackgreen~~
~~death~~. The
      sudden rising. It was **a** Vermont
August, pools of brightness ~~on~~ **dappled** lawn, the
   dance of
      maple leaf

shadows when we heard the phone ring ring ring
   and ~~suddenly~~
      **madly**
drove home.

Lee told us ~~how sweet~~ her sisters had ~~been~~ **cooled**
   ~~in~~ her fevered **face**
~~hours~~, smiled ~~and~~ **then** gently shut us out of her
slow dying. ~~[angry/rage]~~ My woods are ~~filled~~ **lush**
   with
      ~~leaves~~ **blooms, swollen the poison ivy vine**
~~daisies, tall swaying trees but I walk to the rock~~
~~wall, [calm?] not touching the vulnerable blossom~~
   ~~of the~~
**I watch lush August in my woods then** ~~But I Still~~
   **But** ~~eye~~ **the**
      **yellow-orange** ~~the~~ **flame of the**
daylily that opened this hour and will not last
the night.


It is embarrassing to reveal such bad writing, but it is important that
inexperienced writers learn that writers have to write badly to write
well. I have learned to leave alone what I think works—the first
stanza—but I am most excited by those pages where syntax breaks
down, where language is struggling toward meaning.

I need to write this poem on the eve of the anniversary of my
daughter's death, but I do not know what it means. I have no preconceived theme, no idea; if I did, I would not need to write. The meaning
is in the writing of the poem. I don't know if I will end in anger or with
comfort, perhaps neither or both. I hope I will celebrate Lee's brief life,
but I am open to a complex of meanings or a meaning that will change
each time I read the poem. I know my readers will read according to
their own personal history of loss and their own needs at the moment of
reading. The poem—or any other piece of writing—does not belong to
me or to the reader; the magic is that each reading creates a text that
lies between us to which we both contribute.

The next morning I come to my desk eager to type out the poem
anew, knowing it will change. If I am lucky, it will reveal itself to me if I
listen to the evolving lines.

I type through it quickly, paying attention to the organic growth of the
poem, to the lines and how they break. I work on that first stanza that
had been untouched in yesterday's writing. I write easily, hearing the

poem, now looking back, now worrying a bit about its shape—the shorter lines in the first stanza—and copy it out again to work in close, word by word, space by space, line by line.

I print out the poem I have been given, read it once or twice again, then decide I have a poem I can show my wife and mail to Lee's sisters. I have learned to be careful to whom I show my writing and follow one rule: *Show drafts only to those who make me want to write when I leave.*

In the next days I share it with a few poet friends and a poetry group to which I belong. I listen to their response but do not accept all their counsel. I must respect the poem.

I continue, during the day and evening to read the poem lightly, almost casually, to hear what it is saying. I often read what is not yet on the page. In such a reading, I hear myself say, in the fifth line from the bottom, "fear" instead of "hate." "Fear" was a gift, and I am grateful to receive it. I had never felt right about "hate," but "fear" seems just right; it tells me just what I feel as I observe my August woods.

Stepping back from my writing desk after this sequence of drafts, I discover I have:

- Fleshed out the first stanza, making the innocent experience of August more complete. But, of course, it is not so innocent. There is an erasing tide.
- Tried to write with specific details, proper nouns and active verbs. I do not want to tell the reader what to think or how to feel, but to make the reader think and feel.
- Made the lines—usually—end on a solid piece of information but also provide the energy that will drive to the next line—and to the end of the poem.
- Enjoyed, in a mysterious, profound way, the writing of the poem. Although the subject is painful, it was helpful for me to write it. It is a sublime form of fun to play with language, listening to the lines that lead, the words that reveal, to live on the page, a life that may seem, at times, as intense as experience itself. As a writer, I lead the twice—or thrice—lived life.

I will submit the poem for publication and when it returns, put it in the mail again, but the pleasure of publication, if it comes, is nothing compared to those moments of concentration when I was lost in its receiving, when it revealed to me how I feel as August returns.

This is the poem as it is finished—for the moment:

## August is the Month of Leaving

The morning tide at Ocean Park is out and I run
toward the sun to make my last collection: razor
clam shell, seaweed collar, green bottle from Spain
[no message, no Pirate map], my first driftwood
cane. I used its crooked point to draw this summer's
cottage, the next door wolfhound I feared. I know
the incoming

tide will create memory. In August I saw Grandma
for the last time. My wool uniform itched. She ordered
me to defeat Napoleon at Waterloo. Her great-uncle wore
my name into battle, held high the colors his brother
dropped. I would dance on air, swinging in my parachute
but landing would learn his Belgium lesson: we die
alone

as I drowned my ninth August, crystal bright spray,
the rising roof of water and the blackgreen cold before
my rescue. In my thirteenth summer I learned the projectile
dive, to swim under water, holding my breath, to rise.
And thirteen years ago this August we were in Vermont,
sunlight dappled on the long green lawn when the phone
rang

and we madly drove home. In the hospital Lee told us
her sisters had so gently cooled her fevered face, then
shut us out of her five day dying. I fear August
in my woods, so much green, sun, so many dancing shadows
but still I stand by the yellow-orange flame of the daylilly
that blooms that August morning yet will not survive
the night.

440

# 87

## STALKING THE POETIC IMAGE

### BY MIRIAM SAGAN

HOW DO YOU TOUCH, TASTE, AND SMELL A POEM? How do you *see* it? As a poet, you must bring the poem alive for the reader. You can do this by practicing with metaphor, simile, and imagery. With these techniques, you can make your readers "come to their senses"!

*Simile*. Simile is an ancient poetic technique. It is a device of comparison, using the words "as" or "like." In the Greek poem *The Iliad*, the great warrior Achilles comes down on his enemies "like a lion." Don't forget that a simile should work in both directions: Achilles should be like a lion, but a lion should also be like the hero—bold, kingly, dangerous. For the beginning poet, similes may seem flat or clichéd. It is difficult to come up with something fresh. But you want to avoid stale similes like "my true love's lips are like cherries." Try for a comparison that is just a bit new. I was working with this effect at the end of my poem "The Geology of Mercury":

> Even now, hanging out blue towels
> I am waiting for that meteor
> It is like love, the wrong end of the telescope
> Something wants you—
> A stone with wings.

Here I compare a meteor to love, to something viewed far away, and to something unexpected. Meteor-love-telescope-stone with wings is a chain of similes, hopefully fresher than "your cheeks are like roses."

*"Laundry" lists*. One trick for creating fresh similes is to create two lists. For list A, write down ordinary human activities, whatever comes to mind:

441

laundry
riding a bicycle
tickling a child
eating an apple
sharpening a pencil

And for list B, write some observations from the natural world. Try to be as specific as possible:

a sunset over the Atlantic
apricot blossoms
hill of red ants
piece of mica
dandelion in a crack in the sidewalk

Now, for your simile, take one item from list A and one from list B. Maybe the combination will seem silly or useless; maybe it will be unique and interesting. Here are some examples I might use in a poem: "Biting into an apple is like a sunset over the Atlantic." The two images share the color red and a sense of sharpness or pungency. Even wilder: "Biting into an apple is like stepping on a hill of red ants." Try your own combinations. They won't be perfect, but they will give you a new way of playing with comparisons. Don't take this too seriously—it should be fun!

*Metaphor.* The romantic poet and critic Coleridge said that metaphor is the "linking together of disparate elements." Metaphor is a comparison that does not use the words "as" or "like." A metaphor is a delicate balance. There should be just enough tension in the metaphor to avoid making it a cliché, but not so much that it falls apart. (Look back at my two lists. I don't think laundry and a dandelion have much in common, so I wouldn't try to compare them. But laundry on a line might be nice next to a cloud of apricot blossoms.)

Look at the following short poem by Anne Valley-Fox, and watch for the metaphors, both obvious and implied.

## New Year's Resolution

Hike to the nape of Moon Mountain in ice
bright air: stand
on the giant's shoulders and say *thank you*

Here, the mountain is compared to a giant, and the poet is tiny beneath

442

the peak. There is an implied metaphor between the "resolution" of the title and the hike, as if to say that human change is a difficult, if exciting, possibility.

*Image.* An image is any condensed sense perception used in a poem. Poems that depend almost exclusively on images are sometimes called "imagist." Here is a short poem by Elizabeth Searle Lamb that depends on image and contrast for its effect.

## Search

stumbling
onto her body
in the ditch
white butterflies

The sudden image of death is contrasted to the flight of butterflies, an image of life or rebirth. Notice that the poet doesn't come out and say: life and death, what a contrast. Rather, she *shows* us through imagery.

*Elements of haiku.* A haiku is a Japanese poem that depends on image for its effect. In Japanese, it is written in three vertical lines and is composed of approximately seventeen characters or ideograms. Obviously, the form is different when written in English. To try writing a haiku in English, 1) limit yourself to 2, 3, or at most 4 lines; 2) use no more than 17 syllables in total; 3) aim for a sharp image; 4) use contrast. One of Elizabeth Searle Lamb's haikus has all these elements:

this clear morning
a couple of rose petals
in the spider web

See how many contrasts you can find in this poem in terms of color, texture, and the ephemeral nature of things.

*Multiple images.* Most poems, of course, are more than three lines long, and have more than one image. When you work with multiple images, you must apply all the rules of metaphor and simile. Aim for *both* unity and freshness. That's what I tried for in my poem "Black Grapes." The central image of the first stanza is San Francisco Bay:

443

> Where the water is so cold, dark, and salt
> And everything leeches away
> Beneath the bridge's golden span.

By contrast, the second stanza is set in the desert:

> A black and brown dog noses
> Along the dry irrigation ditch

While in the final stanza there is again an image of water and richness:

> But at the greengrocer's
> There are bunches of black grapes
> That taste purple cold, so sweet.

The repetition of the word "cold" ties the grapes back to the ocean and the feeling of the ocean.

*The senses.* Images do not have to be purely visual. I think of Santa Fe poet Mary McGinnis, blind from birth, whose work is full of sense imagery. She once wrote that a woman's voice was "like cherry bark tea." Here a sound and taste are successfully contrasted in a simile. How can you get out of the rut of using only the visual in your poems? Close your eyes. What do you *hear*? *smell*? *feel*? even *taste*?

*Synesthesia.* If you tap your closed eye with your finger, you will sometimes see a flash of light. Your eye translates touch as vision. Synesthesia means that one sense has fused with another. Write a poem that answers some of the following questions: What is the smell of loneliness? What is the sound of a calla lily? What is the taste of rubies? What is the feeling of the Milky Way? Make up your own questions, and answer them. Don't be afraid to be a little bit silly, or daring.

*Stalking the wild image.* It is important to you as a poet to keep yourself refreshed. You want to experience the world in a new way and be able to communicate it. In the midst of a busy life, it is not easy to keep inspiration going. Here are some ways to keep your senses alive.

*A notebook of images.* Get a blank notebook and began filling it with images that appeal to you—details from magazines, art postcards,

444

observations as you go through your daily routines. When I feel stuck, I sometimes buy an architectural or design magazine, cut out pictures, and then jot down lines or contrasting images that come to me. A visit to a museum or a sculpture garden can serve the same purpose.

*A field trip.* In Japan, it is traditional to go view cherry blossoms and then to write a poem. Try this with some seasonal sights—buying pumpkins, putting in flower bulbs, raking leaves. Go for a poetry walk in your own neighborhood, or an ethnic part of the city. What is the weather? What does the moon look like? What can you smell in the air? Look for tiny details, an old woman watering a geranium, a toddler cowgirl waving a pistol. How do the people interact with the environment? Do you notice anything touching, or poignant? Write down what you experience. You may have captured a poem. And now you too can exalt with the poet Wordsworth: "Oh taste and see!"

# 88

## THE POET WITHIN YOU

### BY DAVID KIRBY

I FIGURE POETRY is a way of beating the odds. The world is never going to give you everything you want, so why not look elsewhere? In a wonderful book called *The Crisis of Creativity* (now regrettably out of print) by George Seidel, it is stated that the artist will always have one thing no one else can have: a life within a life.

And that's only the start. If you have talent and luck and you work like a son of a gun, you might even end up, as the poet John Berryman says, adding to "the store of available reality."

But at least you can have a life within a life, no matter who you are. Not all of us can be great poets. If that were so, the Nobel Prize would be in every box of breakfast cereal—you'd get up, write your poem for the day, and collect your prize. But every literate person has it in him- or herself to be a good poet. Indeed, I have wonderful news for you— each of us is a poet already, or at least we used to be. It's just that most of us have gone into early retirement.

Seriously, when interviewers ask the marvelously gifted William Stafford when he started to write poetry, Stafford often replies, "When did you stop?" All children put words together imaginatively; just talk to one and you'll see what I mean. But then they grow up and enter the world of bills and backaches. They start chasing that dollar, and suddenly their time is limited. Poetry is usually the first thing to go. People get so busy with their lives that they forget to have a life within a life. But you have a life anyway, right? So forget about it for a minute—it'll still be there when you come back—and let's talk about the poet within you.

The first thing you need to do is forget that all poets are supposed to be erratic or unstable. Flaubert was quite clear on this point. He said, "Be regular and orderly in your life, like a bourgeois, so that you may be violent and original in your work." In other words, there's no point

446

in sapping your resources by pursuing some phony "artistic" lifestyle. First, the outer person has to be calm and self-disciplined; only then can the inner one be truly spontaneous.

And that means getting organized. Here are a few rules I use to make my life as orderly and bourgeois as possible, so that the poet within me can be as wild as he wants to be.

1) *Start small.* Most beginning writers tackle the big themes: love, death, the meaning of life. But don't we already know everything there is to know about these subjects? Love is wonderful, death is terrible, life is mysterious. So start small and work your way up. Take a phrase you overheard, a snippet of memory, a dream fragment, and make a poem of that. Once the details are in place, the big theme (whatever it is) will follow, but the details have to come first.

2) *Write about what you remember.* It is a commonplace that you should write about what you know, but usually the present is too close for us to see it clearly. We have to move away from the events in our lives before we can see them in such a way that we can write about them engagingly. Don't waste time on the guy you saw talking to his dog this morning; take a few notes, if you like, but if he's memorable, he'll pop into your mind later, when you really need him. Instead, why not write a poem about the girl in your third-grade class who could throw a baseball better than any of the boys and all the problems that caused? By putting these memories down on paper and shaping them, you're enriching not only your own life but also the lives of others.

3) *Be a sponge.* Shakespeare was. His plays are based on historical accounts and on lesser plays by earlier playwrights. So what are you, better than Shakespeare? I once wrote a poem called "The Last Song on the Jukebox" that was published in a magazine and then in a collection of my poetry and now in an anthology that is widely used on college campuses; people seem to like it pretty well. Looking back at the poem, I can hear in it echoes of two country songs that I used to be able to sing in their entireties but have since forgotten. Somebody says something in my poem that is a variation on something a character says in a novel called *Ray,* by the talented Barry Hannah. And the overall tone of "The Last Song on the Jukebox" owes much to a poet I heard reading his own work one night. His voice was perfect—it had just the right twang to it—so I used it for the speaker in my poem. Now that I

447

think about it, I realize that I didn't like the guy's poetry that much. That didn't stop me from adapting his twang to my purpose.

4) *Play dumb*. Just about anything can be turned into a poem if you play dumb about it, because when you're smart, everything makes sense to you and you go about your business, whereas when you're dumb, you have to slow down, stop, figure things out. Recently, in Chicago, I saw a man being arrested. The police had cuffed him and were hauling him away while an elderly woman shook with rage and screamed after them as they all climbed into the paddywagon. "Liar!" she shouted, "liar!" You mean you can get arrested just for lying, I said to myself? Is that only in Chicago, or does the law apply everywhere? Now if I were a smart person, I might have figured out what really happened: Probably the guy grabbed her purse, and she called the cops, and he said he didn't do it, and she said he *did* do it, and so on. But by being dumb, I got a flying start on a poem. I haven't finished the poem yet, but as you can see, I have already given myself a lot to work with, thanks to my astonishingly low IQ.

5) *Reverse your field*. When you catch yourself on the verge of saying something obvious, don't just stop; instead, say the opposite of what you were going to say in the first place. Listen to the poet within you. If you want to eat a chocolate bar, that's not poetry; everybody likes chocolate. But suppose the chocolate bar wanted to eat you? Now that's a poem. Here's another example: I'm thinking of ending my liar-in-Chicago poem with something about husbands and wives and how they have to be truthful to each other, and I can see myself heading toward a stanza in which the speaker wonders what his wife really means when she says (and this would be the last line of the poem), "I love you." The problem is that that's too pat for a last line, too cloying, too sentimental, an easy out. Instead, since people who are really crazy about each other sometimes kid around in a mock-hostile way, why not have the speaker wonder whether the wife is telling the truth or not when she laughs and hits him on the arm and says, "I hate you, you big lug!" Such an unexpected statement would come as a surprise to the reader, although first it will have come as a surprise to me, who was heading in the opposite direction before I realized that I needed to reverse my field.

6) *Work on several poems at once.* For one thing, you won't end up giving too much attention to a poem that doesn't need it—like children, some poems do better if you don't breathe down their necks all the time. For another, if you're working on just one poem and it isn't going anywhere, you're likely to feel terribly frustrated, whereas if one poem is dying on the vine and three others are doing pretty well, you'll feel as though you are ahead of the game (because you will be). Also, sometimes our poems are smarter than we are, and a word or a line or a stanza that isn't right for one poem will often migrate to another and find a home for itself there. Poems are happiest in the company of other poems, so don't try to create them in a vacuum. You probably wouldn't try to write four novels at once, but there's no reason why you shouldn't take advantage of poetry's brevity and get several poems going simultaneously.

7) *Give yourself time.* This is actually related to the preceding rule, since you wouldn't tend to rush a poem if you were working on several of them at once. I have a friend whose daughter is learning how to cook. But she's a little impatient, so when she has a recipe that says you should bake the cake at 350 degrees for thirty minutes, she doesn't see why you can't cook it at 700 degrees for fifteen minutes. If you take this approach to poetry, your poems are going to end up like my friend's daughter's cakes, charred on the outside and raw in the middle. If you saw a stunningly handsome stranger walking down the street, would you run up to him and shout, "Marry me"? Of course not—he might say yes! Poems are the same way, and if you try to make them yours too soon, you won't be happy with the results, I promise you. Be coy, be flirtatious; draw the poem out a little and see what it's really about. There's no hurry, because you've got all those other poems you're working on, remember?

8) *Find a perfect reader.* A perfect reader is like a perfect tennis partner, someone who is a little better than you are (so you feel challenged), but not that much better (so you don't get demoralized). And like an ideal tennis partner, a good reader is going to be hard to find. You don't play tennis with your mother, so don't expect her to critique your writing.

Anyway, what kind of mother would tell her own child that his poetry is terrible? That's what friends are for. So no parents. And no room-mates, either: people are always saying to me, "You're going to love this poem; my roommate says it's the best thing I've ever written." What else would a roommate say? You can hardly go on living with someone after you've told him to throw his notebook away and take up basket-weaving. Just as you would play tennis with a couple of dozen people before you pick the one you want to play with every Saturday, so too should you pass your poems around until you find the one person who can show you their strengths and weaknesses without inflating or deflating your ego too much. If you're lucky, you'll then do what I did when I found my perfect reader—you'll marry her (or him).

If you have a knack for language and you follow these rules and you get a break from time to time and you look both ways whenever you cross the street, after a while you will find you have created for yourself a life within a life. You will have awakened—reawakened, actually—the poet within you. And even if this isn't your year to win the Nobel Prize, I have to say that I never met anybody who didn't break out into a big happy smile when I introduced myself as a poet. I don't know what it is; maybe people associate me with Homer or Milton. At any rate, every-one seems happy to know there is a poet in the neighborhood.

Well, not everybody. Once I was negotiating with a man to buy his house, and I was getting the better of him. So the man lost his temper and said I didn't know what I was doing, I *couldn't* know, because I was a poet and I ought to go back to my poems and leave business affairs to men like him, practical, level-headed men. For a couple of days, I felt pretty rotten, although the whole thing turned out spledidly for me, since I later found another house I liked even better than his. Mean-while, the practical level-headed fellow had lost a great buyer; like Flaubert, I believe in paying my bills on time.

And I got my revenge: I wrote a poem about him.

450

# JUVENILE AND YOUNG ADULT

# 89

## WHAT'S AHEAD FOR CHILDREN'S BOOKS?

### BY JAMES CROSS GIBLIN

As WE MOVE THROUGH THE 90S, THE CHILDREN'S BOOK FIELD is sending out mixed signals.

I'd like to offer a broad overview of some trends I see in the field. It will necessarily be a personal perspective, and somewhat limited, as all such overviews are. But I hope it may provide insights that will be helpful to both beginning and established children's book authors.

The boom in children's books in the last few years has affected every aspect of the field. What caused it? A number of things, in my opinion.

• First, a new generation of enlightened parents wanted their children to be good readers.

• Bookstores specializing in children's books were established to meet these parents' and children's needs, and the major bookstore chains such as B. Dalton and Waldenbooks began to show a new interest in books for children.

• Beginning in California in the mid-1980s, educators proposed a much wider use of children's trade books in the teaching of reading. Instead of getting snippets of children's literature in textbook anthologies, students from preschool through high school were introduced to outstanding examples of picture books, novels, and nonfiction titles.

This innovative method—part of what became known as "the whole language approach"—has since been adopted by educators in many other states and has resulted in greatly increased sales of children's books to schools in both hardcover and paperback editions.

• Children's book publishers responded to this growth in bookstore and school markets by expanding their lists, and many new publishers entered the field in order to get a slice of the pie the boom created. As a result, authors with established reputations have been able to command better contract terms than ever before, and talented new writers have found a more receptive market for their efforts.

However, all is not rosy. Public and school libraries, long the mainstay of the hardcover children's book field, have been hit hard by federal, state, and local budget cuts. They're still buying books, but recently I've noted a disturbing, though understandable, sales pattern. The libraries are purchasing as many if not more copies of the "big" books on a publisher's list: those that have received starred reviews in the library media and won prizes and awards. But they're buying fewer copies of what are sometimes called "midlist" books—the solid, well-done picture books, novels, or nonfiction titles that achieve their goals and deserve to find a readership, even though they may not be of award calibre.

Librarians are also more hesitant about taking a chance on books by unknown authors unless they are greeted by enthusiastic reviews and make a major splash.

In light of these trends, what steps can authors take to insure that their manuscripts will attract first the attention of editors, and then the attention of bookstore customers? What values can they instill in their projects so that librarians will feel they're essential purchases despite tight budgets?

Some answers to these questions can be found by looking in turn at each of the key areas in children's book publishing. Let's start with *picture books.*

1. There's a need for fresh material for children of one to three, but the texts can't be just another introduction to colors and shapes and familiar everyday objects. Editors are looking for more authors who can tell simple but strong stories for this age group, as Cathryn Falwell has done in her books about a little boy named Nicky.

2. Folk and fairy tales attract many writers who retell traditional tales or try to write a new story that follows the classic pattern. But this type of picture book has become more and more the province of illustrators, many of whom write the texts as well as illustrating them. A good example is the 1990 Caldecott Medal winner Ed Young, who

translated and also illustrated his own version of the Chinese Red Riding Hood story, *Lon Po Po.*

Of course, an illustrator who writes his own text receives the entire royalty and doesn't have to share it with a writer.

3. Instead of retelling an old tale, why not think of a fresh variation on a common family or preschool situation? Careful observation of your own children or incidents that occur in your neighborhood can yield appealing new approaches to such themes as sibling rivalry, parent-child relations, and adjusting to the routines of kindergarten and first grade. Editors are always on the lookout for such stories, especially if told with charm and insight.

4. What other sorts of picture book stories would editors like to see more of?

• Stories with real plots and lots of action that suggest exciting illustrations, all presented in a manuscript of no more than four or five double-spaced, typewritten pages. Anything longer won't allow room for illustrations.

• Genuinely funny stories, like Harry Allard's picture books about Miss Nelson and Jon Scieszka's *The True Story of the Three Little Pigs by A. Wolf.*

• Stories with strong endings. Too many picture book manuscripts start off well but end flatly or just stop in a very unsatisfying way for young children. To avoid this, you should have your ending in mind before you begin. Eve Bunting, author of *Scary, Scary Halloween* and *The Wednesday Surprise,* uses this approach. She never begins a picture book until she knows what the last line—the final twist—will be.

5. Another type of picture book in demand today is the story that will lend itself to what I call "beautiful" illustrations. With the bookstore market for children's books growing in importance, especially for picture books, buyers gravitate toward large, strikingly illustrated books that will catch the eye of their customers. Stories set in exotic locales, or in the remote past, or that record dramatic events like a blizzard or a forest fire, all lend themselves to this kind of sweeping pictorial treatment. But they must *first* of all be strong stories in their

own right. No picture book has ever been an enduring success on the strength of its illustrations alone.

6. Editors generally prefer stories written in lyrical prose rather than verse. Far too many authors—especially beginners—make the mistake of thinking they'll have a better chance of placing their picture book manuscripts if they're written in verse. They're wrong. Too often the authors get so involved in maintaining the rhyme scheme that they lose the thread of the stories they're trying to tell. They'd stand a much better chance with editors if they wrote their stories in prose instead.

7. Now for some picture book themes that editors definitely *don't* want to see more of because they've been done to death:
• The story that ends with the protagonist waking up and discovering it was all just a dream.

• The text that personifies an inanimate object or substance—"How Gerald Germ Traveled Through Billy's Body," or some such. In most instances, personification should be limited to human beings.

• The story in which the protagonist wants to be something else and imagines a long list of alternatives. Just once, at the end of one of these stories, I wish the hero *wouldn't* decide he'd rather be himself after all.

What about *nonfiction?* How has the boom affected it and its authors?

1. There's been a proliferation of nonfiction series. Running the gamut from biographies, to sports books, to explorations of topical issues, they are being offered by such relatively new publishers as Chelsea House and Crestwood House, as well as by such established firms as Franklin Watts.

Some of these books are well edited and produced; some aren't. They give many authors the opportunity to be published, some for the first time. But it's difficult for any one title in a series to rise above the rest and get individual critical attention. So if you want your nonfiction book to be noticed, you'll be better off doing it with a house that publishes each title as a separate entity.

2. The boom has also affected the individual book in a positive way. Never has children's nonfiction received as many prestigious prizes and awards as in the past few years. Newbery Honors have gone to Rhoda

Blumberg's *Commodore Perry in the Land of the Shōgun* and Patricia Lauber's *Volcano: The Eruption and Healing of Mt. St. Helens,* and the Newberry Medal itself to Russell Freedman's *Lincoln: A Photobiography.*

3. Why have these and similar nonfiction titles received so much acclaim? It seems to me there are several reasons:

• The texts are not only accurate, but are carefully written with moments of humor and drama, and attention to literary style. They tell true stories that are entertaining as well as informative.

• They find a fresh angle on sometimes familiar subject matter, like Freedman's *Lincoln* with its extensive use of archival photographs that hadn't appeared in other biographies of Lincoln for children. Or else they center on offbeat topics that, for one reason or another, haven't been treated before, like my book *Chimney Sweeps.*

• Where appropriate, they include the contributions of non-Western peoples and cultures. For example, in my book *From Hand to Mouth,* which is a history of eating utensils and table manners, there's a chapter on chopsticks and how to use them. Such multicultural information is much sought after by teachers and librarians.

• Unlike many children's nonfiction titles of the past, books in this category today focus closely on a single topic instead of surveying an entire subject area. They may broaden out to make general points, but they don't attempt to be encyclopedic. For example, Lauber's *Volcano* is about a single volcano, Mt. St. Helens, not volcanoes in general. Such a close focus stands a better chance of getting a reader's attention and making a lasting impression.

• Most important of all, today's nonfiction books are visually inviting. The pages and type are laid out with as much care as a picture book, the paper is of high quality, and the books are elaborately illustrated, usually with photographs. When appropriate to the subject, many of the photographs are being reproduced in full color. But sometimes black-and-white photographs are more effective, like the archival pictures that appear in *Lincoln.*

After most nonfiction writers have finished the texts of their books, they have to do illustration research for them. Finding just the right photos is a time-consuming job, but it is also enjoyable—and it's essential these days if you want your book to be eye-catching and satisfying to readers.

Finally, let's take a look at what's happening in the *fiction* field today.

1. Editors continue to call for chapter books for the 7- to 10-year-old audience. These are short novels divided into six or so chapters, each of which runs to about five or six manuscript pages. They can be any type of story—mystery, adventure, home-and-school—but they all should have appealing characters and fresh dramatic situations at the core. And they don't have to conform to any limited vocabulary lists. Examples of successful chapter books include Jane Resh Thomas's dramatic story, *The Comeback Dog,* Stephen Manes's wacky comedy, *Be a Perfect Person in Just Three Days,* and Sue Alexander's tender story of a lonely girl, *Lila on the Landing.*

A word of warning: Don't make the mistake of thinking a slight, uninvolving story will pass muster with an editor looking for chapter books just because it's short. If anything, a chapter book has to be more compelling than other types of fiction if you want it to catch and hold the attention of beginning readers.

2. Editors are also seeking middle-grade fiction for 8- to 12-year-olds. Contemporary stories featuring characters with whom readers can easily identify dominate this area, but there's room for other types of material including fantasies. However, these must be written with today's young readers in mind and move along at a faster pace than many middle-grade novels of the past. If you're interested in writing for this audience, the novels of Katherine Paterson, Lois Lowry, Betsy Byars, Mary Downing Hahn, and Marion Dane Bauer are excellent models to study.

3. For several reasons, fiction for young adults is a more problematical category today than it was a few years ago. In the paperback area, the fad for teenage romances seems to have run its course, and it isn't clear what new type of story will inspire the same sort of enthusiasm in readers.

Whether published in paperback or hardcover, the "problem novel" has lost its power to shock, since virtually every topic, from drugs to incest to AIDS, has been explored in numerous stories aimed at teenagers. Most damaging of all for the young adult field, library studies show that serious young readers are turning to adult books at earlier ages than ever.

Even so, there continues to be a market, although a limited one, for the hardcover novel for older teens. But to convince an editor to buy your manuscript, you'll need to people it with strong characters, treated in depth, and put them into an unusual dramatic situation. Your writing style will have to be rich and distinctive, too, if it is to win the kind of praise from reviewers that will result in sales to libraries—still the key market for hardcover young adult books. Authors whose novels have earned this kind of critical acceptance, and whose titles merit study in terms of craft, include Richard Peck, Pam Conrad, Bruce Brooks, and M. E. Kerr.

4. Now for two suggestions that can apply to stories for any of the age groups we've discussed:
• Give historical fiction a chance, especially historical novels set during the last forty or so years. The drug scene today may be too unclear and confusing for you to treat in a novel, but what about the choices kids made back in the 1960s, when drugs first became a national concern? You might be able to approach that historical material with the necessary perspective, and use it as the basis of a convincing story.

It's interesting to note that two popular Newbery Medal winners in the last few years—Patricia MacLachlan's *Sarah, Plain and Tall* and Lois Lowry's *Number the Stars*—are both historical novels. And *Number the Stars* takes place in a fairly recent period, the Nazi occupation of Denmark during World War II.

• Don't feel you always have to be serious. Fiction can appeal to a wide range of emotions, and children, like their elders, love to laugh at something funny, or feel a chill run down their spines when something scary happens. In light of this, editors wish more children's fiction writers would turn their attention to humorous stories, to clever mysteries, to ghost stories and stories of suspense—in other words to escape literature. But, of course, it must be done well.

Though the children's book boom may be confusing at times, and authors—especially untried ones—may have a more difficult time placing their manuscripts, I'm sure the majority will rise to the challenge. Knowing the stiff competition they face in the marketplace, they will ask themselves the following questions: Is this a really fresh idea? And will it result in a truly special book manuscript, one that no editor—or child—will be able to resist?

If authors find the right answers to these questions, and incorporate them in their work, chances are they'll be on their way to publishing success.

# 90

## WRITING "HIGH" FANTASY:
## *ONCE UPON A TIME TOO OFTEN*

### BY PATRICIA A. MCKILLIP

THE FORMULA IS SIMPLE. TAKE ONE FIFTEENTH-CENTURY PALACE with high towers and pennants flying, add a hero who talks like a butler, a wizard with fireworks under his fingernails, and a Lurking Evil that threatens the kingdom or the heroine, and there you have it: high fantasy in the making. And there we have all had it up to the proverbial "here." How many times can you repeat the same plot? But how can you write high fantasy without the traditional trappings, characters, and plot that are essential for this kind of fantasy? There are other kinds—fantasies set in the contemporary world, mingling folklore and reality, using familiar language like "rock and roll" and "cholesterol," in which you don't have to worry so much about the clichés of the genre. But this, for perverse reasons I don't fully understand, is not the kind I choose to write. So I am forced to ask myself the same question when I begin a new fantasy: How can it follow the rules of high fantasy and break them at the same time?

### The hero

In the *Riddle-Master* trilogy, my impulse was to be as deliberately traditional as possible: A ruler leaves the comforts of his castle to learn from wizards how to fight a Lurking Evil that threatens to destroy his land. The hero, the magic, the danger, are after all elements of fantasy as old as storytelling. But how do you give the Generic Hero—who only has to be high-born, look passable, and fight really well to be a hero—personality? I discarded quite a number of auditioning heroes before settling on Morgon, Prince of Hed, ruler of a tiny island, who liked to make beer, read books, didn't own a sword, and kept the only crown he possessed under his bed. He did not talk like an English butler, he knew which end of a shovel was up, and only a penchant for wanting to learn odd things kept him from being a sort of placid gentleman farmer. That small detail—among all the details of a prosaic, hard-headed life that included farming, trading, pig-herders, backyard pumps and a couple of strong-willed siblings—became the conflict in his personality but ultimately drove him from his land and set him on his questing path. Before I let him set forth, I placed him against as detailed a background as I possibly could. I wanted the reader to see the land Morgon lived in and how it shaped him before he left it and changed himself. So I let him talk about grain and bulls, beer and plowhorses, and his sister's bare feet, before I let him say fairy tale words like tower, wizard, harp, and king, and state his own driving motivation: to answer the unanswered riddle.

## The heroine

In *The Sorceress and the Cygnet,* my questing hero found himself falling literally into the path of my questing heroine. She is, in one sense, the princess in the tower whom my hero eventually rescues; in other words, she is very much a piece of the familiar storytelling formula. But she has imprisoned herself in a rickety old house in a swamp, trapped there by her own obsession with the darker side of magic. As she defines herself: "I have been called everything from sorceress to bog hag. I know a great many things but never enough. Never enough. I know the great swamp of night, and sometimes I do things for pay if it interests me." She has pursued her quest for knowledge and power into a dangerous backwater of mean, petty magic, from which, it is clear to everyone but her, she must be rescued. The language she uses, like Morgon's, covers a broad territory between palace and pigherder's hut. Her wanderings have freed her tongue, and she can use words like "sorceress" and "bog hag" in the same sentence.

In the same novel, I also used a female point of view, that of a highborn lady, to contrast with the more earthy, gypsyish, view of my hero. She is the female version of the "friend of the hero"; she frets about the sorceress, gives advice, and fights beside her in the end. She is perhaps the toughest kind of character to work with: genuinely good, honest, and dutiful. Making a point-of-view character both good and interesting is a challenge. Traditionally, a "good" character has a limited emotional

462

range, no bad habits to speak of, and a rather bland vocabulary. As the "friend of the heroine," she is also a sounding board for the heroine's more colorful character. I deliberately chose that kind of character because I wanted to see how difficult it would be to make her more than just a device to move the plot along its necessary path. She turned out to be extraordinarily difficult. I wanted her to be elegant, dignified, calm, responsible. That meant whatever humor a situation sparked would not come from her, but from some conjunction of words in her dialogue, and that to keep her from fading completely into the plot, I constantly had to provide her with events that brought out her best qualities. Manipulating the rhythms in the dialogue also helped to keep her from being overwhelmed with blandness, as in this scene when she is in bed with the Gatekeeper—another good but not nearly so difficult character—who is supposed to be watching the gate:

> "Don't," she pleaded, her eyes closed. "Nothing is out there."
> "I must watch." He sounded still asleep.
> "Stay with me. Don't leave me yet. Not even dawn is at the gate."
> "The gate moved."
> "It's only wind at the gate. Only rain."
> "I must watch."
> "I'll watch," she said, and felt him sink back. She pushed against him; he wound his hand into her hair. "I'll watch . . ."

Keeping her dialogue simple and immediate kept her uncomplicated yet responsive as a character; it also moved the plot forward without dragging along the unnecessary baggage of introspection. She is meant to observe and act; the language should not be more complicated than she is.

## The Lurking Evil

Traditionally, the evil in fantasy is personified by someone of extraordinary and perverse power, whose goal in life is to bring the greatest possible misery to the largest number of good honest folk. Sauron of the *Lord of the Rings* trilogy, Darth Vader of the *Star Wars* trilogy, Morgan le Fay of *Le Morte D'Arthur,* are all examples of social misfits from whose destructive powers the hero and heroine must rescue humanity and hobbits and the world as they know it. The problem with the Lurking Evil is that as social misfit, it might become far more interesting than the good and dutiful hero, yet without proper

463

background and personality, the Lurking Evil becomes a kind of un-motivated monster vacuum cleaner that threatens humanity simply because it's plugged in and turned on.

I have trouble coming up with genuinely evil characters who are horrible, remorseless, and deserving of everything the hero can dish out. I always want to give them a human side, which puts them in the social misfit category. In the *Riddle-Master* trilogy, I used various kinds of misfits: the renegade wizard Ohm, who was motivated by an unprincipled desire for magical power; the sea-people, whose intentions and powers seem at first random and obscure until they finally reveal their origins; and the ambiguous character Deth, who may be good and may be evil and who keeps my hero off-balance and guessing until the end of the tale.

In *The Sorceress and the Cygnet,* I used much the same kind of device: allowing my hero to define characters as evil until they, in the end, reveal that the evil is not in them, but in my misguided heroine. I do this because evil as a random event, or as the sole motivation for a character, is difficult for me to work with; it seems to belong in another genre, to horror, or mystery. Jung says that all aspects of a dream are actually faces of the dreamer. I believe that in fantasy, the vanquished evil must be an aspect of the hero or heroine, since by tradition, evil is never stronger than the power of the hero to overcome it—which is where, of course, we get the happy endings in high fantasy.

## Magic

If you put a mage, sorceress, wizard, warlock, witch, or necromancer into fantasy, it's more than likely that they will want, sooner or later, to work some magic. Creating a spell can be as simple or as difficult as you want. You can write: "Mpyxl made a love potion. Hormel drank it and fell in love." Or you can do research into herb lore and medieval recipes for spells and write: "Mpyxl stirred five bay leaves, an owl's eye, a parsnip, six of Hormel's fingernails and some powdered mugwort into some leftover barley soup. Hormel ate it and fell in love." Or you can consider love itself, and how Mpyxl must desire Hormel, how frustrated and rejected she must feel to be obliged to cast a spell over him, what in Hormel generates such overpowering emotions, why he refuses to fall in love with Mpyxl the usual way, and what causes people to fall in love with each other in the first place. Then you will find that Mpyxl herself

464

is under a spell cast by Hormel, and that she must change before his eyes from someone he doesn't want to someone he desires beyond reason. The language of such a spell would be far different from fingernails and barley soup. The Magic exists only in the language; the spell exists only in the reader's mind. The words themselves must create something out of nothing. To invent a convincing love potion you must, for a moment, make even the reader fall in love.

## Why?

Why write fantasy? Because it's there. Fantasy is as old as poetry and myth, which are as old as language. The rules of high fantasy are the rules of the unconscious and the imagination, where good quests, evil lurks, the two clash, and the victor—and the reader—are rewarded. Good might be male or female, so might evil. The battle might be fought with swords, with magic, with wits, on a battlefield, in a tower, or in the quester's heart. At its best, fantasy rewards the reader with a sense of wonder about what lies within the heart of the commonplace world. The greatest tales are told over and over, in many ways, through centuries. Fantasy changes with the changing times, and yet it is still the oldest kind of tale in the world, for it began once upon a time, and we haven't heard the end of it yet.

---

## Author's Postscript

Since I write both fantasy and science fiction, I've often been asked how I deal with the difference between the two. The difference between fantasy and science fiction is like the horizon line, at once very big and very small. There are novels weighted with elements of fantasy which are defined as S/F because they have a technological explanation of how the morning coffee is made. There are nicely researched science fiction novels whose compelling themes of the quest or of the transference of power are straight out of the heritage of fantasy. I tend to weigh the elements in a novel of fantasy or science, and whichever dominate, whichever are most necessary or most moving to me, define its genre for me. I'm not sure that it matters a great deal: Even the contemporary novel is becoming vulnerable to elements of fantasy. For my own purposes, I try to keep the two separate. If I'm writing fantasy I use elements of epic, fantasy, myth, legend; and if I put magic in it, it's magic out of the imagination and out of the heart. When I write S/F, I try to turn my back on traditional fantasy elements and extrapolate a plot from history or everyday life, or whatever science seems to stick in my head. I'm probably more successful at keeping S/F out of my fantasy than keeping fantasy out of my S/F. The heritage, the roots and background of S/F are very different from those of fantasy. The language is different; the images I find in my mind when I contemplate an S/F plot are different. The stars in *Riddle-Master* are a symbol. The stars in science fiction are real.

# ⸨ 91

## Is It Good Enough for Children?

### By Madeleine L'Engle

A while ago when I was teaching a course on techniques of fiction, a young woman came up to me and said, "I do hope you're going to teach us something about writing for children, because that's why I'm taking this course."

"What have I been teaching you?" I asked her.

"Well—writing."

"Don't you write when you write for children?"

"Yes, but—isn't it different?"

No, I assured her, it isn't different. The techniques of fiction are the techniques of fiction, and they hold as true for Beatrix Potter as they do for Dostoevsky.

But the idea that writing for children isn't the same as writing for adults is prevalent indeed, and usually goes along with the conviction that it isn't quite as good. If you're a good enough writer for adults, the implication is, of course, you don't write for children. You write for children only when you can't make it in the real world, because writing for children is easier.

Wrong, wrong, wrong!

I had written several regular trade novels before a publisher asked me to write about my Swiss boarding school experiences. Nobody had told me that you write differently when you write for children, so I didn't. I just wrote the best book I possibly could; it was called *And Both Were Young*. After that I wrote *Camilla*, which has been reissued as a young adult novel, and then *Meet the Austins*. It's hard today for me to understand that this simple little book had a very hard time finding a publisher because it's about a death and how an ordinary family reacts to that death. Death at that time was taboo. Children weren't supposed to know about it. I had a couple of offers of publication if I'd take the death out. But the reaction of the family—children as well as the parents—to the death was the core of the book.

Nowadays what we offer children makes *Meet the Austins* seem pale, and on the whole, I think that's just as well, because children know a lot more than most grown-ups give them credit for. *Meet the Austins* came out of my own family's experience with several deaths. To have tried to hide those deaths from our children would have been blind stupidity. All hiding does is confuse children and add to their fears. It is not subject matter that should be taboo, but the way it is handled.

A number of years ago—the first year I was actually making reasonable money from my writing—my sister-in-law was visiting us, and when my husband told her how much I had earned that year, she was impressed and commented, "And to think most people would have had to word so hard for that!"

Well, it is work, it's most certainly work; wonderful work, but work. Revision, revision, revision. Long hours spent not only in the actual writing, but in research. I think the best thing I learned in college was how to do research, so that I could go right on studying after I had graduated.

Of course, it is not *only* work; it is work that makes the incomprehensible comprehensible. Leonard Bernstein says that for him music is cosmos in chaos. That is true for writing a story, too. Aristotle says that what is plausible and impossible is better than what is possible and implausible.

That means that story must be *true,* not necessarily *factual,* but true. This is not easy for a lot of people to understand. When I was a school child, one of my teachers accused me of telling a story. She was not complimenting me on my fertile imagination; she was accusing me of telling a lie.

Facts are fine; we need facts. But story takes us to a world that is beyond facts, out on the other side of facts. And there is considerable fear of this world.

The writer Keith Miller told me of a young woman who was determined that her three preschool children were going to grow up in the real world. She was not, she vowed, going to sully their minds with myth, fantasy, fairy tales. They were going to know the truth—and for truth, read fact—and the truth would make them free.

One Saturday, after a week of rain and sniffles, the sun came out, so she piled the children into her little red VW bug and took them to the Animal Farm. The parking lot was crowded, but a VW bug is small, and she managed to find a place for it. She and the children had a wonderful day, petting the animals, going on rides, enjoying the sunshine. Suddenly, she looked at her watch and found it was far later than she realized. She and the children ran to where the VW bug was parked, and to their horror, found the whole front end was bashed in.

Outraged, she took herself off to the ranger's office. As he saw her approach, he laughed and said, "I'll bet you're the lady with the red VW bug."

"It isn't funny," she snapped.

"Now, calm down, lady, and let me tell you what happened. You know the elephant your children had such fun riding? She's a circus-trained elephant, and she was trained to sit on a red bucket. When she saw your car, she just did what she was trained to do and sat on it. Your engine's in the back, so you can drive it home without any trouble. And don't worry. Our insurance will take care of it. Just go on home, and we'll get back to you on Monday."

Slightly mollified, she and the kids got into the car and took off. But she was later than ever, so when she saw what looked like a very minor accident on the road, she didn't stop, but drove on.

Shortly, the flashing light and the siren came along, and she was pulled over. "Lady, don't you know that in this state it's a crime to leave the scene of an accident?" the trooper asked.

"But I wasn't in an accident," she protested.

"I suppose your car came that way," she said, pointing to the bashed-in front.

"No. An elephant sat on it."

"Lady, would you mind blowing into this little balloon?"

That taught her that facts alone are not enough; that facts, indeed, do not make up the whole truth. After that she read fairy tales to her children and encouraged them in their games of Make Believe and Let's Pretend.

I learned very early that if I wanted to find out the truth, to find out why people did terrible things to each other, or sometimes wonderful things—why there was war, why children are abused—I was more likely to find the truth in story than in the encyclopedia. Again and again I read *Emily of the New Moon,* by Lucy Maud Montgomery, because

469

Emily's father was dying of diseased lungs, and so was mine. Emily had a difficult time at school, and so did I. Emily wanted to be a writer, and so did I. Emily knew that there was more to the world than provable fact, and so did I. I read fairy tales, the myths of all nations, science fiction, the fantasies and family stories of E. Nesbit. I read Jules Verne and H. G. Wells. And I read my parents' books, particularly those with lots of conversation in them. What was not in my frame of reference went right over my head.

We tend to find what we look for. If we look for dirt, we'll find dirt, whether it's there or not. A very nice letter I received from a reader said that she found *A Ring of Endless Light* very helpful to her in coming to terms with the death of a friend, but that another friend had asked her how it was that I used dirty words. I wrote back saying that I was not going to reread my book looking for dirty words, but that as far as I could remember, the only word in the book that could possibly be construed as dirty was *zuggy,* which I'd made up to avoid using dirty words. And wasn't looking for dirty words an ugly way to read a book?

One of my favorite books is Frances Hodgson Burnett's *The Secret Garden.* I read it one rainy weekend to a group of little girls, and a generation later to my granddaughters up in an old brass bed in the attic. Mary Lennox is a self-centered, spoiled-rotten little heroine, and I think we all recognize at least a little of ourselves in her. The secret garden is as much the garden of Mary's heart as it is the physical walled garden. By the end of the book, warmth and love and concern for others have come to Mary's heart, when Colin, the sick boy, is able to walk and run again. And Dickon, the gardener's boy, looks at the beauty of the restored garden and says, "It's magic!" But "magic" is one of the key words that has become taboo to today's self-appointed censors, so, with complete disregard of content, they would add *The Secret Garden* to the pyre. I shudder. This attitude is extreme. It is also dangerous.

It comes down to the old question of separate standards, separate for adults and children. The only standard to be used in judging a children's book is: *Is it a good book?* Is it good enough for me? Because if a children's book is not good enough for all of us, it is not good enough for children.

# 92

## CALLING IT QUITS

### BY LOIS LOWRY

*"You put __what__ in it?" my son asked, his fork halfway to his mouth.*
*"Ginger snaps," I repeated. "Crushed ginger snaps."*
*"I thought that's what you said." I watched while he put his fork back down on his plate and then pushed the plate away from him. It was clear to me that my son, normally a good sport, was not going to eat my innovative beef stew.*

*It was clear to me, after I tasted it myself, that he had made the right decision.*

SOMETIMES IN THE PROCESS OF CREATING, it is very difficult to know when to quit adding things.

Some years back, I received in the mail the first foreign edition of my first young adult book, *A Summer to Die.* Fortunately it was French. Later I would receive, with a gulp of astonishment, the Finnish, the Afrikaans, the Catalan; but this first one was French. French I can read.

And so I leafed through the pages, savoring the odd, startling sense of recognition that I had, seeing my own words translated into another language.

On the last page, I read the line of dialogue with which I had concluded the book. " 'Meg,' he laughed, putting one arm over my shoulders, 'you were beautiful all along.' " There it was, in French.

But there was something else, as well. I blinked in surprise, seeing it. In French, the book concluded: "They walked on."

They walked on? Of course they *had* walked on, those two characters, Meg and Will. I knew they had, and I had trusted the reader to know that they had. But I hadn't written that line. The translator had.

I don't know why. I can only guess that the translator simply couldn't resist that urge that makes all of us throw a crushed ginger snap into the stew now and then.

Knowing when to stop is one of the toughest tasks a writer faces.

Is there a rule that one can follow? Probably not. But there is, I think, a test against which the writer can measure his ending, his stopping place.

*When something more is going to take place, but the characters have been so fully drawn, and the preceding events so carefully shaped that the reader, on reflection, knows what more will happen, and is satisfied by it—then the book ends.*

In essence, you, as writer, will have successfully taught the reader to continue writing the book in his mind.

What about the concept of resolution, then? Isn't the writer supposed to tie up the loose ends of the story neatly at the conclusion? And if everything is neatly packaged and tied, then how on earth can something more take place?

Your story—your plot—your theme— is only a portion of the lives of the characters you have created. Their lives, if you have made them real to the reader, are going to continue in the reader's mind.

Your role is only a part of that process. And you need to know when and how to get out when your role is finished. As author, you tie up and resolve the piece of a life you have chosen to examine. Then you leave, gracefully. The life continues, but you are no longer looking at it.

You have engaged and directed the imagination of the reader; and then you have turned the reader loose.

Writing this, I looked at the endings of some of my own books, to see if they followed any kind of pattern.

In one, *Anastasia on Her Own,* a mother and daughter are laughing and tap-dancing together up a flight of stairs.

In *Find a Stranger, Say Goodbye,* a young girl is packing to go away; she is deciding what to take and what to leave behind.

The narrator and her mother in *Rabble Starkey* are together in a car, heading into a somewhat uncertain future. (Not coincidentally, that book is published in Great Britain under the title *The Road Ahead.*)

The forms of these endings are different. Some are descriptive, some consist of dialogue. Some are lighthearted, others more introspective.

But they do seem to have a few elements in common:

472

They all include the main character—sometimes more than one—in the final scene.

Each of them, in various forms, reflects a sense of motion, of flow, of moving forward.

And each in its own way contains a kind of conclusive statement.

Anastasia fell in behind her mother and tried to follow the complicated hops, turns, and shuffles her mother was doing. Together they tap-danced down the hall and up the stairs. It was silly, she thought; but it was fun. And it sure felt good, having her mother back in charge.

*—Anastasia on Her Own*

It was the throwing away that was the hardest. But she did it, until the trunk was packed, the trash can was filled, and the room was bare of everything except the memories; those would always be there, Natalie knew.

*—Find a Stranger, Say Goodbye*

She sped up a little, driving real careful, and when we went around the curve I looked, and it was all a blur. But there was nothing there. There was only Sweet Hosanna and me, and outside the whole world, quiet in the early morning, green and strewn with brand new blossoms, like the ones on my very best dress.

*—Rabble Starkey*

The common elements that you can see and hear in those ending paragraphs are a little like the basics in a good stew; maybe you could equate them to a garlic clove, a bay leaf, and a dollop of wine.

As for the crushed ginger snap? The ingredient that qualifies as overkill and makes the whole thing just a little nauseating?

Well, I confess that those three passages have one more thing in common. Each one was tough to end. Like the translator who added another sentence to my book, I wanted to go on, too. I wanted to add crushed ginger snaps: more sentences, more images, embellishments, explanations, embroidery.

And if I had? Take a look:

She sped up a little, driving real careful, and when we went around the curve I looked, and it was all a blur. But there was nothing there. There was only Sweet Hosanna and me, and outside the whole world, quiet in the early morning, green and strewn with brand new blossoms, like the ones on my very best dress.

What would the future hold for us? I had no way of knowing. But I remembered how, in the past years, my mother had worked and saved to bring us this far. I looked at her now, her eyes intent on the road, and I could see the determination . . .

Et cetera. You can't read it—I couldn't *write* it—without a feeling of wanting to push your plate away. It's too much. It's unnecessary. It is, in a word, sickening.

The letters I get so often from kids provide me, unintentionally, with a reminder of the impact of a good ending. Boy, if anyone in the world knows how to *end*, it's a kid writing a letter.

"Well," they say, "I have to quit now."

# PUTTING YOUR CHARACTERS TO WORK IN MYSTERY FICTION

## BY MARY BLOUNT CHRISTIAN

IF WE HAVE DONE OUR JOBS WELL, our characters are real to our young readers. In fact, they are not "characters" at all, but people—living, breathing people who are bumbling through their troubles like the rest of us and who occasionally triumph, making all of us feel better about ourselves.

I gave as much thought to creating that clever Old English Sheepdog, Sebastian (Super Sleuth), as I have to any of my human characters. Detective John Quincy Jones, his human caretaker, is like a single parent. And while Sebastian is a much better detective than John, he, like my young readers, must depend on the kindness of others for his very existence. Sebastian can't open doors or dog food cans. He has no money of his own, and although he thinks in English, he speaks only Canine, which means he has a difficult time putting his ideas across to people.

He is much smarter than others realize. And he is sharply reprimanded when he does something naughty but is rarely, if ever, applauded for accomplishments. My young readers identify with these experiences and readily accept Sebastian as a peer, ignoring the fact that he's hairy and four-footed.

Reader identification is your best tool in making a story believable. It allows the readers to suspend disbelief in some pretty unbelievable adventures.

It's highly improbable that eight- and ten-year-olds, or even teens (and certainly not dogs), will be faced with the sorts of mysteries I confront them with in my stories. I must create people who are so believable, so real that they make the story work, as improbable as it may seem on the surface.

Introducing these people and their peculiarities to readers should never be rushed. Writers are like anthropologists, slowly brushing away the surface clutter to reveal the wondrous secrets, one layer at a time. That is my favorite part of the writing process, because I find surprises at every layer.

Most of my stories begin with a vague situation and only a general idea about whom I need to carry my story: the gender, the age, the surface flaws and strengths.

I carry a small notebook with me all the time, and I jot down brief reminders of people I've observed with potential for characterization. As a "people collector," I may immediately remember someone I've observed—that toothless waitress with the smear of ketchup across the front of her apron, that shifty-eyed guy with hands the size of hams hanging out from his horse blanket coat—from whom I might get the idea for the fictional character I need.

That image remains blurry, however, until I find the right name for him or her, and I am every bit as attentive to my characters' names as I was to naming my offspring.

For contemporary given names I pore through *Name Your Baby* (Bantam). For popular names, there are the school directories and the birth announcements in the newspapers. If I want a name that is rural and rugged or from a past century, I use *Bible Names* (Ark Products) or *Who's Who in the Bible* (Spire). For more unusual names or ethnic names I consult *The New Age Baby Name Book* (Warner). Last names are as important as first names. Just be sure to select names that fit the origins and backgrounds of your characters. This, too, helps in developing your character.

I go through these books until one of the names finally "connects" with that blurry figure, and the features begin to sharpen. I knew I couldn't name my fictional dog hero after our own dog, though he was the inspiration for the character. Who would have believed a hero named Popsicle? The minute I found my name Sebastian, the image of a not-so-perfect Old English sheepdog, an undercover canine, became clear, and the story began to gel for me.

When I wanted to write a near-slapstick mystery with a hero who took himself a little too seriously, I chose Fenton P. Smith for his name, a mix of the usual and unusual and a bit of mystery thrown in, too, just like my character.

Once I'm sure the name and physical image are properly merged, I do the "Baskin-Robbins" test, probably because I'm a perpetual dieter, and this lets me visit vicariously the forbidden ice cream store. I can learn a lot just by observing my character in that setting.

Does he order vanilla, chocolate, or strawberry when confronted with all those luscious choices? He's probably a traditionalist, slow to take risks. As a mystery hero, he'll need to get pushed to the limit before he'll fight back.

Does he go for the raspberry truffles orange blossom flavor-of-the-month—without asking for a sample first? He's easily influenced and ready to follow the suspect down a dark alley. Does he get a dish or a cone, a double or single dip? Draw your own conclusions; there are no calories.

I go home with him and march right into his room, opening drawers and closet doors, peering under the bed. Are things jammed into drawers or divided and neatly stacked? Is that a stack of automotive magazines shoved under the bed? And is that a pair of hockey skates next to the baseball cleats?

The choice of furniture and curtains may be his mom's, but that poster from the movie *Top Gun* is his own.

I've learned a lot about my character, and I haven't even been through his billfold yet. Of course, I will! We carry our identities with us—in our billfolds, in our purses. There are pictures of our loved ones, our special friends, maybe even our pets. We can tell if he has a driver's license, a student I.D., a private pilot's license, membership in specific organizations, whether or not he has one or several credit cards or any cash.

With these tidbits of information, which I'll jot on a sheet of paper, I will list his position in the family (only, middle, oldest child, etc.), his religious background, his attitudes toward children, the elderly, and animals, his ethnic background, his personal ambitions and needs. When I know enough about him, I may write one or more scenes of conflict, just to hear his voice, listen to his inner thoughts, and watch his physical reactions. Does he slouch when he believes himself alone but stand straight in the presence of others? How does he enter a room? Does he repeat a phrase often? How does he sound when he's talking to his best friend, his teacher, his parent, his girlfriend?

And I won't neglect the other members of my little band of characters, either. The anti-hero has a past that has shaped his attitudes and personality, too. And he won't see himself as the villain. He'll have what

477

are to him valid reasons for behaving as he does. Also, he is a villain because of what he does, not because of what he looks like. So I make a sketch for him, too, and for anyone else who will play a major part in the story.

Imagine all the events in our characters' lives, from birth to death, strung together in a chain; our story is about one tiny link of that chain. We see only that section directly in front of us. Yet, everything our characters do that we can see is influenced by their past experiences. Their futures depend on what they do while we observe them, so if we want them to have reasonably happy futures, it's up to us to send our characters on life's journey with the personalities that will make it so.

You wouldn't send a mountain climber up Pike's Peak without a safety rope and pick. Neither should you send a character into a mystery without curiosity, stamina, and a strong feeling of self-preservation. Whether or not he recognizes these qualities in himself in the beginning, they must already be in place when the story starts, or the glue and Band-Aids will show, and your story will lack believability.

The sheet of information will grow as I write the first draft, peeling away the layers of protective covering that my character, like all of us, has built around himself. When a scene isn't working for me, I go back to my information sheet where I had noted, for example, that at the age of five my character was trapped in a burning house until he was rescued by a firefighter. That's how I knew how he would react now to a house fire. And, because my sketch also indicated that his father had died in a hit-and-run accident, I knew he'd feel strongly about catching a hit-and-run driver.

There is more than just knowing how your character would react to a given situation, though. I had sold several stories with only so-so reviews from the critics until I was lucky enough to attend a workshop given by Tony Hillerman. What he said changed my writing technique and my reviews for the better.

He reminded us that it is sensory detail that bonds the reader to the main character and makes the unbelievable seem true. He told us to write our first drafts, then go back and see that every typed page had at least two sensory details observed through the viewpoint character. Now I experience the story with all my senses: taste, smell, touch, sight, sound. I am thus bonded with my character, and so is my reader.

# § 94

# DIALOGUE: LET YOUR CHARACTERS DO THE TALKING

## BY EVE BUNTING

FRANKLY, MY DEAR, I don't give a damn!" So spoke Rhett to Scarlett in one of the best known lines of dialogue ever written. With that statement he signified the end of his patience, his tolerance, and maybe even his love.

Dialogue, real and believable, can say so much. Consider what we learn about the grandmother, come to visit for the first time in Pam Conrad's novel, *My Daniel.*

> "Do you know how to milk a cow, Grandma?"
> "I know how to milk it, feed it, slaughter it, skin it, drain it, quarter it, roast it, and eat it," she answered, getting up from her seat.

The author could have told us that the grandmother was feisty, competent and had a sense of humor. She didn't. She let Grandma speak for herself.

In *Scorpions,* by Walter Dean Myers, the mother of Jamal, Sassy, and Randy reminisces. Randy is in jail, and somehow she has to find the money to bail him out:

> "One day"—Mama's eyes looked far away—"I was walking downtown with Randy in my arms. I was waiting for a light to change when this white lady stopped and looked at him. I looked at her and she was smiling and I smiled back at her, and that was the best feeling in the whole world. You got a baby, and you hope so much for it. . . ."

We don't have to be told of the mother's heartbreak and disappointment and continuing love for her son. Her own words do that more effectively.

But good dialogue can do more than strengthen characterization. It can move your plot along.

In my young adult novel *The Ghost Children,* Matt and his little sister, Abby, have come to live with Aunt Gerda. Aunt Gerda has wooden dolls that she calls her "children." Matt suspects Clay Greeley and his friends, the twins, of vandalizing the house and the dolls. He goes to confront them:

"This bozo's real brave," one twin told the other.
"Well, he'd have to be, wouldn't he, living up there with the witch and the talking dolls."

This is the first time Matt has outside verification of his suspicion that the dolls talk.

"Go ahead and tell them what you heard," Clay Greeley ordered.
"Well, it was real dark. It was just about one in the morning . . ."
"The doll way in back was saying something about the moon and lightning . . ."

Red alert for Matt and for the reader, too. Here the dialogue furthered the plot and heightened the suspense at the same time.

Dialogue can play an important role, even in picture books. In my book *The Mother's Day Mice,* there is a discussion between Biggest Mouse, Middle and Little Mouse. It is right at the beginning, the early morning of Mother's Day:

Biggest studied his watch. "We have two hours before Mother wakes up. Middle and I know what we're getting for her and where to find it." He looked at Little Mouse and waited.
"I know what I'm getting, too," Little Mouse said. "Honeysuckle."
Biggest shook his head. "Little Mouse! Honeysuckle grows only on Honeysuckle Cottage. And we know who lives in Honeysuckle Cottage. You have to find something else for Mother."

In this short exchange, the problem is set up without resorting to exposition. We discover that there is a time limit involved and that a problem lies ahead for Little Mouse. Will he be able to overcome it?

Dialogue can also reveal the theme, or basic truth of your book in a subtle way so that it doesn't seem too much like a Sunday sermon!

There were a lot of important things I wanted to say in my novel *A Sudden Silence.* Jesse's brother, Bry, has been killed by a hit-and-run drunk driver. Jesse believes that if he can find that driver, his own guilt will end. For hadn't he been there when the car struck, and hadn't he saved himself but failed to save his brother? If he finds the driver, won't that exonerate Jesse? I wanted to say to the reader: "Guilt does not go away that easily. Blaming someone else does not mean you ever stop blaming yourself, too."

In this scene, close to the end, Jesse is talking to his dad:

> "Dad?" I began. "I keep thinking that maybe I could have saved Bry somehow. I can't get away from that. If I'd jumped forward. . . . I saved myself, Dad."
> "I don't know what to tell you, Jesse. No use saying you'll get over it. You probably never will. . . . Everybody's left with something to regret, Jesse. We just have to go on the best we can."

There! I let my characters say it for me.

So how does one write vital, meaningful dialogue that deepens characterization, furthers the plot, expands the theme, and sounds real?

First, the author must come out of self and become the characters. Know everything about them before you begin, their likes and dislikes, their strengths and weaknesses, their fears and triumphs. Live with them. Know them so well that a false word coming out of one of their mouths sounds contrived. Not easy, you say? No, not easy. As a "past-young woman" myself who writes books for teenagers and middle graders I have to be constantly alert. I have to remember that "those days" are gone and "these days" are here. I have to adapt. You have to, too.

One way to do this is to eavesdrop. Or, to put it less sneakily, listen, if possible, unobserved.

When I wrote *Sixth Grade Sleepover,* I eavesdropped openly, asking permission to visit a sixth-grade classroom. For the first few days, the children were certainly aware of my presence at the back of the room and on the playground at recess and lunch. But as time passed and I stayed quiet, I became simply a part of the classroom, like their pet rabbit in his cage. That is when I got my truest material. What ten-year-old can you listen to? Which grade school can you go to? Is there a McDonald's where you can sit at a table with a cup of coffee, next to a bunch of teenagers, and make notes in your notebook? Do you have a young child or a grandchild? If you write picture books, then you are lucky. One of my own picture books came straight out of the mouths of my son and my three-year-old granddaughter. He was lying on her bed, trying to get her to take a nap.

481

"Teddy's napping.
The big, yellow dump truck is napping.
Come lie next to Daddy."
"Susie wants a drink of water."
"Susie needs her balloon and her . . ."

Eavesdropping can pay off for those of us lurking outside a grand-daughter's door. My picture book *No Nap* is there to prove it!

Listen! Listen when you are in the mall, or in the market, or waiting in line at the theatre.

One girl, probably junior high, is talking to her friend. "I swear, he's a major babe."

I quickly make a note. So "major babe" is what they say now? However, there is a trap here. Slang dates quickly. But slang used sparingly and judiciously can give a feeling of today to your book. I will probably change the phrase somewhat, keeping the feel but making it more mine. How about "top babe"? Then I'll be safe if "major babe" flares and disappears. There is nothing more out of date than out-of-date slang. An exclamation such as "Out of sight!" is, I believe, out of sight already, and "Far out!" is so far out it is lost in space.

Along with slang, dialect, if used at all, has to be handled cautiously in children's books. It is difficult for many young people—and almost impossible for one who has a reading problem—to understand. In my books with an Irish background, I try for an Irish turn of speech, an Irish cadence, and stay away from the brogue.

Try to avoid pointless chatter that goes nowhere. If your characters use meaningless dialogue in your first draft, take it out of your second draft. It simply slows the action and is a major cause of story sag. And remember, one character never tells a second character something he already knows simply to give information to the reader. For example, two sisters are talking. "We lived in Brigham City for four months. You were three years older than I was. Papa sold insurance." Her sister knows all that. The author must find a better way to tell the reader.

When you are handling several characters in a story, particularly several of the same age and sex, it is important to make each one sound a little different. One way to do this is to give one character a gesture to go with her speech. For instance:

"I did not! How could you think such a thing?" Cassandra pushed back her long, blonde hair.

Let that be her habit. But don't have her overdo it to the point of absurdity. Let one character have a favorite word, or a manner of speaking. Have one always overdramatize, or constantly make rather goofy puns. In my book, *Someone is Hiding on Alcatraz Island*, Jelly Bean talked through his nose, as if he always had a cold. Maxie could never stand still, and his speech was as jerky as his body movements. You can find something that will make your character an individual and keep him distinctive in the reader's mind.

Above all, dialogue must sound natural. Ordinary people and especially ordinary children don't use flowery images in everyday conversation.

"Oh, how beautiful the pool looks. It's almost as if the sun is trapped in the sparkling water."

No. A kid would be more likely to say: "The pool looks great. Last one in's a rotten egg!" Or perhaps now it's "Last one in's a rotten banana." I'll have to eavesdrop and find out.

The repeated use of "he said" and "she said" to identify the speaker is difficult for some authors to accept. Rather than be repetitious they try variations. Some, such as asked, answered, whispered, murmured, are fine. Others are not.

"What a wonderful evening," Tony breathed, moving closer to Kay.
"Isn't it?" she sighed. "Look at the stars."

Try breathing or sighing real words sometime. Much better to stay with "he said," "she said." Better yet, use a tag line.

Tony moved closer to Kay. "What a wonderful evening."
She turned to face him. "Isn't it? Look at the stars."

The tag line identifies who is speaking and also sets the scene more visually.

So many memorable books contain memorable spoken lines.

"I'll huff and I'll puff and I'll blow your house down."
"Who's been sleeping in *my* bed?"
"Don't go into Mr. McGregor's garden; your father had an accident there."

Understand what good dialogue can do for the tale you tell. Train your ear to listen, then step back, and let your characters speak for themselves.

483

# § 95

# WRITING THE WESTERN NOVEL FOR YOUNG ADULTS

## BY JOAN LOWERY NIXON

THE WEST TO ME IS A STATE OF MIND. Those who settled the West were easterners and southerners and immigrants from all over the world, hard-working people who had courage and hope and the imagination to visualize the promise in our vast expanse of unsettled, untamed land. Their lives were difficult and filled with challenges, and it's the uniqueness of these challenges that fascinates young adult readers today. While immersed in stories set west of the Mississippi in the last half of the eighteen-hundreds, modern readers are discovering concepts like *sacrifice* and *self-denial* and *unwavering commitment to an ideal*— concepts that are not too common in today's very different world.

Many authors who write about the West are history buffs with a deep knowledge of the period and place; but for those who are not so knowledgeable, there are three books that can spark ideas and lead to further productive research: *The World Almanac of the American West,* John S. Bowman, General Editor (Ballantine Books); *The Reader's Encyclopedia of the American West,* Edited by Howard R. Lamar (Crowell Publishers); and *Historical Atlas of the Outlaw West,* by Richard Patterson (Johnson Books, Boulder, Colorado).

Plotting the historical western novel usually begins with an event or an important moment in history. For example, in browsing through my copy of *Historical Atlas of the Outlaw West* I read about the town of Leadville, Colorado, during 1879, its worst year. The decent people of Leadville were robbed at gunpoint in broad daylight and beset by "lot jumpers" who'd kill them and take over their property. There were countless unsolved or unpunished murders and an ineffectual law enforcement system. Finally, in desperation, as a warning to *all* outlaws in the area, a group of seven-hundred men who called themselves "The Merchants' Protective Patrol" dragged two prisoners out of the jail and hanged them from the framework of a building under construction across the road from the elegant Tabor Opera House, which was to hold its grand opening that evening. This vigilante action shook up the town. Some thought it was right, because a number of criminals left Leadville; but others felt that killing for any reason was wrong.

With the present-day increase in the crime rate throughout the country and the passionately argued issue of gun control, I thought this event would be an issue that would touch the lives of contemporary young readers, so I decided to set my story in Leadville.

My first step in writing the story was to research Leadville thoroughly. I read everything I could find about the local politics, the civic problems, and the economics of Leadville. It was primarily a mining town, and in 1879 it was the home of the wealthy Horace Tabor. I even found a newspaper account of Jesse and Frank James quietly working a claim at nearby Soda Springs. But reading about a place is never enough for me. I have to discover for myself how it looks and feels. When I discovered that walking in Leadville's thin air made me wheeze, I knew my characters would do the same until they became used to the high altitude.

I bought some books and pamphlets written by residents about Leadville's history. Because of its wonderful local detail, material of this sort is a treasure. Whenever I visit an area to do research, I try to take in all the regional historical museums. Some collections are housed in huge buildings; some fill only a room or two in a tiny restored pioneer house; but I've never failed to learn something of significance at each stop.

A logical question often raised by writers interested in trying their hand at the western historical young adult novel is how to include all the material gathered in the course of your research so the readers will find it interesting. The answer is, you don't. But the research gives you the factual background you need to write a good book.

Even though most western novels are probably sparked by a memorable historical event, you must keep this important point in mind: The main character is always the most important part of any novel—not the period, not the place, not the history—and how she or he reacts to what is taking place. What is she thinking? If she's frightened or curious or angry or unhappy or excited, this is what readers want to know.

An author's goal is to have young readers relate wholeheartedly to the main character of the story, and it's no harder to do in historical novels than in contemporary ones—but the *emotions* of the main characters must be felt and understood by your readers. For example: You could write a contemporary story about a teenage girl named Elizabeth who is furious with her father. He's suddenly become fed up with New York crime, noise, and traffic and has decided to move his family to a small town in Montana, where he is going to open a franchised branch of a popular fast-food restaurant. This means that Liz—note the contemporary nickname—will have to leave her friends, her school; give up her frequent visits to museums, concerts, and theatre, and adapt to a lifestyle she's sure she'll hate.

Or you could move Elizabeth into the mid-eighteen-hundreds, where she'd probably be called Beth. Her father is excited about the fortunes being made in some of the mining towns in California. He decides to share in the boom by packing up his family, moving to Sacramento, and opening a general store to sell supplies to the miners and the families settling the area. Beth is furious that her father has made this choice regardless of the wishes of his family. She doesn't want to leave her friends, her friendly neighborhood, and her grandparents—whom she realizes she may never see again.

The stories would be told through Liz's and Beth's emotional reactions: their emotions are exactly the same, emotions today's readers could understand with no difficulty. Music, clothing, food, manners, family relationships, transportation—everything that would make up life, whether it was lived in 1992 or 1850—are essential to the story, but they provide only background material for Liz or Beth and their emotions.

For the protagonist in my Leadville story, I chose a seventeen-year-old girl. Her father left the family to make his fortune when she was only seven. He has never returned, and the last of his infrequent letters to her mother came from Leadville. The girl remembers her father affectionately as a warm, fun-loving person. He had shared his love of poetry with her, and she treasures that memory.

I gave her a soft name—Sarah—and she's very much like her father—a dreamer and a poet—a fact about which her mother often reminds her. I gave Sarah a fourteen-year-old sister named Susannah, a name with more bounce and spunk. Susannah is a solid, practical person, very much like their mother who has supported her daughters and herself by turning their home in Chicago into a well-run boarding house.

Naming your characters correctly is important. While some period names are found in material being researched, it's also helpful to have at hand *First Names First* by Leslie Alan Dunkling (Universe Books, New York, NY), in which both popular and unusual first names from the past and the present are included.

Before my Leadville story opens, Sarah's and Susannah's mother has died, and a greedy aunt and uncle have moved in, taking over the boarding house. In 1879 the girls would have had no legal rights to their inheritance, so someone needs to find their father and bring him home to straighten things out.

It would have been easy to have Sarah just pack her bag and head West after her father, but that action wouldn't have fit her temperament. *Susannah* is the one who would easily have traveled alone, but Susannah is too young, so she bullies Sarah into making the trip. Through the problems and dangers Sarah encounters on the journey and in Leadville, she discovers some surprising facts about her own capabilities. I told their story through two books: *High Trail to Danger* and *A Deadly Promise* (Bantam).

In the western historical novel, you'll want to make your characters' dialogue true to the period by using colloquialisms, slang, and occasional phrases from that time; but be sure to use contractions so speech patterns won't sound formal and stilted—a turn-off for young readers.

Writing western historical novels for young adults is immensely satisfying. It gives me the opportunity to show that history isn't simply a collection of dates and wars and kings and presidents, but that *children* have always helped make history, that *children* are not only important to the past but are helping to shape history being made today.

And I hope that the characters in my western history-based stories will not only carry today's young readers through stories filled with adventure and excitement, but will also show them that the western state of mind was responsible for handling problems with determination and courage, because in the 1990s, determination and courage may be the qualities our children will need to count on the most.

# 96

## DISCOVERING STORIES FOR PICTURE BOOKS

### By Barbara Abercrombie

YOU ASK YOURSELF WHAT COULD BE SO HARD about writing a picture book? It ought to be easy: a short simple story for little kids . . . kind of an apprenticeship for writing adult fiction. So you write a short simple story you think children will like, but when you send it out to publishers it only generates rejection slips. You wonder if there's some sort of trick to discovering stories that will sell. A right way to do it, maybe a formula.

There isn't a trick, of course, or a formula, and if there's a right way to write picture books for children, it's simply being honest about your own feelings. *Your* feelings, not what you think children should or should not feel.

What were *your* secret fantasies when you were little? Did you want to fly? Did you wish you could talk to your cat, or vice versa? Did you want a larger family, or to be an only child? Were you ever confused about who you were and what was expected of you? Did you sometimes have the best intentions in the world but find your actions misinterpreted? Did you want to be bigger? Better? Braver? Did your parents ever embarrass you? Did you feel guilty about being embarrassed? Did you feel too tall, too short, too thin, too fat?

You may notice that things don't change all that much when we grow up. What we dreamed of, found joy in, hid from, or hoped to change as children often still concerns us as adults, and out of these concerns can come the best stories for picture books. It took me a long time to realize this. When I first attempted writing for children, I believed I could think and plan my way into a story. But instead, the idea for my first picture book, *Amanda & Heather & Company,* came to me as an image, a flash of memory: I remembered how it felt to be a little kid on an elevator and able to see only adult knees.

I can't tell you how or why this image popped into my head. But I can tell you that by paying attention to the feeling it gave me, of being very small and not understanding adults and their strange rituals, a story evolved about two little girls puzzled by the strange ways grownups enjoy themselves at a party. There's nothing about elevators in the story, but there is an illustration (by Mimi Boswell) showing Heather, very small, looking up at a sea of adult knees.

From writing my first picture book, I learned this lesson: Pay attention to your feelings, respect them, and recognize the paradox of thinking that your emotions are unique, yet at the same time *universal*.

One way to get direction into how you felt in the past is through sense memories—concentrating on whatever you absorbed through your five senses during a specific experience. Try it with the following list (you might want to make up your own list later). After each image, shut your eyes for a few moments, relax, and imagine seeing, smelling, tasting, touching, or hearing whatever the image suggests. Choose a specific period in your childhood and pay attention to the feelings that surface with the memory.

Imagine:

* the smell of your classroom the first day of school
* trying on a brand-new pair of shoes
* listening to the sounds of a summer night after you've gone to bed
* eating hot cereal in your kitchen on a cold winter morning
* holding a kitten and running your fingers through its fur
* walking barefoot through grass
* the sound of your parents' voices when they're angry
* opening a present you've longed for (or not getting a present you've longed for)
* your bedroom: what your bed looks like, the things you collect, your favorite toys, the view from the window
* playing a game with your best friend: the sounds, surroundings, feel of the ball or cards or whatever the game is played with

Notice also from this exercise how few words it takes to evoke feelings and memories.

In a picture book as in a poem, each word counts and echoes. In fact, I think a picture book is closer to a poem than to any other form of writing. The story needs to be compressed, yet at the same time each line requires weight and concentration. Dr. Seuss (Theodor Geisel) spoke of "boiling the thing down to the essentials." Simplicity and specific images (including metaphors) are essential. And your story must entertain as well. The sounds and rhythm of the language are vital. Children like to hear a good picture book read over and over again (something rarely true of novels or other forms of written material), but won't want to listen if the story isn't fun.

To understand the power of a picture book, the range and depth and sheer fun it can offer a child, read Maurice Sendak's *Where the Wild Things Are*. Read it over and over, and you'll understand how and why a picture book can endure and resonate, as a poem can. Read *The Story of Ferdinand* by Munro Leaf, too. Written over fifty years ago, this children's classic about a gentle bull who just wants to sit quietly and smell the flowers is an example of what can be done with plot, character, language, humor, and meaning in less than three pages of text. Read and study picture books that were your favorites when you were a child, then read at least fifty examples of picture books that are being published today—not for formulas or rules, but for information and to see what is possible. The best way to learn how to write is to read what you want to write. (This sounds obvious, but I'm always amazed at how many people try to write for children without ever reading what's being published today.)

How do ideas for picture book stories come to you? All I really know for sure is that out of the writing itself comes the story. You take a flash of memory, a true-life incident, a dream, or an observation, and you start writing. You take a cat from your own life and give it to two children in your imagination. You remember what it feels like when a pet is missing. You try what-ifs. What if the father lives in the city with a new wife? What if the girls visit them every weekend? And then suddenly you realize how that situation would connect to the fact that the cat has two homes.

Sometimes inspiration for picture books can come from experiences we have as adults, and then the story itself grows from a blend of reality and imagination. Charlie, the cat in my picture book *Charlie Anderson*, was actually a cat my parents adopted and that, they later discovered, had a second family. I wrote his story through the eyes of two little girls, but only as I wrote did I discover that Sarah and Elizabeth also have two families—a mother in the country and a father and stepmother in the city. I didn't start out to write about children who have two homes because of a divorce; I followed Charlie's life and discovered a more meaningful story as I wrote.

Another source of inspiration for picture books can be an urge to rewrite history, a need to change a sad, factual ending to a happy or more satisfying one. Newspapers can be gold mines for stories you'd like to rewrite. A few years ago I read a letter to Dear Abby about a pet pig named Hamlet who thought he was a dog. His life came to a sad yet predictable end (his name a self-fulfilling prophecy) when his owner had to give him up because of complaints from her suburban neighbors. The grieving owner wrote to Abby to let the world know how good-hearted pigs are and what wonderful pets they make. I was moved by the letter and couldn't get it out of my mind. Finally, I began a story about a pig that would have a happy ending. I worked on it for a long time before I discovered what the story was really about. My pig, renamed Henry, wants to fit into the family that adopted him. He first tries to be a baby, then one of the cats, and then one of the dogs, but he never really belongs or feels appreciated. He can't find happiness because he's always trying to be something he isn't; he feels he's the wrong color, his fur or tail isn't right, or he's too fat. My happy ending has Henry living out the rest of his natural life in a petting zoo, where he's loved and admired for what he is—a magnificent friendly pink pig.

I wrote this story for myself, to make me feel better about the real-life pig who wanted to be a dog. Picture books aren't written for children *out there* in desperate need of being shown the right way to feel and think and live. The child we're really writing for is right inside us. We're writing for the children we were, and the adults we are now. We still want to hear stories that make us laugh at ourselves and the weirdness of the world; stories that tell us we're not the only ones who get into trouble or danger or feel crazy sometimes; stories that will comfort us in the dark.

# 97

## TEN COMMON ERRORS IN WRITING FOR CHILDREN

### BY LINDA LEE MAIFAIR

A STORY FOR CHILDREN must do all the things an adult story does, and do it just as well, but in fewer words and simpler language. Where do would-be authors of juvenile fiction go wrong? The following are among the most common errors in writing for children:

(1) *Adult point of view.* Children want to read about children—children like themselves or as they'd like to be, facing the sort of problems they might face or doing things they've only dreamed about.

They like to identify with the central child characters, living the story's events and facing the characters' problems right along with them. They want to see the situation through the eyes and heart of someone who sees it the way they might see it themselves.

(2) *Multiple point of view.* Although adult fiction sometimes has a multiple point of view, children's stories should not. With less sophisticated reading abilities and very strong identification with the central characters, children are not as willing or able to change viewpoints in the course of a story.

Even shifting back and forth between two equally important characters with relatively the same perspective—like best friends or twin brothers—can be confusing and disconcerting for young readers, requiring them to divide their attention and change personalities vicariously as often as the viewpoint changes.

(3) *Stilted dialogue.* Young readers must be able to accept the youngsters in their stories as "real" children. Part of this reality comes from giving the characters the mannerisms, expressions, and actions of real kids. A great deal of it, however, comes from having young characters *sound* like real children.

Many juvenile characters talk the way authors who have little experience with real children the same age *think* young people talk. This is

492

about as successful as a writer who has never been to England trying to write dialogue for a Scotland Yard detective based on the way he or she *thinks* an Englishman would talk. Awkward, dated, and misused slang and phonetically unreadable dialect are no substitute for plain, spontaneous childlike (as opposed to *childish*) chatter.

Other young characters with flaws are all too often presented merely as miniature adults, stuffy and insufferable. They say things real youngsters would never say in words they would never use. Spouting polysyllabic vocabulary in compound-complex sentences, they never use contractions or utter gross, childish insults or expressions of disgust. Their speech is too mature, too difficult, too wordy and too wise.

(4) *Summaries posing as stories.* Many beginning writers of juvenile fiction leave out the dialogue completely. Because it is extremely difficult to develop both plot and character within the constraints of the juvenile story, they summarize rather than *show* what happened. There is no dialogue, no play-by-play action, no scenes, long or short. The result may, in fact, be a workable, interesting plotline, a place to start, but it isn't a story.

(5) *Lack of conflict.* Stories for young readers should do more than recount an isolated experience, no matter how interesting, pleasant, or "educational." They must have a plot that moves forward, logically and inevitably toward a climax and resolution. A fun day at the zoo or a carefree vacation on Grandpa's farm is seldom enough.

The story must revolve around some sort of problem. The conflict, though not necessarily earth-shattering, must be appropriate and relevant for both the child character and reader. It must also be a conflict that matters, the outcome of which will affect the main character's life and spirit in some way, hopefully for the better.

The plot will evolve from his or her thwarted but persistent efforts to solve the problem. The theme or "lesson" of the story should emerge from the ways the character has changed and what he or she has learned about life in the process.

(6) *Missing climax.* The problem in a juvenile story must be followed through to resolution, building first to a climax, a "darkest moment" and high point of tension, for the character and reader to work and worry through together.

Often the writer uses up the juvenile story's short, strict word limits before he or she reaches this climax, the part the readers would find most exciting. Rather than cutting down the beginning and balancing the development, climax and resolution, the unwary writer tends to rush through the climax or skip it entirely, trying to tie everything together in the few words that remain.

Problems solved too suddenly, too neatly, too miraculously; telling readers what happened after the fact instead of letting them see and hear what goes on as it evolves, leaves readers frustrated, unsatisfied, and cheated, as if someone had fast-forwarded to the end of a really exciting adventure movie without letting the viewers witness the big showdown or how the hero got everything to work out in the end. The climax should be the biggest, strongest scene in the story, the young readers' reward for staying with the character and caring about what happens to him or her.

(7) *Characters uninvolved in the solution of the problem.* In many stories for children, a parent, teacher, coach or other adult intercedes to solve the problems, impart the lesson, and make sure everything ends happily ever after. This is very unsatisfying and unfair to both the young reader and the young character. Young readers expect characters to *do* something about their problems, something the readers themselves may not be able to do, empowerment they may experience only through their stories. It's also one way children learn, safely and vicariously, that actions have consequences, and people must take responsibility for them.

The characters will make mistakes, and there will be obstacles, many of their own creation, all of which makes for a more interesting plot, but the characters have to take action and make decisions that lead logically to the resolution of the story, if not of the conflict itself.

The young protagonists may not, realistically, be able to handle the situation on their own. Ten-year-old sleuths cannot follow, trap and apprehend dangerous criminals singlehandedly. The main child character may need adult assistance, but he must remain an active participant, not merely an observer, throughout the big scene and at the end.

(8) *Starting too soon.* When you have to tell a story in under a thousand words, you don't have the space to go into the history of the character, trace his family back three generations or introduce each cast member in minute, physical and psychological detail, particularly in the critical first paragraph or two of the story.

The story should begin as close to the main action and problem as possible, getting the readers into the thick of things and making them wonder how it's all going to turn out. Necessary background information and details should be woven into the fabric of the story as it moves forward, using bits of dialogue and narration.

A story about a catastrophe on a camping trip shouldn't start when the child is packing his backpack *unless* what he takes or forgets has an impact on the outcome of the story. A story about a Saturday morning basketball game shouldn't start at school on Friday afternoon, *unless* something happens that is crucial to the plot. A story about a new girl who is ostracized by the "in" crowd shouldn't start with Mom's pancake breakfast, but with the opening buzzer of the game, or with the girl's face smarting in angry, embarrassed response to a snubbing remark or action.

(9) *Going on too long.* When the problem is resolved, stop. Don't let the characters stand around analyzing or recapping what happened. Don't follow everyone back home for cookies and milk. Don't lessen the impact of the climax or shift the reader's attention to minor characters or entirely new, unrelated situations. And don't summarize what will happen for the next ten years of the character's life; young readers can't conceptualize that far in the future.

(10) *Sermonizing.* Some editors, especially those of religious and denominational magazines for young people, like their readers to be left with what one calls "moral residue," a "lesson" beyond the simple entertainment value of the story. But such lessons must be handled subtly.

Having an adult character lecture a child who has misbehaved in some way, serious or minor, is not acceptable or appealing to young readers. Equally unacceptable, as well as totally unrealistic, is having the "reformed" young character go on at length about what he or she has learned and how repentant he feels, vowing never to err again.

The writer must let the events of the story—the way a character handles a situation, the consequences of his actions, and the resultant changes in his attitude and behavior—demonstrate the "moral" of the story instead of hitting the reader over the head with it at the end.

Though weaknesses in juvenile fiction take many forms, they are symptomatic of a single underlying, unforgivable sin committed by too many would-be writers: the failure to understand and respect both this unique and special audience and the challenges involved in creating worthwhile stories for children.

# PLAYWRITING

# 98

## BEFORE YOU TRY BROADWAY . . .

### BY ANNA COATES

AS A LOS ANGELES-BASED WRITER, SCRIPT ANALYST, and devotee of community theater, I see a lot of plays that could have been a lot better, and I read a lot of scripts that probably should have been shredded at birth.

Which is not necessarily a bad thing.

One of the functions of little theater is to give the playwright a chance to see what works and what doesn't—not on the page, but on the stage, with living, fumbling, stumbling actors. The playwright's duty—alas, oft-neglected—is to figure out what doesn't work, and why, and if necessary to cut and chop or even to begin again.

And in a world that seems unjustly biased toward screenwriters—from Joe Eszterhas and his three-million-dollar *Basic Instinct* to Joe Schmoe and his twenty-thousand-dollar B-flick advance—the playwright has one wonderful advantage over the screenwriter. In addition to basic moral superiority, of course.

The playwright can learn as he goes.

The playwright may aspire to Broadway, but he has a crack at many lesser triumphs along the way. He can tinker with his work, tightening here and lengthening there. Even after he surrenders a script to a director's interpretation, he may continue to edit and rewrite, with or without the director's blessing.

Markets for a stage script can be divided into four categories: *community theater, experimental theater, "legitimate theater"* (aka, the Big Time), and *publication/TV.*

Of course, the categories aren't mutually exclusive. Community theater can mean a show performed on a makeshift stage in a church basement, or an elaborate and well-funded production staged as part of the regular "season" of a repertory house. (You understand, of course, that the term "well-funded" is relative!) Student productions are another type of community theater, and in some college towns they are eagerly awaited as the only theater available.

Community theaters like to produce well-known plays by established playwrights. That gets a little tired when you're seeing *Our Town* or *Streetcar* for the fifth time in six years, but if you think about it, it makes sense. Working with tiny budgets, directors tend to pick shows that are proven winners with broad appeal. They keep in mind that audiences—not to mention casts—may be unseasoned, and will react most favorably to mainstream fare.

This doesn't mean your original light comedy or social drama can't find a home with a little theater—of course it can. But you may need extra patience to find the right house to handle its premiere.

And yes, local companies will occasionally get crazy and go for *experimental theater.* But you're more likely to come across it in a city like Los Angeles or New York with a heavy concentration of actors and writers, an abundance of venues, and a weird (whoops, I mean *varied*) range of tastes.

If you're slathering to do your play on the Great White Way, or at least on cable TV, back up and slow down.

The road to Broadway (and Off-, and off-Off) wends its way through many a community theater and college campus. Sure, your play might be one of the fifteen selected by the O'Neill Theatre Center's National Playwrights Conference. On the other hand, it might be one of the fifteen hundred they reject. And it's within the realm of possibility—just faintly, there at the border—that you'll zap out your first rough script to a cable television company and get a fat check and a contract by FedEx a week later. Certainly, if you're confident about the quality of your work you should try.

But for most mere mortals the way to earn a few credits and learn the ropes is to have their work produced by a small local theater or an undergraduate director.

And that should be pretty easy. After all, an undergraduate director is really just a college kid. And local theaters pay nothing—or maybe carfare—and ought to be happy to get what they can get. Right?

Well, no.

The great majority of scripts submitted to student directors, to little theaters, and to contests will never be produced or optioned because they are badly written.

It's not because the writers are without talent. There is almost always—no, *always*—something positive I can say about a piece of writing, and I'll go out of my way to figure out what it is. Still, it's frustrating and annoying to read script after script in which plots are direct rip-offs from current movies or standard stage productions, down to characters' names and dialogue. Sure, we all know there are only three basic storylines. The trick is to make yours seem fresh.

What directors and readers and editors look for in a script is a storyline that flows and that is logical *within context*. Think about the eternal *Ten Little Indians*. Now, the idea of a disgruntled murderer gathering nine victims and bumping them off slowly and cleverly, one by one, is a bit preposterous, especially in this day of Uzi machine guns and other high tech timesavers. But so cleverly is this story crafted that contemporary audiences are able to lose themselves in the drama and the terror, and suspend disbelief—for ninety minutes, at least.

## Realistic dialogue

Beyond plot, what you should be most concerned with is that your script be peopled by believable characters who use realistic, interesting dialogue. Trust me, if you write a terrific story and a potential producer thinks it needs a modified end, or an older main character, or a different setting, she will let you know. Those are very fixable flaws and an excellent piece of work won't remain homeless because of them.

What will get "no thanks" is a hackneyed plot, flat, stereotyped characters, and trite, wooden dialogue.

Stilted dialogue is a common problem. If you want to know how real people speak, listen to them.

Don't be afraid of contractions! You'll seldom hear a person say, "I do not know what I am going to do about it." Most people will say "I don't know what I'm going to do about it." (The exceptions might be a person speaking stiffly, for emphasis, or a non-native speaker. For instance, on the television series *Star Trek: the Next Generation,* Mr. Data's "uncontracted" speech helps define his android character. This device is effective because the other cast members speak naturally.)

When in doubt, read your dialogue aloud.

People sometimes—uh, pause, when they speak. And sometimes they begin sentences with *and* or *but*. But I find writers, are, well . . . reluctant to use hesitation in dialogue.

501

If you want your hero to say, "Gloria, I—I'm confused. This feeling is so strong. And I don't know what's happening between us," then don't write "Gloria, I am confused. This feeling is so strong. I do not know what is happening between us."

Remember that theoretically the actor should utter only the lines you write. Yes, he may get fed up and throw in an ad-lib and the director may decide to use it. In that case you, the playwright, have not done your job. Dialogue that *works* doesn't tempt actors to rewrite.

(As I'm chasing you with the hickory switch, remember that an early production of your play is your chance to cut and polish for later audiences. Maybe the church-basement director won't allow you to rewrite dialogue mid-production, but you certainly may do so before you resubmit your play to larger regional companies.)

## The professional look

Budding playwrights I have found avoid commas although I'm not sure why. Without commas the actors may forget to breathe if you follow me or at least they'll be confused.

An occasional *tpyo* is no big deal, but when every other line of a script contains misspellings like "ocaissional," "privledge," "thier," and "perference," can you blame me for concluding that the writer was just too lazy to consult his dictionary?

Grammar mistakes are irksome, too. No, you don't need perfect diction to write a good script. On the other hand, a writer who aspires to be a professional should certainly know the difference between "lie" and "lay." Your heroine may choose to lay on the bed, but that's a pretty good trick if she's alone in the room. And anyway, isn't this a G-rated production?

The writer should know whether his characters are doing well or doing good (or both). He should know whether that cool rebel flaunts rules or flouts them, and why that kid's new puppy can't be a gift from Daddy and I.

He should know if it's proper to contract *it is* as *its* or if it's not.

Of course, people don't speak perfectly, and judiciously placed solecisms make dialogue ring true. But when *every* character confuses literal and figurative, and says fortuitous when he means fortunate, or infer when he means imply, I begin to suspect the blunders aren't the characters' but the writer's own.

502

Get the simple stuff straight: Split infinitives will continue to easily slip by me. Likewise sentence fragments.

Dialect trips up a lot of playwrights. No, you don't have to be African-American to create a character who speaks "Black English," and you don't have to be Chinese to write about a fellow from Beijing. But spare me your "G'wan, man, I be jivin' yo' funky sef' " and your "Solly, no speaky Engrish" and most of all, your Southern Belles who say "y'all" when they're speaking to only one person.

If you must indicate a dialect, do it like this:

BELLE

Why, I declare!
(Belle's thick Southern accent makes this sound like, "wha, ah declayuh.")

You need indicate this only once. The director will get the idea, and so will the actress. And both of them will thank you.

Try to keep your set directions to a minimum. Just tell us we're on a pretty beach at sunset, and let the set designer worry about the golden sun and the cry of the gulls and the sails like white wings against the horizon. And keep in mind that the more sets and props your play calls for, the more it will cost to produce.

Keep blocking—the stage directions that show the actors when and how to move—to a minimum. Entrances and exits must be indicated, of course, and long slow clinches are fun to write. But if Tom enters angry, the director will guess that he might slam the door. If Suzy is doing an audience aside, the director will definitely place her downstage. If the phone rings, he can figure out that Jan will need to cross to answer it. O.K.? So indicate movement when necessary to advance the story, and don't leave your actors rooted in place like young saplings. But do have mercy and let the poor director have something to do.

It's scary for a writer to pack up her work and send it out for strangers to peruse. Presumably the fledgling playwright reminds herself that stage companies—local to pro—*want* to like her work. They, like you, are in this biz for the love of the written and spoken word. And besides, who wouldn't like to discover the next Sam Shepard?

What amazes me is that with this in mind, so many scripts are sent out flawed not only in the ways we've discussed above, but badly typed and poorly photocopied.

Neatness counts. Your third-grade teacher told you that and you probably relearned it in college when your psych professor showed you a study indicating that of two term papers *identical* in content the one typed neatly earned higher grades than one full of typos and cross-outs.

So what's the trouble?

I know. It takes a long time to type a hundred pages, doesn't it? It hardly seems worthwhile to retype the whole thing every time you add a couple of paragraphs or take one away.

Stop! You're breaking my heart!

The fact is, if you want to be taken seriously, your script must look professional. That means 8½″ × 11″ white paper, black ink, margins at the top, bottom, and sides, numbered pages, and invisible corrections or none at all. Absolutely no strike-outs.

Submit a photocopy, never the original. If your script is returned to you clean, there's no reason not to send it out again, but spare us the dog-eared, coffee-ringed, penciled fourth-timers! No one likes to feel like last choice.

The standard format for a play script, adjusted according to number of acts and intended medium and audience, is available from many sources, including books from your local library. But you won't be penalized for indenting dialogue seventeen spaces instead of fifteen, or for numbering your pages at the top center instead of at the top right.

## Cover letters

Whether you are submitting your work to a little theater, a contest committee, a cable television director, or a magazine editor, address your cover letter to a specific person *with whom you have spoken,* and who has agreed to look at your work. And I don't want to hear any whining about the cost of toll calls. First of all, most of these people aren't going to want to sit and chat (until they've read your script and realize you're brilliant and incredibly talented). And secondly, are you interested in getting produced or in sitting around complaining about an unavoidable business expense?

If you're submitting your script to a contest or television company, write ahead to request specific instructions about format, formal copyright registration, and whether a signed release is required. But when you want a local theater director to look at your work, it's still necessary to call ahead. By calling in advance, you can make sure that you have the correct contact name and address and that the director is willing to consider your work. Why waste time if she's not? Many directors will look at new plays only between seasons, and if you mail your script to a college theater department in June, it's likely to gather dust at least until September. And remember that your work should *always* go out with the copyright symbol (©) that indicates "copyright protected" at the right-hand top of the cover page.

Like your call, your cover letter should be brief. "Here's the script we talked about, and thanks for your time" will do. If you want to, add a few lines to mention your credits, if you have any, or your credentials, if they're germane. If your script is a comedy about a dairy farmer, and you happen to live on a dairy farm, say so.

Don't send a script replete with four-letter words to a children's playhouse, no matter how the kids in your neighborhood talk. And keep in mind that an all-nude sex comedy isn't likely to play in Peoria.

If you've done your homework and kept set and prop requirements to a minimum, you can say so in your cover letter. But don't use your cover letter to sell the script; it must sell itself. Don't write, "This is a wonderful, rip-roaring comedy full of hilarious moments in the wacky life of a dairy farmer."

With all the pitfalls I've described, what's the worst mistake aspiring playwrights make?

It's not confused plotting or flat characterization or trite dialogue. It's not sloppy typing or garbled cover letters. It's not even forgetting to put your name and phone number somewhere it can be found.

The worst mistake budding playwrights make is *not trying*. Not writing that script, or not polishing it, or not sending it out. Or sending it out only once, then giving up.

You may place your first script its first time out. Or you may place your tenth, its tenth time out, then watch it move along through little theaters and repertory ensembles. And as you look back on all the rejections, you'll realize that you learned something from every one.

I'm rooting for you, so get busy. And, hey—see you on Broadway!

# ⧙ 99

## TEN GOLDEN RULES FOR PLAYWRIGHTS

### BY MARSHA NORMAN

*Budding playwrights often write to ask me advice on getting started—and succeeding—in writing plays. The following are a few basics that I hope aspiring playwrights will find helpful.—M.N.*

1. Read at least four hours every day, and don't let anybody ask you what you're doing just sitting there reading.

2. Don't write about your present life. You don't have a clue what it's about yet. Write about your past. Write about something that terrified you, something you *still* think is unfair, something that you have not been able to forget in all the time that's passed since it happened.

3. Don't write in order to tell the audience how smart you are. The audience is not the least bit interested in the playwright. The audience only wants to know about the characters. If the audience begins to suspect that the thing onstage was actually written by some other person, they're going to quit listening. So keep yourself out of it!

4. If you have characters you cannot write fairly, cut them out. Grudges have no place in the theatre. Nobody cares about your grudges but you, and you are not enough to fill a house.

5. There must be one central character. One. Everybody write that down. Just one. And he or she must want something. And by the end of the play, he or she must either get it or not. Period. No exceptions.

6. You must tell the audience right away what is at stake in the evening, i.e. how they know when they can go home. They are, in a sense, the jury. You present the evidence, and then they say whether it seems true to them. If it does, it will run, because they will tell all their friends to come see this true thing, God bless them. If it does not seem true to them, try to find out why and don't do it any more.

7. If, while you are writing, thoughts of critics, audience members or family members occur to you, stop writing and go read until you have successfully forgotten them.

8. Don't talk about your play while you are writing it. Good plays are always the product of a single vision, a single point of view. Your friends will be helpful later, after the play's direction is established. A play is one thing you can get too much help with. If you must break this rule, try not to say what you have learned by talking. Or just let other people talk and you listen. Don't talk the play away.

9. Keep pads of paper near all your chairs. You will be in your chairs a good bit (see Rule 1), and you will have thoughts for your play. Write them down. But don't get up from reading to do it. Go right back to the reading once the thoughts are on the paper.

10. Never go to your typewriter until you know what the first sentence is that day. It is definitely unhealthy to sit in front of a silent typewriter for any length of time. If, after you have typed the first sentence, you can't think of a second one, go read. There is only one good reason to write a play, and that is that there is no other way to take care of it, whatever it is. There are too many made-up plays being written these days. So if it doesn't spill out faster than you can write it, don't write it at all. Or write about something that does spill out. Spilling out is what the theatre is about. Writing is for novels.

# ❧100

## NEW WRITING FOR THE THEATRE

### BY SHELLEY BERC AND ROBERT HEDLEY

HAVE YOU EVER FOUND YOURSELF SITTING DOWN to write a play and discovered that the ideas and feelings you wished to convey were not served by the traditional route of exposition, development, and denouement; that the world you were perceiving was plotless, fragmented, and collage-like? Perhaps you even felt defeated before you started because you didn't know the "rules"?

One of the most fascinating things we've discovered working with new playwrights, as we do at the Iowa Playwrights Workshop, is that many of their plays or plays-in-progress do not conform to the usual notion of dramatic writing. In fact, when these students attempt to "fix" their plays in conventional ways—a little character development here, a bit more plot there—the plays fall apart. Many of today's playwrights are mapping out a new dramatic territory and are writing the rules of its domain, rather than trying to superimpose a traditional style or structure upon it.

Not since the end of the nineteenth century has there been less consensus over what playwriting is or should be. The realistic play with its concentration on true-to-life, psychologically motivated action is losing its hold on dramatic writing. Playwrights, in increasing greater numbers, are finding themselves attracted to a variety of theatrical styles and approaches that confound our sense of the linear, character-focused play. Many playwrights find that the subject matter and dramatic structure associated with realism do not reflect the fragmented, multisensory, technologically swift nature of life today.

This new writing for the stage is likely to replace psychologically motivated characters with mercurial ones; linear plot with a series of non-linear events that resemble jam sessions on a theme; realistic, informational dialogue with language arias that exist to create momentary metaphysical landscapes. Actually, such elements in one form

508

or another have been a staple of avant-garde theatre for nearly a century. Now, however, they are becoming part of mainstream dramatic writing and can even be called the new classic style. As the world becomes a place where many things are done simultaneously, in which total communication across hemispheres is just a fax away, playwrights are losing patience with single-minded theatre pieces that systematically follow through a central idea or problem for two or three acts, with characters who consistently respond out of psychological motivation.

Internationally acclaimed playwrights such as Heiner Mueller, Irene Fornes, and Manfred Karge are all in their own unique ways creating scripts that speak to today's concerns in a dramatic language and structure that may wholly disregard plot, conflict, dialogue, even character. What then are the elements of postmodern playwriting, and what do they say about the future place of the playwright in the world and on the stage?

Let's take, for example, Manfred Karge's *Man to Man*. The play has only one character, a woman who impersonates her husband after his death so she can take his job and survive in Nazi Germany. As performed at the Royal Court Theatre in London, it opened with a woman lying on the floor amidst the domestic debris of her life. There is no pretense about making the set look like a real room; we see only fragments of the character's life—a few bottles, a record player, a chair, a TV—as if we were sifting through an archaeological site.

For the next fifty minutes (the length of plays is changing, too) this woman tells us the story of her life in terms of its personal, political, economic, and mythological aspects. No single notion of how to perceive her existence is given weight over another. To this end, the text is mercurial in its transitions rather than causal, fragmented in its plot rather than linear, evocative in its development rather than factual.

The text of *Man to Man* hardly looks like a play at all in the usual sense. It is divided into a series of numbered passages that combine prose, verse, slogans, captions, quotes, puns, political references, and a fairy tale. It is a language picked up and spit out like a grab bag of political and cultural history. Several genres of language, from the literary quotation to the billboard advertisement, create the pastiche of this woman's life. More important, the language here does not exist primarily for the purposes of conveying information, developing character, or tracing a tragic flaw. In *Man to Man,* language is both main character and prime action; its forms comment on each other; its vying genres combust and collide, turning the world as we comfortably know it upside down and freeing us to perceive anew.

In many of the new plays that attract critical attention, conventional playwriting wisdom is inadequate. The idea that to write plays that speak eloquently and powerfully, one must start with Aristotle and spend time with Ibsen has not been true for some time and is now particularly untrue. Linearity and character modesty—that is, the assumption that somebody else must reveal the character's story—are less important than ever. Consistency of tone and authorial absence, bulwarks of realism, are directly refused as today's new plays celebrate verbal fluency and imagination. The audience is not asked to suspend its disbelief or allowed to hide voyeuristically behind a "fourth wall."

This is not to suggest that plays of consequence, beauty, power, or outrageousness are not being written in traditional forms, but that impatience or restlessness with those forms is now a part of the young playwright's make-up. It seems no longer possible, for example, to pretend that stage events are taking place without being observed, that a few hundred eyes are not peering out from the darkness. Likewise, it appears to be impossible for characters to restrain the urge to speak directly to their audience. Verbal literacy—that is, a knowledge of what language can be asked to do and a recognition of what it has done in all its uses, misuses, and variations—is on the rise, leading, yet again, to an impatience with plays whose characters are unaware that they inhabit a stage and hence speak only to the fictional point. In the new plays, the boundaries between what is funny and what is sad, what is tragic or trivial, beautiful or trite have been stretched and blurred to an unprecedented extent in direct reflection of our social and historical times.

While the terms in which many of the new plays address the audience are often abstract and complex, their relationship with the audience is astonishingly direct. Characters often tell the audience flat out what it needs to know, rather than going through a long, slow list of clues that become the plot structure. By getting the facts over with quickly (as the Greeks did ages ago in their plays), the playwright can concentrate on the political, historical, and metaphysical concerns he or she wants to relate. Scenes no longer develop one to another in a storylike trance in which all things lead inevitably to the climax. Rather, they often exist like medieval triptychs in which certain selected images springing from a well-known theme play against each other, illuminating and interpreting the story by its very fracture and incompleteness. Audience response is built through a series of impressions, aural and visceral, carefully arranged to create an idea or image through juxtaposition, irony, parallelism, or repetition.

One of the most interesting trends in new plays is the monodrama, or one-person play. Unlike realism, in which the audience watches the story evolve through key physical and emotional actions, the new monodramas in particular rely heavily on action through language. As storyteller, the playwright uses forms of language in rhythmic variation to provide dynamic action without the trappings of verisimilitude. The monodramas are often a mix of autobiography and cultural mythology. Through a series of impressions, the multiplicity of life is examined, honed down to the microcosm of the lone character. Monodramas examine the self as social creature and the self as mythological hero. Dramatic tension is found in the battle between the disparate identities of the self. Dialogue in the monodrama, when not between these warring selves, is between the character and the audience. Hence, each member of the audience actually becomes a character, and a true dialogue between performer and observer occurs.

The trends and developments are not meant to serve as a prescription nor a set of new rules to replace the old. A play by Irene Fornes, for example, is profoundly different from the Karge play cited here but just as relevant. What is important for the aspiring playwright to recognize is a sense of the freedom and imagination in the newer forms, as well as the reemergence of language as a primary player in the drama.

But let's be more specific. How can beginning playwrights help themselves? First of all it is important to read widely in order to understand what is going on in theater writing today. While publications such as *The Fireside Theatre* are excellent for mainstream writing, the newest pieces can be found in the *Wordplay* collections; the various *PAJ* volumes; *TCG, Plays International, American Theatre,* and other magazines; and in anthologies like *7 Different Plays.* For the inexperienced writer, it is liberating to see the methods and structures used by writers tackling contemporary issues.

In working with their ideas, aspiring playwrights must learn to trust their instincts. While it's not easy for a new playwright to know whether he or she is on the road to creating plays in a nonlinear, lyric, evocative

511

style or merely being sloppy in character delineation and plot development, little good will result from listening to the critical inner voice that compares everything to *Death of a Salesman*. The experience of a new play is a total experience, including its form. Not being a "slice of life," such an experience does not demand consistency of language, place, character, or other normal conditions. Indeed, an impulse or instinct to use multiple forms may indicate the only means of expressing your idea.

But let's conclude with a few basics for you to keep in mind as you write or revise your plays:

1) The one thing traditional playwriting and some of the newer forms have in common is specificity of detail and clarity of expressed ideas.

2) When you are writing a play, make sure you are listening to what *it* is telling *you,* rather than what you think you want to say. Follow your impulses. Listen to your characters. Forget rules, forget doors, forget politeness. Never ask yourself whether it's logical or not.

3) If the play is telling you primarily about the sound and rhythm of a certain day, you must consider that the play may be more of a dramatization of the essence of that day than of the characters or stories you've tried to put in it. The characters and the stories have been there and will be there, at least in your notebook. That day, that flavor, may not. Just because it doesn't resemble plays you know doesn't mean that it won't become a new, important play.

4) Remember that playwrights can and do dramatize anything—from a day to a poem to a piece of architecture. Dramatic action, the mainspring of the theatrical experience, does not necessarily mean physical or psychological action. Action can also mean a movement of ideas or images or words or intentions.

5) Try to put the world you see in your mind on the stage. Explore the thoughts, the words, the visions that own you, and reach for ways to translate them in terms of actors, sets, and audience. Don't settle for what you know or have seen.

512

6) Be courageous. You are individual when you write like yourself. When you try to put your ideas in someone else's form you often betray those ideas.

Many of the new techniques are as old as the Greeks, but the varied and joyous way in which styles and genres of the theatre are being put together is wholly new and magical; an invitation to the mind to explore the farthest reaches of its imaginative strength.

# 101

## AN OBJECT LESSON FOR PLAYWRIGHTS

### BY JEFFREY SWEET

THE EXPERIMENT GOES SOMETHING LIKE THIS: You place a sheet of paper over a magnet. Then you pour iron filings onto the paper. Almost instantly, the filings arrange themselves into a pattern. The pattern indicates the outline of the magnetic field.

You don't *see* the field. You see the *pattern* the filings make because of the *presence* of the field.

And yes, this does have something to do with writing plays.

By way of demonstration, here's a short scene that takes place in a suburban living room between a man and a teenage boy. As it begins, the boy is heading out the door when the man stops him by saying—

MAN: What's that in your hand?
BOY: Nothing.
MAN: Open it, please.
BOY: Dad—
MAN *(Firmly)*: Open your hand. (*The boy opens it to reveal a key.*) Well?
BOY: I'm only going out for an hour.
MAN: Give it to me.
BOY: There's someplace I have to be.
MAN: You give that key to me now or I'll ground you another week. (*The man opens his hand. The boy hesitates, then puts the key into the man's hand.*)

Not a lot of dialogue. But look at how much we learn in this short passage: The man and boy are father and son. The father wields his authority with a firm hand. The son is not above trying to pull a fast one to get around his father's orders. The son wants to go out for an hour and he needs the key to do so, leading to a reasonable guess that the key is for the family car, which he is not supposed to be using. Additionally, from the father's threat to extend the son's grounding, we gather the son is currently being punished.

Just as the pattern the iron filings form indicates the magnetic field acting upon them, so the contest over the car key indicates the dramatic field in existence between the father and son.

To rephrase this into a general principle: You can often dramatize what is going on between your characters through the way they negotiate over an object.

This technique is particularly useful because it allows the audience to figure a good deal out for themselves, obviating the writer from having to go through tedious explanations. Notice, for instance, that in the scene above, the father doesn't say anything like, "I'm very disappointed in your behavior." Nor does the son say, "I'm upset about the way you restrict my movements." Both of these statements indeed would be accurate expressions of their feelings, but how much more effective it is to allow the viewer, by analyzing the negotiation over the key, to arrive at his or her own conclusions as to the nature of the relationship between the characters.

The great plays are filled with brilliant negotiations over objects. Whenever Shakespeare introduces an object onstage, you can be sure it will be used to strong dramatic effect. In fact, according to chroniclers of the time, it was with a scene containing the resourceful use of objects that Shakespeare first established his reputation as a hot young playwright.

Act I, Scene 4 of *Henry VI, Part 3*. The Duke of York, who with his sons has led a revolt against Henry VI, has been captured by Margaret, Henry VI's bloodthirsty queen. Margaret steps forward to taunt York. She shows him a handkerchief with a red stain on it, and informs him in a casual way that it was dipped in the blood of his youngest and much-beloved son Rutland, whom one of her followers has just killed. "And if thine eyes can water for his death," she says, "I give thee this to dry thy cheeks withal," and does indeed offer it to him. (In one particularly effective production I saw, York refused to take the handkerchief, so she draped it over his shoulder.) Continuing with her cruel sport, Margaret goes on to say, in essence, "So you want to be a king, hunh? Well, let's see how you'd look in a crown." And she makes a paper crown and puts it onto his head and remarks sarcastically, "Ay, marry, sir, now looks he like a king!"

Powerful stuff, the power of which derives largely from the *physicalization* of York's downfall and Margaret's sadism by the introduc-

515

tion of two imaginatively chosen objects. The paper crown is a particularly strong choice. Being paper, of course it doesn't have the value of the real crown, an adroit way of conveying the contempt with which Margaret views York's aspirations for the throne.

This use of objects is a technique Shakespeare employed to great advantage in his other plays. Think of Hamlet holding Yorick's skull. Think of the way Iago uses Desdemona's handkerchief (another handkerchief!) to goad Othello. Think of the counterfeit letter used to beguile Malvolio in *Twelfth Night*.

It is a technique that modern playwrights have also employed to great effect. Much of the action in Lillian Hellman's *The Little Foxes* revolves around a safe deposit box and bonds stolen from it. In Frederick Knott's *Wait Until Dark,* the villains' actions are motivated by the desire to get their hands on a doll stuffed with drugs. In William Gibson's *The Miracle Worker,* Annie Sullivan and Helen Keller go head to head over a variety of objects—a key, a plate of food, a pile of silverware and so on.

What's more, the *transformation* or *destruction* of an object introduced onstage can give a scene even greater impact.

At the beginning of the third act of Neil Simon's *The Odd Couple,* Oscar and Felix are feuding. Oscar sees that Felix is eating a plate of pasta and decides to spoil it by spraying it with an aerosol. Oscar makes a derisive remark about Felix's spaghetti. Felix laughs at Oscar's ignorance. "It's not spaghetti. It's linguini!" Whereupon, Oscar picks up the plate, goes to the kitchen door, hurls the food at an unseen wall and announces, "Now it's garbage!" The transformation of the food to garbage graphically dramatizes the disintegration of Felix and Oscar's relationship.

In Tennessee Williams's *The Glass Menagerie,* the shy Laura shows Jim, the gentleman caller, her favorite piece of a collection of glass figures, a unicorn. In an effort to raise her spirits, Jim begins to waltz with Laura, but, during the dance, they bump into the table on which the unicorn is sitting. It falls to the floor and its horn breaks off. Later, when she realizes that Jim's visit will not be the beginning of the relationship between them for which she had hoped (during the scene, he reveals he has recently become engaged), Laura gives him the damaged unicorn as a souvenir. The shattering of the unicorn gives particular emphasis to a scene concerned with the shattering of Laura's illusions.

516

This technique—the negotiation over objects—may be extended to the negotiation over things that are not physical objects. In *A Streetcar Named Desire,* Tennessee Williams has his principals clash memorably over a variety of props (Blanche's trunk, clothes and letters, the deed to Belle Reve, etc.), but they also contest other elements.

At one point, for instance, Blanche turns on the radio. Stanley, in the middle of a poker game with friends, finds the music distracting and orders Blanche to turn it off. A little later, when she turns it on again, Stanley grabs the radio and tosses it out the window. Clearly, then, one can negotiate over sound. (Certainly, as anyone who has had to endure the sound of a boom box on the street, one can negotiate over volume.)

Shortly after she arrives, Blanche covers the naked lightbulbs in Stanley and Stella's apartment with Chinese lanterns. Late in the play, when Mitch confronts her with the truth about her past, he yanks off the lanterns so as to be able to see her clearly. A negotiation over light. (See also the battles between the father and sons over the use of light in Eugene O'Neill's *Long Day's Journey Into Night.*)

In the climactic confrontation, Blanche, feeling threatened by Stanley, wants to walk past him and asks him to move out of her way. He insists she has plenty of room to get by and then backs her into the bedroom. A negotiation over space. (Much of *The Odd Couple,* too, is about the negotiation over space, as two men of different habits and natures try to share one apartment.)

So, characters may negotiate over objects, over sound, over light and over space. Also over time, over temperature, over elevation—over anything, in fact, to which a character might attach value.

Including *people.* Returning to *Streetcar,* notice that Blanche and Stanley carry on a play-long struggle over Stella, and Stanley wins. For that matter, *any* play concerning a triangle, romantic or otherwise, inevitably involves two parties negotiating over the third.

On a more abstract level, the negotiation may be over ideas. Much of David Mamet's *American Buffalo* concerns Teach and Donny arguing over how to steal a set of rare coins from an apartment. Their differing approaches to the plan go a long way toward establishing the differences in their characters and highlighting the ethical issues which are the heart of this remarkable work. And so, too, virtually anything George Bernard Shaw wrote. He almost always defines his characters on the basis of their conflicting opinions on intellectual matters.

Yes, what I'm describing is a technical device. But it's no artificial trick. One of the reasons this technique works so well onstage is that it reflects the way people behave in real life.

For we are constantly negotiating with each other. When two people on a date debate whether to see a kung fu movie or a revival of *Singing in the Rain,* they're revealing their differing tastes through the arguments they advance in support of their respective choices. When children fight over who's going to sleep in the upper bunk, the resolution of their controversy tells a great deal about which child has what powers and prerogatives. When a wife upbraids her husband for constantly leaving the cap off the tube of toothpaste, one may quickly glean something of the health of their marriage.

To bring such negotiations to the stage is to reveal to the audience the ways people use whatever tools are at hand to pursue their objectives with each other. It is to show how, in contests over such seemingly mundane objects as a key, a credit card, a handkerchief, or an alarm clock, human beings often inadvertently reveal the deeper issues between them.

# 102

## CONFLICT: THE HEARTBEAT OF A PLAY

### BY D. R. ANDERSEN

EVERY PLAYWRIGHT is a Dr. Frankenstein trying to breathe life into a page for the stage. In a good play, the heartbeat must be thundering. And the heartbeat of a play is conflict.

Simply put, conflict exists when a character wants something and can't get it. Conflict may sometimes be internal—as when a character struggles to choose between or among opposing desires. For example, Alma in Tennessee Williams's *Summer and Smoke* longs to yield to her sexual yearnings but is prevented by the repressed and conventional side of her nature.

Conflict in drama may also be external—as when a character struggles against another *character* (Oscar and Felix in Neil Simon's *The Odd Couple*); against *society* (Nora in Ibsen's *A Doll's House*); against *nature* (the mountain climbers in Patrick Meyers' *K2*); or against *fate* (Sophocles' *Oedipus*).

In most plays, the conflict is a combination of internal and external struggles. In fact, internal conflict is often externalized for dramatic impact. In Philip Barry's *Holiday,* for instance, the hero's inner dilemma is outwardly expressed in his attraction to two sisters—one who represents the safe but boring world of convention, and the other who is a symbol of the uncertain but exciting life of adventure.

Granted that a conflict may be internal or external; that a character may be in conflict with another character, society, nature or fate; and that most plays are a combination of internal and external conflict, many plays that have these basic elements of conflict do not have a thundering heartbeat. Why? These plays lack one, some, or all of the five magic ingredients of rousing, attention-grabbing-and-holding conflict.

## The five magic ingredients

I. *Never let your audience forget what your protagonist wants.*

You can achieve this in a number of ways. Often the protagonist or another character states and periodically restates in dialogue what is at stake. Or in some plays, he explains what he wants directly to the audience in the form of a monologue. As you read or watch plays you admire, take note of the obvious and ingenious techniques playwrights use to tell the reader or audience what the characters' goals are.

Sometimes the method used to keep your audience alerted to your protagonist's goal/concern/need is a direct reflection of the protagonist's personality. In the following three short passages from my play *Gradua-tion Day,*[1] a mother and father with very traditional values have a conversation while waiting to meet their rebellious daughter, who has told them she has a big surprise. Notice how the protagonist—Mrs. Whittaker—nervously and comically manipulates the conversation, reminding her husband and the audience of her concern for her daughter Jane:

MRS. WHITTAKER
(Knocking on the door)

Jane. Jane. It's Mom and Dad.

(Pause)

No answer. What should we do, Tom?

MR. WHITTAKER

Let's go in.

MRS. WHITTAKER

Suppose we find Jane in a compromising situation?

MR. WHITTAKER

Nobody at Smith College has ever been found in a compromising situation.

* * *

MRS. WHITTAKER

Tom, you know, this was my freshman room.

MR. WHITTAKER

Of course, I know.

MRS. WHITTAKER

And Jane's. It was Jane's freshman room too, Tom. Remember?

* * *

MR. WHITTAKER

Mary, you get in the craziest moods at these reunions. I may never bring you back again.

---

1. First produced by Playwrights Horizons in New York, starring Polly Holliday.

MRS. WHITTAKER

Do you know why you fell in love with me, Tom?

MR. WHITTAKER

I fell in love with you the minute I saw you eat pancakes.

MRS. WHITTAKER

That's a sound basis for a relationship. Tom, where do you suppose Jane is? And more frightening, what do you suppose she wants to tell us? She said just enough on the phone to suggest that she's going to be bringing a boy here for us to meet.

MR. WHITTAKER

A man, Mary, a man.

MRS. WHITTAKER

Oh, God. I never even considered that possibility. Suppose Jane brings a fiancé—our age—like Pia Zadora did.

MR. WHITTAKER

Don't you want Jane to live her own life?

MRS. WHITTAKER

No. Especially not her own life. Practically anyone else's. But not her own.

MR. WHITTAKER

What *do* you want for Jane?

MRS. WHITTAKER

I don't see why Jane can't fall in love with a plain Harvard Business School student, let's say. Someone who'll be steady and dependable.

And so it goes. The protagonist discusses a number of topics, but she inevitably leads the conversation back to her overriding concern. Mrs. Whittaker's desire to see her daughter do the right thing and marry wisely is always uppermost in the mind and conversation of the character.

In this one act, a comic effect is achieved by having Mrs. Whittaker insistently remind the audience what she wants. Once you have clearly established what a character wants, you can then write powerful and often hilarious scenes in which the audience, already knowing the character's point of view, is able to anticipate his reaction.

II. *Show your protagonist struggling to achieve what he wants.*

This principle is, of course, the basic writing advice to *show,* not tell, and it was a major concern for me when I was writing *The House Where I Was Born.*[2]

The plot: A young man, Leo, has returned from the Vietnam War, a psychosomatic mute because of the atrocities he witnessed. He comes back to a crumbling old house in a decaying suburb, a home populated

---

2. First produced by Playwrights Horizons in New York.

by a callous stepfather; a mother who survives on aphorisms and by bending reality to diminish her despair; a half-crazy aunt; and a grand-father who refuses to buckle under to the pressures from his family to sell the home.

I set out to dramatize Leo's painful battle to free himself of memories of the war and to begin a new life. However, each time I worked on the scene in the play when Leo first comes home, his dialogue seemed to trivialize his emotions.

Then it occurred to me that Leo should not speak at all during the first act; that his inability to speak would *show* an audience his suffering and pain far better than his words could.

At the end of the third act, when Leo regains some hope, some strength to go on, every speech I wrote for him also rang false. The problem, I eventually realized, was that as playwright, I was *telling* the audience that a change had taken place, instead of *showing* the change as it took place.

In the final draft, I solved this dramatic problem by having Leo, who had loved music all his life, sit down at the piano and begin playing and singing Christmas carols while his surprised and relieved family joined in.

First silence, then singing, served my play better than mere telling.


III. *Create honest, understandable, and striking obstacles against which your protagonist must struggle.*

Many plays fail because their characters' problems seem too easily solved. I wrestled with this issue when I was writing *Oh Promise Me!*[3] a play that takes place in a private boarding house for the elderly. The play's original title was *Mr. Farner Wants a Double Bed.* The plot involved the attempt of an elderly man and woman—an unmarried couple—to share a double bed in a rooming house run by a repressed and oppressive owner. I wanted to explore contemporary attitudes toward the elderly, particularly as they concerned sexuality.

The more I played with the idea, the more I repeatedly heard an inner voice saying, "Chances are the couple could find some place to live where nobody cared if they were married or not." This voice—like the

---

3. Winner of the Jane Chambers Memorial Playwriting Award.

audience watching a play without an honest, understandable, convincing obstacle for the protagonist—kept saying, "So what?"

The writer's response: "Suppose, instead of a man and a woman, the couple is two men." Here was a real obstacle: Two elderly, gay men, growing feeble, want to sleep together in a double bed under the roof of an unsympathetic and unyielding landlord.

Suddenly, the play was off and running.


IV. *In the final scene or scenes, make sure your protagonist achieves what he wants; comes to understand that there is something else he wants; or accepts (defiantly, humbly, etc.) that he cannot have what he wants.*

If we spend time in the theater watching a character battle for something, we want to know the outcome—whatever it may be.

In my psychological thriller *Trick or Treat*,[4] Kate, a writer in her forties, has been badly burned in a love affair and is unable to decide whether to accept or reject a new relationship. She is involved at present with Toby, a younger man, but—as the following dialogue reveals—she insists on keeping him at a cool distance.

KATE

That does it, Toby. We're getting out of this place.

TOBY

Okay. Tomorrow we'll check into the local Howard Johnson's.

KATE

I want to go home—to New York—to my own apartment.

TOBY

Okay. Okay. If you insist. Besides, Howard Johnson's is not to be entered into lightly.

KATE

Huh?

TOBY

It's an old college rule. You'd never shell out for a room at Howard Johnson's—unless you were *very* serious about the girl.

KATE

I'll remember that. The day I agree to check into a Howard Johnson's—you'll know I've made a serious commitment to our relationship.

In the course of the play, Kate faces a number of trials—including a threat to her life—as she tries to expose the fraudulent leader of a

_____

4. First produced by the Main Street Theater, New York, New York.

religious cult. Through these trials—with Toby by her side—Kate comes to realize that she's ready to forget the past and give herself over to a new relationship. This critical decision is humorously expressed in the last seconds of the play:

KATE
Do you love me, Toby?

TOBY
Yes, I do. I found that out tonight . . . when I thought I might be losing you forever. Do you love me?

KATE
Yes. And I can prove it.

TOBY
How?

KATE
Take me to Howard Johnson's—please! Take me to Howard Johnson's!

The curtain falls and the audience knows that the heroine has made an unequivocal decision.

V. *Make sure that the audience ultimately sympathizes with the protagonist's yearning to achieve his goal, however outlandish his behavior.*

This may be the most important of the five magic ingredients of conflict. It may also be the most elusive. To oversimplify, in a good play, the protagonist must be very likable and/or have a goal that is universal.

In the plays I've had produced, one character seems to win the sympathy of the audience hands down. In my romantic comedy *Funny Valentines*,[5] Andy Robbins, a writer of children's books, is that character. Andy is sloppy, disorganized, and easily distracted, and—this is his likable trait—he's painfully aware of his shortcomings and admits them openly. Here's Andy speaking for himself:

ANDY
Judging by my appearance, you might take me to be a complete physical and emotional wreck. Well, I can't deny it. And it's gotten worse—much worse—since Ellen left. You know that's true.

---

5. Published by Samuel French; winner of the Cummings/Taylor Playwriting Award; produced in Canada under the title *Drôles de Valentins*.

524

Andy is willing to admit his failings to old friends and strangers alike. Here he's talking to an attractive young woman he's just met.

ANDY

You don't have to be consoling just because I haven't finished a book lately. I won't burst into tears or create a scene. No. I lied. I might burst into tears—I'm warning you.

ZAN

I didn't mean to imply . . . (*She laughs.*)

ANDY

Why are you laughing?

ZAN

You stapled your shirt.

ANDY

What's so odd about that? Millions of derelicts do it every day.

ZAN

And your glasses are wired together with a pipe cleaner.

ANDY

I didn't think twine would be as attractive.

In addition to liking Andy, audiences seem to sympathize with his goal of wanting to grow up and get back together with his collaborator and ex-wife, Ellen.

Whether you're wondering where to find an idea for a one-act play or beginning to refine the rough draft of a new full-length work or starting rehearsals of one of your plays, take your cue from the five magic ingredients of conflict. Whatever your experience as a playwright and whatever your current project, understanding the nature of dramatic conflict and how to achieve it will prove invaluable at every point in the writing and staging process.

\* \* \*

### Five exercises for creating dramatic conflict

Try these exercises to develop your skill in handling conflict.

1. Choose five plays you like. Summarize each in one sentence, stating what the protagonist wants. For example, Hamlet wants to avenge his father's murder.

2. Write one page of dialogue in which character A asks character B to do something that character B doesn't want to do. Have character A

make a request in three different ways, each showing a different emotion—guilt, enthusiasm, humility, anger.

3. Write a speech in which a character talks to another character and conveys what he wants without explicitly stating his goal.
4. Choose a famous play you enjoy. Rewrite the last page or two so that the outcome of the conflict for the protagonist is entirely different from the original.
5. Flip through today's newspaper until you find a story about a person—famous or unknown—who interests you. Then summarize the story in one sentence, stating what the person wants. For example: X wants to save an endangered species of bird. Next list the obstacles the person is facing in trying to get what he wants:
   • A developer wants to build a shopping mall where the remaining members of the endangered species live.
   • Pollution from a nearby factory is threatening the birds' food supply.

Finally, write several short scenes in which X (the protagonist) confronts the people (the antagonists) who represent the cause of each obstacle. (In this example, the antagonist would be the developer or the owner of the factory.) Decide which of the scenes you've written is the most dramatically satisfying. Identify the reasons you think it is the best scene.

# EDITING AND MARKETING

# § 103

## AN EDITOR SPEAKS
## FROM THE TRENCHES

### BY PETER RUBIE
#### Fiction Editor, *Walker and Company*

MY FONDEST HOPE IS THAT YOUR NOVEL crosses my desk, I read it, fall in love with it, and help to get it published.

That is the essence of the editor's job. For the less well-known or first-time novelist, however, getting published these days can be fantastically frustrating business.

The trend among the movers and shakers in publishing is toward thinking of books as "units" or "product," and a "Hollywoodization" of opting, because of financial reasons, for predictability and repetition. As a result, as the years go by the publishing industry at the upper levels—with a few notable exceptions—has become more corporate and less comfortable with craft and originality and more concerned with "names," though above all else it is still the editor's job and joy to unearth fresh, well-written material.

Agents may make you money, and in some cases have replaced the old-time editor's job of developing talent, but editors *love* discovering and helping authors get published, though finding them is like panning for gold.

The publishing marketplace has become more demanding of novelists, especially first-time novelists, than ever before. There is much talk of the demise of the mid-list book. Not enough people want to pay $21.95 for a "nice" little novel; they'll get it out of the library instead. So, while there is a market for such "literary" stories, it's limited. These days, publishing houses are looking for "blockbusters," those books that hit the bestseller lists and satisfy a seemingly insatiable corporate craving for ever larger profits, often at the expense of the inexperienced novelist.

What makes it worse—but also, paradoxically, works in an author's

529

favor—is that acquiring a book can be as idiosyncratic as writing one. One major reason in favor of getting an agent is that the good ones know which editor is where and what his or her tastes are, increasing a novel's chances of publication.

It is not the editor's job to teach novelists how to write, and yet at some point in a writer's career, especially early on, that's exactly what the better editors do. More precisely, they help the writer go that last mile.

The editor's work should be invisible. It can be structural, helping the author distinguish *what* the story is, and then helping improve *how* it's told (a difference too many authors seem unaware of); or mechanical, cleaning up a phrase here or there, catching repetition, emphasizing a theme, pointing out a weakness in character development or a hole in the story's logic; but by and large, the novels we buy are 95% ready for publication. We don't have the time to do much else with twenty-four or more books in production a year and reading on average two to three manuscripts a week, on top of all the line editing, conferences, and other work that has to be done.

Another reason behind the need for a finished manuscript is that editors don't make the ultimate decision when accepting a book. The process of acquisition can be frustrating, particularly at the larger houses. Their rules can be arbitrary and from an outsider's point of view, seemingly illogical. At smaller houses, such as the one I work for, editors have more discretion, mainly because we're not concerned with blockbusters, though we *are* concerned with making money on a book.

Editors are constantly surprised, frustrated, and overjoyed by what sells and what doesn't. We always think we know, but the truth is we rely mostly on instinct developed through years of reading, keeping an eye on what sells, and faith in our own educated taste. In the end, an editor can only pin his or her hopes on trying to acquire what inspires them.

Once an editor finds something he or she likes, the editor then has to present it to an editorial board, which in small houses can be limited to only a couple of people, such as the sub rights director, marketing director, and the publisher (who assess the book's commercial potential). In larger houses, the board can include many others. Simply saying a book is good is not enough, as much as that reasoning enrages the idealist in me, because I believe "good" can usually be translated into dollars if the book is handled properly. Not enough people in the industry seem to agree with this point of view, however, so don't take rejection personally: It's not about *you*, but the book, though I know it's often hard to make the distinction.

It's difficult for an editor to convince harried colleagues that while a first novel may not be outstanding, the author is clearly talented and will come across with something wonderful on the second or third go-round. The argument usually goes, "Well, let's see that one, then." The economics of publishing do not allow for this type of "old-fashioned" publishing any longer—except, perhaps, at the smaller hardcover houses. But there, the novelist, especially the first novelist, will get a small advance (rarely more than $5,000, and often less) and a limited print run (perhaps 5,000 copies, and again often less). You'll make a little more money on royalty payments and a share of subsequent sub-rights sales, if any.

For original paperbacks the figures are often higher, both in advances and print runs, but the demands of the company are also more rigid about what they feel comfortable will sell.

The acquisition process can be a bruising experience, so an editor must truly want to go to bat for a book. The canny editor must first find a good book, then find a way of convincing colleagues (who may not have the editor's eye for talent) that the book has a dollars and cents potential. Too often a writer (and sometimes an agent who should know better) adds in the query or manuscript cover letter, "This will make a great movie." Frankly, my dear, to paraphrase a famous literary line, we don't give a fig, because we don't often get to share in the sale of dramatic rights to a film production company. (This kind of sub-right is one good agents will hang on to, unless the publishing company is paying a substantial royalty advance.) Editors will rejoice when one of their writers has a movie sale, but it's *not* a selling point at the submission stage.

Paradoxically, in an industry designed to make money selling books, the majority of published novels die on the vine with little publicity or support from the company. Reviewers are partially responsible for this situation, on the one hand complaining about publishing company hype, but by and large going along with the set up and paying attention

531

only to these "big" books, giving scant attention to other novels, no matter how deserving of attention. Reviews and advanced quotes and publicity are important factors in the success or failure of a book.

All this is not intended to put off would-be novelists, but to tell it as it is.

Tack this on the wall above your word-processor:

DETERMINED NOVELISTS WITH TENACITY AND STAMINA WHO LEARN AND DEVELOP THEIR CRAFT WILL EVENTUALLY GET PUBLISHED.

Don't second-guess what's commercial—that's the editor's job, and we can tell a cynically written piece a mile off. All you can do is pour your heart and soul into the thing, submit it and move on to the next piece, learning the lessons of craft as you go.

Remember:

> The higher calling is not as Writer—
> but as Storyteller.

All this is intended to emphasize, underscore, and reiterate that a finished manuscript (at least to the writer) is the *only* form in which a story should be submitted, and almost certainly it is the only one that may eventually be bought. I get too many letters that accompany submitted manuscripts that say, "I know this needs work, but I don't know where or how to do it. Let me know what to do and I'll be happy to make the changes that are needed." If that's your book, take a class, read a book on writing technique, *learn* how to fix the problems you know are there *before* you submit your manuscript. Don't expect an editor (or agent) to do it for you.

Writing is not putting down words on paper—that's just labor; writing is *editing,* or shaping those words into scenes and images and layers and symbols, making sure each word, be it an "and" or a "but," carries its own weight. Learning to write a good novel, especially a hardcover-quality novel, is *very difficult,* don't let anyone tell you any different. Of the 250 million people in the United States maybe sixty or so make a good living from writing fiction. You figure the odds.

So don't expect to make a living writing fiction: Most of us have to do something else. But that means you are free to take as long as you need on a project, and you won't have to write to a deadline that will force you to compromise on the quality of your work.

Pablo Casals, the world-famous cellist, once badly injured a hand in a mountain climbing expedition, and when told he might never play again told the doctor, "Thank God. At last I'm free." Two years later, he was again giving concerts and playing better than ever. Creative expression is an addiction beyond the creator's control, except in terms of how well we learn the craft. Writers write because they have to, not because they want to.

If you're not put off by all of the above, then you've passed the first hurdle: In the face of absurd odds and difficulties, you have the obdurate determination and attitude it takes to stay the distance and learn what needs to be learned. The odds are that you'll be published eventually.

There's a story that bears telling here. It concerns a young musician who desired more than anything to study with a particular master violinist. One day, the pupil was given his chance to play for the maestro. He arrived for the audition and played his heart out.

After he finished there was a long silence. Then the maestro said, rather offhandedly, "Not enough fire," and with a wave of one hand dismissed the student. Now the student, as you can imagine, was devastated. In disgust he quit the violin and went into commerce, becoming a very successful businessman.

Many years later, when the maestro gave a recital at Carnegie Hall, the former student went backstage and introduced himself. He and the maestro had a pleasant discussion, but finally the student could not resist, and recounted their last meeting, when he had played for the old man and been told, "Not enough fire."

"What did you mean?" the student asked.

"Oh, I say that to everyone," the maestro said disarmingly. The student was stunned, and then became very angry. "I could have been a great musician," he said. "Instead, because of *you,* I gave it up."

The maestro looked up, and with a smile said, "Not really. If you were going to be a great musician you'd have done it anyway, regardless of anything I said."

------------

Walker & Co. is a small independent hardcover house in New York City. In general perhaps half our list is made up of first-time novelists—a bigger percentage than almost any other house, I would venture to suggest. Furthermore, we are one of the few remaining houses that take author submissions. The likelihood is that more readers of this handbook stand a chance of being published by us than probably any other hardcover company. However, we only publish on average 100 books a year, including fiction, non-fiction and children's books.

The importance of hardcover, of course, is one of review notice and quality. A book that is priced at $21.95 obviously must have more to offer than one priced at $5.95. The trend in the industry, however, is to shut out the talented "mid-list" writer as unprofitable. The best bet if you can't get us, or someone like us, to publish you, is to write the best crafted genre novel you can (such as a mystery or science fiction or romance, etc.) and try for an original paperback.

534

# 104

## THE AUTHOR/AGENT RELATIONSHIP

### BY JONATHAN DOLGER

IT USED TO BE TRUE, WHEN I FIRST STARTED working in publishing, that the hardest thing to accomplish was finding a publisher. In those days, publishers still accepted unsolicited manuscripts from authors, and they were read by the editorial staff on a weekly basis. There were fewer agents, and contact between the writer and the editor was on a one-to-one basis, simpler than is currently the case.

With the increasing growth and consolidation of publishing companies, publishing has become a more bureaucratic process. Editors' choices are subjected to a review process that includes looking at "profit and loss statements," input from the marketing and sales staff, etc. Rarely can an editor make the final decision on whether or not to publish a manuscript. Instead, we have judgment by consensus, with editors functioning as *de facto* lobbyists.

It's not productive or helpful for the author to worry about these matters. The "gentlemen's business" has become a real business, and that's not so bad. It has produced, from a variety of viewpoints, a collective approach to publishing, which when it works, can be very successful.

The result of this is that many agents have taken over what used to be seen as part of the editorial side of publishing: i.e., reading and evaluating new work. Agents are not magicians, so it would be unreasonable to expect that if an agent agrees to represent you, you will automatically find a publisher. No one can force an editor to buy a book: There has to be reaction to and interaction with the material itself.

What an agent can do, if your work is accepted for publication, is not only make sure that you get the best possible contract, but also continue to protect your interests with the publisher throughout the entire publication process. This is extremely important, since with so many editors changing from one house to another, it is not at all uncommon to have several editors work on your manuscript. Indeed, a client of mine recently had five different editors at the same house, beginning with the one who acquired the book and ending with the one to whom the book was assigned at the time of actual publication.

Now that I've stated just how important an agent can be for a writer, let me also say that a beginning writer can, and should, begin to establish a career before finding an agent. Magazines and newspapers are still the best places for a beginning writer to get published. Don't confine yourself to the few "brand-name" publications, as they may have many of the same problems as book publishers when it comes to screening and reading unsolicited material. It is possible to begin to build your reputation on a local and regional level, develop contacts, and have a good body of work published, at which point you will be in a better position to approach a potential publisher or agent. I recently attended a writers' conference where there were 450 writers, and many of them began their professional careers in just this manner. A good source book here is *The International Directory of Little Magazines and Small Presses,* published by Dustbooks (P.O. Box 100, Paradise, CA 95967).

If you have already reached the point in your professional career where you think you should have an agent, your next hurdle will be to find the right agent and agency for you. You may have contacts who can personally recommend you to some literary agents. If this isn't the case, there are a number of reliable source books that list literary agents and their requirements, including *Literary Market Place* and *The Writer's Handbook.* Most agencies can easily tell you what kind of material they represent and what types of manuscripts you should submit for their consideration. For example, my agency represents adult trade fiction and nonfiction, as well as illustrated books. We do not accept unsolicited manuscripts, but will consider query letters with sample material, and an SASE. So if you are an author of science fiction or children's books, my agency would not be the best choice for you. In general, you should also be aware that most agencies will not charge a reading fee, so double-check any offers to "evaluate" your material for a price.

Once you find the right agency for you, it's time to consider the question of author/agent contracts. Should authors have contracts with agents, and what happens if things don't work out and you want to break the contract? Some agencies insist on having a contract with every client. Generally, the contract will specify what happens if either the author or the agent wants to end the relationship, but if no such language exists, you should ask that it be inserted into the agreement. The contract between you and any agent should not make you liable for work, or options on your work that continue after the agreement is terminated. There are exceptions to this rule: For example, if an agent sells something before the official termination date of a client's agreement, the agent is entitled to the agreed-upon percentage of proceeds from that sale.

One of the main benefits of a writer's contract with an agent (and the reason many authors request such a contract) is that it makes the agent/client relationship clearer and more professional. There should be little reason for disputes if both parties know the responsibilities of the other, what rights are being negotiated, and what percentages the agent charges (percentages vary with the number of services offered—i.e., sales to foreign publishers, sales of film/television rights, etc.—but usually range between 10% and 20% of the author's gross receipts). A simple letter of agreement spelling out these terms should be sufficient. You don't need to sign away your soul on a document that is more convoluted than the tax information provided *gratis* by the IRS.

One of the most important functions an agent performs before sending your material out to publishers is to make sure that it is in the most intelligible and marketable shape. There is a difference between fiction and nonfiction, and I will address these areas separately.

For a nonfiction book by an unpublished author, the publisher can reasonably expect an outline or proposal, and two or three sample chapters that will give him some sense of how the writer will deal with the chosen subject. It doesn't matter whether it's a self-help book or a sociological study of environmental hazards; what these pages must demonstrate is the tone the book will take. To this exent, the agent acts as a "pre-editor," making sure that the ideas are clearly articulated and presented and that the author clearly has a point of view and knows how to communicate it. Also included should be some information about the author: background, other published articles, education. Equally important, the agent can help the author focus the proposal for its potential market.

The agent will want to know—just as the publisher will—what competition there might be. Are there similar books in the field that have been or are about to be published? If so, does this one have a special handle that will distinguish it from the others? Are there other markets that the publisher should consider with this book—special premium sales, professional groups, etc.—that will give the book added appeal? Has the book been endorsed or recommended by someone prominent in the field? Does the author have personal contacts with other professionals who would help him obtain information that might not be readily available to others? The proposal should be fifty to seventy-five pages of material that is as good as the author and agent can make it. The agent will add his own perspective and information when the material is sent out to the publisher, but this will serve only to highlight the information in the proposal. The author's voice must be heard on its own.

The handling of fiction is often quite different. In the current diminished and very competitive marketplace, it is rare to sell a novel by an unpublished or even published writer on the basis of a few sample chapters and a synopsis. Most publishers want to see a complete manuscript before making a decision to take on a writer. There are exceptions—mostly in "category" books such as romances or male adventure stories—but these novels are written to a specific formula and therefore are not judged by the same standards and criteria. Also, fiction is a *subjective* art: One editor's taste and sensitivity will vary from another's. Only from reading a completed manuscript can an editor judge what a writer is trying to accomplish.

Here again, the agent can help the author by trying to be sure that the pacing is right, the characters well developed, and that the author makes the reader care and sympathize with his story, but there is less involvement by the agent on this level than with a nonfiction proposal. To a certain extent, the agent's view is also subjective; the agent must take into account that his or her reactions may be personal and that an editor might have a different response.

Once an agent has decided to take you on as a client, whether for fiction or nonfiction, there are several ways to submit your manuscript for publication.

The traditional method has been to choose one publishing house and editor at a time and let them consider the book on an exclusive basis. If there is no sale, you move on to the second, third, or fourth choice.

However, because time is so limited and the publishing process so much more complicated by the many editorial committees that often control selection at a publishing house, the agent may want to submit that material to a number of publishers at the same time. Another obvious reason for multiple submissions is that if the book's subject matter is timely (for example, a current political topic), you want to get the widest amount of exposure as quickly as possible. Some publishers used to be offended by the practice of multiple submissions or auctions, but I don't believe that is a valid viewpoint for the current publishing climate. I try to find the best match between editor, author, and publisher and hope that it works. If it doesn't, I will try a few other houses, but if I still haven't been successful, I will make a limited number of multiple submissions, informing each prospective buyer that other publishers are looking at the material at the same time.

Apart from making the best deal and negotiating the most favorable terms for a client, it is the agent's responsibility to know the publishing network—to make the selection and determination of which editor and house are right for your book. As your link to the publishing community, the agent should shepherd you through the publishing process, looking out for your best interests, but also helping you see the publisher's side of any dispute or disagreement. This requires experience, knowledge, intuition, and often just good diplomatic sense. It has been my experience that authors often do not act in their own best interests when they act alone; they require the objective help of an agent.

Negotiating contracts can vary as much as contracts vary from publisher to publisher. The business points, such as advances and royalties, may be similar, but there are many subtleties in such areas of negotiation as subsidiary rights, warranty, and out-of-print clauses that only an experienced agent can handle. A good agent will also be aware of recent changes in publishing agreements, such as those resulting from the united European market, which make it even more imperative to have an agent's solid, professional advice.

Having your work accepted for representation by an agent and obtaining a publishing contract may seem like the end of a road well-traveled, but in truth it's only the beginning. When the sale is concluded, the publishing process begins. Along the way, there are many decisions that will have to be made regarding editorial changes, book design, promotion, and publicity. In the current publishing climate, even the most sophisticated writer can feel like a new arrival in Oz, where the direction of the Yellow Brick Road has changed, and the Wizard has a boss! In these uncertain times, the good counsel of your literary agent means that you won't travel alone and there'll be someone to help you read the map.

# 105

## DEBUNKING THE WRITING-FOR-CHILDREN-IS-EASY MYTH

### BY STEPHANIE OWENS LURIE
Senior Editor, *Little, Brown and Company*

PERHAPS YOU'VE SEEN THEM, THOSE ADS FOR WRITING COURSES that proclaim, "You, too, can be an author. There's no better way to get published than by writing books for children and teenagers." Now, I am in favor of any program that inspires writers, but I do take issue with statements like these. They imply that anyone can get published, and that writing for children is just a stepping stone to getting a contract for a "real" (a.k.a. adult) book. Aspiring writers often fall victim to the myth that children's books are easy to write and even easier to sell. This is a pernicious rumor that has to be stopped, because it bogs down the editorial consideration process for the more dedicated writers out there and also demeans all of us who strive to produce worthwhile children's books.

While the process of writing and publishing a book for children may not be as simple and quick as those ads suggest, it is a rewarding one. If you're serious about breaking into this field, here is some advice that will increase your chances of having your manuscript accepted and published.

1) Don't believe the "writing-for-children-is-easy" myth. The fact that children's books are shorter than books for adults does not mean that they require less time and creative thought. On the contrary, shorter texts are often more difficult to compose, because each word has to be chosen carefully to pack the most punch. Even the most seasoned pro will agree that writing is hard work, no matter how old your intended audience may be.

As for getting that first contract, juvenile editors are just as discriminating as their counterparts in the adult field. In fact, because the market has been inundated with so many children's titles in recent years, booksellers with shrinking shelf space are cutting back their orders, and publishers are being forced to reduce their lists and be even more selective. So, it is more important than ever to try to come up with something strong and unique.

2) One of the best ways you can prepare for the task in front of you is to do research. Understand the market before you approach it. Go to the children's room in your local library and talk to the librarian. Ask him or her which classics you should read. Ask to see some of the recent Caldecott and Newbery Award winners. Ask which books seem to be the most popular with kids today, and what they want but can't find. Next, do the same thing at your local children's bookstore. Watch what parents and kids pick up. Look for the publishers' names on the spines and see if you can get a feel for the kinds of books they produce. Then write to the publishers that appeal to you and ask for their most recent catalogue and their guidelines for submissions. While you're at it, get the name of the children's book editor.

Another important part of your field research is familiarizing yourself with your intended audience—if you don't have children of your own, you can always find some to talk to at a relative's or friend's house, or at a school, library, or day care center. The most successful writers for children have a healthy respect for even the youngest readers. They know better than to condescend or preach to their audience. They avoid writing in a sugary-sweet tone, and they don't automatically choose anthropomorphism or rhyming verse, if a straightforward, true-to-life approach would work better. They know that young children want to learn, are willing to believe, love to laugh, and have boundless imaginations.

3) Although it is important to know what is on the minds of young readers and bookbuyers, I am not suggesting that you write in response to current trends. There are already too many people out there writing about contemporary social issues. By the time you jump on the bandwagon, there will probably be hundreds of manuscripts on the same topic already in circulation, and the trend will be long gone before the typical eighteen months it takes to publish a book are over.

4) When you finally sit down at the keyboard, create for the child in yourself. The information you have gathered in your research will give you a context in which to write, a yardstick against which you can measure yourself. But the bottom line is that you should write about what you as an individual find funny, delightful, important, etc., not what you as an adult think should appeal to kids. Some of the best manuscripts I've seen came out of the authors' direct experience and were not consciously directed toward kids.

5) Once you've finished your piece, play the part of the publisher for a minute. As you read it over, ask yourself, does this picture book text offer plenty of good opportunities for an illustrator? Would this novel speak to a wide audience? Are there any other books like this on the market? Does it offer a fresh perspective? Is the vocabulary appropriate for the intended audience? Is it fast-paced, believable, authentic? Does it have substance? Is the beginning compelling? Is the ending satisfying? Would I pay $15.00 for this?

6) If you feel that your manuscript meets all of the above criteria and you decide to go ahead and submit it, have enough pride in your work to present it as professionally as possible.

Here are some submission do's and don'ts:

## Do . . .

- Type your manuscript (double-spaced).
- Send out a clean, readable photocopy.
- If it is a picture book, it helps to denote page breaks, to show that it will fit into a standard format.
- Include a succinct cover letter, addressed to a specific editor, and listing any publishing credits, credentials, or relevant experience. Briefly explain how your book differs from the competition, if any, and why it would suit this particular publishing house. (This demonstrates your familiarity with the market, and the editor's list.) Mention that you are open to criticism and are willing to revise, if necessary.
- Enclose a self-addressed, stamped envelope.

## Don't . . .

- Send out a letter or manuscript with typos or misspellings. (I remember thinking my creative writing professor in college was too nit-

picky about typos and misspellings, but now that I'm an editor I've seen the negative effects both can have on a reader. They give us the impression that you don't care, and if you don't care, why should we?)
• Use erasable bond, or send out an old, yellowed copy that looks as though it has been in circulation for years.
• Attempt to explain your intentions or, worse, offer to come in to present your manuscript to the editor. It should speak for itself.
• Compare your manuscript to a classic.
• Cite the positive reactions of children. Editors are not particularly impressed by this, considering that children will respond favorably to the phone book if it is read aloud to them.
• Ask that the manuscript you are submitting in September be published in time for Christmas or offer to promote your book on *The Today Show* (this shows that you have unrealistic expectations).
• Include instructions for the illustrator, unless the action is unclear, as we encourage illustrators to interpret the text as they see fit, ideally adding an extra dimension to the story.
• Attempt to do the illustrations yourself, unless you've had professional training. We will choose the illustrator—often we try to pair a new author with a well-known illustrator and vice versa, to ensure that the book receives attention.

7) Even after the manuscript is out of your hands, there are things you can do to increase—or decrease—your chances of getting published. Remember that yours is only one of hundreds of manuscripts that the editors have to read, discuss, and respond to. So refrain from calling the editor within two weeks of submitting your manuscript to check on its status. After three months, you have a right to know where it stands. If you get another offer in the meantime, let everyone know so that competitive offers can be made. If an editor expresses an interest in your piece, express your enthusiasm, indicate your willingness to revise or consider editorial changes, and indicate a professional attitude in your questions about contracts and the publication process.

8) If creating books for children is your first love, we at Little, Brown welcome your submissions, whether they be solicited or unsolicited, agented or unagented, single or simultaneous (just let us know if it's the latter). But if you think of writing for children only as a way to break

into publishing, you'd be better off elsewhere. Children's books should be left to the authors who are truly devoted to reaching young readers (infants through young adults), because children don't deserve anything less.

# 106

## WHEN *NOT* TO TRY, TRY AGAIN

### BY WENDY CORSI STAUB

IT'S HAPPENED AGAIN. I WAS TOO NICE IN A REJECTION LETTER, and a woman I hoped would never darken my editorial doorstep again has not only a) sent me a cute card thanking me for letting her down gently, but b) she said that a revised version will be winging its way toward my desk soon, and c) she has told her writers' group what a humane editor I am, so that d) these friends will be sending me *their* manuscripts that have been rejected elsewhere.

Short of feeding her next submission through a paper shredder and returning it to her, I'm at a loss for a way to get the message across: She will never publish at our house. She simply doesn't have what it takes to sell to us, and if she tried from now until 2091, she couldn't do it. I know this. She should know this so that she won't waste any more of her time or my time. I have to tell her.

Rolling a fresh piece of company letterhead into my typewriter (yes, *typewriter*—contrary to popular belief, many editors don't have word processors in their offices), I contemplate my next step. What can I say that will make her realize future submissions will be futile without totally devastating the poor thing? Is there a way to be nicely brutal?

I do my best, hoping the short, impersonal style of my letter will discourage her. I mention the highly competitive marketplace, suggest that at this point in her writing career she concentrate more on learning and polishing her technique. I thank her for thinking of us and wish her luck. I sign it formally with my full name and title. There—that should do it.

Feeling like Santa Claus informing a hopeful child that he's crossing her off his list, I send it on its grim mission.

Exactly one week later, I receive a second cheerful card from this would-be writer, this one covered with kittens. She is flattered, she says, that I consider her important enough to acknowledge, since I pointed out how competitive our marketplace is. She vows to do her best to live up to my expectations for her writing career—and she's pleased that I referred to it that way, as a "career," because that's how she feels about it, too. She will be sending me a new story proposal soon, to demonstrate how she's been polishing her technique in the two days since she received my letter. She signs the letter, *Love, Marge.*

Obviously, I'm doing something wrong here.

Remember how back when you got dumped by your first real love, the first real love told you it was harder to do the dumping than to be dumped? Remember how you thought, "Yeah, *right.* That's why you're standing there dry-eyed and I'm collapsed on the carpet in tears."

Well, I can vouch for the fact that there's some truth in that theory.

It isn't easy to reject someone in *any* capacity. It's especially taxing when they refuse to take "NO!" for an answer.

As an editor who is also trying to build a writing career, I not only write rejection letters every day—I receive them. Sometimes they're encouraging, sometimes they're standard pre-printed slips, but no matter what format, they're *always* depressing.

But since I'm an editor, and therefore understand the implications of "editor-speak," I am usually able to interpret unwritten messages in letters I receive. When editors offer significant, specific feedback on my work and suggest that I try again, I take them at their word. When someone politely thanks me for trying, but rejects the manuscript with the plain old "it doesn't suit our present needs" line, I know he means exactly that. There is no hidden message there. The person doesn't hope I'll proofread the story, correct a couple of typos, and send it back again. More likely, he means that I'll have better luck selling this type of material elsewhere.

This doesn't rule out occasionally trying these places again, especially if they're major, competitive publishing houses that rarely give personal feedback to *anyone.* It is important in this difficult business not to give up, since even the biggest names have drawers full of early rejection slips. But there's a big difference between not giving up—and making an enormous pest of yourself.

The key lies in learning to interpret what the editor is trying to tell you in his response. And while a personal response is substantially less unpleasant than a standard one, it isn't necessarily an encouraging sign; my own editorial policy is *always* to give an individualized reply, even if the submission was so poorly written I could barely get through the first few pages. After all, the writer went to the trouble of creating this project and giving our publishing house a try—he deserves the courtesy of a personal reply.

How do you tell when an editor will welcome more of your work and when it's just no use continuing to submit to him? You can usually tell from the kind of rejection letter he's written.

One woman, Lynn S., had submitted a manuscript quite a while ago that I found promising. I passed it to my senior editor, who decided the manuscript might work with revisions. We decided to ask Lynn to revise, and I gave her a detailed revision letter with suggestions and detailed notes. She resubmitted the altered manuscript a few months later. When I read it, I felt that it worked, and I passed it again to my senior editor. She hated it!

Now I had to reject Lynn, who I thought was truly a talented author. I knew my senior editor didn't want to see a third version of this manuscript, but I thought Lynn might be capable of hitting the mark with a different project. In my rejection letter, I explained the reasons the manuscript hadn't worked for us. I was specific, outlining the basic problems and pinpointing areas where the characterization grew weak, or the pacing slowed. In the last paragraph I encouraged Lynn to come up with a fresh idea and query me soon.

Lynn did, and she turned in another complete manuscript relatively quickly. Unfortunately, that one wasn't right either. Again, I invited her to try us with a new project. And she did. Twice. And I rejected her. Twice. But each time, I tried to keep the tone of my letter encouraging, and I kept telling her to try again. She kept coming so close, but not managing to make the sale.

I'm happy to say that I finally bought a manuscript from Lynn, and she is now an author under contract. If she'd become discouraged by the trail of rejection letters, she never would have reached this point. But she learned from her mistakes, and fortunately, she believed me when I told her I wanted to see more.

When I genuinely want to hear from an author again, I *always* tell her so. There are people who submit to me repeatedly, and while it's frustrating to keep rejecting them, I am careful to keep my letter optimistic.

If an editor uses phrases like, "you are a talented writer," or "your work has shown promise," or "I look forward to hearing from you again," he means it! March right back to that keyboard, and get started on something new!

Another sign that all is not lost is a rejection that states that your manuscript just didn't "read" like whatever his house publishes, but the editor suggests that you study certain books published by his house so that you'll have a better idea of what he's looking for. When I think that an author might be talented, but is taking his manuscript in the wrong direction, I'll sometimes send him certain books along with my rejection letter, recommending that he read them to learn what kind of material we publish.

Susan L., the author of many young adult novels, recently sent me a proposal for a contemporary adult romance. It was charming, and the writing was professional, but the tone was all wrong. This was a teen story masquerading as women's fiction. Still, I believed the author had potential, so I sent her several recent books by authors who had also published young adult fiction before selling to us. I urged Susan to study them for tone and pacing. If she feels inclined to submit to me again, I'll be glad to consider her work.

What about the lost causes, people who just aren't writing the kind of material we publish? How do I let someone know she isn't cut out for writing a book that will sell to us, without coming right out and saying, "Don't ever send me another submission"?

As I said before, it isn't easy.

There are a number of reasons for writing the ultimate rejection letter, as I've come to think of it. Perhaps the author has written an entire series of bestselling how-to craft books, and she's sent me her latest work—a novel. It's plain to me from page one that, while she is a competent writer, she just isn't suited to writing fiction. She's not going to be able to "fix" this manuscript, and she's not going to be able to write a better one. What do I do? Respond with the ultimate rejection letter.

Maybe my third cousin's eighty-year-old mother-in-law has written a novel, and she's sent it to—who else?—me. While I'm sure dear old Hattie is a lovely person, it would be an understatement to say that her command of the English language leaves something to be desired. It's plain that no matter how hard this woman tries, she just won't be able to sell a book to us. She's another prime candidate for the ultimate rejection letter.

The trick in writing these letters is to keep the tone strictly formal. It's easier for me to reject someone when I maintain the sense that she's a stranger. I stay away from light, chatty phrases and humor, and I always try to get right to the point.

It's necessary for me to first overcome my feeling of guilt about ruining this good person's day. I remind myself that it's not the publisher's place to teach people how to write, so I shouldn't use much space offering advice or suggestions. I remember that my job is to contract books that our readers will buy and enjoy, that raising false hopes by being too kind is cruel in the long run, and it's best just to be as straightforward as possible—without making the rejection seem like an attack.

This strict, no-nonsense mindset allows me to say things that may very well cause the writer pain. "The story lacks vitality and sparkle"; "This work just isn't up to our standards"; "It's too early in your career to be submitting to publishers." *Ouch!*

I try to soften the blows by liberally sprinkling my letter with buffer words like "seems to" and "somewhat"—i.e., "the characters seem self-centered," as opposed to "the characters *are* self-centered," and "the plot came across as somewhat contrived," instead of "the plot is contrived."

I attempt to focus on the project rather than on "I" or "you." I won't say, "I don't find your writing style fresh or compelling," but rather, "The writing seems to lack freshness." This removes both the writer and the editor from the front and diffuses the negative comments as much as possible.

What do you do if you receive one of these letters?

First of all, recognize that the editor is telling you this project isn't right for that particular publishing house, not that it's all wrong for every publishing house in the world and that you should just quit writing.

Accept the fact that it's probably best not to send that project or similar ones back to that editor, and try to learn from any constructive criticism you can glean from the letter. Use this experience to polish the

550

manuscript and send it out again—but to a different publishing house, even a different market.

You might want to look into smaller, less competitive publishing houses if the major houses consistently reject your manuscripts. There's more room for newcomers in those markets, and their editors may prove more willing to work with you on revisions.

Join a writers' group, if you feel that you've been rejected one too many times. Regular feedback can help you hone your skills, and it takes the sting out of rejection to discuss it with other people who know what it's like.

Above all, don't give up if this is something you truly want to do. Keep learning and growing and improving your style; keep researching new outlets for submitting your work. And remember that publishing is a business; you are offering a product for sale. If you handle being turned down with grace and dignity, your chances of eventually succeeding will improve.

What *shouldn't* you do if you receive the ultimate rejection?

It's not a good idea to make a few changes to the manuscript and send it back to the same editor. And it's definitely not wise to call the editor in tears, or make threats. Don't decide that begging or persisting will change the editor's mind.

I wonder whether Marge honestly missed the point in my letters to her, perceiving my discouragement as encouragement, or whether she simply decided to ignore what I was telling her.

Whatever the case, one thing is certain: Marge will never publish a book at our publishing house. That fact has everything to do with the quality of her writing, and no amount of revision, persistence, begging, or threatening could change that.

All I can do is continue to reject her submissions, and hope that eventually she'll tire of sending them to me. I can also practice hardening my heart so that I can make my rejection letters more clear and effective.

And if that doesn't work, I may look into that paper-shredder idea.

# 107

## COMMON QUESTIONS ABOUT COPYRIGHTS

### BY HOWARD ZAHAROFF

TO BE A GOOD WRITER, YOU MUST UNDERSTAND THE BASICS OF WRITING. To be a published writer, you must understand the basics of manuscript submission and the editorial process.

And to be a successful writer, the owner of a portfolio of published manuscripts, you must also understand the basics of copyright law. As a lawyer who practices in the field, I promise that this isn't too hard. Let me prove it by answering a dozen questions that free lancers often ask.

Before doing so, a few comments. First, the answers I give are based on U.S. law. International issues are mostly ignored. Second, my focus is mainly on works first published or created after March 1, 1989, the last major revision of the Copyright Act (which I refer to below as the "Act"). Third, although the Copyright Office cannot provide legal advice, its Circulars and Public Information Office (call 202/479-0700) provide guidance on many of the following issues. (Start with Circular 1, "Copyright Basics.") There are also many excellent books available, such as Ellen Kozak's *Every Writer's Guide to Copyright & Publishing Law* (Owl, 1990).

1. *What can be copyrighted?* Copyright protects nearly every original piece you write (or draw, compose, choreograph, videotape, sculpt, etc.): not just your novel, article, story or poem, but the software program you create, the advertisements and greeting cards you published, and the love letters you wrote in high school. But copyright does not protect your ideas, only the way you *express* them.

2. *What protection does copyright provide?* A "copyright" is really a bundle of rights. The copyright owner (whom we'll call the "proprietor") controls not only the right to copy the work, but also the rights

552

to prepare "derivative works" (i.e., adaptations, translations, and other modifications), to perform or display the work publicly, and to make the "first sale" of each copy of the work.

3. *What is the duration of copyright protection, and is it renewable?* For works created or first published after 1977, copyright generally lasts 50 years after the death of the author. However, for anonymous or pseudonymous works, or works made "for hire" (see below), the term expires 100 years from creation or 75 years from publication. There are no renewals. (For works published before 1978, the term is 28 years, with right to renew for 47 additional years. See Circular 15, "Renewal of Copyright.")

4. *How do you obtain a copyright?* Copyright protection arises *automatically* as soon as you put your ideas into tangible form. Thus, once on paper, canvas, video, or computer disk, your creation is protected by law.

5. *Is a copyright notice required for protection?* No. Until recently a notice was required on all *published* copies of a work. ("Published" simply means distributed to the public; it does not require printing in a periodical or book.) However, on March 1, 1989, the United States joined the international copyright treaty known as the Berne Convention and removed this requirement for works published after that date.

Still, including a copyright notice alerts everyone to your claim and prevents an infringer from pleading "innocence" (that is, that he had no idea your work was copyrighted). Thus, good reasons remain for including notices on all published copies of your work, and for insisting that your publisher do so.

If you are concerned that your *unpublished* work may be used or copied without permission (e.g., you are circulating copies of your most timely and accomplished piece within your newly formed writers group), you can't lose by including a notice.

6. *What should my copyright notice say?* A proper notice has three elements:

- The international copyright symbol © or the word "Copyright." Most publishers use both. (The abbreviation "Copr" is also acceptable.)

553

- The year in which the work is first published. (For unpublished works, you may omit a date.)
- Your name, or a recognizable abbreviation (e.g., International Business Machines Corporation may use "IBM").

In general, notices should be displayed prominently at the beginning of your work, although any reasonable location is acceptable. If your piece will appear in a magazine, anthology, or other collective work, a single notice in the publisher's name will preserve most of your rights. However, including a separate copyright notice in your own name will clarify that only you, *not* the publisher, has the right to authorize further uses of your work.

7. *Must I register my work with the Copyright Office?* Although registration is not required for copyright protection, it is a precondition to suing for infringement of the copyrights in any work first published in the U.S. (and in the unpublished works of U.S. citizens and residents), and enables you to recover both attorneys' fees and "statutory damages" (i.e. damages of up to $100,000, determined by the judge, which the proprietor may elect to recover from the infringer in lieu of proving and recovering actual losses).

You can register your copyrights at any time during the term of copyright. However, registration within three months of publication generally preserves your rights to all infringement remedies, including statutory damages, while registration within five years of publication provides special benefits in legal proceedings.

8. *How do you register a work?* Copyright Office Form TX is the basic form for nondramatic literary works. Form PA is used to register works of the performing arts, including plays and movies. These one-page forms cost $20 to file and are fairly easy to complete (but only if you read the accompanying instructions!). Adjunct Form GR/CP allows writers to reduce costs by making a single registration for all works published in periodicals within a 12-month period. (You can order forms and circulars over the Hotline, 202/707-9100).

When you apply you must submit one copy of the work, if unpublished, and two copies of the "best edition" of the work, if published. (Only one copy of the best edition is required for contributions to collective works.) The "best edition" is the published edition of highest quality, determined by paper quality, binding, and other factors listed by the Copyright Office (see Circular R7b). For example, if the work was published in both hard and soft covers, the hard cover is normally the best edition.

9. *Should I register my work?* In most cases, no. If your work was published, your publisher may have registered it. If not, failure to register costs you mainly the option for *immediate* relief and statutory damages. Moreover, infringement is the exception and, where it occurs, often can be settled without lawsuits or registration. Besides, most writers earn too little to justify the cost of registration (certainly for articles, poems, and other short works).

10. *What is "public domain" and how can you find out what's there?* Works that are not protected by copyright are said to be in the "public domain"—i.e., freely usable by the public, without the need to get permission or pay a fee. This includes works in which copyright has expired or been lost, works for which copyright is not available, and works dedicated to the public. Although there are many exceptions, *in general* the following are in the public domain:

- Works published more than 75 years ago.
- Works published more than 28 years ago, if the copyright was not renewed.
- Works published without a proper copyright notice before 1978.
- Works published without a proper notice between January 1, 1978 and February 28, 1989 (although the Act enables the proprietor to correct this failure).
- Works created by employees of the Federal government as part of their duties.

For a fee the Copyright Office will examine the status of a work. (See Circular 22, "How to Investigate the Copyright Status of a Work.")

11. *What is fair use?* The Act allows the limited use of others' works for research, teaching, news reporting, criticism, and similar purposes. These permitted uses are called "fair use," although the Act never defines that term. Rather, it lists factors to consider, including the purpose and character of the use (e.g., for-profit vs. teaching), the nature of the work (e.g., a science text vs. a poem), the amount and substantiality of the use, and its effect on the market for the work.

Here are some basic rules that should help you stay on the right side of the law (and help you recognize when someone's use of your work doesn't).

- **Copying for noncommercial (e.g., educational) purposes is given wider scope than copying for commercial use.** For example, in general you may quote less of the published writings of a politician in a television docudrama than a history professor may quote in journal articles.

- **Copying factual material gets more latitude than copying fiction.** Fiction contains more of the "originality" protected by the Act: characters and events, sometimes even time and place, derive from the writer's imagination. Facts cannot be copyrighted.

- **Parody is a permissible use, as long as it does not appropriate too much of the original.**

- **Copying from unpublished works without permission is usually considered unfair.** This was illustrated in a 1989 case concerning an unauthorized biography of Scientologist/SF writer L. Ron Hubbard. Referring to an earlier case, in which Random House was enjoined from publishing an unauthorized biography of J. D. Salinger because it infringed copyrights in his unpublished letters, the court wrote that "unpublished works normally enjoy complete protection" from unauthorized publication. (However, legislation is being considered that would expand the application of fair use to unpublished works.)

- **The Act permits certain uses of copyrighted works by libraries, archives, educators, charitable organizations, and others.** See sections 108–110 of the Act and Circular 21.

These rules are complex. Therefore, if you intend to copy more than a negligible amount from another person's work without permission, write to the publisher or copyright owner. Don't take a chance.

12. *What is a "work made for hire," and who owns the rights to these works?* The creator of a work generally owns the copyrights. There is an exception, however, for "works made for hire." Here it is the party who commissions and pays for the work, rather than the actual creator, who owns the copyrights. So when is a work "for hire"?

First, unless expressly excluded by contract, all works created by employees within the scope of their employment are "for hire." (This will normally not include works created on your own time that are unrelated to your employment.) So if you are employed by a newspaper, or hired by a software publisher to write documentation, your employer owns the copyrights in the works you've been paid to create. If you use copies of these works at your next job, you are infringing on your former employer's copyrights.

Second, certain specified categories of works (including translations, compilations, and parts of audiovisual works) are considered "for hire" if they have been specially commissioned and a signed document identifies them as "for hire." Therefore, *if you are not an employee and you haven't agreed in writing that your work is "for hire" (or otherwise assigned your rights), you will generally continue to own the copyrights in your work* even if others paid you to create it (although they will have the right to use your work for the express purposes for which they paid you).

You may wonder about the division of rights when your article, story, or poem is published in a magazine (or other collective work) and there is no written agreement. The Act supplies the answer: The publisher acquires only the right to publish your piece as part of that collective work, of any revision of that work, and of any later collective work in the same series. You retain all other rights, so you are free to revise or remarket your piece.

The above is a *general* discussion of the copyright law as it applies to freelancers. Myriad qualifications and exceptions are not included here. Before making any important copyright decisions consult a knowledgeable copyright lawyer, the Copyright Office, or a trusted publisher or agent with an up-to-date understanding of the law.

# 108

# GETTING STARTED IN THE LITTLE AND LITERARY MAGAZINES

## BY JAMES PLATH

WHEN ERNEST HEMINGWAY WAS A "WANNABE" WRITER living in Chicago, he tried to pen stories for the popular markets, but was turned down by magazines like *Redbook, Argosy,* and *Vanity Fair.* Only after Sherwood Anderson told him to write for non-paying literary magazines did Hemingway find an audience for his work. He also found in them something more valuable than money: acceptance and encouragement.

Many writers have been discovered and nourished by little or literary magazines—so called because their budgets, staff size, circulation, and, all too often, their life spans are short. Yet, many aspiring writers are either unaware of this relatively unfamiliar apprenticeship track to publication, or are reluctant to use it.

As an editor, I recommend the following strategies to those who want to use the small press track instead of sending their early work straight to top markets:

**Read "the bible."** The bible of the small press world, that is. Buy or consult a copy of *The International Dictionary of Little Magazines and Small Presses* at your local library. Even the smallest literary magazines are listed—not just the top-paying and highly selective ones suggested by mass-market guides. At $25.95, the *International Directory* (891 pages, from Dustbooks, P.O. Box 100, Paradise, CA 95967) may seem like a hefty investment, but it lists over 5,000 markets—most of them receptive to new writers.

Publications included in this directory range from mimeographed stapled "magazines" with under 50 readers, to George Plimpton's *Paris Review,* with its 10,000+ readership and international reputation. Each listing gives information on a magazine's format, staff, longevity, publishing schedule, reporting time, payment, current needs, and editorial focus. Such things are helpful when trying to decide what magazine offers you the best chance of publication, given your current stage of development.

**Work your way up.** Small press magazines aren't just the minor leagues of publishing. In many literary magazines, you'll find stories and poems by beginners along with the work of America's top literary writers. To use literary magazines effectively as training ground, writers should recognize that the literary and little magazine world can be divided into three levels.

The leading literary magazines (with circulations of 2,000 plus) are well established, have solid reputations, and pay in cash for the material they use. They've published now-successful writers before they became famous, and their stories and poems are often reprinted in anthologies. This group of publications favors publishing established "name" writers, and their magazines can be found in many independent bookstores and in the larger public libraries. Publication in these magazines carries almost as much prestige in literary circles as publication in *The New Yorker* or *The Atlantic,* but of course, the competition is just as stiff. They receive as many as 100 submissions per day.

The secondary group of little magazines are just as ambitious and attractive as those in the top group, but their circulations are smaller (500 to 1,500), and while they may publish a few big-name writers, they're still receptive to unknowns. In many cases, longevity, reputation, and funding are the only things that keep a magazine in the second tier. Sometimes their publication schedules are less regular and their pages fewer, but the quality of their material is consistently high. Eventually, some will earn their place among the top literary magazines. Even now, they receive an average of 15 to 60 submissions per day.

At the lowest rung are literary magazines that have a limited, mostly regional circulation (50 to 500), and generally do not publish recognizable "name" writers. They are the "entry level" magazines for aspiring authors, and they publish as many new writers as possible. These magazines are often typed and photocopied to keep costs down; the better ones, though, may be set in-house on computers and commercially printed. Writers should be cautioned, however, that magazines in this group may come and go, depending upon their financial support. Sometimes a little magazine will even fold between the time of acceptance and publication of a writer's work, most often for lack of money.

But competition at these entry-level magazines is far less intense than at other small magazines. Their editors favor developing writers who may still be rough around the edges but are full of the energy of discovery, and they receive few submissions from top writers. Hence, they are more willing to offer feedback. Always remember in your cover letter to ask for "comments, if you have the time."

**Pay your dues.** If you want to publish in the little magazines, you need to have some idea of what's *being* published. Subscribe to three different literary magazines each year, and gradually you'll not only build a small press library, but you'll also get a better feel for what constitutes "literary" writing. Beginning writers often justify apprentice work by denying that there *is* such a thing as bad writing. They'll say that their work is too "popular" for a literary magazine (though I don't know many literary magazine editors who would turn down Tony Hillerman or Joyce Carol Oates), or they'll claim it's just a question of editorial taste. That may occasionally be true, but editors read so many manuscripts that they can recognize what's unique and of high quality in terms of imagery, language, character, plot, or form. Read as many literary magazines as you can to give yourself a feel for what makes a story or poem "work."

One trick: Read a literary magazine *as a writer*; instead of reading an entire poem or story, read only until something clicks, and you think, "I could do something like that." Stop reading at that point, and start writing!

**Know the editors.** Most literary magazines are edited by an individual or a group of people with other jobs. Often the magazine is a labor of love published out of an editor's home, and much of his or her time is spent trying to raise money. As a survival technique, editors have learned to spot "indicators" that help them whittle down the stacks of unsolicited manuscripts. Here are some tell-tale signs of writing that's just not ready for their publications yet and would probably prompt a quick rejection:

• No SASE. Editors can't afford to respond to queries or return manuscripts unless a self-addressed stamped envelope is provided.

• Battered or stained manuscripts. These will often go back into the envelope unread, since they have obviously been rejected many times before.

• Origami. Strangely folded manuscripts or poems folded individually take extra time to read. Many editors will read only *one* such poem, and if it shows no promise, they'll slip the rest in the envelope unread.

• Long cover letters. Anything more than a paragraph giving recent publications, background, and a few personal details is unnecessary. The most convincing cover letter is one that says, "I enjoyed so-and-so's story/poem in your last issue. Please consider this one of mine." Never tell what a story or poem is "about." If you have to explain, then your work isn't clear or powerful enough to speak for itself.

• Poor proofreading. Careless mistakes will turn an editor off immediately. If you don't take the time to proofread and check your own work carefully, why should an editor?

• Single-poem submissions. Editors usually suspect that it's the only poem a writer has written. Send batches of six poems or one short story, never more and usually not fewer.

• Poem titles like "Love" or "Death." Such abstractions usually reflect generic treatments of topics or themes that an editor sees too often. Strive to write from your own personal vision or experience.

• Hand-wringing. Some writing is purely therapeutic—and sounds it. Editors see far too many poems and stories that exorcise personal demons, but don't go beyond the pain or self-absorption to make a connection with the reader.

• Small talk. Superficial dialogue is as boring on paper as it is in person. Ask yourself whether it contributes to the reader's understanding of character, creates tension, or advances the plot.

• Building blocks and single strands. Blocks of dialogue, narration, and description are tedious, and are usually the mark of a writer who hasn't developed techniques for integrating these devices smoothly. Similarly, stories that start at point A and move on a single narrative thread toward point Z are usually too closely tied to the writer's experience and include even unimportant details.

Take a character from one aspect of your experience and put him/her into a setting with which you're familiar. Add a personal incident, an object/symbol from memory, and you have the makings of fiction—not a reportorial account.

**Read between the lines.** To use literary magazines as a learning tool, you must read between the lines of rejection slips:

*This isn't right for our magazine* or *This isn't what we're looking for.* In the literary marketplace, while it's possible that a magazine has just accepted a similar story or poem, it's more likely a euphemism that says your writing isn't at the level of quality the magazine publishes.

*It didn't work for us.* Often the compassionate editor tries to fix the blame on his or her editorial judgment. But the bottom line is that the piece didn't work. A form rejection or printed rejection with one word ("Sorry" is popular) indicates that you didn't come close. Go back and study the fiction or poetry in the magazine. Does it seem more readable, more interesting, more complex? If so, what makes it that way? In poetry, compare the imagery and metaphors in your poems with those in the magazine. Are they as vivid, as original? In fiction, if the scenes in your story don't seem as interesting, is your dialogue flat, the conflict trite, or the description lackluster?

*Feel free to try us again.* Encouraging, but it doesn't mean a great deal. *Please try us again* is better. Wait a month, however. A rejection that says such-and-such came close is an attempt to provide some direction. But the best rejections are full sheets of paper (and criticism!) that indicate that *some* editor saw enough merit in your work to take the time to respond to what you've done. You won't get that kind of feedback from commercial publications unless the editor really wants the manuscript. Even if the criticism is negative, you've made an impression and found a supporter.

In the end, most editors of little and literary magazines are willing and eager to "discover" you, if you are willing to serve an apprenticeship and work your way to the top.

# 109

## WHY IT'S HARDER TO FIND AN AGENT THAN A PUBLISHER

### BY EDWARD NOVAK

IF YOU'VE NEVER TRIED TO SECURE the services of a literary agent, you should be forewarned that at times you'll feel as if you are searching for the Holy Grail. Getting published for the first time is no picnic—unless you are a former President of the United States or have slept with Elvis's ghost and can prove it. However, finding an agent who will consider your idea for a novel or nonfiction book, read your manuscript or proposal, answer all your questions, provide encouragement and expertise, and, yes, sell your book, will not only save you time and money, but you will have gained a valuable, much-needed ally in the swirling, shark-infested waters of publishing.

Why do you need an agent? If you are an unpublished author, here's why: One of the duties of my first job in publishing was to read unsolicited manuscripts sent to Macmillan directly from writers. These manuscripts came in all shapes and sizes, but my directive was the same: Unless you saw another *Gone With the Wind,* forget about it. In my two years in that job, I saw a number of admirable manuscripts, but not one unagented manuscript I read caught the fancy of an editor. You see, editors are extremely busy people: They meet with the sales department, the marketing department, the art department, the publicity department, and the editorial department every week. They meet with agents every day. And, in the evenings and on weekends, they squeeze in time to read manuscripts. Every time I meet an editor for the first time, their first complaint is how little time they get to read *published* books, which is something the rest of the world takes for granted.

Which manuscript do you think they are going to spend time considering seriously: the one sent in over the transom and read by an inexperienced, underpaid reader or the one recommended by an experienced agent?

Put another way: The editor's job, redefined over the years, is to publish writers, not discover them. For better or worse, editors simply have come to rely on agents to discover the next Hemingway, Fitzgerald or Welty and bring them to publishers.

If you are already a published author, here's a good reason for you to get an agent: Imagine how much more productive you would be if you didn't have to oversee the details of getting published; it can take weeks or even months to sell an idea to a publisher and negotiate the contract. Wouldn't you rather be writing than worrying?

How do you get an agent, how do they do business, and what can an agent specifically do for you?

The easiest way to get an agent is through the personal recommendation of a close friend, relative or another writer who has or knows an agent. When I first set up shop as an agent, I depended upon referrals from authors I had worked with in my days as an editor; they either became clients or sent authors my way. If you were looking for a lawyer or an accountant, wouldn't you ask your friends first whom they use and if they're happy with them? That's the easy way.

*Step #1:* Do a little research. Go to your local library or bookstore and find a copy of one of the dozens of books (such as the grandfather of reference tools, *The Literary Marketplace*—or *LMP* as we call it) that have lists of reputable agents, the kind of books and/or clients these agents are looking for, and their requirements for submission.

*Step #2:* After you've narrowed down the list of agents to ones who meet your criteria, write a letter describing your book idea and your background and inquire if they would be interested in it (be sure to include a stamped, self-addressed envelope!). I would advise against trying to describe your book over the telephone; a letter doesn't betray nervousness or forget to mention anything or put any sort of pressure on you. This letter will be very important, so spend some time and thought on it—a strong letter stating your case gives you a chance to include all your thoughts cogently and allows the agent to judge your writing. I always tell writers to state why thousands of people would be willing to spend $18.95 to read their book when they can just as easily spend the same amount of money on someone else's book. You don't have to do that exactly, but keep it in the back of your mind as you compose your letter.

Do not get discouraged if you do not receive an answer from every

564

agent. I cannot speak for every agency, but we respond to every query that includes an SASE, and we are not all that different from a lot of other agencies. Do not be surprised if some tell you they are not looking for new clients. To provide a professional level of service to their current clients, agents must devote most of their time to them.

*Step #3:* Keep it up. While many publishers no longer consider unagented work, almost every good agent will consider yours if he or she finds it well written and intriguing. If one agent turns your manuscript down, keep trying. There are any number of reasons for an agent to turn down perfectly good books, some having nothing to do with the quality of your work. We don't all think alike or like the same kinds of books, so maybe the second, third, or tenth agent *will* like your book and take it on. Persistence works! I always like to tell people about one of my clients who had written a fine novel in the seventies and got precious little encouragement. She put the novel away in her closet for fifteen years before finally getting up the nerve to show it to an agent— she showed it to me and I sold it to the second editor who read it. This is a story with a happy ending, but I always think about what this author would have accomplished had she been more persistent from the beginning.

[A few words on multiple submissions: Many agents will not consider multiple submissions because they do not want to spend the time reading an entire manuscript only to discover the author decided on another agent two days earlier. If you are going to submit your work to a number of agents at one time, make sure you inform the agents that it is a multiple submission, and be prepared for some very quick rejections. On the other side of the coin, if you have a strong idea—more likely for a nonfiction book than a novel—you may very well get quicker answers from agents who know they are in a competitive situation. And no, agents do *not* hate each other—some of my best friends are agents!]

A fourth suggestion, which will work for some writers but not all, would be to attend a writers' conference. First of all, this will give your writing exposure to professionals who can critique it and work with you; secondly, agents (like me) and editors attend conferences throughout the year looking for new talent. Though it is often difficult to develop any kind of relationship with an agent at a conference, many published authors got their starts at such conferences.

What kind of manuscripts are agents looking for? In one word:

salable. Few agents I know really specialize in any one type of book, and most will work with both nonfiction and fiction. (I would venture to guess that most agents deal more in nonfiction than fiction.) In nonfiction, we look for subjects of timely nature, written by authors who have solid credentials in their field. If you want to write your autobiography, you had better either be mentioned regularly in *People* magazine or have lived a secret, incredible life. If you want to write a piece of investigative journalism, it helps if you actually are a reporter. Demonstrated expertise cannot be understated. With novels, however, agents simply look for good writing mixed with a good sense of storytelling—and novelists can be *anyone* with talent.

Most agents I know will not consider magazine articles, poetry or children's books. Major magazines solicit or commission most of the pieces they publish. Poetry can be submitted to literary journals directly by the author; book publishers, however, will consider publishing collections of only the most accomplished and published poets. More agents nowadays are considering children's books because publishers are paying larger advances for them, but these agents are still in the minority. You should definitely consult the *LMP* about which agents will consider this kind of work.

I have two pieces of advice for writers looking for subjects: 1) Go to a bookstore and see what is being published. If you see twenty books on a subject, it's a good bet that the market is saturated. For instance, 1990 saw an explosion in the publication of books dealing with the environment; after a while, publishers simply stopped considering new books on this subject, no matter how good their prospects were. 2) Write about something you know about and believe in or care enough about to do the necessary research. If you want to write a novel about soldiering experiences during the Vietnam War, you had better have been there; on the other hand, which science fiction novelist has actually been to Mars or Venus?

Finally, what can you expect from an agent who decides to take on your book? Well, perhaps to become the most important person in your writing life. Years ago, editors such as Maxwell Perkins and publishers such as Bennett Cerf dominated the industry and were the bedrocks of an author's career. Not any more. Certainly, there are many wonderful editors and heady publishers in the business today, but with the rapid and deep changes that have taken place in publishing—takeovers and

566

mergers and "consolidations"—many editors of major firms frequently change jobs and houses before they are able to form close relationships with the authors. Time and time again, I've seen an editor sign up a book and, two months later, announce he or she has landed a new job with another publisher. Nowadays, it is not unusual for an author to write, say, four books and have four or more different editors. The one constant in an author's career is his or her agent.

The most important thing an agent can do for you is to find a publisher for your book and negotiate contract terms and an advance on royalties for you. As a writer, what you want to worry about is your writing; your agent will sweat the details of the business of writing. Successful agents know the industry and will know not to send a first novel to a publisher that specializes in how-to books. A good agent will know not only which publisher is appropriate for your book, but which editor at a particular house is more inclined to consider your book seriously, since editors, unlike agents, tend to specialize in subjects. There are such things as business editors, political editors, fiction editors, and cookbook editors.

Agents can also provide ideas and criticism. Many agents reading a client's new novel, for instance, will suggest changes before submitting it to a publisher. Would you rather have your book submitted to a publisher knowing it was not quite right? Sometimes an agent will read an article in a magazine or newspaper that suggests a book idea and will give the idea to a client who will then write the book. And over the years, we see more books being written by celebrities, but do you think Tip O'Neill took nine months out of his busy schedule to write his memoirs? No, an agent convinced him to get the book done, introduced him to a writer who collaborated with the former Speaker of the House, and negotiated the package with Random House. O'Neill and his collaborator worked together intermittently for a couple of months, and the writer then produced a manuscript, which became a huge bestseller. Without the agent's role in this, the book never would have been published.

Agents also administer the life of a publishing contract, which means this: We keep track of and make sure the publisher pays the advance on time; we also track royalty payments and the issuance of statements. We oversee the selling of various foreign and subsidiary rights to a book: Do you want your book translated and sold in Spain or Japan?

how about getting it excerpted in a magazine or newspaper? recorded on audio cassette? or made into a movie? Literary agents handle all these matters for their authors.

All this is the good news. Agents, quite simply, make an author's life easier and their work more commercially viable in return for a commission on all the deals they handle. These commissions usually range from 10–15 percent on domestic sales and licenses and 15–20 percent on all foreign transactions, which often involve "subagents" in other countries who share the commission.

Then there's the bad news, which you saw in the title of this piece. It's tough to get an agent. The arithmetic is against authors. I personally receive roughly thirty query letters a week from writers who have not been referred to me by close friends, relatives or other writers asking me to consider their books. Of this number, I will ask to see anywhere from two to four manuscripts, and, typically, I take on only one manuscript every two months. This does not mean that everything I reject is bad; actually some of it is good, but even good may not be good enough for publishers. And I'm sure the math works the same for most successful agents. Look at it another way: If only one book were published in this country every year, no matter the subject or the quality, it would sell millions and millions of copies. Actually, about fifty thousand books are published here every year, and for every one of those published, I'd bet there are one hundred that are not.

What this means in practical terms for you and for me is that the struggle to get published is often reduced merely to getting a publisher to sit down and seriously consider your book. And oftentimes, alas, talent simply isn't enough. You *will* need an advocate to give you a fighting chance.

So, in closing and recognizing the self-service I am about to perform, I'll just echo the first piece of sound advice given every writer in this country for the last fifty years: Do everything you can to get an agent, because it's a lot harder to get a publisher!

# 110

## WHEN YOU WRITE FOR *ALFRED HITCHCOCK'S MYSTERY MAGAZINE*

### BY ELANA LORE, MANAGING EDITOR

*ALFRED HITCHCOCK'S MYSTERY MAGAZINE* is a very open market. Two of our policies make it easier for us to discover new talent: We read all submissions, and we don't require stories to be agented. We are looking for good writing and an interesting story more than any particular subgenre of mystery. We publish classic whodunits, police procedurals, private eye stories, suspense, espionage, ghost stories, and tales of the supernatural, to name a few.

We like humor, and occasionally buy stories with elements of fantasy or science fiction. We have no "house style," and in fact encourage authors to develop their own individual "voices." All we ask is that the story be about a crime (or the fear of one).

Except for the one Mystery Classic in each issue, we buy only previously unpublished fiction. Very occasionally, we have reprinted a story that was originally published in England or in a small-circulation regional magazine in the United States.

While most of what we publish is much shorter, we do buy stories of up to 14,000 words. We don't buy excerpts of novels, nor do we serialize them. And we don't buy any poetry.

As a rule, we pay six and a half cents a word, on acceptance.

### Taboos

Keep in mind that we are a family-oriented *fiction* market. Here are some things we *don't* want to see:
- Thinly veiled rewrites of crimes currently in the news.
- Stories in which you have named your characters after your real-life friends or relatives.

569

- Stories in which you have used, under any name, the misdeeds of people you know.
- Stories with graphic sex or egregious violence.

## Cover letters

Cover letters aren't necessary on manuscripts you submit to *AHMM*. If you do send one, here's what we appreciate finding in it:

- Have you been published before? If so, where?

In many publishing houses, prior publication gets you out of the slush pile and onto the desk of a more senior editor. That works with us, too, but it is only a step saved for us, sometimes, in the evaluation process. Prior credits won't ever sell a story; the story must always stand on its own.

- Is this story about a series character you have used in published novels?

If we buy the story, we would like to take this into account in illustrating it. And if our readers enjoyed the novels, they are likely to take a special interest in the short story.

- Have you submitted this particular story to us before?

We don't, as a general rule, like to see resubmissions, unless we've requested specific changes and asked to have the story sent back, and that happens only rarely. But if you have done real revisions on a story we've previously rejected, and resubmit it, please tell us that we've seen it before and explain how you've revised it. (We nearly always remember what we've read before.)

- If some technical detail might seem questionable to readers, please give us the benefit of your own expertise or research unless it's made clear in the manuscript. Tell us, for instance, if you're a doctor, so we can be sure medical details are accurate, or explain that, however unlikely it might seem, X really can be ignited with a match.

## What *not* to include in a cover letter

- "My family and friends think this is the best story I've ever written." For some reason we haven't yet figured out, this is the kiss of death in a cover letter. The manuscript it accompanies is never publishable.
- "You have to publish this. I need the money." We will feel bad

about that, but it just won't sell the story. (Anybody who is in this business for the money has come to the wrong place, unfortunately.)

• "I know you'll like this." Maybe, but then again, maybe not. This kind of statement would be offputting even from one's best friend.

• "Enclosed are three stories I've written." It is in your best interests to submit one story at a time. No matter how noble and fair we try to be, if we don't like the first one, or the second one, it's difficult to greet the third one with the same amount of enthusiasm we started out with.

• You are working on, or have written, unpublished novels. *Everyone* is. Only the story matters.

• A summary of the plot. It does no good—in fact, we skip it. Ditto for descriptions of the characters. A good writer can make a story out of anything; the plot is the least of it. And we would rather have the story unfold for us as it would for our readers.

## Format

We are not rigid about format, but . . .

Your manuscript should be typed double-spaced (not space and a half) on plain white paper. This can be cheap copy machine paper; we don't look for watermarks. The only thing we don't like to work with is erasable paper, since it smears.

You should leave an inch and a half margin on one side or the other of the page, and at least an inch on the top and bottom, to give us room to edit.

It is easier for us if page numbers are on the top right-hand side.

A separate title page is not necessary. In fact, we prefer that you not send one.

The first page of your story should contain your name, address, telephone number, and social security number, plus the title and byline. (We don't mind having people use pen names, but please be sure the byline under the title is the one you want printed. That is, we won't read "J. M. Smith" under the title to mean "John M. Smith" at the top of the page.)

Indent for each new paragraph, and don't leave line spaces between paragraphs. When you do use line spaces to indicate the passage of time or change of point of view, please use only one. It helps us if the number of lines per page is uniform.

If you use a word processor, please don't justify the right-hand margin. (We pay by the word; finding an "average" line isn't easy if the right side is justified. Of course, we might pay more than we should if we don't guess right, but we might also pay less.)

Make sure you have a clean, dark ribbon, no matter what type of machine you are using.

Some computers have the capability of printing italic and large-size characters. Please don't use them on manuscripts you send to us. It makes extra work for us to mark them for the typesetter. Use just one typewriter-sized roman font, with underlined roman characters to indicate italic and no bold-faced words.

If you are using a typewriter, and have to make corrections manually, use common sense about how many you allow. We don't mind reading *some,* but if the page gets really messy, retype it.

Don't staple your story together or put it into a binder. We prefer that you use a *plain* paper clip large enough to hold all the pages together, and mail the story to us flat, not folded. (There's nothing worse than trying to read a once-folded story; it usually won't lie down.)

Enclose a self-addressed envelope large enough and with enough postage to return your entire manuscript, or indicate in your letter that it doesn't need to be returned. Even if you don't want the manuscript back, please enclose a stamped letter-size envelope for our reply.

(I don't know who thought up the idea of the rejection checklist that some authors have started enclosing with their manuscripts, but we prefer to use our own form rejection letter. We don't have the time to write comments about individual manuscripts.)

If you enclose an envelope that isn't large enough for your manuscript, we won't return it. If you enclose an envelope but no postage (or not enough), we won't return it.

We get many submissions from Canada and other countries. If you live outside the United States, note that U.S. postage is required for return mail, or International Reply Coupons, which you can purchase at the post office in your country.

# WHERE TO SELL

# Where to Sell

This year's edition of *The Writer's Handbook* includes a completely revised and updated list of free-lance markets, and writers at all levels of experience should be encouraged by the number and wide variety of opportunities available to them. Editors, publishers, and producers rely on free lancers for a wide range of material, from articles and fiction to play scripts, op-ed pieces, how-tos, and children's books, and they are very receptive to the work of newcomers.

The field of specialized publications, including city and regional magazines, and those covering such areas as science, consumer issues, sports, and hobbies and crafts, remains one of the best markets for beginning free lancers. Editors of these magazines are in constant need of authoritative articles (for which the payment can be quite high), and writers with experience in and enthusiasm for a particular field, whether it's gardening, woodworking, bicycling, stamp collecting, bridge, or car repair, can turn their knowledge into article sales. Such interests and activities can generate more than one article if a different angle is used for each magazine and the writer keeps the audience and editorial content firmly in mind.

The market for technical, computer, health, and personal finance writing is also very strong, with articles on these topics appearing in almost every publication on the newsstands today. For these subjects, editors are looking for writers who can translate technical material into lively, readable prose, often the most important factor in determining a sale.

While some of the more established markets may seem difficult to break into, especially for the beginner, there are thousands of lesser-known publications where editors will consider submissions from first-time free lancers. City and regional publications offer some of the best opportunities, since these editors generally like to work with local writers and often use a wide variety of material, from features to fillers. Many newspapers accept op-ed pieces, and are most receptive to pieces on topics not covered by syndicated columnists (politics, economics, and foreign affairs); pieces with a regional slant are particularly welcome here.

It is important for writers to keep in mind the number of opportunities that exist for nonfiction, because the paying markets for fiction are somewhat limited. Many general-interest and women's magazines do publish short stories; however, beginners will find these markets extremely competitive, with their work being judged against that of experienced professionals. We highly recommend that new writers look into the small, literary, and college publications, which always welcome the work of talented beginners. Payment usually is made only in copies, but publication in literary journals can lead to recognition by editors of larger circulation magazines, who often look to the smaller publications for new talent. A growing number of regional, specialized, and Sunday magazines use short stories and are particularly interested in local writers.

The market for poetry in general-interest magazines continues to be tight, and the advice for poets, as for fiction writers, is to try to get established and build up a list of publishing credits by submitting material to literary journals. Poets should look also to local newspapers, which often use verse, especially if it is related to holidays or other special occasions.

Community, regional, and civic theaters and college dramatic groups offer new playwrights the best opportunities for staged production in this competitive market. Indeed, many of today's well-known playwrights received their first recognition in regional theaters, and aspiring writers who can get their work produced by one of these have taken a significant step toward breaking into this field. In addition to producing plays and giving dramatic readings, many theaters also sponsor competitions or new play festivals.

The market for television scripts is limited, and most writers break into it only after a careful study of the medium and a long apprenticeship. Writers should be aware of the fact that this market is inaccessible without an agent, and for this reason, we've listed several agents who are willing to read queries for TV scripts, as well as screenplays.

While the book publishing field remains competitive, beginners should be especially encouraged by the many first novels published over the past few years, with more editors than ever before seeking out new works of fiction. An increasing number of publishers are broadening their nonfiction lines as well, and editors at many hardcover and paperback houses are on the lookout for new authors, especially those with a knowledge of or training in a particular field. Writers of juvenile and young-adult books will be pleased to hear that in response to a growing audience of young readers and increased sales, many publishers are greatly expanding their lists of children's books.

Small presses across the country continue to flourish—in fact, they are currently publishing more books by name authors and more books on mainstream subjects than at any other time in recent years—offering writers an attractive alternative for their manuscripts.

All information in these lists concerning the needs and requirements of magazines, book publishing companies, and theaters comes directly from the editors, publishers, and directors, but editors move and addresses change, as do requirements. No published listing can give as clear a picture of editorial needs and tastes as a careful study of several issues of a magazine or a book catalogue, and writers should never submit material without first thoroughly researching the prospective market. If a magazine is not available in the local library, write directly to the editor for a sample copy (often sent free or at a small cost). Contact the publicity department of a book publisher for an up-to-date catalogue or a theater for a current schedule. Many companies also offer a formal set of writers guidelines, available for an SASE upon request.

# ARTICLE MARKETS

The magazines in the following list are in the market for free-lance articles of many types. Unless otherwise stated in these listings, a writer should submit a query first, including a brief description of the proposed article and any relevant qualifications or credits. A few editors want to see samples of published work, if available. Manuscripts must be typed double-space on good white bond paper (8 ½ × 11), with name, address, and telephone number at the top left- or right-hand corner of the paper. Do not use erasable or onion skin paper, since it is difficult to work with, and always keep a copy of the manuscript, in case it is lost in the mail. Submit photos or slides *only* if the editor has specifically requested them. A self-addressed envelope with sufficient postage to cover the return of the manuscript or the answer to a query should accompany all submissions. Response time may vary from two to eight weeks, depending on the size of the magazine and the volume of mail it receives. If an editor doesn't respond within what seems to be a reasonable amount of time, it's perfectly acceptable to send a polite inquiry. Many publications have writers guidelines, outlining their editorial requirements and submission procedures; these can be obtained by sending a self-addressed, stamped envelope (SASE) to the editor. Also, be sure to ask for a sample copy: Editors indicate the most consistent mistake free lancers make is failing to study several issues of the magazine to which they are submitting material.

## GENERAL-INTEREST PUBLICATIONS

**ACCENT/TRAVELOG**—P.O. Box 10010, Ogden, UT 84409. Caroll Shreeve, V.P. of Pub. Articles, 1,200 words, about travel, having fun, fitness, sightseeing, the ordinary and the unusual in foreign and domestic destinations. "Avoid budget approaches and emphasize the use of travel professionals." Must include excellent transparencies. Queries required. Guidelines with SASE. Pays 15¢ a word, $35 for photos, $50 for cover photo, on acceptance.

**ALLIED PUBLICATIONS**—2176 Jog Rd., West Palm Beach, FL 33415. Articles, to 1,500 words: business, management, fashion, careers, travel (foreign and domestic), beauty, hairstyling, general interest, home, and family. Photos, cartoons, humor. Write for terms of payment. Guidelines. Publishes *Trip & Tour, Modern Office, Woman Beautiful, Home.*

**AMERICAN HERITAGE**—60 Fifth Ave., New York, NY 10011. Richard F. Snow, Ed. Articles, 750 to 5,000 words, on U.S. history and background of American life and culture from the beginning to recent times. No fiction. Pays $300 to $1,500, on acceptance. Query. SASE.

**AMERICAN HISTORY ILLUSTRATED**—6405 Flank Dr., P.O. Box 8200, Harrisburg, PA 17105. Well-researched articles, 3,000 to 5,000 words. Style should be popular, not scholarly. No travelogues, fiction, or puzzles. Pays $200 to $1,000, on acceptance. Query.

**THE AMERICAN LEGION**—Box 1055, Indianapolis, IN 46206. John

Greenwald, Ed. Articles, 750 to 2,000 words, on current world affairs, public policy, and subjects of contemporary interest. Pays $400 to $1,500, on acceptance. Query.

**AMERICAN VISIONS, THE MAGAZINE OF AFRO-AMERICAN CUL-TURE**—The Carter G. Woodson House, 1538 9th St. N.W., Washington, DC 20001. Joanne Harris, Ed. Articles, 1,500 to 2,500 words, and columns, 750 to 2,000 words, on African-American history and culture with a focus on the arts. Pays from $100 to $1,000, on publication. Query first.

**THE ATLANTIC**—745 Boylston St., Boston, MA 02116. William Whitworth, Ed. Non-polemical, meticulously researched articles on public issues, politics, social sciences, education, business, literature, and the arts. Ideal length: 3,000 to 6,000 words, though short pieces, 1,000 to 2,000 words, are also welcome and longer text pieces will be considered. Pays excellent rates.

**BON APPETIT**—5900 Wilshire Blvd., Los Angeles, CA 90036. Barbara Fairchild, Exec. Ed. Articles on fine cooking (menu format or single focus), cooking classes, and gastronomically focused travel. Query with samples of published work. Pays varying rates, on acceptance.

**BOSTONIA**—10 Lenox St., Brookline, MA 02146. Keith Botsford, Ed. Articles, to 3,000 words, on politics, literature, music, art, travel, food, and wine. Pays $150 to $1,000, on acceptance. Queries required.

**CAPPER'S**—616 Jefferson St., Topeka, KS 66607–1188. Nancy Peavler, Ed. Articles, 300 to 500 words: human-interest, personal experience for women's section, historical. Pays $2 to $6, on publication.

**CAR AUDIO AND ELECTRONICS**—21700 Oxnard St., Woodland Hills, CA 91367. Bill Neill, Ed. Features, 1,000 to 2,000 words, on electronic products for the car: audio systems, security systems, CBs, radar detectors, cellular telephones, etc. Pays $300 to $1,000, on acceptance.

**CHANGE**—1319 18th St. N.W., Washington, DC 20036. Well-researched features, 2,500 to 3,500, words, on programs, people, and institutions of higher education; and columns, 700 to 2,000 words. "We can't usually pay for unsolicited articles."

**CHATELAINE**—MacLean Hunter Bldg., 777 Bay St., Toronto, Ont., Canada M5W 1A7. Articles, 1,500 to 2,500 words, for Canadian women, on current issues, personalities, medicine, psychology, etc., covering all aspects of Canadian life; send queries to Ivor Shapiro, Exec. Ed. "Upfront" columns, 500 words, on relationships, health, nutrition, fitness, parenting; send queries to Diane Merlevede, Man. Ed. Pays from $350 for columns, from $1,250 for features, on acceptance.

**THE CHRISTIAN SCIENCE MONITOR**—One Norway St., Boston, MA 02115. Greg Lamb, Features Ed. Articles, 800 words, on arts, education, food, sports, science, and lifestyle; interviews, literary essays for "Home Forum" page; guest columns for "Opinion Page." Pay varies, on acceptance. Original material only.

**COLUMBIA**—1 Columbus Plaza, New Haven, CT 06510–0901. Richard McMunn, Ed. Journal of the Knights of Columbus. Articles, 500 to 1,500 words, on a wide variety of topics of interest to K. of C. members, their families, and the Catholic layman: current events, religion, education, art, etc., illustrated with color photos. Pays $250 to $500, including art, on acceptance.

**THE COMPASS**—Grand Central Towers, 230 E. 44th St., Suite 14B, New York, NY 10017. J.A. Randall, Ed. True stories, to 2,500 words, on the sea, sea trades, and aviation. Pays to $600, on acceptance. Query with SASE.

**CONSUMERS DIGEST**—5705 N. Lincoln Ave., Chicago, IL 60659. John Manos, Ed. Articles, 500 to 3,000 words, on subjects of interest to consumers: products and services, automobiles, health, fitness, consumer legal affairs, and personal money management. Photos. Pays from 35¢ to 50¢ a word, extra for photos, on publication. Buys all rights. Query with resumé and published clips.

**COSMOPOLITAN**—224 W. 57th St., New York, NY 10019. Helen Gurley Brown, Ed. Guy Flatley, Man. Ed. Articles, to 3,000 words, and features, 500 to 2,000 words, on issues affecting young career women. Query.

**COUNTRY**—5400 S. 60th, Greendale, WI 53129. Dan Matel, Man. Ed. People-centered articles, 500 to 1,000 words, for a rural audience. (No articles on farm production techniques.) Taboos: tobacco, liquor, and sex. Pays $75 to $100, on acceptance. Query.

**COUNTRY JOURNAL**—P.O. Box 8200, Harrisburg, PA 17105. Peter V. Fossel, Ed. Articles, 1,000 to 3,000 words, for country and small-town residents. Helpful, authoritative pieces; issues, humor, how-to, preserving the countryside. Pays $300 to $1,000, on acceptance. Send SASE for guidelines. Query with SASE.

**DALLAS LIFE MAGAZINE**—*The Dallas Morning News*, Communications Center, P.O. Box 655237, Dallas, TX 75265. Mike Maza, Man. Ed. Well-researched articles and profiles, 1,000 to 3,000 words, on contemporary local issues and personalities. Pays from 20¢ a word, on acceptance. Query.

**DIVERSION MAGAZINE**—60 E. 42nd St., Suite 2424, New York, NY 10165. Tom Passavant, Ed.-in-Chief. Articles, 1,200 to 2,500 words, on travel, sports, hobbies, entertainment, food, etc., of interest to physicians at leisure. Photos. Pays from $500, on acceptance. Query.

**EBONY**—820 S. Michigan, Chicago, IL 60603. Lerone Bennett, Jr., Exec. Ed. Articles, with photos, on blacks: achievements, civil rights, etc. Pays from $150, on publication. Query.

**THE ELKS MAGAZINE**—425 W. Diversey Parkway, Chicago, IL 60614. Fred D. Oakes, Ed. Articles, 3,000 words, on business, sports, and topics of current interest, for non-urban audience with above-average income. Informative or humorous pieces, to 2,500 words. Pays $150 to $400 for articles, on acceptance. Query.

**ESQUIRE**—1790 Broadway, New York, NY 10019. Terry McDonell, Ed.-in-Chief. David Hirshey, Articles Ed. Articles, 2,500 to 4,000 words, for intelligent adult audience. Pay varies, on acceptance. Query with published clips; complete manuscripts from unpublished writers. SASE required.

**ESSENCE**—1500 Broadway, New York, NY 10036. Stephanie Stokes Oliver, Ed. Provocative articles, 800 to 2,500 words, about black women in America today: self-help, how-to pieces, business and finance, health, celebrity profiles, and political issues. Short items, 500 to 750 words, on work, parenting, and health. Query required. Pays varying rates, on acceptance.

**FAMILY CIRCLE**—110 Fifth Ave., New York, NY 10011. Susan Ungaro, Deputy Ed. Articles, to 2,000 words, on "women who have made a difference," marriage, family, and child-rearing issues; consumer affairs, health and fitness, humor and psychology. Query required. Pays top rates, on acceptance.

**GLAMOUR**—350 Madison Ave., New York, NY 10017. Ruth Whitney, Ed.-in-Chief. Susan Pelzer, Articles Ed. Editorial approach is "how-to" for women, 18 to 35. Articles on careers, health, psychology, interpersonal relationships, etc. Fashion, health, and beauty material staff-written. Pays from $1,000 for 1,500- to 2,000-word articles, from $1,500 for longer pieces, on acceptance.

**GLOBE**—5401 N.W. Broken Sound Blvd., Boca Raton, FL 33487. Robert Taylor, Man. Ed. Factual articles, 500 to 1,000 words, with photos: exposés, celebrity interviews, consumer and human-interest pieces. Pays $50 to $1,500.

**GOLDEN YEARS**—P.O. Box 537, Melbourne, FL 32902–0537. Carol Brenner Hittner, Ed. Bimonthly for people over the age of 50. Pieces on unique hobbies, beauty and fashion, sports, and travel, 600 words. Pays 10¢ a word, on publication.

**GOOD HOUSEKEEPING**—959 Eighth Ave., New York, NY 10019. Joan Thursh, Articles Ed. Personal-experience articles, 2,500 words, on a unique or trend-setting event; family relationships; personal medical pieces dealing with an unusual illness, treatment, and result; personal problems and how they were solved. Short essays, 750 to 1,000 words, on family life or relationships. Pays top rates, on acceptance. Queries preferred. Guidelines.

**GOOD READING MAGAZINE**—Litchfield, IL 62056. Peggy Kuethe, Assoc. Ed. Articles, 500 to 1,000 words, with B&W photos, on current subjects of general interest: travel, business, personal experiences, relationships. Pays $10 to $100.

**GRIT**—208 W. Third St., Williamsport, PA 17701. Alvin Elmer, Assoc. Ed. Articles, to 800 words, with photos, on interesting people, communities, jobs, recreation, families, and coping. Also, short fiction, 3,500 to 4,000 words. Pays 15¢ a word, extra for photos, on acceptance.

**HARPER'S MAGAZINE**—666 Broadway, New York, NY 10012. Address Editor. Articles, 2,000 to 5,000 words. Query first. SASE required.

**HG: HOUSE & GARDEN**—350 Madison Ave., New York, NY 10017. "Check recent issue of magazine to become familiar with our needs. We rarely buy unsolicited manuscripts." Query.

**HISTORIC PRESERVATION**—1785 Massachusetts Ave. N.W., Washington, DC 20036. Anne Elizabeth Powell, Ed. Feature articles from published writers, 1,500 to 4,000 words, on residential restoration, preservation issues, and people involved in preserving America's heritage. Mostly staff-written. Query.

**HOME**—See *Allied Publications.*

**HOUSE BEAUTIFUL**—1700 Broadway, New York, NY 10019. Elaine Greene, Ed. Articles related to the home. Pieces on architecture, design, travel, and gardening; mostly staff written. Pays varying rates, on acceptance. Query with detailed outline and SASE. Guidelines.

**INQUIRER MAGAZINE**—*Philadelphia Inquirer*, P.O. Box 8263, 400 N. Broad St., Philadelphia, PA 19101. Ms. Avery Rome, Ed. Local-interest features, 500 to 7,000 words. Profiles of national figures in politics, entertainment, etc. Pays varying rates, on publication. Query.

**INSIDE MAGAZINE**—226 S. 16th St., Philadelphia, PA 19102–3392. Jane Biberman, Ed. Articles, 1,500 to 3,000 words, on Jewish issues, health, finance, and the arts. Queries required; send clips if available. Pays $75 to $600, within four weeks of acceptance.

**KEY HORIZONS**—Gateway Plaza, 950 N. Meridian, Suite 1200, Indianapolis, IN 46204. Joan Todd, Man. Ed. General-interest articles and department pieces, 300 to 3,000 words, for readers over 50. Topics include personal finance, cooking, family trends, travel, and puzzles. No nostalgia, domestic humor, fillers, or poetry. Pays $25 to $500, $25 to $50 for photos, on publication.

**KIWANIS**—3636 Woodview Trace, Indianapolis, IN 46268. Chuck Jonak,

Exec. Ed. Articles, 2,500 to 3,000 words, on home; family; international issues; the social, health, and emotional needs of youth (especially under age six); career and community concerns of business and professional people. No travel pieces, interviews, profiles. Pays $400 to $1,000, on acceptance. Query. Send SASE for guidelines.

**LADIES' HOME JOURNAL**—100 Park Ave., New York, NY 10017. Lynn Langway, Exec. Ed. Jane Farrell, Articles Ed. Articles on contemporary subjects of interest to women. Query required. Not responsible for unsolicited manuscripts.

**LIFE IN THE TIMES**—Army Times Publishing Co., Springfield, VA 22159–0200. Margaret Roth, Ed. Features, to 2,000 words, on aspects of military life. Personal-experience pieces, 750 words, of interest to military people and their families around the world. Special interest supplements cover careers after the military, books and home entertainment, finance, fitness and health, and education. Travel articles, 750 to 900 words, narrowly focused. "Rather than an article on New York City, we'd prefer one on some particular aspect of the trip." Pays $125 for travel articles, $100 to $150 for short pieces, to $350 for features, on acceptance.

**LISTEN MAGAZINE**—Pacific Press Pub. Assn., P.O. Box 7000, Boise, ID 83707. Lincoln Steed, Ed. Articles, 1,200 to 1,500 words, on problems of alcohol and drug abuse, for teenagers; personality profiles; self-improvement articles, and drug-free activities. Photos. Pays 5¢ to 7¢ a word, extra for photos, on acceptance. Query. Guidelines.

**MCCALL'S**—110 Fifth Ave., New York, NY 10011. Kate White, Ed.-in-Chief. Andrea Thompson, Articles Ed. Interesting, unusual, and topical narratives, reports on social trends relating to women of all ages, 1,000 to 3,000 words. Human-interest stories. Pays top rates, on acceptance.

**MADEMOISELLE**—350 Madison Ave., New York, NY 10017. Liz Logan, Articles Ed. Articles, 1,500 to 2,500 words, on subjects of interest to single, working women in ther 20s. Reporting pieces, essays, first-person accounts, and humor. No how-to or fiction. Query with clips. Pays from $1,750 for full-length articles, on acceptance. Query.

**MD MAGAZINE**—55 Fifth Ave., New York, NY 10003. Helen Smith, Ed. Articles, 750 to 2,500 words, for doctors, on the arts, travel, history, other aspects of culture; fresh angle required. Payment varies, on publication. Query by mail only.

**METROPOLITAN HOME**—750 Third Ave., New York, NY 10017. Service and informational articles for residents of houses, co-ops, lofts, and condominiums, on real estate, equity, wine and spirits, collecting, trends, travel, etc. Interior design and home furnishing articles with emphasis on lifestyle. Pay varies. Query.

**MODERN MATURITY**—3200 E. Carson St., Lakewood, CA 90712. J. Henry Fenwick, Ed. Articles, 1,000 to 2,000 words, on careers, workplace, human interest, living, finance, relationships, and consumerism, for persons over 50 years. Photos. Pays $500 to $2,500, on acceptance. Query first.

**MODERN OFFICE**—See *Allied Publications.*

**THE MOTHER EARTH NEWS**—24 E. 23rd St., 5th Fl., New York, NY 10010. Karen Bokram, Sr. Ed. Articles for rural and urban readers: home improvements, how-tos, indoor and outdoor gardening, family pastimes, health, food, ecology, energy, and consumerism. Pays varying rates, on acceptance.

**MOVING HOME**—(formerly *The New Homeowner*) DIR Communications, 6198 Butler Pike, Suite 135, Blue Bell, PA 19422. Articles, of varying lengths, on resources, home care, interior design, and decorating for the affluent new home-owner. Pays varying rates, on acceptance.

**MS.: THE WORLD OF WOMEN**—230 Park Ave., 7th Fl., New York, NY 10169. Address Manuscript Ed. Articles relating to feminism, women's roles, and social change; reporting, profiles, essays, theory, and analysis. Pays market rates. Query with resumé, clips, and SASE required.

**NATIONAL ENQUIRER**—Lantana, FL 33464. Articles, of any length, for mass audience: topical news, the occult, how-to, scientific discoveries, human drama, adventure, personalities. Photos. Pays from $325. Query or send complete manuscript.

**THE NEW HOMEOWNER**—See *Moving Home*.

**NEW WOMAN**—215 Lexington Ave., New York, NY 10016. Karen Walden, Ed.-in-Chief. Articles on personal and professional relationships, health, fitness, lifestyle, money and career issues. Editorial focus is on self-discovery, self-develop-ment, and self-esteem. "Read the magazine to become familiar with our needs, and request guidelines with SASE. We look for originality, solid research, and a friendly, accessible style." Pays varying rates, on acceptance.

**NEW YORK**—755 Second Ave., New York, NY 10017. Edward Kosner, Ed. Laurie Jones, Man. Ed. Feature articles of interest to New Yorkers; focus is on current events in the metropolitan New York area. Pays $850 to $3,500, on accept-ance. Query required; not responsible for unsolicited material.

**THE NEW YORK ANTIQUE ALMANAC**—Box 335, Lawrence, NY 11559. Carol Nadel, Ed. Articles on antiques, shows, shops, art, investments, collectibles, collecting suggestions, nostalgia, related humor. Photos. Pays $5 to $75, extra for photos, on publication.

**THE NEW YORK TIMES MAGAZINE**—229 W. 43rd St., New York, NY 10036. Address Articles Ed. Timely articles, approximately 3,000 words, on news items, forthcoming events, trends, culture, entertainment, etc. Pays to $2,500 for major articles, on acceptance. Query with clips.

**NEWSWEEK**—444 Madison Ave., New York, NY 10022. Original opinion essays, 1,000 to 1,100 words, for "My Turn" column: must contain verifiable facts. Submit manuscript with SASE. Pays $1,000, on publication.

**OMNI**—324 W. Wendover Ave., Suite 205, Greensboro, NC 27408. Keith Ferrell, Ed. Articles, 2,500 to 3,000 words, on scientific aspects of the future: space, machine intelligence, ESP, origin of life, future arts, lifestyles, etc. Pays $750 to $2,500, less for short features, on acceptance. Query.

**PARADE**—750 Third Ave., New York, NY 10017. Fran Carpentier, Sr. Articles Ed. National Sunday newspaper supplement. Factual and authoritative articles, 1,000 to 1,500 words, on subjects of national interest: health, consumer and environmental issues, science, the family, sports, etc. Profiles of well-known person-alities and service pieces. No fiction, poetry, games, or puzzles. Pays from $1,000. Query.

**PENTHOUSE**—1965 Broadway, New York, NY 10023–5965. Peter Bloch, Ed. Nanette Varian, Articles Ed. General-interest or controversial articles, to 5,000 words. Pays to $1 a word, on acceptance.

**PEOPLE IN ACTION/SPORTS PARADE**—Box 10010, Ogden, UT 84409. Caroll Shreeve, Pub. Personality profiles, 1,200 words, of celebrities in sports, entertainment, fine arts, science, etc. Celebrities must be nationally or internationally known for their participation in their field, have positive values, and be making a contribution to society. "High quality color transparencies are a must; query for details." Pays 15¢ a word, $35 for photos, $50 for cover photos, on acceptance.

**PEOPLE WEEKLY**—Time-Life Bldg., Rockefeller Ctr., New York, NY 10020. John Saar, Asst. Man. Ed. Considers article proposals only, three to four paragraphs, on timely, entertaining, and topical personalities. Pays good rates, on acceptance. "Vast majority of material is staff written."

**PHILIP MORRIS MAGAZINE**—153 Waverly Pl., 3rd Floor, New York, NY 10014. Frank Gannon, Ed. Profiles of American innovators, entertainers, sports figures, animal conservationists. Also U.S. travel destinations, food. Pays on publication.

**PLAYBOY**—680 N. Lakeshore Dr., Chicago, IL 60611. John Rezek, Articles Ed. Sophisticated articles, 4,000 to 6,000 words, of interest to urban men. Humor: satire. Pays to $3,000, on acceptance. Query.

**PLAYGIRL**—801 Second Ave., New York, NY 10017. Barbara Haigh, Ed.-in-Chief. Articles, 2,000 to 2,500 words, for women ages 18 to 34. Query with clips to Nonfiction Editor. No fiction. Pays negotiable rates.

**PRIME TIMES**—2802 International Ln., Suite 120, Madison, WI 53704. Rod Clark, Exec. Ed. Articles, 500 to 1,800 words, for dynamic, creative mid-lifers. Departments, 850 to 1,000 words. Pays $125 to $750, on publication. Query or send partial manuscript. Guidelines with SASE.

**PSYCHOLOGY TODAY**—24 E. 23rd St., 5th Floor, New York, NY 10010. Karen Bokram, Features Ed. Articles, 3,000 words, on timely subjects and people. Pays varying rates, on publication; published bimonthly.

**QUEEN'S QUARTERLY**—Queens Univ., Kingston, Ont., Canada K7L 3N6. Boris Castel, Ed. Articles, to 8,000 words, on a wide range of topics, and fiction, to 5,000 words. Poetry; send no more than 6 poems. B&W art. Pays to $400, on publication.

**READER'S DIGEST**—Pleasantville, NY 10570. Kenneth O. Gilmore, Ed.-in-Chief. Unsolicited manuscripts will not be read or returned. General-interest articles already in print and well-developed story proposals will be considered. Send reprint or query to any editor on the masthead.

**REAL PEOPLE**—950 Third Ave., New York, NY 10022–2705. Alex Polner, Ed. True stories, to 500 words, on the bizarre: occult, UFOs, strange occurrences, everyday weirdness, etc. Pays $50, on publication; send submissions to "Real Bizarre" column. Query for interviews, 1,000 to 1,800 words, with movie or TV actors, musicians, and other entertainment celebrities: Pays $100 to $350, on publication. SASE required.

**REDBOOK**—224 W. 57th St., New York, NY 10019. Diane Salvatore, Sr. Ed. Sally Lee, Sr. Ed. Toni Gerber Hope, Articles Ed. Articles, 1,000 to 3,500 words, on subjects related to relationships, sex, current social issues, psychology, marriage, the family, and parenting. Payment varies, on acceptance. Query.

**ROLLING STONE**—1290 Ave. of the Americas, 2nd Fl., New York, NY 10104. Magazine of American music, culture, and politics. No fiction. Query. "We rarely accept free-lance material."

**THE ROTARIAN**—1560 Sherman Ave., Evanston, IL 60201. Willmon L. White, Ed. Articles, 1,200 to 2,000 words, on international social and economic issues, business and management, human relationships, travel, sports, environment, science and technology; humor. Pays good rates, on acceptance. Query.

**SATELLITE ORBIT**—8330 Boone Blvd., Suite 600, Vienna, VA 22182. Mike Doan, Ed. Television-related articles, 750 to 2,500 words, personality profiles, general sports pieces, items on hardware, and articles of interest to the satellite and cable TV viewer. Query with clips. Pay varies, on acceptance.

**THE SATURDAY EVENING POST**—1100 Waterway Blvd., Indianapolis, IN 46202. Ted Kreiter, Exec. Ed. Family-oriented articles, 1,500 to 3,000 words: humor, preventive medicine, destination-oriented travel pieces (not personal experience), celebrity profiles, the arts, and sciences. Pieces on sports and home repair (with photos). Pays varying rates, on publication. Queries preferred.

**SELF**—350 Madison Ave., New York, NY 10017. Alexandra Penney, Ed.-in-Chief. Articles for young women with a particular interest in health, nutrition, fitness, relationships, fashion and beauty, and related lifestyle subjects. Pays from $1 a word. Query.

**SMITHSONIAN MAGAZINE**—900 Jefferson Dr., Washington, DC 20560. Marlane A. Liddell, Articles Ed. Articles on history, art, natural history, physical science, profiles, etc. Query with SASE.

**SOAP OPERA DIGEST**—45 W. 25th St., New York, NY 10010. Jason Bonderoff, Man. Ed. Investigative reports and profiles, to 1,500 words, about New York- or Los Angeles-based soaps. Pays from $250, on acceptance. Query with clips.

**SPORTS ILLUSTRATED**—1271 Ave. of the Americas, New York, NY 10020. Chris Hunt, Articles Ed. Query.

**SPORTS PARADE**—See *People in Action*.

**STAR**—660 White Plains Rd., Tarrytown, NY 10591. Topical articles, 50 to 800 words, on human-interest subjects, show business, lifestyles, the sciences, etc., for family audience. Pays varying rates.

**SUCCESS**—230 Park Ave., #7, New York, NY 10169–0014. Scott DeGarmo, Pub./Ed.-in-Chief. Profiles of successful executives, entrepreneurs; management science, psychology, behavior, and motivation articles, 500 to 3,500 words. Query.

**SUNDAY JOURNAL MAGAZINE**—*Providence Sunday Journal*, 75 Fountain St., Providence, RI 02902. Elliot Krieger, Ed. Features on some aspect of life in New England, especially Rhode Island and S.E. Massachusetts. No fiction. Pays $100 to $500, on publication.

**THE TOASTMASTER**—P.O. Box 9052, Mission Viejo, CA 92690. Suzanne Frey, Ed. Member-supported monthly. Articles, 1,500 to 2,500 words, on decision making, leadership, language, interpersonal and professional communication, humor, logical thinking, rhetorical devices, public speaking in general, profiles of guest orators, speaking techniques, etc. Pays $100 to $250, on acceptance.

**TOWN & COUNTRY**—1700 Broadway, New York, NY 10019. Address Ed.-in-Chief. Considers one-page proposals for articles. Include clips and resumé. Rarely buys unsolicited manuscripts.

**TRAVEL & LEISURE**—1120 Ave. of the Americas, New York, NY 10036. Ila Stanger, Ed.-in-Chief. Articles, 800 to 3,000 words, on destinations and leisure-time activities. Regional pieces for regional editions. Pays $600 to $3,000, on acceptance. Query.

**TRIP & TOUR**—See *Allied Publications.*

**TROPIC**—*The Miami Herald*, One Herald Plaza, Miami, FL 33132. Tom Shroder, Exec. Ed. Essays and articles, 1,000 to 4,000 words, on current trends and issues, light or heavy, for sophisticated audience. No fiction or poetry. Limited humor. Pays $200 to $1,000, on publication. SASE. Allow four to six weeks for response.

**TV GUIDE**—Radnor, PA 19088. Barry Golson, Exec. Ed. Short, light, brightly written pieces about humorous or offbeat angles of television and industry trends. (Majority of personality pieces are staff written.) Pays on acceptance. Query.

**VANITY FAIR**—350 Madison Ave., New York, NY 10017. Pamela McCarthy, Man. Ed. Articles. Pays on acceptance. Query.

**VILLAGE VOICE**—36 Cooper Sq., New York, NY 10003. Sarah Jewler, Man. Ed. Articles, 500 to 2,000 words, on current or controversial topics. Pays $75 to $450, on acceptance. Query or send manuscript with SASE.

**VISTA**—999 Ponce, Suite 600, Coral Gables, FL 33134. Renato Perez, Ed. Articles, to 1,500 words, for English-speaking Hispanic Americans, on job advancement, bilingualism, immigration, the media, fashion, education, medicine, sports, and food. Profiles, 100 words, of Hispanic Americans in unusual jobs; photos welcome. Pays 20¢ a word, on acceptance. Query required. "Sample copy and guidelines free on request."

**VOGUE**—350 Madison Ave., New York, NY 10017. Address Proposals to Features Ed. Articles, to 1,500 words, on women, entertainment and the arts, travel, medicine, and health. General features. Query.

**VOLKSWAGEN WORLD**—Volkswagen of America, Mail Code 3C03, 3800 Hamlin Rd., Auburn, MI 48326. No free-lance material.

**WASHINGTON JOURNALISM REVIEW**—4716 Pontiac St., #310, College Park, MD 20740–2493. Rem Rieder, Ed. Articles, 500 to 3,000 words, on print or electronic journalism. Pays 20¢ a word, on publication. Query.

**WASHINGTON POST MAGAZINE**—*The Washington Post*, 1150 15th St. N.W., Washington, DC 20071. Linton Weeks, Man. Ed. Essays, profiles, and Washington-oriented general-interest pieces, to 5,000 words, on business, arts and culture, politics, science, sports, education, children, relationships, behavior, etc. Pays from $1,000, after acceptance.

**WISCONSIN**—*The Milwaukee Journal Magazine*, P.O. Box 661, Milwaukee, WI 53201. Alan Borsuk, Ed. Trend stories, essays, humor, personal-experience pieces, profiles, 500 to 2,500 words, with strong Wisconsin emphasis. Pays $75 to $650, on publication.

**WOMAN BEAUTIFUL**—See *Allied Publications.*

**WOMAN'S DAY**—1633 Broadway, New York, NY 10019. Rebecca Greer, Articles Ed. Articles, 500 to 2,500 words, on subjects of interest to women: marriage, education, family health, child rearing, money management, interpersonal relationships, changing lifestyles, etc. Dramatic first-person narratives about women who have experienced medical miracles or other triumphs, or have overcome common problems, such as alcoholism. Query first. Pays top rates, on acceptance.

**YANKEE**—Dublin, NH 03444. Judson D. Hale, Ed. Articles, to 3,000 words, with New England angle. Photos. Pays $150 to $1,000 (average $750), on acceptance.

**YOUR HOME/INDOORS & OUT**—Box 10010, Ogden, UT 84409. Caroll Shreeve, V.P. of Pub. Articles, 1,200 words, on fresh ideas in home decor, ranging from floor and wall coverings to home furnishings. Latest in home construction (exteriors, interiors, building materials, design, entertaining, and lifestyle), the outdoors at home (landscaping, pools, patios, gardens, etc.), home management, and home buying and selling. Avoid do-it-yourself approaches. Emphasis on the use of home-improvement professionals. Must include excellent transparencies. Queries required. Guidelines. Pays 15¢ a word and $35 for photos, $50 for cover photo, on acceptance.

## CURRENT EVENTS, POLITICS

**AFRICA REPORT**—833 U.N. Pl., New York, NY 10017. Margaret A. Novicki, Ed. Well-researched articles by specialists, 1,000 to 2,500 words, with photos, on current African affairs. Pays $150 to $250, on publication.

**THE AMERICAN LEGION**—Box 1055, Indianapolis, IN 46206. John Greenwald, Ed. Articles, 750 to 1,800 words, on current world affairs, public policy, and subjects of contemporary interest. Pays $500 to $1,000, on acceptance. Query.

**THE AMERICAN SCHOLAR**—1811 Q St. N.W., Washington, DC 20009–9974. Joseph Epstein, Ed. Non-technical articles and essays, 3,500 to 4,000 words, on current affairs, the American cultural scene, politics, arts, religion, and science. Pays to $500, on acceptance.

**THE AMICUS JOURNAL**—Natural Resources Defense Council, 40 W. 20th St., New York, NY 10011. Peter Borrelli, Ed. Investigative articles, book reviews, and poetry related to national and international environmental policy. Pays varying rates, on acceptance. Queries required.

**THE ATLANTIC**—745 Boylston St., Boston, MA 02116. William Whitworth, Ed. In-depth articles on public issues, politics, social sciences, education, business, literature, and the arts, with emphasis on information rather than opinion. Ideal length is 3,000 to 6,000 words, though short pieces, 1,000 to 2,000 words, are also welcome. Pays excellent rates, on acceptance.

**CHRISTIANITY AND CRISIS**—537 W. 121st St., New York, NY 10027. Leon Howell, Ed. Tom Kelly, Assoc. Ed. Articles, 800 to 1,200 words or 2,000 to 3,000 words, on theology, politics, ethics, economics, civil rights, foreign and domestic affairs. "We are a progressive Christian journal of opinion. We carry no 'devotional' material but welcome solid contemplative reflections." Payment varies, to $150, on publication. Guidelines.

**CHURCH & STATE**—8120 Fenton St., Silver Spring, MD 20910. Joseph L. Conn, Man. Ed. Articles, 600 to 2,600 words, on religious liberty and church-state relations. Pays varying rates, on acceptance. Query.

**COMMENTARY**—165 E. 56th St., New York, NY 10022. Norman Podhoretz, Ed. Articles, 5,000 to 7,000 words, on contemporary issues, Jewish affairs, social sciences, community life, religious thought, culture. Serious fiction; book reviews. Pays on publication.

**COMMONWEAL**—15 Dutch St., New York, NY 10038. Margaret O'Brien Steinfels, Ed. Catholic. Articles, to 3,000 words, on political, social, religious, and literary subjects. Pays 3¢ a word, on acceptance.

**THE CRISIS**—4017 24th St., #8, San Francisco, CA 94114. Fred Beauford, Ed. Articles, to 1,500 words, on the arts, civil rights, and problems and achievements of blacks and other minorities. Pays $75 to $500, on acceptance.

**CURRENT HISTORY**—4225 Main St., Philadelphia, PA 19127. Country-specific political science articles, to 20 pages. "We devote each issue to a specific region or country. Writers should be experts with up-to-date knowledge of the region, who can deliver sharp analysis of recent events in a clear, entertaining manner." Queries preferred. Pays $300, on publication.

**ENVIRONMENT**—1319 18th St. N.W., Washington, DC 20036–1802. Barbara T. Richman, Man. Ed. Articles, 2,500 to 5,000 words, on environmental, scientific, and technological policy and decision-making issues. Pays $100 to $300, on publication. Query.

**FOREIGN SERVICE JOURNAL**—2101 E St. N.W., Washington, D.C. 20037. Articles on American diplomacy, foreign affairs, and subjects of interest to Americans representing U.S. abroad. Query.

**THE FREEMAN**—Foundation for Economic Education, Irvington-on-Hudson, NY 10533. Brian Summers, Sr. Ed. Articles, to 3,500 words, on economic, political, and moral implications of private property, voluntary exchange, and individual choice. Pays 10¢ a word, on publication.

**INQUIRER MAGAZINE**—*Philadelphia Inquirer*, P.O. Box 8263, 400 N. Broad St., Philadelphia, PA 19101. Ms. Avery Rome, Ed. Local-interest features, 500 to 7,000 words. Profiles of national figures in politics, entertainment, etc. Pays varying rates, on publication. Query.

**IRISH AMERICA**—432 Park Ave. S., Suite 1000, New York, NY 10016. Patricia Harty, Ed. Articles, 1,500 to 2,000 words, of interest to Irish-American audience; preferred topics include history, sports, the arts, and politics. Pays 10¢ a word, after publication. Query.

**LABOR'S HERITAGE**—10000 New Hampshire Ave., Silver Spring, MD 20903. Stuart Kaufman, Ed. Quarterly journal of The George Meany Memorial Archives. Publishes 15- to 30-page articles to be read by labor scholars, labor union members, and the general public. Pays in copies.

**MIDSTREAM**—110 E. 59th St., New York, NY 10022. Joel Carmichael, Ed. Articles of international and Jewish concern. Pays 5¢ a word, after publication. Allow three months for response.

**MOMENT**—3000 Connecticut Ave. N.W., Suite 300, Washington, DC 20008. Suzanne Singer, Man. Ed. Sophisticated articles and some fiction, 2,500 to 5,000 words, on Jewish topics. Columns, to 1,500 words, on current issues in the Mideast, American Jewry, Israel, pluralism. Pays $50 to $400, on publication.

**THE NATION**—72 Fifth Ave., New York, NY 10011. Victor Navasky, Ed. Articles, 1,500 to 2,500 words, on politics and culture from a liberal/left perspective. Pays $75 per published page, to $300, on publication. Query.

**NATIONAL REVIEW**—150 E. 35th St., New York, NY 10016. Mark Cunningham, Articles Ed. Articles, 1,000 to 5,000 words. "We use very few unsolicited pieces. The overwhelming majority of our articles are written by professional established writers." Pays to $200, on publication.

**THE NEW COMBAT**—168 Rivington St., New York, NY 10002. William Ney, Ed. "A Journal of Reason and Resistance." Political feature articles. Short pieces, to 1,500 words, that comment on public life. "Our journal is meant to inform general citizens, in detail, rather than to influence leaders." Query for feature articles. Pays $75 to $200 for features; $40 for short pieces.

**THE NEW YORK TIMES MAGAZINE**—229 W. 43rd St., New York, NY 10036. Address Articles Ed. Timely articles, approximately 4,000 words, on news items, trends, culture, etc. Pays $1,000 for short pieces, $2,500 for major articles, on acceptance. Query with clips.

**THE NEW YORKER**—20 W. 43rd St., New York, NY 10036. Address the Editors. Factual and biographical articles, for "Profiles," "Reporter at Large," "Annals of Crime," "Onward and Upward with the Arts," etc. Pays good rates, on acceptance. Query.

**NUCLEAR TIMES: ISSUES & ACTIVISM FOR GLOBAL SURVIVAL**—P.O. Box 351, Kenmore Sta., Boston, MA 02215. Sonia Shah, Man. Ed. News and feature articles, 500 to 4,000 words, on peace, justice, the environment, nuclear disarmament, military policy, and militarization of American culture. Pays from 25¢ a word, two to four weeks after acceptance.

**ON THE ISSUES**—Choices Women's Medical Center, Inc., 97–77 Queens Blvd., Forest Hills, NY 11374–3317. Beverly Lowy, Man. Ed. "The Magazine of Substance for Progressive Women." Articles, up to 2,500 words, on political or social issues. Movie, music, and book reviews, 500 to 750 words. Query. Payment varies, on publication.

**THE PROGRESSIVE**—409 E. Main St., Madison, WI 53703. Erwin Knoll, Ed. Articles, 1,000 to 3,500 words, on political and social problems. Pays $100 to $300, on publication.

**PUBLIC CITIZEN MAGAZINE**—2000 P St. N.W., Suite 610, Washington, DC 20036. Ana Radelat, Ed. Investigative reports and articles of timely political interest, for members of Public Citizen: consumer rights, health and safety, environmental protection, safe energy, tax reform, and government and corporate accountability. Photos, illustrations. Pays to $500.

**ROLL CALL: THE NEWSPAPER OF CAPITOL HILL**—900 2nd St. N.E., Washington, DC 20002. James K. Glassman, Ed. Factual, breezy articles with political or Congressional angle: Congressional history, human-interest subjects, political lore, etc. Political satire and humor. Pays on publication.

**THE ROTARIAN**—1560 Sherman Ave., Evanston, IL 60201. Willmon L. White, Ed. Articles, 1,200 to 2,000 words, on international social and economic issues, business and management, environment, science and technology. "No direct political or religious slants." Pays good rates, on acceptance. Query.

**SATURDAY NIGHT**—36 Toronto St., Suite 1160, Toronto, Ont., Canada M5C 2C5. John Fraser, Ed. Canada's oldest magazine of politics, social issues, culture, and business. Features, 1,000 to 3,000 words, and columns, 800 to 1,000 words; fiction, to 3,000 words. Must have Canadian tie-in. Payment varies, on acceptance.

**VFW MAGAZINE**—406 W. 34th St., Kansas City, MO 64111. Richard K. Kolb, Ed. Magazine for Veterans of Foreign Wars and their families. Articles, 1,500 words, on current issues and history, with veteran angle. Photos. Pays to $500, extra for photos, on acceptance. Guidelines.

**VILLAGE VOICE**—842 Broadway, New York, NY 10003. Sarah Jewler, Man. Ed. Articles, 500 to 2,000 words, on current or controversial topics. Pays $75 to $450, on publication. Query or send manuscript with SASE.

**WASHINGTON POST MAGAZINE**—*The Washington Post,* 1150 15th St. N.W., Washington, DC 20071. Linton Weeks, Man. Ed. Essays, profiles, and general-interest pieces, to 5,000 words, on Washington-oriented politics and related issues. Pays from $1,000, after acceptance. SASE required.

# REGIONAL AND CITY PUBLICATIONS

**ADIRONDACK LIFE**—P.O. Box 97, Jay, NY 12941. Tom Hughes, Ed. Features, to 4,000 words, on outdoor and environmental activities and issues, arts, wilderness, profiles, history, and fiction; focus is on the Adirondack region and North Country of New York State. Pays to 25¢ a word, 30 days after acceptance. Query.

**ALASKA**—808 E St., Suite 200, Anchorage, AK 99501. Tobin Morrison, Ed. Articles, 2,000 words, on life in Alaska and northwestern Canada. Pays varying rates, on acceptance. Guidelines.

**ALOHA, THE MAGAZINE OF HAWAII**—49 South Hotel St., #309, Honolulu, HI 96813. Cheryl Chee Tsutsumi, Ed. Articles, 1,500 to 2,500 words, on the life, customs, and people of Hawaii and the Pacific. Poetry. Fiction. Pays $150 to $500 for full-length features, on publication. Query first.

**APPRISE**—P.O. Box 2954, 1982 Locust Ln., Harrisburg, PA 17105. Jim Connor, Ed. Articles, 1,500 to 3,500 words, of regional (Central Pennsylvania) interest, including profiles of notable Pennsylvanians, and broadly based articles of social interest that "enlighten and inform." Pays 10¢ a word, on acceptance; published monthly.

**ARIZONA HIGHWAYS**—2039 W. Lewis Ave., Phoenix, AZ 85009. Robert J. Early, Ed. Articles, 1,500 to 2,000 words, on travel in Arizona; pieces on adventure, humor, lifestyles, nostalgia, history, archaeology, nature, etc. Departments using personal experience pieces include "Milestones," "Focus on Nature," "Along the Way," "Event of the Month," "Outdoor Recreation," "Back Road Adventures," "Legends of the Lost," "Hiking," and "Arizona Humor." Pays 30¢ to 50¢ a word, on acceptance. Guidelines. Query first.

**ARKANSAS TIMES**—Box 34010, Little Rock, AR 72203. John Brummett, Ed. Articles, to 6,000 words, on Arkansas history, people, travel, politics. All articles must have strong AR orientation. Pays to $500, on acceptance.

**ATLANTA**—1360 Peachtree St., Suite 1800, Atlanta, GA 30309. Lee Walburn, Ed. Articles, 1,500 to 5,000 words, on Atlanta subjects or personalities. Pays $300 to $2,000, on publication. Query.

**ATLANTIC CITY MAGAZINE**—P.O. Box 2100, Pleasantville, NJ 08232. Ken Weatherford, Ed. Lively articles, 200 to 4,000 words, on Atlantic City and the southern New Jersey shore, for locals and tourists: entertainment, casinos, business, recreation, personalities, lifestyle, local color. Pays $50 to $700, on publication. Query.

**BACK HOME IN KENTUCKY**—P.O. Box 681629, Franklin, TN 37068–1629. Nanci P. Gregg, Man. Ed. Articles on Kentucky history, travel, craftsmen and artisans, Kentucky cooks, "colorful" characters, and limited personal nostalgia specifically related to Kentucky. Pays $25 to $100 for articles with B&W or color photos. Queries preferred.

**BAJA EXPLORER**—4180 La Jolla Village Dr., La Jolla, CA 92037. Landon S. Crumpton, Ed.-in-Chief. Articles, 800 to 1,200 words, on fishing, sailing, surfing, windsurfing, camping, and natural history, and cultural events of interest to tourists visiting Baja California. Pays 25¢ a word, $50 per slide, on publication; published bimonthly.

**THE BIG APPLE PARENTS' PAPER**—928 Broadway, Suite 709, New York, NY 10010. Helen Rosengren Freedman, Ed. Articles, 600 to 750 words, for

New York City parents. Pays $50 to $75, on publication, plus $25 cover bonus. Buys first NY-area rights.

**BIRMINGHAM**—2027 First Ave. N., Birmingham, AL 35203. Joe O'Donnell, Ed. Personality profiles, features, business, and nostalgia pieces, to 2,500 words, with Birmingham tie-in. Pays $50 to $175, on publication.

**BLUE RIDGE COUNTRY**—P.O. Box 21535, Roanoke, VA 24018. Kurt Rheinheimer, Ed. Bimonthly. Regional articles, 1,200 to 2,000 words, that "explore and extol the beauty, history, and travel opportunities in the mountain regions of Virginia, North Carolina, West Virginia, Tennessee, Kentucky, Maryland, South Carolina, and Georgia." Color slides or B&W prints considered. Pays $200 for photo/features, on publication. Queries preferred.

**BOCA RATON**—JES Publishing, Amtec Center, Suite 100, 6413 Congress Ave., Boca Raton, FL 33487. Marie Speed, Ed. Articles, 800 to 3,000 words, on Florida topics, personalities, and travel. Pays $50 to $500, on publication. Query with clips required.

**THE BOSTON GLOBE MAGAZINE**—*The Boston Globe*, Boston, MA 02107. Ande Zellman, Ed. General-interest articles on local, national, and international topics and profiles, 2,500 to 5,000 words. Query and SASE required.

**BOSTON MAGAZINE**—300 Massachusetts Ave., Boston, MA 02115. Art Jahnke, Man. Ed. Informative, entertaining features, 1,000 to 3,000 words, on Boston-area personalities, institutions, and phenomena. Query. Pays to $2,000, on publication.

**BOUNDARY WATERS JOURNAL**—9396 Rocky Ledge Rd., Ely, MN 55731. Stuart Osthoff, Ed. Articles, 2,000 to 3,000 words, on wilderness recreation, nature, and conservation in Minnesota's Boundary Waters region, including canoe routes, fishing, wildlife, history, and lifestyles of residents. Pays $200 to $400, on publication.

**BUFFALO SPREE MAGAZINE**—Box 38, Buffalo, NY 14226. Johanna Shotell, Ed. Articles, to 1,800 words. Pays $75 to $100, $25 for poetry, on publication.

**BUSINESS IN BROWARD**—2455 E. Sunrise Blvd., Suite 300, Ft. Lauderdale, FL 33304. Beva Weinlaub, Ed. Small business regional bimonthly; 1,000-word articles for eastern Florida county. Pay varies, on acceptance. Same address and requirements for *Business in Palm Beach County*.

**BUSINESS IN PALM BEACH COUNTY**—See *Business in Broward*.

**CAPE COD LIFE**—P.O. Box 767, Cataumet, MA 02534–0767. Brian F. Shortsleeve, Pub. Articles on Cape Cod current events, business, art, history, gardening, and lifestyle, 2,000 words. Pays $40 per column, 30 days after publication. Queries preferred.

**CARIBBEAN TRAVEL AND LIFE**—8403 Colesville Rd., Silver Spring, MD 20910. Veronica Gould Stoddart, Ed. Articles, 500 to 3,000 words, on all aspects of travel, recreation, leisure, and culture in the Caribbean, Bahamas, and Bermuda. Pays $75 to $550, on publication. Query with published clips.

**CAROLOGUE**—South Carolina Historical Society, 100 Meeting St., Charleston, SC 29401–2299. Stephen Hoffius, Ed. General-interest articles, to 10 pages, on South Carolina history. Queries preferred. Payment is six copies.

**CHICAGO**—414 N. Orleans, Chicago, IL 60610. Joanne Trestrail, Man. Ed.

591

Articles, 1,000 to 5,000 words, related to Chicago. Pays varying rates, on acceptance. Query.

**CHICAGO HISTORY**—Clark St. at North Ave., Chicago, IL 60614. Russell Lewis, Ed. Articles, to 4,500 words, on Chicago's urban, political, social, and cultural history. Pays to $250, on publication. Query.

**CITY NEWS**—2 Park Ave., Suite 2012, New York, NY 10016. Leslie Elgort, Ed. Bimonthly. Articles, 750 to 1,500 words, poetry, fillers, and humor of interest to New York City teenagers; B&W photos. Payment varies, on publication.

**CITY SPORTS MAGAZINE**—P.O. Box 193693, San Francisco, CA 94119. Chris Newbound, Ed. Articles, 500 to 2,000 words, on participant sports, family recreation, travel, and the active lifestyle. Pays $100 to $650, on publication. Query. Limited market.

**CLINTON STREET**—Box 3588, Portland, OR 97208. David Milholland, Ed. Articles, to 15 pages, and creative fiction, 2 to 20 pages. "Eclectic blend of politics, culture, humor, and art." Compelling first-person accounts welcome. Pays $50 to $200, on publication.

**COLORADO HOMES & LIFESTYLES**—7009 S. Potomac, Englewood, CO 80112. Anne McGregor Parsons, Ed. Articles, 1,200 to 1,500 words, on topics related to Colorado: travel, home design and decorating, architecture, gardening, art, antiques, collecting, and entertaining. Pays $125 to $200, on acceptance.

**COMMON GROUND MAGAZINE**—P.O. Box 99, McVeytown, PA 17051–0099. Ruth Dunmire and Pam Brumbaugh, Eds. General-interest articles, 500 to 5,000 words, related to Central Pennsylvania's Juniata River Valley and its rural lifestyle. Related fiction, 1,000 to 2,000 words. Poetry, 12 lines or fewer. Fillers, photos, and cartoons.Pays $25 to $200 for articles, $5 to $15 for fillers, and $5 to $25 for photos, on quarterly publication. Guidelines.

**CONCORD AND THE NORTH**—See *Network Publications*.

**CONNECTICUT**—789 Reservoir Ave., Bridgeport, CT 06606. Charles Monagan, Ed. Articles, 1,500 to 3,500 words, on Connecticut topics, issues, people, and lifestyles. Pays $500 to $1,200, within 30 days of acceptance.

**CONNECTICUT FAMILY**—See *New York Family*.

**CRAIN'S DETROIT BUSINESS**—1400 Woodbridge, Detroit, MI 48207. Mary Kramer, Ed. Business articles, 500 to 1,000 words, about Detroit, for Detroit business readers. Pays $100 to $200, on publication. Query required.

**D**—3988 N. Central Expressway, Suite 1200, Dallas, TX 75204. Melissa Houtte, Ed. In-depth investigative pieces on current trends and problems, personality profiles, and general-interest articles on the arts, travel, and business, for upperclass residents of Dallas. Pays $350 to $500 for departments, $800 to $1,200 for features. Written queries only.

**DALLAS LIFE MAGAZINE**—*The Dallas Morning News*, P.O. Box 655237, Communications Center, Dallas, TX 75265. Mike Maza, Man. Ed. Well-researched articles and profiles, 1,000 to 3,000 words, on contemporary local issues and personalities. Pays from 25¢ a word, on acceptance. Query required.

**DELAWARE TODAY**—P.O. Box 4440, Wilmington, DE 19807. Lise Monty, Ed. Service articles, profiles, news, etc., on topics of local interest. Pays $75 to $125 for department pieces, $50 to $500 for features, on publication. Queries with clips required.

**DETROIT FREE PRESS MAGAZINE**—*Detroit Free Press*, 321 W. Lafayette Blvd., Detroit, MI 48231. Articles, to 5,000 words, on issues, lifestyles. Personality profiles; essays; humor. Pays from $150. Query appreciated.

**DETROIT MONTHLY**—1400 Woodbridge, Detroit, MI 48207. John Barron, Ed. Articles on Detroit-area people, issues, lifestyles, and business. Payment varies. Query required.

**DOWN EAST**—Camden, ME 04843. Davis Thomas, Ed. Articles, 1,500 to 2,500 words, on all aspects of life in Maine. Photos. Pays to 20¢ a word, extra for photos, on acceptance. Query.

**ERIE & CHAUTAUQUA MAGAZINE**—Charles H. Strong Bldg., 1250 Tower Ln., Erie, PA 16505. K. L. Kalvelage, Man. Ed. Feature articles, to 2,500 words, on issues of interest to upscale readers in the Erie, Warren, and Crawford counties (PA), and Chautauqua (NY) county. Pieces with regional relevance. Pays after publication. Query preferred, with writing samples. Buys all rights. Guidelines available.

**FLORIDA GULF COAST HOMEBUYER'S GUIDE**—1715 N. Westshore Blvd., #244, Tampa, FL 33607–3926. Paula L. Maguire, Relocation/Production Dir. Articles, 750 to 1,200 words, for the active home buyer on the Gulf Coast: home-related articles, moving tips, financing, etc. Pays 7¢ to 10¢ a word, on acceptance. Query preferred.

**FLORIDA HOME & GARDEN**—800 Douglas Rd., Suite 500, Coral Gables, FL 33134. Kathryn Howard, Ed. Articles, 1,000 words, on Florida interior design, architecture, travel (Florida and Caribbean), and home entertaining. Pays $200 to $300, photos extra.

**FLORIDA KEYS MAGAZINE**—P.O. Box 2921, Key Largo, FL 33037. Gibbons Cline, Ed. Articles, 1,000 to 2,000 words, on the Florida Keys: history, environment, natural history, profiles, etc. Fillers, humor. Photos. Pays varying rates, on publication.

**FLORIDA TREND**—Box 611, St. Petersburg, FL 33731–0611. Matt Walsh, Ed. Articles on Florida business and businesspeople. Query letter required.

**FLORIDA WILDLIFE**—620 S. Meridian St., Tallahassee, FL 32399–1600. Andrea H. Blount, Ed. Bimonthly of the Florida Game and Fresh Water Fish Commission. Articles, 800 to 1,500 words, that promote native flora and fauna, hunting, fishing in Florida's fresh waters, outdoor ethics, and conservation of Florida's natural resources. Pays $50 to $300, on publication.

**GEORGIA JOURNAL**—Grimes Publications, P.O. Box 27, Athens, GA 30603–0027. Millard B. Grimes, Ed. and Pub. Articles, 1,000 to 2,000 words, on people, history, events, travel, etc., in and around Georgia. Poetry, to 20 lines. Pays $50 to $350, on publication.

**GOLDENSEAL**—The Cultural Center, 1900 Kanawha Blvd. East, Charleston, WV 25305–0300. Ken Sullivan, Ed. Articles, 1,000 and 3,000 words, on West Virginia history, folklife, folk art and crafts, and music of a traditional nature. Pays to $175, on publication. Guidelines.

**GRAND RAPIDS**—549 Ottawa N.W., Grand Rapids, MI 49503. Carole Valade Smith, Ed. Service articles (dining guide, travel, personal finance, humor) and issue-oriented pieces related to Grand Rapids, Michigan. Pays $35 to $200, on publication. Query.

**GULF COAST GOLFER**—See *North Texas Golfer*.

**GULFSHORE LIFE**—2975 S. Horseshoe Dr., Naples, FL 33942. Janis Lyn Johnson, Ed. Articles, 800 to 3,000 words, on southwest Florida personalities, travel, sports, business, interior design, arts, history, and nature. Pays $150 to $300. Query.

**HAMPSHIRE EAST**—See *Network Publications*.

**HAWAII**—Box 6050, Mission Viejo, CA 92690–6050. Dennis Shattuck, Ed. Bimonthly. Articles, 1,000 to 5,000 words, related to Hawaii. Pays 10¢ a word, on publication. Query.

**HIGH COUNTRY NEWS**—Box 1090, Paonia, CO 81428. Betsy Marston, Ed. Articles on environmental issues, public lands management, energy, and natural resource issues; profiles of western innovators; pieces on western politics. "Writers must take regional approach." Poetry. B&W photos. Pays $2 to $4 per column inch, on publication, for 750-word roundups and 2,000-word features. Query first.

**HONOLULU**—36 Merchant St., Honolulu, HI 96813. Ed Cassidy, Ed. Features highlighting contemporary life in the Hawaiian islands: politics, sports, history, people, arts, events. Pays $500, on publication. Columns and department pieces are mostly staff-written. Queries required.

**HOUSTON METROPOLITAN MAGAZINE**—P.O. Box 25386, Houston, TX 77265–5386. Maria Moss, Man. Ed. Chris Kelly, Ed. Articles with strong Houston-area angles. Issue-oriented features, profiles, lifestyle pieces; gardening and design pieces; department columns ("About Town," "Art Beat," "Metropolitan Marketplace"). Pays $50 to $500 for columns; $600 to $1,000 for features.

**ILLINOIS ENTERTAINER**—2250 E. Devon, Suite 150, Des Plaines, IL 60018. Michael C. Harris, Ed. Articles, 500 to 1,500 words, on local and national entertainment (emphasis on alternative music) in the greater Chicago area. Personality profiles; interviews; reviews. Photos. Pays varying rates, on publication. Query preferred.

**ILLINOIS MAGAZINE**—P.O. Box 40, Litchfield, IL 62056. Peggy Kuethe, Ed. Bimonthly. Regional articles, 100 to 2,000 words, on travel, history, current events, points of interest, and biography. No exposés or personal experience pieces. Pays $15 to $150, on publication.

**INDIANAPOLIS MONTHLY**—950 N. Meridian St., Suite 1200, Indianapolis, IN 46204. Deborah Paul, Ed./Pub. Sam Stall, Man. Ed. Articles, 1,000 words, on health, sports, politics, business, interior design, travel, and Indiana personalities. All material must have a regional focus. Pays varying rates, on publication.

**INSIDE CHICAGO**—2501 W. Peterson Ave., Chicago, IL 60659. Shane Tritsch, Sr. Ed. Features, to 3,500 words, on Chicago-related trends, profiles of Chicagoans, nightlife, arts, and lifestyle. Short reports, 150 to 300 words. Department pieces, 800 to 1,000 words. Pays varying rates. Query.

**THE IOWAN MAGAZINE**—108 Third St., Suite 350, Des Moines, IA 50309. Karen Massetti-Miller, Ed. Articles, 1,000 to 3,000 words, on business, arts, people, and history of Iowa. Photos a plus. Pays $200 to $600, on publication. Query required.

**JACKSONVILLE MAGAZINE**—9550 Regency Square Blvd., #801, Jacksonville, FL 32225. Kathy Blum, Ed. Articles of interest to the Northeast Florida community: strong regional slant a must. Pays $100 to $300, two weeks after publication. Experienced writers only. Query required.

**JOURNAL OF THE WEST**—Box 1009, Manhattan, KS 66502–4228. Robin

Higham, Ed. Articles, to 15 pages, on the history and culture of the West, then and now. Payment is 10 copies.

**KANSAS!**—Kansas Dept. of Commerce, 400 W. Eighth Ave., 5th Fl., Topeka, KS 66603–3957. Andrea Glenn, Ed. Quarterly. Articles, 5 to 7 typed pages, on the people, places, history, and events of Kansas. Color slides. Pays to $250, on acceptance. Query.

**KENTUCKY LIVING**—P.O. Box 32170, Louisville, KY 40232. Gary Luhr, Ed. Articles, 800 to 2,000 words, with strong Kentucky angle: profiles (of people, places, events), history, biography, recreation, travel, leisure or lifestyle, and book excerpts. Pays $125 to $300, on acceptance. Guidelines available.

**KEY HORIZONS**—Gateway Plaza, 950 N. Meridian, Suite 1200, Indianapolis, IN 46204. Joan Todd, Man. Ed. Quarterly. General-interest articles and department pieces, 300 to 2,500 words, for readers 50 and older. Topics include personal finance, cooking, family trends, and travel. Pays $75 to $500, $25 to $50 for photos, on publication.

**L.A. WEST**—462 Stevens Ave. #302, Solana Beach, CA 92075. Mary Daily, Ed. Features, 850 to 1,200 words, relating to western Los Angeles; humorous essays on current lifestyles; profiles, 350 to 500 words, on westside professionals; travel pieces, 800 words, on foreign and domestic destinations. Queries preferred. Guidelines.

**LAKE SUPERIOR MAGAZINE**—P.O. Box 16417, Duluth, MN 55816–0417. Paul Hayden, Ed. Articles with emphasis on Lake Superior regional subjects: historical pieces that highlight the people, places, and events that affect the Lake Superior region. Pictorial essays; humor and occasional fiction. Quality photos enhance submission. "Writers must have a thorough knowledge of the subject and how it relates to our region." Pays to $400, extra for photos, after publication. Query first.

**THE LOOK**—P.O. Box 272, Cranford, NJ 07016–0272. John R. Hawks, Pub. Articles, 1,500 to 3,000 words, on fashion, student life, employment, relationships, and profiles of interest to local (NJ) readers ages 16 to 26. Also, beach stories and articles about the New Jersey shore. Pays $30 to $200, on publication.

**LOS ANGELES MAGAZINE**—1888 Century Park E., Suite 920, Los Angeles, CA 90067. Lew Harris, Ed. Articles, to 3,000 words, of interest to sophisticated, affluent southern Californians, preferably with local focus on a lifestyle topic. Pays from 10¢ a word, on acceptance. Query.

**LOS ANGELES READER**—5550 Wilshire Blvd., Suite 301, Los Angeles, CA 90036. James Vowell, Ed. Articles, 750 to 5,000 words, on subjects relating to the Los Angeles area; special emphasis on feature journalism, entertainment, and the arts. Pays $25 to $300, on publication. Query preferred.

**LOS ANGELES TIMES MAGAZINE**—Times Mirror Sq., Los Angeles, CA 90053. Linda Mathews, Ed. Articles, to 5,000 words: general-interest news features, photo spreads, profiles, and narratives focusing on current events of the southern California region and the world. Pays to $3,000, on acceptance. Query required.

**LOUISVILLE**—One Riverfront Plaza, Louisville, KY 40202. James Oppel, Jr., Ed. Articles, 1,000 to 2,000 words, on community issues, personalities, and entertainment in the Louisville area. Photos. Pays from $50, on acceptance. Query; articles on assignment only. Limited free-lance market.

**MANCHESTER**—See *Network Publications*.

**MEMPHIS**—MM Corp., Box 256, Memphis, TN 38101. Leanne Kleinmann, Ed. Articles, 1,500 to 4,000 words, on a wide variety of topics related to Memphis and the Mid-South region: politics, education, sports, business, etc. Profiles; investigative pieces. Pays $75 to $500, on publication. Query. Guidelines available.

**MICHIGAN BUSINESS**—26111 Evergreen, Suite 303, Southfield, MI 48076. Ron Garbinski, Ed. Business news features on Michigan businesses. Query. Pay varies, on publication.

**MICHIGAN LIVING**—1 Auto Club Dr., Dearborn, MI 48126–9982. Len Barnes, Ed. Travel articles, 500 to 1,500 words, on tourist attractions and recreational opportunities in the U.S. and Canada, with emphasis on Michigan: places to go, things to do, costs, etc. Color photos. Pays $150 to $380, extra for photos, on acceptance.

**MID-WEST OUTDOORS**—111 Shore Dr., Hinsdale, IL 60521–5885. Gene Laulunen, Ed. Articles, 1,500 words, with photos, on where, when, and how to fish and hunt, within 500 miles of Chicago. Pays $25, on publication.

**MILWAUKEE MAGAZINE**—312 E. Buffalo, Milwaukee, WI 53202. David Fryxell, Ed. Profiles, investigative articles, and service pieces, 3,000 to 6,000 words; local tie-in a must. No fiction. Pays from $500, on publication. Query preferred.

**MINNESOTA MONTHLY**—15 S. Ninth St., Suite 320, Minneapolis, MN 55402. Jodie Ahern, Man. Ed. Articles, to 4,000 words, on the people, places, events, and issues in Minnesota; fiction, to 3,000 words; poetry, to 50 lines. Pays $50 to $800, on acceptance. Query for nonfiction only.

**MONTANA MAGAZINE**—P.O. Box 5630, Helena, MT 59604. Carolyn Cunningham, Ed. Where-to-go items, regional profiles, photo essays. Montana-oriented only. B&W prints, color slides. Pays $75 to $350, on publication.

**MPLS. ST. PAUL**—12 S. 6th St., Suite 400, Minneapolis, MN 55402. Claude Peck, Man. Ed. In-depth articles, features, profiles, and service pieces, 400 to 3,000 words, with Minneapolis-St. Paul focus. Pays to $1,000.

**MUSEUM OF SCIENCE MAGAZINE**—Publications Dept., Museum of Science, Science Park, Boston, MA 02114–1099. Attn: Editorial Offices. Published bimonthly for Museum of Science members. Articles, 1,200 to 1,500 words, on general science topics related to exhibits and shows at Boston's Museum of Science. Send SASE for list of upcoming exhibits. Pays to $500, on publication.

**NASHUA**—See *Network Publications*.

**NEBRASKA HISTORY**—P.O. Box 82554, Lincoln, NE 68501. James E. Potter, Ed. Articles, 3,000 to 7,000 words, on the history of Nebraska and the Great Plains. B&W line drawings. Payment is six copies. Cash prize awarded to one article each year.

**NETWORK PUBLICATIONS**—100 Main St., Nashua, NH 03060. Kate Binder, Man. Ed. Lifestyle and business articles with a New Hampshire angle, with sources from all regions of the state, for the company's four regional monthlies: *Nashua, Manchester, Concord and the North,* and *Hampshire East*. Query. Payment varies, on acceptance.

**NEVADA**—1800 East Hwy. 50, Suite 200, Carson City, NV 89710. David Moore, Ed. Articles, 500 to 700 or 1,500 to 1,800 words, on topics related to Nevada: travel, history, profiles, humor, and place. Special section on Nevada events. Photos. Pay varies, on publication.

**NEW ALASKAN**—8339 Snug Harbor Ln. N., Ketchikan, AK 99901. R.W.

Pickrell, Ed. Articles, 1,000 to 5,000 words, and fiction, must be related to southern Alaska. Pays 1 ½¢ a word, on publication.

**NEW DOMINION**—2000 N. 14th St., Suite 750, Arlington, VA 22201. Philip Hayward, Ed. "The Magazine for and about Northern Virginia." Articles, 600 to 2,000 words, on regional business and lifestyles. Query with writing samples. Pays $5.50 per column inch, on publication.

**NEW JERSEY MONTHLY**—P.O. Box 920, Morristown, NJ 07963–0920. Jan Bresnick, Ed. Articles, profiles, and service pieces, 2,000 to 3,000 words; department pieces on health, business, education, travel, sports, local politics, and arts with New Jersey tie-in, 1,000 to 1,500 words. Pays $35 to $100 for shorts, $400 to $600 for departments, $600 to $1,750 for features, on acceptance. Query with SASE and magazine clips. Guidelines.

**NEW JERSEY REPORTER**—The Center for Analysis of Public Issues, 16 Vandeventer Ave., Princeton, NJ 08542. Neil Upmeyer, Ed. Lee Seglem, Man. Ed. In-depth articles, 2,000 to 6,000 words, on New Jersey politics and public affairs. Pays $250 to $500, on publication. Query required.

**NEW MEXICO MAGAZINE**—Joseph M. Montoya Bldg., 1100 St. Francis Dr., Santa Fe, NM 87503. Address Ed. Articles, 250 to 2,000 words, on New Mexico subjects. No poetry or fiction. Pays about 25¢ a word, on acceptance.

**NEW ORLEANS MAGAZINE**—111 Veterans Blvd., Metairie, LA 70005. Errol Laborde, Ed. Articles, 3 to 15 triple-spaced pages, on New Orleans area people and issues. Photos. Pays $15 to $500, extra for photos, on publication. Query.

**NEW YORK**—755 Second Ave., New York, NY 10017. Edward Kosner, Ed. Laurie Jones, Man. Ed. Feature articles on subjects of interest to New Yorkers. Payment negotiated, made on acceptance. Query required.

**NEW YORK FAMILY**—141 Halstead Ave., Suite 30, Mamaroneck, NY 10543. Felice Shapiro, Susan Ross, Eds. Stephen Morison, Assoc. Ed. Articles related to family life in New York City. Pays $50 to $100, on publication. Same requirements for *Westchester Family*, for parents in Westchester County, NY. and *Connecticut Family*.

**NORTH DAKOTA HORIZONS**—P.O. Box 2467, Fargo, ND 58108. Sheldon Green, Ed. Quarterly. Articles, about 3,000 words, on the people, places, and events that affect life in North Dakota. Photos. Pays $75 to $300, on publication.

**NORTH GEORGIA JOURNAL**—65 Roswell St., Bldg. 400, Alpharetta, GA 30201. Olin Jackson, Pub./Ed. History, travel, and lifestyle features, 2,000 to 3,000 words, on North Georgia. History features need human-interest approach and must be written in first person; include interviews. Photos a plus. Pays $75 to $250, on acceptance. Query.

**NORTH TEXAS GOLFER**—9182 Old Katy Rd., Suite 212, Houston, TX 77055. Bob Gray, Ed. Articles, 800 to 1,500 words, involving local golfers or related directly to north Texas. Pays from $50 to $425, on publication. Query. Same requirements for *Gulf Coast Golfer* (related to south Texas).

**NORTHEAST MAGAZINE**—*The Hartford Courant*, 285 Broad St., Hartford, CT 06115. Lary Bloom, Ed. Articles and short essays, 750 to 3,000 words, that reflect the concerns of Connecticut residents. Pays $250 to $1,000, on acceptance.

**NORTHERN LIGHTS**—Box 8084, Missoula, MT 59807–8084. Address Editor. Thoughtful articles, 500 to 3,000 words, about the contemporary West. Occasional fiction. "We're open to virtually any subject as long as it deals with our region (the Rocky Mountains) in some way." Pays to 10¢ a word, on publication.

**NORTHWEST LIVING!**—130 Second Ave. S., Edmonds, WA 98020–3512. Terry W. Sheely, Ed. Lively, informative articles, 400 to 1,000 words, on the natural resources of the Northwest: homes, gardens, people, travel, history, etc. Color photos essential. Shorts, 100 to 400 words. Pays to $300, on publication. Query with SASE for guidelines.

**NORTHWEST PRIME TIMES**—10829 N.E. 68th St., Kirkland, WA 98033. Neil Strother, Pub./Ed. News and features aimed at 50 and up audience. Pays $25 to $50, on publication. Limited market.

**NORTHWEST REGIONAL MAGAZINES**—P.O. Box 18000, Florence, OR 97439–0130. Address Dave Peden or Judy Fleagle. All submissions considered for use in *Oregon Coast, Northwest Travel*, and *Northwest Parks & Wildlife*. Articles, 1,200 to 3,000 words, pertaining to the Pacific Northwest, on travel, history, town/ city profiles, and nature. News releases, 200 to 500 words. Articles with photos preferred. Pays $75 to $350, on publication. Guidelines.

**NORTHWEST TRAVEL**—See *Northwest Regional Magazines*.

**OH! IDAHO**—Peak Media, Box 925, Hailey, ID 83333–0925. Laurie Sammis, Ed. "Articulate, image-oriented" features, 1,500 to 2,000 words, on Idaho's residents, recreation, and other Idaho topics. Department pieces, 1,200 words, on a wide variety of subjects, including food and travel in Idaho. Pays from 10¢ a word, on publication. Query. Guidelines.

**OHIO MAGAZINE**—62 E. Broad St., Columbus, OH 43215. Ellen Stein Burbach, Ed. Profiles of people, cities, and towns of Ohio; pieces on historic sites, tourist attractions, little-known spots. Lengths and payment vary. Query.

**OKLAHOMA TODAY**—Box 53384, Oklahoma City, OK 73152–9971. Jeanne M. Devlin, Ed. Travel articles; profiles, history, nature and outdoor recreation, and arts articles. All material must have regional tie-in. Queries for 1,000- to 2,000-word articles preferred. Pays $75 to $750, on acceptance. SASE for guidelines.

**ORANGE COAST**—245-D Fischer Ave., Suite 8, Costa Mesa, CA 92626. Palmer Jones, Ed. Articles of interest to educated Orange County residents. Pieces, 1,000 to 1,500 words, for regular departments: "Escape" (local travel), "Access" (local services and products), "Selects" (local phenomena), "Guide" (local private schools, weight control centers, art galleries, etc.), and "Focus" (local personality profiles). Feature articles, 1,500 to 2,500 words: investigative, social issues, business trends, and other local topics. Query. Pays $250 for features, $100 for columns, on acceptance. Guidelines.

**OREGON COAST**—See *Northwest Regional Magazines*.

**ORLANDO MAGAZINE**—P.O. Box 2207, Orlando, FL 32802. Nancy Long, Michael Candelaria, Eds. Articles and profiles, 1,200 to 1,500 words, on business, lifestyle, home and garden. Photos a plus. Pays $350, on publication. Query required.

**OTTAWA MAGAZINE**—192 Bank St., Ottawa, Ont., Canada K2P 1W8. Marion Soubliere, Sr. Ed. Articles, investigative journalism, and profiles, 2,000 to 2,500 words, relating to the social issues and cultural and consumer interests of Ottawa City. Query with five or six article ideas, with resumé and published clips. Payment varies, on publication.

**PALM SPRINGS LIFE**—Desert Publications, 303 North Indian Canyon

Dr., P.O. Box 2724, Palm Springs, CA 92263. Jamie Lee Pricer, Ed. Articles, 1,000 to 2,000 words, of interest to "wealthy, upscale people who live and/or play in the desert": food, interior design, luxury cars, shopping, sports, homes, personalities, desert issues, arts, and culture. Pays $150 to $400 for features, $30 to $60 for short profiles, on publication. Query required.

**PARENTGUIDE NEWS**—475 Park Ave. S., New York, NY 10016. Leslie Elgort, Ed. Monthly. Articles, 750 to 1,500 words, related to New York families and parenting: trends, profiles, issues, special programs, special products. Payment varies, on publication.

**PENNSYLVANIA HERITAGE**—P.O. Box 1026, Harrisburg, PA 17108–1026. Michael J. O'Malley III, Ed. Quarterly of the Pennsylvania Historical Museum Commission. Articles, 3,000 to 4,000 words, on fine and decorative arts, architecture, archaeology, oral history, exhibits, industry and technology, travel, and folklore, written with an eye toward illustration. Photographic essays. Pieces should "introduce readers to the state's rich culture and historic legacy." Pays $300 to $500 for articles; up to $100 for photos and drawings, on acceptance.

**PENNSYLVANIA MAGAZINE**—Box 576, Camp Hill, PA 17011. Albert E. Holliday, Ed. General-interest features with a Pennsylvania flavor. All articles must be accompanied by illustrations or photos. Send photocopies of possible illustrations. Photos. SASE required. Guidelines.

**PERSIMMON HILL**—1700 N.E. 63rd St., Oklahoma City, OK 73111. M.J. Van Deventer, Ed. Published by the National Cowboy Hall of Fame. Articles, 1,500 to 3,000 words, on Western history and art, cowboys, ranching, and nature. Top-quality illustrations a must. Pays from $100 to $250, on publication.

**PHILADELPHIA**—1818 Market St., Philadelphia, PA 19103. Laurence Stains, Articles Ed. Articles, 1,000 to 5,000 words, for sophisticated audience, relating to Philadelphia area. No fiction or poetry. Pays on acceptance. Query.

**PHOENIX MAGAZINE**—4707 N. 12th St., Phoenix, AZ 85014. Richard Vonier, Ed. Articles, 1,000 to 3,000 words, on topics of interest to Phoenix-area residents. Pays $300 to $1,500, on publication. Queries preferred.

**PITTSBURGH**—4802 Fifth Ave., Pittsburgh, PA 15213. Bruce VanWyngarden, Ed. Articles, 850 to 3,000 words, with western Pennsylvania slant, two- to four-month lead time. Pays on publication.

**PORTLAND MONTHLY MAGAZINE**—578 Congress St., Portland, ME 04101. Colin Sargent, Ed. Articles on local people, fashion, culture, and trends. Fiction, to 750 words. Pays on publication. Query preferred.

**RECREATION NEWS**—P.O. Box 32335, Washington, DC 20007–0635. Sam E. Polson, Ed. Articles, 1,500 to 2,000 words, on recreation for government workers in the Washington, D.C. area. Light, first-person accounts, 800 words, for "Sporting Life" column. "Articles should have a conversational tone that's lean and brisk." Queries preferred. Pays $50 for reprints to $350 for cover articles, on publication. Send SASE for guidelines.

**RHODE ISLAND MONTHLY**—18 Imperial Pl., Providence, RI 02903. Vicki Sanders, Man. Ed. Features, 1,000 to 4,000 words, ranging from investigative reporting and in-depth profiles to service pieces and visual stories, on Rhode Island and southeastern Massachusetts. Seasonal material, 1,000 to 2,000 words. Fillers, 150 to 250 words, on places, customs, people, events, products and services, restaurants and food. Pays $250 to $1,000 for features; $25 to $50 for shorts, on publication. Query.

**ROCKFORD MAGAZINE**—331 E. State St., Box 678, Rockford, IL 61105. Eileen Townsend, Ed. General-interest magazine covering Rockford and northern Illinois. Feature articles, 2,500 to 3,500 words, and departments, 1,500 to 2,000 words, on city and area personalities, politics, events, business, family, travel destinations, home improvement and decor, dining, etc. "Nothing predictable or routine." Query with samples and clips. Pays from 5¢ a word, on acceptance.

**RUNNER TRIATHLETE NEWS**—P.O. Box 19909, Houston, TX 77224. Karissa G. Strong, Ed. Articles on running for road racing and multi-sport enthusiasts in Texas, Louisiana, and Arkansas. Published monthly. Payment varies, on publication.

**RURAL LIVING**—4201 Dominion Blvd., Suite 101, Glen Allen, VA 23060. Richard G. Johnstone, Jr., Ed. Features, 1,000 to 1,500 words, on people, places, historic sites in Virginia and Maryland's Eastern Shore. Queries preferred. Pays $100 to $150 for articles, on publication.

**RURALITE**—P.O. Box 558, Forest Grove, OR 97116. Address Ed. or Feature Ed. Articles, 800 to 2,000 words, of interest to a primarily rural and small-town audience in Oregon, Washington, Idaho, Nevada, northern California, and Alaska. "Think pieces" affecting rural/urban interests, regional history and celebrations, self-help, profiles, etc. No fiction or poetry. No sentimental nostalgia. Pays $30 to $400, on acceptance. Queries required. Guidelines.

**SACRAMENTO MAGAZINE**—P.O. Box 2424, Sacramento, CA 95811. Karen Coe, Man. Ed. Features, 2,500 words, on a broad range of topics related to the region. Department pieces, 1,200 to 1,500 words, and short pieces, 400 words, for "City Lights" column. Pays $150 to $300, on acceptance. Query first.

**SAN DIEGO MAGAZINE**—4206 W. Point Loma Blvd., P.O. Box 85409, San Diego, CA 92138. Virginia Butterfield, Assoc. Ed. Articles, 1,500 to 3,000 words, on local personalities, politics, lifestyles, business, history, etc., relating to San Diego area. Photos. Pays $250 to $600, on publication. Query with clips.

**SAN DIEGO READER**—P.O. Box 85803, San Diego, CA 92186. Jim Holman, Ed. Articles, 2,500 to 10,000 words, on the San Diego region. Literate nonfiction. Pays $500 to $2,000, on publication.

**SAN FRANCISCO FOCUS**—2601 Mariposa St., San Francisco, CA 94110–1400. Mark Powelson, Ed. Service features, profiles of local newsmakers, and investigative pieces of local issues, 2,500 to 3,000 words. Payment is negotiated, on acceptance. Query required.

**SEATTLE**—701 Dexter Ave. N., Suite 101, Seattle, WA 98109. Giselle Smith, Ed. City, home, and lifestyle articles, 500 to 2,000 words, relating directly to the greater Seattle area. Pays $100 to $800, on publication. Guidelines.

**SEATTLE HOME AND GARDEN**—See *Seattle*.

**SEATTLE'S CHILD**—Northwest Parent Publishing, 2107 Elliott Ave., #303, Seattle, WA 98121. Ann Bergman, Ed. Articles, 400 to 2,500 words, of interest to parents, educators, and childcare providers of children under 12, and investigative reports and consumer tips on issues affecting families in the Puget Sound region. Pays $75 to $400, on publication. Query required.

**SENIOR MAGAZINE**—3565 S. Higuera St., San Luis Obispo, CA 93401. Personality profiles and health articles, 600 to 900 words, and book reviews (of new books or outstanding older titles) of interest to senior citizens of California. Pays $1.50 per inch, $10 to $25 for B&W photos, on publication.

**SILENT SPORTS**—717 10th St., P.O. Box 152, Waupaca, WI 54981. Upper Midwest monthly with regional focus on bicycling, cross-country skiing, running, canoeing, hiking, backpacking, and other "silent" sports; articles, 1,000 to 2,000 words. Pays $40 to $100 for features; $20 to $50 for fillers, on publication. Query.

**SOUTH CAROLINA HISTORICAL MAGAZINE**—South Carolina Historical Society, 100 Meeting St., Charleston, SC 29401–2299. Stephen Hoffius, Ed. Scholarly articles, to 25 pages with footnotes, on all areas of South Carolina history. Payment is five copies.

**SOUTH CAROLINA WILDLIFE**—P.O. Box 167, Columbia, SC 29202–0167. Address Man. Ed. Articles, 1,000 to 3,000 words, with regional outdoors focus: conservation, natural history and wildlife, recreation. Profiles, natural history. Pays from 10¢ a word. Query.

**SOUTH FLORIDA MAGAZINE**—800 Douglas Rd., Suite 500, Coral Gables, FL 33134. Marilyn A. Moore, Ed. Features, 1,100 to 3,500 words, and department pieces, 900 to 1,300 words, on news, profiles, and hot topics related to south Florida. Short, bright items, 200 to 400 words. Pays $75 to $900, within 30 days of acceptance.

**SOUTHWEST ART**—Franklin Tower, 5444 Westheimer, Suite 1440, Houston, TX 77056. Susan McGarry, Ed. Articles, 1,800 to 2,200 words, on the artists, art collectors, museum exhibitions, gallery events and dealers, art history, and art trends west of the Mississippi River. Particularly interested in representational or figurative arts. Pays from $400, on acceptance. Query with slides of artwork to be featured.

**THE STATE: DOWN HOME IN NORTH CAROLINA**—128 S. Tryon St., Suite 2200, Charlotte, NC 28202. Angela Terez, Man. Ed. Articles, 750 to 2,000 words, on people, history, and places in North Carolina. Photos. Pays on publication.

**SUNDAY JOURNAL MAGAZINE**—*Providence Sunday Journal*, 75 Fountain St., Providence, RI 02902. Elliot Krieger, Ed. Nonfiction, 1,000 to 3,000 words, with a New England focus. Pays $100 to $500, on publication.

**SUNSET MAGAZINE**—80 Willow Rd., Menlo Park, CA 94025. William Marken, Ed. Western regional. Limited free-lance market.

**SUNSHINE: THE MAGAZINE OF SOUTH FLORIDA**—*The Sun-Sentinel*, 200 E. Las Olas Blvd., Ft. Lauderdale, FL 33301–2293. John Parkyn, Ed. Articles, 1,000 to 3,000 words, on topics of interest to south Floridians. Pays $250 to $1,000, on acceptance. Query first. Guidelines.

**TALLAHASSEE MAGAZINE**—P.O. Box 1837, Tallahassee, FL 32302–1837. Dave Fiore, Ed. Articles, 800 to 1,500 words, with a positive outlook on the life, people, and history of the north Florida area. Pays on acceptance. Query.

**TAMPA BAY LIFE: THE BAY AREA'S MAGAZINE**—6200 Courtney Campbell Causeway, Suite 580, Tampa, FL 33607–1458. Larry Marscheck, Ed. Dir. Articles, 850 to 3,000 words, on the people, events, and issues shaping the Tampa Bay region's future. Pays $125 to $300 for department pieces; $400 to $600 for features, on publication. Guidelines.

**TEXAS HIGHWAYS MAGAZINE**—Texas Dept. of Transportation, P.O. Box 141009, Austin, TX 78714–1009. Tommie Pinkard, Ed. Texas travel, history, and scenic features, 200 to 1,800 words. Pays 40¢ to 50¢ a word, $80 to $500 per photo, on acceptance. Query. Guidelines for writers and photographers.

**TEXAS MONTHLY**—P.O. Box 1569, Austin, TX 78767–1569. Gregory Curtis, Ed. Features, 2,500 to 5,000 words, and departments, to 2,500 words, on art, architecture, food, education, business, politics, etc. "We like solidly researched pieces that uncover issues of public concern, reveal offbeat and previously unreported topics, or use a novel approach to familiar topics." Pays varying rates, on acceptance. Queries required.

**TIMELINE**—1982 Velma Ave., Columbus, OH 43211–2497. Christopher S. Duckworth, Ed. Articles, 1,000 to 6,000 words, on history of Ohio (politics, economics, social, and natural history) for lay readers in the Midwest. Pays $100 to $900, on acceptance. Queries preferred.

**TROPIC**—*The Miami Herald*, One Herald Plaza, Miami, FL 33132. Tom Shroder, Exec. Ed. General-interest articles, 750 to 3,000 words, for south Florida readers. Pays $200 to $1,000, on acceptance. Send SASE.

**TUCSON LIFESTYLE**—Old Pueblo Press, 7000 E. Tanque Verde, Tucson, AZ 85715. Sue Giles, Ed.-in-Chief. Features on local businesses, lifestyles, the arts, homes, fashion, and travel in the Southwest. Payment varies, on acceptance. Query preferred.

**VALLEY MAGAZINE**—16800 Devonshire, Suite 275, Granada Hills, CA 91344. Barbara Wernik, Ed. Articles, 1,000 to 1,500 words, on celebrities, issues, education, health, business, dining, and entertaining, etc., in the San Fernando Valley. Pays $100 to $350, within eight weeks of acceptance.

**VENTURA COUNTY & COAST REPORTER**—1583 Spinnaker Dr., Suite 213, Ventura, CA 93001. Nancy Cloutier, Ed. Articles, 3 to 5 pages, on any locally slanted topic. Pays $10, on publication.

**VERMONT LIFE**—61 Elm St., Montpelier, VT 05602. Tom Slayton, Ed.-in-Chief. Articles, 500 to 3,000 words, on Vermont subjects only. Pays 20¢ a word, extra for photos. Query preferred.

**VIRGINIA BUSINESS**—411 E. Franklin St., Suite 105, Richmond, VA 23219. James Bacon, Ed. Articles, 1,000 to 2,500 words, related to the business scene in Virginia. Pays varying rates, on acceptance. Query required.

**VIRGINIA SOUTHWEST**—P.O. Box 4244, Roanoke, VA 24015. Attn: J. Johnson. "Written for and about people, places, events, and activities in, around, and affecting southwestern Virginia." Features, 2,000 to 2,500 words; articles, 1,200 to 1,800 words; humor, folklore, and legend, to 2,000 words; fiction, 1,000 to 1,500 words, with regional setting or reference; related poetry, to 32 lines. Department pieces, 500 to 700 words. Photos. Pays to $600, on bimonthly publication or within 6 months, whichever comes first.

**VIRGINIA WILDLIFE**—P.O. Box 11104, Richmond, VA 23230–1104. Monthly publication of the Commission of Game and Inland Fisheries. Articles, 1,500 to 2,500 words, with Virginia tie-in, on conservation and related topics, including fishing, hunting, wildlife management, outdoor safety and ethics, etc. Articles must be accompanied by color photos. Query with SASE. Pays 10¢ a word, extra for photos, on publication.

**WASHINGTON POST MAGAZINE**—*The Washington Post*, 1150 15th St. N.W., Washington, DC 20071. Linton Weeks, Man. Ed. Personal-experience essays, profiles, and general-interest pieces, to 6,000 words, on business, arts and culture, politics, science, sports, education, children, relationships, behavior, etc. Articles should be of interest to people living in Washington, D.C. area. Pays from $100, on acceptance. Limited market.

**THE WASHINGTONIAN**—1828 L St. N.W., Suite 200, Washington, DC 20036. John Limpert, Ed. Helpful, informative articles, 1,000 to 4,000 words, on DC-related topics. Pays 50¢ a word.

**WE ALASKANS MAGAZINE**—Anchorage Daily News, Box 149001, Anchorage, AK 99514–9001. George Bryson, Ed. Articles, 500 to 1,000 words, and features, 3,000 to 4,000 words, on Alaska topics only. Profiles, narratives, fiction, and humor. Pays $50 to $150 for short articles, $300 to $600 for features, on publication.

**THE WEEKLY, SEATTLE'S NEWS MAGAZINE**—1931 Second Ave., Seattle, WA 98101. David Brewster, Ed. Articles, 700 to 4,000 words, with a Northwest perspective. Pays $75 to $800, on publication. Query. Guidelines.

**WESTCHESTER FAMILY**—See *New York Family*.

**WESTERN SPORTSMAN**—P.O. Box 737, Regina, Sask., Canada S4P 3A8. Roger Francis, Ed. Informative articles, to 2,500 words, on hunting, fishing, and outdoor experiences in Alberta, Saskatchewan, and Manitoba. How-tos, humor, cartoons. Photos. Pays $75 to $400, on publication.

**WESTWAYS**—2601 S. Figueroa St., Los Angeles, CA 90007. Eric Seyfarth, Man. Ed. Articles, 1,000 to 2,000 words, and photo essays, on California, western U.S., Canada, and Mexico: history, contemporary living, travel, personalities, etc. Photos. Pays from 25¢ a word, extra for photos, 30 days before publication. Query.

**WINDY CITY SPORTS**—1450 W. Randolph, Chicago, IL 60607. Mary Thorne, Pub./Ed. Articles, to 1,500 words, on amateur sports in the Chicago area. Queries required. Pays $100, on publication.

**WISCONSIN**—*The Milwaukee Journal Magazine*, Journal/Sentinel, Inc., Box 661, Milwaukee, WI 53201. Alan Borsuk, Ed. Articles, 500 to 2,500 words, on business, politics, arts, environment, and social issues with strong Wisconsin emphasis. Personal-experience essays, profiles and investigative articles. Pays $75 to $600, on publication. Query.

**WISCONSIN TRAILS**—P.O. Box 5650, Madison, WI 53705. Patricia H. McKeown, Assoc. Ed. Articles, 1,500 to 3,000 words, on regional topics: outdoors, lifestyle, events, history, arts, adventure, travel; profiles of artists, craftspeople, and regional personalities. Fillers. Pays $150 to $500, on acceptance and on publication. Query with SASE.

**WISCONSIN WEST MAGAZINE**—2645 Harlem St., Eau Claire, WI 54703. Articles on current issues for residents of western Wisconsin; profiles of restaurants, weekend leisure activities and getaways, and famous people of western Wisconsin; and historical pieces. Short humor. Payment varies, on publication.

**YANKEE**—Yankee Publishing Co., Dublin, NH 03444. Judson D. Hale, Ed. Articles and fiction, about 2,500 words, on New England and residents. Pays about $800 for features, on acceptance.

**YANKEE MAGAZINE'S TRAVEL GUIDE TO NEW ENGLAND**—Main St., Dublin, NH 03444. Janice Brand, Ed. Articles, 500 to 2,000 words, on activities, attractions, places to visit in New England. Photos. Pays on acceptance. Query with outline and writing samples required.

## TRAVEL ARTICLES

**AAA WORLD**—1000 AAA Dr., Heathrow, FL 32746–5063. Douglas Damerst, Ed. Articles, 600 to 1,500 words, on consumer automotive and travel concerns. Pays $200 to $800, on acceptance. Query with writing samples required. Articles by assignment only.

**ACCENT/TRAVELOG**—Box 10010, Ogden, UT 84409. Caroll Shreeve, V.P./Pub. Articles, 1,200 words, on travel destinations, ways to travel, and travel tips. Pays 15¢ a word, $35 for color photos, on acceptance. Query first.

**ADVENTURE ROAD**—M & A Publishing, 122 E. 25th St., New York, NY 10010. Marilyn Holstein, Ed. Official publication of the Amoco Motor Club. Articles, 1,500 words, on destinations in North America, Mexico, and the Caribbean. Photos. Pays $500 to $1,000, on acceptance. Query required.

**AIRFARE: THE MAGAZINE FOR AIRLINE EMPLOYEES**—6401 Congress #100, Boca Raton, FL 33487. Roland Little, Ed. Travel articles, 2,000 words, with photos, on shopping, sightseeing, dining, and nightlife for airline employees. Prices, discount information, and addresses must be included. Pays $250, after publication.

**ARIZONA HIGHWAYS**—2039 W. Lewis Ave., Phoenix, AZ 85009. Richard G. Stahl, Man. Ed. Informal, well-researched travel articles, 2,000 to 2,500 words, focusing on a specific city or region in Arizona and environs. Also articles dealing with nature, environment, flora and fauna, history, anthropology, archaeology, hiking, boating, industry. Departments for personal-experience pieces include "Milestones," "Focus on Nature," "Along the Way," "Event of the Month," "Outdoor Recreation," Back Road Adventures," "Legends of the Lost," "Hiking," and "Arizona Humor." Pays 30¢ to 45¢ a word, on acceptance. Query with published clips. Guidelines.

**ASIA PACIFIC TRAVEL**—(formerly *Pacific Travel*) 1540 Gilbreth Rd., Burlingame, CA 94010. Kumar Pati, Pub. Articles, 4 to 6 pages, about travel, tourism, entertainment, fashion, culture, and business in Asia and the Pacific Rim countries. Departments include: news in brief, business opportunities, vacation information, etc. Profiles of hotels and restaurants, tourist information, and transportation. "Articles should be written in first person, about personal experience. Submit 8 photos, of which we'll publish about 4." Payment varies, on publication. Guidelines.

**BAJA EXPLORER**—4180 La Jolla Village Dr., La Jolla, CA 92037. Landon S. Crumpton, Ed.-in-Chief. Bimonthly. Articles, 800 to 1,200 words, on fishing, sailing, surfing, windsurfing, camping, natural history, and cultural events, of interest to tourists visiting Baja California. Pays 25¢ a word, $50 per slide, on publication.

**BLUE RIDGE COUNTRY**—P.O. Box 21535, Roanoke, VA 24018. Kurt Rheinheimer, Ed. Regional travel articles, 750 to 1,200 words, on destinations in the mountain regions of Virginia, North Carolina, West Virginia, Tennessee, Kentucky, Maryland, South Carolina, and Georgia. Color slides and B&W prints considered. Pays to $200 for photo-features, on publication. Queries preferred.

**BRITISH HERITAGE**—P.O. Box 8200, Harrisburg, PA 17105–8200. Gail Huganir, Ed. Travel articles on places to visit in the British Isles, 800 to 1,500 words. Include detailed historical information with a "For the Visitor" sidebar. Pays $100 to $200, on acceptance.

**CALIFORNIA HIGHWAY PATROLMAN**—2030 V St., Sacramento, CA 95818–1730. Carol Perri, Ed. Travel articles, to 2,000 words, focusing on places in

California and the West Coast. "We prefer out-of-the-way stops with California Highway Patrol tie-in instead of regular tourist destinations." Query or send completed manuscript with photos. SASE required. Pays 2 ½¢ a word, $5 for B&W photos, on publication.

**CANADIAN**—111 Avenue Rd., Suite 801, Toronto, Ontario, Canada M5R 3J8. Grant N. R. Geall, Pres./Pub. Inflight magazine of Canadian Airlines International. Travel pieces, 1,000 to 1,500 words. Payment varies, on acceptance. Query.

**CARIBBEAN TRAVEL AND LIFE**—8403 Colesville Rd., Suite 830, Silver Spring, MD 20910. Veronica Gould Stoddart, Ed. Lively, informative articles, 500 to 2,500 words, on all aspects of travel, leisure, recreation, and culture in the Caribbean, Bahamas, and Bermuda, for upscale, sophisticated readers. Photos. Pays $75 to $550, on publication. Query.

**CHILE PEPPER**—P.O. Box 4278, Albuquerque, NM 87196. Melissa Jackson, Ed. First-person food and travel articles, 1,000 to 1,500 words, about spicy world cuisine. Queries required. Payment varies, on publication.

**COLORADO HOMES & LIFESTYLES**—7009 S. Potomac, Englewood, CO 80112. Anne McGregor Parsons, Ed. Travel articles, 1,200 to 1,500 words, on cities, regions, establishments in Colorado; roundups and travel pieces with unusual angles, 1,000 to 1,500 words. Pays $150, on acceptance. Query.

**CRUISE TRAVEL**—990 Grove St., Evanston, IL 60201. Robert Meyers, Ed. Charles Doherty, Man. Ed. Ship-, port-, and cruise-of-the-month features, 800 to 2,000 words; cruise guides; cruise roundups; cruise company profiles; travel suggestions for one-day port stops. Payment varies, on acceptance. Query with sample color photos.

**EARLY AMERICAN LIFE**—Box 8200, Harrisburg, PA 17105–8200. Frances Carnahan, Ed. Travel features about historic sites and country inns, 1,000 to 3,000 words. Pays $100 to $600, on acceptance. Query.

**ENDLESS VACATION**—Box 80260, Indianapolis, IN 46280. Helen W. O'Guinn, Ed. Travel features, to 1,500 words; international scope. Pays on acceptance. Query preferred. Send SASE for guidelines. Limited market.

**FAMILY CIRCLE**—110 Fifth Ave., New York, NY 10011. Sylvia Barsotti, Sr. Ed. Travel articles, to 1,500 words. Concept travel pieces should appeal to a national audience and focus on affordable activities for families; prefer service-filled, theme-oriented travel pieces or first-person family vacation stories. Pay rates vary, on acceptance. Query first.

**FRIENDLY EXCHANGE**—Locust at 17th, Des Moines, IA 50336. Adele Malott, Ed. Articles, 1,000 to 1,500 words, of interest to active midwestern and western families, on travel and leisure. Photos. Pays $300 to $800, extra for photos. Query preferred. Send SASE for guidelines.

**GREAT EXPEDITIONS**—Box 18036, Raleigh, NC 27609. George Kane, Ed. Articles, 700 to 2,500 words, on independent, adventurous, budget-conscious travel and unusual destinations. Pays $30 to $80, on publication. Guidelines.

**GULFSHORE LIFE**—Collier Park of Commerce, 2975 S. Horseshoe Dr., Naples, FL 33942. Janis Lyn Johnson, Ed. Florida travel articles focusing on the unusual and unique, 500 to 2,000 words. Don't want "typical" Sunshine-State destinations. Pay negotiable, on publication. Queries required.

**INDIA CURRENTS**—P.O. Box 21285, San Jose, CA 95151. Arvind Kumar, Submissions Ed. First-person accounts, 800 words, of trips to India or the subcontinent. Helpful tips for first-time travelers. Prefer descriptions of people-to-people interactions. Pays $20 to $25 per 1,000 words, on publication.

**INTERNATIONAL LIVING**—824 E. Baltimore St., Baltimore, MD 21202. Kathleen Peddicord, Ed. Newsletter. Short pieces and features, 200 to 2,000 words, with useful information on investing, shopping, travel, employment, education, real estate, and lifestyles overseas. Pays $100 to $400, after publication.

**ISLANDS**—3886 State St., Santa Barbara, CA 93105. Destination features, 1,000 to 3,000 words, on islands around the world as well as department pieces and front-of-the-book items on island-related topics. Pays about 50¢ a word, on publication. Query required. Guidelines.

**LIFE IN THE TIMES**—Army Times Publishing Co., Springfield, VA 22159–0200. Margaret Roth, Ed. Travel articles, 750 to 900 words, narrowly focused. "Rather than an article on New York City, we'd prefer one on some particular aspect of the trip." Also short, personal-experience pieces, 750 words, of interest to military people and their families around the world. Special interest supplements cover careers after the military, books, home entertainment, finance, fitness and health, and education. Pays $125 for travel articles; $100 to $150 for short pieces; to $350 for 2,000-word features on aspects of military life, on acceptance.

**MICHIGAN LIVING**—Automobile Club of Michigan, 1 Auto Club Dr., Dearborn, MI 48126. Len Barnes, Ed. Informative travel articles, 500 to 1,500 words, on U.S. and Canadian tourist attractions and recreational opportunities; special interest in Michigan.

**THE MIDWEST MOTORIST**—12901 N. Forty Dr., St. Louis, MO 63141. Michael Right, Ed. Articles 1,000 to 1,500 words, with color slides, on domestic and foreign travel. Pays from $150, on acceptance.

**NATIONAL GEOGRAPHIC**—17th and M Sts. N.W., Washington, DC 20036. William P.E. Graves, Ed. First-person articles on geography, exploration, natural history, archaeology, and science. Half staff-written; half written by recognized authorities and published authors. Does not consider unsolicited manuscripts.

**NATIONAL MOTORIST**—Bayside Plaza, 188 The Embarcadero, San Francisco, CA 94105. Jane Offers, Ed. Illustrated articles, 500 to 1,100 words, for California motorists, on motoring in the West, car care, roads, personalities, places, etc. Color slides. Pays from 10¢ a word, on acceptance. Pays for photos on publication. SASE required.

**NEW WOMAN**—215 Lexington Ave., New York, NY 10016. Karen Walden, Ed.-in-Chief. Armchair travel pieces; women's personal-experience and "what I learned from this experience" pieces, 1,000 to 2,000 words. Pays $500 to $2,000, on acceptance. Query required.

**NEW YORK DAILY NEWS**—220 E. 42nd St., New York, NY 10017. Gunna Bitee Dickson, Travel Ed. Articles, 500 to 700 words, on all manner of travel. Price information must be included. B&W or color photos. Pays $100 to $200, extra for photos, on publication.

**THE NEW YORK TIMES**—229 W. 43rd St., New York, NY 10036. Nancy Newhouse, Travel Ed. Considers queries only; include writer's background, description of proposed article. No unsolicited manuscripts or photos. Pays on acceptance.

**NORTHWEST LIVING!**—130 Second Ave. S., Edmonds, WA 98020–3512. Terry W. Sheely, Ed. Articles, 400 to 1,500 words, on regional travel and natural resources. Color slides or B&W prints. Query with SASE required. Payment varies, on publication.

**NORTHWEST PARKS & WILDLIFE**—See *Northwest Regional Magazines.*

**NORTHWEST REGIONAL MAGAZINES**—P.O. Box 18000, Florence, OR 97439. Address Dave Peden or Judy Fleagle. All submissions considered for use in *Oregon Coast, Northwest Travel,* and *Northwest Parks & Wildlife.* Articles, 1,200 to 2,000 words, on travel, history, town/city profiles, and nature. News releases, 200 to 500 words. Articles with photos or slides preferred. Pays $75 to $300, on publication. Send SASE for guidelines.

**NORTHWEST TRAVEL**—See *Northwest Regional Magazines.*

**OREGON COAST**—See *Northwest Regional Magazines.*

**PACIFIC TRAVEL**—See *Asia Pacific Travel.*

**RV TIMES MAGAZINE**—Royal Productions, Inc., Box 6294, Richmond, VA 23230. Alice P. Supple, Ed. Articles and fiction, 500 to 2,000 words, related to outdoor or leisure activities, travel attractions in the Maryland, Virginia, New Jersey, New York, Delaware, and Pennsylvania areas. Pays 7¢ a word (to $90), on publication.

**SACRAMENTO MAGAZINE**—P.O. Box 2424, Sacramento, CA 95812–2424. Jan Haag, Ed. Articles, 1,000 to 1,500 words, on destinations within a six-hour drive of Sacramento. Pay varies, on acceptance. Query.

**SPECIALTY TRAVEL INDEX**—305 San Anselmo Ave., #313, San Anselmo, CA 94960. C. Steen Hansen, Co-Publisher/Ed. Semiannual directory of adventure vacation tour companies, destinations, and vacation packages. Articles, 1,000 to 2,000 words, with how-to travel information, humor, and opinion. Pays 20¢ per word, on publication. Slides and photos considered. Queries preferred.

**TEXAS HIGHWAYS MAGAZINE**—Texas Dept. of Transportation, P.O. Box 141009, Austin, TX 78714–1009. Tommie Pinkard, Ed. Travel, historical, cultural, scenic features on Texas, 200 to 1,800 words. Pays 40¢ to 50¢, on acceptance; photos $80 to $500. Guidelines.

**TOURS & RESORTS**—World Publishing Co., 990 Grove St., Evanston, IL 60201–4370. Randy Mink, Man. Ed. Robert Meyers, Ed. Features on U.S. and international vacation destinations and resorts, 1,000 to 1,500 words; also essays, nostalgia, humor, tour company profiles, travel tips, and service articles, 800 to 1,500 words. Pays up to $350, on acceptance. Top-quality color slides a must. Query.

**TRANSITIONS ABROAD**—18 Hulst Rd., Box 344, Amherst, MA 01004. Dr. Clayton A. Hubbs, Ed. Articles for overseas travelers who seek an in-depth experience of the culture: work, study, travel, budget tips. Include practical, first-hand information. Emphasis on establishing meaningful contact with people and socially responsible, ecology-minded travel. "Eager to work with inexperienced writers who travel to learn and want to share information." B&W photos a plus. Pays $1.50 per column inch, after publication. Query preferred. Guidelines.

**TRAVEL & LEISURE**—1120 Ave. of the Americas, New York, NY 10036. Ila Stanger, Ed.-in-Chief. Articles, 800 to 3,000 words, on destinations and travel-related activities. Regional pieces for regional editions. Short pieces for "The Last Word" and "Taking Off." Pays on acceptance: $2,000 to $3,000 for features; $500 to $1,200 for regionals; $50 to $300 for short pieces. Query; articles on assignment.

**TRAVEL SMART**—Dobbs Ferry, NY 10522. Short pieces, 250 to 1,000 words, about interesting, unusual and/or economical places. Give specific details on hotels, restaurants, transportation, and costs. Pays on publication. Query first.

**VISTA/USA**—Box 161, Convent Station, NJ 07961. Matha J. Mendez, Ed. Travel articles, 1,200 to 2,000 words, on U.S., Canada, Mexico, and the Caribbean. Also, general-interest topics, hobby/collecting, culture, and Americana. "Flavor of the area, not service oriented." Shorts, 500 to 1,000 words, on "Minitrips," "CloseFocus," "American Vignettes." Pays from $500 for features, from $150 for shorts, on acceptance. Query with writing sample and outline. Limited market.

**VOLKSWAGEN WORLD**—Volkswagen of America, Inc., Mail Code 3C03, 3800 Hamlin Rd., Auburn Hills, MI 48326. Marlene Goldsmith, Ed. Travel articles on unique places or with a unique angle, to 750 words. Pays $300, on acceptance. Query.

**WESTWAYS**—2601 S. Figueroa St., Los Angeles, CA 90007. Eric Seyfarth, Man. Ed. Travel articles on where to go, what to see, and how to get there, 1,300 to 2,000 words. Domestic travel articles are limited to western U.S., and Hawaii; foreign travel articles are also of interest. Quality color transparencies should be available. Pays 25¢ a word, 30 days before publication.

**YANKEE MAGAZINE'S TRAVEL GUIDE TO NEW ENGLAND**—Main St., Dublin, NH 03444. Janice Brand, Ed. Articles, 500 to 2,000 words, on destinations in New England. Photos. Pays on acceptance. Query with outline and writing samples.

## INFLIGHT MAGAZINES

**ABOARD**—North-South Net, Inc., 100 Almeria Ave., Suite 220, Coral Gables, FL 33134. Pedro Gonzalez, Ed. Inflight magazine of eight Latin American international airlines in Chile, Dominican Republic, Ecuador, Guatemala, El Salvador, Bolivia, Nicaragua, Honduras, Peru, and Paraguay. Articles, 1,200 to 1,500 words, with photos, on science, sports, home, fashion, and gastronomy. No political stories. Pays $150, with photos, on acceptance and on publication. Query required.

**ALASKA AIRLINES MAGAZINE**—2701 First Ave., Suite 250, Seattle, WA 98121. Paul Frichtl, Ed. Articles, 800 to 2,500 words, on lifestyle topics, business, travel, and profiles of regional personalities for West Coast business travelers. Query. Payment varies, on publication.

**AMERICA WEST AIRLINES MAGAZINE**—Skyword Marketing, Inc., 7500 N. Dreamy Draw Dr., Suite 240, Phoenix, AZ 85020. Michael Derr, Ed. Articles celebrating creativity, 500 to 2,000 words; regional angle helpful. Pays from $250, on acceptance. Query with clips required. Guidelines.

**CANADIAN**—111 Avenue Rd., Suite 807, Toronto, Ontario, Canada M5R 3J8. Grant N. R. Geall, Pres./Pub. Articles, 1,000 to 1,500 words, on travel and business for Canadian Airlines International travelers. Payment varies, on acceptance. Query.

**SKY**—12955 Biscayne Blvd., North Miami, FL 33181. Lidia de Leon, Ed. Delta Air Lines' inflight magazine. Articles on business, lifestyle, high tech, sports, the arts, etc. Color slides. Pays varying rates, on acceptance. Query with SASE. Guidelines.

**USAIR MAGAZINE**—1301 Carolina St., Greensboro, NC 27401. Terri Barnes, Ed. Articles, 1,500 to 2,500 words, on travel, business, sports, entertainment, food, health, and other general-interest topics. No downbeat or extremely controversial subjects. Pays $350 to $800, before publication. Query first.

**VIS A VIS**—Pace Communications, 1301 Carolina St., Greensboro, NC 27401. Mary Ellis, Acting Ed. First-person articles, 600 to 700 words, on profiles, resorts, and luxury vacations. Pays varying rates, on acceptance. No photos. Queries required. Guidelines.

## WOMEN'S PUBLICATIONS

**BBW: BIG BEAUTIFUL WOMAN**—9171 Wilshire Blvd., Suite 300, Beverly Hills, CA 90210. Carole Shaw, Ed.-in-Chief. Articles, 1,500 words, of interest to women ages 25 to 50, especially large-size women, including interviews with successful large-size women and personal accounts of how to cope with difficult situations. Tips on restaurants, airlines, stores, etc., that treat large women with respect. Payment varies, on publication. Query.

**BLACK ELEGANCE**—475 Park Ave. S., New York, NY 10016. Sharyn J. Skeeter, Ed. Articles, 1,000 to 2,000 words, on fashion, beauty, relationships, home design, careers, personal finance, and personalities, for black women ages 25 to 45. Short interviews. Include photos if available. Pays $150 to $225, on publication. Query. Guidelines.

**BRIDAL GUIDE**—Globe Communications Corp., 441 Lexington Ave., New York, NY 10017. Deborah Harding, Ed. Susan Sulich, Articles Ed. Bimonthly. Articles, 900 to 1,900 words, covering wedding planning, fashion, beauty, contemporary relationships, honeymoon travel, and plans for the first home. Regular departments include: finance, sex, remarriage, and advice for the groom. Prefers queries for articles. Pays $350 to $650, on acceptance.

**BRIDE'S & YOUR HOME**—(formerly *Bride's Magazine*) 350 Madison Ave., New York, NY 10017. Andrea Feld, Man. Ed. Articles, 800 to 3,000 words, for engaged couples or newlyweds, on communication, sex, housing, redecorating, finances, careers, remarriage, step-parenting, health, birth control, pregnancy, babies, religion, in-laws, relationships, and wedding planning. Three major editorial subjects: home, wedding, and honeymoon travel. Pays $300 to $1,000, on acceptance.

**CHATELAINE**—Maclean Hunter Bldg., 777 Bay St., Toronto, Ont., Canada M5W 1A7. Elizabeth Parr, Sr. Ed. Articles, 2,500 words, on current issues and personalities of interest to Canadian women. Pays from $1,200 for 1,500 to 3,000 words; from $350 for 500-word "Up-front" columns (relationships, health, parents/kids), on acceptance. Send query with international reply coupon and outline or manuscript.

**COMPLETE WOMAN**—1165 N. Clark, Chicago, IL 60610. Susan Handy, Man. Ed. Articles, 1,500 to 2,000 words, with how-to sidebars, giving practical advice to women on careers, health, personal relationships, etc. Also interested in reprints. Pays varying rates, on publication. Send manuscript or query with SASE.

**COSMOPOLITAN**—224 W. 57th St., New York, NY 10019. Helen Gurley Brown, Ed. Betty Nichols Kelly, Fiction and Books Ed. Articles, to 3,000 words, and features, 500 to 2,000 words, on issues affecting young career women, with emphasis on jobs and personal life. Fiction on male-female relationships: short shorts, 1,500 to 3,000 words; short stories, 3,000 to 4,000 words; condensed published novels, 25,000 words. SASE required.

**COUNTRY WOMAN**—P.O. Box 643, Milwaukee, WI 53201. Kathy Pohl, Man. Ed. Profiles of country women (photo/feature packages), inspirational, reflective pieces. Personal-experience, nostalgia, humor, service-oriented articles, original crafts, and how-to features, to 1,000 words, of interest to country women. Pays $40 to $150, on acceptance.

**ELLE**—1633 Broadway, New York, NY 10019. Ruth La Ferla, Exec. Ed. Articles, varying lengths, for fashion-conscious women, ages 20 to 50. Subjects include beauty, health, fitness, travel, entertainment, and lifestyles. Pays top rates, on publication. Query required.

**ESSENCE**—1500 Broadway, New York, NY 10036. Stephanie Stokes Oliver, Ed. Provocative articles, 800 to 2,500 words, about black women in America today: self-help, how-to pieces, business and finance, health, celebrity profiles, art, travel, and political issues. Short items, 500 to 750 words, on work, parenting, and health. Features and fiction, 800 to 2,500 words. Pays varying rates, on acceptance. Query for articles.

**EXECUTIVE FEMALE**—127 W. 24th St., New York, NY 10011. Basia Hellwig, Ed.-in-Chief. Articles, 750 to 2,500 words, on managing people, time, money, and careers, for women in business. Pays varying rates, on acceptance. Query.

**FAMILY CIRCLE**—110 Fifth Ave., New York, NY 10011. Susan Ungaro, Deputy Ed. Articles, to 2,000 words, on "women who have made a difference," marriage, family, and child-care and elder-care issues; consumer affairs, psychology, humor, health, nutrition, and fitness. Query required. Pays top rates, on acceptance.

**FIRST FOR WOMEN**—P.O. Box 1649, Englewood Cliffs, NJ 07632. Dennis Neeld, Ed. Mainstream stories, 2,000 words, reflecting the concerns of contemporary women; no formula or experimental fiction. "A humorous twist is welcome in fiction." Pay varies, on acceptance. Query first for articles. Send manuscript for fiction. Allow 8 to 12 weeks for response. SASE required.

**GLAMOUR**—350 Madison Ave., New York, NY 10017. Ruth Whitney, Ed.-in-Chief. Barbara Coffey, Man. Ed. How-to articles, from 1,500 words, on careers, health, psychology, interpersonal relationships, etc., for women ages 18 to 35. Fashion and beauty pieces staff written. Submit queries to Lisa Bain, Articles Ed. Pays from $500, on acceptance.

**GOOD HOUSEKEEPING**—959 Eighth Ave., New York, NY 10019. Joan Thursh, Articles Ed. Lee Quarfoot, Fiction Ed. In-depth articles and features on controversial problems, topical social issues; dramatic personal narratives of unusual experiences of average families; new or unusual medical information, personal medical stories. No submissions on food, beauty, needlework, or crafts. Short stories, 2,000 to 5,000 words, with strong identification for women, by published writers and "beginners with demonstrable talent." Unsolicited fiction not returned; if no response in 6 weeks, assume work was unsuitable. Include SASE with nonfiction submissions. Pays top rates, on acceptance.

**IDEALS**—P.O. Box 140300, Nashville, TN 37214–0300. Dorothy Morley, Ed. Articles, 600 to 800 words; poetry, 12 to 50 lines. Light, nostalgic pieces. Payment varies. Guidelines.

**LADIES' HOME JOURNAL**—100 Park Ave., New York, NY 10017. Myrna Blyth, Pub. Dir./Ed.-in-Chief. Articles of interest to women. Send queries with outlines to: Lynn Langway, Exec. Ed. (news/general interest); Jane Farrell, Articles Ed. (news/human interest); Nadia Zonis (health/medical); Jill Rachlin (celebrity/entertainment); Pamela Guthrie O'Brien (psychology); Lois Johnson (beauty/fashion/fitness); Jan Hazard (food); Shana Aborn (personal experience); Mary Mohler, Man. Ed. (children and families). Fiction accepted through literary agents only. Humorous poetry accepted for "Last Laughs" column. Brief, true anecdotes about the amusing things children say, for "Kidspeak"; anecdotes will not be returned. True, first-person accounts, 1,000 words, "about the most intimate aspects of our lives" for "Woman to Woman": Submit typed, double-spaced manuscript with SASE to Box WW, c/o address above; pays $750. Guidelines.

**LADY'S CIRCLE**—152 Madison Ave., Suite 906, New York, NY 10016. Mary F. Bemis, Ed. How-to, food, and crafts articles for homemakers. Short fiction. "Upbeat" pieces for over-50 audience. Pays $125 for articles, $10 for pet peeves, $5 for recipes or helpful hints, on publication.

**LEAR'S**—655 Madison Ave., New York, NY 10021. "Literate, lively, and compelling" articles, 800 to 1,200 words, for women, on health, finance, contemporary issues, personalities, and leisure. Query with clips and SASE.

**MCCALL'S**—110 Fifth Ave., New York, NY 10011. Andrea Thompson, Articles Ed. Articles, 1,000 to 3,000 words, on current issues, human interest, family relationships. Pays top rates, on acceptance.

**MADEMOISELLE**—350 Madison Ave., New York, NY 10017. Liz Logan, Articles Ed. Articles, 1,500 to 2,500 words, on work, relationships, health, and trends of interest to single, working women in their mid-twenties. Reporting pieces, essays, first-person accounts, and humor. No how-to or fiction. Submit query with clips and SASE. Pays excellent rates, on acceptance. SASE required.

**MODERN BRIDE**—249 W. 17th St., New York, NY 10011. Mary Ann Cavlin, Man. Ed. Articles, 1,800 to 2,000 words, for bride and groom, on wedding planning, financial planning, juggling career and home, etc. Query Travel Editor Geri Bain with articles on honeymoon travel. Pays $600 to $1,200, on acceptance.

**MS.: THE WORLD OF WOMEN**—230 Park Ave., 7th Fl., New York, NY 10169. Address Manuscript Editor with SASE. Articles relating to feminism, women's roles, and social change; national and international news reporting, profiles, essays, theory, and analysis. Query with resumé, published clips, and SASE required. No fiction or poetry accepted, acknowledged, or returned.

**NA'AMAT WOMAN**—200 Madison Ave., Suite 2120, New York, NY 10016. Judith A. Sokoloff, Ed. Articles on Jewish culture, women's issues, social and political topics, and Israel, 1,500 to 2,500 words. Short stories with a Jewish theme. Pays 8¢ a word, on publication. Query or send manuscript.

**NEW WOMAN**—215 Lexington Ave., New York, NY 10016. Karen Walden, Ed.-in-Chief. Articles for women ages 25 to 49, on self-improvement, self-esteem, self-discovery. Features: relationships, careers, health and fitness, money, fashion, beauty, food and nutrition, travel features with self-discovery angle, and essays by and about women pacesetters. Pays about $1 a word, on acceptance. Query with SASE.

**ON THE ISSUES**—Choices Women's Medical Center, Inc., 97–77 Queens Blvd., Forest Hills, NY 11374–3317. Beverly Lowy, Man. Ed. "The Magazine of Substance for Progressive Women." Articles, to 2,500 words, on political or social issues. Movie, music, and book reviews, 500 to 750 words. Query. Payment varies, on publication.

**PLAYGIRL**—801 Second Ave., New York, NY 10017. Barbara Haigh, Ed.-in-Chief. In-depth articles for contemporary women. Humor, celebrity interviews. No free-lance fiction. Pays varying rates. Query first with clips. Guidelines.

**RADIANCE: THE MAGAZINE FOR LARGE WOMEN**—P.O. Box 30246, Oakland, CA 94604. Alice Ansfield, Ed./Pub. Quarterly. Articles, 1,500 to 2,500 words, that provide information, inspiration, and resources for women all sizes of large. Features include information on health, media, fashion, and politics that relate to issues of body size. Fiction and poetry also welcome. Pays to $100, on publication.

**REDBOOK**—224 W. 57th St., New York, NY 10019. Dawn Raffel, Fiction Ed. Toni Hope, Articles Ed. For women ages 25 to 40. Short stories, to 25 typed pages, and personal-experience pieces, 1,000 to 2,000 words, on solving problems in marriage, family life, or community, for "A Mother's Story." Pays $1,000 for short stories, $750 for personal-experience pieces. Query for articles only. SASE required.

**SELF**—350 Madison Ave., New York, NY 10017. Alexandra Penney, Ed.-in-Chief. Query for articles on current women's issues. No poetry. Payment varies. Include SASE.

**TODAY'S CHRISTIAN WOMAN**—465 Gundersen Dr., Carol Stream, IL 60188. Julie A. Talerico, Ed. Jan Senn, Asst. Ed. Articles, 1,500 words, that are "warm and personal in tone, full of real-life anecdotes that deal with the following relationships: marriage, parenting, friendship, spiritual life, and self." Humorous anecdotes, 150 words, that have a Christian slant. Queries required. Payment varies, on acceptance. Guidelines.

**VOGUE**—350 Madison Ave., New York, NY 10017. Address Features Ed. Articles, to 1,500 words, on women, entertainment and the arts, travel, medicine, and health. General features. No unsolicited manuscripts. Query first. Pays good rates, on acceptance.

**WOMAN OF POWER**—P.O. Box 2785, Orleans, MA 02653. Char McKee, Ed. A magazine of feminism, spirituality, and politics. Articles, to 3,500 words. Each issue explores a special theme. Send SASE for themes and guidelines. Pays in copies and subscription.

**WOMAN'S DAY**—1633 Broadway, New York, NY 10019. Rebecca Greer, Articles Ed. Human-interest or helpful articles, to 2,500 words, on marriage, child-rearing, health, careers, relationships, money management. Dramatic first-person narratives of medical miracles, rescues, women's experiences, etc. "We will read and respond to queries; unsolicited manuscripts will be returned unread." Pays top rates, on acceptance. Query.

**WOMAN'S TOUCH**—1445 Boonville, Springfield, MO 65802–1894. Sandra G. Clopine, Ed. Aleda Swartzendruber, Assoc. Ed. Inspirational articles, 500 to 1,200 words, for Christian women. Uses some poetry, 50 to 150 words. Pays on acceptance. Allow 3 months for response. Guidelines and editorial calendar.

**WOMAN'S WORLD**—270 Sylvan Ave., Englewood Cliffs, NJ 07632. Marilyn Webb, Feature Ed. Fast-moving short stories, about 1,900 words, with light romantic theme. (Specify "short story" on outside of envelope.) Mini-mysteries, 950 words, with "whodunit" or "howdunit" theme. No science fiction, fantasy, or historical romance and no horror, ghost stories, or gratuitous violence. Pays $1,000 for short stories, $500 for mini-mysteries, on acceptance. Submit manuscript with SASE.

**WOMEN IN BUSINESS**—American Business Women's Assn., 9100 Ward Pkwy., Box 8728, Kansas City, MO 64114–0728. Wendy S. Myers, Ed. Features, 1,000 to 1,500 words, for working women ages 35 to 55. No profiles. Pays on acceptance. Written query required.

**WOMEN'S CIRCLE**—P.O. Box 299, Lynnfield, MA 01940. Marjorie Pearl,

Ed. Success stories on home-based female entrepreneurs. How-to articles on contemporary craft and needlework projects. Unique money-saving ideas and recipes. Pays varying rates, on acceptance.

**WOMEN'S HOUSEHOLD**—306 E. Parr Rd., Berne, IL 46711. Allison Ballard, Ed. Profiles, 1,200 to 1,500 words, of women in history, crafts, and pieces on relationships, fiction, and nostalgia. Pieces on pen pals (arranging meetings, reunions, etc.). Pays $40 to $250, on publication.

**WOMEN'S SPORTS & FITNESS**—2025 Pearl St., Boulder, CO 80302. Marjorie McCloy, Ed. How-tos, profiles, active travel, and controversial issues in women's sports, 500 to 3,000 words. Fitness, nutrition, and health pieces also considered. Pays on publication.

**WORKING MOTHER**—Lang Communications, 230 Park Ave., New York, NY 10169. Address Editorial Dept. Articles, to 2,000 words, that help women in their task of juggling job, home, and family. "We like pieces that solve or illuminate a problem unique to our readers." Payment varies, on acceptance.

## MEN'S PUBLICATIONS

**ESQUIRE**—1790 Broadway, New York, NY 10019. Terry McDonell, Ed.-in-Chief. David Hirshey, Articles Ed. Articles, 2,500 to 4,000 words, for intelligent audience. Pays varying rates, on acceptance. Query with clips and SASE.

**GALLERY**—401 Park Ave. S., New York, NY 10016–8802. Barry Janoff, Ed.-in-Chief. Peter Emshwiller, Man. Ed. Articles, investigative pieces, interviews, profiles, to 2,500 words, for sophisticated men. Short humor, satire, service pieces, and fiction. Photos. Pays varying rates, half on acceptance, half on publication. Query.

**MEN'S FITNESS**—21100 Erwin St., Woodland Hills, CA 91367. Jim Rosenthal, Fitness Ed. Articles, 1,500 to 2,500 words, and department pieces, 1,000 to 1,500 words: "authoritative and practical articles dealing with fitness, health, and men's lifestyles." Pays $350 to $1,000, on acceptance.

**MEN'S HEALTH**—Rodale Press, 33 E. Minor Dr., Emmaus, PA 18098. Steve Slon, Man. Ed. Articles, 1,000 to 2,500 words, on fitness, diet, health, relationships, sports, and travel for men ages 25 to 55. Pays from 50¢ a word, on acceptance. Query.

**PLAYBOY**—680 N. Lakeshore Dr., Chicago, IL 60611. John Rezek, Articles Ed. Articles, 3,500 to 6,000 words, and sophisticated fiction, 1,000 to 10,000 words (5,000 preferred), for urban men. Humor; satire. Science fiction. Pays to $5,000 for articles and fiction, $1,000 for short-shorts, on acceptance.

**PLAYERS**—8060 Melrose Ave., Los Angeles, CA 90046. Joe Nazel, Ed. Articles, 1,000 to 3,000 words, for black men: politics, economics, travel, fashion, grooming, entertainment, sports, interviews, fiction, humor, satire, health, and sex. Photos a plus. Pays on publication.

## HOME AND GARDEN PUBLICATIONS

**THE AMERICAN ROSE MAGAZINE**—P.O. Box 30,000, Shreveport, LA 71130. Kathy Hamm, Man. Ed. Articles on home rose gardens: varieties, products, helpful advice, rose care, etc.

**BETTER HOMES AND GARDENS**—1716 Locust St., Des Moines, IA 50309–3023. David Jordan, Ed. Articles, to 2,000 words, on money management, health, travel, pets, and cars. Pays top rates, on acceptance. Query.

**BRIDE'S & YOUR HOME**—(formerly *Bride's Magazine*) 350 Madison Ave., New York, NY 10017. Andrea Feld, Man. Ed. Articles, 800 to 3,000 words, for engaged couples or newlyweds on housing, redecorating, etc. Three major editorial subjects: home, wedding, and honeymoon travel. Pays $300 to $1,000, on acceptance.

**CANADIAN WORKSHOP MAGAZINE**—130 Spy Ct., Markham, Ont., Canada L3R 5H6. Erina Kelly, Ed. Articles, 1,500 to 5,000 words, on do-it-yourself home renovations, energy saving projects, etc., with photos. Payment varies, on publication.

**CHILE PEPPER**—P.O. Box 4278, Albuquerque, NM 87196. Melissa Jackson, Ed. Food and travel articles, 1,000 to 1,500 words. "No general and obvious articles, such as 'My Favorite Chile Con Carne.' We want first-person articles about spicy world cuisine." Queries required. Payment varies, on publication.

**THE CHRISTIAN SCIENCE MONITOR**—One Norway St., Boston, MA 02115. Greg Lamb, Features Ed. Newspaper. Articles on lifestyle trends, women's rights, family, and parenting. Pays varying rates, on acceptance.

**ELLE DECOR**—1633 Broadway, New York, NY 10019. Charles Bricker, Exec. Ed. Articles, 300 to 1,000 words, on designers and craftspeople and their work. "Query with photos of the designers you want to write about and their work." Query. Pays $1.25 a word, on publication.

**FARM AND RANCH LIVING**—5400 S. 60th St., Greendale, WI 53129. Bob Ottum, Ed. Articles, 2,000 words, on rural people and situations; nostalgia pieces, profiles of interesting farms and farmers, ranches and ranchers. Pays $15 to $400, on acceptance and on publication.

**FLORIDA HOME & GARDEN**—800 Douglas Rd., Suite 500, Coral Gables, FL 33134. Marilyn Moore, Ed. Features, 800 to 1,000 words, and department pieces, 500 to 750 words, about Florida interior design, architecture, landscape architecture, gardening, trendy new products, art. Published as a section in South Florida, Orlando, and other Florida regional magazines. Pays $200 to $400, extra for photos.

**FLOWER & GARDEN MAGAZINE**—4251 Pennsylvania, Kansas City, MO 64111. Practical how-to articles, 1,000 words, on lawn and garden advice. Query first. Good photos enhance submission. Pays varying rates, on acceptance (payment for photos on publication).

**FOOD & WINE**—1120 Ave. of the Americas, New York, NY 10036. Carole Lalli, Ed.-in-Chief. Warren Picower, Man. Ed. Current culinary or beverage ideas for dining and entertaining at home and out. Food-related travel pieces. Submit detailed proposal.

**GARDEN DESIGN**—Society of American Landscape Architects, 4401 Connecticut Ave. N.W., Fifth Fl., Washington, DC 20008. Karen D. Fishler, Ed. Garden-related features. Articles, 800 to 1,500 words, on "private and public gardens, interviews with landscape designers and other personalities, and stories on art, architecture, furniture and fashion as they relate to the garden." Pays from 50¢ a word, on publication. Guidelines.

**HARROWSMITH COUNTRY LIFE**—Ferry Rd., Charlotte, VT 05445. Address Editorial Dept. Investigative pieces, 4,000 to 5,000 words, on issues of ecology and the environment, rural life, gardening, energy-efficient housing, and healthful food. Short pieces for "Screed" (opinions) and "Gazette" (news briefs). Pays $500 to $1,500 for features, from $50 to $600 for department pieces, on acceptance. Query required. Send SASE for guidelines.

**THE HERB QUARTERLY**—P. O. Box 548, Boiling Springs, PA 17007. Linda Sparrowe, Ed. Articles, 2,000 to 4,000 words, on herbs: practical uses, cultivation, gourmet cooking, landscaping, herb tradition, medicinal herbs, crafts ideas, unique garden designs, profiles of herb garden experts, practical how-tos for the herb businessperson. Include garden design when possible. Pays on publication. Guidelines; send SASE.

**HG: HOUSE & GARDEN**—350 Madison Ave., New York, NY 10017. "Check a recent issue of our magazine to become familiar with our needs. We rarely buy unsolicited manuscripts." Query.

**HOME MECHANIX**—2 Park Ave., New York, NY 10016. Michael Morris, Ed. Home improvement articles. Time- or money-saving tips for the home, garage, or yard; seasonal reminders for homeowners. Pays $50, on acceptance.

**HORTICULTURE**—Statler Bldg., 20 Park Plaza, Suite 1220, Boston, MA 02116. Deborah Starr, Exec. Ed. Authoritative, well-written articles, 500 to 2,500 words, on all aspects of gardening. Pays competitive rates. Query first.

**HOUSE BEAUTIFUL**—1700 Broadway, New York, NY 10019. Elaine Greene, Features Ed. Service articles related to the home. Pieces on design, travel, and gardening; mostly staff-written. Send for guidelines. Query with detailed outline. SASE required.

**HOUSEPLANT MAGAZINE**—1449 Ave. William, Sillery, Quebec, Canada G1S 4G5. Larry Hodgson, Ed.-in-Chief. Plant portraits and personal experiences about growing houseplants, 1,000 to 2,000 words, for amateur houseplant enthusiasts. Organic solutions should be proposed for any pest problems. Queries preferred. Pays $25 per page, on publication.

**LOG HOME GUIDE FOR BUILDERS & BUYERS**—164 Middle Creek Rd., Cosby, TN 37722. Articles, 500 to 1,500 words, on building new, or restoring old log homes, especially with solar or alternative heating systems, as well as pieces on decorating or profiles of interesting builders of log homes. Pays 20¢ a word, extra for photos, on publication. Limited market. Query first.

**LOG HOME LIVING**—P.O. Box 220039, Chantilly, VA 22022. Roland Sweet, Ed. Articles, 1,000 to 1,500 words, on modern manufactured and hand-crafted kit log homes: homeowner profiles, design and decor features. Pays $200 to $500, on acceptance.

**METROPOLITAN HOME**—750 Third Ave., New York, NY 10017. Barbara Graustark, Articles Ed. Service and informational articles for residents of houses, co-ops, lofts, and condominiums, on real estate, equity, wine and spirits, collecting, trends, travel, etc. Interior design and home furnishing articles with emphasis on lifestyle. Pay varies. Query.

**MILITARY LIFESTYLE MAGAZINE**—4800 Montgomery Ln., Suite 710, Bethesda, MD 20814. Hope Daniels, Ed. Articles, 1,000 to 2,000 words, for military families in the U.S. and overseas; pieces on child raising, marriage, health, fitness, food, and issues concerning young military families; home decor and "portable" or "instant" gardening articles; fiction. Pays $300 to $700, on publication. Query first.

**THE MOTHER EARTH NEWS**—24 E. 23rd St., 5th Fl., New York, NY 10010. Karen Bokram, Sr. Ed. Articles on country living: home improvement and construction, how-tos, indoor and outdoor gardening, crafts and projects, etc. Also health, ecology, energy, and consumerism pieces; profiles. Pay varies.

**NATIONAL GARDENING MAGAZINE**—180 Flynn Ave., Burlington, VT 05401. Warren Schultz, Ed. Articles, 300 to 3,000 words for advanced and beginning gardeners: seed-to-table profiles of major crops; firsthand reports from experienced gardeners in this country's many growing regions; easy-to-follow gardening techniques; garden food recipes; coverage of fruits, vegetables, and ornamentals. Pays $75 to $450, extra for photos, on acceptance. Query preferred.

**PALM SPRINGS LIFE**—Desert Publications, 303 North Indian Canyon Dr., P.O. Box 2724, Palm Springs, CA 92263. Jamie Pricer, Ed. Articles, 1,000 to 3,000 words, of interest to "wealthy, upscale people who live and/or play in the desert." Pays $150 to $400 for features, $30 to $75 for short profiles, on publication. Query required.

**SEATTLE**—701 Dexter Ave. N., Suite 101, Seattle, WA 98109. Giselle Smith, Ed. Articles, 500 to 2,000 words, on home and garden, personalities, arts and entertainment, events, social issues, business, fashion, and other features relating directly to the greater Seattle area. Pays $100 to $800, on publication. Guidelines.

**SELECT HOMES**—50 Holly St., Toronto, Canada M4S 3B3. Lynette Jennings, Ed. How-to articles, profiles of Canadian homes, renovation features, 800 to 1,500 words. Pays from $400 to $800 (Canadian), on acceptance. Query with international reply coupons. Send SAE with international reply coupons for guidelines.

**WINE TIDINGS**—5165 Sherbrooke St. W., Suite 414, Montreal, Quebec, Canada H4A 1T6. Barbara Leslie, Ed. Published eight times a year. Articles, 1,000 to 1,500 words, and 400- to 1,000-word shorts, with accurate wine information and written for a Canadian audience. Pays $100 to $300 for features, $30 to $150 for shorts, on publication. Photos, $20 to $50 for B&W or color; $200 to $400 for covers.

**WORKBENCH**—700 West 47th St., Suite 310, Kansas City, MO 64112. Robert N. Hoffman, Exec. Ed. Illustrated how-to articles on home improvement and woodworking, with detailed instructions. Pays from $150 per printed page, on acceptance. Send SASE for guidelines.

**YOUR HOME/INDOORS & OUT**—P.O. Box 10010, Ogden, UT 84409. Articles, 1,200 words with quality color transparencies, and fresh ideas in all areas of home decor: the latest in home construction (exteriors, interiors, building materials, design); the outdoors at home (landscaping, pools, patios, gardening); home management, buying and selling. "We are especially interested in articles on choosing a realtor or home builder." No do-it-yourself pieces. Query first with SASE to Editor.

## LIFESTYLE AND FAMILY PUBLICATIONS

**AMERICAN BABY**—475 Park Ave. S., New York, NY 10016. Judith Nolte, Ed. Articles, 1,000 to 2,000 words, for new or expectant parents on prenatal and infant care. Pays varying rates, on acceptance.

**AMERICAN HEALTH**—28 West 23rd. St., New York, NY 10010. Address Editorial Dept. Lively, authoritative articles, 1,000 to 3,000 words, on scientific and lifestyle aspects of health and fitness; 100- to 500-word news reports. Query with clips. Pays $250 ($50 kill fee) for news stories; 75¢ per word for features (kill fee is 25% of assigned fee), on acceptance.

**BABY TALK**—636 Ave. of the Americas, New York, NY 10011. Susan Strecker, Ed. Articles, 1,500 to 3,000 words, by parents or professionals, on babies, baby care, etc. Pays varying rates, on acceptance. SASE required.

**THE BIG APPLE PARENTS' PAPER**—928 Broadway, Suite 709, New York, NY 10010. Helen Rosengren Freedman, Ed. Articles, 600 to 750 words, for NYC parents. Pays $50 to $75 (plus $25 cover bonus), on publication. Buys first NY-area rights.

**CAPPER'S**—616 Jefferson St., Topeka, KS 66607–1188. Nancy Peavler, Ed. Human-interest, personal-experience, historical articles, 300 to 700 words. Poetry, to 15 lines, on nature, home, family. Novel-length fiction for serialization. Letters on women's interests, recipes, hints, for "Heart of the Home." Jokes. Children's writing and art section. Pays varying rates, on publication.

**CHRISTIAN HOME & SCHOOL**—3350 East Paris Ave. S.E., Grand Rapids, MI 49512. Gordon L. Bordewyk, Ed. Articles for parents in Canada and the U.S. who send their children to Christian schools and are concerned about the challenges facing Christian families today. Pays $50 to $110, on publication. Guidelines.

**CHRISTIAN PARENTING**—P.O. Box 850, Sisters, OR 97759. David Kopp, Ed. Articles, 900 to 1,500 words, dealing with raising children with Christian principles. Departments: "Parent Exchange," 25 to 100 words, on problem-solving ideas that have worked for parents; "My Story," 800 to 1,500 words, in first person, of how one family or parent faced a parenting challenge; "Life in our House," insightful anecdotes, 25 to 100 words, about humorous things said at home. Queries preferred. Pays 15¢ to 25¢ a word, on acceptance for assigned articles, on publication for unsolicited articles. Pays $40 for "Parent Exchange," $25 for "Life in our House." Guidelines.

**CONNECTICUT FAMILY**—See *New York Family.*

**COUNTRY**—5400 S. 60th St., Greendale, WI 53129. Dan Matel, Man. Ed. Pieces on interesting rural and country people who have unusual hobbies or businesses, 500 to 1,500 words; liberal use of direct quotes. Good, candid, color photos required. Pays on acceptance. Queries preferred.

**EAST WEST: THE JOURNAL OF NATURAL HEALTH & LIVING**—See *Natural Health: The Guide to Well-Being.*

**EASTSIDE PARENT**—Northwest Parent Publishing, 2107 Elliott Ave., #303, Seattle, WA 98121. Ann Bergman, Ed. Articles, 300 to 2,500 words, for parents of children under 12. Readers tend to be professional, two-career families. Queries are preferred. Pays $150 to $500, on publication. Also publishes *Portland Parent* and *Pierce County Parent.*

**EXCEPTIONAL PARENT**—1170 Commonwealth Ave., Boston, MA 02134–4646. Stanley D. Klein, Ed. Maxwell J. Schleifer, Ed. Articles, 1,000 to 1,500 words, for parents raising children with disabilities. Practical ideas and techniques on parenting, as well as the latest in technology, research, and rehabilitation. Query. Pays $25, on publication.

**FATE**—P.O. Box 64383, St. Paul, MN 55164–0383. Phyllis Galde, Ed. Factual fillers and true stories, to 300 words, on strange or psychic happenings and mystic personal experiences. Pays 10¢ a word.

**GROWING CHILD/GROWING PARENT**—22 N. Second St., Lafayette, IN 47902–0620. Nancy Kleckner, Ed. Articles, to 1,500 words, on subjects of interest to parents of children under 6. No personal experience pieces or poetry. Guidelines.

**HOME LIFE**—127 Ninth Ave. N., Nashville, TN 37234. Charlie Warren, Ed. Southern Baptist. Articles, to 1,500 words, on Christian marriage, parenting, and family relationships. Pays to 5 ½¢ a word, on acceptance.

**INDEPENDENT LIVING**—44 Broadway, Greenlawn, NY 11740. Anne Kelly, Ed. Articles, 1,000 to 2,000 words, addressing lifestyles of persons who have disabilities. Possible topics: home health care, travel, sports, family life, and sexuality. Pays 10¢ a word, on publication. Query.

**JEWISH CURRENTS**—22 E. 17th St., #601, New York, NY 10003. Morris U. Schappes, Ed. Articles, 2,400 to 3,000 words, on Jewish culture and social progress. "We are a secular Jewish magazine." No payment.

**LIVING WITH CHILDREN**—MSN 140, 127 Ninth Ave. N., Nashville, TN 37234. Articles, 800 to 1,200 words, on parent-child relationships, told from a Christian perspective. Pays 5 ½¢ a word, after acceptance.

**LIVING WITH PRESCHOOLERS**—MSN 140, 127 Ninth Ave. N., Nashville, TN 37234. Articles, 800 to 1,200 words, on Christian family issues. Pays 5 ½¢ a word, on acceptance.

**LIVING WITH TEENAGERS**—127 Ninth Ave. N., Nashville, TN 37234. Articles told from a Christian perspective for parents of teenagers; first-person approach preferred. Poetry, 4 to 16 lines. Pays 5 ½¢ a word, on acceptance, for articles.

**MAGICAL BLEND**—Box 421130, San Francisco, CA 94142. Jerry Snider, Literary Ed. Positive, uplifting articles on spiritual exploration, lifestyles, occult, white magic, new age thought, and fantasy. Fiction and features, to 5,000 words.

**NATIVE PEOPLES MAGAZINE**—5333 N. 7th St., Suite C-224, Phoenix, AZ 85014–2804. Gary Avey, Ed. Quarterly. Articles, 1,800 to 2,800 words, on the "arts and lifeways" of the native peoples of the Americas; authenticity and positive portrayals of present traditional and cultural practices necessary. Query, including availability of photos. Pays 25¢ a word, on publication.

**NATURAL HEALTH: THE GUIDE TO WELL-BEING**—(formerly *East West: The Journal of Natural Health & Living*) 17 Station St., Box 1200, Brookline, MA 02147. Features, 1,500 to 2,500 words, on holistic health, natural foods, herbal remedies, etc. Interviews. Photos. Pays 20¢ a word, extra for photos, on acceptance.

**NEW AGE JOURNAL**—342 Western Ave., Brighton, MA 02135. Peggy Taylor, Ed. Articles for readers who take an active interest in social change, personal growth, health, and contemporary issues. Features, 2,000 to 4,000 words; columns, 750 to 1,500 words; short news items, 50 words; and first-person narratives, 750 to 1,500 words. Pays varying rates.

**NEW CHOICES FOR RETIREMENT LIVING**—28 W. 23rd St., New York, NY 10010. David A. Sendler, Ed.-in-Chief. News and service magazine for people ages 50 to 65. Articles on planning for retirement, health and fitness, financial strategies, housing options, travel, profiles/interviews (celebrities and newsmakers), relationships, leisure pursuits, etc. Query or send complete manuscript. SASE required. Payment varies, on acceptance.

**NEW YORK FAMILY**—141 Halstead Ave., Suite 30, Mamaroneck, NY 10543. Felice Shapiro, Susan Ross, Eds. Articles related to family life in New York City and general parenting topics. Pays $50 to $100. Same requirements for *Westchester Family* and *Connecticut Family.*

**PARENTGUIDE NEWS**—475 Park Ave. S., New York, NY 10016. Leslie Elgort, Ed. Monthly. Articles, 1,000 to 1,500 words, related to New York families and parenting: trends, profiles, issues, special programs and products, etc. Humor, jokes, puzzles, and photos also considered. Payment varies, on publication.

**PARENTING**—301 Howard St., 17th Fl., San Francisco, CA 94105. Rachael Grossman, Ed. Articles, 500 to 3,500 words, on education, health, fitness, nutrition, child development, psychology, and social issues for parents of young children. Query.

**PIERCE COUNTY PARENT**—See *Eastside Parent.*

**PORTLAND PARENT**—See *Eastside Parent.*

**SEATTLE'S CHILD**—Northwest Parent Publishing, 2107 Elliott Ave., #303, Seattle, WA 98121. Ann Bergman, Ed. Articles, 400 to 2,500 words, of interest to parents, educators, and childcare providers of children under 12, plus investigative reports and consumer tips on issues affecting families in the Puget Sound region. Pays $75 to $400, on publication. Query required.

**THE SINGLE PARENT**—Parents Without Partners, Inc., 8807 Colesville Rd., Silver Spring, MD 20910–4346. Rene McDonald, Ed. Bimonthly. Articles, 1,500 to 2,200 words, addressing the concerns of single parents, including physical and emotional wellness, careers (for adults and youths), and intergenerational issues. Fillers, 300 to 500 words. Prefers pieces that "enlighten and entertain busy people"; no "cutesy or sob stories." Pays $75 to $125 for articles, $25 to $50 for fillers, on publication.

**TODAY'S FAMILY**—27 Empire Dr., St. Paul, MN 55103. Valerie Hockert, Pub./Man. Ed. Bimonthly. Articles, 750 to 2,000 words, "directed toward the nontraditional family, the good teenager, the step family, and the single parent family." Pays $10 to $50, on publication. Query preferred.

**VIRTUE**—P. O. Box 850, Sisters, OR 97759. Marlee Alex, Ed. Articles, 1,000 to 1,500 words, on family, marriage, self-esteem, working mothers, opinions, food, crafts. Fiction and poetry. Pays 15¢ to 25¢ a word, on acceptance. Query required.

**WESTCHESTER FAMILY**—See *New York Family.*

**WILDFIRE**—Bear Tribe Publishing, P.O. Box 9167, Spokane, WA 99209–9167. Matthew Ryan, Ed. Articles, 1,000 to 2,500 words, with a strong nature-based focus on spirituality, personal development, alternative lifestyles, natural healings, and ecology. Poetry, 20 lines. Pay varies, on publication.

**WORKING MOTHER**—Lang Communications, 230 Park Ave., New York, NY 10169. Address Editorial Dept. Articles, to 2,000 words, that help women in their task of juggling job, home, and family. Payment varies, on acceptance.

**YOGA JOURNAL**—2054 University Ave., Berkeley, CA 94704. Stephan Bodian, Ed. Articles, 1,200 to 4,000 words, on holistic health, spirituality, yoga, and transpersonal psychology; new age profiles; interviews. Pays $50 to $400, on publication.

## SPORTS AND RECREATION

**THE AMERICAN FIELD**—542 S. Dearborn, Chicago, IL 60605. B.J. Matthys, Man. Ed. Yarns about hunting trips, bird-shooting; articles to 1,500 words, on dogs and field trials, emphasizing conservation of game resources. Pays varying rates, on acceptance.

**AMERICAN HANDGUNNER**—591 Camino de la Reina, Suite 200, San Diego, CA 92108. Cameron Hopkins, Ed. Semi-technical articles on shooting sports, gun repair and alteration, handgun matches and tournaments, for lay readers. Pays $100 to $500, on publication. Query.

**AMERICAN HUNTER**—470 Spring Park Place, Suite 1000, Herndon, VA 22070–5227. Tom Fulgham, Ed. Articles, 1,400 to 2,000 words, on hunting. Photos. Pays on acceptance. Guidelines.

**AMERICAN MOTORCYCLIST**—American Motorcyclist Assn., Box 6114, Westerville, OH 43081–6114. Greg Harrison, Ed. Articles and fiction, to 3,000 words, on motorcycling: news coverage, personalities, tours. Photos. Pays varying rates, on publication. Query with SASE.

**THE AMERICAN RIFLEMAN**—470 Spring Park Place, Suite 1000, Herndon, VA 22070. Bill Parkerson, Ed. Factual articles on use and enjoyment of sporting firearms. Pays on acceptance.

**ATLANTIC SALMON JOURNAL**—P.O. Box 429, St. Andrews, N.B., Canada E0G 2X0. Harry Bruce, Ed. Material related to Atlantic salmon: fishing, conservation, ecology, travel, politics, biology, how-tos, anecdotes, cuisine. Articles, 1,500 to 3,000 words. Pays $100 to $400, on publication.

**BACKPACKER MAGAZINE**—Rodale Press, 33 E. Minor St., Emmaus, PA 18098. John Viehman, Exec. Ed. Articles, 250 to 3,000 words, on self-propelled backcountry travel: backpacking, technique, kayaking/canoeing, mountaineering, nordic skiing, health, natural science. Photos. Pays varying rates. Query.

**THE BACKSTRETCH**—19899 W. 9 Mile Rd., Southfield, MI 48075–3960. Harriet Randall, Ed. United Thoroughbred Trainers of America. Feature articles, with photos, on subjects related to thoroughbred horse racing. Pays after publication. Sample issue and guidelines on request.

**BAJA EXPLORER**—11760 Sorrento Valley Rd., Suite K, San Diego, CA 92121. Landon S. Crumpton, Ed.-in-Chief. Articles, 800 to 1,200 words, on fishing sailing, surfing, windsurfing, camping, and natural history, of interest to tourists visiting Baja California. Pays 25¢ a word, $50 per slide, on publication; published bimonthly.

**BASEBALL FORECAST, BASEBALL ILLUSTRATED, BASEBALL PREVIEW**—See *Hockey Illustrated.*

**BASKETBALL ANNUAL, BASKETBALL FORECAST**—See *Hockey Illustrated.*

**BASSIN'**—15115 S. 76th E. Ave., Bixby, OK 74008. Gordon Sprouse, Exec. Ed. Articles, 1,500 to 1,800 words, on how and where to bass fish, for the amateur fisherman. Pays $275 to $400, on acceptance.

**BC OUTDOORS**—1132 Hamilton St., #202, Vancouver, B.C., Canada V6B 2S2. George Will, Ed. Articles, to 2,000 words, on fishing, hunting, conservation, and all forms of non-competitive outdoor recreation in British Columbia and Yukon. Photos. Pays from 20¢ to 27¢ a word, on acceptance.

**BIKEREPORT**—Bikecentennial, P.O. Box 8308, Missoula, MT 59807. Daniel D'Ambrosio, Ed. Accounts of bicycle tours in the U.S. and overseas, interviews, personal-experience pieces, humor, and news shorts, 1,200 to 2,500 words. Pays $25 to $65 per published page.

**BIRD WATCHER'S DIGEST**—P.O. Box 110, Marietta, OH 45750. Mary B. Bowers, Ed. Articles, 600 to 2,500 words, for bird watchers: first-person accounts;

how-tos; pieces on endangered species; profiles. Cartoons. Pays from $50, on publication.

**BLACK BELT**—P.O. Box 918, Santa Clarita, CA 91380–9018. Articles related to self-defense: how-tos on fitness and technique; historical, travel, philosophical subjects. Pays $100 to $250, on publication. Guidelines.

**BOAT PENNSYLVANIA**—Pennsylvania Fish and Boat Commission, P.O. Box 67000, Harrisburg, PA 17106–7000. Art Michaels, Ed. Articles, 200 to 2,500 words, with photos, on boating in Pennsylvania: motorboating, sailing, waterskiing, canoeing, kayaking, and personal watercraft. No pieces on fishing. Pays $50 to $250, on acceptance. Query. Guidelines.

**BOUNDARY WATERS JOURNAL**—9396 Rocky Ledge Rd., Ely, MN 55031. Stuart Osthoff, Ed. Articles, 2,000 to 3,000 words, on wilderness recreation, nature, and conservation in Minnesota's Boundary Waters Canoe Area Wilderness and Ontario's Quetico Provincial Park. Regular features include canoe-route journals, fishing, camping, hiking, cross-country skiing, wildlife and nature, regional lifestyles, history, and events. Pays $200 to $400, on publication; $50 to $150 for photos.

**BOW & ARROW HUNTING**—Box HH, 34249 Camino Capistrano, Capistrano Beach, CA 92624. Roger Combs, Ed. Dir. Articles, 1,200 to 2,500 words, with B&W photos, on bowhunting; profiles and technical pieces. Pays $50 to $300, on acceptance. Same address and mechanical requirements for *Gun World*.

**BOWHUNTER MAGAZINE**—Box 8200, Harrisburg, PA 17105–8200. M.R. James, Ed. Informative, entertaining features, 500 to 2,000 words, on bow-and-arrow hunting. Fillers. Photos. Pays $25 to $300, on acceptance. Study magazine first.

**BOWHUNTING WORLD**—319 Barry Ave. S., Suite 101, Wayzata, MN 55391. Tim Dehn, Ed. Articles, 1,800 to 3,000 words, on all aspects of bowhunting and competitive archery, with photos. Pays from $250, on acceptance, with premium for features available on double-density 5 ¼-inch disks, ASCII format preferred.

**BOWLERS JOURNAL**—200 S. Michigan Ave., Chicago, IL 60604. Mort Luby, Ed. Trade and consumer articles, 1,200 to 2,200 words, with photos, on bowling. Pays $75 to $200, on acceptance.

**BOWLING**—5301 S. 76th St., Greendale, WI 53129. Bill Vint, Ed. Articles, to 1,500 words, on amateur league and tournament bowling. Profiles. "Looking for unique, unusual stories about bowling people and places." Pays varying rates, on publication.

**CALIFORNIA ANGLER**—1921 E. Carnegie St., Suite N, Santa Ana, CA 92705. How-to and where-to articles, 2,000 words, for freshwater and saltwater anglers in California: travel, new products, fishing techniques, profiles. Photos. Pays $75 to $400, on acceptance. Query first.

**CANOE**—P.O. Box 3146, Kirkland, WA 98083. Les Johnson, Man. Ed. Features, 1,100 to 2,000 words; department pieces, 500 to 1,000 words. Topics include canoeing or kayaking adventures, destinations, boat and equipment reviews, techniques and how-tos, short essays, camping, environment, humor, health, history, etc. Pays $5 per column inch, on publication. Query preferred. Guidelines.

**CAR AND DRIVER**—2002 Hogback Rd., Ann Arbor, MI 48105. William Jeanes, Ed. Articles, to 2,500 words, for enthusiasts, on new cars, classic cars, industry topics. "Ninety percent staff written. Query with clips. No unsolicited manuscripts." Pays to $2,500, on acceptance.

**CAR CRAFT**—8490 Sunset Blvd., Los Angeles, CA 90069. John Baechtel, Ed. Articles and photo features on high performance street machines, drag cars, racing events; technical pieces; action photos. Pays from $150 per page, on publication.

**CARIBBEAN SPORTS & TRAVEL**—(formerly *Pleasure Boating*) 1995 N.E. 150th St., North Miami, FL 33181. Vic Hanna, Exec. Ed. Articles, 1,000 to 2,500 words, on cruising, recreational boating, golf, travel, covering the Bahamas and the Caribbean. Special sections on the Bahamas, Jamaica, Cayman Islands, and Puerto Rico. Pays varying rates, on publication. Query first. Study sample copies. Guidelines.

**CASCADES EAST**—716 N.E. Fourth St., P.O. Box 5784, Bend, OR 97708. Geoff Hill, Ed./Pub. Articles, 1,000 to 2,000 words, on outdoor activities (fishing, hunting, golfing, backpacking, rafting, skiing, snowmobiling, etc.), history, special events, and scenic tours in Central Oregon Cascades. Photos. Pays 5¢ to 10¢ a word, extra for photos, on publication.

**CASINO PLAYER**—2524 Arctic Ave., Atlantic City, NJ 08401. Roger Gros, Ed. Articles, 500 to 1,000 words, accompanied by photos, for beginning to intermediate gamblers, on slots, video poker, and table games. No first-person or real-life gambling stories. Pays $100, on monthly publication.

**CHESAPEAKE BAY MAGAZINE**—1819 Bay Ridge Ave., Annapolis, MD 21403. Jean Waller, Ed. Technical and how-to articles, to 1,500 words, on boating and fishing on Chesapeake Bay. Photos. Pays $85 to $150, on publication.

**CITY SPORTS MAGAZINE**—P.O. Box 193693, San Francisco, CA 94119. Chris Newbound, Ed. Articles, 200 to 2,000 words, on the active lifestyle, including service pieces, trend pieces, profiles, and nutrition. Pays $50 to $650, on publication. Query editor.

**CROSS COUNTRY SKIER**—1823 Fremont Ave. S., Minneapolis, MN 55403. Jim Chase, Ed. Articles, to 3,000 words, on all aspects of cross-country skiing. Departments, 1,000 to 1,500 words, on ski maintenance, skiing techniques, health and fitness. Published October through February. Pays $300 to $700 for features, $100 to $350 for departments, on publication. Query.

**CURRENTS**—P.O. Box 6847, 314 N. 20th St., Suite 200, Colorado Springs, CO 80904. Address Greg Moore. Quarterly. "Voice of the National Organization for River Sports." Articles, 500 to 2,000 words, for kayakers, rafters, and river canoeists, pertaining to whitewater rivers and/or river running. Fillers. B&W action photos. Pays $40 and up for articles, $30 to $50 for photos, on publication. Queries preferred.

**CYCLING U.S.A.**—U.S. Cycling Federation, 1750 E. Boulder St., Colorado Springs, CO 80909. Nancy Moore, Ed. Articles, 300 to 500 words, on bicycle racing. Pays 12¢ to 15¢ a word, on publication. Query first.

**THE DIVER**—P.O. Box 313, Portland, CT 06480. Bob Taylor, Ed. Articles on divers, coaches, officials, springboard and platform techniques, training tips, etc. Pays $15 to $50, extra for photos ($5 to $25 for cartoons), on publication.

**EQUUS**—Fleet Street Corp., 656 Quince Orchard Rd., Gaithersburg, MD 20878. Laurie Prinz, Ed. Articles, 1,000 to 3,000 words, on all breeds of horses, covering their health, care, the latest advances in equine medicine and research. "Attempt to speak as one horseperson to another." Pays $100 to $400, on publication.

622

**FAMILY MOTOR COACHING**—8291 Clough Pike, Cincinnati, OH 45244–2796. Pamela Wisby Kay, Ed. Monthly. Articles, 1,500 to 2,000 words, on technical topics and travel routes and destinations accessible by motorhome. Query preferred. Payment varies, on acceptance.

**FIELD & STREAM**—2 Park Ave., New York, NY 10016. Duncan Barnes, Ed. Articles, 1,500 to 2,000 words, with photos, on hunting, fishing. Fillers, 75 to 1,000 words. Cartoons. Pays from $800 for feature articles with photos, $75 to $500 for fillers, $100 for cartoons, on acceptance. Query for articles.

**FISHING WORLD**—51 Atlantic Ave., Floral Park, NY 11001. Keith Gardner, Ed. Features, to 1,500 words, with color transparencies, on fishing sites, technique, equipment. Pays to $350 for major features. Query preferred.

**THE FLORIDA HORSE**—P.O. Box 2106, Ocala, FL 32678. F. J. Audette, Ed. Articles, 1,500 words, on Florida thoroughbred breeding and racing. Also veterinary articles, financial articles, and articles of general interest. Pays $100 to $200, on publication.

**FLY FISHERMAN**—6405 Flank Dr., Box 8200, Harrisburg, PA 17105. Philip Hanyok, Man. Ed. Query.

**FLY ROD & REEL**—P.O. Box 370, Camden, ME 04843. James E. Butler, Man. Ed. Flyfishing pieces, 2,000 to 2,500 words, and occasional fiction; articles on the culture and history of the areas being fished. Pays on publication. Query.

**FOOTBALL DIGEST**—Century Publishing Co., 990 Grove St., Evanston, IL 60201. Vince Aversano, Ed. Profiles of pro and college stars, nostalgia, trends in the sport, 1,500 to 2,500 words, aimed at the hard-core football fan. Pays on publication.

**FOOTBALL FORECAST**—See *Hockey Illustrated.*

**FUR-FISH-GAME**—2878 E. Main St., Columbus, OH 43209. Mitch Cox, Ed. Illustrated articles, 800 to 2,500 words, preferably with how-to angle, on hunting, fishing, trapping, dogs, camping, or other outdoor topics. Some humorous or where-to articles. Pays $40 to $150, on acceptance.

**GAME AND FISH PUBLICATIONS**—P.O. Box 741, Marietta, GA 30061. Publishes 30 monthly outdoors magazines for 48 states. Articles, 1,500 to 2,500 words, on hunting and fishing. How-tos, where-tos, and adventure pieces. Profiles of successful hunters and fishermen. No hiking, canoeing, camping, or backpacking pieces. Pays $125 to $175 for state-specific articles, $200 to $250 for multi-state articles, before publication. Pays $25 to $75 for photos.

**GOAL**—650 Fifth Ave., 33rd Fl., New York, NY 10019. Michael A. Berger, Ed. Official magazine of the National Hockey League. Player profiles and trend stories, 1,000 to 1,800 words, for hockey fans with knowledge of the game, by writers with understanding of the sport. Pays $150 to $300, on acceptance. Query.

**GOLF DIGEST**—5520 Park Ave., Trumbull, CT 06611. Jerry Tarde, Ed. Instructional articles, tournament reports, and features on players, to 2,500 words. Fiction, 1,000 to 2,000 words. Poetry, fillers, humor, photos. Pays varying rates, on acceptance. Query preferred.

**GOLF FOR WOMEN**—2130 Jackson Ave. W., Oxford, MS 38655. George Kehoe, Ed.-in-Chief. Golf-related articles of interest to women; fillers and humor. Instructional pieces are staff written. Pays from 40¢ a word, on publication. Query first.

**GOLF JOURNAL**—Golf House, P.O. Box 708, Far Hills, NJ 07931–0708.

David Earl, Ed. U.S. Golf Assn. Articles on golf personalities, history, travel. Humor. Photos. Pays varying rates, on publication.

**GOLF MAGAZINE**—2 Park Ave., New York, NY 10016. Jim Frank, Ed. Articles, 1,000 words with photos, on golf history and travel (places to play around the world); profiles of professional tour players. Shorts, to 500 words. Pays 75¢ a word, on acceptance. Queries preferred.

**THE GREYHOUND REVIEW**—National Greyhound Assoc., Box 543, Abilene, KS 67410. Tim Horan, Man. Ed. Articles, 1,000 to 10,000 words, pertaining to the greyhound racing industry: how-to, historical nostalgia, interviews. Pays $85 to $150, on publication.

**GULF COAST GOLFER**—See *North Texas Golfer.*

**GUN DIGEST**—4092 Commercial Ave., Northbrook, IL 60062. Ken Warner, Ed. Well-researched articles, to 5,000 words, on guns and shooting, equipment, etc. Photos. Pays from 10¢ a word, on acceptance. Query.

**GUN DOG**—P.O. Box 35098, Des Moines, IA 50315. Bob Wilbanks, Man. Ed. Features, 1,000 to 2,500 words, with photos, on bird hunting: how-tos, where-tos, dog training, canine medicine, breeding strategy. Fiction. Humor. Pays $50 to $150 for fillers and short articles, $150 to $350 for features, on acceptance.

**GUN WORLD**—See *Bow & Arrow Hunting.*

**GUNS & AMMO**—8490 Sunset Blvd., Los Angeles, CA 90069. E. G. Bell, Jr., Ed. Technical and general articles, 1,500 to 3,000 words, on guns, ammunition, and target shooting. Photos, fillers. Pays from $150, on acceptance.

**HANG GLIDING**—U.S. Hang Gliding Assn., P.O. Box 8300, Colorado Springs, CO 80933–8300. Gilbert Dodgen, Ed. Articles, two to three pages, on hang gliding. Pays to $50, on publication. Query.

**HOCKEY ILLUSTRATED**—Lexington Library, Inc., 355 Lexington Ave., New York, NY 10017. Stephen Ciacciarelli, Ed. Articles, 2,500 words, on hockey players, teams. Pays $125, on publication. Query. Same address and requirements for *Baseball Illustrated, Wrestling World, Pro Basketball Illustrated, Pro Football Illustrated, Basketball Annual* (college), *Baseball Preview, Baseball Forecast, Pro Football Preview, Football Forecast,* and *Basketball Forecast.*

**HORSE & RIDER**—1060 Calle Cordillera, Suite 103, San Clemente, CA 92673. Juli S. Thorson, Ed. Articles, 500 to 1,700 words, with photos, on Western riding and general horse care geared to the performance horse: training, feeding, grooming, health, etc. Pays varying rates, on publication. Buys one-time rights. Guidelines.

**HORSEMEN'S YANKEE PEDLAR**—785 Southbridge St., Auburn, MA 01501. Nancy L. Khoury, Pub. News and feature-length articles, about horses and horsemen in the Northeast. Photos. Pays $2 per published inch, on publication. Query.

**HORSEPLAY**—P.O. Box 130, Gaithersburg, MD 20884. Cordelia Doucet, Ed. Articles, 700 to 3,000 words, on eventing, show jumping, horse shows, dressage, driving, and fox hunting for horse enthusiasts. Pays 10¢ a word for all rights, 9¢ a word for first American rights, after publication. Query. SASE required.

**THE IN-FISHERMAN**—Two In-Fish Dr., Brainerd, MN 56401–0999. Doug Stange, Ed. Published seven times yearly. How-to articles, 1,500 to 4,500 words, on all aspects of freshwater fishing. Humorous or nostalgic looks at fishing, 1,000 to 1,500 words, for "Reflections" column. Pays $250 to $1,000, on acceptance.

624

**INSIDE SPORTS**—990 Grove St., Evanston, IL 60201. Vince Aversano, Ed. In-depth, insightful sports articles, player profiles, fillers, and humor. Payment varies, on acceptance. Query.

**INSIDE TEXAS RUNNING**—9514 Bristlebrook Dr., Houston, TX 77083–6193. Joanne Schmidt, Ed. Articles and fillers on running, cycling, and triathlons in Texas. Pays $35 to $100, $10 for photos, on acceptance.

**LAKELAND BOATING**—1560 Sherman Ave., Suite 1220, Evanston, IL 60201–5047. Sarah Wortham, Ed. Articles for powerboat owners on the Great Lakes and other area waterways, on long-distance cruising, short trips, maintenance, equipment, history, regional personalities and events, and environment. Photos. Pays on publication. Query first. Guidelines.

**MEN'S FITNESS**—21100 Erwin St., Woodland Hills, CA 91367. Jim Rosenthal, Fitness Ed. Ted Mason, Health Ed. Features, 1,500 to 2,500 words, and department pieces, 1,000 to 1,500 words: authoritative and practical articles dealing with fitness, health, and men's lifestyles. Pays $350 to $1,000, on acceptance.

**MEN'S HEALTH**—Rodale Press, 33 E. Minor Dr., Emmaus, PA 18098. Steven Slon, Man. Ed. Articles, 1,000 to 2,500 words, on fitness, diet, health, nutrition, relationships, sports, and travel, for men ages 25 to 55. Pays from 50¢ a word, on acceptance. Query first.

**MICHIGAN OUT-OF-DOORS**—P.O. Box 30235, Lansing, MI 48909. Kenneth S. Lowe, Ed. Features, 1,500 to 2,500 words, on hunting, fishing, camping, and conservation in Michigan. Pays $75 to $150, on acceptance.

**MID-WEST OUTDOORS**—111 Shore Dr., Hinsdale, IL 60521–5885. Gene Laulunen, Ed. Articles, 1,000 to 1,500 words, with photos, on where, when, and how to fish and hunt in the Midwest. No Canadian material. Pays $15 to $35, on publication.

**MOUNTAIN BIKE**—Rodale Press, 33 E. Minor St., Emmaus, PA 18098. Nelson Pena, Man. Ed. Articles, 500 to 2,000 words, on mountain-bike touring; major off-road cycling events; political, sport, or land-access issues; riding techniques; fitness and training tips. Pays $100 to $650, on publication. Query first.

**MUSCULAR DEVELOPMENT**—505-H Saddle River Rd., Saddle Brook, NJ 07662. Alan Paul, Ed. Articles, 1,000 to 3,000 words, personality profiles, training features, and diet and nutrition pieces. Photos. Pays $100 to $300 for articles; $35 for color photos, $20 for B&W, and $300 to $500 for cover photos.

**MUSHING**—P.O. Box 149, Ester, AK 99725–0149. Todd Hoener, Ed. Dog-driving how-tos, profiles, and features, 1,500 to 2,000 words; and department pieces, 500 to 1,000 words, for competitive and recreational dog-sled drivers, weight pullers, and skijorers. International audience. Photos. Pays $20 to $250, on publication. Queries preferred. Guidelines.

**NATIONAL PARKS MAGAZINE**—1776 Massachusetts Ave., Washington, DC 20002. Sue E. Dodge, Ed. Articles, 1,000 to 2,000 words, on natural history, wildlife, and conservation as they relate to national parks; illustrated features on the natural, historic, and cultural resources of the National Park System. Pieces about legislation and other issues and events related to the parks. Pays $100 to $800, on acceptance. Query. Send for guidelines.

**THE NEW ENGLAND SKIERS GUIDE**—Box 1125, Waitsfield, VT 05673. Andrew Bigford, Ed. Annual (June deadline for submissions). Articles on alpine and nordic skiing, equipment, and winter vacations at New England resorts. Rates vary.

**NORTH TEXAS GOLFER**—9182 Old Katy Rd., Suite 212, Houston, TX 77055. Steve Hunter, Ed./Pub. Articles, 800 to 1,500 words, of interest to golfers in north Texas. Pays $50 to $250, on publication. Queries required. Same requirements for *Gulf Coast Golfer.*

**NORTHEAST OUTDOORS**—P.O. Box 2180, Waterbury, CT 06722-2180. John Florian, Ed. Dir. Articles, 500 to 1,800 words, preferably with B&W photos, on camping in Northeast U.S.: recommended private campgrounds, camp cookery, recreational vehicle hints. Stress how-to, where-to. Cartoons. Pays $20 to $80, on publication. Guidelines.

**OFFSHORE**—220 Reservoir St., Needham Heights, MA 02194. Herbert Gliick, Ed. Articles, 1,200 to 2,500 words, on boats, people, and places along the New England, New York, and New Jersey coasts. Writers should be knowledgeable boaters. Photos a plus. Pays 15¢ to 20¢ a word.

**ON TRACK**—17165 Newhope St., "M," Fountain Valley, CA 92708. Andrew Crask and Tim Tuttle, Eds. Features and race reports, 500 to 2,500 words. Pays $4 per column inch, on publication.

**OPEN WHEEL**—P.O. Box 715, Ipswich, MA 01938. Dick Berggren, Ed. Articles, to 6,000 words, on open wheel drivers, races, and vehicles. Photos. Pays to $400 on publication.

**OUTDOOR AMERICA**—1401 Wilson Blvd., Level B, Arlington, VA 22209. Quarterly publication of the Izaak Walton League of America. Articles, 1,500 to 2,500 words, on natural resource conservation issues and outdoor recreation; especially fishing, hunting, and camping. Pays 20¢ a word. Query Articles Ed. with published clips.

**OUTDOOR CANADA**—703 Evans Ave., Suite 202, Toronto, Ont., Canada M9C 5E9. Ms. Teddi Brown, Ed. Published nine times yearly. Articles, 1,500 to 2,000 words, on outdoor sports, with an emphasis on fishing, for sportsmen and their families. Pays $200 to $600, on publication.

**PENNSYLVANIA ANGLER**—Pennsylvania Fish and Boat Commission, P.O. Box 67000, Harrisburg, PA 17106-7000. Address Art Michaels, Ed. Articles, 250 to 2,500 words, with photos, on freshwater fishing in Pennsylvania. Pays $50 to $250, on acceptance. Must send SASE with all material. Query. Guidelines.

**PENNSYLVANIA GAME NEWS**—Game Commission, 2001 Elmerton Ave., Harrisburg, PA 17110-9797. Bob Mitchell, Ed. Articles, to 2,500 words, with photos, on outdoor subjects, except fishing and boating. Photos. Pays from 6¢ a word, extra for photos, on acceptance.

**PETERSEN'S BOWHUNTING**—8490 Sunset Blvd., Los Angeles, CA 90069. Greg Tinsley, Ed. How-to articles, 2,000 to 2,500 words, on bowhunting. Also pieces on where to bowhunt, unusual techniques and equipment, and profiles of successful bowhunters will also be considered. Photos must accompany all manuscripts. Query. Pays $300 to $400, on acceptance.

**PETERSEN'S HUNTING**—8490 Sunset Blvd., Los Angeles, CA 90069. Craig Boddington, Ed. How-to articles, 2,500 words, on all aspects of sport hunting. B&W photos; color slides. Pays $300 to $500, on acceptance. Query.

**PGA MAGAZINE**—The Quartron Group, 2155 Butterfield, Suite 200, Troy, MI 48084. Articles, 1,500 to 2,500 words, on golf-related subjects. Pays $300 to $500, on acceptance. Query.

**PLEASURE BOATING**—See *Caribbean Sports & Travel.*

**POWERBOAT**—15917 Strathern St., Van Nuys, CA 91406. Lisa Nordskog, Ed. Articles, to 1,500 words, with photos, for high performance powerboat owners, on outstanding achievements, water-skiing, competitions; technical articles on hull and engine developments; how-to pieces. Pays $300 to $1,000, on acceptance. Query.

**PRACTICAL HORSEMAN**—Box 589, Unionville, PA 19375. Mandy Lorraine, Ed. How-to articles on English riding, training, and horse care. Pays on acceptance. Query.

**PRIVATE PILOT**—P.O. Box 6050, Mission Viejo, CA 92690–6050. Mary F. Silitch, Ed. Technically based aviation articles for general aviation pilots and aircraft owners, 1,000 to 4,000 words, for aviation enthusiasts. Photos. Pays $75 to $250, on publication. Query.

**PRO BASKETBALL ILLUSTRATED**—See *Hockey Illustrated.*

**PRO FOOTBALL ILLUSTRATED, PRO FOOTBALL PREVIEW**—See *Hockey Illustrated.*

**RIDER**—29901 Agoura Rd., Agoura Hills, CA 91301. Mark Tuttle Jr., Ed. Articles, with slides, to 3,000 words, with emphasis on travel, touring, commuting, and camping motorcyclists. Pays $100 to $500, on publication. Query.

**RUNNER TRIATHLETE NEWS**—P.O. Box 19909, Houston, TX 77224. Karissa G. Strong, Ed. Articles on running for road racing and multi-sport enthusiasts in Texas, Oklahoma, New Mexico, Louisiana, and Arkansas. Payment varies, on publication.

**RUNNER'S WORLD**—Rodale Press, 33 E. Minor St., Emmaus, PA 18098. Bob Wischnia, Sr. Ed. Articles for "Human Race" (submit to Eileen Shovlin), "Finish Line" (to Cristina Negron), and "Health Watch" (to Megan Othersen) columns. Send feature articles or queries to Bob Wischnia. Payment varies, on acceptance. Query.

**SAFARI**—4800 West Gates Pass Rd., Tucson, AZ 85745. William Quimby, Publications Dir. Articles, 2,000 words, on big game hunting. Pays $200, on publication. Pays extra for photos.

**SAIL**—275 Washington St., Newton, MA 02158–1630. Patience Wales, Ed. Articles, 1,500 to 3,500 words, features, 1,000 to 2,500 words, with photos, on sailboats, equipment, racing, and cruising. How-tos on navigation, sail trim, etc. Pays $75 to $1,000 on publication. Guidelines sent on request.

**SAILING**—125 E. Main St., Port Washington, WI 53074. M. L. Hutchins, Ed. Features, 700 to 1,500 words, with photos, on cruising and racing; first-person accounts; profiles of boats and regattas. Query for technical or how-to pieces. Pays varying rates, 30 days after publication. Guidelines.

**SALT WATER SPORTSMAN**—280 Summer St., Boston, MA 02210. Barry Gibson, Ed. Articles, 1,200 to 1,500 words, on how anglers can improve their skills, and on new places to fish off the coast of the U.S. and Canada, Central America, the Caribbean, and Bermuda. Photos a plus. Pays $350 to $700, on acceptance. Query.

**SCORE, CANADA'S GOLF MAGAZINE**—287 MacPherson Ave., Toronto, Ont., Canada M4V 1A7. Bob Weeks, Man. Ed. Articles, 800 to 2,000 words, on travel, golf equipment, golf history, personalities, and prominent professionals. Canadian content only. Pays $125 to $600 for features, on assignment and publication. Query with published clips and SAS with IRC.

**SEA, BEST OF BOATING IN THE WEST**—17782 Cowan, Suite C, Irvine,

CA 92714. John Vigor, Ed. Features, 800 to 1,500 words, and news articles, 200 to 250 words, of interest to West Coast powerboaters: profiles of boating personalities, cruise destinations, analyses of marine environmental issues, technical pieces on navigation and seamanship, news from western harbors. No fiction, poetry, or cartoons. Pays varying rates, on publication.

**SEA KAYAKER**—6327 Seaview Ave. N.W., Seattle, WA 98107–2664. Christopher Cunningham, Ed. Articles, 400 to 4,500 words, on ocean kayaking. Related fiction. Pays about 10¢ a word, on publication. Query with clips and international reply coupons.

**SHOTGUN SPORTS**—P.O. Box 6810, Auburn, CA 95604. Frank Kodl, Ed. Official publication of The United States Sporting Clays Assoc. Articles with photos, on trap and skeet shooting, sporting clays, hunting with shotguns, reloading, gun tests, and instructional shooting. Pays $25 to $200, on publication.

**THE SHOW**—100 W. Harrison, North Tower, 5th Fl., Seattle, WA 98119. Kenneth Leiker, Ed. Annual. Articles, 1,000 to 3,500 words, on the past, present, and future of baseball. Payment negotiable, on publication. Queries required.

**SILENT SPORTS**—717 10th St., P.O. Box 152, Waupaca, WI 54981–9990. Upper Midwest monthly with regional focus on bicycling, cross country skiing, running, canoeing, hiking, backpacking, and other "silent" sports; articles, 1,000 to 2,000 words. Pays $50 to $100 for features; $20 to $50 for fillers, on publication. Query.

**SKI MAGAZINE**—2 Park Ave., New York, NY 10016. Dick Needham, Ed. Articles, 1,300 to 2,000 words, for experienced skiers: profiles, humor, it-happened-to-me stories, and destination articles. Short, 100- to 300-word, news items for "Ski Life" column. Equipment and racing articles are staff written. Query first (with clips) for articles. Pays from $200, on acceptance.

**SKI RACING**—Box 1125, Rt. 100, Waitsfield, VT 05673. Articles on alpine and nordic racing, training, personalities. Photos. Rates vary.

**SKYDIVING MAGAZINE**—1725 N. Lexington Ave., DeLand, FL 32724. Michael Truffer, Ed. Timely news articles, 300 to 800 words, relating to sport and military parachuting. Fillers. Photos. Pays $25 to $200, extra for photos, on publication.

**SNOWBOARDER**—P.O. Box 1028, Dana Point, CA 92629. Doug Palladini, Assoc. Pub. Published 5 times yearly. Articles, 1,000 to 1,500 words, on snowboarding personalities, techniques, and events; color transparencies or B&W prints. Limited marked for fiction, 1,000 to 1,500 words. Pays $150 to $800, on acceptance and on publication.

**SNOWEST**—520 Park Ave., Idaho Falls, ID 83402. Steve Janes, Ed. Articles, 1,200 words, on snowmobiling in the western states. Pays to $100, on publication.

**SNOWMOBILE**—319 Barry Ave., S., Suite. 101, Wayzata, MN 55391. Dan Hauser, Ed. Articles, 700 to 2,000 words, with color or B&W photos, related to snowmobiling: races and rallies, trail rides, personalities, travel. How-tos; humor; cartoons. Pays to $500, on publication. Query.

**SOCCER AMERICA MAGAZINE**—P. O. Box 23704, Oakland, CA 94623. Paul Kennedy, Ed. Articles, to 500 words, on soccer: news, profiles. Pays $50, for features, within 60 days of publication.

**SOCCER JR.**—27 Unquowa Rd., Fairfield, CT 06430. Joe Provey, Ed. Articles, fiction, and fillers related to soccer for readers in 5th and 6th grade. Query. Pays $450 for features; $250 for department pieces, on acceptance.

**SOUTH CAROLINA WILDLIFE**—P. O. Box 167, Columbia , SC 29202–0167. John E. Davis, Ed. Articles, 1,000 to 3,000 words, with state and regional outdoor focus: conservation, natural history, wildlife, and recreation. Profiles, how-tos. Pays on acceptance.

**SOUTHERN OUTDOORS**—5845 Carmichael Pkwy., Montgomery, AL 36117. Larry Teague, Ed. Essays, 1,200 to 1,500 words, related to the outdoors. Pays 15¢ to 20¢ a word, on acceptance.

**SPORT MAGAZINE**—8490 Sunset Blvd., Los Angeles, CA 90069. Cam Benty, Ed. Dir. Query with clips. No fiction, poetry, or first person.

**THE SPORTING NEWS**—1212 N. Lindbergh Blvd., St. Louis, MO 63132. John D. Rawlings, Ed. Articles, 250 to 2,000 words, on baseball, football, basketball, hockey, and other sports. Queries must be timely. "We publish highly personal guest columns, but do not submit a guest column without reading back issues." Pays $150 to $1,000, on publication.

**SPORTS ILLUSTRATED**—1271 Avenue of the Americas, New York, NY 10020. Chris Hunt, Articles Ed. Query.

**SPUR MAGAZINE**—P. O. Box 85, Middleburg, VA 22117. Address Editorial Dept. Articles, 300 to 5,000 words, on thoroughbred racing, breeding, polo, show jumping, eventing, and steeplechasing. Profiles of people and farms. Historical and nostalgia pieces. Pays $50 to $400, on publication. Query.

**STARTING LINE**—P.O. Box 19909, Houston, TX 77224. Karissa G. Strong, Ed. Quarterly. Articles, to 800 words, for coaches, parents, and children, 8 to 18, on training for track and field, cross country, and racewalking, including techniques, health and fitness, nutrition, sports medicine, and related issues. Payment varies, on publication.

**STOCK CAR RACING**—P. O. Box 715, Ipswich, MA 01938. Dick Berggren, Feature Ed. Articles, to 6,000 words, on stock car drivers, races, and vehicles. Photos. Pays to $400, on publication.

**SURFER MAGAZINE**—P. O. Box 1028, Dana Point, CA 92629. Court Overin, Pub. Steve Hawk, Ed. Articles, 500 to 5,000 words, on surfing, surfers, etc. Photos. Pays 10¢ to 15¢ a word, $10 to $600 for photos, on publication.

**SURFING**—P. O. Box 3010, San Clemente, CA 92674. Nick Carroll, Ed. Eric Fairbanks, Man. Ed. Short newsy and humorous articles, 200 to 500 words. No first-person travel articles; knowledge of sport essential. Pays varying rates, on publication.

**TENNIS**—5520 Park Ave., P. O. Box 0395, Trumbull, CT 06611–0395. Donna Doherty, Ed. Instructional articles, features, profiles of tennis stars, grass-roots articles, humor, 800 to 2,000 words. Photos. Pays from $300, on publication. Query.

**TENNIS WEEK**—124 E. 40th St., Suite 1101, New York, NY 10016. Eugene L. Scott, Pub. Julie Tupper, Nina Talbot, Merrill Chapman, Man. Eds. In-depth, researched articles, from 1,000 words, on current issues and personalities in the game. Pays $125, on publication.

**TRAILER BOATS**—20700 Belshaw Ave., P. O. Box 5427, Carson, CA 90249–5427. Randy Scott, Ed. Technical and how-to articles, 500 to 2,000 words, on boat, trailer, or tow vehicle maintenance and operation; skiing, fishing, and cruising. Fillers, humor. Pays $100 to $700 a word, on acceptance.

**TRAILER LIFE**—29901 Agoura Rd., Agoura, CA 91301. Bill Estes, Ed. Articles, to 2,500 words, with photos, on trailering, truck campers, motorhomes, hobbies, and RV lifestyles. How-to pieces. Pays to $600, on acceptance. Send for guidelines.

**TRAILS-A-WAY**—Compass Publishing Group, P.O. Box 5000, Lake Forest, IL 60045–5000. Ann Emerson, Ed. RV-related travel articles, 1,000 to 1,200 words, for "the monthly magazine dedicated to Midwest camping families." Pay varies, on publication.

**TRIATHLETE**—1415 Third St., Suite 303, Santa Monica, CA 90401. Richard Graham, Ed. Published 11 times yearly. Articles, varying lengths, pertaining to the sport of triathlon. Color slides. Pays 20¢ to 30¢ a word, on publication.

**VELONEWS**—1830 North 55th St., Boulder, CO 80301. John Wilcockson, Ed. Articles, 500 to 1,500 words, on competitive cycling, training, nutrition; profiles, interviews. No how-to or touring articles. "We focus on the elite of the sport." Pay varies, on publication.

**THE WATER SKIER**—799 Overlook Dr., Winter Haven, FL 33884. Greg Nixon, Ed. Feature articles on waterskiing. Pays varying rates, on acceptance.

**THE WESTERN HORSEMAN**—P.O. Box 7980, Colorado Springs, CO 80933–7980. Pat Close, Ed. Articles, about 1,500 words, with photos, on care and training of horses; farm, ranch, and stable management; health care and veterinary medicine. Pays to $350, on acceptance.

**WESTERN OUTDOORS**—3197-E Airport Loop, Costa Mesa, CA 92626. Timely, factual articles on fishing and hunting, 1,200 to 1,500 words, of interest to western sportsmen. Pays $400 to $500, on acceptance. Query. Send first-class stamp for guidelines.

**WESTERN SPORTSMAN**—P.O. Box 737, Regina, Sask., Canada S4P 3A8. Roger Francis, Ed. Articles, to 2,500 words, on outdoor experiences in Alberta, Saskatchewan, and Manitoba; how-to pieces. Photos. Pays $75 to $325, on publication.

**WIND SURFING**—(formerly *Windrider*) P.O. Box 2456, Winter Park, FL 32790. Debbie Snow, Ed. Features, instructional pieces, and tips, by experienced boardsailors. Fast action photos. Pays $50 to $75 for tips, $250 to $300 for features, extra for photos. Send SASE for guidelines first.

**WINDRIDER**—See *Wind Surfing*.

**WINDY CITY SPORTS**—1450 W. Randolph, Chicago, IL 60607. Shelly Berryhill, Ed. Articles, 1,500 words, on amateur sports in Chicago. Query required. Pays $100, on publication.

**WOMAN BOWLER**—5301 S. 76th St., Greendale, WI 53129–1191. Jeff Nowak, Ed. Profiles, interviews, and news articles, to 1,000 words, for women bowlers. Pays varying rates, on acceptance. Query with outline.

**WOMEN'S SPORTS & FITNESS**—2025 Pearl St., Boulder, CO 80302. Marjorie McCloy, Ed. How-tos, profiles, active travel, and controversial issues in women's sports, 500 to 3,000 words. Fitness, nutrition, and health pieces also considered. Pays on publication.

**WRESTLING WORLD**—See *Hockey Illustrated*.

**YACHTING**—2 Park Ave., New York, NY 10016. Charles Barthold, Exec. Ed. Articles, 1,500 words, on upscale recreational power and sail boating. How-to and personal-experience pieces. Photos. Pays $350 to $1,000, on acceptance. Queries preferred.

# AUTOMOTIVE MAGAZINES

**AAA WORLD**—AAA Headquarters, 1000 AAA Dr., Heathrow, FL 32746–5063. Douglas Damerst, Ed. Automobile and travel concerns, including automotive travel, purchasing, and upkeep, 750 to 1,500 words. Pays $300 to $600, on acceptance. Query with clips; articles are by assignment only.

**AMERICAN MOTORCYCLIST**—American Motorcyclist Assn., Box 6114, Westerville, OH 43081–6114. Greg Harrison, Ed. Articles and fiction, to 3,000 words, on motorcycling: news coverage, personalities, tours. Photos. Pays varying rates, on publication. Query with SASE.

**CAR AND DRIVER**—2002 Hogback Rd., Ann Arbor, MI 48105. William Jeanes, Ed. Articles, to 2,500 words, for enthusiasts, on new cars, classic cars, industry topics. "Ninety percent staff-written. Query with clips. No unsolicited manuscripts." Pays to $2,500, on acceptance.

**CAR AUDIO AND ELECTRONICS**—21700 Oxnard St., Woodland Hills, CA 91367. Bill Neill, Ed. Features, 1,000 to 2,000 words, on electronic products for the car: audio systems, cellular telephones, security systems, CBs, radar detectors, etc.; how to buy them; how they work; how to use them. "To write for us, you must know this subject thoroughly." Pays $200 to $1,000, on acceptance. Send manuscript or query.

**CAR CRAFT**—8490 Sunset Blvd., Los Angeles, CA 90069. John Baechtel, Ed. Articles and photo features on high performance street machines, drag cars, racing events; technical pieces; action photos. Pays from $150 per page, on publication.

**HOT ROD**—8490 Sunset Blvd., Los Angeles, CA 90069. Jeff Smith, Ed. How-to pieces and articles, 500 to 5,000 words, on auto mechanics, hot rods, track and drag racing. Photo features on custom or performance-modified cars. Pays $250 per page, on publication.

**MOTOR TREND**—8490 Sunset Blvd., Los Angeles, CA 90069. Jeff Karr, Ed. Articles, 250 to 2,000 words, on autos, racing, events, and profiles. Photos. Pay varies, on acceptance. Query.

**OPEN WHEEL**—See *Stock Car Racing.*

**RESTORATION**—P.O. Box 50046, Tucson, AZ 85703–1046. W.R. Haessner, Ed. Articles, 1,200 to 1,800 words, on restoration of autos, trucks, planes, trains, etc., and related building (bridges, structures, etc.). Photos. Pays varying rates, from $25 per page, on publication. Queries required.

**RIDER**—29901 Agoura Rd., Agoura Hills, CA 91301. Mark Tuttle Jr., Ed. Articles, to 3,000 words, with color slides, with emphasis on travel, touring, commuting, and camping motorcyclists. Pays $100 to $500, on publication. Query.

**ROAD & TRACK**—1499 Monrovia Ave., Newport Beach, CA 92663. Ellida Maki, Man. Ed. Short automotive articles, to 450 words, of "timeless nature," for knowledgeable car enthusiasts. Pays on publication. Query.

**STOCK CAR RACING**—P.O. Box 715, Ipswich, MA 01938. Dick Berggren, Ed. Features, technical automotive pieces, up to ten typed pages, for oval track racing enthusiasts. Fillers. Pays $75 to $350, on publication. Same requirements for *Open Wheel*.

**TRUCKERS/USA**—P.O. Box 323, Windber, PA 15963. David Adams, Ed. Articles, 500 to 1,000 words, on the trucking business and marketing. Poetry and trucking-related fiction. Pay is negotiable, on acceptance.

# FITNESS MAGAZINES

**AMERICAN FITNESS**—15250 Ventura Blvd., Suite 310, Sherman Oaks, CA 91403. Peg Jordan, Ed. Rhonda Wilson, Man. Ed. Articles, 500 to 1,500 words, on exercise, health, sports, nutrition, etc. Illustrations, photos, cartoons.

**EAST WEST: THE JOURNAL OF NATURAL HEALTH & LIVING**—See *Natural Health: The Guide to Well-Being*.

**FITNESS**—The New York Times Company Women's Magazines, 110 Fifth Ave., New York, NY 10011. Karen Larson, Deputy Ed. Articles, 500 to 2,000 words, on health, exercise, sports, nutrition, diet, psychological well-being, sex, and beauty for 28-year-old readers. Profiles of athletes and fit celebrities. Queries required. Pays $1 per word, on acceptance.

**IDEA TODAY**—6190 Cornerstone Ct. East, Suite 204, San Diego, CA 92121–3773. Patricia Ryan, Ed. Practical articles, 1,000 to 3,000 words, on new exercise programs, business management, nutrition, sports medicine, dance-exercise, and one-to-one training techniques. Articles must be geared toward the aerobics instructor, exercise studio owner or manager, or personal trainer. Don't query for consumer or general health articles. Payment is negotiable, on acceptance. Query preferred.

**MEN'S FITNESS**—21100 Erwin St., Woodland Hills, CA 91367. Jim Rosenthal, Fitness Ed. Features, 1,500 to 2,500 words, and department pieces, 1,000 to 1,500 words: "authoritative and practical articles dealing with fitness, health, and men's lifestyles." Pays $350 to $1,000, on acceptance.

**MUSCULAR DEVELOPMENT**—505-H Saddle River Rd., Saddle Brook, NJ 07662. Alan Paul, Ed. Articles, 1,000 to 2,500 words, on competitive bodybuilding, power lifting, sports, and nutrition for serious weight training athletes: personality profiles, training features, and diet and nutrition pieces. Photos. Pays $100 to $300 for articles; $35 for color photos; $20 for B&W; and $300 to $500 for cover photos.

**NATURAL HEALTH: THE GUIDE TO WELL-BEING**—(formerly *East West: The Journal of Natural Health & Living*) 17 Station St., Box 1200, Brookline, MA 02147. Features, 1,500 to 2,500 words, on holistic health, natural foods, herbal remedies, etc. Interviews. Photos. Pays 20¢ a word, extra for photos, on acceptance.

**NEW BODY**—1700 Broadway, New York, NY 10019. Nicole Dorsey, Ed. Lively, readable service-oriented articles, 800 to 1,500 words, on exercise, nutrition, lifestyle, diet, and health for women ages 18 to 35. Writers should have some background in or knowledge of the health field. Also considers 500- to 600-word essays for "How I Lost It" column by writers who have lost weight and kept it off. Pays $100 to $300, on publication. Query.

**THE PHYSICIAN AND SPORTSMEDICINE**—4530 W. 77th St., Minneapolis, MN 55435. Terry Monahan, Man. Ed. News and feature articles. Clinical articles must be co-authored by physicians. Sports medicine angle necessary. Pays $150 to $1,000, on acceptance. Query first. Guidelines.

**SHAPE**—21100 Erwin St., Woodland Hills, CA 91367–3772. Elizabeth Turner, Asst. Ed. Articles, 1,200 to 1,500 words, with new and interesting ideas on the physical and mental side of getting and staying in shape; reports, 300 to 400 words, on journal research. Mostly expert bylines. Payment varies, on publication. Guidelines. Limited market.

**VEGETARIAN TIMES**—P.O. Box 570, Oak Park, IL 60303. Paul Obis, Pub.

Articles, 1,200 to 2,500 words, on vegetarian cooking, nutrition, health and fitness, and profiles of prominent vegetarians. "News Items" and "In Print" (book reviews), to 500 words. "Herbalist" pieces, to 1,800 words, on medicinal uses of herbs. Queries preferred. Pays $75 to $375, on acceptance. Guidelines.

**VIM & VIGOR**—8805 N. 23rd Ave., Suite 11, Phoenix, AZ 85021. Fred Petrovsky, Ed. Positive articles, with accurate medical facts, on health and fitness, 1,200 to 2,000 words, by assignment only. Pays $450, on acceptance. Query.

**WOMEN'S SPORTS & FITNESS**—2025 Pearl St., Boulder, CO 80302. Marjorie McCloy, Ed. How-tos, profiles, active travel, and controversial issues in women's sports, 500 to 3,000 words. Fitness, nutrition, and health pieces also considered. Pays on publication.

**YOGA JOURNAL**—2054 University Ave., Berkeley, CA 94704. Stephan Bodian, Ed. Articles, 1,200 to 4,000 words, on holistic health, meditation, consciousness, spirituality, and yoga. Pays $50 to $500, on publication.

## CONSUMER/PERSONAL FINANCE

**BETTER HOMES AND GARDENS**—750 Third Ave., New York, NY 10017. Margaret V. Daly, Exec. Features Ed. Articles, 750 to 1,000 words, on "any and all topics that would be of interest to family-oriented, middle-income people."

**BLACK ENTERPRISE**—130 Fifth Ave., New York, NY 10011. Earl G. Graves, Ed. Articles on money management, careers, political issues, entrepreneurship, high technology, and lifestyles for black professionals. Profiles. Pays on acceptance. Query.

**CONSUMERS DIGEST**—5705 N. Lincoln Ave., Chicago, IL 60659. John Manos, Ed. Articles, 500 to 3,000 words, on subjects of interest to consumers: products and services, automobiles, travel, health, fitness, consumer legal affairs, and personal money management. Photos. Pays from 35¢ to 50¢ a word, extra for photos, on acceptance. Query with resumé and clips.

**FAMILY CIRCLE**—110 Fifth Ave., New York, NY 10011. Susan Ungaro, Exec. Ed. Susan Sherry, Sr. Ed. Enterprising, creative, and practical articles, 1,000 to 1,500 words, on investing, starting a business, secrets of successful entrepreneurs, and consumer news on smart shopping. Query first with clips. Pays $1 a word, on acceptance.

**GOLDEN YEARS**—P.O. Box 537, Melbourne, FL 32902–0537. Carol Brenner Hittner, Ed. "We consider articles, to 600 words, on preretirement, retirement planning, real estate, travel, celebrity profiles, humor, and contemporary issues of particular interest to affluent people over 50." Pays on publication.

**KIPLINGER'S PERSONAL FINANCE MAGAZINE**—1729 H St. N.W., Washington, DC 20006. Articles on personal finance (i.e., buying a stereo, mutual funds). Length and payment vary. Query required. Pays on acceptance.

**KIWANIS**—3636 Woodview Trace, Indianapolis, IN 46468. Chuck Jonak, Exec. Ed. Articles, 2,500 to 3,000 words, on financial planning for younger families and retirement planning for older people. Pays $400 to $1,000, on acceptance. Query required.

**MODERN MATURITY**—3200 E. Carson St., Lakewood, CA 90712. J. Henry Fenwick, Ed. Articles, 1,000 to 2,000 words, on a wide range of financial topics of interest to people over 50. Pays to $2,500. Queries required.

**MONEY MAKER**—See *Your Money.*

**THE MONEYPAPER**—1010 Mamaroneck Ave., Mamaroneck, NY 10543. Vita Nelson, Ed. Financial news and money-saving ideas. Brief, well-researched articles on personal finance, money management: saving, earning, investing, taxes, insurance, and related subjects. Pays $75 for articles, on publication. Query with resumé and writing sample.

**SELF**—350 Madison Ave., New York, NY 10017. Anne Field, Money/Careers Ed. Articles, 1,200 to 1,500 words, on money matters for career women in their 20s and 30s. Pays from $1,000, on acceptance. Query first.

**WOMAN'S DAY**—1633 Broadway, New York, NY 10019. Rebecca Greer, Articles Ed. Articles, to 2,500 words, on financial matters of interest to a broad range of women. Pays top rates, on acceptance. Query first.

**WORTH**—82 Devonshire St., R25A, Boston, MA 02109. Sheryl Argiro, Ed. Asst. Articles on personal finance for "sophisticated people who are not necessarily sophisticated investors." Possible topics: taking control of your finances; achieving financial well-being; balancing family and career; coping with aging and health; understanding the impact of government, the financial markets, and other institutions on your financial life. Payment varies, on acceptance. Query with clips and SASE.

**YOUR MONEY**—(formerly *Money Maker*) 5705 N. Lincoln Ave., Chicago, IL 60659. Dennis Fertig, Ed. Informative, jargon-free personal finance articles, to 2,500 words, for the general reader, on investment opportunities and personal finance. Pays 25¢ a word, on acceptance. Query with clips for assignment. (Do not send manuscripts on disks.)

## BUSINESS AND TRADE PUBLICATIONS

**ABA JOURNAL**—American Bar Association, 750 N. Lake Shore Dr., Chicago, IL 60611. Gary A. Hengstler, Ed./Pub. Articles, to 3,000 words, on law-related topics: current events in the law and ideas that will help lawyers practice better and more efficiently. Writing should be in an informal, journalistic style. Pays from $1,000, on acceptance; buys all rights.

**ACCESS CONTROL**—6255 Barfield Rd., Atlanta, GA 30328. John Brady, Ed. Comprehensive case studies on large-scale access control installations in industrial, commercial, governmental, retail, and transportational environments: door and card entry, gates and operators, turnstiles and portals, perimeter security fencing and its accessories, perimeter and interior sensors, CCTV technology, system design strategies, integration of hardware, and guard services. Photos. Pays from 20¢ a word, extra for photos, on publication. Query.

**ACCESSORIES MAGAZINE**—50 Day St., Norwalk, CT 06854. Reenie Brown, Ed. Dir. Articles, with photos, for women's fashion accessories buyers and manufacturers. Profiles of retailers, designers, manufacturers; articles on merchandising and marketing. Pays $75 to $100 for short articles, from $100 to $300 for features, on publication. Query.

**ACROSS THE BOARD**—845 Third Ave., New York, NY 10022. John Ramos, Asst. Ed. Articles, to 5,000 words, on a variety of topics of interest to business executives; straight business angle not required. Pays $100 to $1,000, on publication.

**ALTERNATIVE ENERGY RETAILER**—P.O. Box 2180, Waterbury, CT

06722. John Florian, Ed. Dir. Feature articles, 1,000 words, for retailers of alternative energy products: wood, coal, and fireplace products and services. Interviews with successful retailers, stressing the how-to. B&W photos. Pays $200, extra for photos, on publication. Query first.

**AMERICAN COIN-OP**—500 N. Dearborn St., Chicago, IL 60610–9988. Laurance Cohen, Ed. Articles, to 2,500 words, with photos, on successful coin-operated laundries: management, promotion, decor, maintenance, etc. Pays from 8¢ a word, $8 per B&W photo, 2 weeks prior to publication. Query. Send SASE for guidelines.

**AMERICAN DEMOGRAPHICS**—P.O. Box 68, Ithaca, NY 14851–9989. Brad Edmondson, Ed.-in-Chief. Articles, 500 to 2,000 words, on the four key elements of a consumer market (its size, its needs and wants, its ability to pay, and how it can be reached), with specific examples of how companies market to consumers. Readers include marketers, advertisers, and strategic planners. Pays $100 to $500, on acceptance. Query.

**AMERICAN FARRIERS JOURNAL**—P.O. Box 624, Brookfield, WI 53008–0624. Frank Lessiter, Ed. Articles, 800 to 2,000 words, on general farriery issues, hoof care, tool selection, equine lameness, and horse handling. Pays 30¢ per published line, $10 per published illustration or photo, on publication. Query.

**AMERICAN MEDICAL NEWS**—515 N. State St., Chicago, IL 60610. Ronni Scheier, Asst. Exec. Ed. Features, 1,000 to 3,000 words, on socioeconomic developments of interest to physicians across the country. No pieces on health, clinical treatments, or research. Query required. Pays $500 to $1,500, on acceptance. Guidelines.

**THE AMERICAN SALESMAN**—424 N. Third St., P.O. Box 1, Burlington, IA 52601–0001. Barbara Boeding, Ed. Articles, 900 to 1,200 words, on techniques for increasing sales. Author photos requested on article acceptance. Buys all rights. Pays 3¢ a word, on publication. Guidelines.

**AMERICAN SALON**—7500 Old Oak Blvd., Cleveland, OH 44130. Angela Watkins, Ed. Official publication of the National Cosmetology Assoc. Business and fashion articles of varying lengths for salon professionals. Payment varies, on publication. Query.

**AMERICAN SCHOOL & UNIVERSITY**—401 N. Broad St., Philadelphia, PA 19108. Joe Agron, Ed. Articles and case studies, 1,200 to 1,500 words, on design, construction, operation, and management of school and college facilities.

**ARCHITECTURE**—1130 Connecticut Ave. N.W., Suite 625, Washington, DC 20036. Address Man. Ed. Articles, to 3,000 words, on architecture, building technology, professional practice. Pays 50¢ a word.

**AREA DEVELOPMENT MAGAZINE**—400 Post Ave., Westbury, NY 11590. Tom Bergeron, Ed. Articles for top executives of industrial companies on sites and facility planning. Pays $60 per manuscript page. Query.

**ART BUSINESS NEWS**—777 Summer St., P.O. Box 3837, Stamford, CT 06905. Fergus Reid, Ed. Articles, 1,000 words, for art dealers and framers, on trends and events of national importance to the art industry, and relevant business subjects. Pays from $100, on publication. Query preferred.

**ART MATERIAL TRADE NEWS**—6255 Barfield Rd., Atlanta, GA 30328–4369. Tom Cooper, Ed. Articles, from 800 words, for dealers, wholesalers, and manufacturers of artist materials; must be specific to trade. Pays to 15¢ a word, on publication. Query.

635

**AUTOMATED BUILDER**—P.O. Box 120, Carpinteria, CA 93014. Don Carlson, Ed. Articles, 500 to 750 words, on various types of home manufacturers and dealers. Query required. Pays $300, on acceptance, for articles with slides.

**BARRISTER**—American Bar Assn., 750 N. Lake Shore Dr., Chicago, IL 60611–4403. Vicki Quade, Ed. Articles, 250 to 3,000 words, on legal and social issues, for young lawyers. Pays $250 to $1,000, on acceptance. Query.

**BARRON'S**—200 Liberty St., New York, NY 10281. Alan Abelson, Ed. National-interest articles, 1,200 to 2,500 words, on business and finance. Query.

**BEAUTY EDUCATION**—2 Computer Dr. W., Albany, NY 12212. Catherine Frangie, Pub. Articles, 750 to 1,000 words, that provide beauty educators, trainers, and professionals in the cosmetology industry with information, skills, and techniques on such topics as hairstyling, makeup, aromatherapy, retailing, massage, and beauty careers. Send SASE for editorial calendar with monthly themes. Pays $50 to $75, on publication. Query.

**BICYCLE RETAILER AND INDUSTRY NEWS**—1444-C South St. Francis Dr., Santa Fe, NM 87501. Marc Sani, Ed. Articles, 50 to 1,200 words, on employee management, employment strategies, and general business subjects for bicycle manufacturers, distributors, and retailers. Monthly. Pays 20¢ a word, plus expenses, on acceptance; fee is negotiable for complex stories. Query.

**BOATING INDUSTRY**—5 Penn Plaza, 13th Floor, New York, NY 10001–1810. Richard W. Porter, Ed. Articles, 1,000 to 2,500 words, on marine products, management, merchandising and selling, for boat dealers. Photos. Pays varying rates, on publication. Query.

**BUILDER**—Hanley-Wood, Inc., 655 15th St. N.W., Suite 475, Washington, DC 20005. Mitchell B. Rouda, Ed. Articles, to 1,500 words, on trends and news in home building: design, marketing, new products, etc. Pays negotiable rates, on acceptance. Query.

**BUSINESS AND COMMERCIAL AVIATION**—4 International Dr., Rye Brook, NY 10573. John W. Olcott, Ed. Articles, 2,500 words, with photos, for pilots, on use of private aircraft for business transportation. Pays $100 to $500, on acceptance. Query.

**BUSINESS ATLANTA**—6151 Powers Ferry Rd., Atlanta, GA 30339–2941. John Sequerth, Ed. Articles, 1,000 to 3,000 words, with Atlanta business angle, strong marketing slant that will be useful to top Atlanta executives and business people. Pays $300 to $1,000, on publication. Query with clippings.

**BUSINESS MARKETING**—740 N. Rush St., Chicago, IL 60611. Steve Yahn, Ed. Articles on selling, advertising, and promoting products and services to business buyers. Pays competitive rates, on acceptance. Queries are required.

**BUSINESS TIMES**—P.O. Box 580, 315 Peck St., New Haven, CT 06513. Joel MacClaren, Ed. Articles on Connecticut-based businesses and corporations. Query.

**BUSINESS TODAY**—P.O. Box 10010, 1720 Washington Blvd., Ogden, UT 84409. Caroll Shreeve, Pub./Ed.-in-Chief. Informative articles, 1,200 words, on business concerns of the businessperson/entrepreneur in U.S. and Canada. Color photos. Pays 15¢ a word, $35 for photos, $50 for cover photos, on acceptance. Query. Send SASE for guidelines.

**CALIFORNIA BUSINESS**—4221 Wilshire Blvd., Suite 400, Los Angeles, CA 90010. G.B. Engel, Ed. Articles, 1,200 to 3,000 words, on business and econometric issues in California. Pays varying rates, on acceptance. Query.

**CALIFORNIA LAWYER**—1390 Market St., Suite 1210, San Francisco, CA 94102. Thomas Brom, Man. Ed. Articles, 2,500 to 3,000 words, for attorneys in California, on legal subjects (or the legal aspects of a given political or social issue); how-tos on improving legal skills and law office technology. Pays $300 to $1,200, on acceptance. Query.

**CAMPGROUND MANAGEMENT**—P.O. Box 5000, Lake Forest, IL 60045–5000. Mike Byrnes, Ed. Detailed articles, 500 to 2,000 words, on managing recreational vehicle campgrounds. Photos. Pays $50 to $200, after publication.

**CHEESE MARKET NEWS**—See *Dairy Foods Magazine*.

**CHIEF EXECUTIVE**—233 Park Ave. S., New York, NY 10003. J.P. Donlon, Ed. CEO bylines. Articles, 2,500 to 3,000 words, on management, financial, or business strategy. Departments on investments, amenities, and travel, 1,200 to 1,500 words. Features on CEOs at leisure, Q&A's with CEOs, other topics. Pays varying rates, on acceptance. Query required.

**CHINA, GLASS & TABLEWARE**—P.O. Box 2147, Clifton, NJ 07015. Amy Stavis, Ed. Case histories and interviews, 1,500 to 2,500 words, with photos, on merchandising of china and glassware. Pays $50 per page, on publication. Query.

**CHRISTIAN RETAILING**—600 Rinehart Rd., Lake Mary, FL 32746. Brian Peterson, Ed. Articles, 1,000 to 2,000 words, on new products, industry news, or topics related to running a profitable Christian retail store. Pays $50 to $300, on publication.

**CLEANING MANAGEMENT MAGAZINE**—13 Century Hill Dr., Latham, NY 12110–2197. Tom Williams, Ed. Articles, 500 to 1,200 words, on managing efficient cleaning and custodial/maintenance operations, profiles, photo features, or general-interest articles directly related to the industry; also technical/mechanical how-tos. Photos encouraged. Query first. Pays to $200 for features, on publication. Guidelines.

**COMMERCIAL CARRIER JOURNAL**—Chilton Way, Radnor, PA 19089. Jerry Standley, Ed. Thoroughly researched, focused articles on private fleets and for-hire trucking operations. Pays from $50, on acceptance. Queries required.

**COMPUTER GRAPHICS WORLD**—One Technology Park Dr., Westford, MA 01886. Stephen Porter, Ed. Articles, 1,000 to 3,000 words, on computer graphics technology and its use in science, engineering, architecture, film and broadcast, and graphic arts areas. Photos. Pays $600 to $1,200 per article, on acceptance. Query.

**CONCORD AND THE NORTH**—See *Network Publications.*

**CONCRETE INTERNATIONAL**—Box 19150, 22400 W. Seven Mile Rd., Detroit, MI 48219–1849. William J. Semioli, Assoc. Pub. & Ed. Articles, 6 to 12 double-spaced pages, on concrete construction and design, with drawings and/or photos. Pays $100 per printed page, on publication. Query.

**THE CONSTRUCTION SPECIFIER**—Construction Specifications Institute, 601 Madison St., Alexandria, VA 22314. Kristina A. Kessler, Ed. Technical articles, 1,000 to 3,000 words, on the "nuts and bolts" of commercial construction, for architects, engineers, specifiers, contractors, and manufacturers. Pays 15¢ per word, on publication.

**CONVENIENCE STORE NEWS**—7 Penn Plaza, New York, NY 10001. Barbara Francella, Ed. Features and news items, 500 to 750 words, for convenience store owners, and operators. Photos, with captions. Pays $3 per column inch or negotiated price for features; extra for photos, on publication. Query.

**COOKING FOR PROFIT**—P.O. Box 267, Fond du Lac, WI 54936–0267. Colleen Phalen, Ed. Practical how-to articles, 1,000 words, on commercial food preparation, gas energy management; case studies, etc. Pays $75 to $250, on publication.

**CORPORATE CASHFLOW**—6255 Barfield Rd., Atlanta, GA 30328. Richard Gamble, Ed. Articles, 1,250 to 2,500 words, for treasury managers in public and private institutions: cash management; investments; domestic and international financing; credit and collection management; developments in law, economics, and tax. Pays $125 per published page, on publication. Query.

**CRAIN'S CHICAGO BUSINESS**—740 Rush St., Chicago, IL 60611. David Snyder, Man. Ed. Business articles about the Chicago metropolitan area exclusively. Pays $12 per column inch, on acceptance.

**CREDIT AND COLLECTION MANAGER'S LETTER**—(formerly *Credit and Collection Management Bulletin*) Bureau of Business Practice, 24 Rope Ferry Rd., Waterford, CT 06386. Russell Case, Ed. Interviews, 500 to 1,250 words, for commercial and consumer credit managers, on innovations, successes, and problem solving. Query.

**DAIRY FOODS MAGAZINE**—Delta Communications, 455 N. Cityfront Pl., Chicago, IL 60611. Mike Pehanich, Ed. Articles, to 2,500 words, on innovative dairies, dairy processing operations, marketing successes, new products, for milk handlers and makers of dairy products. Fillers, 25 to 150 words. Pays $25 to $300, $5 to $25 for fillers, on publication. Same requirements for *Cheese Market News*.

**DEALERSCOPE MERCHANDISING**—North American Publishing Co., 401 N. Broad St., Philadelphia, PA 19108. Murray Slovick, Ed. Articles, 750 to 3,000 words, for dealers and distributors of audio, video, personal computers for the home, office; satellite TV systems for the home; major appliances on sales, marketing, and finance. How-tos for retailers. Pays varying rates, on publication. Query with clips.

**DENTAL ECONOMICS**—P.O. Box 3408, Tulsa, OK 74101. Dick Hale, Ed. Articles, 1,200 to 3,500 words, on business side of dental practice, patient and staff communication, personal investments, etc. Pays $100 to $400, on acceptance.

**DRUG TOPICS**—Five Paragon Dr., Montvale, NJ 07645–1742. Valentine A. Cardinale, Ed. News items, 500 words, with photos, on drug retailers and associations. Merchandising features, 1,000 to 1,500 words. Pays $100 to $150 for news, $200 to $400 for features, on acceptance. Query for features.

**EMERGENCY**—6300 Yarrow Dr., Carlsbad, CA 92009–1597. Rhonda Foster, Ed. Features, to 3,000 words, and department pieces, to 2,000 words, of interest to paramedics, emergency medical technicians, flight nurses, and other pre-hospital personnel: disaster management, advanced and basic life support, assessment, treatment. Pays $100 to $400 for features, $50 to $250 for departments. Photos are a plus. Guidelines and editorial calendar available.

**EMPLOYEE SERVICES MANAGEMENT**—NESRA, 2400 S. Downing, Westchester, IL 60154–5199. Cynthia M. Helson, Ed. Articles, 1,200 to 2,500 words, for human resource, fitness, and employee service professionals.

**THE ENGRAVERS JOURNAL**—26 Summit St., P.O. Box 318, Brighton, MI 48116. Rosemary Farrell, Man. Ed. Articles, of varying lengths, on topics related to the engraving industry or small business. Pays $60 to $175, on acceptance. Query.

**ENTREPRENEUR**—2392 Morse Ave., Irvine, CA 92714. Rieva Lesonsky,

638

Ed.-in-Chief. Articles for established and aspiring independent business owners, on all aspects of running a business. Pay varies, on acceptance. Query required.

**ENTREPRENEURIAL WOMAN**—2392 Morse Ave., Irvine, CA 92714. Rieva Lesonsky, Ed.-in-Chief. Profiles, 1,800 words, of female entrepreneurs; how-tos on running a business; and pieces on coping as a woman owning a business. Payment varies, on acceptance.

**EQUIPMENT WORLD**—P.O. Box 2029, Tuscaloosa, AL 35403. Marcia Gruver, Ed. Features, 500 to 1,500 words, for contractors who buy, sell, and use heavy equipment; articles on equipment selection, application, maintenance, management, and replacement. Pay varies, on acceptance.

**EXECUTIVE FEMALE**—127 W. 24th St., New York, NY 10011. Basia Hellwig, Ed.-in-Chief. Articles, 750 to 2,500 words, on managing people, time, money, and careers, for women in business. Pays varying rates, on acceptance. Query.

**FARM JOURNAL**—230 W. Washington Sq., Philadelphia, PA 19106. Earl Ainsworth, Ed. Practical business articles, 500 to 1,500 words, with photos, on growing crops and raising livestock. Pays 20¢ to 50¢ a word, on acceptance. Query required.

**FARM STORE**—P.O. Box 2400, 12400 Whitewater Dr., Suite 160, Minnetonka, MN 55343. Julie Emnett, Ed. Articles, 500 to 1,500 words, of interest to farm store owners and managers. Payment varies, on publication. Query.

**FISHING TACKLE RETAILER MAGAZINE**—P.O. Box 17151, Montgomery, AL 36141–0151. Dave Ellison, Ed. Articles, 300 to 1,250 words, for merchants who carry angling equipment. Business focus is required, and writers should provide practical information for improving management and merchandising. Pays varying rates, on acceptance.

**FITNESS MANAGEMENT**—P.O. Box 1198, Solana Beach, CA 92075. Edward H. Pitts, Ed. Authoritative features, 750 to 2,500 words, and news shorts, 100 to 750 words, for owners, managers, and program directors of fitness centers. Content must be in keeping with current medical practice; no fads. Pays 8¢ a word, on publication. Query.

**FLORIST**—29200 Northwestern Hwy., P.O. Box 2227, Southfield, MI 48037–1099. Susan Nicholas, Man. Ed. Articles, to 2,000 words, with photos, on retail florist business improvement. Photos.

**FLOWERS &**—Teleflora Plaza, Suite 118, 12233 W. Olympic Blvd., Los Angeles, CA 90064. Marie Moneysmith, Ed.-in-Chief. Articles, 1,000 to 3,500 words, with how-to information for retail florists. Pays from $500, on acceptance. Query with clips.

**FOOD MANAGEMENT**—270 Madison Ave., 5th Fl., New York, NY 10016. Donna Boss, Ed. Articles on food service in hospitals, nursing homes, schools, colleges, prisons, businesses, and industrial sites. Trends and how-to pieces, with management tie-in; legislative issues. Query.

**FREQUENT FLYER**—1775 Broadway, New York, NY 10019. Joe Brancatelli, Exec. Ed. Articles, 1,000 to 3,000 words, on all aspects of frequent business travel, international trade, aviation, etc. Few pleasure travel articles; no personal experience pieces. Pays to $500, on acceptance. Query.

**THE FUTURE, NOW: INNOVATIVE VIDEO**—Blue Feather Co., N8494 Poplar Grove Rd., P.O. Box 669, New Glarus, WI 53574–0669. Becky Hustad, Ed.

Articles, to 2 pages, on new ideas in the video industry. Pays from $75 to $150, on bimonthly publication.

**GENERAL AVIATION NEWS & FLYER**—P.O. Box 98786, Tacoma, WA 98498–0786. Dave Sclair, Pub. Articles, 500 to 2,500 words, of interest to "general aviation" pilots. "Best shot for non-pilot writers is 'destination' series: attractions and activities near airports not necessarily aviation oriented." Pays to $3 per column inch (approximately 40 words); $10 for B&W photos; to $50 for color photos; within the first month of publication.

**GENETIC ENGINEERING NEWS**—1651 Third Ave., New York, NY 10128. John Sterling, Man. Ed. Features and news articles on all aspects of biotechnology. Pays varying rates, on acceptance. Query.

**GLOBAL PRODUCTION**—1301 Spruce St., Boulder, CO 80302. Victoria Cooper, Ed. "We are looking for Spanish-speaking writers who have an interest in writing about manufacturing issues in the Caribbean, Mexico, and Central America." Articles, 500 to 2,500 words. Published bimonthly for manufacturing managers and support services in the U.S., Canada, Europe, Asia, and Latin America. Pays 30¢ a word, on acceptance. Query for assignment.

**GOLF COURSE NEWS**—38 Lafayette St., P.O. Box 997, Yarmouth, ME 04096. Hal Phillips, Ed. Features, 500 to 1,500 words, on all aspects of golf course maintenance, design, building, and management. Payment varies, on acceptance.

**GREENHOUSE MANAGER**—P.O. Box 1868, Fort Worth, TX 76101–1868. David Kuack, Ed. How-to articles, success stories, 500 to 1,800 words, accompanied by color slides, of interest to professional greenhouse growers. Profiles. Pays $50 to $300, on acceptance. Query required.

**HAMPSHIRE EAST**—See *Network Publications.*

**HARDWARE AGE**—Chilton Way, Radnor, PA 19089. Terrence V. Gallagher, Chief Ed. Articles on merchandising methods in hardware outlets. Photos. Pays on acceptance.

**HARDWARE TRADE**—2965 Broadmoor Valley Rd., Suite B, Colorado Springs, CO 80906. Edith Briggs, Ed. Dir. Articles, 800 to 1,000 words, on unusual hardware and home center stores and promotions in the Northwest and Midwest. Photos. Query.

**HARVARD BUSINESS REVIEW**—Harvard Graduate School of Business Administration, Boston, MA 02163. Query editors, in writing, on new ideas about management of interest to senior executives.

**HEALTH FOODS BUSINESS**—567 Morris Ave., Elizabeth, NJ 07208. Gina Geslewitz, Ed. Articles, 1,200 words, with photos, profiling health food stores. Shorter pieces on trends, research findings, preventive medicine, alternative therapies. Interviews with doctors and nutritionists. Pays on publication. Query. Send for guidelines.

**HEALTH PROGRESS**—4455 Woodson Rd., St. Louis, MO 63134–3797. Judy Cassidy, Ed. Journal of the Catholic Health Association. Features, 2,000 to 4,000 words, on hospital and nursing home management and administration, medical-moral questions, health care, public policy, technological developments in health care and their effects, nursing, financial and human resource management for health-care administrators, and innovative programs in hospitals and long-term care facilities. Payment negotiable. Query.

**HEARTH & HOME**—P.O. Box 2008, Laconia, NH 03247. Kenneth E. Daggett, Pub./Ed. Profiles and interviews, 1,000 to 1,800 words, with specialty retailers selling both casual furniture and hearth products (fireplaces, woodstoves, accessories, etc.). Pays $150 to $250, on acceptance.

**HEATING/PIPING/AIR CONDITIONING**—2 Illinois Center, Chicago, IL 60601. Robert T. Korte, Ed. Articles, to 5,000 words, on heating, piping, and air conditioning systems in industrial plants and large buildings; engineering information. Pays $60 per printed page, on publication. Query.

**HOME OFFICE COMPUTING**—Scholastic, Inc., 730 Broadway, New York, NY 10003. Mike Espindle, Man. Ed. Articles of interest to people operating businesses out of their homes: product roundups, profiles of successful businesses, marketing, and financial tips and advice. Payment varies, on acceptance.

**HOSPITAL SUPERVISOR'S BULLETIN**—24 Rope Ferry Rd., Waterford, CT 06386. Michele Dunaj, Ed. Interviews, articles with non-medical hospital supervisors on departmental problem solving. Pays 12¢ to 15¢ a word. Query.

**HOSPITALS**—737 N. Michigan Ave., Chicago, IL 60611. Mary Grayson, Ed. Articles, 800 to 3,200 words, for hospital administrators. Pays varying rates, on acceptance. Query.

**HUMAN RESOURCE EXECUTIVE**—Axon Group, 747 Dresher Rd., Horsham, PA 19044–0980. David Shadovitz, Ed. Profiles and case stories, 1,800 to 2,200 words, of interest to people in the personnel profession. Pays varying rates, on acceptance. Queries required.

**INC.**—38 Commercial Wharf, Boston, MA 02110. George Gendron, Ed. No free-lance material.

**INCOME OPPORTUNITIES**—1500 Broadway, New York, NY 10036–4015. Stephen Wagner, Ed. Helpful articles, 1,000 to 2,500 words, on how to make money full- or part-time; how to start a successful small business, improve sales, etc. Pays varying rates, on acceptance.

**INCOME PLUS**—73 Spring St., Suite 303, New York, NY 10012. Roxane Farmanfarmaian, Ed. How-to articles on starting a small business, franchise, or mail-order operation. Payment varies, on publication. Query.

**INDEPENDENT BUSINESS**—875 S. Westlake Blvd., Suite 211, Westlake Village, CA 91361. Daniel Kehrer, Ed. Articles, 500 to 2,000 words, of practical interest and value to small business owners. Pays $200 to $1,500, on acceptance. Query.

**INSTANT & SMALL COMMERCIAL PRINTER**—P.O. Box 1387, Northbrook, IL 60065. Jeanette Clinkunbroomer, Ed. Articles, 3 to 6 typed pages, for operators and employees of printing businesses specializing in retail printing and/or small commercial printing: case histories, how-tos, technical pieces, small-business management. Pays $150 to $250, extra for photos, on publication. Query.

**INTERNATIONAL BUSINESS**—500 Mamaroneck Ave., Suite 314, Harrison, NY 10528. David E. Moore, Pres./Ed. Dir. Articles, 1,000 to 1,500 words, on global marketing strategies. Short pieces, 500 words, with tips on operating abroad. Profiles, 750 to 3,000 words, on individuals or companies. Pays 50¢ to $1 a word, on acceptance and on publication. Query with clips.

**INTERNATIONAL DESIGN**—330 W. 42nd St., New York, NY 10036. Annetta Hanna, Ed. Articles to 2,000 words, on product development, design management, graphic design, design history, fashion, art, and environments for designers and marketing executives. Profiles of designers and corporations that use design effectively. Pays $250 to $600, on publication.

**JEMS, JOURNAL OF EMERGENCY MEDICAL SERVICES**—P.O. Box 2789, Carlsbad, CA 92018. Tara Regan, Man. Ed. Articles, 1,500 to 3,000 words, of interest to emergency medical providers (from EMTs to paramedics to nurses and physicians) who work in the EMS industry worldwide.

**LLAMAS**—P.O. Box 100, Herald, CA 95638. Susan Ley, Asst. Ed. "The International Camelid Journal," published 8 times yearly. Articles, 300 to 3,000 words, of interest to llama and alpaca owners. Pays $25 to $300, extra for photos, on acceptance. Query.

**LOTUS**—P.O. Box 9123, Cambridge, MA 02139. Peter Bartolik, Ed.-in-Chief. Articles, 1,500 to 2,000 words, for business and professional people using electronic spreadsheets. Query with outline required. Pay varies, on final approval.

**MACHINE DESIGN**—Penton Publications, 1100 Superior Ave., Cleveland, OH 44114. Leland E. Teschler, Exec. Ed. Articles, to 10 typed pages, on design-related topics for engineers. Pays varying rates, on publication. Submit outline or brief description.

**MAGAZINE DESIGN & PRODUCTION**—8340 Mission Rd., Suite 106, Prairie Village, KS 66206. Maureen Waters, Man. Ed. Articles, 6 to 10 typed pages, on magazine design and production: printing, typesetting, design, computers, lay-out, etc. Pays $100 to $200, on acceptance. Query required.

**MAINTENANCE TECHNOLOGY**—1300 S. Grove Ave., Barrington, IL 60010. Robert C. Baldwin, Ed. Technical articles with how-to information on maintenance of electrical and electronic systems, mechanical systems and equip-ment, and plant facilities. Readers are maintenance managers, supervisors, and engineers in all industries and facilities. Payment varies, on acceptance. Query.

**MANAGE**—2210 Arbor Blvd., Dayton, OH 45439. Doug Shaw, Ed. Articles, 1,500 to 2,200 words, on management and supervision for first-line and middle managers. "Please indicate word count on manuscript and enclose SASE." Pays 5¢ a word.

**MANCHESTER**—See *Network Publications.*

**MANUFACTURING SYSTEMS**—191 S. Gary, Carol Stream, IL 60188. Tom Inglesby, Ed. Articles, 500 to 2,000 words, on computer and information systems for industry executives seeking to increase productivity in manufacturing firms. Pays 10¢ to 20¢ a word, on acceptance. Query required.

**MEDICAL INDUSTRY EXECUTIVE**—1130 Hightower Trail, Atlanta, GA 30350–2910. Elizabeth R. Porter, Ed. Articles, 750 to 4,000 words, on business, marketing, management, and medical manufacturing, for medical equipment manu-facturers and suppliers. Payment varies, on acceptance. Bimonthly. Query.

**MEMPHIS BUSINESS JOURNAL**—88 Union, Suite 102, Memphis, TN 38103. Barney DuBois, Ed. Articles, to 2,000 words, on business, industry trade, agri-business and finance in the mid-South trade area. Pays $80 to $200, on accept-ance.

**MIX MAGAZINE**—6400 Hollis St., Suite 12, Emeryville, CA 94608. David Schwartz, Ed. Articles, varying lengths, for professionals, on audio, video, and music entertainment technology. Pay varies, on publication. Query.

**MODERN HEALTHCARE**—740 N. Rush St., Chicago, IL 60611. Clark Bell, Ed. Features on management, finance, building design and construction, and new technology for hospitals, health maintenance organizations, nursing homes, and other health care institutions. Pays $200 to $400, on publication. Very limited free-lance market.

**MODERN OFFICE TECHNOLOGY**—1100 Superior Ave., Cleveland, OH 44114. Lura Romei, Ed. Articles, 3 to 4 double-spaced, typed pages, on new concepts, management techniques, technologies, and applications for management executives. Payment varies, on acceptance. Query preferred.

**MODERN TIRE DEALER**—P.O. Box 8391, 341 White Pond Dr., Akron, OH 44320. Lloyd Stoyor, Ed. Tire retailing and automotive service articles, 1,000 to 1,500 words, with photos, on independent tire dealers and retreaders. Query; articles by assignment only. Pays $300 to $350, on publication.

**NASHUA**—See *Network Publications.*

**NATIONAL FISHERMAN**—120 Tillson Ave., Rockland, ME 04841. James W. Fullilove, Ed. Articles, 200 to 2,000 words, aimed at commercial fishermen and boat builders. Pays $4 to $6 per inch, extra for photos, on publication. Query preferred.

**NATION'S BUSINESS**—1615 H St. N.W., Washington, DC 20062. Articles on small-business topics, including management advice and success stories. Pays negotiable rates, on acceptance. Guidelines available.

**NEPHROLOGY NEWS & ISSUES**—13901 N. 73rd St., Suite 214, Scottsdale, AZ 85260. Mark E. Neumann, Ed. "We publish news articles, human-interest features, and opinion essays on dialysis, kidney transplants, and kidney disease." No payment.

**NETWORK PUBLICATIONS**—100 Main St., Nashua, NH 03060. Kate Binder, Man. Ed. Lifestyle and business articles with a New Hampshire angle, with sources from all regions of the state, for the company's four regional monthlies: *Nashua, Manchester, Concord and the North,* and *Hampshire East.* Payment varies, on acceptance.

**NEVADA BUSINESS JOURNAL**—3800 Howard Hughes Pkwy., Suite 120, Las Vegas, NV 89109. Lyle Brennan, Ed. Business articles, 1,500 to 2,500 words, of interest to Nevada readers; profiles, how-to articles. Pays $75 to $150 on publication. Query. Guidelines.

**NEW CAREER WAYS NEWSLETTER**—67 Melrose Ave., Haverhill, MA 01830. William J. Bond, Ed. How-to articles, 1,500 to 2,000 words, on new ways to succeed at work in the 1990s. Pays varying rates, on publication. Query with outline and SASE. Same address and requirements for *Workskills Newsletter.*

**THE NORTHERN LOGGER AND TIMBER PROCESSOR**—Northeastern Logger's Assn., Inc., P.O. Box 69, Old Forge, NY 13420. Eric A. Johnson, Ed. Features, 1,000 to 2,000 words, of interest to the forest product industry. Photos. Pays varying rates, on monthly publication. Query preferred.

**NSGA RETAIL FOCUS**—National Sporting Goods Assoc., 1699 Wall St., Suite 700, Mt. Prospect, IL 60056. Cindy Savio, Man. Ed. Members magazine. Articles, 700 to 1,000 words, on sporting goods industry news and trends, the latest in new product information, and management and store operations. Payment varies, on publication. Query.

**NURSINGWORLD JOURNAL**—470 Boston Post Rd., Weston, MA 02193. R. Patrick Gates, Ed. Articles, 800 to 1,500 words, for nurses, nurse educators, and students of nursing, etc., on all aspects of nursing. B&W photos. Pays $35, on publication.

**OPPORTUNITY MAGAZINE**—73 Spring St., Suite 303, New York, NY 10012. Donna Ruffini, Ed. Articles, 900 to 1,500 words, on sales psychology, sales techniques, successful small business careers, self-improvement. Pays $25 to $50, on publication.

**OPTOMETRIC ECONOMICS**—American Optometric Assn., 243 N. Lindbergh Blvd., St. Louis, MO 63141–7881. Dr. Jack Runninger, Ed. Monthly. Articles, 1,000 to 2,000 words, on private practice management for optometrists; direct, conversational style with how-to advice on how optometrists can build, improve, better manage, and enjoy their practices. Short humor and photos. Query. Payment varies, on acceptance.

**PARTY & PAPER RETAILER**—70 New Canaan Ave., Norwalk, CT 06850. Trisha McMahon Drain, Ed. Monthly. Articles, 800 to 1,000 words, that offer employee and store management, and retail marketing advice to the party or stationery store owner: display ideas, success stories, financial advice, legal advice. "Articles grounded in facts and anecdotes are appreciated." Pay varies, on publication. Query with published clips.

**PET BUSINESS**—P.O. Box 2300, Miami, FL 33243–2300. Karen Payne, Ed. Brief, documented articles on animals and products found in pet stores; research findings; legislative/regulatory actions; business and marketing tips and trends. Pays $4 per column inch, on publication. Photos, $10 to $20. Also publishes *Pet Care Times*, a quarterly consumer tabloid.

**PET CARE TIMES**—See *Pet Business.*

**PETS/SUPPLIES/MARKETING**—One E. First St., Duluth, MN 55802. Hugh Bishop, Ed. Articles, 1,000 to 1,200 words, with photos, on pet shops, and pet and product merchandising. Pays 10¢ a word, extra for photos. No fiction or news clippings. Query.

**PHOTO MARKETING**—3000 Picture Pl., Jackson, MI 49201. Margaret Hooks, Man. Ed. Business articles, 1,000 to 3,500 words, for owners and managers of camera/video stores or photo processing labs. Pays $150 to $500, extra for photos, on publication.

**PHYSICIAN'S MANAGEMENT**—7500 Old Oak Blvd., Cleveland, OH 44130. Bob Feigenbaum, Ed. Articles, about 2,500 words, on finance, investments, malpractice, and office management for primary care physicians. No clinical pieces. Pays $125 per printed page, on acceptance. Query with SASE.

**P.O.B.**—5820 Lilley Rd., Suite 5, Canton, MI 48187–3623. Victoria L. Dickinson, Ed. Technical and business articles, 1,000 to 4,000 words, for professionals and technicians in the surveying and mapping fields. Technical tips on field and office procedures and equipment maintenance. Pays $150 to $400, on acceptance.

**POLICE MAGAZINE**—6300 Yarrow Dr., Carlsbad, CA 92009–1597. Dan Burger, Ed. Articles and profiles, 1,000 to 3,000 words, on specialized groups, equipment, issues and trends of interest to people in the law enforcement profession. Pays $100 to $300, on acceptance.

**POOL & SPA NEWS**—3923 W. Sixth St., Los Angeles, CA 90020. News articles for the swimming pool, spa, and hot tub industry. Pays from 10¢ to 15¢ a word, extra for photos, on publication. Query first.

**PRIVATE PRACTICE**—Box 890547, Oklahoma City, OK 73189–0547.

Brian Sherman, Ed. Articles, 1,500 to 2,000 words, on anything that affects doctors' ability to treat their patients. Pays $150 to $300, on publication.

**PRO**—1233 Janesville Ave., Fort Atkinson, WI 53538. Karla Raye Cuculi, Ed. Articles, 1,000 to 1,500 words, on business management for owners of lawn maintenance firms. Pays $150 to $250, on publication. Query.

**PROGRESSIVE GROCER**—Four Stamford Forum, Stamford, CT 06901. Priscilla Donegan, Man. Ed. Articles related to retail food operations; ideas for successful merchandising, promotions, and displays. Short pieces preferred. Pay varies, on acceptance.

**QUICK PRINTING**—1680 S. W. Bayshore Blvd., Port St. Lucie, FL 34984. Bob Hall, Ed. Articles, 1,500 to 3,000 words, of interest to owners and operators of quick print shops, copy shops, and small commercial printers, on how to make their businesses more profitable; include figures. Pays from $75, on acceptance.

**REAL ESTATE TODAY**—National Association of Realtors, 430 N. Michigan Ave., Chicago, IL 60611–4087. Educational, how-to articles on all aspects of residential, finance, commercial-investment, and brokerage-management real estate, to 1,500 words. Query required.

**REMODELING**—Hanley-Wood, Inc., 655 15th St., Suite 475, Washington, DC 20005. Wendy A. Jordan, Ed. Articles, 250 to 1,700 words, on remodeling and industry news for residential and light commercial remodelers. Pays 20¢ a word, on acceptance. Query.

**RESEARCH MAGAZINE**—2201 Third St., P.O. Box 77905, San Francisco, CA 94107. Anne Evers, Ed. Articles of interest to stockbrokers, 1,000 to 3,000 words, on financial products, selling, how-tos, and financial trends. Pays from $300 to $900, on publication. Query.

**RESTAURANTS USA**—1200 17th St. N.W., Washington, DC 20036–3097. Paul Moomaw, Ed. Publication of the National Restaurant Association. Articles, 1,000 to 1,500 words, on the food service and restaurant business. Restaurant experience preferred. Pays $350 to $750, on acceptance. Query.

**ROOFER MAGAZINE**—6719 Winkler Rd., Suite 214, Ft. Myers, FL 33919. Mr. Shawn Holiday, Ed. Technical and non-technical articles, human-interest pieces, 1,000 to 1,500 words, on roofing-related topics: new roofing concepts, energy savings, pertinent issues, roofing contractor profiles, industry concern. Humorous items welcome. No general business or computer articles. Include photos. Pays negotiable rates, on publication. Guidelines.

**RV BUSINESS**—29901 Agoura Rd., Agoura, CA 91301. Katherine Sharma, Ed. Articles, to 1,500 words, on manufacturing, financing, selling, and servicing recreational vehicles. Articles on legislative matters affecting the industry. Pays varying rates.

**THE SAFETY COMPLIANCE LETTER**—24 Rope Ferry Rd., Waterford, CT 06386. Shelley Wolf, Ed. Interview-based articles, 800 to 1,250 words, for corporate safety managers, on solving safety and health problems in the workplace. Pays to 15¢ a word, on acceptance. Query.

**SAFETY MANAGEMENT**—24 Rope Ferry Rd., Waterford, CT 06386. Margot Loomis, Ed. Interview-based articles, 1,100 to 1,500 words, for safety professionals, on improving workplace safety and health. Pays to 15¢ a word, on acceptance. Query.

**SALES & MARKETING MANAGEMENT**—Bill Communications, Inc.,

633 Third Ave., New York, NY 10017. Richard Kern, Ed. Short and feature articles of interest to sales and marketing executives. Looking for practical "news you can use." Pays varying rates, on acceptance. Queries preferred.

**SIGN BUSINESS**—P.O. Box 1416, Broomfield, CO 80038. Glen Richardson, Ed. Articles specifically targeted to the sign business. Pays $50 to $200, on publication.

**SNACK FOOD MAGAZINE**—131 W. First St., Duluth, MN 55802. Jerry Hess, Ed. Articles, 600 to 1,500 words, on trade news, personalities, promotions, production in snack food manufacturing industry. Short pieces; photos. Pays 12¢ to 15¢ a word, $15 for photos, on acceptance. Query.

**SOFTWARE MAGAZINE**—1900 W. Park Dr., Westborough, MA 01581. John Desmond, Ed. Technical features, to 3,000 words, for computer-literate audience, on how software products can be used. Pays about $500 to $750, on publication. Query required. Calendar of scheduled editorial features available.

**SOUTHERN LUMBERMAN**—P.O. Box 681629, Franklin, TN 37068–1629. Nanci P. Gregg, Man. Ed. Articles on sawmill operations, interviews with industry leaders, how-to technical pieces with an emphasis on increasing sawmill production and efficiency. "Always looking for 'sweetheart' mill stories; we publish one per month." Pays $100 to $250 for articles with B&W photos. Queries preferred.

**SOUVENIRS AND NOVELTIES**—7000 Terminal Square, Suite 210, Upper Darby, PA 19082. Articles, 1,500 words, quoting souvenir shop managers on items that sell, display ideas, problems in selling, industry trends. Photos. Pays from $1 per column inch, extra for photos, on publication.

**TEA & COFFEE TRADE JOURNAL**—130 W. 42nd St., New York, NY 10036. Jane P. McCabe, Ed. Articles, 3 to 5 pages, on trade issues reflecting the tea and coffee industry. Query first. Pays $5 per published inch, on publication.

**TEXTILE WORLD**—4170 Ashford-Dunwoody Rd. N.E., Suite 420, Atlanta, GA 30319. L.A. Christiansen, Ed. Articles, 500 to 2,000 words, with photos, on manufacturing and finishing textiles. Pays varying rates, on acceptance.

**TILE WORLD/STONE WORLD**—320 Kinderkamack Rd., Oradell, NJ 07649–2102. John Sailer, Ed. Articles, 750 to 1,500 words, on new trends in installing and designing with tile and stone. For architects, interior designers, and design professionals. Pays $115 per printed page, on publication. Query.

**TODAY'S O.R. NURSE**—6900 Grove Rd., Thorofare, NJ 08086. Mary Jo Krey, Man. Ed. Clinical or general articles, from 2,000 words, of direct interest to operating room nurses.

**TOURIST ATTRACTIONS AND PARKS**—7000 Terminal Square, Suite 210, Upper Darby, PA 19082. Articles, 1,500 words, on successful management of parks and leisure attractions. News items, 250 and 500 words. Pays 7¢ a word, on publication. Query.

**TRAILER/BODY BUILDERS**—P.O. Box 66010, Houston, TX 77266. Paul Schenck, Ed. Articles on engineering, sales, and management ideas for truck body and truck trailer manufacturers. Pays from $100 per printed page, on acceptance.

**TRAINING MAGAZINE**—(formerly *Training, the Magazine of Human Resources Development*) 50 S. Ninth St., Minneapolis, MN 55402. Jack Gordon, Ed. Articles, 1,000 to 2,500 words, for managers of training and development activities in corporations, government, etc. Pays to 20¢ a word, on acceptance. Query.

**TRAVEL COUNSELOR**—(formerly *Travel People*) CMP Publications, 600 Community Dr., Manhasset, NY 11030. Linda Ball, Ed. Business and management how-to articles, 1,000 to 1,500 words, of successful travel industry workers. Pay varies, on acceptance.

**TRAVEL PEOPLE**—See *Travel Counselor.*

**TRAVELAGE EAST/SOUTHEAST**—555 N. Birch Rd., Ft. Lauderdale, FL 33304. Marylyn Springer, Ed. Articles, 1,500 to 2,000 words, for travel agents and other travel industry personnel. Pays $2 per column inch, on publication.

**TREASURY**—253 Summer St., Boston, MA 02210. Ms. Maile Hulihan, Ed. Robert Lessor, Art Dir. Quarterly. Articles, 200 to 3,000 words, on treasury management for corporate treasurers, CFOs, and vice presidents of finance. Pays 50¢ to $1 a word, on acceptance. Query.

**TRUCKERS/USA**—P.O. Box 323, Windber, PA 15963. David Adams, Ed. Monthly. Articles, 500 to 1,000 words, on the trucking business and marketing. Trucking-related poetry and fiction. Payment varies, on publication.

**VENDING TIMES**—545 Eighth Ave., New York, NY 10018. Arthur E. Yohalem, Ed. Features and news articles, with photos, on vending machines. Pays varying rates, on acceptance. Query.

**WINES & VINES**—1800 Lincoln Ave., San Rafael, CA 94901. Philip E. Hiaring, Man. Ed. Articles, 1,000 words, on grape and wine industry, emphasizing marketing and production. Pays 5¢ a word, on acceptance.

**WOODSHOP NEWS**—Pratt St., Essex, CT 06426–1185. Ian C. Bowen, Ed. Features, 1 to 3 typed pages, for and about people who work with wood: business stories, profiles, news. Pays from $3 per column inch, on publication. Queries preferred.

**WORKBOAT**—P.O. Box 1348, Mandeville, LA 70470. Don Nelson, Ed. Features, to 2,000 words, and shorts, 500 to 1,000 words, providing current, lively information for work boat owners, operators, crew, suppliers, and regulators. Topics include construction and conversion; diesel engines and electronics; politics and industry; unusual vessels; new products; and profiles. Payment varies, on acceptance and on publication. Queries preferred.

**WORKSKILLS NEWSLETTER**—See *New Career Ways Newsletter.*

**WORLD OIL**—Gulf Publishing Co., P.O. Box 2608, Houston, TX 77252–2608. T.R. Wright, Jr., Ed. Engineering and operations articles, 3,000 to 4,000 words, on petroleum industry exploration, drilling, or production. Photos. Pays from $50 per printed page, on acceptance. Query.

**WORLD SCREEN NEWS**—49 E. 21st St., 8th Fl., New York, NY 10010. Gregory P. Fagan, Ed. Features and short pieces on trends in the business of international television programming (network, syndication, cable, and pay). Pays to $750, after publication.

**WORLD WASTES**—6151 Powers Ferry Rd. N.W., Atlanta, GA 30339. Bill Wolpin, Ed./Pub. Katya Andresen, Assoc. Ed. Case studies, market analysis, and how-to articles, 1,000 to 2,000 words, with photos, of refuse haulers, recyclers, landfill operators, resource recovery operations, and transfer stations, with solutions to problems in field. Pays from $125 per printed page, on publication. Query preferred.

## IN-HOUSE/ASSOCIATION MAGAZINES

Publications circulated to company employees (sometimes called house magazines or house organs) and to members of associations and organizations are excellent, well-paying markets for writers at all levels of experience. Large corporations publish these magazines to promote good will, familiarize readers with the company's services and products, and interest customers in these products. And, many organizations publish house magazines designed to keep their members abreast of the issues and events concerning a particular cause or industry. Always read an in-house magazine before submitting an article; write to the editor for a sample copy (offering to pay for it) and the editorial guidelines. Stamped, self-addressed envelopes should be enclosed with any query or manuscript. The following list includes a sampling of publications in this large market.

**AMERICAN DANE**—The Danish Brotherhood of America, National Headquarters, 3717 Harney St., Omaha, NE 68131–3844. Jennifer Denning-Kock, Ed. Articles and fiction, to 1,500 words, with a Danish "flavor." Queries are preferred. Submit from May through August. Payment varies, to $50, on publication.

**CALIFORNIA HIGHWAY PATROLMAN**—2030 V St., Sacramento, CA 95818–1730. Carol Perri, Ed. Articles on transportation safety, California history, travel, consumerism, past and present vehicles, humor, general items, etc. Photos a plus. Pays 2 ½ ¢ a word, $5 for B&W photos, on publication. Guidelines and/or sample copy with 9″ × 11″ SASE.

**CATHOLIC FORESTER**—P.O. Box 3012, 355 Shuman Blvd., Naperville, IL 60566–7012. Barbara Cunningham, Ed. Official publication of the Catholic Order of Foresters, a fraternal life insurance company for Catholics. General-interest articles, to 2,000 words. Fiction, to 3,000 words (prefer shorter), that deals with contemporary issues; no moralizing, explicit sex or violence. Pays from 10¢ a word, on acceptance.

**COLUMBIA**—1 Columbus Plaza, New Haven, CT 06510–0901. Richard McMunn, Ed. Journal of the Knights of Columbus. Articles, 1,500 words, for Catholic families. Must be accompanied by color photos or transparencies. No fiction. Pays to $500 for articles and photos, on acceptance.

**THE COMPASS**—Grand Central Towers, 230 E. 44th St., Suite 14B, New York, NY 10017. J.A. Randall, Ed. Articles, to 2,500 words, on the sea and deep sea trade; also articles on aviation. Pays to $600, on acceptance. Query with SASE.

**THE ELKS MAGAZINE**—425 W. Diversey Pkwy., Chicago, IL 60614. Judith L. Keogh, Man. Ed. Articles, to 2,500 words, on business, sports, and topics of current interest; for non-urban audience with above-average income. Informative or humorous pieces, to 2,500 words. Pays $150 to $400 for articles, on acceptance. Query.

**FIREHOUSE**—PTN Publishing Company, 445 Broad Hollow Rd., Melville, NY 11747. Barbara Dunleavy, Ed.-in-Chief. Articles, 500 to 2,000 words: on-the-scene accounts of fires, trends in firefighting equipment, controversial fire-service issues, and lifestyles of firefighters. Pays $100 per typeset page; extra for photos. Query.

**FOCUS**—Turnkey Publishing, P.O. Box 200549, Austin, TX 78720. Doug Johnson, Ed. Magazine of the North American Data General Users Group. Articles, 700 to 4,000 words, on Data General computers. Photos a plus. Pays to $50, on publication. Query required.

**FORD NEW HOLLAND NEWS**—Ford New Holland, Inc., P.O. Box 1895, New Holland, PA 17557. Attn: Ed. Articles, to 1,500 words, with strong color photo support, on production, agriculture, research, and rural living. Pays on acceptance. Query.

**FRIENDS, THE CHEVY OWNERS' MAGAZINE**—30400 Van Dyke, Warren, MI 48093. Jerry Burton, Ed. Feature articles, 800 to 1,200 words, auto-travel related with specific focus; outdoor/adventure oriented; lifestyle; celebrity profiles; entertainment. Pays varying rates, extra for photos, on acceptance. Query.

**THE FURROW**—Deere & Company, John Deere Rd., Moline, IL 61265. George R. Sollenberger, Exec. Ed. Specialized, illustrated articles on farming. Pays to $1,000, on acceptance.

**GEOBYTE**—P.O. Box 979, Tulsa, OK 74101–0979. Ken Milam, Man. Ed. Publication of the American Association of Petroleum Geologists. Articles, 20 typed pages, on computer applications in exploration and production of oil, gas, and energy minerals for geophysicists, geologists, and petroleum engineers. Pay varies, on acceptance. Queries preferred.

**KIWANIS**—3636 Woodview Trace, Indianapolis, IN 46268. Chuck Jonak, Exec. Ed. Articles, 2,500 words (sidebars, 250 to 350 words), on lifestyle, relationships, world view, education, trends, small business, religion, health, etc. No travel pieces, interviews, profiles. Pays $400 to $1,000, on acceptance. Query.

**THE LION**—300 22nd St., Oak Brook, IL 60521. Robert Kleinfelder, Sr. Ed. Official publication of Lions Clubs International. Articles, 800 to 2,000 words, and photo essays, on club activities. Pays from $100 to $700, including photos, on acceptance. Query.

**MOTOR CLUB NEWS**—484 Central Ave., Newark, NJ 07107. Marlene Timm, Man. Ed. Magazine of the Motor Club of America. Articles, 2,500 words, on automotive travel inside and outside the U.S., auto safety, and trends in the auto industry. "Issues are seasonal; articles often reflect travel destinations appropriate to the season." Queries are preferred; address Christy Colato, Ed. Asst. Pays $150, on acceptance.

**MUSEUM OF SCIENCE MAGAZINE**—Publications Dept., Museum of Science, Science Park, Boston, MA 02114–1099. Attn: Editorial Offices. Bimonthly. Articles, 1,200 to 1,500 words, on general science topics related to exhibits and shows at Boston's Museum of Science. Send SASE for list of upcoming exhibits. Pays to $500, on publication.

**NATURE CONSERVANCY**—1815 N. Lynn St., Arlington, VA 22209. Mark Cheater, Ed. Membership publication. Articles on wildlife, people, trends in conservation or ecology. Pieces must have connection to The Nature Conservancy's activities or mission. No poetry or fiction. Query with clips required; article lengths, deadlines, and payment determined at time of assignment. Pays on acceptance.

**OPTIMIST MAGAZINE**—4494 Lindell Blvd., St. Louis, MO 63108. Gary S. Bradley, Ed. Articles, to 1,500 words, on activities of local Optimist Club, and techniques for personal and club success. Pays from $100, on acceptance. Query.

**RESTAURANTS USA**—1200 17th St. N.W., Washington, DC 20036–3097. Paul Moomaw, Ed. Publication of the National Restaurant Association. Articles, 1,000 to 1,500 words, on the food service and restaurant business. Restaurant experience preferred. Pays $350 to $750, on acceptance. Query.

**THE RETIRED OFFICER MAGAZINE**—201 N. Washington St., Alexandria, VA 22314. Articles, 800 to 2,000 words, of interest to military retirees and their families. Current military/national affairs: recent military history, health/medicine, and second-career opportunities. No fillers. Photos a plus. Pays to $500, on acceptance. Query Manuscripts Ed. Guidelines.

**THE ROTARIAN**—1560 Sherman Ave., Evanston, IL 60201–3698. Willmon L. White, Ed. Publication of Rotary International, world service organization of business and professional men and women. Articles, 1,200 to 2,000 words, on international social and economic issues, business and management, human relationships, travel, sports, environment, science and technology; humor. Pays good rates, on acceptance. Query.

**SILVER CIRCLE**—4900 Rivergrade Rd., Irwindale, CA 91706. Jay Binkly, Ed. National consumer-interest quarterly. Consumer service articles, 800 to 2,000 words, on money, health, home, gardening, food, travel, hobbies, etc. Query. Pays $250 to $1,500 (20% kill fee), on acceptance.

**VFW MAGAZINE**—406 W. 34th St., Kansas City, MO 64111. Richard K. Kolb, Ed. Magazine for Veterans of Foreign Wars and their families. Articles, to 1,500 words, on current issues and military history, with veteran angle. Photos. Pays to $500 for unsolicited articles, extra for photos, on acceptance. Guidelines.

**WOODMEN MAGAZINE**—1700 Farnam St., Omaha, NE 68102. Scott J. Darling, Asst. V.P. Articles on history, insurance, family, health, science, etc. Photos. Pays 10¢ a word, extra for photos, on acceptance.

# RELIGIOUS MAGAZINES

**ADVANCE**—1445 Boonville Ave., Springfield, MO 65802. Harris Jansen, Ed. Articles, 1,200 words, slanted to ministers, on preaching, doctrine, practice; how-to features. Pays to 6¢ a word, on acceptance.

**AMERICA**—106 W. 56th St., New York, NY 10019–3893. George W. Hunt, S.J., Ed. Articles, 1,000 to 2,500 words, on current affairs, family life, literary trends. Pays $75 to $150, on acceptance.

**AMERICAN BIBLE SOCIETY RECORD**—1865 Broadway, New York, NY 10023. Clifford P. Macdonald, Man. Ed. Material related to work of American Bible Society: translating, publishing, distributing. Pays on acceptance. Query.

**AMERICAN JEWISH HISTORY**—American Jewish Historical Society, 2 Thornton Rd., Waltham, MA 02154. Dr. Marc Lee Raphael, Ed. Academic articles, 15 to 30 typed pages, on the settlement, history, and life of Jews in North America. Queries preferred. No payment.

**AMIT WOMAN**—817 Broadway, New York, NY 10003–4761. Micheline Ratzersdorfer, Ed. Articles, 1,000 to 2,000 words, of interest to Jewish women: Middle East, Israel, history, holidays, travel. Pays to $75, on publication.

**ANGLICAN JOURNAL**—600 Jarvis St., Toronto, Ont., Canada M4Y 2J6. Carolyn Purden, Ed. National newspaper of the Anglican Church of Canada. Articles, 1,500 words, on current events and human-interest subjects. Pays $200 to $500, on acceptance. Query.

**ANNALS OF ST. ANNE DE BEAUPRÉ**—P.O. Box 1000, St. Anne de Beaupré, Quebec, Canada G0A 3C0. Roch Achard, C.Ss.R., Ed. Articles, 1,100 to 1,200 words, on Catholic subjects and on St. Anne. Pays 3¢ to 4¢ a word, on acceptance.

**BAPTIST LEADER**—American Baptist Churches-USA, P.O. Box 851, Valley Forge, PA 19482–0851. L. Isham, Ed. Practical how-to or thought-provoking articles, 1,200 to 1,600 words, for local church lay leaders and teachers.

**BIBLE ADVOCATE**—P.O. Box 33677, Denver, CO 80233. Roy Marrs, Ed. Articles, 1,000 to 2,500 words, and fillers, 100 to 500 words, on Bible passages and Christian living. Poetry, 5 to 25 lines, on religious themes. "Be familiar with the doctrinal beliefs of the Church of God (Seventh Day). For example, they don't celebrate a traditional Easter or Christmas." Pays $10 per page (to $25), on publication. Guidelines.

**BRIGADE LEADER**—Box 150, Wheaton, IL 60189. Deborah Christensen, Assoc. Ed. Inspirational articles, 1,000 to 1,800 words, for Christian men who lead boys, with an emphasis on issues pertaining to men. Pays $60 to $150. Query only.

**CATHOLIC DIGEST**—P.O. Box 64090, St. Paul, MN 55164–0090. Address Articles Ed. Articles, 1,000 to 3,500 words, on Catholic and general subjects. Fillers, to 300 words, on instances of kindness rewarded, for "Hearts Are Trumps"; accounts of good deeds, for "People Are Like That." Pays from $200 for original articles, $100 for reprints, on acceptance; $4 to $50 for fillers, on publication. Guidelines.

**CATHOLIC NEAR EAST MAGAZINE**—1011 First Ave., New York, NY 10022–4195. Michael La Civita, Ed. A quarterly publication of Catholic Near East Welfare Assoc., a papal agency for humanitarian and pastoral support. Articles, 1,500 to 2,000 words, on people of the Balkans, Eastern Europe, Egypt, Russia, Ethiopia, Middle East, and India; their religious affairs, heritage, culture, and current state of affairs. Special interest in Eastern Christian churches. Color photos for all articles. Query. Pays 15¢ a word, on publication.

**CATHOLIC TWIN CIRCLE**—12700 Ventura Blvd., Suite 200, Studio City, CA 91604. Loretta G. Seyer, Ed. Articles and interviews of interest to Catholics, 1,000 to 2,000 words, with photos. Opinions or inspirational columns, 800 words. Strict attention to Catholic doctrine required. Enclose SASE. Pays 10¢ a word, $50 a column, on publication.

**CHARISMA & CHRISTIAN LIFE**—600 Rinehart Rd., Lake Mary, FL 32746. John Archer, Assoc. Ed. Charismatic/evangelical Christian articles, 1,500 to 2,500 words, for developing the spiritual life. Photos. Pays varying rates, on publication.

**THE CHRISTIAN CENTURY**—407 S. Dearborn St., Chicago, IL 60605. James M. Wall, Ed. Ecumenical. Articles, 1,500 to 2,500 words, with a religious angle, on political and social issues, international affairs, culture, the arts. Poetry, to 20 lines. Photos. Pays about $25 per printed page, extra for photos, on publication.

**CHRISTIAN HOME & SCHOOL**—3350 East Paris Ave. S.E., Grand Rapids, MI 49512. Gordon L. Bordewyk, Ed. Articles for parents in Canada and the U.S. who send their children to Christian schools and are concerned about the challenges facing Christian families today. Pays $50 to $110, on publication. Guidelines.

**CHRISTIAN MEDICAL & DENTAL SOCIETY JOURNAL**—P.O. Box 830689, Richardson, TX 75083–0689. Hal Habecker, D. Min., Ed. Articles, 8 to 10 double-spaced pages, for Christian medical and dental professionals. Queries preferred. Pays to $50, on publication. Guidelines.

**CHRISTIAN PARENTING TODAY**—P.O. Box 850, Sisters, OR 97759. David Kopp, Ed. Articles, 900 to 1,500 words, dealing with raising children with Christian principles. Departments: "Parent Exchange," 25 to 100 words on problem-solving ideas that have worked for parents; "My Story," 800 to 1,500 words, in first person of how one family or parent faced a parenting challenge; "Life in Our House," insightful anecdotes, 25 to 100 words, about humorous things said at home.

Pays 15¢ to 25¢ a word, on acceptance for assigned articles, on publication for unsolicited articles. Pays $40 for "Parent Exchange," $25 for "Life in our House." Guidelines.

**CHRISTIAN SINGLE**—MSN 140, 127 Ninth Ave. N., Nashville, TN 37234. Articles, 600 or 1,200 words, for single adults about leisure activities, issues related to single parents, inspiring personal experiences, humor, life from a Christian perspective. Pays 5 ½¢ a word, on acceptance, plus 3 complimentary copies. Query or send complete manuscript. Guidelines.

**CHRISTIANITY AND CRISIS**—537 W. 121st St., New York, NY 10027. Leon Howell, Ed. Virginia Lindermayer, Man. Ed. Tom Kelly, Assoc. Ed. Articles, 800 to 1,200 words and 2,000 to 3,000 words, on theology, ethics, politics, and economics for progressive Christian readers. "We carry no 'devotional' material but welcome solid contemplative reflections." Payment varies, to $150, on publication. Guidelines.

**CHRISTIANITY TODAY**—465 Gundersen Dr., Carol Stream, IL 60188. David Neff, Man. Ed. Doctrinal, social issues and interpretive essays, 1,500 to 3,000 words, from evangelical Protestant perspective. No fiction or poetry. Pays $200 to $500, on acceptance. Query.

**CHURCH & STATE**—8120 Fenton St., Silver Spring, MD 20910. Joseph L. Conn, Man. Ed. Articles, 600 to 2,600 words, on religious liberty and church-state relations issues. Pays varying rates, on acceptance. Query.

**CHURCH ADMINISTRATION**—127 Ninth Ave. N., Nashville, TN 37234. Southern Baptist. How-to articles, 1,500 to 1,800 words, on administrative planning, staffing, pastoral ministry, organization, and financing. Pays 5 ½¢ a word, on acceptance. Query.

**CHURCH EDUCATOR**—Educational Ministries, Inc., 165 Plaza Dr., Prescott, AZ 86303. Robert G. Davidson, Ed. How-to articles, to 1,750 words, on Christian education: activity projects, crafts, learning centers, games, bulletin boards, etc., for all church school, junior and high school programs, and adult study group ideas. Allow 3 months for response. Pays 3¢ a word, on publication.

**THE CHURCH HERALD**—6157 28th St. S.E., Grand Rapids, MI 49546–6999. Jeffrey Japinga, Ed. Reformed Church in America. Articles, 500 to 1,500 words, on Christianity and culture, politics, marriage, and home. Pays $50 to $125, on acceptance. Query.

**CHURCH MANAGEMENT: THE CLERGY JOURNAL**—P.O. Box 162527, Austin, TX 78716. Manfred Holck, Jr., Ed. How-to articles, 1,500 words, on subjects such as church administration and personal finance for protestant clergy readers. Avoid sexist language. Queries preferred. Pays $40, on publication.

**CHURCH RECREATION MAGAZINE**—127 Ninth Ave. N., Nashville, TN 37234. Lisa Wilson, Asst. Ed. Articles, 4 to 9 double-spaced pages, on drama, sports, clowning, puppetry, crafts, camping, retreats, travel, wellness/fitness, games, outdoor education, and administration. Also cartoons and puzzles. "The magazine is produced to guide churches, denominational leaders, and church volunteers in the effective use of recreation in the church and in daily Christian living." Query preferred. Pays 5 ½¢ a word, after acceptance. Guidelines.

**CHURCH TEACHERS**—1119 Woodburn Road, Durham, NC 27705. Shirley H. Strobel, Ed. Articles, 1,500 words, that offer classroom-tested teaching strategies and curriculum ideas for church schools. Book reviews. No simultaneous submissions. Pays $30 to $40 per page, on publication. Guidelines.

**CIRCUIT RIDER**—P.O. Box 801, Nashville, TN 37202–0801. Keith Pohl, Ed. Articles for United Methodist pastors, 800 to 1,600 words. Pays $50 to $200, on acceptance. Query preferred.

**COLUMBIA**—1 Columbus Plaza, New Haven, CT 06510–0901. Richard McMunn, Ed. Knights of Columbus. Articles, 1,500 words, for Catholic families. Must be accompanied by color photos or transparencies. No fiction. Pays to $500 for articles with photos, on acceptance.

**COMMENTARY**—165 E. 56th St., New York, NY 10022. Norman Podhoretz, Ed. Articles, 5,000 to 7,000 words, on contemporary issues, Jewish affairs, social sciences, religious thought, culture. Serious fiction; book reviews. Pays on publication.

**COMMONWEAL**—15 Dutch St., New York, NY 10038. Margaret O'Brien Steinfels, Ed. Catholic. Articles, to 3,000 words, on political, religious, social, and literary subjects. Pays 3¢ a word, on acceptance.

**COMPASS: A JESUIT JOURNAL**—10 St. Mary St., #300, Toronto, Ont., Canada M4Y 1P9. Robert Chodos, Ed. Essays, 1,500 to 2,500 words, on current religious, political, and cultural topics. "We are ecumenical in spirit and like to provide a forum for lively debate and an ethical perspective on social and religious questions." Query preferred. Pays $250 to $750, on publication.

**CONFIDENT LIVING**—Box 82808, Lincoln, NE 68501. Jan Reeser, Man. Ed. Articles, to 1,200 words, on relating biblical truths to daily living. Photos. Pays 7¢ to 15¢ a word, on acceptance. No simultaneous submissions. SASE required. Photos paid on publication.

**CRUSADER**—P.O. Box 7259, Grand Rapids, MI 49510. G. Richard Broene, Ed. Fiction, 900 to 1,500 words, and articles, 400 to 1,000 words, for boys ages 9 to 14 that show how God is at work in their lives and in the world around them. Also, short fillers. Pays 4¢ to 5¢ a word, on acceptance.

**DAILY WORD**—Unity Village, MO 64065. Colleen Zuck, Ed. Daily lessons, 25 lines (double-spaced), that may be based on an affirmation, a Bible text, or an idea that has been helpful in meeting some situation in your life. Pays $30, on acceptance, plus copies. Guidelines.

**DAUGHTERS OF SARAH**—3801 N. Keeler Ave., Chicago, IL 60641. Reta Finger, Ed. Fiction, 750 to 2,000 words, and poetry, to 500 words, from a Christian feminist perspective. Articles, 750 to 2,000 words, on theology and social issues of Christian feminism. Guidelines.

**DECISION**—Billy Graham Evangelistic Association, 1300 Harmon Pl., Minneapolis, MN 55403–0779. Roger C. Palms, Ed. Christian testimonials and teaching articles on evangelism and Christian nurturing, 1,500 to 1,800 words. Vignettes, 400 to 1,000 words. Pays varying rates, on publication.

**DISCOVERIES**—See *Power and Light*.

**DREAMS & VISIONS**—Skysong Press, RR1, Washago, Ontario, Canada L0K 2B0. Wendy Stanton, Manuscript Ed. New frontiers in Christian fiction. Eclectic fiction, 2,000 to 7,500 words, that "has literary value and is unique and relevant to Christian readers today." Pays in copies and $100 reward to best of the year.

**EVANGEL**—Light and Life Press, Box 535002, Indianapolis, IN 46253–5002. Vera Bethel, Ed. Free Methodist. Personal experience articles, 1,000 words; short devotional items, 300 to 500 words; fiction, 1,200 words, showing personal faith in

Christ to be instrumental in solving problems. Pays $10 to $25 for articles, $45 for fiction, $10 for poetry, on publication.

**EVANGELICAL BEACON**—901 E. 78th St., Minneapolis, MN 55420. Carol Madison, Ed. Evangelical Free Church. Articles, 500 to 2,000 words, that fit with the editorial theme. Send SASE for guidelines and editorial calendar. Pays 7¢ a word (3¢ a word for reprints), on publication.

**EVANGELIZING TODAY'S CHILD**—Warrenton, MO 63383. Articles, 1,200 to 1,500 words, for Sunday school teachers, Christian education leaders, and children's workers. Feature articles should include teaching principles, instruction for the reader, and classroom illustrations. "Impact" articles, 700 to 900 words, show the power of the gospel in or through the life of a child; "Resource Center" short, original teaching tips. Also short stories, 800 to 1,000 words, of contemporary children dealing with problems; must have a scriptural solution. Pays 8¢ to 10¢ a word for articles; $15 to $25 for "Resource Center" pieces; 6¢ a word for short stories, on publication. Guidelines.

**FAITH TODAY**—Box 8800, Sta. B, Willowdale, Ontario, Canada M2K 2R6. Brian C. Stiller, Ed. Audrey Dorsch, Man. Ed. Articles, 1,500 words, on current issues relating to the church in Canada. Pays negotiable rates, on publication. Queries are preferred.

**FELLOWSHIP IN PRAYER**—291 Witherspoon St., Princeton, NJ 08542. Articles, to 1,500 words, and poems, to 35 lines, relating to prayer, meditation, and the spiritual life as practiced by any of the world's religions. Pays in copies. Guidelines.

**FOURSQUARE WORLD ADVANCE**—1910 W. Sunset Blvd., Suite 200, Los Angeles, CA 90026. Ronald D. Williams, Ed. Official publication of the International Church of the Foursquare Gospel. Religious fiction and nonfiction, 1,000 to 1,200 words, and religious poetry. Pays $75, on publication. Guidelines.

**FRIENDS JOURNAL**—1501 Cherry St., Philadelphia, PA 19102–1497. Vinton Deming, Ed. Articles and fiction, to 2,000 words, reflecting Quaker life today: commentary on social issues, experimental articles, Quaker history, world affairs. Poetry, to 25 lines, and Quaker-related humor and crossword puzzles also considered. Pays in copies. Guidelines.

**THE GEM**—Box 926, Findlay, OH 45839–0926. Marilyn Rayle Kern, Ed. Articles, 300 to 1,600 words, and fiction, 1,000 to 1,600 words: true-to-life experiences of God's help, of healed relationships, and of growing maturity in faith. For adolescents through senior citizens. Pays $15 for articles and fiction, $5 to $10 for fillers, after publication.

**GROUP, THE YOUTH MINISTRY MAGAZINE**—Box 481, Loveland, CO 80539. Rick Lawrence, Ed. Interdenominational magazine for leaders of junior and senior high school Christian youth groups. Articles, 500 to 1,700 words, about practical youth ministry principles, techniques, or activities. Short how-to pieces, to 300 words, for "Try This One." Pays to $150 for articles, $15 to $25 for department pieces, on acceptance. Guidelines.

**GUIDE**—Review and Herald Publishing Co., 55 W. Oak Ridge Dr., Hagerstown, MD 21740. Stories and articles, to 1,200 words, for Christian youth, ages 10 to 14. Pays 3¢ to 4¢ a word, on acceptance.

**GUIDEPOSTS**—16 E. 34th St., New York, NY 10016. Rick Hamlin, Features Ed. True first-person stories, 250 to 1,500 words, stressing how faith in God helps people cope with life. Anecdotal fillers, to 250 words. Pays $100 to $400, $50 for fillers, on acceptance.

654

**HERALD OF HOLINESS**—6401 The Paseo, Kansas City, MO 64131. Address Man. Ed. Church of the Nazarene. Articles, 800 to 2,000 words, about distinctive Nazarenes, Christian family life and marriage, a Christian approach to social issues, seasonal material, and short devotional articles. Submit complete manuscript. Pays 4¢ to 5¢ a word, within 30 days of acceptance. Guidelines.

**HOME LIFE**—127 Ninth Ave. N., Nashville, TN 37234. Charlie Warren, Ed. Mary P. Darby, Asst. Ed. Southern Baptist. Articles, preferably personal-experience, and fiction, to 1,500 words, on Christian marriage, parenthood, and family relationships. Human-interest pieces, 200 to 500 words; cartoons and short verse. Pays to 5 ½¢ a word, on acceptance.

**INDIAN LIFE**—Box 3765, Sta. B, Winnipeg, MB, Canada R2W 3R6. Linda Fortin, Ed. Biographies of North American Indians and fiction, 1,500 words; poetry, to 20 lines. "Our magazine is designed to help the North American Indian Church speak to the social, cultural, and spiritual needs of native people." Writing should be at an eighth grade reading level. Queries preferred. Pays 4¢ a word, on publication.

**INSIDE MAGAZINE**—226 S. 16th St., Philadelphia, PA 19102–3392. Jane Biberman, Ed. Articles, 1,500 to 3,000 words, and fiction, 2,000 to 3,000 words, of interest to Jewish adults. Pays $100 to $500, on acceptance. Query.

**JEWISH CURRENTS**—22 E. 17th St., #601, New York, NY 10003. Morris U. Schappes, Ed. Articles, 2,400 to 3,000 words, on Jewish history, secularism, progressivism, labor struggle, Holocaust resistance, Black-Jewish relations, Israel, Yiddish culture. "We are pro-Israel though non-Zionist and a secular magazine; no religious articles." Overstocked with fiction and poetry. No payment.

**THE JEWISH MONTHLY**—B'nai B'rith International, 1640 Rhode Island Ave. N.W., Washington, DC 20036. Jeff Rubin, Ed. Articles, 500 to 3,000 words, on politics, religion, history, culture, and social issues of Jewish concern with an emphasis on people. Pays 10¢ to 25¢ a word, on publication. Query with clips.

**JOURNAL OF CHRISTIAN NURSING**—P.O. Box 700, Frederick, PA 19435. Judy Shelly, Sr. Ed. Articles, 8 to 12 double-spaced pages, that help Christian nurses view nursing practice through the eyes of faith: spiritual care, ethics, values, healing and wholeness, psychology and religion, personal and professional ethics, etc. Priority given to nurse authors, though work by non-nurses will be considered. Opinion pieces, to 4 pages, for "Speaking Out" section. Pays $25 to $80. Guidelines and editorial calendar.

**JOURNEY**—Christian Board of Publication, Box 179, St. Louis, MO 63166. Michael E. Dixon, Ed. Fiction, 100 to 1,200 words; articles, 600 to 1,000 words; and poetry, to 20 lines. Accepts material for 12- to 16-year-olds. Pays 3¢ a word for prose, from $3 for poetry, on acceptance. Guidelines.

**KEY TO CHRISTIAN EDUCATION**—8121 Hamilton Ave., Cincinnati, OH 45231–2396. Barbara Bolton and Lowellette Lauderdale, Eds. Articles, to 1,200 words, on teaching methods, and success stories for workers in Christian education. Pays varying rates, on acceptance.

**LEADERSHIP**—465 Gundersen Dr., Carol Stream, IL 60188. Marshall Shelley, Ed. Articles, 500 to 3,000 words, on administration, finance, and/or programming of interest to ministers and church leaders. Personal stories of crisis in ministry. "We deal mainly with the how-to of running a church. We're not a theological journal but a practical one." Pays $50 to $350, on acceptance.

**LIBERTY MAGAZINE**—12501 Old Columbia Pike, Silver Spring, MD 20904–1608. Roland R. Hegstad, Ed. Timely articles, to 2,500 words, and photo essays, on religious freedom and church-state relations. Pays 6¢ to 8¢ a word, on acceptance. Query.

**LIGHT AND LIFE**—P.O. Box 535002, Indianapolis, IN 46253–5002. Robert Haslam, Ed. Fresh, lively articles about practical Christian living, and sound treatments of vital issues facing the Evangelical in contemporary society. Pays 4¢ a word, on publication.

**LIGUORIAN**—Liguori, MO 63057–9999. Rev. Allan Weinert, Ed. Francine O'Connor, Man. Ed. Catholic. Articles and short stories, 1,500 to 2,000 words, on Christian values in modern life. Pays 10¢ to 12¢ a word, on acceptance.

**THE LIVING LIGHT**—U.S. Catholic Conference, Dept. of Education, 3211 4th St. N.W., Washington, DC 20017–1194. Berard L. Marthaler, Exec. Ed. Theoretical and practical articles, 1,500 to 4,000 words, on religious education, catechesis, and pastoral ministry.

**LIVING WITH CHILDREN**—MSN 140, 127 Ninth Ave. N., Nashville, TN 37234. Informative articles and personal experience pieces, 800 to 1,200 words, on family relationships and child-related issues, from a Christian perspective. Pays 5 ½¢ a word, after acceptance.

**LIVING WITH PRESCHOOLERS**—MSN 140, 127 Ninth Ave. N., Nashville, TN 37234. Informative articles and personal experience pieces, 800 to 1,200 words, relating to family and the preschool child, written with a Christian perspective. Pays 5 ½¢ a word, on acceptance.

**LIVING WITH TEENAGERS**—127 Ninth Ave. N., Nashville, TN 37234. Articles told from a Christian perspective for parents of teenagers; first-person approach preferred. Poetry, 4 to 16 lines. Pays 5 ½¢ a word, on acceptance, for articles.

**THE LOOKOUT**—8121 Hamilton Ave., Cincinnati, OH 45231. Simon J. Dahlman, Ed. Articles, 500 to 2,000 words, on family issues, Christian education, applying Christian faith to current issues, and people overcoming problems with Christian principles. Inspirational or humorous shorts, 500 to 800 words; fiction, to 2,000 words. Pays 4¢ to 7¢ a word, on acceptance.

**THE LUTHERAN**—8765 W. Higgins Rd., Chicago, IL 60631. Edgar R. Trexler, Ed. Articles, to 2,000 words, on Christian ideology, personal religious experiences, social and ethical issues, family life, church, and community. Pays $100 to $600, on acceptance. Query.

**MARYKNOLL**—Maryknoll, NY 10545. Frank Maurovich, Man. Ed. Magazine of the Catholic Foreign Mission Society of America. Articles, 800 to 1,000 words, and photos relating to missions or missioners overseas. Pays $150, on acceptance. Payment for photos made on publication.

**MATURE LIVING**—127 Ninth Ave. N., Nashville, TN 37234. Leisure magazine for senior adults. "Unique, creative manuscripts, to 900 words, characterized by human interest, Christian warmth, and humor." Pays 5 ½¢ a word (or per line for poetry). Buys all rights.

**MATURE YEARS**—201 Eighth Ave. S., P.O. Box 801, Nashville, TN 37202. Marvin W. Cropsey, Ed. United Methodist quarterly. Articles on retirement or related subjects, 1,500 to 2,000 words. Humorous and serious fiction, 1,500 to 1,800 words, for adults. Travel pieces with religious slant. Poetry, to 14 lines. Include Social Security no. with manuscript.

**THE MENNONITE**—P.O. Box 347, Newton, KS 67114. Gordon Houser,

Ed. Larry Penner, Asst. Ed. Articles, 1,000 words, that emphasize Christian themes. Pays 5¢ a word, on publication. Guidelines.

**MESSENGER OF THE SACRED HEART**—661 Greenwood Ave., Toronto, Ont., Canada M4J 4B3. Articles and short stories, about 1,500 words, for American and Canadian Catholics. Pays from 4¢ a word, on acceptance.

**MIDSTREAM**—110 E. 59th St., New York, NY 10022. Joel Carmichael, Ed. Jewish-interest articles and book reviews. Fiction, to 3,000 words, and poetry. Pays 5¢ a word, after publication. Allow 3 months for response.

**THE MIRACULOUS MEDAL**—475 E. Chelten Ave., Philadelphia, PA 19144–5785. John W. Gouldrick, C.M., Ed. Dir. Catholic. Fiction, to 2,400 words. Religious verse, to 20 lines. Pays from 2¢ a word for fiction, from 50¢ a line for poetry, on acceptance.

**MODERN LITURGY**—160 E. Virginia St., #290, San Jose, CA 95112. Ken Guentert, Ed. Plays, parables, fables (for teaching and preaching). "Articles making the connection between imagination and celebration (faith expression) or worship and 'real' life." Material must be related to Roman Catholic liturgy. Query only. Pays in copies and subscription.

**MOMENT**—3000 Connecticut Ave. N.W., Suite 300, Washington, DC 20008. Suzanne Singer, Man. Ed. Sophisticated, issue-oriented articles, 2,000 to 4,000 words, on Jewish topics. Pays $150 to $400, on publication.

**MOMENTUM**—National Catholic Educational Assn., 1077 30th St. N.W., Suite 100, Washington, DC 20007–3852. Patricia Feistritzer, Ed. Articles, 500 to 1,500 words, on outstanding programs, issues, and research in education. Book reviews. Pays 4¢ a word, on publication. Query.

**MOODY MAGAZINE**—820 N. La Salle Blvd., Chicago, IL 60610. Andrew Scheer, Man. Ed. Anecdotal articles, 1,200 to 2,000 words, on the evangelical Christian experience in the home, the community, and the workplace. Pays 15¢ to 20¢ a word, on acceptance. Query.

**THE NATIONAL CHRISTIAN REPORTER**—See *The United Methodist Reporter.*

**NEW COVENANT**—P.O. Box 7009, Ann Arbor, MI 48107. Jim Manney, Ed. Articles and testimonials, 1,000 to 4,000 words, that foster renewal in the Catholic Church, especially the charismatic, ecumenical, and evangelical dimensions of that renewal. Queries preferred. Pays from 15¢ a word, on acceptance.

**NEW ERA**—50 E. North Temple, Salt Lake City, UT 84150. Richard M. Romney, Man. Ed. Articles, 150 to 2,000 words, and fiction, to 2,000 words, for young Mormons. Poetry; photos. Pays 5¢ to 10¢ a word, 25¢ a line for poetry, on acceptance. Query.

**NEW WORLD OUTLOOK**—475 Riverside Dr., Rm. 1351, New York, NY 10115–0122. Alma Graham, Ed. Articles, 500 to 1,500 words, on United Methodist missions and Methodist-related programs and ministries. Focus on national, global, and women's and children's issues, and on men and youth in missions. Photos a plus. Pays on publication.

**OBLATES**—15 S. 59th St., Belleville, IL 62223–4694. Priscilla Kurz, Manuscripts Ed. Jacqueline Lowery Corn, Man. Ed. Articles, 500 to 600 words, that inspire, uplift, and motivate through positive Christian values in everyday life. Inspirational poetry, to 16 lines. Pays $80 for articles, $30 for poems, on acceptance. Send complete manuscript only. Send 52¢ SASE for guidelines and sample copy.

**THE OTHER SIDE**—300 W. Apsley, Philadelphia, PA 19144. Doug Davidson, Nonfiction Ed. Jennifer Wilkins, Fiction Ed. Independent, ecumenical Christian magazine devoted to issues of peace, justice, and faith. Fiction, 500 to 5,000 words, that deepens readers' encounter with the mystery of God and the mystery of ourselves. Nonfiction, 500 to 4,000 words (most under 2,000 words), on contemporary social, political, economic, or racial issues in the U.S. or abroad. Poems, to 50 lines; submit up to 3 poems. Pays 2 complimentary copies plus $20 to $350 for articles; $75 to $250 for fiction; $15 for poems, on acceptance. Guidelines.

**OUR FAMILY**—Box 249, Battleford, Sask., Canada S0M 0E0. Nestor Gregoire, Ed. Articles, 1,000 to 3,000 words, for Catholic families, on modern society, family, marriage, current affairs, and spiritual topics. Humor; verse. Pays 7¢ to 10¢ a word for articles, 75¢ to $1 a line for poetry, on acceptance. SAE with international reply coupons required with all submissions. Guidelines.

**OUR SUNDAY VISITOR**—Huntington, IN 46750. Greg Erlandson, Ed. In-depth features, 1,000 to 1,200 words, on the Catholic church in America today. Pays $150 to $250, on acceptance

**PARISH FAMILY DIGEST**—200 Noll Plaza, Huntington, IN 46750. Corine B. Erlandson, Ed. Articles, 750 to 1,000 words, on family life, Catholic subjects, seasonal, parish life, prayer, inspiration, etc., for the Catholic reader. Also publishes short humorous anecdotes and light-hearted cartoons. Pays 5¢ a word, on acceptance.

**PASTORAL LIFE**—Box 595, Canfield, OH 44406–0595. Anthony L. Chenevey, Ed. Articles, 2,000 to 2,500 words, addressing the problems of pastoral ministry. Pays 4¢ a word, on publication. Guidelines.

**PENTECOSTAL EVANGEL**—1445 Boonville Ave., Springfield, MO 65802. Richard Champion, Ed. Assemblies of God. Religious, personal experience, and devotional articles, 400 to 1,000 words. Verse, 12 to 30 lines. Pays 7¢ a word, on acceptance.

**THE PENTECOSTAL MESSENGER**—P.O. Box 850, Joplin, MO 64802. Peggy Allen, Man. Ed. Articles, 500 to 2,000 words, that deal with Christian commitment: human interest, inspiration, social and religious issues, Bible topics, and seasonal material. Pays 1 ½¢ per word, on publication. Guidelines.

**PERSPECTIVE**—Pioneer Clubs, Box 788, Wheaton, IL 60189. Rebecca Powell Parat, Ed. Articles, 750 to 1,500 words, that provide growth for adult club leaders in leadership and relationship skills and offer encouragement and practical support to club leaders. Readers are lay leaders of Pioneer Clubs for boys and girls (ages 2 to 12th grade). "Most articles written on assignment; writers familiar with Pioneer Clubs who would be interested in working on assignment should contact us." Queries preferred. Pays $40 to $75, on acceptance. Guidelines.

**PIME WORLD**—35750 Moravian Dr., Clinton, MI 48035. Paul W. Witte, Man. Ed. Articles, 600 to 1,200 words, on Catholic missionary work in Hong Kong, India, Latin America, Africa. Color photos. No fiction or poetry. Pays 6¢ a word, extra for photos, on publication.

**POWER AND LIGHT**—6401 The Paseo, Kansas City, MO 64131. Beula J. Postlewait, Preteen Ed. Fiction, 400 to 800 words, for children (grades 5 and 6), defining Christian experiences and demonstrating Christian values and beliefs. Pays 3 ½¢ a word for first rights; 5¢ a word for multi-use rights, on acceptance or publication. Also publishes *Discoveries* for readers in grades 3 and 4.

**THE PREACHER'S MAGAZINE**—10814 E. Broadway, Spokane, WA

99206. Randal E. Denny, Ed. Scholarly and practical articles, 700 to 2,500 words, on areas of interest to Christian ministers: church administration, pastoral care, professional and personal growth, church music, finance, evangelism. Pays 3 ½¢ a word, on publication. Guidelines.

**THE PRESBYTERIAN RECORD**—50 Wynford Dr., Don Mills, Ont., Canada M3C 1J7. John Congram, Ed. Fiction and nonfiction, 1,500 words, and poetry, any length. Short items, to 800 words, of a contemporary and often controversial nature for "Full Count." The purpose of the magazine is to provide news, not only from our church but the church at large, and to fulfill both a pastoral and prophetic role among our people. Queries preferred. Pays $50 (Canadian), on publication. Guidelines.

**PRESBYTERIAN SURVEY**—100 Witherspoon, Louisville, KY 40202–1396. Kenneth E. Little, Ed./Pub. Articles, 1,200 words, of interest to members of the Presbyterian Church or ecumenical individuals. Pays to $150, on acceptance.

**THE PRIEST**—200 Noll Plaza, Huntington, IN 46750–4304. Robert A. Willems, Assoc. Ed. Viewpoints, to 1,500 words, and articles, to 5,000 words, on life and ministry of priests, current theological developments, etc., for priests, permanent deacons, and seminarians. Pays $50 to $300, on acceptance.

**PURPOSE**—616 Walnut Ave., Scottdale, PA 15683–1999. James E. Horsch, Ed. Fiction and fillers, to 800 words, on Christian discipleship and church-year related themes, with good photos; pieces of history, biography, science, hobbies, from a Christian perspective; Christian problem solving. Poetry, to 12 lines. "Send complete manuscript; no queries." Pays to 5¢ a word, to $1 a line for poetry, on acceptance.

**QUAKER LIFE**—Friends United Meeting, 101 Quaker Hill Dr., Richmond, IN 47374–1980. James R. Newby, Ed. Carol Beals, Man. Ed. Articles and news for members of the Society of Friends. Brief poetry considered. "Almost all material solicited to match theme format." Pays in copies.

**QUEEN**—26 S. Saxon Ave., Bay Shore, NY 11706–8993. J. Patrick Gaffney, S.M.M., Ed. Publication of Montfort Missionaries. Articles and fiction, 1,000 to 2,000 words, related to the Virgin Mary. Poetry. Pay varies, on acceptance.

**THE QUIET HOUR**—850 N. Grove Ave., Elgin, IL 60120. Gary Wilde, Ed. Short devotionals. Pays $15, on acceptance. By assignment only; query.

**RESPONSE: A CONTEMPORARY JEWISH REVIEW**—27 W. 20th St., 9th Fl., New York, NY 10011–3707. Bennett Lovett-Graff, Ed. Adam Margolis, Ed. Fiction, to 25 double-spaced pages, in which Jewish experience serves as controlling influence. Articles, to 25 pages, with a focus on Jewish issues. Poetry, to 80 lines, and book reviews. Pays in 5 copies per article or story; 2 copies per poem. Guidelines.

**REVIEW FOR RELIGIOUS**—3601 Lindell Blvd., St. Louis, MO 63108. David L. Fleming, S.J., Ed. Informative, practical, or inspirational articles, 1,500 to 5,000 words, from a theological or spiritual point of view. Pays $6 per page, on publication. Guidelines.

**ST. ANTHONY MESSENGER**—1615 Republic St., Cincinnati, OH 45210–1298. Norman Perry, O.F.M., Ed. Articles, 2,000 to 3,000 words, on personalities, major movements, education, family, religious and church issues, spiritual life, and social issues. Human-interest pieces. Humor; fiction, 2,000 to 3,000 words. Pays 14¢ a word, on acceptance. Articles and stories should have religious implications. Query for nonfiction.

**ST. JOSEPH'S MESSENGER**—P.O. Box 288, Jersey City, NJ 07303–0288. Sister Ursula Maphet, Ed. Inspirational articles, 500 to 1,000 words, and fiction, 1,000 to 1,500 words. Verse, 4 to 40 lines.

**SEEK**—8121 Hamilton Ave., Cincinnati, OH 45231. Eileen H. Wilmoth, Ed. Articles and fiction, to 1,200 words, on inspirational and controversial topics and timely religious issues. Christian testimonials. Pays 5¢ to 7¢ a word, on acceptance. SASE for guidelines.

**SHARING THE VICTORY**—Fellowship of Christian Athletes, 8701 Leeds Rd., Kansas City, MO 64129. John Dodderidge, Ed. Articles, interviews, and profiles, to 1,000 words, for co-ed Christian athletes and coaches in high school, college, and pros. Pays from $50, on publication. Query required.

**SIGNS OF THE TIMES**—P. O. Box 7000, Boise, ID 83707. Greg Brothers, Ed. Seventh-Day Adventists. Feature articles on Christians who have performed community services; current issues from a biblical perspective; health, home, marriage, human-interest pieces; inspirational articles, 500 to 2,000 words. Pays 20¢ a word, on acceptance. Send 9×12 SASE for sample and guidelines.

**SISTERS TODAY**—The Liturgical Press, St. John's Abbey, Collegeville, MN 56321–7500. Articles, 500 to 3,500 words, on theology, social justice issues, and religious issues for women and the Church. Poetry, to 34 lines. Pays $5 per printed page, $10 per poem, on publication; $50 for color cover photos and $25 for B&W inside photos. Send articles to: Sister Mary Anthony Wagner, O.S.B., Ed., St. Benedict's Convent, St. Joseph, MN 56374–2099. Send poetry to: Sister Virginia Micka, C.S.J., College of Saint Catherine, Box 4162, St. Paul, MN 55105.

**SOCIAL JUSTICE REVIEW**—3835 Westminster Pl., St. Louis, MO 63108–3409. Rev. John H. Miller, C.S.C., Ed. Articles, 2,000 to 3,000 words, on social problems in light of Catholic teaching and current scientific studies. Pays 2¢ a word, on publication.

**SPIRITUAL LIFE**—2131 Lincoln Rd. N.E., Washington, DC 20002–1199. Steven Payne, O.C.D., Ed. Professional religious journal. Religious essays, 3,000 to 5,000 words, on spirituality in contemporary life. Pays from $50, on acceptance. Send 7×10 SASE with 4 first-class stamps for guidelines and sample issue.

**STANDARD**—6401 The Paseo, Kansas City, MO 64131. Articles, 300 to 1,700 words; true experiences; poetry, to 20 lines; fiction with Christian emphasis but not overtly preachy; fillers; short articles with devotional emphasis; cartoons in good taste. Pays 3 ½¢ a word, on acceptance.

**SUNDAY DIGEST**—850 N. Grove Ave., Elgin, IL 60120. Christine Dallman, Ed. Articles, 1,000 to 1,800 words, on Christian faith in contemporary life; inspirational and how-to articles; free-verse poetry. Anecdotes, 500 words. Pays on acceptance.

**SUNDAY SCHOOL COUNSELOR**—1445 Boonville Ave., Springfield, MO 65802–1894. Sylvia Lee, Ed. Articles, 1,000 to 1,500 words, on teaching and Sunday school people, for local Sunday school teachers. Pays 3¢ to 5¢ a word, on acceptance.

**SUNSHINE MAGAZINE**—Sunshine Press, Litchfield, IL 62056. Peggy Kuethe, Ed. Inspirational articles, to 600 words. Short stories, 1,000 words, and juveniles, 400 words. No heavily religious material or "born again" pieces. Pays varying rates, on acceptance.

**TEACHERS INTERACTION**—3558 S. Jefferson Ave., St. Louis, MO 63118. Jean Haas, Ed. Articles, 800 to 1,200 words; how-to pieces, to 100 words, for

Lutheran volunteer church school teachers. Pays $10 to $35, on publication. Limited free-lance market.

**TEENS TODAY**—Church of the Nazarene, 6401 The Paseo, Kansas City, MO 64131. Karen DeSollar, Ed. Short stories that deal with teens demonstrating Christian principles, 1,200 to 1,500 words. Pays 4¢ a word for first rights, 3 ½¢ a word for reprints, on acceptance. Guidelines.

**THEOLOGY TODAY**—Box 29, Princeton, NJ 08542. Thomas G. Long, Ed. Patrick D. Miller, Ed. Articles, 1,500 to 3,500 words, on theology, religion, and related social issues. Literary criticism. Pays $75 to $200, on publication.

**TODAY'S CHRISTIAN WOMAN**—465 Gundersen Dr., Carol Stream, IL 60188. Julie A. Talerico, Ed. Jan Senn, Asst. Ed. Articles, 1,500 words, that are "warm and personal in tone, full of real-life anecdotes that deal with the following relationships: marriage, parenting, friendship, spiritual life, and self." Humorous anecdotes, 150 words, that have a Christian slant. Queries required. Payment varies, on acceptance. Guidelines.

**THE UNITED CHURCH OBSERVER**—84 Pleasant Blvd., Toronto, Ont., Canada M4T 2Z8. Factual articles, 1,500 to 2,500 words, on religious trends, human problems, social issues. No poetry. Pays after publication. Query.

**THE UNITED METHODIST REPORTER**—P.O. Box 660275, Dallas, TX 75266–0275. John Lovelace, Man. Ed. United Methodist newspaper. Religious features, to 500 words. Religious verse, 4 to 12 lines. Photos. "Tight-deadline, time-sensitive, nationally circulated weekly newspaper." Pays 4¢ a word, on publication. Send for guidelines. Same address and requirements for *The National Christian Reporter* (interdenominational).

**UNITED SYNAGOGUE REVIEW**—155 Fifth Ave., New York, NY 10010. Lois Goldrich, Ed. Articles, 1,000 to 1,200 words, on issues of interest to Conservative Jewish community. Query.

**UNITY MAGAZINE**—Unity School of Christianity, Unity Village, MO 64065. Philip White, Ed. Articles and poems: inspirational, religious, metaphysical, Bible interpretation, 500 to 1,500 words. Pays 20¢ a word, on acceptance.

**VIRTUE**—P. O. Box 850, Sisters, OR 97759–0850. Marlee Alex, Ed. Articles and fiction for Christian women. Query for articles. Guidelines. Send 9 × 12 SASE with 5 stamps for sample copy.

**VISTA MAGAZINE**—P. O. Box 50434, Indianapolis, IN 46250–0434. Articles and adult fiction, on current Christian concerns and issues. First-person pieces, 500 to 1,200 words. Opinion pieces from an evangelical perspective, 500 to 650 words. Pays 4¢ a word for first rights, 2¢ a word for reprint. Send SASE for guidelines before submitting material.

**WITH**—722 Main St., Box 347, Newton, KS 67114. Eddy Hall and Carol Duerksen, Eds. Fiction, 500 to 2,000 words; nonfiction, 500 to 1,500 words; and poetry, to 50 lines for Anabaptist-Mennonite teenagers. "Wholesome humor always gets a close read." B&W 8 × 10 photos accepted. Payment is 4¢ a word, on acceptance (2¢ a word for reprints).

**WOMAN'S TOUCH**—1445 Boonville, Springfield, MO 65802–1894. Sandra G. Clopine, Ed. Aleda Swartzendruber, Assoc. Ed. Articles, 500 to 1,200 words, that provide help and inspiration to Christian women, strengthening family life, and reaching out in witness to others. Uses some poetry and fillers, 50 to 150 words. Allow 3 months for response. Payment varies, on acceptance. Guidelines and editorial calendar.

**WORLD VISION MAGAZINE**—919 W. Huntington Dr., Monrovia, CA 91016. Larry Wilson, Man. Ed. Thoroughly researched articles, 1,200 to 2,000 words, on worldwide poverty, evangelism, the environment, and justice. Include reputable sources and strong anecdotes. "Turning Points," first-person articles, 450 to 700 words, about a life-changing, spiritual experience related to Third World issues. "We like articles to offer positive ways Christians can make a difference." Query required. Payment negotiable, made on acceptance or publication.

**YOUNG SALVATIONIST**—The Salvation Army, 615 Slaters Ln., P.O. Box 269, Alexandria, VA 22313. M. Lesa Salyer, Ed. Articles, 600 to 1,200 words, teach the Christian view to everyday living, for teenagers. Short shorts, first-person testimonies, 600 to 800 words. Pays 10¢ a word, on acceptance. SASE required. Send 8 ½ × 11 SASE (3 stamps) for theme list, guidelines, and sample copy.

**YOUR CHURCH**—465 Gundersen Dr., Carol Stream, IL 60188. James D. Berkley, Ed. Articles, to 1,000 words, about church business administration. Query required. Pays about 10¢ a word, on acceptance. Guidelines.

# HEALTH

**ACCENT ON LIVING**—P. O. Box 700, Bloomington, IL 61702. Raymond C. Cheever, Pub. Betty Garee, Ed. Articles, 250 to 1,000 words, about physically disabled people, including their careers, recreation, sports, self-help devices, and ideas that can make daily routines easier. Good photos a plus. Pays 10¢ a word, on publication. Query.

**AMERICAN BABY**—475 Park Ave. S., New York, NY 10016. Judith Nolte, Ed. Articles, 1,000 to 2,000 words, for new or expectant parents on prenatal or infant care. Pays varying rates, on acceptance.

**AMERICAN FITNESS**—15250 Ventura Blvd., Suite 310, Sherman Oaks, CA 91403. Peg Jordan, Ed. Rhonda Wilson, Man. Ed. Articles, 500 to 1,500 words, on exercise, health, sports, nutrition, etc. Illustrations, photos, cartoons.

**AMERICAN HEALTH**—28 West 23rd St., New York, NY 10010. Address Editorial Dept. Lively, authoritative articles, 1,000 to 3,000 words, on scientific and lifestyle aspects of health and fitness; 100- to 500-word news reports. Query with clips. Pays $250 ($50 kill fee) for news stories; 75¢ per word for features (kill fee is 25% of assigned fee), on acceptance.

**AMERICAN JOURNAL OF NURSING**—555 W. 57th St., New York, NY 10019. Florence L. Huey, Ed. Articles, 1,500 to 2,000 words, with photos, on nursing. Query.

**ARTHRITIS TODAY**—The Arthritis Foundation, 1314 Spring St. N.W., Atlanta, GA 30309. Cindy McDaniel, Ed. Self-help, how-to, general interest, and inspirational articles, 1,000 to 2,000 words, and short fillers, 100 to 250 words, to help people with arthritis live more productive, independent, and pain-free lives. Pays from $450, on acceptance.

**BABY TALK**—636 Ave. of the Americas, New York, NY 10011. Susan Strecker, Ed. Articles, 1,500 to 3,000 words, by parents or professionals, on babies and baby care, etc. Pay varies, on acceptance. SASE required.

**BETTER HEALTH**—1384 Chapel St., New Haven, CT 06511. James F. Malerba, Pub. Dir. Wellness and prevention magazine affiliated with The Hospital of Saint Raphael of New Haven. Upbeat articles, 2,000 to 2,500 words, that encourage a healthier lifestyle. Pays $200 to $400, on acceptance. Query with SASE.

**EAST WEST: THE JOURNAL OF NATURAL HEALTH & LIVING**—See *Natural Health: The Guide to Well-Being*.

**EXPECTING**—685 Third Ave., New York, NY 10017. Evelyn A. Podsiadlo, Ed. Articles, 700 to 1,800 words, for expectant mothers. Pays $300 to $500, on acceptance.

**FITNESS**—The New York Times Company Women's Magazine, 110 Fifth Ave., New York, NY 10011. Karen Larson, Deputy Ed. Articles, 500 to 2,000 words, on health, exercise, sports, nutrition, diet, psychological well-being, sex, and beauty. Average reader is 28 years old. Profiles of athletes and fit celebrities. Query required. Pays $1 a word, on acceptance.

**HEALTH**—(formerly *In Health*) 301 Howard St., 18th Fl., San Francisco, CA 94105. Cassandra Wrightson, Ed. Asst. Articles, 1,200 words, for "Food," "Fitness," "Vanities," "Drugs," "Mind," and "Family" departments. Pays $1,500 for departments, on acceptance. Query with clips required.

**HEALTH WATCH**—Baker Communications, 3106 First National Tower, Louisville, KY 40202. Olive Herman, Ed. Bimonthly. Articles on issues of consumer health and physician relocation. "Strong reporting and research required." Mention availability of color slides in query. Payment varies, on acceptance.

**IDEA TODAY**—6190 Cornerstone Ct. East, Suite 204, San Diego, CA 92121–3773. Patricia Ryan, Ed. Practical articles, 1,000 to 3,000 words, on new exercise programs, business management, nutrition, sports medicine, dance-exercise and one-to-one training techniques. Articles must be geared toward the aerobics instructor, exercise studio owner or manager, or personal trainer. No queries on topics for the consumer. No general health ideas wanted. Payment negotiable, on acceptance. Query preferred.

**IN HEALTH**—See *Health*.

**LET'S LIVE**—P.O. Box 74908, Los Angeles, CA 90004. Court van Rooten, Ed.-in-Chief. Articles, 1,000 to 1,500 words, on preventive medicine and nutrition, alternative medicine, diet, exercise, recipes, and natural beauty. Pays $150, on publication. Query.

**MUSCULAR DEVELOPMENT**—505-H Saddle River Rd., Saddle Brook, NJ 07662. Alan Paul, Ed. Articles, 5 to 10 double-spaced typed pages, geared to serious weight training athletes, on any aspect of competitive body building, power-lifting, sports, and nutrition. Photos. Pays $50 to $300, on publication. Query.

**NATURAL HEALTH: THE GUIDE TO WELL-BEING**—(formerly *East West: The Journal of Natural Health & Living*) 17 Station St., Box 1200, Brookline, MA 02147. Features, 1,500 to 2,500 words, on holistic health, natural foods, herbal remedies, etc. Interviews. Photos. Pays 20¢ a word, extra for photos, on acceptance.

**NEW BODY**—1700 Broadway, New York, NY 10019. Nicole Dorsey, Ed. Well-researched, service-oriented articles, 800 to 1,500 words, on exercise, nutrition, lifestyle, diet, and health for women ages 18 to 35. Also considers submissions, 500 to 600 words, for "How I Lost It" column in which writers tell how they lost weight and have kept it off. Writers should have some background in or knowledge of the health field. Pays $100 to $300, on publication. Send detailed query.

**NURSING 93**—1111 Bethlehem Pike, Springhouse, PA 19477. Maryanne Wagner, Ed. Most articles are clinically oriented, and are written by nurses for nurses. Covers legal, ethical, management, and career aspects of nursing. Also includes narratives about personal nursing experiences. No poetry. Pays $25 to $300, on publication. Query.

**NURSINGWORLD JOURNAL**—470 Boston Post Rd., Weston, MA 02193. R. Patrick Gates, Man. Ed. Articles, 500 to 1,500 words, for and by nurses and nurse-educators, on aspects of current nursing issues. Pays $35, on publication.

**PATIENT CARE**—5 Paragon Dr., Montvale, NJ 07645. Robert L. Edsall, Ed. Articles on medical care, for physicians; mostly staff written. Pays varying rates, on publication. Query; all articles assigned.

**THE PHYSICIAN AND SPORTSMEDICINE**—4530 W. 77th St., Minneapolis, MN 55435. Terry Monahan, Man. Ed. News and feature articles; clinical articles coauthored with physician. Sports medicine angle necessary. Pays $150 to $1,000, on acceptance. Guidelines. Query required.

**A POSITIVE APPROACH**—P.O. Box 910, Millville, NJ 08332. Ann Miller, Ed. Articles, 500 words, on all aspects of the positive-thinking disabled/handicapped person's private and business life. Well-researched articles of interest to the visually and hearing impaired, veterans, the arthritic, and all categories of the disabled and handicapped, on interior design, barrier-free architecture, gardening, wardrobe, computers, and careers. No fiction or poetry. Pays in copies.

**PSYCHOLOGY TODAY**—24 E. 23rd St., 5th Floor, New York, NY 10010. Hara E. Marano, Consulting Ed. Bimonthly. Articles, 3,000 words, on timely subjects and news. Pays varying rates, on publication.

**TODAY'S O.R. NURSE**—6900 Grove Rd., Thorofare, NJ 08086. Mary Jo Kray, Man. Ed. Clinical or general articles, from 2,000 words, of direct interest to operating room nurses.

**VEGETARIAN TIMES**—P.O. Box 570, Oak Park, IL 60303. Paul Obis, Pub. Articles, 1,200 to 2,500 words, on vegetarian cooking, nutrition, health and fitness, and profiles of prominent vegetarians. "News items" and "In Print" (book reviews), to 500 words. "Herbalist" pieces, to 1,800 words, on medicinal uses of herbs. Queries preferred. Pays $75 to $375, on acceptance. Guidelines.

**VIBRANT LIFE**—55 W. Oak Ridge Dr., Hagerstown, MD 21740. Features, 750 to 1,500 words, on total health: physical, mental, and spiritual. Seeks upbeat articles on the family and how to live happier and healthier lives; Christian slant. Pays $80 to $250, on acceptance.

**VIM & VIGOR**—8805 N. 23rd Ave., Suite 11, Phoenix, AZ 85021. Fred Petrovsky, Ed. Positive health and fitness articles, 1,200 to 2,000 words, with accurate medical facts. By assignment only. Pays $450, on acceptance. Query.

**YOGA JOURNAL**—2054 University Ave., Berkeley, CA 94704. Stephan Bodian, Ed. Articles, 1,200 to 4,000 words, on holistic health, meditation, consciousness, spirituality, and yoga. Pays $50 to $500, on publication.

**YOUR HEALTH**—5401 N.W. Broken Sound Blvd., Boca Raton, FL 33487. Susan Gregg, Ed.-in-Chief. Health and medical articles, 1,000 to 2,000 words, for a lay audience. Queries preferred. Pays $75 to $100, on publication.

**YOUR HEALTH**—1720 Washington Blvd., Box 10010, Ogden, UT 84409. Caroll Shreeve, Pub. Articles, 1,200 words, on individual health care needs: prevention, treatment, low-impact aerobics, fitness, nutrition, etc. Color photos required. Pays 15¢ a word, on acceptance. Guidelines.

# EDUCATION

**AMERICAN SCHOOL & UNIVERSITY**—401 N. Broad St., Philadelphia, PA 19108. Joe Agron, Ed. Articles and case studies, 1,200 to 1,500 words, on design, construction, operation, and management of school and college facilities.

**THE BOOK REPORT**—Linworth Publishing, 480 E. Wilson Bridge Rd., Suite L, Worthington, OH 43085–2372. Carolyn Hamilton, Ed./Pub. "The Journal for Secondary School Librarians." Articles by school librarians or other educators about practical aspects of running a school library." Write for themes. Also publishes *Library Talk,* "The Magazine for Elementary School Librarians." Payment is one copy plus one free book.

**CAREER WOMAN**—See *Minority Engineer.*

**CAREERS AND THE DISABLED**—See *Minority Engineer.*

**CHANGE**—1319 18th St. N.W., Washington, DC 20036. Columns, 700 to 2,000 words, and in-depth features, 2,500 to 3,500 words, on programs, people, and institutions of higher education. "We can't usually pay for unsolicited articles."

**CHRISTIAN EDUCATION JOURNAL**—Scripture Press Ministries, P.O. Box 650, Glen Ellyn, IL 60138. Ronald R. Ramsey, Exec. Ed. Articles, 5 to 15 typed pages, on Christian education topics. Pays $100, on publication. Guidelines.

**CHURCH TEACHERS**—1119 Woodburn Rd., Durham, NC 27705. Shirley H. Strobel, Ed. Articles, 1,000 words, on classroom-tested teaching strategies for church school. Book reviews and poetry related to teaching. Pays $30 to $40 per page, on publication. Guidelines.

**EQUAL OPPORTUNITY**—See *Minority Engineer.*

**FOUNDATION NEWS**—1828 L St. N.W., Washington, DC 20036. Arlie W. Schardt, Ed. Articles, to 2,000 words, on national or regional activities supported by, or of interest to, grant makers and the nonprofit sector. Pays to $1,500, on acceptance. Query.

**GIFTED EDUCATION PRESS NEWSLETTER**—P.O. Box 1586, 10201 Yuma Ct., Manassas, VA 22110. Maurice Fisher, Pub. Articles, to 4,000 words, written by educators, laypersons, and parents of gifted children, on the problems of identifying and teaching gifted children and adolescents. "Interested in incisive analyses of current programs for the gifted and recommendations for improving the education of gifted students. Particularly interested in the problems of teaching humanities, science, ethics, literature, and history to the gifted. Looking for highly imaginative and knowledgeable writers." Query required. Pays with subscription.

**THE HISPANIC OUTLOOK IN HIGHER EDUCATION**—P.O. Box 362, Paramus, NJ 07652. Articles, 1,500 to 2,000 words, on the issues, concerns, and potential models for furthering the academic results of Hispanics in higher education. Queries are preferred. Payment is negotiable, on publication.

**HOME EDUCATION MAGAZINE**—P.O. Box 1083, Tonasket, WA 98855–1083. Helen E. Hegener, Man. Ed. Informative articles, 750 to 2,000 words, on all aspects of the growing homeschool movement. Send complete manuscript or detailed query with SASE. Pays about 2¢ a word, on publication.

**INDEPENDENT LIVING MAGAZINE**—See *Minority Engineer.*

**INSTRUCTOR MAGAZINE**—Scholastic, Inc., 730 Broadway, New York,

NY 10003. Debra Martorelli, Ed. Articles, 300 to 1,500 words, for teachers in grades K through 8. Payment varies, on acceptance.

**ITC COMMUNICATOR**—International Training in Communication, 4249 Elzevir Rd., Woodland Hills, CA 91364. JoAnn Levy, Ed. Educational articles, 200 to 800 words, on leadership, language, speech presentation, procedures for meetings, personal and professional development, written and spoken communication techniques. SASE required. Pays in copies.

**KEY TO CHRISTIAN EDUCATION**—8121 Hamilton Ave., Cincinnati, OH 45231–2396. Barbara Bolton and Lowellette Lauderdale, Eds. Articles, to 1,200 words, on Christian education; tips for teachers in the local church. Pays varying rates, on acceptance.

**LEADERSHIP PUBLISHERS, INC.**—P.O. Box 8358, Des Moines, IA 50301–8358. Lois F. Roets, Ed. Educational materials for talented and gifted students, grades K to 12. Send SASE for catalogue and guidelines before submitting. Pays in royalty for books, and flat fee for short pieces or booklets. Query or send complete manuscript.

**LEARNING 92/93**—1111 Bethlehem Pike, Springhouse, PA 19477. Charlene Gaynor, Ed. How-to, why-to, and personal-experience articles, to 3,000 words, for teachers of grades K through 8. Tested classroom ideas for curriculum roundups, to 600 words. Pays to $300 for features, on acceptance.

**LIBRARY TALK**—See *The Book Report.*

**MEDIA & METHODS**—1429 Walnut St., Philadelphia, PA 19102. Michele Sokoloff, Ed. Articles, 800 to 1,000 words, on media, technologies, and methods used to enhance instruction and learning in high school and university classrooms. Pays $50 to $200, on publication. Query required.

**MINORITY ENGINEER**—150 Motor Parkway, Suite 420, Hauppauge, NY 11788–5145. James Schneider, Exec. Ed. Articles, 1,000 to 1,500 words, for college students, on career opportunities in engineering, techniques of job hunting, and role-model profiles of professional minority engineers. Interviews. Pays 10¢ a word, on publication. Query. Same address and requirements for *Equal Opportunity, Career Woman* (query Eileen Nester), and *Careers and the Disabled.* For *Independent Living Magazine* and *Woman Engineer* query Editor Anne Kelly.

**MOMENTUM**—National Catholic Educational Assn., 1077 30th St. N.W., Suite 100, Washington, DC 20007–3852. Patricia Feistritzer, Ed. Articles, 500 to 1,500 words, on outstanding programs, issues, and research in education. Book reviews. Query or send complete manuscript. No simultaneous submissions. Pays 4¢ a word, on publication.

**PHI DELTA KAPPAN**—8th and Union St., Box 789, Bloomington, IN 47402–0789. Pauline Gough, Ed. Articles, 1,000 to 4,000 words, on educational research, service, and leadership; issues, trends, and policy. Pays from $250, on publication.

**SCHOOL ARTS MAGAZINE**—50 Portland St., Worcester, MA 01608. Kent Anderson, Ed. Articles, 800 to 1,000 words, on art education with special application to the classroom. Photos. Pays varying rates, on publication.

**SCHOOL SAFETY**—National School Safety Center, 4165 Thousand Oaks Blvd., Suite 290, Westlake Village, CA 91362. Ronald D. Stephens, Exec. Ed. Published eight times during the school year. Articles, 2,000 to 3,000 words, of use to educators, law enforcers, judges, and legislators on the prevention of drugs, gangs, weapons, bullying, discipline problems, and vandalism; also on-site security and character development as they relate to students and schools. No payment.

**SCHOOL SHOP/TECH DIRECTIONS**—See *Tech Directions*.

**TEACHING K-8**—40 Richards Ave., Norwalk, CT 06854. Patricia Boderick, Ed. Dir. Articles, 1,200 words, on the profession of teaching children. Queries are not necessary. Pays to $35, on publication.

**TECH DIRECTIONS**—(formerly *School Shop/Tech Directions*) Box 8623, Ann Arbor, MI 48107. Paul J. Bamford, Man. Ed. Articles, 1 to 10 double-spaced typed pages, for teachers and administrators in industrial, technological, and vocational educational fields, with particular interest in classroom projects, computer users, and political issues. Pays $10 to $150, on publication. Guidelines.

**TECHNOLOGY & LEARNING**—Peter Li, Inc., 2169 E. Francisco Blvd. E., Suite A-4, San Rafael, CA 94901. Holly Brady, Ed. Articles, to 3,000 words, for teachers of grades K through 12, about uses of computers and related technology in the classroom: human-interest and philosophical articles, how-to pieces, software reviews, and hands-on ideas. Pay varies, on acceptance.

**TODAY'S CATHOLIC TEACHER**—330 Progress Rd., Dayton, OH 45449. Stephen Brittan, Ed. Articles, 600 to 800 words, 1,000 to 1,200 words, and 1,200 to 1,500 words, on education, parent-teacher relationships, innovative teaching, teaching techniques, etc., of use to educators. Pays $15 to $175, on publication. SASE required. Query first. Guidelines.

**WILSON LIBRARY BULLETIN**—950 University Ave., Bronx, NY 10452. Mary Jo Godwin, Ed. Articles, 1,800 to 3,600 words, on libraries, communications, and information systems. News, reports, features. Pays from $150, extra for photos, on publication.

**WOMAN ENGINEER**—See *Minority Engineer*.

## FARMING AND AGRICULTURE

**ACRES USA**—10008 E. 60 Terrace, Kansas City, MO 64133. Charles Walters, Ed. Articles on biological agriculture: technology, economics, public policy, and current events. "Our emphasis is on production of quality food without the use of toxic chemicals." Pays 6¢ a word, on acceptance. Query.

**AGRI-BOOK MAGAZINE**—Exeter, Ont., Canada N0M 1S3. Attn: The Editors. Articles, 700 to 1,000 words, dealing with all phases of agriculture and trade, with photos. Pays $150 to $250, on publication. Query.

**AMERICAN BEE JOURNAL**—51 N. Second St., Hamilton, IL 62341. Joe M. Graham, Ed. Articles on beekeeping, for professionals. Photos. Pays 75¢ a column inch, extra for photos, on publication.

**BEEF**—7900 International Dr., Minneapolis, MN 55425. Paul D. Andre, Ed. Articles on beef cattle feeding, cowherds, stocker operations, and related phases of the cattle industry. Pays to $300, on acceptance.

**BUCKEYE FARM NEWS**—Ohio Farm Bureau Federation, Two Nationwide Plaza, Box 479, Columbus, OH 43216–0479. Susie Taylor, Copy Ed. Articles, to 600 words, related to agriculture. Pays on publication. Query. Limited market.

**DAIRY GOAT JOURNAL**—W. 2997 Markert Rd., Helenville, WI 53137. Dave Thompson, Ed. Articles, to 1,500 words, on successful dairy goat owners, youths and interesting people associated with dairy goats. "Especially interested in practical husbandry ideas." Photos. Pays $50 to $250, on publication. Query.

**FARM AND RANCH LIVING**—5400 S. 60th St., Greendale, WI 53129. Bob Ottum, Ed. Articles, 2,000 words, on rural people and situations; nostalgia pieces; profiles of interesting farms and farmers, ranches and ranchers. Pays $15 to $400, on acceptance and on publication.

**FARM INDUSTRY NEWS**—7900 International Dr., Minneapolis, MN 55425. Joe Degnan, Ed. Articles for farmers, on new products, machinery, equipment, chemicals, and seeds. Pays $175 to $400, on acceptance. Query required.

**FARM JOURNAL**—230 W. Washington Sq., Philadelphia, PA 19106. Earl Ainsworth, Ed. Articles, 500 to 1,500 words, with photos, on the business of farming. Pays 20¢ to 50¢ a word, on acceptance. Query.

**FLORIDA GROWER & RANCHER**—1331 N. Mills Ave., Orlando, FL 32803. Frank Garner, Ed. Articles and case histories on Florida farmers, growers, and ranchers. Pays on publication. Query; buys little freelance material.

**THE FURROW**—Deere & Company, John Deere Rd., Moline, IL 61265. George Sollenberger, Exec. Ed. Specialized, illustrated articles on farming. Pays to $1,000, on acceptance.

**HARROWSMITH**—Telemedia Publishing, Inc., Camden East, Ont., Canada K0K 1J0. Michael Webster, Ed. Articles, 700 to 4,000 words, on country life, homesteading, husbandry, organic gardening, and alternative energy with a Canadian slant. Pays $150 to $1,500, on acceptance. Query with SAE/international reply coupon.

**HARROWSMITH COUNTRY LIFE**—Ferry Rd., Charlotte, VT 05445. Address Ed. Dept. Investigative pieces, 4,000 to 5,000 words, on ecology, energy, health, gardening, energy-efficient housing, do-it-yourself projects, and the food chain. News briefs for "Gazette." Pays $500 to $2,000 for features, $50 to $600 for department pieces, on acceptance. Query required. Send SASE for guidelines.

**THE OHIO FARMER**—1350 W. Fifth Ave., Columbus, OH 43212. Tim White, Ed. Articles on farming, rural living, etc., in Ohio. Pays $20 per column, on publication.

**PEANUT FARMER**—P.O. Box 95075, Raleigh, NC 27625. Mary Evans, Man. Ed. Articles, 500 to 2,000 words, on production and management practices in peanut farming. Pays $50 to $350, on publication.

**PENNSYLVANIA FARMER**—704 Lisburn Rd., Camp Hill, PA 17011. John R. Vogel, Ed. Articles on farmers in Pennsylvania, New Jersey, Delaware, Maryland, and West Virginia; timely business-of-farming concepts and successful farm management operations.

**SHEEP! MAGAZINE**—W. 2997 Markert Rd., Helenville, WI 53137. Dave Thompson, Ed. Articles, to 1,500 words, on successful shepherds, woolcrafts, sheep raising, and sheep dogs. "Especially interested in people who raise sheep successfully as a sideline enterprise." Photos. Pays $80 to $300, extra for photos, on publication. Query first.

**SMALL ACREAGE MANAGEMENT**—Rt. 1, Box 146, Silex, MO 63377. Kelly Klober, Ed. Articles, 500 to 800 words, on land uses for small farm owners. Pays 1¢ to 3¢ a word, on publication. Query.

**SMALL FARMER'S JOURNAL**—P.O. Box 2805, Dept. 106, Eugene, OR 97402–0318. Address the Editors. How-tos, humor, practical work horse information, livestock and produce marketing, gardening information, and articles appropriate to the independent family farm. Pays negotiable rates, on publication. Query first.

**TOPICS IN VETERINARY MEDICINE**—812 Springdale Dr., Exton, PA 19341–2803. Kathleen Etchison, Ed. Technical articles, 1,200 to 1,500 words, and clinical features, 500 words, on veterinary medicine. Photos. Pays $300, $150 for shorter pieces, extra for photos, on publication.

**WALLACES FARMER**—1501 42nd St., #501, W. Des Moines, IA 50266. Monte Sesker, Ed. Features, 600 to 700 words, on farming in Iowa; methods and equipment; interviews with farmers. Query.

**THE WESTERN PRODUCER**—Box 2500, Saskatoon, Saskatchewan, Canada S7K 2C4. Address Man. Ed. Articles, to 800 words (prefer under 600 words), on agricultural and rural subjects, preferably with a Canadian slant. Photos. Pays from 15¢ a word; $20 to $40 for B&W photos; to $100 for color photos, on acceptance.

## ENVIRONMENT AND CONSERVATION

**THE AMERICAN FIELD**—542 S. Dearborn, Chicago, IL 60605. B.J. Matthys, Man. Ed. Yarns about hunting trips, bird-shooting; articles, to 1,500 words, on dogs and field trials, emphasizing conservation of game resources. Pays varying rates, on acceptance.

**AMERICAN FORESTS**—1516 P St. N.W., Washington, DC 20005. Bill Rooney, Ed. Well-documented articles, to 2,000 words, with photos, on recreational and commercial uses and management of forests. Photos. Pays on acceptance.

**THE AMICUS JOURNAL**—Natural Resources Defense Council, 40 W. 20th St., New York, NY 10011. Francesca Lyman, Ed. Investigative articles, opinions, features, profiles, essays, book reviews, and poetry on subjects related to national and international environmental issues. Pays varying rates, on acceptance. Queries required.

**ANIMALS**—Massachusetts Society for the Prevention of Cruelty to Animals, 350 S. Huntington Ave., Boston, MA 02130. Marjorie Kinder, Ed. Asst. Informative, well-researched articles, to 3,000 words, on animal welfare and pet care, conservation, international wildlife, and environmental issues affecting animals; no personal accounts or favorite pet stories. Pays to $300, on publication. Query.

**ATLANTIC SALMON JOURNAL**—P.O. Box 429, St. Andrews, N.B., Canada E0G 2X0. Harry Bruce, Ed. Articles, 1,500 to 3,000 words, related to Atlantic salmon: fishing, conservation, ecology, travel, politics, biology, how-tos, anecdotes, cuisine. Pays $100 to $400, on publication.

**AUDUBON**—700 Broadway, New York, NY 10003. Michael W. Robbins, Ed. Bimonthly. Articles, 1,800 to 4,500 words, on conservation and environmental issues, natural history, ecology, and related subjects. Payment varies, on acceptance. Query.

**BIRD WATCHER'S DIGEST**—P.O. Box 110, Marietta, OH 45750. Mary B. Bowers, Ed. Articles, 600 to 2,500 words, for bird watchers: first-person accounts; how-tos; pieces on endangered species; profiles. Cartoons. Pays from $50, on publication.

**BUZZWORM**—2305 Canyon Blvd., Suite 206, Boulder, CO 80302. Ilana Kotin, Man. Ed. Bimonthly. Articles on environmental and natural resources issues worldwide: endangered species, new ideas in conservation, personalities, etc. Query with clips and resumé. Pays $50 to $1,500, after publication.

**EQUINOX**—7 Queen Victoria Rd., Camden East, Ont., Canada K0K 1J0. Jody Morgan, Asst. Ed. Articles, 3,000 to 6,000 words, on popular geography, wildlife, astronomy, science, the arts, travel, and adventure. Department pieces, 300 to 800 words, for "Nexus" (science and medicine) and "Habitat" (synthetic and natural environment). Pays $1,500 to $3,000 for features, $100 to $500 for short pieces, on acceptance.

**FLORIDA WILDLIFE**—620 S. Meridian St., Tallahassee, FL 32399–1600. Andrea H. Blount, Ed. Bimonthly of the Florida Game and Fresh Water Fish Commission. Articles, 800 to 1,200 words, that promote native flora and fauna, hunting, fishing in Florida's fresh waters, outdoor ethics, and conservation of Florida's natural resources. Pays $50 to $400, on publication.

**GARBAGE: THE PRACTICAL JOURNAL FOR THE ENVIRONMENT** —2 Main St., Gloucester, MA 01930. Patricia Poore, Ed. Articles, 1,500 to 3,000 words, that tailor scientific and technical information to the environmental interests of a lay audience. Topics include food/health; gardening; how-to methods for improving efficiency and cutting down on waste; environmental science and technology. Occasionally publish short news items. Query with published clips or relevant resumé. Payment varies, on acceptance.

**HARROWSMITH COUNTRY LIFE**—Ferry Rd., Charlotte, VT 05445. Address Editorial Dept. Feature articles, 3,000 to 4,000 words, on environment, energy, gardening, rural issues, shelter. How-to and do-it-yourself projects. Short opinion pieces and profiles of country careers, news briefs, and natural history. Pays $500 to $1,500 for features, from $50 to $600 for department pieces, on acceptance. Query with SASE required. Guidelines.

**HOUSEPLANT MAGAZINE**—1449 Ave. William, Sillery, Quebec, Canada G1S 4G5. Larry Hodgson, Ed.-in-Chief. Personal experiences and plant profiles, 700 to 1,500 words, for amateur houseplant enthusiasts. Organic solutions should be proposed for any pest problems.

**INTERNATIONAL WILDLIFE**—8925 Leesburg Pike, Vienna, VA 22184. Donna Johnson, Assoc. Ed. Short features, 700 words, and 1,500- to 2,500-word articles that make nature, and human use and stewardship of it, understandable and interesting. Pays $500 for one-page features, $1,800 for full-length articles, on acceptance. Query. Limited free-lance needs. Guidelines.

**NATIONAL GEOGRAPHIC**—17th and M Sts. N.W., Washington, DC 20036. William P.E. Graves, Ed. First-person, general-interest, heavily illustrated articles on science, natural history, exploration, and geographical regions. Written query required.

**NATIONAL PARKS MAGAZINE**—1776 Massachusetts Ave., Washington, DC 20002. Sue E. Dodge, Ed. Articles, 1,000 to 2,000 words, on natural history, wildlife, and conservation as they relate to national parks; illustrated features on the natural, historic, and cultural resources of the national park system. Pieces about legislation and other issues and events related to the parks. Pays $100 to $800, on acceptance. Query. Send for guidelines.

**NATIONAL WILDLIFE**—8925 Leesburg Pike, Vienna, VA 22184. Mark Wexler, Ed. Articles, 1,000 to 2,500 words, on wildlife, conservation, environment; outdoor how-to pieces. Photos. Pays on acceptance. Query.

**NATURE CONSERVANCY**—1815 N. Lynn St., Arlington, VA 22209. Mark

Cheater, Ed. Membership publication. Articles on wildlife, people, trends in conservation or ecology. Pieces must have connection to The Nature Conservancy's activities or mission. No poetry or fiction. Query with clips required; article lengths, deadlines, and payment determined at time of assignment. Pays on acceptance.

**OUTDOOR AMERICA**—1401 Wilson Blvd., Level B, Arlington, VA 22209. Quarterly publication of the Izaak Walton League of America. Articles, 1,500 to 2,500 words, on natural resource conservation issues and outdoor recreation; especially fishing, hunting, and camping. Pays 20¢ a word. Query Articles Ed. with published clips.

**SEA FRONTIERS**—400 S.E. Second Ave., 4th Fl., Miami, FL 33131. Bonnie Bilyeu Gordon, Ed. Illustrated articles, 500 to 3,000 words, on scientific advances related to the sea, biological, physical, chemical, or geological phenomena, ecology, conservation, etc., written in a popular style for lay readers. Send SASE for guidelines. Pays 25¢ a word, on acceptance. Query.

**SIERRA**—730 Polk St., San Francisco, CA 94109. Jonathan F. King, Ed.-in-Chief. Articles, 750 to 2,500 words, on environmental and conservation topics, politics, travel, hiking, backpacking, skiing, rafting, cycling. Photos. Pays from $500 to $2,000, extra for photos, on acceptance. Query with SASE and clips.

**SMITHSONIAN MAGAZINE**—900 Jefferson Dr., Washington, DC 20560. Marlane A. Liddell, Articles Ed. Articles on history, art, natural history, physical science, profiles, etc. Query.

**SPORTS AFIELD**—250 W. 55th St., New York, NY 10019. Tom Paugh, Ed. Articles, 500 to 2,000 words, with quality photos, on hunting, fishing, natural history, conservation, ecology, personal experiences. How-to pieces; humor, fiction. Pays top rates, on acceptance.

**VIRGINIA WILDLIFE**—P.O. Box 11104, Richmond, VA 23230–1104. Monthly magazine of the Commission of Game and Inland Fisheries. Articles, 1,500 to 2,500 words, on conservation and related topics, including fishing, hunting, wildlife management, outdoor safety, ethics, etc. All material must have Virginia tie-in and be accompanied by color photos. Query with SASE. Pays 10¢ a word, extra for photos, on acceptance.

**WILDLIFE CONSERVATION**—New York Zoological Society, Bronx, NY 10460. Nancy Simmons, Sr. Ed. First-person articles, 1,500 to 2,000 words, on "popular" natural history, "based on author's research and experience as opposed to textbook approach." Payment varies, on acceptance. Guidelines.

**ZOO LIFE**—11661 San Vicente Blvd., Suite 402, Los Angeles, CA 90049. Audrey Tawa, Ed. Quarterly. Articles, 1,500 to 2,000 words, on the work zoos and aquariums are doing in the fields of animal conservation and education. Mention possibility of photos when querying. Pays 30¢ a word, on publication. Payment for photos negotiable. Guidelines.

**ZOOMIN'**—c/o Friends of the Zoo, 3515 Broadway, Suite 103, Kansas City, MO 64111. Aimée Larrabee, Ed. Articles of varying lengths on wildlife and the environment, geared toward family readership; profiles. Each issue focuses on a specific animal species and its ecosystem. Pays in copies.

## MEDIA AND THE ARTS

**AHA! HISPANIC ARTS NEWS**—Assoc. of Hispanic Arts, 173 E. 116th St., New York, NY 10029–1302. Dolores Prida, Ed. Editorials, reviews, monthly calendars, feature articles, and listings by artistic discipline. Query required.

**AIRBRUSH ACTION**—P.O. Box 73, 1985 Swarthmore Ave., Lakewood, NJ 08701. Address the Editors. Articles, 500 to 3,000 words, on airbrush, graphics, and art-related topics. Pays $75 to $300, on publication. Query.

**THE AMERICAN ART JOURNAL**—40 W. 57th St., 5th Fl., New York, NY 10019–4044. Jayne A. Kuchna, Ed. Scholarly articles, 2,000 to 10,000 words, on American art of the 17th through the early 20th centuries. Photos. Pays $200 to $500, on acceptance.

**AMERICAN INDIAN ART MAGAZINE**—7314 E. Osborn Dr., Scottsdale, AZ 85251. Roanne P. Goldfein, Ed. Detailed articles, 10 typed pages, on American Indian arts: painting, carving, beadwork, basketry, textiles, ceramics, jewelry, etc. Pays varying rates, on publication. Query.

**AMERICAN THEATRE**—355 Lexington Ave., New York, NY 10017. Jim O'Quinn, Ed. Features, 500 to 4,000 words, on the theater and theater-related subjects. Payment negotiable, on publication. Query.

**AMERICAN VISIONS, THE MAGAZINE OF AFRO-AMERICAN CULTURE**—The Carter G. Woodson House, 1538 9th St. N.W., Washington, DC 20001. Joanne Harris, Ed. Articles, 1,500 words, and columns, 750 to 2,000 words, on African-American culture with a focus on the arts. Pays from $100 to $1,000, on publication. Query.

**ART & ANTIQUES**—919 Third Ave., 15th Fl., New York, NY 10022. Jeffrey Schaire, Ed. Investigative pieces or personal narratives, 1,500 words, and news items, 300 to 500 words, on art or antiques. Pays $1 a word, on publication. Query first.

**THE ARTIST'S MAGAZINE**—1507 Dana Ave., Cincinnati, OH 45207. Michael Ward, Ed. Features, 1,200 to 2,500 words, and department pieces for the working artist. Poems, to 20 lines, on art and the creative process. Single-panel cartoons. Pays $150 to $350 for articles; $50 for cartoons, on acceptance. Guidelines. Query.

**ARTS ATLANTIC**—P.O. Box 848, Charlottetown, P.E.I., Canada C1A 7L9. Joseph Sherman, Ed. Articles and reviews, 600 to 3,000 words, on visual, performing, and literary arts in Atlantic Canada. Also, "idea and concept" articles of universal appeal. Pays from 15¢ a word, on publication; flat rates for reviews. Query.

**BLUEGRASS UNLIMITED**—Box 111, Broad Run, VA 22014–0111. Peter V. Kuykendall, Ed. Articles, to 3,500 words, on bluegrass and traditional country music. Photos. Pays 6¢ to 8¢ a word, extra for photos.

**CAMERA & DARKROOM**—(formerly *Darkroom Photography*) 9171 Wilshire Blvd., Suite 300, Beverly Hills, CA 90210. Ana Jones, Ed. Articles on photographic techniques and photographic portfolios, 1,000 to 2,500 words, with photos, for all levels of photographers. Pays $100 to $750. Query.

**CLAVIER MAGAZINE**—200 Northfield Rd., Northfield, IL 60093. Kingsley Day, Ed. Practical articles, interviews, master classes, and humor pieces, 2,000 words, for keyboard performers and teachers. Pays $40 to $80 per published page, on publication.

**DANCE MAGAZINE**—33 W. 60th St., New York, NY 10023. Richard Philp, Ed.-in-Chief. Features on dance, personalities, techniques, health issues, and trends. Photos. Query; limited free-lance market.

**DANCE TEACHER NOW**—3020 Beacon Blvd., West Sacramento, CA 95691–3436. K.C. Patrick, Ed. Articles, 1,000 to 3,000 words, for professional dance educators, senior students, and other dance professionals on practical information for the teacher and/or business owner, economic and historical issues related to the profession. Profiles of schools, methods, and people who are leaving their mark on dance. Must be thoroughly researched. Pays $200 to $350, on acceptance. Query preferred.

**DARKROOM PHOTOGRAPHY**—See *Camera & Darkroom.*

**DRAMATICS**—Educational Theatre Assoc., 3368 Central Pkwy., Cincinnati, OH 45225–2392. Don Corathers, Ed. Articles, interviews, how-tos, 750 to 4,000 words, for high school students on the performing arts with an emphasis on theater practice: acting, directing, playwriting, technical subjects. Prefer articles that "could be used by a better-than-average high school teacher to teach students something about the performing arts." Pays $15 to $200 honorarium. Complete manuscripts preferred; graphics and photos accepted.

**THE ENGRAVERS JOURNAL**—26 Summit St., P. O. Box 318, Brighton, MI 48116. Rosemary Farrell, Man. Ed. Articles, varying lengths, on topics related to the engraving industry and small business operations. Pays $60 to $175, on acceptance. Query first.

**FILM QUARTERLY**—Univ. of California Press Journals, 2120 Berkeley Way, Berkeley, CA 94720. Ann Martin, Ed. Historical and critical articles, film reviews, book reviews, to 6,000 words. Pays on publication. Guidelines.

**FLUTE TALK**—Instrumentalist Publishing Co., 200 Northfield Rd., Northfield, IL 60093. Kathleen Goll-Wilson, Ed. Articles, 6 to 12 typed pages, on flute performance, music, and pedagogy; fillers; photos and line drawings. Thorough knowledge of music or the instrument a must. Pays honorarium, on publication. Queries preferred.

**THE FUTURE, NOW: INNOVATIVE VIDEO**—Blue Feather Co., N8494 Poplar Grove Rd., P.O. Box 669, New Glarus, WI 53574–0669. Becky Hustad, Ed. Articles, to 2 pages, on new ideas in the video business. Pays from $75 to $150, on bimonthly publication.

**GUITAR PLAYER MAGAZINE**—20085 Stevens Creek, Cupertino, CA 95014. Articles, 1,500 to 5,000 words, on guitarists, guitars, and related subjects. Pays $100 to $400, on acceptance. Buys one-time and reprint rights.

**INDIA CURRENTS**—P.O. Box 21285, San Jose, CA 95151. Arvind Kumar, Submissions Ed. Fiction, to 2,000 words, and articles, to 800 words, on Indian culture in the United States and Canada. Articles on Indian arts, entertainment, and dining. Also music reviews, 300 to 400 words; book reviews, 300 to 400 words; commentary on national or international events affecting the lives of Indians, 800 words. Pays $20 to $25 per 1,000 words, on publication. Pays $2 to $5 for photos. Guidelines.

**INDUSTRIAL PHOTOGRAPHY**—445 Broadhollow Rd., Melville, NY 11747. Steve Shaw, Ed. Articles on techniques and trends in current professional photography; audiovisuals, etc., for industrial photographers and executives. Query.

**INTERNATIONAL MUSICIAN**—Paramount Bldg., 1501 Broadway, Suite 600, New York, NY 10036. Articles, 1,500 to 2,000 words, for professional musicians. Pays varying rates, on acceptance. Query.

**JAZZIZ**—3620 N.W. 43rd St., #D, Gainesville, FL 32606. Roy Parkhurst, Sr. Ed. Feature articles on all aspects of adult contemporary music: interviews, profiles, concept pieces. "Departments include reviews of a variety of music genres, radio, and video." Emphasis on new releases. Query with resumé. Pays varying rates, on acceptance.

**KEYBOARD MAGAZINE**—20085 Stevens Creek, Cupertino, CA 95014. Dominic Milano, Ed. Articles, 1,000 to 5,000 words, on keyboard instruments, MIDI and computer technology, and players. Photos. Pays $175 to $500, on acceptance. Query.

**MEDIA HISTORY DIGEST**—c/o Editor & Publisher, 11 W. 19th St., New York, NY 10011. Hiley H. Ward, Ed. Articles, 1,500 to 2,000 words, on the history of media, for wide consumer audience. Puzzles and humor related to media history. Pays varying rates, on publication. Query.

**MODERN DRUMMER**—870 Pompton Ave., Cedar Grove, NJ 07009. Ronald L. Spagnardi, Ed. Articles, 500 to 2,000 words, on drumming: how-tos, interviews. Pays $50 to $500, on publication.

**NEW ENGLAND ENTERTAINMENT DIGEST**—P.O. Box 313, Portland, CT 06480. Bob Taylor, Ed. News, features and reviews on the arts and entertainment industry in New England. Pays $10 to $25, on publication.

**NOIR**—P.O. Box 1838, New York, NY 10009. Duane Thomas, Pub. Dir. Articles, 750 to 1,500 words, for young African-Americans interested in the arts and politics. Queries are preferred. No payment.

**OPERA NEWS**—The Metropolitan Opera Guild, 70 Lincoln Center Plaza, New York, NY 10023–6593. Patrick J. Smith, Ed. Articles, 600 to 2,500 words, on all aspects of opera. Pays 20¢ a word, on publication. Query.

**PERFORMANCE**—1203 Lake St., Suite 200, Fort Worth, TX 76102–4504. Don Waitt, Pub./Ed.-in-Chief. Reports on the touring industry: concert promoters, booking agents, concert venues and clubs, as well as support services, such as lighting, sound and staging companies. Pays 35¢ per column line, on publication.

**PETERSEN'S PHOTOGRAPHIC**—8490 Sunset Blvd., Los Angeles, CA 90069. Bill Hurter, Ed. Articles and how-to pieces, with photos, on travel, video, and darkroom photography, for beginners, advanced amateurs, and professionals. Pays $60 per printed page, on publication.

**PHOTO: ELECTRONIC IMAGING MAGAZINE**—(formerly *Photomethods*) 1090 Executive Way, Des Plaines, IL 60010. Kimberly Brady, Ed.-in-Chief. Articles, 1,000 to 3,000 words, on silver-halide still and cine photography, video, electronic imaging, and multimedia. Material must be directly related to professional imaging techniques for business, military, government, education, scientific, and industrial photographers. Query required; all articles on assignment only. Payment varies, on publication.

**PHOTOMETHODS**—See *Photo: Electronic Imaging Magazine.*

**PLAY**—3620 N.W. 43rd St., #D, Gainesville, FL 32606. Roy Parkhurst, Sr. Ed. Articles and departments for parents covering entertainment products for children: music, spoken word, video, electronics, books, computers, games and interactive toys, profiles of children's entertainers. Query with resumé. Pays varying rates, on acceptance.

**PLAYBILL**—52 Vanderbilt Ave., New York, NY 10017. Joan Alleman, Ed.-in-Chief. Sophisticated articles, 700 to 1,800 words, with photos, on theater and subjects of interest to theater goers. Pays $100 to $500, on acceptance.

**POPULAR PHOTOGRAPHY**—1633 Broadway, New York, NY 10019.

Jason Schneider, Ed.-in-Chief. How-to articles, 500 to 2,000 words, for amateur photographers. Query first with outline and photos.

**PREVUE**—P.O. Box 974, Reading, PA 19603. J. Steranko, Ed. Lively articles, 4 to 25 pages, on films and filmmakers, entertainment features, and celebrity interviews. Pays varying rates, on acceptance. Query with clips.

**PROFESSIONAL STAINED GLASS**—Route 6 at Dingle Ridge Rd., Brewster, NY 10509. Joe Porcelli, Man. Ed. Practical articles of interest to stained glass professionals and home owners. Abundant opportunity for energetic and enterprising free lancers. Pays $100 to $250, on publication. Query required.

**RIGHTING WORDS**—Frerdonna Communications, Box 9808, Knoxville, TN 37940. Michael Ward, Pub. Journal of Language and Editing. Articles, 3,000 words, on topics of interest to professional editors. Pays from $100, on acceptance.

**ROLLING STONE**—1290 Ave. of the Americas, 2nd Fl., New York, NY 10104. Magazine of American music, culture, and politics. No fiction. Query. Rarely accepts free-lance material.

**SHEET MUSIC MAGAZINE**—223 Katonah Ave., Katonah, NY 10536. Josephine Sblendorio, Man. Ed. Pieces, 1,000 to 2,000 words, for pianists and organists, on musicians and composers, how-tos, and book reviews, to 500 words; no hard rock or heavy metal subjects. Pays $75 to $200, on publication.

**STORYTELLING MAGAZINE**—P.O. Box 309, Jonesborough, TN 37659. Articles, 800 words, related to storytelling. Profiles, 600 to 800 words, on people who tell stories via various arts and media. "We publish articles about the people, applications, traditions, and impact of storytelling. No personal essays, travel pieces, fiction, how-tos, or poetry." Pays 5¢ to 10¢ a word.

**SUN TRACKS**—Box 2510, Phoenix, AZ 85002. Robert Baird, Music Ed. Music section of *New Times*. Long and short features, record reviews, and interviews. Pays $25 to $500, on publication. Query.

**TDR (THE DRAMA REVIEW): A JOURNAL OF PERFORMANCE STUDIES**—721 Broadway, 6th Fl., New York, NY 10003. Michael Barnwell, Man. Ed. Eclectic articles on experimental performance and performance theory; cross-cultural, examining the social, political, historical, and theatrical contexts in which performance happens. Submit query or manuscript with SASE. Pays $100 to $250, on publication.

**U.S. ART**—12 S. Sixth St., Suite 400, Minneapolis, MN 55402. Frank J. Sisser, Ed./Pub. Features and artist profiles, 2,000 words, for collectors of limited-edition art prints. Published monthly. Query. Pays $400 to $450, within 30 days of acceptance.

**VIDEO MAGAZINE**—460 W. 34th St., New York, NY 10001. Stan Pinkwas, Man. Ed. How-to and service articles on home video equipment, technology, and programming. Human-interest features related to above subjects, from 500 to 2,500 words. Pays varying rates, on acceptance. Query.

**VIDEOMAKER**—P.O. Box 4591, Chico, CA 95927. Stephen Muratore, Ed. Authoritative, how-to articles geared at hobbyist and professional video camera/camcorder users: instructionals, editing, desktop video, audio and video production, innovative applications, tools and tips, industry developments, new products, etc. Pays varying rates, on publication. Queries preferred.

**WASHINGTON JOURNALISM REVIEW**—4716 Pontiac St., #310, College Park, MD 20740–2493. Rem Rieder, Ed. Articles, 500 to 3,000 words, on print or electronic journalism. Pays 20¢ a word, on publication. Query.

## HOBBIES, CRAFTS, COLLECTING

**AMERICAN WOODWORKER**—Rodale Press, 33 E. Minor St., Emmaus, PA 18098. David Sloan, Ed. "A how-to bimonthly for the woodworking enthusiast." Technical or anecdotal articles, to 2,000 words, relating to woodworking or furniture design. Fillers, drawings, slides and photos considered. Pays from $150 per published page, on publication; regular contributors paid on acceptance. Queries preferred. Guidelines.

**ANTIQUE MONTHLY**—2100 Powers Ferry Road, Atlanta, GA 30339. Kenna Simmons, Man. Ed. Articles, 750 to 1,200 words, on trends and the exhibition and sales (auctions, antique shops, etc.) of decorative arts and antiques, with B&W photos or color slides. Heavy emphasis on news and timely material. Pays varying rates, on publication.

**THE ANTIQUE TRADER WEEKLY**—Box 1050, Dubuque, IA 52004. Kyle D. Husfloen, Ed. Articles, 1,000 to 2,000 words, on all types of antiques and collectors' items. Photos. Pays from $25 to $200, on publication. Query preferred. Buys all rights.

**ANTIQUES & AUCTION NEWS**—P.O. Box 500, Mount Joy, PA 17552. Weekly newspaper. Factual articles, 600 to 1,500 words, on antiques, collectors, and collections. Query required. Photos. Pays $5 to $20, after publication.

**ANTIQUEWEEK**—P.O. Box 90, Knightstown, IN 46148. Tom Hoepf, Ed., Central Edition; Connie Swaim, Ed., Eastern Edition. Weekly antique, auction, and collectors' newspaper. Articles, 500 to 1,500 words, on antiques, collectibles, restorations, genealogy, auction and antique show reports. Photos. Pays from $40 to $150 for in-depth articles, on publication. Query. Guidelines.

**AOPA PILOT**—421 Aviation Way, Frederick, MD 21701. Mark R. Twombly, Ed. Magazine of the Aircraft Owners and Pilots Assn. Articles, to 2,500 words, with photos, on general aviation for beginning and experienced pilots. Pays to $750.

**AQUARIUM FISH**—P.O. Box 6050, Mission Viejo, CA 92690. Edward Bauman, Ed. Articles, 2,000 to 4,000 words, on freshwater, saltwater, and pond fish, with or without color transparencies. (No "pet fish" stories, please.) Payment varies, on publication.

**AUTOGRAPH COLLECTOR'S MAGAZINE**—541 N. Main St., Suite 104–352, Corona, CA 91720. Joe Kraus, Ed. Articles, 100 to 1,500 words, on all areas of autograph collecting: preservation, framing, and storage, specialty collections, documents and letters, collectors and dealers. Queries preferred. Payment varies.

**BIRD TALK**—Box 6050, Mission Viejo, CA 92690. Julie Rach, Ed. Articles for pet bird owners: care and feeding, training, safety, outstanding personal adventures, exotic birds in their native countries, profiles of celebrities' pet birds, travel to bird parks or shows. Pays 10¢ a word, after publication. Query or send manuscript; good transparencies a plus.

**BIRD WATCHER'S DIGEST**—P.O. Box 110, Marietta, OH 45750. Mary B. Bowers, Ed. Articles, 600 to 3,000 words, on bird-watching experiences and expeditions: information about rare sightings; updates on endangered species. Pays from $50, on publication. Allow eight weeks for response.

**THE BLADE MAGAZINE**—P.O. Box 22007, Chattanooga, TN 37422.

J. Bruce Voyles, Ed. Articles, 500 to 1,500 words: historical pieces on knives and old knife factories, etc.; interviews; celebrities who use/collect knives; knife trends, handmade and factory; values on collectible knives and knife accessories; how to use knives, sharpen; etc. Study magazine first. Pays from $150, on publication.

**CANADIAN STAMP NEWS**—103 Lakeshore Rd., Suite 202, St. Catharines, Ont., Canada L2N 2T6. Ellen Rodger, Ed. Biweekly. Articles, 1,000 to 2,000 words, on stamp collecting news, rare and unusual stamps and auction and club reports. Special issues throughout the year; ask for guidelines. Photos. Pays from $70, on publication.

**CANADIAN WORKSHOP MAGAZINE**—130 Spy Ct., Markham, Ont., Canada L3R 5H6. Erina Kelly, Ed. Articles, 1,500 to 5,000 words, on do-it-yourself home renovations, energy saving projects, etc., with photos. Payment varies, on publication.

**CARD COLLECTOR'S PRICE GUIDE**—3 Fairchild Ct., Plainview, NY 11803. Address Editorial Office. Articles, from 800 words, related to non-sports, auto racing, boxing, golf, minor league baseball, and soccer cards; collecting and investing; fillers. Queries preferred. Pays 10¢ a word, on publication.

**CARD PLAYER**—1455 E. Tropicana Ave., Suite 450, Las Vegas, NV 89119. June Field, Ed./Pub. "The Magazine for Those Who Play to Win." Articles on events, personalities, legal issues, new casinos, tournaments, and prizes. Also articles on strategies, theory and game psychology to improve play. Occasionally use humor, cartoons, puzzles, or anecdotal material. Pays $50, on publication; $25 to $35 for fillers. (For longer stories, features, or special coverage, pays $75 to $200.) Guidelines.

**CHESS LIFE**—186 Route 9W, New Windsor, NY 12553–7698. Glenn Petersen, Ed. Articles, 500 to 3,000 words, for members of the U.S. Chess Federation, on news, profiles, technical aspects of chess. Features on all aspects of chess: history, humor, puzzles, etc. Fiction, 500 to 2,000 words, related to chess. Photos. Pays varying rates, on acceptance. Query; limited free-lance market.

**COLLECTOR EDITIONS**—170 Fifth Ave., New York, NY 10010. Joan Muyskens Pursley, Ed. Articles, 750 to 1,500 words, on collectibles, mainly contemporary limited-edition figurines, plates, and prints. Pays $150 to $350, within 30 days of acceptance. Query with photos.

**COLLECTORS NEWS**—P.O. Box 156, Grundy Center, IA 50638. Linda Kruger, Ed. Articles, to 1,500 words, on private collections, antiques, and collectibles, especially 20th-century nostalgia, Americana, glass and china, music, furniture, transportation, timepieces, jewelry, farm-related collectibles, and lamps; include B&W photos. Pays $1 per column inch; $25 for front-page color photos, on publication.

**COUNTED CROSS-STITCH PLUS**—See *Cross-Stitch Plus.*

**COUNTRY FOLK ART MAGAZINE**—8393 E. Holly Rd., Holly, MI 48442–8819. Julie L. Semrau, Man. Ed. Historical, gardening, collectibles, and how-to pieces, 750 to 2,000 words, with a creative slant on American country folk art. Pays $150 to $300, on acceptance. Submit pieces on seasonal topics one year in advance.

**COUNTRY HANDCRAFTS**—5400 S. 60th St., Greendale, WI 53129. Kathy Pohl, Exec. Ed. All types of craft designs (needlepoint, quilting, woodworking, etc.) with complete instructions and full-size patterns. Pays from $50 to $300, on acceptance, for all rights.

**CRAFTS 'N THINGS**—Dept. W, 701 Lee St., Suite 1000, Des Plaines, IL 60016–4570. Julie Stephani, Ed. How-to articles on all kinds of crafts projects, with instructions. Send manuscript with instructions and photograph of the finished item. Pays $50 to $250, on acceptance.

**CROSS-STITCH PLUS**—(formerly *Counted Cross-Stitch Plus*) 306 E. Parr Rd., Berne, IN 46711. Lana Schurb, Ed. How-to and instructional counted cross-stitch. Book and product reviews. Pays varying rates.

**CROSS-STITCH SAMPLER**—P.O. Box 413, Chester Heights, PA 19017. Deborah N. DeSimone, Ed. Articles, 500 to 1,500 words, about counted cross-stitch, drawn thread, or themes revolving around stitching (samplers, needlework tools, etc.). Queries required. Payment varies, on acceptance.

**DOG FANCY**—P.O. Box 6050, Mission Viejo, CA 92690. Kim Thornton, Ed. Articles, 1,500 to 3,000 words, on dog care, health, grooming, breeds, activities, events, etc. Photos. Payment varies, on acceptance.

**DOLL LIFE**—243 Newton-Sparta Rd., Newton, NJ 07860. Michele Epstein, Ed. Articles, 500 to 1,500 words, on antique, nostalgic, folk, and craft dolls. Profiles of doll artists and how-to pieces for doll makers. Bimonthly. Pays 15¢ a word, on publication.

**DOLLS, THE COLLECTOR'S MAGAZINE**—170 Fifth Ave., New York, NY 10010. Joan Muyskens Pursley, Ed. Articles, 500 to 2,500 words, for knowledgeable doll collectors; sharply focused with a strong collecting angle, and concrete information (value, identification, restoration, etc.). Pays $100 to $350, after acceptance. Query.

**FIBERARTS**—50 College St., Asheville, NC 28801. Ann Batchelder, Ed. Published five times yearly. Articles, 400 to 1,200 words, on contemporary trends in fiber sculpture, weaving, surface design, quilting, stitchery, papermaking, felting, basketry, and wearable art. Query with photos of subject, outline, and synopsis. Pays varying rates, on publication.

**FINESCALE MODELER**—P.O. Box 1612, Waukesha, WI 53187. Bob Hayden, Ed. How-to articles for people who make nonoperating scale models of aircraft, automobiles, boats, figures. Photos and drawings should accompany articles. One-page model-building hints and tips. Pays from $30 per published page, on acceptance. Query preferred.

**GAMES**—19 W. 21st St., New York, NY 10010. Will Shortz, Ed. Articles on games and playful, offbeat subjects. Quizzes, tests, brainteasers, etc. Pays top rates, on publication.

**THE HOME SHOP MACHINIST**—2779 Aero Park Dr., Box 1810, Traverse City, MI 49685. Joe D. Rice, Ed. How-to articles on precision metalworking and foundry work. Accuracy and attention to detail a must. Pays $40 per published page, extra for photos and illustrations, on publication. Send SASE for writer's guidelines.

**INTERNATIONAL DOLL WORLD**—306 E. Parr Rd., Berne, IN 46711. Beth Schwartz, Ed. Informational articles about doll collecting.

**KITPLANES**—P.O. Box 6050, Mission Viejo, CA 92690. Dave Martin, Ed. Articles geared to the growing market of aircraft built from kits and plans by home craftsmen, on all aspects of design, construction, and performance, 1,000 to 4,000 words. Pays $60 per page, on publication.

**LOST TREASURE**—P.O. Box 1589, Grove, OK 74344. Grace Michael,

Man. Ed. Factual articles, 1,000 to 1,800 words, on treasure hunting, metal detecting, prospecting techniques, and legendary lost treasure. Profiles. Pays 4¢ a word; preference given to stories with photos. Pays $5 for B&W photos, $100 for color slides used on cover. Send SASE with 52¢ postage for guidelines.

**MILITARY HISTORY**—602 S. King St., Suite 300, Leesburg, VA 22075. C. Brian Kelly, Ed. Bimonthly on the strategy, tactics, and personalities of military history. Department pieces, 2,000 words, on espionage, weaponry, personality, and travel. Features, 4,000 words, with 500-word sidebars. Pays $200 to $400, on publication. Query. Guidelines.

**MODEL RAILROADER**—21027 Crossroads Cir., Waukesha, WI 53187. Russ Larson, Ed. Articles, with photos of layout and equipment, on model railroads. Pays $75 per printed page, on acceptance. Query.

**NEEDLEWORK RETAILER**—117 Alexander Ave., P.O. Box 724, Ames, IA 50010. Anne Bradford, Ed. Articles, 500 to 1,000 words, on how to run a small needlework business or anything related to the needlework trade. "Writers must have a background in needlework; we don't want general articles about small businesses." Payment varies, on acceptance.

**NEW ENGLAND ANTIQUES JOURNAL**—4 Church St., Ware, MA 01082. Jody Young, Gen. Mgr. Well-researched articles, to 2,500 words, on antiques of interest to collectors and/or dealers, auction and antiques show reviews, to 1,000 words, antiques market news, to 500 words; photos desired. Pays to $150, on publication. Query or send manuscript. Reports in 2 to 4 weeks.

**THE NEW YORK ANTIQUE ALMANAC**—Box 335, Lawrence, NY 11559. Carol Nadel, Ed. Articles on antiques, shows, shops, art, investments, collectibles, collecting suggestions; related humor. Photos. Pays $5 to $75, extra for photos, on publication.

**NOSTALGIA WORLD**—Box 231, North Haven, CT 06473. Richard Mason, Jr., Ed. Features, 3,000 words, and other articles, 1,500 words, on all kinds of collectibles: records, TV memorabilia (Munsters, Star Trek, Dark Shadows, Elvira, etc.), comics, gum cards, toys, sheet music, monsters, magazines, dolls, movie posters, etc. Pays $10 to $50, on publication.

**NUTSHELL NEWS**—21027 Crossroads Cir., P.O. Box 1612, Waukesha, WI 53187. Sybil Harp, Ed. Articles, 1,200 to 1,500 words, for dollhouse-scale miniatures enthusiasts, collectors, craftspeople, and hobbyists. Interested in artisan profiles, tours of collections, and how-to projects. "Writers must be knowledgeable miniaturists." Color slides or B&W prints required. Pays $50 per published page, on acceptance. Query first.

**PETERSEN'S PHOTOGRAPHIC**—8490 Sunset Blvd., Los Angeles, CA 90069. Bill Hurter, Ed. How-to articles on all phases of still photography of interest to the amateur and advanced photographer. Pays $60 per printed page for article accompanied by photos, on publication.

**POPULAR MECHANICS**—224 W. 57th St., New York, NY 10019. Deborah Frank, Man. Ed. Articles, 300 to 2,000 words, on latest developments in mechanics, industry, science; features on hobbies with a mechanical slant; how-tos on home, shop, and crafts projects; features on outdoor adventures, boating, and electronics. Photos and sketches a plus. Pays to $1,000, $25 to $100 for short pieces, on acceptance. Buys all rights.

**POPULAR WOODWORKING**—1320 Galaxy Way, Concord, CA 94520. David M. Camp, Ed. Project articles, to 2,000 words; techniques pieces, to 1,500 words; anecdotes and essays, to 1,000 words, for the "modest production wood-worker, small shop owner, wood craftsperson, advanced hobbyist and woodcarver." Pays $500 to $1,000 for large, complicated projects; $100 to $500 for small projects and other features; half made on acceptance, half on publication. Query with brief outline and photo of finished project.

**QUICK & EASY CRAFTS**—306 E. Parr Rd., Berne, IN 46711. Beth Schwartz, Ed. How-to and instructional needlecrafts and other arts and crafts, book reviews, and tips. Photos. Pays varying rates, before publication.

**RAILROAD MODEL CRAFTSMAN**—P.O. Box 700, Newton, NJ 07860–0700. William C. Schaumburg, Ed. How-to articles on scale model railroading; cars, operation, scenery, etc. Pays on publication.

**R/C MODELER MAGAZINE**—P.O. Box 487, Sierra Madre, CA 91025. Patricia E. Crews, Ed. Technical and semi-technical how-to articles on radio-controlled model aircraft, boats, helicopters, and cars. Query.

**RESTORATION**—P.O. Box 50046, Tucson, AZ 85703–1046. W.R. Haessner, Ed. Articles, 1,200 to 1,800 words, on restoring autos, trucks, planes, trains, etc. Photos and art required. Pays $50 per page, on publication. Query.

**THE ROBB REPORT**—1 Acton Pl., Acton, MA 01720. Attn: Toby Perelmuter. Feature articles on investment opportunities, classic and collectible autos, entrepreneurship, technology, lifestyles, home interiors, boats, travel, etc. Pays on publication. Query with SASE and published clips.

**SCHOOL MATES**—U.S. Chess Federation, 186 Route 9W, New Windsor, NY 12553–7698. Jennie L. Simon, Ed. Articles and fiction, to 1,000 words, and short fillers, related to chess for beginning chess players (not necessarily children). "Instructive, but room for fun puzzles, anecdotes, etc. All chess related. Articles on chessplaying celebrities are always of interest to us." Pays about $40 per 1,000 words, on publication. Query; limited free-lance market.

**73 AMATEUR RADIO**—WGI, 70 Route 202N, Peterborough, NH 03458. Bill Brown, Ed. Articles, 1,500 to 3,000 words, for electronics hobbyists and amateur radio operators. Pays $50 to $250.

**SEW NEWS**—P.O. Box 1790, News Plaza, Peoria, IL 61656. Linda Turner Griepentrog, Ed. Articles, to 3,000 words, "that teach a specific technique, inspire a reader to try new sewing projects, or inform a reader about an interesting person, company, or project related to sewing, textiles, or fashion." Emphasis is on fashion (not craft) sewing. Pays $25 to $400, on acceptance. Queries required; no unsolicited manuscripts accepted.

**SPORTS CARD TRADER**—3 Fairchild Ct., Plainview, NY 11803. Address Editorial Office. Articles, from 1,000 words, related to baseball, football, basketball, and hockey cards; collecting and investing and fillers. Queries preferred. Pays 10¢ per word, on publication.

**SPORTS COLLECTORS DIGEST**—Krause Publications, 700 E. State St., Iola, WI 54990. Tom Mortenson, Ed. Articles, 750 to 2,000 words, on old baseball card sets and other sports memorabilia and collectibles. Pays $50 to $100, on publication.

**TEDDY BEAR REVIEW**—P.O. Box 1239, Hanover, PA 17331. Chris Revi, Ed. Articles on antique and contemporary teddy bears for makers, collectors, and enthusiasts. Pays $50 to $200, within 30 days of acceptance. Query with photos.

**THREADS MAGAZINE**—Taunton Press, 63 S. Main St., Box 5506, Newtown, CT 06470. Address the Editors. Bimonthly. Articles and department pieces about materials, tools, techniques, people, and design in sewing and textile arts, especially garment making, knitting, quilting, and stitchery. Pays $150 per published page, on publication.

**TREASURE**—31970 Yucaipa Blvd., Yucaipa, CA 92399. Jim Williams, Ed. Articles, to 2,500 words, and fillers, 300 words, of interest to treasure hunters: "How-to" (building projects and hunting techniques); "Search" (where to look for treasure); and "Found" (stories of discovered treasure). Photos and illustrations welcome. Pays from $30 for fillers, to $125 for features, on publication. Same address and requirements for *Treasure Search* and *Treasure Found*.

**TREASURES IN NEEDLEWORK**—Craftways, Inc., 4118 Lakeside Dr., Richmond, CA 94806. Kit Schlich, Text Ed. Anecdotal, descriptive, and concrete articles on heirloom-quality needlework, including embroidery, quilting, cross-stitch, and crocheting. Departments, 2,000 words: "Treasures in Our Communities," highlights of collections; "Material Things," stories on fabrics and accessories; "Meet the Artist," interviews with designers and needleworkers. Fillers, 100 to 800 words. Query. Pays $150 to $300 for departments; $15 to $150 for fillers; buys all rights, on acceptance. Guidelines.

**TROPICAL FISH HOBBYIST**—1 T.F.H. Plaza, Neptune City, NJ 07753. Ray Hunziker, Ed. Articles, 500 to 3,000 words, for beginning and experienced tropical and marine fish enthusiasts. Photos. Pays $35 to $250, on acceptance. Query.

**WEST ART**—Box 6868, Auburn, CA 95604–6868. Martha Garcia, Ed. Features, 350 to 700 words, on fine arts and crafts. No hobbies. Photos. Pays 50¢ per column inch, on publication. SASE required.

**WESTERN & EASTERN TREASURES**—P.O. Box 1095, Arcata, CA 95521. Rosemary Anderson, Man. Ed. Illustrated articles, to 1,500 words, on treasure hunting and how-to metal detecting tips. Pays 2¢ a word, extra for photos, on publication.

**WIN MAGAZINE**—16760 Stagg St., #213, Van Nuys, CA 91406–1642. Cecil Suzuki, Ed. Gambling-related articles, 1,000 to 3,000 words, and fiction. Pays on publication.

**THE WINE SPECTATOR**—Opera Plaza, Suite 2014, 601 Van Ness Ave., San Francisco, CA 94102. Jim Gordon, Man. Ed. Features, 600 to 2,000 words, preferably with photos, on news and people in the wine world. Pays from $100, extra for photos, on publication. Query required.

**WOODENBOAT MAGAZINE**—P.O. Box 78, Brooklin, ME 04616. Jonathan Wilson, Ed. How-to and technical articles, 4,000 words, on construction, repair, and maintenance of wooden boats; design, history, and use of wooden boats; and profiles of outstanding wooden boat builders and designers. Pays $150 to $200 per 1,000 words. Query preferred.

**WOODWORK**—42 Digital Dr., Suite 5, Novato, CA 94949. Graham Blackburn, Ed. Published 6 times yearly. Articles on all aspects of woodworking (simple, complex, technical, or aesthetic) with illustrations and cut lists. Topics include personalities, joinery, shows, carving, how-to, finishing, etc. Pays $150 per published page; $35 for "Techniques" department pieces, on publication. Queries or outlines preferred.

**WORKBASKET MAGAZINE**—700 West 47th St., Suite 310, Kansas City, MO 64112. Roma Jean Rice, Ed. Instructions and models for original knit, crochet, and tat items. (Designs must fit theme of issue.) How-tos on crafts and gardening, 400 to 1,200 words, with photos. Pays 7¢ a word for articles, extra for photos, on acceptance; negotiable rates for instructional items.

**WORKBENCH**—700 West 47th St., Suite 310, Kansas City, MO 64112. Robert N. Hoffman, Exec. Ed. Articles on do-it-yourself home improvement and maintenance projects and general woodworking articles for beginning and expert craftsmen. Complete working drawings with accurate dimensions, step-by-step instructions, lists of materials, in-progress photos, and photos of the finished product must accompany submission. Queries welcome. Pays from $150 per published page, on acceptance.

**YELLOWBACK LIBRARY**—P.O. Box 36172, Des Moines, IA 50315. Gil O'Gara, Ed. Articles, 300 to 2,000 words, on boys/girls series literature (Hardy Boys, Nancy Drew, Tom Swift, etc.) for collectors, researchers, and dealers. "Especially welcome are interviews with, or articles by past and present writers of juvenile series fiction." Pays in copies.

**YESTERYEAR**—P.O. Box 2, Princeton, WI 54968. Michael Jacobi, Ed. Articles on antiques and collectibles, for readers in Wisconsin, Illinois, Iowa, Minnesota, and surrounding states. Photos. Will consider regular columns on collecting or antiques. Pays from $10, on publication.

**ZYMURGY**—Box 1679, Boulder, CO 80306–1679. Charles N. Papazian, Ed. Articles appealing to beer lovers and homebrewers. Pays in merchandise and books. Query.

## POPULAR & TECHNICAL SCIENCE, COMPUTERS

**A+/INCIDER**—IDG Communications/Peterborough, 80 Elm St., Peterborough, NH 03458. Paul Statt, Sr. Ed. Features, 2,000 to 2,500 words, and product reviews, 1,000 to 1,500 words, of interest to Apple II and Macintosh computer users. Short hints and news, to 100 words. Pays from $25 to $500, on acceptance. Query.

**AD ASTRA**—National Space Society, 922 Pennsylvania Ave. S.E., Washington, DC 20003–2140. Richard Wagner, Ed.-in-Chief. Lively, non-technical features, to 3,000 words, on all aspects of international space program. Particularly interested in "Living in Space" articles; space settlements; lunar and Mars bases. Pays $150 to $200, on publication. Query; guidelines available.

**AIR & SPACE**—370 L'Enfant Promenade, 10th Fl., Washington, DC 20024–2518. George Larson, Ed. General-interest articles, 1,000 to 3,500 words, on aerospace experience, past, present, and future; travel, space, history, biographies, essays, commentary. Pays varying rates, on acceptance. Query first.

**AMERICAN HERITAGE OF INVENTION & TECHNOLOGY**—60 Fifth Ave., New York, NY 10011. Frederick Allen, Ed. Articles, 2,000 to 5,000 words, on history of technology in America, for the sophisticated general reader. Query. Pays on acceptance.

**AMIGA WORLD**—IDG Communications, 80 Elm St., Peterborough, NH 03458. Barbara Gefvert, Sr. Ed. Linda Laflamme, Reviews Ed. Articles, 1,500 to 3,000 words: product roundups and comparisons of major products, explanations of new technologies, applications and programming tutorials relating to Amiga systems. Single and comparative reviews, 300 to 1,500 words, on just-released Amiga hardware and software products, and 500-word news pieces on Amiga-related events. Pays $75 to $800, on publication. Query preferred; include credentials.

**ARCHAEOLOGY**—135 William St., New York, NY 10038. Peter A. Young, Ed.-in-Chief. Articles on archaeology by professionals or lay people with a solid knowledge of the field. Pays $500 to $1,000, on acceptance. Query required.

**ASTRONOMY**—P.O. Box 1612, Waukesha, WI 53187. Robert Burnham, Ed. Articles on astronomy, astrophysics, space programs, research. Hobby pieces on equipment; short news items. Pays varying rates, on acceptance.

**BIOSCIENCE**—American Institute of Biological Science, 730 11th St. N.W., Washington, DC 20001. Anna Maria Gillis, Features Ed. Articles, 2 to 4 journal pages, on new developments in biology or on science policy, for professional biologists. Style should be journalistic. Pays $300 per journal page, on publication. Query required.

**BYTE MAGAZINE**—One Phoenix Mill Ln., Peterborough, NH 03458. Dennis Allen, Ed. Features on new technology, how-to articles, and reviews of computers and software, varying lengths, for technically advanced users of personal computers. Payment is competitive. Query. Guidelines.

**CBT DIRECTIONS**—Weingarten Publications, 38 Chauncy St., Boston, MA 02111. Floyd Kemske, Ed. Articles, 1,500 words, on computer-based training, interactive video, and multimedia for industry and government professionals in program development and administration. Pays $100 to $600, on acceptance. Query.

**COMPUTE**—324 W. Wendover Ave., Suite 200, Greensboro, NC 27408–8439. Clifton Karnes, Ed. In-depth feature articles on using the personal computer at home, work, and school. Industry news, interviews with leaders in the PC field, product information, hardware and software reviews. For users of Amiga, Commodore 64/128, IBM, Tandy, and compatibles.

**COMPUTERCRAFT**—76 N. Broadway, Hicksville, NY 11801. Art Salsberg, Ed.-in-Chief. How-to features, technical tutorials, and construction projects related to personal computer and microcontroller equipment. Emphasizes enhancements, modifications, and applications. Lengths vary. Query with outline required. Pays $90 to $150 per published page, on acceptance.

**DIGITAL NEWS**—33 West St., Boston, MA 02111. Charles Babcock, Ed. Newspaper articles of varying lengths, covering products, applications, and events related to Digital's VAX line of computers. Pay varies, on acceptance. Query required.

**ELECTRONICS NOW**—(formerly *Radio-Electronics*) 500-B Bi-County Blvd., Farmingdale, NY 11735. Brian C. Fenton, Ed. Technical articles, 1,500 to 3,000 words, on all areas related to electronics. Pays $50 to $500 or more, on acceptance.

**ENVIRONMENT**—1319 18th St. N.W., Washington, DC 20036–1802. Barbara T. Richman, Man. Ed. Factual articles, 2,500 to 5,000 words, on scientific, technological, and environmental policy and decision-making issues. Pays $100 to $300. Query.

**FOCUS**—Turnkey Publishing, Inc. P.O. Box 200549, Austin, TX 78720. Doug Johnson, Ed. Articles, 700 to 4,000 words, on Data General computers. Photos a plus. Pays to $50, on publication. Query required.

**THE FUTURIST**—World Future Society, 7910 Woodmont Ave., Suite 450, Bethesda, MD 20814. Cynthia G. Wagner, Man. Ed. Features, 1,000 to 5,000 words, on subjects pertaining to the future: environment, education, business, science, technology, etc. Submit complete manuscript with brief bio (or CV) and SASE. Pays in copies.

**GENETIC ENGINEERING NEWS**—1651 Third Ave., New York, NY 10128. John Sterling, Man. Ed. Articles on all aspects of biotechnology; feature articles and news articles. Pays varying rates, on acceptance. Query.

**HOME OFFICE COMPUTING**—Scholastic, Inc., 730 Broadway, New York, NY 10003. Mike Espindle, Man. Ed. Articles of interest to people operating businesses out of their homes: product roundups, profiles of successful businesses, marketing and financial tips and advice. Payment varies, on acceptance.

**INFOMART MAGAZINE**—Infomart Corporate Communications, 1950 Stemmons Fwy., Suite 6038, Dallas, TX 75207. Aaron Woods, Ed. Articles, 800 to 1,200 words, on business applications of information systems and data processing mangers. Query. Payment is negotiable.

**LINK-UP**—143 Old Marlton Pike, Medford, NJ 08055. Joseph A. Webb, Ed. Dir. How-to pieces, hardware and software reviews, and current trends, 600 to 2,500 words, for business and education professionals who use computers and modems at work and at home. Pays $90 to $220, on publication. Book reviews, 500 to 800 words, $55. Photos a plus.

**MACWORLD**—Editorial Proposals, 501 Second St., Suite 600, San Francisco, CA 94107. Reviews, news, consumer, and how-to articles relating to Macintosh personal computers; varying lengths. Query or send outline with screen shots, if applicable. Pays from $300 to $3,500, on acceptance. Send SASE for writers guidelines.

**MOBILE OFFICE**—21800 Oxnard St., Suite 250, Woodland Hills, CA 91367. Jeff Hecox, Ed. Articles, 1,500 to 2,000 words, on applications for mobile electronics. Query. Payment varies, on publication.

**MUSEUM OF SCIENCE MAGAZINE**—Publications Dept., Museum of Science, Science Park, Boston, MA 02114–1099. Attn: Editorial Offices. Published bimonthly for Museum of Science members. Articles, 1,200 to 1,500 words, on general science topics related to exhibits and shows at Boston's Museum of Science. Send SASE for list of upcoming exhibits. Pays to $500, on publication.

**NETWORK WORLD**—161 Worcester Rd., Framingham, MA 01701-9171. John Gallant, Ed. Articles, to 2,500 words, about applications of communications technology for management level users of data, voice, and video communications systems. Pays varying rates, on acceptance.

**OMNI**—324 W. Wendover Ave., Suite 205, Greensboro, NC 27408. Keith Ferrell, Ed. Articles, 750 to 3,500 words, on scientific aspects of the future: space colonies, cloning, machine intelligence, ESP, origin of life, future arts, lifestyles, etc. Pays $800 to $3,500, $175 for short items, on acceptance. Query.

**POPULAR ELECTRONICS**—500-B Bi-County Blvd., Farmingdale, NY 11735. Carl Laron, Ed. Features, 1,500 to 2,500 words, for electronics hobbyists and experimenters. "Our readers are science oriented, understand computer theory and operation, and like to build electronics projects." Fillers and cartoons. Pays $25 to $350, on acceptance.

**PUBLISH**—Integrated Media, Inc., 501 Second St., San Francisco, CA 94107. Stan Augarten, Ed.-in-Chief. Features, 1,200 to 2,000 words, and reviews, 300 to 800 words, on all aspects of computerized publishing. Pays $400 for short articles and reviews, $900 and up for full-length features and reviews, on acceptance.

**RADIO-ELECTRONICS**—See *Electronics Now.*

**SCIENCE PROBE!**—500-B Bi-County Blvd., Farmingdale, NY 11735. Forrest M. Mims III, Ed. Quarterly. Articles, 2,500 to 3,000 words, geared toward amateur scientists of all ages; color slides should be available with all articles. Pays $350 to $1,000, on acceptance.

**THE SCIENCES**—2 E. 63rd St., New York, NY 10021. Peter G. Brown, Ed. Essays and features, 2,000 to 4,000 words, and book reviews, on all scientific disciplines. Pays honorarium, on publication. Query.

**SEA FRONTIERS**—400 S.E. Second Ave., 4th Fl., Miami, FL 33131. Bonnie Bilyeu Gordon, Ed. Illustrated articles, 500 to 3,000 words, on scientific advances related to the sea, biological, physical, chemical, or geological phenomena, ecology, conservation, etc., written in a popular style for lay readers. Send SASE for guidelines. Pays 25¢ a word, on acceptance. Query.

**SHAREWARE MAGAZINE**—1030D E. Duane Ave., Sunnyvale, CA 94086. Michael Callahan, Ed.-in-Chief. Reviews of shareware programs and articles on related topics, 1,000 to 4,000 words. Payment varies, on publication. Query.

**TECHNOLOGY & LEARNING**—Peter Li, Inc., 2169 E. Francisco Blvd., Suite A-4, San Rafael, CA 94901. Holly Brady, Ed. Articles, to 3,000 words, on computer use in the classroom: human-interest, philosophical articles, how-to pieces, software reviews, and hands-on ideas, for teachers of grades K through 12. Pay varies, on acceptance.

**TECHNOLOGY REVIEW**—MIT, W59–200, Cambridge, MA 02139. Steven J. Marcus, Ed. General-interest articles on technology and its implications. Pay varies, on publication. Query.

**WORDPERFECT MAGAZINE**—270 W. Center St., Orem, UT 84057. Gayle Humpherys, Ed. Asst. Features, 1,400 to 1,800 words, and columns, 1,200 to 1,400 words, on how-to subjects with easy-to-follow instructions that familiarize readers with WordPerfect software. Humorous essays, 750 words, for "Final Keystrokes." Pays $400 to $700, on acceptance. Query.

## SENIORS MAGAZINES

**DOWN MEMORY LANE**—3816 Industry Blvd., Lakeland, FL 33811. Adrian Hoff, Man. Ed. Articles relating to the '40s, '50s, and '60s. Focus on the human element. Lead features, 800 to 1,500 words; features, 500 to 800 words; and 200- to 500-word pieces. Photos. Also personal anecdotes, remembrances, and articles on collectibles for departments. Pays $75 to $200 per page for articles; to $200 departments. Payment made within 30 days of publication. Guidelines.

**GOLDEN YEARS**—P.O. Box 537, Melbourne, FL 32902–0537. Carol Brenner Hittner, Ed. Bimonthly for people over 50. Pieces on unique hobbies, beauty and fashion, sports, and travel, 600 words. Pays 10¢ a word, on publication.

**KEY HORIZONS**—Gateway Plaza, 950 N. Meridian, Suite 1200, Indianapolis, IN 46204. Joan Todd, Ed. General-interest articles and department pieces, 300 to 3,000 words, for readers over 50 who live in Indiana and western Pennsylvania. Departments include: Personal Finance; Wellness; Cooking; Nostalgia (restrospectives on Midwestern people, places, and events); Generations (family trends); and Travel (no first-person pieces). Pays $25 to $500, on publication.

**MATURE LIVING**—127 Ninth Ave. N., Nashville, TN 37234. Judy Pregel, Asst. Ed. Fiction and human-interest articles, to 900 words, for senior adults. Must be consistent with Christian principles. Pays 5 ½¢ a word, on acceptance.

**MATURE YEARS**—201 Eighth Ave. S., P.O. Box 801, Nashville, TN 37202.

Marvin W. Cropsey, Ed. Anecdotes, to 300 words, poems, cartoons, jokes, and puzzles for older adults. Allow two months for response. "A Christian magazine that seeks to build faith. We always show older adults in a favorable light." Include name, address, and Social Security number with all submissions.

**MODERN MATURITY**—3200 E. Carson St., Lakewood, CA 90712. J. Henry Fenwick, Ed. Articles, to 2,000 words, on careers, workplace, human interest, living, finance, relationships, and consumerism for readers over 50 years old. Photos. Query first. Pays $500 to $2,500, extra for photos, on acceptance.

**PRIME TIMES**—2802 International Ln., Suite 120, Madison, WI 53704. Rod Clark, Exec. Ed. Articles, 500 to 800 words, for dynamic, creative mid-lifers. Departments, 850 to 1,000 words. Pays $125 to $750, on publication.

**THE RETIRED OFFICER MAGAZINE**—201 N. Washington St., Alexandria, VA 22314. Articles, 800 to 2,000 words, of interest to military retirees and their families. Current military/political affairs, recent military history (especially Vietnam and Korea), humor, travel, hobbies, military family lifestyles, wellness, second careers. Photos a plus. Pays $500, on acceptance. Queries required; address Manuscript Editor. Guidelines.

**SAGACITY**—560 Lincoln St., P.O. Box 7187, Worcester, MA 01605–0187. Marcia Wilson, Ed. Personal experience, memoirs, wit, and reflections, 750 to 850 words. Sonnets, free verse, light verse, and traditional poetry, to 30 lines. (Submit poetry to Dorothy Wilder Halleran, 30 Chestnut St., Peabody, MA 01960.) " Our magazine is by, for and about mature people of any age." SASE required. Pays $10 for articles; $25 for cover story; $15 for reflections; $10 to $15 for poetry, on acceptance.

**SENIOR MAGAZINE**—3565 S. Higuera St., San Luis Obispo, CA 93401. Personality profiles and health articles, 600 to 900 words, and book reviews of interest to senior citizens in California. Pays $1.50 per inch, $10 to $25 for B&W photos, on publication.

**YESTERDAY'S MAGAZETTE**—P.O. Box 15126, Sarasota, FL 34277. Ned Burke, Ed. Articles and stories, 500 to 1,000 words, set in the '20s to '70s. "Stories with photos have the best chance of acceptance here." Traditional poetry, to 24 lines. Pays $5 to $25, for articles, on publication. Pays in copies for short pieces and poetry.

# ANIMALS

**AMERICAN FARRIERS JOURNAL**—P.O. Box 624, Brookfield, WI 53008–0624. Frank Lessiter, Ed. Articles, 800 to 2,000 words, on general farrier issues, hoof care, tool selection, equine lameness, and horse handling. Pays 30¢ per published line, $10 per published illustration or photo, on publication. Query.

**AQUARIUM FISH**—P.O. Box 6050, Mission Viejo, CA 92690. Edward Bauman, Ed. Articles, 2,000 to 4,000 words, on freshwater, saltwater, and pond fish, with or without color transparencies. (No "pet fish" stories, please.) Payment varies, on publication.

**BIRD TALK**—Box 6050, Mission Viejo, CA 92690. Julie Rach, Ed. Articles for pet bird owners: care and feeding, training, safety, outstanding personal adventures, exotic birds in their native countries, profiles of celebrities' birds, travel to bird parks or bird shows. Pays 7¢ to 10¢ a word, after publication. Query or send manuscript; good transparencies a plus.

**CAT FANCY**—P.O. Box 6050, Mission Viejo, CA 92690. K.E. Segnar, Ed. Fiction and nonfiction, to 3,000 words, on cat care, health, grooming, etc. Pays 5¢ to 10¢ a word, on acceptance.

**DAIRY GOAT JOURNAL**—W. 2997 Markert Rd., Helenville, WI 53137. Dave Thompson, Ed. Articles, to 1,500 words, on successful dairy goat owners, youths and interesting people associated with dairy goats. "Especially interested in practical husbandry ideas." Photos. Pays $50 to $250, on publication. Query.

**DOG FANCY**—P. O. Box 6050, Mission Viejo, CA 92690. Kim Thornton, Ed. Articles, 1,500 to 3,000 words, on dog care, health, grooming, breeds, activities, events, etc. Photos. Payment varies, on acceptance.

**EQUUS**—Fleet Street Corp., 656 Quince Orchard Rd., Gaithersburg, MD 20878. Laurie Prinz, Ed. Articles, 1,000 to 3,000 words, on all breeds of horses, covering their health, care, the latest advances in equine medicine and research. "Attempt to speak as one horse-person to another." Pays $100 to $400, on acceptance.

**HORSE & RIDER**—1060 Calle Cordillera, Suite 103, San Clemente, CA 92673. Juli Thorson, Ed. Sue M. Copeland, Man. Ed. Articles, 500 to 3,000 words, with photos, on western riding and general horse care: training, feeding, health, grooming, etc. Pays varying rates, on publication. Buys one-time rights. Guidelines.

**HORSE ILLUSTRATED**—P.O. Box 6050, Mission Viejo, CA 92690. Susan Wells, Ed. Articles, 1,500 to 2,500 words, on all aspects of owning and caring for horses. Photos. Pays 7¢ to 10¢ a word, on publication.

**HORSEMEN'S YANKEE PEDLAR**—785 Southbridge St., Auburn, MA 01501. Nancy L. Khoury, Pub. News and feature-length articles, about horses and horsemen in the Northeast. Photos. Pays $2 per published inch, on publication. Query.

**HORSEPLAY**—P.O. Box 130, Gaithersburg, MD 20884. Cordelia Doucet, Ed. Articles, 700 to 3,000 words, on eventing, show jumping, horse shows, dressage, driving, and fox hunting for horse enthusiasts. Pays 10¢ a word, buys all rights, after publication.

**LLAMAS**—P.O. Box 100, Herald, CA 95638. Susan Ley, Asst. Ed. "The International Camelid Journal," published 8 times yearly. Articles, 300 to 3,000 words, of interest to llama and alpaca owners. Pays $25 to $300, extra for photos, on acceptance. Query.

**MUSHING**—P.O. Box 149, Ester, AK 99725–0149. Todd Hoener, Pub. How-tos, profiles, interviews, and features, 1,500 to 2,000 words, and department pieces, 500 to 1,000 words, for competitive and recreational dog drivers and skijorers. International audience. Photos. Pays $20 to $250, after acceptance. Queries preferred. Guidelines.

**PRACTICAL HORSEMAN**—Box 589, Unionville, PA 19375. Mandy Lorraine, Ed. How-to articles on horse care, English riding, and training. Pays on acceptance. Query.

**PURE-BRED DOGS/AMERICAN KENNEL GAZETTE**—51 Madison Ave., New York, NY 10010. Elizabeth Bodner, DVM, Exec. Ed. Audrey Pavia, Sr. Ed. Articles, 1,000 to 2,500 words, relating to pure-bred dogs. Pays from $100 to $300, on acceptance. Query preferred.

**SHEEP! MAGAZINE**—W. 2997 Markert Rd., Helenville, WI 53137. Dave Thompson, Ed. Articles, to 1,500 words, on successful shepherds, woolcrafts, sheep

687

raising, and sheep dogs. "Especially interested in people who raise sheep successfully as a sideline enterprise." Photos. Pays $80 to $300, extra for photos, on publication. Query.

**TROPICAL FISH HOBBYIST**—1 T.F.H. Plaza, Neptune City, NJ 07753. Ray Hunziker, Ed. Articles, 500 to 3,000 words, for beginning and experienced tropical and marine fish enthusiasts. Photos. Pays $35 to $250, on acceptance. Query.

**WILDLIFE CONSERVATION**—New York Zoological Society, Bronx, NY 10460. Nancy Simmons, Sr. Ed. Articles, 1,500 to 2,000 words, that "probe conservation controversies to search for answers and help save threatened species." Payment varies, on acceptance. Guidelines.

**ZOOMIN'**—c/o Friends of the Zoo, 3515 Broadway, Suite 103, Kansas City, MO 64111. Aimée Larrabee, Ed. Articles, varying lengths, on wildlife and the environment, geared toward family readership; profiles. Each issue focuses on a specific animal species and its ecosystem. Pays in copies.

# MILITARY

**ARMY MAGAZINE**—2425 Wilson Blvd., Arlington, VA 22201–3385. L. James Binder, Ed.-in-Chief. Features, to 4,000 words, on military subjects. Essays, humor, history, news reports, first-person anecdotes. Pays 12¢ to 18¢ a word, $25 to $50 for anecdotes, on publication.

**ARMY RESERVE MAGAZINE**—1815 N. Ft. Myer Dr., #501, Arlington, VA 22209–1805. Lt. Col. B. R. Devlin, Ed. Articles, 900 to 1,200 words, for readers in the Army Reserves. Some training-related items; family support pieces. Queries preferred. No payment.

**LEATHERNECK**—Box 1775, Quantico, VA 22134–0776. William V.H. White, Ed. Articles, to 3,000 words, with photos, on U.S. Marines. Pays $50 per printed page, on acceptance. Query.

**LIFE IN THE TIMES**—Army Times Publishing Co., Springfield, VA 22159–0200. Margaret Roth, Ed. Travel articles, 900 words; and general-interest features, up to 3,000 words, of interest to military people and their families around the world. Personal experience pieces, 750 words, articles for special interest supplements on careers after military service, books and home entertainment, finance, fitness and health, and education. Pays $100 to $350, on acceptance. Query first.

**MARINE CORPS GAZETTE**—Box 1775, Quantico, VA 22134. Col. John E. Greenwood, Ed. Military articles, 500 to 2,000 and 2,500 to 5,000 words. "Our magazine serves primarily as a forum for active duty officers to exchange news on professional, Marine Corps related topics. Opportunity for 'outside' writers is limited." Queries preferred. Pays $50 to $100 for short articles; $200 to $400 for features, on publication.

**MILITARY**—2122 28th St., Sacramento, CA 95818. Lt. Col. Michael Mark, Ed. Articles, 600 to 2,500 words, on firsthand experience in military service: World War II, Korea, Vietnam, and all current services. "Our magazine is about military history by the people who served. They are the best historians." No payment.

**MILITARY HISTORY**—602 S. King St., Suite 300, Leesburg, VA 22075. C. Brian Kelly, Ed. Bimonthly on the strategy, tactics, and personalities of military history. Department pieces, 2,000 words, on espionage, weaponry, personality, and travel. Features, 4,000 words, with 500-word sidebars. Pays $200 to $400, on publication. Query. Guidelines.

**MILITARY LIFESTYLE MAGAZINE**—4800 Montgomery Ln., Suite 710, Bethesda, MD 20814–5341. Hope Daniels, Ed. Articles, 1,000 to 1,800 words, for active-duty military families in the U.S. and overseas, on lifestyles, child-raising, health, food, fashion, travel, sports and leisure; short fiction. Pays $300 to $800, on publication. Query first. No poetry, no historical reminiscences.

**THE RETIRED OFFICER MAGAZINE**—201 N. Washington St., Alexandria, VA 22314. Articles, 800 to 2,000 words, of interest to military retirees and their families. Current military/political affairs: recent military history (especially Vietnam and Korea), humor, travel, hobbies, military family lifestyles, wellness, and second-career job opportunities. Photos a plus. Pays to $500, on acceptance. Queries required, no unsolicited manuscripts; address Manuscript Ed. Guidelines.

**VFW MAGAZINE**—406 W. 34th St., Kansas City, MO 64111. Richard K. Kolb, Ed. Magazine for Veterans of Foreign Wars and their families. Articles, 1,500 words, on current events, veteran affairs, and military history, with veteran angle. Photos. Pays to $500, extra for photos, on acceptance. Guidelines. Query first.

# HISTORY

**AMERICAN HERITAGE**—60 Fifth Ave., New York, NY 10011. Richard F. Snow, Ed. Articles, 750 to 5,000 words, on U.S. history and background of American life and culture from the beginning to recent times. No fiction. Pays from $300 to $1,500, on acceptance. Query. SASE.

**AMERICAN HERITAGE OF INVENTION & TECHNOLOGY**—60 Fifth Ave., New York, NY 10011. Frederick Allen, Ed. Articles, 2,000 to 5,000 words, on history of technology in America, for the sophisticated general reader. Query. Pays on acceptance.

**AMERICAN HISTORY ILLUSTRATED**—6405 Flank Dr., P.O. Box 8200, Harrisburg, PA 17105. Articles, 3,000 to 5,000 words, soundly researched. Style should be popular, not scholarly. No travelogues, fiction, or puzzles. Pays $300 to $650, on acceptance. Query with SASE required.

**AMERICAN JEWISH HISTORY**—American Jewish Historical Society, 2 Thornton Rd., Waltham, MA 02154. Dr. Marc Lee Raphael, Ed. Articles, 15 to 30 typed pages, on Jewish history in general and particularly American Jewish history. Queries preferred. No payment made.

**BACKWOODSMAN**—P.O. Box 627, Westcliffe, CO 81252. Charlie Richie, Ed. Articles for the twentieth-century frontiersman: muzzleloading, primitive weapons, black powder cartridge guns, woodslore, survival, homesteading, trapping, etc. Historical and how-to articles. No payment.

**CAROLOGUE**—South Carolina Historical Society, 100 Meeting St., Charleston, SC 29401–2299. Stephen Hoffius, Ed. General-interest articles, to 10 pages, on South Carolina history. Queries preferred. Payment is six copies.

**CHICAGO HISTORY**—Clark St. at North Ave., Chicago, IL 60614. Russell Lewis, Ed. Articles, to 4,500 words, on political, social, and cultural history. Pays to $250, on publication. Query.

**CURRENT HISTORY**—4225 Main St., Philadelphia, PA 19127. William W. Finan, Jr. Country-specific political science articles, to 20 pages. Hard analysis written in a lively manner. "We devote each issue to a specific region or country. Writers should be experts with up-to-date knowledge of the region." Queries preferred. Pays $300, on publication.

**EARLY AMERICAN LIFE**—Box 8200, Harrisburg, PA 17105–8200.

Frances Carnahan, Ed. Illustrated articles, 1,000 to 3,000 words, on early American life: arts, crafts, furnishings, architecture; travel features about historic sites and country inns. Pays $50 to $500, on acceptance. Query.

**EIGHTEENTH CENTURY STUDIES**—1938 Mt. Vernon, Ft. Wright, KY 41011. Diane M. Coldiron, Ed. Quarterly. Articles, to 6,500 words, on all aspects of the eighteenth century, especially those that are interdisciplinary or that are of general interest to scholars working in other disciplines. Blind submission policy: Submit two copies of manuscript; author's name and address should appear only on separate title page. No payment.

**GOLDENSEAL**—The Cultural Center, 1900 Kanawha Blvd. East, Charleston, WV 25305–0300. Ken Sullivan, Ed. Features, 3,000 words, and shorter articles, 1,000 words, on traditional West Virginia culture and history. Oral histories, old and new B&W photos, research articles. Pays to $175, on publication. Guidelines.

**THE HIGHLANDER**—P.O. Box 397, Barrington, IL 60011. Angus Ray, Ed. Bimonthly. Articles, 1,300 to 1,900 words, related to Scottish history. "We are not concerned with modern Scotland or current problems in Scotland." Pays $100 to $150, on acceptance.

**HISTORIC PRESERVATION**—1785 Massachusetts Ave. N.W., Washington, DC 20036. Anne Elizabeth Powell, Ed. Feature articles from published writers, 1,500 to 4,000 words, on residential restoration, preservation issues, and people involved in preserving America's heritage. Mostly staff-written. Query required.

**HISTORY NEWS**—AASLH, 172 2nd Ave. N., Suite 202, Nashville, TN 37201. Susan Cantrell, Ed. History-related articles, 2,500 to 3,500 words, geared to museums, historical societies and sites, libraries, etc. No payment made. Guidelines.

**JOURNAL OF THE WEST**—P.O. Box 1009, Manhattan, KS 66502–4228. Robin Higham, Ed. Articles, to 15 pages, devoted to the history and the culture of the West, then and now. B&W photos. Pays in copies.

**LABOR'S HERITAGE**—10000 New Hampshire Ave., Silver Spring, MD 20903. Stuart Kaufman, Ed. Quarterly journal of The George Meany Memorial Archives. Articles, 15 to 30 pages, for labor scholars, labor union members, and the general public. Pays in copies.

**MILITARY**—2122 28th St., Sacramento, CA 95818. Lt. Col. Michael Mark, Ed. Military history by people who served in the military. Firsthand experiences, 600 to 2,500 words, of service in World War II, Korea, Vietnam, and more recent times. No payment.

**MILITARY HISTORY**—602 S. King St., Suite 300, Leesburg, VA 22075. C. Brian Kelly, Ed. Bimonthly on the strategy, tactics, and personalities of military history. Department pieces, 2,000 words, on espionage, weaponry, personality, and travel. Features, 4,000 words, with 500-word sidebars. Pays $200 to $400, on publication. Query. Guidelines.

**MONTANA, THE MAGAZINE OF WESTERN HISTORY**—225 N. Roberts St., Helena, MT 59620. Charles E. Rankin, Ed. Authentic articles, 3,500 to 5,500 words, on the history of the American and Canadian West; new interpretive approaches to major developments in western history. Footnotes or bibliography must accompany article. "Strict historical accuracy is essential." No fiction. Queries preferred. No payment made.

**NEBRASKA HISTORY**—P.O. Box 82554, Lincoln, NE 68501. James E. Potter, Ed. Articles, 3,000 to 7,000 words, relating to the history of Nebraska and the Great Plains. B&W line drawings. Allow 60 days for response. Pays in six copies. Cash prize awarded to one article each year.

**OLD WEST**—P.O. Box 2107, Stillwater, OK 74076. John Joerschke, Ed. Thoroughly researched and documented articles, 1,500 to 4,500 words, on the history of the American West. B&W 5×7 photos to illustrate articles. Queries are preferred. Pays 3¢ to 6¢ a word, on acceptance.

**PENNSYLVANIA HERITAGE**—P.O. Box 1026, Harrisburg, PA 17108–1026. Michael J. O'Malley III, Ed. Quarterly of the Pennsylvania Historical and Museum Commission. Articles, 3,000 to 4,000 words, that "introduce readers to the state's rich culture and historic legacy and involve them in such a way as to ensure that Pennsylvania past has a future." Pays $300 to $500, up to $100 for photos or drawings, on acceptance.

**PERSIMMON HILL**—1700 N.E. 63rd St., Oklahoma City, OK 73111. M.J. Van Deventer, Ed. Published by the National Cowboy Hall of Fame. Articles, 1,500 to 3,000 words, on Western history and art, cowboys, ranching, and nature. Top-quality illustrations a must. Pays from $100 to $250, on publication.

**SOUTH CAROLINA HISTORICAL MAGAZINE**—South Carolina Historical Society, 100 Meeting St., Charleston, SC 29401–2299. Stephen Hoffius, Ed. Scholarly articles, to 25 pages including footnotes, on South Carolina history. "Authors are encouraged to look at previous issues to be aware of previous scholarship." Payment is five copies.

**TRUE WEST**—P.O. Box 2107, Stillwater, OK 74076–2107. John Joerschke, Ed. True stories, 500 to 4,500 words, with photos, about the Old West to 1930. Some contemporary stories with historical slant. Source list required. Pays 3¢ to 6¢ a word, extra for B&W photos, on acceptance.

**THE WESTERN HISTORICAL QUARTERLY**—Utah State Univ., Logan, UT 84322–0740. Anne M. Butler, Ed. Original articles about the American West, the Westward movement from the Atlantic to the Pacific, twentieth-century regional studies, Spanish borderlands, Canada, northern Mexico, Alaska, and Hawaii. No payment made.

**YESTERDAY'S MAGAZETTE**—P.O. Box 15126, Sarasota, FL 34277. Ned Burke, Ed. Articles and fiction, to 1,000 words, on the '20s through '70s, nostalgia and memories of people, places, and things. Traditional poetry, to 24 lines. Pays $5 to $25, on publication. Pays in copies for poetry and short pieces. Guidelines.

## COLLEGE, CAREERS

**THE BLACK COLLEGIAN**—1240 S. Broad St., New Orleans, LA 70125. K. Kazi-Ferrouillet, Man. Ed. Articles, to 2,000 words, on experiences of African-American students, careers, and how-to subjects. Pays on publication. Query.

**BYLINE**—Box 130596, Edmond, OK 73013. Marcia Preston, Ed.-in-Chief. General fiction, 2,000 to 4,000 words. Nonfiction: 1,500- to 1,800-word features and 300- to 800-word special departments. Poetry, 10 to 30 lines preferred. Nonfiction and poetry must be about writing. Humor, 400 to 800 words, about writing. "We seek practical and motivational material that tells writers how they can succeed, not why they can't. Overdone topics: writers' block, the muse, rejection slips." Pays $5 to $10 for poetry; $15 to $35 for departments; $50 for features and short fiction, on acceptance.

**CAREER WOMAN**—See *Minority Engineer*.

**CAREER WORLD**—General Learning Corp., 60 Revere Dr., Northbrook, IL 60062–1563. Carole Rubenstein, Man. Ed. Gender-neutral articles about specific occupations and career development for junior and senior high school audience.

Published monthly, September through May. Query. Payment varies, on publication.

**CAREERS AND THE DISABLED**—See *Minority Engineer*.

**CIRCLE K**—3636 Woodview Trace, Indianapolis, IN 46268–3196. Nicholas K. Drake, Exec. Ed. Serious and light articles, 1,700 to 2,000 words, on careers, college issues, trends, leadership development, self-help, community service and involvement. Pays $225 to $400, on acceptance. Queries preferred.

**COLLEGE BROADCASTER**—National Assn. of College Broadcasters, Box 1955, 71 George St., 2nd Fl., Providence, RI 02906. Bimonthly. Articles, 500 to 2,000 words, on college radio and TV station operations and media careers. Query. Pays in copies.

**EQUAL OPPORTUNITY**—See *Minority Engineer*.

**JOURNAL OF CAREER PLANNING & EMPLOYMENT**—62 Highland Ave., Bethlehem, PA 18017. Mimi Collins, Ed. Bill Beebe, Assoc. Ed. Quarterly. Articles, 3,000 to 4,000 words, on topics related to career planning, placement, recruitment, and employment of new college graduates. Pays $100 to $200, on acceptance. Query first with clips. Guidelines.

**MINORITY ENGINEER**—44 Broadway, Greenlawn, NY 11740. James Schneider, Exec. Ed. Articles, 1,000 to 1,500 words, for college students, on career opportunities in engineering fields; techniques of job hunting; developments in and applications of new technologies. Interviews. Profiles. Pays 10¢ a word, on publication. Query. Same address and requirements for *Woman Engineer, Equal Opportunity, Career Woman*, and *Careers and the Disabled*.

**STUDENT LEADERSHIP**—P.O. Box 7895, Madison, WI 53707–7895. Jeff Yourison, Ed. Articles, to 2,000 words, and poetry for Christian college students. All material should reflect a Christian world view. Queries required.

**UCLA MAGAZINE**—405 Hilgard Ave., Los Angeles, CA 90024–1391. Mark Wheeler, Ed. Quarterly. Articles, 2,000 words, must be related to UCLA through research, alumni, students, etc. Queries required. Pays to $2,000, on acceptance.

**WOMAN ENGINEER**—See *Minority Engineer*.

# OP-ED MARKETS

Op-ed pages in newspapers (those that run opposite the editorials) offer writers an excellent opportunity to air their opinions, views, ideas, and insights on a wide spectrum of subjects and in styles, from the highly personal and informal essay to the more serious commentary on politics, foreign affairs, and news events. Humor and nostalgia often find a place here.

**THE ARGUS LEADER**—P.O. Box 5034, Sioux Falls, SD 57117–5034. Rob Swenson, Editorial Page Ed. Articles, to 850 words, on a wide variety of subjects for "Different Voices" column. Prefer local writers with an expertise on their subject. No payment.

**THE BALTIMORE SUN**—P.O. Box 1377, Baltimore, MD 21278–0001. Hal Piper, Opinion-Commentary Page Ed. Articles, 600 to 1,500 words, on a wide range of topics: politics, education, foreign affairs, lifestyles, etc. Humor. Payment varies, on publication. Exclusive rights: MD and DC.

**THE BOSTON GLOBE**—P.O. Box 2378, Boston, MA 02107–2378. Marjorie Pritchard, Ed. Articles, to 700 words, on economics, education, environment, foreign affairs, and regional interest. Send complete manuscript. Pays $100, on publication. Exclusive rights: New England.

**BOSTON HERALD**—One Herald Sq., Boston, MA 02106. Editorial Page Ed. Pieces, 600 to 800 words, on economics, foreign affairs, politics, regional interest, and seasonal topics. Prefer submissions from regional writers. Payment varies, on publication. Exclusive rights: MA, RI, and NH.

**THE CHARLOTTE OBSERVER**—P.O. Box 32188, Charlotte, NC 28232. Jane McAlister Pope, Ed. Well-written, thought-provoking articles, to 700 words. "We are only interested in articles on local (Carolinas) issues or that use local examples to illustrate other issues." Pays $50, on publication. No simultaneous submissions in NC or SC.

**THE CHICAGO TRIBUNE**—435 N. Michigan Ave., Chicago, IL 60611. Ruby Scott, Op-Ed Page Ed. Pieces, 800 to 1,000 words, on domestic and international affairs, environment, regional interest, and personal essays. "Writers must be experts in their fields." Pays about $150, on publication. SASE required.

**THE CHRISTIAN SCIENCE MONITOR**—One Norway St., Boston, MA 02115. Blithe Holcomb, Opinion Page Coordinator. Pieces, 700 to 800 words, on domestic and foreign affairs, economics, education, environment, foreign affairs, law, and politics. Pays $100, on acceptance. "We retain all rights for 90 days after publication. Submissions must be exclusive."

**THE CLEVELAND PLAIN DEALER**—1801 Superior Ave., Cleveland, OH 44114. Jim Strang, Op-Ed Ed. Pieces, 700 to 900 words, on a wide variety of subjects. Pays $50, on publication.

**DALLAS MORNING NEWS**—Communications Center, P.O. Box 655237, Dallas, TX 75265. Carolyn Barta, "Viewpoints" Ed. Pieces, 750 words, on politics, education, foreign and domestic affairs, seasonal and regional issues. No humor. Pay averages $75, on publication. SASE required. Exclusive rights: Dallas/Ft. Worth area.

**DES MOINES REGISTER**—P.O. Box 957, Des Moines, IA 50304. "Opinion" Page Ed. Articles, 500 to 850 words, on all topics. Pays $35 to $75, on publication. Exclusive rights: IA.

**DETROIT FREE PRESS**—321 W. Lafayette Blvd., Detroit, MI 48226. Address Op-Ed Editor. Opinion pieces, to 800 words, on domestic and foreign affairs, economics, education, environment, law, politics, and regional interest. Priority given to local writers or topics of local interest. Pays $50 to $100, on publication. Query. Exclusive rights: MI and northern OH.

**THE DETROIT NEWS**—615 Lafayette Blvd., Detroit, MI 48226. Richard Burr, Ed. Pieces, 600 to 900 words, on a wide variety of subjects. Pays $75, on publication.

**THE FLINT JOURNAL**—200 E. First St., Flint, MI 48502–1925. David J. Fenech, Opinion Dept. Ed. Articles, 650 words, of regional interest by local writers. Non-local writers should query first. No payment. Limited market.

**THE HOUSTON POST**—P.O. Box 4747, Houston, TX 77210–4747. Fred King, Ed. Opinions and current affairs pieces, 900 words, on wide variety of topics. Send complete manuscript. Pays $40, on publication. Exclusive rights: Houston area.

693

**INDIANAPOLIS STAR**—P.O. Box 145, Indianapolis, IN 46206–0145. John H. Lyst, Ed. Articles, 700 to 800 words. Pays $40, on publication. Exclusive rights: IN.

**LONG BEACH PRESS-TELEGRAM**—604 Pine Ave., Long Beach, CA 90844. Larry Allison, Ed. Articles, 750 to 900 words, on lifestyles and regional topics. Writers must be local. "Articles on baby boomer issues are of interest to us." Pays $75, on publication. Exclusive rights: Los Angeles area.

**LOS ANGELES TIMES**—Times Mirror Sq., Los Angeles, CA 90053. Bob Berger, Op-Ed Ed. Commentary pieces, to 750 words, on many subjects. "Not interested in nostalgia or first-person reaction to faraway events. Pieces must be exclusive." Payment varies, on publication. Limited market. SASE required.

**NEWSDAY**—"Viewpoints," 235 Pinelawn Rd., Melville, NY 11747. Noel Rubinton, "Viewpoints" Ed. Pieces, 700 to 800 words, on a variety of topics. Pays $150, on publication.

**THE OAKLAND TRIBUNE**—Box 24424, Oakland, CA 94623. Mary Ellen Butler, Editorial Page Ed. Articles, 750 words, on a wide range of political and social topics affecting East Bay residents; no humor or lifestyle materials. No payment.

**THE ORANGE COUNTY REGISTER**—P.O. Box 11626, Santa Ana, CA 92711. K.E. Grubbs, Jr., Ed. Articles on a wide range of local and national issues and topics. Pays $50 to $100, on publication.

**THE OREGONIAN**—1320 S.W. Broadway, Portland, OR 97201. Address Forum Ed. Articles, 900 to 1,000 words, of news analysis. Send complete manuscript. Pays $100, on publication.

**PITTSBURGH POST GAZETTE**—50 Blvd. of the Allies, Pittsburgh, PA 15222. Editorial Page Ed. Articles, to 800 words, on a variety of subjects. No humor. Pays $75 to $150, on publication. SASE required.

**PORTLAND PRESS HERALD**—P.O. Box 1460, Portland, ME 04104. Op-Ed Page Ed. Articles, 750 words, on any topic with regional tie-in. Writers must live in Maine. Pays $50, on publication. Query. Exclusive rights: ME.

**THE REGISTER GUARD**—P.O. Box 10188, Eugene, OR 97440. Don Robinson, Editorial Page Ed. All subjects; regional angle preferred. Pays $10 to $25, on publication. Very limited use of non-local writers.

**THE SACRAMENTO BEE**—2100 Q St., Sacramento, CA 95852. Rhea Wilson, Opinion Ed. Op-ed pieces, to 750 words, on state and regional topics only. Pays $150, on publication.

**ST. LOUIS POST-DISPATCH**—900 N. Tucker Blvd., St. Louis, MO 63101. Donna Korando, Ed. Articles, 700 words, on economics, education, science, politics, foreign and domestic affairs, and the environment. Pays $70, on publication. "Goal is to have half of the articles by local writers."

**ST. PAUL PIONEER PRESS DISPATCH**—345 Cedar St., St. Paul, MN 55101. Ronald D. Clark, Ed. Articles, to 750 words, on a variety of topics. Strongly prefer authors with a connection to the area. Pays $50, on publication.

**ST. PETERSBURG TIMES**—Box 1121, 490 First Ave. S., St. Petersburg, FL 33731. Jeanne Grinstead, "Perspective" Section Ed. Authoritative articles, to 2,000 words, on current political, economic, and social issues. Payment varies, on publication. Query first.

**THE SAN FRANCISCO CHRONICLE**—901 Mission St., San Francisco, CA 94103. Marsha Vande Berg, Open Forum Ed. Articles, 500 and 700 words, "that are relevant to public policy debates and push the debate forward." Also, well-crafted humor pieces. Pays to $150 (usually $75 for unsolicited pieces), on publication.

**SAN FRANCISCO EXAMINER**—110 5th St., San Francisco, CA 94103. Op-Ed Ed. Well-written articles, 500 to 650 words, on any subject. Payment varies, on publication.

**SEATTLE POST-INTELLIGENCER**—P.O. Box 1109, Seattle, WA 98111. Charles J. Dunsire, Editorial Page Ed. Articles, 750 to 800 words, on foreign and domestic affairs, environment, education, politics, regional interest, religion, science, and seasonal material. Prefer writers who live in the area. Pays $75 to $150, on publication. SASE required. Very limited market.

**TULSA WORLD**—P.O. Box 1770, Tulsa, OK 74102. Articles, about 750 words, on subjects of local or regional interest. Exclusive rights: Tulsa area.

**USA TODAY**—1000 Wilson Blvd., Arlington, VA 22229. Sid Hurlburt, Ed./ Columns. Articles, 380 to 530 words. Very limited market. Query. Pays $125, on publication.

**THE WALL STREET JOURNAL**—Editorial Page, 200 Liberty St., New York, NY 10281. Amity Shlaes, Op-Ed Ed. Articles, to 1,500 words, on politics, economics, law, education, environment, humor (occasionally), and foreign and domestic affairs. Articles must be timely, heavily reported, and of national interest by writers with expertise in their field. Pays $150 to $300, on publication.

**WASHINGTON TIMES**—3600 New York Ave. N.E., Washington, DC 20002. John McCaslin, Articles and Opinion Page Ed. Articles, 800 to 1,000 words, on a variety of subjects. No pieces written in the first-person. "Syndicated columnists cover the 'big' issues; find an area that is off the beaten path." Pays $150, on publication. Exclusive rights: Washington, DC and Baltimore area.

## ADULT MAGAZINES

**CHIC**—9171 Wilshire Blvd., Suite 300, Beverly Hills, CA 90210. Doug Oliver, Exec. Ed. Sex-related articles, interviews, erotic fiction, 2,500 to 3,500 words. Query for articles. Pays $750 for articles, $500 for fiction, on acceptance.

**GALLERY**—401 Park Ave. S., New York, NY 10016–8802. Barry Janoff, Ed.-in-Chief. Peter Emshwiller, Man. Ed. Articles, investigative pieces, interviews, profiles, to 2,500 words, for sophisticated men. Short humor, satire, service pieces, and fiction. Photos. Pays varying rates, half on acceptance, half on publication. Query.

**GENESIS**—1776 Broadway, 20th Fl., New York, NY 10019. Michael Banka, Ed. Articles, 2,500 words; celebrity interviews, 2,500 words. Sexually explicit nonfiction features, 2,000 to 3,000 words. Photo essays. Pays 60 days after acceptance. Query with clips.

**PENTHOUSE**—1965 Broadway, New York, NY 10023. Peter Bloch, Ed. General-interest profiles, interviews, or investigative articles, to 5,000 words. Interviews, 5,000 words, with introductions. Pays to $1 a word, on acceptance.

**PLAYBOY**—680 N. Lakeshore Dr., Chicago, IL 60611. John Rezek, Articles Ed. Alice K. Turner, Fiction Ed. Articles, 3,500 to 6,000 words, and sophisticated fiction, 1,000 to 10,000 words (5,000 preferred), for urban men. Humor; satire.

Science fiction. Pays to $5,000 for articles and fiction, $1,000 for short-shorts, on acceptance.

**PLAYERS**—8060 Melrose Ave., Los Angeles, CA 90046. Joe Nazel, Ed. Articles, 1,000 to 3,000 words, for black men: politics, economics, travel, fashion, grooming, entertainment, sports, interviews, fiction, humor, satire, health, and sex. Photos a plus. Pays on publication.

**PLAYGIRL**—801 Second Ave., New York, NY 10017. Susan Bax, Man. Ed. Articles, 1,500 words, for women 18 to 34. Celebrity interviews, 1,500 to 2,000 words. Humor. Pays varying rates, on acceptance.

# FICTION MARKETS

This list gives the fiction requirements of general- and special-interest magazines, including those that publish detective and mystery, science fiction and fantasy, romance and confession stories. Other good markets for short fiction are the *College, Literary and Little Magazines* where, though payment is modest (usually in copies only), publication can help a beginning writer achieve recognition by editors at the larger magazines. Juvenile fiction markets are listed under *Juvenile, Teenage, and Young Adult Magazines*. Publishers of book-length fiction manuscripts are listed under *Book Publishers*.

All manuscripts must be typed double-space and submitted with self-addressed envelopes bearing postage sufficient for the return of the material. Use good white paper; onion skin and erasable bond are not acceptable. *Always* keep a copy of the manuscript, since occasionally a manuscript is lost in the mail. Magazines may take several weeks—often longer—to read and report on submissions. If an editor has not reported on a manuscript after a reasonable amount of time, write a brief, courteous letter of inquiry.

**ABORIGINAL SF**—P.O. Box 2449, Woburn, MA 01888–0849. Charles C. Ryan, Ed. Stories, 2,500 to 6,000 words, with a unique scientific idea, human or alien character, plot, and theme of lasting value; "must be science fiction; no fantasy, horror, or sword and sorcery." Pays $250. Send SASE for guidelines.

**AIM MAGAZINE**—P.O. Box 20554, Chicago, IL 60620. Ruth Apilado, Ed. Short stories, 800 to 3,000 words, geared to promoting racial harmony and peace. Pays from $15 to $25, on publication. Annual contest.

**ALFRED HITCHCOCK'S MYSTERY MAGAZINE**—380 Lexington Ave., New York, NY 10168–0035. Cathleen Jordan, Ed. Well-plotted, plausible mystery, suspense, detection and crime stories, to 14,000 words; "ghost stories, humor, futuristic or atmospheric tales are all possible, as long as they include a crime or the suggestion of one." Pays 6 ½¢ a word, on acceptance. Guidelines with SASE.

**ALOHA, THE MAGAZINE OF HAWAII AND THE PACIFIC**—49 S. Hotel St., Suite 309, Honolulu, HI 96813. Cheryl Tsutsumi, Ed. Fiction to 4,000 words, with a Hawaii focus. Pays $150 to $300, on publication. Query.

**AMAZING STORIES**—Box 111, Lake Geneva, WI 53147. Mr. Kim Mohan, Ed. Janis Wells, Asst. Ed. Monthly. Original, previously unpublished science fiction, fantasy, and horror, 1,000 to 25,000 words. Pays 6¢ to 10¢ a word, on acceptance.

**ANALOG: SCIENCE FICTION/SCIENCE FACT**—380 Lexington Ave., New York, NY 10168–0035. Stanley Schmidt, Ed. Science fiction, with strong characters in believable future or alien setting: short stories, 2,000 to 7,500 words; novelettes, 10,000 to 20,000 words; serials, to 70,000 words. Pays 5¢ to 8¢ a word, on acceptance. Query for novels.

**THE ATLANTIC**—745 Boylston St., Boston, MA 02116. William Whitworth, Ed. Short stories, 2,000 to 6,000 words, of highest literary quality, with "fully developed narratives, distinctive characterization, freshness in language, and a resolution of some kind." SASE required. Pays excellent rates, on acceptance.

**THE BOSTON GLOBE MAGAZINE**—*The Boston Globe*, Boston, MA 02107. Ande Zellman, Ed. Short stories, to 3,000 words. Include SASE. Pays on acceptance.

**BOYS' LIFE**—1325 W. Walnut Hill Ln., P.O. Box 152079, Irving, TX 75015–2079. Kathleen Vilim DaGroomes, Fiction Ed. Publication of the Boy Scouts of America. Humor, mystery, SF, adventure, 500 to 1,200 words, for 8- to 18-year-old boys; study back issues. Pays from $750, on acceptance. Send SASE for guidelines.

**BUFFALO SPREE MAGAZINE**—Box 38, Buffalo, NY 14226. Johanna V. Shotell, Ed. Fiction and humor, to 2,000 words, for readers in the western New York region. Pays $100 to $125, on publication.

**BYLINE**—Box 130596, Edmond, OK 73013. Marcia Preston, Ed.-in-Chief. Kathryn Fanning, Man. Ed. General fiction, 2,000 to 4,000 words. Nonfiction, 1,500- to 1,800-word features and 300- to 800-word special departments. Poetry, 10 to 30 lines preferred. Nonfiction and poetry must be about writing. Humor, 400 to 800 words, about writing. "We seek practical and motivational material that tells writers how they can succeed, not why they can't. Overdone topics: writers' block, the muse, rejection slips." Pays $5 to $10 for poetry; $15 to $35 for departments; $50 for features and short fiction, on acceptance.

**CAMPUS LIFE**—465 Gundersen Dr., Carol Stream, IL 60188. James Long, Ed. Fiction and humor, reflecting Christian values (no overtly religious material), 1,000 to 4,000 words, for high school and college students. Pays from $150 to $400, on acceptance. Limited free-lance market. Published writers only. Queries required; SASE.

**CAPPER'S**—616 Jefferson Ave., Topeka, KS 66607–1188. Nancy Peavler, Ed. Short novel-length family-oriented or romance stories. Also very limited market for short stories, 7,500 to 12,000 words, that can be divided into two installments. Pays $75 to $250. Submit complete manuscript.

**CAT FANCY**—P.O. Box 6050, Mission Viejo, CA 92690. K.E. Segnar, Ed. Fiction and nonfiction, to 3,000 words, about cats. Pays 5¢ to 10¢ a word, on acceptance.

**CATHOLIC FORESTER**—P.O. Box 3012, 425 W. Shuman Blvd., Naperville, IL 60566–7012. Barbara A. Cunningham, Ed. Official publication of the Catholic Order of Foresters. Fiction, to 3,000 words (prefer shorter); "looking for more contemporary, meaningful stories dealing with life today." No sex or violence or "preachy" stories; religious angle not required. Pays 10¢ a word, on acceptance.

**COBBLESTONE**—7 School St., Peterborough, NH 03458–1454. Carolyn P. Yoder, Ed.-in-Chief. Fiction must relate to monthly theme, 500 to 1,200 words, for children aged 8 to 14 years. Pays 10¢ to 17¢ a word, on publication. Send SASE for editorial guidelines.

**COMMENTARY**—165 E. 56th St., New York, NY 10022. Marion Magid, Ed. Fiction, of high literary quality, on contemporary social or Jewish issues. Pays on publication.

**COMMON GROUND MAGAZINE**—P.O. Box 99, McVeytown, PA 17051–0099. Ruth Dunmire and Pam Brumbaugh, Eds. Fiction, 1,000 to 2,000 words, related to Central Pennsylvania's Juniata River Valley. Pays $25 to $200, on quarterly publication. Guidelines.

**COSMOPOLITAN**—224 W. 57th St., New York, NY 10019. Betty Kelly, Fiction and Books Ed. Short shorts, 1,500 to 3,000 words, and short stories, 4,000 to 6,000 words, focusing on contemporary man-woman relationships. Solid, upbeat plots, sharp characterization; female protagonists preferred. "Submission cannot be returned without SASE." Pays $800 for short shorts; from $1,000 for short stories.

**COUNTRY WOMAN**—P.O. Box 643, Milwaukee, WI 53201. Kathy Pohl, Man. Ed. Fiction, 750 to 1,000 words, of interest to rural women; protagonist must be a country woman. "Stories should focus on life in the country, its problems and joys, as experienced by country women; must be upbeat and positive." Pays $90 to $125, on acceptance.

**CRICKET**—Box 300, Peru, IL 61354–0300. Marianne Carus, Pub./Ed.-in-Chief. Fiction, 200 to 1,500 words, for 6- to 14-year-olds. Pays to 25¢ a word, on publication. Return envelope and postage required.

**DISCOVERIES**—See *Power and Light.*

**DIVER MAGAZINE**—295–10991 Shellbridge Way, Richmond, B.C., Canada V6X 3C6. Peter Vassilopoulos, Pub./Ed. Fiction related to diving. Humor. Pays $2.50 per column inch, on publication. Query.

**EASYRIDERS MAGAZINE**—P. O. Box 3000, Agoura Hills, CA 91301–0800. Keith R. Ball, Ed. Fiction, 500 to 1,500 words. Pays from 15¢ a word, on acceptance.

**ELLERY QUEEN'S MYSTERY MAGAZINE**—380 Lexington Ave., New York, NY 10168. Janet Hutchings, Ed. High-quality detective, crime, and mystery stories, to 7,000 words. Also "Minute Mysteries," 250 words, short verses, limericks, and novellas, to 17,000 words. "We like a mix of classic detection and suspenseful crime." "First Stories" by unpublished writers. Pays 3¢ to 8¢ a word, on acceptance.

**ESQUIRE**—1790 Broadway, New York, NY 10019. Terry McDonell, Ed.-in-Chief. Send finished manuscript of short story; submit one at a time. No full-length novels. No pornography, science fiction, or "true romance" stories.

**EVANGEL**—Light and Life Press, Box 535002, Indianapolis, IN 46253–5002. Vera Bethel, Ed. Free Methodist. Fiction, 1,200 words, with personal faith in Christ shown as instrumental in solving problems. Pays $45, on publication.

**FAITH 'N STUFF**—c/o *Guideposts*, 747 Third Ave., New York, NY 10017. Mary Lou Carney, Ed. Bible-based bimonthly for 7- to 12-year-olds. Problem fiction, mysteries, historicals, 1,500 words, with "realistic dialogue and sharp imagery. No preachy stories about Bible-toting children." Pays $125 to $300 for all rights, on acceptance. No reprints.

**FAMILY CIRCLE**—110 Fifth Ave., New York, NY 10011. Kathy Sagan,

Fiction Ed. We no longer publish fiction on any regular basis. No manuscripts are currently being considered.

**FICTION INTERNATIONAL**—English Dept., San Diego State Univ., San Diego, CA 92182–0295. Harold Jaffe and Larry McCaffery, Eds. Post-modernist and politically committed fiction and theory. Submit between September 1st and December 15th.

**FIRST FOR WOMEN**—P.O. Box 1649, Englewood Cliffs, NJ 07632. Bibi Wein, Fiction Ed. Well-written, mainstream stories, 2,000 words, reflecting the concerns of contemporary women; no formula or experimental fiction. A humorous twist is welcome. Pay varies, on acceptance. SASE required. Do not query for fiction. Allow 8 to 10 weeks for response. Guidelines.

**FLY ROD & REEL**—P.O. Box 370, Camden, ME 04843. James E. Butler, Man. Ed. Occasional fiction, 2,000 to 2,500 words, related to fly fishing. Special annual fiction issue published in summer. Payment varies, on publication.

**GALLERY**—401 Park Ave. S., New York, NY 10016–8802. Barry Janoff, Ed. Dir. Peter Emshwiller, Fiction Ed. Fiction, to 3,000 words, for sophisticated men. "We are not looking for SF, mystery, 40s-style detective, or stories involving aliens from other planets. We do look for interesting stories that enable readers to view life in an off-beat, unusual, or insightful manner: fiction with believable characters and actions." Pays varying rates, half on acceptance, half on publication.

**GLIMMER TRAIN PRESS**—812 S.W. Washington St., Suite 1205, Portland, OR 97205. Susan Burmeister, Ed. Fiction, 1,200 to 5,500 words. "Twelve stories in each quarterly magazine." Pays $300, on acceptance.

**GOLF DIGEST**—5520 Park Ave., Trumbull, CT 06611. Jerry Tarde, Ed. Unusual or humorous stories, to 2,000 words, about golf; golf "fables," to 1,000 words. Pays 50¢ a word, on acceptance.

**GOOD HOUSEKEEPING**—959 Eighth Ave., New York, NY 10019. Lee Quarfoot, Fiction Ed. Short stories, 1,000 to 3,000 words, with strong identification figures for women, by published writers and "beginners with demonstrable talent." Novel condensations or excerpts. "Writers whose work interests us will hear from us within 4 to 5 weeks of receipt of manuscript. Please send inexpensive copies of your work; and do not enclose SASEs or postage. We can no longer return or critique manuscripts. We do accept multiple submissions." Pays top rates, on acceptance.

**GRIT**—208 W. Third St., Williamsport, PA 17701. Alvin Elmer, Assoc. Ed. Short stories, 3,500 to 4,000 words. Articles, 400 to 800 words, with photos, on interesting people. Pays 15¢ a word, extra for photos, on acceptance.

**GUN DOG**—1901 Bell Ave., Des Moines, IA 50315. Bob Wilbanks, Man. Ed. Occasional fiction, humor related to gun dogs and bird hunting. Pays $100 to $350, on acceptance.

**HICALL**—1445 Boonville Ave., Springfield, MO 65802–1894. Deanna Harris, Ed. Fiction, to 1,500 words, for 15- to 19-year-olds. Strong evangelical emphasis a must: believable characters working out their problems according to biblical principles. Pays 3¢ a word for first rights, on acceptance. Reprints considered.

**HIGHLIGHTS FOR CHILDREN**—803 Church St., Honesdale, PA 18431–1824. Kent L. Brown Jr., Ed. Fiction on sports, humor, adventure, mystery, etc., 800 words, for 9- to 12-year-olds. Easy rebus form, 100 to 150 words, and easy-to-read stories, to 500 words, for beginning readers. "We are partial to stories in which the protagonist solves a dilemma through his or her own resources, rather than through luck or magic." Pays from 14¢ a word, on acceptance. Buys all rights.

**HOMETOWN PRESS**—2007 Gallatin St., Huntsville, AL 35801. Jeffrey C. Hindman, M.D., Ed.-in-Chief. Fiction, 800 to 2,500 words, well-crafted and tightly written, suitable for family reading. New and unpublished writers welcome. SASE for guidelines.

**ISAAC ASIMOV'S SCIENCE FICTION MAGAZINE**—380 Lexington Ave., New York, NY 10168–0035. Gardner Dozois, Ed. Short science fiction and fantasies, to 15,000 words. Pays 6¢ to 8¢ a word, on acceptance.

**LADIES' HOME JOURNAL**—100 Park Ave., New York, NY 10017. Fiction accepted through agents only.

**LOLLIPOPS**—Good Apple, Inc., P. O. Box 299, Carthage, IL 62321–0299. Sharon Thompson, Ed. Teaching ideas and activities covering all areas of the curriculum for preschool to second-grade children. Rates vary.

**THE LOOKOUT**—8121 Hamilton Ave., Cincinnati, OH 45231. Simon J. Dahlman, Ed. Inspirational short-shorts, 500 to 2,000 words. Pays to 7¢ a word, on acceptance. No historical fiction, science fiction, or fantasy.

**MCCALL'S**—110 Fifth Ave., New York, NY 10011. Does not accept fiction submissions.

**MADEMOISELLE**—350 Madison Ave., New York, NY 10017. Eileen Schnurr, Fiction Ed. No longer accepts fiction.

**THE MAGAZINE OF FANTASY AND SCIENCE FICTION**—Box 11526, Eugene, OR 97440. Kristine Kathryn Rusch, Ed. Fantasy and science fiction stories, to 15,000 words. Pays 5¢ to 7¢ a word, on acceptance.

**MATURE LIVING**—127 Ninth Ave. N., Nashville, TN 37234. Judy Pregel, Asst. Ed. Fiction, 900 to 1,200 words, for senior adults. Must be consistent with Christian principles. Pays 5 ½¢ a word, on acceptance.

**MIDSTREAM**—110 E. 59th St., New York, NY 10022. M. S. Solow, Asst. Ed. Fiction on Jewish themes, to 3,000 words. Pays 5¢ a word, after publication. Allow three months for response.

**MILITARY LIFESTYLE MAGAZINE**—4800 Montgomery Ln., Suite 710, Bethesda, MD 20814–5341. Hope Daniels, Ed. Fiction, to 2,000 words, for military families in the U.S. and overseas. Pays from $500, on publication. Annual fiction contest.

**NA'AMAT WOMAN**—200 Madison Ave., 21st Fl., New York, NY 10016. Judith A. Sokoloff, Ed. Short stories, approximately 2,500 words, with Jewish theme. Pays 8¢ a word, on publication.

**THE NEW YORKER**—20 W. 43rd St., New York, NY 10036. Fiction Dept. Short stories, humor, and satire. Payment varies, on acceptance. Include SASE.

**OMNI**—1965 Broadway, New York, NY 10023. Ellen Datlow, Fiction Ed. Strong, realistic science fiction, to 12,000 words. Some contemporary hard-edged fantasy. Pays to $2,250, on acceptance.

**PENTHOUSE**—1965 Broadway, New York, NY 10023. No unsolicited manuscripts.

**PLAYBOY**—680 N. Lakeshore Dr., Chicago, IL 60611. Alice K. Turner, Fiction Ed. Quality fiction, 1,000 to 8,000 words (average 6,000): suspense, mystery, adventure, and sports short stories; stories about contemporary relationships; science fiction. Active plots, masterful pacing, and strong characterization. Pays from $2,000 to $5,000, on acceptance.

**PLOUGHSHARES**—Emerson College, 100 Beacon St., Boston, MA 02116–1596. Address Editors. Serious fiction, to 6,000 words. Poetry. Pays $10 to $50, on publication. Reading periods and themes vary; send SASE for guidelines.

**POWER AND LIGHT**—6401 The Paseo, Kansas City, MO 64131. Beula J. Postlewait, Preteen Ed. Fiction, 500 to 700 words, for children grades 5 to 6, defining Christian experiences and values. Pays 5¢ a word for multiple-use rights, on publication. Also publishes *Discoveries* for grades 3 and 4.

**PURPOSE**—616 Walnut Ave., Scottdale, PA 15683–1999. James E. Horsch, Ed. Fiction, 800 words, on problem solving from a Christian point of view. Poetry, 3 to 12 lines. Pays up to 5¢ a word, to $1 per line for poetry, on acceptance.

**QUEEN'S QUARTERLY**—Queens Univ., Kingston, Ont., Canada K7L 3N6. Fiction, to 4,000 words, in English and French. Pays to $300, on publication.

**RANGER RICK**—8925 Leesburg Pike, Vienna, VA 22184–0001. Deborah Churchman, Fiction Ed. Action-packed nature- and conservation-related fiction, for 6- to 12-year-olds. Maximum: 900 words. No anthropomorphism. "Multi-cultural stories welcome." Pays to $550, on acceptance. Buys all rights.

**REDBOOK**—224 W. 57th St., New York, NY 10019. Dawn Raffel, Fiction Ed. Fresh, distinctive short stories, of interest to women. Pays from $1,500 for short stories (to 30 pages). Allow 6 weeks for reply. Manuscripts without SASE will not be returned. No unsolicited novellas or novels accepted.

**ROAD KING**—P.O. Box 250, Park Forest, IL 60466. George Friend, Ed. Short stories, to 1,200 words, for and/or about truck drivers. Pays to $400, on acceptance.

**ST. ANTHONY MESSENGER**—1615 Republic St., Cincinnati, OH 45210–1298. Norman Perry, O.F.M., Ed. Barbara Beckwith, Man. Ed. Fiction that makes readers think about issues, lifestyles, and values. Pays 14¢ a word, on acceptance. Queries or manuscripts accepted.

**SASSY**—230 Park Ave., New York, NY 10169. Christina Kelly, Fiction Ed. Short stories written in the magazine's style, 1,000 to 3,000 words, for girls age 14 to 19. Pays $1,000, on acceptance.

**SEA KAYAKER**—6327 Seaview Ave. N.W., Seattle, WA 98107–2664. Christopher Cunningham, Ed. Short stories exclusively related to ocean kayaking, 1,000 to 3,000 words. Pays on publication.

**SEVENTEEN**—850 Third Ave., New York, NY 10022. Fiction Ed. High-quality, literary short fiction, to 4,000 words. Pays on acceptance.

**SPORTS AFIELD**—250 W. 55th St., New York, NY 10019. Tom Paugh, Ed. Occasional fiction, 1,500 words, on hunting, fishing, and related topics. Humor. Pays top rates, on acceptance.

**STRAIGHT**—8121 Hamilton Ave., Cincinnati, OH 45231. Carla Crane, Ed. Well-constructed fiction, 1,000 to 1,500 words, showing Christian teens using Bible principles in everyday life. Contemporary, realistic teen characters a must. Most interested in school, church, dating, and family life stories. Pays 3¢ to 7¢ a word, on acceptance. Send SASE for guidelines.

**SUNDAY DIGEST**—850 N. Grove Ave., Elgin, IL 60120. Christine Dallman, Ed. Short stories, 400 to 1,800 words, with evangelical religious slant. Payment varies, on acceptance.

**SUNSHINE MAGAZINE**—Sunshine Press, Litchfield, IL 62056. Peggy Kuethe, Ed. Wholesome fiction, 900 to 1,200 words; short stories for youths, 400 words. Pays $10 to $100, on acceptance. Guidelines. Include SASE.

**TAMPA BAY LIFE: THE BAY AREA'S MAGAZINE**—6200 Courtney Campbell Causeway, Suite 580, Tampa, FL 33607–1458. Larry Marscheck, Ed. Fiction, 1,200 to 2,000 words. Stories must have a Tampa Bay region base/flavor. Payment varies, on publication.

**'TEEN**—8490 Sunset Blvd., Los Angeles, CA 90069. Address Fiction Dept. Short stories, 2,500 to 4,000 words: mystery, teen situations, adventure, romance, humor for teens. Pays from $200, on acceptance.

**TEENS TODAY**—Nazarene Publishing House, 6401 The Paseo, Kansas City, MO 64131. Karen DeSollar, Ed. Short stories, 1,000 to 1,200 words, that deal with teens demonstrating Christian principles in real-life situations. Pays 4¢ a word (3 ½¢ a word for reprints), on acceptance.

**TQ/TEEN QUEST**—Box 82808, Lincoln, NE 68501. Lisa Thompson, Man. Ed. Fiction, 1,000 to 2,000 words, for Christian teens. Pays 8¢ to 15¢ a word, on acceptance.

**TRUCKERS/USA**—P.O. Box 323, Windber, PA 15963. David Adams, Ed. Monthly. Trucking related articles, poetry, and fiction. Payment varies, on acceptance.

**VIRGINIA SOUTHWEST**—P.O. Box 4244, Roanoke, VA 24015. Attn: J. Johnson. Fiction, 1,000 to 1,500 words, with southwestern Virginia setting or reference. Pays to $600, on bimonthly publication or within 6 months, whichever comes first.

**VIRTUE**—P.O. Box 850, Sisters, OR 97759–0850. Marlee Alex, Ed. Fiction with a Christian slant. Pays 15¢ to 25¢ a word, on acceptance. Query required.

**WESTERN PEOPLE**—Box 2500, Saskatoon, Sask., Canada S7K 2C4. Short stories, 850 to 1,800 words, on subjects or themes of interest to rural readers in western Canada. Pays $100 to $175, on acceptance. Enclose international reply coupons and SAE.

**WOMAN'S WORLD**—270 Sylvan Ave., Englewood Cliffs, NJ 07632. Jeanne Muchnick, Fiction Ed. Fast-moving short stories, about 1,900 words, with light romantic theme. (Specify "short story" on outside of envelope.) Mini-mysteries, 950 words, with "whodunit" or "howdunit" theme. No science fiction, fantasy, or historical romance and no horror, ghost stories, or gratuitous violence. Pays $1,000 for short stories, $500 for mini-mysteries, on acceptance. Submit manuscript with SASE.

**WOMEN'S HOUSEHOLD**—306 E. Parr Rd., Berne, IN 46711. Allison Ballard, Ed. Pen pal stories or other stories, 1,000 to 1,500 words, about friendships and family relationships. Pays $40 to $250, on publication.

**YANKEE**—Yankee Publishing Co., Dublin, NH 03444. Judson Hale, Ed. Edie Clark, Fiction Ed. High-quality, literary short fiction, to 1,500 words, with setting in or compatible with New England; no sap buckets or lobster pot stereotypes. Pays $1,000, on acceptance.

## DETECTIVE AND MYSTERY

**ALFRED HITCHCOCK'S MYSTERY MAGAZINE**—380 Lexington Ave., New York, NY 10168–0035. Cathleen Jordan, Ed. Well-plotted mystery, detective, suspense, and crime fiction, to 14,000 words. Submissions by new writers strongly encouraged. Pays from 6 ½¢ a word, on acceptance. Guidelines with SASE.

**ARMCHAIR DETECTIVE**—129 W. 56th St., New York, NY 10019. Kathy Daniel, Ed. Articles on mystery and detective fiction; short stories; biographical sketches, reviews, etc. Pays $10 a printed page for nonfiction; fiction payment varies; reviews are unpaid.

**DETECTIVE CASES**—See *Globe Communications Corp.*

**DETECTIVE DRAGNET**—See *Globe Communications Corp.*

**DETECTIVE FILES**—See *Globe Communications Corp.*

**ELLERY QUEEN'S MYSTERY MAGAZINE**—380 Lexington Ave., New York, NY 10168. Janet Hutchings, Ed. Detective, crime, and mystery fiction, approximately 1,500 to 12,000 words. No sex, sadism, or sensationalism. Particularly interested in new writers and "first stories." Pays 3¢ to 8¢ a word, on acceptance.

**FRONT PAGE DETECTIVE**—Reese Communications, Inc., 460 W. 34th St., New York, NY 10001. Rose Mandelsberg, Ed.-in-Chief. True detective stories, 5,000 to 6,000 words. Fiction, to 3,000 words, with detective work, mystery, and some kind of twist. Artwork may accompany story and is paid for separately. Pays $250 to $500 for articles, $150 for stories. Query.

**FUGITIVE!**—848 Dodge Ave., Suite 420, Evanston, IL 60202. Lawrence Shulruff, Ed. Articles, 600 to 800 words, on unsolved crime and criminals at large. "Provide details about case. We encourage readers to contact police with tips about cases. Articles shouldn't be gory. Provide photos or composites of suspect, if possible." Query required. Pays $50 to $150, on acceptance.

**GLOBE COMMUNICATIONS CORP.**—1350 Sherbrooke St. West, Suite 600, Montreal, Quebec, Canada H3G 2T4. Dominick A. Merle, Ed. Factual accounts, 3,500 to 6,000 words, of "sensational crimes, preferably sex crimes, either pre-trial or after conviction." All stories will be considered for *Startling Detective, True Police Cases, Detective Files, Headquarters Detective, Detective Dragnet,* and *Detective Cases.* Query with pertinent information, including dates, site, names, etc. Pays $250 to $350, on acceptance; buys all rights.

**HEADQUARTERS DETECTIVE**—See *Globe Communications Corp.*

**INSIDE DETECTIVE**—Reese Communications, Inc., 460 W. 34th St., New York, NY 10001. Rose Mandelsberg, Ed.-in-Chief. Timely, true detective stories, 5,000 to 6,000 words, or 10,000 words. No fiction. Pays $250 to $500, extra for photos, on acceptance. Query.

**MASTER DETECTIVE**—460 W. 34th St., New York, NY 10001. Rose Mandelsberg, Ed. Detailed articles, 5,000 to 6,000 words, with photos, on current cases, emphasizing human motivation and detective work. No fiction. Pays to $250, on acceptance. Query.

**OFFICIAL DETECTIVE STORIES**—460 W. 34th St., New York, NY 10001. Rose Mandelsberg, Ed. True detective stories, 5,000 to 6,000 words, on current investigations, strictly from the investigator's point of view. No fiction. Photos. Pays $250, extra for photos, on acceptance. Query.

**P.I. MAGAZINE**—755 Bronx Ave., Toledo, OH 43609. Bob Mackowiak, Ed. Fiction, 2,500 to 5,000 words, and profiles of professional investigators containing true accounts of their most difficult cases; puzzles. Pays $10 to $25, plus copies, on publication.

703

**STARTLING DETECTIVE**—See *Globe Communications Corp.*

**TRUE DETECTIVE**—460 W. 34th St., New York, NY 10001. Rose Mandelsberg, Ed.-in-Chief. Articles, from 5,000 words, with photos, on current police cases, emphasizing detective work and human motivation. No fiction. Pays $250, extra for photos, on acceptance. Query.

**TRUE POLICE CASES**—See *Globe Communications Corp.*

## SCIENCE FICTION AND FANTASY

**ABORIGINAL SF**—P.O. Box 2449, Woburn, MA 01888–0849. Charles C. Ryan, Ed. Short stories, 2,500 to 5,500 words, and poetry, 1 to 2 typed pages, with strong science content, lively, unique characters, and well-designed plots. No sword and sorcery or fantasy. Pays $250 for fiction, $20 for poetry, $4 for SF jokes, and $20 for cartoons, on publication.

**ALTERNATE REALITIES**—1712A Ridgewood Ln., Sanford, FL 32773. Jane Finkbohner, Man. Ed. "The Magazine for the Southeastern Science Fiction/ Fantasy Fan." News about fan organizations, including Doctor Who, Star Trek, Beauty and The Beast, and Dark Shadows. Also SF/fantasy related articles, 200 to 1,000 words; sidebars and B&W photos encouraged. Pays 3¢ a word, $2 per photo, on publication. Query preferred.

**AMAZING STORIES**—Box 111, Lake Geneva, WI 53147. Mr. Kim Mohan, Ed. Janis Wells, Asst. Ed. Original, previously unpublished science fiction, fantasy, and horror, 1,000 to 25,000 words. Pays 6¢ to 10¢ a word, on acceptance.

**ANALOG: SCIENCE FICTION/SCIENCE FACT**—380 Lexington Ave., New York, NY 10168–0035. Stanley Schmidt, Ed. Science fiction with strong characters in believable future or alien setting: short stories, 2,000 to 7,500 words; novelettes, 10,000 to 20,000 words; serials, to 80,000 words. Also uses future-related articles. Pays to 7¢ a word, on acceptance. Query on serials and articles.

**ARGONAUT**—P.O. Box 4201, Austin, TX 78765. Michael E. Ambrose, Ed. "Hard" science fiction, to 7,500 words, and SF dealing with the sciences, intergalactic or interplanetary adventure. Poetry, to 30 lines, with a SF focus. No fantasy, horror, interviews, reviews, or seasonal material. Pays in 2 copies.

**BEYOND: SCIENCE FICTION & FANTASY**—P.O. Box 1124, Fair Lawn, NJ 07410. Roberta Rogow, Ed. Science fiction and fantasy: original, exciting, thought-provoking fiction, 3,000 to 5,000 words, and poems, 10 to 20 lines. Pays ¼¢ a word, on publication.

**DRAGON MAGAZINE**—P.O. Box 111, Lake Geneva, WI 53147. Roger E. Moore, Ed. Barbara G. Young, Fiction Ed. Articles, 1,500 to 7,500 words, on fantasy and SF role-playing games. Fantasy, 1,500 to 8,000 words. Pays 6¢ to 8¢ a word for fiction, on acceptance. Pays 4¢ a word for articles, on publication. Guidelines (specify article or fiction).

**FANGORIA**—475 Park Ave. S., 8th Fl., New York, NY 10016. Anthony Timpone, Ed. Published 10 times yearly. Movie previews and interviews, 1,800 to 2,500 words, in connection with upcoming horror films. "A strong love of the genre and an appreciation and understanding of the magazine are essential." Pays $150 to $200, on publication.

**FANTASY AND SCIENCE FICTION**—Mercury Press, Inc., P.O. Box 11526, Eugene, OR 97440. Kristine Kathryn Rusch, Ed. Short stories, to 20,000 words. "We have no formula, but you should be familiar with the magazine before submitting"; for sample copies, write to 14 Jewell St., Cornwall, CT 06753. Pays 5¢ to 7¢ a word, on acceptance.

**FANTASY MACABRE**—P.O. Box 20610, Seattle, WA 98102. Jessica Salmonson, Ed. Fiction, to 3,000 words, including translations. "We look for a tale that is strong in atmosphere, with menace that is suggested and threatening rather than the result of dripping blood and gore." Pays 1¢ a word, to $30 per story, on publication. Also publishes *Fantasy & Terror* for poetry-in-prose pieces.

**FIGMENT: TALES FROM THE IMAGINATION**—Figment Press, P.O. Box 3128, Moscow, ID 83843–0477. Barb and J.C. Hendee, Eds. Mark Coen, Assoc. Ed. Science fiction and fantasy, to 10,000 words, hard or soft, light or dark. Nonfiction, to 2,000 words, of interest to SF readers, not writers. SF and fantasy poems, all styles. Pays ½¢ to 1¢ a word, $3 to $5 for poems, within 30 days of acceptance. Send SASE for guidelines before submitting.

**FOOTSTEPS PRESS**—P.O. Box 75, Round Top, NY 12473. Bill Munster, Ed. Horror, mystery, and ghost story chapbooks, 3,000 to 5,000 words. Royalty (usually from $350 to $500).

**GRUE MAGAZINE**—Box 370, Times Square Sta., New York, NY 10108. Peggy Nadramia, Ed. Fiction, 6,000 words, and macabre/surreal poetry of any length. "We seek very visceral, original horror stories with an emphasis on characterization and motivation." Pays ½¢ a word for fiction, $5 per poem, on publication. Allow 3 to 6 months for response.

**HAUNTS**—Nightshade Publications, Box 3342, Providence, RI 02906. Joseph K. Cherkes, Ed. Horror, science/fantasy, and supernatural short stories with strong characters, 1,500 to 8,000 words. No explicit sexual scenes or gratuitous violence. Pays ¼¢ to 1¢ a word, on publication.

**ISAAC ASIMOV'S SCIENCE FICTION MAGAZINE**—380 Lexington Ave., New York, NY 10168–0035. Gardner Dozois, Ed. Short, character-oriented science fiction and fantasy, to 15,000 words. Pays 5¢ to 8¢ a word, on acceptance. Send SASE for requirements.

**THE LEADING EDGE**—3163 JKHB, Provo, UT 84602. Marny Parkin, Ed. Published 3 times a year. Short stories, 3,000 to 12,000 words, and some experimental fiction; poems, to 200 lines; and articles, to 8,000 words, on science, scientific speculation, and literary criticism. Fillers and comics. "Do not send originals; manuscripts are marked and critiqued by staff." Pays ½¢ a word (minimum of $5) for fiction; $5 per published page of poetry; $2 to $4 for fillers, on publication. Guidelines.

**THE MAGAZINE OF FANTASY AND SCIENCE FICTION**—P.O. Box 11526, Eugene, OR 97440. Kristine K. Rusch, Ed. Fantasy and science fiction stories, to 10,000 words. Pays 5¢ to 7¢ a word, on acceptance.

**MAGIC REALISM**—P.O. Box 620, Orem, UT 84059–0620. C. Darren Butler, Ed. Julie Thomas, Ed. Published 3 times a year. Stories, to 7,500 words (4,000 words preferred), of magic realism, exaggerated realism, some genre fantasy/dark fantasy. Occasionally publish glib fantasy like that found in folk, fairy tales, and myths. No occult, sleight-of-hand magicians, or wizards/witches. Pays in 1 copy.

**MARION ZIMMER BRADLEY'S FANTASY MAGAZINE**—P.O. Box 249, Berkeley, CA 94701. Marion Zimmer Bradley, Ed. Quarterly. Well-plotted stories, 3,500 to 4,000 words. Action and adventure fantasy "with no particular objection to modern settings." Send SASE for guidelines before submitting. Pays 3¢ to 10¢ a word, on acceptance.

**OMNI**—1965 Broadway, New York, NY 10023. Ellen Datlow, Ed. Strong, realistic science fiction, 2,000 to 10,000 words, with good characterizations. Some fantasy. No horror, ghost, or sword and sorcery tales. Pays $1,250 to $2,250, on acceptance.

**PULPHOUSE: A FICTION MAGAZINE**—P.O. Box 1227, Eugene, OR 97440. Dean Wesley Smith, Ed./Pub. Fantasy, SF, horror, and mysteries, 5,000 words. Articles, essays, interviews, and news items, to 5,000 words. Query for nonfiction only. Pays 4¢ to 7¢, on publication. Overstocked; closed to submissions until September 93.

**QUANTUM: SCIENCE FICTION & FANTASY REVIEW**—8217 Langport Terrace, Gaithersburg, MD 20877. D. Douglas Fratz, Ed. Articles, interviews, 2,000 to 6,000 words, for readers familiar with SF and related literary and scientific topics. Book reviews, 100 to 900 words. Pays 1¢ to 2¢ a word, on publication. Query preferred. SASE for guidelines.

**SCIENCE FICTION CHRONICLE**—P.O. Box 2730, Brooklyn, NY 11202. Andrew Porter, Ed. News items, 200 to 500 words, for SF and fantasy readers, professionals, and booksellers. Interviews with authors, 2,500 to 4,000 words. No fiction. Pays 3¢ to 5¢ a word, on publication. Query first.

**TWISTED**—P.O. Box 1249, Palmetto, GA 30268–1249. Christine Hoard, Ed. Fiction and articles, to 5,000 words; poetry, to 1 page. "No sword and sorcery or hard science fiction. We prefer adult-oriented horror and dark fantasy. Best to query first. Send SASE for guidelines." Pays in copies.

**2AM MAGAZINE**—P.O. Box 6754, Rockford, IL 61125–1754. Gretta M. Anderson, Ed. Fiction, of varying lengths. "We prefer dark fantasy/horror; great science fiction and sword and sorcery stories are welcome." Profiles and intelligent commentaries. Poetry, to 50 lines. Pays from ½¢ a word, on acceptance. Guidelines.

**WEIRD TALES**—P.O. Box 13418, Philadelphia, PA 19101. George Scithers, Pub. Darrell Schweitzer, Ed. Fantasy and horror (no SF), to 20,000 words. Pays 3¢ to 8¢ a word, on acceptance. Guidelines.

## CONFESSION AND ROMANCE

**BLACK CONFESSIONS**—See *Black Secrets.*

**BLACK ROMANCE**—See *Black Secrets.*

**BLACK SECRETS**—355 Lexington Ave., New York, NY 10017. Tonia L. Shakespeare, Ed. Romance fiction, 5,800 words to 6,700 words, and service articles on beauty, health, etc., 800 to 1,000 words, for black female readers. "We like romance and confession stories with upbeat endings." Queries preferred. Pays $75 to $125, on publication. Also publishes *Black Romance, Bronze Thrills*, and *Black Confessions*.

**BRONZE THRILLS**—See *Black Secrets.*

**INTIMACY**—355 Lexington Ave., New York, NY 10017. I. Sang, Ed. Fiction, 5,000 to 5,800 words, for black women ages 18 to 45; must have contemporary plot and contain two romantic and intimate love scenes. Pays $75 to $100, on publication. Same address for *Jive*, geared toward younger women seeking adventure, glamour, and romance. Guidelines.

**JIVE**—See *Intimacy.*

**MODERN ROMANCES**—233 Park Ave. S., New York, NY 10003. Cherie

Clark King, Ed. Confession stories with reader-identification and strong emotional tone, 2,000 to 10,000 words. Pays 5¢ a word, after publication. Buys all rights.

**TRUE CONFESSIONS**—233 Park Ave. S., New York, NY 10003. Jean Sharbel, Ed. Timely, emotional, first-person stories, 2,000 to 10,000 words, on romance, family life, and problems of today's young blue-collar women. Pays 5¢ a word, after publication.

**TRUE EXPERIENCE**—233 Park Ave. S., New York, NY 10003. Jean Press Silberg, Ed. Cynthia Di Martino, Assoc. Ed. Realistic first-person stories, 4,000 to 10,000 words (short shorts, to 2,000 words), on family life, single life, love, romance, overcoming hardships, psychic/occult occurrences, mysteries. Pays 3¢ a word, after publication.

**TRUE LOVE**—233 Park Ave. South, New York, NY 10003. Mary Lou Lang, Ed. Fresh, young, true-to-life romance stories, on love and topics of current interest. Must be written in the past tense and first person. Pays 3¢ a word, a month after publication. Buys all rights. Guidelines.

# POETRY MARKETS

The following list includes markets for both serious and light verse. Although major magazines pay good rates for poetry, the competition to break into print is very stiff, since editors use only a limited number of poems in each issue. On the other hand, college, little, and literary magazines use a great deal of poetry, and though payment is modest—usually in copies—publication in these journals can establish a beginning poet's reputation, and can lead to publication in the major magazines. Poets will also find a number of competitions offering cash awards for unpublished poems in the *Literary Prize Offers* list.

Poets should also consider local newspapers as possible verse markets. Although they may not specifically seek poetry from free lancers, newspaper editors often print verse submitted to them, especially on holidays and for special occasions.

The market for book-length collections of poetry at commercial publishers is extremely limited. There are, however, a number of university presses that publish poetry collections (see *University Presses*), and many of them sponsor annual competitions. Consult the *Literary Prize Offers* list for more information.

**ALOHA, THE MAGAZINE OF HAWAII**—49 South Hotel St., #309, Honolulu, HI 96813. Cheryl Chee Tsutsumi, Ed. Poetry relating to Hawaii. Pays $25 per poem, on publication.

**AMERICA**—106 W. 56th St., New York, NY 10019. Patrick Samway, S.J., Literary Ed. Serious poetry, preferably in contemporary prose idiom, 10 to 25 lines.

Occasional light verse. Submit 2 or 3 poems at a time. Pays $1.40 per line, on publication. SASE for guidelines.

**THE AMERICAN SCHOLAR**—1811 Q St. N.W., Washington, DC 20009–9974. Joseph Epstein, Ed. Highly original poetry, 10 to 32 lines, for college-educated, intellectual readers. Pays $50, on acceptance.

**THE ATLANTIC**—745 Boylston St., Boston, MA 02116. Peter Davison, Poetry Ed. Previously unpublished poetry of highest quality. Limited market; only 2 to 3 poems an issue. Interested in new poets. Occasionally uses light verse. "No simultaneous submissions; we make prompt decisions." Pays excellent rates, on acceptance.

**CAPPER'S**—616 Jefferson St., Topeka, KS 66607–1188. Nancy Peavler, Ed. Traditional poetry and free verse, 4 to 16 lines, with simple everyday themes. Submit up to 6 poems at a time, with SASE. Pays $3 to $6, on acceptance.

**CHILDREN'S PLAYMATE**—P.O. Box 567, Indianapolis, IN 46206. Elizabeth A. Rinck, Ed. Poetry for children, 6 to 8 years old, on good health, nutrition, exercise, safety, seasonal and humorous subjects. Pays from $15, on publication. Buys all rights.

**THE CHRISTIAN SCIENCE MONITOR**—One Norway St., Boston, MA 02115. Alice Hummer, The Home Forum. Fresh, vigorous nonreligious poems of high quality, on various subjects. Short poems preferred. Pays varying rates, on acceptance. Submit no more than 3 poems at a time.

**COMMONWEAL**—15 Dutch St., New York, NY 10038. Rosemary Deen, Poetry Ed. Catholic. Serious, witty poetry. Pays 50¢ a line, on publication. SASE required.

**COMPLETE WOMAN**—Dept. P, 1165 N. Clark St., Chicago, IL 60610. Address Assoc. Ed Send poetry with SASE. Pays $10, on publication.

**COSMOPOLITAN**—224 W. 57th St., New York, NY 10019. Rachel Zalis, Poetry Ed. Poetry about relationships and other topics of interest to young, active women. Pays from $25, on acceptance. SASE required.

**COUNTRY WOMAN**—P.O. Box 643, Milwaukee, WI 53201. Kathy Pohl, Man. Ed. Traditional rural poetry and light verse, 4 to 30 lines, on rural experiences and country living. Poems must rhyme. Pays $10 to $40, on acceptance.

**EVANGEL**—Box 535002, Indianapolis, IN 46253–5002. Vera Bethel, Ed. Free Methodist. Devotional or nature poetry, 8 to 16 lines. Pays $10, on publication.

**FAMILY CIRCLE**—110 Fifth Ave., New York, NY 10011. No unsolicited poetry.

**GOOD HOUSEKEEPING**—"Light Housekeeping" Page, 959 8th Ave., New York, NY 10019. Rosemary Leonard, Ed. Light, humorous verses, quips, and poems. Pays $25 for 4 lines, $50 for 6 to 8 lines, on acceptance. All unused submissions to "Light Housekeeping" page will be returned to author when accompanied by SASE.

**JOURNEY**—Christian Board of Publication, Box 179, St. Louis, MO 63166. Short poems for 12- to 15-year-olds. Pays 30¢ a line, on publication.

**LADIES' HOME JOURNAL**—100 Park Ave., New York, NY 10017. Short, humorous poetry for "Last Laughs" page only. Must be accessible to women in general. Pays $100 for accepted poetry.

**MCCALL'S**—110 Fifth Ave., New York, NY 10011. No unsolicited poetry.

**MATURE YEARS**—201 Eighth Ave. S., P.O. Box 801, Nashville, TN 37202. Marvin W. Cropsey, Ed. United Methodist. Poetry, to 14 lines, on preretirement, retirement, seasonal subjects, aging. No "saccharine" poetry. Pays 50¢ to $1 per line.

**MIDSTREAM**—110 E. 59th St., New York, NY 10022. Joel Carmichael, Ed. Poetry of Jewish interest. Pays $25, on publication. Allow 3 months for response.

**THE MIRACULOUS MEDAL**—475 E. Chelten Ave., Philadelphia, PA 19144–5785. John W. Gouldrick, C.M., Ed. Catholic. Religious verse, to 20 lines. Pays 50¢ a line, on acceptance.

**MODERN BRIDE**—249 West 17th St., New York, NY 10011. Mary Ann Cavlin, Man. Ed. Short verse of interest to bride and groom. Pays $25 to $35, on acceptance.

**THE NATION**—72 Fifth Ave., New York, NY 10011. Grace Schulman, Poetry Ed. Poetry of high quality. Pays after publication. SASE requried.

**NATIONAL ENQUIRER**—Lantana, FL 33464. Michele Cooke, Asst. Ed. Short poems, with traditional rhyming verse, of an amusing, philosophical, or inspirational nature. No experimental poetry. Original epigrams, humorous anecdotes, and "daffynitions." Submit seasonal/holiday material at least 2 months in advance. Pays $25, after publication. SASE required.

**NEW ENGLAND ENTERTAINMENT DIGEST**—P.O. Box 313, Portland, CT 06480. Bob Taylor, Ed. Light verse, of any length, related to the entertainment field. Pays $3, on publication.

**THE NEW REPUBLIC**—1220 19th St. N.W., Washington, DC 20036. Mary Jo Salter, Poetry Ed. Poetry for intellectual readers. Pays $75, after publication.

**THE NEW YORKER**—20 W. 43rd St., New York, NY 10036. First-rate poetry. Pays top rates, on acceptance. Include SASE.

**PENTECOSTAL EVANGEL**—1445 Boonville, Springfield, MO 65802. Richard G. Champion, Ed. Journal of Assemblies of God. Religious and inspirational verse, 12 to 30 lines. Pays to 50¢ a line, on acceptance.

**PURPOSE**—616 Walnut Ave., Scottdale, PA 15683–1999. James E. Horsch, Poetry Ed. Poetry, to 8 lines, with challenging Christian discipleship angle. Pays 50¢ to $1 a line, on acceptance.

**ST. JOSEPH'S MESSENGER**—P.O. Box 288, Jersey City, NJ 07303–0288. Sister Ursula Maphet, Ed. Light verse and traditional poetry, 4 to 40 lines. Pays $5 to $15, on publication.

**THE SATURDAY EVENING POST**—P.O. Box 567, Indianapolis, IN 46206. Address Post Scripts Ed. Light verse and humor. Pays $15, on publication.

**THE UNITED METHODIST REPORTER**—P.O. Box 660275, Dallas, TX 75266–0275. John Lovelace, Man. Ed. Religious verse, 4 to 16 lines. Pays $2, on acceptance.

**WESTERN PEOPLE**—P.O. Box 2500, Saskatoon, Sask., Canada S7K 2C4. Michael Gillgannon, Man. Ed. Short poetry, with Western Canadian themes. Pays on acceptance. Send International Reply Coupons.

**YANKEE**—Yankee Publishing Co., Dublin, NH 03444. Jean Burden, Poetry Ed. Serious poetry of high quality, to 30 lines. Pays $50 per poem for all rights, $35 for first rights, on publication.

# POETRY SERIES

The market for books of poetry is limited, confined mostly to university presses that publish poetry series, and to foundations that sponsor contests for book-length poetry manuscripts. The following organizations publish book-length collections of poetry, many by writers who have never had a book of poems published. Each has specific rules for submission, so before submitting any material, be sure to write well ahead of the deadline dates for further information. Some organizations sponsor competitions for groups of poems; see *Literary Prize Offers*.

**ACADEMY OF AMERICAN POETS**—584 Broadway, Suite 1208, New York, NY 10012. Offers Walt Whitman Award of publication and a $1,000 cash prize for a book-length poetry manuscript by a poet who has not yet published a volume of poetry. Closes in November.

**AMPERSAND PRESS**—Women Poets Series, Creative Writing Program, School of Fine and Performing Arts, Roger Williams University, One Old Ferry Rd., Bristol, RI 02809–2921. National contest awards $500 and publication to a female poet who has not yet published a full-length collection. Manuscripts should be 48 to 64 pages; single, previously published poems are eligible. Closes in December.

**BARNARD COLLEGE**—Women Poets at Barnard, Columbia University, 3009 Broadway, New York, NY 10027–6598. Celeste Schenck and Christopher Baswell, Co-Directors. The Barnard New Women Poets Prize offers $1,500 and publication by Beacon Press for an unpublished poetry manuscript, 50 to 100 pages, by a female poet who has never published a book of poetry. Closes in September.

**CLEVELAND STATE UNIVERSITY POETRY CENTER**—Dept. of English, Rhodes Tower, Room 1815, Cleveland, OH 44115. The writer of the best volume of poetry submitted between December 1 and March 1 receives publication in the CSU Poetry Series and $1,000. Runners-up are considered for publication in the series under standard royalty contract. The CSU Poetry Center also publishes a Cleveland Poets Series, open only to Ohio poets; write for details.

**NATIONAL POETRY SERIES**—P.O. Box G, Hopewell, NJ 08525. Attn: The Coordinator. Sponsors Annual Open Competition for unpublished book-length poetry manuscripts. Five manuscripts are selected for publication. Closes in February.

**NEW YORK UNIVERSITY**—Elmer Holmes Bobst Awards, Bobst Library, New York University, 70 Washington Sq. S., New York, NY 10012. Rhonda Zangwill, Coord. Winning book-length fiction (novel or short stories) and poetry manuscripts, by writers who have not yet had a book published, will be published by New York University Press. Closes in March.

**NORTHEASTERN UNIVERSITY PRESS**—English Dept., 406 Holmes, Northeastern Univ., Boston, MA 02115. Guy Rotella, Chairman. Offers Samuel French Morse Poetry Prize of $500 plus publication for a full-length poetry manuscript by a U.S. poet who has published no more than one book of poems. August is the deadline for inquiries; contest closes in September.

**NORTHWESTERN UNIVERSITY**—*TriQuarterly*, 2020 Ridge Ave., Evanston, IL 60208. The Terrence des Pres Prize for Poetry offers $3,000 plus publication for a poetry manuscript, 48 to 64 pages. Closes in June of even-numbered years.

**PEREGRINE SMITH POETRY SERIES**—Gibbs Smith, Publisher, P.O.

Box 667, Layton, UT 84041. Offers a $500 prize plus publication for a 64-page poetry manuscript. Closes in April.

**PURDUE UNIVERSITY PRESS**—1131 South Campus Courts-D, W. Lafayette, IN 47907–1131. Attn: Managing Editor. The Verna Emery Poetry Competition for an unpublished collection of poetry (50 to 90 pages) awards $500 plus publication for original poems. Closes in January.

**UNIVERSITY OF ARKANSAS PRESS**—Arkansas Poetry Award, Fayetteville, AR 72701. Awards publication of a 50- to 80-page poetry manuscript to a writer who has never had a book of poetry published. Closes in May.

**UNIVERSITY OF GEORGIA PRESS**—Contemporary Poetry Series, Athens, GA 30602–1743. Poets who have never had a book of poems published may submit book-length poetry manuscripts during the month of September each year for possible publication. Manuscripts from poets who have published at least one volume of poetry (chapbooks excluded) are considered during the month of January. Send SASE for guidelines before submitting. Manuscripts will not be returned.

**UNIVERSITY OF IOWA PRESS**—The Edwin Ford Piper Poetry Awards, 119 W. Park Rd., 100 Kuhl House, Iowa City, IA 52242–1000. Two $1,000 prizes, plus publication, will be awarded for poetry manuscripts, 50 to 120 pages, by writers who have published at least one book of poetry. Closes in March.

**UNIVERSITY OF MASSACHUSETTS PRESS**—Juniper Prize, Amherst, MA 01003. Offers the annual Juniper Prize of $1,000, plus publication, for a book-length manuscript of poetry; awarded in odd-numbered years to writers who have never published a book of poetry, and in even-numbered years to writers who have published a book or chapbook of poetry. Closes in September.

**UNIVERSITY OF MISSOURI PRESS**—2910 LeMone Blvd., Columbia, MO 65201–8227. Mr. Clair Willcox, Poetry Ed. Publishes several volumes of poetry in each seasonal list. From the manuscripts accepted for publication in a given year, one outstanding collection is the recipient of the $500 Devins Award. Submit 4 to 6 sample poems, table of contents for entire manuscript, and brief cover letter giving manuscript length and other appropriate information. Submissions accepted year round.

**UNIVERSITY OF PITTSBURGH PRESS**—Pitt Poetry Series, Pittsburgh, PA 15260. Poets who have never had a full-length book of poetry published may enter a 48- to 100-page collection of poems to the Agnes Lynch Starrett Poetry Prize in March and April. Publication in the Pitt Poetry Series and $2,000 is offered. SASE required.

**UNIVERSITY OF WISCONSIN PRESS**—Poetry Series, 114 N. Murray St., Madison, WI 53715. Ronald Wallace, Administrator. Manuscripts may be submitted during the month of September to the Brittingham Prize in Poetry competition, which offers $500, plus publication in the poetry series, for an unpublished book-length poetry manuscript. Send SASE for details. Manuscripts will not be returned.

**WESLEYAN UNIVERSITY PRESS**—Wesleyan Poetry Program, 110 Mt. Vernon St., Middletown, CT 06459. Considers unpublished poetry manuscripts, 64 to 82 pages, by poets who have never had a book published. Response time is 2 to 3 months. There is no deadline. Submit manuscript and SASE.

**WORD WORKS**—P. O. Box 42164, Washington, DC 20015. Offers the Washington Prize of $1,000 plus publication for an unpublished volume of poetry by an American poet. Closes in March.

**YALE UNIVERSITY PRESS**—Box 92A, Yale Sta., New Haven, CT 06520.

Attn: Editor, Yale Series of Younger Poets. Conducts Yale Series of Younger Poets Competition, in which the prize is publication of a book-length manuscript of poetry, written by a poet under 40 who has not previously published a volume of poems. Manuscripts are accepted only during the month of February.

# GREETING CARD MARKETS

Greeting card companies often have their own specific requirements for submitting ideas, verse, and artwork. In general, however, each verse or message should be typed, double-spaced, on a $3 \times 5$ or $4 \times 6$ card. Use only one side of the card, and be sure to put your name and address in the upper left-hand corner. Keep a copy of every verse or idea you send. (It's also advisable to keep a record of what you've submitted to each publisher.) Always enclose an SASE, and do not send out more than ten verses or ideas in a group to any one publisher. Never send original artwork.

**AMBERLEY GREETING CARD COMPANY**—11510 Goldcoast Dr., Cincinnati, OH 45249–1695. Ned Stern, Ed. Humorous ideas for birthday, illness, friendship, anniversary, congratulations, "miss you," etc. No seasonal or holiday ideas. Send SASE for market letter before submitting ideas. Pays $150. Buys all rights.

**AMERICAN GREETINGS**—10500 American Rd., Cleveland, OH 44144. Lynne Shlonsky, Dir., Creative Resources and Development. Study current offerings and query before submitting.

**BLUE MOUNTAIN ARTS, INC.**—P.O. Box 1007, Boulder, CO 80306. Attn: Editorial Staff, Dept. TW. Poetry and prose about love, friendship, family, philosophies, etc. Also material for special occasions and holidays: birthdays, get well, Christmas, Valentine's Day, Easter, etc. Submit seasonal material four months in advance. No artwork or rhymed verse. Pays $200 per poem.

**DAYSPRING GREETING CARDS**—Outreach Publications, P.O. Box 1010, Siloam Springs, AR 72761. David Taylor, Ed. Inspirational messages that minister love, encouragement, and comfort to the receiver. Holidays, everyday occasions, and special-occasion cards. SASE for guidelines. Allow 4 to 6 weeks for response. Pays $30, on acceptance.

**FREEDOM GREETING CARD COMPANY**—P.O. Box 715, Bristol, PA 19007. Submit to Jay Levitt. Traditional and humorous verse and love messages. Inspirational poetry for all occasions. Pays negotiable rates, on acceptance. Query with SASE.

**HALLMARK CARDS, INC.**—Box 419580, Mail Drop 216, Kansas City, MO 64141–6580. Write Carol King for submission agreement and guidelines; include SASE, no samples. Not currently soliciting new writers or sentiments. Work is on assignment basis only. Free lancers must show exceptional originality and style not available from in-house employees and must have previous writing experience.

**KALAN**—97 S. Union Ave., Lansdowne, PA 19050. Attn: Editor. Unique and wildly funny messages for birthday and love greeting cards. Send humorous card ideas for Christmas and Valentine's Day 9 or 10 months before holiday. One-liners (risqué O.K.) about school, dating, money (or lack thereof), life, sex, etc., for key rings. Pays $75 per idea purchased. Very selective; send SASE for guidelines.

**NOBLE WORKS**—113 Clinton St., Hoboken, NJ 07030. Christopher Noble, Ed. Humorous greeting card ideas and copy. "No smut, no verse, nothing sweet or sentimental. We like 'Saturday Night Live' style humor." Pays $150 per complete idea against royalties, on publication. (Other deals and licensing agreements available depending on artist and quality of work.) SASE required.

**OATMEAL STUDIOS**—Box 138 TW, Rochester, VT 05767. Attn: Editor. Humorous, clever, and new ideas needed for all occasions. Send SASE for guidelines.

**PARAMOUNT CARDS**—P.O. Box 6546, Providence, RI 02940–6546. Attn: Editorial Freelance. Humorous card ideas for birthday, relative's birthday, friendship, romance, get well, Christmas, Valentine's Day, Easter, Mother's Day, Father's Day, and Graduation. Submit each idea (5 to 10 per submission) on 3 × 5 card with name and address on each. Enclose SASE. Payment varies, on acceptance.

**RAINBOW JUNGLE**—29 Van Zandt St., Albany, NY 12207. Greeting-card text for holidays, birthdays, anniversaries, personal messages, etc. Send #10 SASE for guidelines. Pays to $100, on acceptance.

**RED FARM STUDIO**—1135 Roosevelt Ave., P.O. Box 347, Pawtucket, RI 02862. Traditional cards for graduation, wedding, birthday, get well, anniversary, friendship, new baby, sympathy, and Christmas. No studio humor. Pays varying rates. SASE required.

**SANGAMON COMPANY**—Route 48 West, P.O. Box 410, Taylorville, IL 62568. Address Editorial Dept. "We will send writer's guidelines to experienced free lancers before reviewing any submissions. We work on assignment." Pays competitive rates, on acceptance.

**SUNRISE PUBLICATIONS, INC.**—P.O. Box 4699, Bloomington, IN 47402. Address Editorial Coordinator. Original copy for holiday and everyday cards. "Submit up to 20 verses, 1 to 4 lines; simple, to-the-point ideas that could be serious, humorous, or light-hearted, but sincere, without being overly sentimental. Rhymed verse not generally used." SASE required. Allow 4 to 6 weeks for response. Send #10-size SASE for guidelines. Pays standard rates.

**TLC GREETINGS**—615 McCall Rd., Manhattan, KS 66502–8512. Michele Johnson, Creative Dir. Humorous and traditional sewing and craft-related cards. General humor cards for women for everyday, Christmas, and Valentine's Day. Very few risqué cards purchased. Pays on acceptance. Guidelines.

**VAGABOND CREATIONS, INC.**—2560 Lance Dr., Dayton, OH 45409. George F. Stanley, Jr., Ed. Greeting cards with graphics only on cover (no copy) and short tie-in copy punch line on inside page: birthday, everyday, Valentine's Day, Christmas, and graduation. Mildly risqué humor with double entendre acceptable. Ideas for illustrated theme stationery. Pays $15, on acceptance.

**WARNER PRESS PUBLISHERS**—1200 E. Fifth St., Anderson, IN 46012. Robin Fogle, Product Ed. New free-lance system has been developed; send SASE for guidelines before submitting. Religious themes, sensitive prose, and inspirational verse for boxed cards, posters, and calendars. Pays $20 to $35, on acceptance. Also accepts ideas for coloring and activity books.

**WEST GRAPHICS PUBLISHING**—238 Capp St., San Francisco, CA

94110. Attention: Editorial Dept. Outrageous humor concepts, all occasions (especially birthday) and holidays, for photo and illustrated card lines. Submit on 3×5 cards: concept on one side; name, address, and phone number on other. Pays $100, 30 days after publication.

**WILLIAMHOUSE-REGENCY, INC.**—28 W. 23rd St., New York, NY 10010. Query Nancy Boecker with SASE for writing specs. Captions for wedding invitations only. Pays $25 per caption, on acceptance. SASE required.

**CAROL WILSON FINE ARTS, INC.**—P.O. Box 17394, Portland, OR 97217. Gary Spector, Ed. Carol Wilson, Ed. Humorous copy for greeting cards. Queries preferred. Pays $75 or negotiated royalties, on publication. Guidelines.

# COLLEGE, LITERARY, AND LITTLE MAGAZINES

## FICTION, NONFICTION, POETRY

The thousands of literary journals, little magazines, and college quarterlies published today welcome work from novices and pros alike; editors are always interested in seeing traditional and experimental fiction, poetry, essays, reviews, short articles, criticism, and satire, and as long as the material is well-written, the fact that a writer is a beginner doesn't adversely affect his or her chances for acceptance.

Most of these smaller publications have small budgets and staffs, so they may be slow in their reporting time—several months is not unusual. In addition, they usually pay only in copies of the issue in which published work appears and some—particularly college magazines—do not read manuscripts during the summer.

Publication in the literary journals can, however, lead to recognition by editors of large-circulation magazines, who read the little magazines in their search for new talent. There is also the possibility of having one's work chosen for reprinting in one of the prestigious annual collections of work from the little magazines.

Because the requirements of these journals differ widely, it is always important to study recent issues before submitting work to one of them. Copies of magazines may be in large libraries, or a writer may send a postcard to the editor and ask the price of a sample copy. When submitting a manuscript, always enclose a self-addressed envelope, with sufficient postage for its return.

For a complete list of literary and college publications and little magazines, writers may consult such reference works as *The International Directory of Little Magazines and Small Presses*, published annually by Dustbooks (P.O. Box 100, Paradise, CA 95967).

**THE AGNI REVIEW**—Dept. TW, Boston University, Creative Writing Pro-

714

gram, 236 Bay State Rd., Boston, MA 02215. Askold Melnyczuk, Ed. Short stories, poetry, essays, and artwork. Reading period October 1 to June 1 only.

**ALABAMA LITERARY REVIEW**—Troy State Univ., Smith 253, Troy, AL 36082. Theron Montgomery, Chief Ed. Contemporary, literary fiction and nonfiction, 3,500 words, and poetry, to two pages. Thought provoking B&W photos. Published semi-annually. Pays in copies. Responds in up to three months.

**ALASKA QUARTERLY REVIEW**—College of Arts & Sciences, Univ. of Alaska, 3211 Providence Dr., Anchorage, AK 99508. Address Eds. Short stories, novel excerpts, poetry (traditional and unconventional forms). Submit manuscripts between August 15 and May 15. Pays in copies.

**ALBATROSS**—125 Horton Ave., Englewood, FL 34223. Richard Smyth, Richard Brobst, Eds. High-quality poetry; especially interested in ecological and nature poetry written in narrative form. Interviews with well-known poets. Submit 3 to 5 poems at a time with brief bio. Pays in copies.

**THE AMARANTH REVIEW**—P.O. Box 56235, Phoenix, AZ 85079. Dana L. Yost, Ed. Semiannual. Fiction, to 7,500 words, and poetry, any length. Query with #10 SASE for issue themes and contest information. Pays in copies and subscription.

**AMELIA**—329 E St., Bakersfield, CA 93304. Frederick A. Raborg, Jr., Ed. Poetry, to 100 lines; critical essays, to 2,000 words; reviews, to 500 words; belles lettres, to 1,000 words; fiction, to 4,500 words; fine pen-and-ink sketches; photos. Pays $35 for fiction and criticism, $10 to $25 for other nonfiction and artwork, $2 to $25 for poetry. Annual contest.

**THE AMERICAN BOOK REVIEW**—Publications Center, Univ. of Colorado, English Dept., Box 494, Boulder, CO 80309. Don Laing, Man. Ed. Literary book reviews, 700 to 1,200 words. Pays $50 honorarium and copies. Query first.

**AMERICAN LITERARY REVIEW**—Univ. of North Texas, P.O. Box 13615, Denton, TX 76203. J.F. Kobler, Ed. Short stories, to 20 double-spaced pages, and poetry (submit up to five poems). Pays in copies.

**THE AMERICAN POETRY REVIEW**—1721 Walnut St., Philadelphia, PA 19103. Address Eds. Highest quality contemporary poetry. Responds in 10 weeks. SASE a must.

**AMERICAN QUARTERLY**—National Museum of American History, Smithsonian Institution, Washington, DC 20560. Gary Kulik, Ed. Scholarly essays, 5,000 to 10,000 words, on any aspect of U.S. culture. Pays in copies.

**THE AMERICAN SCHOLAR**—1811 Q St. N.W., Washington, DC 20009–9974. Joseph Epstein, Ed. Articles, 3,500 to 4,000 words, on science, politics, literature, the arts, etc. Book reviews. Pays to $500 for articles, $100 for reviews, on publication.

**AMERICAN WRITING**—4343 Manayunk Ave., Philadelphia, PA 19128. Alexandra Grilikhes, Ed. Semiannual that "encourages experimentation in writing." Fiction and nonfiction, to 3,000 words, and poetry. Pays in copies.

**AMHERST REVIEW**—P.O. Box 1811, Amherst College, Amherst, MA 01002–5000. Bryant Rousseau, Ed. Fiction and other prose, to 6,000 words; poetry to 160 lines. Photos, paintings, drawings, and graphic art. Submit material September through March. SASE required.

**ANOTHER CHICAGO MAGAZINE**—3709 N. Kenmore, Chicago, IL

60613. Semiannual. Fiction, essays on literature, and poetry. "We want writing that's urgent, new, and lives in the world." Pays $5 to $25, on acceptance.

**ANTAEUS**—100 West Broad, Hopewell, NJ 08525. Daniel Halpern, Ed. Short stories, essays, documents, excerpts, translations, poems. Pays on publication.

**ANTIETAM REVIEW**—82 W. Washington St., Hagerstown, MD 21740. Susanne Kass and Ann Knox, Eds.-in-Chief. Fiction, to 5,000 words; poetry and photography. Submissions from regional artists only (MD, PA, WV, VA, DE, DC), from October through February. Pays from $20 to $100. Guidelines.

**THE ANTIGONISH REVIEW**—St. Francis Xavier Univ., Antigonish, N.S., Canada B2G 1C0. George Sanderson, Ed. Poetry; short stories, essays, book reviews, 1,800 to 2,500 words. Pays in copies.

**ANTIOCH REVIEW**—P.O. Box 148, Yellow Springs, OH 45387-0148. Robert S. Fogarty, Ed. Timely articles, 2,000 to 8,000 words, on social sciences, literature, and humanities. Quality fiction. Poetry. No inspirational poetry. Pays $15 per printed page, on publication.

**APALACHEE QUARTERLY**—Apalachee Press, P.O. Box 20106, Tallahassee, FL 32316. Barbara Hamby, Pamela Ball, Mary Jane Ryals, Bruce Boehrer, Paul McCall, Eds. Fiction, to 30 manuscript pages; poems (submit 3 to 5). Pays in copies.

**APPALACHIA**—299 Gunstock Hill Rd., Gilford, NH 03246-7563. Helen Howe, Poetry Ed. Semiannual publication of the Appalachian Mountain Club. Oldest mountaineering journal in the country covers nature, conservation, climbing, hiking, canoeing, and ecology. Poems, to 30 lines. Pays in copies.

**ARACHNE**—162 Sturges St., Jamestown, NY 14701-3233. Susan L. Leach, Ed. Fiction, to 1,500 words. Poems (submit up to 7). "We are looking for rural material and would like first publication rights." No simultaneous submissions. Quarterly. Pays in copies.

**ARIZONA QUARTERLY**—Univ. of Arizona, Main Library B-541, Tucson, AZ 85721. Edgar A. Dryden, Ed. Criticism of American literature and culture from a theoretical perspective. No poetry or fiction. Pays in copies.

**ARTFUL DODGE**—College of Wooster, Wooster, OH 44691. Daniel Bourne and Karen Kovacik, Eds. Annual. Fiction, to 20 pages. Literary essays "based on a balance of analysis and insight," to 10 pages. Poetry, including translations of contemporary poets; submit 3 to 6 poems at a time; long poems encouraged. Pays $5 per page, on publication, plus 2 copies.

**AURA LITERARY/ARTS REVIEW**—P.O. Box 76, Univ. Center, UAB, Birmingham, AL 35294. Nan Smith, Ed. Fiction and essays on literature, to 7,000 words; book reviews, to 4,000 words; poetry; photos. Pays in copies.

**BAD HAIRCUT**—1055 Adams S.E. #4, Olympia, WA 98501-1443. Ray and Kim Gofroth, Eds. Articles and fiction, to 4,000 words (2,000 words preferred): Focus on politics, human rights, and environmental themes. Unrhymed poetry, to one page, and drawings also accepted. "We hope that by creating art with these themes we can influence society and help create a better world." Pays in copies.

**BAMBOO RIDGE, THE HAWAII WRITERS' QUARTERLY**—Bamboo Ridge Press, P.O. Box 61781, Honolulu, HI 96839-1781. Eric Chock, Ed. Welcomes poetry (10 pages) and short stories (25 pages) of writers in U.S. and abroad. Submit with SASE. Reports in 3 to 6 months. Pays in small honorarium and 2 copies.

**BELLES LETTRES**—11151 Captain's Walk Ct., North Potomac, MD

20878–0441. Janet Mullaney, Ed. Reviews and essays, 250 to 2,000 words, on literature by women. Literary puzzles, interviews, rediscoveries, retrospectives, and fiction. Query required. Pays in copies and subscription.

**THE BELLINGHAM REVIEW**—The Signpost Press, Inc., 1007 Queen St., Bellingham, WA 98226. Susan Hilton, Ed. Semiannual. Fiction, to 5,000 words, and poetry, any length. Pays in copies and subscription. Reading period is from September 1 to June 30.

**BELLOWING ARK**—P.O. Box 45637, Seattle, WA 98145. Robert R. Ward, Ed. Short fiction, and poetry and essays of varying lengths, that portray life as a positive, meaningful process. B&W photos; line drawings. Pays in copies.

**THE BELOIT FICTION JOURNAL**—Box 11, Beloit College, Beloit, WI 53511. Clint McCown, Ed. Short fiction, one to 35 pages, on all themes. No pornography, political propaganda, religious dogma. Manuscripts read September to May. Pays in copies.

**BELOIT POETRY JOURNAL**—RFD 2, Box 154, Ellsworth, ME 04605. Strong contemporary poetry, of any length or in any mode. Pays in copies. Send SASE for guidelines.

**BLACK AMERICAN LITERATURE FORUM**—Dept. of English, Indiana State Univ., Terre Haute, IN 47809. Joe Weixlmann, Ed. Essays on black American literature, art, and culture; bibliographies; interviews; poems; and book reviews. Submit up to 6 poems. Address queries for book review assignments to: Henry Louis Gates, Jr., Book Review Ed., Black American Literature Forum, Dept. of English, Duke Univ., Durham, NC 27706. Send 2 copies of all other submissions to Indiana State Univ. address above. Pays in copies.

**BLACK BEAR REVIEW**—Black Bear Publications, 1916 Lincoln St., Croydon, PA 19021–8026. Ave Jeanne, Ed. Book reviews and contemporary poetry. "We publish poems with social awareness, but any well-written piece is considered." Semiannual. Pays in one copy.

**BLACK RIVER REVIEW**—855 Mildred Ave., Lorain, OH 44052–1213. Deborah Glaefke Gilbert, Ed. Contemporary poetry, fiction, essays, short book reviews, B&W artwork. No greeting card verse or slick magazine prose. Submit between January 1 and May 1. Pays in copies. Guidelines. SASE required.

**THE BLACK WARRIOR REVIEW**—The Univ. of Alabama, P.O. Box 2936, Tuscaloosa, AL 35486–2936. Glenn Mott, Ed. Fiction; poetry; translations; reviews and essays. Pays per printed page. Annual awards. SASE required.

**THE BLOOMSBURY REVIEW**—1028 Bannock St., Denver, CO 80204–4037. Tom Auer, Ed. Marilyn Auer, Assoc. Ed. Book reviews, publishing features, interviews, essays, poetry. Pays $5 to $25, on publication.

**BLUE UNICORN**—22 Avon Rd., Kensington, CA 94707. Address the Editors. Published in October, February, and June. "We are looking for originality of image, thought, and music; we rarely use poems over a page long." Submit up to 5 poems with SASE. Artwork used occasionally. Pays in one copy.

**BLUELINE**—English Dept., SUNY, Potsdam, NY 13676. Alan Steinberg, Ed. Reading period September 1 to December 1. Essays, fiction, to 2,500 words, on Adirondack region or similar areas. Poetry, to 44 lines. Submit no more than 5 poems. Pays in copies.

**BOSTON REVIEW**—33 Harrison Ave., Boston, MA 02111–2008. Josh

Cohen, Ed.-in-Chief. Reviews and essays, 800 to 3,000 words, on literature, art, music, film, photography. Original fiction, to 5,000 words. Poetry. Pays $40 to $150.

**BOTTOMFISH**—21250 Stevens Creek Blvd., Cupertino, CA 95014. Robert Scott, Ed. Annual. Stories, vignettes, and experimental fiction, to 5,000 words. Free verse or traditional poetry, any subject, any length. "Our purpose is to give national exposure to new writers and new styles of creative writing. We publish at the end of March each year; manuscripts received after March 1 may be held as long as 9 months." Pays in copies.

**BOULEVARD**—P.O. Box 30386, Philadelphia, PA 19103. Richard Burgin, Ed. Published three times a year. High-quality fiction and articles, to 30 pages; poetry. Pays to $250, on publication.

**THE BRIDGE**—14050 Vernon St., Oak Park, MI 48237. Jack Zucker, Ed. Helen Zucker, Fiction Ed. Mitzi Alvin, Poetry Ed. Manom Meilgaard, Assoc. Fiction Ed. Semiannual. Fiction, 7,500 words, and poetry, to 300 lines. Pays in copies.

**BUCKNELL REVIEW**—Bucknell Univ., Lewisburg, PA 17837. Interdisciplinary journal in book form. Scholarly articles on arts, science, and letters. Pays in copies.

**CACANADADADA REVIEW**—P.O. Box 1283, Port Angeles, WA 98362. R.L. Hurt, Ed. Short-shorts, to 800 words, and poetry. Drawings and B&W photos. Pays in 2 copies.

**CALLIOPE**—Creative Writing Program, Roger Williams College, Bristol, RI 02809–2921. Martha Christina, Ed. Short stories, to 2,500 words; poetry. Pays in copies and subscription. No submissions April through July.

**CALYX, A JOURNAL OF ART & LITERATURE BY WOMEN**—P.O. Box B, Corvallis, OR 97339. M. Donnelly, Man. Ed. Fiction, 5,000 words; book reviews, 1,000 words (please query with SASE about reviews); poetry, to 6 poems. Pays in copies. Submissions accepted March 1 to April 15 and October 1 to November 15. Include short bio and SASE. Guidelines.

**CANADIAN FICTION MAGAZINE**—Box 946, Sta. F, Toronto, Ontario, Canada M4Y 2N9. High-quality short stories, novel excerpts, and experimental fiction, to 5,000 words, by Canadians. Interviews with Canadian authors; translations. Pays $10 per page, on publication. Annual prize, $500.

**THE CAPE ROCK**—Dept. of English, Southeast Missouri State Univ., Cape Girardeau, MO 63701. Harvey E. Hecht, Ed. Semiannual. Poetry, to 70 lines, and B&W photography. (One photographer per issue; pays $100.) Pays in copies and $200 for best poem in each issue.

**THE CAPILANO REVIEW**—2055 Purcell Way, N. Vancouver, B.C., Canada V7J 3H5. Pierre Coupey, Ed. Fiction; poetry; visual arts. SASE required. Pays $30 to $120.

**THE CARIBBEAN WRITER**—Univ. of the Virgin Islands, RR 02, Box 10,000, Kingshill, St. Croix, Virgin Islands, U.S. 00850. Erika J. Waters, Ed. Annual. Fiction (to 15 pages, submit up to 2 stories) and poems (no more than 5); the Caribbean should be central to the work. Blind submissions policy: place title only on manuscript; name, address, and title of ms. on separate sheet. Reading period is through September for spring issue of the following year. Pays in copies.

**CAROLINA QUARTERLY**—Greenlaw Hall CB#3520, Univ. of North Carolina, Chapel Hill, NC 27599–3520. David Kellogg, Ed. Fiction, to 7,000 words, by new or established writers. Poetry (no restrictions on length, though limited space makes inclusion of works of more than 300 lines impractical). Pays $15 for fiction and poetry, on publication.

**CATALYST**—Atlanta-Fulton Public Library, 1 Margaret Mitchell Sq., Carnegie & Forsyth Sq., Atlanta, GA 30303–1089. Pearl Cleage, Ed. Semiannual. Fiction, to 3,000 words, and poetry, primarily by Southern black writers. Pays to $200, on publication. Send SASE for guidelines and themes.

**THE CENTENNIAL REVIEW**—312 Linton Hall, Michigan State Univ., East Lansing, MI 48824–1044. R.K. Meiners, Ed. Articles, 3,000 to 5,000 words, on sciences, humanities, and interdisciplinary topics. Pays in copies.

**THE CHARITON REVIEW**—Northeast Missouri State Univ., Kirksville, MO 63501. Jim Barnes, Ed. Highest quality poetry and fiction, to 6,000 words. Modern and contemporary translations. "The only guideline is excellence in all matters."

**THE CHICAGO REVIEW**—5801 S. Kenwood Ave., Chicago, IL 60637. David Nicholls, Ed. Essays, interviews, reviews, fiction, translations, poetry. Pays in copies plus one year's subscription.

**CHIRON REVIEW**—1514 Stone, Great Bend, KS 67530–4025. Michael Hathaway, Ed. Contemporary fiction, to 4,000 words; articles, 500 to 1,000 words; and poetry, to 30 lines. Photos. Pays in copies.

**CICADA**—329 E St., Bakersfield, CA 93304. Frederick A. Raborg, Jr., Ed. Single haiku, sequences or garlands, essays about the forms, haibun and fiction related to haiku or Japan. Pays in copies.

**CIMARRON REVIEW**—205 Morrill Hall, Oklahoma State Univ., Stillwater, OK 74078–0135. Gordon Weaver, Ed. Poetry, fiction, essays. Seeks an individual, innovative style that focuses on contemporary themes. Pays $50 for stories and essays; $15 for poems, plus one-year subscription.

**CINCINNATI POETRY REVIEW**—Dept. of English, 069, Cincinnati, OH 45221. Dallas Wiebe, Ed. Published fall and spring. Poetry of all types. Pays in copies.

**CLOCKWATCH REVIEW**—Dept. of English, Illinois Wesleyan Univ., Bloomington, IL 61702–2900. James Plath, Ed. Semiannual. Fiction, to 4,000 words, and poetry, to 36 lines. "Our preference is for fresh language, a believable voice, a mature style, and a sense of the unusual in the subject matter." Pays currently $50 for fiction, $10 for poetry, on acceptance, plus copies.

**COLLAGES & BRICOLAGES**—Office of Int'l Programs, 212 Founders Hall, Clarion Univ. of Pennsylvania, Clarion, PA 16214. Marie-José Fortis, Ed. Annual. Fiction and nonfiction, plays, interviews, book reviews, and poetry. Surrealistic and expressionistic drawings in ink. "I seek writers who are politically and socially aware and whose writing is not egocentric." Pays in copies.

**COLORADO REVIEW**—English Dept., 359 Eddy, Colorado State Univ., Fort Collins, CO 80523. Bill Tremblay, Ed. Poetry, short fiction, translations, interviews, articles on contemporary themes. Submit from September through April 1. Pays $20 per printed page.

**COLUMBIA: A MAGAZINE OF POETRY & PROSE**—404 Dodge, Columbia Univ., New York, NY 10027. Address the Editors. Semiannual. Fiction and nonfiction; poetry; essays; interviews; visual art. Pays in copies. SASE required. Guidelines and annual awards.

719

**THE COMICS JOURNAL**—Fantagraphics, Inc., 7563 Lake City Way, Seattle, WA 98115. Address Man. Ed. Monthly journal, 90 percent written by freelancers with "working knowledge of the diversity and history of the comics medium." Reviews, 2,500 to 5,000 words; domestic and international news, 500 to 7,000 words; "Opening Shots" editorials, 500 to 1,500 words; interviews; and features, 2,500 to 5,000 words. Query for news and interviews. Pays 1 ½¢ a word, on publication. Guidelines.

**CONFRONTATION**—Dept. of English, C.W. Post of L. I. U., Brookville, NY 11548. Martin Tucker, Ed. Serious fiction, 750 to 6,000 words. Crafted poetry, 10 to 200 lines. Pays $10 to $100, on publication.

**THE CONNECTICUT POETRY REVIEW**—P.O. Box 3783, New Haven, CT 06525. J. Claire White and James Wm. Chichetto, Eds. Poetry, 5 to 20 lines, and reviews, 700 words. Pays $5 per poem, $10 per review, on acceptance.

**CONNECTICUT RIVER REVIEW**—P.O. Box 2171, Bridgeport, CT 06608. Robert Isaacs, Ed. Semiannual. Poetry. Submit 3 to 5 poems, 40 lines or less. Pays in one copy. Guidelines.

**CRAB CREEK REVIEW**—4462 Whitman N., Seattle, WA 98103. Linda Clifton, Ed. Carol Orlock, Fiction Ed. Published three times a year. Clear, dynamic fiction, to 4,000 words, with strong voice and imagery. Nonfiction, to 4,000 words, that "uses image and occasion as a reason to share ideas with an intelligent reader." Poetry, to 80 lines. Pays in copies.

**CRAZY QUILT**—P.O. Box 632729, San Diego, CA 92163–2729. Address the Editors. Fiction, to 4,000 words, poetry, one-act plays, and literary criticism. Also B&W art, photographs. Pays in copies.

**THE CREAM CITY REVIEW**—Box 413, Univ. of Wisconsin, Milwaukee, WI 53201. Sandra Nelson and Kathlene Postma, Co-Eds. "We serve a national audience interested in a diversity of writing (in terms of style, subject, genre) and writers (gender, race, class, publishing history, etc.). Both well-known and newly published writers of fiction, poetry, and essays are featured, along with B&W artwork and a debate among 3 or more writers on a contemporary literary issue." Payment varies.

**THE CRESCENT REVIEW**—1445 Old Town Rd., Winston-Salem, NC 27106–3143. Guy Nancekeville, Ed. Semiannual. Short stories only. No submissions May to June or November to December. Pays in copies.

**CRITICAL INQUIRY**—Univ. of Chicago Press, Wieboldt Hall, 1050 E. 59th St., Chicago, IL 60637. W. J. T. Mitchell, Ed. Critical essays that offer a theoretical perspective on literature, music, visual arts, and popular culture. No fiction, poetry, or autobiography. Pays in copies.

**CUMBERLAND POETRY REVIEW**—P.O. Box 120128, Acklen Sta., Nashville, TN 37212. Address Eds. High-quality poetry and criticism; translations. No restrictions on form, style, or subject matter. Pays in copies.

**DENVER QUARTERLY**—Univ. of Denver, Denver, CO 80208. Donald Revell, Ed. Literary, cultural essays and articles; poetry; book reviews; fiction. Pays $5 per printed page, after publication.

**DESCANT**—Texas Christian Univ., T.C.U. Sta., Fort Worth, TX 76129. Betsy Colquitt, Stanley Trachtenberg, Eds. Fiction, to 6,000 words. Poetry, to 40 lines. No restriction on form or subject. Pays in copies. Submit September through May only. Frank O'Connor Award ($500) is given each year for best short story published in the volume.

**THE DEVIL'S MILLHOPPER**—The Devil's Millhopper Press, Coll. of Humanities, USC/Aiken, 171 University Pkwy., Aiken, SC 29801–6399. Stephen Gardner, Ed. Poetry. Pays in copies. Send SASE for guidelines and contest information.

**DOG RIVER REVIEW**—5976 Billings Rd., Parkdale, OR 97041. Laurence F. Hawkins, Jr. Fiction, to 2,500 words, and articles on literature, to 2,500 words. Poetry, to 30 lines. No religious verse. Pays in copies.

**DREAMS & VISIONS**—Skysong Press, RR1, Washago, Ontario, Canada L0K 2B0. Wendy Stanton, Manuscript Ed. Eclectic fiction, 2,000 to 7,500 words, that is "in some way unique and relevant to Christian readers today." Pays in copies, with $100 award to best of the year.

**EARTH'S DAUGHTERS**—Box 622, Station C, Buffalo, NY 14209. Published three times a year. Fiction, to 1,000 words, poetry, to 40 lines, and B&W photos or drawings. "Finely crafted work with a feminist theme." Pays in copies. SASE for guidelines.

**ELF: ECLECTIC LITERARY FORUM**—Elf Associates, P.O. Box 392, Tonawanda, NY 14150. C. K. Erbes, Ed. Fiction, 3,500 words. Essays on literary themes, 3,500 words. Poetry, to 30 lines. Allow 4 to 6 weeks for response. Pays in two copies.

**EMBERS**—Box 404, Guilford, CT 06437. Katrina Van Tassel, Mark Johnston, Charlotte Garrett, Eds. Semiannual. Poetry. Interested in original new voices as well as published poets.

**EVENT**—Douglas College, Box 2503, New Westminster, BC, Canada V3L 5B2. Dale Zieroth, Ed. Short fiction, reviews, poetry. Pays $20 per printed page, on publication.

**FARMER'S MARKET**—P.O. Box 1272, Galesburg, IL 61402. Short stories, essays, and novel excerpts, to 40 pages, and poetry. Pays in copies.

**FICTION INTERNATIONAL**—English Dept., San Diego State Univ., San Diego, CA 92182–0295. Harold Jaffe, Larry McCaffery, Eds. Post-modernist and politically committed fiction and theory. Manuscripts read from September 1 to December 15. Payment in copies.

**THE FIDDLEHEAD**—Campus House Univ. of New Brunswick, Fredericton, N.B., Canada E3B 5A3. Serious fiction, 2,500 words, preferably by Canadians. Pays about $10 per printed page, on publication. SAE with international reply coupons required.

**FIELD**—Rice Hall, Oberlin College, Oberlin, OH 44074. Stuart Friebert, David Young, Eds. Serious poetry, any length, by established and unknown poets; essays on poetics by poets. Translations by qualified translators. Pays $20 per page, on publication.

**FINE MADNESS**—P.O. Box 31138, Seattle, WA 98103–1138. Poetry, any length; short fiction. Pays varying rates. Guidelines.

**FOLIO**—Dept. of English, American Univ., Washington, DC 20016. Elizabeth Poliner, Ed. Semiannual. Fiction, poetry, translations, and essays. Photos and drawings. Submissions read August through April. Pays in 2 copies. Contest.

**FOOTWORK, THE PATERSON LITERARY REVIEW**—Cultural Affairs Dept., Passaic County Comm. College, College Blvd., Paterson, NJ 07509–9976. Maria Mazziotti Gillan, Ed. High quality fiction, to 8 pages, and poetry, to 3 pages, any style. Pays in copies.

**FREE INQUIRY**—P.O. Box 5, Buffalo, NY 14215–0005. Paul Kurtz, Ed. Tim Madigan, Exec. Ed. Articles, 500 to 5,000 words, for "literate and lively readership. Focus is on criticisms of religious belief systems, and how to lead an ethical life without a supernatural basis." Pays in copies.

**THE GEORGIA REVIEW**—Univ. of Georgia, Athens, GA 30602. Stanley W. Lindberg, Ed. Stephen Corey, Assoc. Ed. Short fiction; personal and interdisciplinary essays; book reviews; poetry. Novel excerpts discouraged. No submissions in June to September.

**THE GETTYSBURG REVIEW**—Gettysburg College, Gettysburg, PA 17325. Peter Stitt, Ed. Quarterly. Poetry, fiction, essays, and essay-reviews, 1,000 to 20,000 words. "Review sample copy before submitting." Pays $2 a line for poetry; $25 per printed page for fiction and nonfiction. Allow 3 to 6 months for response.

**GLIMMER TRAIN PRESS**—812 S.W. Washington St., Suite 1205, Portland, OR 97205. Susan Burmeister, Ed. Quarterly. Fiction, 1,200 to 5,500 words. Twelve stories in each issue. Pays $300, on acceptance.

**GRAHAM HOUSE REVIEW**—Box 5000, Colgate Univ., Hamilton, NY 13346. Peter Balakian, Ed. Bruce Smith, Ed. Poetry and essays on modern poets. Payment depends on grants.

**GRAIN**—Box 1154, Regina, Sask., Canada S4P 3B4. Geoffrey Ursell, Ed. Short stories, to 20 typed pages; poems, send up to 8; visual art. Pays $30 to $100 for stories, $100 for cover art, $30 for other art. Self-addressed envelope with international reply coupons required.

**GREAT RIVER REVIEW**—211 W. 7th St., Winona, MN 55987. Orval Lund, Jr., Ed. Fiction and creative prose, 2,000 to 10,000 words. Quality contemporary poetry; send 4 to 8 poems. Special interest in midwestern writers and themes.

**GREEN'S MAGAZINE**—P.O. Box 3236, Regina, Sask., Canada S4P 3H1. David Green, Ed. Fiction for family reading, 1,500 to 4,000 words. Poetry, to 40 lines. Pays in copies. International reply coupons must accompany U.S. manuscripts.

**THE GREENSBORO REVIEW**—Dept. of English, Univ. of North Carolina, Greensboro, NC 27412–5001. Jim Clark, Ed. Semiannual. Poetry and fiction. Submission deadlines: September 15 and February 15. Pays in copies. Writer's guidelines and guidelines for literary awards issue available on request.

**HALF TONES TO JUBILEE**—Pensacola Junior College, English Dept., 1000 College Blvd., Pensacola, FL 32504. Walter F. Spara, Ed. Fiction, to 1,500 words, and poetry, to 60 lines. Pays in copies.

**HAUNTS**—Nightshade Publications, Box 3342, Providence, RI 02906–0742. Joseph K. Cherkes, Ed. Short stories, 1,500 to 8,000 words: horror, science-fantasy, and supernatural tales with strong characters. Pays ¼ ¢ to ½ ¢ a word, on publication.

**HAWAII REVIEW**—Dept. of English, Univ. of Hawaii, 1733 Donagho Rd., Honolulu, HI 96822. Tamara Moan, Ed.-in-Chief. Quality fiction, poetry, interviews, essays, and literary criticism reflecting both regional and global concerns.

**HAYDEN'S FERRY REVIEW**—Matthew's Center, Arizona State Univ., Tempe, AZ 85287–1502. Salima Keegan, Ed. Semiannual. Fiction, essays, and poetry (submit up to 6 poems). Include brief bio and SASE. Deadline for Spring/Summer issue is September 30; Fall/Winter issue, February 28. Pays in copies.

**HERESIES: A FEMINIST PUBLICATION ON ART AND POLITICS—** Box 1306, Canal Street Sta., New York, NY 10013. Thematic issues. Fiction, to 20 double-spaced typed pages; nonfiction; poetry; art; photography. SASE required.

**THE HIGHLANDER—**P.O. Box 397, Barrington, IL 60011. Angus Ray, Ed. Bimonthly. Articles, 1,300 to 1,900 words, related to Scottish history. "We are not concerned with modern Scotland or current problems in Scotland." Pays $100 to $150, on acceptance.

**THE HOLLINS CRITIC—**P.O. Box 9538, Hollins College, VA 24020. John Rees Moore, Ed. Published 5 times a year. Poetry, to 2 pages. Pays $25, on publication.

**HOME LIFE—**127 Ninth Ave. N., Nashville, TN 37234. Charlie Warren, Ed. Southern Baptist. Short lyrical verse: humorous, marriage and family, seasonal, and inspirational. Pays to $24 for poetry, 5 ½¢ a word for articles, on acceptance.

**HOME PLANET NEWS—**P.O. Box 415, Stuyvesant Sta., New York, NY 10009. Enid Dame and Donald Lev, Eds. Quarterly art tabloid. Fiction, to 8 typed pages; reviews, 3 to 5 pages; and poetry, any length. "We are looking for quality poetry, fiction and discerning literary and art reviews." Query for nonfiction. Pays in copies and gift subscription.

**HOWLING DOG—**8419 Rhode, Utica, MI 48317. Mary Donovan, Ed. Semiannual. "Strange" fiction, to 1,000 words. Free verse, avant-garde, wild poetry to 5 pages. "We are looking for pieces with a humorous perspective toward society's problems." Pays in copies.

**HURRICANE ALICE: A FEMINIST QUARTERLY—**207 Lind Hall, 207 Church St. S.E., Minneapolis, MN 55455. Articles, fiction, essays, interviews, and reviews, 500 to 3,000 words, with feminist perspective. Pays in copies.

**ILLINOIS WRITERS REVIEW—**English Dept., Illinois State Univ., Normal, IL 61761–6901. Kevin Stein and Jim Elledge, Eds. Semiannual. Critical reviews, essays, and commentary on contemporary writing, 750 to 2,500 words. B&W cover art and photos. Pays to $25, on publication.

**IN THE COMPANY OF POETS—**P.O. Box 10786, Oakland, CA 94610. Jacalyn Robinson, Ed./Pub. Fiction and creative essays, to 2,500 words, for a wide multicultural range of readers. Poems of any length. Drawings and photos. Published bimonthly. Pays in three copies. Guidelines available.

**INDIANA REVIEW—**316 N. Jordan Ave., Indiana Univ., Bloomington, IN 47405. Allison Joseph, Ed. Dorian Gessy, Assoc. Ed. Fiction with an emphasis on storytelling and sophistication of language. Poems that are well-executed and ambitious. Pays $5 per page. SASE required.

**INTERIM—**Dept. of English, Univ. of Nevada, Las Vegas, NV 89154–5034. A. Wilber Stevens, Ed. Semiannual. Fiction, to 6,000 words, and poetry. Pays in copies and 2-year subscription.

**THE IOWA REVIEW—**EPB 308, Univ. of Iowa, Iowa City, IA 52242. David Hamilton, Ed. Essays, poems, stories, reviews. Pays $10 a page for fiction and nonfiction, $1 a line for poetry, on publication.

**JACARANDA REVIEW—**Dept. of English, Univ. of California, Los Angeles, CA 90024. Bruce Kijewski, Ed. Katherine Swiggart, Fiction Ed. Laurence Roth, Poetry Ed. Semiannual. Fiction, to 50 pages, and poetry (submit up to 3 poems). No payment.

**KALEIDOSCOPE—**United Cerebral Palsy & Services for the Handicapped, 326 Locust St., Akron, OH 44302–1876. Darshan Perusek, Ph.D., Ed.-in-Chief.

Semiannual. Fiction, essays, interviews, articles, and biographies relating to disability and the arts, to 5,000 words. Poetry any length. Photos a plus. "We present balanced, realistic images of people with disabilities and like to publish pieces that challenge stereotypes." Submissions accepted from disabled or nondisabled writers. Pays $50 for fiction; to $50 for poetry; to $25 for book reviews; to $25 for photos. Guidelines recommended.

**KANSAS QUARTERLY**—Dept. of English, Denison Hall 122, Kansas State Univ., Manhattan, KS 66506. Literary criticism, art, and history. Fiction and poetry. Pays in copies. Two series of annual awards.

**KARAMU**—Dept. of English, Eastern Illinois Univ., Charleston, IL 61920. Peggy Brayfield, Ed. Contemporary or experimental fiction. Creative nonfiction prose, personal essays, and memoir pieces. Poetry. Pays in copies.

**THE KENYON REVIEW**—Kenyon College, Gambier, OH 43022. Marilyn Hacker, Ed. Quarterly. Fiction, poetry, essays, literary criticism, and reviews. Manuscripts read September to March. "We appreciate manuscripts from writers who read the magazine." Pays $10 a printed page for prose, $15 a printed page for poetry and reviews, on publication.

**KIOSK**—c/o English Dept., 302 Clemens Hall, SUNY Buffalo, Buffalo, NY 14260. N. Gillespie, Ed. "Quirky experimental fiction and poetry." SASE required. Pays in copies.

**THE LEADING EDGE**—3163 JKHB, Provo, UT 84602. Marny Parkin, Ed. Science fiction and fantasy magazine published 3 times a year. Short stories, 3,000 to 12,000 words; poetry, to 200 lines; and articles, to 8,000 words, on science, scientific speculation, and literary criticism. Fillers and comics. "Do not send originals; manuscripts are marked and critiqued by staff." Pays ½¢ per word with $5 minimum for fiction; $5 per published page of poetry; $2 to $4 for fillers; on publication. SASE for guidelines.

**LILITH, THE JEWISH WOMEN'S MAGAZINE**—250 W. 57th St., New York, NY 10107. Susan Weidman Schneider, Ed. Fiction, 1,500 to 2,000 words, on issues of interest to Jewish women.

**THE LION AND THE UNICORN**—Ed. Offices, English Dept., Brooklyn College, Brooklyn, NY 11210. Geraldine DeLuca, Roni Natov, Eds. Articles, from 2,000 words, offering criticism of children's and young-adult books, for teachers, scholars, artists, and parents. Query preferred. Pays in copies.

**LITERARY MAGAZINE REVIEW**—English Dept., Kansas State Univ., Manhattan, KS 66506. Reviews and articles concerning literary magazines, 1,000 to 1,500 words, for writers and readers of contemporary literature. Pays modest fees and in copies. Query.

**THE LITERARY REVIEW**—Fairleigh Dickinson Univ., 285 Madison Ave., Madison, NJ 07940. Walter Cummins, Martin Green, Harry Keyishian, William Zander, Jill Kushner, Eds. Serious fiction; poetry; translations; essays and reviews on contemporary literature. Pays in copies.

**LONG SHOT**—P.O. Box 6231, Hoboken, NJ 07030. Danny Shot, Jack Wiler, Jessica Chosid, Tom Pulhamus, Eds. Fiction, poetry, and nonfiction, to 10 pages. B&W photos and drawings. Pays in copies.

**THE LONG STORY**—11 Kingston St., N. Andover, MA 01845. Stories, 8,000 to 20,000 words; prefer committed fiction. Pays in copies.

**LOST CREEK LETTERS**—Lost Creek Publications, RR 2, Box 373A, Rushville, MO 64484. Pamela Montgomery, Ed. Fiction, to 3,000 words, and poetry, any length. "We are looking for shining gems of contemporary literature. We will not read material sent without SASE." Pays $5 for short stories, $2 for poems, or two contributor's copies.

**LYRA**—P.O. Box 3188, Guttenberg, NJ 07093. Lourdes Gil, Iraida Iturralde, Eds. Fiction, to 12 double-spaced pages. Essays, translations, interviews, and reviews, 3 to 15 pages. Poetry, any length. Quarterly. Pays $25 to $30 per book review, on acceptance, plus copies.

**MAGIC REALISM**—P.O. Box 620, Orem, UT 84059–0620. C. Darren Butler and Julie Thomas, Eds. Published three times a year. Stories, to 7,500 words (4,000 words preferred), of magic realism, exaggerated realism, some genre fantasy/dark fantasy. Occasionally publish glib fantasy like that found in folk, fairy tales, and myths. No occult, sleight-of-hand magicians, or wizards/witches. Pays in one copy.

**THE MALAHAT REVIEW**—Univ. of Victoria, P.O. Box 3045, Victoria, BC, Canada V8W 3P4. Derk Wynard, Ed. Fiction and poetry, including translations. Pays from $20 per page, on acceptance.

**THE MANHATTAN REVIEW**—440 Riverside Dr., #45, New York, NY 10027. Highest quality poetry. Pays in copies.

**MASSACHUSETTS REVIEW**—Memorial Hall, Univ. of Massachusetts, Amherst, MA 01003. Literary criticism; articles on public affairs, scholarly disciplines. Short fiction. Poetry. No submissions between June and October. Pays modest rates, on publication. SASE required.

**MICHIGAN HISTORICAL REVIEW**—Clarke Historical Library, Central Michigan Univ., Mt. Pleasant, MI 48859. Address Ed. Scholarly articles related to Michigan's political, social, economic, and cultural history; articles on American, Canadian, and Midwestern history that directly or indirectly explore themes related to Michigan's past. SASE required.

**MID-AMERICAN REVIEW**—Dept. of English, Bowling Green State Univ., Bowling Green, OH 43403. George Looney, Ed. Wayne Burham, Assoc. Ed. High-quality fiction, poetry, articles, translations, and reviews of contemporary writing. Fiction to 5,000 words, (query for longer work). Reviews, articles, 500 to 2,500 words. Pays to $50, on publication. No manuscripts read June through August.

**MIDWEST QUARTERLY**—Pittsburg State Univ., Pittsburg, KS 66762. James B. M. Schick, Ed. Scholarly articles, 2,500 to 5,000 words, on contemporary academic and public issues. Pays in copies.

**THE MINNESOTA REVIEW**—Dept. of English, East Carolina Univ., Greenville, NC 27858. Address the Editors. "Politically committed fiction, 3,000 to 6,000 words, nonfiction, 5,000 to 7,500 words, and poetry, 3 pages maximum, for socialist, marxist, or feminist audience." Pays in copies.

**MISSISSIPPI REVIEW**—Center for Writers, Univ. of Southern Mississippi, Southern Sta., Box 5144, Hattiesburg, MS 39406–5144. Frederick Barthelme, Ed. Serious fiction, poetry, criticism, interviews. Pays in copies.

**THE MISSISSIPPI VALLEY REVIEW**—Dept. of English, Western Illinois Univ., Macomb, IL 61455. John Mann and Tama Baldwin, Eds. Short fiction, to 20 typed pages. Poetry; send 3 to 5 poems. Pays in copies.

**THE MISSOURI REVIEW**—1507 Hillcrest Hall, Univ. of Missouri-Columbia, Columbia, MO 65211. Greg Michalson, Man. Ed. Speer Morgan, Ed. Poems, of any length. Fiction and essays. Pays $20 per printed page, on contract.

725

**MODERN HAIKU**—P.O. Box 1752, Madison, WI 53701–1752. Robert Spiess, Ed. Haiku and articles about haiku. Pays $1 per haiku, $5 a page for articles.

**MONTHLY REVIEW**—122 W. 27th St., New York, NY 10001. Paul M. Sweezy, Harry Magdoff, Eds. Analytical articles, 5,000 words, on politics and economics, from independent socialist viewpoint. Pays $50, on publication.

**MOVING OUT**—P.O. Box 21249, Detroit, MI 48221. Poetry, fiction, articles, and art by women. Submit 4 to 6 poems at a time. Pays in copies.

**NEBO: A LITERARY JOURNAL**—Dept. of English and Foreign Languages, Arkansas Tech. Univ., Russellville, AR 72801–2222. Poems (submit up to 5); mainstream fiction, to 3,000 words; critical essays, to 10 pages. Pays in one copy. SASE required. Offices closed May through August. SASE for guidelines.

**NEGATIVE CAPABILITY**—62 Ridgelawn Dr. E., Mobile, AL 36608. Sue Walker, Ed. Poetry, any length; fiction, essays, art. Pays $20 per story. Contests.

**NEW AUTHOR'S JOURNAL**—1542 Tibbits Ave., Troy, NY 12180. Mario V. Farina, Ed. Fiction, to 3,000 words, and poetry. Topical nonfiction, to 1,000 words. Pays in copies and subscription.

**NEW DELTA REVIEW**—c/o Dept. of English, Louisiana State Univ., Baton Rouge, LA 70803–5001. Janet Wondra, Ed. Semiannual. Fiction and nonfiction, 500 to 5,000 words. Submit up to 4 poems, any length. Also essays, interviews, reviews, and B&W photos or drawings. "We want to see your best work, even if it's been rejected elsewhere." Pays in copies.

**NEW ENGLAND REVIEW**—Middlebury College, Middlebury, VT 05753. T.R. Hummer, Ed. Devon Jersild, Assoc. Ed. Fiction, nonfiction, and poetry of varying lengths. "National, international, literary, political, effectively radical writing." Pays $10 per page, on acceptance, and in copies and subscription.

**NEW LAUREL REVIEW**—828 Lesseps St., New Orleans, LA 70117. Lee Meitzen Grue, Ed. Annual. Fiction, 20 to 40 pages; nonfiction, to 10 pages; poetry, any length. Library market. No inspirational verse. International readership. Pays in one copy.

**NEW LETTERS**—5100 Rockhill Rd., Kansas City, MO 64110–2499. James McKinley, Ed. Fiction, 10 to 25 pages. Poetry, submit 3 to 6 at a time. Send SASE for literary awards guidelines. Manuscripts read October 15 to May 15.

**NEW MEXICO HUMANITIES REVIEW**—Box A, New Mexico Tech., Socorro, NM 87801. Poetry and fiction, to 30 pages, any theme; personal and scholarly essays; articles dealing with southwestern and Native American themes; book reviews. Pays in subscriptions. Annual contests.

**NEW ORLEANS REVIEW**—Loyola Univ., New Orleans, LA 70118. John Mosier, Ed. Literary or film criticism, to 6,000 words. Serious fiction and poetry.

**THE NEW PRESS**—87–40 Francis Lewis Blvd., A44, Queens Village, NY 11427. Bob Abramson, Pub. Quarterly. Fiction and nonfiction, to 2,500 words. Poetry to 200 lines. Pays in copies and occasional honorarium. Annual poetry contest; send SASE for details.

**THE NEW RENAISSANCE**—9 Heath Rd., Arlington, MA 02174. Louise T. Reynolds, Ed. An international magazine of ideas and opinions, emphasizing literature and the arts. Query with SASE, outline, and writing sample for articles; send complete manuscript for essays. "Fiction and poetry must be submitted from January through June. All poetry accepted in 1992 will be for the 1993 and 1994 issues." SASE required. Payment varies, after publication.

726

**THE NEW YORK QUARTERLY**—P.O. Box 693, Old Chelsea Sta., New York, NY 10011. William Packard, Ed. Published three times yearly by The National Poetry Foundation. Poems of any style and persuasion, well written and well intentioned. Pays in copies.

**NEXUS**—Wright State Univ., 006 Univ. Center, Dayton, OH 45435. Kevin Keavney, Ed. Poetry, hard-hitting fiction, photography. Essays on obscure poets, artists, and musicians. Pays in copies.

**NIMROD**—2210 S. Main St., Tulsa, OK 74114–1190. Publishes two issues annually, one awards and one thematic. Quality poetry and fiction, experimental and traditional. Pays $5 a page (to $25) and copies. Annual awards for poetry and fiction. Send #10 SASE for guidelines.

**THE NORTH AMERICAN REVIEW**—Univ. of Northern Iowa, Cedar Falls, IA 50614–0516. Peter Cooley, Poetry Ed. Poetry of high quality. Pays 50¢ a line, on acceptance.

**NORTH ATLANTIC REVIEW**—15 Arbutus Lane, Stony Brook, NY 11790–1408. John Gill, Ed. Annual. Fiction and nonfiction, to 5,000 words; poetry, any length; fillers, humor, photographs and illustrations. A special section on the 60s will be part of each issue. Pays in copies.

**THE NORTH DAKOTA QUARTERLY**—Univ. of North Dakota, Grand Forks, ND 58202–8237. Essays in the humanities; fiction, reviews, graphics, and poetry. Limited market. Pays in copies and subscription.

**NORTHEASTARTS**—Boston Arts Organization, Inc., JFK Sta., P.O. Box 6061, Boston, MA 02114. Mr. Leigh Donaldson, Ed. Fiction and nonfiction, to 750 words; poetry, to 30 lines; and brief humor. "Both professional and beginning writers are considered. No obscene or offensive material." Payment is one copy.

**NORTHWEST REVIEW**—369 PLC, Univ. of Oregon, Eugene, OR 97403. Hannah Wilson, Fiction Ed. Fiction, commentary, essays, and poetry. Reviews. Pays in copies. Send SASE for guidelines.

**THE OHIO REVIEW**—Ellis Hall, Ohio Univ., Athens, OH 45701–2979. Wayne Dodd, Ed. Short stories, poetry, essays, reviews. Pays $5 per page for prose, $1 a line for poetry, plus copies, on publication. SASE required. Submissions not read in June, July, or August.

**ONIONHEAD**—Arts on the Park, Inc., 115 N. Kentucky Ave., Lakeland, FL 33801–5044. Address the Editorial Council. Short stories, to 4,000 words; essays, to 2,500 words; and poetry, to 60 lines; on provocative social, political, and cultural observations and hypotheses. Pays in copies. Send SASE for Wordart poetry contest information.

**ORANGE COAST REVIEW**—Dept. of English, Orange Coast College, 2701 Fairview Rd., Costa Mesa, CA 92628–5005. Short stories, poetry, essays, and interviews, any length. Submit material from December 1 to April 1. Allow six to eight weeks for response. Payment is 2 copies.

**OREGON EAST**—Hoke College Center, EOSC, La Grande, OR 97850. Short fiction, nonfiction, to 3,000 words, poetry, to 60 lines, and high-contrast graphics. Pays in copies. Submissions by March 1, notification by June.

**ORPHIC LUTE**—526 Paul Pl., Los Alamos, NM 87544. Patricia Doherty Hinnebusch, Ed. Brief, structured poems and free verse, to 40 lines. Especially welcome: humorous poetry that is not ribald. Submit 4 to 6 poems at a time. Pays in copies.

**OTHER VOICES**—Univ. of Illinois at Chicago, Dept. of English (M/C 162), Box 4348, Chicago, IL 60680. Lois Hauselman, Sharon Fiffer, Eds. Semiannual. Fresh, accessible short stories, one-act plays, and novel excerpts, to 5,000 words. Pays in copies and modest honorarium. Reading period is from September 1 to May 1.

**OUTERBRIDGE**—College of Staten Island, English Dept. A324, 715 Ocean Terr., Staten Island, NY 10301. Charlotte Alexander, Ed. Annual. Well-crafted stories, about 20 pages, and poetry, to 4 pages, "directed to a wide audience of literate adult readers." Reading period: September to June. Pays in 2 copies.

**PAINTBRUSH**—Language & Literature, Northeast Missouri State Univ., Kirksville, MO 63501. Ben Bennani, Ed. Semiannual. Book reviews, to 1,500 words, and serious, sophisticated poems (submit 3 to 5). Query preferred for book reviews. Pays in copies.

**PAINTED BRIDE QUARTERLY**—230 Vine St., Philadelphia, PA 19106. Fiction and poetry, varying lengths. Pays in subscription.

**PAINTED HILLS REVIEW**—P.O. Box 494, Davis, CA 95617. Michael Ishii, Ed. Kara Kosmatka, Ed. Well-crafted fiction, to 3,500 words and creative nonfiction, to 3,500 words. Poetry, to 100 lines. Pays in one or two copies.

**PANDORA**—2844 Grayson, Ferndale, MI 48220. Meg Mac Donald, Ed. Ruth Berman, Poetry Ed. (2809 Drew Ave. S., Minneapolis, MN 55416). Science fiction and speculative fantasy, to 5,000 words; poetry. "Looking for stories about people, not just ideas or futuristic settings. No futile endings, 'It was a dream/joke, etc.' Avoid contemporary fantasy; we want traditional fantasy." Pays to 2¢ a word for fiction, on publication. Payment varies for poetry and artwork.

**PANHANDLER**—English Dept., Univ. of West Florida, Pensacola, FL 32514–5751. Michael Yots and Stanton Millet, Eds. Semiannual. Fiction, 1,500 to 3,000 words, "that tells a story"; poetry, any length, with a strong sense of colloquial language. Pays in copies.

**THE PARIS REVIEW**—541 E. 72nd St., New York, NY 10021. Address Fiction and Poetry Eds. Fiction and poetry of high literary quality. Pays on publication.

**PARNASSUS**—41 Union Sq. W., Rm. 804, New York, NY 10003. Herbert Leibowitz, Ed. Critical essays and reviews on contemporary poetry. International in scope. Pays in cash and copies.

**PARTISAN REVIEW**—Boston Univ., 236 Bay State Rd., Boston, MA 02215. William Phillips, Ed. Serious fiction, poetry, and essays. Payment varies. No simultaneous submissions.

**PASSAGES NORTH**—Kalamazoo College, 1200 Academy St., Kalamazoo, MI 49007. Ben Mitchell, Ed. Mark Cox, Poetry Ed. Mary LaChapelle, Fiction Ed. Published twice a year in December and June. Poetry, fiction, criticism, essays, visual art. Pays in copies. Frequent prizes and honoraria.

**PEQUOD**—New York Univ. English Dept., 19 University Pl., 2nd Fl., New York, NY 10003. Mark Rudman, Ed. Semiannual. Short stories, essays, and literary criticism, to 10 pages; poetry and translations, to 3 pages. Pays $10 to $25, on publication.

**PERMAFROST**—English Dept., Univ. of Alaska, Fairbanks, AK 99775. Poetry, short fiction to 7,500 words, creative nonfiction and essays, and B&W photos and graphics. Reading periods: September 1 to December 1 and January 15 to April 1. Pays in copies.

**PIEDMONT LITERARY REVIEW**—Bluebird Lane, Rt. #1, Box 512, Forest, VA 24551. Evelyn Miles, Man. Ed. Quarterly. Prose, to 2,500 words. Submit prose to Dr. Olga Kronmeyer, 25 West Dale Dr., Lynchburg, VA 24501. Poems, any length and style. Submit up to 5 poems to Gail White, 1017 Spanish Moss Ln., Breaux Bridge, LA 70517. Submit Asian verse to Dorothy McLaughlin, 10 Atlantic Rd., Somerset, NJ 08873. No pornography. Pays one copy.

**PIG IRON PRESS**—P.O. Box 237, Youngstown, OH 44501–0237. Jim Villani, Ed. Fiction and nonfiction, to 8,000 words. Write for upcoming themes. Poetry, to 100 lines. Pays $5 per published page, on publication.

**THE PINEHURST JOURNAL**—Pinehurst Press, P.O. Box 360747, Milpitas, CA 95036–0747. Michael K. McNamara, Ed. Quarterly. Contemporary and experimental fiction, 750 to 4,000 words. Articles, 1,500 to 3,500 words, on art, music, literature, theater, and opinion; profiles and essays. Poetry to 24 lines. Line art (no photos). Pays $5, on publication, plus one copy, for fiction and nonfiction; pays in one copy for poetry and art. Send #10 SASE for guidelines.

**PIVOT**—250 Riverside Dr., #23, New York, NY 10025. Martin Mitchell, Ed. Poetry, to 75 lines. Reading period is January 1 to June 1. Annual. Pays two copies.

**PLAINS POETRY JOURNAL**—Box 2337, Bismarck, ND 58502–2337. Jane Greer, Ed. Poetry using traditional conventions in vigorous, compelling ways; no greeting card-type verse or prosaic verse. No subject is taboo. Pays in copies.

**PLOUGHSHARES**—Emerson College, 100 Beacon St., Boston, MA 02116–1523. Pays $10 to $50, on publication, and 2 copies. Reading periods vary, check current issue or send #10 SASE for guidelines.

**POEM**—c/o English Dept., U.A.H., Huntsville, AL 35899. Nancy Frey Dillard, Ed. Serious lyric poetry. Pays in copies.

**POET AND CRITIC**—203 Ross Hall, Iowa State Univ., Ames, IA 50011–1201. Neal Bowers, Ed. Poetry, reviews, essays on contemporary poetry. No manuscripts read June through August. Pays in copies.

**POET LORE**—7815 Old Georgetown Rd., Bethesda, MD 20814. Sunil Freeman, Man. Ed. Original poetry, all kinds. Translations, reviews, and critical essays. Pays in copies. Annual narrative poetry contest.

**POET MAGAZINE**—Submission Dept., P.O. Box 54947, Oklahoma City, OK 73154. "Dedicated to publishing new and experienced poets and writers." Submit copies of up to five poems, any subject, form, or length, and articles of any length on subjects related to poetry. Include SASE for editorial reply; manuscripts will not be returned. There is no payment; contributors receive tearsheets of their published work. Published quarterly.

**POETRY**—60 West Walton St., Chicago, IL 60610. Joseph Parisi, Ed. Poetry of highest quality. Submit 3 to 4 poems. Allow 8 to 10 weeks for response. Pays $2 a line, on publication.

**POETRY EAST**—DePaul University, 802 W. Belden Ave., Chicago, IL 60614–3214. Marilyn Woitel, Man. Ed. Published in spring and fall. Poetry, essays, and translations. "Please send a sampling of your best work. Do not send book-length manuscripts without querying first." Pays in copies.

**PORTLAND REVIEW**—c/o Portland State Univ., P.O. Box 751, Portland, OR 97207. Semiannual. Short fiction, essays, poetry, one-act plays (to 5 pages), photography, and artwork. "Please include a bio." Payment is one copy.

**PRAIRIE SCHOONER**—201 Andrews Hall, Univ. of Nebraska, Lincoln, NE 68588–0334. Hilda Raz, Ed. Short stories, poetry, essays, book reviews, and translations. Pays in copies. Annual contests. SASE required.

**PRIMAVERA**—Box 37–7547, Chicago, IL 60637. Attn: Editorial Board. Fiction and poetry that focuses on the experiences of women; "author need not be female." B&W photos and drawings. Published annually. Pays in two copies.

**PRISM INTERNATIONAL**—E459–1866 Main Mall, Dept. of Creative Writing, Univ. of British Columbia, Vancouver, B.C., Canada V6T 1Z1. High-quality fiction, poetry, drama, creative nonfiction, and literature in translation, varying lengths. Include international reply coupons. Pays $20 per published page. Annual short fiction contest.

**PROOF ROCK**—P.O. Box 607, Halifax, VA 24558. Don Conner, Fiction Ed. Serena Fusek, Poetry Ed. Fiction, to 2,500 words. Poetry, to 32 lines. Reviews. Pays in copies.

**PUCKERBRUSH REVIEW**—76 Main St., Orono, ME 94473. Constance Hunting, Ed. Literary fiction, criticism, and poetry of various lengths, "to bring literary Maine news to readers." Pays in two copies; published semiannually.

**PUDDING MAGAZINE**—c/o Pudding House Bed & Breakfast for Writers, 60 N. Main St., Johnstown, OH 43031. Jennifer Bosveld, Ed. "The International Journal of Applied Poetry." Poems on popular culture, social concerns, personal struggle; poetry therapy that has been revised for art's sake; articles/essays on poetry in the human services.

**PUERTO DEL SOL**—New Mexico State Univ., Box 3E, Las Cruces, NM 88003–0001. Kevin McIlvoy, Ed. Short stories and personal essays, to 30 pages; novel excerpts, to 65 pages; articles, to 45 pages, and reviews, to 15 pages. Poetry, photos. Pays in copies.

**PULPHOUSE: A FICTION MAGAZINE**—P.O. Box 1227, Eugene, OR 97440. Dean Wesley Smith, Ed./Pub. Fiction, 5,000 words: SF, fantasy, horror, mystery, romance, western, and mainstream. Nonfiction, to 5,000 words: articles, essays, interviews, and news items that are controversial or innovative with a futuristic slant. Occasionally uses poetry. Query for nonfiction only. Pays 4¢ to 7¢, on publication. Overstocked; closed to submissions until September 93.

**THE QUARTERLY**—201 East 50th, New York, NY 10022. Gordon Lish, Ed. "The Magazine of New Writing." Fiction, nonfiction, poetry, and humor, no limits on length. Payment varies, after publication.

**QUARTERLY WEST**—317 Olpin Union, Univ. of Utah, Salt Lake City, UT 84112. Tom Hazuka and Bernard Wood, Eds. Short shorts and poetry. Biennial novella competition in even-numbered years. Pays $25 to $50 for stories, $25 for poems.

**RACCOON**—Ion Books, Inc., Box 111327, Memphis, TN 38111–1327. David Spicer, Ed. Poetry and poetic criticism, varying lengths. Pays in subscription for poetry, $50 for criticism, fiction.

**RAG MAG**—P.O. Box 12, Goodhue, MN 55027–0188. Beverly Voldseth, Ed. Semiannual. Fiction and nonfiction, to 1,000 words. Poetry any length. No religious writing. Pays in copies.

**RAMBUNCTIOUS REVIEW**—1221 W. Pratt Blvd., Chicago, IL 60626. Mary Dellutri, Richard Goldman, Nancy Lennon, Beth Hausler, Eds. Fiction, to 12 pages; poems, submit up to 5 at a time. Pays in copies. Submit material September through May. Contests.

**RECONSTRUCTION**—1563 Massachusetts Ave., Cambridge, MA 02138. Randall Kennedy, Pub. Quarterly. Articles, 2,000 to 40,000 words, on "important political, social, and cultural issues involving race relations. It is particularly concerned with providing a forum for uninhibited commentary on African-American politics, society, and culture." Payment is negotiable. Queries preferred.

**RED CEDAR REVIEW**—Dept. of English, 17-C Morrill Hall, Michigan State Univ., East Lansing, MI 48824–1036. Fiction, to 15 pages; poetry (submit up to 5); interviews; book reviews; graphics; and one-act dramas. Pays in copies.

**THE REDNECK REVIEW OF LITERATURE**—2919 N. Downer Ave., Milwaukee, WI 53211. Penelope Reedy, Ed. Semiannual. Fiction, to 2,500 words, of the contemporary American West; essays and book reviews, 300 to 1,500 words; poetry. Pays in copies.

**RELIGION AND PUBLIC EDUCATION**—E261 Lagomarcino Hall, Iowa State Univ., Ames, IA 50011. Charles R. Kniker, Ed.-in-Chief. Paul Blakely, Poetry Ed. Poems with mythological or religious values or themes. Pays in copies.

**RESONANCE**—P.O. Box 215, Beacon, NY 12508. Evan Pritchard, Ed. Published three times a year. Fiction, to 1,200 words; thematic nonfiction, to 1,200 words; poetry, to 46 lines. Pays one copy.

**REVIEW: LATIN AMERICAN LITERATURE AND ARTS**—Americas Society, 680 Park Ave., New York, NY 10021. Alfred J. MacAdam, Ed. Published twice yearly. Work in English translation by and about young and established Latin American writers; essays and book reviews considered. Send queries for 1,000- to 1,500-word manuscripts, and short poem translations. Payment varies, on acceptance.

**RHINO**—8403 W. Normal Ave., Niles, IL 60648. Kay Meier and Martha Vertreace, Eds. "Authentic emotion in well-crafted poetry." January to June reading period. Pays in copies.

**RIVER CITY**—Dept. of English, Memphis State Univ., Memphis, TN 38152. Amy Palughi, Man. Ed. Poems, short stories, essays and interviews. No novel excerpts. Pay varies according to grants. No reading May through August. Contests.

**RIVER STYX**—14 S. Euclid, St. Louis, MO 63108. Lee Fournier, Ed. Published 3 times a year. Fiction, personal essays, literary interviews, poetry, and B&W photos. Submit between September 1st and October 31st; reports in 12 weeks. Payment is $8 per printed page and two copies.

**RIVERSIDE QUARTERLY**—Box 5507, Drew Sta., Lake Charles, LA 70606. Leland Sapiro, Ed. Science fiction and fantasy, to 3,500 words; reviews, criticism, any maximum length; poetry and letters. "Read magazine before submitting." Send poetry to Sheryl Smith, 515 Saratoga #2, Santa Clara, CA 95050; fiction to Redd Boggs, Box 1111, Berkeley, CA 94701. Buys first rights only. Pays in copies.

**ROANOKE REVIEW**—Roanoke College, Salem, VA 24153. Robert R. Walter, Ed. Quality short fiction, to 7,500 words, and poetry, to 100 lines. Pays in copies.

**ROMANCING THE PAST**—17239 S. Oak Park Ave. #207, Tinley Park, IL 60477. Michelle Regan, Ed. Bimonthly. Nostalgia and historical material: fiction and nonfiction, to 10 pages, and poetry. Pays in copies.

**SAN FERNANDO POETRY JOURNAL**—18301 Halstead St., Northridge, CA 91325. Richard Cloke, Ed. Quality poetry, 20 to 100 lines, with social content; scientific, philosophic, and historical themes. Pays in copies.

**SAN JOSE STUDIES**—c/o English Dept., San Jose State Univ., San Jose,

CA 95192. Fauneil J. Rinn, Ed. Poetry, fiction, and essays on interdisciplinary topics. Occasionally publishes photos and art. Pays in copies. Annual awards.

**SANSKRIT LITERARY/ART PUBLICATION**—Univ. of North Carolina/Charlotte, Charlotte, NC 28223–0001. Jeff Byers, Ed.-in-Chief. Annual. Poetry, short fiction, photos, and fine art.

**SCANDINAVIAN REVIEW**—725 Park Ave., New York, NY 10021. Essays on contemporary Scandinavia. Fiction and poetry, translated from Nordic languages. Pays from $100, on publication.

**SCRIVENER**—McGill Univ., 853 Sherbrooke St. W., Montreal, Quebec, Canada H3A 2T6. Sam Anson, Thea Boyanowsky, Eds. Poem, submit 5 to 15; prose, to 20 pages; reviews, to 5 pages; essays, to 10 pages. Photography and graphics. Pays in copies.

**THE SEATTLE REVIEW**—Padelford Hall, GN-30, Univ. of Washington, Seattle, WA 98195. Donna Gerstenberger, Ed. Short stories, to 20 pages, poetry, essays on the craft of writing, and interviews with northwest writers. Payment varies. Reading period: September 1 through May 31.

**SENECA REVIEW**—Hobart & William Smith Colleges, Geneva, NY 14456. Deborah Tall, Ed. Poetry, translations, and essays on contemporary poetry. Pays in copies.

**SHOOTING STAR REVIEW**—7123 Race St., Pittsburgh, PA 15208. Sandra Gould Ford, Pub. Fiction and folktales, to 3,500 words, essays, to 2,500 words, and poetry, to 50 lines, on the African-American experience. Query for book reviews only. Pays from $4 and in copies. Send SASE for topic deadlines.

**SHORT FICTION BY WOMEN**—Box 1276, Stuyvesant Station, New York, NY 10009. Rachel Whalen, Ed. Short stories, novellas, and novel excerpts, to 20,000 words, by women writers. "Stories do not need a feminist slant to be acceptable." No horror, romance, or mystery fiction. Published three times yearly. Payment varies, on acceptance.

**SHORT STORY DIGEST**—Caldwell Publishing, P.O. Box 1183, Richardson, TX 87083. Wayne Caldwell, Ed. Fiction, to 3,000 words. Drawings and B&W photos. Quarterly. Pays 1¢ per word, on publication.

**SING HEAVENLY MUSE! WOMEN'S POETRY & PROSE**—P.O. Box 13320, Minneapolis, MN 55414. Short stories and essays, to 5,000 words. Poetry. Query for themes and reading periods. Pays in copies.

**SKYLARK**—2200 169th St., Hammond, IN 46323–2094. Pamela Hunter, Ed. "The Fine Arts Annual of Purdue Calumet." Fiction and articles, to 5,000 words. Poetry, to 25 lines. B&W prints and drawings. Deadline is May 15th for fall publication. Pays in one copy.

**SLIPSTREAM**—Box 2071, Niagara Falls, NY 14301. Contemporary poetry, any length. Pays in copies. Query for themes. (Also accepting cassette tape submissions for audio poetics tape series: spoken word, collaborations, songs, audio experimentation.) Guidelines. Annual poetry chapbook contest has a December 1 deadline; send SASE for details.

**THE SMALL POND MAGAZINE**—P.O. Box 664, Stratford, CT 06497–0664. Napoleon St. Cyr, Ed. Published three times a year. Fiction, to 2,500 words; poetry, to 100 lines. Query for nonfiction. SASE required. Include short bio. Pays in copies.

**SMALL PRESS REVIEW**—Box 100, Paradise, CA 95967. Len Fulton, Ed.

News pieces and reviews, to 200 words, about small presses and little magazines. Pays in copies.

**SNOWY EGRET**—P.O. Box 9, Bowling Green, IN 47833. Karl Barnebey and Michael Aycock, Eds. Poetry, fiction, and nonfiction, to 10,000 words. Natural history from artistic, literary, philosophical, and historical perspectives. Pays $2 per page for prose; $2 to $4 for poetry, on publication.

**SONORA REVIEW**—Dept. of English, Univ. of Arizona, Tucson, AZ 85721. Address Fiction, Poetry, or Nonfiction Editor. Fiction, poetry, translations, interviews, literary nonfiction. Personal essays, memoirs, creative nonfiction. Pays in copies. Annual prizes for fiction and poetry.

**THE SOUTH CAROLINA REVIEW**—Dept. of English, Clemson Univ., Clemson, SC 29634–1503. Richard J. Calhoun, Exec. Ed. Published twice a year. Fiction, essays, reviews, and interviews of up to 4,000 words. Short poems. Send complete ms.; query Mark Royden Winchell for book reviews. Pays in copies. Response time is 6 to 9 months. No manuscripts read in summer or December.

**SOUTH COAST POETRY JOURNAL**—English Dept., CSUF, Fullerton, CA 92634. John J. Brugaletta, Ed. Semiannual. Poetry, to 40 lines. Only unpublished and uncommitted poetry, please. "Our editorial tastes are eclectic, ranging from the strictly metered and rhymed to free verse and including virtually every mixture in between." Payment is in one copy.

**SOUTH DAKOTA REVIEW**—Box 111, Univ. Exchange, Vermillion, SD 57069–2390. John R. Milton, Ed. Exceptional fiction, 3,000 to 5,000 words, and poetry, 10 to 25 lines. Critical articles, especially on American literature, Western American literature, theory and esthetics, 3,000 to 5,000 words. Pays in copies.

**THE SOUTHERN CALIFORNIA ANTHOLOGY**—c/o Master of Professional Writing Program, WPH 404, Univ. of Southern California, Los Angeles, CA 90089–4034. James Ragan, Ed.-in-Chief. Richard Aloia, Man. Ed. Fiction, to 20 pages, and poetry, to 5 pages. Pays in copies.

**SOUTHERN EXPOSURE**—P.O. Box 531, Durham, NC 27702. Eric Bates, Ed. Quarterly forum on "Southern movements for social change." Short stories, to 4,500 words, essays, investigative journalism, and oral histories, 500 to 4,500 words. Pays $25 to $200, on publication. Query.

**SOUTHERN HUMANITIES REVIEW**—9088 Haley Center, Auburn Univ., Auburn, AL 36849. Dan R. Latimer, R. T. Smith, Eds. Short stories, essays, and criticism, 3,500 to 5,000 words; poetry, to 2 pages.

**SOUTHERN POETRY REVIEW**—Dept. of English, Univ. of North Carolina, Charlotte, NC 28223. Lucinda Grey and Ken McLaurin, Eds. Poems. No restrictions on style, length, or content. No manuscripts read in the summer.

**THE SOUTHERN REVIEW**—43 Allen Hall, Louisiana State Univ., Baton Rouge, LA 70803. James Olney and Dave Smith, Eds. Emphasis on contemporary literature in United States and abroad with special interest in southern culture and history. Fiction and essays, 4,000 to 8,000 words. Serious poetry of highest quality. Pays $12 a page for prose, $20 a page for poetry, on publication.

**SOUTHWEST REVIEW**—307 Fondren Library West, Box 4374, Southern Methodist Univ., Dallas, TX 75275. Willard Spiegelman, Ed. "A quarterly that serves the interests of the region but is not bound by them." Fiction, essays, and interviews with well-known writers, 3,000 to 7,500 words. Poetry. Pays varying rates.

**SOU'WESTER**—Southern Illinois Univ. at Edwardsville, Edwardsville, IL 62026–1438. Fred W. Robbins, Man. Ed. Fiction, to 8,000 words. Poetry, any length. Pays in copies.

**SPECTRUM**—Anna Maria College, Box 72-A, Paxton, MA 01612–1198. Robert H. Goepfert, Ed. Scholarly articles, 3,000 to 15,000 words; short stories, to 10 pages; and poetry, to 2 pages; book reviews, photos, and artwork. Pays $20 plus 2 copies. SASE required.

**THE SPOON RIVER QUARTERLY**—Dept. of English, Stevenson Hall, Illinois State Univ., Normal, IL 61761. Lucia Cordell Getsi, Ed. Poetry, any length. Pays in copies.

**SPSM&H**—329 E St., Bakersfield, CA 93304. Frederick A. Raborg, Jr., Ed. Single sonnets, sequences, essays about the sonnet, short fiction in which the sonnet plays a part, books, and anthologies. Pays $10, plus copies.

**STAND MAGAZINE**—P.O. Box 2812, Huntsville, AL 35804. Jessie Emerson, Ed. Fiction, 3,500 to 4,000 words, and poetry to 100 lines. No formulaic verse. Pays varying rates, on publication.

**STORY QUARTERLY**—P.O. Box 1416, Northbrook, IL 60065. Anne Brashler, Diane Williams, Eds. Short stories and interviews. Pays in copies.

**STUDIES IN AMERICAN FICTION**—English Dept., Northeastern Univ., Boston, MA 02115. James Nagel, Ed. Reviews, 750 words; scholarly essays, 2,500 to 6,500 words, on American fiction. Pays in copies.

**THE SUN**—The Sun Publishing Co., 107 N. Roberson St., Chapel Hill, NC 27516. Sy Safransky, Ed. Articles, essays, interviews, and fiction, to 10,000 words; poetry; photos, illustrations, and cartoons. "We're interested in all writing that makes sense and enriches our common space." Pays $100 for fiction and essays, $25 for poetry, on publication.

**SWAMP ROOT**—Route 2, Box 1098, Hiwassee One, Jacksboro, TN 37757. Al Masarik, Ed. Published three times a year. Poetry, any length, any style. Essays, reviews, letters, and interviews related to poetry. Query for artwork. SASE required. Pays in copies and subscription.

**SYCAMORE REVIEW**—Purdue Univ., Dept. of English, West Lafayette, IN 47907. Michael D. Kiser, Ed.-in-Chief. Semiannual. Poetry, short fiction (no genre fiction), personal essays, and translations, to 10,000 words. Pays in copies. Reading period: September to April.

**TAR RIVER POETRY**—Dept. of English, East Carolina Univ., Greenville, NC 27834. Peter Makuck, Ed. Poetry and reviews. "Interested in skillful use of language, vivid imagery. Less academic, more powerful poetry preferred." Submit from September to November or January to April. Pays in copies.

**THE TEXAS REVIEW**—English Dept., Sam Houston State Univ., Huntsville, TX 77341. Paul Ruffin, Ed. Fiction, poetry, articles, to 20 typed pages. Reviews. Pays in copies and subscription.

**THEMA**—Box 74109, Metairie, LA 70033–4109. Virginia Howard, Ed. Fiction, to 20 pages, and poetry to 2 pages, related to theme. Pays $25 per story; $10 per short-short, poem, or B&W artwork or photo, on acceptance. Send SASE for themes and guidelines.

**THIRTEEN**—Box 392, Portlandville, NY 13834–0392. Ken Stone, Ed. Quarterly. Thirteen-line poetry. Pays in one copy.

**THE THREEPENNY REVIEW**—P.O. Box 9131, Berkeley, CA 94709. Wendy Lesser, Ed. Fiction, to 5,000 words. Poetry, to 100 lines. Essays, on books, theater, film, dance, music, art, television, and politics, 1,500 to 3,000 words. Pays to $100, on acceptance. Limited market. Query first with SASE for guidelines.

**TIGHTROPE**—323 Pelham Rd., Amherst, MA 01002. Ed Rayher, Ed. Limited-edition, letterpress semiannual. Fiction and nonfiction, to 10 pages; poetry, any length. Pays in copies.

**TRANSLATION**—The Translation Center, 412 Dodge Hall, Columbia Univ., New York, NY 10027. Frank MacShane, Dir. Semiannual. New translations of contemporary foreign fiction and poetry.

**TRIQUARTERLY**—Northwestern Univ., 2020 Ridge Ave., Evanston, IL 60208–4302. Serious, aesthetically informed and inventive poetry and prose, for an international and literate audience. Pays $20 per page for prose, $1.50 per line for poetry. Reading period October 1 to April 30. Allow 10 to 12 weeks for reply.

**TRIVIA**—P.O. Box 606, N. Amherst, MA 01059. Erin Rice, Kay Parkhurst, Eds. Semiannual journal of feminist writing. Literary essays, experimental prose, translations, interviews, and reviews. "After readings": essay reviews on books written by women. Pays in copies. Guidelines.

**2AM MAGAZINE**—P.O. Box 6754, Rockford, IL 61125–1754. Gretta Anderson, Ed. Poetry, articles, reviews, and personality profiles, 500 to 2,000 words, as well as fantasy, horror, and some science fiction/sword-and-sorcery short stories, 500 to 5,000 words. Pays ½¢ a word, on acceptance.

**VANDELOECHT'S FICTION MAGAZINE**—P.O. Box 515, Montross, VA 22520. Mike Vandeloecht, Ed. Quarterly. Fiction, to 2,500 words: adventure, contemporary, experimental, fantasy, horror, mystery, science fiction, suspense. No pornography. Free verse and traditional poetry, to 25 lines. Pays one copy.

**THE UNIVERSITY OF PORTLAND REVIEW**—Univ. of Portland, Portland, OR 97203. Thompson M. Faller, Ed. Scholarly articles and contemporary fiction, 500 to 2,500 words. Poetry. Book reviews. Pays in copies.

**UNIVERSITY OF WINDSOR REVIEW**—Dept. of English, Univ. of Windsor, Windsor, Ont., Canada N9B 3P4. Joseph A. Quinn, Ed. Short stories, poetry. Pays $10 to $50, on publication.

**VERVE**—P.O. Box 3205, Simi Valley, CA 93093. Ron Reichick, Ed. Contemporary fiction and nonfiction, to 1,000 words, that fits the theme of the issue. Poetry, to two pages; submit up to 5 poems. Pays in one copy. Query for themes.

**THE VILLAGER**—135 Midland Ave., Bronxville, NY 10708. Amy Murphy, Ed. Fiction, 900 to 1,500 words: mystery, adventure, humor, romance. Short, preferably seasonal poetry. Pays in copies.

**VIRGINIA QUARTERLY REVIEW**—One West Range, Charlottesville, VA 22903. Quality fiction and poetry. Serious essays and articles, 3,000 to 6,000 words, on literature, science, politics, economics, etc. Pays $10 per page for prose, $1 per line for poetry, on publication.

**VISIONS INTERNATIONAL**—1110 Seaton Lane, Falls Church, VA 22046. Bradley R. Strahan, Ed. Published 3 times a year. Poetry, to 40 lines, and B&W drawings. (Query first for artwork.) "Nothing amateurish or previously published." Pays in copies.

**WASCANA REVIEW**—c/o Dept. of English, Univ. of Regina, Regina, Sask.,

Canada S4S 0A2. Joan Givner, Ed. Short stories, 2,000 to 6,000 words; critical articles; poetry. Pays $3 per page for prose, $10 for poetry, after publication.

**WASHINGTON REVIEW**—P.O. Box 50132, Washington, DC 20091–0132. Clarissa Wittenberg, Ed. Poetry; articles on literary, performing and fine arts in the Washington, D.C., area. Fiction, 1,000 to 2,500 words. Area writers preferred. Pays in copies.

**WEBSTER REVIEW**—Webster Univ., 470 E. Lockwood, Webster Groves, MO 63119. Nancy Schapiro, Ed. Fiction; poetry; interviews; essays; translations. Pays in copies.

**WEST**—Bluestone Press, P.O. Box 1186, Hampshire College, Amherst, MA 01002. John C. Horoschak, Ed. Short fiction, to 30 pages, and poetry, to 15 pages. "We are open to all kinds of short fiction and poetry, although overtly political submissions are discouraged. Pen-and-ink drawings. Pays in copies.

**WEST BRANCH**—Bucknell Hall, Bucknell Univ., Lewisburg, PA 17837. Karl Patten, Robert Taylor, Eds. Poetry and fiction. Pays in copies and subscriptions.

**WESTERN HUMANITIES REVIEW**—Univ. of Utah, Salt Lake City, UT 84112. Kristoffer Jacobson, Man. Ed. Quarterly. Fiction and essays, to 30 pages, and poetry. Pays $50 for poetry, $150 for short stories and essays, on acceptance.

**THE WESTMINSTER REVIEW**—Dept. of English, Westminster College, New Wilmington, PA 16172. David Swerdlow, Ed. Poetry and fiction. "Interested in writing that explores the frontier between knowledge and mystery." No traditional verse forms, sentimentality, or work that is merely experimental. Submissions accepted September 15 to May 15. Pays in copies. SASE required. Allow 8 to 12 weeks for response.

**THE WILLIAM AND MARY REVIEW**—P.O. Box 8795, College of William and Mary, Williamsburg, VA 23187–8795. Alexandra Nemecek, Ed. Annual. Fiction, critical essays, and interviews, 2,500 to 7,500 words; poetry, all genres (submit 5 to 8 poems). Submissions accepted September through December 31. Responds in 3 months. Pays in copies.

**WIND**—RFD #1-Box 809K, Pikeville, KY 41501. Quentin Howard, Ed. Semiannual. Short stories and poems. Reviews of books from small presses, to 250 words. Pays in copies.

**WINDFALL**—Dept. of English, UW-Whitewater, Whitewater, WI 53190. Ron Ellis, Ed. Semiannual. Intense, highly crafted, lyric poetry. (Occasionally consider poems longer than one page.) No dot matrix or poor copies will be considered. Pays in one copy.

**THE WINDLESS ORCHARD**—Dept. of English, Indiana-Purdue Univ., Ft. Wayne, IN 46805. Robert Novak, Ed. Contemporary poetry. Pays in copies. SASE required.

**WITHOUT HALOS**—Ocean County Poets Collective, P.O. Box 1342, Point Pleasant Beach, NJ 08742. Frank Finale, Ed. Submit 3 to 5 poems (to 2 pages) between January 1 and June 30. Pays in copies.

**WITNESS**—Oakland Community College, 27055 Orchard Lake Rd., Farmington Hills, MI 48334. Peter Stine, Ed. Thematic journal. Fiction and essays, 5 to 20 pages, and poems (submit up to 3). Pays $6 per page for prose, $10 per page for poetry, on publication.

**WOMAN OF POWER**—P.O. Box 2785, Orleans, MA 02653. Char McKee,

Ed. A magazine of feminism, spirituality, and politics. Nonfiction, to 3,500 words. Send SASE for issue themes and guidelines. Pays in copies and subscription.

**THE WORCESTER REVIEW**—6 Chatham St., Worcester, MA 01609. Rodger Martin, Ed. Poetry (submit up to 5 poems at a time), fiction, critical articles about poetry, and articles and reviews with a New England connection. Pays in copies.

**THE WORMWOOD REVIEW**—P.O. Box 4698, Stockton, CA 95204–0698. Marvin Malone, Ed. Quarterly. Poetry and prose-poetry, 4 to 400 lines. "We encourage wit and conciseness." Pays 3 to 20 copies or cash equivalent.

**WRITERS FORUM**—Univ. of Colorado, Colorado Springs, CO 80933–7150. Alex Blackburn, Ed. Annual. Mainstream and experimental fiction, 1,000 to 10,000 words. Poetry (one to five poems per submission). Emphasis on western themes and writers. Send material October through May. Pays in copies.

**WRITERS ON THE RIVER**—P.O. Box 40828, Memphis, TN 38174. Miss Demaris C. Smith, Ed. Peggy Burdick, Prose Ed. Pansy Shirley, Poetry Ed. Fiction (adventure, fantasy, historical, humor, mainstream, mystery/suspense) and nonfiction (profiles, scholarly essays, regional history), to 2,500 words. "We try to promote good writing and act as a sounding board for Southern writers." Submit two copies of manuscripts. Submissions accepted from: Arkansas, Alabama, Mississippi, Louisiana, Tennessee, Kentucky, and Missouri. Pays in copies.

**WYOMING, THE HUB OF THE WHEEL**—The Willow Bee Publishing House, Box 9, Saratoga, WY 82331. Dawn Senior, Man. Ed. Fiction and nonfiction, to 1,500 words; poetry, to 80 lines. "An international literary/art magazine devoted to peace, the human race, positive relationships, and the human spirit and possibilities." Pays in copies. Query first with SASE.

**XANADU**—Box 773, Huntington, NY 11743–0773. Pat Nesbitt, Mildred Jeffrey, Barbara Lucas, Eds. Barry Fruchter, Articles Ed. Weslea Sidon, Asst. Ed. Poetry on a variety of topics; no length restrictions. Pays in copies.

**YALE REVIEW**—1902A Yale Sta., New Haven, CT 06520. J.D. McClatchy, Ed. Serious poetry, to 200 lines, and fiction, 3,000 to 5,000 words. Pays average of $300.

**YARROW**—English Dept., Lytle Hall, Kutztown State Univ., Kutztown, PA 19530. Harry Humes, Ed. Semiannual. Poetry. "Just good, solid, clear writing. We don't have room for long poems." Pays in copies.

**ZYZZYVA**—41 Sutter, Suite 1400, San Francisco, CA 94104. Howard Junker, Ed. Publishes work of West Coast writers only: fiction, essays, and poetry. Pays $50 to $250, on acceptance.

# HUMOR, FILLERS, AND SHORT ITEMS

Magazines noted for their excellent filler departments, plus a cross-section of publications using humor, short items, jokes, quizzes, and cartoons, follow. However, almost all magazines use some type of filler material, and writers can find dozens of markets by studying copies of magazines at a library or newsstand.

**THE AMERICAN FIELD**—542 S. Dearborn, Chicago, IL 60605. B.J. Matthys, Ed. Short fact items and anecdotes on hunting dogs and field trials for bird dogs. Pays varying rates, on acceptance.

**THE AMERICAN NEWSPAPER CARRIER**—P.O. Box 2225, Kernersville, NC 27285. W.H. Lowry, Ed. Short, humorous pieces, to 1,200 words, for preteen, teenage, and adult newspaper carriers. Pays $25, on publication.

**ARMY MAGAZINE**—2425 Wilson Blvd., Arlington, VA 22201-3385. L. James Binder, Ed.-in-Chief. True anecdotes on military subjects. Pays $25 to $50, on publication.

**THE ATLANTIC**—745 Boylston St., Boston, MA 02116. Sophisticated humorous or satirical pieces, 1,000 to 3,000 words. Some light poetry. Pays from $500 for prose, on acceptance.

**ATLANTIC SALMON JOURNAL**—P.O. Box 429, St. Andrews, N.B., Canada E0G 2X0. Harry Bruce, Ed. Fillers, 50 to 100 words, on salmon politics, conservation, and nature. Pays $25 for fillers, on publication.

**BICYCLING**—33 E. Minor St., Emmaus, PA 18098. Anecdotes, helpful cycling tips, and other items for "Paceline" section, 150 to 250 words. Pays $50, on acceptance.

**BIKEREPORT**—Bikecentennial, P.O. Box 8308, Missoula, MT 59807. Daniel D'Ambrosio, Ed. News shorts from the bicycling world for "In Bicycle Circles." Pays $5 to $10, on publication.

**BYLINE**—Box 130596, Edmond, OK 73013. Marcia Preston, Ed.-in-Chief. Humor, 400 to 800 words, about writing. Pays $50 for humor, on acceptance.

**CAPPER'S**—616 Jefferson St., Topeka, KS 66607-1188. Nancy Peavler, Ed. Household hints, recipes, jokes. Pays varying rates, on publication.

**CASCADES EAST**—716 N. E. 4th St., P. O. Box 5784, Bend, OR 97708. Geoff Hill, Ed. Fillers related to travel, history, and recreation in central Oregon. Pays 3¢ to 10¢ a word, extra for photos, on publication.

**CATHOLIC DIGEST**—P.O. Box 64090, St. Paul, MN 55164-0090. No fiction. Articles, 200 to 500 words, on instances of kindness rewarded, for "Hearts Are Trumps." Stories about conversions, for "Open Door." Reports of tactful remarks or actions, for "The Perfect Assist." Accounts of good deeds, for "People Are Like That." Humorous pieces, 50 to 300 words, on parish life, for "In Our Parish." Amusing signs, for "Signs of the Times." Jokes; fillers. Pays $4 to $50, on publication. Manuscripts cannot be acknowledged or returned.

**CHICKADEE**—56 The Esplanade, Suite 306, Toronto, Ont., Canada M5E 1A7. Humorous juvenile poetry, 10 to 15 lines, about animals and nature. (Also humorous fiction, 800 words.) Pays on acceptance. Enclose international reply coupons.

**CHILDREN'S PLAYMATE**—1100 Waterway Blvd., P. O. Box 567, Indianapolis, IN 46206. Elizabeth Rinck, Ed. Puzzles, games, mazes for children, ages six to eight, emphasizing health, safety, and nutrition. Pays about 10¢ a word (varies on puzzles), on acceptance.

**THE CHURCH MUSICIAN**—127 Ninth Ave. N., Nashville, TN 37234.

738

W. M. Anderson, Ed. For Southern Baptist music leaders. Humorous fillers with a music slant. No clippings. Pays around 5¢ a word, on acceptance. Same address and requirements for *Glory Songs* and *The Senior Musician*.

**COLUMBIA JOURNALISM REVIEW**—Columbia University, 700 Journalism Bldg., New York, NY 10027. Gloria Cooper, Man. Ed. Amusing mistakes in news stories, headlines, photos, etc. (original clippings required), for "Lower Case." Pays $25, on publication.

**CORPORATE CASHFLOW**—6255 Barfield Rd., Atlanta, GA 30328. Dick Gamble, Ed. Fillers, to 1,000 words, on varied aspects of treasury management and corporate finance, for treasury managers in public and private companies. Pays on publication. Query.

**COUNTRY WOMAN**—P. O. Box 643, Milwaukee, WI 53201. Kathy Pohl, Man. Ed. Short rhymed verse, 4 to 20 lines, and fillers, to 250 words, on the rural experience. All material must be positive and upbeat. Pays $10 to $50, on acceptance.

**CRACKED**—Globe Communications, Inc., 441 Lexington Ave., 2nd Fl., New York, NY 10017. Andy Simmons, Ed. Humor, to 5 pages, for 12- to 15-year-old readers. "Queries are not necessary, but read the magazine before submitting material!" Pays from $100 per page, on acceptance.

**CURRENT COMEDY**—165 W. 47th St., New York, NY 10036. Gary Apple, Ed. Original, funny, performable one-liners and brief jokes on news, fads, topical subjects, business, etc. Jokes for roasts, retirement dinners, and for speaking engagements. Humorous material specifically geared for public speaking situations such as microphone feedback, hecklers, etc. Also interested in longer original jokes and anecdotes that can be used by public speakers. Pays $12, after publication. SASE for guidelines.

**CYCLE WORLD**—1499 Monrovia Ave., Newport Beach, CA 92663. David Edwards, Ed. News items on motorcycle industry, legislation, trends. Pays on publication.

**THE ELKS MAGAZINE**—425 W. Diversey Pkwy., Chicago, IL 60614. Fred D. Oakes, Ed. Informative or humorous pieces, to 2,500 words. No fillers. Pays from $150, on acceptance. Query required.

**FACES**—30 Grove St., Peterborough, NH 03458. Carolyn Yoder, Ed. Puzzles, mazes, crosswords, and picture puzzles, related to monthly themes, for children. Send SASE for list of themes before submitting.

**FATE**—P.O. Box 64383, St. Paul, MN 55164–0383. Phyllis Galde, Ed. Factual fillers, to 300 words, on strange or psychic happenings. True stories, to 300 words, on psychic or mystic personal experiences. Pays 10¢ a word. Send SASE for guidelines.

**FIELD & STREAM**—2 Park Ave., New York, NY 10016. Duncan Barnes, Ed. Fillers on hunting, fishing, camping, etc., to 1,000 words. Cartoons. Pays $75 to $250 for fillers, $100 for cartoons, on acceptance.

**GALLERY**—401 Park Ave. S., New York, NY 10016–8802. Barry Janoff, Ed. Dir. Peter Emshwiller, Man. Ed. Short humor, satire, and short service features for men. Pays varying rates, half on acceptance and half on publication. Query.

**GAMES**—19 W. 21st St., New York, NY 10010. Will Shortz, Ed. Pencil puzzles, visual brainteasers, and pop culture tests. Humor and playfulness a plus; quality a must. Pays top rates, on publication.

739

**GLAMOUR**—350 Madison Ave., New York, NY 10017. Articles, 1,000 words, for "Viewpoint" section: opinion pieces for women. Pays $500, on acceptance. Send SASE.

**GLORY SONGS**—See *The Church Musician.*

**GOOD HOUSEKEEPING**—959 Eighth Ave., New York, NY 10019. Rosemary Leonard, Ed. Two to eight lines of witty poetry, light verse, and quips with broad appeal, easy to illustrate for "Light Housekeeping" page. Seasonal material welcome. SASE required for return of material. Pays $25 to $50, on acceptance.

**GUIDEPOSTS**—16 E. 34th St., New York, NY 10016. Rick Hamlin, Features Ed. Inspirational anecdotes, to 250 words. Pays $10 to $50, on acceptance.

**HEARTH & HOME**—P. O. Box 2008, Laconia, NH 03247. Ken Daggett, Ed. Profiles and interviews, 1,000 to 1,800 words, with specialty retailers selling both casual furniture and hearth products (fireplaces, woodstoves, accessories, etc.). Pays $150 to $250, on acceptance.

**HUMOR MAGAZINE**—Box 41070, Philadelphia, PA 19127. Edward Savaria, Jr., Ed. Quarterly. Fiction, interviews, and profiles, up to 1,000 words; short poetry, jokes, and fillers. "We would edit out all truly gross humor and anything that elicits loud groans. Please, no X-rated jokes or stories." Pays $50 to $300 for stories and articles, $5 to $25 for jokes and fillers, on acceptance.

**INDEPENDENT LIVING**—44 Broadway, New York, NY 11740. Anne Kelly, Ed. Short humor, to 500 words, and cartoons for magazine addressing lifestyles and home health care of persons who have disabilities. Pays 10¢ a word, on publication. Query.

**JUST FOR LAUGHS**—22 Miller Ave., #G, Mill Valley, CA 94941. Jon Fox, Ed. Satirical pieces, 1,500 words, and articles, 1,000 to 2,000 words. Cartoons. "The only publication dedicated to the artform of stand-up comedy." Queries preferred. Pays $50 to $250, 30 days after publication.

**LADIES' HOME JOURNAL**—"Kidspeak," 100 Park Ave., 3rd Fl., New York, NY 10017. Brief, true anecdotes about the amusing things children say for "Out of the Mouths of Babes" column. All material must be original. Pays $50 for children's anecdotes. Due to the volume of mail received, submissions cannot be acknowledged or returned.

**MAD MAGAZINE**—485 Madison Ave., New York , NY 10022. Address Editors. Humorous pieces on a wide variety of topics. Two- to eight-panel cartoons (not necessary to include sketches with submission). SASE for guidelines strongly recommended. Pays top rates, on acceptance.

**MATURE LIVING**—127 Ninth Ave. N., MSN 140, Nashville, TN 37234. Brief, humorous, original items; 25-line profiles with action photos; "Grandparents Brag Board" items; Christian inspirational pieces for senior adults, 125 words. Pays $5 to $15.

**MATURE YEARS**—201 Eighth Ave. S., P.O. Box 801, Nashville, TN 37202. Marvin W. Cropsey, Ed. Poems, cartoons, puzzles, jokes, anecdotes, to 300 words, for older adults. Allow two months for manuscript evaluation. "A Christian magazine that seeks to build faith. We always show older adults in a favorable light." Include name, address, Social Security number with all submissions.

**MID-WEST OUTDOORS**—111 Shore Dr., Hinsdale, IL 60521–5885. Gene Laulunen, Man. Ed. Where to and how to fish and hunt in the Midwest, 400 to 1,500 words, with two photos. Pays $15 to $35, on publication.

**MODERN BRIDE**—249 West 17th St., New York, NY 10011. Mary Ann Cavlin, Man. Ed. Humorous pieces, 500 to 1,000 words, for brides. Pays on acceptance.

**MODERN MATURITY**—3200 E. Carson St., Lakewood, CA 90712. J. Henry Fenwick, Ed. Money-saving tips. Submit seasonal material six months in advance. Pays from $50, on acceptance. Query.

**MOUNTAIN BIKE**—33 E. Minor St., Emmaus, PA 18098. Tim Blumenthal, Man. Ed. Descriptions, 500 words, detailing the routes of off-road rides. Pays $75, on acceptance.

**NATIONAL ENQUIRER**—Lantana, FL 33464. Michele Cooke, Asst. Ed. Short, humorous or philosophical fillers, witticisms, anecdotes, jokes, tart comments. Original items only. Short poetry with traditional rhyming verse, amusing, philosophical, or inspirational in nature. No obscure or artsy poetry. Submit seasonal/holiday material at least three months in advance. SASE required with all submissions. Pays $25, after publication.

**NEW CHOICES FOR RETIREMENT LIVING**—28 W. 23rd St., New York, NY 10010. David A. Sendler, Ed.-in-Chief. Short humor pieces for news/service magazine for people ages 50 to 65. Payment varies, on acceptance.

**NEW JERSEY MONTHLY**—P.O. Box 920, Morristown, NJ 07963–0920. Jan Bresnick, Ed. Short pieces related to life in New Jersey. Pays $400 for about 750 words.

**NEW YORK**—755 Second Ave., New York, NY 10017. Chris Smith, Assoc. Ed. Short, lively pieces, to 400 words, highlighting events and trends in New York City for "Fast Track." Profiles, to 300 words, for "Brief Lives." Pays $25 to $300, on publication. Include SASE.

**THE NEW YORKER**—20 West 43rd St., New York, NY 10036. Amusing mistakes in newspapers, books, magazines, etc. Pays from $10, extra for headings and tags, on acceptance. Address Newsbreaks Dept. Material returned only with SASE.

**THE NOSE**—Acme Publishing Co., Inc., 1095 Market St., Suite 812, San Francisco, CA 94103. Jack Boulware, Ed. Humorous pieces with "a shoot-from-the-hip attitude." Features, 1,500 to 4,000 words, on some facet of the bizarre world of the West. Interviews, 1,000 to 3,000 words, that bring out the humorous and outrageous side of the subject. "The Beat," 350 words, on lifestyle categories. "Wild West," 300 words, random satirical pieces, rewrites of actual news items. Also short, witty reviews of recent videos and books, 150 words. No payment made. Guidelines.

**OPTOMETRIC ECONOMICS**—American Optometric Assn., 243 N. Lindbergh Blvd., St. Louis, MO 63141. Dr. Jack Runninger, Ed. Short humor for monthly magazine on private practice management for optometrists. Payment varies, on acceptance.

**OUTDOOR LIFE**—2 Park Ave., New York, NY 10016. Vin T. Sparano, Ed.-in-Chief. Short instructive items, 900 to 1,100 words, on hunting, fishing, boating, and outdoor equipment. Photos. No fiction or poetry. Pays $300 to $350, on acceptance.

**PARISH FAMILY DIGEST**—200 Noll Plaza, Huntington, IN 46750. Corine B. Erlandson, Ed. Family- or Catholic parish-oriented humor. Anecdotes, to 250 words, of funny or unusual parish and family experiences. Pays $5, on acceptance.

**PLAYBOY**—680 N. Lakeshore Dr., Chicago, IL 60611. Address Party Jokes

Ed. or After Hours Ed. Jokes; short original material on new trends, lifestyles, personalities; humorous news items. Pays $100 for jokes, on publication; $50 to $350 for "After Hours" items, on publication.

**PLAYGIRL**—801 Second Ave., New York, NY 10017. Humorous looks at daily life and relationships from male or female perspective, to 800 words, for "The Men's Room" and "The Women's Room." Query Managing Ed. Pays varying rates.

**POPULAR MECHANICS**—224 W. 57th St., New York, NY 10019. Deborah Frank, Man. Ed. How-to pieces, from 300 words, with photos and sketches, on home improvement and shop and craft projects. Pays $25 to $300, on acceptance. Buys all rights.

**PUNCH DIGEST FOR CANADIAN DOCTORS**—14845 Yonge St., Suite 300, Aurora, Ontario, Canada L4G 6H8. Simon Hally, Ed. Humorous pieces, 250 to 2,000 words, for physicians. "Most articles have something to do with medicine and most are by doctors." Short humorous verse and original jokes. Pays 30¢ to 40¢ a word; $50 for cartoons (Canadian), on publication.

**READER'S DIGEST**—Pleasantville, NY 10570. True, original anecdotes for "Life in These United States," "Humor in Uniform," "Campus Comedy," and "All in a Day's Work." Pays $400, on publication. Original short items for "Toward More Picturesque Speech." Pays $50. Anecdotes, original items, for "Laughter, the Best Medicine," "Personal Glimpses," "Points to Ponder," "Quotable Quotes," etc. Pays $30 per two-column line. No submissions acknowledged or returned. Consult "Contributor's Corner" page for guidelines.

**REAL PEOPLE**—950 Third Ave., 16th Fl., New York, NY 10022. Alex Polner, Ed. True stories, to 500 words, for "Real Bizarre" column, on the occult, UFOs, strange occurrences, everyday weirdness, etc.; may be funny, sad, or hair-raising. Pays $50, on publication. Buys all rights.

**REDBOOK**—"Check Out," 224 West 57th St., New York, NY 10019. Tips about crafts or family-fun ideas, brief anecdotes, and poems. Also witty, warm, and wonderful quotes from children. (Enclose a snapshot of the child.) Include your name, address, and daytime phone number with submissions. Submissions will not be acknowledged or returned. Pays $50.

**RHODE ISLAND MONTHLY**—18 Imperial Pl., Providence, RI 02903. Vicki Sanders, Man. Ed. Short pieces, to 250 words, on Rhode Island and southeastern Massachusetts: places, customs, people and events; pieces to 150 words on products and services; to 200 words on food, chefs, and restaurants. Pays $25 to $50, on publication.

**ROAD & TRACK**—1499 Monrovia Ave., Newport Beach, CA 92663. Ellida Maki, Man. Ed. Monthly for knowledgeable car enthusiasts. Short automotive articles, to 450 words, of "timeless nature." Pays on publication. Query.

**ROAD KING**—P. O. Box 250, Park Forest, IL 60466. Address Features Ed. Trucking-related cartoons and anecdotes, to 200 words, for "Trucker's Life." Pays $25 for cartoons, $25 for anecdotes, on publication. SASE required.

**THE ROTARIAN**—1560 Sherman Ave., Evanston, IL 60201. Willmon L. White, Ed. Occasional humor articles. Payment varies, on acceptance.

**RURAL HERITAGE**—P. O. Box 516, Albia, IA 52531. Allan Young, Pub. Current articles, 100 to 750 words, related to draft horses, rural events, or crafts. Pays 3¢ to 10¢ a word, on publication.

**SACRAMENTO**—1021 Second St., Sacramento, CA 95814. "City Lights,"

742

interesting and unusual people, places, and behind-the-scenes news items, 100 to 350 words. All material must have Sacramento tie-in. Pays $60 to $100, on publication.

**THE SATURDAY EVENING POST**—P.O. Box 567, Indianapolis, IN 46206. Steven Pettinga, Post Scripts Ed. Humor and satire, to 100 words; light verse, cartoons, jokes, for "Post Scripts." Pays $15, on publication.

**SCHOOL SHOP/TECH DIRECTIONS**—See *Tech Directions.*

**SCORE, CANADA'S GOLF MAGAZINE**—287 MacPherson Ave., Toronto, Ont., Canada M4V 1A4. Bob Weeks, Man. Ed. Fillers, 50 to 100 words, related to Canadian golf scene. Rarely uses humor or poems. Pays $10 to $25, on publication. Unused submissions not returned.

**THE SENIOR MUSICIAN**—See *The Church Musician.*

**THE SINGLE PARENT**—Parents Without Partners, Inc., 8807 Colesville Rd., Silver Spring, MD 20910–4346. Rene McDonald, Ed. Fillers, 300 to 500 words, addressing the concerns of the single parent. Pays $25 to $50, on publication; published bimonthly.

**SKI MAGAZINE**—2 Park Ave., New York, NY 10016. Dick Needham, Ed. Short, 100- to 300-word items on events and people in skiing for "Ski Life" department. Humor, 300 to 2,000 words, related to skiing. Pays on acceptance.

**SNOWMOBILE**—319 Barry Ave. S., Suite 101, Wayzata, MN 55391. Dick Hendricks, Ed. Short humor and cartoons on snowmobiling and winter "Personality Plates" sighted. Pays varying rates, on publication.

**SPORTS AFIELD**—250 W. 55th St., New York, NY 10019. Unusual, useful tips, anecdotes, 100 to 300 words, for "Almanac" section: hunting, fishing, camping, boating, etc. Photos. Pays 10¢ per column inch, on publication.

**SPORTS CARD TRADER**—3 Fairchild Ct., Plainview, NY 11803. Douglas Kale, Ed. Fillers related to collecting and investing in baseball, football, basketball, and hockey cards. (Also articles on investing in sports cards or memorabilia.) Pays 10¢ a word, on publication.

**STAR**—660 White Plains Rd., Tarrytown, NY 10591. Topical articles, 50 to 800 words, on human-interest subjects, show business, lifestyles, the sciences, etc., for family audience. Pays varying rates.

**TECH DIRECTIONS**—(formerly *School Shop/Tech Directions*) Box 8623, Ann Arbor, MI 48107. Paul J. Bamford, Man. Ed. Articles, to 10 double-spaced pages, for teachers and administrators in industrial, technical, and vocational fields, with particular interest in classroom projects, computer uses, and policy issues. Also humorous anecdotes, brain teasers, and crossword puzzles related to these educational fields. Pays $10 to $150, on publication.

**THOUGHTS FOR ALL SEASONS: THE MAGAZINE OF EPIGRAMS** —11530 S.W. 99th St., Miami, FL 33176. Michael P. Richard, Ed. Epigrams and puns, one to two lines, and poetry, to one page. "Writers are advised not to submit material until they have examined a copy of the magazine." No payment.

**TOUCH**—Box 7259, Grand Rapids, MI 49510. Carol Smith, Man. Ed. Puzzles based on the NIV Bible, for Christian girls aged 8 to 14. Pays $5 to $10 per puzzle, on acceptance. Send SASE for theme update.

**TRAVEL SMART**—Dobbs Ferry, NY 10522. Interesting, unusual travel-related tips. Practical information for vacation or business travel. Query for over 250 words. Pays $5 to $150.

**TREASURES IN NEEDLEWORK**—Craftways, Inc., 4118 Lakeside Dr., Richmond, CA 94806. Kit Schlich, Text Ed. Fillers, 100 to 800 words, for quarterly on heirloom-quality needlework. Pays $15 to $150; buys all rights, on acceptance. Guidelines.

**TRUE CONFESSIONS**—233 Park Ave. S., New York, NY 10003. Jean Sharbel, Ed. Warm, inspirational first-person fillers, 300 to 700 words, about love, marriage, family life, for "The Feminine Side of Things." Pays after publication. Buys all rights.

**VOLKSWAGEN WORLD**—Volkswagen of America, Mail Code 3C03, 3800 Hamlin Rd., Auburn Hills, MI 48326. Marlene Goldsmith, Ed. Anecdotes, to 100 words, about Volkswagen owners' experiences; humorous photos of current model Volkswagens. Pays $100, on acceptance.

**WISCONSIN TRAILS**—P.O. Box 5650, Madison, WI 53705. Short fillers about Wisconsin: places to go, things to see, etc., 300 words. Pays $75, on publication.

**WOMAN'S DAY**—1633 Broadway, New York, NY 10019. Address "Neighbors" editor. Heartwarming anecdotes about the public service work of a "good neighbor," creative solutions to common community or family problems, true humorous anecdotes. For "Tips to Share": short personal tips, experiences, and practical suggestions for homemakers. Pays $75, on publication.

**WOMEN'S GLIB**—P.O. Box 259, Bala Cynwyd, PA 19004. Rosalind Warren, Ed. Annual. Feminist humor, 2 to 10 pages, and brief, rhymed poems. No pieces on diet, weight loss, body image, or romance. Cartoons. Pays from $5 per page, on publication, and copies. Accepts material by women only.

**WOODENBOAT MAGAZINE**—Box 78, Brooklin, ME 04616. Jon Wilson, Ed. Address Peter Spectre. News of wooden boat-related activities and projects. Pays $5 to $50, on publication.

# JUVENILE, TEENAGE, AND YOUNG ADULT MAGAZINES

## JUVENILE MAGAZINES

**BEAR ESSENTIAL NEWS FOR KIDS**—See *Essential News for Kids*

**CALLIOPE: WORLD HISTORY FOR YOUNG PEOPLE**—Cobblestone Publishing, Inc., 30 Grove St., Peterborough, NH 03458. Carolyn P. Yoder, Ed.-in-Chief. Theme-based magazine, published five times yearly. Articles, 750 words, with lively, original approach to world history (East/West) through the Renaissance. Shorts, 200 to 750 words, on little-known information related to issue's theme. Fiction, to 1,200 words: historical, biographical, adventure, or retold legends. Activities for children, to 800 words. Poetry, to 100 lines. Puzzles and games. Send SASE for guidelines and themes. Pays 10¢ to 17¢ per word, on publication.

**CHICKADEE**—The Young Naturalist Foundation, 56 The Esplanade, Suite 306, Toronto, Ont., Canada M5E 1A7. Catherine Ripley, Ed. Animal and adventure stories, 200 to 800 words, for children ages 3 to 8. Also, puzzles, activities, and observation games, 50 to 100 words. Pays varying rates, on acceptance. Send complete manuscript and $1 check or money order for return postage.

**CHILDREN'S ALBUM**—P.O. Box 6086, Concord, CA 94524. Margo M. Lemas, Ed. Fiction and poetry by children 8 to 14. Workbook and crafts projects, with step-by-step instructions. Guidelines.

**CHILDREN'S DIGEST**—1100 Waterway Blvd., P.O. Box 567, Indianapolis, IN 46202. Elizabeth Rinck, Ed. Health publication for preteens. Informative articles, 500 to 1,200 words, and fiction (especially realistic, adventure, mystery, and humorous), 500 to 1,500 words, with health, safety, exercise, nutrition, sports, or hygiene as theme. Historical and biographical articles. Poetry activities. Pays 10¢ a word, from $15 for poems, on publication.

**CHILDREN'S PLAYMATE**—Editorial Office, 1100 Waterway Blvd., P.O. Box 567, Indianapolis, IN 46206. Elizabeth Rinck, Ed. Humorous and health-related short stories, 500 to 700 words, for 6- to 8-year-olds. Simple science articles and how-to crafts pieces with brief instructions. "All About" features, about 500 words, on health, fitness, nutrition, safety, and exercise. Poems, puzzles, dot-to-dots, mazes, hidden pictures. Pays about 10¢ a word, $10 minimum for poetry, on publication.

**CLUBHOUSE**—Box 15, Berrien Springs, MI 49103. Elaine Trumbo, Ed. Action-oriented Christian stories: features, 800 to 1,200 words. Children in stories should be wise, brave, funny, kind, etc. Pays $30 to $35 for stories.

**COBBLESTONE**—7 School St., Peterborough, NH 03458–1454. Carolyn Yoder, Ed.-in-Chief. Theme-related articles, biographies, fiction, and short accounts of historical events, to 1,000 words, for children ages 8 to 15. Pays 10¢ to 17¢ a word, on publication. Send SASE for editorial guidelines with monthly themes.

**CRICKET**—Box 300, Peru, IL 61354–0300. Marianne Carus, Pub./Ed.-in-Chief. Articles and fiction, 200 to 1,500 words, for 6- to 14-year-olds. Poetry, to 30 lines. Pays to 25¢ a word, to $3 a line for poetry, on publication. SASE required. Guidelines.

**DISCOVERIES**—See *Power and Light.*

**THE DOLPHIN LOG**—The Cousteau Society, 8440 Santa Monica Blvd., Los Angeles, CA 90069. Pam Stacey, Ed. Articles, 500 to 1,000 words, on a variety of topics related to our global water system: marine biology, ecology, natural history, and water-related subjects, for children ages 7 to 15. No fiction. Pays $25 to $150, on publication. Query.

**ESSENTIAL NEWS FOR KIDS**—(formerly *Bear Essential News for Kids*) P.O. Box 26908, Tempe, AZ 85285–6908. Educational and entertaining articles, 300 to 600 words, for children in grades K through 3, and 4 through 8, including: world news in kids' terms; unique school projects; profiles of interesting achievers; family entertainment; science; youth sports and health; bilingual and multicultural topics; hobbies/young careers; pets and pet care; cartoon humor; activities, trivia, or puzzles that are educational. Also uses 50- to 150-word companion pieces for a teachers guide, providing classroom-use ideas related to articles. Payment is 10¢ a word, on publication; $10 to $35 for photos. Buys all rights. SASE required.

**FACES**—30 Grove St., Peterborough, NH 03458. Carolyn P. Yoder, Ed.-in-Chief. In-depth feature articles, 800 to 1,200 words, with an anthropology theme.

Shorts, 200 to 800 words, related to monthly themes. Fiction, to 1,500 words, on legends, folktales, stories from around the world, etc., related to theme. Activities, to 1,000 words, including recipes, crafts, games, etc., for children. Pays 13¢ to 17¢ a word for features; 10¢ to 12¢ a word for shorts; 10¢ to 15¢ a word for fiction. Send for guidelines and themes.

**FAITH 'N STUFF**—c/o Guideposts, 747 Third Ave., New York, NY 10017. Mary Lou Carney, Ed. Bible-based bimonthly. Problem fiction, mysteries, historicals, 1,500 words; articles, 1,500 words, on issues of interest to kids ages 7 to 12; profiles, 200 to 500 words, of kids doing interesting and unusual activities. "No preachy stories and no Bible games." Pays $125 to $300 for features; $75 to $250 for fiction and fillers; buys all rights, on acceptance. No reprints. Query.

**FREE SPIRIT: NEWS & VIEWS ON GROWING UP**—Free Spirit Publishing, Inc., 400 First Ave. N., Suite 616, Minneapolis, MN 55401–1724. Judy Galbraith, Ed. Published five times a year. Nonfiction, 800 to 1,200 words, related to the lives of teens and preteens (school, peer relationships, family, health, etc.). Annual cartoon and writing contests for kids. Readers are 10 to 14 years old. No fiction. Queries preferred. Pays to $100, on publication.

**THE FRIEND**—50 E. North Temple, 23rd Floor, Salt Lake City, UT 84150. Vivian Paulsen, Man. Ed. Stories and articles, 1,000 to 1,200 words. Stories, to 250 words, for younger readers and preschool children. Pays from 9¢ a word, from $25 per poem, on acceptance. Prefers completed manuscripts.

**HIGHLIGHTS FOR CHILDREN**—803 Church St., Honesdale, PA 18431–1824. Kent L. Brown, Ed. Fiction and articles, to 800 words, for 2- to 12-year-olds. Fiction should have strong plot, believable characters, story that holds reader's interest from beginning to end. No crime or violence. For articles, cite references used and qualifications. Easy rebus-form stories. Easy-to-read stories, 300 to 500 words, with strong plots. Pays from 14¢ a word, on acceptance.

**HOPSCOTCH, THE MAGAZINE FOR GIRLS**—P.O. Box 164, Bluffton, OH 45817–0164. Marilyn Edwards, Ed. Bimonthly. Articles and fiction, 600 to 1,200 words, and short poetry for girls ages 6 to 12. "We believe young girls deserve the right to enjoy a season of childhood before they become young adults; we are not interested in such topics as sex, romance, cosmetics, hairstyles, etc." Pays 5¢ per word; $150 for cover photos, made on acceptance.

**HUMPTY DUMPTY'S MAGAZINE**—1100 Waterway Blvd., P.O. Box 567, Indianapolis, IN 46206. Christine French Clark, Ed. General-interest publication with an emphasis on health and fitness for children ages 4 to 6. Easy-to-read fiction, to 600 words, some with health and nutrition, safety, exercise, or hygiene as theme; humor and light approach preferred. Creative nonfiction, including photo stories. Crafts with clear, brief instructions. No-cook recipes using healthful ingredients. Short verse, narrative poems. Pays about 10¢ a word, from $15 for poems, on publication. Buys all rights.

**JACK AND JILL**—Box 567, Indianapolis, IN 46206. Steve Charles, Ed. Articles, 500 to 1,200 words, for 6- to 8-year-olds, on sports, fitness, health, safety, exercise. Features, 1,000 to 1,200 words, on history, biography, life in other countries, etc. Fiction, to 1,500 words. Short poems, games, puzzles, projects, recipes. Photos. Pays about 10¢ a word, extra for photos, varying rates for fillers, on publication.

**JUNIOR TRAILS**—1445 Boonville Ave., Springfield, MO 65802–1894. Sinda Zinn, Ed. Fiction, 1,000 to 1,500 words, with a Christian focus, believable characters, and moral emphasis. Articles, 500 to 800 words, on science, nature, biography. Pays 2¢ or 3¢ a word, on acceptance.

**KID CITY**—See *3–2–1 Contact.*

**LADYBUG**—P.O. Box 300, Peru, IL 61354. Marianne Carus, Pub./Ed.-in-Chief. Paula Morrow, Assoc. Ed. Picture stories, read-aloud stories, fantasy, folk and fairy tales, 300 to 750 words; poetry, to 20 lines; songs and rhymes; crafts, activities, and games, to 4 pages. Pays on publication: to 25¢ a word for stories and articles; to $3 a line for poetry. SASE required. Guidelines.

**LOLLIPOPS**—Good Apple, Inc., P.O. Box 299, Carthage, IL 62321–0299. Learning games and activities covering all areas of the curriculum; arts and crafts ideas; stories, for ages 4 to 7. Pays varying rates, on publication. Query first.

**MY FRIEND**—Daughters of St. Paul, 50 St. Paul's Ave., Boston, MA 02130. Sister Anne Joan, Ed. "The Catholic Magazine for Kids." Readers are 6 to 12 years old. Fiction, to 400 words, for primary readers; 400 to 600 words for intermediate readers. Nonfiction: general-information articles, lives of saints, etc., 150 to 600 words. Some humorous poetry, 6 to 8 lines. Buys first rights. Pays $20 to $150 for stories and articles, $5 to $20 for fillers. Query for artwork. Guidelines available.

**NATIONAL GEOGRAPHIC WORLD**—1145 17th St. N.W., Washington, DC 20036. Pat Robbins, Ed. Picture magazine for young readers, ages 8 and older. Proposals for picture stories only. No unsolicited manuscripts.

**ODYSSEY: SCIENCE THAT'S OUT OF THIS WORLD**—Cobblestone Publishing, 30 Grove St., Peterborough, NH 03458. Carolyn P. Yoder, Ed.-in-Chief. Eleanor Cochrane, Assoc. Ed. Features, 250 to 750 words, on astronomy and space science for 8- to 14-year-old readers. Short experiments, projects, and games. Pays 10¢ to 17¢ a word, on publication.

**OH!ZONE**—Project Oh!Zone, 420 E. Hewitt Ave., Marquette, MI 49855. Jessica Gray, Man. Ed. Articles, 200 to 2,000 words, on environmental news, art, and opinion for youths in grades 7 to 12. Special attention given to student submissions. Published five times yearly. Send SASE for guidelines and list of upcoming themes. Pays $30 to $100 for articles, $10 to $25 for photos or illustrations, and $100 for covers, on publication. Contributors receive ten copies and a subscription.

**ON THE LINE**—616 Walnut, Scottdale, PA 15683–1999. Mary Clemens Meyer, Ed. Weekly paper for 10- to 14-year-olds. Uses nature and how-to articles, 350 to 500 words; fiction, 900 to 1,200 words; poetry, puzzles, cartoons. Pays to 4¢ a word, on acceptance.

**OWL**—The Young Naturalist Foundation, 56 The Esplanade, Suite 306, Toronto, Ont., Canada M5E 1A7. Debora Pearson, Ed. Articles, 500 to 1,000 words, for children ages 8 to 12 about animals, science, people, technology, new discoveries, activities. Pays varying rates, on acceptance. Send for guidelines.

**PLAYS, THE DRAMA MAGAZINE FOR YOUNG PEOPLE**—120 Boylston St., Boston, MA 02116–4615. Elizabeth Preston, Man. Ed. One-act plays, skits, creative dramatic material, suitable for school productions at junior high, middle, and lower grade levels. Plays with one set preferred. Uses comedies, dramas, satires, farces, dramatized classics, folktales and fairy tales, puppet plays. Pays good rates, on acceptance. Buys all rights. Guidelines; send SASE.

**POCKETS**—1908 Grand Ave., Box 189, Nashville, TN 37202–0189. Janet McNish, Ed. Ecumenical magazine for children ages 6 to 12. Fiction and scripture stories, 600 to 1,500 words; short poems; and articles about the Bible, 400 to 600 words. Pays from 12¢ a word, $25 to $50 for poetry, on acceptance. Guidelines and themes. Annual fiction contest; send SASE for details.

**POWER AND LIGHT**—6401 The Paseo, Kansas City, MO 64131. Beula J. Postlewait, Preteen Ed. Stories, 600 to 900 words, for 3rd to 6th graders, with Christian emphasis. Poetry, 4 to 20 lines. Cartoons and puzzles. Pays 5¢ a word for multi-use rights, 3 ½¢ a word for first rights, 1 ¾¢ a word for reprints, 25¢ a line for poetry (minimum of $3), on acceptance. Pays $15 for cartoons and puzzles. Send SASE with manuscript. Also publishes *Discoveries* for grades 3 and 4.

**RADAR**—8121 Hamilton Ave., Cincinnati, OH 45231. Margaret Williams, Ed. Articles, 400 to 650 words, on nature, hobbies, crafts. Short stories, 900 to 1,000 words: mystery, sports, school, family, with 12-year-old as main character; serials of 2,000 words. Christian emphasis. Poems to 12 lines. Pays to 7¢ a word, to 50¢ a line for poetry, on acceptance.

**RANGER RICK**—1400 16th St. N.W., Washington, DC 20036–2266. Gerald Bishop, Ed. Articles, to 900 words, on wildlife, conservation, natural sciences, and kids in the outdoors, for 6- to 12-year-olds. Nature-related fiction, mysteries, fantasies, and science fiction welcome. Games (no crosswords or word-finds), crafts, humorous poems, outdoor activities, and puzzles. For nonfiction, query with sample lead, list of references, and names of experts you plan to contact. Pays to $550, on acceptance.

**REFLECTIONS**—P.O. Box 368, Duncan Falls, OH 43734. Dean Harper, Ed. "A National Magazine Publishing Student Writing." Published twice a year. Fiction and nonfiction, 300 to 2,000 words; poetry, any length. "Our magazine is published for students in grades K through 12. The purpose is to encourage writing." Queries not necessary. Pays in copies.

**SESAME STREET MAGAZINE**—See *3–2–1 Contact.*

**SHOFAR**—43 Northcote Dr., Melville, NY 11747. Gerald H. Grayson, Ed. Short stories, 500 to 750 words; articles, 250 to 750 words; poetry, to 50 lines; short fillers, games, puzzles, and cartoons for Jewish children, 8 to 13. All material must have a Jewish theme. Pays 10¢ a word, on publication. Submit holiday pieces at least six months in advance.

**SKIPPING STONES**—P.O. Box 3939, Eugene, OR 97403. Arun N. Toké, Man. Ed. "A Multi-Cultural Children's Quarterly." Articles, approximately 500 words, relating to cultural celebrations, life in other countries, and traditions for children ages 7 to 13. "Especially invited to submit are children from cultural backgrounds other than European-American and/or those with physical challenges. We print art, poetry, songs, games, stories, and photographs from anywhere in the world and include many different languages." Payment is one copy, on publication. Send SASE for guidelines.

**SOCCER JR.**—27 Unquowa Rd., Fairfield, CT 06430. Joe Provey, Ed. Fiction and fillers about soccer for readers ages 8 and up. Pays $450 for a feature story; $250 for department pieces, on publication. Query.

**STONE SOUP, THE MAGAZINE BY CHILDREN**—Box 83, Santa Cruz, CA 95063–0083. Gerry Mandel, Ed. Stories, poems, plays, book reviews by children under 14. Pays $10.

**STORY FRIENDS**—Mennonite Publishing House, Scottdale, PA 15683. Marjorie Waybill, Ed. Stories, 350 to 800 words, for 4- to 9-year-olds, on Christian faith and values in everyday experiences. Poetry. Pays to 5¢ a word, to $10 per poem, on acceptance.

**SUPERSCIENCE BLUE**—Scholastic, Inc., 730 Broadway, New York, NY 10003. Science news and hands-on experiments for grades 4 through 6. Article topics are staff-generated and assigned to writers. For consideration, send children's and science writing clips to Editor. Include SASE for editorial calendar. Pays $100 to $500, on acceptance.

**3–2–1 CONTACT**—Children's Television Workshop, 1 Lincoln Plaza, New York, NY 10023. Curtis Slepian, Ed. Entertaining and informative articles, 600 to 1,000 words, for 8- to 14-year-olds, on all aspects of science, computers, scientists, and children who are learning about or practicing science. Pays $75 to $500, on acceptance. No fiction. Also publishes *Kid City* and *Sesame Street Magazine*. Query.

**TOUCH**—Box 7259, Grand Rapids, MI 49510. Carol Smith, Man. Ed. Upbeat fiction and features, 500 to 1,000 words, for Christian girls ages 8 to 14; personal life, nature, crafts. Poetry, puzzles. Pays 2 ½¢ a word, extra for photos, on acceptance. Query with SASE for theme update.

**TURTLE MAGAZINE FOR PRESCHOOL KIDS**—1100 Waterway Blvd., Box 567, Indianapolis, IN 46202. Christine French Clark, Ed. Stories about safety, exercise, health, and nutrition for preschoolers. Humorous, entertaining fiction. Simple poems. Stories-in-rhyme and read-aloud stories, to 500 words. Pays about 10¢ a word, on publication. Buys all rights. Send SASE for guidelines.

**U.S. KIDS**—1100 Waterway Blvd., P.O. Box 567, Indianapolis, IN 46206. Christine French Clark, Ed. Dir. Articles, 200 to 400 words, on issues related to kids ages 5 to 10, true-life adventures, science and nature topics. Special emphasis on health and fitness. Fiction with real-world focus; no fantasy.

**VENTURE**—Christian Service Brigade, P.O. Box 150, Wheaton, IL 60189. Deborah Christensen, Man. Ed. Fiction and nonfiction, 1,000 to 1,500 words, for 10- to 15-year-old boys involved in Stockade and Battalion. "Articles and stories should reflect the simple truths of the gospel and its life-changing power." Humor and fillers and B&W 8×10 photos also accepted. Pays 5¢ to 10¢ a word, on publication.

**WONDER TIME**—6401 The Paseo, Kansas City, MO 64131. Evelyn J. Beals, Ed. Stories, 200 to 550 words, for 6- to 8-year-olds, with Christian emphasis to correlate with Sunday school curriculum. Poetry, 4 to 12 lines. Pays 5¢ a word for stories ($25 minimum); 25¢ a line for verse ($3 minimum), on acceptance.

**ZILLIONS**—Consumers Union of the United States, 101 Truman Ave., Yonkers, NY 10703–9925. Jeanne Kiefer, Man. Ed. Bimonthly. Articles, 1,000 to 1,500 words, on consumer education (money, product testing, health, etc.), for children, preteens, and young teens. "We are the *Consumer Reports* for kids." Pays $500 to $1,000, on publication. Guidelines.

## TEENAGE AND YOUNG ADULT

**ALIVE NOW!**—P.O. Box 189, Nashville, TN 37202. Short essays, 250 to 400 words, with Christian emphasis for adults and young adults. Poetry, one page. Photos. Pays $20 to $30, on publication.

**BOYS' LIFE**—P.O. Box 152079, 1325 W. Walnut Hill Ln., Irving, TX 75015–2079. William B. McMorris, Ed.-in-Chief. Publication of Boy Scouts of America. Articles and fiction, 500 to 1,500 words, for 8- to 18-year-old boys. Pays from $350 for major articles, $750 for fiction, on acceptance. Query first for articles; send complete manuscript for fiction.

**CAMPUS LIFE**—465 Gundersen Dr., Carol Stream, IL 60188. Jim Long, Ed. Articles reflecting Christian values and world view, for high school and college students. Humor, general fiction, and true, first-person experiences. "If we have a choice of fiction, how-to, and a strong first-person story, we'll go with the true story every time." Photo essays, cartoons. Pays 10¢ to 20¢ a word, on acceptance. Query.

**CHALLENGE MAGAZINE**—See *Pioneer.*

**CITY NEWS**—2 Park Ave., Suite 2012, New York, NY 10016. Leslie Elgort, Ed. Bimonthly. Articles, 750 to 1,500 words, poetry, fillers, and humor of interest to New York City teenagers; B&W photos. Payment varies, on publication.

**CRACKED**—Globe Communications, Inc., 441 Lexington Ave., 2nd Fl., New York, NY 10017. Andy Simmons, Ed. Humor, to 5 pages, for 12- to 15-year-old readers. "Read magazine before submitting." Pays $100 per page, on acceptance.

**EXPLORING**—1325 W. Walnut Hill Ln., P.O. Box 152079, Irving, TX 75015–2079. Scott Daniels, Exec. Ed. Publication of Boy Scouts of America. Articles, 500 to 1,500 words, for 14- to 21-year-old boys and girls, on teenage trends, college, computer games, music, education, careers, "Explorer" activities (hiking, canoeing, camping) and program ideas for meetings. No controversial subjects. Pays $150 to $500, on acceptance. Query. Send SASE for guidelines.

**FREEWAY**—Box 632, Glen Ellyn, IL 60138. Kyle Lennart Olund, Ed. First-person true stories, personal experience, how-tos, fillers, humor, fiction, to 1,200 words, for 15- to 22-year-olds. Send photos, if available. Occasionally publishes poetry. Must have Christian emphasis. Pays to 8¢ a word.

**HICALL**—1445 Boonville Ave., Springfield, MO 65802–1894. Deanna Harris, Ed. Articles, 500 to 1,000 words, fiction, to 1,500 words, and short poetry, for 13- to 17-year-olds; strong evangelical emphasis. Pays on acceptance.

**I.D.**—850 N. Grove, Elgin, IL 60120. Douglas C. Schmidt, Ed. Articles and fiction, 750 to 1,000 words, of interest to Christian teens. Don't preach. Pays 10¢ a word, on acceptance.

**KEYNOTER**—3636 Woodview Trace, Indianapolis, IN 46268. Tamara P. Burley, Exec. Ed. Articles, 1,500 to 2,500 words, for high school leaders: general-interest features; self-help; contemporary teenage problems. No fillers, poetry, first-person accounts, or fiction. Photos. Pays $75 to $250, extra for photos, on acceptance. Query preferred.

**LISTEN MAGAZINE**—Pacific Press Publishing, P.O. Box 7000, Boise, ID 83707. Lincoln Steed, Ed. Articles, 1,200 to 1,500 words, providing teens with "a vigorous, positive, educational approach to the problems arising out of the use of tobacco, alcohol, and other drugs." Pays 5¢ to 7¢ a word, on acceptance.

**MERLYN'S PEN: THE NATIONAL MAGAZINE OF STUDENT WRITING**—P.O. Box 1058, Dept. WR, East Greenwich, RI 02818. R. James Stahl, Ed. Writing by students in grades 7 through 10 only. Short stories, to 3,500 words; reviews; travel pieces; and poetry, to 100 lines. Pays in copies. Guidelines available.

**NEW ERA**—50 E. North Temple, Salt Lake City, UT 84150. Richard M. Romney, Ed. Articles, 150 to 2,000 words, and fiction, to 2,000 words, for young Mormons. Poetry. Photos. Pays 5¢ to 20¢ a word, 25¢ a line for poetry, on acceptance. Query.

**PIONEER**—1548 Poplar Ave., Memphis, TN 38104–2493. Jeno Smith, Ed. Southern Baptist. Articles, to 800 words, for 12- and 14-year-old boys, on teen issues, current events. Photo essays on Christian sports personalities. Pays 4 ½¢ a word, extra for photos, on acceptance. Same address and requirements for *Challenge Magazine*.

**SEVENTEEN**—850 Third Ave., New York, NY 10022. Roberta Myers, Articles Ed. Articles, to 2,500 words, on subjects of interest to teenagers. Sophisticated, well-written fiction, 1,500 to 3,500 words, for young adults. Short news and features, to 500 words, for "Talk." Articles, 1,200 words, by teenagers, for "View." Pays varying rates, on acceptance.

**STRAIGHT**—8121 Hamilton Ave., Cincinnati, OH 45231. Carla J. Crane, Ed. Articles on current issues, and humor, for Christian teens. Well-constructed fiction, 1,000 to 1,200 words, showing teens using Christian principles. Poetry by teenagers. Photos. Pays about 3¢ to 7¢ a word, on acceptance. Send SASE for guidelines.

**SUPERTEEN'S LOUD MOUTH**—c/o Sterling's Magazines, 355 Lexington Ave., New York, NY 10017. Louise Barile, Ed. Light celebrity fan pieces and interviews (pop/rock, movies, and TV); occasional serious articles on topics of interest to teens. Query.

**'TEEN**—8490 Sunset Blvd., Los Angeles, CA 90069. Short stories, 2,500 to 4,000 words: mystery, teen situations, adventure, romance, humor for teens. Pays $200, on acceptance. Buys all rights.

**TEEN POWER**—Box 632, Glen Ellyn, IL 60138. Amy Cox, Ed. True-to-life fiction or first person (as told to), true teen experience stories with Christian insights and conclusion, 700 to 1,000 words. Include photos. Pays 7¢ to 10¢ a word, extra for photos, on acceptance.

**TEENS TODAY**—Nazarene Headquarters, 6401 The Paseo, Kansas City, MO 64131. Karen DeSollar, Ed. Short stories, 1,000 to 1,200 words, dealing with teens demonstrating Christian principles in real-life situations. Stories about relationships and ethics. Pays 3 ½¢ a word, on acceptance.

**TIGER BEAT**—Sterling's Magazines, 355 Lexington Ave., New York, NY 10017. Louise Barile, Ed. Articles, to 4 pages, on young people in show business and music industry. Pays varying rates, on acceptance. Query. Unsolicited manuscripts sent without SASE will not be returned.

**TQ/TEEN QUEST**—Box 82808, Lincoln, NE 68501. Lisa Thompson, Ed. Articles, to 1,800 words, and well-crafted fiction, to 2,500 words, for conservative Christian teens. Cartoons and B&W photos and color slides. Pays 10¢ to 15¢ a word, on publication.

**WRITING!**—60 Revere Dr., Northbrook, IL 60062–1563. Alan Lenhoff, Ed. Interviews, 1,200 words, for "Writers at Work" department, for junior high and high school students. Pays $200, on publication. Query.

**YM**—685 Third Ave., New York, NY 10017. Peter McQuaid, Entertainment Ed. Cathy Cavender, Man. Ed. Articles, to 2,500 words, on entertainment, lifestyle, fashion, beauty, relationships, health, for women ages 14 to 19. Query with clips. SASE. Payment varies, on acceptance.

**YOUNG AND ALIVE**—4444 S. 52nd St., Lincoln, NE 68506. Richard Kaiser, Ed. Feature articles, 800 to 1,400 words, for blind and visually impaired young adults, on adventure, biography, camping, health, hobbies, and travel. Photos. Pays 3¢ to 5¢ a word, extra for photos, on acceptance. Write for guidelines.

**YOUNG SALVATIONIST**—The Salvation Army, 615 Slaters Ln., P.O. Box

269, Alexandria, VA 22313. Capt. M. Lesa Salyer, Ed. Articles for teens, 800 to 1,200 words, with Christian perspective; fiction, 800 to 1,200 words; short fillers. Pays 10¢ a word, on acceptance.

# THE DRAMA MARKET

Community, regional, and civic theaters and college dramatic groups offer the best opportunities today for playwrights to see their plays produced, whether for staged production or for dramatic readings. Indeed, aspiring playwrights who can get their work produced by any of these have taken an important step toward breaking into the competitive dramatic field —many well-known playwrights received their first recognition in the regional theaters. Payment is generally nominal, but regional and university theaters usually buy only the right to produce a play, and all further rights revert to the author. Since most directors like to work closely with the authors on any revisions necessary, theaters will often pay the playwright's expenses while in residence during rehearsals. The thrill of seeing your play come to life on the stage is one of the pleasures of being on hand for rehearsals and performances.

Aspiring playwrights should query college and community theaters in their region to find out which ones are interested in seeing original scripts. Dramatic associations of interest to playwrights include the Dramatists Guild (234 W. 44th St., New York, NY 10036), Theatre Communications Group, Inc. (355 Lexington Ave., New York, NY 10017), which publishes the annual *Dramatists Sourcebook*, and The International Society of Dramatists (1638 Euclid Ave., Miami Beach, FL 33139), publishers of *The Dramatist's Bible*. *The Playwright's Companion*, published by Feedback Theatrebooks, 305 Madison Ave., Suite 1146, New York, NY 10165, is an annual directory of theaters and prize contests seeking scripts. See the *Organizations for Writers* list for other dramatists' associations.

Some of the theaters on the following list require that playwrights submit all or some of the following with scripts—cast list, synopsis, resumé, recommendations, return postcard—and with scripts and queries, SASEs must always be enclosed. Playwrights may also wish to register their material with the U.S. Copyright Office. For additional information about this, write Register of Copyrights, Library of Congress, Washington, DC 20559.

## REGIONAL AND UNIVERSITY THEATERS

**ACADEMY THEATRE**—P.O. Box 191306, Atlanta, GA 31119. Elliott J. Berman, Lit. Mgr. Comedies and dramas that "stretch the boundaries of imagination, with poetic language, and imagery." Prefers local and regional playwrights or subjects relating to the Southeast. Considers regional and national playwrights for new play premieres. Royalty is negotiable.

**ACTORS THEATRE OF LOUISVILLE**—316 W. Main St., Louisville, KY 40202. Michael Bigelow Dixon, Lit. Mgr. Ten-minute comedies and dramas, to 10 pages; include SASE. Annual contest. Guidelines.

**A. D. PLAYERS**—2710 W. Alabama, Houston, TX 77098. Jeannette Clift George, Artistic Dir. Martha Doolittle, Lit. Mgr. Full-length or one-act comedies, dramas, musicals, children's plays, and adaptations with Christian world view. Submit resumé, cast list, and synopsis with SASE. Readings. Pays negotiable rates.

**ALABAMA SHAKESPEARE FESTIVAL**—The State Theatre, #1 Festival Drive, Montgomery, AL 36117–4605. Kent Thompson, Artistic Dir. Full-length adaptations and plays dealing with southern or black issues. Send resumé and synopsis in June.

**ALLEY THEATRE**—615 Texas Ave., Houston, TX 77002. Christopher Baker, Lit. Dir. Full-length plays and musicals, including translations and adaptations. Query with synopsis, 10 sample pages, and resumé. No unsolicited scripts.

**ALLIANCE THEATRE COMPANY**—1280 Peachtree St. N.E., Atlanta, GA 30309. Walter Bilderback, Dramaturg. Full-length comedies and dramas. Query with synopsis and cast list. Pay varies.

**AMERICAN LIVING HISTORY THEATER**—P.O. Box 2677, Hollywood, CA 90078. Dorene Ludwig, Artistic Dir. One-act, historically accurate (primary source materials only) dramas dealing with American people and events. Submit script with SASE. Reports in one to six months. Pays varying rates.

**AMERICAN PLACE THEATRE**—111 W. 46th St., New York, NY 10036. Elise Thoron, Dramaturg. "No unsolicited manuscripts accepted. We welcome scripts from writers who have had full or workshop productions of their plays by professional theaters. Writers may send a synopsis and the first 20 pages with SASE. We seek challenging, innovative works and do not favor obviously commercial material."

**AMERICAN REPERTORY THEATRE**—64 Brattle St., Cambridge, MA 02138. Robert Scanlan, Lit. Dir. No unsolicited manuscripts. Submit one-page description of play, 10-page sample; nothing returned without SASE; allow four to six months for response.

**AMERICAN STAGE**—P.O. Box 1560, St. Petersburg, FL 33731. Victoria Holloway, Artistic Dir. Full-length comedies and dramas. Send synopsis with short description of cast and production requirements with SAS postcard. Pays negotiable rates. Submit Sept. to Jan.

**AMERICAN STAGE COMPANY**—FDU, Box 336, Teaneck, NJ 07666. James Vagias, Exec. Prod. Full-length comedies, dramas, and musicals for cast of five or six and single set. Submit synopsis with resumé, cast list, and return postcard. Reads in spring; reports in three to four months. No unsolicited scripts.

**AMERICAN STANISLAVSKI THEATRE**—485 Park Ave., #6A, New York, NY 10022. Sonia Moore, Artistic Dir. Full-length or one-act dramas with important message. No offensive language. For cast ages 16 to 45. Submit script with SAS postcard in April and May; reports in Sept. No payment.

**AMERICAN THEATRE OF ACTORS**—314 W. 54th St., New York, NY 10019. James Jennings, Artistic Dir. Full-length dramas for a cast of two to six. Submit complete play and SASE. Reports in one to two months.

**MAXWELL ANDERSON PLAYWRIGHTS SERIES, INC.**—11 Esquire Rd., Norwalk, CT 06851. Muriel Nussbaum, Artistic Dir. Produces six to eight professional staged readings of new plays each year. Send complete script with SASE.

**ARENA STAGE**—Sixth and Maine Ave. S.W., Washington, DC 20024. Chiori Miyagawa, Lit. Mgr. No unsolicited manuscripts; send synopsis and first 10 pages of dialogue. Allow three to six months for reply.

**ARKANSAS REPERTORY THEATRE COMPANY**—601 S. Main, P.O. Box 110, Little Rock, AR 72203–0110. Brad Mooy, Lit. Mgr. Full-length comedies, dramas, and musicals; prefer up to eight characters. Send synopsis, cast list, resumé, and return postage. Reports in five to six months.

**ARTREACH TOURING THEATRE**—3074 Madison Rd., Cincinnati, OH 45209. Kathryn Schultz Miller, Artistic Dir. One-act dramas and adaptations for touring children's theater; cast to three, simple sets. Submit script with synopsis, cast list, resumé, recommendations, and SASE. Payment varies.

**BARTER THEATER**—P.O. Box 867, Abingdon, VA 24210. Rex Partington, Producing Dir. Full-length dramas, comedies, adaptations, musicals, and children's plays. Full workshop and reading productions. Allow six to eight months for report. Payment rates negotiable.

**BERKELEY REPERTORY THEATRE**—2025 Addison St., Berkeley, CA 94704. Sharon Ott, Artistic Dir. No unsolicited manuscripts; agent submissions or professional recommendations only. Reporting time: three to four months.

**BERKSHIRE THEATRE FESTIVAL**—Box 797, Stockbridge, MA 01262. Richard Dunlap, Artistic Dir. Full-length comedies, musicals, and dramas; cast to eight. Submit through agent only.

**BOARSHEAD THEATER**—425 S. Grand Ave., Lansing, MI 48933. John Peakes, Artistic Dir. Full-length comedies and dramas with simple sets and cast to 10. Send precis, five to 10 pages of dialogue, cast list with descriptions, and resumé. SAS postcard for reply.

**BRISTOL RIVERSIDE THEATRE**—Box 1250, Bristol, PA 19007. Susan D. Atkinson, Producing/Artistic Dir. Full-length plays with up to 10 actors on simple set. Submit synopsis with return postcard in summer. Offers workshops and readings.

**CALIFORNIA UNIVERSITY THEATRE**—California, PA 15419. Dr. Roger C. Emelson, Chairman. Unusual, avant-garde, and experimental one-act and full-length comedies and dramas, children's plays, and adaptations. Cast size varies. Submit synopsis with short, sample scene(s). Payment available.

**CHILDSPLAY, INC.**—Box 517, Tempe, AZ 85280. David Saar, Artistic Dir. Plays running 45 to 120 minutes: dramas, musicals, children's plays, and adaptations. Productions may need to travel. Cast size, four to eight. Submissions accepted July through November. Reports in two to six months. Payment varies.

**CIRCLE IN THE SQUARE/UPTOWN**—1633 Broadway, New York, NY 10019–6795. Theodore Mann, Artistic Dir. Full-length comedies, dramas, and adaptations. Send synopsis with resumé, cast list, and 10-page dialogue sample to Nancy Bosco, Lit. Advisor. No unsolicited scripts. SASE required.

**CIRCLE REPERTORY COMPANY**—161 Ave. of the Americas, New York, NY 10013. Lynn Thomson, Lit. Mgr. "We accept scripts submitted by agents or accompanied by professional recommendation only." Offers criticism "as often as possible." Reports in five months. Readings.

754

**CLASSIC STAGE COMPANY**—136 E. 13th St., New York, NY 10003. Patricia Taylor, Man. Dir. David Esbjornson, Artistic Dir. Full-length adaptations and translations of existing classic literature. Submit synopsis with cast list and SASE, September to May. Offers readings. Pays on royalty basis.

**CREATIVE THEATRE**—102 Witherspoon St., Princeton, NJ 08540. Eloise Bruce, Artistic Dir. Participatory plays for children, grades K through six; cast of four to six; arena or thrust stage. Submit manuscript with synopsis and cast list. Pay varies.

**THE CRICKET THEATRE**—1407 Nicollet Ave., Minneapolis, MN 55403. William Partlan, Artistic Dir. Send synopsis, resumé, and 10-page sample of work; "prefer contemporary plays." Cast to eight. Reports in six months.

**CROSSROADS THEATRE CO.**—7 Livingston Ave., New Brunswick, NJ 08901. Ricardo Khan, Artistic Dir. Sydné Mahone, Dir. of Play Development. Full-length and one-act dramas, comedies, musicals, and adaptations; issue-oriented experimental pieces that offer honest, imaginative, and insightful examinations of the African-American experience. Also interested in African, Caribbean, and inter-racial plays. Queries only, with synopsis, cast list, resumé, and SASE.

**DELAWARE THEATRE COMPANY**—200 Water St., Wilmington, DE 19801–5030. Cleveland Morris, Artistic Dir. Full-length comedies, dramas, musicals, and adaptations, with cast to 10; prefer single set. Send cast list, synopsis, and SASE. Reports in six months. Pays royalty.

**DENVER CENTER THEATRE COMPANY**—1050 13th St., Denver, CO 80204. Send full-length, previously unproduced scripts with cast to 12, June through November. Stipend and housing. Annual New Play Festival, "US West Theatre-Fest."

**DETROIT REPERTORY THEATRE**—13103 Woodrow Wilson Ave., Detroit, MI 48238. Barbara Busby, Lit. Mgr. Full-length comedies and dramas. Enclose SASE. Pays royalty.

**STEVE DOBBINS PRODUCTIONS**—650 Geary Blvd., San Francisco, CA 94102. Chuck Hilbert, Lit. Dir. Full-length comedies, dramas, and musicals. Cast to 12. Query with synopsis and resumé. No unsolicited manuscripts. Reports in six months. Offers workshops and readings. Pays 6% of gross.

**DORSET THEATRE FESTIVAL**—Box 519, Dorset, VT 05251. Jill Charles, Artistic Dir. Full-length comedies, musicals, dramas, and adaptations; cast to eight; simple set preferred. Agent submissions and professional recommendations only. Pays varying rates. Residencies at Dorset Colony House for Writers available October to June; see listing in "Writers Colonies" for details.

**DRIFTWOOD SHOWBOAT**—Box 1032, Kingston, NY 12401. Fred Hall, Resident Company Artistic Dir. Full-length family comedies for two- to six-person cast, single setting. No profanity. Submit cast list, synopsis, and return postcard September to June.

**EAST WEST PLAYERS**—4424 Santa Monica Blvd., Los Angeles, CA 90029. Nobu McCarthy, Artistic Dir. Brian Nelson, Dramaturg. Produces two to three new plays annually. Original plays, translations, adaptations, musicals, and youth theater. Readings. Prefer to see query letter with synopsis and 10 pages of dialogue; complete scripts also considered. Reports in five to six weeks for query; six months for complete script.

**ECCENTRIC CIRCLES THEATRE**—400 W. 43rd St., #4N, New York, NY 10036. Rosemary Hopkins, Artistic Dir. Full-length and one-act comedies and dramas with simple sets and a cast size to 10. Submit manuscript with resumé and SASE. Reports in six weeks.

**THE EMPTY SPACE THEATRE**—P.O. Box 1748, Seattle, WA 98111–1748. Kurt Beattie, Art. Dir. Unsolicited scripts accepted only from WA, OR, WY, MT, and ID. Outside five-state N.W. region: scripts accepted through agents or established theater groups only.

**ENSEMBLE STUDIO THEATRE**—549 W. 52nd St., New York, NY 10019. Address Lit. Mgr. Send full-length or one-act comedies and dramas, with resumé and SASE, September to April. Rarely pays for scripts. Fifteen readings of new plays per year.

**ENSEMBLE THEATRE COMPANY OF MARIN**—c/o Tamalpais High School, 700 Miller Ave., Mill Valley, CA 94941. Daniel Caldwell, Artistic Dir. Comedies, dramas, children's plays, adaptations, and scripts addressing high school issues for largely female cast (approx. three women per man). Send synopsis and resumé.

**FLORIDA STUDIO THEATRE**—1241 N. Palm Ave., Sarasota, FL 33577. Steve Ramay, New Play Development. Innovative smaller cast plays that are pertinent and contemporary. Query first with synopsis and SASE. Also accepting musicals.

**GEER THEATRICUM BOTANICUM, WILL**—Box 1222, Topanga, CA 90290. All types of scripts for outdoor theater, with large playing area. Submit synopsis with SASE. Pays varing rates.

**EMMY GIFFORD CHILDREN'S THEATER**—3504 Center St., Omaha, NE 68105. James Larson, Artistic Dir. Referrals only.

**THE GOODMAN THEATRE**—200 S. Columbus Dr., Chicago, IL 60603. Tom Creamer, Dramaturg. Queries required for full-length comedies or dramas submitted through recognized literary agents or producing organizations. No unsolicited scripts or synopses accepted.

**THE GUTHRIE THEATER**—725 Vineland Pl., Minneapolis, MN 55403. Full-length comedies, dramas, and adaptations. Manuscripts accepted only from recognized theatrical agents. Query with detailed synopsis and cast size. Reports in one to two months.

**HARRISBURG COMMUNITY THEATRE**—513 Hurlock St., Harrisburg, PA 17110. Thomas G. Hostetter, Artistic Dir. Full-length comedies, dramas, musicals, and adaptations; cast to 20; prefers simple set. Submit script with cast list, resumé, synopsis, and SAS postcard. Best time to submit: June to August. Reporting time: six months. Pays negotiable rates.

**HIPPODROME STATE THEATRE**—25 S.E. Second Pl., Gainesville, FL 32601. David Boyce, Dramaturg. Full-length plays with unit sets and casts to 10. Submit synopsis and resumé in summer and fall. Enclose return postcard.

**HOLLYWOOD THEATER COMPANY**—12838 Kling St., Studio City, CA 91604–1127. Rai Tasco, Artistic Dir. Full-length comedies and dramas for integrated cast. Include cast list and stamped return postcard with submission.

**HONOLULU THEATRE FOR YOUTH**—2846 Ualena St., Honolulu, HI 96819. Pam Sterling, Artistic Dir. Plays, 60 to 90 minutes playing time, for young people and family audiences. Adult casts. Contemporary issues, Pacific themes, etc. Unit sets, small cast. Query or send cover letter with synopsis, cast list, and SASE. Royalties negotiable.

**HORIZON THEATRE COMPANY**—P. O. Box 5376, Station E, Atlanta, GA 30307. Jeffrey and Lisa Adler, Artistic Directors. Full-length comedies, dramas, and satires. Encourages submissions by women writers. Cast to 10. Submit synopsis with cast list, resumé, and recommendations. Pays percentage. Readings. Reports in six months.

**HUNTINGTON THEATRE COMPANY**—252 Huntington Ave., Boston, MA 02115. Full-length comedies and dramas. Query with synopsis, cast list, resumé, recommendations, and return postcard.

**ILLINOIS THEATRE CENTER**—400 Lakewood Blvd., Park Forest, IL 60466. Steve S. Billig, Artistic Dir. Full-length comedies, dramas, musicals, and adaptations, for unit/fragmentary sets, and cast to eight. Send summary and return postcard. No unsolicited manuscripts. Pays negotiable rates. Workshops and readings offered.

**ILLUSTRATED STAGE COMPANY**—Box 640063, San Francisco, CA 94164–0063. Steve Dobbins, Artistic Dir. Full-length comedies, dramas, and musicals for a cast to 18. Query with synopsis and SASE. No unsolicited manuscripts. Offers workshops and readings.

**INVISIBLE THEATRE**—1400 N. First Ave, Tucson, AZ 85719. Deborah Dickey, Lit. Mgr. Reads queries for full-length comedies, dramas, musicals, and adaptations, January to May. Cast to 10; simple set. Pays royalty.

**JEWISH REPERTORY THEATRE**—344 E. 14th St., New York, NY 10003. Ran Avni, Artistic Dir. Full-length comedies, dramas, musicals, and adaptations, with cast to 10, relating to the Jewish experience. Pays varying rates. Enclose SASE.

**THE JULIAN THEATRE**—New College of California, 777 Valencia St., San Francisco, CA 94110. Address New Plays. Full-length comedies and dramas with a social statement. Send five- to 10-page scene, synopsis, cast description, and SASE. Pays on contractual basis. Allow two to nine months for reply. Readings offered.

**KUMU KAHUA**—Kennedy Theatre, Univ. of Hawaii at Manoa, 1770 East-West Rd., Honolulu, HI 96822. Dennis Carroll, Man. Dir. Full-length plays specially relevant to life in Hawaii. Prefer simple sets for arena and in-the-round productions. Submit resumé and synopsis January through April. Pays $35 per performance. Readings. Contests.

**LIVE OAK THEATRE**—311 Nueces, Austin, TX 78701. Mari Marchbanks, Lit. Mgr. Full-length plays, one-acts, translations, adaptations, musicals, and plays for young audiences. "Special interest in producing works of Texan and southern topics and new American plays." No unsolicited scripts; send synopsis, letter of inquiry, and 10 pages of dialogue. Contest. Guidelines.

**LOS ANGELES DESIGNERS' THEATRE**—P. O. Box 1883, Studio City, CA 91614–0883. Richard Niederberg, Artistic Dir. Full-length comedies, dramas, musicals, fantasies, or adaptations. Religious, political, social, and controversial themes encouraged. Nudity, "adult" language, etc., O.K. "Please detail in the cover letter what the writer's proposed involvement with the production would be." Payment varies.

**THE MAGIC THEATRE**—Fort Mason Center, Bldg. D, San Francisco, CA 94123. Mary DeDanan, Lit. Mgr. Comedies and dramas. "Special interest in poetic, non-linear, and multicultural work for mainstage productions, workshops, and readings." Query with synopsis, resumé, first 10 to 20 pages of script, and SASE. No unsolicited manuscripts. Pays varying rates.

**MANHATTAN THEATRE CLUB**—453 W. 16th, New York, NY 10011. Address Kate Loewald. Full-length and one-act comedies, dramas, and musicals. No unsolicited manuscripts. Send synopsis with 10 to 15 pages of dialogue, cast list, resumé, and SASE. Pays negotiable rates. Allow six months for reply.

**MILL MOUNTAIN THEATRE**—One Market Sq., Second Fl., Roanoke, VA 24011–1437. Jo Weinstein, Lit. Mgr. One-act comedies and dramas, 25 to 40 minutes long. No full-length plays. Send letter, resumé, and synopsis. Payment varies.

**MISSOURI REPERTORY THEATRE**—4949 Cherry St., Kansas City, MO 64110. Felicia Londré, Dramaturg. Full-length comedies and dramas. Query with synopsis, cast list, resumé, and return postcard. Pays standard royalty.

**MUSIC-THEATRE GROUP**—29 Bethune St., New York, NY 10014. Innovative works of music-theatre, to one and a half hours. Query only, with synopsis and return postcard. Best submission time: September to December.

**MUSICAL THEATRE WORKS**—440 Lafayette St., New York, NY 10003. Gary Littman, Lit. Mgr. Full-length musicals, cast to 15. Submit manuscript and cassette score with SASE. Responds in two months.

**NATIONAL BLACK THEATRE**—2033 Fifth Ave., Harlem, NY 10035. Submit to Tunde Samuel. Drama, musicals, and children's plays. "Scripts should reflect African and African-American lifestyle. Historical, inspirational, and ritualistic forms appreciated." Workshops and readings.

**NATIONAL PLAYWRIGHTS CONFERENCE, EUGENE O'NEILL THEATRE CENTER**—234 W. 44th St., Suite 901, New York, NY 10036. Annual competition to select new stage and television screenplays for development during the summer at organization's Waterford, CT, location. Submission deadline: December 1. Send #10-size SASE in the fall for guidelines to National Playwright's Conference, c/o above address. Pays stipend, plus travel/living expenses during conference.

**NEW EHRLICH THEATRE**—See New Theatre, Inc.

**NEW THEATRE, INC.**—(formerly New Ehrlich Theatre) 755 Boylston St., Suite 309, Boston, MA 02116. New full-length scripts (no musicals) by Massachusetts playwrights for readings and workshop productions. Include SASE. Address to NEWorks Submissions Program.

**NEW TUNERS/PERFORMANCE COMMUNITY**—1225 W. Belmont Ave., Chicago, IL 60657. Allan Chambers, Dramaturg. Full-length musicals only, for cast to 15; no wing/fly space. Send query with brief synopsis, cassette tape of score, cast list, resumé, SASE, and return postcard. Pays on royalty basis.

**NEW YORK SHAKESPEARE FESTIVAL/JOSEPH PAPP PUBLIC THEATER**—425 Lafayette St., New York, NY 10003. Jason Fogelson, Lit. Mgr. Plays and musical works for the theater, translations, and adaptations. Submit manuscript, cassette (with musicals), and SASE. Allow three to four months for response.

**NEW YORK STATE THEATRE INSTITUTE**—PAC 266, 1400 Washington Ave., Albany, NY 12222. Query for new musicals and plays for family audiences, with synopsis, cast list. Submit between June and August. Payment varies.

**ODYSSEY THEATRE ENSEMBLE**—2055 South Sepulveda Blvd., Los Angeles, CA 90025. Ron Sossi, Artistic Dir. Full-length comedies, dramas, musicals, and adaptations: provocative subject matter, or plays that stretch and explore the possibilities of theater. Query Jan Lewis, Lit. Mgr., with synopsis, eight to 10 pages of sample dialogue, and resumé. Pays variable rates. Allow two to six months for reply to script; two to four weeks reply for queries. Workshops and readings.

**OLD GLOBE THEATRE**—Simon Edison Center for the Performing Arts, Box 2171, San Diego, CA 92112. Address Mark Hofflund. Full-length comedies, dramas, and musicals. No unsolicited manuscripts. Submit through agent, or query with synopsis.

**OLDCASTLE THEATRE COMPANY**—Southern Vermont College, Box 1555, Bennington, VT 05201. Eric Peterson, Dir. Full-length comedies, dramas, and musicals for a small cast (up to 10) and a single stage set. Submit synopsis and cast list in the winter. Reports in two months. Offers workshops and readings. Pays expenses for playwright to attend rehearsals. Royalty.

**PENGUIN REPERTORY COMPANY**—Box 91, Stony Point, Rockland County, NY 10980. Joe Brancato, Artistic Dir. Full-length comedies and dramas with cast size to five. Submit script, resumé, and SASE. Payment varies.

**PENNSYLVANIA STAGE COMPANY**—837 Linden St., Allentown, PA 18101. Full-length plays with cast to eight; one set. Send synopsis, cast list, and SASE to Literary Dept. Pays negotiable rates. Allow six months for reply. Readings.

**PEOPLE'S LIGHT AND THEATRE COMPANY**—39 Conestoga Rd., Malvern, PA 19355. Alda Cortese, Lit. Mgr. One-act or full-length comedies, dramas, adaptations. No unsolicited manuscripts; query with synopsis, 10 pages of script required. Reports in six months. Payment negotiable.

**PIER ONE THEATRE**—Box 894, Homer, AK 99603. Lance Petersen, Lit. Dir. Full-length and one-act comedies, dramas, musicals, children's plays, and adaptations. Submit complete script; include piano score with musicals. New works given staged readings. "We think new works in the theater are extremely important!" Pays 8% of ticket sales for mainstage musicals; other payment varies.

**PLAYHOUSE ON THE SQUARE**—51 S. Cooper in Overton Sq., Memphis, TN 38104. Jackie Nichols, Artistic Dir. Full-length comedies, dramas; cast to 15. Southern playwrights given preference. Contest deadline is April for fall production. Pays $500. Sponsors Mid-South Playwrighting Contest; see listing in "Literary Prize Offers" section.

**PLAYWRIGHTS HORIZONS**—416 W. 42nd St., New York, NY 10036. Address Literary Dept. Full-length, original comedies, dramas, and musicals by American authors. Send resumé and SASE. Pays varying rates.

**PLAYWRIGHTS' PLATFORM**—164 Brayton Rd., Boston, MA 02135. Script development workshops and public readings for New England playwrights only. Full-length and one-act plays of all kinds. No sexist or racist material accepted. Residents of New England send scripts with short synopsis, resumé, return postcard, and SASE. Readings conducted at Mass. College of Art.

**POPLAR PIKE PLAYHOUSE**—7653 Old Poplar Pike, Germantown, TN 38138. Frank Bluestein, Artistic Dir. Full-length and one-act comedies, dramas, musicals, and children's plays. Submit synopsis with return postcard and resumé. Pays $300.

**PORTLAND STAGE COMPANY**—Box 1458, Portland, ME 04104. Not accepting unsolicted material at this time.

**PRINCETON REPERTORY COMPANY**—33A Hulfish St., Palmer Sq. North, Princeton, NJ 08542. Victoria Liberatori, Artistic Dir. Full-length comedies

759

and dramas for a cast to eight. One set. Submit synopsis with resumé and cast list, or complete manuscript. "Scripts with socially relevant themes that move beyond domestic drama preferred. The treatment of these themes might be lyrical, surreal, realistic, or high concept." Workshops and readings offered. Response within one year.

**THE REPERTORY THEATRE OF ST. LOUIS**—Box 191730, St. Louis, MO 63119. Query with brief synopsis, technical requirements, and cast size. Unsolicited manuscripts will be returned unread.

**THE ROAD COMPANY**—Box 5278 EKS, John City, TN 37603. Robert H. Leonard, Artistic Dir. Christine Murdock, Lit. Mgr. Full-length and one-act comedies, dramas with social/political relevance to small-town audiences. Send synopsis, cast list, and production history, if any. Pays negotiable rates. Reports in six to 12 months.

**ROUND HOUSE THEATRE**—12210 Bushey Dr., Silver Spring, MD 20902. Address Production Office Mgr. Full-length comedies, dramas, adaptations, and musicals; cast to 10; prefer simple set. Send one-page synopsis. No unsolicited manuscripts.

**SALT AND PEPPER MIME COMPANY/NEW ENSEMBLE ACTORS THEATRE**—320 E. 90th St., #1B, New York, NY 10128. Ms. Scottie Davis, Man. Prod. One-acts, all types, especially those conducive to "nontraditional" casting. "Very interested in pieces suitable to surrealistic or mimetic concept in philosophy or visual style." Cast size to 2. Send resumé, return postcard, cast list, and synopsis. Scripts reviewed from May to September. Payment of royalties based on rates established at beginning of run. Works also considered for readings, storyplayers, experimental development, and readers theater.

**SEATTLE GROUP THEATRE**—P.O. Box 45430, Seattle, WA 98105–0430. Full-length satires, dramas, musicals, and translations, cast to 10; simple set. Special interest in plays suitable for multi-ethnic cast; serious plays on social/cultural issues; satires and comedies with bite. Query with synopsis, sample dialogue, resumé, and SASE required. Reporting time: six weeks.

**SEATTLE REPERTORY THEATRE**—155 Mercer St., Seattle, WA 98109. Daniel Sullivan, Artistic Dir. Full-length comedies, dramas, and adaptations. Submit synopsis, 10-page sample, return postcard, and resumé to Mark Bly, Artistic Assoc. New plays series with workshops each spring.

**SOCIETY HILL PLAYHOUSE**—507 S. 8th St., Philadelphia, PA 19147. Walter Vail, Dramaturg. Full-length dramas and comedies; cast to six; simple set. Submit synopsis and SASE. Reports in six months. Nominal payment.

**SOUTH COAST REPERTORY**—P. O. Box 2197, Costa Mesa, CA 92628. John Glore, Lit. Mgr. Full-length comedies, dramas, musicals, juveniles. Query first with synopsis and resumé. Payment varies.

**SOUTHERN APPALACHIAN REPERTORY THEATRE**—P.O. Box 620, Mars Hill, NC 28754. James W. Thomas, Artistic Dir. Full-length comedies, dramas, musicals, and plays with Appalachian theme. Submit resumé, recommendations, full script, and SASE to Jan W. Blalock, Asst. Man. Dir. Send SASE for information on Southern Appalachian Playwright's Conference (held in January each year). Pays $500 royalty if play is selected for production during the summer season. Deadline for submissions is 1st of October each year.

**STAGE LEFT THEATRE**—3244 N. Clark, Chicago, IL 60657. Mike Troccoli and Sandra Verthein, Artistic Dirs. Full-length comedies, dramas, and adaptations for cast of one to 12. "We are committed to producing material that is politically and socially conscious." Offers workshops and readings. No unsolicited scripts. Payment varies.

**STAGE ONE: THE LOUISVILLE CHILDREN'S THEATRE**—425 W. Market St., Louisville, KY 40202. Adaptations of classics and original plays for children ages four to 18. Submit script with resumé and SASE. Reports in four months.

**STAGES REPERTORY THEATRE**—3201 Allen Pkwy., #101, Houston, TX 77019. Peter Bennett, Artistic Dir. Unproduced new works: full-length dramas, comedies, translations, and adaptations, with small casts and simple sets. Texas playwrights' festival held in the spring. Send for guidelines on submitting scripts to the festival.

**MARK TAPER FORUM**—135 N. Grand Ave., Los Angeles, CA 90012. Oliver Mayer, Lit. Assoc. Full-length comedies, dramas, musicals, juveniles, adaptations. Query first.

**THE TEN MINUTE MUSICALS PROJECT**—Box 461194, West Hollywood, CA 90046. Michael Koppy, Prod. One-act musicals. Include audio cassette, libretto, and lead sheets with submission. "We are looking for complete short musicals." Pays $250.

**THEATER ARTISTS OF MARIN**—Box 150473, San Rafael, CA 94915. Charles Brousse, Artistic Dir. Full-length comedies, dramas, and musicals for a cast of two to eight. Submit complete script with SASE. Reports in four to six months. Three showcase productions each year.

**THEATRE ON THE SQUARE**—450 Post St., San Francisco, CA 94102. Jonathan Reinis, Artistic Dir. Full-length comedies, dramas, and musicals for 15-person cast. Submit cast list and script with SASE. Reports in 30 days.

**THEATRE/TEATRO**—Bilingual Foundation for the Arts, 421 N. Ave., #19, Los Angeles, CA 90031. Margarita Galban, Artistic Dir. Full-length plays about Hispanic experience; small casts. Submit manuscript with SASE. Pays negotiable rates.

**THEATREWORKS/USA**—890 Broadway, 7th Fl., New York, NY 10003. Barbara Pasternack, Lit. Mgr. One-hour children's musicals for five-person cast. Playwrights must be within commutable distance to New York City. Submit outline or treatment, sample scenes, and song in spring, summer. Pays royalty.

**WALNUT STREET THEATRE COMPANY**—9th and Walnut Sts., Philadelphia, PA 19107. Alexa Kelly, Lit. Mgr. Full-length comedies, dramas, musicals, and adaptations; also, one- to five-character plays for studio stage. Submit 20 sample pages with return postcard, cast list, and synopsis. Musical submissions must include an audio tape. Reports in five months. Payment varies.

**THE WESTERN STAGE**—156 Homestead Ave., Salinas, CA 93901. Tom Humphrey, Artistic Dir. Joyce Lower, Dramaturg. The Salinas River Playwriting Festival. Prizewinner receives $2,000, royalties for the production, and a subsidized residency during development and rehearsal. Write for guidelines and required application.

**WISDOM BRIDGE THEATRE**—1559 W. Howard St., Chicago, IL 60626. Jeffrey Ortmann, Prod. Dir. Jose Calleja, Lit. Mgr. Plays dealing with contemporary social/political issues; small-scale musicals, literary adaptations; cast to 12. Synopsis only. No unsolicited scripts.

**WOOLLY MAMMOTH THEATRE COMPANY**—1401 Church St. N.W., Washington, DC 20005. Greg Tillman, Lit. Mgr. Looking for offbeat material, unusual writing. Unsolicited scripts accepted. Pay negotiable.

**GARY YOUNG MIME THEATRE**—23724 Park Madrid, Calabasas, CA 91302. Gary Young, Artistic Dir. Comedy monologues and two-person vignettes, for children and adults, one minute to 90 minutes in length; casts of one or two, and portable set. Pays varying rates. Enclose return postcard, resumé, recommendations, cast list, and synopsis.

## PLAY PUBLISHERS

**ART CRAFT PLAY COMPANY**—Box 1058, Cedar Rapids, IA 52406. Three-act comedies, mysteries, musicals, and farces, and one-act comedies or dramas, with one set, for production by junior or senior high schools. Pays on royalty basis or by outright purchase.

**BAKER'S PLAYS**—100 Chauncy St., Boston, MA 02111. Scripts for amateur production: one-act plays, children's plays, musicals, religious drama, full-length plays for high school production. Three- to four-month reading period. Include SASE.

**CHILDREN'S PLAYMATE**—1100 Waterway Blvd., P. O. Box 567, Indianapolis, IN 46206. Elizabeth A. Rinck, Ed. Plays, 200 to 600 words, for children ages 6 to 8: special emphasis on health, nutrition, exercise, and safety. Pays about 15¢ a word, on publication.

**CONTEMPORARY DRAMA SERVICE**—Meriwether Publishing Co., Box 7710, 885 Elkton Dr., Colorado Springs, CO 80903. Arthur Zapel, Ed. Books on theater arts subjects and anthologies. Textbooks for speech and drama. Easy-to-stage comedies, skits, one-acts, musicals, puppet scripts, full-length plays for schools and churches. (Junior high through college level; no elementary level material.) Adaptations of classics and improvised material for classroom use. Comedy monologues and duets. Chancel drama for Christmas and Easter church use. Enclose synopsis. Pays by fee arrangement or on royalty basis.

**THE DRAMATIC PUBLISHING CO.**—311 Washington St., Woodstock, IL 60098. Sarah Clark, Ed. Full-length and one-act plays and musicals for the stock, amateur, and children's theater market. Pays on royalty basis. Reports within 12 to 16 weeks.

**DRAMATICS**—Educational Theatre Assoc., 3368 Central Pkwy., Cincinnati, OH 45225–2392. Don Corathers, Ed. One-act and full-length plays for high school production. Pays $100 to $400, on acceptance.

**ELDRIDGE PUBLISHING COMPANY**—P. O. Drawer 216, Franklin, OH 45005. Nancy Vorhis, Ed. Dept. One-, two-, and three-act plays and operettas for schools, churches, community groups, etc. Special interest in comedies and Christmas plays. Include cassette for operettas. Pays varying rates. Responds in 2 to 3 months.

**SAMUEL FRENCH, INC.**—45 W. 25th St., New York, NY 10010. Lawrence R. Harbison, Ed. Full-length plays for dinner, community, stock, college, and high school theaters. One-act plays (30 to 45 minutes). Children's plays, 45 to 60 minutes. Pays on royalty basis.

**HEUER PUBLISHING COMPANY**—Drawer 248, Cedar Rapids, IA 52406. C. Emmett McMullen, Ed. One-act comedies and dramas for contest work;

three-act comedies, mysteries, or farces, and musicals, with one interior setting, for high school production. Pays royalty or flat fee.

**PIONEER DRAMA SERVICE**—P. O. Box 22555, Denver, CO 80222. Full-length and one-act plays; plays for young audiences; musicals, melodramas, and Christmas plays. No unproduced plays or plays with largely male casts or multiple sets. Query. Outright purchase or royalty.

**PLAYS, THE DRAMA MAGAZINE FOR YOUNG PEOPLE**—120 Boylston St., Boston, MA 02116–4615. Elizabeth Preston, Man. Ed. One-act plays, with simple settings, for production by young people, 7 to 17: comedies, dramas, farces, skits, holiday plays, adaptations of classics and folktales, biography plays, puppet plays, and creative dramatics. Maximum lengths: lower grades, 10 double-spaced pages; middle grades, 15 pages; junior and senior high, 20 pages. Send SASE for manuscript specification sheet. Query first for adaptations. Pays good rates, on acceptance. Buys all rights.

**THE RADIO PLAY**—Suite 230, 100 Boylston St., Boston, MA 02116. Stanley Richardson, Lit. Mgr. Original radio plays and radio adaptations of American classics in the public domain, 30 to 34 pages, to fit a thirty-minute program format. Query for adaptations only. Responds in up to 4 months for complete manuscripts. Pays $250 per script, on acceptance. Send SASE for style sheet.

## THE TELEVISION MARKET

The almost round-the-clock television offerings on commercial, educational, and cable TV stations may lead free-lance writers to believe that opportunities to sell scripts or program ideas are infinite. Unfortunately, this is not true. With few exceptions, producers and programmers do not consider scripts submitted directly to them, no matter how good they are. In general, free lancers can achieve success in this nearly closed field by concentrating on getting their fiction (short stories and novels) and nonfiction published in magazines or books, combed diligently by television producers for possible adaptations. A large percentage of the material offered over all types of networks (in addition to the motion pictures made in Hollywood) is in the form of adaptations of published material.

Writers who want to try their hand at writing directly for this very limited market should be prepared to learn the special techniques and acceptable format of scriptwriting. Also, experience in playwriting and a knowledge of dramatic structure gained through working in amateur, community, or professional theaters can be helpful.

Since virtually all TV producers will read scripts and queries submitted only through recognized agents, we've included a list of agents who have indicated to us that they are willing to read queries for TV scripts or screenplays. Association of Authors' Representatives (10 Astor Pl., 3rd Floor, New York, NY 10003) will send a list of member agents upon receipt of an SASE and a $5.00 check or money order. *Literary Market Place* (Bowker), available in most libraries, has list of agents; and *Literary Agents of North America* (Author Aid/Research Associates International, 340 E. 52nd St., New York, NY 10022) provides the most detailed information on agents and their needs. Before submitting scripts to producers or to agents, authors should query to learn whether they prefer to see the material in

763

script form, or as an outline or summary. A list of network (ABC, NBC, CBS, FOX) shows and production companies may be found in *Ross Reports Television*, published monthly by Television Index, Inc., (40–29 27th St., Long Island City, NY 11101; (718) 937–3990).

Writers may wish to register their story, treatment, series format, or script with the Writers Guild of America. This registration does not confer statutory rights, but it does supply evidence of authorship and date of authorship. Registration is effective for five years (and is renewable after that). The WGA's registration service is available to guild members and non-members for a reasonable fee. For more information, write to the Writers Guild of America Registration Service East, Inc., 555 W. 57th St., New York, NY 10019. Dramatic material can also be registered with the U.S. Copyright Office (Register of Copyrights, Library of Congress, Washington, DC 20559). Finally, those interested in writing for television may want to read such daily trade newspapers as *Daily Variety* (5700 Wilshire Blvd., Suite 120, Los Angeles, CA 90036) and *Hollywood Reporter* (6715 Sunset Blvd., Hollywood, CA 90028).

## TELEVISION SCRIPT AGENTS

**MICHAEL AMATO AGENCY**—1650 Broadway, Rm. 307, New York, NY 10019. Attn: Susan Tomkins. Screenplays, teleplays, and stage plays. Query with bio, one-page outline, 5 pages of dialogue, and SASE.

**MARCIA AMSTERDAM AGENCY**—41 W. 82nd St., #9A, New York, NY 10024. Screenplays and teleplays: comedy, romance, psychological suspense. Query with resumé and SASE.

**LOIS BERMAN**—240 W. 44th St., New York, NY 10036. Dramatic material. Query with SASE.

**DON BUCHWALD & ASSOCIATES**—10 E. 44th St., New York, NY 10017. Attn: Michael Traum. Screenplays, teleplays, and stage plays. Query with resumé and two-paragraph synopsis.

**EARTH TRACKS ARTISTS AGENCY**—4712 Avenue N, Suite 286, Brooklyn, NY 11234. Screenplays and teleplays. Query with SASE and syopsis no longer than one page; proposed material should have copyright.

**ROBERT A. FREEDMAN DRAMATIC AGENCY, INC.**—1501 Broadway, #2310, New York, NY 10036. Screenplays, teleplays, and stage plays. Query with SASE.

**BRIAN KEITH MOODY MANAGEMENT**—G.P.O. Box 7996, New York, NY 10116. Attn: Script Dept. Screenplays and teleplays. Query with outline. "Responds to queries only if interested in material."

**ARCHER KING, LTD.**—10 Columbus Cir., Rm. 1492, New York, NY 10019. Screenplays, teleplays, and stage plays. Query with SASE, outline, and resumé.

**OTTO R. KOZAK LITERARY AGENCY**—P.O. Box 152, Long Beach, NY 11561. Screenplays and teleplays. Query with outline or treatment and SASE.

**THE SHUKAT COMPANY, LTD.**—340 W. 55th St., #1A, New York, NY 10019—Attn: Patricia McLaughlin. Screenplays, teleplays, and stage plays. Query with outline, sample pages, and bio. "Since this is a small office, we will reply *only* if we are interest in the material. SASE not necessary."

**ANN WRIGHT REPRESENTATIVES, INC.**—136 E. 56th St., New York, NY 10022–3615. Dan Wright, Literary Dept. Screenplays with strong motion picture potential and stage plays; teleplays (no episodic material). Query with SASE.

**E.M. ZAHLER AGENCY**—181 Eighth Ave., Suite 6, New York, NY 10011. Screenplays: drama, comedy, action adventure, etc. Material for all TV series; teleplays. Query with SASE, outline, and bio.

# BOOK PUBLISHERS

The following list includes the major book publishers (adult and juvenile fiction and nonfiction) and a representative number of small publishers from across the country.

Before sending a complete manuscript to an editor, it is advisable to send a brief query letter describing the proposed book. The letter should also include information about the author's special qualifications for dealing with a particular topic and any previous publication credits. An outline of the book (or a synopsis for fiction) and a sample chapter may also be included.

It is common practice to submit a book manuscript to only one publisher at a time, although it is becoming more and more acceptable for writers, even those without agents, to submit the same query or proposal to more than one editor at the same time.

Book manuscripts may be sent in typing paper boxes (available from a stationer) and sent by first-class mail, or, more common and less expensive, by "Special Fourth Class Rate—Manuscript." For rates, details of insurance, and so forth, inquire at your local post office. With any submission to a publisher, be sure to enclose sufficient postage for the manuscript's return.

Royalty rates for hardcover books usually start at 10% of the retail price of the book and increase after a certain number of copies have been sold. Paperbacks generally have a somewhat lower rate, about 5% to 8%. It is customary for the publishing company to pay the author a cash advance against royalties when the book contract is signed or when the finished manuscript is received. Some publishers pay on a flat-fee basis.

**ABBEY PRESS**—St. Meinrad, IN 47577. Karen Katafiasz, Books Ed. Nonfiction books on self-care, pastoral care, spiritual growth, and inspirational themes guided by Judeo-Christian values rooted in the Catholic tradition. Query with outline/synopsis, sample chapters, and SASE.

**ABINGDON PRESS**—Imprint of The United Methodist Publishing House, P.O. Box 801, Nashville, TN 37202. Mary Catherine Dean, Ed. General-interest books: mainline, social issues, marriage/family, self-help, exceptional persons. Query with outline and one or two sample chapters. Guidelines.

**ACADEMIC PRESS**—Harcourt, Brace, Jovanovich, Inc., 1250 Sixth St., San Diego, CA 92101. Scientific and technical books for professionals; upper-level undergraduate and graduate science texts. Query.

**ACCENT BOOKS**—Box 15337, 12100 W. 6th Ave., Denver, CO 80215. Mary Nelson, Exec. Ed. Nonfiction church resources from evangelical Christian perspective; no trade books. "Request guidelines before querying." Query with sample chapters and SASE. Royalty. Paperback only.

**ACCESS PUBLISHERS**—1078 E. Otero Ave., Littleton, CO 80122. Kathy Fanchi, Ed. Novels on disk. Science fiction, mystery, adventure, fantasy, and mainstream novels, from 40,000 words. "We are looking for highly readable manuscripts that entertain." Query with outline and sample chapters. Royalty.

**ACE BOOKS**—Imprint of Berkley Publishing Group, 200 Madison Ave., New York, NY 10016. Susan Allison, V.P., Ed.-in-Chief. Science fiction and fantasy. Royalty. Query with first three chapters and outline to Laura Anne Gilman, Asst. Ed.

**ADAMA BOOKS**—See Modan Publishing.

**ADDISON-WESLEY PUBLISHING CO.**—Rt. 128, Reading, MA 01867–3999. General Publishing Group: Adult nonfiction on current topics including science, health, psychology, computers, software, business, biography, child care, etc. Specializing in literary nonfiction. Royalty.

**ALADDIN BOOKS**—See Macmillan Children's Book Group.

**ALASKA NORTHWEST BOOKS**—A Div. of GTE Discovery Publications, 22026 20th Ave. S.E., Bothell, WA 98021. Marlene Blessing, Ed.-in-Chief. Nonfiction, 50,000 to 100,000 words, with an emphasis on natural world and history of Alaska, Western Canada, Pacific Northwest, and Pacific Rim: travel books; cookbooks; field guides; children's books; outdoor recreation; natural history; native culture; lifestyle. Send query or sample chapters with outline. Guidelines available.

**ALGONQUIN BOOKS OF CHAPEL HILL**—Div. of Workman Publishing Co., Inc., Box 2225, Chapel Hill, NC 27515. Shannon Ravenel, Ed. Dir. Trade books, fiction and nonfiction, for adults.

**THE AMERICAN PSYCHIATRIC PRESS**—1400 K St. N.W., Washington, DC 20005. Carol C. Nadelson, M.D., Ed.-in-Chief. Books that interpret scientific and medical aspects of psychiatry for a lay audience and that address specific psychiatric problems. Authors must have appropriate credentials to write on medical topics. Query required. Royalty.

**ANCHOR BOOKS**—Imprint of Doubleday and Co., 666 Fifth Ave., New York, NY 10103. Martha K. Levin, Pub. Adult trade paperbacks. General fiction and nonfiction, sociology, psychology, philosophy, women's interest, etc. No unsolicited manuscripts.

**AND BOOKS**—702 S. Michigan, South Bend, IN 46618. Janos Szebedinsky, Ed. Adult nonfiction. Topics include computers, fine arts, health, philosophy, regional subjects, and social justice.

**APPALACHIAN MOUNTAIN CLUB BOOKS**—5 Joy St., Boston, MA 02108. Regional (New England) and national nonfiction titles, 250 to 400 pages, for adult audience; juvenile and young-adult nonfiction. Topics include guidebooks on non-motorized backcountry recreation, nature, mountain history/biography, search and rescue, conservation, and environmental management. Query with outline and sample chapters. Multiple queries considered. Royalty.

**APPLE BOOKS**—See Scholastic, Inc.

**ARCADE PUBLISHING**—Subsidiary of Little, Brown, and Co., 141 Fifth Ave., New York, NY 10010. Richard Seaver, Pub./Ed. Fiction, nonfiction, and children's books. Query first.

**ARCHWAY PAPERBACKS**—Pocket Books, 1230 Ave. of the Americas, New York, NY 10020. Patricia MacDonald, Exec. Ed. Young-adult contemporary fiction (suspense thrillers, survival adventure, strong boy/girl stories) and nonfiction (popular current topics), for ages 11 and up. Query and SASE required; include outline and sample chapter.

**ARCO PUBLISHING**—Div. of Simon & Schuster, Paramount Communications Bldg., 15 Columbus Cir., New York, NY 10023. Charles Wall, Ed.-in-Chief. Nonfiction, originals and reprints, from 50,000 words. Career guides, test preparation. Royalty. Query; unsolicited manuscripts not accepted.

**ASTARTE SHELL PRESS**—P.O. Box 10453, Portland, ME 04104. Elly Haney, Ed. Books on theology, politics, and social issues from a feminist/woman's perspective. Send sample chapters or complete manuscripts. Royalty.

**ATHENEUM PUBLISHERS**—Subsidiary of Macmillan Publishing Co., 866 Third Ave., New York, NY 10022. Mr. Lee Goerner, Pub. General nonfiction, biography, history, current affairs, fiction, belles lettres. Query with sample chapters and outline.

**THE ATLANTIC MONTHLY PRESS**—19 Union Square West, New York, NY 10003. Morgan Entrekin, Pub. Fiction, general nonfiction. Hardcover and trade paperback. Royalty. SASE required.

**AVALON BOOKS**—Imprint of Thomas Bouregy & Co., Inc., 401 Lafayette St., New York, NY 10003. Barbara J. Brett, Ed. Hardcover library books, 40,000 to 50,000 words: wholesome contemporary romances and mystery romances about young single (never married) women; wholesome westerns. Query with first chapter and outline. SASE required. Guidelines for SASE.

**AVERY PUBLISHING GROUP**—120 Old Broadway, Garden City Park, NY 11040. Nonfiction, from 40,000 words, on health, childbirth, child care, healthful cooking. Query first with SASE. Royalty.

**AVIATION PUBLISHERS**—See Markowski International Publishers.

**AVON BOOKS**—1350 Ave. of the Americas, New York, NY 10019. Robert Mecoy, Ed.-in-Chief. Genre fiction, general nonfiction, historical romance, 60,000 to 200,000 words. Science fiction, 75,000 to 100,000 words. Query with synopsis and sample chapters. Ellen Edwards, Historical Romance; John Douglas, Science Fiction; Chris Miller, Fantasy. *Camelot Books*: Ellen Krieger, Ed. Fiction and nonfiction for 7- to 10-year-olds. Query. *Flare Books*: Ellen Krieger, Ed. Fiction and nonfiction for 12-year-olds and up. Query. Royalty. Paperback only.

**BACKCOUNTRY PUBLICATIONS**—Div. of The Countryman Press, Inc., P. O. Box 175, Woodstock, VT 05091. Robin Dutcher-Bayer, Man. Ed. Regional guidebooks, 150 to 250 pages, on hiking, walking, canoeing, bicycling, mountain biking, cross-country skiing, and fishing covering New England, the mid-Atlantic states, and the Midwest. Send outline and sample chapter with SASE. Royalty.

**BAEN BOOKS**—Baen Enterprises, P.O. Box 1403, Riverdale, NY 10471–1403. Jim Baen, Pres. and Ed.-in-Chief. Strongly plotted science fiction; innovative fantasy. Query with synopsis and manuscript. Advance and royalty. Guidelines available for letter-sized SASE.

**BAKER BOOK HOUSE**—P. O. Box 6287, Grand Rapids, MI 49516–6287. Allan Fisher, Dir. of Publications. Religious nonfiction: books for trade, clergy, seminarians, collegians. Religious fiction. Royalty.

**BALLANTINE BOOKS**—201 E. 50th St., New York, NY 10022. Clare Ferraro, Ed.-in-Chief. General fiction and nonfiction. Query.

**BALSAM PRESS**—One Madison Ave., 25th Fl., New York, NY 10010. Barbara Krohn, Exec. Ed. General and illustrated adult nonfiction. Query. Royalty.

**BANTAM BOOKS**—Div. of Bantam, Doubleday, Dell, 666 Fifth Ave., New York, NY 10103. Linda Grey, Pres. Matthew Shear, Pub. Adult fiction and nonfiction. Mass-market titles, submit queries to the following imprints: *Crime Line*, crime and mystery fiction; *Domain*, frontier fiction, historical sagas, traditional westerns; *Falcon*, high-tech action, suspense, espionage, adventure; *Bantam Nonfiction*, wide variety of commercial nonfiction, including true crime, health and nutrition, sports, reference. Judy Gitenstein, Ed. Dir., *Books for Young Readers*: fiction and science fiction, ages 6 to 12. Beverly Horowitz, Ed. Dir., Books for Young Adults: fiction and non-formula romance for teens. Agented queries and manuscripts only.

**BARRICADE/DEMBNER BOOKS**—61 4th Ave., New York, NY 10003. Lyle Stuart, Pub. Popular reference books, popular medicine, controversial subjects. No first-person tragedy, no romance or pornography, no fads. Send synopsis and two sample chapters with SASE. Modest advances against royalties.

**BARRON'S**—250 Wireless Blvd., Hauppauge, NY 11788. Grace Freedson, Acquisitions Ed. Nonfiction for juveniles (science, nature, history, hobbies, and how-to) and picture books for ages 3 to 6. Nonfiction for adults (business, childcare, sports). Queries required. Guidelines.

**BAUHAN, PUBLISHER, WILLIAM L.**—Dublin, NH 03444. William L. Bauhan, Ed. Biographies, fine arts, gardening, and history books with an emphasis on New England. Submit query with outline and sample chapter.

**BEACON PRESS**—25 Beacon St., Boston, MA 02108. Wendy Strothman, Dir. Lauren Bryant, Sr. Ed. General nonfiction: world affairs, women's studies, anthropology, history, philosophy, religion, gay and lesbian studies, environment, nature writing, African-American studies, Asian-American studies, Native-American studies. Series: *Concord Library* (nature writing); *Asian Voices* (fiction and nonfiction); *Barnard New Women Poets*; *Black Women Writers* (fiction); *Men and Masculinity* (nonfiction); *Night Lights* (juveniles). Query first. SASE required.

**BEAR & COMPANY, INC.**—P.O. Drawer 2860, Santa Fe, NM 87504. Barbara Clow, Ed. Nonfiction "that will help transform our culture philosophically, environmentally, and spiritually." Query with outline and sample chapters. SASE required. Royalty.

**BEECH TREE BOOKS**—See William Morrow and Co., Inc.

**BERKLEY PUBLISHING GROUP**—200 Madison Ave., New York, NY 10016. Roger Cooper, Pub. General-interest fiction and nonfiction; science fiction, suspense and espionage novels; romance. Submit through agent only. Publishes both reprints and originals. Paperback only.

**BETHANY HOUSE PUBLISHERS**—6820 Auto Club Rd., Minneapolis, MN 55438. Address Editorial Dept. Religious fiction, nonfiction. Query with SASE required. Royalty.

**BETTER HOMES AND GARDENS BOOKS**—See Meredith Corporation.

**BINFORD & MORT PUBLISHING**—1202 N.W. 17th Ave., Portland, OR 97209. J. F. Roberts, Ed. Books on subjects related to the Pacific Coast and the Northwest. Lengths vary. Query first. Royalty.

**BLAIR, PUBLISHER, JOHN F.**—1406 Plaza Dr., Winston-Salem, NC 27103. Stephen D. Kirk, Ed. Dept. Biography, history, fiction, folklore, and guidebooks, with Southeastern tie-in. Length: at least 50,000 words. Query. Royalty.

**BLUEMOON BOOKS, INC.**—(formerly Rosset & Co.) 61 Fourth Ave., New York, NY 10003. Barney Rosset, Pub. Fiction and nonfiction on a variety of topics. Send complete manuscript or sample chapters and SASE.

**BONUS BOOKS**—160 E. Illinois St., Chicago, IL 60611. Larry Razbadouski, Ed. Nonfiction; topics vary widely. Query with sample chapters and SASE. Royalty.

**BOOKS FOR PROFESSIONALS**—See Harcourt Brace Jovanovich, Publishers.

**BOYDS MILL PRESS**—*Highlights for Children*, 910 Church St., Honesdale, PA 18431. Beth Troop, Manuscript Coordinator. Hardcover trade books for children. Fiction: picture books; middle-grade fiction with fresh ideas and involving story; young-adult novels of literary merit. Nonfiction should be "fun, entertaining, and informative." Send outline and sample chapters for young-adult novels and nonfiction, complete manuscripts for all other categories. Royalty.

**BRADBURY PRESS**—866 Third Ave., New York, NY 10022. Barbara Lalicki, Ed. Hardcover: fiction (general, humor, mysteries), grades 4 to 12; nonfiction (science, sports, history) up to grade 6; picture books, to age 8. Submit complete manuscript. Royalty.

**BRANDEN PUBLISHING COMPANY**—17 Station St., Box 843, Brookline Village, MA 02147. Novels, biographies, and autobiographies. Especially books by or on women, 250 to 350 pages. Also considers queries on history, computers, business, performance arts, and translations. Query only with SASE. Royalty.

**BRICK HOUSE PUBLISHING**—Francestown Turnpike, New Boston, NH 03070. Richard Katzenberg, Ed. Books on New England travel, energy, and environment. Query with outline and sample chapters. Royalty.

**BRISTOL PUBLISHING ENTERPRISES**—P.O. Box 1737, San Leandro, CA 94577. Patricia J. Hall, Ed. Mature reader series: nonfiction for 50+ population, approximately 40,000 words. *Nitty Gritty Cookbooks*: 120-recipe manuscripts. Query with outline, sample chapters, SASE. Royalty.

**BROADMAN PRESS**—127 Ninth Ave. N., Nashville, TN 37234. Harold S. Smith, Mgr. Religious and inspirational fiction and nonfiction. Query. Royalty.

**BROWNDEER PRESS**—Imprint of Harcourt Brace Jovanovich Children's Books, P.O. Box 80160, Portland, OR 97280–1160. Linda Zuckerman, Ed. Dir. Picture books, humorous middle-grade fiction, and young-adult material written from an unusual perspective or about an unusual subject. Query for nonfiction with cover letter, resumé, and sample chapter; send complete manuscript for picture books (avoid rhyming text). For longer fiction, send first three chapters, synopsis, and short cover letter with biographical information. SASE required.

**BUCKNELL UNIVERSITY PRESS**—Bucknell University, Lewisburg, PA 17837. Mills F. Edgerton, Jr., Dir. Scholarly nonfiction. Query. Royalty.

**BULFINCH PRESS**—Div. of Little, Brown and Co., 34 Beacon St., Boston,

MA 02108. Books on fine arts and photography. Query with outline or proposal and vita.

**C&T PUBLISHING**—5021 Blum Rd., #1, Martinez, CA 94553. Diane Pedersen, Ed. Quilting books, 64 to 200 finished pages. "Our focus is how-to, although we will consider picture, inspirational, or history books on quilting." Send query, outline, or sample chapters. Multiple queries considered. Royalty.

**CAMELOT BOOKS**—See Avon Books.

**CANDLEWICK PRESS**—2067 Massachusetts Ave., Cambridge, MA 02140. Address Editors. Children's books: baby books, picture books, easy-to-reads and read-alouds, middle-grade fiction and nonfiction, and young-adult novels. Poetry and all genres of fiction and nonfiction considered. Query or send complete manuscript. Royalty.

**CANE HILL PRESS**—225 Varick St., New York, NY 10014. Steven Schrader, Ed./Pub. Trade paperbacks. "Our purpose is to publish and encourage excellent writers who haven't clicked commercially." Query. Pays $1,500 flat fee for 1,000-copy first printings.

**CAPSTONE PRESS, INC.**—P.O. Box 669, N. Mankato, MN 56001–0669. Juvenile theme-books for children in preschool to grade 6. Send SASE for catalogue of series themes. Query required. Pays in flat fee.

**CAROLRHODA BOOKS**—241 First Ave. N., Minneapolis, MN 55401. Rebecca Poole, Ed. Complete manuscripts for ages 4 to 12: biography, science, nature, history, photo essays; historical fiction, 10 to 15 pages, for ages 6 to 10. Guidelines. Hardcover.

**CARROLL AND GRAF PUBLISHERS, INC.**—260 Fifth Ave., New York, NY 10001. Kent E. Carroll, Exec. Ed. General fiction and nonfiction. Query with SASE. Royalty.

**CASSANDRA PRESS**—P.O. Box 868, San Rafael, CA 94915. New Age, holistic health, metaphysical, and psychological books. Query with outline and sample chapters, or complete manuscript. Include SASE. Royalty.

**THE CATHOLIC UNIVERSITY OF AMERICA PRESS**—620 Michigan Ave. N.E., Washington, DC 20064. David J. McGonagle, Dir. Scholarly nonfiction: American and European history (both ecclesiastical and secular); Irish studies; American and European literature; philosophy; political theory; theology. Query with prospectus, annotated table of contents, or introduction and resumé. Royalty.

**CHARIOT FAMILY PUBLISHING**—A Div. of David C. Cook Publishing Co., 850 N. Grove Ave., Elgin, IL 60120. Catherine Davis, Exec. Ed., *Chariot Children's Books*: fiction that "helps children better understand themselves and their relationship with God"; nonfiction that illuminates the Bible; picture books, ages 1 to 7; fiction for ages 8 to 10, 10 to 12, and 12 to 14. Life *Journey General Titles*: fiction with underlying spiritual theme; books on parenting from a Christian perspective. Lengths and payment vary. Query required. Guidelines.

**CHARTER/DIAMOND BOOKS**—Imprint of Berkley Publishing Co., 200 Madison Ave., New York, NY 10012. Leslie Gelbman, Ed.-in-Chief. Adventure, suspense fiction, historical romances, regencies, women's contemporary fiction, family sagas, and historical novels. Westerns. Paperback.

**CHATHAM PRESS**—P. O. Box A, Old Greenwich, CT 06870. Roger H. Lourie, Man. Dir. Books on the Northeast coast, New England maritime subjects, and the ocean. Large photography volumes. Query with outline, sample chapters, illustrations, and SASE large enough for the return of material. Royalty.

**CHELSEA GREEN PUBLISHING CO.**—Route 113, P.O. Box 130, Post Mills, VT 05058–0130. Ian Baldwin, Jr., Ed. Primarily nonfiction: natural history, environmental issues, outdoor recreation, and travel. Occasional fiction with northern New England or environmental focus. Query with outline and SASE. Royalty.

**CHICAGO REVIEW PRESS**—814 N. Franklin St., Chicago, IL 60610. Amy Teschner, Ed. Nonfiction: project books for young people ages 10 to 18, architecture, anthropology, travel, nature, and regional topics. Query with outline and sample chapters.

**CHRONICLE BOOKS**—275 Fifth St., San Francisco, CA 94103. Topical nonfiction, history, biography, fiction, art, photography, architecture, nature, food, regional, and children's books. Send proposal with SASE.

**CLARION BOOKS**—215 Park Ave. S., New York, NY 10003. Dorothy Briley, Ed.-in-Chief/Pub. Fiction, nonfiction, and picture books: short novels and lively stories for ages 6 to 10 and 8 to 12, historical fiction, humor; picture books for infants to age 7; biography, natural history, social studies, American and world history for readers 5 to 8, and 9 and up. Royalty. Hardcover.

**CLARK CITY PRESS**—P.O. Box 1358, Livingston, MT 59047. Collections of poems, short stories, and essays, novels, biographies, and occasional children's books. No unsolicited manuscripts. Royalty.

**CLEIS PRESS**—P.O. Box 14684, San Francisco, CA 94114. Frédérique Delacoste, Ed. Fiction and nonfiction, 200 pages, by women. No poetry. Send SASE with two first-class stamps for catalogue before querying. Pays in royalties.

**CLIFFHANGER PRESS**—P.O. Box 29527, Oakland, CA 94604–9527. Nancy Chirich, Ed. Mystery and suspense. Unagented authors only. Send SASE for guidelines before querying. Unsolicited manuscripts returned unopened. Quality trade paperbacks. Royalty. Guidelines.

**CLOVERDALE PRESS**—109 W. 17th St., New York, NY 10011. Book packager. Adult nonfiction; YA, middle- and lower-grade fiction and nonfiction. "Since our requirements vary considerably and frequently according to our publishers' needs, please send query letter before submitting material." Address YA and juvenile to Marion Vaarn; adult to Lisa Howell.

**COBBLEHILL BOOKS**—375 Hudson St., New York, NY 10014. Joe Ann Daly, Ed. Dir. Rosanne Lauer, Sr. Ed. Fiction and nonfiction for preschoolers through junior high school. Query with outline and sample chapters. For picture books send complete manuscript. Royalty.

**COFFEE HOUSE PRESS**—27 N. 4th St., Suite 400, Minneapolis, MN 55401. Address M. Wiegers. Fiction (no genres) and literary essays. Query or send complete manuscript. Allow six months for response. Royalty.

**COLLIER BOOKS**—See Macmillan Publishing Co. and Macmillan Children's Book Group.

**COMPCARE PUBLISHERS**—2415 Annapolis Ln., Minneapolis, MN 55441. Margaret Marsh, Man. Ed. Adult nonfiction; young-adult nonfiction: books on recovery from addictive/compulsive behavior; emotional health; growth in personal, couple, and family relationships. Submit proposal and two sample chapters or complete manuscript. Royalty.

**COMPUTE BOOKS**—324 West Wendover Ave., Greensboro, NC 27408. PC game books, video game books. Also specializes in Amiga and PC application books.

**CONCORDIA PUBLISHING HOUSE**—3558 S. Jefferson Ave., St. Louis, MO 63118. Practical nonfiction with explicit religious content, conservative Lutheran doctrine. Children's fiction with explicit Christian content. No poetry. Query. Royalty.

**CONFLUENCE PRESS**—Spalding Hall, Lewis Clark State College, 8th Ave. and 6th St., Lewiston, ID 83502–2698. James Hepworth, Dir. Fiction, nonfiction, and poetry, of varying lengths, "to promote and nourish young writers in particular, to strive for literary and artistic excellence." Flat fee or royalty. Send query, outline, and sample chapters.

**CONSUMER REPORTS BOOKS**—101 Truman Ave., Yonkers, NY 10703. Address Exec. Ed. Medicine/health, finances, automotive, homeowners, food and cooking topics. Submit complete manuscript, or send contents, outline, three chapters, and resumé.

**CONTEMPORARY BOOKS, INC.**—180 N. Michigan Ave., Chicago, IL 60601. Nancy Crossman, Ed. Dir. Trade nonfiction, 100 to 400 pages, on health, fitness, sports, cooking, humor, business, popular culture, biography, real estate, finance, women's issues. Query with outline and sample chapters. Royalty.

**CRAFTSMAN BOOK COMPANY**—6058 Corte del Cedro, P.O. Box 6500, Carlsbad, CA 92018. Laurence D. Jacobs, Ed. How-to construction and estimating manuals and software for builders, 450 pages. Query. Royalty. Softcover.

**CREATIVE ARTS BOOK CO.**—833 Bancroft Way, Berkeley, CA 94710. Donald S. Ellis, Pub. Adult nonfiction: women's issues, music, and California topics. Query with outline and sample chapters. Include SASE. Royalties.

**THE CROSSING PRESS**—P.O. Box 1048, Freedom, CA 95019. Elaine Goldman Gill, John Gill, Pubs. Health, men's studies, feminist studies, spiritual works, gay topics, cookbooks; fiction. Royalty.

**CROWELL, THOMAS Y.**—See HarperCollins Children's Books.

**CROWN BOOKS FOR YOUNG READERS**—225 Park Ave. S., New York, NY 10003. Simon Boughton, Ed.-in-Chief. Children's nonfiction (biography, science, sports, nature, music, and history), and picture books for ages 3 and up. Query with outline and sample chapter; send manuscript for picture books. Guidelines.

**DANIEL AND COMPANY, JOHN**—P.O. Box 21922, Santa Barbara, CA 93121. John Daniel, Pub. Books, to 200 pages, in the field of belles lettres and literary memoirs; stylish and elegant writing; essays and short fiction dealing with social issues; one poetry title per year. Send synopsis or outline with no more that 50 sample pages and SASE. Allow 6 to 8 weeks for response. Royalty.

**DAW BOOKS, INC.**—375 Hudson St., 3rd Fl., New York, NY 10014–3658. Elizabeth R. Wollheim, Ed.-in-Chief. Sheila E. Gilbert, Sr. Ed. Peter Stampfel, Submissions Ed. Science fiction and fantasy, 60,000 to 120,000 words. Royalty.

**DEARBORN FINANCIAL PUBLISHING, INC.**—Div. of Dearborn Publishing Group Inc., 520 N. Dearborn St., Chicago, IL 60610. Anita A. Constant, Sr. V.P. Books on financial services, real estate, banking, etc. Query with outline and sample chapters. Royalty and flat fee.

**DEL REY BOOKS**—201 E. 50th St., New York, NY 10022. Shelly Shapiro, Exec. Ed. Veronica Chapman, Sr. Ed. Science fiction and fantasy, 60,000 to 120,000 words; first novelists welcome. Material must be well paced with logical resolutions. Fantasy with magic basic to plotline. Complete manuscripts preferred, or send outline with three sample chapters. Royalty.

**DELACORTE PRESS**—666 Fifth Ave., New York, NY 10103. Brian DeFiore, Jackie Farber, Emily Reichert, Dan Levy, Eds. Adult fiction and nonfiction.

Juvenile and YA fiction (George Nicholson, Ed.). Accepts fiction (mystery, YA, romance, fantasy, etc.) from agents only.

**DELANCEY PRESS**—P.O. Box 40285, Philadelphia, PA 19106. Wesley Morrison, Ed. Dir. Adult genre fiction and all types of nonfiction, 60,000 words. Query. Royalty.

**DELL BOOKS**—666 Fifth Ave., New York, NY 10103. Family sagas, historical romances, war action, general fiction, occult/horror/psychological suspense, true crime, men's adventure. Send four-page narrative synopsis for fiction, or an outline for nonfiction. Enclose SASE. Address submissions to Dell Books, Editorial Dept., Book Proposal. Allow 2 to 3 months for response.

**DELTA BOOKS**—666 Fifth Ave., New York, NY 10103. General-interest nonfiction: psychology, feminism, health, nutrition, child care, science, self-help, and how-to. Send an outline with SASE. Address Editorial Dept., Book Proposal.

**DEVIN-ADAIR PUBLISHERS, INC.**—6 N. Water St., Greenwich, CT 06830. C. de la Belle Issue, Pub. J. Andrassi, Ed. Books on conservative affairs, Irish topics, photography, Americana, self-help, health, gardening, cooking, and ecology. Send outline, sample chapters, and SASE. Royalty.

**DIAL BOOKS FOR YOUNG READERS**—375 Hudson St., New York, NY 10014. Phyllis Fogelman, Pub./Ed.in-Chief. Picture books; easy-to-read books; middle-grade readers; young-adult fiction and some nonfiction. Submit complete manuscript for picture books and easy-to-reads; outline and sample chapters for nonfiction and novels. Enclose SASE. Royalty.

**DILLON PRESS**—Macmillan Publishing Co. 866 Third Ave., New York, NY 10022. Joyce Stanton, Ed. Juvenile nonfiction, 10 to 90 pages: U.S. history and social studies, Third World countries, world geography/places of interest, environmental and science topics, unusual or remarkable animals, contemporary and historical biographies for middle-grade levels. Royalty and outright purchase. Query.

**DORLING KINDERSLEY, INC.**—232 Madison Ave., New York, NY 10016. Attn: B. Alison Weir. Preschool and children's picture books that encourage independence and learning. Submit complete manuscripts or sample chapters.

**DOUBLE D. WESTERN**—See Doubleday and Co.

**DOUBLEDAY AND CO.**—666 Fifth Ave., New York, NY 10103. Stephen Rubin, Pub./Pres. David Gernert, Ed.-in-Chief. Hardcover: *Perfect Crime, Double D. Western*, romance fiction, mystery/suspense fiction, science fiction, 70,000 to 80,000 words. Send query and outline. Paperback: *Currency* line, business books for a general audience on "the art of getting things done." No unsolicited manuscripts.

**DUNNE BOOKS, THOMAS**—Imprint of St. Martin's Press, 175 Fifth Ave., New York, NY 10010. Thomas L. Dunne, Ed. Adult fiction (mysteries, trade, SF, etc.) and nonfiction (history, biographies, science, politics, etc.). Query with outline, sample chapters, and SASE. Royalty.

**DUQUESNE UNIVERSITY PRESS**—600 Forbes Ave., Pittsburgh, PA 15282–0101. Scholarly publications in the humanities and social sciences.

**DUTTON ADULT**—Div. of Penguin USA, 375 Hudson St., New York, NY 10014. Kevin Mulroy, Ed. Dir. Fiction and nonfiction books. Manuscripts accepted only from agents or on personal recommendation.

**DUTTON CHILDREN'S BOOKS**—Div. of Penguin USA, 375 Hudson St., New York, NY 10014. Lucia Monfried, Ed.-in-Chief. Picture books, easy-to-read books; fiction and nonfiction for preschoolers to young adults. Submit outline and sample chapters with query for fiction and nonfiction, complete manuscripts for picture books and easy-to-read books. Manuscripts should be well-written with fresh ideas and child appeal.

**EERDMANS PUBLISHING COMPANY, INC., WM. B**—255 Jefferson Ave. S.E., Grand Rapids, MI 49503. Jon Pott, Ed.-in-Chief. Protestant, Roman Catholic, and Orthodox theological nonfiction; American religious history; some fiction. For children's religious books, query Amy Eerdmans, Children's Book Ed. Royalty.

**EMC CORP.**—300 York Ave., St. Paul, MN 55101. Eileen Slater, Ed. Vocational, career, and consumer education textbooks. Royalty. No unsolicited manuscripts.

**ENSLOW PUBLISHERS, INC.**—Bloy St. & Ramsey Ave., Box 777, Hillside, NJ 07205. Brian D. Enslow, Ed./Pub. Nonfiction books for young people. Areas of emphasis are children's and young-adult books for ages 10 to 18 in the fields of science, social studies, and biography. Other specialties for young people are reference books for all ages and easy reading books for teenagers.

**ERDMANN PUBLISHING, ROBERT**—810 W. Los Vallecitos Blvd., Suite 210, San Marcos, CA 92069. Glenn Austin, Ed. Nonfiction books: business/personal finance, child care/parenting, marriage/relationships, hobby/crafts, psychology, and travel. Royalty. Send outline and sample chapters or complete manuscript.

**ERIKSSON, PUBLISHER, PAUL S.**—208 Battell Bldg., Middlebury, VT 05753. General nonfiction (send outline and cover letter); some fiction (send three chapters with query). Royalty.

**ESTRIN PUBLISHING**—2811 Wilshire Blvd., Suite 707, Santa Monica, CA 90403. Dana Graves, Ed. Books, 300 to 400 pages, for paralegal professionals. Query with outline and sample chapters; multiple queries considered. Royalty.

**EVANS & CO., INC., M.**—216 E. 49th St., New York, NY 10017. Books on humor, health, self-help, popular psychology, and cookbooks. Western fiction for adults; fiction and nonfiction for young adults. Query with outline, sample chapter, and SASE. Royalty.

**EVENT HORIZON PRESS**—P.O. Box 867, Desert Hot Springs, CA 92240. Joseph Cowles, Ed. Adult fiction and nonfiction. Poetry books, from 50 pages. Juvenile fiction and nonfiction for 7- to 10-year-olds. Query with outline and sample chapters, or send complete manuscript. Royalty.

**FABER AND FABER**—50 Cross St., Winchester, MA 01890. Novels, anthologies, and nonfiction books on topics of popular culture and general interest. Query with SASE. Royalty.

**FACTS ON FILE PUBLICATIONS**—460 Park Ave. S., New York, NY 10016. Susan Schwartz, Ed. Dir. Reference and trade books on nature, business, science, health, language, history, the performing arts, etc. (No fiction, poetry, computer books, technical books or cookbooks.) Query with outline, sample chapter, and SASE. Royalty. Hardcover.

**FANFARE**—Imprint of Bantam Books, 666 Fifth Ave., New York, NY 10103. Nita Taublib, Assoc. Pub. Mass-market women's fiction of all kinds, from historical to contemporary, from romantic suspense to romantic fantasy. No word limit. Study field before submitting. Query required.

**FARRAR, STRAUS & GIROUX**—19 Union Sq. West, New York, NY 10003. Adult and juvenile fiction and nonfiction.

**FAWCETT/IVY BOOKS**—Imprint of Ballantine Books, 201 E. 50th St., New York, NY 10022. Barbara Dicks, Ed. Adult mysteries, regencies and historical romances, 75,000 to 120,000 words. Mysteries and problem novels, 60,000 to 70,000 words, for middle readers to young adults. Query with outline and sample chapters. Average response time is 2 to 4 months. Royalty.

**FELL PUBLISHERS, INC.**—See Lifetime Books, Inc.

**THE FEMINIST PRESS AT THE CITY UNIVERSITY OF NEW YORK** —311 E. 94th St., New York, NY 10128. Florence Howe, Pub. Reprints of significant "lost" fiction, original memoirs, autobiographies, biography; intercultural anthologies; handbooks; bibliographies. "We are especially interested in international literature, women and peace, women and music, and women of color." Royalty.

**FIELDING TRAVEL BOOKS**—See William Morrow and Co., Inc.

**FINE, INC., DONALD I.**—19 W. 21st St., New York, NY 10010. Literary and commercial fiction. General nonfiction. No queries or unsolicited manuscripts. Submit through agent only.

**FIREBRAND BOOKS**—141 The Commons, Ithaca, NY 14850. Nancy K. Bereano, Ed. Feminist and lesbian fiction and nonfiction. Royalty. Paperback and library edition cloth.

**FLARE BOOKS**—See Avon Books.

**FORTRESS PRESS**—426 S. Fifth St., Box 1209, Minneapolis, MN 55440. Dr. Marshall D. Johnson, Dir. Books in the areas of biblical studies, theology, ethics, and church history for academic and professional markets, including libraries. Query first.

**FOUR WINDS PRESS**—Imprint of Macmillan Publishing Co., 866 Third Ave., New York, NY 10022. Virginia Duncan, Ed.-in-Chief. Juveniles: picture books, nonfiction for all ages. Fiction for young children. Query with SASE required for nonfiction. Hardcover only.

**THE FREE PRESS**—See Macmillan Publishing Co.

**FRIENDS UNITED PRESS**—101 Quaker Hill Dr., Richmond, IN 47374. Ardith Talbot, Ed. Nonfiction and fiction, 200 pages, on Quaker history, biography, and Quaker faith experience. Query with outline and sample chapters. Royalty.

**GARDEN WAY PUBLISHING COMPANY**—Storey Communications, Schoolhouse Rd., Pownal, VT 05261. Galen Stege, Ed. How-to books on gardening, cooking, crafts, building, animals, country living. Royalty or outright purchase. Query with outline and sample chapter.

**GARRETT PARK PRESS**—P.O. Box 190, Garrett Park, MD 20896. Robert Calvert, Jr., Pub. Reference books on career education, occupational guidance, and financial aid only. Query required. Multiple queries considered but not encouraged. Royalty.

**GEORGIA STATE UNIVERSITY BUSINESS PRESS**—University Plaza, Atlanta, GA 30303-3093. Books, software, research monographs, and directories in the business sciences and related disciplines.

**GERINGER BOOKS, LAURA**—See HarperCollins Children's Books.

**GIBBS SMITH PUBLISHER/PEREGRINE SMITH BOOKS**—P. O. Box 667, Layton, UT 84401. Steve Chapman, Fiction Ed. Madge Baird, Nonfiction Ed. Adult fiction and nonfiction. Query. Royalty.

**GINIGER CO. INC., THE K.S.**—250 W. 57th St., Suite 519, New York, NY 10107. General nonfiction. Query with SASE; no unsolicited manuscripts. Royalty.

**GLENBRIDGE PUBLISHING**—4 Woodland Ln., Macomb, IL 61455. James A. Keene, Ed. Nonfiction books on a variety of topics, including business, history, and psychology. Query with sample chapter. Royalty.

**GLOBE PEQUOT PRESS, THE**—6 Business Park Rd., Box 833, Old Saybrook, CT 06475. Laura Strom, Assoc. Ed. Nonfiction with national and regional focus; nature and outdoor guides; travel; environment and natural sciences; how-tos; gardening; journalism and media. Query with sample chapter, contents, and one-page synopsis. SASE required. Royalty.

**GOLD EAGLE BOOKS**—See Worldwide Library.

**GOLDEN PRESS**—See Western Publishing Co., Inc.

**GOLDEN WEST PUBLISHERS**—4113 N. Longview, Phoenix, AZ 85014. Hal Mitchell, Ed. Cookbooks and Western history and travel books. Query first. Pays royalty or flat fee.

**GRAYWOLF PRESS**—2402 University Ave., Suite 203, St. Paul, MN 55114. Scott M. Walker, Ed. Literary fiction (short story collections and novels), poetry, and essays. Query with sample chapters.

**GREEN TIGER PRESS**—See Simon & Schuster Books for Young Readers.

**GREENWILLOW BOOKS**—Imprint of William Morrow and Co., Inc., 1350 Ave. of the Americas, New York, NY 10019. Susan Hirschman, Ed.-in-Chief. Children's books for all ages. Picture books.

**GROSSET AND DUNLAP, INC.**—Div. of Putnam & Grosset Books, 200 Madison Ave., New York, NY 10016. Craig Walker, Ed.-in-Chief.

**GROVE PRESS, INC.**—(formerly Grove Weidenfeld) 841 Broadway, New York, NY 10003–4793. Walter Bode, Ed.-in-Chief. "Looking to publish distinguished fiction and nonfiction." Query required.

**GULLIVER BOOKS**—See Harcourt Brace Jovanovich.

**HBJ PROFESSIONAL PUBLISHING**—(formerly Miller Accounting Publications) Imprint of Harcourt Brace Jovanovich, 1250 Sixth Ave., San Diego, CA 92101. Professional books for practitioners in accounting and finance, information systems, human resource management. Query required. Royalty.

**H.P. BOOKS**—Div. of Price Stern Sloan, Inc., 11150 Olympic Blvd., Los Angeles, CA 90064. Illustrated how-tos on cooking, gardening, photography, automotive topics. Query with SASE. Royalty.

**HAMMOND, INC.**—Maplewood, NJ 07040. Charles Lees, Ed. Nonfiction: cartographic reference, travel. Payment varies. Query with outline and sample chapters. SASE required.

**HARBINGER HOUSE**—2802 N. Alvernon Way, Tucson, AZ 85712. Laurel Gregory, Pub. Adult nonfiction focusing on personal growth, self-development, family/social issues. Children's picture books; stories for middle readers; nonfiction series (Natural History, Science). Submit resumé, outline/synopsis, two sample chapters, and SASE. For short children's book, submit entire manuscript with SASE. Royalty.

**HARCOURT BRACE JOVANOVICH**—1250 Sixth Ave., San Diego, CA 92101. Adult trade nonfiction and fiction. Books for Professionals: test preparation guides and other student self-help materials. Juvenile fiction and nonfiction for beginning readers through young adults under the following imprints: *HBJ Children's Books, Gulliver Books, Jane Yolen Books, Odyssey Paperbacks*, and *Voyager Paperbacks*. Adult books: no unsolicited manuscripts or queries. Children's books: unsolicited manuscripts accepted by *HBJ Children's Books* only. No simultaneous submissions. Send query or manuscript to Manuscript Submissions, Children's Book Division. SASE required.

**HARLEQUIN BOOKS/CANADA**—225 Duncan Mill Rd., Don Mills, Ont., Canada M3B 3K9. Harlequin Romance: Paula Eykelhof, Ed. Contemporary romance novels, 50,000 to 55,000 words, any setting, ranging in plot from the traditional and gentle to the more sophisticated. Query first. *Harlequin Regency*: Marmie Charndoff, Ed. Short traditional novels set in 19th century Europe, 50,000 to 60,000 words. Query first. *Harlequin Superromance*: Marsha Zinberg, Sr. Ed. Contemporary romance, 85,000 words, with a mainstream edge. Query first. *Harlequin Temptation*: Birgit Davis-Todd, Sr. Ed. Sensuous, humorous contemporary romances, 60,000 words. Query first.

**HARLEQUIN BOOKS/U.S.**—300 E. 42nd St., 6th Fl., New York, NY 10017. Debra Matteucci, Sr. Ed. Contemporary romances, 70,000 to 75,000 words. Send for tip sheets. Paperback. *Harlequin American Romances*: bold, exciting romantic adventures set in America,"where anything is possible and dreams come true." *Harlequin Intrigue*: set against a backdrop of mystery and suspense, worldwide locals. Query.

**HARPER PAPERBACKS**—HarperCollins, 10 E. 53rd St., New York, NY 10022. Geoff Hannell, Pub. Karen Solem, Ed.-in-Chief. Carolyn Marino, Sr. Ed. Jessica Kovar, Ed. Katie Smith, Ed. Submissions from agents only.

**HARPERCOLLINS CHILDREN'S BOOKS**—10 E. 53rd St., New York, NY 10022–5299. Katrin Magnusson, Admin. Coord. West Coast: 8948 S.W. Barbur Blvd., Suite 154, Portland, OR 92719. Linda Zuckerman, Exec. Ed. (Query one address only.) Juvenile fiction, nonfiction, and picture books imprints include *Thomas Y. Crowell Co.*, Publishers: juveniles, etc.; *J. B. Lippincott Co.*: juveniles, picture books, etc.; *Harper & Row*: juveniles, picture books, etc.; *HarperTrophy Books*: paperback juveniles; *Laura Geringer*, juvenile books. All publish from preschool to young-adult titles. Guidelines available. Query, send sample chapters, or complete manuscript. Royalty.

**HARPERCOLLINS PUBLISHERS**—(formerly Harper & Row) 10 E. 53rd St., New York, NY 10022–5299. Adult Trade Department: Tracy Behar, Man. Ed. Fiction, nonfiction (biography, economics, history, etc.), reference. Submissions from agents only. College texts: address College Dept. Religion, theology, etc., address Harper San Francisco, Ice House One-401, 151 Union St., San Francisco, CA 94111–1299. No unsolicited manuscripts; query only.

**HARVARD COMMON PRESS**—535 Albany St., Boston, MA 02118. Bruce Shaw, Ed. Adult nonfiction: cookbooks, travel guides, books on family matters, small business, etc. Send outline and sample chapters or complete manuscript. Royalty.

**HARVEST HOUSE PUBLISHERS**—1075 Arrowsmith, Eugene, OR 97402. Eileen L. Mason, V.P. Editorial. Nonfiction with evangelical theme: how-tos, education, counseling, marriage, women, contemporary issues. No biographies, autobiographies, history, fiction, music books, or poetry. Query first. SASE required.

**HAZELDEN EDUCATIONAL MATERIALS**—Box 176, Center City, MN 55012. Attn: Editorial Dept. Self-help books, 100 to 400 pages, relating to addiction, recovery, and wholeness. Query with outline and sample chapters. Multiple queries considered. Royalty.

**HEALTH COMMUNICATIONS, INC.**—3201 S.W. 15th St., Deerfield Beach, FL 33442. Marie Stilkind, Ed. Books on self-help recovery for adults (250 pages) and juveniles (100 pages). "Looking for children's books (ages 8 to 13) stressing good self-esteem and healthy feelings, 40 to 60 pages." Query with outline and sample chapter, or send manuscript. Royalty.

**HEALTH PLUS PUBLISHERS**—P.O. Box 1027, Sherwood, OR 97140. Paula E. Clure, Ed. Books on health and fitness. Query with outline and sample chapters.

**HEALTH PRESS**—P.O. Box 1388, Santa Fe, NM 87501. Kathleen Schwartz, Ed. Health-related adult books, 100 to 300 finished pages. "We're seeking cutting-edge, original manuscripts that will excite and help readers. Author must have credentials, or preface/intro must be written by M.D., Ph.D., etc. Controversial topics are desired; must be well researched and documented." Prefer completed manuscript, but will consider queries with outline and sample chapters. Multiple queries considered. Royalty.

**HEARST BOOKS/HEARST MARINE BOOKS**—See William Morrow and Co.

**HEARTFIRE ROMANCES**—See Zebra Books.

**HEATH & COMPANY, D. C.**—125 Spring St., Lexington, MA 02173. Text-books for school and college. Query Bruce Zimmerli.

**HEMINGWAY WESTERN STUDIES SERIES**—Boise State University, 1910 University Dr., Boise, ID 83725. Tom Trusky, Ed. Nonfiction relating to the Inter-Mountain West (Rockies) in areas of history, political science, anthropology, natural sciences, film, fine arts, literary history or criticism.

**HERALD PRESS**—616 Walnut Ave., Scottdale, PA 15683. Christian books for adults and children: inspiration, Bible study, self-help, devotionals, current issues, peace studies, church history, missions, evangelism, family life, fiction, and personal experience. Send one-page summary and two sample chapters. Royalty.

**HIPPOCRENE BOOKS**—171 Madison Ave., New York, NY 10016. George Blagowidow, Ed. Dir. Language instruction books and foreign language dictionaries, travel guides, and military history. Send outline and sample chapters. Multiple queries considered. Royalty.

**HOLIDAY HOUSE, INC.**—425 Madison Ave., New York, NY 10017. Margery S. Cuyler, Vice Pres. Alyssa Chase, Assoc. Ed. General juvenile and young-adult fiction and nonfiction. Submit three sample chapters and summary for novels and nonfiction. (Buys very few unsolicited picture books.) Hardcover only. Royalty.

**HOLT AND CO., HENRY**—115 W. 18th St., New York, NY 10011. William Strachan, Ed.-in-Chief. Fiction and nonfiction (mysteries, history, biographies, natural history, travel, and how-to) of highest literary quality. Query with SASE required. Royalty.

**HOME BUILDER PRESS**—Nat'l Assoc. of Home Builders, 1201 15th St., N.W., Washington, DC 20005–2800. Doris M. Tennyson, Sr. Ed. How-to and business management books, 150 to 250 words, for builders and remodelers on

"How to Design and Build Homes for First-Time Home Buyers," "How to Customize Standard Plans," "Frame Carpentry," and "Residential Concrete." Proposals accepted from authors with building industry knowledge and experience. Query with outline and sample chapters. Royalty. Guidelines.

**HOUGHTON MIFFLIN COMPANY**—2 Park St., Boston, MA 02108. Fiction: literary, historical, suspense. Nonfiction: history, biography, psychology. No unsolicited submissions. Children's Book Division, address Children's Trade Books: picture books, fiction, and nonfiction for all ages. Query. Royalty.

**HUNTER PUBLISHING, INC.**—300 Raritan Center Pkwy., Edison, NJ 08818. Michael Hunter, Ed. Travel guides. Query with outline.

**HYPERION**—114 Fifth Ave., New York, NY 10011. Material accepted from agents only. No unsolicited manuscripts considered.

**INDIANA UNIVERSITY PRESS**—601 N. Morton St., Bloomington, IN 47404–3797. Scholarly nonfiction, especially cultural studies, literary criticism, music, history, women's studies, African-American studies, African studies, Middle East studies, Russian studies, anthropology, regional, etc. Query with outline and sample chapters. Royalty.

**ISLAND PRESS**—1718 Connecticut Ave. N.W., Suite 300, Washington, DC 20009. Charles C. Savitt, Pub. Nonfiction focusing on the west, natural history, the environment, and natural resource management. "We want solution-oriented material to solve environmental problems." Query or send manuscript, with SASE.

**JAMES BOOKS, ALICE**—33 Richdale Ave., Cambridge, MA 02140. Kinereth Gensler, Pres. "Shared-work cooperative" publishes books of poetry (64 to 72 pages) by writers living in New England. Manuscripts read in September and February. "We emphasize the publication of poetry by women, but also welcome and publish manuscripts by men." Authors paid with 100 copies of their books. Guidelines available.

**JOHNSON BOOKS, INC.**—1880 S. 57th Court, Boulder, CO 80301. Barbara Mussil, Pub. Nonfiction: environmental subjects, archaeology, geology, natural history, astronomy, travel guides, outdoor guidebooks, fly fishing, regional. Query. Royalty.

**JONATHAN DAVID PUBLISHERS, INC.**—68–22 Eliot Ave., Middle Village, NY 11379. Alfred J. Kolatch, Ed.-in-Chief. General nonfiction (how-to, sports, cooking and food, self-help, etc.) and specializing in Judaica. Query with outline, sample chapter, and resumé required. SASE. Royalty or outright purchase.

**JOY STREET BOOKS**—Imprint of Little, Brown & Co., 34 Beacon St., Boston, MA 02108. Melanie Kroupa, Ed.-in-Chief. Juvenile picture books; fiction and nonfiction for middle readers and young adults. Especially interested in fiction for 8- to 12-year-olds and innovative nonfiction. Query with outline and sample chapters for nonfiction; complete manuscript for fiction. Royalty.

**JUST US BOOKS**—301 Main St., Suite 22–24, Orange, NJ 07050. Cheryl Hudson, Ed. Children's books celebrating African-American heritage. Picture books, 24 to 32 pages. Chapter books and biographies, from 2,500 words. Queries required. Royalty or flat fee.

**KAR-BEN COPIES**—6800 Tildenwood Lane, Rockville, MD 20852. Judye Groner, Ed. Books on Jewish themes for pre-school and elementary-age children (to age 9): picture books, fiction, and nonfiction. Complete manuscript preferred. Flat fee and royalty.

**KEATS PUBLISHING, INC.**—27 Pine St., Box 876, New Canaan, CT 06840. Nathan Keats, Pub. Nonfiction: health, how-to. Query. Royalty.

**KENT STATE UNIVERSITY PRESS**—Kent State University, Kent, OH 44242. John T. Hubbel, Dir. Julia Morton, Sr. Ed. Publishes hardcover and paperback originals and some reprints. Especially interested in scholarly works in history and literary studies of high quality, any titles of regional interest for Ohio, scholarly biographies, archaeological research, the arts, and general nonfiction.

**KNOPF, INC., ALFRED A.**—201 E. 50th St., New York, NY 10022. Ashbel Green, V.P./Sr. Ed. Distinguished adult fiction and general nonfiction; query. Royalty. Guidelines.

**KNOPF BOOKS FOR YOUNG READERS, ALFRED A.**—225 Park Ave. S., New York, NY 10003. Janet Schulman, Pub. Stephanie Spinner, Assoc. Pub. Frances Foster, Ed. at Large. Anne Schwartz, Exec. Ed. Reg Kahney, Sr. Ed., Nonfiction. Sherry Gerstein, Paperback Ed. Distinguished juvenile fiction and nonfiction; query. Royalty. Guidelines.

**KODANSHA INTERNATIONAL**—114 Fifth Ave., New York, NY 10011. Attn: Editorial Dept. Books, 50,000 to 200,000 words, on Asian and other international subjects. Query with outline and sample chapters. Royalty.

**LARK BOOKS**—50 College St., Asheville, NC 28801. Rob Pulleyn, Pub. Publishes "distinctive books for creative people" in crafts, how-to, leisure activities, and "coffee table" categories. Query with outline. Royalty.

**LAUREL-LEAF**—Imprint of Bantam, Doubleday, Dell Publishing Co., 666 Fifth Ave., New York, NY 10103. Address Editors. Books for children grades 7 through 12. Submissions accepted from agents only.

**LEADERSHIP PUBLISHERS, INC.**—P.O. Box 8358, Des Moines, IA 50301–8358. Lois F. Roets, Ed. Educational materials for talented and gifted students, grades K to 12, and teacher reference books. No fiction or poetry. Send SASE for catalogue and writer's guidelines before submitting. Royalty for books; flat fee for short pieces or booklets. Query or send complete manuscript.

**LEISURE BOOKS**—Div. of Dorchester Publishing Co., Inc., 276 Fifth Ave., New York, NY 10001. Frank Walgren, Ed. Historical romance novels, from 100,000 words; futuristic and time-travel romances, from 90,000 words. Query with synopsis, sample chapters, and SASE. Royalty.

**LIFE JOURNEY GENERAL TITLES**—See Chariot Family Publishing.

**LIFETIME BOOKS, INC.**—(formerly Fell Publishers, Inc.) 2131 Hollywood Blvd., Hollywood, FL 33020. Joyce Sweeney, Ed. Nonfiction, 100 to 300 pages: general interest, how-tos, business, health, and inspirational. Query with letter or outline and sample chapter; include SASE. Royalty.

**LION PUBLISHING**—1705 Hubbard Ave., Batavia, IL 60510. Robert Bittner, Ed. Fiction and nonfiction written from a Christian viewpoint for a general audience. Guidelines. Royalty.

**LIPPINCOTT COMPANY, J.B.**—See HarperCollins Children's Books.

**LITTLE, BROWN & CO.**—1271 Ave. of the Americas, New York, NY 10020. Maria Modugno, Ed.-in-Chief. Fiction, general nonfiction, sports books; divisions for law and medical texts. Royalty. Query Children's Book Dept. (34 Beacon St., Boston, MA 02106) for juvenile fiction and nonfiction (science, history, and nature) and picture books (ages 3 to 8). Guidelines.

**LITTLE ROOSTER BOOKS**—Imprint of Bantam Doubleday Dell, 666 Fifth Ave., New York, NY 10103. Diane Arico, Exec. Ed. Hardcover picture books for ages 4 to 8. Send complete manuscript suitable for 32-page book; indicate multiple submissions. Royalty.

**LITTLE SIMON**—See Simon & Schuster Books for Young Readers.

**LLEWELLYN PUBLICATIONS**—P.O. Box 64383, St. Paul, MN 55164–0383. Nancy J. Mostad, Acquisitions Mgr. Books, around 300 pages, on subjects of self-help, astrology, metaphysics, new age, and the occult. Royalty. Query with sample chapters. Multiple queries considered.

**LODESTAR**—An affiliate of Dutton Children's Books, a Div. of Penguin Books USA, Inc., 375 Hudson St., New York, NY 10014. Virginia Buckley, Ed. Dir. Fiction (picture books to YA, mystery, fantasy, science fiction, western) and nonfiction (science, contemporary issues, nature, history) considered for ages 9 to 11, 10 to 14, and 12 and up. Also fiction and nonfiction picture books for ages 4 to 8. "We're looking for strong multicultural books by African Americans, Hispanics, Asian, and Native American writers." Send query and sample chapters.

**LONGMEADOW PRESS**—P.O. Box 10218, 201 High Ridge Rd., Stamford, CT 06904. Attn: Juvenile Ed. Board books, picture books, fiction, and nonfiction for children and young adults. Send complete manuscript. Royalty or flat fee.

**LOTHROP, LEE & SHEPARD BOOKS**—Imprint of William Morrow & Co., Inc., 1350 Ave. of the Americas, New York, NY 10016. Susan Pearson, Ed.-in-Chief. Juvenile, picture books, fiction, and nonfiction. Does not review unsolicited material. Royalty.

**LOVEGRAM ROMANCES**—See Zebra Books.

**LOVESWEPT**—Imprint of Bantam Books, 666 Fifth Ave., New York, NY 10103. Nita Taublib, Assoc. Pub. Highly sensual, adult contemporary romances, approximately 55,000 words. Study field before submitting. Query required. Paperback only.

**LOYOLA UNIVERSITY PRESS**—3441 N. Ashland Ave., Chicago, IL 60657–1397. Joseph Downey, S.J., Ed. Religious material for college-educated Christian readers. *Campion Book Series*: art, literature, and religion; contemporary Christian concerns; Jesuit studies; Chicago books. Nonfiction, 200 to 400 pages. Query with outline. Royalty.

**LYONS & BURFORD, PUBLISHERS**—31 W. 21st St., New York, NY 10010. Peter Burford, Ed. Books, 100 to 300 pages, related to the outdoors (camping, natural history, etc.). Query with outline. Royalty.

**MCELDERRY BOOKS, MARGARET K.**—Macmillan Children's Book Group, 866 Third Ave., New York, NY 10022. Margaret K. McElderry, Ed. Picture books; quality fiction, including fantasy, science fiction, beginning chapter books, humor, and realism; nonfiction. For ages 3 to 5, 6 to 9, 8 to 12, 10 to 14, and 12 and up.

**MCFARLAND & COMPANY, INC., PUBLISHERS**—Box 611, Jefferson, NC 28640. Robert Franklin, Ed. Scholarly and reference books in many fields, except mathematical sciences. Please do not send new age, inspirational, children's, poetry, fiction, or exposés. Submit double spaced manuscripts, 225 pages and up, or query with outline and sample chapters. Royalty.

**MACMILLAN CHILDREN'S BOOK GROUP**—866 Third Ave., New York, NY 10022. Leslie Ward, Ed. *Aladdin Books*: paperback fiction (except problem novels) for middle grades (age 8 to 12) and young adults (age 12 and up). *Collier Books for Young Adults*: young-adult novels. Query with outline; no multiple queries. Royalty.

**MACMILLAN PUBLISHING CO., INC.**—866 Third Ave., New York, NY 10022. General Books Division: Religious, sports, science, and reference books. No fiction. Paperbacks: *Collier Books*. College texts and professional books in social sciences, humanities: Address The Free Press. Royalty.

**MADISON BOOKS**—4720 Boston Way, Lanham, MD 20706. James E. Lyons, Pub. Full-length nonfiction: history, biography, contemporary affairs, trade reference. Query required. Royalty.

**MARKOWSKI INTERNATIONAL PUBLISHERS**—(formerly Aviation Publishers) One Oakglade Cir., Hummelstown, PA 17036. Michael A. Markowski, Ed. Nonfiction, from 30,000 words: aviation, cars, model cars and planes, boats, trains, health, self-help, personal development, relationships, sales, marketing, success, motivation, and inspiration. Query with outline and sample chapters. Royalty.

**MEADOWBROOK PRESS**—18318 Minnetonka Blvd., Deephaven, MN 55391. Upbeat, useful books on pregnancy, childbirth and parenting, travel, humor, cooking, environmental guides, children's activities, 60,000 words. Query with outline, sample chapters, and qualifications. Royalty or flat fee.

**MEGA-BOOKS**—116 E. 19th St., New York, NY 10003. Matthew Debord, Asst. Man. Ed. Book packager. Young-adult books, 150 pages. Submit outline and sample chapters with resumé. Flat fee.

**MERCURY HOUSE**—201 Filbert St., Suite 400, San Francisco, CA 94133. Thomas Christensen, Exec. Ed. Quality fiction and nonfiction (international politics, literary travel, environment, philosophy/personal growth, and performing arts). Query with outline, sample chapters, and SASE. Limited fiction market.

**MEREDITH CORP. BOOK GROUP**—(Better Homes and Gardens Books) 1716 Locust St., Des Moines, IA 50336. David A. Kirchner, Man. Ed. Books on gardening, crafts, health, decorating, etc., mostly staff written. "Interested in freelance writers with expertise in these areas." Limited market. Query with SASE.

**MESSNER, JULIAN**—Simon & Schuster Bldg., 1230 Ave. of the Americas, New York, NY 10020. George Rubich, Assoc. Pub. Curriculum-oriented nonfiction. General nonfiction, ages 8 to 14: science, nature, biography, history, and hobbies. Lengths vary. Royalty.

**METAMORPHOUS PRESS**—P.O. Box 10616, Portland, OR 97210. Nancy Wyatt-Kelsey, Acquisitions Ed. Business, education, health, how-to, performance arts, psychology, neurolinguistics, body work, nutrition/weight control, and women's topics. Also children's books that promote self-esteem and self-reliance. "We select books that provide the tools to help people improve their lives and the lives of those around them." Query with sample chapter and outline.

**METEOR PUBLISHING**—3369 Progress Dr., Bensalem, PA 19020. Kate Duffy, Ed.-in-Chief. Contemporary romance novels, 65,000 words, sold through direct mail only. Royalty.

**THE MICHIGAN STATE UNIVERSITY PRESS**—1405 S. Harrison Rd., Suite 25, Manly Miles Bldg., E. Lansing, MI 48823–5202. Scholarly nonfiction. Submit prospectus, table of contents, and sample chapter. Authors should refer to *The Chicago Manual of Style, 13th Edition*, for formats and styles.

**MILKWEED EDITIONS**—528 Hennepin Ave., Suite 505, Minneapolis, MN

55403. Emilie Buchwald, Ed. "We publish excellent fiction, poetry, essays, and collaborative books, the kind of writing that makes for good reading." Publishes about 12 books a year. Query first with sample chapters. Royalty.

**THE MILLBROOK PRESS**—2 Old New Milford Rd., Brookfield, CT 06804. Tricia Bauer, Manuscript Coord. Nonfiction for early elementary grades through grades 7 and up, appropriate for the school and public library market, encompassing curriculum-related topics and extracurricular interests. Query with outline and sample chapter. Royalty.

**MILLER ACCOUNTING PUBLICATIONS, INC.**—See HBJ Professional Publishing.

**MILLS & SANDERSON, PUBLISHERS**—41 North Rd., #201, Bedford, MA 01730. Georgia Mills, Pub. Books, 250 pages, on family problem-solving. Query. Royalty.

**MINSTREL BOOKS**—Imprint of Pocket Books, 1230 Ave. of the Americas, New York, NY 10020. Patricia MacDonald, Exec. Ed. Fiction for girls and boys ages 6 to 11: scary stories, fantasies, funny stories, school stories, adventures, animal stories. No picture books. Query first with detailed plot outline, sample chapter, and SASE. Royalty.

**THE MIT PRESS**—Acquisitions Dept., 55 Hayward St., Cambridge, MA 02142. Books on computer science/artificial intelligence; cognitive sciences; economics; architecture; aesthetic and social theory; linguistics; technology studies; environmental studies; and neuroscience.

**MODAN PUBLISHING**—P.O. Box 1202, Bellmore, NY 11710. Bennett Shelkowitz, Man. Dir. Adult nonfiction. Young-adult fiction and nonfiction. Children's picture books. Books with international focus or related to political or social issues. Judaica and Hebrew books from Israel. *Adama Books*.

**MOON HANDBOOKS**—Moon Publications, Inc., 722 Wall St., Chico, CA 95928. Taran March, Ed. Travel guides of varying lengths. Will consider multiple submissions. Query. Royalty.

**MOREHOUSE PUBLISHING**—871 Ethan Allen Hwy., Suite 204, Ridgefield, CT 06877. E. Allen Kelley, Pub. Theology, pastoral care, church administration, spirituality, Anglican studies, history of religion, books for children, youth, elders, etc. Query with outline, contents, and sample chapter. Royalty.

**MORROW AND CO., INC., WILLIAM**—1350 Avenue of the Americas, New York, NY 10019. Adrian Zackheim, Ed. Dir. Adult fiction and nonfiction: no unsolicited manuscripts. *Beech Tree* and *Mulberry Books* (children's paperbacks) Amy Cohn, Ed. Dir.; *Fielding Travel Books*, Randy Ladenheim-Gil, Ed.; *Hearst Books* (general nonfiction) and *Hearst Marine Books*, Ann Bramsom, Ed. Dir.; *Morrow Junior Books* (children's books for all ages) David Reuther, Ed.-in-Chief.

**MOUNTAIN PRESS PUBLISHING**—2016 Strand Ave., P.O. Box 2399, Missoula, MT 59806. Address John Rimel. Nonfiction, 300 pages: natural history, geology, horses, Western history, Americana, outdoor guides, and fur trade lore. Query with outline and sample chapters; multiple queries considered. Royalty.

**THE MOUNTAINEERS BOOKS**—1011 S.W. Klickitat Way, Suite 107, Seattle, WA 98134. Margaret Foster, Ed. Mgr. Nonfiction books on noncompetitive aspects of outdoor sports such as mountaineering, backpacking, canoeing, kayaking, bicycling, skiing. Field guides, how-to and where-to guidebooks, biographies of outdoor people; accounts of expeditions. Nature books. Submit sample chapters and outline. Royalty.

**MUIR PUBLICATIONS, JOHN**—P.O. Box 613, Santa Fe, NM 87504–0613. Ken Luboff, Ed. Travel guidebooks for adults. Nonfiction books for children, 8 to 12, primarily in the areas of science and intercultural issues. Send manuscript or query with sample chapters. Royalty or work for hire.

**MULBERRY BOOKS**—See William Morrow and Co., Inc.

**MULTNOMAH PRESS**—10209 S.E. Division St., Portland, OR 97266. Conservative, evangelical nonfiction. Send SASE for guidelines and manuscript questionnaire. Royalty.

**MUSTANG PUBLISHING CO., INC.**—Box 3004, Memphis, TN 38173. Rollin A. Riggs, Pres. Nonfiction for 18- to 40-year-olds. Send queries for 100- to 300-page books, with outlines and sample chapters. Royalty. SASE required.

**THE MYSTERIOUS PRESS**—Imprint of Warner Books, Time and Life Bldg., 1271 Ave. of the Americas, New York, NY 10020. William Malloy, Ed.-in-Chief. Mystery/suspense novels. Agented manuscripts only.

**NAIAD PRESS, INC.**—Box 10543, Tallahassee, FL 32302. Barbara Grier, Ed. Adult fiction, 52,000 to 60,000 words, with lesbian themes and characters: mysteries, romances, gothics, ghost stories, westerns, regencies, spy novels, etc. Query with letter and one-page précis only. Royalty.

**NATIONAL PRESS**—7200 Wisconsin Ave., Suite 212, Bethesda, MD 20814. G. Edward Smith, Ed. Nonfiction: history, criminology, reference, and health (*Zenith Editions*); cookbooks; sports and parenting; business, management, and automotive titles (*Plain English Press*). Royalty. Query with outline and sample chapters.

**NATUREGRAPH PUBLISHERS**—P. O. Box 1075, Happy Camp, CA 96039. Barbara Brown, Ed. Nonfiction: Native American culture, natural history, outdoor living, land and gardening, holistic learning and health, Indian lore, crafts, and how-to. Query. Royalty.

**THE NAVAL INSTITUTE PRESS**—Annapolis, MD 21402. Nonfiction, 60,-000 to 100,000 words: how-tos on boating and navigation; battle histories; biography; ship guides. Occasional fiction, 75,000 to 110,000 words. Query with outline and sample chapters. Royalty.

**NELSON, INC., THOMAS**—Nelson Place at Elm Hill Pike, P. O. Box 141000, Nashville, TN 37214–1000. Religious adult nonfiction. Teen and adult nonfiction. Query with outline and sample chapter.

**NEW DIRECTIONS**—80 Eighth Ave., New York, NY 10011. Stephen Moran, Ed. Stylistically experimental fiction and poetry. "Writers should look at our catalogue and backlist first." Submit sample chapters or complete manuscript. Royalty.

**NEW HORIZON PRESS**—P.O. Box 669, Far Hills, NJ 07931. Joan Dunphy, Ed.-in-Chief. True stories, 96,000 words, dealing with contemporary issues that revolve around a hero or heroine. Royalty. Query.

**NEW RIVERS PRESS**—420 N. 5th St., Suite 910, Minneapolis, MN 55401. C.W. Truesdale, Ed./Pub. Collections of short stories, essays, and poems from emerging writers. Query. Royalty or flat fee.

**NEW SOCIETY PUBLISHERS**—4527 Springfield Ave., Philadelphia, PA 19143. Nonfiction books on fundamental social change through nonviolent social action. Request guidelines before submitting proposal. SASE required.

**NEW WORLD LIBRARY**—58 Paul Dr., San Rafael, CA 94903. Submissions Ed. Nonfiction to 300 pages, especially high quality, inspirational/self-help books, environmental awareness. "Aim for intelligent, aware audience, interested in personal and planetary transformation." Query with outline. Multiple queries accepted. Royalty.

**NEWCASTLE PUBLISHING**—13419 Saticoy St., N. Hollywood, CA 91605. Al Saunders, Pub. Nonfiction manuscripts, 200 to 250 pages, for older adults on personal health, health care issues, and relationships. "We are not looking for fads or trends. We want books with a long shelf life." Multiple queries considered. Royalty.

**NEWMARKET PRESS**—18 E. 48th St., New York, NY 10017. Keith Hollaman, Man. Ed. Nonfiction on health, self-help, child care, parenting, and music. Query first. Royalty.

**NORTH COUNTRY PRESS**—P.O. Box 440, Belfast, ME 04915. William M. Johnson, Pub. Nonfiction with a Maine and/or New England tie-in with emphasis on the outdoors. "Our goal is to publish high-quality books for people who love New England." Query with SASE, outline, and sample chapters. Royalty.

**NORTHWORD PRESS, INC.**—Box 1360, 7520 Highway 51, Minocqua, WI 54548. Tom Klein, Ed. Natural history and natural heritage books, from 25,000 words. Send outline with sample chapters, or complete manuscript. Royalty or flat fee.

**NORTON AND CO., INC., W.W.**—500 Fifth Ave., New York, NY 10110. Liz Malcolm, Ed. High-quality fiction and nonfiction. No occult, paranormal, religious, genre fiction (formula romance, SF, westerns), cookbooks, arts and crafts, YA, or children's books. Query with synopsis, two to three chapters (including first chapter), and resumé. Return postage and packaging required. Royalty.

**ODYSSEY PAPERBACKS**—See Harcourt Brace Jovanovich.

**OLD RUGGED CROSS PRESS**—1160 Alpharetta St., Suite K, Roswell, GA 30075. Jay Walton, Assoc. Ed. Adult fiction, 150 to 300 pages, and nonfiction, 100 to 400 pages. Juvenile fiction, 100 to 150 pages, and nonfiction, 100 to 200 pages. Young-adult books, 150 to 225 pages. "We publish books that honor the Lord and reflect God's truth, beauty, and holiness." Submit sample chapters. Royalty.

**OPEN COURT PUBLISHING COMPANY**—Box 599, Peru, IL 61354. Scholarly books on philosophy, psychology, religion, eastern thought, history, public policy, education, science, and related topics. Send sample chapters with outline and resumé. Royalty.

**ORCHARD BOOKS**—387 Park Ave., New York, NY 10016. Norma Jean Sawicki, Pres./Pub. Hardcover picture books. Fiction for middle grades and young adults. Nonfiction and photo essays for young children. Submit complete manuscript. Royalty.

**OREGON STATE UNIVERSITY PRESS**—101 Waldo Hall, Corvallis, OR 97331. Scholarly books in a limited range of disciplines and books of particular importance to the Pacific Northwest. Query with summary of manuscript.

**THE OVERLOOK PRESS**—149 Wooster St., New York, NY 10012. Tracy Carns, Ed. Dir. General nonfiction, including biography, carpentry, architecture, how-to, crafts, martial arts, Hudson Valley regionals, and history. Query with outline and sample chapters. Royalty.

**OWEN PUBLISHERS, INC., RICHARD C.**—135 Katonah Ave., Katonah,

NY 10536. Janice Boland, Ed. Fiction, nonfiction, and poetry. Brief storybooks of 8, 12, and 16 pages (including illustration) suitable for 5-, 6-, and 7-year-old beginning readers for the "Ready to Read" program. Royalties for writers. Flat fee for illustrators. Send SASE for guidelines before submitting.

**OXFORD UNIVERSITY PRESS**—200 Madison Ave., New York, NY 10016. Authoritative books on literature, history, philosophy, etc.; college textbooks, medical, and reference books. Query. Royalty.

**PACER BOOKS FOR YOUNG ADULTS**—Imprint of Berkley Publishing Group, 200 Madison Ave., New York, NY 10016. Fiction: adventure, fantasy, and role-playing fantasy gamebooks. No unsolicited manuscripts; queries only. Address Melinda Metz. Paperback only.

**PANTHEON BOOKS**—Div. of Random House, 201 E. 50th St., New York, NY 10022. Quality fiction and nonfiction. Query required. Royalty.

**PAPIER-MACHE PRESS**—795 Via Mansana, Watsonville, CA 95076. Sandra Martz, Ed. Short stories, 8 to 20 pages, and poetry for anthologies and single-author books. "We emphasize, but are not limited to, the publication of books and related items for midlife and older women." Query. Royalties for single-author books; pays in copies for anthologies, plus royalties if book goes into second printing.

**PARA PUBLISHING**—P.O. Box 4232, Santa Barbara, CA 93140–4232. Dan Poynter, Ed. Adult nonfiction books on parachutes and skydiving only. Author must present evidence of having made at least 1,000 jumps. Query. Royalty.

**PARAGON HOUSE**—90 Fifth Ave., New York, NY 10011. Arthur Samuelson, Ed.-in-Chief. Serious nonfiction, including biography, history, reference, parenting, self-help, military history, politics and current affairs, and how-to. Query or send manuscript. Royalty.

**PASSPORT BOOKS**—4255 W. Touhy Ave., Lincolnwood, IL 60646–1975. Constance Rajala, Ed. Dir. Adult nonfiction, 200 to 400 pages, picture books up to 120 pages, and juvenile nonfiction. Send outline and sample chapters for books on foreign language, travel, and culture. Multiple queries considered. Royalty and flat fee.

**PATH PRESS**—53 W. Jackson Blvd., Chicago, IL 60604. Bennett Johnson, Pres. Herman C. Gilbert, Ed. Quality books by and about African-Americans and Third-World peoples. Submit outline, sample chapters, or complete manuscript. Royalty.

**PEACHTREE PUBLISHERS, LTD.**—494 Armour Circle N.E., Atlanta, GA 30324. Wide variety of children's books, humor, and nonfiction. Contemporary southern fiction. No religious material, SF/fantasy, romance, mystery/detective, historical fiction; no business, scientific, or technical books. Send outline and sample chapters for fiction and nonfiction. SASE required. Royalty. No unsolicited submissions at this time.

**PELICAN PUBLISHING CO., INC.**—1101 Monroe St., Gretna, LA 70053. Nina Kooij, Ed. General nonfiction: Americana, regional, architecture, how-to, travel, cookbooks, inspirational, motivational, music, parenting, etc. Juvenile fiction. Royalty.

**PELION PRESS**—See Rosen Publishing Group.

**PENGUIN BOOKS**—Imprint of Penguin USA, 375 Hudson St., New York, NY 10014. Address Editors. Adult fiction and nonfiction paperbacks. Royalty.

**PERFECT CRIME**—See Doubleday and Co.

**THE PERMANENT PRESS**—Noyac Rd., Sag Harbor, NY 11963. Judith Shepard, Ed. Seeks original and arresting novels, biographies. Query. Royalty.

**PHAROS BOOKS**—200 Park Ave., New York, NY 10166. Hana Umlauf Lane, Kevin McDonough, Eileen Schlesinger, Eds. Current issues, personal finance, food, health, history, true crime, how-to, humor, politics, reference, and sports. Reference books for children, ages 6 and up. Query with sample chapter and outline. Royalty.

**PHILOMEL BOOKS**—Div. of The Putnam & Grosset Group, 200 Madison Ave., New York, NY 10016. Patricia Lee Gauch, Ed. Dir. Paula Wiseman, Ed.-in.-Chief. Picture books, young-adult fiction, and some biographies. Fresh, original work with compelling characters and "a truly childlike spirit." Query required.

**PINEAPPLE PRESS**—P.O. Drawer 16008, Southside Sta., Sarasota, FL 34239. June Cussen, Ed. Serious fiction and nonfiction, 60,000 to 125,000 words. Query with outline, sample chapters, and SASE. Royalty.

**PIPPIN PRESS**—229 E. 85th St., Gracie Sta., Box 92, New York, NY 10028. Barbara Francis, Pub. High-quality picture books for pre-schoolers; middle-group fiction, humor and mysteries; imaginative nonfiction for children of all ages. Query required. Royalty.

**PLAIN ENGLISH PRESS**—See National Press.

**PLENUM PUBLISHING CORP.**—233 Spring St., New York, NY 10013. Linda Greenspan Regan, Sr. Ed. Trade nonfiction, approximately 300 pages, on science, criminology, psychology, sociology, and health. Query required. Royalty. Hardcover.

**PLUME BOOKS**—Imprint of Penguin USA, 375 Hudson St., New York, NY 10014. Address Editors. Nonfiction: hobbies, business, health, cooking, child care, psychology, history, popular culture, biography, and politics. Fiction: serious literary and gay.

**POCKET BOOKS**—Div. of Simon and Schuster, 1230 Ave. of the Americas, New York, NY 10020. William R. Grose, Ed. Dir. Original fiction and nonfiction. Mystery line: police procedurals, private eye, and amateur sleuth novels; query with outline and sample chapters to Jane Chelius, Sr. Ed. Royalty.

**POINT**—See Scholastic, Inc.

**POPULAR PRESS**—Bowling Green State University, Bowling Green, OH 43403. Ms. Pat Browne, Ed. Nonfiction, 250 to 400 pages, examining some aspect of popular culture. Query with outline. Flat fee or royalty.

**POSEIDON PRESS**—Imprint of Simon & Schuster, 1230 Ave. of the Americas, New York, NY 10020. Ann Patty, V.P./Pub. General fiction and nonfiction. No unsolicited material. Royalty.

**POTTER, CLARKSON**—201 E. 50th St., New York, NY 10022. Carol Southern, Assoc. Pub./Ed.-in-Chief. General trade books. Submissions accepted through agents only.

**PRAEGER PUBLISHERS**—Imprint of Greenwood Publishing Group, One Madison Ave., New York, NY 10010. Ron Chambers, Pub. General nonfiction; scholarly and reference books. Query with outline. Royalty.

**PREISS VISUAL PUBLICATIONS, BYRON**—24 W. 25th St., New York, NY 10010. Book packager. "We are primarily interested in seeing samples from established authors willing to work to specifications on firm deadlines." Genres:

science fiction, fantasy, horror, juvenile, young adult, nonfiction. Pays competitive advance against royalties for commissioned work.

**PRESIDIO PRESS**—505B San Marin Dr., Suite 300, Novato, CA 94945–1340. Nonfiction: military history, from 90,000 words. Fiction: selected military and action-adventure works, from 120,000 words. Query. Royalty.

**PRICE STERN SLOAN, INC.**—11150 Olympic Blvd., Los Angeles, CA 90064. Children's books; adult trade nonfiction, including humor and calendars. Query with SASE required. Royalty.

**PRIMA PUBLISHING**—P.O. Box 1260, Rocklin, CA 95677. Ben Dominitz, Pub. Nonfiction on variety of subjects, including business, health, and cookbooks. "We want books with originality, written by highly qualified individuals." Royalty.

**PRUETT PUBLISHING COMPANY**—2928 Pearl, Boulder, CO 80301. Jim Pruett, Pres. Nonfiction: outdoors and recreation, western U.S. history, travel, natural history and the environment, fly fishing. Query. Royalty.

**PUFFIN BOOKS**—Imprint of Penguin USA, 375 Hudson St., New York, NY 10014. Address Editors. Children's fiction and nonfiction paperbacks. Query required. Royalty.

**PUTNAM'S SONS, G.P. (BOOKS FOR YOUNG READERS)**—Div. of The Putnam & Grosset Book Group, 200 Madison Ave., New York, NY 10016. Margaret Frith, Ed.-in-Chief. Picture books, fiction and nonfiction. No unsolicited manuscripts. Query with sample required.

**QUARRY PRESS**—P.O. Box 1061, Kingston, Ontario, Canada K7L 4Y5. Adult and juvenile fiction and nonfiction. Picture books, 32 pages. "We are known for publishing new and innovative Canadian writing." Query with outline, synopsis, and sample chapters. Royalty.

**QUEST BOOKS**—Imprint of The Theosophical Publishing House, 306 W. Geneva Rd., P. O. Box 270, Wheaton, IL 60189–0270. Shirley Nicholson, Sr. Ed. Nonfiction books on Eastern and Western religion and philosophy, holism, healing, meditation, yoga, ancient wisdom. Query. Royalty.

**QUILL TRADE PAPERBACKS**—Imprint of William Morrow and Co., Inc., 105 Madison Ave., New York, NY 10019. Andrew Dutter, Ed. Trade paperback adult nonfiction. Submit through agent only.

**RAINTREE STECK-VAUGHN PUBLISHERS**—Div. of Steck-Vaughn Co., National Education Corp., 11 Prospect St., Madison, NJ 07940. Walter Kossmann, Ed. Nonfiction books, 5,000 to 30,000 words, for school and library market: biographies for grades 6 and up; and science, social studies, and history books for primary grades through high school. Query with outline and sample chapters; SASE required. Flat fee and royalty.

**RANDOM HOUSE, INC.**—201 E. 50th St., New York, NY 10022. General fiction and nonfiction. Query with three chapters and outline for nonfiction; complete manuscript for fiction. SASE required. Royalty.

**RANDOM HOUSE JUVENILE DIV.**—225 Park Ave. S., New York, NY 10003. Kate Klimo, Ed.-in-Chief. Fiction and nonfiction for beginning readers; paperback fiction line for 7- to 9-year-olds; 35 pages maximum. Query with three chapters and outline for nonfiction; complete manuscript for fiction. SASE for all correspondence. Royalty.

**REGNERY GATEWAY**—1130 17th St. N.W., Suite 600, Washington, DC 20036. Nonfiction books on public policy. Query. Royalty.

**RENAISSANCE HOUSE**—541 Oak St., P. O. Box 177, Frederick, CO 80530. Eleanor H. Ayer, Ed. Regional guidebooks. Currently publishing guidebooks on Colorado, Arizona, California, and the Southwest. "We use only manuscripts written to our specifications for new or ongoing series." Submit outline and short bio. Royalty.

**RIZZOLI INTERNATIONAL PUBLICATIONS, INC.**—300 Park Ave. S., New York, NY 10010. Kimberly Harbour, Children's Book Ed. Books that lend themselves to illustration, for children of all ages: original stories (no novels), poetry anthologies, and retellings of classics and myths. Artist and architect biographies for children. Query; send complete manuscripts for picture books only. Pays in royalties.

**RODALE PRESS**—33 E. Minor St., Emmaus, PA 18098. Pat Corpora, Pub. Books on health, gardening, homeowner projects, cookbooks, inspirational topics, pop psychology, woodworking, natural history. Query with outline and sample chapter. Royalty and outright purchase. In addition: "We're always looking for truly competent free lancers to write chapters for books conceived and developed in-house"; payment on a write-for-hire basis; address Bill Gottlieb, V.P.

**ROSEN PUBLISHING GROUP**—29 E. 21st St., New York, NY 10010. Roger Rosen, Pres. Ruth C. Rosen, Ed. Young-adult books, 8,000 to 40,000 words, on career and personal guidance, journalism, self-help, etc. *Pelion Press*: music, art, history. Pays varying rates.

**ROSSET & CO.**—See Bluemoon Books, Inc.

**RUTGERS UNIVERSITY PRESS**—109 Church St., New Brunswick, NJ 08901. Literary fiction.

**RUTLEDGE HILL PRESS**—513 Third Ave. S., Nashville, TN 37210. Ronald E. Pitkin, V.P. Southern-interest fiction and market-specific nonfiction. Query with outline and sample chapters. Royalty.

**ST. ANTHONY MESSENGER PRESS**—1615 Republic St., Cincinnati, OH 45210–1298. Lisa Biedenbach, Man. Ed. Inspirational nonfiction for Catholics, supporting a Christian lifestyle in our culture; prayer aids, education, practical spirituality, parish ministry, liturgy resources. Query with 500-word summary. Royalty.

**ST. MARTIN'S PRESS**—175 Fifth Ave., New York, NY 10010. General adult fiction and nonfiction. Query first. Royalty.

**SANDLAPPER PUBLISHING, INC.**—P.O. Drawer 730, Orangeburg, SC 29116–0730. Frank N. Handal, Book Ed. Nonfiction books on South Carolina history, culture, cuisine; fiction set in South Carolina. Query with outline, sample chapters, and SASE.

**SASQUATCH BOOKS**—1931 Second Ave., Seattle, WA 98101. Books by Pacific Northwest authors on a wide range of nonfiction topics: travel, natural history, gardening, cooking, history, and public affairs. Books must have a Pacific Northwest angle; length is 60,000 to 80,000 words. Query with SASE. Royalty.

**SCARECROW PRESS**—P.O. Box 4167, Metuchen, NJ 08840. Norman Horrocks, V.P./Editorial. Reference works and bibliographies, from 150 pages, especially in the areas of cinema, TV, radio, and theater, mainly for use by libraries. Query or send complete manuscript; multiple queries considered. Royalty.

**SCHOCKEN BOOKS**—Div. of Pantheon Books, 201 E. 50th St., New York,

NY 10022. General nonfiction: Judaica, women's studies, education, art history. Query with outline and sample chapter. Royalty.

**SCHOLASTIC, INC.**—730 Broadway, New York, NY 10003. *Point*: Regina Griffin, Sr. Ed. Young-adult fiction for readers 12 and up. *Apple Books*: Regina Griffin, Sr. Ed. Fiction for readers ages 8 to 12. Submit complete manuscript with cover letter and SASE. Royalty. *Sunfire*: Ann Reit, Exec. Ed.: Fiction and nonfiction for readers 8 to 14, mysteries, "horror" books, and romances. *Cartwheel Books*: Bernette Ford, Exec. Ed. General fiction and nonfiction for 2- to 6-year-olds. Query with resumé. Write for tip sheets.

**SCHOLASTIC PROFESSIONAL BOOKS**—730 Broadway, New York, NY 10003. Attn: Laureen Harris. Books by and for teachers of kindergarten through eighth grade. *Instructor Books*: practical, activity/resource books on teaching reading, science, math, etc. *Teaching Strategies Books*: 64 to 96 pages on new ideas, practices, and approaches to teaching. Query with outline, sample chapters or activities, contents page, and resumé. Flat fee or royalty. Multiple queries considered. SASE for guidelines.

**SCOTT, FORESMAN AND CO.**—1900 E. Lake Ave., Glenview, IL 60025. Richard E. Peterson, Pres. Elementary and secondary textbooks. Royalty or flat fee.

**SCRIBNER'S SONS, CHARLES**—866 Third Ave., New York, NY 10022. Barbara Grossman, Pub. Fiction, general nonfiction, science, history, and biography; query first. Clare Costello, Ed., *Books for Young Readers*: fantasy, mystery, SF, and problem novels; picture books, ages 5 and up; and nonfiction (science and how-tos). Query with outline and sample chapter.

**SEVEN SEAS PRESS**—International Marine, Box 220, Camden, ME 04843. Jonathan Eaton, VP/Ed. James Babb, Acquisitions Ed. Books on boating (sailing and power), outdoor recreation, and alternative travel.

**SHAW PUBLISHERS, HAROLD**—388 Gunderson Dr., Box 567, Wheaton, IL 60189. Ramona Cramer Tucker, Dir. of Ed. Services. Nonfiction, 120 to 220 pages, with an evangelical Christian perspective. Some teen and adult fiction and literary books. Query. Flat fee.

**SHOE TREE PRESS**—Betterway Publications, Inc. P.O. Box 219, Crozet, VA 22932. Susan Morris, Sr. Ed. Fiction for young people, ages 12 and up; nonfiction, 120 pages, for ages 10 and up; young-adult titles, 160 pages. Especially interested in biographies, historical fiction, history, and nonfiction on such topics as math, writing, and geography. Multiple queries accepted. Royalty.

**SIERRA CLUB BOOKS**—100 Bush St., San Francisco, CA 94104. Nonfiction: environment, natural history, the sciences, outdoors and regional guidebooks, nature photography; juvenile fiction and nonfiction. Query with SASE. Royalty.

**SILHOUETTE BOOKS**—300 E. 42nd St., New York, NY 10017. Isabel Swift, Ed. Dir. *Silhouette Romances*: Valerie Hayward, Sr. Ed. Contemporary romances, 53,000 to 58,000 words. *Special Edition*: Tara Gavin, Sr. Ed. Sophisticated contemporary romances, 75,000 to 80,000 words. *Silhouette Desire*: Lucia Macro, Sr. Ed. Sensuous contemporary romances, 53,000 to 60,000 words. *Intimate Moments*: Leslie Wainger, Sr. Ed./Ed. Coord. Sensuous, exciting contemporary romances, 80,000 to 85,000 words. Historical romance: 95,000 to 105,000 words, set in England, France, and North America between 1700 and 1900; query with synopsis and three sample chapters to Tracy Farrell, Sr. Ed. Query with synopsis and SASE to appropriate editor. Tipsheets available.

**SIMON & SCHUSTER**—1230 Ave. of the Americas, New York, NY 10020. Adult books: No unsolicited material.

**SIMON & SCHUSTER BOOKS FOR YOUNG READERS**—15 Columbus Cir., New York, NY 10023. Grace Clarke, Ed.-in-Chief. *Books for Young Readers*: Books for ages preschool through 14. Picture books, fiction from first chapter books to young adult, and nonfiction at all age levels. *Little Simon*: Books for children under 8. Board books, novelty books, picture books, nursery tales, and concept books with a broad market base. *Green Tiger Press*: Illustrated books for all ages. Special content, special art. Unusual fantasy, lyrical prose, offbeat subject matter. "Unsolicited material discouraged for all three imprints. Long wait for replies. Identify multiple submissions."

**SINGER MEDIA CORPORATION**—Seaview Business Park, 1030 Calle Cordillera #106, San Clemente, CA 92672. Kurt Singer, Pres. Foreign reprint rights to books in fields of business, management, self-help, and psychology. Also, unpublished modern romance novels for foreign licensing. Pays on percentage basis, or outright purchase.

**SLAWSON COMMUNICATIONS, INC.**—165 Vallecitos de Oro, San Marcos, CA 92069–1436. Ron Tucker, Asst. to the Pub. *Microtrend*: high-level computer books, 160 to 256 pages. *Avant*: business titles. Query with sample chapters. Royalty.

**THE SMITH**—69 Joralemon St., Brooklyn, NY 11201. Harry Smith, Ed. Fiction and nonfiction, from 64 pages, and poetry, 48 to 112 pages. "While publishing at a high level of craftsmanship, we have pursued the increasingly difficult, expensive and now relatively rare policy of keeping our titles in print over the decades." Query with outline and sample chapters. Royalty.

**SOHO PRESS**—853 Broadway, New York, NY 10003. Juris Jurjevics, Ed. Adult fiction, mysteries, thrillers, and nonfiction, from 60,000 words. Send SASE and complete manuscript. Royalty.

**SOUTHERN ILLINOIS UNIVERSITY PRESS**—Box 3697, Carbondale, IL 62902–3697. Curtis L. Clark, Ed. Nonfiction in the humanities, 200 to 400 pages. Query with outline and sample chapters. Royalty.

**SOUTHERN METHODIST UNIVERSITY PRESS**—Box 415, Dallas, TX 75275. Kathryn Lang, Sr. Ed. Serious literary fiction. Nonfiction: scholarly studies in religion, medical ethics (death and dying); film, theater; scholarly works on Texas or Southwest. No juvenile material, SF, or poetry. Query. Royalty or flat fee.

**SPECTRA BOOKS**—Imprint of Bantam Books, 666 Fifth Ave., New York, NY 10103. Lou Aronica, Pub. Science fiction and fantasy, with emphasis on storytelling and characterization. Query with SASE; no unsolicited manuscripts. Royalty.

**STANDARD PUBLISHING**—8121 Hamilton Ave., Cincinnati, OH 45231. Address Mark Plunkett. Fiction: juveniles, based on Bible or with moral tone. Nonfiction: biblical, Christian education. Conservative evangelical. Query preferred.

**STANFORD UNIVERSITY PRESS**—Stanford University, Stanford, CA 94305–2235. Norris Pope, Ed. "For the most part, we publish academic scholarship." No original fiction or poetry. Query with outline and sample chapters. Royalty.

**STEMMER HOUSE PUBLISHERS, INC.**—2627 Caves Rd., Owings Mills,

MD 21117. Barbara Holdridge, Ed. Juvenile fiction and adult fiction and nonfiction. Specializes in art, design, cookbooks, and horticultural titles. Query with SASE. Royalty.

**STERLING PUBLISHING CO., INC.**—387 Park Ave. S., New York, NY 10016. Sheila Anne Barry, Acquisitions Mgr. How-to, hobby, woodworking, health, fiber arts, craft, wine, nature, oddities, new age, puzzles, juvenile humor and activities, juvenile science, sports and games books, reference, and military topics. Query with outline, sample chapter, and sample illustrations. Royalty.

**STONE WALL PRESS, INC.**—1241 30th St. N.W., Washington, DC 20007. Nonfiction manuscripts on natural history, outdoors, conservation, 200 to 300 pages. Query first. Royalty.

**STONEYDALE PRESS**—205 Main St., Drawer B, Stevensville, MT 59870. Dale A. Burk, Ed. Adult nonfiction, primarily how-to on outdoor recreation with emphasis on big game hunting. "We're a very specialized market. Query with outline and sample chapters essential." Royalty.

**STORY LINE PRESS**—Three Oaks Farm, Brownsville, OR 97327–9718. Robert McDowell, Ed. Fiction, nonfiction, and poetry of varying lengths. Query. Royalty.

**STRAWBERRY HILL PRESS**—3848 S.E. Division St., Portland, OR 97202–1641. Carolyn Soto, Ed. Nonfiction: biography, autobiography, history, cooking, health, how-to, philosophy, performance arts, and Third World. Query first with sample chapters, outline, and SASE. Royalty.

**SUNFIRE**—See Scholastic, Inc.

**TSR, INC.**—P.O. Box 756, Lake Geneva, WI 53147. Address Manuscript Ed. Highly original works, 100,000 words, of fantasy, science fiction, horror, or mystery related to those genres. Query required.

**TAB BOOKS**—A Div. of McGraw-Hill, Inc., Blue Ridge Summit, PA 17294. Ron Powers, Dir. of Acquisitions, Ed. Dept. Nonfiction: electronics, computers, how-to, aviation, science fair projects, self-help, business, solar and energy, science and technology, back to basics, automotive, marine and outdoor life, hobby and craft, military history, graphic design, and engineering. Fiction: military. Royalty or flat fee.

**TAMBOURINE BOOKS**—Imprint of William Morrow & Co., Inc., 1350 Ave. of the Americas, New York, NY 10019. Paulette C. Kaufmann, V.P./Ed.-in-Chief. Picture books, fiction, and nonfiction for all ages in general trade market. "We hope to find new talented writers and illustrators who are working outside the New York area."

**TAYLOR PUBLISHING CO.**—1550 W. Mockingbird Ln., Dallas, TX 75235. Jim Donovan, Sr. Ed. Adult nonfiction: gardening, sports and recreation, health, popular culture, parenting, home improvement, nature/outdoors. Query with outline, sample chapters, relevant author bio, and SASE. Royalty.

**TEMPLE UNIVERSITY PRESS**—Broad and Oxford Sts., Philadelphia, PA 19122. Michael Ames, Ed. Adult nonfiction. Query with outline and sample chapters. Royalty.

**TEN SPEED PRESS**—P.O. Box 7123, Berkeley, CA 94707. Mariah Bear, Ed. Self-help and how-to on careers, recreation, etc.; natural science, history, cookbooks. Query with outline and sample chapters. Royalty. Paperback.

**THUNDER'S MOUTH PRESS**—54 Greene St., Suite 4S, New York, NY

10013. Neil Ortenberg, Ed. Mainly nonfiction: popular culture, current affairs, memoir, and biography, to 200 pages. Royalty.

**TICKNOR & FIELDS**—Subsidiary of Houghton Mifflin Company, 215 Park Ave. S., New York, NY 10003. John Herman, Ed. Dir. General nonfiction and fiction. Send query letters to Cindy Spiegel. No unsolicited manuscripts accepted. Royalty.

**TIMES BOOKS**—Div. of Random House, Inc., 201 E. 50th St., New York, NY 10022. Steve Wasserman, Ed. Dir. General nonfiction specializing in business, science, and current affairs. No unsolicited manuscripts or queries accepted.

**TOR BOOKS**—49 W. 24th St., New York, NY 10010. Robert Gleason, Ed.-in-Chief. Patrick Nielsen Hayden, Sr. Ed., science fiction and fantasy. Melissa Ann Singer, Sr. Ed., general fiction. Length: from 60,000 words. Query with outline and sample chapters. Royalty.

**TROLL ASSOCIATES**—100 Corporate Dr., Mahwah, NJ 07430. M. Francis, Ed. Juvenile fiction and nonfiction. Query preferred. Royalty or flat fee.

**TROUBADOR PRESS**—Imprint of Price Stern Sloan, Inc., 11150 Olympic Blvd., Los Angeles, CA 90064. Juvenile illustrated game, activity, paper doll, coloring, and cut-out books. Query with outline and SASE. Royalty or flat fee.

**TUDOR PUBLISHERS, INC.**—P.O. Box 38366, Greensboro, NC 27438. Eugene E. Pfaff, Jr., Ed. Helpful nonfiction books for senior citizens, teenagers, and minorities. Reference library titles. Occasional high-quality fiction. Send proposal or query with sample chapters. Royalty.

**TYNDALE HOUSE**—351 Executive Dr., Box 80, Wheaton, IL 60189. Ron Beers, V.P. Juvenile and adult fiction and nonfiction on subjects of concern to Christians. Picture books with religious focus for preschool and early readers. Query only.

**UNITED RESOURCE PRESS**—4521 Campus Dr., #388, Irvine, CA 92715. Charlene Brown, Ed. Personal finance books, 50,000 to 80,000 words, and poetry arts project, varying lengths. Send SASE for guidelines. Submit outline and sample chapters with SASE. Royalty.

**UNIVERSE BOOKS**—300 Park Ave. S., New York, NY 10010. Adele J. Ursone, Ed. Dir. Fine arts, art history, and art criticism with a concentration in women's studies and the 20th century. Query with SASE. Royalty.

**UNIVERSITY OF ALABAMA PRESS**—P.O. Box 870380, Tuscaloosa, AL 35487–0380. Scholarly and general regional nonfiction. Submit to appropriate editor: Malcolm MacDonald, Ed. (history, public administration, political science); Nicole Mitchell, Ed. (English, rhetoric and communication, Judaic studies, women's studies); Judith Knight, Ed. (archaeology, anthropology). Send complete manuscript. Royalty.

**UNIVERSITY OF ARIZONA PRESS**—1230 N. Park Ave., Suite 102, Tucson, AZ 85719. Joanne O'Hare, Sr. Ed. Christine R. Szuter, Acquiring Ed. Scholarly nonfiction: Arizona, American West, anthropology, archaeology, environmental science, global change, Latin America, Native Americans, natural history, space sciences, women's studies. Query with outline and sample chapters or send complete manuscript. Royalty.

**UNIVERSITY OF CALIFORNIA PRESS**—2120 Berkeley Way, Berkeley, CA 94720. Address Acquisitions Dept. Scholarly nonfiction. Query with cover letter, outline, sample chapters, curriculum vitae, and SASE.

**UNIVERSITY OF GEORGIA PRESS**—University of Georgia, Athens, GA 30602. Karen Orchard, Ed. Short story collections and poetry, scholarly nonfiction and literary criticism, Southern and American history, regional studies, biography and autobiography. For nonfiction, query with outline and sample chapters. Poetry collections considered in Sept. and Jan. only; short fiction in June and July only. A $10 fee is required for all poetry and fiction submissions. Royalty. SASE for competition guidelines.

**UNIVERSITY OF ILLINOIS PRESS**—54 E. Gregory Dr., Champaign, IL 61820. Richard L. Wentworth, Ed.-in-Chief. Short story collections, 140 to 180 pages; nonfiction; and poetry, 70 to 100 pages. Rarely considers multiple submissions. Query. Royalty.

**UNIVERSITY OF MINNESOTA PRESS**—2037 University Ave. S.E., Minneapolis, MN 55414. Biodun Iginla, Ed. Janaki Bakhlé, Ed. Nonfiction: media studies, literary theory, critical aesthetics, philosophy, cultural criticism, regional titles, 50,000 to 225,000 words. Query with detailed prospectus or introduction, table of contents, sample chapter, and recent resumé. Royalty.

**UNIVERSITY OF MISSOURI PRESS**—2910 LeMone Blvd., Columbia, MO 65201-8227. Scholarly books on American and European history; American, British, and Latin American literary criticism; political philosophy; intellectual history; regional studies; and poetry and short fiction. Query Beverly Jarrett, Dir. and Ed.-in-Chief, for scholarly studies and creative nonfiction. Query Mr. Clair Willcox, Poetry and Fiction Editor, with 4 to 6 sample poems or one short story, table of contents for entire manuscript, and cover letter describing the work and author's professional background.

**UNIVERSITY OF NEBRASKA PRESS**—901 N. 17th St., Lincoln, NE 68588-0520. Address the Editors. Specializes in the history of the American West. Send proposals with summary, two sample chapters, and resumé.

**UNIVERSITY OF NEW MEXICO PRESS**—University of New Mexico, Albuquerque, NM 87131. Elizabeth C. Hadas, Ed. Dir. David V. Holtby, Andrea Otanez, Dana Asbury, and Barbara Guth, Eds. Scholarly nonfiction on social and cultural anthropology, archaeology, Western history, art, and photography. Query. Royalty.

**UNIVERSITY OF NORTH CAROLINA PRESS**—P.O. Box 2288, Chapel Hill, NC 27515-2288. David Perry, Ed. General-interest books (75,000 to 125,000 words) on the lore, crafts, cooking, gardening, travel, and natural history of the Southeast. No fiction or poetry. Query preferred. Royalty.

**UNIVERSITY OF OKLAHOMA PRESS**—1005 Asp Ave., Norman, OK 73019-0445. John Drayton, Asst. Dir. Books, to 300 pages, on the history of the American West, Indians of the Americas, congressional studies, classical studies, literary criticism, and natural history. Query. Royalty.

**UNIVERSITY OF TENNESSEE PRESS**—293 Communications Bldg., Knoxville, TN 37996-0325. Nonfiction, 200 to 300 pages. Query with outline and sample chapters. Royalty.

**UNIVERSITY PRESS OF COLORADO**—P.O. BOX 849, Niwot, CO 80544. Scholarly books in the humanities, social sciences, and applied sciences. No fiction or poetry.

**UNIVERSITY PRESS OF FLORIDA**—15 N.W. 15th St., Gainesville, FL 32611-2079. Walda Metcalf, Sr. Ed. and Asst. Dir. Nonfiction, 150 to 450 manuscript pages, on regional studies, Native Americans, folklore, women's studies, Latin American studies, contemporary literary criticism, sociology, anthropology, archaeology, international affairs, labor studies, and history. Poetry. Royalty.

**THE UNIVERSITY PRESS OF KENTUCKY**—663 S. Limestone St., Lexington, KY 40508–4008. William Jerome Crouch, Ed.-in-Chief. Scholarly books in the major fields. Serious nonfiction of general interest. Books related to Kentucky and the Ohio Valley, the Appalachians, and the South. No fiction, drama, or poetry. Query.

**UNIVERSITY PRESS OF MISSISSIPPI**—3825 Ridgewood Rd., Jackson, MS 39211–6492. Seetha Srinivasan, Ed.-in-Chief. Scholarly and trade titles in American literature, history, and culture; southern studies; African-American, women's and American studies; social sciences; popular culture; folklife; art and architecture; natural sciences; reference; and other liberal arts.

**UNIVERSITY PRESS OF NEW ENGLAND**—23 S. Main St., Hanover, NH 03755–2048. General and scholarly nonfiction. American, British, and European history, literature, literary criticism, creative fiction and nonfiction, and cultural studies. Jewish studies, women's studies, and studies of the New England region.

**VAN NOSTRAND REINHOLD**—115 Fifth Ave., New York, NY 10003. Judith R. Joseph, Pres./C.E.O. Business, professional, scientific, and technical publishers of applied reference works: hospitality; architecture; graphic and interior design; gemology; chemistry; industrial and environmental health and safety; food science and technology; computer science and engineering. Royalty.

**VANDAMERE PRESS**—P.O. Box 5243, Arlington, VA 22205. Arthur F. Brown, Ed.-in-Chief. General trade books, fiction and nonfiction. History, military, parenting and children, career guides, and travel. Also books about the nation's capital for a national audience. Prefer to see outline with sample chapter for nonfiction; for fiction send 4 or 5 sample chapters. Multiple queries considered. Royalty.

**VIKING BOOKS**—Imprint of Penguin USA, 375 Hudson St., New York, NY 10014. No unagented manuscripts.

**VIKING CHILDREN'S BOOKS**—Imprint of Penguin USA, 375 Hudson St., New York, NY 10014. Address Editors. Fiction and nonfiction, including biography, history, and sports, for ages 7 to 14. Humor and picture books for ages 2 to 6. Query Children's Book Dept. with outline and sample chapter. SASE required. Royalty.

**VILLARD BOOKS**—Div. of Random House, 201 E. 50th St. , New York, NY 10022. Diane Reverand, V.P/Pub./Ed.-in-Chief. "We look for good books we can sell: fiction, sports, inspiration, how-to, biography, humor, etc. We do look for authors who are promotable and books we feel we can market well." Royalty.

**VOYAGER PAPERBACKS**—See Harcourt Brace Jovanovich.

**WALKER AND COMPANY**—720 Fifth Ave., New York, NY 10019. Fiction: mysteries, suspense, westerns, regency romance, and espionage. Nonfiction: Americana, biography, history, science, natural history, medicine, psychology, parenting, sports, outdoors, reference, popular science, self-help, business, and music. Juvenile nonfiction, including biography, science, history, music, and nature. Fiction and young-adult problem novels. Query with synopsis and SASE. Royalty.

**WARNER BOOKS**—1271 Ave. of the Americas, New York, NY 10020. Mel Parker, Pub., Warner Paperbacks. Fiction: historical romance, contemporary women's fiction, unusual big-scale horror and suspense. Nonfiction: business books, health and nutrition, self-help. Query with sample chapters.

**WASHINGTON WRITERS PUBLISHING HOUSE**—4901 N. 17th St., Arlington, VA 22209. Naomi Thiers, Ed. Poetry books, 50 to 60 pages, by writers in the greater Washington, DC, area. Send SASE for guidelines.

**WATERSTON PRODUCTIONS, INC.**—1019 N.W. Brooks St., Bend, OR 97701. Carey Vendrame, Ed. Picture books, 200 words, for preschoolers to 8-year-olds; books for young readers, 5 to 8 years old, up to 1,500 words. "We welcome all manuscripts but have particular interest in those with a Northwest focus. Manuscripts must be well written, entertaining and have a unique and endearing quality about them. Cute, condescending or preachy stories are not acceptable." Payment is negotiable. Submit complete manuscript with SASE.

**WATTS, INC., FRANKLIN**—95 Madison Ave., New York, NY 10016. Philippe Gray, Submissions. Curriculum-oriented nonfiction for grades 7 to 12, including science, history, social studies, and biography. Query with SASE required.

**WESLEYAN UNIVERSITY PRESS**—110 Mt. Vernon St., Middletown, CT 06459–0433. Terry Cochran, Dir. *Wesleyan Poetry*: new poets, 64 pages; published poets, 64 to 80 pages. Query. Royalty.

**WESTERN PUBLISHING CO., INC.**—850 Third Ave., New York, NY 10022. Robin Warner, V.P./Pub., Children's Books; Margo Lundell, Marilyn Salomon, Ed. Dirs., Children's Books. Children's books, fiction and nonfiction: picture books, storybooks, concept books, novelty books. Adult nonfiction: field guides. No unsolicited manuscripts. Same address and requirements for *Golden Press*. Royalty or flat fee.

**WESTMINSTER/JOHN KNOX PRESS**—100 Witherspoon St., Louisville, KY 40202. Davis Perkins, Ed. Dir. Books that inform, interpret, challenge, and encourage Christian faith and living. Royalty. Send SASE for "Guidelines for a Book Proposal."

**WHITMAN, ALBERT**—6340 Oakton, Morton Grove, IL 60053. Kathleen Tucker, Ed. Picture books for preschool children; novels, biographies, mysteries, and general nonfiction for middle-grade readers. Submit complete manuscript for picture books, three chapters and outline for longer fiction; query for nonfiction. Royalty.

**WILDERNESS PRESS**—2440 Bancroft Way, Berkeley, CA 94704. Thomas Winnett, Ed. Nonfiction: sports, recreation, and travel in the western U.S. Royalty.

**WILEY & SONS, JOHN**—605 Third Ave., New York, NY 10158–0012. Nonfiction manuscripts, 250 to 350 pages: science/nature; business/management; real estate; travel; cooking; biography; psychology; microcomputers; language; history; current affairs; health; finance. Send proposals with outline, author vita, market information, and sample chapter. Royalty.

**WILLOWISP PRESS, INC.**—10100 SBF Dr., Pinellas Park, FL 34666. Address Acquisitions Ed. Juvenile books for children in grades K through 8. Picture books, 300 to 800 words. Fiction, 14,000 to 18,000 words for grades 3 through 5; 20,000 to 24,000 words for grades 5 through 8. Requirements for nonfiction vary. Query with outline, sample chapter, and SASE. Guidelines. Royalty or flat fee.

**WILSHIRE BOOK COMPANY**—12015 Sherman Rd., N. Hollywood, CA 91605. Melvin Powers, Pub. Nonfiction: self-help, motivation, inspiration, psychology, how-to, entrepreneurship, mail order, and horsemanship. Fiction: adult fables, 35,000 to 45,000 words, that teach principles of psychological growth or offer guidance in living. Send synopsis/detailed chapter outline, 3 chapters, and SASE. Royalty.

**WINDSWEPT HOUSE PUBLISHERS**—Mt. Desert, ME 04660. Jane Weinberger, Pub. Carl Little, Ed. Children's picture books. Query first for how-to and young-adult novels.

**WINGBOW PRESS**—7900 Edgewater Dr., Oakland, CA 94621. Randy Fingland, Ed. Nonfiction: women's interests, health, psychology. Query preferred. Royalty.

**WOODBINE HOUSE**—5615 Fishers Lane, Rockville, MD 20852. Susan Stokes, Ed. "Emphasis is increasingly on books for or about people with disabilities, but will consider nonfiction of all types. No personal accounts or books that can be marketed only through bookstores." Query or submit complete manuscript with SASE. Guidelines for SASE. Royalty.

**WORDWARE PUBLISHING**—1506 Capital Ave., Plano, TX 75074. Russell A. Stultz, Ed. Computer reference books and Texas regional books. Query with outline and sample chapters. Royalty.

**WORKMAN PUBLISHING CO., INC.**—708 Broadway, New York, NY 10003. Address Editors. General nonfiction. Normal contractual terms based on agreement.

**WORLDWIDE LIBRARY**—Div. of Harlequin Books, 225 Duncan Mill Rd., Don Mills, Ont., Canada M3B 3K9. Randall Toye, Ed. Dir. Action adventure series and futuristic fiction for *Gold Eagle* imprint; mystery fiction reprints only, no originals. Query. Paperback only.

**YANKEE BOOKS**—Rodale Press, 33 E. Minor St., Emmaus, PA 18098. Edward Claflin, Sr. Ed. Books relating specifically to New England: travel in the Northeast; New England cooking and recipes; New England crafts. "We are looking for accurate, informative, and practical books that can be used by visitors and would-be visitors to New England, as well as residents of the Northeast. Send proposals only, addressed to Editor. Royalty.

**YEARLING BOOKS**—Imprint of Dell Publishing Co., 666 Fifth Ave., New York, NY 10103. Address Editors. Books for kindergarten through 6th grade. Manuscripts accepted from agents only.

**YOLEN BOOKS, JANE**—See Harcourt Brace Jovanovich.

**ZEBRA BOOKS**—475 Park Ave. S., New York, NY 10016. Ann LaFarge, Sr. Ed. Carin Cohen Ritter, Exec. Ed. Popular fiction: horror; historical romance (*Heartfire Romances*, 107,000 words, and *Lovegram Romances*, 130,000 words); traditional gothics (first person, 100,000 words); regencies (80,000 to 120,000 words); sagas (150,000 words); glitz (100,000 words); men's adventure; westerns; thrillers, etc. Query with synopsis and sample chapters preferred.

**ZENITH EDITIONS**—See National Press.

**ZONDERVAN PUBLISHING HOUSE**—5300 Patterson SE, Grand Rapids, MI 49530. Christian titles. General fiction and nonfiction; academic and professional books. Address Manuscript Review. Query with outline, sample chapter, and SASE. Royalty. Guidelines.

# UNIVERSITY PRESSES

University presses generally publish books of a scholarly nature or of specialized interest by authorities in a given field. A few publish fiction and poetry. Many publish only a handful of titles a year. Always query first. Do not send a manuscript until you have been invited to do so by the editor. Several of the following presses and their detailed editorial submission requirements are included in the *Book Publishers* list.

**BRIGHAM YOUNG UNIVERSITY PRESS**—205 University Press Bldg., Provo, UT 84602.

**BUCKNELL UNIVERSITY PRESS**—Bucknell University, Lewisburg, PA 17837.

**CAMBRIDGE UNIVERSITY PRESS**—40 W. 20th St., New York, NY 10011-4211.

**THE CATHOLIC UNIVERSITY OF AMERICA PRESS**—620 Michigan Ave. N.E., Washington, DC 20064.

**COLUMBIA UNIVERSITY PRESS**—562 W. 113th St., New York, NY 10025.

**DUKE UNIVERSITY PRESS**—Box 6697, College Sta., Durham, NC 27708.

**DUQUESNE UNIVERSITY PRESS**—600 Forbes Ave., Pittsburgh, PA 15282-0101.

**GEORGIA STATE UNIVERSITY BUSINESS PRESS**—University Plaza, Atlanta, GA 30303-3093.

**HARVARD UNIVERSITY PRESS**—79 Garden St., Cambridge, MA 02138.

**INDIANA UNIVERSITY PRESS**—601 N. Morton St., Bloomington, IN 47404-3797.

**THE JOHNS HOPKINS UNIVERSITY PRESS**—701 W. 40th St., Suite 275, Baltimore, MD 21211-2190.

**KENT STATE UNIVERSITY PRESS**—Kent State Univ., Kent, OH 44242.

**LOUISIANA STATE UNIVERSITY PRESS**—LSU, Baton Rouge, LA 70893.

**LOYOLA UNIVERSITY PRESS**—3441 N. Ashland Ave., Chicago, IL 60657-1397.

**THE MICHIGAN STATE UNIVERSITY PRESS**—1405 S. Harrison Rd., Suite 25, Manly Miles Bldg., E. Lansing, MI 48823-5202.

**THE MIT PRESS**—Acquisitions Dept., 55 Hayward St., Cambridge, MA 02142.

**NEW YORK UNIVERSITY PRESS**—Washington Sq., New York, NY 10003.

**OHIO STATE UNIVERSITY PRESS**—180 Pressey Hall, 1070 Carmack Rd., Columbus, OH 43210.

**OREGON STATE UNIVERSITY PRESS**—101 Waldo Hall, Corvallis, OR 97331.

**THE PENNSYLVANIA STATE UNIVERSITY PRESS**—Barbara Bldg., Suite C, 820 N. University Dr., University Park, PA 16802.

**PRINCETON UNIVERSITY PRESS**—41 William St., Princeton, NJ 08540.

**RUTGERS UNIVERSITY PRESS**—109 Church St., New Brunswick, NJ 08901.

**SOUTHERN ILLINOIS UNIVERSITY PRESS**—Box 3697, Carbondale, IL 62902–3697.

**SOUTHERN METHODIST UNIVERSITY PRESS**—Box 415, Dallas, TX 75275.

**STANFORD UNIVERSITY PRESS**—Stanford University, Stanford, CA 94305–2235.

**STATE UNIVERSITY OF NEW YORK PRESS**—State University Plaza, Albany, NY 12246–0001.

**SYRACUSE UNIVERSITY PRESS**—1600 Jamesville Ave., Syracuse, NY 13244–5160.

**TEMPLE UNIVERSITY PRESS**—Broad and Oxford Sts., Philadelphia, PA 19122.

**UNIVERSITY OF ALABAMA PRESS**—P.O. Box 870380, Tuscaloosa, AL 35487–0380.

**UNIVERSITY OF ARIZONA PRESS**—1230 N. Park Ave., Suite 102, Tucson, AZ 85719.

**UNIVERSITY OF CALIFORNIA PRESS**—2120 Berkeley Way, Berkeley, CA 94720.

**UNIVERSITY OF CHICAGO PRESS**—5801 Ellis Ave., Chicago, IL 60637–1496.

**UNIVERSITY OF GEORGIA PRESS**—University of Georgia, Athens, GA 30602.

**UNIVERSITY OF ILLINOIS PRESS**—54 E. Gregory Dr., Champaign, IL 61820.

**UNIVERSITY OF MASSACHUSETTS PRESS**—Box 429, Amherst, MA 01004.

**UNIVERSITY OF MICHIGAN PRESS**—839 Greene St., P.O. Box 1104, Ann Arbor, MI 48106–1104.

**UNIVERSITY OF MINNESOTA PRESS**—2037 University Ave. S.E., Minneapolis, MN 55414.

**UNIVERSITY OF MISSOURI PRESS**—2910 LeMone Blvd., Columbia, MO 65201–8227.

**UNIVERSITY OF NEBRASKA PRESS**—901 North 17th St., Lincoln, NE 68588–0520.

**UNIVERSITY OF NEW MEXICO PRESS**—University of New Mexico, Albuquerque, NM 87131.

**UNIVERSITY OF NORTH CAROLINA PRESS**—P.O. Box 2288, Chapel Hill, NC 27515–2288.

**UNIVERSITY OF OKLAHOMA PRESS**—1005 Asp Ave., Norman, OK 73019–0445.

**UNIVERSITY OF PITTSBURGH PRESS**—127 North Bellefield Ave., Pittsburgh, PA 15260.

**UNIVERSITY OF SOUTH CAROLINA PRESS**—1716 College St., Columbia, SC 29208.

**UNIVERSITY OF TENNESSEE PRESS**—293 Communications Bldg., Knoxville, TN 37996–0325.

**UNIVERSITY OF UTAH PRESS**—101 U.S.B., Salt Lake City, UT 84112.

**UNIVERSITY OF WASHINGTON PRESS**—P.O. Box 50096, Seattle, WA 98145–5096.

**UNIVERSITY OF WISCONSIN PRESS**—114 N. Murray St., Madison, WI 53715–1199.

**UNIVERSITY PRESS OF COLORADO**—P.O. Box 849, Niwot, CO 80544.

**UNIVERSITY PRESS OF FLORIDA**—15 N.W. 15th St., Gainesville, FL 32611–2079.

**THE UNIVERSITY PRESS OF KENTUCKY**—663 S. Limestone St., Lexington, KY 40508–4008.

**UNIVERSITY PRESS OF MISSISSIPPI**—3825 Ridgewood Rd., Jackson, MS 39211–6492.

**UNIVERSITY PRESS OF NEW ENGLAND**—23 S. Main St., Hanover, NH 03755–2048.

**THE UNIVERSITY PRESS OF VIRGINIA**—Box 3608, University Sta., Charlottesville, VA 22903.

**WAYNE STATE UNIVERSITY PRESS**—5959 Woodward Ave., Detroit, MI 48202.

**WESLEYAN UNIVERSITY PRESS**—110 Mt.Vernon St., Middletown, CT 06459–0433.

**YALE UNIVERSITY PRESS**—92A Yale Sta., New Haven, CT 06520.

# SYNDICATES

Syndicates are business organizations that buy material from writers and artists to sell to newspapers all over the country and the world. Authors are paid either a percentage of the gross proceeds or an outright fee.

Of course, features by people well known in their fields have the best chance of being syndicated. In general, syndicates want columns that have been popular in a local newspaper, perhaps, or magazine. Since most syndicated fiction has been published previously in magazines or books, beginning fiction writers should try to sell their stories to magazines before submitting them to syndicates.

Always query syndicates before sending manuscripts, since their needs change frequently, and be sure to enclose SASEs with queries and manuscripts.

**ARKIN MAGAZINE SYNDICATE**—1817 N.E. 164th St., N. Miami Beach, FL 33162. Joseph Arkin, Ed. Dir. Articles, 750 to 2,200 words, for trade and professional magazines. Must have small-business slant, be written in layman's language, and offer solutions to business problems. Articles should apply to many businesses, not just a specific industry. No columns. Pays 3¢ to 10¢ a word, on acceptance. Query not necessary.

**CONTEMPORARY FEATURES SYNDICATE**—P.O. Box 1258, Jackson, TN 38302–1258. Lloyd Russell, Ed. Articles, 1,000 to 10,000 words: how-tos, money savers, business, etc. Self-help pieces for small business. Pays from $25, on acceptance.

**HARRIS & ASSOCIATES FEATURES**—12084 Caminito Campana, San Diego, CA 92128. Dick Harris, Ed. Sports- and family-oriented features, to 1,200 words; fillers and short humor, 500 to 800 words. Queries preferred. Pays varying rates.

**HISPANIC LINK NEWS SERVICE**—1420 N St. N.W., Washington, DC 20005. Charles A. Ericksen, Ed. Trend articles, opinion and personal experience pieces, and general features with Hispanic focus, 650 to 700 words; editorial cartoons. Pays $25 for op-ed columns and cartoons, on acceptance. Send SASE for guidelines.

**THE HOLLYWOOD INSIDE SYNDICATE**—Box 49957, Los Angeles, CA 90049. John Austin, Dir. Feature articles, 750 to 2,500 words, on TV and film personalities with B&W photo(s). Story suggestions for three-part series. Pieces on unusual medical and scientific breakthroughs. Pays on percentage basis for features, negotiated rates for ideas, on publication.

**KING FEATURES SYNDICATE**—235 E. 45th St., New York, NY 10017. Thomas E. Pritchard, Exec. Ed. Columns, comics. "We do not consider or buy individual articles. We are interested in ideas for nationally syndicated columns." Submit cover letter, six sample columns of 650 words each, bio sheet and any additional clips, and SASE. No simultaneous submissions. Query with SASE for guidelines.

**LOS ANGELES TIMES SYNDICATE**—Times Mirror Sq., Los Angeles, CA 90053. Commentary, features, columns, editorial cartoons, comics, puzzles and games; news services. Send SASE for submission guidelines.

**NATIONAL NEWS BUREAU**—P.O. Box 5628, Philadelphia, PA 19129. Harry Jay Katz, Ed. Articles, 500 to 1,500 words, interviews, consumer news, how-tos, travel pieces, reviews, entertainment pieces, features, etc. Pays on publication.

**NEW YORK TIMES SYNDICATION SALES**—130 Fifth Ave., New York, NY 10011. Barbara Gaynes, Man. Ed. Previously published health, lifestyle, and entertainment articles only, to 2,000 words. Query with published article or tear sheet and SASE. Pays varying rates, on publication.

**NEWSPAPER ENTERPRISE ASSOCIATION**—200 Park Ave., New

York, NY 10166. Diana Loevy, Exec. Ed. Ideas for new concepts in syndicated columns. No single stories or stringers. Payment by contractual arrangement.

**OCEANIC PRESS SERVICE**—Seaview Business Park, 1030 Calle Cordillera, Unit #106, San Clemente, CA 92673. Peter Carbone, General Mgr. Buys reprint rights for foreign markets, on previously published novels, self-help, and how-to books; interviews with celebrities; illustrated features on celebrities, family, health, beauty, personal relationships, etc.; cartoons, comic strips. Pays on acceptance or half on acceptance, half on syndication. Query.

**SINGER MEDIA CORP.**— #106, 1030 Calle Cordillera, San Clemente, CA 92672. Kurt D. Singer, Ed. U.S. and/or foreign reprint rights to romantic short stories, historical and romantic novels, gothics, westerns, and mysteries published during last 25 years; business management titles. Biography, women's-interest material, all lengths. Home repair, real estate, crosswords, psychological quizzes. Interviews with celebrities. Illustrated columns, humor, cartoons, comic strips. Pays on percentage basis or by outright purchase.

**TRIBUNE MEDIA SERVICES**—64 E. Concord St., Orlando, FL 32801. Michael Argirion, Ed. Continuing columns, comic strips, features, electronic databases.

**UNITED FEATURE SYNDICATE**—200 Park Ave., New York, NY 10166. Diana Loevy, V.P./Exec. Ed. Syndicated columns; no one-shots or series. Payment by contractual arrangement. Send samples with SASE.

**UNITED PRESS INTERNATIONAL**—1400 Eye St. N.W., Washington, DC 20005. Bill G. Ferguson, Man. Ed. No free-lance material.

**UNIVERSAL PRESS SYNDICATE**—4900 Main St., Kansas City, MO 64112. Attn: Doris Richetti Nolan. Articles for "High Impact" feature service, covering lifestyles, trends, health, fashion, parenting, business, humor, the home, entertainment, and personalities. Query. Pays advances or flat fee.

# LITERARY PRIZE OFFERS

Each year many important literary contests are open to free-lance writers. The short summaries given below are intended merely as guides. Closing dates, requirements, and rules are tentative. Every effort has been made to ensure the accuracy of information provided here. However, due to the ever-changing nature of literary competitions, writers should send SASE for guidelines before submitting to any contest. Writers are also advised to check the monthly "Prize Offers" column of *The Writer* Magazine (120 Boylston St., Boston, MA 02116–4615) for additional contest listings and up-to-date contest requirements.

**ACADEMY OF AMERICAN POETS**—584 Broadway, Suite 1208, New York, NY 10012. Offers Walt Whitman Award of publication and a $1,000 cash prize for a book-length poetry manuscript by a poet who has not yet published a volume of poetry. Closes in November.

**ACADEMY OF MOTION PICTURE ARTS AND SCIENCES**—The Nicholl Fellowships, Dept. WR, 8949 Wilshire Blvd., Beverly Hills, CA 90211–1972. Up to 5 fellowships of $20,000 each will be awarded for original screenplays that display exceptional craft and engaging storytelling. Closes in May.

**ACTORS THEATRE OF LOUISVILLE**—316 W. Main St., Louisville, KY 40202. Conducts Ten-Minute Play Contest. Offers $1,000 for previously unproduced 10-page script. Closes in December.

**THE AMARANTH REVIEW**—Spring Edition and Fall Edition Contests, P.O. Box 56235, Phoenix, AZ 85079. Unpublished fiction, under 7,500 words, and poetry of any length may be entered to win $150, $100, and $50 in each category; winning entries are published. Spring Edition Contest closes in March; Fall Edition Contest closes in September.

**AMELIA MAGAZINE AWARDS**—329 "E" St., Bakersfield, CA 93304. Frederick A. Raborg, Jr., Ed. Offers writing awards year round in poetry, short fiction, and nonfiction, with prizes of up to $250. Contest closings vary.

**AMERICAN ACADEMY OF ARTS AND LETTERS**—633 W. 155th St., New York, NY 10032. Offers Richard Rodgers Production Award, which consists of subsidized production in New York City by a non-profit theater for a musical, play with music, thematic review, or any comparable work other than opera. Closes in November.

**AMPERSAND PRESS**—Women Poets Series, Creative Writing Program, School of Fine and Performing Arts, Roger Williams University, One Old Ferry Rd., Bristol, RI 02809–2921. National contest awards $500 and publication to a female poet who has not yet published a full-length collection. Manuscripts should be 48 to 64 pages; single, previously published poems are eligible. Closes in December.

**THE ASSOCIATED WRITING PROGRAMS AWARDS SERIES**—c/o Old Dominion University, Norfolk, VA 23529–0079. Conducts Annual Awards Series in Poetry, Short Fiction, the Novel, and Nonfiction. In each category the prize is book publication and a $1,500 honorarium. Closes in February.

**ASSOCIATION OF JEWISH LIBRARIES**—15 Goldsmith St., Providence, RI 02906. Address Lillian Schwartz, Coordinator. The Sydney Taylor Manuscript Competition offers $1,000 for the best fiction manuscript by an unpublished author, for readers 8 to 11. Stories must have a positive Jewish focus. Closes in January.

**BAKER'S PLAYS**—High School Playwriting Contest, 100 Chauncy St., Boston, MA 02111. Plays about the high school experience, written by high school students, are eligible for awards of $500, $250, and $100. Closes in January.

**BARNARD COLLEGE**—Women Poets at Barnard, Columbia University, 3009 Broadway, New York, NY 10027–6598. Celeste Schenck and Christopher Baswell, Co-Directors. The Barnard New Women Poets Prize offers $1,500 and publication by Beacon Press for an unpublished poetry manuscript, 50 to 100 pages, by a female poet who has never published a book of poetry. Closes in September.

**THE BELLINGHAM REVIEW**—Contest Entry, The 49th Parallel Poetry Contest, 1007 Queen St., Bellingham, WA 98226. A first prize of $150 plus publication, a second prize of $100, and a third prize of $50 will go to the winning poems, up to 40 lines. Closes in December.

**BEVERLY HILLS THEATRE GUILD/JULIE HARRIS PLAYWRIGHT AWARD**—2815 N. Beachwood Dr., Los Angeles, CA 90068. Address Marcella Meharg. Offers prize of $5,000, plus possible $2,000 for productions in Los Angeles area, for previously unproduced and unpublished full-length play. A $1,000 second prize and $500 third prize are also offered. Closes in November.

**BIRMINGHAM-SOUTHERN COLLEGE WRITER'S CONFERENCE**—Hackney Literary Awards, BSC A-3, Birmingham, AL 35254. The Hackney Literary Awards offers $2,000 for an unpublished novel, any length. Closes in September. Also, a $2,000 prize is shared for the winning short story, to 5,000 words, and poem of up to 50 lines. Closes in December.

**BOSTON MAGAZINE**—Fiction Contest, 300 Massachusetts Ave., Boston, MA 02115. Publication and $500 are awarded for the best short story, up to 3,000 words, set in or around Boston. Closes in September.

**CITY OF CARDIFF INTERNATIONAL POETRY COMPETITION**—P.O. Box 438, Cardiff, Wales CF1 6YA. Prizes totalling 4,000 pounds British will be awarded for poems of up to 50 lines, written in English. Closes in August.

**THE CLAUDER COMPETITION**—Theaterworks, Inc., P.O. Box 635, Boston, MA 02117. Awards $3,000 plus professional production for a full-length play by a New England writer. Runner-up prizes of $500 and a staged reading also awarded. Closes in June of even-numbered years.

**CLEVELAND STATE UNIVERSITY POETRY CENTER**—Dept. of English, Rhodes Tower, Room 1815, Cleveland, OH 44115. Publication in the CSU Poetry Series and $1,000 will be awarded for the best volume of poetry. The CSU Poetry Center also publishes a Cleveland Poets Series, open only to Ohio poets. Closes in March.

**COLONIAL PLAYERS, INC.**—99 Great Lake Dr., Annapolis, MD 21403. Attn: Frank Moorman. A prize of $750 plus possible production will be awarded for the best full-length play. Closes in December of even-numbered years.

**COLORADO CHRISTIAN UNIVERSITY**—New Christian Plays Competition, 180 S. Garrison St., Lakewood, CO 80226. Attn: Patrick Rainville Dorn, Theatre Coordinator. Biblical adaptations, holiday plays, historical/traditional plays, and contemporary drama will be considered for a prize of $200. Four finalists receive full or partial production or staged readings. Closes in January.

**COMMUNITY CHILDREN'S THEATRE OF KANSAS CITY**—8021 E. 129th Terrace, Granview, MO 64030. Mrs. Blanche Sellens, Dir. A prize of $500, plus production, are awarded for the best play, up to one hour long, written for elementary school children. Closes in January.

**CONNECTICUT POETRY SOCIETY**—Joseph E. Brodine Contest, P.O. Box 4827, Waterbury, CT 06704–1992. Awards of $175, $75, and $50, plus publication in the *Connecticut River Review* are offered for unpublished poems, to 40 lines. Closes in July.

**THE CRITIC SHORT STORY CONTEST**—Thomas More Assoc., 205 W. Monroe St., 6th Floor, Chicago, IL 60606–5097. Original, upublished short stories are eligible for the prize of $1,000 plus publication. Closes in September of even-numbered years.

**EUGENE V. DEBS FOUNDATION**—Dept. of History, Indiana State Univ., Terre Haute, IN 47809. Offers the Bryant Spann Memorial Prize of $1,000 for a published or unpublished article or essay on themes relating to social protest or human equality. Closes in April.

**DEEP SOUTH WRITERS CONFERENCE**—Contest Clerk, Drawer 44691, Univ. of Southwestern Louisianna, Lafayette, LA 70504–4691. Prizes ranging from

$50 to $300 are offered for unpublished manuscripts in the following categories: short fiction, novel, nonfiction, poetry, drama, and French literature. Closes in July.

**DELACORTE PRESS**—Dept. BFYR, 666 Fifth Ave., New York, NY 10103. Sponsors Delacorte Press Prize for outstanding first young adult novel. The prize consists of one Delacorte hardcover and one Dell paperback contract, an advance of $6,000 on royalties, and a $1,500 cash prize. Closes in December.

**DOUBLEDAY BOOKS FOR YOUNG READERS**—Doubleday BFYR, 666 Fifth Ave., New York, NY 10103. The Marguerite de Angeli Prize awards a $1,500 cash prize and a $3,500 advance against royalties for middle-grade fiction that concerns the diversity of the American experience. Closes in June.

**DRURY COLLEGE**—Playwriting Contest, c/o Sandy Asher, Writer-in-Residence, 900 N. Benton Ave., Springfield, MO 65802. Original, unproduced, unpublished one-act plays are eligible to enter the Drury College Playwriting Contest. Awards are possible production, a $300 first prize, and two $150 honorable mentions. Closes in December of even-numbered years.

**DUBUQUE FINE ARTS PLAYERS**—One-Act Playwriting Contest, 569 S. Grandview Ave., Dubuque, IA 52003. Attn: Sally T. Ryan. Prizes of $300, $200, and $100, plus possible production are awarded for unproduced, original one-act plays of up to 40 minutes. Closes in January.

**DUKE UNIVERSITY**—Center for Documentary Studies at Duke University, College Sta., Box 7727, Durham, NC 27708–7727. The Dorothea Lange/Paul Taylor Prize awards up to $10,000 in grant money to a writer and photographer in the formative stages of a documentary project that will ultimately result in a publishable work. Closes in January.

**ELF: ECLECTIC LITERARY FORUM**—Poetry Competition, P.O. Box 392, Tonawanda, NY 14150. Awards of $350, $150, and three $50 prizes are given for poems up to 60 lines. Closes in March.

**ELMIRA COLLEGE**—Dept. of Theatre, Elmira College, Elmira, NY 14901. Prof. Amnon Kabatchnik, Artistic Dir. The Elmira College Playwriting Award of $1,000 plus production is awarded for the best original full-length play. Closes in June of even-numbered years.

**FLORIDA STATE UNIVERSITY**—Richard Eberhart Prize in Poetry, 406 Williams, English Dept., F.S.U., Tallahassee, FL 32306. A $300 prize and publication in *Sun Dog: The Southeast Review*, are awarded for the best unpublished poem of 30 to 100 lines. Closes in March.

**FOUNDATION OF THE DRAMATISTS GUILD**—Young Playwrights Festival, 321 W. 44th St., Suite 906, New York, NY 10036. Playwrights under the age of 19 are eligible to submit scripts. Winning plays will be given production or staged readings. Closes in October.

**HELICON NINE EDITIONS**—9000 W. 64th Terrace, Merriam, KS 66202. Attn: Gloria Hickok. Offers the Marianne Moore Poetry Prize of $1,000 for an original unpublished poetry manuscript of at least 50 pages, as well as the Willa Cather Fiction Prize of $1,000 for an original full-length fiction manuscript (novella or short stories) from 150 to 350 pages. Both close in December.

**HEMINGWAY SHORT STORY COMPETITION**—Hemingway Days Festival, P.O. Box 4045, Key West, FL 33041. A $1,000 first prize, and two $500 runner-up prizes are offered for short stories, up to 2,500 words, any form or style. Closes in July.

**O. HENRY FESTIVAL, INC.**—P.O. Box 29484, Greensboro, NC 27429. Publication plus a $1,000 first prize and a $500 second prize is awarded for short stories of under 5,000 words. Closes in August of even-numbered years.

**HIGHLIGHTS FOR CHILDREN**—803 Church St., Honesdale, PA 18431. Conducts children's short fiction contest, with three $1,000 prizes and publication for stories up to 900 words. Closes in February.

**L. RON HUBBARD'S WRITERS OF THE FUTURE CONTEST**—P.O. Box 1630, Los Angeles, CA 90078. Awards of $1,000, $750, and $500 are given quarterly for science fiction or fantasy short stories or novelettes written by writers with no more than three short stories or one novelette published. Closes in March, June, September, and December.

**THE HUMANIST**—Essay Contest, 7 Harwood Dr., P.O. Box 146, Amherst, NY 14226–0146. Writers under the age of 29 are eligible to submit essays, to 2,000 words, on the most pressing social, political, or ethical issues facing the world today, for prizes of $500, $250, and $100, plus possible publication. Closes in October.

**HUMBOLDT STATE UNIVERSITY**—English Dept., Arcata, CA 95521–4957. Sponsors Raymond Carver Short Story Contest, with a prize of $500, plus publication in the literary journal *Toyon*, and a $250 second prize for an unpublished short story by a writer living in the U.S. Closes in November.

**INTERNATIONAL SOCIETY OF DRAMATISTS**—ISD Fulfillment Center, 1638 Euclid Ave., Miami, FL 33139. Sponsors Adriatic Award: $250 is awarded for an unproduced full-length play. Closes in November. Also sponsors the Perkins Playwriting Contest: $500 is awarded for an unproduced full-length play. Closes in December.

**IUPUI CHILDREN'S THEATRE PLAYWRITING COMPETITION**—Indiana University-Purdue University at Indianapolis, 525 N. Blackford St., Indianapolis, IN 46202–3120. Offers four $1,000 prizes plus staged readings for plays for young people. Closes in September of even-numbered years.

**JEROME PLAYWRIGHT-IN-RESIDENCE FELLOWSHIPS**—The Playwrights' Center, 2301 Franklin Ave. East, Minneapolis, MN 55406. Annually awards six emerging playwrights each a $5,000 stipend and 12-month residency; housing and travel are not provided. Closes in January.

**JEWISH COMMUNITY CENTER THEATRE IN CLEVELAND**—3505 Mayfield Rd., Cleveland Heights, OH 44118. Elaine Rembrandt, Dir. Offers cash award of $1,000 and a staged reading in the Dorothy Silver Playwriting Competition for an original, previously unproduced full-length play, on some aspect of the Jewish experience. Closes in December.

**THE CHESTER H. JONES FOUNDATION**—P. O. Box 498, Chardon, OH 44024. Conducts the National Poetry Competition, with more than $1,900 in cash prizes (including a $1,000 first prize) for original, unpublished first poems, to 32 lines. Closes in March.

**THE JOURNAL: THE LITERARY MAGAZINE OF O.S.U.**—The Ohio State University Press, 180 Pressey Hall, 1070 Carmack Rd. Attn: David Citino, Poetry Editor. Awards $1,000 plus publication for at least 48 pages of original, unpublished poetry. Closes in September.

**KEATS/KERLAN MEMORIAL FELLOWSHIP**—The Ezra Jack Keats/Kerlan Collection Memorial Fellowship Committee, 109 Walter Library, 117 Pleasant St. S.E., Univ. of Minnesota, Minneapolis, MN 55455. A $1,500 fellowship is awarded to a talented writer and/or illustrator of children's books who wishes to use the Kerlan Collection to further his or her artistic development. Closes in May.

**JACK KEROUAC LITERARY PRIZE**—Lowell Historical Preservation Commission, 222 Merrimack St., Suite 310, Lowell, MA 01852. A $500 honorarium and festival reading are awarded for an unpublished work of fiction, nonfiction, or poetry relating to themes expressed in Kerouac's work. Closes in May.

**MARC A. KLEIN PLAYWRITING AWARD**—Case Western Reserve Univ., Dept. of Theater Arts, 10900 Euclid Ave., Cleveland, OH 44106–7077. A $1,000 prize plus production are offered for an original, previously unproduced, full-length play by a student currently enrolled at an American college or university. Closes in May.

**LIGHT AND LIFE MAGAZINE**—Writing Contest, P.O. Box 535002, Indianapolis, IN 46253–5002. Awards of up to $100 and possible publication for first-person stories and essays on Christian themes. Closes in April.

**LINCOLN COLLEGE**—Lincoln, IL 62656. Address Janet Overton. The Billee Murray Denny Poetry Award offers $1,000, $500, and $250 for an original poem by a poet who has not previously published a volume of poetry. Closes in May.

**LIVE OAK THEATRE NEW PLAY AWARDS**—311 Nueces St., Austin, TX 78701. Offers $1,000 each plus possible production for Best American Play and Best Play by a Texas Playwright for unproduced, unpublished, full-length scripts. Closes in November.

**LOVE CREEK PRODUCTIONS**—Short Play Festival, 42 Sunset Dr., Croton-on-Hudson, NY 10520. At least 30 scripts, up to 40 minutes long, are chosen for festival performance; the winner receives a $300 prize. Closes in September.

**LYCEUM THEATRE**—Main St., Arrow Rock, MO 65320. Michael Bollinger, Artistic Dir. A $1,000 prize plus possible production are awarded for a full-length play relating to rural, small-town America. Closes in December.

**THE MADISON REVIEW**—Dept. of English, Univ. of Wisconsin-Madison, Madison, WI 53706. Awards the $500 Felix Pollack Prize in Poetry for a group of 3 unpublished poems, and the $250 Chris O'Malley Prize in Fiction for an unpublished short story. Winners are published in *The Madison Review*. Closes in September.

**MID-SOUTH PLAYWRITING CONTEST**—Playhouse-on-the-Square, 51 S. Cooper, Memphis, TN 38104. Mr. Jackie Nichols, Exec. Dir. A stipend plus production is awarded for a full-length, previously unproduced play or musical; Southern playwrights given preference. Closes in April.

**MIDWEST RADIO THEATRE WORKSHOP**—MRTW Script Contest, 915 E. Broadway, Columbia, MO 65201. Offers $800 in prizes, to be divided among 2 to 4 winners, for contemporary radio scripts, 15 to 56 minutes long. Winners also receive $200 scholarship to the annual MRTW conference. Closes in July.

**MILKWEED NATIONAL FICTION PRIZE**—P.O. Box 3226, Minneapolis, MN 55403. Annual contest for a novel, novella, or collection of short fiction, for which the winner receives $3,000 advance plus publication. Open to writers who have previously published a book-length collection of fiction or at least three short stories or a novella in commercial or literary journals with national distribution. Closes in September.

**MILL MOUNTAIN THEATRE NEW PLAY COMPETITION**—2nd Floor, One Market Square, Roanoke, VA 24011–1437. Jo Weinstein, Lit. Mgr.

Sponsors New Play Competition with a $1,000 prize and staged reading, with possible full production, for unpublished, unproduced, full-length or one-act play. Cast size to 10. Closes in January.

**THE MISSOURI REVIEW**—Editors' Prize, 1507 Hillcrest Hall, UMC, Columbia, MO 65211. Publication plus $750 are awarded for short fiction and essay manuscripts, 25 pages, and $250 for the winning poetry manuscript, 10 pages. Closes in October.

**THE MOUNTAINEERS BOOKS**—1011 S. W. Klickitat Way, Seattle, WA 98134. Address Donna DeShazo, Dir. Offers the Barbara Savage/"Miles From Nowhere" Memorial Award for a book-length, nonfiction personal-adventure narrative. The prize consists of a $3,000 cash award, plus publication and a $12,000 guaranteed advance against royalties. Closes in February of even-numbered years.

**MULTICULTURAL PLAYWRIGHTS' FESTIVAL**—The Group Theatre, 3940 Brooklyn Ave. N.E., Seattle, WA 98105. Awards each of up to 2 American citizens of Asian, African-American, Chicano/Latino, or Native American ethnicity $1,000 plus production for a previously unproduced one-act or full-length play. Closes in November.

**NATIONAL ENDOWMENT FOR THE ARTS**—Nancy Hanks Center, 1100 Pennsylvania Ave. N.W., Room 722, Washington, DC 20506. Address Director, Literature Program. Offers fellowships to writers and translators of poetry, fiction, and creative nonfiction. Deadlines vary; write for guidelines.

**NATIONAL PLAY AWARD**—630 N. Grand Ave., Suite 405, Los Angeles, CA 90012. The National Play Award consists of a $5,000 first prize, plus five runner-up awards of $500 each, for an original, previously unproduced play. Sponsored by National Repertory Theatre Foundation. Closes in June of even-numbered years.

**NATIONAL POETRY SERIES**—P.O. Box G, Hopewell, NJ 08525. Attn: The Coordinator. Sponsors Annual Open Competition for unpublished book-length poetry manuscripts. Five manuscripts are selected for publication. Closes in February.

**NEGATIVE CAPABILITY MAGAZINE**—62 Ridgelawn Dr. East, Mobile, AL 36608. Attn: Sue Walker. Sponsors the $1,000 Short Fiction Award for previously unpublished stories, 1,500 to 4,500 words. Closes in December. Also sponsors the Eve of St. Agnes Poetry Competition of $1,000 plus publication for an original, unpublished poem. Closes in January.

**NEW DRAMATISTS**—L. Arnold Weissberger Playwriting Competition, 424 W. 44th St., New York, NY 10036. Sponsors competition for full-length, unpublished, unproduced scripts; the winning playwright receives $5,000. Closes in May.

**NEW ENGLAND THEATRE CONFERENCE**—50 Exchange St., Waltham, MA 02154. A $500 first prize and a $250 second prize are offered for unpublished and unproduced one-act plays in the John Gassner Memorial Playwriting Award Competition. Closes in April.

**NEW LETTERS**—University of Missouri-Kansas City, Kansas City, MO 64110. Offers $750 for the best short story, to 5,000 words; $750 for the best group of 3 to 6 poems; $500 for the best essay, to 5,000 words. The work of each winner and first runner-up will be published. Closes in May.

**NEW YORK UNIVERSITY**—Elmer Holmes Bobst Awards, Bobst Library, New York University, 70 Washington Sq. S., New York, NY 10012. Rhonda Zangwill, Coord. Winning book-length fiction (novel or short stories) and poetry manuscripts, by writers who have not yet had a book published, will be published by New York University Press. Closes in March.

**NILON AWARD FOR MINORITY FICTION**—Fiction Collective Two, English Dept. Publications Ctr., University of Colorado, Campus Box 494, Boulder, CO 80309–0494. Awards $1,000 plus joint publication by Fiction Collective Two and CU-Boulder for original, unpublished, book-length fiction (novels, novellas, short story collections), in English, by U.S. citizens of the following ethnic minorities: African-American, Hispanic, Asian, Native American or Alaskan Native, and Pacific Islander. Closes in November.

**NIMROD/HARDMAN AWARDS**—Arts and Humanities Council of Tulsa, 2210 S. Main St., Tulsa, OK 74114. Awards a $1,000 first prize and $500 second prize to winners of the Katherine Anne Porter Prize for Fiction (to 7,500 words) and the Pablo Neruda Prize for Poetry (one long poem, or a group of poems). Closes in April.

**NORTH CAROLINA WRITERS' NETWORK**—Randall Jarrell Poetry Prize, c/o Coyla Barry, Chair, 516 Dogwood Dr., Chapel Hill, NC 27516. A $500 prize is awarded for a previously unpublished poem. Closes in November.

**NORTHEASTERN UNIVERSITY PRESS**—English Dept., 406 Holmes, Northeastern Univ., Boston, MA 02115. Guy Rotella, Chairman. Offers Samuel French Morse Poetry Prize of $500 plus publication for a full-length poetry manuscript by a U.S. poet who has published no more than one book of poems. August is the deadline for inquiries; contest closes in September.

**NORTHERN KENTUCKY UNIVERSITY**—Dept. of Theatre, Highland Heights, KY 41076. Joe Conger, Project Dir. Awards three $400 prizes, plus production in the Year End Series New Play Festival, for previously unproduced full-length plays, one-acts, and musicals. Closes in November of even-numbered years.

**NORTHERN MICHIGAN UNIVERSITY**—Playwriting Award Information, Forest Roberts Theatre, Northern Michigan Univ., Marquette, MI 49855. Conducts annual Shiras Institute/Albert & Mildred Panowski Playwriting Competition, with prize of $2,000, plus production, for original, full-length, previously unproduced and unpublished play. Closes in November.

**NORTHWESTERN UNIVERSITY**—*TriQuarterly*, 2020 Ridge Ave., Evanston, IL 60208. The Terrence des Pres Prize for Poetry offers $3,000 plus publication for a poetry manuscript, 48 to 64 pages. Closes in June of even-numbered years.

**O'NEILL THEATER CENTER**—234 W. 44th St., Suite 901, New York, NY 10036. Offers stipend, staged readings, and room and board at the National Playwrights Conference, for new stage and television plays. Send SASE for guidelines. Closes in December.

**THE PARIS REVIEW**—541 E. 72nd St., New York, NY 10021. Sponsors 3 annual prizes: The Aga Khan Prize for Fiction awards $1,000, plus publication, for a previously unpublished short story; closes in June. The Bernard F. Connors Prize awards $1,000, plus publication, for a previously unpublished poem; closes in May. The John Train Humor Prize awards $1,500, plus publication, for an unpublished work of humorous fiction, nonfiction, or poetry; closes in March.

**PEN/JERARD FUND AWARD**—568 Broadway, New York, NY 10012. Address John Morrone, Programs & Publications. Offers $4,000 to beginning female writers for a work-in-progress of general nonfiction. Applicants must have published

809

at least one article in a national magazine or major literary magazine, but not more than one book of any kind. Closes in January of odd-numbered years.

**PEN WRITING AWARDS FOR PRISONERS**—PEN American Center, 568 Broadway, New York, NY 10012. County, state, and federal prisoners are eligible to enter one published manuscript in each of four categories: poetry, fiction, drama, and nonfiction. Prizes of $100, $50, and $25 are awarded in each category. Closes in September.

**PEREGRINE SMITH POETRY SERIES**—Gibbs Smith, Publisher, P.O. Box 667, Layton, UT 84041. Offers a $500 prize plus publication for a 64-page poetry manuscript. Closes in April.

**PETERLOO POETS OPEN COMPETITION**—Peterloo Poets, c/o Administrator, 2 Kelly Gardens, Calstock, Cornwall PL18 9SA, U.K. Prizes totalling 4,100 pounds British, including a grand prize of 2,000 pounds, plus publication, are awarded for poems up to 40 lines. Closes in March.

**PLAYBOY MAGAZINE COLLEGE FICTION CONTEST**—680 N. Lakeshore Dr., Chicago, IL 60611. Sponsors college fiction contest, with first prize of $3,000 and publication in *Playboy*, for a short story by a college student; second prize is $500. Closes in January.

**PLAYWRIGHTS' FORUM AWARDS**—Theatreworks, Univ. of Colorado, P.O. Box 7150, Colorado Springs, CO 80933–7150. Whit Andrews, Producing Dir. Two unpublished, unproduced one-act plays are selected for production; playwrights are awarded $250 plus travel expenses. Closes in December.

**POCKETS FICTION-WRITING CONTEST**—c/o Lynn W. Gilliam, Assoc. Ed., P.O. Box 189, Nashville, TN 37202–1089. A $1,000 prize goes to the author of the winning 1,000- to 1,600-word story for children in grades one to six. Closes in October.

**POET LORE NARRATIVE POETRY CONTEST**—The Writer's Center, 7815 Old Georgetown Rd., Bethesda, MD 20814–2415. The best unpublished, original narrative poem to 100 lines, receives $350 John Williams Andrews prize, plus publication. Closes in November.

**POETRY SOCIETY OF AMERICA**—15 Gramercy Park, New York, NY 10003. Conducts annual contests (The Celia B. Wagner Memorial Award, the John Masefield Memorial Award, the Elias Lieberman Student Poetry Award, the George Bogin Memorial Award, the Robert H. Winner Memorial Award, and the Ruth Lake Memorial Award) for non-members in which cash prizes are offered for unpublished poems. Closes in December.

**PRISM INTERNATIONAL**—Short Fiction Contest, Creative Writing Dept., Univ. of B.C., E466–1866 Main Mall, Vancouver, B.C., Canada V6T 1Z1. A $2,000 first prize and five $200 prizes are awarded for stories of up to 25 pages long. Winning stories are published in Prism International. Closes in December.

**PURDUE UNIVERSITY PRESS**—1131 South Campus Courts-D, W. Lafayette, IN 47907–1131. Attn: Managing Editor. The Verna Emery Poetry Competition for an unpublished collection of poetry (50 to 90 pages) awards $500 plus publication for original poems. Closes in January.

**RANDOM HOUSE JUVENILE BOOKS**—225 Park Ave. S., New York, NY 10003. The Dr. Seuss Picturebook Award offers $25,000 plus publication for a picturebook manuscript by an author/illustrator who has not published more than one book. Closes in December.

**RIVER CITY WRITING AWARDS**—*River City*, Dept. of English, Memphis State University, Memphis, TN 38152. Sharon Bryan, Ed. Awards a $2,000 first prize, plus publication, a $500 second prize, and a $300 third prize, for previously unpublished short stories, to 7,500 words. Closes in December.

**THE H.G. ROBERTS FOUNDATION**—Roberts Writing Awards, P.O. Box 1868, Pittsburg, KS 66762. Publication plus a $500 first prize, $200 second prize, $100 third prize, and $25 honorable mention are awarded in each category of poetry, short fiction, and informal essay. Closes in September.

**ST. MARTIN'S PRESS/MALICE DOMESTIC CONTEST**—Thomas Dunne Books, 175 Fifth Ave., New York, NY 10010. Co-sponsored by Macmillan London, offers publication plus a $10,000 advance against royalties, for Best First Traditional Mystery Novel. Closes in November.

**ST. MARTIN'S PRESS/PRIVATE EYE CONTEST**—Thomas Dunne Books, 175 Fifth Ave., New York, NY 10010. Attn: Ruth Cavin, Sr. Ed. Co-sponsored by Private Eye Writers of America, offers publication with St. Martin's Press plus $10,000 against royalties for a previously unpublished first private eye novel. Closes in August.

**SIENA COLLEGE**—International Playwrights' Competition, Fine Arts Dept., Siena College, Loudonville, NY 12211–1462. Offers $2,000 plus campus residency expenses for the best full-length script; contemporary settings preferred; no musicals. Closes in June of even-numbered years.

**SIERRA REPERTORY THEATRE**—P. O. Box 3030, Sonora, CA 95370. Attn: Dennis Jones, Producing Dir. Offers annual playwriting award of $500, plus possible production, for full-length plays or musicals that have received no more than two productions or staged readings. Closes in August.

**SOCIETY OF AMERICAN TRAVEL WRITERS**—1155 Connecticut Ave. N.W., Suite 500, Washington, DC 20036. Sponsors Lowell Thomas Travel Journalism Award for published and broadcast work by U.S. and Canadian travel journalists. Prizes total $11,000. Closes in February.

**SONS OF THE REPUBLIC OF TEXAS**—5942 Abrams Rd., Suite 222, Dallas, TX 75231. Sponsors the Summerfield G. Roberts Award of $2,500 for published or unpublished creative writing (fiction, nonfiction, poetry) on the Republic of Texas. Closes in January.

**SOUTH COAST POETRY JOURNAL**—English Dept., California State University at Fullerton, Fullerton, CA 92634. Previously unpublished, original poems, to 40 lines, will be considered for prizes of $200, $100, and $50, plus publication. Closes in March.

**SOUTHERN APPALACHIAN REPERTORY THEATRE**—P.O. Box 620, Mars Hill, NC 28754–0620. Attn: Mrs. Jan W. Blalock. Invites writers of selected scripts to the Southern Appalachian Playwrights' Conference. All scripts are given readings and considered for full production. Closes in October.

**STAND MAGAZINE**—Short Story Competition, 179 Wingrove Rd., Newcastle upon Tyne, NE4 9DA, U.K. Prizes totalling 2,250 pounds British, including a first prize of 1,250 pounds, are awarded for previously unpublished stories under 8,000 words; winning stories are published. Closes in March.

**STANLEY DRAMA AWARD**—Wagner College, Dept. of Humanities, 631 Howard Ave., Staten Island, NY 10301. Awards $2,000 plus possible production for an original, previously unpublished and unproduced full-length play. Closes in September.

**AGNES LYNCH STARRETT POETRY PRIZE**—University of Pittsburgh Press, Pittsburgh, PA 15260. Poets who have never had a full-length book of poetry published may enter a book-length collection of poems, 48 to 100 pages. The prize is $2,500 and publication. Closes in April.

**STORY LINE PRESS**—27006 Gap Rd., Three Oaks Farm, Brownsville, OR 97327–9718. Sponsors the Nicholas Roerich Prize of $1,000 plus publication for an original, unpublished book of poetry by a poet who has never been published in book form. Closes in October.

**SUNY FARMINGDALE**—Visiting Writers Series, Knapp Hall, SUNY Farmingdale, Farmingdale, NY 11735. The Paumanok Poetry Award offers $750 plus reading expenses for 7 to 10 poems. There is an entry fee. Closes in September.

**SYNDICATED FICTION PROJECT**—P.O. Box 15650, Washington, DC 20003. Offers $500 for rights to previously unpublished short fiction, to 2,500 words, and $100 each time stories appear in print. All selected stories are used on the Project's radio show, "The Sound of Writing." Closes in January.

**SYRACUSE UNIVERSITY PRESS**—1600 Jamesville Ave., Syracuse, NY 13244–5160. Address Director. Sponsors John Ben Snow Prize: a $1,500 royalty advance, plus publication, for an unpublished book-length nonfiction manuscript about New York State, especially upstate or central New York. Closes in December.

**TAKESHI KAIKO AWARD**—Takeshi Kaiko Award Secretariat, c/o TBS Britannica Co., Ltd., Shuwa Sanbancho Bldg., 28–1 Sanbancho, Chiyoda-ku, Tokyo 102, Japan. Three million yen is awarded for a previously unpublished manuscript relating to the observation of human nature; fiction, nonfiction, reviews, or reports from 8,250 to 82,500 words are eligible. Closes in October.

**TEN-MINUTE MUSICALS PROJECT**—Box 461194, W. Hollywood, CA 90046. Michael Koppy, Producer. Musicals of 8 to 14 minutes are eligible for a $250 advance against royalties and musical anthology productions at theaters in the U.S. and Canada. Closes in October.

**THEATRE MEMPHIS**—New Play Competition, P.O. Box 240117, Memphis, TN 38124–0117. Conducts New Play Competition for a full-length play or related one-acts. The prize is $1,500 and production. Contest closes in July 1993 and is held every 3 years.

**THURBER HOUSE RESIDENCIES**—The Thurber House, 77 Jefferson Ave., Columbus, OH 43215. Michael J. Rosen, Lit. Dir. Three-month residencies and stipends of $5,000 each will be awarded in the categories of writing, playwriting, and journalism. Winners have limited teaching responsibilities with The Ohio State University. Closes in January.

**TOWNGATE THEATRE PLAYWRITING CONTEST**—Oglebay Institute, Oglebay, Wheeling, WV 26003. Offers $300 plus production for an unproduced, full-length, non-musical play. Closes in January.

**TRITON COLLEGE**—Salute to the Arts Poetry Contest, 2000 Fifth Ave., River Grove, IL 60171–1995. Winning original, unpublished poems, to 60 lines, on designated themes, are published by Triton College. Closes in March.

**U.S. NAVAL INSTITUTE**—A.B.E.C., 118 Maryland Ave., Annapolis, MD 21402–5035. Attn: Publisher. Conducts the Arleigh Burke Essay Contest, with prizes of $2,000, $1,000, and $750, plus publication, for essays on the advancement of professional, literary or scientific knowledge in the naval or maritime services, and the advancement of the knowledge of sea power. Closes in December.

**UNIVERSITY OF ARKANSAS PRESS**—Arkansas Poetry Award, Fayetteville, AR 72701. Awards publication of a 50- to 80-page poetry manuscript to a writer who has never had a book of poetry published. Closes in May.

**UNIVERSITY OF CENTRAL FLORIDA**—Florida Poetry Contest, Sigma Tau Delta, Dept. of English, University of Central Florida, Orlando, FL 32816. Attn: Jonathan Harrington. The National English Honor Society awards $500 plus publication for the best poem submitted. Closes in November.

**UNIVERSITY OF GEORGIA PRESS**—Athens, GA 30602. Offers Flannery O'Connor Award for Short Fiction: two prizes of $1,000, plus publication, for a book-length collection of short fiction. Closes in July.

**UNIVERSITY OF HAWAII AT MANOA**—Dept. of Drama and Theatre, 1770 East-West Rd., Honolulu, HI 96822. Conducts annual Kumu Kahua Playwriting Contest with $500 prize for a full-length play, and $200 for a one-act, set in Hawaii and dealing with some aspect of the Hawaiian experience. Also conducts contest for plays written by Hawaiian residents. Write for conditions-of-entry brochure. Closes in January.

**UNIVERSITY OF IOWA**—Iowa Short Fiction Awards, Dept. of English, 308 English Philosophy Bldg., Iowa City, IA 52242–1492. The John Simmons Short Fiction Award and the Iowa Short Fiction Award each offers $1,000, plus publication, for an unpublished full-length collection of short stories, at least 150 pages. Closes in September.

**UNIVERSITY OF IOWA PRESS**—The Edwin Ford Piper Poetry Awards, 119 W. Park Rd., 100 Kuhl House, Iowa City, IA 52242–1000. Two $1,000 prizes, plus publication, will be awarded for poetry manuscripts, 50 to 120 pages, by writers who have published at least one book of poetry. Closes in March.

**UNIVERSITY OF MASSACHUSETTS PRESS**—Juniper Prize, Amherst, MA 01003. Offers the annual Juniper Prize of $1,000, plus publication, for a book-length manuscript of poetry; awarded in odd-numbered years to writers who have never published a book of poetry, and in even-numbered years to writers who have published a book or chapbook of poetry. Closes in September.

**UNIVERSITY OF MISSOURI PRESS**—2910 LeMone Blvd., Columbia, MO 65201–8227. Mr. Clair Willcox, Poetry Ed. The $500 Devins Award goes to the best manuscript of poetry selected for publication during the year. Submissions accepted year round.

**UNIVERSITY OF PITTSBURGH PRESS**—127 N. Bellefield Ave., Pittsburgh, PA 15260. Sponsors Drue Heinz Literature Prize of $10,000, plus publication and royalty contract, for unpublished collection of short stories. Closes in August. Also sponsors the Agnes Lynch Starrett Poetry Prize of $2,000, plus publication, for a book-length collection of poems by a poet who has not yet published a volume of poetry. Closes in April.

**UNIVERSITY OF WISCONSIN PRESS**—Poetry Series, 114 N. Murray St., Madison, WI 53715. Ronald Wallace, Administrator. The Brittingham Prize in Poetry awards $500, plus publication for an unpublished book-length poetry manuscript. Closes in September

**THE UNTERBERG POETRY CENTER OF THE 92ND STREET Y**— "Discovery"/*The Nation*, 1395 Lexington Ave., New York, NY 10128. Four prizes of $200, publication in *The Nation* Magazine, and a reading at the Poetry Center are offered for original 10-page manuscripts by poets who have not yet had a book of poems published. Closes in February.

**WASHINGTON PRIZE FOR FICTION**—1301 S. Scott St., Arlington, VA 22204. Larry Kaltman, Dir. Offers $1,000, $500, and $250 for unpublished novels, short story or novella collections, at least 65,000 words. Closes in November.

**ANN WHITE THEATRE**—5266 Gate Lake Rd., Ft. Lauderdale, FL 33319. The New Playwrights Contest offers $500 plus production for the winning unpublished, unproduced full-length play. Closes in November.

**TENNESSEE WILLIAMS FESTIVAL**—Suite 217, 5500 Prytania St., New Orleans, LA 70115. A $1,000 prize plus a reading at the festival are offered for an original, unpublished one-act play on an American subject. Closes in January.

**WORD WORKS**—P. O. Box 42164, Washington, DC 20015. Offers the Washington Prize of $1,000 plus publication for an unpublished volume of poetry by a living American poet. Closes in March.

**WORLD'S BEST SHORT SHORT STORY COMPETITION**—Short Short, English Dept., Florida State University, Tallahassee, FL 32306. Attn: Jerome Stern. A prize of $100, a box of Florida oranges, and publication are offered for the best short short story, under 250 words. Closes in February.

**YALE UNIVERSITY PRESS**—Box 92A, Yale Sta., New Haven, CT 06520. Attn: Editor, Yale Series of Younger Poets Competition. Conducts contest for publication of a book-length manuscript of poetry, written by a poet under 40 who has not previously published a volume of poems. Closes in February.

# WRITERS COLONIES

Writers colonies offer isolation and freedom from everyday distractions and a quiet place for writers to concentrate on their work. Though some colonies are quite small, with space for just three or four writers at a time, others can provide accommodations for as many as thirty or forty. The length of a residency may vary, too, from a couple of weeks to five or six months. These programs have strict admissions policies, and writers must submit a formal application or letter of intent, a resumé, writing samples, and letters of recommendation. As an alternative to the traditional writers colony, a few of the organizations listed offer writing rooms for writers who live nearby. Write for application information first, enclosing a stamped, self-addressed envelope. Residency fees listed are subject to change.

**THE EDWARD F. ALBEE FOUNDATION, INC.**
14 Harrison St.
New York, NY 10013
(212) 266–2020
David Briggs, *Foundation Secretary*

"The Barn," or the William Flanagan Memorial Creative Persons Center, on Long Island, is maintained by the Albee Foundation. "The standards for admission are, simply, talent and need." Sixteen writers are accepted each season for one-month residencies, available from June 1 to October 1; applications, including writing samples, project description, and resumé, are accepted from January 1 to April 1. There is no fee, though residents are responsible for their own food and travel expenses.

## ATLANTIC CENTER FOR THE ARTS
1414 Art Center Ave.
New Smyrna Beach, FL 32168
(904) 427-6975
James Murphy, *Program Director*
The center is located on the east coast of central Florida, with 67 acres of pristine hammockland on a tidal estuary. All buildings, connected by raised wooden walkways, are handicapped accessible and air conditioned. The center provides a unique environment for sharing ideas, learning, and collaborating on interdisciplinary projects. Master artists meet with mid-career artists for readings and critiques, with time out for individual work. Residencies are three weeks. Fees are $600 for private room/bath; $200 for off-site (tuition only); financial aid is limited. Application deadlines vary.

## BLUE MOUNTAIN CENTER
Blue Mountain Lake, NY 12812
(518) 352-7391
Harriet Barlow, *Director*
Hosts month-long residencies for artists and writers from mid-June to mid-October. Fiction and nonfiction writers of "fine work which evinces social and ecological concern" are among the 14 residents accepted per session. Apply by sending a brief biographical sketch, a statement of your plan for work at Blue Mountain, names and phone numbers of three references, five slides or approximately 10 pages of work, an indication of your preference for an early summer, late summer, or fall residence, and a $20 application fee; applications due February 1. There is no charge to residents for their time at Blue Mountain, although all visitors are invited to contribute to the studio construction fund. Brochure available upon request.

## CAMARGO FOUNDATION/CASSIS, FRANCE
c/o 64 Main St.
Box 32
East Haddam, CT 06423
Attn: Jane M. Viggiani
The Camargo Foundation offers academics, writers, artists, and composers the opportunity to complete a work-in-progress. Residents are provided a furnished apartment with equipped kitchen on property belonging to the Foundation in the town of Cassis, France. Minimum residency is three months; terms are September to December, or January to May. There are no fees. Applicants chosen on the basis of writing sample, project description, resumé, and three letters of recommendation. Applications due March 1.

## CENTRUM
P.O. Box 1158
Port Townsend, WA 98368
(206) 385-3102
Sarah Muirhead, *Program Coordinator*
Centrum sponsors month-long residencies at Fort Worden State Park, a Victorian fort on the Strait of Juan De Fuca in Washington. The program "provides a working retreat for selected artists to create, without distractions, in a beautiful setting." Nonfiction, fiction, and poetry writers may apply for residency awards, which include housing and a $75 a week stipend. Families are welcome, but no separate working space is provided. Application deadlines: October 1 and April 1.

**CHATEAU DE LESVAULT**
Writers Retreat Program
58370 Onlay
Villapourcon, France
(33) 86–84–32–91
Bibbi Lee, *Director*
    This French country residence is located in western Burgundy, in the national park of Le Morvan. Five large rooms, fully equipped for living and working, are available October through April, for one month or longer. Residents in this small artists' community have access to the entire chateau, including the salon, library, and grounds. The fee is 4,500 francs per month, for room, board, and utilities. Applications handled on a first-come basis.

**COTTAGES AT HEDGEBROOK**
2197 E. Millman Rd.
Langley, WA 98260
(206) 321–4786
Holly Galt, *Project Coordinator*
    Cottages at Hedgebrook provides for women writers, published or not, of all ages and from all cultural backgrounds, a natural place to work. Established in 1988, the retreat is part of Hedgebrook Farm, thirty acres of farmland and woods located on Whidbey Island in Washington State. Each writer has her own cottage, equipped with electricity and woodstove; one cottage is wheelchair accessible. A bathhouse serves all six cottages. Writers gather for dinner in the farmhouse every evening and frequently read in the living room/library afterwards. Limited travel scholarships are available. Residencies range from one week to three months. April 1 is the application deadline for residencies from July 1 to December 10; October 1 for January 11 to June 14. Applicants are chosen by a selection committee composed of writers.

**CUMMINGTON COMMUNITY OF THE ARTS**
RR#1, Box 145
Cummington, MA 01026
(413) 634–2172
Kirk Stephens, *Executive Director*
    Residencies for artists of all disciplines. Artists enjoy private living spaces and studios for residencies ranging from two weeks to three months, on 110 acres in the Berkshires. Open year round. Work exchange available. Artists with children are encouraged to apply for stays during July and August; there is a children's program with supervised activities. Fees are $500 to $600 per month (children extra); financial aid available. Application deadlines: February 1 for April, May, June; March 15 for July, August; June 1 for September and October; and August 1 for November, December.

**CURRY HILL/GEORGIA**
c/o 404 Crestmont Ave.
Hattiesburg, MS 39401
Mrs. Elizabeth Bowne, *Director*
    This retreat for eight fiction and nonfiction writers is offered for one week each April by writer/teacher Elizabeth Bowne. "I care about writers and am delighted and enthusiastic when I can help develop talent." A $400 fee covers meals and lodging at Curry Hill, a family plantation home near Bainbridge, Georgia. Applications should be sent in early January; qualified applicants accepted on a first-come basis.

## DJERASSI RESIDENT ARTISTS PROGRAM
2325 Bear Gulch Rd.
Woodside, CA 94062–4405
(415) 851–8395
Attn: *Executive Director*

The Djerassi Foundation offers living and work spaces in a rural, isolated setting, plus all meals, to writers, visual artists, choreographers, and composers, to provide undisturbed time for creative work. Residencies range from one to six months; 30 artists are accepted each year. There are no fees, other than the $15 application fee. Applications, with resumé and documentation of recent creative work, are due March 31.

## DORLAND MOUNTAIN ARTS COLONY
Box 6
Temecula, CA 92593
(714) 676–5039
Attn: *Admissions Committee*

Novelists, playwrights, poets, nonfiction writers, composers, and visual artists are encouraged to apply for residencies of two weeks to three months. Dorland is a nature preserve located in the Palomar Mountains of Southern California. "A primitive retreat for creative people. Without electricity, residents find a new, natural rhythm for their work." Fee of $150 a month includes cottage, fuel, and firewood. Application deadlines are March 1 and September 1.

## DORSET COLONY HOUSE
Box 519
Dorset, VT 05251
(802) 867–2223
John Nassivera, *Director*

Writers and playwrights are offered low-cost room with kitchen facilities at the historic Colony House in Dorset, Vermont. Residencies are one week to two months, and are available between September 15 and June 1. Applications are accepted year round, and up to eight writers stay at a time. The fee is $75 per week; financial aid is limited. For more information, send SASE.

## FINE ARTS WORK CENTER IN PROVINCETOWN
P.O. Box. 565
24 Pearl St.
Provincetown, MA 02657
John Skoyles, *Executive Director*

Fellowships, including living and studio space and monthly stipends, are available at the Fine Arts Work Center on Cape Cod, for writers to work independently. Residencies are for seven months (October to May); apply before February 1 deadline. Eight first-year fellows and two second-year fellows are accepted. Send SASE for details.

## THE GUTHRIE CENTRE
Annaghmakerrig, Newbliss
County Monaghan, Ireland
Bernard Loughlin, *Director*

Set on a 400-acre country estate, the Tyrone Guthrie Centre offers peace and seclusion to writers and other artists to enable them to get on with their work. All art forms are represented. One- to three-month residencies are offered throughout the year, at the rate of 1,500 Irish pounds per month; financial assistance available to Irish citizens only. A number of longer term self-catering houses in the old farmyard are also available at 150 pounds per week. Writers may apply for acceptance year round.

## THE HAMBIDGE CENTER
P.O. Box 339
Rabun Gap, GA 30568
(404) 746–5718
Judy Barber, *Director*

An environment for those in search of creative excellence in the arts, humanities, and sciences. Six private cottages are available for fellows, who are asked to contribute about $125 per week. Two-week to two-month residencies, from May to October, are offered to writers, artists, composers, historians, humanists, and scientists at the Hambidge Center for Creative Arts and Sciences located on 600 acres of quiet woods in the north Georgia mountains. Send SASE for application form. Application reviews begin in March.

## HAWTHORNDEN CASTLE INTERNATIONAL RETREAT FOR WRITERS
Hawthornden Castle
Lasswade, Midlothian EH18 1EG
Scotland
Attn: *Administrator*

Hawthornden Castle stands on a secluded crag overlooking the valley of the River North Esk. The retreat provides a peaceful setting where creative writers can work without disturbance. The castle houses five writers at a time, and is open ten months out of the year. Writers from any part of the world may apply for full fellowships. Apply with writing sample, project description, resumé, and two references by September 15.

## KALANI HONUA
Artist-in-Residence Program
RR2, Box 4500
Pahoa-Kalapana, HI 96778
Richard Koob, *Program Coordinator*

Located in a country, coastal setting of 20 botanical acres, Kalani Honua "provides participants with quality educational programs and the aloha experience that is its namesake: harmony of heaven and earth." Residencies range from two weeks to two months and are available throughout the year. Fees range from $20 to $80 per day, depending on accommodations; fee subsidies are available. Applications accepted year round.

## LEIGHTON ARTIST COLONY
The Banff Centre
Box 1020-Station 22
Banff, Alberta T0L 0C0
Canada
(403) 762–6180
Shirley Feragen, *Registrar*

Located at the Banff Centre's inspirational Rocky Mountain setting, Banff National Park, the colony provides time and space for artists to produce new work. Residencies last from one week to three months. Applicants are accepted on the basis of project description, resumé, reviews, and writing samples. Three writing studios, and three writing/composing studios are available. Fee is $81.83 per day. Financial subsidy in the form of a discount is available for those who demonstrate need. Apply at least four months in advance of desired dates or residencies.

**THE MACDOWELL COLONY**
100 High St.
Peterborough, NH 03458
(603) 924–3886
Pat Dodge, *Admissions Coordinator*
Studios, room, and board at the MacDowell Colony of Peterborough, New Hampshire, are available for writers to work without interruption in a woodland setting. Selection is competitive. Apply by January 15 for stays May through August; April 15 for September through December; and September 15 for January through April. Residencies last up to eight weeks, and 80 to 90 writers are accepted each year. Send SASE for details and application form.

**THE MILLAY COLONY FOR THE ARTS**
Steepletop
P.O. Box 3
Austerlitz, NY 12017–0003
(518) 392–3103
Gail Giles, *Assistant Director*
At Steepletop in Austerlitz, New York (former home of Edna St. Vincent Millay), studios, living quarters, and meals are provided to writers at no cost. Residencies are for one month. Application deadlines are February 1, May 1, and September 1. Send SASE for more information and an application form.

**THE NORTHWOOD INSTITUTE**
Alden B. Dow Creativity Center
3225 Cook Rd.
Midland, MI 48640–2398
(517) 837–4478
Carol B. Coppage, *Director*
The Fellowship Program allows individuals time away from their ongoing daily routines to pursue their project ideas without interruption. A project idea should be innovative, creative, and have potential for impact in its field. Four ten-week residencies, lasting from mid-June to mid-August, are awarded yearly. There are no fees and a modest stipend is provided. No spouses or families. Applications are due December 31.

**PALENVILLE INTERARTS COLONY**
2 Bond St.
New York, NY 10012
(518) 678–3332
Joanna Sherman, *Artistic Director*
Support is provided for artists of the highest calibre in all disciplines, either working alone or in groups. The admissions panel is interested in interartistic collaboration and intercultural projects. Residencies last from one to eight weeks, and fees range from $125 to $260 per week; scholarships are available. About 50 applicants are accepted for May through October season. Applications due in April; send SASE for details.

**RAGDALE FOUNDATION**
1260 N. Green Bay Rd.
Lake Forest, IL 60045
(708) 234–1063
Michael Wilkerson, *Director*
Uninterrupted time and peaceful space allow writers a chance to finish works in progress, to begin new works, to solve thorny creative problems, and to experiment in new genres. Located in Lake Forest, Illinois, 30 miles north

of Chicago, on 40 acres of prairie. Residencies from two weeks to two months are available for writers, artists, and composers. Fee is $10 per day; some full and partial fee waivers available. Application deadlines are January 15 for May to August; April 15 for September to December; and September 15 for January to April. Special fellowship program for older women writers has March 1 deadline. Late applications considered when space is available. Application fee: $20.

## THE JOHN STEINBECK ROOM
Long Island University
Southampton Campus Library
Southampton, NY 11968
(516) 283–4000, ext. 379
Robert Gerbereux, *Library Director*

The John Steinbeck Room at Long Island University provides a basic research facility to writers who have either a current contract with a book publisher or a confirmed assignment from a magazine editor. Use of the room is for a period of six months with one six-month renewal permissible. Send SASE for application.

## SYVENNA FOUNDATION
Rte. 1, Box 193
Linden, TN 75563
(903) 835–8252
Barbara Carroll, *Associate Director*

Our purpose is to offer beginning and intermediate women writers the time and space to devote themselves totally to their work. Private cottages with work space, located in the piney woods of Northeast Texas, are provided at no cost; writers receive stipend of $300 per month, and writers are responsible for their personal needs. Residencies last two to three months; eight writers accepted per year. Application deadlines: April 1 for fall residency; August 1, winter; October 1, spring; December 1, summer.

## THE THURBER HOUSE RESIDENCIES
c/o Thurber House
77 Jefferson Ave.
Columbus, OH 43215
(614) 464–1032
Michael J. Rosen, *Literary Director*

Residencies in the restored home of James Thurber are awarded to journalists, writers, and playwrights. Residents work on their own writing projects, and in addition to other duties, teach one class at The Ohio State University. A stipend of $5,000 per quarter is provided. Applications must be received by January 1.

## UCROSS FOUNDATION
Residency Program
2836 US Hwy 14–16 East
Clearmont, WY 82835
(307) 737–2291
Elizabeth Guheen, *Executive Director*

Residencies, two weeks to two months, in the foothills of the Big Horn Mountains in Wyoming, "with lots of open spaces," allow writers, artists, and scholars to concentrate on their work without interruptions. Two residency sessions are scheduled annually: January to May and August to November. There is no charge for room, board, or studio space. Application deadlines are

820

March 1 for fall session and October 1 for spring session. Send SASE for more information.

**VERMONT STUDIO CENTER**
P.O. Box 613
Johnson, VT 05656
(802) 635-2727
Susan Kowalsky, *Registrar*
The Vermont Studio Center offers two-week writing studio sessions led by prominent writers/teachers focusing on the craft of writing. Independent writers' retreats are also available year round for those wishing more solitude. Room, working studio, and meals are included in all programs. Work-exchange fellowships are available. Send SASE for more information and application.

**VILLA MONTALVO ARTIST RESIDENCY PROGRAM**
P.O. Box 158
Saratoga, CA 95071
(408) 741-3421
Lori A. Wood, *Artist Residency Coordinator*
One- to three-month, free residencies at Villa Montalvo in the foothills of the Santa Cruz Mountains south of San Francisco, for writers working on specific projects. Several merit-based fellowships available. September 1 and March 1 are the application deadlines. Send SASE for application forms.

**VIRGINIA CENTER FOR THE CREATIVE ARTS**
Sweet Briar, VA 24595
(804) 946-7236
William Smart, *Director*
A working retreat for writers, composers, and visual artists in Virginia's Blue Ridge Mountains. Residencies of one to three months are available year round. Application deadlines are the 25th of January, May, and September; about 300 residents are accepted each year. A limited amount of financial assistance is available. Send SASE for more information.

**THE WRITERS ROOM**
153 Waverly Pl., 5th Floor
New York, NY 10014
(212) 807-9519
Renata Rizzo-Harvi, *Executive Director*
Located in Greenwich Village, The Writers Room provides "highly subsidized work space to all types of writers at all stages of their careers. We offer urban writers a quiet, benevolent oasis, a place to escape from noisy neighbors, children, roommates, and other distractions of city life." The Room holds 24 desks separated by partitions, a smokers room with four desks, a kitchen, library, and lounge. Open 24 hours a day, 365 days a year. Fee is $165 quarter; several scholarships are available.

**THE WRITERS STUDIO**
The Mercantile Library Association
17 E. 47th St.
New York, NY 10017
(212) 755-6710
Harold Augenbraum, *Membership*
The Studio is a business-like place in which writers can rent quiet space conducive to the production of good work. A carrel, locker, small reference collection, electrical outlets, and membership in The Mercantile Library of

New York are available at the cost of $200 per three-month residency. Submit application, resumé, and writing samples; applications considered year round.

**HELENE WURLITZER FOUNDATION OF NEW MEXICO**
Box 545, Taos, NM 87571
(505) 758–2413
Henry A. Sauerwein, Jr., *Executive Director*
Rent-free and utility-free studios at the Helene Wurlitzer Foundation in Taos, New Mexico, are offered to creative writers and artists in all media. All artists are given the opportunity to be free of the shackles of a 9-to-5 routine. Length of residency varies from three to six months. The Foundation is closed from October 1 through March 31.

**YADDO**
Box 395
Saratoga Springs, NY 12866–0395
(518) 584–0746
Attn: Admissions Committee
Artists, writers, and composers are invited for stays from two weeks to two months. Voluntary payment of $20 a day is suggested. No artist deemed worthy of admission by the judging panels will be denied admission on the basis of an inability to contribute. Deadlines are January 15 and August 1. Send SASE for application. An application fee of $20 is required.

# WRITERS CONFERENCES

Each year, hundreds of writers conferences are held across the country. The following list, arranged geographically, represents a sampling of conferences; each listing includes the location of the conference, the month during which it is usually held, and the name of the person from whom specific information may be received. Additional conferences are listed annually in the May issue of *The Writer* Magazine (120 Boylston St., Boston, MA 02116–4615).

## ALASKA

**SITKA SYMPOSIUM ON HUMAN VALUES AND THE WRITTEN WORD**—Sitka, AK. June. Write Carolyn Servid, Island Institute, Box 2420-W, Sitka, AK 99835.

**ANNUAL ALASKA ADVENTURE IN TRAVEL WRITING**—Juneau, AK. June. Write Mike Miller, Travel Writing, Box 21494, Juneau, AK 99802.

## ARIZONA

**PIMA WRITERS' WORKSHOP**—Tucson, AZ. May. Write Peg Files, Dir., Pima College, 2202 W. Anklam Rd., Tucson, AZ 85709.

**ANNUAL ARIZONA CHRISTIAN WRITER'S CONFERENCE**—Phoenix, AZ. November. Write Reg Forder, Dir., P.O. Box 5168, Phoenix, AZ 85010.

## ARKANSAS

**OZARK CREATIVE WRITERS, INC.**—Eureka Springs, AR. October. Write Peggy Vining, Dir., 6817 Gingerbread Ln., Little Rock, AR 72204.

## CALIFORNIA

**SAN DIEGO STATE UNIVERSITY WRITERS CONFERENCE**—San Diego, CA. January. Write Diane Dunaway, Dir., SDSU, 8465 Jane St., San Diego, CA 92129.

**THIRD ANNUAL IWWG SAN DIEGO CONFERENCE**—San Diego, CA. January. Write Hannelore Hahn, International Women's Writing Guild, P.O. Box 810, Gracie Station, New York, NY 10028.

**MOUNT HERMON CHRISTIAN WRITERS CONFERENCE**—Mount Hermon, CA. April. Write David Talbott, Mount Hermon Christian Writers Conference, P.O. Box 413, Mount Hermon, CA 95041–0413.

**SIERRA NEVADA WRITING INSTITUTE**—North Lake Tahoe, CA. June. Write Stephen Tchudi, Dept. of English, Univ. of Nevada, Reno, NV 89557–0031.

**BIOLA UNIVERSITY WRITERS INSTITUTE**—La Mirada, CA. July. Write Gretchen Passantino, Biola Univ. Writers Institute, 13800 Biola Ave., La Mirada, CA 90639.

**"WRITE TO BE READ" WORKSHOP**—Hume Lake, CA. July. Write Norman B. Rohrer, 260 Fern Ln., Hume Lake, CA 93628.

**ROUND TABLE COMEDY WRITERS CONVENTION**—Palm Springs, CA. July. Write Linda Perret, 2135 Huntington Dr., #205, San Marino, CA 91108.

**CALIFORNIA WRITERS' CONFERENCE**—Pacific Grove, CA. July. Write Carol O'Hara, California Writers' Club, 2214 Derby St., Berkeley, CA 94705.

**ANNUAL WRITERS CONFERENCE IN CHILDREN'S LITERATURE**—Marina Del Rey, CA. August. Write Lin Oliver, Dir., SCBW, P.O. Box 66296, Mar Vista Station, Los Angeles, CA 90066.

**NAPA VALLEY WRITERS' CONFERENCE**—Napa, CA. August. Write John Leggett, NVWC, 2277 Napa-Vallejo Hwy., Napa, CA 94558.

**SANTA BARBARA PUBLISHING WORKSHOP**—Santa Barbara, CA. Various weekend dates throughout year. Write Dan Poynter, Dir., Para Publishing, P.O. Box 4232–196, Santa Barbara, CA 93140.

## COLORADO

**NATIONAL WRITERS CLUB ANNUAL CONFERENCE**—Denver, CO. June. Write Sandy Whelchel, Dir., National Writers Club, 1450 S. Havana, Suite 620, Aurora, CO 80012.

**ASPEN WRITERS' CONFERENCE**—Aspen, CO. July. Write Kurt Brown, Dir., Box 5840, Snowmass Village, CO 81615.

**SCBW ANNUAL ROCKY MOUNTAIN SUMMER RETREAT**—Colorado Springs, CO. July. Write Linda White, 1712 Morning Dr., Loveland, CO 80537.

**STEAMBOAT SPRINGS WRITERS CONFERENCE**—Steamboat Springs, CO. August. Write Harriet Freiberger, Dir., P.O. Box 774284, Steamboat Springs, CO 80477.

**ROCKY MOUNTAIN FICTION WRITERS COLORADO GOLD**—Denver,CO. September. Write Linda Herbert, Rocky Mountain Fiction Writers, P.O. Box 260244, Denver, CO 80226-0244.

## Connecticut

**SCBW: NEW ENGLAND ANNUAL CONFERENCE**—New Britain, CT. March. Write Donald Gallo, 857 Mountain Rd., West Hartford, CT 06117.

**WESLEYAN WRITERS CONFERENCE**—Middletown, CT. June. Write Anne Greene, Dir., Wesleyan Writers Conference, Wesleyan Univ., Middletown, CT 06457.

## Florida

**KEY WEST LITERARY SEMINAR**—Key West, FL. January. Write Monica Haskell, Dir., Key West Literary Seminar, Inc., 419 Petronia St., Dept. TW, Key West, FL 33040.

**SPACE COAST WRITERS GUILD**—Cocoa Beach, FL. November. Write Dr. Edwin J. Kirschner, Space Coast Writers Guild, Box 804, Melbourne, FL 32902.

**ANNUAL FLORIDA STATE WRITERS CONFERENCE**—Orlando, FL. May. Write Dana K. Cassell, Dir., Florida Freelance Writers Assoc., P.O. Box 9844, Ft. Lauderdale, FL 33310.

## Georgia

**SANDHILLS WRITERS' CONFERENCE**—Augusta, GA. May. Write Tony Kellman, Div. of Cont. Education, Augusta College, 2500 Walton Way, Augusta, GA 30910.

**SOUTHEASTERN WRITERS CONFERENCE**—St. Simons Island, GA. June. Write Pat Laye, Rt. 1, Box 102, Cuthbert, GA 31740.

## Illinois

**CHRISTIAN WRITERS CONFERENCE**—Wheaton, IL. May. Write Dottie McBroom, 177 E. Crystal Lake Ave., Lake Mary, FL 32746.

**20TH ANNUAL MISSISSIPPI VALLEY WRITERS CONFERENCE**—Rock Island, IL. June. Write David R. Collins, 3403 45th St., Moline, IL 61265.

**MOODY WRITE-TO-PUBLISH CONFERENCE**—Chicago, IL. June. Write Lin Johnson, Dir., Moody Bible Institute, 820 N. LaSalle Blvd., Chicago, IL 60610.

**AUTUMN AUTHORS' AFFAIR XI**—Oak Brook, IL. October. Write Pat Wilson, Love Designers Writers' Club, 1507 Burnham Ave., Calumet City, IL 60409.

## Indiana

**BUTLER UNIVERSITY MIDWINTER CHILDREN'S LITERATURE CONFERENCE**—Indianapolis, IN. February. Write Valiska Gregory, Butler Writers Studio, Dept. of English, 4600 Sunset Ave., Indianapolis, IN 46208.

**INDIANA SOCIETY OF CHILDREN'S BOOK WRITER'S RETREAT**—Madison, IN. June. Write Betsy Storey, Dir., 4810 Illinois Rd., Ft. Wayne, IN 46804.

**MIDWEST WRITERS WORKSHOP**—Muncie, IN. August. Write Earl L. Conn, Dept. of Journalism, Ball State Univ., Muncie, IN 47306.

## Iowa

**IOWA SUMMER WRITING FESTIVAL**—Iowa City, IA. June, July. Write Peggy Houston, Dir., Cont. Ed., 116 International Center, Univ. of Iowa, Iowa City, IA 52242.

## Kansas

**WRITERS WORKSHOP IN SCIENCE FICTION**—Lawrence, KS. July. Write James Gunn, English Dept., Univ. of Kansas, Lawrence, KS 66045.

## Kentucky

**16TH ANNUAL APPALACHIAN WRITERS WORKSHOP**—Hindman, KY. August. Write Mike Mullins, Box 844, Hindman Settlement School, Hindman, KY 41822.

**WRITERS' ROUNDTABLE AT AUGUSTA**—Augusta, KY. October. Write Ed McClanahan, Augusta Roundtable, P.O. Box 127, Augusta, KY 41002.

## Louisiana

**WRITERS' GUILD OF ACADIANA**—Lafayette, LA. February. Write Rosalind Foley, WGA, P.O. Box 51535, Lafayette, LA 70505–1532.

## Maine

**WELLS WRITERS' WORKSHOP**—Wells Beach, ME. May, September. Write Victor A. Levine, 69 Broadway, Concord, NH 03301.

**ANNUAL STONECOAST WRITERS' CONFERENCE**—Portland, ME. July, August. Write Barbara Hope, Univ. of Southern Maine, Summer Session, 98 Falmouth St., Portland, ME 04103.

**ANNUAL STATE OF MAINE WRITERS' CONFERENCE**—Ocean Park, ME. August. Write Richard F. Burns, Dir., P.O. Box 296, Ocean Park, ME 04063.

## MARYLAND

**FAIRVIEW SUMMIT WRITERS SANCTUARY**—Cumberland, MD. March, June, October. Write Petrina Aubol, Fairview Summit, Rt. 9, Box 351, Cumberland, MD 21502.

**SANDY COVE CHRISTIAN WRITERS CONFERENCE**—North East, MD. October. Write Gayle Roper, RD 6, Box 112, Coatesville, PA 19320.

## MASSACHUSETTS

**MARTHA'S VINEYARD WRITERS WORKSHOP IN POETRY**—Vineyard Haven, MA. July. Write The Nathan Mayhew Seminars, P.O. Box 1125, Vineyard Haven, MA 02568.

**CAPE LITERARY ARTS WORKSHOPS**—Barnstable, MA. July, August. Write Marion Vuilleumier, Dir., Cape Literary Arts Workshops, c/o Cape Cod Writers Conference, Cape Cod Conservatory, Rt. 132, West Barnstable, MA 02668.

**CAPE COD WRITERS' CONFERENCE**—Craigville, MA. August. Write Marion Vuilleumier, Dir., CCWC, c/o Cape Cod Conservatory, Rt.132, West Barnstable, MA 02668.

## MICHIGAN

**CHRISTIAN WRITERS AND COMMUNICATORS WORKSHOP**—Berrien Springs, MI. June. Write Kermit Netteburg, Dir., Lifelong Learning, Andrews Univ., Berrien Springs, MI 49104–0800.

**MIDLAND WRITERS CONFERENCE**—Midland, MI. June. Write Eileen Finzel and Margaret Allen, Dirs., Grace A. Dow Memorial Library, 1710 W. St. Andrews, Midland, MI 48640.

**BAY VIEW FALL WRITERS' RETREAT**—Bay View, MI. October. Write Claire Korn, Bay View Fall Writers' Retreat, c/o Terrace Inn, P.O. Box 266, Petoskey, MI 49770.

## MINNESOTA

**SPLIT ROCK ARTS PROGRAM**—Duluth, MN. July, August. Write Andrea Gilats, 306 Wesbrook Hall, 77 Pleasant St. S.E., Minneapolis, MN 55455.

**9TH ANNUAL WRITERS' WORKSHOP**—Minneapolis, MN. August. Write Colleen Campbell, P.O. Box 24356, Minneapolis, MN 55424.

## MISSOURI

**ANNUAL MARK TWAIN WRITERS CONFERENCE**—Hannibal, MO. June. Write Dr. James C. Hefley, Dir., Hannibal-LaGrange College, 921 Center St., Hannibal, MO 63401.

**ROMANCE WRITERS OF AMERICA ANNUAL CONFERENCE**—St. Louis, MO. July, August. Write Romance Writers of America, 13700 Veterans Memorial, Suite 315, Houston, TX 77014.

**WRITING FOR CHILDREN WORKSHOP**—Springfield, MO. November. Write Sandy Asher, Dir., Drury College, 900 N. Benton, Springfield, MO 65802.

## Montana

**ANNUAL "GATHERING AT BIGFORK"**—Bigfork, MT. April, May. Write Malcolm Hillgartner, Dir., P.O. Box 1230, Bigfork, MT 59911.

**YELLOW BAY WRITERS' WORKSHOP**—Flathead Lake, MT. August. Write Annick Smith and Judy Jones, Dirs., Center for Cont. Ed., Univ. of Montana, Missoula, MT 59812.

## Nebraska

**BOUCHERCON XXIV-WORLD MYSTERY CONVENTION**—Omaha, NE. October. Write Charles Levitt, Bouchercon XXIV, P.O. Box 540516, Omaha, NE 68154–0516.

## New Hampshire

**ANNUAL SEACOAST WRITERS CONFERENCE**—Portsmouth, NH. October. Write Rae Francover, Dir., Registrar, Seacoast Writers, P.O. Box 6553, Portsmouth, NH 03802–6553.

## New Jersey

**NJ AUTHORS' PANELS LUNCHEON**—Newark, NJ. March. Write Dr. Herman Estrin, NJ Institute of Technology, Newark, NJ 07102.

**WRITING BY THE SEA**—Cape May, NJ. October, November. Write Natalie Newton, Cape May Institute, Inc., 1511 New York Ave., Cape May, NJ 08204.

## New Mexico

**SOUTHWEST CHRISTIAN WRITERS ASSOCIATION**—Farmington, NM. September. Write Kathy Cordell, Dir., P.O. Box 2635, Farmington, NM 87499–2635.

**SOUTHWEST WRITERS WORKSHOP 11TH ANNUAL CONFERENCE**—Albuquerque, NM. September. Write Southwest Writers Workshop, 1336-C Wyoming Blvd. N.E., Albuquerque, NM 87112.

## New York

**WRITING TO SELL IN 1993**—New York, NY. May. Write Florence Isaacs, Dir., American Society of Journalists & Authors, Inc., 1501 Broadway, #302, New York, NY 10036.

**WRITERS ON WRITING AT BARNARD**—New York, NY. June. Write Ann Birstein, Dir., Barnard College, 3009 Broadway, New York, NY 10027.

**WRITERS' WEEK**—Purchase, NY. June, July. Write Ruth Dowd, Manhattanville College, 2900 Purchase St., Purchase, NY 10577.

**ROBERT QUACKENBUSH'S CHILDREN'S BOOK WRITING AND ILLUSTRATING WORKSHOP**—New York, NY. July. Write Robert Quackenbush, Dir., 460 East 79th St., New York, NY 10021.

**CATSKILL POETRY WORKSHOP**—W. Davenport, NY. July. Write

Carol Frost, Dir., Office of Special Programs, Hartwick College, Oneonta, NY 13820.

**HIGHLIGHTS FOUNDATION WRITERS WORKSHOP**—Chautauqua, NY. July. Write Jan Keen, Dir., Highlights Foundation, Dept. WFL, 711 Court St., Honesdale, PA 18431.

**HOFSTRA UNIVERSITY SUMMER WRITERS' CONFERENCE**— Hempstead, NY. July. Write Lewis Shena, Hofstra Univ., UCCE, Davison Hall, Rm. 205, Hempstead, NY 11550.

## NORTH CAROLINA

**DUKE UNIVERSITY WRITERS WORKSHOP**—Durham, NC. June. Write Marilyn Hartman, Dir., The Bishop's House, Duke Univ., Durham, NC 27708.

**WILDACRES WRITERS WORKSHOP**—Little Switzerland, NC. July. Write Judith Hill, 233 S. Elm St., Greensboro, NC 27401.

## OHIO

**10TH ANNUAL WESTERN RESERVE WRITERS & FREELANCE CONFERENCE**—Mentor, OH. March, September. Write Lea Leever Oldham, 34200 Ridge Rd., #110, Willoughby, OH 44094.

**2ND ANNUAL CLEVELAND HTS./UNIVERSITY MINI WRITERS CONFERENCE**—University Hts., OH. May. Write Lea Leever Oldham, 34200 Ridge Rd., #110, Willoughby, OH 44094.

**25TH ANNUAL MIDWEST WRITERS' CONFERENCE**—Canton, OH. October. Write Gregg L. Andrews, Dir., 6000 Frank Ave. N.W., Canton, OH 44720.

## OKLAHOMA

**25TH ANNUAL OKLAHOMA WRITERS FEDERATION CONFERENCE**—Oklahoma City, OK. April. Write Deborah Bouziden, 8416 Huckleberry, Edmond, OH 73034.

**ANNUAL WRITERS OF CHILDREN'S LITERATURE CONFERENCE** —Lawton, OK. June. Write Dr. George E. Stanley, P.O. Box 16355, Cameron Univ., Lawton, OK 73505.

**OKLAHOMA FALL ARTS INSTITUTE**—Lone Wolf, OK. October. Write Laura Anderson, P.O. Box 18154, Oklahoma City, OK 73154.

## OREGON

**HAYSTACK PROGRAM IN THE ARTS AND SCIENCES**—Cannon Beach, OR. July, August. Write Portland State Univ., Summer Session, P.O. Box 751, Portland, OR 97207.

## PENNSYLVANIA

**PENNWRITERS, INC.**—Pittsburgh, PA. May. Write Colleen Kulikowski, 122 Westward Ho Dr., Pittsburgh, PA 15235.

**CUMBERLAND VALLEY WRITERS WORKSHOP**—Carlisle, PA. June. Write Judy Gill, Dir., Dept. of English, Dickinson College, Carlisle, PA 17013–2896.

## SOUTH CAROLINA

**FRANCIS MARION WRITERS' CONFERENCE**—Florence, SC. June. Write David Starkey, Dir., Francis Marion College, English Dept., Florence, SC 29501–0547.

## TENNESSEE

**RHODES COLLEGE WRITING CAMP**—Memphis, TN. June. Write Dr. Beth Kamhi, Dir., Dept. of English, Rhodes College, 2000 N. Parkway, Memphis, TN 38112.

**WRITERS WORKSHOP**—Nashville, TN. July. Write Bob Dean, Dir., Church Program Training Center, P.O. Box 24001, Nashville, TN 37203.

## TEXAS

**ANNUAL CRAFT OF WRITING CONFERENCE**—Richardson, TX. September. Write Janet Harris, Dir., UTD Center for Cont. Ed., P.O. Box 830688, CN1.1, Richardson, TX 75083–0688.

**AMERICAN MEDICAL WRITERS ASSOCIATION 53RD ANNUAL CONFERENCE**—Houston, TX. November. Write AMWA, 9650 Rockville Pike, Bethesda, MD 20814.

**WORLD OF WRITING WORKSHOPS**—Various dates and locations throughout year. Write Pamela Renner, Coord., World of Writing Enterprises, P.O. Box 870335, Dallas, TX 75287.

## VERMONT

**TRAVEL WRITING WORKSHOP**—Various locations throughout Vermont. May, June, September. Write Jules and Effin Older, Dirs., Box 163, Albany, VT 05820.

**BENNINGTON WRITING WORKSHOPS**—Bennington, VT. July. Write Liam Rector, Bennington Writing Workshops, Bennington College, Bennington, VT 05201.

**NEW ENGLAND WRITERS CONFERENCE**—Windsor, VT. July. Write Dr. Frank Anthony, Dir., P.O. Box 483, Windsor, VT 05089.

**ANNUAL BREAD LOAF WRITERS' CONFERENCE**—Ripton, VT. August. Write Robert Pack, Dir., Bread Loaf Writers' Conference, Middlebury College, Middlebury, VT 05753.

## VIRGINIA

**12TH ANNUAL WRITERS' CONFERENCE & CONTEST**—Newport News, VA. April. Write Doris Gwaltney, Conference Coord., Christopher Newport Univ., Office of Cont. Educ., 50 Shoe Ln., Newport News, VA 23606.

**SHENANDOAH VALLEY WRITERS' GUILD**—Middletown, VA. May, November. Write F. Cogan, Dir., Writers' Guild, Lord Fairfax College, P.O. Box 47, Middletown, VA 22645.

**ANNUAL HIGHLAND SUMMER CONFERENCE**—Radford, VA. June. Write Dr. Grace Toney Edwards, Dir., Box 5917, Radford Univ., Radford, VA 24142.

**APPALACHIAN WRITERS ASSOCIATION**—Radford, VA. July. Write Dr. Parks Lanier, Dir., Box 6935 RU, Radford, VA 24142.

**SHENANDOAH PLAYWRIGHTS RETREAT**—Staunton, VA. July, August. Write Robert Graham Small, Dir., Pennyroyal Farm, Rt. 5, Box 167F, Staunton, VA 24401.

**MID-ATLANTIC REGION SCBW CONFERENCE**—Richmond, VA. Fall. Write T.R. Hollingsworth, Reg. Advisor, SCBW, P.O. Box 1707, Midlothian, VA 23112.

### WASHINGTON

**WRITER'S WEEKEND AT THE BEACH**—Ocean Park, WA. February. Write Birdie Etchison, P.O. Box 877, Ocean Park, WA 98640.

**SEATTLE PACIFIC CHRISTIAN WRITERS' CONFERENCE**—Seattle, WA. June. Write Linda Wagner, Dir., Humanities Dept., Seattle Pacific Univ., Seattle, WA 98119.

**CLARION WEST WRITER'S WORKSHOP**—Seattle, WA. June, July. Write Leslie Howle, Clarion West Writer's Workshop, 340 15th Ave. E., Suite 350, Seattle, WA 98112.

**PACIFIC NORTHWEST WRITERS CONFERENCE**—Olympia, WA. July. Write Mary Sikkema, Dir., PNWC, 2033 6th Ave., #804, Seattle, WA 98121.

**PORT TOWNSEND WRITERS' CONFERENCE**—Port Townsend, WA. July. Write Carol Jane Bangs, Dir., Centrum, Box 1158, Port Townsend, WA 98368.

**WASHINGTON CHRISTIAN WRITERS**—Seattle, WA. Various dates throughout year. Write Elaine Wright Colvin, Dir., Washington Christian Writers, P.O. Box 11337, Bainbridge Island, WA 98110.

### WISCONSIN

**GREEN LAKE CHRISTIAN WRITERS CONFERENCE**—Green Lake, WI. July. Write Dr. Arlo Reichter, American Baptist Assembly, Green Lake, WI 54941.

**SCBW WISCONSIN 3RD ANNUAL FALL RETREAT**—Racine, WI. November. Write to Sheri Cooper Sinykin, Dir., 26 Lancaster Ct., Madison, WI 53719–1433.

### CANADA

**MARITIME WRITERS' WORKSHOP**—Fredericton, New Brunswick. July. Write Glenda Turner, Dir., Dept. of Extension, Univ. of New Brunswick, P.O. Box 4400, Fredericton, NB, Canada E3B 5A3.

# STATE ARTS COUNCILS

State arts councils sponsor grants, fellowships, and other programs for writers. To be eligible for funding, a writer *must* be a resident of the state in which he is applying. For more information, write to the addresses below. Telephone numbers are listed; numbers preceded by TDD indicate Telecommunications Device for the Deaf.

**ALABAMA STATE COUNCIL ON THE ARTS**
Albert B. Head, Executive Director
One Dexter Ave.
Montgomery, AL 36130
(205) 242–4076

**ALASKA STATE COUNCIL ON THE ARTS**
Christine D'Arcy, Executive Director
Jean Palmer, Grants Officer
411 W. 4th Ave., Suite 1E
Anchorage, AK 99501–2343
(907) 279–1558

**ARIZONA COMMISSION ON THE ARTS**
Tonda Gorton, Literature Director
417 W. Roosevelt
Phoenix, AZ 85003
(602) 255–5882

**ARKANSAS ARTS COUNCIL**
The Heritage Center, Suite 200
225 E. Markham
Little Rock, AR 72201
(501) 324–9337

**CALIFORNIA ARTS COUNCIL**
Public Information Office
2411 Alhambra Blvd.
Sacramento, CA 95817
(916) 739–3186

**COLORADO COUNCIL ON THE ARTS**
Barbara Neal, Executive Director
750 Pennsylvania St.
Denver, CO 80203–3699
(303) 894–2617

**CONNECTICUT COMMISSION ON THE ARTS**
John Ostrout, Executive Director
227 Lawrence St.
Hartford, CT 06106
(203) 566–4770

**DELAWARE DIVISION OF THE ARTS**
Cecelia Fitzgibbon, Director
Carvel State Building
820 N. French St.
Wilmington, DE 19801
(302) 577–3540

**FLORIDA ARTS COUNCIL**
Ms. Peyton Fearington
Dept. of State
Div. of Cultural Affairs
The Capitol
Tallahassee, FL 32399–0250
(904) 487–2980

**GEORGIA COUNCIL FOR THE ARTS**
Betsey Weltner, Executive Director
530 Means St. N.W., Suite 115
Atlanta, GA 30318
(404) 651–7920

**HAWAII STATE FOUNDATION ON CULTURE AND THE ARTS**
Wendell P.K. Silva, Executive Director
335 Merchant St., Room 202
Honolulu, HI 96813
(808) 548–4145

**IDAHO COMMISSION ON THE ARTS**
304 W. State St.
Boise, ID 83720
(208) 334–2119

**ILLINOIS ARTS COUNCIL**
Richard Gage, Communication Arts Program Director
State of Illinois Center
100 W. Randolph, Suite 10–500
Chicago, IL 60601
(312) 814–6750/(800) 237–6994

**INDIANA ARTS COMMISSION**
402 W. Washington St., Rm. 072
Indianapolis, IN 46204–2741
(317) 232–1268/TDD: (317) 233–3001

**IOWA STATE ARTS COUNCIL**
Iowa Literary Awards
Capitol Complex
Des Moines, IA 50319
(515) 281–6787

**KANSAS ARTS COMMISSION**
Robert T. Burtch, Editor
Jayhawk Tower
700 Jackson, Suite 1004
Topeka, KS 66603–3758
(913) 296–3335

**KENTUCKY ARTS COUNCIL**
31 Fountain Pl.
Frankfort, KY 40601
(502) 564–3757/TDD: (502) 564–3757

**LOUISIANA STATE ARTS COUNCIL**
Emma Burnett, Executive Director
Box 44247
Baton Rouge, LA 70804
(504) 342–8180

832

**MAINE ARTS COMMISSION**
David Cadigan
State House, Station 25
Augusta, ME 04333
(207) 287-2724

**MARYLAND STATE ARTS COUNCIL**
Linda Vlasak, Program Director
Artists-in-Education
601 N. Howard St.
Baltimore, MD 21201
(410) 333-8232

**MASSACHUSETTS CULTURAL COUNCIL**
James McCullough, Literature Coordinator
80 Boylston St., 10th Fl.
Boston, MA 02116
(617) 727-3668/(800) 232-0960
TDD: (617) 338-9153

**MICHIGAN COUNCIL FOR ARTS AND CULTURAL AFFAIRS**
Betty Boone, Interim Director
1200 Sixth Ave., Suite 1180
Detroit, MI 48226-2461
(313) 256-3735

**MINNESOTA STATE ARTS BOARD**
Karen Mueller
Artist Assistance Program Associate
432 Summit Ave.
St. Paul, MN 55102
(612) 297-2603

**COMPAS: WRITERS AND ARTISTS IN THE SCHOOLS**
Molly LaBerge, Executive Director
Daniel Gabriel, Director
305 Landmark Center
75 W. 5th St.
St. Paul, MN 55102
(612) 292-3249

**MISSISSIPPI ARTS COMMISSION**
Jane Crater Hiatt, Executive Director
239 N. Lamar St., Suite 207
Jackson, MS 39201
(601) 359-6030

**MISSOURI ARTS COUNCIL**
Autry Jackson, Program Administrator for Literature
Wainwright Office Complex
111 N. 7th St., Suite 105
St. Louis, MO 63101-2188
(314) 340-6845

**MONTANA ARTS COUNCIL**
Martha Sprague, Director, Artists Services Programs
316 N. Park Ave, Room 252
Helena, MT 59620
(406) 444-6430

833

**NEBRASKA ARTS COUNCIL**
Jennifer S. Clark, Executive Director
1313 Farnam On-the-Mall
Omaha, NE 68102-1873
(402) 595-2122

**NEVADA STATE COUNCIL ON THE ARTS**
William L. Fox, Executive Director
329 Flint St.
Reno, NV 89501
(702) 688-1225

**NEW HAMPSHIRE STATE COUNCIL ON THE ARTS**
Phenix Hall, 40 N. Main St.
Concord, NH 03301-4974
(603) 271-2789

**NEW JERSEY STATE COUNCIL ON THE ARTS**
Grants Office
4 N. Broad St. CN-306
Trenton, NJ 08625
(609) 292-6130

**NEW MEXICO ARTS DIVISION**
Arts in Education Program
228 E. Palace Ave.
Santa Fe, NM 87501
(505) 827-6490

**NEW YORK STATE COUNCIL ON THE ARTS**
Jewelle L. Gomez, Director, Literature Program
915 Broadway
New York, NY 10010
(212) 387-7020

**NORTH CAROLINA ARTS COUNCIL**
Deborah McGill, Literature Director
Dept. of Cultural Resources
Raleigh, NC 27601-2807
(919) 733-2111

**NORTH DAKOTA COUNCIL ON THE ARTS**
Vern Goodin, Executive Director
Black Building, Suite 606
Fargo, ND 58102
(701) 239-7150

**OHIO ARTS COUNCIL**
727 E. Main St.
Columbus, OH 43205-1796
(614) 466-2613

**STATE ARTS COUNCIL OF OKLAHOMA**
Suzanne Tate, Assistant Director
Jim Thorpe Bldg., Room 640
Oklahoma City, OK 73105
(405) 521-2931

**OREGON ARTS COMMISSION**
550 Airport Rd.
Salem, OR 97301
(503) 378–3625

**PENNSYLVANIA COUNCIL ON THE ARTS**
Marcia Salvatore, Literature and Theatre Programs
Diane Young, Artists-in-Education Program
Room 216, Finance Bldg.
Harrisburg, PA 17120
(717) 787–6883

**RHODE ISLAND STATE COUNCIL ON THE ARTS**
Iona B. Dobbins, Executive Director
95 Cedar St., Suite 103
Providence, RI 02903
(401) 277–3880

**SOUTH CAROLINA ARTS COMMISSION**
Steven Lewis, Director, Literary Arts Program
1800 Gervais St.
Columbia, SC 29201
(803) 734–8696

**SOUTH DAKOTA ARTS COUNCIL**
230 S. Phillips Ave., Suite 204
Sioux Falls, SD 57102–0788
(605) 339–6646

**TENNESSEE ARTS COMMISSION**
320 Sixth Ave., N., Suite 100
Nashville, TN 37243–0780
(615) 741–1701

**TEXAS COMMISSION ON THE ARTS**
P.O. Box 13406
Austin, TX 78711–3406
(512) 463–5535

**UTAH ARTS COUNCIL**
G. Barnes/Mark Preiss, Literary Coordinators
617 East South Temple
Salt Lake City, UT 84102
(801) 533–5895

**VERMONT COUNCIL ON THE ARTS**
Cornelia Carey, Grants Officer
136 State St.
Montpelier, VT 05602
(802) 828–3291

**VIRGINIA COMMISSION FOR THE ARTS**
Peggy J. Baggett, Executive Director
223 Governor St.
Richmond, VA 23219
(804) 225–3132

**WASHINGTON STATE ARTS COMMISSION**
110 9th & Columbia Bldg.
P.O. Box 42675
Olympia, WA 98504–2675
(206) 753–3860

**WEST VIRGINIA DEPT. OF EDUCATION AND THE ARTS**
Larkin Ray Cook, Executive Director
Culture and History Division
Arts and Humanities Section
The Cultural Center, Capitol Complex
Charleston, WV 25305
(304) 558–0220

**WISCONSIN ARTS BOARD**
Dean Amhaus, Executive Director
101 E. Wilson St., 1st Floor
Madison, WI 53703
(608) 266–0190

**WYOMING ARTS COUNCIL**
John Coe, Director
2320 Capitol Ave.
Cheyenne, WY 82002
(307) 777–7742

# ORGANIZATIONS FOR WRITERS

**THE ACADEMY OF AMERICAN POETS**
584 Broadway, Suite 1208
New York, NY 10012
(212) 274–0343
Mrs. Edward T. Chase, *President*
    The Academy of American Poets was founded in 1934 to promote American poetry through fellowships, awards programs, public programs, and publications. The Academy offers an annual fellowship for distinguished poetic achievement, the Peter I. B. Lavan Younger Poet Awards, three major book awards, and sponsors prizes for poetry at 181 universities and colleges nationwide. The Academy's readings, lectures, and regional symposia take place at various New York City locations and other locations in the United States. Membership is open to all: $45 annual fee includes subscription to the bimonthly newsletter, *Poetry Pilot*, and complimentary copies of prize book selections.

## AMERICAN CRIME WRITERS LEAGUE

12 St. Ann Dr.
Santa Barbara, CA 93109
Barbara Mertz, *President*
Michael Collins, *Membership Chair*

A national organization of working professional mystery authors. To be eligible for membership in ACWL you must have published at least one of the following: one full-length work of crime fiction or nonfiction; three short stories; or three nonfiction crime articles. The bimonthly *ACWL BULLETin* features articles by reliable experts and an exchange of information and advice among professional writers. Annual dues: $35.

## AMERICAN MEDICAL WRITERS ASSOCIATION

9650 Rockville Pike
Bethesda, MD 20814
(301) 493-0003
Lillian Sablack, *Executive Director*

Members of this association are engaged in biomedical communications. Any person actively interested in or professionally associated with any medium of medical communication is eligible for membership. Annual dues: $65.

## AMERICAN SOCIETY OF JOURNALISTS AND AUTHORS, INC.

1501 Broadway, Suite 302
New York, NY 10036
(212) 997-0947
Alexandra Cantor, *Executive Director*

This nationwide organization of independent writers of nonfiction is dedicated to promoting high standards of nonfiction writing through monthly meetings, annual writers' conferences, etc. ASJA offers extensive benefits and services including referral services, numerous discount services, and the opportunity to explore professional issues and concerns with other writers. Members also receive a monthly newsletter with confidential market information. Membership is open to professional free-lance writers of nonfiction; qualifications are judged by Membership Committee. Call or write for application details.

## ASSOCIATION OF HISPANIC ARTS, INC.

173 E. 116th St.
New York, NY 10029
(212) 860-5445
Jane Arce Bello, *Executive Director*

Founded in 1975, the AHA serves both Hispanic arts organizations and individual artists at various stages of development, to ensure that the rich array of Hispanic arts and cultural expressions will be preserved. Publishes *Hispanic Arts News*, providing information on events, job opportunities, and other issues. Annual dues: $20.

## THE AUTHORS GUILD, INC.

330 W. 42nd St.
New York, NY 10036-6902
(212) 563-5904
Attn: *Membership Committee*

A writer who has published a book in the last seven years with an established publisher, or one who has published several magazine pieces with periodicals of general circulation within the last eighteen months, may be eligible for active voting membership in The Authors Guild. A new writer may be eligible for associate membership. All members of the Authors Guild automatically become members of its parent organization, The Authors League of America, Inc. Annual dues: $90.

## THE AUTHORS LEAGUE OF AMERICA, INC.
330 W. 42nd St.
New York, NY 10036–6902
(212) 564–8350

The Authors League of America is a national organization of over 14,000 authors and dramatists, representing them on matters of joint concern, such as copyright, taxes, and freedom of expression. Membership in the league is restricted to authors and dramatists who are members of The Authors Guild and The Dramatists Guild. Matters such as contract terms and subsidiary rights are in the province of the two guilds.

## BLACK THEATRE NETWORK
Box 11502
Fisher Bldg. Sta.
Detroit, MI 48211
(714) 880–5892
Kathryn Ervin, *President*

The BTN's every activity is to expose all people to the beauty and complexity of Black theater, and to preserve the art form so future generations may inherit a theater worthy of its African roots. BTN serves as coordinator of panels and workshops for the National Black Theatre Festival. Publications include *BTNews* newsletter and *The Black Theatre* directory. Membership is open to playwrights, performers, directors, teachers, and researchers. Annual dues: $25 to $75.

## BRITISH AMERICAN ARTS ASSOCIATION
116 Commercial St.
London E1 6NF
England
(071) 247–5385
Jennifer Williams, *Executive Director*

An information service and clearing house for exchange between British and American cultural activities in all arts fields, the BAAA provides advocacy and technical assistance to professional artists. The BAAA does not give funds and is not a membership organization.

## COUNCIL OF AUTHORS & JOURNALISTS, INC.
1214 Laurel Hill Dr.
Decatur, GA 30033
Attn: *CAJ Membership*

The CAJ is a writers' network established to encourage high standards of creative writing and to promote interest in writers, their books, and other literary works. A summer conference in St. Simons Island, Georgia, attended by about 100 members, is the Council's main event. Annual dues: $15 to $100.

## THE DRAMATISTS GUILD
234 W. 44th St.
New York, NY 10036
(212) 398–9366
Peter Stone, *President*

America's only professional association of playwrights, composers, and lyricists, the Dramatists Guild was established to protect dramatists' rights and to improve working conditions. Services include use of the Guild's contracts, business counseling, publications, and symposia in major cities. All playwrights (produced or not) are eligible for membership. All Active or Associate members of the Dramatists Guild automatically become members of its parent organization, the Authors League. Annual dues: $100, *active*; $65, *associate/ subscribing*; $25, *student*.

## INTERNATIONAL ASSOCIATION OF THEATRE FOR CHILDREN AND YOUNG PEOPLE
c/o The Open Eye: New Stagings
270 W. 89th St.
New York, NY 10024
Harold Oaks, *President*
   The only theater organization in the U.S. that has the development of professional theater for young audiences and international exchange as its primary mandates. Provides a link between professional theaters, artists, directors, training institutions, and arts agencies; sponsors festivals and forums for interchange among theaters and theater artists. Annual dues: $50, *individual*; $25, *student and retiree*.

## THE INTERNATIONAL SOCIETY OF DRAMATISTS
1638 Euclid Ave.
Miami Beach, FL 33139
(305) 538–3111
   Open to playwrights, agents, producers, screenwriters, and others involved in the theater. Publishes *Dramatist's Bible*, a directory of script opportunities, and *The Globe*, a newsletter with information and news of theaters across the country. Also provides free referral service for playwrights. Annual dues: $24.

## THE INTERNATIONAL WOMEN'S WRITING GUILD
Box 810
Gracie Sta.
New York, NY 10028
(212) 737–7536
Hannelore Hahn, *Executive Director*
   The IWWG is a network for the personal and professional empowerment of women through writing. Services include a newsletter, a list of literary agents and publishing services, access to health insurance plans at group rates, annual events, regional writing clusters, and year-round supportive networking. Membership is open to anyone, regardless of writing accomplishments. Annual dues: $35.

## MIDWEST RADIO THEATRE WORKSHOP
KOPN
915 E. Broadway
Columbia, MO 65201
(314) 874–5676
Diane Huneke, *Director*
   Founded in 1979, MRTW is the only national resource for American radio dramatists, providing information (referral, technical assistance, educational materials) and workshops. MRTW coordinates an annual national radio script contest, publishes an annual radio scriptbook, and distributes a script anthology with primer. Send SASE for more information.

## MYSTERY WRITERS OF AMERICA, INC.
17 E. 47th St., 6th Floor
New York, NY 10017
Priscilla Ridgway, *Executive Director*
   The MWA exists for the purpose of raising the prestige of mystery and

detective writing, and of defending the rights and increasing the income of all writers in the field of mystery, detection, and fact crime writing. Each year, the MWA presents the Edgar Allan Poe Awards for the best mystery writing in a variety of fields. The four classifications of membership are: *active* (open to any writer who has made a sale in the field of mystery, suspense, or crime writing); *associate* (for professionals in allied fields/writers in other fields); *corresponding* (for writers living outside the U.S.); *affiliate* (for unpublished writers and mystery enthusiasts). Annual dues: $65; $32.50 for corresponding members.

## NATIONAL ASSOCIATION OF SCIENCE WRITERS, INC.
P.O. Box 294
Greenlawn, NY 11740
(516) 757–5664

The NASW promotes the dissemination of accurate information regarding science through all media, and conducts a varied program to increase the flow of news from scientists, to improve the quality of its presentation, and to communicate its meaning to the reading public.

Anyone who has been actively engaged in the dissemination of science information is eligible to apply for membership. Active members must be principally involved in reporting on science through newspapers, magazines, TV, or other media that reach the public directly. Associate members report on science through limited-circulation publications and other media. Annual dues: $50.

## NATIONAL LEAGUE OF AMERICAN PEN WOMEN
1300 17th St. N.W.
Washington, DC 20036–1973
(202) 785–1997
Mary Latka, *Secretary*

Founded in 1897. Offers networking opportunities and workshops through local branches for the purpose of receiving manuscript critiques, exchange of ideas, and marketing news. Members receive the national *PEN Woman* Magazine as well as statewide newsletters. Annual dues: $25.

## THE NATIONAL WRITERS CLUB
1450 S. Havana, Suite 620
Aurora, CO 80012
(303) 751–7844
Sandy Whelchel, *Executive Director*

New and established writers, poets, and playwrights throughout the U.S. and Canada may become members of The National Writers Club, a full-time, customer-service-oriented association founded in 1937. Membership includes bimonthly newsletter, *Authorship*. Annual dues: $60, *professional*; $50, *regular*; plus a $15 one-time initiation fee; add $20 outside the USA, Canada, and Mexico.

## NATIONAL WRITERS UNION
873 Broadway, #203
New York, NY 10003
(212) 254–0279

The National Writers Union is dedicated to bringing about equitable payment and fair treatment of free-lance writers through collective action. Its membership is over 3,000 and includes book authors, poets, free-lance journalists, and technical writers in eleven chapters nationwide. The NWU offers its members contract and agent information, health insurance plans, press credentials, grievance handling, a union newspaper, and sponsors events across the country. Membership is open to writers who have published a book, play, three articles, five poems, one short story or an equivalent amount of newsletter, publicity, technical, commercial, government or institutional copy, or have written an equivalent amount of unpublished material and are actively seeking publication. Dues range from $60 to $150.

## NEW DRAMATISTS
424 W. 44th St.
New York, NY 10036
(212) 757–6960
New Dramatists is dedicated to finding gifted playwrights and giving them the time, space, and tools to develop their craft. Services include readings and workshops; a director-in-residence program; national script distribution for members; artist work spaces; international playwright exchange programs; script copying facilities; and a free ticket program. Membership is open to residents of New York City and the surrounding tri-state area. National memberships are offered to those outside the area who can spend time in NYC in order to take advantage of programs. Apply between July 15 and September 15. No annual dues.

## NORTHWEST PLAYWRIGHTS GUILD
Box 95259
Seattle, WA 98145
(206) 545–7955
Barbara Callander, *Executive Director*
Carl Sander, *Artistic Director*
NWPG supports and promotes playwrights living in the Northwest through play development, staged readings, and information networking for play competitions and production opportunities. Members receive monthly and quarterly newsletters. Dues: $25 initiation fee; $15 annual renewal.

## OUTDOOR WRITERS ASSOCIATION OF AMERICA, INC.
2017 Cato Ave., Suite 101
State College, PA 16801–2768
(814) 234–1011
Sylvia G. Bashline, *Executive Director*
The OWAA is a non-profit, international organization representing professional communicators who report and reflect upon America's diverse interests in the outdoors. Membership (by nomination only) includes a monthly publication, *Outdoors Unlimited*; annual conference; annual membership directory; contests. OWAA also provides scholarships to qualified students.

## PEN AMERICAN CENTER
568 Broadway
New York, NY 10012
(212) 334–1660
PEN American Center is one of more than 104 centers in 69 countries that make up International PEN, a worldwide association of literary writers, offering conferences, writing programs, and financial and educational assistance. Membership is open to writers who have published two books of literary merit, as well as editors, agents, playwrights, and translators who meet specific standards. (Apply to nomination committee.) PEN sponsors annual awards and grants and publishes the quarterly *PEN Newsletter* and the biennial directory, *Grants and Awards Available to American Writers*.

## THE PLAYWRIGHTS' CENTER
2301 Franklin Ave. East
Minneapolis, MN 55406
(612) 332–7481
David Moore, Jr., *Executive Director*
The Playwrights' Center fuels the contemporary theater by providing services that support the development and public appreciation of playwrights and playwriting. Members receive applications for all Center programs, a calendar of events, eligibility to participate in special activities, including classes, outreach programs, and PlayLabs. Annual dues: $35.

## THE POETRY SOCIETY OF AMERICA
15 Gramercy Park
New York, NY 10003
(212) 254–9628
Elise Paschen, *Executive Director*
Founded in 1910, The Poetry Society of America seeks through a variety of programs to gain a wider audience for American poetry. The Society offers 19 annual prizes for poetry (with many contests open to non-members as well as members), and sponsors workshops, poetry readings, and publications. Maintains the Van Vooris Library of American Poetry. Annual dues: $40.

## POETS AND WRITERS, INC.
72 Spring St.
New York, NY 10012
(212) 226–3586
Elliot Figman, *Executive Director*
Poets & Writers, Inc., was founded in 1970 to foster the development of poets and fiction writers and to promote communication throughout the literary community. A non-membership organization, it offers a nationwide information center for writers; *Poets & Writers Magazine* and other publications; as well as sponsored readings and workshops.

## PRIVATE EYE WRITERS OF AMERICA
1750 Fourth St., #607
Cuyahoga Falls, OH 44221
(216) 923–0986
Dick Stodghill, *Membership Chairman*
Robert J. Randisi, *Executive Director*
Private Eye Writers of America is a national organization that seeks to promote a wider recognition and appreciation of private eye literature. Sponsors the annual Shamus Award for the best in P.I. fiction. Writers who have published a work of fiction (short story, novel, TV script, or movie screenplay) with a private eye as the central character are eligible to join as active members. Serious devotees of the P.I. story may become associate members. Annual dues: $30, *active; $24,* associate; $30, *international*.

## ROMANCE WRITERS OF AMERICA
13700 Veterans Memorial Dr., Suite 315
Houston, TX 77014
(713) 440–6885
Linda Fisher, *Office Supervisor*
The RWA is an international organization with over 104 local chapters across the U.S. and Canada, open to any writer, published or unpublished, interested in the field of romantic fiction. Annual dues of $45, plus $10 applica-

tion fee for new members; benefits include annual conference, contest, market information, and bimonthly newsmagazine, *Romance Writers' Report*.

## SCIENCE FICTION AND FANTASY WRITERS OF AMERICA, INC.
5 Winding Brook Dr., #1B
Guilderland, NY 12084
Peter Dennis Pautz, *Executive Secretary*

Science Fiction and Fantasy Writers of America (formerly Science Fiction Writers of America) is a professional organization of science fiction and fantasy writers whose purpose is to foster and further the interests of writers of fantasy and science fiction. SFWA presents the Nebula Award annually for excellence in the field and publishes the *Bulletin* for its members.

Any writer who has sold a work of science fiction or fantasy is eligible for membership. Annual dues: $50, *active* ; $35, *affiliates*; plus $10 installation fee; send for application and information. The *Bulletin* is available to nonmembers for $15 (four issues) within the U.S.; $18.50 overseas.

## SMALL PRESS WRITERS AND ARTISTS ORGANIZATION
615 N. 187th Ave.
Buckeye, AZ 85326
Cathy Hicks, *Secretary*

Founded in 1977, the SPWAO is an international service organization of 400 writers, artists, poets, and publishers dedicated to the promotion of excellence in the small-press fields of science fiction, fantasy, and horror. Members receive the bimonthly *SPWAO Newsletter*, critiques by fellow members, grievance arbitration, and research assistance. Annual dues: $15, plus $17.50 one-time initiation fee.

## SOCIETY FOR TECHNICAL COMMUNICATION
901 N. Stuart St., #304
Arlington, VA 22203
(703) 522–4114
William C. Stolgitis, *Executive Director*

The Society for Technical Communication is a professional organization dedicated to the advancement of the theory and practice of technical communication in all media. The 17,000 members in the U.S. and other countries include technical writers and editors, publishers, artists and draftsmen, researchers, educators, and audiovisual specialists.

## SOCIETY OF AMERICAN TRAVEL WRITERS
1155 Connecticut Ave. N.W., Suite 500
Washington, DC 20036
(202) 429–6639
Ken Fischer, *Administrative Coordinator*

The Society of American Travel Writers represents writers and other professionals who strive to provide travelers with accurate reports on destinations, facilities, and services.

Membership is by invitation. Active membership is limited to salaried travel writers and free lancers who have a steady volume of published or distributed work about travel. Initiation fees: $200, *active*; $400, *associate*. Annual dues: $120, *active*; $240 *associate*.

## SOCIETY OF CHILDREN'S BOOK WRITERS & ILLUSTRATORS

P.O. Box 66296
Mar Vista Station
Los Angeles, CA 90066
(818) 347-2849
Lin Oliver, *Executive Director*

This national organization of authors, editors, publishers, illustrators, filmmakers, librarians, and educators offers a variety of services to people who write, illustrate for or share an interest in children's literature. Full memberships are open to those who have had at least one children's book or story published. Associate memberships are open to all those with an interest in children's literature. Yearly dues are $40.

## SOCIETY OF ENVIRONMENTAL JOURNALISTS

370-D Willowbrook Dr.
Jeffersonville, PA 19403
(215) 630-9147
Amy Gahran, *SEJ Records Manager*

Dedicated to enhancing the quality and accuracy of environmental reporting, the SEJ has 780 members and services include a quarterly newsletter, an annual conference, computer bulletin board, mentoring program, annual directory. Annual dues: $30.

## SOCIETY OF PROFESSIONAL JOURNALISTS

16 S. Jackson St.
Greencastle, IN 46135-0077
(317) 653-3333
Ernie Ford, *Executive Director*

With over 16,000 members and 300 chapters, SPJ serves the interests of print, broadcast, and wire journalists. Services include legal counsel on journalism issues, jobs-for-journalists career search program, professional development seminars, and awards that encourage journalism. Members receive *The Quill*, a monthly magazine that explores current issues in the field. SPJ promotes ethics and freedom of information programs.

Members must spend at least 50 percent of their working hours in journalism. Annual dues: $57, *professional*; $28.50, *student*.

## THE SONGWRITERS GUILD OF AMERICA

276 Fifth Ave., Suite 306
New York, NY 10001
(212) 686-6820
George Wurzbach, *Director*

Open to published and unpublished songwriters, the Guild provides members with contracts, reviews contracts, collects royalties from publishers, offers group health and life insurance plans, conducts workshops and critique sessions, and provides a songwriting collaboration service. Annual dues: $45, *associate*; $55 and up, *full member*.

## THEATRE COMMUNICATIONS GROUP

355 Lexington Ave.
New York, NY 10017
(212) 697-5230
Peter Zeisler, *Executive Director*

TCG, the national organization for the nonprofit professional theater, provides services to facilitate the work of playwrights, literary managers, and other theater professionals and journalists. Programs include *Plays in Process*, which circulates manuscripts of new plays, translations, and adaptations to an international subscribership of individuals and organizations involved in producing new work. Publishes a bimonthly bulletin of new American plays, and the annual *Dramatists Sourcebook*. No fees for individual theater artists.

**WESTERN WRITERS OF AMERICA, INC.**
2800 N. Campbell
El Paso, TX 79902–2522
(915) 532–3222
Francis L. Fugate, *Secretary/Treasurer*
Published writers of fiction, nonfiction, and poetry pertaining to the traditions, legends, development, and history of the American West may join the nonprofit Western Writers of America. Its chief purpose is to promote a more widespread distribution, readership, and appreciation of the West and its literature. Annual dues: $60. Sponsors annual Spur Awards, Owen Wister Award, and Medicine Pipe Bearer's Award for Published Work.

**WRITERS GUILD OF AMERICA, EAST, INC.**
555 W. 57th St.
New York, NY 10019
(212) 767–7800
Mona Mangan, *Executive Director*

**WRITERS GUILD OF AMERICA, WEST, INC.**
8955 Beverly Blvd.
West Hollywood, CA 90048
(310) 550–1000
Brian Walton, *Executive Director*
The Writers Guild of America (East and West) represents writers in the fields of radio, television, and motion pictures in both news and entertainment. In order to qualify for membership, a writer must fulfill current requirements for employment or sale of material in one of these three fields.
The basic dues are $25 per quarter for the Writers Guild West and $12.50 per quarter for Writers Guild East. In addition, there are quarterly dues based on percentage of the member's earnings in any one of the fields over which the Guild has jurisdiction. The initiation fee is $1,000 for Writers Guild East and $1,500 for Writers Guild West. (Writers living east of the Mississippi join Writers Guild East, and those living west of the Mississippi, Writers Guild West.)

# LITERARY AGENTS

The following is a sampling of agents that handle literary and/or dramatic material. Most literary agents do not accept new writers as clients. Since the agent's income is a percentage (10% to 20%) of the amount he receives from the sales he makes for his clients, he must have as clients writers who are selling fairly regularly to good markets. Always query an agent first. Do not send any manuscripts until the agent has asked you to do so; and be wary of agents who charge fees for reading manuscripts.

The Association of Authors' Representatives, Inc. is a recent merger of the Society of Authors' Representatives with the Independent Literary Agents Association, Inc.; for the most up-to-date list of AAR members and their code of ethics, send a 52¢ legal-size SASE, and a $5.00 check or money order to defray handling costs to: Association of Authors' Representatives, Inc., 10 Astor Pl., 3rd Floor, New York, NY 10003.

Addresses that include zip codes in parentheses are located in New York City (many agents in this list are in New York). Individual agents within an agency are listed in italics. An extensive list of agents and their policies can be found in *Literary Market Place*, a directory found in most libraries, and in *Literary Agents of North America* (Author Aid/Research Associates International, 340 E. 52nd St., New York, NY 10022).

**CAROLE ABEL LITERARY AGENT** 160 W. 87th St. (10024) *Carole Abel*

**DOMINICK ABEL LITERARY AGENCY** 498 West End Ave. (10024) *Dominick Abel, Claire Israel*

**ACTON & DYSTEL** 928 Broadway, Suite 301 (10010) *Edward Acton*

**BRET ADAMS LIMITED** 448 W. 44th St. (10036) *Bret Adams, Mary Harden*

**MICHAEL AMATO AGENCY** 1650 Broadway, Rm. 307 (10019) *Michael Amato*

**MARCIA AMSTERDAM AGENCY** 41 W. 82nd St., #9A (10024) *Marcia Amsterdam*

**ARCADIA, INC.** 221 W. 82nd St., Suite 7D (10024) *Victoria Pryor*

**THE AXELROD AGENCY** 66 Church St., Lenox, MA 01240 *Steve Axelrod*

**THE BALKIN AGENCY** P.O. Box 222, Amherst, MA 01004 *Richard Balkin*

**VIRGINIA BARBER AGENCY, INC.** 353 W. 21st St. (10011) *Virginia Barber*

**LORETTA BARRETT** 121 W. 27th St., #601 (10001) *Loretta Barrett*

**LOIS BERMAN** The Little Theatre Bldg., 240 W. 44th St. (10036) *Lois Berman, Judy Boals*

**MEREDITH G. BERNSTEIN** 2112 Broadway, Suite 503A (10023) *Meredith G. Bernstein*

**VICKY BIJUR** 333 West End Ave. (10023) *Vicky Bijur*

**DAVID BLACK LITERARY AGENCY** 220 Fifth Ave., Suite 1400 (10001) *David Black*

**THE BOOK PEDDLERS** 18326 Minnetonka Blvd., Deephaven, MN 55391 *Vicki Lansky*

**GEORGES BORCHARDT, INC.** 136 E. 57th St. (10022) *Anne Borchardt, Georges Borchardt, Wendy Schacher Finn, Alexandra Harding, Cindy Klein, Denise Shannon*

**BRANDT & BRANDT LITERARY AGENTS, INC.** 1501 Broadway (10036) *Carl Brandt, Gail Hochman, Marianne Merola, Charles Schlessinger*

**THE HELEN BRANN AGENCY, INC.** 94 Curtis Rd., Bridgewater, CT 06752 *Helen Brann*

**BROADWAY PLAY PUBLISHING** 357 W. 20th St. (10011) *Christopher Gould*

**ANDREA BROWN** 1081 Alameda, Suite 71, Belmont, CA 94002 *Andrea Brown*

**CURTIS BROWN, LTD.** 10 Astor Pl. (10003) *Laura Blake, Emilie Jacobson, Ginger Knowlton, Perry Knowlton, Timothy Knowlton, Marilyn Marlow, Irene Skolnick, Emma Sweeney, Clyde Taylor, Jess Taylor, Maureen Walters*

**CURTIS BROWN, LTD.** 606 Larchmont Blvd., Suite 309, Los Angeles, CA 90004 *Jeannine Edmunds*

**CURTIS BROWN, LTD.** 1750 Montgomery St., San Francisco, CA 94111 *Peter Ginsberg*

**DON BUCHWALD & ASSOCIATES** 10 E. 44th St. (10017) *Don Buchwald*

**KNOX BURGER ASSOCIATES, LTD.** 39 ½ Washington Square S. (10012) *Knox Burger, Katherine Preminger, Kitty Sprague*

**MARIA CARVAINIS AGENCY, INC.** 235 West End Ave. (10023) *Maria Carvainis*

**MARTHA CASSELMAN** Box 342, Calistoga, CA 94515–0342 *Martha Casselman*

**RUTH COHEN, INC., LITERARY AGENCY** P.O. Box 7626, Menlo Park, CA 94025 *Ruth Cohen*

**COLLIER ASSOCIATES** 2000 Flat Run Rd., Seaman, OH 45679 *Oscar Collier*

**FRANCES COLLIN LITERARY AGENCY** 110 W. 40th St., Suite 1403 (10018) *Frances Collin*

**COLUMBIA LITERARY ASSOCIATES** 7902 Nottingham Way, Ellicott City, MD 21043 *Linda Hayes*

**DON CONGDON ASSOCIATES, INC.** 156 Fifth Ave., Suite 625 (10010) *Don Congdon, Michael Congdon, Susan Ramer*

**ROBERT CORNFIELD LITERARY AGENCY** 145 W. 79th St. (10024) *Robert Cornfield*

**RICHARD CURTIS ASSOCIATES, INC.** 171 E. 74th St. (10021) *Richard Curtis*

**DARHANSOFF & VERRILL** 1220 Park Ave. (10128) *Liz Darhansoff*

**JOAN DAVES** 21 W. 26th St. (10010–1003) *Joan Daves*

**ANITA DIAMANT AGENCY, INC.** 310 Madison Ave., #1508 (10017) *Anita Diamant, Robin Rue*

**SANDRA DIJKSTRA LITERARY AGENCY** 1155 Camino Del Mar, Suite 515, Del Mar, CA 92014 *Sanda Dijkstra*

**THE JONATHAN DOLGER AGENCY** 49 E. 96th St., 9B (10128) *Jonathan Dolger*

**DONADIO & ASHWORTH, INC.** 231 W. 22nd St. (10011) *Eric Ashworth, Candida Donadio*

**ANNE EDELSTEIN LITERARY AGENCY** 137 Fifth Ave. (10010) *Anne Edelstein*

**JOSEPH ELDER AGENCY** 150 W. 87th St., 6D (10024) *Joseph Elder*

**ETHAN ELLENBERG LITERARY AGENCY** 548 Broadway, 5-E (10012) *Ethan Ellenberg*

**ANN ELMO AGENCY, INC.** 60 E. 42nd St. (10165) *Ann Elmo, Lettie Lee*

**FELICIA ETH** 555 Bryant St., Suite 350, Palo Alto, CA 94301 *Felicia Eth*

**FALLON LITERARY AGENCY** 301 W. 53rd St., 13B (10019) *Eileen Fallon*

**JOHN FARQUHARSON, LTD.** 250 W. 57th St., (10107) *Jane Gelfman, Deborah Schneider*

**MARJE FIELDS, INC.** 165 W. 46th St., Suite 1205 (10036) *Marje Fields*

**JOYCE FLAHERTY** 816 Lynda Ct., St. Louis, MO 63122 *Joyce Flaherty*

**THE FOX CHASE AGENCY, INC.** Public Ledger Bldg. #930, Independence Square, Philadelphia, PA 19106 *A.L. Hart, Jo C. Hart*

**ROBERT A. FREEDMAN DRAMATIC AGENCY, INC.** 1501 Broadway, #2310 (10036) *Robert Freedman, Selma Luttinger*

**SAMUEL FRENCH, INC.** 45 W. 25th St. (10010) *Lawrence Harbison, William Talbot, Charles R. Van Nostrand, Abbott Van Nostrand*

**JAY GARON-BROOKE ASSOCIATES** 415 Central Park West (10025) *Jay Garon*

**FRANCES GOLDIN** 305 E. 11th St. (10003) *Frances Goldin*

**GOODMAN ASSOCIATES** 500 West End Ave. (10024) *Arnold Goodman, Elise Simon Goodman*

**IRENE GOODMAN LITERARY AGENCY** 521 Fifth Ave., 17th Fl. (10017) *Irene Goodman*

**GRAHAM AGENCY** 311 W. 43rd St. (10036) *Earl Graham*

**SANFORD J. GREENBURGER ASSOCIATES** 55 Fifth Ave., 15th Floor (10003) *Francis Greenburger, Faith Hornby Hamlin, Heide Lange*

**MAXINE GROFFSKY LITERARY AGENCY** 2 Fifth Ave. (10011) *Maxine Groffsky*

**JEANNE K. HANSON LITERARY AGENCY** 511 Wooddale Ave. S., Edina, MN 55424 *Jeanne K. Hanson*

**HELEN HARVEY** 410 W. 24th St., (10011) *Helen Harvey*

**JOHN W. HAWKINS & ASSOCIATES, INC.** 71 W. 23rd St., Suite 1600 (10010) *Sharon Friedman, John Hawkins, William Reiss*

**HEACOCK LITERARY AGENCY, INC.** 1523 Sixth St., Suite 14, Santa Monica, CA 90401 *James Heacock*

**THE JEFF HERMAN AGENCY, INC.** 500 Greenwich St., Suite 501C (10013) *Jeff Herman*

**JOHN L. HOCHMAN BOOKS** 320 E. 58th St. (10022) *John L. Hochman*

**BERENICE HOFFMAN LITERARY AGENCY** 215 W. 75th St. (10023) *Berenice Hoffman*

**IMG/JULIAN BACH LITERARY AGENCY** 747 Third Ave. (10017) *Julian Bach*

**INTERNATIONAL CREATIVE MANAGEMENT, INC.** 40 W. 57th St. (10019) *Bridget Aschenberg, Lisa Bankoff, Jill Bock, Sam Cohn, Kristine Dahl, Arlene Donovan, Mitch Douglas, Suzanne Gluck, Wiley Hausam, Esther Newberg, Bob Tabian, Amanda Urban, Timothy Flannigan*

**SHARON JARVIS & CO.** 260 Willard Ave., Staten Island, NY 10314 *Sharon Jarvis*

**JCA LITERARY AGENCY, INC.** 27 W. 20th St., Suite 1103 (10011) *Jane Cushman, Jeff Gerecke, Tony Outhwaite*

**NATASHA KERN LITERARY AGENCY** 13147 N.W. Cheerio, Portland, OR 97229 *Natasha Kern*

**KIDDE, HOYT & PICARD** 335 E. 51st St. (10022) *Katharine Kidde*

**BARBARA S. KOUTS LITERARY AGENT** P.O. Box 558, Bellport, NY 11713 *Barbara S. Kouts*

**OTTO R. KOZAK LITERARY AGENCY** P.O. Box 152, Long Beach, NY 11561 *Otto R. Kozak*

**LUCY KROLL AGENCY** 390 West End Ave. (10024) *Barbara Hogenson, Lucy Kroll*

**PINDER LANE PRODUCTIONS, LTD.** 159 W. 53rd St. (10019) *Dick Duane, Robert Thixton*

**THE LANTZ OFFICE** 888 Seventh Ave. (10106) *Joy Harris, Robert Lantz*

**MICHAEL LARSEN/ELIZABETH POMADA LITERARY AGENTS** 1029 Jones St., San Francisco, CA 94109 *Michael Larsen*

**LESCHER & LESCHER, LTD.** 67 Irving Pl. (10003) *Michael Choate, Robert Lescher, Susan Lescher*

**ELLEN LEVINE LITERARY AGENCY, INC.** 15 E. 26th St., Suite 1801 (10010–1505) *Anne Dubuisson, Diana Finch, Ellen Levine*

**WENDY LIPKIND AGENCY** 165 E. 66th St. (10021) *Wendy Lipkind*

849

**LONDON STAR PROMOTIONS** 7131 Owensmouth Ave., #C116, Canoga Park, CA 91303 *Lore London*

**NANCY LOVE LITERARY AGENCY** 250 E. 65th St. (10021) *Nancy Love*

**BARBARA LOWENSTEIN ASSOCIATES, INC.** 121 W. 27th St., Suite 601 (10001) *Barbara Lowenstein*

**DONALD MAASS LITERARY AGENCY** 304 W. 92nd St., 8P (10025) *Donald Maass*

**MARGARET MCBRIDE LITERARY AGENCY** 4350 Executive Dr., Suite 225, San Diego, CA 92121 *Margaret McBride*

**GERARD MCCAULEY AGENCY, INC.** P.O. Box AE, Katonah, NY 10536 *Gerard McCauley*

**ANITA D. MCCLELLAN ASSOCIATES** 50 Stearns St., Cambridge, MA 02138 *Anita D. McClellan*

**MCINTOSH & OTIS, INC.** 310 Madison Ave. (10017) *Julie Fallowfield, Dorothy Markinko, Evva Pryor, Louisa Quayle, Eugene Winick*

**CAROL MANN LITERARY AGENCY** 55 Fifth Ave. (10003) *Carol Mann*

**JANET WILKENS MANUS LITERARY AGENCY** 417 E. 57th St., Suite 5D (10022) *Janet Wilkens Manus*

**DENISE MARCIL LITERARY AGENCY, INC.** 685 West End Ave. (10025) *Denise Marcil*

**BETTY MARKS** 176 E. 77th St., Suite 9F (10021) *Betty Marks*

**ELAINE MARKSON LITERARY AGENCY, INC.** 44 Greenwich St. (10011) *Elaine Markson*

**MILDRED MARMUR ASSOCIATES LTD.** 310 Madison Ave., Suite 607 (10017) *Mildred Marmur, Naomi H. Wittes*

**EVAN MARSHALL LITERARY AGENCY** 22 South Park St., Suite 216, Montclair, NJ 07042 *Lisa Healy, Evan Marshall*

**ELISABETH MARTON** 96 Fifth Ave. (10011) *Elisabeth Marton, Tonda Marton*

**HAROLD MATSON COMPANY, INC.** 276 Fifth Ave. (10001) *Ben Camardi, Jonathan Matson, Elizabeth McKee*

**CLAUDIA MENZA LITERARY AGENCY** 1170 Broadway (10001) *Claudia Menza*

**HELEN MERRILL, LTD.** 435 W. 23rd St., #1A (10011) *Mary Lou Aleskie, Helen Merrill*

**MARTHA MILLARD LITERARY AGENCY** 204 Park Ave., Madison, NJ 07940 *Martha Millard*

**HOWARD MORHAIM LITERARY AGENCY** 175 Fifth Ave., Suite 709 (10010) *Howard Morhaim*

**WILLIAM MORRIS AGENCY, INC.** 1350 Ave. of the Americas (10019) *Mel Berger, Pam Bernstein, Matthew Bialer, Michael Carlisle, Peter Franklin, Robert Gottlieb, Peter Hagan, George Lane, Owen Laster,*

Samuel Liff, Gilbert Parker, Marcy Posner, Esther Sherman, James Stein, Dan Strone

**MULTIMEDIA PRODUCT DEVELOPMENT, INC.** 410 S. Michigan Ave., Rm. 724, Chicago, IL 60605 *Jane Jordan Browne*

**JEAN V. NAGGAR LITERARY AGENCY, INC.** 216 E. 75th St. (10021) *Teresa Cavanaugh, Jean V. Naggar*

**RUTH NATHAN AGENCY** c/o Van Horn Co., 80 Fifth Ave., Suite 705 (10016) *Ruth Nathan*

**NEW ENGLAND PUBLISHING ASSOCIATES, INC.** P.O. Box 5, Chester, CT 06412 *Elizabeth Frost Knappman*

**THE BETSY NOLAN LITERARY AGENCY** 1700 California, Suite 707, San Francisco, CA 94109 *Betsy Nolan*

**HAROLD OBER ASSOCIATES, INC.** 425 Madison Ave. (10017) *Henry Dunow, Patricia Powell, Wendy Schmalz, Peter Shephard, Claire Smith, Craig Tenney, Phyllis Westberg*

**FIFI OSCARD AGENCY, INC.** 24 W. 40th St. (10018) *Carmen LaVia, Kevin McShane, Nancy Murray, Fifi Oscard, Peter Sawyer, Ivy Fisher Stone*

**THE RICHARD PARKS AGENCY** 138 E. 16th St., 5B (10003) *Richard Parks*

**L. PERKINS & ASSOCIATES** 330 Haven Ave., Apt. E (10033) *Lori Perkins*

**JAMES PETER ASSOCIATES, INC.** P.O. Box 772, Tenafly, NJ 07670 *Bert Holtje*

**BELLA POMER AGENCY, INC.** 22 Shallmar Blvd., PH2, Toronto, Ont. M5N 2Z8, Canada *Bella Pomer*

**SUSAN ANN PROTTER** 110 W. 40th St., Suite 1408 (10018) *Susan Ann Protter*

**ROBERTA PRYOR, INC.** 24 W. 55th St. (10019) *Roberta Pryor*

**RAINES & RAINES** 71 Park Ave. (10016) *Mrs. Joan Raines, Theron Raines*

**HELEN REES LITERARY AGENCY** 308 Commonwealth Ave., Boston, MA 02116 *Helen Rees*

**RHODES LITERARY AGENCY** 140 West End Ave. (10023) *Joseph Rhodes*

**FLORA ROBERTS, INC.** 157 W. 57th St., Penthouse A (10019) *Sarah Douglas, Flora Roberts*

**ROSENSTONE/WENDER** 3 E. 48th St. (10017) *Renata Cobbs, Suzie Perlman Cohen, Howard Rosenstone, Phyllis Wender*

**JANE ROTROSEN AGENCY** 318 E. 51st St. (10022) *Jane Rotrosen*

**RUSSELL & VOLKENING, INC.** 50 W. 29th St. (10001) *Miriam Altshuler, Timothy Seldes*

**RAPHAEL SAGALYN, INC.** 1520 New Hampshire Ave. N.W., Washington, DC 20036 *Raphael Sagalyn*

851

**SCHAFFNER AGENCY, INC.** 6625 Casas Adobes Rd., Tucson, AZ 85704 *Timothy Schaffner*

**HAROLD SCHMIDT** 668 Greenwich St., Apt. 1005 (10014) *Harold Schmidt*

**SUSAN SCHULMAN LITERARY AGENCY** 454 W. 44th St. (10036) *Susan Schulman*

**ARTHUR P. SCHWARTZ LITERARY AGENT** 16 Winton St., P.O. Box 9132, St. Albans, Christchurch 1, New Zealand *Arthur P. Schwartz*

**EDYTHEA GINIS SELMAN LITERARY AGENT** 14 Washington Pl. (10003) *Edythea Ginis Selman*

**CHARLOTTE SHEEDY LITERARY AGENCY** 41 King St. (10014) *Ellen Geiger, Charlotte Sheedy*

**THE SHUKAT COMPANY, LTD.** 340 W. 55th St., Suite 1A (10019) *Scott Shukat*

**ROSALIE SIEGEL INTERNATIONAL LITERARY AGENCY, INC.** 111 Murphy Dr., Pennington, NJ 08543 *Rosalie Siegel*

**IRENE SKOLNIK** Curtis Brown Agency, 10 Astor Pl. (10003)

**SMITH/SKOLNIK LITERARY AGENCY** 23 E. 10th St., #712 (10003) *Nikki Smith*

**ELYSE SOMMER, INC.** 110–34 73rd Rd., P.O. Box 1133, Forest Hills, NY 11375 *Elyse Sommer*

**PHILIP G. SPITZER LITERARY AGENCY** 788 Ninth Ave. (10019) *Philip Spitzer*

**STEPPING STONE LITERARY AGENCY** 59 W. 71st St., Apt. 9B (10023) *Sarah Jane Freymann*

**STERLING LORD LITERISTIC, INC.** 1 Madison Ave. (10010) *Philippa Brophy, Elizabeth Grossman, Elizabeth Kaplan, Stuart Krichevsky, Peter Matson*

**GLORIA STERN AGENCY** 1230 Park Ave. (10128) *Gloria Stern*

**ROBIN STRAUS AGENCY, INC.** 229 E. 79th St. (10021) *Robin Straus*

**TAMS-WITMARK MUSIC LIBRARY, INC.** 560 Lexington Ave. (10022) *Louis H. Aborn, Sargent L. Aborn, Kenneth Duffy, Peter A. Hut, Robert Aborn Hut*

**ROSLYN TARG LITERARY AGENCY, INC.** 105 W. 13th St., #15E (10011) *Roslyn Targ*

**PATRICIA TEAL LITERARY AGENCY** 2036 Vista del Rosa, Fullerton, CA 92631 *Patricia Teal*

**SUSAN P. URSTADT** 103 Brushy Ridge Rd., New Canaan, CT 06840 *Susan P. Urstadt*

**RALPH VICINANZA LTD.** 111 Eighth Ave., Suite 1501 (10011) *Ralph Vicinanza*

**THE WALLACE AGENCY** 177 E. 70th St. (10021) *Karina Gee, Lois Wallace, Thomas C. Wallace*

**WATERSIDE PRODUCTIONS, INC.** 2191 San Elijo Ave., Cardiff-by-the-Sea, CA 92024 *Julie Castiglia*

**THE WENDY WEIL AGENCY, INC.** 232 Madison Ave., Suite 1300 (10016) *Wendy Weil*

**RHODA WEYR AGENCY** 151 Bergen St., Brooklyn, NY 11217 *Rhoda Weyr*

**AUDREY A. WOLF LITERARY AGENCY** 1001 Connecticut Ave. N.W., Suite 1210, Washington, DC 20036 *Audrey A. Wolf*

**ANN WRIGHT REPRESENTATIVES, INC.** 136 E. 56th St. (10022–3615) *Ann Wright*

**WRITERS AND ARTISTS AGENCY** 19 W. 44th St., Suite 1000 (10036) *William Craver, Scott Hudson*

**WRITERS HOUSE, INC.** 21 W. 26th St. (10010) *Amy Berkower, Susan Cohen, Merilee Heifetz, Fran Lebowitz, Albert Zuckerman*

**MARY YOST ASSOCIATES, INC.** 59 E. 54th St., #72 (10022) *Mary Yost*

**E.M. ZAHLER AGENCY** 181 Eighth Ave., Suite 6 (10011) *E.M. Zahler*

**SUSAN ZECKENDORF ASSOCIATES, INC.** 171 W. 57th St. (10019) *Susan Zeckendorf*

# INDEX TO MARKETS

A. D. Players .................... 753
A+/Incider .................... 682
AAA World ................. 604, 631
ABA Journal .................... 634
Abbey Press .................... 765
Abingdon Press .................. 765
Aboard ........................ 608
Aboriginal SF ............... 696, 704
Academic Press ................. 766
Academy of American Poets .... 710, 836
Academy Theatre ................ 752
Accent Books ................... 766
Accent on Living ............... 662
Accent/Travelog .............. 578, 604
Access Control ................. 634
Access Publishers .............. 766
Accessories Magazine ........... 634
Ace Books ..................... 766
Acres USA .................... 667
Across the Board ............... 634
Actors Theatre of Louisville ....... 753
Ad Astra ..................... 682
Adama Books .................. 766
Addison-Wesley Publishing Co. ..... 766
Adirondack Life ................ 590
Advance ...................... 650
Adventure Road ................ 604
Africa Report ................. 587
Agni Review, The .............. 714
Agri-Book Magazine ............. 667
Aha! Hispanic Arts News ......... 671
Aim Magazine ................. 696
Air & Space .................. 682
Airbrush Action ............... 672
Airfare: The Magazine for Airline
    Employees .................. 604
Alabama Literary Review ......... 715
Alabama Shakespeare Festival ...... 753
Aladdin Books ................. 766
Alaska ....................... 590
Alaska Airlines Magazine ......... 608
Alaska Northwest Books .......... 766
Alaska Quarterly Review .......... 715
Albatross ..................... 715
Albee Foundation, Inc., The Edward F. 814
Alfred Hitchcock's Mystery
    Magazine ................. 696, 702
Algonquin Books of Chapel Hill .... 766
Alive Now! .................... 749
Alley Theatre ................. 753
Alliance Theatre Company ......... 753
Allied Publications ............. 578
Aloha, the Magazine of Hawaii and the
    Pacific .............. 590, 696, 707
Alternate Realities .............. 704
Alternative Energy Retailer ......... 634
Amaranth Review, The ........... 715

Amazing Stories .............. 697, 704
Amberley Greeting Card Company .. 712
Amelia ....................... 715
America ..................... 650, 707
America West Airlines Magazine .... 608
American Art Journal, The ........ 672
American Baby ............... 616, 662
American Bee Journal ............ 667
American Bible Society Record ..... 650
American Book Review, The ....... 715
American Coin-Op ............... 635
American Crime Writers League .... 837
American Dane .................. 648
American Demographics ........... 635
American Farriers Journal ..... 635, 686
American Field, The ..... 619, 669, 738
American Fitness ............. 632, 662
American Forests ............... 669
American Greetings .............. 712
American Handgunner ............ 620
American Health ............. 616, 662
American Heritage ............ 578, 689
American Heritage of Invention &
    Technology .............. 682, 689
American History Illustrated ... 578, 689
American Hunter ............... 620
American Indian Art Magazine ..... 672
American Jewish History ....... 650, 689
American Journal of Nursing ....... 662
American Legion, The ......... 578, 587
American Literary Review ........ 715
American Living History Theater .... 753
American Medical News .......... 635
American Medical Writers Association 837
American Motorcyclist ........ 620, 631
American Newspaper Carrier, The ... 738
American Place Theatre .......... 753
American Poetry Review, The ..... 715
American Psychiatric Press, The .... 766
American Quarterly .............. 715
American Repertory Theatre ....... 753
American Rifleman, The .......... 620
American Rose Magazine, The ...... 613
American Salesman, The .......... 635
American Salon ................. 635
American Scholar, The .... 587, 708, 715
American School & University .. 635, 665
American Society of Journalists and
    Authors, Inc. ................. 837
American Stage ................. 753
American Stage Company .......... 753
American Stanislavski Theatre ...... 753
American Theatre ............... 672
American Theatre of Actors ........ 753
American Visions, the Magazine of
    Afro-American Culture ..... 579, 672
American Woodworker ............ 676

American Writing . . . . . . . . . . . . . . . . 715
Amherst Review . . . . . . . . . . . . . . . . . 715
Amicus Journal, The . . . . . . . . . . 587, 669
Amiga World . . . . . . . . . . . . . . . . . . . . 682
Amit Woman . . . . . . . . . . . . . . . . . . . . 650
Ampersand Press . . . . . . . . . . . . . . . . 710
Analog: Science Fiction/Science
    Fact . . . . . . . . . . . . . . . . . . . . . 697, 704
Anchor Books . . . . . . . . . . . . . . . . . . . 766
And Books . . . . . . . . . . . . . . . . . . . . . 766
Anderson Playwrights Series, Inc.,
    Maxwell . . . . . . . . . . . . . . . . . . . . . 753
Anglican Journal . . . . . . . . . . . . . . . . 650
Animals . . . . . . . . . . . . . . . . . . . . . . . 669
Annals of St. Anne de Beaupré . . . . . 650
Another Chicago Magazine . . . . . . . . 715
Antaeus . . . . . . . . . . . . . . . . . . . . . . . 716
Antietam Review . . . . . . . . . . . . . . . . 716
Antigonish Review, The . . . . . . . . . . . 716
Antioch Review . . . . . . . . . . . . . . . . . 716
Antique Monthly . . . . . . . . . . . . . . . . 676
Antique Trader Weekly, The . . . . . . . 676
Antiques & Auction News . . . . . . . . . 676
Antiqueweek . . . . . . . . . . . . . . . . . . . 676
AOPA Pilot . . . . . . . . . . . . . . . . . . . . 676
Apalachee Quarterly . . . . . . . . . . . . . 716
Appalachia . . . . . . . . . . . . . . . . . . . . . 716
Appalachian Mountain Club Books . . 766
Apple Books . . . . . . . . . . . . . . . . . . . 767
Apprise . . . . . . . . . . . . . . . . . . . . . . . 590
Aquarium Fish . . . . . . . . . . . . . . 676, 686
Arachne . . . . . . . . . . . . . . . . . . . . . . . 716
Arcade Publishing . . . . . . . . . . . . . . . 767
Archaeology . . . . . . . . . . . . . . . . . . . . 683
Architecture . . . . . . . . . . . . . . . . . . . . 635
Archway Paperbacks . . . . . . . . . . . . . 767
Arco Publishing . . . . . . . . . . . . . . . . . 767
Area Development Magazine . . . . . . . 635
Arena Stage . . . . . . . . . . . . . . . . . . . . 754
Argonaut . . . . . . . . . . . . . . . . . . . . . . 704
Argus Leader, The . . . . . . . . . . . . . . . 692
Arizona Highways . . . . . . . . . . . 590, 604
Arizona Quarterly . . . . . . . . . . . . . . . 716
Arkansas Repertory Theatre Company 754
Arkansas Times . . . . . . . . . . . . . . . . . 590
Arkin Magazine Syndicate . . . . . . . . . 801
Armchair Detective . . . . . . . . . . . . . . 703
Army Magazine . . . . . . . . . . . . . 688, 738
Army Reserve Magazine . . . . . . . . . . 688
Art & Antiques . . . . . . . . . . . . . . . . . 672
Art Business News . . . . . . . . . . . . . . . 635
Art Craft Play Company . . . . . . . . . . 762
Art Material Trade News . . . . . . . . . . 635
Artful Dodge . . . . . . . . . . . . . . . . . . . 716
Arthritis Today . . . . . . . . . . . . . . . . . . 662
Artist's Magazine, The . . . . . . . . . . . . 672
Artreach Touring Theatre . . . . . . . . . 754
Arts Atlantic . . . . . . . . . . . . . . . . . . . 672
Asia Pacific Travel . . . . . . . . . . . . . . . 604
Association of Hispanic Arts, Inc. . . . 837
Astarte Shell Press . . . . . . . . . . . . . . . 767

Astronomy . . . . . . . . . . . . . . . . . . . . . 683
Atheneum Publishers . . . . . . . . . . . . . 767
Atlanta . . . . . . . . . . . . . . . . . . . . . . . . 590
Atlantic, The . . . . . 579, 587, 697, 708, 738
Atlantic Center for the Arts . . . . . . . . 815
Atlantic City Magazine . . . . . . . . . . . 590
Atlantic Monthly Press, The . . . . . . . . 767
Atlantic Salmon Journal . . . 620, 669, 738
Audubon . . . . . . . . . . . . . . . . . . . . . . . 669
Aura Literary/Arts Review . . . . . . . . . 716
Authors Guild, Inc., The . . . . . . . . . . . 837
Authors League of America, Inc., The 838
Autograph Collector's Magazine . . . . 676
Automated Builder . . . . . . . . . . . . . . . 636
Avalon Books . . . . . . . . . . . . . . . . . . . 767
Avery Publishing Group . . . . . . . . . . . 767
Aviation Publishers . . . . . . . . . . . . . . 767
Avon Books . . . . . . . . . . . . . . . . . . . . 767

Baby Talk . . . . . . . . . . . . . . . . . . 617, 662
Back Home in Kentucky . . . . . . . . . . . 590
Backcountry Publications . . . . . . . . . . 767
Backpacker Magazine . . . . . . . . . . . . . 620
Backstretch, The . . . . . . . . . . . . . . . . . 620
Backwoodsman . . . . . . . . . . . . . . . . . . 689
Bad Haircut . . . . . . . . . . . . . . . . . . . . 716
Baen Books . . . . . . . . . . . . . . . . . . . . 767
Baja Explorer . . . . . . . . . . . 590, 604, 620
Baker Book House . . . . . . . . . . . . . . . 768
Baker's Plays . . . . . . . . . . . . . . . . . . . 762
Ballantine Books . . . . . . . . . . . . . . . . 768
Balsam Press . . . . . . . . . . . . . . . . . . . 768
Baltimore Sun, The . . . . . . . . . . . . . . 692
Bamboo Ridge, the Hawaii Writers'
    Quarterly . . . . . . . . . . . . . . . . . . . . 716
Bantam Books . . . . . . . . . . . . . . . . . . 768
Baptist Leader . . . . . . . . . . . . . . . . . . 650
Barnard College . . . . . . . . . . . . . . . . . 710
Barricade/Dembner Books . . . . . . . . . 768
Barrister . . . . . . . . . . . . . . . . . . . . . . . 636
Barron's . . . . . . . . . . . . . . . . . . . . 636, 768
Barter Theater . . . . . . . . . . . . . . . . . . 754
Baseball Forecast, Baseball Illustrated,
    Baseball Preview . . . . . . . . . . . . . . 620
Basketball Annual, Basketball Forecast 620
Bassin' . . . . . . . . . . . . . . . . . . . . . . . . 620
Bauhan, Publisher, William L. . . . . . . 768
BBW: Big Beautiful Woman . . . . . . . . 609
BC Outdoors . . . . . . . . . . . . . . . . . . . 620
Beacon Press . . . . . . . . . . . . . . . . . . . 768
Bear & Company, Inc. . . . . . . . . . . . . 768
Bear Essential News for Kids . . . . . . . 744
Beauty Education . . . . . . . . . . . . . . . . 636
Beech Tree Books . . . . . . . . . . . . . . . . 768
Beef . . . . . . . . . . . . . . . . . . . . . . . . . . 667
Belles Lettres . . . . . . . . . . . . . . . . . . . 716
Bellingham Review, The . . . . . . . . . . . 717
Bellowing Ark . . . . . . . . . . . . . . . . . . 717
Beloit Fiction Journal, The . . . . . . . . . 717
Beloit Poetry Journal . . . . . . . . . . . . . 717
Berkeley Repertory Theatre . . . . . . . . 754

Berkley Publishing Group .......... 768
Berkshire Theatre Festival .......... 754
Bethany House Publishers .......... 768
Better Health ................... 662
Better Homes and Gardens ..... 614, 633
Better Homes and Gardens Books ... 769
Beyond: Science Fiction & Fantasy .. 704
Bible Advocate ................... 651
Bicycle Retailer and Industry News .. 636
Bicycling ....................... 738
Big Apple Parents' Paper, The .. 590, 617
Bikereport ................... 620, 738
Binford & Mort Publishing ........ 769
Bioscience ...................... 683
Bird Talk .................... 676, 686
Bird Watcher's Digest ..... 620, 669, 676
Birmingham ..................... 591
Black American Literature Forum ... 717
Black Bear Review ............... 717
Black Belt ...................... 621
Black Collegian, The ............. 691
Black Confessions ................ 706
Black Elegance .................. 609
Black Enterprise ................. 633
Black River Review .............. 717
Black Romance ................... 706
Black Secrets .................... 706
Black Theatre Network ............ 838
Black Warrior Review, The ........ 717
Blade Magazine, The ............. 676
Blair, Publisher, John F. .......... 769
Bloomsbury Review, The .......... 717
Blue Mountain Arts, Inc. .......... 712
Blue Mountain Center ............ 815
Blue Ridge Country .......... 591, 604
Blue Unicorn ................... 717
Bluegrass Unlimited .............. 672
Blueline ....................... 717
Bluemoon Books, Inc. ............ 769
Boarshead Theater ............... 754
Boat Pennsylvania ............... 621
Boating Industry ................ 636
Boca Raton ..................... 591
Bon Appetit .................... 579
Bonus Books .................... 769
Book Report, The ................ 665
Books for Professionals ........... 769
Boston Globe, The ............... 693
Boston Globe Magazine, The ... 591, 697
Boston Herald ................... 693
Boston Magazine ................. 591
Boston Review ................... 717
Bostonia ....................... 579
Bottomfish ..................... 718
Boulevard ...................... 718
Boundary Waters Journal ...... 591, 621
Bow & Arrow Hunting ........... 621
Bowhunter Magazine .............. 621
Bowhunting World ............... 621
Bowlers Journal ................. 621
Bowling ....................... 621

Boyds Mill Press ................. 769
Boys' Life ................... 697, 749
Bradbury Press .................. 769
Branden Publishing Company ....... 769
Brick House Publishing ........... 769
Bridal Guide ................... 609
Bride's & Your Home ......... 609, 614
Bridge, The .................... 718
Brigade Leader .................. 651
Brigham Young University Press .... 798
Bristol Publishing Enterprises ....... 769
Bristol Riverside Theatre .......... 754
British American Arts Association ... 838
British Heritage ................. 604
Broadman Press ................. 769
Bronze Thrills .................. 706
Browndeer Press ................ 769
Buckeye Farm News .............. 667
Bucknell Review ................ 718
Bucknell University Press ...... 769, 798
Buffalo Spree Magazine ....... 591, 697
Builder ........................ 636
Bulfinch Press .................. 769
Business and Commercial Aviation .. 636
Business Atlanta ................. 636
Business in Broward .............. 591
Business in Palm Beach County ..... 591
Business Marketing .............. 636
Business Times .................. 636
Business Today .................. 636
Buzzworm ...................... 669
Byline ................... 691, 697, 738
Byte Magazine .................. 683

C&T Publishing ................. 770
Cacanadadada Review ............ 718
California Angler ................ 621
California Business ............... 636
California Highway Patrolman .. 604, 648
California Lawyer ................ 637
California University Theatre ....... 754
Calliope ....................... 718
Calliope: World History for Young
  People ...................... 744
Calyx, a Journal of Art & Literature
  by Women ................... 718
Camargo Foundation/Cassis, France . 815
Cambridge University Press ........ 798
Camelot Books .................. 770
Camera & Darkroom ............. 672
Campground Management ......... 637
Campus Life ................ 697, 750
Canadian ................... 605, 608
Canadian Fiction Magazine ........ 718
Canadian Stamp News ............ 677
Canadian Workshop Magazine .. 614, 677
Candlewick Press ................ 770
Cane Hill Press ................. 770
Canoe ........................ 621
Cape Cod Life .................. 591
Cape Rock, The ................. 718

Capilano Review, The .............. 718
Capper's ........ 579, 617, 697, 708, 738
Capstone Press, Inc. ................ 770
Car and Driver ................. 621, 631
Car Audio and Electronics ..... 579, 631
Car Craft ..................... 622, 631
Card Collector's Price Guide ....... 677
Card Player ...................... 677
Career Woman ................ 665, 691
Career World .................... 691
Careers and the Disabled ....... 665, 692
Caribbean Sports & Travel ......... 622
Caribbean Travel and Life ...... 591, 605
Caribbean Writer, The ............. 718
Carolina Quarterly ................ 718
Carologue ................... 591, 689
Carolrhoda Books ................. 770
Carroll and Graf Publishers, Inc. .... 770
Cascades East ................ 622, 738
Casino Player .................... 622
Cassandra Press .................. 770
Cat Fancy ................... 687, 697
Catalyst ........................ 719
Catholic Digest .............. 651, 738
Catholic Forester ............ 648, 697
Catholic Near East Magazine ....... 651
Catholic Twin Circle ............. 651
Catholic University of America Press,
   The ..................... 770, 798
CBT Directions ................... 683
Centennial Review, The ............ 719
Centrum ........................ 815
Challenge Magazine ............... 750
Change ...................... 579, 665
Chariot Family Publishing ......... 770
Charisma & Christian Life .......... 651
Chariton Review, The ............. 719
Charlotte Observer, The ........... 693
Charter/Diamond Books ........... 770
Chateau de Lesvault .............. 816
Chatelaine ................... 579, 609
Chatham Press ................... 770
Cheese Market News .............. 637
Chelsea Green Publishing Co. ....... 771
Chesapeake Bay Magazine .......... 622
Chess Life ...................... 677
Chic ........................... 695
Chicago ........................ 591
Chicago History .............. 592, 689
Chicago Review, The .............. 719
Chicago Review Press ............. 771
Chicago Tribune, The ............. 693
Chickadee ................... 738, 745
Chief Executive .................. 637
Children's Album ................. 745
Children's Digest ................. 745
Children's Playmate ... 708, 738, 745, 762
Childsplay, Inc. .................. 754
Chile Pepper ................. 605, 614
China, Glass & Tableware .......... 637
Chiron Review ................... 719

Christian Century, The ............ 651
Christian Education Journal ........ 665
Christian Home & School ...... 617, 651
Christian Medical & Dental Society
   Journal ...................... 651
Christian Parenting ............... 617
Christian Parenting Today ......... 651
Christian Retailing ............... 637
Christian Science Monitor,
   The ............. 579, 614, 693, 708
Christian Single ................. 652
Christianity and Crisis ......... 587, 652
Christianity Today ................ 652
Chronicle Books ................. 771
Church & State ............... 587, 652
Church Administration ............ 652
Church Educator ................. 652
Church Herald, The .............. 652
Church Management: The Clergy
   Journal ...................... 652
Church Musician, The ............. 738
Church Recreation Magazine ....... 652
Church Teachers .............. 652, 665
Cicada ......................... 719
Cimarron Review ................. 719
Cincinnati Poetry Review .......... 719
Circle in the Square/Uptown ....... 754
Circle K ........................ 692
Circle Repertory Company ......... 754
Circuit Rider .................... 653
City News .................. 592, 750
City Sports Magazine .......... 592, 622
Clarion Books ................... 771
Clark City Press ................. 771
Classic Stage Company ............ 755
Clavier Magazine ................. 672
Cleaning Management Magazine .... 637
Cleis Press ...................... 771
Cleveland Plain Dealer, The ........ 693
Cleveland State University Poetry
   Center ...................... 710
Cliffhanger Press ................. 771
Clinton Street ................... 592
Clockwatch Review ............... 719
Cloverdale Press ................. 771
Clubhouse ...................... 745
Cobblehill Books ................. 771
Cobblestone ................. 697, 745
Coffee House Press ............... 771
Collages & Bricolages ............. 719
Collector Editions ................ 677
Collectors News .................. 677
College Broadcaster .............. 692
Collier Books .................... 771
Colorado Homes & Lifestyles ... 592, 605
Colorado Review ................. 719
Columbia ............. 579, 648, 653
Columbia: A Magazine of Poetry &
   Prose ....................... 719
Columbia Journalism Review ....... 739
Columbia University Press ......... 798

Comics Journal, The .............. 720
Commentary ............. 587, 653, 698
Commercial Carrier Journal ........ 637
Common Ground Magazine .... 592, 698
Commonweal ............ 587, 653, 708
Compass, The ................ 579, 648
Compass: A Jesuit Journal ......... 653
Compcare Publishers .............. 771
Complete Woman ............. 609, 708
Compute ......................... 683
Compute Books ................... 771
Computer Graphics World ......... 637
Computercraft .................... 683
Concord and the North ........ 592, 637
Concordia Publishing House ........ 771
Concrete International ............. 637
Confident Living .................. 653
Confluence Press ................. 772
Confrontation .................... 720
Connecticut ...................... 592
Connecticut Family ........... 592, 617
Connecticut Poetry Review, The .... 720
Connecticut River Review .......... 720
Construction Specifier, The ........ 637
Consumer Reports Books .......... 772
Consumers Digest ............. 580, 633
Contemporary Books, Inc. .......... 772
Contemporary Drama Service ....... 762
Contemporary Features Syndicate ... 801
Convenience Store News ........... 637
Cooking for Profit ................ 638
Corporate Cashflow ........... 638, 739
Cosmopolitan ........ 580, 609, 698, 708
Cottages at Hedgebrook ........... 816
Council of Authors & Journalists, Inc. 838
Counted Cross-Stitch Plus .......... 677
Country ...................... 580, 617
Country Folk Art Magazine ........ 677
Country Handcrafts .............. 677
Country Journal .................. 580
Country Woman ...... 609, 698, 708, 739
Crab Creek Review .............. 720
Cracked ...................... 739, 750
Crafts 'n Things .................. 678
Craftsman Book Company .......... 772
Crain's Chicago Business .......... 638
Crain's Detroit Business .......... 592
Crazy Quilt ...................... 720
Cream City Review, The ........... 720
Creative Arts Book Co. ............ 772
Creative Theatre ................. 755
Credit and Collection Manager's Letter 638
Crescent Review, The ............. 720
Cricket ...................... 698, 745
Cricket Theatre, The ............. 755
Crisis, The ...................... 587
Critical Inquiry .................. 720
Cross Country Skier .............. 622
Crossing Press, The .............. 772
Crossroads Theatre Co. ........... 755
Cross-Stitch Plus ................ 678

Cross-Stitch Sampler ............. 678
Crowell, Thomas Y. ............... 772
Crown Books for Young Readers .... 772
Cruise Travel ................... 605
Crusader ....................... 653
Cumberland Poetry Review ........ 720
Cummington Community of the Arts 816
Current Comedy .................. 739
Current History ............. 587, 689
Currents ........................ 622
Curry Hill/Georgia .............. 816
Cycle World .................... 739
Cycling U.S.A. .................. 622

D .............................. 592
Daily Word ..................... 653
Dairy Foods Magazine ............ 638
Dairy Goat Journal .......... 667, 687
Dallas Life Magazine .......... 580, 592
Dallas Morning News ............ 693
Dance Magazine ................. 672
Dance Teacher Now ............. 672
Daniel and Company, John ........ 772
Darkroom Photography ........... 673
Daughters of Sarah .............. 653
DAW Books, Inc. ................ 772
Dayspring Greeting Cards ......... 712
Dealerscope Merchandising ........ 638
Dearborn Financial Publishing, Inc. .. 772
Decision ....................... 653
Del Rey Books .................. 772
Delacorte Press ................. 772
Delancey Press ................. 773
Delaware Theatre Company ....... 755
Delaware Today ................. 592
Dell Books ..................... 773
Delta Books .................... 773
Dental Economics ............... 638
Denver Center Theatre Company .... 755
Denver Quarterly ................ 720
Des Moines Register ............. 693
Descant ........................ 720
Detective Cases ................. 703
Detective Dragnet .............. 703
Detective Files ................. 703
Detroit Free Press ............... 693
Detroit Free Press Magazine ...... 593
Detroit Monthly ................. 593
Detroit News, The .............. 693
Detroit Repertory Theatre ........ 755
Devil's Millhopper, The .......... 721
Devin-Adair Publishers, Inc. ...... 773
Dial Books for Young Readers ...... 773
Digital News ................... 683
Dillon Press ................... 773
Discoveries ........... 653, 698, 745
Diver, The ..................... 622
Diver Magazine ................. 698
Diversion Magazine ............. 580
Djerassi Resident Artists Program ... 817
Dog Fancy ................. 678, 687

Dog River Review ................ 721
Doll Life ........................ 678
Dolls, the Collector's Magazine ..... 678
Dolphin Log, The ................ 745
Dorland Mountain Arts Colony ..... 817
Dorling Kindersley, Inc. ........... 773
Dorset Colony House .............. 817
Dorset Theatre Festival ............ 755
Double D. Western ............... 773
Doubleday and Co. ............... 773
Down East ...................... 593
Down Memory Lane .............. 685
Dragon Magazine ................. 704
Dramatic Publishing Co., The ...... 762
Dramatics .................. 673, 762
Dramatists Guild, The ............ 838
Dreams & Visions ............ 653, 721
Driftwood Showboat .............. 755
Drug Topics ..................... 638
Duke University Press ............. 798
Dunne Books, Thomas ............. 773
Duquesne University Press ..... 773, 798
Dutton Adult .................... 773
Dutton Children's Books .......... 773

Early American Life .......... 605, 689
Earth's Daughters ............... 721
East West Players ................ 755
East West: The Journal of Natural Health
   & Living ............. 617, 632, 663
Eastside Parent .................. 617
Easyriders Magazine .............. 698
Ebony ......................... 580
Eccentric Circles Theatre .......... 755
Eerdmans Publishing Company, Inc.,
   Wm. B ...................... 774
Eighteenth Century Studies ......... 690
Eldridge Publishing Company ....... 762
Electronics Now ................. 683
ELF: Eclectic Literary Forum ...... 721
Elks Magazine, The ....... 580, 648, 739
Elle ........................... 610
Elle Decor ...................... 614
Ellery Queen's Mystery Magazine 698, 703
Embers ........................ 721
EMC Corp. ..................... 774
Emergency ...................... 638
Employee Services Management ..... 638
Empty Space Theatre, The ......... 756
Endless Vacation ................. 605
Engravers Journal, The ........ 638, 673
Ensemble Studio Theatre .......... 756
Ensemble Theatre Company of Marin 756
Enslow Publishers, Inc. ............ 774
Entrepreneur .................... 638
Entrepreneurial Woman ............ 639
Environment ................. 588, 683
Equal Opportunity ............ 665, 692
Equinox ........................ 670
Equipment World ................. 639
Equus ...................... 622, 687

Erdmann Publishing, Robert ........ 774
Erie & Chautauqua Magazine ....... 593
Eriksson, Publisher, Paul S. ........ 774
Esquire ................. 580, 613, 698
Essence .................... 580, 610
Essential News for Kids ........... 745
Estrin Publishing ................. 774
Evangel ................. 653, 698, 708
Evangelical Beacon ................ 654
Evangelizing Today's Child ......... 654
Evans & Co., Inc., M. ............. 774
Event .......................... 721
Event Horizon Press .............. 774
Exceptional Parent ............... 617
Executive Female ............. 610, 639
Expecting ...................... 663
Exploring ...................... 750

Faber and Faber ................. 774
Faces ..................... 739, 745
Facts On File Publications ......... 774
Faith 'n Stuff ................. 698, 746
Faith Today .................... 654
Family Circle 580, 605, 610, 633, 698, 708
Family Motor Coaching ........... 623
Fanfare ........................ 774
Fangoria ....................... 704
Fantasy and Science Fiction ........ 704
Fantasy Macabre ................. 705
Farm and Ranch Living ....... 614, 668
Farm Industry News .............. 668
Farm Journal ................ 639, 668
Farm Store ..................... 639
Farmer's Market ................. 721
Farrar, Straus & Giroux ........... 774
Fate ...................... 617, 739
Fawcett/Ivy Books ............... 775
Fell Publishers, Inc. .............. 775
Fellowship in Prayer .............. 654
Feminist Press at The City University of
   New York, The ................ 775
Fiberarts ....................... 678
Fiction International .......... 699, 721
Fiddlehead, The ................. 721
Field .......................... 721
Field & Stream .............. 623, 739
Fielding Travel Books ............. 775
Figment: Tales from the Imagination . 705
Film Quarterly .................. 673
Fine Arts Work Center in Provincetown 817
Fine, Inc., Donald I. .............. 775
Fine Madness ................... 721
Finescale Modeler ................ 678
Firebrand Books ................. 775
Firehouse ...................... 648
First for Women .............. 610, 699
Fishing Tackle Retailer Magazine ... 639
Fishing World ................... 623
Fitness .................... 632, 663
Fitness Management ............... 639
Flare Books .................... 775

Flint Journal, The ................ 693
Florida Grower & Rancher ......... 668
Florida Gulf Coast Homebuyer's Guide 593
Florida Home & Garden ....... 593, 614
Florida Horse, The ................ 623
Florida Keys Magazine ............ 593
Florida Studio Theatre ............ 756
Florida Trend ................... 593
Florida Wildlife .............. 593, 670
Florist ........................ 639
Flower & Garden Magazine ........ 614
Flowers & ...................... 639
Flute Talk ..................... 673
Fly Fisherman .................. 623
Fly Rod & Reel ............. 623, 699
Focus ...................... 648, 683
Folio ......................... 721
Food & Wine ................... 614
Food Management ............... 639
Football Digest ................. 623
Football Forecast ............... 623
Footsteps Press ................. 705
Footwork, the Paterson Literary Review 721
Ford New Holland News ......... 648
Foreign Service Journal ........... 588
Fortress Press .................. 775
Foundation News ................ 665
Four Winds Press ............... 775
Foursquare World Advance ....... 654
Free Inquiry ................... 722
Free Press, The ................ 775
Free Spirit: News & Views on Growing
   Up ........................ 746
Freedom Greeting Card Company ... 712
Freeman, The .................. 588
Freeway ...................... 750
Frequent Flyer ................. 639
Friend, The ................... 746
Friendly Exchange .............. 605
Friends Journal ................. 654
Friends, the Chevy Owners' Magazine 649
Friends United Press ............. 775
Front Page Detective ............ 703
Fugitive! ...................... 703
Fur-Fish-Game ................. 623
Furrow, The ............... 649, 668
Future, Now: Innovative Video,
   The .................... 639, 673
Futurist, The .................. 683

Gallery ............ 613, 695, 699, 739
Game and Fish Publications ....... 623
Games ..................... 678, 739
Garbage: The Practical Journal for the
   Environment ................ 670
Garden Design ................. 614
Garden Way Publishing Company ... 775
Garrett Park Press .............. 775
Geer Theatricum Botanicum, Will ... 756
Gem, The ..................... 654
General Aviation News & Flyer ..... 640

Genesis ....................... 695
Genetic Engineering News ..... 640, 684
Geobyte ....................... 649
Georgia Journal ................ 593
Georgia Review, The ............ 722
Georgia State University Business
   Press ................... 775, 798
Geringer Books, Laura ........... 775
Gettysburg Review, The .......... 722
Gibbs Smith Publisher/Peregrine
   Smith Books ................ 775
Gifford Children's Theater, Emmy ... 756
Gifted Education Press Newsletter ... 665
Giniger Co. Inc., The K.S. ........ 776
Glamour .............. 580, 610, 740
Glenbridge Publishing ............ 776
Glimmer Train Press .......... 699, 722
Global Production ............... 640
Globe ......................... 581
Globe Communications Corp........ 703
Globe Pequot Press, The .......... 776
Glory Songs .................... 740
Goal ......................... 623
Gold Eagle Books ............... 776
Golden Press ................... 776
Golden West Publishers ........... 776
Golden Years ............ 581, 633, 685
Goldenseal ................. 593, 690
Golf Course News .............. 640
Golf Digest ................. 623, 699
Golf for Women ................ 623
Golf Journal ................... 623
Golf Magazine ................. 624
Good Housekeeping 581, 610, 699, 708, 740
Good Reading Magazine .......... 581
Goodman Theatre, The .......... 756
Graham House Review ........... 722
Grain ......................... 722
Grand Rapids .................. 593
Graywolf Press ................. 776
Great Expeditions .............. 605
Great River Review ............. 722
Green Tiger Press ............... 776
Greenhouse Manager ............ 640
Green's Magazine ............... 722
Greensboro Review, The ......... 722
Greenwillow Books ............. 776
Greyhound Review, The ......... 624
Grit ...................... 581, 699
Grosset and Dunlap, Inc. ......... 776
Group, the Youth Ministry Magazine 654
Grove Press, Inc. ............... 776
Growing Child/Growing Parent ..... 617
Grue Magazine ................. 705
Guide ......................... 654
Guideposts ................. 654, 740
Guitar Player Magazine .......... 673
Gulf Coast Golfer ........... 593, 624
Gulfshore Life ............... 594, 605
Gulliver Books ................. 776
Gun Digest .................... 624

Gun Dog .................... 624, 699
Gun World ..................... 624
Guns & Ammo .................. 624
Guthrie Centre, The ............. 817
Guthrie Theater, The ............ 756

Half Tones to Jubilee ............ 722
Hallmark Cards, Inc. ............. 712
Hambidge Center, The ........... 818
Hammond, Inc. ................. 776
Hampshire East .............. 594, 640
Hang Gliding .................... 624
Harbinger House ................ 776
Harcourt Brace Jovanovich ........ 776
Hardware Age .................. 640
Hardware Trade ................. 640
Harlequin Books/Canada .......... 777
Harlequin Books/U.S. ............ 777
Harper Paperbacks ............... 777
HarperCollins Children's Books .... 777
HarperCollins Publishers .......... 777
Harper's Magazine ............... 581
Harris & Associates Features ....... 801
Harrisburg Community Theatre ..... 756
Harrowsmith .................... 668
Harrowsmith Country Life . 614, 668, 670
Harvard Business Review ......... 640
Harvard Common Press .......... 777
Harvard University Press ......... 798
Harvest House Publishers ......... 777
Haunts .................... 705, 722
Hawaii ........................ 594
Hawaii Review .................. 722
Hawthornden Castle International
  Retreat for Writers ............ 818
Hayden's Ferry Review ........... 722
Hazelden Educational Materials ..... 778
HBJ Professional Publishing ....... 776
Headquarters Detective ........... 703
Health ........................ 663
Health Communications, Inc. ....... 778
Health Foods Business ........... 640
Health Plus Publishers ........... 778
Health Press ................... 778
Health Progress ................. 640
Health Watch ................... 663
Hearst Books/Hearst Marine Books .. 778
Heartfire Romances .............. 778
Hearth & Home .............. 640, 740
Heath & Company, D. C. ......... 778
Heating/Piping/Air Conditioning .... 641
Hemingway Western Studies Series .. 778
Herald of Holiness .............. 655
Herald Press ................... 778
Herb Quarterly, The ............ 615
Heresies: A Feminist Publication on Art
  and Politics .................. 723
Heuer Publishing Company ........ 762
HG: House & Garden ........ 581, 615
HiCall ..................... 699, 750
High Country News .............. 594

Highlander, The .............. 690, 723
Highlights for Children ........ 699, 746
Hippocrene Books ............... 778
Hippodrome State Theatre ........ 756
Hispanic Link News Service ....... 801
Hispanic Outlook in Higher Education,
  The ........................ 665
Historic Preservation .......... 581, 690
History News ................... 690
Hockey Illustrated .............. 624
Holiday House, Inc. ............. 778
Hollins Critic, The .............. 723
Hollywood Inside Syndicate, The .... 801
Hollywood Theater Company ....... 756
Holt and Co., Henry ............ 778
Home ......................... 581
Home Builder Press ............. 778
Home Education Magazine ......... 665
Home Life ............... 618, 655, 723
Home Mechanix ................. 615
Home Office Computing ....... 641, 684
Home Planet News ............... 723
Home Shop Machinist, The ........ 678
Hometown Press ................ 700
Honolulu ...................... 594
Honolulu Theatre for Youth ....... 756
Hopscotch, the Magazine for Girls .. 746
Horizon Theatre Company ......... 757
Horse & Rider .............. 624, 687
Horse Illustrated ................ 687
Horsemen's Yankee Pedlar ..... 624, 687
Horseplay .................. 624, 687
Horticulture ................... 615
Hospital Supervisor's Bulletin ...... 641
Hospitals ..................... 641
Hot Rod ...................... 631
Houghton Mifflin Company ....... 779
House Beautiful ............. 581, 615
Houseplant Magazine ......... 615, 670
Houston Metropolitan Magazine .... 594
Houston Post, The .............. 693
Howling Dog ................... 723
H.P. Books .................... 776
Human Resource Executive ........ 641
Humor Magazine ................ 740
Humpty Dumpty's Magazine ....... 746
Hunter Publishing, Inc. .......... 779
Huntington Theatre Company ...... 757
Hurricane Alice: A Feminist Quarterly 723
Hyperion ...................... 779

I.D. .......................... 750
Idea Today ................. 632, 663
Ideals ........................ 610
Illinois Entertainer ............. 594
Illinois Magazine ............... 594
Illinois Theatre Center .......... 757
Illinois Writers Review .......... 723
Illustrated Stage Company ........ 757
In Health ..................... 663
In the Company of Poets ......... 723

Inc................................ 641
Income Opportunities .............. 641
Income Plus ....................... 641
Independent Business .............. 641
Independent Living ....... 618, 665, 740
India Currents ................ 605, 673
Indian Life ....................... 655
Indiana Review .................... 723
Indiana University Press ....... 779, 798
Indianapolis Monthly .............. 594
Indianapolis Star ................. 694
Industrial Photography ............ 673
In-Fisherman, The ................. 624
Infomart Magazine ................. 684
Inquirer Magazine ............ 581, 588
Inside Chicago .................... 594
Inside Detective .................. 703
Inside Magazine ............. 581, 655
Inside Sports ..................... 625
Inside Texas Running .............. 625
Instant & Small Commercial Printer . 641
Instructor Magazine ............... 665
Interim............................ 723
International Association of Theatre for
    Children and Young People ..... 839
International Business ............. 641
International Design............... 641
International Doll World .......... 678
International Living .............. 606
International Musician ............ 673
International Society of Dramatists, The  839
International Wildlife ............. 670
International Women's Writing Guild,
    The .......................... 839
Intimacy .......................... 706
Invisible Theatre ................. 757
Iowa Review, The .................. 723
Iowan Magazine, The .............. 594
Irish America ..................... 588
Isaac Asimov's Science Fiction
    Magazine .................. 700, 705
Island Press ...................... 779
Islands ........................... 606
ITC Communicator ................. 666

Jacaranda Review .................. 723
Jack and Jill ..................... 746
Jacksonville Magazine ............. 594
James Books, Alice ............... 779
Jazziz ............................ 673
Jems, Journal of Emergency Medical
    Services ..................... 642
Jewish Currents .............. 618, 655
Jewish Monthly, The .............. 655
Jewish Repertory Theatre .......... 757
Jive............................... 706
Johns Hopkins University Press, The . 798
Johnson Books, Inc. .............. 779
Jonathan David Publishers, Inc. ..... 779
Journal of Career Planning &
    Employment ................. 692

Journal of Christian Nursing ...... 655
Journal of the West ........... 594, 690
Journey ..................... 655, 708
Joy Street Books .................. 779
Julian Theatre, The .............. 757
Junior Trails ..................... 746
Just for Laughs ................... 740
Just Us Books ..................... 779

Kalan ............................. 712
Kalani Honua ...................... 818
Kaleidoscope ...................... 723
Kansas! ........................... 595
Kansas Quarterly .................. 724
Karamu ............................ 724
Kar-Ben Copies ................... 779
Keats Publishing, Inc. ............ 780
Kent State University Press .... 780, 798
Kentucky Living ................... 595
Kenyon Review, The ............... 724
Key Horizons ............ 581, 595, 685
Key to Christian Education .... 655, 666
Keyboard Magazine ................ 674
Keynoter .......................... 750
Kid City .......................... 747
King Features Syndicate ........... 801
Kiosk ............................. 724
Kiplinger's Personal Finance Magazine 633
Kitplanes ......................... 678
Kiwanis ................. 581, 633, 649
Knopf Books for Young Readers,
    Alfred A...................... 780
Knopf, Inc., Alfred A. ............ 780
Kodansha International ............ 780
Kumu Kahua ....................... 757

L.A. West ......................... 595
Labor's Heritage .............. 588, 690
Ladies' Home
    Journal ...... 582, 610, 700, 708, 740
Ladybug ........................... 747
Lady's Circle ..................... 611
Lake Superior Magazine ........... 595
Lakeland Boating .................. 625
Lark Books ........................ 780
Laurel-Leaf ....................... 780
Leadership ........................ 655
Leadership Publishers, Inc. ..... 666, 780
Leading Edge, The ............ 705, 724
Learning 92/93 .................... 666
Lear's ............................ 611
Leatherneck ....................... 688
Leighton Artist Colony ............ 818
Leisure Books ..................... 780
Let's Live ........................ 663
Liberty Magazine .................. 655
Library Talk ...................... 666
Life in the Times ......... 582, 606, 688
Life Journey General Titles ......... 780
Lifetime Books, Inc. .............. 780
Light and Life..................... 656

Liguorian .......................... 656
Lilith, The Jewish Women's Magazine 724
Link-Up ........................... 684
Lion, The ......................... 649
Lion and the Unicorn, The ......... 724
Lion Publishing ................... 780
Lippincott Company, J.B. .......... 780
Listen Magazine .............. 582, 750
Literary Magazine Review .......... 724
Literary Review, The .............. 724
Little, Brown & Co. ............... 780
Little Rooster Books .............. 781
Little Simon ...................... 781
Live Oak Theatre .................. 757
Living Light, The ................. 656
Living With Children .......... 618, 656
Living With Preschoolers ...... 618, 656
Living With Teenagers ......... 618, 656
Llamas ....................... 642, 687
Llewellyn Publications ............ 781
Lodestar .......................... 781
Log Home Guide for Builders & Buyers 615
Log Home Living ................... 615
Lollipops .................... 700, 747
Long Beach Press-Telegram ......... 694
Long Shot ......................... 724
Long Story, The ................... 724
Longmeadow Press .................. 781
Look, The ......................... 595
Lookout, The ................. 656, 700
Los Angeles Designers' Theatre .... 757
Los Angeles Magazine .............. 595
Los Angeles Reader ................ 595
Los Angeles Times ................. 694
Los Angeles Times Magazine ........ 595
Los Angeles Times Syndicate ....... 801
Lost Creek Letters ................ 724
Lost Treasure ..................... 678
Lothrop, Lee & Shepard Books ...... 781
Lotus ............................. 642
Louisiana State University Press ... 798
Louisville ........................ 595
Lovegram Romances ................. 781
Loveswept ......................... 781
Loyola University Press ....... 781, 798
Lutheran, The ..................... 656
Lyons & Burford, Publishers ....... 781
Lyra .............................. 725

McCall's ............ 582, 611, 700, 708
MacDowell Colony, The ............. 819
McElderry Books, Margaret K. ...... 781
McFarland & Company, Inc.,
  Publishers ...................... 781
Machine Design .................... 642
Macmillan Children's Book Group ... 781
Macmillan Publishing Co., Inc. .... 782
Macworld .......................... 684
Mad Magazine ...................... 740
Mademoiselle ............ 582, 611, 700
Madison Books ..................... 782

Magazine Design & Production ..... 642
Magazine of Fantasy and Science
  Fiction, The .............. 700, 705
Magic Realism ................ 705, 725
Magic Theatre, The ............... 757
Magical Blend .................... 618
Maintenance Technology ........... 642
Malahat Review, The .............. 725
Manage ........................... 642
Manchester ................... 595, 642
Manhattan Review, The ............ 725
Manhattan Theatre Club ........... 758
Manufacturing Systems ............ 642
Marine Corps Gazette ............. 688
Marion Zimmer Bradley's Fantasy
  Magazine ...................... 705
Markowski International Publishers .. 782
Maryknoll ........................ 656
Massachusetts Review ............. 725
Master Detective ................. 703
Mature Living ....... 656, 685, 700, 740
Mature Years ........ 656, 685, 709, 740
MD Magazine ...................... 582
Meadowbrook Press ................ 782
Media & Methods .................. 666
Media History Digest ............. 674
Medical Industry Executive ....... 642
Mega-Books ....................... 782
Memphis .......................... 596
Memphis Business Journal ......... 642
Mennonite, The ................... 656
Men's Fitness ............ 613, 625, 632
Men's Health ................ 613, 625
Mercury House .................... 782
Meredith Corp. Book Group ........ 782
Merlyn's Pen: The National Magazine
  of Student Writing ............ 750
Messenger of the Sacred Heart .... 657
Messner, Julian .................. 782
Metamorphous Press ............... 782
Meteor Publishing ................ 782
Metropolitan Home ........... 582, 615
Michigan Business ................ 596
Michigan Historical Review ....... 725
Michigan Living .............. 596, 606
Michigan Out-of-Doors ............ 625
Michigan State University Press,
  The ....................... 782, 798
Mid-American Review .............. 725
Midstream ........... 588, 657, 700, 709
Midwest Motorist, The ............ 606
Mid-West Outdoors ....... 596, 625, 740
Midwest Quarterly ................ 725
Midwest Radio Theatre Workshop ... 839
Military ..................... 688, 690
Military History .......... 679, 688, 690
Military Lifestyle Magazine . 615, 689, 700
Milkweed Editions ................ 782
Mill Mountain Theatre ............ 758
Millay Colony for the Arts, The .... 819
Millbrook Press, The ............. 783

Miller Accounting Publications, Inc. . 783
Mills & Sanderson, Publishers ...... 783
Milwaukee Magazine .............. 596
Minnesota Monthly ............... 596
Minnesota Review, The ........... 725
Minority Engineer ............ 666, 692
Minstrel Books ................... 783
Miraculous Medal, The ........ 657, 709
Mississippi Review ............... 725
Mississippi Valley Review, The ...... 725
Missouri Repertory Theatre ........ 758
Missouri Review, The ............. 725
MIT Press, The ............. 783, 798
Mix Magazine .................... 642
Mobile Office .................... 684
Modan Publishing ................ 783
Model Railroader ................. 679
Modern Bride ............ 611, 709, 741
Modern Drummer ................. 674
Modern Haiku ................... 726
Modern Healthcare .............. 642
Modern Liturgy ................. 657
Modern Maturity ..... 582, 633, 686, 741
Modern Office ................... 582
Modern Office Technology ......... 643
Modern Romances ............... 706
Modern Tire Dealer ............. 643
Moment ................... 588, 657
Momentum ................. 657, 666
Money Maker .................... 634
Moneypaper, The ................ 634
Montana Magazine ............... 596
Montana, The Magazine of Western
    History ...................... 690
Monthly Review .................. 726
Moody Magazine ................. 657
Moon Handbooks ................ 783
Morehouse Publishing ............ 783
Morrow and Co., Inc., William ..... 783
Mother Earth News, The ...... 582, 615
Motor Club News ................. 649
Motor Trend .................... 631
Mountain Bike .............. 625, 741
Mountain Press Publishing ........ 783
Mountaineers Books, The .......... 783
Moving Home ................... 582
Moving Out ..................... 726
Mpls. St. Paul .................. 596
Ms.: The World of Women ..... 583, 611
Muir Publications, John ........... 784
Mulberry Books ................. 784
Multnomah Press ................ 784
Muscular Development .... 625, 632, 663
Museum of Science Magazine 596, 649, 684
Mushing ................... 625, 687
Musical Theatre Works ........... 758
Music-Theatre Group ............. 758
Mustang Publishing Co., Inc. ....... 784
My Friend ...................... 747
Mysterious Press, The ............ 784
Mystery Writers of America, Inc. ... 839

Na'amat Woman ............. 611, 700
Naiad Press, Inc. ................. 784
Nashua .................... 596, 643
Nation, The ................. 588, 709
National Association of Science Writers,
    Inc. ........................ 840
National Black Theatre ........... 758
National Christian Reporter, The .... 657
National Enquirer ........ 583, 709, 741
National Fisherman .............. 643
National Gardening Magazine ...... 616
National Geographic .......... 606, 670
National Geographic World ........ 747
National League of American Pen
    Women ..................... 840
National Motorist ................ 606
National News Bureau ............ 801
National Parks Magazine ..... 625, 670
National Playwrights Conference, Eugene
    O'Neill Theatre Center ......... 758
National Poetry Series ............ 710
National Press ................... 784
National Review ................. 588
National Wildlife ................ 670
National Writers Club, The ........ 840
National Writers Union ........... 840
Nation's Business ................ 643
Native Peoples Magazine ........... 618
Natural Health: The Guide to
    Well-Being ......... 618, 632, 663
Nature Conservancy .......... 649, 670
Naturegraph Publishers ........... 784
Naval Institute Press, The ......... 784
Nebo: A Literary Journal .......... 726
Nebraska History ............. 596, 690
Needlework Retailer .............. 679
Negative Capability .............. 726
Nelson, Inc., Thomas ............. 784
Nephrology News & Issues ......... 643
Network Publications .......... 596, 643
Network World .................. 684
Nevada ........................ 596
Nevada Business Journal ........... 643
New Age Journal ................ 618
New Alaskan ................... 596
New Author's Journal ............ 726
New Body ................. 632, 663
New Career Ways Newsletter ...... 643
New Choices for Retirement Living 618, 741
New Combat, The ............... 588
New Covenant .................. 657
New Delta Review ............... 726
New Directions ................. 784
New Dominion .................. 597
New Dramatists ................. 841
New Ehrlich Theatre ............. 758
New England Antiques Journal .... 679
New England Entertainment
    Digest ................... 674, 709
New England Review ............. 726
New England Skiers Guide, The .... 625

New Era ................... 657, 750
New Homeowner, The ............. 583
New Horizon Press .............. 784
New Jersey Monthly .......... 597, 741
New Jersey Reporter ............. 597
New Laurel Review ............... 726
New Letters .................... 726
New Mexico Humanities Review .... 726
New Mexico Magazine ............ 597
New Orleans Magazine ............ 597
New Orleans Review .............. 726
New Press, The ................. 726
New Renaissance, The ............ 726
New Republic, The .............. 709
New Rivers Press ................ 784
New Society Publishers ........... 784
New Theatre, Inc. ............... 758
New Tuners/Performance Community 758
New Woman ............. 583, 606, 611
New World Library .............. 785
New World Outlook .............. 657
New York ............... 583, 597, 741
New York Antique Almanac, The 583, 679
New York Daily News ............ 606
New York Family ............ 597, 618
New York Quarterly, The .......... 727
New York Shakespeare Festival/
　Joseph Papp Public Theater ..... 758
New York State Theatre Institute ... 758
New York Times, The ............ 606
New York Times Magazine, The 583, 588
New York Times Syndication Sales .. 801
New York University ............. 710
New York University Press ........ 798
New Yorker, The ..... 589, 700, 709, 741
Newcastle Publishing ............. 785
Newmarket Press ................ 785
Newsday ....................... 694
Newspaper Enterprise Association ... 801
Newsweek ...................... 583
Nexus ......................... 727
Nimrod ........................ 727
Noble Works ................... 713
Noir .......................... 674
North American Review, The ...... 727
North Atlantic Review ........... 727
North Country Press ............. 785
North Dakota Horizons ........... 597
North Dakota Quarterly, The ...... 727
North Georgia Journal ........... 597
North Texas Golfer ........... 597, 626
Northeast Magazine .............. 597
Northeast Outdoors .............. 626
NortheastArts .................. 727
Northeastern University Press ....... 710
Northern Lights ................ 597
Northern Logger and Timber Processor,
　The .......................... 643
Northwest Living! .......... 598, 606
Northwest Parks & Wildlife ........ 607
Northwest Playwrights Guild ....... 841

Northwest Prime Times ........... 598
Northwest Regional Magazines .. 598, 607
Northwest Review ............... 727
Northwest Travel ............. 598, 607
Northwestern University .......... 710
Northwood Institute, The ......... 819
Northword Press, Inc. ............ 785
Norton and Co., Inc., W.W. ........ 785
Nose, The ..................... 741
Nostalgia World ................. 679
NSGA Retail Focus .............. 643
Nuclear Times: Issues & Activism for
　Global Survival ................ 589
Nursing 93 .................... 663
Nursingworld Journal ......... 643, 664
Nutshell News .................. 679

Oakland Tribune, The ............ 694
Oatmeal Studios ................. 713
Oblates ....................... 657
Oceanic Press Service ............ 802
Odyssey Paperbacks ............. 785
Odyssey: Science That's Out of This
　World ....................... 747
Odyssey Theatre Ensemble ......... 758
Official Detective Stories .......... 703
Offshore ...................... 626
Oh! Idaho ..................... 598
Oh!Zone ...................... 747
Ohio Farmer, The ............... 668
Ohio Magazine .................. 598
Ohio Review, The ............... 727
Ohio State University Press ........ 798
Oklahoma Today ................ 598
Old Globe Theatre .............. 759
Old Rugged Cross Press .......... 785
Old West ...................... 691
Oldcastle Theatre Company ....... 759
Omni ............... 583, 684, 700, 706
On the Issues ............... 589, 611
On the Line.................... 747
On Track ...................... 626
Onionhead ..................... 727
Open Court Publishing Company .... 785
Open Wheel ................. 626, 631
Opera News .................... 674
Opportunity Magazine ............ 644
Optimist Magazine .............. 649
Optometric Economics ......... 644, 741
Orange Coast ................... 598
Orange Coast Review ............. 727
Orange County Register, The ....... 694
Orchard Books .................. 785
Oregon Coast ............... 598, 607
Oregon East ................... 727
Oregon State University Press ... 785, 798
Oregonian, The ................. 694
Orlando Magazine ............... 598
Orphic Lute ................... 727
Other Side, The ................ 658
Other Voices .................. 728

Ottawa Magazine ................. 598
Our Family ...................... 658
Our Sunday Visitor .............. 658
Outdoor America ............. 626, 671
Outdoor Canada ................. 626
Outdoor Life .................... 741
Outdoor Writers Association of
  America, Inc. ................. 841
Outerbridge ..................... 728
Overlook Press, The ............. 785
Owen Publishers, Inc., Richard C. ... 785
Owl ............................ 747
Oxford University Press .......... 786

Pacer Books for Young Adults ...... 786
Pacific Travel ................... 607
Paintbrush ...................... 728
Painted Bride Quarterly .......... 728
Painted Hills Review ............. 728
Palenville Interarts Colony ........ 819
Palm Springs Life ............ 598, 616
Pandora ........................ 728
Panhandler ..................... 728
Pantheon Books ................. 786
Papier-Mache Press ............. 786
Para Publishing ................. 786
Parade ......................... 583
Paragon House .................. 786
Paramount Cards ................ 713
Parentguide News ............ 599, 619
Parenting ...................... 619
Paris Review, The .............. 728
Parish Family Digest .......... 658, 741
Parnassus ...................... 728
Partisan Review ................. 728
Party & Paper Retailer .......... 644
Passages North .................. 728
Passport Books .................. 786
Pastoral Life ................... 658
Path Press ..................... 786
Patient Care ................... 664
Peachtree Publishers, Ltd. ......... 786
Peanut Farmer .................. 668
Pelican Publishing Co., Inc. ....... 786
Pelion Press .................... 786
PEN American Center ............. 841
Penguin Books .................. 786
Penguin Repertory Company ....... 759
Pennsylvania Angler ............. 626
Pennsylvania Farmer ............. 668
Pennsylvania Game News ......... 626
Pennsylvania Heritage ........ 599, 691
Pennsylvania Magazine ........... 599
Pennsylvania Stage Company ....... 759
Pennsylvania State University Press,
  The ........................... 799
Pentecostal Evangel .......... 658, 709
Pentecostal Messenger, The ........ 658
Penthouse ............. 583, 695, 700
People in Action/Sports Parade ..... 583
People Weekly .................. 584

People's Light and Theatre Company  759
Pequod .......................... 728
Peregrine Smith Poetry Series ....... 710
Perfect Crime ................... 786
Performance .................... 674
Permafrost ..................... 728
Permanent Press, The ........... 787
Persimmon Hill ............. 599, 691
Perspective .................... 658
Pet Business ................... 644
Pet Care Times ................. 644
Petersen's Bowhunting ........... 626
Petersen's Hunting .............. 626
Petersen's Photographic ....... 674, 679
Pets/Supplies/Marketing .......... 644
PGA Magazine ................... 626
Pharos Books ................... 787
Phi Delta Kappan ............... 666
Philadelphia ................... 599
Philip Morris Magazine .......... 584
Philomel Books ................. 787
Phoenix Magazine ............... 599
Photo: Electronic Imaging Magazine . 674
Photo Marketing ................ 644
Photomethods ................... 674
Physician and Sportsmedicine, The  632, 664
Physician's Management .......... 644
P.I. Magazine ................... 703
Piedmont Literary Review ......... 729
Pier One Theatre ................ 759
Pierce County Parent ............ 619
Pig Iron Press .................. 729
PIME World ..................... 658
Pineapple Press ................. 787
Pinehurst Journal, The .......... 729
Pioneer ........................ 750
Pioneer Drama Service ........... 763
Pippin Press ................... 787
Pittsburgh ..................... 599
Pittsburgh Post Gazette ......... 694
Pivot .......................... 729
Plain English Press .............. 787
Plains Poetry Journal ............ 729
Play ........................... 674
Playbill ....................... 674
Playboy ........ 584, 613, 695, 700, 741
Players ..................... 613, 696
Playgirl ............. 584, 611, 696, 742
Playhouse on the Square .......... 759
Plays, The Drama Magazine for Young
  People .................... 747, 763
Playwrights' Center, The ......... 842
Playwrights Horizons ............ 759
Playwrights' Platform ........... 759
Pleasure Boating ................ 626
Plenum Publishing Corp. ......... 787
Ploughshares ................ 701, 729
Plume Books ................... 787
P.O.B. ......................... 644
Pocket Books ................... 787
Pockets ........................ 747

Poem .......................... 729
Poet and Critic .................. 729
Poet Lore ...................... 729
Poet Magazine .................. 729
Poetry ......................... 729
Poetry East .................... 729
Poetry Society of America, The ..... 842
Poets and Writers, Inc. ........... 842
Point .......................... 787
Police Magazine ................. 644
Pool & Spa News ................ 644
Poplar Pike Playhouse ............ 759
Popular Electronics .............. 684
Popular Mechanics ........... 679, 742
Popular Photography .............. 674
Popular Press ................... 787
Popular Woodworking ............. 679
Portland Monthly Magazine ........ 599
Portland Parent ................. 619
Portland Press Herald ............ 694
Portland Review ................. 729
Portland Stage Company .......... 759
Poseidon Press .................. 787
Positive Approach, A ............. 664
Potter, Clarkson ................. 787
Power and Light .......... 658, 701, 748
Powerboat ...................... 627
Practical Horseman ........... 627, 687
Praeger Publishers ............... 787
Prairie Schooner ................ 730
Preacher's Magazine, The ......... 658
Preiss Visual Publications, Byron .... 787
Presbyterian Record, The ......... 659
Presbyterian Survey .............. 659
Presidio Press .................. 788
Prevue ......................... 675
Price Stern Sloan, Inc. ........... 788
Priest, The ..................... 659
Prima Publishing ................ 788
Primavera ...................... 730
Prime Times ................ 584, 686
Princeton Repertory Company ...... 759
Princeton University Press ........ 799
Prism International .............. 730
Private Eye Writers of America ..... 842
Private Pilot .................... 627
Private Practice ................. 644
Pro ............................ 645
Pro Basketball Illustrated ......... 627
Pro Football Illustrated, Pro Football
    Preview ..................... 627
Professional Stained Glass ........ 675
Progressive, The ................ 589
Progressive Grocer .............. 645
Proof Rock ..................... 730
Pruett Publishing Company ........ 788
Psychology Today ........... 584, 664
Public Citizen Magazine .......... 589
Publish ........................ 684
Puckerbrush Review .............. 730
Pudding Magazine ............... 730
Puerto Del Sol .................. 730

Puffin Books .................... 788
Pulphouse: A Fiction Magazine . 706, 730
Punch Digest for Canadian Doctors . 742
Purdue University Press ........... 711
Pure-Bred Dogs/American Kennel
    Gazette ..................... 687
Purpose .................. 659, 701, 709
Putnam's Sons, G.P. (Books for Young
    Readers).................... 788

Quaker Life..................... 659
Quantum: Science Fiction & Fantasy
    Review ..................... 706
Quarry Press ................... 788
Quarterly, The .................. 730
Quarterly West .................. 730
Queen.......................... 659
Queen's Quarterly ........... 584, 701
Quest Books .................... 788
Quick & Easy Crafts ............. 680
Quick Printing .................. 645
Quiet Hour, The ................. 659
Quill Trade Paperbacks .......... 788

R/C Modeler Magazine ........... 680
Raccoon........................ 730
Radar.......................... 748
Radiance: The Magazine for Large
    Women ..................... 611
Radio Play, The ................. 763
Radio-Electronics ............... 684
Rag Mag ....................... 730
Ragdale Foundation .............. 819
Railroad Model Craftsman ......... 680
Rainbow Jungle ................. 713
Raintree Steck-Vaughn Publishers ... 788
Rambunctious Review ............ 730
Random House, Inc. ............. 788
Random House Juvenile Div. ...... 788
Ranger Rick ................ 701, 748
Reader's Digest .............. 584, 742
Real Estate Today ............... 645
Real People ................. 584, 742
Reconstruction .................. 731
Recreation News................. 599
Red Cedar Review ............... 731
Red Farm Studio ................ 713
Redbook ........... 584, 612, 701, 742
Redneck Review of Literature, The .. 731
Reflections ..................... 748
Register Guard, The ............. 694
Regnery Gateway ................ 788
Religion and Public Education ...... 731
Remodeling ..................... 645
Renaissance House ............... 789
Repertory Theatre of St. Louis, The . 760
Research Magazine................ 645
Resonance ...................... 731
Response: A Contemporary Jewish
    Review ..................... 659
Restaurants USA ............. 645, 649
Restoration ................. 631, 680

Retired Officer Magazine, The 649, 686, 689
Review for Religious .............. 659
Review: Latin American Literature and
   Arts ........................ 731
Rhino ......................... 731
Rhode Island Monthly ......... 599, 742
Rider ...................... 627, 631
Righting Words ................. 675
River City ..................... 731
River Styx ..................... 731
Riverside Quarterly ............. 731
Rizzoli International Publications, Inc. 789
Road & Track ................. 631, 742
Road Company, The .............. 760
Road King .................. 701, 742
Roanoke Review ................. 731
Robb Report, The .............. 680
Rockford Magazine ............... 600
Rodale Press ................... 789
Roll Call: The Newspaper of Capitol
   Hill ....................... 589
Rolling Stone ............... 584, 675
Romance Writers of America ...... 842
Romancing the Past ............. 731
Roofer Magazine ................ 645
Rosen Publishing Group .......... 789
Rosset & Co. ................... 789
Rotarian, The ........ 584, 589, 650, 742
Round House Theatre ............. 760
Runner Triathlete News ....... 600, 627
Runner's World ................. 627
Rural Heritage ................. 742
Rural Living ................... 600
Ruralite ...................... 600
Rutgers University Press ....... 789, 799
Rutledge Hill Press ............. 789
RV Business ................... 645
RV Times Magazine ............. 607

Sacramento .................... 742
Sacramento Bee, The ............ 694
Sacramento Magazine ......... 600, 607
Safari ........................ 627
Safety Compliance Letter, The ...... 645
Safety Management .............. 645
Sagacity ...................... 686
Sail ......................... 627
Sailing ...................... 627
St. Anthony Messenger ....... 659, 701
St. Anthony Messenger Press ...... 789
St. Joseph's Messenger ......... 660, 709
St. Louis Post-Dispatch .......... 694
St. Martin's Press .............. 789
St. Paul Pioneer Press Dispatch ..... 694
St. Petersburg Times ............ 694
Sales & Marketing Management ..... 645
Salt and Pepper Mime Company/New
   Ensemble Actors Theatre ........ 760
Salt Water Sportsman ........... 627
Samuel French, Inc. ............. 762
San Diego Magazine ............. 600
San Diego Reader ............... 600

San Fernando Poetry Journal ....... 731
San Francisco Chronicle, The ....... 695
San Francisco Examiner .......... 695
San Francisco Focus ............. 600
San Jose Studies ................ 731
Sandlapper Publishing, Inc. ........ 789
Sangamon Company .............. 713
Sanskrit Literary/Art Publication .... 732
Sasquatch Books ................ 789
Sassy ........................ 701
Satellite Orbit ................. 585
Saturday Evening Post, The 585, 709, 743
Saturday Night ................. 589
Scandinavian Review ............. 732
Scarecrow Press ................ 789
Schocken Books ................ 789
Scholastic, Inc. ................. 790
Scholastic Professional Books ....... 790
School Arts Magazine ............ 666
School Mates ................... 680
School Safety .................. 666
School Shop/Tech Directions ... 667, 743
Science Fiction and Fantasy Writers
   of America, Inc. .............. 843
Science Fiction Chronicle ......... 706
Science Probe! ................. 684
Sciences, The .................. 685
Score, Canada's Golf Magazine . 627, 743
Scott, Foresman and Co. .......... 790
Scribner's Sons, Charles ........... 790
Scrivener ..................... 732
Sea, Best of Boating in the West .... 627
Sea Frontiers ............... 671, 685
Sea Kayaker ................. 628, 701
Seattle ..................... 600, 616
Seattle Group Theatre ............ 760
Seattle Home and Garden ......... 600
Seattle Post-Intelligencer ......... 695
Seattle Repertory Theatre ......... 760
Seattle Review, The ............. 732
Seattle's Child ............... 600, 619
Seek ......................... 660
Select Homes .................. 616
Self ................... 585, 612, 634
Seneca Review ................. 732
Senior Magazine ............. 600, 686
Senior Musician, The ............ 743
Sesame Street Magazine .......... 748
Seven Seas Press ............... 790
Seventeen .................. 701, 751
73 Amateur Radio .............. 680
Sew News ..................... 680
Shape ........................ 632
Shareware Magazine ............. 685
Sharing the Victory ............. 660
Shaw Publishers, Harold .......... 790
Sheep! Magazine ............. 668, 687
Sheet Music Magazine ........... 675
Shoe Tree Press ................ 790
Shofar ....................... 748
Shooting Star Review ............ 732
Short Fiction by Women .......... 732

Short Story Digest ................ 732
Shotgun Sports .................. 628
Show, The ...................... 628
Sierra .......................... 671
Sierra Club Books ............... 790
Sign Business ................... 646
Signs of the Times .............. 660
Silent Sports ................ 601, 628
Silhouette Books ................ 790
Silver Circle .................... 650
Simon & Schuster ............... 791
Simon & Schuster Books for Young
  Readers ...................... 791
Sing Heavenly Muse! Women's Poetry &
  Prose ....................... 732
Singer Media Corp. ........... 791, 802
Single Parent, The ............ 619, 743
Sisters Today ................... 660
Ski Magazine ................ 628, 743
Ski Racing ...................... 628
Skipping Stones .................. 748
Sky ............................ 608
Skydiving Magazine .............. 628
Skylark ........................ 732
Slawson Communications, Inc. ...... 791
Slipstream ...................... 732
Small Acreage Management ........ 668
Small Farmer's Journal ........... 668
Small Pond Magazine, The ........ 732
Small Press Review .............. 732
Small Press Writers and Artists
  Organization ................. 843
Smith, The ..................... 791
Smithsonian Magazine ......... 585, 671
Snack Food Magazine ............ 646
Snowboarder .................... 628
Snowest ........................ 628
Snowmobile .................. 628, 743
Snowy Egret .................... 733
Soap Opera Digest .............. 585
Soccer America Magazine .......... 628
Soccer Jr. ................... 628, 748
Social Justice Review ............. 660
Society for Technical Communication 843
Society Hill Playhouse ............ 760
Society of American Travel Writers .. 843
Society of Children's Book Writers &
  Illustrators ................... 844
Society of Environmental Journalists . 844
Society of Professional Journalists ... 844
Software Magazine ................ 646
Soho Press ..................... 791
Songwriters Guild of America, The .. 844
Sonora Review .................. 733
South Carolina Historical
  Magazine ................ 601, 691
South Carolina Review, The ........ 733
South Carolina Wildlife ....... 601, 629
South Coast Poetry Journal ......... 733
South Coast Repertory ............ 760
South Dakota Review ............. 733
South Florida Magazine .......... 601

Southern Appalachian Repertory
  Theatre ...................... 760
Southern California Anthology, The . 733
Southern Exposure ............... 733
Southern Humanities Review ....... 733
Southern Illinois University
  Press ..................... 791, 799
Southern Lumberman ............ 646
Southern Methodist University
  Press ..................... 791, 799
Southern Outdoors .............. 629
Southern Poetry Review .......... 733
Southern Review, The ............ 733
Southwest Art ................... 601
Southwest Review ............... 733
Souvenirs and Novelties ........... 646
Sou'wester ..................... 734
Specialty Travel Index ............ 607
Spectra Books .................. 791
Spectrum ....................... 734
Spiritual Life ................... 660
Spoon River Quarterly, The ........ 734
Sport Magazine .................. 629
Sporting News, The .............. 629
Sports Afield ............. 671, 701, 743
Sports Card Trader .......... 680, 743
Sports Collectors Digest ........... 680
Sports Illustrated ............ 585, 629
Sports Parade ................... 585
SPSM&H ....................... 734
Spur Magazine .................. 629
Stage Left Theatre ............... 760
Stage One: The Louisville Children's
  Theatre ...................... 761
Stages Repertory Theatre .......... 761
Stand Magazine ................. 734
Standard ....................... 660
Standard Publishing .............. 791
Stanford University Press ...... 791, 799
Star ....................... 585, 743
Starting Line ................... 629
Startling Detective ............... 704
State: Down Home in North Carolina,
  The .......................... 601
State University of New York Press .. 799
Steinbeck Room, The John ......... 820
Stemmer House Publishers, Inc. ..... 791
Sterling Publishing Co., Inc. ....... 792
Steve Dobbins Productions ........ 755
Stock Car Racing ............. 629, 631
Stone Soup, the Magazine by Children 748
Stone Wall Press, Inc. ............ 792
Stoneydale Press ................ 792
Story Friends ................... 748
Story Line Press ................ 792
Story Quarterly ................. 734
Storytelling Magazine ............. 675
Straight ................... 701, 751
Strawberry Hill Press ............. 792
Student Leadership ............... 692
Studies in American Fiction ........ 734
Success ........................ 585

Sun, The ........................ 734
Sun Tracks ..................... 675
Sunday Digest ................ 660, 701
Sunday Journal Magazine ...... 585, 601
Sunday School Counselor .......... 660
Sunfire ........................ 792
Sunrise Publications, Inc. .......... 713
Sunset Magazine ................. 601
Sunshine Magazine ............ 660, 702
Sunshine: The Magazine of South
    Florida ....................... 601
Superscience Blue ................ 749
Superteen's Loud Mouth .......... 751
Surfer Magazine ................. 629
Surfing ........................ 629
Swamp Root ..................... 734
Sycamore Review ................ 734
Syracuse University Press ......... 799
Syvenna Foundation .............. 820

Tab Books ...................... 792
Tallahassee Magazine .............. 601
Tambourine Books ............... 792
Tampa Bay Life: The Bay Area's
    Magazine ................. 601, 702
Taper Forum, Mark ............... 761
Tar River Poetry ................ 734
Taylor Publishing Co. ............ 792
TDR (The Drama Review): A Journal of
    Performance Studies .......... 675
Tea & Coffee Trade Journal ....... 646
Teachers Interaction .............. 660
Teaching K-8 ................... 667
Tech Directions .............. 667, 743
Technology & Learning ........ 667, 685
Technology Review .............. 685
Teddy Bear Review .............. 680
'Teen ...................... 702, 751
Teen Power .................... 751
Teens Today .............. 661, 702, 751
Temple University Press ....... 792, 799
Ten Minute Musicals Project, The ... 761
Ten Speed Press ................. 792
Tennis ......................... 629
Tennis Week .................... 629
Texas Highways Magazine ..... 601, 607
Texas Monthly .................. 602
Texas Review, The ............... 734
Textile World ................... 646
Theater Artists of Marin .......... 761
Theatre Communications Group .... 844
Theatre on the Square ............ 761
Theatre/Teatro .................. 761
Theatreworks/USA .............. 761
Thema ......................... 734
Theology Today .................. 661
Thirteen ....................... 734
Thoughts for All Seasons: The Magazine
    of Epigrams ................. 743
Threads Magazine ............... 680
3-2-1 Contact .................. 749
Threepenny Review, The .......... 735

Thunder's Mouth Press ............ 792
Thurber House Residencies, The .... 820
Ticknor & Fields ................. 793
Tiger Beat ...................... 751
Tightrope ...................... 735
Tile World/Stone World .......... 646
Timeline........................ 602
Times Books .................... 793
TLC Greetings .................. 713
Toastmaster, The ................ 585
Today's Catholic Teacher ......... 667
Today's Christian Woman ...... 612, 661
Today's Family .................. 619
Today's O.R. Nurse .......... 646, 664
Topics in Veterinary Medicine ...... 669
TOR Books ..................... 793
Touch ...................... 743, 749
Tourist Attractions and Parks ....... 646
Tours & Resorts ................. 607
Town & Country ................ 585
TQ/Teen Quest .............. 702, 751
Trailer Boats ................... 629
Trailer/Body Builders ............ 646
Trailer Life .................... 629
Trails-A-Way ................... 630
Training Magazine ............... 646
Transitions Abroad .............. 607
Translation .................... 735
Travel & Leisure ............. 585, 607
Travel Counselor ................ 646
Travel People ................... 647
Travel Smart ................ 607, 743
Travelage East/Southeast .......... 647
Treasure ....................... 681
Treasures in Needlework ....... 681, 744
Treasury ....................... 647
Triathlete ...................... 630
Tribune Media Services ........... 802
Trip & Tour .................... 585
Triquarterly .................... 735
Trivia ......................... 735
Troll Associates ................. 793
Tropic ..................... 585, 602
Tropical Fish Hobbyist ........ 681, 688
Troubador Press ................. 793
Truckers/USA .......... 631, 647, 702
True Confessions ............ 707, 744
True Detective .................. 704
True Experience ................. 707
True Love ...................... 707
True Police Cases ............... 704
True West ...................... 691
TSR, Inc....................... 792
Tucson Lifestyle ................ 602
Tudor Publishers, Inc. ........... 793
Tulsa World .................... 695
Turtle Magazine for Preschool
    Kids ........................ 749
TV Guide ...................... 586
Twisted ....................... 706
2AM Magazine .............. 706, 735
Tyndale House .................. 793

UCLA Magazine ................. 692
Ucross Foundation .............. 820
United Church Observer, The ....... 661
United Feature Syndicate .......... 802
United Methodist Reporter, The   661, 709
United Press International ......... 802
United Resource Press ............ 793
United Synagogue Review .......... 661
Unity Magazine ................. 661
Universal Press Syndicate .......... 802
Universe Books ................. 793
University of Alabama Press .... 793, 799
University of Arizona Press .... 793, 799
University of Arkansas Press ....... 711
University of California Press ... 793, 799
University of Chicago Press ....... 799
University of Georgia Press . 711, 794, 799
University of Illinois Press ..... 794, 799
University of Iowa Press .......... 711
University of Massachusetts Press 711, 799
University of Michigan Press ....... 799
University of Minnesota Press ... 794, 799
University of Missouri Press  711, 794, 799
University of Nebraska Press ... 794, 799
University of New Mexico Press   794, 799
University of North Carolina Press  794, 799
University of Oklahoma Press ... 794, 800
University of Pittsburgh Press .. 711, 800
University of Portland Review, The .. 735
University of South Carolina Press ... 800
University of Tennessee Press ... 794, 800
University of Utah Press .......... 800
University of Washington Press ..... 800
University of Windsor Review ...... 735
University of Wisconsin Press ... 711, 800
University Press of Colorado ... 794, 800
University Press of Florida ..... 794, 800
University Press of Kentucky, The  795, 800
University Press of Mississippi .. 795, 800
University Press of New England  795, 800
University Press of Virginia, The .... 800
U.S. Art ...................... 675
U.S. Kids ..................... 749
USA Today .................... 695
USAir Magazine ................ 608

Vagabond Creations, Inc. ......... 713
Valley Magazine ................ 602
Van Nostrand Reinhold ........... 795
Vandamere Press ................ 795
Vandeloecht's Fiction Magazine ..... 735
Vanity Fair .................... 586
Vegetarian Times ............ 632, 664
Velonews ...................... 630
Vending Times ................. 647
Ventura County & Coast Reporter ... 602
Venture ....................... 749
Vermont Life .................. 602
Vermont Studio Center ........... 821
Verve ........................ 735
VFW Magazine .......... 589, 650, 689
Vibrant Life .................. 664

Video Magazine ................. 675
Videomaker .................... 675
Viking Books .................. 795
Viking Children's Books .......... 795
Villa Montalvo Artist Residency
    Program ................... 821
Village Voice .............. 586, 589
Villager, The .................. 735
Villard Books .................. 795
Vim & Vigor ............... 633, 664
Virginia Business ............... 602
Virginia Center for the Creative Arts . 821
Virginia Quarterly Review ......... 735
Virginia Southwest ............ 602, 702
Virginia Wildlife ............. 602, 671
Virtue ................. 619, 661, 702
Vis a Vis ..................... 609
Visions International ............. 735
Vista ........................ 586
Vista Magazine ................. 661
Vista/USA .................... 608
Vogue .................... 586, 612
Volkswagen World ........ 586, 608, 744
Voyager Paperbacks ............. 795

Walker and Company ............ 795
Wall Street Journal, The .......... 695
Wallaces Farmer ................ 669
Walnut Street Theatre Company .... 761
Warner Books .................. 795
Warner Press Publishers .......... 713
Wascana Review ................ 735
Washington Journalism Review . 586, 675
Washington Post Magazine . 586, 589, 602
Washington Review .............. 736
Washington Times ............... 695
Washington Writers Publishing House 796
Washingtonian, The ............. 603
Water Skier, The ............... 630
Waterston Productions, Inc. ....... 796
Watts, Inc. ............. Franklin, 796
Wayne State University Press ....... 800
We Alaskans Magazine ........... 603
Webster Review ................ 736
Weekly, Seattle's News Magazine, The 603
Weird Tales ................... 706
Wesleyan University Press .. 711, 796, 800
West ........................ 736
West Art ..................... 681
West Branch ................... 736
West Graphics Publishing ......... 713
Westchester Family .......... 603, 619
Western & Eastern Treasures ...... 681
Western Historical Quarterly, The ... 691
Western Horseman, The .......... 630
Western Humanities Review ....... 736
Western Outdoors .............. 630
Western People ............. 702, 709
Western Producer, The ........... 669
Western Publishing Co., Inc. ....... 796
Western Sportsman .......... 603, 630
Western Stage, The ............. 761

Western Writers of America, Inc. ... 845
Westminster/John Knox Press ...... 796
Westminster Review, The .......... 736
Westways ..................... 603, 608
Whitman, Albert ................. 796
Wilderness Press ................. 796
Wildfire ........................ 619
Wildlife Conservation ......... 671, 688
Wiley & Sons, John .............. 796
William and Mary Review, The ..... 736
Williamhouse-Regency, Inc. ........ 714
Willowisp Press, Inc. .............. 796
Wilshire Book Company .......... 796
Wilson Fine Arts, Inc., Carol ...... 714
Wilson Library Bulletin ........... 667
Win Magazine................... 681
Wind ......................... 736
Wind Surfing .................... 630
Windfall ....................... 736
Windless Orchard, The ........... 736
Windrider ...................... 630
Windswept House Publishers ....... 797
Windy City Sports ............ 603, 630
Wine Spectator, The.............. 681
Wine Tidings.................... 616
Wines & Vines .................. 647
Wingbow Press .................. 797
Wisconsin .................. 586, 603
Wisconsin Trails .............. 603, 744
Wisconsin West Magazine ......... 603
Wisdom Bridge Theatre ........... 761
With.......................... 661
Without Halos ................. 736
Witness ....................... 736
Woman Beautiful ............... 586
Woman Bowler .................. 630
Woman Engineer ............ 667, 692
Woman of Power ............. 612, 736
Woman's Day ....... 586, 612, 634, 744
Woman's Touch .............. 612, 661
Woman's World ............. 612, 702
Women in Business .............. 612
Women's Circle ................. 612
Women's Glib .................. 744
Women's Household ......... 613, 702
Women's Sports & Fitness . 613, 630, 633
Wonder Time ................... 749
Woodbine House ................ 797
Woodenboat Magazine ......... 681, 744
Woodmen Magazine............... 650
Woodshop News.................. 647
Woodwork...................... 681
Woolly Mammoth Theatre Company . 762
Worcester Review, The ........... 737
Word Works .................... 711
WordPerfect Magazine............. 685
Wordware Publishing ............. 797
Workbasket Magazine ............ 681

Workbench ................. 616, 682
Workboat ...................... 647
Working Mother ............. 613, 619
Workman Publishing Co., Inc. ...... 797
Workskills Newsletter ............ 647
World Oil ...................... 647
World Screen News ............... 647
World Vision Magazine ............ 662
World Wastes ................... 647
Worldwide Library ............... 797
Wormwood Review, The .......... 737
Worth ........................ 634
Wrestling World ................. 630
Writers Forum .................. 737
Writers Guild of America, East, Inc. . 845
Writers Guild of America, West, Inc. 845
Writers on the River ............. 737
Writers Room, The .............. 821
Writers Studio, The .............. 821
Writing! ....................... 751
Wurlitzer Foundation of New Mexico,
  Helene ...................... 822
Wyoming, the Hub of the Wheel .... 737

Xanadu ........................ 737

Yachting ...................... 630
Yaddo ........................ 822
Yale Review .................... 737
Yale University Press .......... 711, 800
Yankee ............. 586, 603, 702, 709
Yankee Books ................... 797
Yankee Magazine's Travel Guide to New
  England ................... 603, 608
Yarrow ....................... 737
Yearling Books .................. 797
Yellowback Library .............. 682
Yesterday's Magazette ......... 686, 691
Yesteryear ..................... 682
YM .......................... 751
Yoga Journal ........... 619, 633, 664
Yolen Books, Jane ............... 797
Young and Alive ................ 751
Young Mime Theatre, Gary ........ 762
Young Salvationist ............ 662, 751
Your Church ................... 662
Your Health ................... 664
Your Home/Indoors & Out .... 586, 616
Your Money ................... 634

Zebra Books ................... 797
Zenith Editions ................. 797
Zillions ....................... 749
Zondervan Publishing House ....... 797
Zoo Life....................... 671
Zoomin' .................. 671, 688
Zymurgy ...................... 682
Zyzzyva ...................... 737